Photoshop® CS3
Bible

Photoshop® CS3
Bible

Laurie Ulrich Fuller & Robert C. Fuller

Wiley Publishing, Inc.

Photoshop® CS3 Bible

Published by
Wiley Publishing, Inc.
10475 Crosspoint Boulevard
Indianapolis, IN 46256
www.wiley.com

Copyright © 2007 by Wiley Publishing, Inc., Indianapolis, Indiana

Published simultaneously in Canada

ISBN: 978-0-470-11541-1

Manufactured in the United States of America

10 9 8 7 6 5 4 3 2 1

For general information on our other products and services or to obtain technical support, please contact our Customer Care Department within the U.S. at (800) 762-2974, outside the U.S. at (317) 572-3993 or fax (317) 572-4002.

Library of Congress Control Number: 2007926393

About the Authors

Laurie Ulrich Fuller. Drawing and writing since she could pick up a crayon, and telling people what to do (and how to do it) since she was able to speak, Laurie Ulrich Fuller is a graphic artist, computer trainer, and the author and co-author of more than 25 books on computers, software, and the Web. Laurie has written hundreds of training manuals for universities and corporate training centers, and in the past 16 years, she's personally trained thousands of people to make more creative and effective use of their computers. Her classroom has expanded in recent years to include total strangers around the world — through CD-based training products and online courses.

In the early 1990s, after spending way too many years working for other people, Laurie started her own firm, Limehat & Company. This venture allowed her to put her experience, ideas, and contacts to good use, providing consulting, training, Web development, and Web hosting services with a focus on the special needs of growing companies and non-profit organizations. If you're wondering where the name "Limehat" came from, it's a long story, but suffice to say it goes back to a childhood taunt, regarding a plaid hat she involuntarily wore to school. She still gets flashbacks.

When not writing about or teaching people to use computers, Laurie can be found working for a variety of animal and environmental advocacy groups, including the League of Humane Voters (www.lohvpa.org). You can find out more about Laurie's work, experiences, and both personal and professional interests at www.planetlaurie.com. You can find out more about Photoshop and the Photoshop Bibles and check out online Photoshop tutorials, tips, tricks, and expert advice at www.photoshopbible.com. Laurie welcomes reader mail at authors@photoshop bible.com. She can't promise an immediate response, but all mail will be answered.

Robert C. Fuller. Another year, another Photoshop update. True to form, Mr. Fuller still shuns the daylight, but just like the last time around, it took only a shiny new iMac to bring him up from the basement. While the rejuvenating effects of last year's run-in with the eMac did not have long-standing positive effects on his mental health, at least this year he's been speaking in complete sentences. "I really like this iMac" is all we've heard out of him, but at least he's smiling and the faceless apparitions don't seem to plague him as much.

Robert is the author of the *Dreamweaver 4* and *HTML Virtual Classroom* books (McGraw-Hill/Osborne), as well as *HTML in 10 Steps or Less* (Wiley Publishing, Inc.). He has contributed to *The Photoshop 7 Complete Reference* (McGraw-Hill/Osborne), *The Photoshop 2 Elements Bible*, and *Restoration and Retouching with Photoshop Elements 2* (both Wiley Publishing, Inc.), as well as last year's *Photoshop CS2 Bible Professional Edition*. Robert also teaches computer topics at colleges and through online courses. You can write to him at authors@photoshopbible.com.

We'd like to thank **Peter Simon**, photographer and author, for his interest in our book — his artist's eye and technical perspective are greatly appreciated. Readers can check out Peter's work at www.petersimon.com. His magnificent images of everything from Martha's Vineyard to the Mets are a must-see, as is his book, I and EYE: Pictures of My Generation, which you can order through his Web site.

We'd also like to thank the artists who contributed images for this book:

Krisha Martzall
KLM Photography
(717)808-5503
www.krishamartzall.com

Terri Shadle
Terri Shadle Photography
(570)337-5754
pear725@yahoo.com
www.tshadle.info

A special thank you is also extended to **Grant Stokke** of The Pennsylvania State University, whose wonderful photo of a crow being fitted with a radio collar was used in this book. We're grateful to Grant for this image and for his work — along with his colleague, David Burkett — in helping study Lancaster, Pennsylvania's migratory crow population and the impact of humane, non-lethal wildlife management techniques. For more information, visit www.lancastercrows.org.

Credits

Acquisitions Editor
Stephanie McComb

Project Editor
Martin V. Minner

Technical Editor
Dennis R. Cohen

Copy Editor
Gwenette Gaddis Goshert

Editorial Manager
Robyn Siesky

Business Manager
Amy Knies

Vice President and Executive Group Publisher
Richard Swadley

Vice President and Publisher
Barry Pruett

Project Coordinator
Adrienne Martinez

Graphics and Production Specialists
Jennifer Mayberry
Barbara Moore
Alicia B. South
Ronald Terry
Christine Williams

Quality Control Technicians
Laura Albert
John Greenough
Christy Pingleton

Proofreading
Aptara

Indexing
Aptara

Cover Design
Michael Trent

Cover Illustration
Joyce Haughey

Contents at a Glance

Contents

Contents

Part II: Painting and Retouching 181

Chapter 4: Defining Colors 183

Contents

Contents

Contents

Contents

Part V: Color and Output   861

Chapter 17: Essential Color Management. 863

xxi

Contents

Contents

Preface

Welcome to the *Photoshop CS3 Bible*, the latest edition of the bestselling book on Photoshop in publishing history. We've done our best to cover everything thoroughly, accurately, and whenever we could, in such a way as to remind you that even though Photoshop is a powerful tool, it's also fun to use. Of course, we hope you learn lots of good stuff, but we also hope you have a wonderful time while you're at it, because if you're not having a good time, what's the point?

Before you begin delving into the actual Photoshop portion of this book, let us tell you a little something about this book overall. Now in its 13th year, the *Photoshop Bible* is the longest continuously published title on Adobe Photoshop. Not coincidentally, it also happens to be the best-selling reference guide on the topic, with more than 15 U.S. editions, dozens of localized translations around the globe, and more than a million copies in print worldwide. This makes it not only the most successful book of its kind, but also one of the most successful books on any electronic publishing topic ever printed.

We've made it our mission to address every topic directly, and we haven't always spared you our personal opinions and experience, even if they're not entirely flattering to the software. We believe this is a good thing, because you're not buying a brochure or some marketing piece from Adobe here — you're buying a book about Photoshop from people who use it, teach it, and dive into all its features, every day. If something works well and is a great feature, we say so. If it doesn't do what you'd expect or it's not the most elegant tool in the toolbox, we say that, too. We share workarounds, tips, tricks, and give you the benefit of our experience wherever we feel it will be helpful.

About This Edition of the Book

This particular edition has undergone a design overhaul, including new front and back covers, new interior design, and new graphics throughout the book. Couple this with the large-scale update that Photoshop has undergone with the release of CS3, and you've got a book that's in many ways nothing like its predecessors. Of course, legacy material remains, for areas of the software that haven't changed in years — and the quality, scope, and depth of the coverage remains a positive constant. And good news for more advanced users — we've also brought in much of the content found in the CS2 *Professional Edition*, which means that more of the specialized and in-depth coverage deemed "for professionals only" last year is now found within this enlarged, enhanced, *"for everyone"* edition for Photoshop CS3.

We've also added a CD that contains many of the images used in the book, as well as tutorials for a wide variety of Photoshop's tools and features. You don't need to use the CD to learn Photoshop, but it's there as a visual backup for people who like to learn by doing, not just reading. To find out what's on the CD-ROM, check out Appendix B, where the individual tutorials and the tools, features, and skills they cover are discussed in detail.

Conventions

Every computer book conforms to its own special brand of logic, and this one is no exception. While we generally find conformity and convention to be annoying and well, conventional, the book does have some features that we figured you'd want to find and be able to count on — so here they are:

Vocabulary

Call it *computerese*, call it *technobabble*, call it the indecipherable gibberish of incorrigible propeller head geeks. Whatever you call it, we can't explain Photoshop in graphic (pardon the pun) detail without occasionally reverting to the specialized language of the trade. However, to help you keep up, we can and have italicized vocabulary words (such as *bit depth*) with which you may not be familiar or which are used in an unusual context. An italicized term is followed by a definition.

If you come across a strange word that is *not* italicized (*that* bit of italics was for emphasis), look it up in the index to find the first reference to the word in the book.

Commands and options

To distinguish the literal names of commands, dialog boxes, buttons, and so on, we capitalize the first letter in each word (for example, *click the Cancel button*). The only exceptions are option names, which can be six or seven words long and filled with prepositions such as *to* and *of*. Traditionally, prepositions and articles (*a, an, the*) don't appear in initial caps, and this book follows that time-honored rule, too.

When discussing menus and commands, we use an arrow symbol to indicate hierarchy. For example, *Choose File ➪ Open* means to choose the Open command from the File menu. If you have to display a submenu to reach a command, we list the command used to display the submenu between the menu name and the final command. *Choose Image ➪ Adjustments ➪ Invert* means to choose the Adjustments command from the Image menu and then choose the Invert command from the Adjustments submenu.

The whole platform thing

This is a cross-platform book, which means it's written for both Windows and Macintosh users. Photoshop is virtually identical on the two platforms, so it makes little difference. However, the PC and Mac keyboards are different. The Ctrl key on the PC translates to the Command key (⌘) on the Mac. Alt translates to Option, and because Apple's mice do not always include right mouse buttons, right-clicking on the PC becomes Control-clicking on the Mac. Throughout this book, we try to make things as unambiguous as possible by mentioning the Windows keystroke first with the Macintosh equivalent second, usually in parentheses. You'll also find that select figures of dialog boxes and other parts of the Photoshop workspace were shot in both operating systems; there are Mac figures and Windows figures where the two differ greatly. We don't want anyone to feel left out, unrepresented, unloved, or unappreciated.

Version names and numbers

A new piece of software comes out every 15 minutes. That's not a real statistic, mind you, but it's probably not far off. When it comes to Photoshop, it started (surprisingly enough) with version 1.0, and the numbering of versions ended with Photoshop 7. With the release of Photoshop CS in 2003, Adobe abandoned numbering, but has gone back to it now (sort of) by calling last year's model Photoshop CS2, and this year's CS3. This book refers to older versions, but without being overly specific. While there were multiple releases of the major versions, when we write *Photoshop 7*, we mean versions 7.0 and 7.0.1, and so on.

It's important to note that Photoshop CS3 comes in two flavors — an Extended version, which is what is documented in this book, and a Standard version, which sells for a slightly lower price than the Extended. The Extended version has a few "bells and whistles" that the Standard version does not, and these include:

- Enhanced cloning and healing with overlay preview
- Enhanced 32-bit HDR support
- Enhanced Vanishing Point (basic Vanishing Point features are included in the Standard version)
- 3D editing
- Motion graphics and video layers
- Enhanced animation (basic animation is in the Standard version)
- Measurement and data
- DICOM support
- MATLAB support
- Enhanced Image Stack processing (basic stack processing is present in the Standard version)

If you have purchased the Standard version of CS3, you'll find this book completely useful and appropriate — very few core features vary between the two versions, and many of the things that exist only or are enhanced in the Extended version are highly specialized — the video and 3D features, for example. If you must have those features, you'll want to buy the Extended version of Photoshop CS3. If you don't care about those things, or have other software to deal with your need to edit video layers or create movies, then you'll be perfectly happy with the Standard version *and* this book.

Icons

Like just about every computer book currently, this one includes compelling and visually arresting icons that focus your peepers on important information. The icons make it easy for people who like to just skim books to figure out what the heck's going on, to "cut to the chase" in some cases, or to just provide "the highlights." Icons exist not only for those with short attention spans, but for people who are just so darn busy that reading an entire page is just unimaginable. On the whole, the icons are self-explanatory, but here's an explanation of them anyway.

CAUTION The Caution icon warns you that a step you're about to take may produce disastrous results. Well, perhaps "disastrous" is an exaggeration. Inconvenient, then. Uncomfortable. For heaven's sake, be careful.

NOTE The Note icon highlights some little tidbit of information we've decided to share with you that seemed at the time to be at least remotely related to the topic at hand. You might learn how an option came into existence, why a feature is implemented the way it is, or how you might use the feature in an unconventional way or skip its use altogether.

NEW FEATURE The New Feature icon explains an option, a command, or a feature that is either bright, shiny, and new to this latest revision, or it's something that's been changed more than slightly. If you're already familiar with previous versions of Photoshop, you might just want to plow through the book looking for Photoshop CS3 icons and see what new stuff is out there. A description of what's new also can be found at the beginning of Chapter 2, if you're interested in a quick tour. Again, those in search of instant gratification need not be put off by the girth of this book; we've accommodated both the cover-to-cover reader and those of you who'll hardly crack the binding, but will want to know that when they need us, we're there.

TIP This book is bursting with tips and techniques. If we were to highlight every one of them, entire pages would be gray with light bulbs popping out all over the place. The Tip icon calls attention to shortcuts that are specifically applicable to the Photoshop application. For the bigger, more useful power tips, you'll have to — gasp — actually read the text.

CROSS-REF The Cross-Ref icon tells you where to go for information related to the current topic. It's about as straightforward as an icon can get, so you won't have any trouble with this one.

Contact

Even in its millionth edition, scanned by the eyes of hundreds of thousands of readers and scrutinized intensely for months at a time by the authors and our editors, we bet someone, somewhere, will still manage to locate errors and oversights. If you notice those kinds of things and have a few spare moments, please let us know what you think. We always appreciate readers' comments. Really, we do.

If you want to share your insights, comments, or corrections, send a note to authors@photoshop bible.com. Don't worry if you don't get a response immediately. While every letter does get read and every constructive idea is considered, it would be impossible, due to volume, to respond immediately or at great length. We will endeavor to respond to all emails, however, and thank you in advance for your patience.

NOTE Please, do not write to ask why your copy of Photoshop is misbehaving on your specific computer. Neither of the authors of this book was involved in developing Photoshop, we are not employed by Adobe, and we cannot possibly provide product support via email or phone. Adobe can answer your technical support questions way better than anyone can, so leave it to the experts.

Okay, that's enough out of us. Now you need to get on with things and start reading the actual book part of this book. Soon, you'll know much more about Photoshop CS3 than you did before, and you'll feel more like you can become a real expert — at least in terms of the features that are most important and useful to you. We thank you for your time and your confidence in us by purchasing this book, and we wish you all the best. Enjoy the book!

Part I

Welcome to Photoshop

Chapter 1

Welcome to Photoshop CS3

Photoshop has been around long enough that the name has become a verb in our cultural lexicon ("You can tell THAT'S been Photoshopped!"). But simply because a term gets bandied about in general parlance doesn't mean everyone knows what Photoshop truly is or does. Granted, you may be one of the many graphics professionals who have been using this program for years. But you may just as likely be one of the greater majority who, while having a general idea of Photoshop's capabilities, has little or no experience using it — and with this book have decided to change all that.

As you move forward and get to "What's New in Photoshop CS3," the playing field should level out, and as you move through the rest of the book, no matter what level of user you are now, you'll find a great deal of new and useful information throughout.

So what exactly is Photoshop and what does it do? Adobe Photoshop — Photoshop is the name of the software, Adobe Systems is the name of the company that develops and sells it — is a professional-level image-editing application. It allows you to create images from whole cloth or, more likely, modify scanned artwork and digital photographs. Photoshop is available for use on computers equipped with either Microsoft Windows or Apple's Macintosh operating system.

Of course, Photoshop isn't just an image-editing application. It's the most powerful, most ubiquitous image-editing application in the world. Despite hefty competition, where professional image editing is concerned, Photoshop's not just the market leader — it's the only game in town — and as you'll discover (or you may already know), that status is well deserved.

Such a lack of competition is rarely a good thing, because stagnation can often result. But in Photoshop's case, the historically lopsided sales advantage has provided Adobe with a clear incentive to reinvest in Photoshop and regularly enhance, and even overhaul, its capabilities. Photoshop CS3 is no exception, and in fact, it may be one of the most significant upgrades in the past few years.

It's as if each new version of Photoshop is competing with its own previous versions for the hearts and minds of the digital art community. Meanwhile, other vendors have had to devote smaller resources to playing catch-up. Some, such as Jasc Software, with its Windows-only Paint Shop Pro, have hung in there and remained commercially viable. But such success stories are few and far between. Although competitors have provided some interesting and sometimes amazing capabilities, the sums of their parts have — more often than not — fallen well short of Photoshop's.

As a result, Photoshop rides a self-perpetuating wave of market leadership. It wasn't always the best image editor, nor was it the first. But its deceptively straightforward interface combined with a few terrific core functions made it a hit from the moment of its first release. More than a dozen years later — thanks to substantial capital injections from Adobe and highly creative programming on the parts of Photoshop's engineering staff and its originator, Thomas Knoll — Photoshop has evolved into the most popular program of its kind.

Image-Editing Concepts

Like any *image editor*, Photoshop enables you to alter photographs and other scanned artwork. You can retouch an image, apply special effects, swap details between photos, introduce text and logos, adjust color balance, and sharpen the details — to name just a few of your options. Photoshop also provides everything you need to create artwork from scratch. These tools are fully compatible with pressure-sensitive tablets, so you are not limited to creating only those images that you can successfully draw with a mouse.

Raster versus vector

Graphics programs tend to fall into two broad categories: painting programs and drawing programs. While these terms are nice, it's better to think of graphics programs in terms of the type of images they produce: raster images or vector images.

Raster images

A raster image creates a picture on your screen by mapping color values to a rectangular grid of pixels (short for picture elements). As with all computer data, the color or grayscale values are stored in bits. The bits correspond to the grid of pixels, and this is where the term *bitmap* comes from. If you look at the code behind an image, it represents a map of all the bits devoted to the individual pixels — left to right, top to bottom.

For example, JPEG, GIF, and PNG files are all raster (bitmap) graphic filetypes. By dragging one of these filetypes to a text editor capable or rendering hex code, you get a window into what that map of bits looks like, as shown in Figure 1.1.

FIGURE 1.1

The code underlying a GIF file shows you the map of the bits that make up the image.

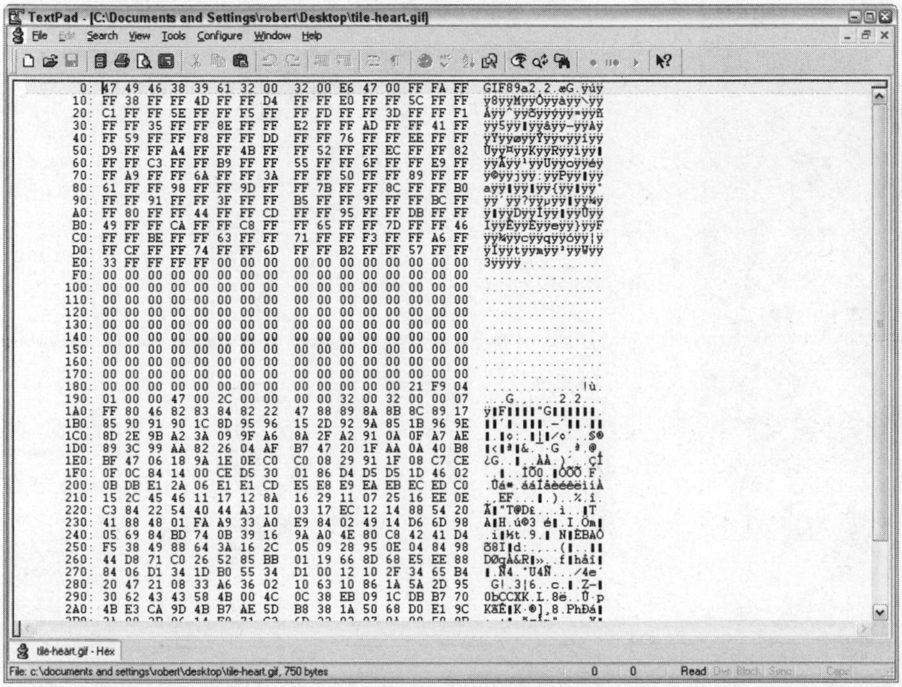

Raster images contain a fixed number of pixels, which makes them resolution-dependent. This means when you attempt to enlarge them, they "pixelate" — a fancy way of saying they become all jagged looking. Figure 1.2 gives an example.

FIGURE 1.2

At its original size, the JPEG on the left is sharp and clear. After being enlarged by 500 percent (on the right), the image becomes pixelated.

A continuous-tone image

Same image, increased 500 percent

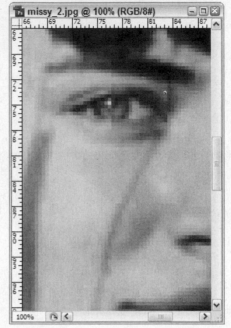

Vector images

A vector image creates a picture using mathematical statements. Instead of mapping out data bits to specific pixels, a vector image describes the geometric properties (points, lines, curves, and polygons) that need to be constructed to render the image. For example, if a vector image contains a circle, the data in the file keeps track of the circle's radius, where the center point is, and any stroke or fill colors to be used.

Vector files are not resolution dependent. If you increase the dimensions, the objects described by the mathematical statement are simply redefined. In the case of our circle example, instead of trying to enlarge pixels, the vector file simply changes the radius value — and viola! You get a larger circle that's just as clear the second time around. Figure 1.3 provides a demonstration.

While painting programs have been traditionally raster-centric and drawing programs vector-centric, Photoshop bridges the gap quite nicely, providing many of the best features of both. In addition to its wealth of image-editing and organic-painting capabilities, Photoshop permits you to add vector-based text and shapes to your photographic images. These features may not altogether take the place of a drawing program (though Photoshop keeps incorporating many of the vector tools found in Adobe's drawing program Illustrator), but they help to make Photoshop an increasingly flexible and dynamic image-creation environment.

FIGURE 1.3

This image, originally created in Adobe Illustrator, and opened here in Photoshop CS3, looks just as good regardless of the size it's resampled to.

A vector image

Same image, increased 500 percent

NOTE You should realize that even when working with vectors, everything you see onscreen is in a rasterized state — because monitors (for the most part) are raster output devices. Printers, on the other hand, are where the benefit of vector imagery is seen most clearly — literally and figuratively. This explains why you tend to find print designers singing the praises of applications like Adobe Illustrator (a vector image editor) and Web graphic designers (who design for a monitor-based experience) siding with Photoshop.

The ups and downs of painting

As you might expect, painting programs and drawing programs have their own strengths and weaknesses. The strength of a painting program is that it offers a straightforward approach to creating images. For example, although many of Photoshop's features are complex — some of them extremely so — its core painting tools are as easy to use and familiar as a pencil. You alternately draw and erase until you reach a desired effect, just as you've been doing since childhood with pencil and paper.

In addition to being simple to use, each of Photoshop's main painting tools — include paint brushes, pencils, and erasers — is fully customizable. It's as if you have access to an infinite variety of crayons, colored pencils, pastels, airbrushes, watercolors, and so on, all of which are erasable — and even the eraser is customizable, so you can erase in any one of hundreds of ways. The simplicity and customization potential make these tools fun to use, and you'll find yourself creating artwork that you might never have had the time or patience to attempt manually. Of course, if you still find you're more facile with a pencil and paper (or ink and paper or any other artist's medium, for that matter), you can always scan the manual drawing/painting into Photoshop and then use Photoshop's tools to enhance and edit it — zooming in very close for fine adjustments, which you could never do to the same extent if you remained in the manual world.

Because painting programs rely on pixels, they are ideally suited to electronic photography. Whether captured with a scanner or digital camera, an electronic photograph is composed of thousands or even tens of millions of colored pixels. A drawing program such as Illustrator may let you import such a photograph and apply very simple edits, but Photoshop gives you complete control over every pixel, entire collections of pixels, or independent elements of pixels. If you just leaf quickly through this book, you'll see that a photograph can become anything, and the options for what you can do to a photo are virtually unlimited.

The downside of paintings and electronic photos is that they are ultimately finite in scale. Because a bitmap contains a fixed number of pixels, the *resolution* of an image — the number of pixels in an inch, a centimeter, or some other defined space — changes with respect to the size at which the image is printed. Print the image small, and the pixels become tiny, which increases the resolution of the image. Like the millions of cells in your body, tiny pixels become too small to see and thus blend together to form a cohesive whole, as in the first image in Figure 1.2. Print the image large, and the pixels grow, which decreases the resolution. Large pixels are like cells viewed through a microscope; once you can distinguish them independently, the image falls apart, as in the second example in the figure. The results are jagged edges and blocky transitions. The only way to remedy this problem is to increase the number of pixels in the image, which increases the size of the file.

CROSS-REF   Remember, this is a very basic explanation of how images work. For a more complete description that includes techniques for maximizing image resolution and quality, check out Chapter 3.

The downs and ups of drawing

A better way to describe the process of creating a vector-based drawing might be "constructing." Why? Because you actually build each of the lines and shapes, point by point, and stack them on top of each other to create a finished image. Each of these objects is independently editable — one of the main advantages of an object-oriented approach — but you're still faced with the task of building your artwork one chunk at a time.

Because a drawing program defines lines, shapes, and text as mathematical equations, these objects automatically conform to the full resolution of the output device, whether it's a laser printer, an image setter, or a film recorder. The drawing program sends the math to the printer and the printer *renders* the math to paper or film. In other words, the printer converts the drawing program's equations to printer pixels. Your printer offers far more pixels than your screen — a 600-dots-per-inch (dpi) laser printer, for example, offers 600 pixels per inch (dots equal pixels), whereas most screens are limited to 150 pixels per inch or fewer. So the printed drawing appears smooth and sharply focused regardless of the size at which you print it.

Another advantage of drawings is that they take up relatively little space on a hard drive. The file size of a drawing depends on the quantity and complexity of the objects the drawing contains. Thus, the file size has almost nothing to do with the size of the printed image, which is just the opposite of the way bitmapped images work. A thumbnail drawing of a garden that contains hundreds of leaves and petals consumes several times more space than a poster-sized drawing made up of three rectangles.

When to use Photoshop

Because of their specialized tools and methods, painting programs and drawing programs fulfill distinct and divergent purposes. Photoshop and other painting programs are best suited to creating and editing the following kinds of artwork:

- Scanned photos, including photographic collages and embellishments that originate from scans
- Images captured with any type of digital camera
- Still frames captured from videotape or film
- Realistic artwork that relies on the play among naturalistic highlights, midranges, and shadows
- Impressionistic artwork and other images created for purely personal or aesthetic purposes
- Logos and other display type featuring soft edges, reflections, or tapering shadows
- Special effects that require the use of filters and color enhancements that you simply can't achieve in a drawing program

When to use a drawing program

You're probably better off using Illustrator or some other drawing program if you're interested in creating more stylized artwork, such as the following:

- Architectural plans, product designs, or other precise line drawings
- Business graphics, such as graphs, charts, and diagrams that reflect data or show how things work
- Traditional logos and text effects that require crisp, ultra-smooth edges
- Brochures, flyers, and other single-page documents that mingle artwork, logos, and body-copy text (such as the text you're reading now)

If you're serious about computer graphics, you should own at least one painting program and one drawing program. This enables you to create and edit images that are best suited to each of the different program types, potentially mixing and mingling the content you create and/or edit in each program for projects that require, for example, photographic content as well as crisp line art. For simplicity's sake, you may consider owning both Photoshop and Illustrator, so that you can benefit from the products' common elements—similar menus, commands, buttons, and common keyboard shortcuts. The key, though, is to have tools that suit your needs and work the way you think. Of course, as you'll learn later, another of Photoshop's benefits is that you can customize it to work the way you do, making it a highly effective tool for just about anyone.

What's New in Photoshop CS3

If you used Photoshop CS2 or CS, you'll notice some big changes in Photoshop CS3 right away. There are big changes to the toolbox layout and the way palettes (those boxes of tools and settings on the workspace) look and interact — with you and the tools you're using at any given time. So the look and feel of Photoshop has changed with the release of CS3, and you'll spot that immediately.

What you may not realize immediately are many of the feature changes and enhancements. These you won't find until you start working with a particular tool or fire up a particular command via a menu or keyboard shortcut. Some of them may take you weeks to find, just based on which features you typically use when you sit down to work with Photoshop. Some you may never find on your own, if they reside in feature areas that you never, ever use.

That's the neat thing about Photoshop, too. It's so vast that you can use it and love it and be really productive with it without ever using certain parts of it. It's like living in a big state or province: All the things you ever need are probably right there near your house, and you may never need to venture very far for anything. Of course, the adventurous among you will feel compelled to poke around and play with features you may not need on a daily basis, and hopefully this book will encourage that sort of pioneer spirit.

To give you an idea of the magnitude of the upgrade that CS3 represents, this section includes a list of just some of the new and enhanced features. You'll find a chapter number reference (though some features are mentioned in more than one chapter), along with a description of the new/enhanced feature and how you'll benefit from it. Remember, there are many changes, both large and small (and each person's idea of "large" versus "small" may vary), so this isn't everything:

- **New toolbox layout (Chapter 2):** The toolbox can now be displayed in a single vertical column of tools, or the old two-column arrangement many of us have come to know and love. Of course, the tools themselves look the same and those that are grouped under a single button location are in those same groupings, so you won't be struggling to figure out where things are. The idea behind this change is to simplify access to the tools, making grabbing a particular tool with the mouse easier. You're less likely to click the tool's neighbor when the only neighbors are above and below, not side by side as well.

- **No ImageReady button on the toolbox (Chapters 19 and 20):** ImageReady is gone. Now, now, wipe those tears and keep reading. While the application is gone, its features are not. They're now housed completely within Photoshop. We've seen many of ImageReady's tools for animation migrate to Photoshop in the previous two versions, but the assimilation is now complete. Between the new Timeline palette (a version of the Animation palette, both of which are discussed later) and the Save for Web dialog box, there's nothing you did with ImageReady that you can't do within Photoshop.

■ **Changed palettes (Chapter 2):** The palettes are in roughly the same spots as they were in CS2, but their connection to the workspace has changed. The palettes are affixed to the right side of the workspace as part of a static dock and can be collapsed and expanded individually, in groups, or you can choose to expand the dock so that all the palettes and palette groups are displayed at the same time. You can still separate a particular palette from the dock and drag it anywhere onscreen, though, so don't think you can't bring your tools with you when you go to work, because you can. You also can drag the one or two palettes you need with you and collapse the rest to make as much room for your image as needed. You'll also notice tabs on the left side of the palette dock (when the palettes are in their default arrangement, with just one column of palettes visible). You can click the tabs to display different palettes and palette groups, providing yet another way to get at the palette you need, when you need it.

■ **The Analysis menu (Chapter 3):** Now you can really control how your image measurements are made — visually, by you, using the displayed rulers, or with measurement features implemented within your image. Through the Analysis menu, you can set up a measurement scale, set data points within your image, measure elements within your image, customize your rulers and counting tools, and apply scale markers. For those images where the distance between points A and B is important, and where you need to determine for yourself where points A and B are, this development is a big benefit.

■ **The Animation/Timeline palette (Chapter 19):** The ability to create animations and movies, with tools that will remind some of you of Macromedia's Flash application (now that Adobe and Macromedia are one and the same), are housed in the new Timeline palette, which is part of the Animation palette. You'll use this palette for many of the things you used to do in ImageReady, and in Photoshop CS2 with the Animation palette that premiered with that version of the software. In addition to creating animations and movies, you also can use this timeline to view video frame by frame, and with the enhanced Clone tool (described below), you can clone between frames in a video.

■ **The Clone Source palette (Chapter 7):** You can plot up to five clone sources, from locations within one or more images, and after setting them, use this new palette to switch between them when using the Clone Stamp. The palette also allows you to set offsets, horizontal and vertical scale, angles, overlay, and opacity for the cloned content from each clone source.

■ **The Measure Tool (Chapter 3):** Used along with the new Measurement Scale command, you can set a measurement scale by dragging within your image. You also can drag to measure any distance within the image, and the value appears in the Info palette. Measurements made with this tool (and the Measurement Scale command) find their way into the Measurement Log palette, which is also new.

■ **The Measurement Log palette (Chapter 3):** Keep track of your measurements (made with the new Measurement tool) with this palette, through which you can also track your measurements, use measurements from one image in another, select all stored measurements, or delete them.

■ **Smart Filters (Chapter 10):** If you've turned any layer in your image into a Smart Object (or opened an image as a Smart Object), your filters are applied as Smart Filters. What's so smart about them? They appear, after you apply them, in the Layers palette, where you can turn them on and off and delete them entirely. This makes filtering something much more flexible than ever, because filters can be applied and then un-applied later — without having to rely on the History Palette or Undo to get rid of their effects.

■ **More support for video (Chapter 19):** Photoshop CS3 supports new formats and allows you to import and expert image sequences and frames. You also can take advantage of expanded QuickTime export capabilities, which include exporting to Flash Video (FLV). Layered video is now also supported in the Timeline palette, and you can work with them in grayscale, RGB, CMYK, and Lab document modes, at 16-bit, as well as 32-bit depth.

This list covers just some of the big changes you'll find in CS3 — there are lots of smaller changes throughout, many applying to existing tools. For example, you'll find enhancements to the Brightness/Contrast dialog box and improvements in the selection tools, in terms of the addition of a Refine Edge option that allows you to do just that — clean up the edges of a selection. You'll find support for creating graphics for use on handheld devices in the new version of the Save for Web dialog box (now called the Save for Web and Devices dialog box), and of course, the Bridge has changed, too — in many ways for the better.

Summary

Photoshop CS3 is a major upgrade, made up of significant interface changes and several big changes and enhancements throughout the application. This chapter's goal has been to familiarize you with what to expect from CS3 and where you can find coverage of the new features throughout this book. You're now ready to move forward and focus, chapter by chapter, on exploring Photoshop CS3 — the features that have always been part of Photoshop but may be new to you, and the new and changed features that will be new for everyone. See you in Chapter 2!

Chapter 2

Photoshop Inside Out

D espite the sometimes enigmatic quality of computers and software, we can count on certain things in just about any computer application—toolbars, menus, keyboard shortcuts (some of them common to many applications), and dialog boxes that appear when the toolbar buttons and menu commands are used. All these common features do two things: They help us feel more comfortable with different applications, which shortens our overall learning curve, and they help us devote our time to the features that vary by application—the things that make each application unique.

You'll find all the aforementioned familiar features in Photoshop, which should put you at ease. At first glance, the workspace—the default arrangement of the Toolbox, menu bar, and a handful of palettes—looks simple enough, and in fact, Photoshop *can* be simple to use. Upon further inspection, of course, you'll find that Photoshop has much more going on than many applications. Photoshop has lots of palettes, some unique menus, and options bars. Photoshop CS3 also continues to offer the Bridge, which premiered in CS2, which provides a separate application workspace for file management. Add to that the fact that some of the dialog boxes can be a little intimidating to a new user, and you may wonder if you can really learn to use it all—but don't worry; you can.

For new users, the Photoshop workspace can seem like lots to absorb, but absorb it you will, and through this chapter, you get more comfortable with the program, its tools, menus, and the process of navigating it all. If you're not new to Photoshop, this chapter shows you some new features Adobe has added to the workspace, and you may even discover some things that aren't new to Photoshop but that are new to you.

The aforementioned Bridge — that name is a trifle dramatic, but fear not — is covered in Chapter 3, where its role as an image file management tool is thoroughly discussed. In Chapter 20, you see the Bridge used to print and publish various multiple-image creations. For now, though, let's fire up Photoshop CS3 and start poking around!

Diving in with the Splash Screen

Shortly after you launch Photoshop, the *splash screen* appears. A splash screen is not a phenomenon unique to Photoshop — many applications have one. The splash screen's role is to announce the application's launch, maybe offer some marketing information (here, it's simply the name of the software and a cool graphic to assure you that you're in the right place to create cool graphics), and to explain the launching process by showing the names of plug-in modules as they load and listing the various initialization procedures. In Photoshop, the splash also lists the names of Photoshop's developers, going all the way back (note the first names in the list) to the beginning, when Photoshop 1.0 was just a baby.

TIP   If you're a Windows user, you can access the splash screen at any time by choosing Help ⇨ About Photoshop. On the Mac, choose About Photoshop from the Photoshop menu. After a few seconds, the list of programmers and copyright statements at the bottom of the screen starts to scroll. Press Alt (Option on the Mac) to make the list scroll more quickly. To make the splash screen go away, just click it or press the Esc key.

NOTE   If you've ever tried to launch Photoshop on a networked computer while another computer on the network is already running a copy of Photoshop using the same serial number, you're familiar with the message "Could not initialize Photoshop because So-and-So is already running a copy of Adobe Photoshop with this serial number." There are two important things to note here: One is that you can work around this by simply detaching the second computer from the network before you launch Photoshop. After the application is open, re-network the computer, and you'll be up and running. And the other important thing to note is that with Mac OS X, this network problem doesn't occur.

Using the Photoshop Workspace

After the launch process is complete, the Photoshop workspace appears in the foreground. Figure 2.1 shows the Photoshop CS3 workspace as it appears for a Windows user when an image is open and the default palettes are visible. You'll use the Window menu to select additional palettes to view, or use the techniques discussed later in this chapter for displaying, minimizing, and closing palettes. Figure 2.2 shows the same scenario as it appears on a Mac running Mac OS X.

Many of the elements that make up the Photoshop workspace are familiar to people who are acquainted with the Windows or Macintosh operating system environments. For example, the menu bar lives at the top of the workspace (as it lives at the top of the window for virtually all applications) and provides access to menus and commands. Even the way the menus work should be comfortable to users of both operating systems. At the top of the window, you have a title bar, and you can drag the title bar to move the application window (assuming it's not already maximized). In either operating system, you have scroll bars in your windows if there's more to be seen than will fit in the window at its current size.

These other Photoshop workspace features may be less familiar:

■ **Image window:** Photoshop lets you open multiple images at one time — you can open them simultaneously from the Open dialog box, or one at a time, over the course of a work session. The nice thing is that each open image resides in its own window. On the Mac, click the green zoom button in the upper-left corner of the title bar to resize the window to fit the image. Also worth noting are the special boxes in the lower-left corner of the image window (see Figure 2.2). The magnification box tells you the current view size, and the Info palette can tell you important things about image size and computer resources.

FIGURE 2.1

The Photoshop CS3 workspace as it looks for a user running Windows

- **Status bar:** In each image window, you find the Status bar, which provides running commentary on the active tool and image. (If your image is maximized, it appears above the Windows taskbar.) The left end of the Status bar features the magnification box (type a new number into the box and that becomes the zoom percentage), an Open icon, the current size of the image file, and a right-pointing triangle that displays a list of additional information you can choose to see in the Status bar. This list includes the default information about the document size, the document profile, dimensions, measurement scale, scratch sizes, efficiency, timing, the name of the active tool, and the option to preview an HDR (High Dynamic Range) image at 32-bit exposure. To access these options, click the aforementioned triangle and select Show from the resulting pop-up menu.

CROSS-REF   For complete information on the magnification box, read the section "Navigating in Photoshop" later in this chapter.

FIGURE 2.2

The Photoshop CS3 workspace as it looks on a Mac.

- **Toolbox:** The Toolbox, which is somewhat changed in CS3, gives you access to all of Photoshop's tools. Each tool is represented by an icon, and the icons are activated with a single click or the press of a keyboard shortcut (single characters, such as V for the Move tool, or B for the paintbrush). Some tools share a single spot in the Toolbox, and to access the "hidden" tools (as only one tool can be displayed in a spot at once), you can use keyboard shortcuts or your mouse to get at them. Once activated, you can use a tool by clicking or dragging with it inside the image window. When you click on any tool, observe the Options bar, across the top of the workspace, below the menus. The Options bar changes with each tool selected, offering choices for how the active tool operates.

   The bottom five buttons on the Toolbox (at the bottom of the last section of tools) contain controls for changing your foreground and background paint colors, entering and exiting the quick mask mode, and changing the screen area available for image display. In CS2, there was also a button for launching ImageReady, but as we've discussed, that application is gone, its powers absorbed and assimilated into Photoshop, so there is no ImageReady button on the Toolbox anymore.

- **Palettes:** Photoshop CS3 offers a total of 21 palettes, not including the Toolbox and the Options bar, which are technically palettes as well. Each palette is part of the larger palette dock, which is a fixed part of the workspace that resides on the right side of the workspace. You can separate palettes from the dock and make them float, which means that the palette becomes independent of the image window and of other palettes. Palettes can be grouped together or dragged apart to float separately according to your needs — you may want a specific palette or group of palettes on hand for a particular image and have no need for some of the default palettes at all. Photoshop makes it easy to customize the workspace, as you find later on in this chapter and as you work through the rest of the book. To see the whole list of palettes, click your Window menu.

The Info palette

The Info palette, one of the default palettes that are displayed when Photoshop is opened for the first time, is Photoshop's way of keeping you informed of important things. It provides one-stop shopping for all your image information needs. These important things include the size of the image, the tool that's in use, where your image is on the page (if it were to be printed), how much memory you're using — lots of stuff you may or may not want to know at any given time. You don't have to display the Info palette if you don't want to (it's displayed in Figure 2.3), or you may be thrilled that it's there and feel anxious when you can't see it — but it's there if you need it. The following sections explain all the useful things it can tell you.

FIGURE 2.3

Click the palette menu button to display the Info Palette Options dialog box, which shows the info you can choose to see.

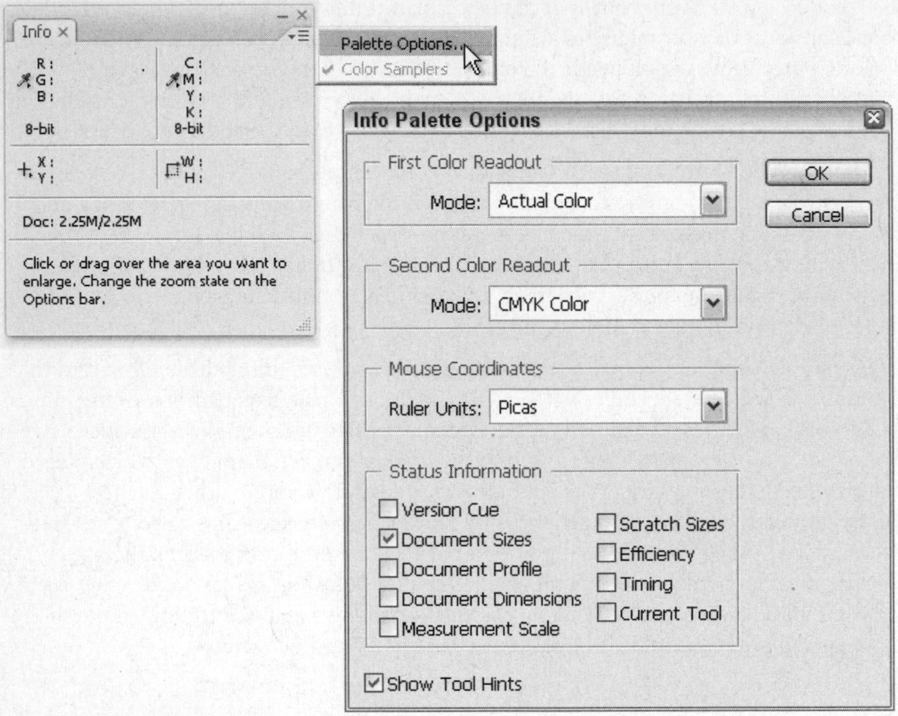

Document size

By default, the Info palette contains two numbers divided by a slash. The first number is the size of the base image in memory. The second number takes into account any additional layers in your image. If you're interested in how the values are calculated, here goes:

Photoshop calculates the first value by multiplying the height and width of the image (both in pixels) by the *bit depth* of the image, which is the size of each pixel in memory. Consider a typical, full-color, 640×480-pixel image. A full-color image takes up 24 bits of memory per pixel (which is why it's called a 24-bit image). There are 8 bits in a byte, so 24 bits translates to 3 bytes. Multiply that by the number of pixels, and you get 640×480×3 = 921,600 bytes. Because there are 1,024 bytes in a kilobyte, 921,600 bytes is exactly 900K. Try it yourself — open a 640×480-pixel RGB image, and you'll see that the first number in the Info palette reads 900K. Now you know why.

It's the second value — the one that factors in the layers — that represents the real amount of memory that Photoshop needs. If the image contains one layer only, the numbers before and after the slash are the same. Otherwise, Photoshop measures the opaque pixels in each layer and adds approximately 1 byte of overhead per pixel to calculate the transparency. The second number also grows to accommodate paths, masks, spot-color channels, undoable operations, and miscellaneous data required by the image cache.

Of course, it's not necessary that you be able to predict these values, which is a good thing, because predicting the second value is virtually impossible. Photoshop asks no help when calculating the values in the information, but you should know what's going on as you start adding layers to an image. The larger the preview numbers grow, the more work Photoshop has to do and the slower it's likely to perform, depending on your system configuration — memory, processor, available hard-drive space, and so on.

Image position

If you want to position a picture precisely on a page before printing, use the Print command in the File menu (see Chapter 20 for details). New to Photoshop CS3, the Print command contains not only options for determining how your image will print, but a preview of the print job as well. This combines the Print and Print with Preview commands from CS2 into a single command.

> **TIP**   Speaking of "Info," for more information, you can Ctrl-click (⌘-click on the Mac) the status bar's display of the document size to see the tile sizes. Photoshop uses *tiles* to calculate pixel manipulations. If you confine your work to a single tile, it probably will go faster than if you allow a little to run over into a second tile.

To see a pop-up menu of other information the Info palette can provide, click the Info palette's palette menu to display a pop-up menu of display options. The first option — Document Sizes — is selected by default. This option displays the image-size values described in the preceding section. You find out what information the other choices provide in the next few sections.

Image color

If you work regularly with many different color modes, you may find the Document Profile option quite useful. When you select this option, the name of the current color mode (such as "RGB 8bpc") appears in the Info palette.

> **CROSS-REF**   For more information on color profiles, see Chapter 17, where you can find everything you need to know about color profiles — how to apply them and what they do.

Document measurements

Choosing to view Document Dimensions gives you a quick readout of the width-by-height measurements of your document. The unit of measurement is set in the Units & Rulers panel of Photoshop's Preferences dialog box, and conveniently enough, you learn more about setting such preferences later on in this chapter.

Memory consumption and availability

When you select Scratch Sizes, Photoshop changes the values in the Info palette to represent memory consumption and availability. The first value is the amount of room required to hold the currently open images in RAM. The second value indicates the total amount of RAM that Photoshop has to work with. For the program to run at top efficiency, the first number must be smaller than the second.

In earlier versions of Photoshop, the number before the slash was generally equal to between three and five times the size of all open images, including layers. Since we have had the ability to undo multiple levels (going back multiple states through the History palette), however, this value can grow to more than 100 times as big as any one image. This is because Photoshop has to store each operation in memory on the off chance that you may want to undo to a previous point in time. For each and every action, Photoshop nudges the first value upward until you reach the ceiling of undoable operations.

The second value is simply equal to the amount of memory available to your images after the Photoshop application itself has loaded. For example, suppose Photoshop has 100MB of RAM at its disposal. The code that makes up the Photoshop application consumes about 15MB, so that leaves 85MB to hold and edit images.

If the second value is bigger than the first, all is happiness and Photoshop is running as fast as your particular brand of computer permits. But if the first value is larger, Photoshop has to dig into its supply of *virtual memory*, a disk-bound adjunct to RAM. Virtual memory makes Photoshop run more slowly because the program must swap portions of the image on and off your hard drive. The simple fact is, hard drives have moving parts and RAM does not. That means disk-bound virtual memory is slower than real memory.

To increase the size of the value after the slash, you have to get more RAM to your images in one of the following ways:

- Purchase more RAM. Installing an adequate supply of memory is the single best way to make Photoshop run more quickly. Not sure how? Consult your manufacturer, or get help from the company from whom you buy the RAM.
- Quit other applications so that only Photoshop is running.
- Quit Photoshop, and remove any filters you don't need from the Plug-Ins folder (which resides in the same folder as the Photoshop application). But don't throw the filters away! Just move them to a location outside the Plug-Ins folder so they don't load into RAM when you launch Photoshop.
- Choose Performance in the Preferences submenu, and increase the Memory Usage value as explained later in this chapter.

Operating efficiency

When you select the Efficiency option, Photoshop lists the amount of time it spends running operations in RAM compared with swapping data back and forth between the hard drive. A value of

100 percent is the best-case scenario. It means Photoshop never has to rely on scratch files. Low values indicate higher reliance on the hard drive and, as a result, slower operations. Adobe recommends that if the value falls below 75 percent, you should either assign more memory to Photoshop or purchase more RAM for your computer.

The Efficiency option is a reality check. If it seems Photoshop is dragging its feet, and you hear it writing to your hard drive a little too often, you can refer to the Efficiency rating to see whether performance is as bad as you suspect. Keep in mind that hearing Photoshop occasionally write to disk is not cause for concern. All versions of Photoshop since 3.0 automatically copy open images to a disk buffer in case using virtual memory is later warranted. In fact, this is the reason Adobe added the Efficiency option to Version 3.0.1 — to quash fears that a few sparks from your hard drive indicated anything less than peak performance.

Photoshop operations timing

If you select Timing, the Info palette tells how long Photoshop took to perform the last operation (including background tasks, such as transferring an image to the system Clipboard). Adobe may have added this option to help testing facilities run their Photoshop tests. But built-in timing helps you as well.

For example, suppose you're trying to decide whether to purchase a new computer. You read a magazine article detailing the newest super-fast system. You can run the same filters with the same settings on your computer and see how much slower your results are, all without picking up a stopwatch.

Measurement Scale

New to Photoshop CS3, the Measurement Scale option for the Info palette shows the status of the currently set Measurement Scale. You can set this using the Set Measurement Scale command in the Analysis menu. You learn more about this command and all the other ways the new Measurement Scale feature is used in Chapter 3. If you haven't set a custom scale for the open image, the Info palette doesn't display anything pertaining to this. After you have set a scale, however, the status of what you set appears in the next-to-last position.

The active tool

Select the Current Tool option, and Photoshop displays the name of the active tool. Why do you need information on what seems to be so obvious? Of course you know which tool you're using, right? Adobe's intention is not to insult your intelligence or short-term memory with redundant information, but to remind you which tool is active, especially if something you've selected has changed the active tool. For example, if you choose Analysis ➪ Measurement Scale, the active tool changes to Ruler, regardless of what you were using before issuing the command. The active tool returns to the one you were using as soon as the Measurement Scale dialog box closes, but you see the switch reflected in the Info palette while the dialog box is open. Of course, you may find that having all this information displayed in the Info palette is of limited use. Maybe you only want to see Timing or Efficiency information and you choose to use the Status bar to show you the Document size. Whatever you want to see, however, you can customize the palette quickly, making it provide just what interests you in any given image.

The tools

When multiple tools share a single Toolbox slot, you select the tool you want from a menu-style list, as shown in Figure 2.4. A tiny triangle in the lower-right corner of a Toolbox button indicates that multiple tools share that button. You can click the triangle and then click the name of the tool you want to use. Or, to do the job with one less click, just drag from the icon onto the name of the tool and then release the mouse button.

FIGURE 2.4

Drag from any tool icon with a triangle to display a pop-up menu of alternate tools.

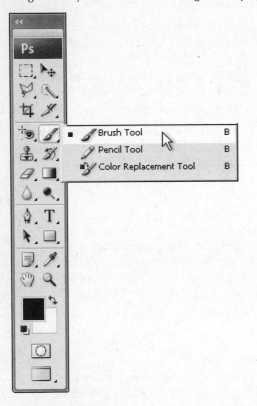

TIP   You can cycle between the tools in the pop-up menu by Alt-clicking (Win) or Option-clicking (Mac) a tool icon. Pressing the key that appears to the right of the tool names also does the trick — however, depending on a tool setting that you establish in the Preferences dialog box, you may need to press Shift (see the section "General preferences").

Also, when you position your cursor over a tool, Photoshop tells you the name of the tool and how to select it from the keyboard. If you find the tool tips irritating, see the section "General preferences" to find out how to turn them off.

Each tool has been cataloged in the following list, with tool icons, quick summaries, and the chapter (if any) to which you can refer for more information. There's no need to read the list word for word; instead, just use it as a reference to get acquainted with the program or specific tools with which you may be unfamiliar. Unless otherwise noted, each of the following descriptions tells how to use the tool in the image window. For example, if an item says drag, you click the tool's icon to select the tool, and then click and drag in the image window; you don't drag on the tool icon itself. Of course, you probably knew that!

 Move (Chapter 8): Drag to move a selection or layer. In fact, the Move tool is the exclusive means for moving and cloning portions of an image. You also can Ctrl-drag (Win) or ⌘-drag (Mac) selections with any tools except the Shape, Path, and Slicing tools, but only because Ctrl (⌘ on the Mac) temporarily accesses the Move tool.

 Rectangular marquee (Chapter 8): Drag with this tool to enclose a portion of the image in a rectangular *marquee*, which is a pattern of moving dash marks indicating the boundary of a selection.

Shift-drag to add to a selection; Alt-drag (Win) or Option-drag (Mac) to delete from a selection. The same goes for the other marquee tools, as well as the lassos and the Magic Wand. As an alternative to using these time-honored shortcuts, you can click mode icons in the Options bar to change the behavior of the selection tools.

 Elliptical Marquee (Chapter 8): Drag with the Elliptical Marquee tool to enclose a portion of the window in an elliptical marquee.

 Single-Row Marquee (Chapter 8): Click with the Single-Row Marquee tool to select an entire horizontal row of pixels that stretches all the way across the image. You also can drag with the tool to position the selection. You rarely need the Single-Row Marquee, but when you do, here it is.

 Single-Column Marquee (Chapter 8): Same as the Single-Row Marquee, except the Single-Column Marquee tool selects an entire vertical column of pixels. Again, not a particularly useful tool.

 Lasso (Chapter 8): Drag with the Lasso tool to select a free-form portion of the image. You also can Alt-click (Win) or Option-click (Mac) with the Lasso to create a straight-sided selection outline.

Polygonal Lasso (Chapter 8): Click hither and yon with this tool to draw a straight-sided selection outline (just like Alt-clicking or Option-clicking with the standard lasso). Each click sets a corner point in the selection.

Magnetic Lasso (Chapter 8): As you drag with the Magnetic Lasso tool, the selection outline automatically sticks to the edge of the foreground image. Bear in mind, however, that Photoshop's idea of an edge may not jibe with yours. Like any automated tool, the Magnetic Lasso sometimes works wonders, and other times it's more trouble than it's worth.

 TIP   The Magnetic Lasso automatically lays down points as you drag. If you don't like a point and want to get rid of it, press Backspace (Win) or Delete (Mac).

Quick Selection Tool (Chapter 8): This selection tool allows you to paint a selection, sampling pixels on one or all layers as you drag the mouse. It shares a spot in the Toolbox with the Magic Wand because it also works by sampling pixels, and that process is customized with the Options bar and the Refine Edge dialog box, which allows you to control the selection process as it pertains to the edges of the selection.

NEW FEATURE The Quick Selection Tool is new in Photoshop CS3.

 Magic Wand (Chapter 8): Click with the Magic Wand tool to select a contiguous area of similarly colored pixels. To select noncontiguous areas, click in one area and then Shift+click in another. Deselect the Contiguous tool option, and click once to select similar colors throughout the image.

 Crop (Chapter 3): Drag with the Crop tool to enclose the portion of the image you want to retain in a rectangular boundary. Photoshop tints areas outside the boundary to help you better see which image areas will go and which will stay when you apply the crop. The crop boundary sports several square handles that you can drag to resize the cropped area. Drag outside the boundary to rotate it; drag inside to move it. Press Enter or Return to apply the crop or Esc to cancel.

 Slice (Chapter 20): The Slice tool and its companion, the Slice Select tool, come into play when you're creating Web graphics. You can cut images into rectangular sections — known as slices — so you can apply Web effects, such as links, rollovers, and animations, to different areas of the same image. Drag with the Slice Tool to define the area that you want to turn into a slice.

 Slice Select (Chapter 20): If you don't get the boundary of your slice right the first time, click the slice with this tool and drag one of the side or corner handles that appear. Or drag inside the boundary to relocate it.

Press Ctrl (Win) or ⌘ (Mac) when the Slice tool is active to temporarily access the Slice Select tool, and vice versa.

 Spot Healing Brush (Chapter 7): This tool is new to Photoshop CS2 and works similarly to the Healing Brush — it clones other content over offending material and makes it match the new surroundings. It's different from the Healing Brush in that it is simpler to use, fixes one spot at a time, and is best used for small problems — small stains, cuts, scratches, or small items in the image itself that you want to eradicate.

 Healing Brush (Chapter 7): The Clone Stamp tool (also known to longtime Photoshop users as the Rubber Stamp tool) has always seemed like a miracle worker when removing unwanted elements from images. Although excellent results were possible, you still had to be careful that the texture and shading of the cloned area matched the area you were replacing. Although the Healing Brush tool seems at first use just like the Clone Stamp tool, its special "healing" process lets you clone details from one area without obscuring the texture and shading of the other.

 Patch (Chapter 7): Similar to the Healing Brush, the Patch tool lets you use the same "healing" technology by making selections and dragging them to new locations. It's generally useful for healing larger areas of the image.

Red Eye Removal (Chapter 7): Click the offending demonic pool of red, yellow, or green, and based on your Options bar settings, remove the glow in favor of a dark pupil. This isn't the cure-all for red-eye (or the yellow-eye or green-eye you get when photographing animals' eyes), and you may find that it still pays to remove red-eye manually, using one or more of Photoshop's other painting tools, but for a quick fix, this certainly lives up to its name.

 Brush (Chapter 5): Drag with the Brush tool to paint soft lines. If you're thinking that sounds kind of dull, wait until you learn about the multitude of settings available to you in the Brushes palette.

 Pencil (Chapter 5): Drag with the Pencil tool to paint jagged, hard-edged lines. Its main purpose is to clean up individual pixels when you want to zoom in and really tidy up an edge or create details to augment the existing pixels' impact on the image.

 Color Replacement (Chapter 5): Hailing from Photoshop's younger sibling, Photoshop Elements, the Color Replacement tool lets you paint over an existing color in the image to replace it with the foreground color. Its main reason for existence is to make it easy to fix red-eye — but now that there is also a tool specifically for that purpose, you may have to find another reason to use it.

 Clone Stamp (Chapter 7): Greatly enhanced in Photoshop CS3, this tool copies one portion of the image onto another. Alt-click (Win) or Option-click (Mac) the part of your image you want to clone, and then drag to clone that area to another portion of the image. The enhancement comes in the form of a new palette, called Clone Source, which allows you to set up to five clone sources and customize their size, position, and impact on the image.

Pattern Stamp (Chapter 6): The Pattern Stamp tool lets you paint with a pattern. Either choose a preset pattern (several come with Photoshop) or define your own pattern using Edit ➪ Define Pattern command. Either way, after your pattern is selected and your brush settings established (for size, among other settings you learn about in Chapter 7), you can paint to your pattern-loving heart's content.

 History Brush (Chapter 7): The History Brush reverts portions of the image to any of a handful of previous states throughout the recent history of the image. To specify the state that you want to revert to, click in the first column of the History palette. It's like an undo brush but way, way better.

 Art History Brush (Chapter 7): Like the History Brush, the Art History Brush paints with pixels from a previous image state. But with this brush, you get a variety of brush options that create different artistic effects.

 Eraser (Chapter 7): Drag with the Eraser tool to paint in the background color or erase areas in a layer to reveal the layers below. Alt-drag (Win) or Option-drag (Mac) to switch to the Erase to History mode, which reverts the image to a previous state just as if you were using the History Brush.

 Background Eraser (Chapter 9): The Background Eraser rubs away the background from an image as you drag along the border between the background and foreground. If you don't wield this tool carefully, though, you wind up erasing both background and foreground.

Magic Eraser (Chapter 9): The Magic Eraser came from the same gene pool that produced the Magic Wand. When you click with the Magic Wand, Photoshop selects a range of similarly colored pixels; click with the Magic Eraser, and you erase instead of select.

 Gradient (Chapter 6): Drag with this tool to fill a selection with a gradual transition of colors, commonly called a *gradient.* You can click the gradient icon in the Toolbox and select a gradient style from the Options bar.

Paint Bucket (Chapter 6): Click with the Paint Bucket tool to fill a contiguous area of similarly colored pixels with the foreground color or a predefined pattern.

 Blur (Chapter 5): Drag with the Blur tool to diffuse the contrast between neighboring pixels, which blurs the focus of the image. You also can Alt-drag (Win) or Option-drag (Mac) to sharpen the image.

 Sharpen (Chapter 5): Drag with this tool to increase the contrast between pixels, which sharpens the focus. Alt-drag (Win) or Option-drag (Mac) when this tool is active to blur the image.

 Smudge (Chapter 5): The Smudge tool works just as its name implies; drag with the tool to smear colors inside the image.

 Dodge (Chapter 5): Drag with the Dodge tool to lighten pixels in the image. Alt-drag (Win) or Option-drag (Mac) to darken the image.

 Burn (Chapter 5): Drag with the Burn tool to darken pixels. Press Alt (Win) or Option (Mac) to temporarily access the Dodge tool and lighten pixels.

 Sponge (Chapter 5): Drag with the Sponge tool to decrease the amount of saturation in an image so the colors appear more drab and eventually gray. You also can increase color saturation by changing the Mode setting in the Options bar from Desaturate to Saturate.

 Path Selection (Chapter 8): Click anywhere inside a path to select the entire path. If you click inside a path that contains multiple subpaths, Photoshop selects the subpath under the tool cursor. Shift+click to select additional paths or subpaths. You also use this tool and the Direct Selection tool, described next, to select and manipulate lines and shapes drawn with the shape tools.

 Direct Selection (Chapter 8): To select and edit a segment in a selected path or shape, click it or drag over it with this tool. Press Shift while using the tool to select additional segments. Or Alt-click (Option-click on the Mac) inside a path or shape to select and edit the entire object.

 Horizontal Type (Chapter 16): Also known simply as the Type tool, click with this tool to add vector text to your image.

Vertical Type (Chapter 16): The Vertical Type tool behaves just like the Horizontal Type tool, except that your text is oriented vertically in the image.

Horizontal Type Mask (Chapter 16): As you might expect, this tool creates horizontal type. The twist is that the type appears not directly in the image but rather as a mask, with an active selection around the shapes of the letters.

Vertical Type Mask (Chapter 16): Combine the verticality of the Vertical Type tool with the maskiness of the Horizontal Type Mask tool, and you have — what else? — the Vertical Type Mask tool. Use it to create an active selection of vertically oriented text.

Pen (Chapter 8): Click and drag with the Pen tool to set points in the image window. Photoshop draws an editable path outline — much like a path in Illustrator — that you can convert to a selection outline or stroke with color.

 Freeform Pen (Chapter 8): Drag with this tool to draw freehand paths or vector masks. Photoshop automatically adds points along the path as it sees fit. If you select the Magnetic option in the Options bar, the Freeform Pen morphs into the Magnetic Pen. Deselect the option to return to the Freeform Pen.

 Add Anchor Point (Chapter 8): To insert a point in a path, click a path segment with this tool.

 Delete Anchor Point (Chapter 8): Click a point to remove it without interrupting the outline of the path. Photoshop automatically draws a new segment between the neighboring points.

 Convert Point (Chapter 8): Points in a path come in different varieties, some indicating corners and others indicating smooth arcs. The Convert Point tool enables you to change one kind of point to another. Drag a point to convert it from a corner to an arc. Click a point to convert it from an arc to a sharp corner.

 Rectangle (Chapter 15): One of the five vector drawing tools, this tool draws rectangles filled with the foreground color. Just click and drag to create a rectangle; Shift-drag to draw a square.

 Rounded Rectangle (Chapter 15): Prefer your boxes with nice, curved corners instead of sharp, 90-degree angles? Drag or Shift-drag with the Rounded Rectangle tool.

CROSS-REF You can opt to create rasterized shapes and lines with the Rectangle, Rounded Rectangle, Ellipse, Polygon, Line, and Custom Shape tools. See Chapter 15 for details.

 Ellipse (Chapter 15): You look pretty smart to me, so you probably already figured out that you drag with this tool to draw an ellipse and Shift-drag to draw a circle.

Polygon (Chapter 15): By default, dragging with this tool creates a five-sided polygon. Controls available in the Options bar enable you to change the number of sides or set the tool to create star shapes.

Line (Chapter 15): Drag with the Line tool to create a straight line. But before you do, travel to the Options bar to set the line thickness and specify whether you want arrowheads at the ends of the line.

Custom Shape (Chapter 15 Draw any of a vast array of custom shapes, from paw prints to cartoon bubbles, from arrows to starbursts.

Notes (Chapter 3): Use this tool to create a little sticky note on which you can jot down thoughts, ideas, and other pertinent info that you want to share with other people who work with the image — or that you simply want to remember the next time you open the image. After you create the note, Photoshop displays a note icon in the image window; double-click the icon to see what you had to say.

Audio Annotation (Chapter 3): If you prefer the spoken word to the written one, you can annotate your images with an audio clip, assuming that you have a microphone and sound card for your computer. As with the Notes tool, an audio icon appears in the image window after you record your message. Clicking the icon plays the audio clip.

Eyedropper (Chapter 4): Click with the Eyedropper tool on a color in the image window to make that color the foreground color. Alt-click (Win) or Option-click (Mac) a color to make that color the background color.

 Color Sampler (Chapter 4): Click as many as four locations in an image to evaluate the colors of those pixels in the Info palette. After you set a point, you can move it by dragging it to a different pixel.

 Ruler (Chapter 3): The Ruler tool lets you measure distances and directions inside the image window. Just drag from one point to another, and note the measurement data in the Info palette or the Options bar. You also can drag the endpoints of your line to take new measurements. And by Alt-dragging (Win) or Option-dragging (Mac) an endpoint, you can create a sort of virtual protractor that measures angles.

 Count (Chapter 3): Use the Count tool to mark and number locations in your image, on any layer. As you use the Count tool, you can see the information about the exact location that you've clicked in the Info palette.

 Hand (Chapter 2): Drag inside the image window with the Hand tool to scroll the window so you can see a different portion of the image. Double-click the Hand tool icon to magnify or reduce the image so it fits on the screen in its entirety. When the Hand tool is active, you can click buttons in the Options bar to display the image at the actual-pixels, fit-onscreen, or print-size view sizes.

 Zoom (Chapter 2): Click with the Zoom tool to magnify the image so you can see individual pixels more clearly. Alt-click (Win) or Option-click (Mac) to step back from the image and take in a broader view. Drag to enclose the specific portion of the image you want to magnify. And finally, double-click the Zoom tool icon inside the Toolbox to restore the image to 100 percent view size.

You can modify the performance of any tool except the Ruler tool (the "options" shown for this tool simply note the measurements between the locations on which you've clicked the tool) by adjusting the settings in the Options bar. To change the unit of measurement used by the Ruler tool, double-click the ruler or choose Edit ⇨ Preferences ⇨ Units & Rulers (Photoshop ⇨ Preferences ⇨ Units & Rulers in Mac OS X) to display the Units & Rulers panel of the Preferences dialog box. Then select the unit from the Rulers pop-up menu. Or even quicker, right-click (Win) or Control-click (Mac) the ruler or click the plus sign in the lower-left corner of the Info palette and select a measurement unit from the resulting pop-up menu.

The Toolbox controls

So that's about it for the Photoshop CS3 tools — except for a few more tools that are actually known as controls. These controls are used for selecting colors, views of the workspace, and working in a masking mode.

 Foreground color: Click the foreground color icon to bring up the Color Picker dialog box. Select a color and press Enter or Return to change the foreground color, which is used by the Pencil, Paintbrush, Airbrush, Gradient, and shape tools.

Background color: Click the background color icon to display the Color Picker and change the background color, which is used by the Eraser and Gradient tools. Photoshop also uses the background color to fill a selected area on the background layer when you press the Backspace or Delete key.

Switch colors: Click the switch colors icon to exchange the foreground and background colors.

Default colors: Click this icon to return to the default foreground and background colors — black and white, respectively.

> **TIP** At any time, you can quickly make the foreground color white by clicking the default colors icon and then clicking the switch colors icon. Or just press D (for default colors) and then X (for switch colors).

 Quick Mask: Click here to enter the Quick Mask mode, which enables you to edit selection boundaries using painting tools. If you make a selection prior to entering this mode, the selection's "marching ants" (those flashing dashes that surround your selection) vanish and the image appears covered by a translucent layer of red, like a rubylith in traditional paste-up. The red layer covers the deselected — or masked — portions of the image. Paint with black to extend the masked areas, thereby subtracting from the selection. Paint with white to erase the mask, thereby adding to the selection.

> **CROSS-REF** The Quick Mask mode is too complex a topic to sum up in a few sentences. If you can't wait to find out what it's all about, check out Chapter 9.

Screen Modes

Regardless of the program in question, a workspace is all about getting work done. Photoshop gives you four screen modes to suite various workflows.

Standard Screen mode: This is the default display mode, as shown earlier in Figures 2.1 and 2.2. In this mode, your images appear in a standard window, and you have access to all title and menu bars.

Maximized Screen mode: Sometimes you just need a little more space. This mode explodes the standard window, losing its title bar, allowing it to fill all available space not occupied by the palettes.

> **NOTE** This is similar to the effect that you get when you click the Maximize button in the upper-right corner of the image window on a PC. However, you probably want to avoid maximizing images; use the Toolbox controls instead. Photoshop has a habit of resizing a maximized window whenever you zoom with the commands on the View menu. If you use the Toolbox controls, you don't have that problem.

 Full Screen with Menu Bar mode: If Maximized Screen mode doesn't do it for you, perhaps this mode will. In Full Screen with Menu Bar mode, shown in Figure 2.5, the title bars and scroll bars disappear. Only the menu bar and palettes remain visible, and the image area also occupies space behind the palettes, whose dock becomes partially transparent. To access other open images, you simply choose their names from the Window menu.

FIGURE 2.5

Full Screen with Menu Bar mode gives you a bit more elbow room for your image.

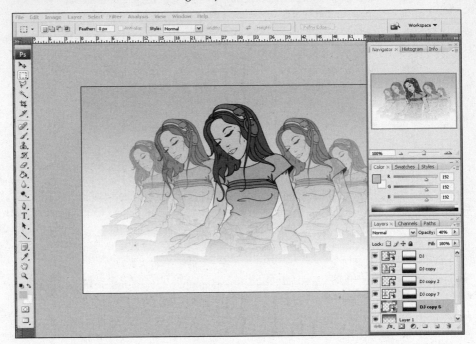

 **TIP**   In any of the screen modes, when the image doesn't consume the entire area devoted to its display, the empty portion of the window or screen appears gray. To change the gray area to a different color — such as black — select a color (using the Foreground color icon), then switch to the Paint Bucket tool, and finally Shift+click in the gray area surrounding the image. Bear in mind that the color you choose becomes the default for all image window backgrounds — so you'll have to reset it to gray (using the same procedure) if you want to go back to that.

Full Screen mode: Still need more space? Try Full Screen mode. This mode is just like Full Screen with Menu Bar, without — you guessed it — the menu bar. You even lose the Windows taskbar and the Mac's dock with this mode. Granted, this does limit your access to menu commands, but you still can access many commands using keyboard shortcuts.

As noted in the tool tips, pressing F lets you cycle through the different modes. If you need access to a menu command when working in Full Screen mode, press Shift+F to display the menu bar. Press Shift+F again to hide it.

TIP   If Photoshop's screen elements interfere with your view of an image, you can hide all palettes — including the Toolbox and Options bar — by pressing Tab. To bring the hidden palettes back into view, press Tab again.

You can hide the palettes but leave the Toolbox and Options bar onscreen by pressing Shift+Tab. Press Shift+Tab again to bring the palettes back. (Pressing Tab while the standard palettes are gone hides the Toolbox and Options bar.) If the rulers are turned on, they remain visible at all times. Press Ctrl+R (⌘-R on the Mac) to toggle the ruler display off and on.

> **TIP** If you don't want to hide the palettes, you can reposition an image in either Full Screen mode by dragging it with the Hand tool. Or press the spacebar and drag when any other tool is selected.

> **TIP** Here's one more workspace display tip: Shift+click the icon for Full Screen to switch the display mode for all open images. Then press Ctrl+Tab (Control-Tab on the Mac) to cycle through the open images. This same trick works for the Standard Screen and Full Screen with Menu Bar modes.

The Options bar

Spanning the width of the Photoshop window, and found just below the menu bar, the Options bar (refer to Figures 2.1 and 2.2) contains the major controls for the tools in the Toolbox. There's an Options bar for every tool, and through them, you establish settings for the active tool by selecting options, clicking icons, dragging sliders, and choosing options from pop-up menus in the bar. You can think of the Options bar as just another floating palette, albeit a long, skinny one. There is a difference, though — you use different tactics to hide, display, and relocate the Options bar than you do a regular palette:

- Choose Window ➪ Options or double-click any tool icon in the Toolbox to toggle on the display of the Options bar. (You should see a check mark to the left of the command when the Options bar is visible.) Of course, if the Options bar is already displayed, double-clicking a Toolbox icon has no impact. Choose Window ➪ Options again to toggle off the display of the Options bar. You also can press Tab to toggle on and off the display of the Options bar and all other palettes.

- By default, the Options bar is docked at the top of the program window. Drag the vertical handle at the left end of the bar to relocate it. If you drag the Options bar to the top or bottom of the window, the bar becomes docked again. It can be hard to re-dock the Options bar at the top of the window, so if you find that you can't get it to really return to the docked position, just choose Window ➪ Workspace ➪ Default Workspace. Everything snaps back into place, although your current palette arrangement is lost in favor of the default selection.

- Unfortunately, you can't change the size or shape of the Options bar.

> **TIP** You also can get back to the default workspace — or view any of a series of preset workspaces, designed for specific types of projects and images — by clicking the Workspace button at the far-right end of the Options bar (to the right of the Go to Bridge button). If you click the drop-down list, you can choose Default Workspace (the first command in the menu) and watch as the default palettes appear (and any you've opened that aren't among the defaults disappear) and the Toolbox positions itself tight against the left side of the workspace. Check out some of the other available workspace options to see if any of them provide the perfect set of palettes and workspace element positions for your needs.

Tool presets

For tools that you use the same way every time you use them, you can establish presets that save you the time of resetting the tool to your favorite options each time you select the tool. For example, imagine that you often use a Brush set to a particular shape, size, and opacity. Rather than having to use the Options bar and Brushes palette every time you want to use those particular settings, you can call up a preset group of settings for the tool and know that the exact same settings are now in force, and you can save lots of time and be assured that your settings are consistent, enabling you to create identical effects with that brush.

To create a tool preset, select a tool and adjust the settings until they're perfect. You may want to choose an ideal gradient and direction settings for the Gradient tool, a frequently used tolerance for the Magic Wand, or a combination of font, size, and alignment options for the Type tool. After setting up your "dream" tool, use any of these techniques to make it a preset you can call upon at any time:

- Choose Window ➪ Tool Presets to display the Tool Presets palette, which appears attached to the docked palettes on the right side of the workspace. Then click the new tool preset icon at the bottom of the palette (labeled in Figure 2.6).

- Click the current tool icon in the Options bar; then click the new tool preset icon below the flyout menu arrow in the upper-right corner of the drop-down palette.

- Choose New Tool Preset from either the Tool Presets palette menu or the palette menu accessible from the drop-down palette in the Options bar (shown in Figure 2.6).

FIGURE 2.6

Click the current tool icon in the Options bar or choose Window ➪ Tool Presets to display options for creating new tool presets.

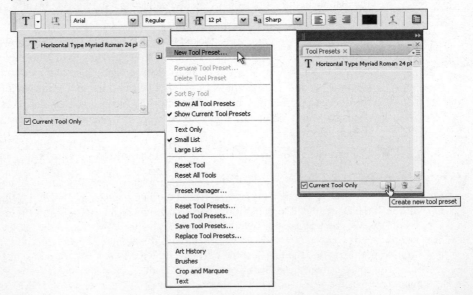

Any of these methods takes you to a small dialog box where you can type a descriptive name for your tool settings. When naming your preset, be sure to give it a name that reminds you what the goal or purpose for the preset is. You can give the preset a descriptive name, such as "complexion brush," a name that describes what the tool does ("softens skin"), or a name that associates the preset with a particular project, such as "ABC Company Type," for Type tool settings that you use for a particular client's artwork.

Some tools also have a check box where you can choose to include or exclude a particular setting from the preset, such as the color for the Brush tool or the pattern for the Pattern Stamp tool. Click OK (after making the choice to exclude a setting or not), and your newly named group of tool settings appears in the list. From here on out, clicking the preset loads that group of settings into the Options bar. If you're having a hard time finding a preset, make sure the Current Tool Only option is checked; this makes presets for only the current tool appear in the list.

Whether you access the Tool Presets menu from the Options bar or from the Tool Presets palette, you can choose from the following additional options:

- Rename Tool Preset and Delete Tool Preset let you perform those functions on the currently selected tool preset. If you want to do this from the Options bar, right-click the preset you want to rename or delete and choose the command from the pop-up menu. You also can click the options menu button and make selections from that menu instead. The Tool Presets palette offers buttons at the bottom for these two activities.

- Sort By Tool is active only if the Current Tool Only option is deselected; it groups the presets in the list by tool.

- Show All Tool Presets and Show Current Tool Presets toggle off and on the Current Tool Only check box.

- You have three options for viewing the list: Text Only, which lets you see the most options onscreen at one time; Small List, which adds a small icon; and Large List, which gives you the icon along with larger text.

- Reset Tool and Reset All Tools are carryovers from Photoshop 6, letting you restore either the current tool or all tools to their default settings. This has no effect on your collection of tool presets.

- Reset Tool Presets, Load Tool Presets, Save Tool Presets, and Replace Tool Presets all let you deal with groups of presets. Reset takes you back to the default set of tool presets, giving you the option to append the default set to the current set or to replace it entirely with the default set; Load gives you access to previously saved groups of presets; Save lets you save the group of presets to disk for future use; and Replace wipes out the current group of presets in favor of the pre-saved group of your choice.

- Preset Manager takes you to Adobe's gift to the obsessively organized: the Preset Manager dialog box. Here you can store and manage all your preset collections, as explained in the next section.

The Preset Manager

Tool presets are a recent addition to the Preset Manager, which was introduced in Photoshop 6. With the added ability to create presets for tools, you can organize and store presets in eight categories: Brushes, Swatches, Gradients, Styles, Patterns, Contours, Custom Shapes, and Tools. In addition to choosing Preset Manager from the palette menus of the Tool Presets, Brushes, Swatches, and Styles palettes, you can always access the Preset Manager dialog box, shown in Figure 2.7, by choosing Edit ➪ Preset Manager. Then choose a category from the Preset Type pop-up menu.

FIGURE 2.7

The Preset Manager dialog box lets you store and organize presets for eight categories.

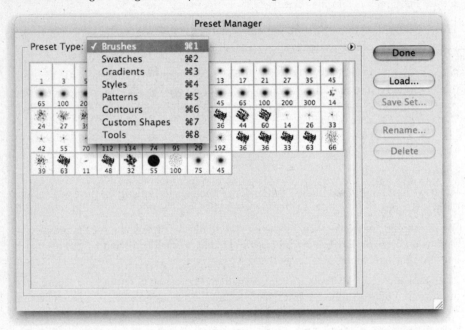

If you click the right-pointing arrow to the left of the Done button, a pop-up menu appears with some of the same options found in the Tool Presets palette menu. For example, you can choose to replace the current preset collection with another or return to the default collection. To append a collection, click Load. Alternatively, click a collection name in the pop-up menu, in which case you have the choice of appending or replacing the current collection with the new one. In addition, you can click a preset and then click Delete to remove the preset or Rename to change the preset's name. If you want to delete or rename a series of presets, Shift+click them and then click Delete or Rename. Of course, you also can use the Ctrl key (⌘ on the Mac) to select non-sequential presets for renaming or deletion.

To select all presets, press Ctrl+A (⌘-A on the Mac). If you press Alt (Option on the Mac), you get a scissors cursor with which you can click a preset to delete it.

TIP Probably the best reason for using the Preset Manager is to create a new preset collection out of presets from an existing set or sets. Load the collection that you want to use as a basis for the new set, and then Shift+click to select presets for the new set — or press Ctrl+A (⌘-A on the Mac) to select all presets — and click Save Set. Give the collection a name and store it in the suggested folder. You also can also store the presets in a folder outside of the main Photoshop CS3 application folder or folders, so that if you reinstall or upgrade Photoshop later, you don't risk losing your presets.

NOTE To protect you from yourself, Photoshop has set it up so that you can't overwrite any existing preset files. Also, after you add a new preset, you must save it as part of a collection, either through the palette menu or the Preset Manager. Otherwise, Photoshop deletes the preset if you replace the current preset collection with another.

Docked and floating palettes

The first time you launch Photoshop CS3, all the default palettes are attached to the dock on the right side of the workspace. The default palettes are the Navigator, Histogram, Info, Color, Swatches, Styles, Layers, Channels, and Paths palettes. To see other palettes, and have them attach to the right-hand dock or to the left-hand dock from which the Toolbox hangs, you need to use the Window menu or press the appropriate keyboard shortcut (see the Appendix for a complete list of these handy items). The appearance of this dock and the way the palettes are connected to it is one of the big interface changes in Photoshop CS3. You can still make palettes float, dragging them from their groupings at the dock, but by default, none of them are floating when first selected, and none of the groups are free-floating either.

Unto themselves, the palettes look and behave just as they have in previous versions, except for how they're collapsed. You can collapse them all at once by clicking the dock (see the long, black bar at the top of the palettes in Figure 2.8), or you can right-click (⌘-click on the Mac) the dock and choose Collapse to Icons.

While they're expanded, each palette contains most or all elements shown in Figure 2.9 (note that on the Mac, the Close button is positioned on the far left side of the title bar), but some palettes have a few kinks. For example, some palettes don't let you resize them, and some palettes have scroll bars while others don't. These aren't huge, glaring differences, but they're enough to keep things interesting. Sort of.

FIGURE 2.8

The dock's appearance and functioning, along with the palettes and their relationship to it, are a big change in CS3.

Expanded view

Collapsed view

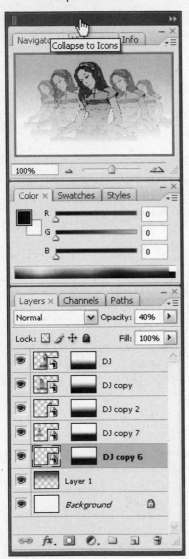

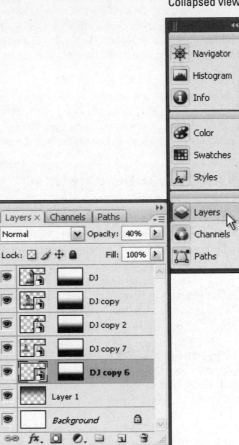

FIGURE 2.9

Most palettes include the same basic elements as the Layers palette, shown here.

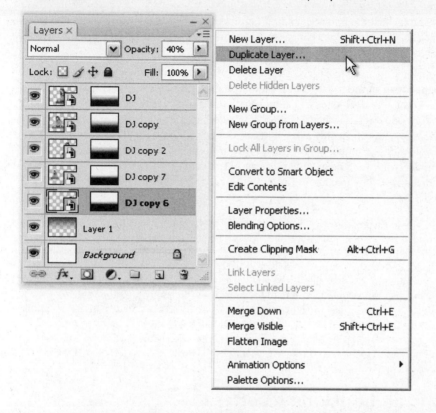

Whether floating (after you've dragged them from the dock) or still docked, palettes generally offer the following options for their display and use:

- **Palette options:** Each palette offers its own collection of options. These options may include icons, pop-up menus, and sliders.

- **Palette menu:** Click the button below the X in the upper-right corner of the palette (it's a stack of lines with a down-pointing arrow) to display a menu of commands specific to the palette. These commands enable you to manipulate the palette options and adjust preference settings.

- **Palette tabs:** When palettes appear in groups, you can click a palette tab to move it to the front of that group. (You also can select the palette commands from the Window menu, but clicking a tab is more convenient.)

- **Close palette button:** When a palette is active (in the front of the group), its tab bears an X or Close button. This is new to Photoshop CS3 and pretty handy. Click the X to close that palette entirely. To bring the palette back, re-select it from the Window menu.

- **Collapse box:** Click the minimize button (an underscore) to reduce the palette to a title bar. Once clicked, this button changes to a maximize button (a small box), which, when clicked, redisplays the palette at full size.

- **Resize options:** If a palette has a size icon (a set of diagonal lines in a triangle in the lower-right corner of the palette), and you mouse over that icon, you can resize that palette — within the dock or as a floating palette out on the workspace. Note that some palettes don't allow resizing at all (and no sizing icon appears in the lower-right corner if this is the case) and others only allow it in one direction — horizontally or vertically. You won't know until you mouse over the icon; if your pointer becomes a diagonal two-headed arrow, you can resize in either direction. If it becomes a vertical or horizontal two-headed arrow, the direction the arrows point tells you what sizing limitations you're faced with.

NOTE If you previously enlarged a palette by dragging the size box, your first click reduces the palette back to its default size. After that, clicking the collapse box hides all but the most essential palette options.

TIP Collapsing a palette hides all options and leaves only the tabs visible, as shown in Figure 2.10. You also can double-click one of the tabs or in the empty area to the right of the tabs — and either technique works like a toggle: Double-click once, and the palettes are hidden; double-click again, and they're redisplayed. And if your palette is located at the bottom edge of the screen, collapsing the palette makes it collapse downward, leaving the visible part of the collapsed palette hugging the bottom of the screen. These tricks work even if you've enlarged the palette by dragging the size box.

Rearranging and docking palettes

Despite the changes to the way palettes are automatically docked in Photoshop CS3, dragging them around and changing their groupings as a floating group of palettes or within the dock is still easy. This, of course, enables you to customize the workspace so it's the most efficient arrangement for your specific needs.

To undock a palette and make it a floating palette, grab the palette's tab within the dock and drag out onto the workspace, as shown in Figure 2.11. The palette comes with you, and wherever you release the mouse, there floats the palette. You can drag others out of the dock and group them with the first floating palette, or you can have one or more individual floating palettes on the workspace.

FIGURE 2.10

When collapsed, a palette (or group of palettes) shows only the tabs and the palette/group title bar.

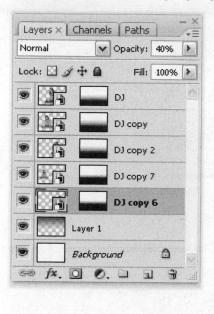

If you want to make one of those custom groupings out on the workspace or within the dock, just drag a palette from its current location onto the other palette or palettes. When the target palette's title bar becomes highlighted, release the mouse. If you release before this happens, you've simply placed a palette on top of another and have not achieved an actual group.

If you want to go back to the default arrangement for your palettes — the way Photoshop CS3's workspace looks "out of the box," choose Window ➪ Workspace ➪ Reset Palette Locations, or click the Workspace button on the far-right end of the Options bar and choose Default Workspace from the resulting menu. Either way allows you to easily restore your palette setup to the neat and tidy defaults — a fixed set of palettes in their default groupings, all in the dock, and the Toolbox on the left side of the workspace.

Of course, in addition to restoring the workspace to its default arrangement, you can create your own custom workspace, an arrangement you can go to at any time, with a simple menu selection.

FIGURE 2.11

Undock a palette by dragging it off the dock.

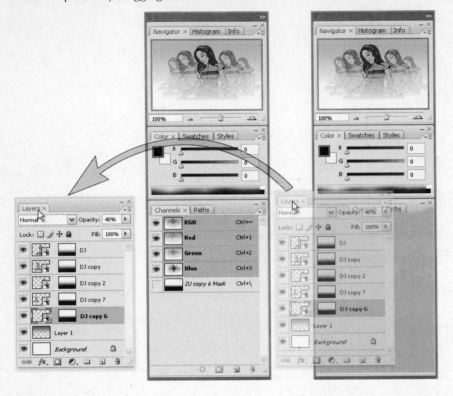

These workspace presets, created by you, allow you to easily create workspace arrangements that suit particular images, projects, or people. For example, if you're working on a series of images that require the use of a particular Action all the time, or in which you use the History palette often to save snapshots of your image (more about these features in Chapters 3 and 7), choose Window ⇨ Workspace ⇨ Save Workspace. You also can click the aforementioned Workspace button (on the Options bar) and choose Save Workspace from the menu. In the resulting dialog box, name the workspace something that will make sense later and remind you of why you created it in the first place, and click Save. From then on, you (or another user who shares your computer) can access the saved workspace in the Window ⇨ Workspace menu. If and when a workspace you've saved outlives its usefulness, you can get rid of it quickly and easily — just choose Window ⇨ Workspace ⇨ Delete Workspace, and choose from a pop-up list of all saved workspaces.

> **NOTE** Wherever you initiate the command to select a workspace (or save one), you also can choose from a series of task-specific presets already built in to the software. Choose from presets like Color and Tonal Correction, Painting and Retouching, Web Design, Working with Type, and Video and Film — plus several others, from a group of eight presets. Simply choose Window ⇨ Workspace (or click the Workspace button on the Options bar), and make a selection from the menu, as shown in Figure 2.12.

FIGURE 2.12

Not sure how to group your palettes and arrange your onscreen tools for a particular job? Let Photoshop take a whack at it, and choose one of the built-in workspace presets.

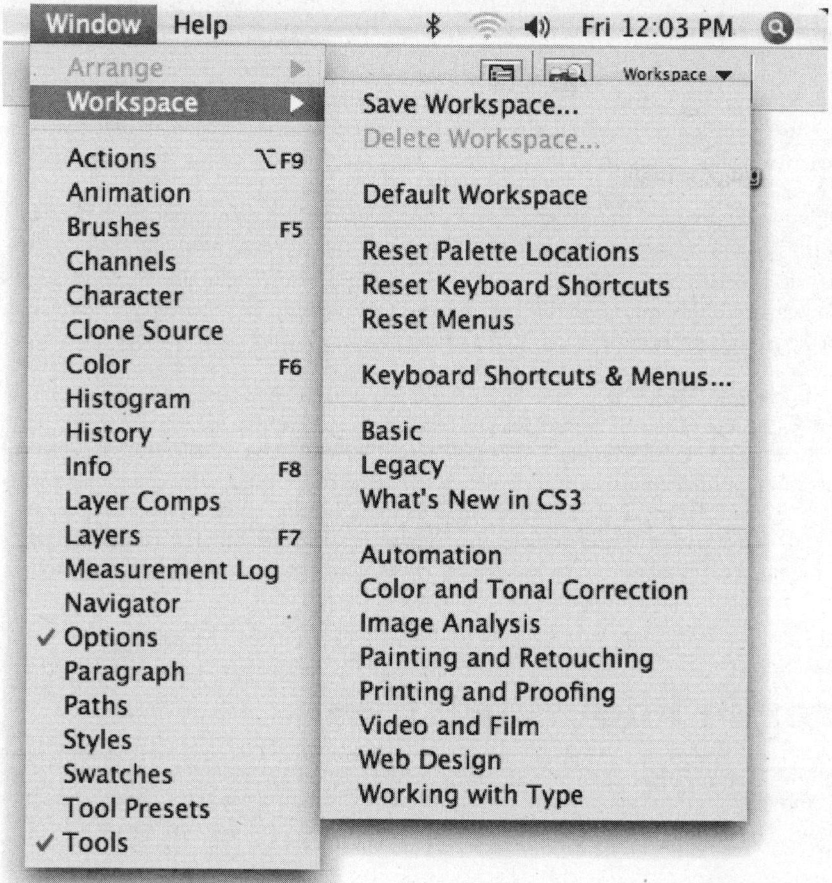

Window	Help		✳ 🛜 🔊 Fri 12:03 PM 🔍

Arrange ▶
Workspace ▶

Actions ⌥F9
Animation
Brushes F5
Channels
Character
Clone Source
Color F6
Histogram
History
Info F8
Layer Comps
Layers F7
Measurement Log
Navigator
✓ Options
Paragraph
Paths
Styles
Swatches
Tool Presets
✓ Tools

Save Workspace...
Delete Workspace...

Default Workspace

Reset Palette Locations
Reset Keyboard Shortcuts
Reset Menus

Keyboard Shortcuts & Menus...

Basic
Legacy
What's New in CS3

Automation
Color and Tonal Correction
Image Analysis
Painting and Retouching
Printing and Proofing
Video and Film
Web Design
Working with Type

Tabbing through the options

As mentioned earlier, you can hide the palettes by pressing Shift+Tab and you can hide the palettes, Toolbox, and Options bar by pressing Tab. This keyboard trick doesn't work, however, if one of the fields in the Options bar is active, or if the Type tool is in use (with an active text cursor in the image window).

For example, suppose you click in the R (Red) option box in the Color palette. This activates the option. Now press Tab. Rather than hiding the palettes, Photoshop advances you to the next option box in the palette, G. This function of the Tab key is common to virtually all Windows and Mac-based software, whenever you're working in a dialog box: The dialog box functions like a form (like those you might fill in at a Web site, for example), and the Tab key moves you from field to field. To move backward through the options, press Shift+Tab. This "trick" applies to the Options bar as well as to the standard palettes.

To apply an option box value and return focus to the image window, press Enter or Return. This deactivates the palette options. You also can simply click outside of the palette to refocus Photoshop on either an image window or on nothing specific, if you choose to click the gray background of the Photoshop desktop rather than on any particular workspace component. Either way, you want to refocus Photoshop's "attention" so that you can continue to work elsewhere and rely on keyboard shortcuts to work as expected. Otherwise, Photoshop assumes whatever keys you press relate to the active palette's options.

While you're working in the image window, you can return focus to the Options bar from the keyboard. When you press Enter or Return, Photoshop displays the Options bar, if it's not already visible. If the Options bar offers an option box for the active tool, Photoshop highlights the contents of the option box. You can then tab around to reach the option you want to change, type a new value, and press Enter or Return to get out.

> **TIP** You can see your open images side by side — for comparison, to drag layers from one to the other, or just to see all the images you have open without having to drag them around and resize them manually. This is done by choosing Window ➪ Arrange ➪ Tile Horizontally or Tile Vertically. Your other options in this submenu include Cascade, which stacks the open image windows with their title bars visible. You also can open a new window for the active image by choosing New Window for X, where "X" is the name of the active image. What about the Arrange Icons command in the same menu? It takes all the icons for your minimized images (one title bar for each open, minimized image) and arranges them along the bottom of the workspace.

Navigating in Photoshop CS3

All graphics and desktop publishing programs provide a variety of navigational tools and functions that enable you to move around the screen. You can jump from place to place, switching between open image windows, between tools and their options, and to change your view of the images themselves.

The view size

Using the Zoom tool's Options bar, the View menu's various Zoom commands (Zoom In, Zoom Out, Fit On Screen, Actual Pixels, and Print Size), or the Navigator palette's Zoom percentage field and slider, you can change the *view size* for your image. The *view size* is the size at which an image appears onscreen — so you can either step back to see more of an image or all of it at once or get in really close to concentrate on individual pixels. Each change in view size is expressed as a *zoom ratio*, which is the ratio between screen pixels and image pixels. Photoshop displays the zoom ratio as a percentage value in the title bar as well as in the magnification box — and in the lower-left corner of the image window. The 100 percent zoom ratio shows one image pixel for each screen pixel, a 200 percent zoom ratio doubles the size of the image pixels onscreen, and a 300 percent zoom triples the size, and so on.

Actual pixels

Photoshop calls the 100 percent zoom ratio the *actual-pixels* view. This is the most accurate view size because you can see the image as it really is. Reduced view sizes drop pixels; magnified view sizes stretch pixels. Only the actual-pixels view displays each pixel without a trace of screen distortion — good to know if you think your image looks a bit choppy or noisy, and you're not sure if that's how it really looks or if it's just the screen size you're using at the time. A quick change to Actual Pixels view ends all doubt.

You can switch to this most accurate of view sizes at any time using one of the following techniques:

- Choose View ⇨ Actual Pixels.
- Press Ctrl+Alt+0 (⌘-Option-0 on the Mac). That's the number 0, not the letter *O*.
- Double-click the Zoom tool icon in the Toolbox.
- Click the Actual Pixels button, which appears in the Options bar when the Zoom tool is selected.

Fit on screen

When you first open an image, Photoshop displays it at a zoom ratio that permits the entire image to fit onscreen. Assuming you don't change the size of the image, you can return to this "fit-onscreen" view size in one of the following ways:

- Choose View ⇨ Fit on Screen.
- Press Ctrl+0 (or ⌘-0 on the Mac).
- Double-click the Hand tool icon in the Toolbox.
- Select the Zoom tool, and then click the Fit on Screen button in the Options bar.

Strangely, any of these techniques may magnify the image beyond the 100 percent view size. When working on a very small image, for example, Photoshop enlarges the image to fill the screen, even if this means maxing out the zoom to 1,600 percent. Personally, I prefer to use the fit-onscreen view only when working on very large images, because it usually causes a good deal of distortion — not to the image in reality, but to its display in the image window.

You may not love Fit on Screen view because while Photoshop does the best job of previewing an image when you can see all pixels — that is, at 100 percent view size, in Fit on Screen view, the percentage you get is rather arbitrary. You never know what percentage you'll get when you choose this command; all you know is that the entire image is visible within the image window.

Print size

You can switch to yet another predefined view size by choosing View ⇨ Print Size. This command theoretically displays the image onscreen at the size it will print. (You set the print size using Image ⇨ Image Size, as explained in Chapter 3.) When the Zoom tool is active, you also can click the Print Size button in the Options bar to turn on the print-size view.

In practice, "print-size" view isn't particularly reliable. Photoshop assumes that your monitor displays exactly 72 pixels per inch, even on the PC, where the accepted screen resolution is 96 pixels per inch. But it's all complete nonsense, whatever the assumption. Monitor resolutions vary all over the map. And high-end monitors let you change screen resolutions without Photoshop even noticing.

The long and the short of it is this: Don't expect to hold up your printed image and have it exactly match the print-size view onscreen. It's a rough approximation, designed to show you how the image will look when imported into InDesign, QuarkXPress, PageMaker, or some other publishing program — nothing more.

The Zoom tool

Obviously, the aforementioned zoom ratios aren't the only ones available to you. You can zoom in as close as 1,600 percent and zoom out to 0.2 percent.

The most straightforward way to zoom in and out of your image is to use the Zoom tool, and here are some techniques to try:

■ Click in the image window with the Zoom tool to magnify the image in preset increments — from 33.33 percent to 50 to 66.67 to 100 to 200 and so on. Photoshop centers the zoomed view at the point where you click (or comes as close as possible).

■ Go the other way, and Alt-click (Win) or Option-click (Mac) with the Zoom tool to reduce the image incrementally — 200 to 100 to 66.67 to 50 to 33.33 and so on. Again, Photoshop tries to center the new view on the click point.

TIP   Drag with the Zoom tool to draw a rectangular marquee around the portion of the image you want to magnify. Photoshop magnifies the image so the marqueed area fits just inside the image window. (If the horizontal and vertical proportions of the marquee do not match those of your screen — for example, if you draw a tall, thin marquee or a really short, wide one — Photoshop favors the smaller of the two possible zoom ratios to avoid hiding any detail inside the marquee.)

■ If you want Photoshop to resize the window when you click with the Zoom tool, select the Resize Windows to Fit option in the Options bar. The check box appears only when the Zoom tool is the active tool.

■ Turn off the Ignore Palettes check box in the Options bar if you want Photoshop to stop resizing the window when the window bumps up against a palette anchored against the side of the program window. Select the option to resize the window regardless of the palettes. The palettes then float over the resized window.

■ If you have multiple image windows open, you can control the zoom ratio on all of them at the same time. Simply Shift+click with the Zoom tool in any image window. Alternatively, you can eliminate the need for the Shift key by selecting the Zoom All Windows option in the Options bar.

■ Use the Window, Arrange, Match Zoom, Match Location, or Match Zoom and Location commands to control the zoom on two or more open images. Zoom in on (or out from) one of your open images, and maybe even pan the image to one side or another. Then choose Window, Arrange, Match Zoom and Location, and voila! Both images are zoomed to the same percentage, and the image content is placed in the same position within the image window.

TIP To access the Zoom tool temporarily when some other tool is selected, press and hold Ctrl (⌘ on the Mac) and the spacebar. Release both to return control of the cursor to the selected tool. To access the Zoom Out cursor, press Alt (Option on the Mac) with the spacebar. These keyboard equivalents work from inside many dialog boxes, enabling you to modify the view of an image while applying a filter or color correction.

The Zoom commands

You can also zoom in and out using the following commands and keyboard shortcuts:

■ Choose View ⇨ Zoom In, or press Ctrl+plus (+) (⌘-plus on the Mac) to zoom in. This command works exactly like clicking with the Zoom tool except that you can't specify the center of the new view size. Photoshop merely centers the zoom in keeping with the previous view size.

■ Choose View ⇨ Zoom Out, or press Ctrl+minus (–) (⌘-minus on the Mac) to zoom out.

TIP The General panel of the Preferences dialog box (Ctrl+K on the PC; ⌘-K on the Mac) includes an option called Zoom Resizes Windows. If you select this option, Photoshop resizes the image window when you use the Zoom commands. To override the setting temporarily, press Alt (Option on the Mac) as you press the keyboard shortcut or select the menu command. Similarly, if you deselect the option in the Preferences dialog box, you can add Alt or Option to turn window-zooming on temporarily.

If Photoshop is unresponsive to these or any other keyboard shortcuts, it's probably because the image window has somehow become inactive. (It can happen in Windows if you so much as click the taskbar.) Just click the image window's title bar and try again; you also may want to momentarily minimize the window and then restore it, which can aid in refreshing the window to give you the view you want if it wasn't responding properly before.

The Navigator palette's magnification field

Another way to zoom in and out without changing the window size is to type a value into the magnification box, located in the lower-left corner of the image window. Select the magnification value, type a new one, and press Enter or Return. Photoshop zooms the view without zooming the window. (Neither the Resize Windows to Fit option in the Options bar nor the Zoom Resizes Windows option in the Preferences dialog box affect the magnification box.)

Figure 2.13 starts with a specially sized window at 50 percent. Two different percentages are typed in the magnification box — 100 percent and 25 percent — alternately enlarging and reducing the image in the confines of a static window.

You may like to know more about the magnification box:

- You can type values in the magnification box as percentages, ratios, or "times" values. To switch to a zoom value of 250 percent, for example, you can type 250%, 5:2, or 2.5x.

- You can specify a zoom value in increments as small as 0.01 percent. So if a zoom value of 250.01 doesn't quite suit your fancy, you can try 250.02. It's unlikely that you'll need this kind of precision, but isn't it great to know that it's there?

> **TIP**   When you press Enter or Return after typing a magnification value, Photoshop changes the view size and returns focus to the image window. If you aren't exactly certain what zoom ratio you want to use, press Shift+Enter (Shift+Return on the Mac) instead. This changes the view size while keeping the magnification value active; this way, you can type a new value and try again.

Creating a reference window

In the past, paint programs provided a cropped view of your image at the actual-pixels view size to serve as a reference when you worked in a magnified view. Photoshop does not, but you can easily create a second view of your image by choosing Window ⇨ Arrange ⇨ New Window, as in Figure 2.14. Use one window to maintain a 100 percent view of your image while you zoom and edit inside the other window. Both windows track the changes to the image.

FIGURE 2.13

To zoom an image without changing the window size, type a zoom ratio in the magnification box and press Enter or Return. You also can deselect the Resize Windows to Fit option in the Options bar when working with the Zoom tool.

FIGURE 2.14

You can create multiple windows to track the changes made to a single image by choosing Window ⇨ Arrange ⇨ New Window.

Scrolling in the window

In the standard window mode, you have access to scroll bars, as you do in just about every other major application. But as you become more proficient with Photoshop, you'll use the scroll bars less and less. One way to bypass the scroll bars is to use the keyboard equivalents listed in Table 2.1.

TABLE 2.1

Scrolling from the Keyboard

Scrolling Action	Keystroke	Alternate Keystroke (Mac Standard Keyboard Only)
Up one screen	Page Up	Control+K
Up slightly	Shift+Page Up	Control+Shift+K
Down one screen	Page Down	Control+L
Down slightly	Shift+Page Down	Control-Shift+L
Left one screen	Ctrl+Page Up (⌘-Page Up)	⌘-Control+K
Left slightly	Ctrl+Shift+Page Up (⌘-Shift+Page Up)	⌘-Control+Shift+K
Right one screen	Ctrl+Page Down (⌘-Page Down)	⌘-Control+L
Right slightly	Ctrl+Shift+Page Down (⌘-Shift+Page Down)	⌘-Control+Shift+L
To upper-left corner	Home	Control+A
To lower-right corner	End	Control+D

TIP Try using the Page Up and Page Down shortcuts to comb through very large images at 100 percent view size. This way, you can make sure all the pixels are in order before going to print.

TIP To access the Hand tool temporarily when some other tool is selected, press and hold the spacebar. Releasing the spacebar returns the cursor to its original appearance. This keyboard equivalent even works in many dialog boxes.

TIP You can scroll multiple image windows at the same time by Shift-dragging in any one image with the Hand tool. If you don't want to use the Shift key, select the Scroll All Windows option in the Options bar. You also can use the spacebar+Shift-drag method if you want to scroll multiple image windows without first selecting the Hand tool.

The Navigator palette

As referenced earlier when we started the whole discussion of zooming in and out, the Navigator palette, shown in Figure 2.15, is the best thing to happen to zooming and scrolling since Photoshop was introduced. If you routinely work on large images that extend beyond the confines of your relatively tiny screen, you'll want to get up and running with this palette as soon as possible: It makes life so much easier that you won't know how you got along without it.

FIGURE 2.15

You can navigate, preview, and zoom, all in one palette.

While the Navigator palette is one of Photoshop CS3's default palettes, you or another user may have closed it at some point, and it may not be showing. Or you may have invoked a saved workspace that doesn't include it. In any case, if the Navigator palette isn't visible, choose Window ➪ Navigator. You can then use the palette options as follows:

- **View box:** Drag the view box (see the red box encompassing some of the image thumbnail inside the palette) to reveal some hidden portion of the photograph. Of course, if the entire image is currently visible in the image window, the red view box border encompasses the entire thumbnail. If the entire image is *not* visible within the image window, you can drag the red bordered view box around inside the palette and watch the displayed portion of the image in the image window change to match your movements. Even fans of the Hand tool (for panning an image within the image window) will find this technique really helpful, despite having to leave the image window with your mouse to use it.

> **TIP**   As if the View box and its panning powers weren't enough, try this: Press Ctrl (⌘ on the Mac) to get a Zoom cursor in the Navigator palette. Then Ctrl-drag (⌘-drag on the Mac) to resize the view box and zoom the photo in the image window. You also can Shift-drag to constrain dragging the view box to only horizontal or vertical movement.

- **Box color:** You can change the color of the view box by choosing the Palette Options command from the palette menu. The default is red, but if your image has lots of red in it or if you just don't like red, try yellow or bright lime green — something that stands out against even a bright color image.

- **Magnification box:** This value works like the one in the lower-left corner of the image window — just type a new zoom ratio, and press Enter or Return.

- **Zoom out:** Click the zoom out button (it looks like a tiny set of mountains) to reduce the view size in the same predefined increments as the Zoom tool. This button doesn't alter the size of the image window, regardless of any window resizing options you set for the other zoom controls.

- **Zoom slider:** Move the slider triangle, and watch what happens. Drag to the left to zoom out; drag right to zoom in. Again, Photoshop dynamically tracks your changes in the image window.

- **Zoom in:** Click the big mountains to incrementally magnify the view of the image without altering the window size. Of course, the small mountains zoom out, and they, too, do not alter the window size.

- **Size box:** If you have a large monitor, you don't have to settle for that teeny thumbnail of the image. While docked, the palette can be dragged only vertically, making it taller, but not wider. If you want to widen it as well, drag the palette away from its default group and release it as a floating palette on the workspace. Then drag the size box to enlarge both palette and thumbnail to a more appropriate size for your needs.

Customizing the Interface

Just about every program gives you access to a few main settings — things you can modify about the way the program looks or works to make it more useful for your way of doing things. Typically, these settings are called *preferences*, and Photoshop is no exception. Photoshop ships with certain recommended preference settings already in force — settings known as *factory defaults* — that were put in place in the hopes of meeting the needs of the average user. Of course, the fact that these settings are the default doesn't mean they're right or appropriate for most people. If you find that some of Photoshop's settings aren't making your life easier, they're easy to change, and the following coverage shows you how to change them, what the change will do, and of course, how to restore the defaults if you decide your tinkering was a mistake.

You can modify preference settings in two ways. You can make environmental adjustments in Windows by using Edit ⇨ Preferences ⇨ General; on the Mac, that's Photoshop ⇨ Preferences ⇨ General. Or you can change the operation of specific tools by adjusting settings in the Options bar. Photoshop remembers environmental preferences, tool settings, and even the file format under which you saved the last image by storing this information to a file each time you exit the program.

> **TIP**   You can dump the preferences file using this trick: Close the program, and then relaunch it. Immediately after you launch the program, press and hold Ctrl+Shift+Alt (⌘-Shift-Option on the Mac). Photoshop displays a dialog box asking for your permission to delete the preferences file. Click Yes.

Meanwhile, Back at the Factory...

To restore Photoshop's factory default settings, delete the Adobe Photoshop *Prefs.psp* (simply *Prefs* on the Mac) file when the application is *not* running. The next time you launch Photoshop, it creates a new preferences file automatically. On the PC, you can find the preferences file in the Application Data\Adobe\Adobe Photoshop CS3\Adobe Photoshop CS3 Settings folder. Under Windows XP, the Application Data folder is located in the Documents and Settings/*User Name* folder. In earlier versions of Windows, the Application Data folder is in the Windows folder. In Mac OS X, follow this path: Home folder ➪ Library ➪ Preferences ➪ Adobe Photoshop CS3 Settings. (Depending on your system setup, the program may choose a different storage folder.) You also can search for the preferences file by name using Spotlight on the Mac or the built-in search tool in Windows. Under Windows XP, you must first turn on the visibility of hidden files. To do so, choose Tools ➪ Folder Options, click the View tab, and then select the Show Hidden Files and Folders option.

Deleting the preferences file is also a good idea if Photoshop starts acting funny. Photoshop's preferences file has always been highly susceptible to corruption, possibly because the application writes to it so often. Whatever the reason, if Photoshop starts behaving erratically, trash the preferences file. You have to reset your preferences, but a smooth-running program is worth the few minutes of extra effort. It's a good thing that Photoshop saves actions, color settings, custom shapes, contours, and the like separately from the *Prefs* file. This means that you can delete your *Prefs* file without worrying about harming your scripts, color conversions, and other custom settings.

TIP   After you get your preferences set as you like them, you can prevent Photoshop from altering them further by locking the file. On the PC, right-click the Adobe Photoshop *Prefs.psp* file in Windows Explorer, and choose Properties from the pop-up menu. Then select the Read Only option in the Properties dialog box, and press Enter. On the Mac, go to the Finder, track down the Adobe Photoshop *Prefs* file, and choose File ➪ Show Info (⌘-I on the Mac). Then select the Locked option in the Info dialog box. From then on, Photoshop starts up with a consistent set of default settings.

That's a good tip, and it's included in the name of comprehensive coverage. But you may not want to lock your *Prefs* file because you may periodically want to modify your settings and want Photoshop to remember the latest and greatest. Instead, make a backup copy of your favorite settings. After a few weeks of working in the program and customizing it to a more or less acceptable level, copy the preferences file to a separate folder on your hard drive (someplace you'll remember!). Then if the preferences file becomes corrupt, you can replace it quickly with your backup.

The Preference Panels

Under Windows, the Preferences command appears on the Edit menu. In Mac OS X, it's found on the Photoshop menu. Choosing the command displays a long submenu of commands, but you needn't ever use them if you remember a simple keyboard shortcut: Ctrl+K (⌘-K on the Mac).

This shortcut brings up the Preferences dialog box, which provides access to 10 panels of options representing every one of the Edit ⇨ Preferences commands. Select the desired panel from the list on the left side of the dialog box, as demonstrated in Figure 2.16. You also can click the Prev and Next buttons or press Alt+P and Alt+N, respectively (⌘-Option+P and ⌘-Option+N on the Mac) to cycle from one panel to the next.

FIGURE 2.16

Select a panel of options from the pop-up menu, or click the Prev and Next buttons to advance from one panel to the next.

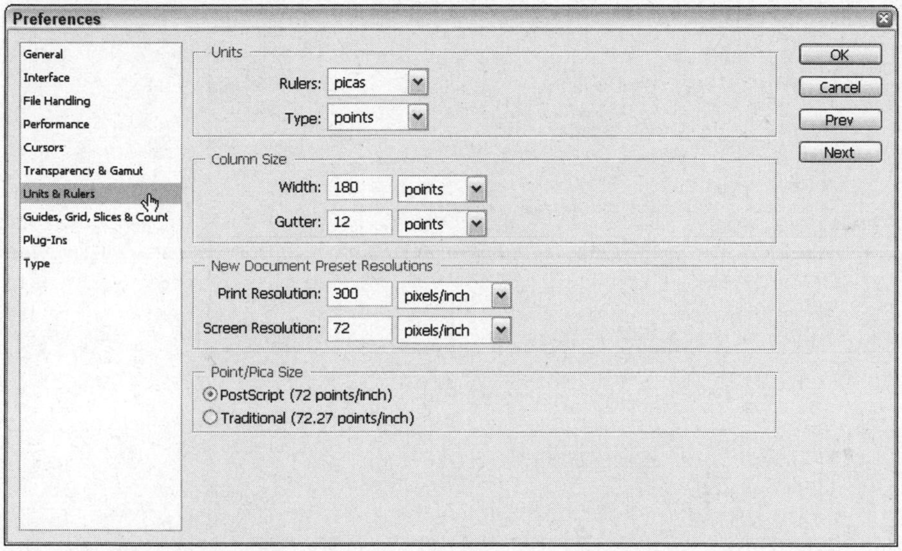

TIP Photoshop always displays the first panel, General, when you press Ctrl+K (or ⌘-K on the Mac). If you prefer to go to the panel you were last using, press Ctrl+Alt+K (⌘-Option+K on the Mac).

To accept your settings and exit the Preferences dialog box, press Enter or Return. Or press Escape to cancel any changes you've made to your settings. Okay, so you already knew that, but here's one you may not know: Press and hold Alt (Option on the Mac) to change the Cancel button to Reset. Then click the button to restore the settings that were in force before you entered the dialog box.

The following sections examine the Preferences panels in the order in which they appear in the Figure 2.16 dialog box (see the left-hand panel). How each option works is explained, and what are considered the optimal settings are included in parentheses. (The figures, however, show the default settings.) Out of context like this, Photoshop's preference settings can be a bit confusing. In later chapters, some additional light is shed on the settings you may find most useful.

General preferences

The General panel, shown in Figure 2.17, contains a miscellaneous supply of what are arguably the most important Preferences options. For those of you who worked with Photoshop CS2, you'll find some of the General panel's options have been moved to the new Interface panel, which is discussed later in this chapter.

FIGURE 2.17

The General panel provides access to the most important environmental preference settings.

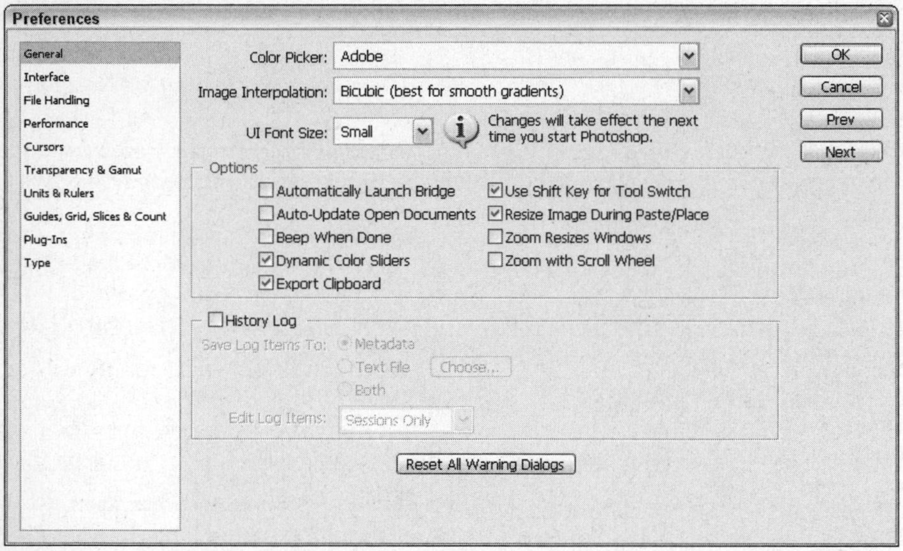

- **Color Picker (Adobe):** When you click the foreground or background color control icon in the Toolbox, Photoshop displays any Color Picker plug-ins that you may have installed, plus one of two standard Color Pickers: the Adobe Color Picker or the one provided by the operating system. If you're familiar with other Windows graphics programs, the system's color picker may at first seem more familiar. But Photoshop's color picker is better suited to photographic work.

- **Image Interpolation (Bicubic):** When you resize an image using Image ➪ Image Size or transform it using Layer ➪ Free Transform or one of the commands in the Layer ➪ Transform submenu, Photoshop has to make up — or *interpolate* — pixels to fill in the gaps. You can change how Photoshop calculates the interpolation by choosing one of five options from the Image Interpolation pop-up menu.

  If you select Nearest Neighbor (Faster), Photoshop simply copies the next-door pixel when creating a new one. This is the fastest setting (hence the label "Faster"), but it invariably results in jagged effects.

The second option, Bilinear, smoothes the transitions between pixels by creating intermediate shades. Photoshop averages the color of each pixel with four neighbors — the pixel above, the one below, and the two to the left and right. Bilinear takes more time but, typically, the softened effect is worth it.

Still more time-intensive is the default setting, Bicubic, which averages the color of a pixel with its eight closest neighbors — one up, one down, two on the sides, and four in the corners. The Bicubic setting boosts the amount of contrast between pixels to offset the blurring effect that generally accompanies interpolation.

You also have two Image Interpolation settings: Bicubic Smoother and Bicubic Sharper. Based on the standard Bicubic option, these settings are further optimized for different sizing operations. Bicubic Smoother is designed to produce the smoothest possible transitions between pixels, ideal when resizing a grainy or noisy image. It is also the option of choice on those rare occasions when you decide to enlarge an image. Bicubic Sharper is designed to preserve the sharpness and detail of an image when you reduce it, eliminating the need to apply Unsharp Mask after downsampling. Although these new interpolation options can be useful, they're best used on a case-by-case basis from inside the Image Size dialog box (see Chapter 3).

TIP The moral is this: Select Bicubic to turn Photoshop's interpolation capabilities on and select Nearest Neighbor to turn them off. The Bilinear setting is a poor compromise between the other options — too slow for roughing out effects and too remedial to be worth your time.

- **UI Font Size:** This sets the font size to use for Small User Interface fonts, which are fonts used in small devices, such as handheld organizers, cell phones, and so forth. It's set to Small by default, and your alternates are Medium and Large. As the "i" ("!" on the Mac) balloon indicates, changes take effect the next time you start Photoshop.

- **Automatically Launch Bridge (off):** The Bridge can be started automatically when Photoshop is launched; if you select this option, the Bridge opens and runs in the background. Because the very powerful Bridge saps much of the system resources, you may prefer to deselect this option and activate it only when you need it.

CROSS-REF The Bridge is discussed fully in Chapters 3 and 20.

- **Auto-Update Open Documents (off):** This option creates and maintains a link between an open image and the image file on disk. Anytime the image on disk updates, Photoshop updates the image onscreen in kind. This feature is an amazing help when you're editing images with another artist over a network. Imagine that you and a coworker each have the same server file open in separate copies of Photoshop. Your coworker makes a change and saves it. Seconds later, your copy of Photoshop automatically updates the image on your screen. Then you make a change and save it, and Photoshop relays your modifications to your coworker's screen.

So what happens if you're both editing the image simultaneously? Whoever saves first gets the glory. If your coworker saves the image before you do, any changes that you haven't saved are overwritten by the other person's work.

TIP   However, you can snatch victory from the jaws of defeat simply by pressing Ctrl+Alt+Z
(⌘-Option+Z on the Mac), which undoes your coworker's edits and retrieves yours.
Quickly save your image to lob your changes over the net. Ooh, psych! With any luck, your coworker
won't understand Photoshop well enough to know that your changes can be undone just as easily. But
just to be safe, better hide this book from prying eyes.

■ **Beep When Done (off):** You can instruct Photoshop to beep at you whenever it finishes
an operation that displays a Progress window. This option may be useful if you doze off
during particularly time-consuming operations.

■ **Dynamic Color Sliders (on):** When selected, this option instructs Photoshop to preview
color effects in the slider bars of the Color palette. When the option is turned off, the
slider bars show the same colors regardless of your changes. Unless you're working on a
slow computer, leave this option on. On a fast machine, Photoshop takes a billionth of a
second longer to calculate the color effects and it's well worth it.

■ **Export Clipboard (on):** When selected, this option tells Photoshop to transfer a copied
image from the program's internal Clipboard to the operating system's Clipboard whenever you switch applications. This enables you to paste the image into another running
program. Turn this option off if you plan to use copied images only within Photoshop
and want to reduce the lag time that occurs when you switch from Photoshop to another
program. Even with this option off, you can paste images copied from other programs
into Photoshop.

■ **Use Shift Key for Tool Switch (on):** When two or more tools share the same slot in the
Toolbox, you can press the keyboard shortcut associated with the tools to cycle through
the tools. This Preferences option determines whether you must press Shift along with
the shortcut. I recommend that you turn this option off: One extra keystroke per function
adds up over the course of a day, you know.

NOTE   In this book, it is assumed that you have deselected the Use Shift Key for Tool Switch
option when tool shortcuts are presented.

■ **Resize Image During Paste/Place (on):** This option determines whether your image is
resized when you paste content or place a layer from another image into the image window. I usually turn this option off, because I find that I don't remember it's on and am
then surprised (rarely pleasantly so) when the image resizes.

■ **Zoom Resizes Windows (off):** Select this option to force Photoshop to resize the image
window when you zoom in on or out from your image by choosing a Zoom command
from the View menu or by using the keyboard shortcuts, Ctrl+plus (⌘-plus on the Mac)
and Ctrl+minus (⌘-minus on the Mac). This one's really a matter of personal choice —
you'll do no harm to yourself or the planet if you leave it off, as it is by default in
Windows, or leave it on, as it is by default on the Mac. Either way, you can temporarily
choose the opposite setting by pressing Alt (Option on the Mac) as you choose the Zoom
command.

- **Zoom with Scroll Wheel (off):** Because this is off by default, you can use the scroll wheel (predominantly for Windows users) to move up and down in an image window that's not set to Fit on Screen or where whatever zoom you're using allows the entire image to be seen in the image window. If you turn this on, scrolling forward with the scroll wheel zooms in and scrolling backward zooms out. If you use the scroll wheel often in Photoshop and other applications, turning this on can be annoying, because you'll keep forgetting it's on and then wonder why the stupid image keeps growing whenever you scroll up.

- **History Log (your call):** This option lets you save information about the list of edits and operations applied to your images. For starters, select the History Log option and select a radio button to specify whether you want to save the log along with the image's metadata, in a separate text file, or both. If you select the Metadata option, you can view the log information in the History panel of the File Info dialog box (Ctrl+Alt+I or ⌘-Option+I). If you select the Text File radio button, Photoshop prompts you to specify a name and location for the log file. Naturally, the Both radio button saves the log information to metadata and a text tile.

  Use the Edit Log Items pop-up menu to specify the type of information you want to save to the log. The Sessions Only option simply keeps track of every time you launch and quit Photoshop and open and close files. Choose the Concise option to log the session information plus the data that's recorded in the History palette. Choose Detailed to log detailed information about every edit performed on an image, giving you a permanent record of the steps you took to achieve the final results.

- **Reset All Warning Dialogs:** Every now and then, Photoshop displays a warning dialog box to let you know that the course you're on may have consequences you hadn't considered. Some dialog boxes include an option that you can select to tell Photoshop that you don't want to see the current warning anymore. This can be a good thing, if the prompt in question isn't one you typically listen to — so rather than having to acknowledge and then ignore it over and over, you won't be bothered again. On the other hand, sometimes that "Leave me alone!" response can be regrettable later — especially if the prompt you no longer choose to see was advice you really needed to heed. If you're afraid you've silenced some useful warnings, click the Reset All Warning Dialogs button in the Preferences dialog box. Photoshop clears all the Don't Show This Warning Again options so that you once again get all available warnings. Photoshop responds to your click of the reset button by displaying a warning dialog box telling you that all warning dialog boxes will be enabled if you go forward.

Interface

The Interface panel, as the name leads us to believe, pertains to the settings that control how Photoshop reveals itself to the user. You can press Ctrl+2 to access this panel while the Preferences dialog box is open (⌘+2 on a Mac). The panel appears in Figure 2.18.

FIGURE 2.18

The Interface panel allows you to tweak the color of various workspace elements and whether Photoshop remembers where you left your palettes.

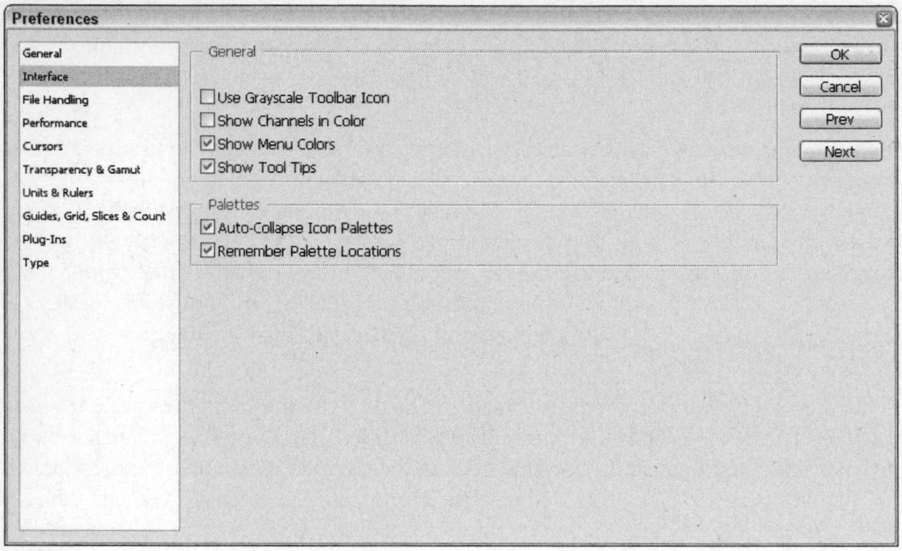

```
Preferences                                                    ⊠
┌──────────────┬─────────────────────────────────────┬─────────┐
│ General      │ ┌─General──────────────────────────┐ │   OK    │
│ Interface    │ │                                   │ │         │
│ File Handling│ │ ☐ Use Grayscale Toolbar Icon      │ │ Cancel  │
│ Performance  │ │ ☐ Show Channels in Color          │ │         │
│ Cursors      │ │ ☑ Show Menu Colors                │ │  Prev   │
│ Transparency & Gamut │ ☑ Show Tool Tips            │ │         │
│ Units & Rulers │                                   │ │  Next   │
│ Guides, Grid, Slices & Count │ ┌─Palettes────────┐ │ │         │
│ Plug-Ins     │ │ ☑ Auto-Collapse Icon Palettes     │ │         │
│ Type         │ │ ☑ Remember Palette Locations      │ │         │
│              │ └───────────────────────────────────┘ │         │
└──────────────┴─────────────────────────────────────┴─────────┘
```

Divided into two sections, General and Palettes, you have the following options:

- **Show Background Drop Shadow (on):** If you want to be able to see a drop shadow on the canvas in the document window, leave this Windows-only option on.

- **Use Grayscale Toolbar Icon (off):** Here's a real dilemma: Do you want to see a color icon at the top of the Toolbox or a grayscale one? If you prefer grayscale for some reason, turn this option on. Otherwise, the gloom of a grayscale icon is replaced with the excitement of color.

- **Show Channels in Color (off):** An individual color channel contains just 8 bits of data per pixel, which makes it equivalent to a grayscale image. Photoshop provides you with the option of colorizing the channel according to the primary color it represents. For example, when this option is selected, the Red color channel looks like a grayscale image viewed through red acetate. Most experts agree the effect isn't helpful, though, and it does more to obscure your image than to make it easier for you to see what's happening. Leave this option deselected, and read Chapter 4 for more information.

- **Show Menu Colors (on):** This option, which was new in Photoshop CS2, allows you to take advantage of the ability to apply colors to menu commands (Edit ➪ Menus). If this is off, your settings through that feature don't show.

- **Show Tool Tips (on):** When on, this option displays little labels and keyboard shortcuts when you hover your cursor over a tool or palette option. The tool tips don't impede Photoshop's performance, so there is no reason to turn off this option.

- **Auto-Collapse Icon Palettes (off):** Given that the palettes are now docked and permanently attached to the dock, which now resides within the workspace (rather than above it, as it was in CS2), the ability to have the palettes respond to our activities is paramount. With this option on, palettes collapse to an icon if you click onto another image or another area of the workspace. In its OFF state, this option requires you to minimize a palette (collapsing it to an icon) if you no longer want to see it open. If you find that you're often hopping between palettes or using particular palettes for just a second and then you move on, you may want to turn this on. Otherwise, it may be a pain to keep re-opening a palette that you use frequently.

- **Remember Palette Locations (on):** When this option is selected, Photoshop keeps track of the location of the Toolbox and palettes (open palettes in the dock and those you've chosen to make floating palettes) from one session to the next. If you deselect this option, Photoshop restores the default palette positions the next time you start the program.

File Handling

When in the Preferences dialog box, press Ctrl+3 (⌘-3 on the Mac) to advance to the File Handling panel. Figures 2.19 and 2.20 show the panel as it appears on the PC and the Mac, respectively.

FIGURE 2.19

The File Handling panel as it appears on the PC

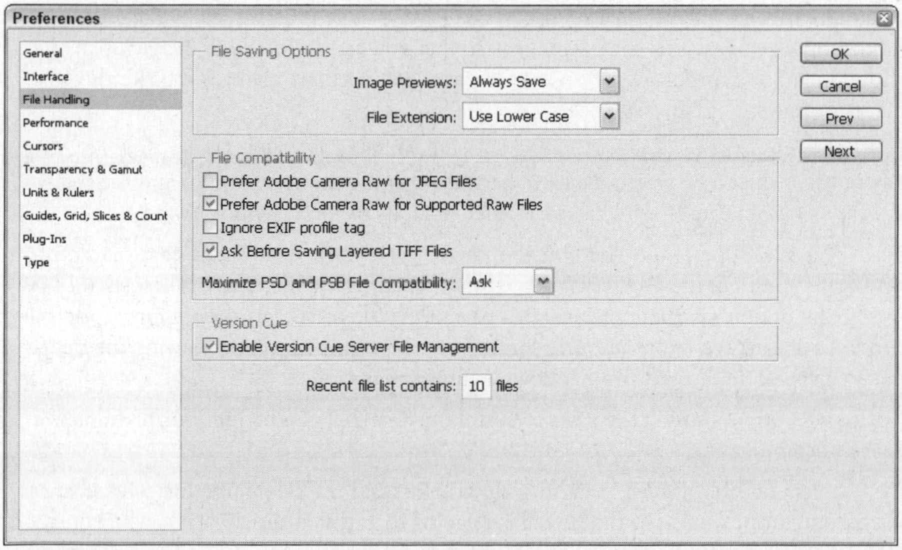

FIGURE 2.20

The File Handling panel as it appears on the Mac

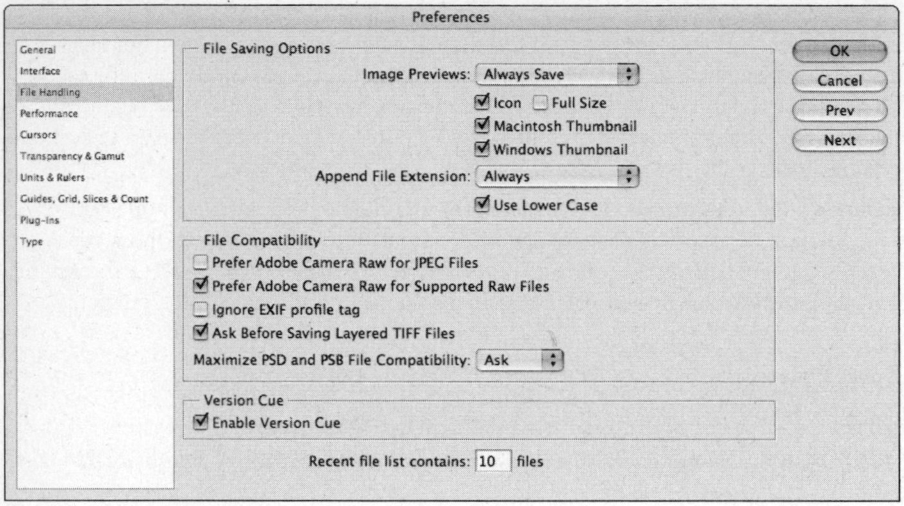

Every option in the File Handling panel affects how Photoshop saves images to disk. The following list explains how the options work and the recommended settings:

- **Image Previews (Ask When Saving):** When Always Save is active (as by default), Photoshop saves a postage-stamp preview so that you can see what an image looks like before opening or importing it. On the Mac, you can select as many as four kinds of image previews, as follows:

The Icon option creates a preview icon that you can view from the Finder desktop. You may not find this to be worth the extra hard drive space that it takes up, and too many custom icons can cause problems with older versions of the system software.

When you select one of the Thumbnail options, Photoshop creates a postage-stamp preview that appears in the Open dialog box when you select a file. The Macintosh Thumbnail option saves the preview in a part of the file known as the resource fork, but Windows doesn't recognize resource forks. So if you ever plan on previewing the image on a PC, you should select the Windows Thumbnail option as well.

The fourth option, Full Size, creates a 72-dpi preview that can be used for placement in a page-layout program.

The problem with previews is that they slightly increase the size of the file. This is fine when doing print work — a thumbnail isn't going to add that much — but when creating Web graphics, every byte counts. That's why we recommend Ask When Saving from the Image Previews pop-up menu. This option makes the preview options available in the Save dialog box so that you can specify whether you want previews on a case-by-case basis when you save your images.

- **File Extension (Use Lower Case)/Use Lower Case (on):** Called File Extension for Windows users (see the File Extension list) and Use Lower Case on the Mac (see checkbox beneath "Append File Extension"), this option decides whether the three-character extension at the end of a file name is uppercase or lowercase. Lowercase is the better choice because it ensures compatibility with other platforms, particularly UNIX, the primary operating system for Web servers. (UNIX is case-sensitive, so a file called *Image.psd* is different than *Image.PSD*. Lowercase extensions eliminate confusion.)

- **Append File Extension (Ask When Saving):** Available only on the Mac, this option adds a three-character extension to the end of a file name to make your Mac images compatible with Windows and DOS programs. For example, a layered composition saved in the Photoshop format gets a *.psd* extension. You may want to set this option to Ask When Saving; that way, you can decide whether to include a PC-style extension from inside the Save dialog box on a file-by-file basis.

> **TIP** You can set the Append File Extension option to Never and still access extensions when saving images. Just press Option when selecting a file format, and Photoshop automatically slaps on an extension. Read more about this process in Chapter 3.

- **Prefer Adobe Camera Raw for JPEG Files (off):** This option uses Adobe's Camera Raw settings for JPEG files.

- **Prefer Adobe Camera Raw for supported raw files (on):** If you'd rather use Adobe's Camera Raw format for all RAW files you open, leave this option on. When RAW files are opened, the Photoshop Raw dialog box opens, which you can use to change the image settings for pixel dimensions, channels, bit depth, and header size. Read more about Camera RAW files in Chapter 18.

- **Ignore EXIF sRGB tag (off)/Ignore EXIF profile tag (off):** This is a controversial feature, but I'm coming down on the side of the default. Virtually every modern digital camera embeds information about when and how a photo was captured (date, f-stop, flash setting, and so on) in the image file. Part of this so-called EXIF data (short for Exchangeable Image File) is a color profile, which is meant to convey the source of the photo so Photoshop knows how to handle its colors. It's a great idea, but there's a big problem. Most vendors make no attempt to profile their specific cameras, instead defaulting to sRGB (the color profile of last resort for just about every printer and scanner sold today). It's also been said that there is so little quality control that the profile is nearly meaningless. However, "nearly meaningless" is better than nothing. Better to have a vague sense of where your images come from than no sense at all. So it is recommended that you leave this option deselected.

- **Ask Before Saving Layered TIFF Files (on):** If you add a layer to a TIFF file that formerly consisted of only a background layer and then try to save the file, having this option selected opens the TIFF Options dialog box. This dialog box lets you choose between JPEG, ZIP, and the traditional LZW compression for TIFFs, as well as other options discussed in Chapter 3. These are useful options, so I say leave this turned on. You also are prompted that saving a TIFF with layers may create a larger file, at which point you can accept that and move on, or stop the process and go back to merge your layers.

■ **Maximize PSD File Compatibility (Ask):** This option is pure evil, yet it is set to "Ask" by default, which means that you are prompted about maximizing file compatibility when saving a new PSD file. If you never change another preference setting, you should set this one to Never. Of course, this begs the question, "Why did Adobe set it to Ask by default if it's so evil?" The answer? Who knows, but this option should be named Double My File Sizes Just Because.

Even Adobe's designers would be hard-pressed to defend use of this option, but here's the tragic backstory: The option ensures backward compatibility between Photoshop CS2 and programs that support the Photoshop file format but don't recognize layers. It's a nice idea, but it comes at a very steep price. To ensure compatibility, Photoshop has to insert an additional flattened version of a layered image into every native Photoshop file. As you can imagine, this takes up a considerable amount of hard drive space, doubling the file size in the most extreme situations.

So set this option to Never. And when you want cross-application compatibility, save an extra TIFF version of your file (as explained in Chapter 3). It's worth the extra time, and it only has to be done when you want that cross-application compatibility, not every single time you save a PSD file.

NOTE   Actually, there is one situation where you may find the Maximize PSD File Compatibility option useful. It permits older versions of After Effects or Illustrator to open files that contain layer effects that were added to Photoshop after those products shipped. If this rare scenario applies to you, then Ask may be the appropriate setting for this otherwise evil option.

■ **Enable Version Cue (on):** This option invokes a spinoff of WebDAV technology, which is a means for multiple users to share and modify documents over a network. Although not currently widely implemented, Adobe and others hope to see WebDAV (or just DAV, as it's sometimes called) grow into a standard means of collaboration. We're not just talking about interoffice networks here; in the DAV world of the future, artists can collaborate with each other remotely from points around the globe.

Probably, most of you won't need this option, and those of you who do will be forced into it by some maniacal IT manager. For those in such a position, here's how it works. Selecting this option inserts a Version Cue icon in the Open dialog box. Clicking the Version Cue icon enables you to check out files and work on collaborative efforts. If, after clicking the Version Cue icon, you need to work on a local file, simply click the Local Files icon in the Open dialog box.

■ **Recent file list contains (10) files (your call):** This option determines how many file names appear when you choose the Open Recent command, which displays a list of the images that you worked on most recently. You can simply click an image name to open the image. The default number of file names is 10, but you can raise it to 30. Raising the value doesn't use resources that would otherwise be useful to Photoshop, so type whatever value makes you happy — the more images you tend to work with in a given day, the higher a value you may want to set for this option.

Performance

Displayed by pressing Ctrl+4 while the Preferences dialog box is open (⌘+4 on the Mac), this panel is divided into four sections: Memory Usage, History & Cache, Scratch Disks, and GPU Settings. Shown in Figure 2.21, this is a new panel in the Preferences dialog box, and you may recognize some of the options from their former homes in other panels in CS2 and previous versions of Photoshop. Suffice to say, the purpose of this panel is to control and improve Photoshop's efficiency with respect to memory and the underlying resources that give the application the ability to respond to your changes. Your options are explained in the following sections.

FIGURE 2.21

How memory is used, where and how big your scratch disks are, and your history and cache settings are all controlled through the Performance panel.

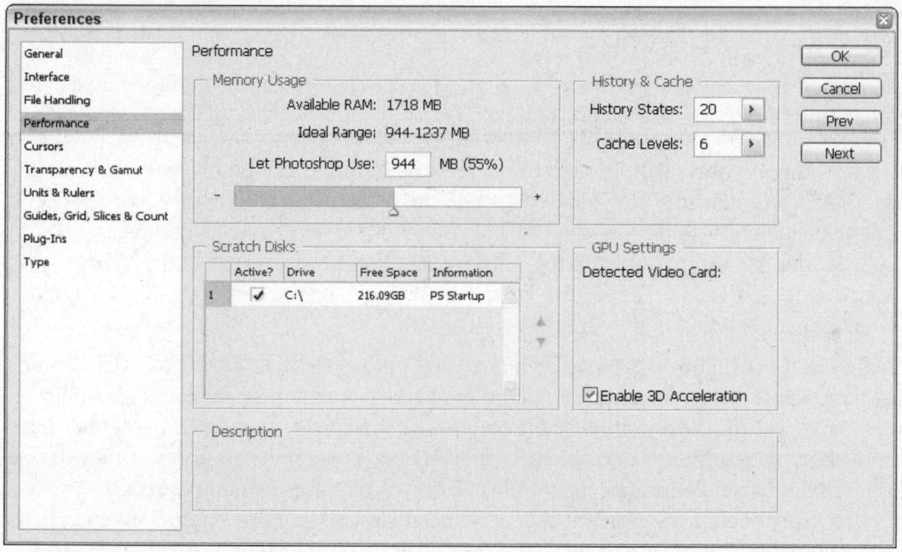

Memory Usage

Mac OS X and Windows 2000 and XP offer dynamic memory allocation, which means that each application gets the memory it needs as it needs it. But Photoshop has a habit of using every spare bit of RAM it can get its hands on, which can cause problems in such an environment. Left to its own devices, it might gobble up all the RAM and bleed over into the operating system's virtual memory space, which is less efficient than Photoshop's own scratch disk scheme.

The Memory Usage option helps you place some limits on Photoshop's ravenous appetite. The option lists the amount of RAM available to all applications after the operating system loads into memory. You can then decide how much of that memory should go to Photoshop. If you like to run lots of applications at the same time — your word processor, Web browser, spreadsheet program, drawing program, and Photoshop, for example — set the Maximum Used by Photoshop value to 50 percent or lower. But if Photoshop is the only program running — and if you have less than 256MB of RAM — raise the value to 70 to 80 percent.

CAUTION   It is recommended that you not take the Maximum Used by Photoshop value any higher than 80 percent, particularly on a low-capacity machine (less than 1 GB). Doing so permits Photoshop to fill up RAM that the operating system may need, which makes for a less stable working environment. As noted earlier, if Photoshop is going too slow for you and hitting the scratch disk too often, buy more RAM — don't play dangerous games with the little RAM you do have.

- **Let Photoshop Use (367 MB (55%)):** This option follows the stated Available RAM and Ideal Range settings, which are not editable directly in this dialog box. You also can use the slider beneath the option, to increase (drag to the right) or decrease (drag to the left) the amount of RAM you want Photoshop to use.

History & Cache

Here you can control how far back in time you can go with the History palette and how repeated saves of an image are stored. These are your options:

- **History States (your call):** Located in the History & Cache section of the Performance panel, this value controls how many steps you can undo using the History palette. The right value depends on the amount of RAM you're willing to devote to Photoshop. If you're working with limited memory, I suggest that you lower the value to 5 or 10. Otherwise, raise the value as you see fit, remembering that the more states the program retains, the more you strain your system.

- **Cache Levels (6):** Photoshop has been criticized for its lack of a "pyramid-style" file format capable of storing an image several times over at progressively smaller and smaller image sizes, called downsamplings. Photoshop's alternative is image caching. Rather than saving the downsamplings to disk, Photoshop generates the reduced images in RAM. The Cache Levels value determines the number of downsamplings, which permits the program to apply operations more quickly at reduced view sizes. For example, if you choose a color correction command at the 50 percent view size, it previews much faster than normal because Photoshop has to modify a quarter as many pixels onscreen.

  However, Photoshop must cache downsamplings in RAM, which takes away memory that could be used to hold the image. If you have lots of RAM (say, 2 GB or more) and you frequently work on large images (20MB or larger), you'll probably want to raise the value to the maximum, 8. The lost memory is worth the speed boost. If you have little RAM (say 256MB or less) and you usually work on small images or Web graphics (4MB or smaller), you may want to reduce the Cache Levels value to 1 or 2. When files are small, RAM is better allocated to storing images rather than caching them.

Scratch Disks

By default, Photoshop assumes you have only one hard drive, so it stores its temporary virtual memory documents — called *scratch files* — on the same drive that contains your system software. If you have more than one drive available, though, you may want to tell Photoshop to look elsewhere. In fact, Photoshop can use up to four drives.

Changes affect the next session

As the note at the bottom of the Performance panel states, "Changes will take effect the next time you start Photoshop." (Don't see it? Mouse over the Scratch Disks settings.) This means that you have to exit and restart Photoshop in order to see your new settings here go into effect. Potentially annoying, yes, but necessary given that Photoshop has to reacquaint itself with your hardware if you're suddenly informing it of an additional drive or partition and want it to make use of it as a scratch disk or location for your plug-ins.

TIP If you find restarting simply unacceptable, there is a workaround. To access the plug-ins and scratch disk settings during the launch cycle, after double-clicking the Photoshop application icon or choosing Photoshop from the Windows Start menu, press and hold Ctrl and Alt (⌘ and Option on the Mac). If you're using a Mac, Photoshop greets you with a message requesting that you locate the Plug-Ins folder. After you do so, press and hold ⌘ and Option again. After a few seconds, a screen of the scratch disk options appears. Specify the disks as desired, and press Enter or Return. Your new settings now work for the current session — no restarting necessary. In order to use this workaround, you need to know that you want to make these changes before you start Photoshop.

- **Enable 3D Acceleration (on):** This option is on by default because it enhances your video display and rendering capabilities.

Cursors

Press Ctrl+5 (⌘-5 on the Mac) to check out the Cursors options (formerly known as the Display & Cursors options in Photoshop CS2), which appear in Figure 2.22. These options affect the way colors and cursors appear onscreen. Here's how the options work, along with recommended settings:

- **Painting Cursors (Brush Size):** When you use a paint or edit tool, Photoshop can display one of four cursors — Standard, Precise, Normal Brush Tip, or Full Size Brush Tip. The Standard cursor looks like a paintbrush, a pencil, a finger (if you're smudging), or whatever tool you're using. These cursors are great if you have problems keeping track of what tool you selected, but otherwise they border on childish and make precision nearly impossible — imagine trying to erase a row of single pixels with a cursor that looks like a big picture of an eraser. Not easy.

  The Precise and two Brush Size options are more functional. The Precise option displays a cross-shaped cursor — called a cross hair — regardless of which tool is active. The cross hair is great because it prevents the cursor from blocking your view as you edit, but it has a significant drawback — sometimes it's hard to see your cursor unless you're zoomed in very close to your image. On the other hand, the Normal Brush Size option displays a circle that's 50 percent of the size and shape of the active brush in the Brushes palette, and allows you to be precise as well as providing a sense of the effect the Brush tool in question will have, at least in terms of how wide a swath you'll be painting, smudging, blurring, sharpening, or erasing. The Full Size Brush Tip option is the default setting, and shows your brush tip in the actual size you have set. Most artists prefer this final setting to the others because it comes the closest to showing the cursor the way it really is, and because it's a circle (and you can see through it), it affords more accuracy in tight spots and where a high level of precision is required. You also can add to the precision by selecting the Show Crosshair in Brush Tip option, which does just that — it places a cross hair in the middle of the Normal or Full Size brush tip cursor.

> **TIP** When Standard or Brush Size is selected, you can access the cross-hair cursor by pressing the Caps Lock key. When Precise is selected from the Painting Cursors options, pressing Caps Lock displays the brush size.

- **Other Cursors (Standard):** Again, you can select Standard to get the regular cursors or Precise to get cross hairs. You may want to leave this option set to Standard because you can always access the cross-hair cursor by pressing Caps Lock. The Precise option locks you into the cross hair whether you like it or not.

FIGURE 2.22

The Cursors options control the way images and cursors appear onscreen. Here we see the default settings.

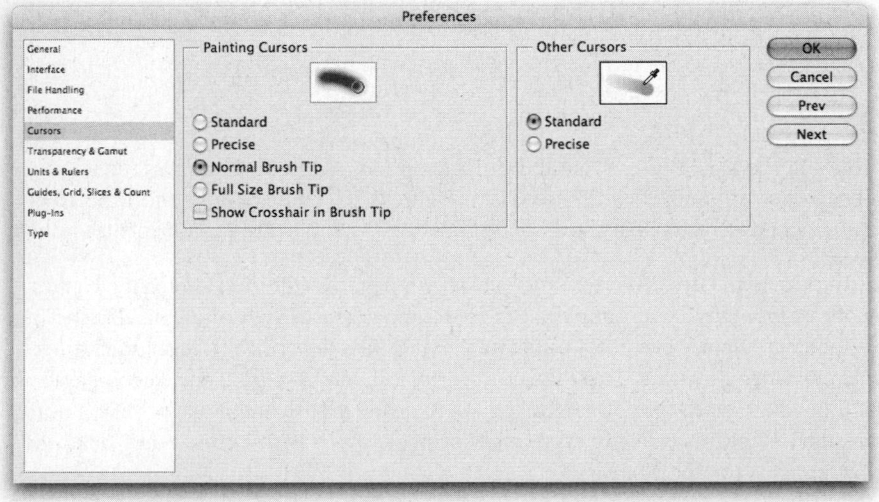

Transparency & Gamut

Press Ctrl+6 (⌘-6 on the Mac) to switch to the Transparency & Gamut panel shown in Figure 2.23. The options in this panel change how Photoshop displays two conceptual items — transparent space behind layers and RGB colors that can't be expressed in CMYK printing.

FIGURE 2.23

The options in this panel affect how Photoshop represents transparency and out-of-gamut colors. Try to select colors that you don't often see in your images, so you can tell Transparency from an actual pattern in your image.

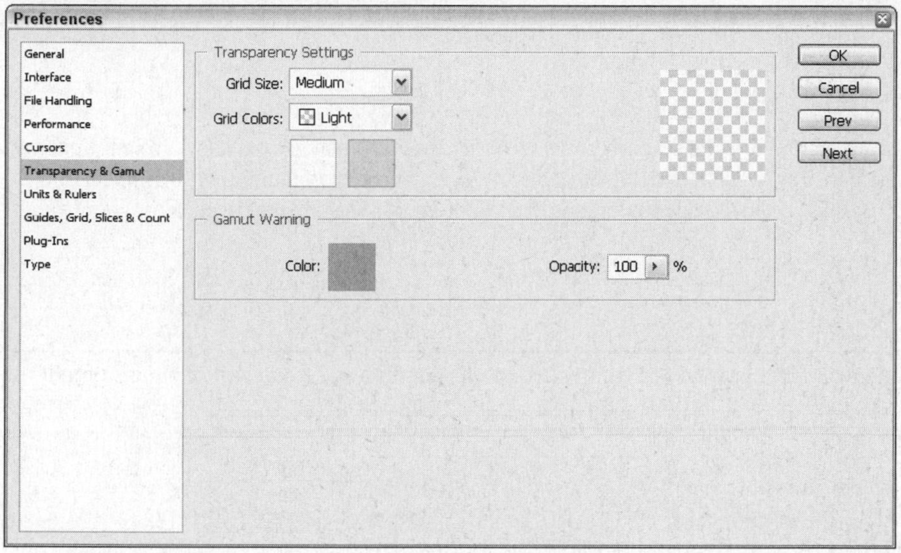

The options are arranged into two groups — Transparency Settings and Gamut Warning — as explained in the following sections.

Transparency settings

Photoshop images rest on a layer of absolute transparency, and by default, Photoshop represents this transparency as a gray checkerboard pattern. When you view a layer independently of others, Photoshop fills the see-through portions of the layer with the checkerboard, so having the checkerboard stand out from the layer itself is essential. You can customize the size of the checkers and the color of the squares using the Grid Size and Grid Colors pop-up menus, and you also can set the Opacity of the checkerboard (it's set to 100 percent by default). You also can click the color swatches to define your own colors: When you click either one, the Color Picker opens.

TIP To lift colors from the image window (for use in your checkerboard, or anything else you're coloring, for that matter), move your cursor outside the Color Picker (if that dialog box is open) or the Preferences dialog box to get the Eyedropper. Click a color to change the color of the white checkers; Alt-click (or Option-click on the Mac) to change the gray ones.

If you own a 32-bit device that enables chroma keying, you can select the Use Video Alpha option to view a television signal in the transparent area behind a layer. Unless you work in video production, you needn't worry about this option.

Gamut warning

If Photoshop can display a color onscreen but can't accurately print the color, the color is said to be *out of gamut*. You can choose View ⇨ Gamut Warning to coat all out-of-gamut colors with gray (or any other color you choose by clicking the Color block in the dialog box). You may find that you prefer using the View ⇨ Proof Colors (Ctrl+Y or ⌘-Y) command instead — but if you use View ⇨ Gamut Warning, you don't have to accept gray as the out-of-gamut coating.

Units & Rulers

The Units & Rulers panel is the seventh panel in the Preferences dialog box; as you might imagine, you reach the panel by pressing Ctrl+7 (⌘-7 on the Mac). Shown in Figure 2.24, this panel offers options that enable you to change the predominant system of measurement used throughout the program.

FIGURE 2.24

Go to the Units & Rulers panel to change the column and pica settings and set the unit of measurement.

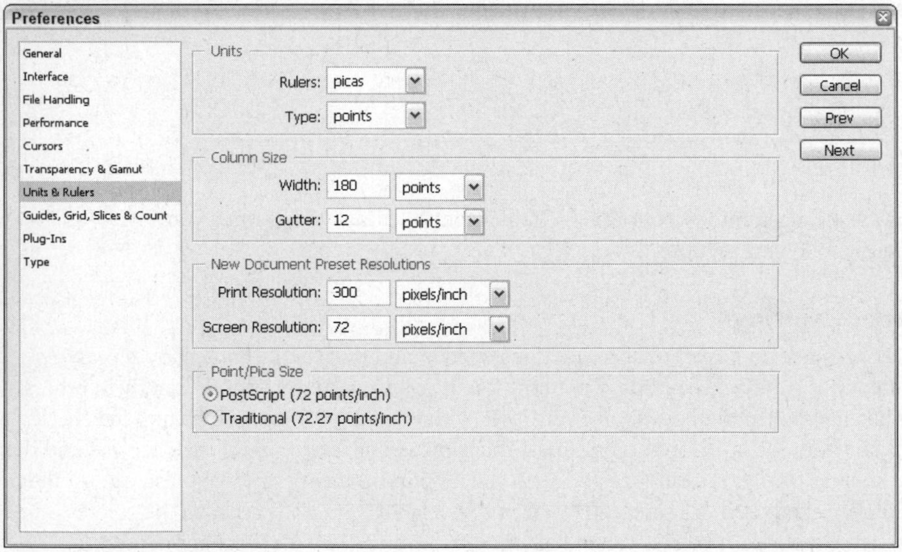

> **TIP**   Whenever the rulers are visible, the Units & Rulers panel is only a double-click away. Choose View ⇨ Rulers (Ctrl+R or ⌘-R) to display the rulers (if they're not already showing), and then double-click either the horizontal or vertical ruler to open the dialog box.

Rulers

You can set the unit of measurement with the Units option in the Preferences dialog box. But there's an easier way: Just right-click (Control-click on the Mac) anywhere on the ruler to display a pop-up menu of unit options, and then click the unit you want to use. You can display the same pop-up menu by clicking the plus sign next to the X and Y coordinates that appear in the Info palette.

When you're first learning Photoshop, and if you're coming from the print design world, you may be tempted to go with inches or picas as your Unit of choice. Another option? Use pixels. Why? Because you can change the resolution of an image at any time and the only constant is pixels. An image measures a fixed number of pixels high by a fixed number of pixels wide — that's it. You can print those pixels as large or as small as you want, but the pixels are the one constant. Another reason? If your images might ever end up on the Web, you'll want to be thinking in pixels because that's how Web pages are measured, too.

CROSS-REF To learn more about resolution, read Chapter 3.

Type

Photoshop enables you to set the unit of measure used for the Type tool independently of the ruler units. You can work in points, pixels, and millimeters; select your unit of choice from the Type pop-up menu.

CROSS-REF Check out Chapter 16 for more information and insights about type in Photoshop.

Column Size

The Column Size options enable you to size images according to columns in a newsletter or magazine. Type the width of your columns and the size of the gutter in the Width and Gutter option boxes. Then use File ⇨ New or Image ⇨ Image Size to specify the number of columns assigned to the width of the image. You can read more about these commands in more detail in Chapter 3.

New Document Preset Resolutions

One nifty feature, first introduced in Photoshop 7, is the listing of preset sizes you get when you create a new document by choosing File ⇨ New. The New Document Preset Resolutions preferences let you set a default resolution for these presets for both print and screen. This can be especially helpful for setting different print resolutions if you commonly work at something other than the default of 300 pixels per inch. Adjusting the Print Resolution preference changes the number of pixels in the document when you choose the Letter preset, for example. For general purposes though, the defaults are just fine here.

Point/Pica Size

The last option in the Units & Rulers panel, Point/Pica Size, may be the most obscure of all Photoshop options. To interpret the information displayed here, you need to know that exactly 12 points are in a pica, and about 6.06 picas are in an inch.

Because picas are almost evenly divisible into inches, the people who came up with the PostScript printing language decided to throw out the difference and define a pica as exactly ⅙ inch. This makes a point exactly ¹⁄₇₂ inch.

But a few purists didn't take to it — you know those purists, they're always making trouble. They found their new electronic documents weren't quite matching their old paste-up documents, and apparently this was more than they could bear. So Adobe caved and had to go back and add the Traditional (72.27 points/inch) option to keep everyone happy.

You may find that you prefer the nontraditional PostScript definition of points. This way, a pixel onscreen translates to a point on paper when you print an image at 72 ppi (the standard screen resolution).

Guides, Grid, Slices & Count

The Guides, Grid, Slices & Count version of the Preferences dialog box can be accessed by pressing Ctrl+8 (⌘-8 on the Mac). If your computer isn't on and glowing at your side right now, you can see the dialog box in Figure 2.25. This dialog box lets you modify the colors of any guides you place in the image window and specify the size of the grid that you use to help line things up. It also provides tools for customizing Smart Guides, which you can read more about in Chapter 13.

> **TIP**   You can display the Preferences dialog box and go directly to the Guides, Grid, Slices & Count panel by double-clicking a guide with the Move tool or Ctrl+double-clicking (⌘-double-clicking on the Mac) with another tool. (To create a guide, drag from the horizontal or vertical ruler into the image.)

These options are explained in more detail in Chapter 13, but for the moment, here are some brief descriptions.

Guides

Select a color for horizontal and vertical ruler guides from the Color pop-up menu. To lift a color from the image, move your cursor outside the Preferences dialog box and click in the image window with the Eyedropper. You also can view guides as solid lines or dashes by selecting an option from the Style pop-up menu.

Smart Guides

These snappy little guides appear when you have Smart Guides turned on through the View ⇨ Show submenu. Pink by default, they show up to help you line up one layer's content with another, letting you know when the top, bottom, sides, and/or center of the content in transit is aligned to nearby content in the image. Through this portion of the dialog box, you can change the

Color of the Smart Guides, using the list to choose from eight alternatives to the default Magenta, or click the color swatch to the right of the Color option and use the Color Picker to make your selection. What should you do? Pick a color that doesn't occur in your image (or that doesn't appear in great quantity) because the Smart Guides appear fleetingly — just as you're moving the layers around, and only while you're close to perfect alignment — so you need to be able to spot them quickly and easily.

FIGURE 2.25

Use these options to adjust the size of the grid and change the way that ruler guides, Smart Guides, the grid, and your slices appear onscreen.

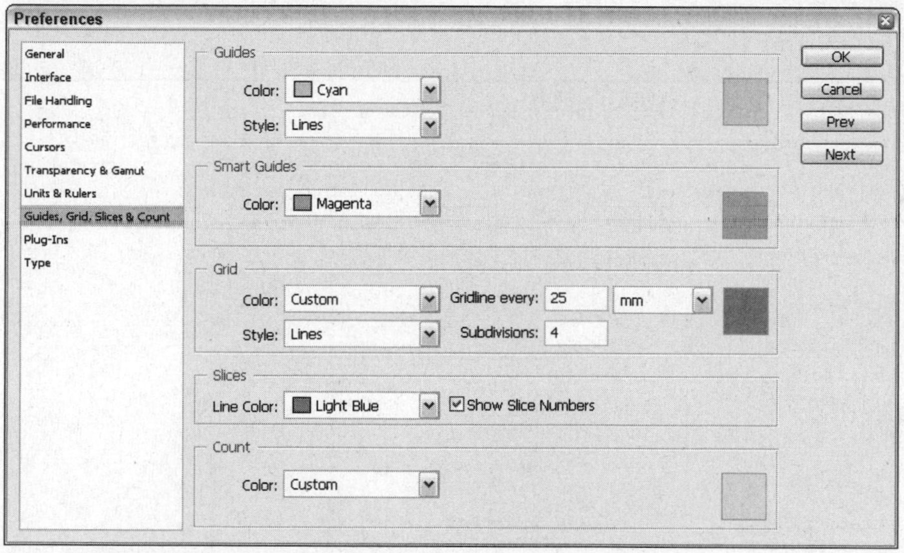

Grid

Choose a color for the grid from the Color menu, or Alt+click (Option-click on the Mac) in the image window to lift a color from the image. Then decide how the grid lines look by selecting a Style option. The Dots setting is the least intrusive.

The Gridline Every value determines the increments for the visible grid marks onscreen. But the Subdivisions value sets the real grid. For example, if you request a grid mark every 1 inch with four subdivisions, Photoshop snaps selections and layers in ¼-inch increments (1 inch divided by 4).

Slices

Like setting the color for guides and the grid, the Slices preference lets you choose a color for the lines that illustrate exactly where you've sliced up your image for posting on the Web. You can turn on and off the visibility of the slice numbers here as well.

Count

The color in which your numbers and tiny blocks appear when you use the Count tool to numerically label locations in your image is set here. The default is the same color as the Guides default, so if you use the Count feature often (see Chapter 3 for more information on this tool), you may want to choose an alternate color, should a guide and a count marker overlap.

Plug-Ins

Press Ctrl+9 (⌘-9 on the Mac) to advance to the panel shown in Figure 2.26. Each time you launch Photoshop, the program searches for plug-in modules, and you have to tell Photoshop where to find them.

FIGURE 2.26

Tell Photoshop where to find plug-ins using these options.

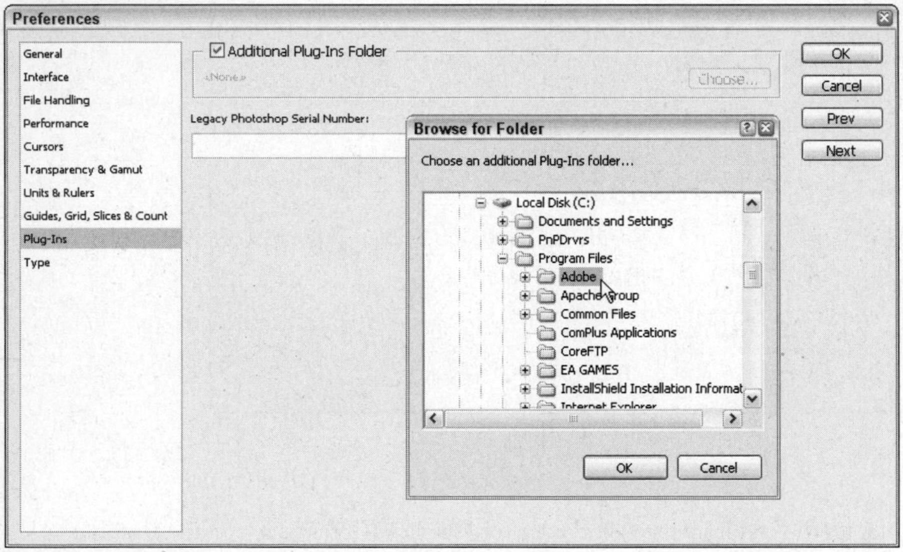

Additional Plug-Ins Folder

By default, the plug-ins are located in a folder cleverly disguised with the name Plug-Ins, which resides in the same folder as the Photoshop application. But you can tell Photoshop to also look for plug-ins in some other folder — a useful option if you install all your third-party plug-ins to some central location outside the Photoshop folders. To specify the second plug-ins location, select the option and then click Choose to select the folder.

Legacy Photoshop Serial Number

As you may have noticed when you installed it, Photoshop CS3 continues the new era in Adobe serial numbers first introduced with Photoshop 7. No longer are they a mixture of numbers and letters; it's all just numbers and dashes now. Some third-party plug-ins, however, serialize themselves to the old-style Photoshop serial number format. So if you're upgrading to Photoshop CS3 and you have an old serial number from Photoshop 6 or earlier, you can type it here.

Type

Housing just four simple options, the Type preferences dialog box, shown in Figure 2.27, lets you choose from the following:

FIGURE 2.27

Tell Photoshop a thing or two about how you want to work with type.

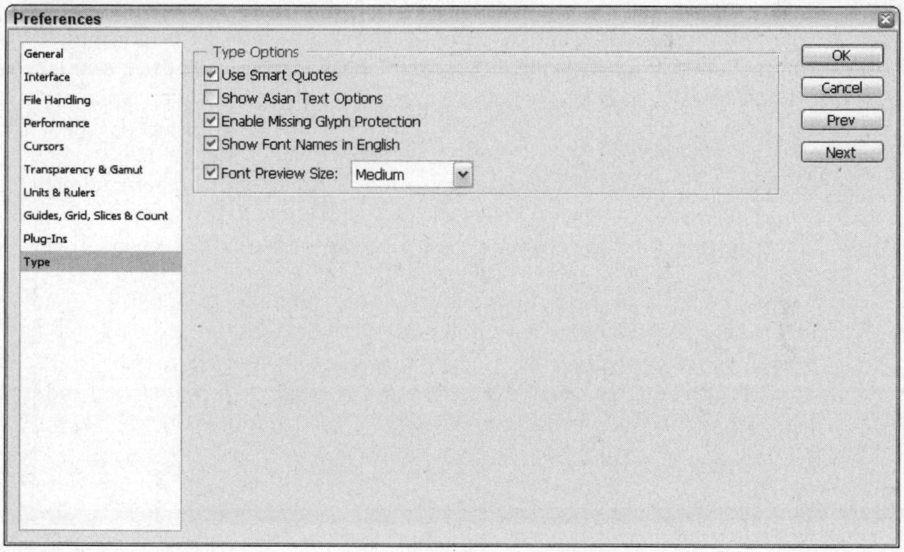

- **Use Smart Quotes:** On by default, Smart Quotes that "know" they're at the beginning or end of a word or phrase curl accordingly. If you turn this off, you get straight quotes. Straight quotes can be useful if you're typing measurements, where a single straight quote means feet and two straight quotes mean inches.

- **Show Asian Text Options:** Off by default, if you want to see Chinese, Japanese, and Korean type options in the Character and Paragraph palettes, turn this option on. If you don't, don't.

- **Enable Missing Glyph Protection:** When this option is on, which it is by default, Photoshop makes font substitutions for any missing glyphs — especially useful if you type in various languages that employ non-English alphabets, such as Chinese, Japanese, Russian, Greek, or Arabic.

- **Show Font Names in English:** This option, which is on by default, really pertains to non-Roman fonts and whether you want to see their Roman names. You do, for familiarity's sake, so leave this on.

- **Font Preview Size:** This option lets you choose between Small, Medium (the default), and Large. The preview is found in the Type tool's Options bar, and certainly Small is going to be less visually effective than Medium, and Large is great for people with their monitors set to a high resolution — say 1024×768 or greater.

Summary

In this chapter, you received a friendly introduction to the Photoshop desktop, tools, palettes, and the interface in general. For the new user, this was hopefully a comfort-inducing experience where you found out how helpful Photoshop can be in helping you move around the interface and your images. If you're a more experienced user, you may have found out what some of the tools you've looked at but not explored can do for you — a common experience for the self-taught.

No matter what level user you are, you also learned about new tools and preference settings (and found out where in-depth coverage can be found elsewhere in the book) and discovered how to view your tool options and save presets for tools, presets, and the workspace.

Key to getting to know Photoshop is getting around in Photoshop, and toward that end you also learned about zooming in on your images, scrolling from the keyboard, and navigating the workspace. Finally, you learned how to use Photoshop's Preferences to make yourself at home — so hopefully by now, you have your feet up and are ready to move forward and find out about file management, covered in the next chapter.

Chapter 3

Image Management

The colored pixels that make up an *image* work much like the tiles in a mosaic. When you view a mosaic up close, you may not be able to tell what the overall image is supposed to be — move far enough away, however, and the mosaic's tiles blend together to make a complete image. If you enlarge the pixels in an image in Photoshop, they look like an unrelated collection of colored squares. Reduce the size of the pixels, and they blend together to form an image that looks like a standard photograph. Photoshop deceives the eye, counting on the distance that printing or normal onscreen viewing puts between the person's eye and the image pixels, and in most cases, the deception works quite well.

Of course, there are differences between pixels and mosaic tiles. Pixels come in 16 million distinct colors. Also, you can resample, color separate, and crop electronic images, often working at a very zoomed-in, you-can-see-the-individual-pixels level. Luckily, you can get extremely close to the image to make changes that have a very subtle impact when viewed at that aforementioned eye-deceiving distance.

In this chapter, you learn about how images are constructed, how to change their resolution, how to crop out what you don't want, how to save your files (including an exhaustive discussion of file formats and choosing the right ones for the way your files will be used), and ways to better organize and view your saved images. You also learn about automating the use of Photoshop, finding out more about actions and how you can use them to record often-performed and/or complex tasks over and over again, with the press of a button or the click of an icon.

Size versus Resolution

If you haven't already guessed, the term *image size* describes the physical dimensions of an image. *Resolution* is the number of pixels per linear inch in the final printed image. The term *linear* is used because you measure pixels in a straight line. If the resolution of an image is 72 *ppi* — that is, pixels per inch — you get 5,184 pixels per square inch (72 pixels wide × 72 pixels tall = 5,184).

Assuming the number of pixels in an image is fixed, increasing the size of an image decreases its resolution, and vice versa. An image that looks good when printed on a postage stamp, therefore, probably looks jagged when printed as an 11×17-inch poster.

Figure 3.1 shows a single image printed at three different sizes and resolutions. The smallest image is printed at twice the resolution of the medium-sized image; the medium-sized image is printed at twice the resolution of the largest image.

FIGURE 3.1

These three images contain the same number of pixels but are printed at different resolutions. Doubling the resolution of an image reduces it to 25 percent of its original size.

One inch in the smallest image includes twice as many pixels vertically and twice as many pixels horizontally as an inch in the medium-sized image, for a total of four times as many pixels per square inch. Therefore, the smallest image covers one-fourth the area of the medium-sized image.

The same relationships exist between the medium-sized image and the largest image. An inch in the medium-sized image comprises four times as many pixels as an inch in the largest image. Consequently, the medium-sized image consumes one-fourth the area of the largest image.

Changing the Printing Resolution

When printing an image, a higher resolution translates to a sharper image with greater clarity. Photoshop lets you change the resolution of a printed image in one of two ways:

- Choose Image ⇨ Image Size to access the controls that enable you to change the pixel dimensions and resolution of an image. Then type a value into the Resolution option box, either in pixels per inch or pixels per centimeter.

  A good idea (although not essential) is to deselect the Resample Image option, as demonstrated in Figure 3.2. If you leave it selected, Photoshop may add or subtract pixels, as discussed later in this chapter. Of course, if you're shrinking an image for posting on the Web, resampling the image is necessary. For non-Web images, deselecting resampling instructs Photoshop to leave the pixels intact but change how many of them print per inch. This is especially important when going from a lower resolution to a higher one.

FIGURE 3.2

Deselect the Resample Image option to maintain a constant number of pixels in an image and to change only the printed resolution.

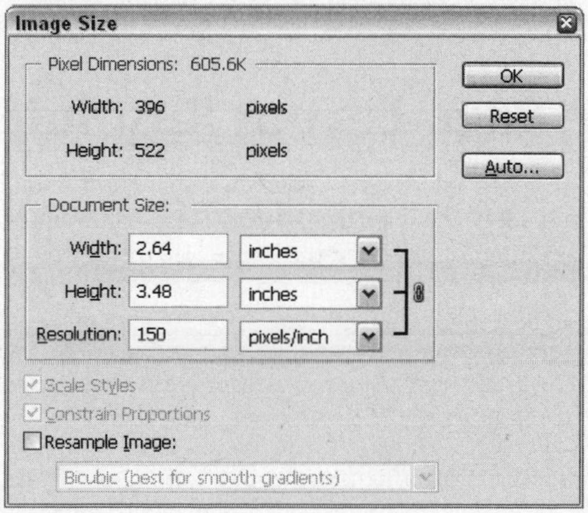

- Alternatively, you can ask Photoshop to scale an image during the print cycle. You hand down this edict with the Print command. Choose File ➪ Print or press Ctrl+P (⌘+P on the Mac) to open the dialog box. You can type specific Width and Height values or type a percentage value into the Scale option box. Lower values reduce the size of the printed image and thereby increase the resolution; higher values lower the resolution. (Chapter 20 contains more information about scaling images as well as the other settings in the Print dialog box.)

Photoshop saves the Resolution setting with the image; the scale settings in the Print dialog box affect only the current print job. Together, the two determine the printed resolution. Photoshop divides the Resolution value in the Image Size dialog box by the Scale percentage from the Print dialog box. For example, if the image resolution is set to 72 ppi and you reduce the image to 48 percent, the final printed image has a resolution of 150 ppi (72 divided by 0.48).

NOTE   With apologies to the non-mathematically inclined readers out there, it's important to remind you that whenever you use a percentage in an equation, you first convert it to a decimal. For example, 100 percent is 1.0, 64 percent is 0.64, and 5 percent is 0.05. This little tip can help you make sense of the discussions of image size, resolution, and so on throughout this chapter and the rest of the book.

TIP   To avoid confusion, most people rely exclusively on the Resolution value and leave the Print dialog box Scale value set to 100 percent. The only exception is when printing tests and proofs. Because inkjet and other consumer printers offer lower-resolution output than high-end commercial devices, you may find it helpful to proof larger images so that you can see more pixels. Raising the Scale value lets you accomplish this without upsetting the Resolution value. Just be sure to restore the value to 100 percent after you make your test print.

NEW FEATURE   When you view the list of Resample Image options in the Image Size dialog box, you now get tips as to which resampling method might work best for your current image or goals for resizing it. For example, you are reminded that Bicubic resampling works well for smooth gradients, while Bicubic Smoother is your best choice if you're enlarging an image.

Changing the Page-Layout Resolution

The Scale value in the Print dialog box value has no effect on the size and resolution of an image imported into an object-oriented application, such as QuarkXPress or Illustrator. But these same applications do observe the Resolution setting from the Image Size dialog box.

Specifying the resolution in Photoshop is a handy way to avoid resizing operations and printing complications in your page-layout program. For example, when images were created for this book, their resolution was preset so the production team had only to import the images in preparation for the printing process.

Photoshop is as good as or better than any other program at adjusting pixels. It's a good idea, therefore, to take advantage of its considerable powers and prepare your images as completely as possible in Photoshop before importing them into another program.

Knowing the Best Resolution

After all this explanation of pixels and resolution, you may still be wondering what the best resolution would be for any image — images that will be printed, displayed onscreen, or both. The answer is a frustrating "non-answer" to some and a liberating "whatever you want!" to others: The resolution is entirely up to you, and there's no hard and fast rule. You're best off using the highest resolution possible, of course, because the higher the resolution, the cleaner, crisper, and more detailed the image is, but there are no absolute right answers. The images in this book vary from 150 ppi for figures that show black-and-white images, dialog boxes, and other parts of the workspace to 300 ppi for the images that appear in color. Now, despite the lack of an established rule for determining resolution, here's a little help to assist you in making effective choices for your images:

- Most experts recommend that you set the Resolution value to somewhere between 150 percent and 200 percent of the screen frequency of the final output device. The *screen frequency* is the number of halftone dots per linear inch, measured in *lpi* (short for *lines per inch*). So ask your commercial printer what screen frequency he uses — generally 120 lpi to 150 lpi — and multiply that times 1.5 or 2.

- More specifically, for high-end photographic print work, it's hard to go wrong with the standard Resolution value of 267 ppi. That's around 200 percent of 133 lpi, arguably the most popular screen frequency. When in doubt, most professionals aim for 267 ppi.

- If you're printing on a home or small-office printer, the rules change slightly. Different manufacturers recommend different optimum resolutions for their various models, but the average is 250 to 300 ppi. Experiment to see how low you can go, though — sometimes you can get by with fewer pixels than the manufacturer suggests. And don't forget that the quality of the paper you use may be more to blame than a lack of pixels for a lousy print — copier-quality paper absorbs the ink and colors, and detail can be lost to that. You want bright white paper that won't suck up all the ink. Most papers you can buy at the office-supply store or printer will be marked clearly as to what kind of printing they're best used for — photos, brochures, flyers, informal publications, and so on.

- What if you don't have enough pixels for 267 ppi? Say that you shoot a digital photograph that measures 768×1024 pixels and you want to print it at 6×8 inches. That works out to a measly 128 ppi. Won't that look grainy? Probably. Should you add pixels with Image Size or some other command? No, that typically won't help. You have a finite number of pixels to work with, so you can print the image large and a little grainy, or sharp and small. The choice is yours.

- What if you have a photograph or slide and you can scan it at any resolution you want? Flatbed scanners typically offer two maximum resolutions: a true optical maximum and an interpolated digital enhancement. The lower of the two values is invariably the true optical resolution. Scan at this lower maximum setting. Then use Image ⇨ Image Size to resample the image down to the desired size and resolution, as explained in the section "Resampling and Cropping" near the end of this chapter.

Finally, just take the pixels you have and try to make them look the best you can. Then print the image at the size you want it to appear, or for images that will be viewed solely online or onscreen, make sure they look good on the monitor and leave it at that — the Save for Web dialog box (discussed later in this chapter and again in Chapter 20) can help you make sure your image is both visually appealing *and* browser-friendly in terms of fast-loading for your onsite patrons. Overall, if you focus on the function of your image first and worry about resolution and other technical issues second, you'll produce better art.

> **TIP**   While it's often a case of making the best of what you've got, you *can* improve images prior to printing and onscreen display. Check out Chapters 10, 11, and 12 for ideas on using filters to blur, sharpen, and otherwise manipulate your image content — from subtle changes that smooth out noise and graininess to others that apply fancy-schmancy artistic effects, some of which can creatively mask a low-resolution, otherwise shabby-looking image.

The Resolution of Screen Images

Regardless of the Resolution and Scale values, Photoshop displays each pixel onscreen according to the zoom ratio (covered in Chapter 2). If the zoom ratio is 100 percent, for example, each image pixel takes up a single screen pixel. Zoom ratio and printer output are unrelated.

This same rule applies outside Photoshop as well. Other programs that display screen images — including multimedia development applications, presentation programs, and Web browsers — default to showing one image pixel for every screen pixel. This means that when you're creating an image for the screen, the Resolution value has limited impact. Some people might recommend that screen images should be set to 72 ppi on the Mac or 96 ppi for Windows, and while there's nothing wrong with doing this, anything at or over 72 ppi should be fine, considering that the load time is king when it comes to Web images — unlike print, where the image quality is primary. On the Web, you want the image to look good, but to load fast — even if that means sacrificing image quality somewhat.

When publishing for the screen, just scan or capture at a high resolution — 300 ppi or more — make your corrections, retouches, edits, and so on — and then use the Save for Web dialog box to optimize the image for the Web. The dialog box contains a preview that lets you choose the right format, quality, and color range, and the software does the work of setting the resolution for you. You also get a load-time estimate so you can decide whether you want to sacrifice some of the clarity in order for your image to load in under a minute. The Save for Web dialog box is discussed later in this chapter, and also in Chapter 20.

So, in the end, all that counts is the 100 percent view. That means you want the image to fit inside the prospective monitor when you choose View ➪ Actual Pixels (Ctrl+Alt+0 on the PC or ⌘+Option+0 on the Mac) inside Photoshop. The term *prospective monitor* is used because although you may use a 17-inch monitor when you create the image, you may need the final image to fit on a 13-inch display. So even though your monitor probably displays at least 1,024×768 pixels, many Web and screen artists prepare for some worst-case scenarios — 800×600 pixels for a computer screen, or 640×480 for a hand-held device.

Opening, Duplicating, and Saving Images

Believe it or not, before you can work on an image in Photoshop—whether you're creating a brand-new document or opening an image from disk—you must first load the image into an image window. Here are the basic ways to create an image window:

- **File ⇨ New:** Create a new window by choosing File ⇨ New or by pressing Ctrl+N (⌘+N on the Mac). After you fill out the desired size and resolution specifications (or accept the defaults, based on any content from another image you may have copied to the Clipboard) in the New dialog box, Photoshop confronts you with a stark, white, empty canvas. You then face the ultimate test of your artistic abilities—painting from scratch, unless you have content in other images that you can bring in and play with in the new image window. For information on how to click and drag layers and selections from one image into another image, see Chapter 13.

> **NOTE** If you opt to choose Transparent or Background Color from the Background Contents drop list, you'll either see a dim checkerboard effect or the currently-selected background color (see the toolbox for what's currently chosen).

- **File ⇨ Open:** Choose File ⇨ Open or press Ctrl+O (⌘+O on the Mac) to open images scanned in other applications, images purchased from stock photo agencies, slides and transparencies digitized to a Kodak Photo CD, or an image you previously edited in Photoshop. Photoshop CS3's Bridge feature also gives you access to Adobe Stock Photos. While you're in the Open dialog box, click the Use Adobe Dialog button, and see the dialog box shown in Figure 3.3. The dialog box functions nearly identically to the default dialog box (see the Use OS Dialog button that appears when you're in the Adobe version), but it provides a few more tools, such as opening images into the Bridge (Photoshop CS3's enhanced file organization workspace).

- **File ⇨ Browse:** This command opens the Bridge, a separate workspace that allows you to organize and print your images.

> **NOTE** You also can open the Bridge by clicking the Go To Bridge button (found just to the left of the Workspace drop list on the Options bar). The Bridge is discussed later in this chapter and also in Chapter 20.

- **File ⇨ Open Recent:** A variation on the Open command, Open Recent displays a list of the images that you recently opened. Click an image name to crack open the image file without taking that tedious trip to the Open dialog box. You can set the number of files that you want to appear in this list in the File Handling panel of the Preferences dialog box.

- **Edit ⇨ Paste:** Photoshop automatically adapts a new image window to the contents of the Clipboard (provided that those contents are bitmapped). So if you copy an image in a different application or in Photoshop and then choose File ⇨ New, Photoshop enters the dimensions and resolution of the image into the New dialog box. You can just accept the settings and choose Edit ⇨ Paste to introduce the image into a new window. Photoshop pastes the Clipboard contents as a new layer. This technique is useful for editing screen shots captured to the Clipboard or for testing effects on a sample of an image without harming the original.

FIGURE 3.3

The Adobe Open dialog box is an alternative for opening files in Photoshop CS3; if you want a "totally Adobe" experience, it's great. Otherwise, just stick with the default OS version of the box.

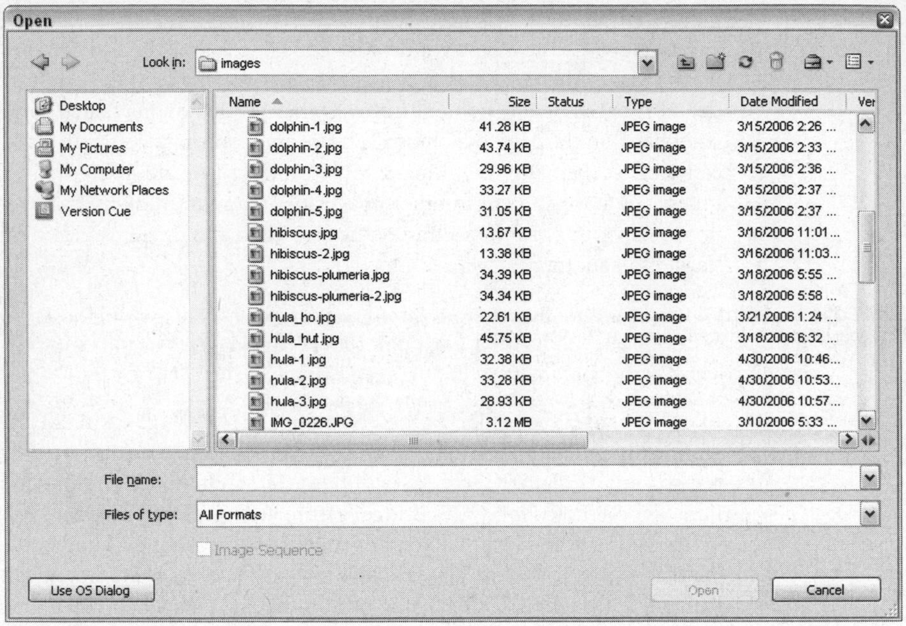

- **File ➪ Import:** This command's submenu, as it relates to opening images, includes commands for opening a digital camera image, grabbing an image from your scanner, or bringing in video frames as layers. Typically, if you have a scanner or camera, your installation of that device (for using the device with your computer) has made Photoshop "aware" of the device and enabled it to support it. You also may have to deal with the device's plug-in module, which lets you transfer an image directly into Photoshop. Just copy the module into Photoshop's Plug-Ins folder and then run or relaunch the Photoshop application. To initiate a scan or to load an image into Photoshop, choose the already set-up scanner from the File ➪ Import submenu.

After you choose the command, Photoshop launches the device's download software. If you're scanning, select the scanner settings and initiate the scan as usual; the scanned picture appears in a new image window in Photoshop. If you're transferring images from a digital camera, the camera software typically creates thumbnail previews of images in the camera's memory so that you can select the ones you want to transfer to Photoshop. If you're bringing in video frames to be viewed as layers in an image, you are presented with a dialog box through which you can choose the video file and the frames within that video for import.

Save your images to disk immediately after you scan or download them; unlike some other programs, Photoshop doesn't automatically take this step for you. Also, if your digital camera stores images on removable memory cards (CompactFlash, SmartMedia, Memory Stick, and the like), it's a good idea to invest in a card reader or adapter that enables your computer to see the memory card as just another hard drive — if your computer didn't already come with a built in reader. You can then just drag and drop images from the memory card to your computer's hard drive, a process that, depending on your camera, may be much faster and more convenient than transferring images using a cable connection.

NOTE Open as Smart Object is another command on the File menu, and it does two jobs. It opens an image, but it also opens it as a Smart Object, which prepares the image for use with Smart Filters, among other benefits. Find out more about Smart Objects as they relate to Blend Modes in Chapter 14 and as they relate to Filters in Chapter 10.

Creating a new image

Whether you're creating an image from scratch or transferring the contents of the Clipboard to a new image window, choose File ⇨ New or press Ctrl+N (⌘+N on the Mac) to open the New dialog box shown in Figure 3.4. If the Clipboard contains a selection or a layer within another image, the Width, Height, and Resolution option boxes show the size and resolution of this content. Otherwise, you can type your own values in one of six units of measurement: pixels, inches, centimeters, millimeters, picas, or points. If you're uncertain exactly what size image you want to create, enter a rough approximation. You can always change your settings later.

FIGURE 3.4

Use the New dialog box to specify the size, resolution, and color mode of your new image. You can even give the file a name at this stage, if you want.

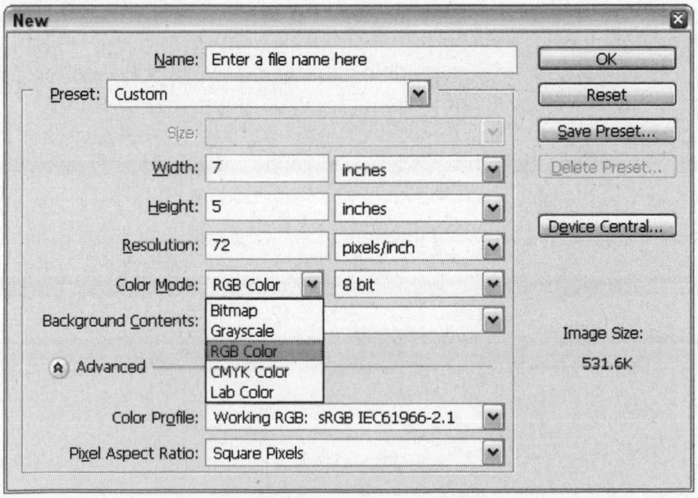

TIP   When in doubt about the size of your new image, go for bigger rather than smaller. If you have a general sense that the image needs to print at 3 inches by 4 inches, go for 4 inches by 5 inches, or even use one of the preset sizes, such as 4×6. You can always crop away unwanted periphery, and it's better to have too much room than not enough.

The Preset pop-up menu gives you easy access to several popular document sizes, common settings for working in print or on the Web, and several presets for video and film formats such as NTSC, PAL, and HDTV. Photoshop also lets you select the pixel aspect ratio of your document. You find more information about pixel aspect ratios later in this chapter.

TIP   You also have the New Document Preset Resolutions settings in the Units & Rulers panel of the Preferences dialog box, which let you set a default resolution for print or screen; the resolutions you set in the Preferences dialog box appear when you select certain options from the Preset menu.

NOTE   When you select one of the video presets from the Preset pop-up menu, Photoshop automatically adds guides to your image that are specific to that setting. These guides delineate areas known in the video industry as the action-safe and title-safe zones. Because most television screens crop a certain amount off the borders of a video image, it's extremely helpful to be aware of what will and won't be visible on any given television set. These days, you'll be safe on most televisions if you keep your graphics within the outermost, or action-safe, zone. You can quickly toggle the visibility of these guides on and off by pressing Ctrl+; (semicolon) (⌘+; on the Mac). You find a more in-depth look at guides in Chapter 13.

NEW FEATURE   Device Central, represented by a button in the New dialog box as well as the File menu (File ➪ Device Central), is a new application added to Photoshop CS3. What does it do? It enables you to create and view images for mobile devices (cell phones, mainly). You can preview the mobile-device-bound image through the Save for Web dialog box (see Chapter 20). After Device Central is open, select a device and click the Create button to open a new image window in Photoshop.

If you don't like Photoshop's preset document sizes, you can easily create your own. The moment you make any sort of change to one of Photoshop CS3's predefined presets, you get access to the Save Preset button. Click it to open the New Document Preset dialog box, shown in Figure 3.5. Here you can type a name for the new preset and specify which of your current settings you'd like to include. This is a great feature that can be a huge timesaver when you're creating a large batch of identically sized files. If you later decide that you want to delete a custom document preset, simply select it from the Preset pop-up menu in the New dialog box and click Delete Preset.

Size and Resolution Tips

Although Photoshop matches the contents of the Clipboard by default, you also can match the size and resolution of other images:

- Press Alt (Option on the Mac) when choosing File ➪ New or press Ctrl+Alt+N (⌘+Option+N on the Mac) to override the contents of the Clipboard. Photoshop displays the size and resolution of the last image you created, whether or not it came from the Clipboard. Use this technique when creating many same-sized images in a row.

- You also can match the size and resolution of the new image to any other open image. Any images you currently have open appear at the bottom of the Preset pop-up menu.

FIGURE 3.5

The New Document Preset dialog box lets you name and save custom document presets for future convenient use.

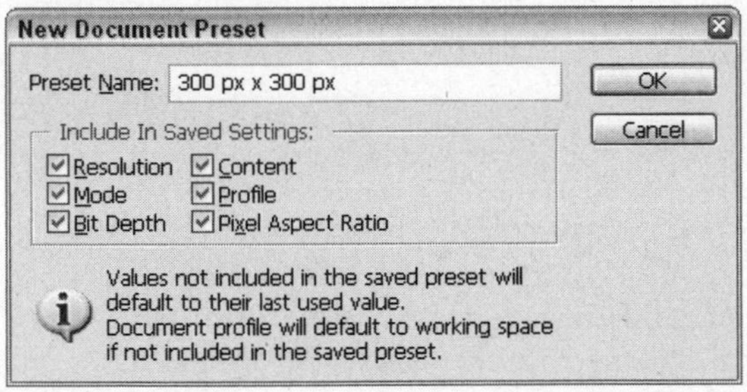

Units of measure

The Width and Height pop-up menus contain the six common units of measure mentioned earlier: pixels, inches, centimeters, millimeters, points, and picas. But the Width pop-up menu offers one more: Columns. If you want to create an image that fits exactly within a certain number of columns when it's imported into a desktop-publishing program, select this option. You can specify the width of a column and the gutter between columns by pressing Ctrl+K and Ctrl+6 (⌘+K and ⌘+6 on the Mac) to display the Units & Rulers preferences. Then type values into the Column Size option boxes.

Setting the Unit of Measure

You can set the default unit of measurement for the Width and Height pop-up menus in the Units & Rulers panel of the Preferences dialog box. (Select the value from the Rulers pop-up menu; the Type menu sets the measurement unit for text-related controls.) But if the dialog box isn't already open, here are two quicker options:

- Press Ctrl+R (or ⌘+R on the Mac) to display the rulers, and then right-click (Control-click on the Mac) anywhere in the rulers to display a pop-up menu of units. Click the unit you want to use.

- If you're a Windows users, you can display the same pop-up menu by pressing F8 to display the Info palette and then click or drag the cross icon (next to the X and Y coordinate values) in the palette's lower-left corner. Click the unit you prefer.

The Gutter value affects multiple-column images. For example, if you accept the default setting of a 15-pica column width and a 1-pica gutter, and you specify a one-column image in the New dialog box, Photoshop makes it 15 picas wide. If you ask for a two-column image, Photoshop adds the width of the gutter to the width of the two columns and creates an image 31 picas wide.

The Height pop-up menu in the New dialog box lacks a Column option because vertical columns have nothing to do with the image height.

New image size

In most cases, the onscreen dimensions of an image depend on your entries in the Width, Height, and Resolution option boxes. If you set both the Width and Height values to 10 inches and the Resolution to 72 ppi, the new image measures 720×720 pixels. An exception occurs if you choose pixels as your unit of measurement. In this case, the onscreen dimensions depend solely on the Width and Height options, and the Resolution value only determines the size at which the image prints.

Color Mode

Use the Color Mode pop-up menu to specify the number of colors that can appear in your image. Choose Bitmap to create an image consisting of only black and white pixels, and choose Grayscale to access only gray values. RGB Color, CMYK Color, and Lab Color all provide access to a full range of colors, although their methods of doing so differ. You can read all about these color modes and how they work in Chapters 4, 17, and 18.

In addition to specifying the color mode, Photoshop lets you set the bit depth of your image in the New dialog box. The bit depth determines the amount of color information available to each individual pixel in the image. Choosing 1 bit limits your image to black and white pixels and thus can be used only in Bitmap mode. The option you'll probably use most often is 8 bit, which is standard fare for most full-color images. Choosing 16 bit gives your image a much greater number of available colors, providing you with a more accurate color representation and finer color controls. But the 16-bit option also greatly increases the file size and limits your editing options. For more information on using 16-bit mode, see Chapter 4, where you also can read about taking an existing image and bumping it up to 32-bit mode, using the Image ⇨ Mode ⇨ 32 Bits/Channel command.

CROSS-REF RGB stands for red-green-blue, CMYK for cyan-magenta-yellow-black, and Lab for luminosity and two abstract color variables: *a* and *b*. To learn how each of these color modes work, read Chapter 4.

Background Contents

The New dialog box also provides a Background Contents pop-up menu that enables you to change the color of the background for the new image. You can fill the new image with white, with the current background color (which may be white anyway, of course), or with no color at all. This last setting, Transparent, results in a floating layer with no background image whatsoever (represented by a gray and white checkerboard pattern), which can be useful when editing one layer independently of the rest of an image or when preparing a layer to be composited with an image. For an in-depth examination of layering, see Chapter 13.

If you do select a transparent background, you must later flatten the layers if you want to save the image to a format that doesn't support layers. (See the upcoming discussion on saving an image to disk for information about options that retain layers when saving.) The advantage of the Transparent setting, however, is that Photoshop doesn't create a new layer when you press Ctrl+V (⌘+V on the Mac) to paste the contents of the Clipboard. In the long run, you don't gain much — you still must flatten the image before you save it to some formats — but at least you needn't fuss with two layers, one of which may be an unwanted background layer.

Color Profile

At the very bottom of the New dialog box, you find an Advanced option (click the button to the left of the word Advanced). The Advanced settings offer options for selecting a Color Profile and the Pixel Aspect Ratio for your image.

In the first option, Color Profile, you can determine the color space in which your new image will exist. Essentially, the color profile of an image provides the information necessary to make sense of how an image should be displayed or printed based on the circumstances under which the image was created. For an in-depth look at the sometimes daunting world of color management, check out Chapter 17.

Pixel Aspect Ratio

The second and final setting in the Advanced section of the New dialog box lets you set the Pixel Aspect Ratio for your image. Computer monitors display images with an assortment of perfectly square pixels. The pixels that make up an image on a television, however, are of a more rectangular nature. The result is that an image created with square pixels in Photoshop looks somewhat squashed when imported into video-editing software and output onto a television screen.

Luckily, Photoshop can help. By selecting a non-square pixel aspect ratio or choosing any of the non-square video presets, you can work with a preview of the image that more accurately represents its appearance in your final film or video project. It's important to note, however, that these settings don't actually alter the pixels in your image. They simply present them to you in a way that more closely matches your specific destination. You always have the option of displaying the pixels in a square ratio by choosing View ➪ Pixel Aspect Ratio Correction to turn the option off. Toggling this option off can be helpful at times because it eliminates the need for Photoshop to do any scaling and provides you with a higher-quality preview.

 If you decide to change the pixel aspect ratio of an image after you've begun to edit it, simply choose Image ➪ Pixel Aspect Ratio and select a new setting from the submenu.

It's important to note that choosing a non-square aspect ratio affects the behavior of many tools. For example, if you Shift-drag with the Elliptical Marquee tool to draw a circular selection outline, a different number of pixels are selected depending on whether you're working with square or non-square pixels. This pertains to all shape tools and even brushes. A 90-pixel circular brush used on an NTSC image, for example, paints a circle 90 pixels tall and 100 pixels wide.

Naming the new image

The New dialog box provides a Name option. If you know what you want to call your new image, you can type the name now. You don't have to, of course, because you won't be officially naming the file until you save it with the File ➪ Save command. Through the resulting Save As dialog box, Photoshop asks you to specify the location of the file and confirm the file's name. Therefore, don't feel compelled to name your image anything in the New dialog box — the only reason to use this option is to help you keep your images organized onscreen, because the name you provide in the New dialog box appears on the image window title bar, replacing the generic "Untitled."

Opening an image

Photoshop provides a File menu command, Open Recent, which displays a list of the images you worked on in recent Photoshop sessions. Click the name of the image you want to open. You set the number of files that appear on the list by typing a value in the Recent File List Contains option box, found on the File Handling panel of the Preferences dialog box, which you access by pressing Ctrl+K and then Ctrl+3 (⌘+K and ⌘+3 on the Mac). The maximum value is 30.

Some tricks for Mac people: ⌘-click the title bar of an open image to display a pop-up menu showing the folder hierarchy for the image file. Click any folder to open it and display all image files therein. Then simply double-click the image file you want to open. (In Mac OS 10.X, this trick works in virtually any application, not just Photoshop.)

Also, the icon in the title bar gives you an instant hint as to whether your image has been edited since it was last saved. If the image has unsaved changes, the title bar icon appears faded. (Mac OS 10.X users also can look at the red Close button in the title bar; if it contains a black dot, the image has been edited since it was last saved.)

Of course, you can always open images the old-fashioned way by choosing File ⇨ Open or pressing its keyboard shortcut, Ctrl+O (⌘+O on the Mac), to display the Open dialog box. On the PC, you also can double-click an empty spot in the Photoshop program window to open the dialog box.

The default Open dialog box behaves just like the ones in other Windows and Macintosh applications, with a folder bar at the top, a scrolling list of files, and the usual file management and navigation options. You also can open multiple files at one time. To select a range of files on the PC and in Mac OS 10.X, click the first file name and then Shift-click the last file in the range. Ctrl-click (⌘-click in Mac OS 10.X) to add a single file to the group you want to open. Ctrl-click or ⌘-click again to deselect a file from the group.

The Photoshop version of the Open dialog box (not to be confused with the Adobe Open dialog box, discussed just a few paragraphs from here) also includes a few controls that most other programs lack. You can read about these options in the next sections. But first, a few other brief notes about opening files:

- When you choose File ⇨ Open, Photoshop displays the folder that contained the last file you opened. Similarly, when you save a file, the folder you saved last is selected automatically.

- When you open an image, Photoshop may display a dialog box telling you that the color profile of the image doesn't match the default color profile you've established. You have the option of converting the image to the default profile or leaving well enough alone. See Chapter 17 for help with this issue.

TIP When opening an image, you may occasionally encounter a dialog box warning you that some data in the file cannot be read and will be ignored. Well, it's a bunch of bunk. If this happens to you, just click OK to dismiss the warning and open the image as usual.

The Adobe Open dialog box (displayed by clicking the Use Adobe Dialog button in the lower-left corner of the default Open dialog box) offers the same options as the default Open dialog box. You can click the Look in drop-down list to choose from disks, drives, and other places to look for your file. You also can click the icons on the left side of the dialog box to look on the Desktop and in particular folders. In the main area of the dialog box, shown in Figure 3.6, you can view the images in the open folder or drive in the same ways that you can in the default Open dialog box — in Details view, where file name, size, status, type, and date modified are displayed, Icons, Thumbnails, or Tiles view. Wait — Tiles? Yes, as shown in Figure 3.6, Tiles view shows an icon for the image — indicating format — and some basic stats for the image, including name, size, and date/time modified.

TIP Click the Tools button (looks like a little briefcase) in the upper right of the dialog box to access a menu that includes commands for accessing the Bridge, creating a new project, editing file properties, creating new folders, and looking at or restoring deleted files. This menu also offers a command for going back to the "OS Dialog" (OS standing for Operating System), which you also can do by clicking the Use OS Dialog button that has replaced the Use Adobe Dialog button in the lower-left corner of the dialog box. There also is an Adobe dialog version of the Save and Save As dialog boxes — look for coverage of these later in this chapter.

FIGURE 3.6

The Tiles view in the Adobe version of the Open dialog box offers enlarged image icons and file information that rivals the familiar Details view's list of file statistics.

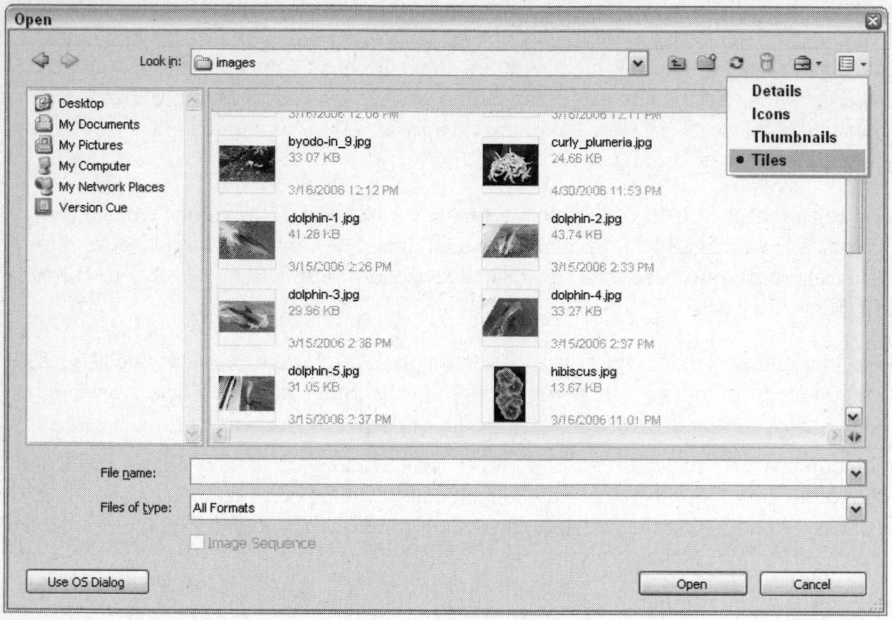

Viewing the thumbnail

To help you assess an image before you open it, Photoshop displays a thumbnail preview of the selected file in the Open dialog box, as shown in Figure 3.7. On the Mac, the column view found in Open dialog boxes automatically displays a preview of graphic files. On the PC, Photoshop automatically displays thumbnails for any files saved in the native format (PSD). If you're running Windows XP, the operating system may generate thumbnails for files saved in other formats.

On the Mac, the thumbnail space may appear empty, which means the file does not contain a Photoshop-compatible preview. The file may have been created by a piece of hardware or software that doesn't support thumbnails, or the thumbnail feature may have simply been turned off when the image file was saved. To generate thumbnails when saving images in Photoshop, press Ctrl+K and then Ctrl+3 (⌘+K and ⌘+3 on the Mac) to display the File Handling panel of the Preferences dialog box. Then select the Macintosh Thumbnail option if you're using a Mac, or set the Image Previews pop-up menu to Always Save if you're using a PC. Alternatively, you can set the Image Previews pop-up menu to Ask When Saving, in which case Photoshop gives you the option of adding a thumbnail to the image inside the Save dialog box.

FIGURE 3.7

You can see a preview of an image if you previously saved it in Photoshop with the thumbnails option selected.

NOTE What's that Image Sequence check box in the Open dialog box all about? This option pertains to video and image sequence files. Photoshop CS3 allows users to open and edit video, frame by frame, and to open sequential image files. Find out more about Photoshop CS3's video image support in Chapter 19.

Previewing outside Photoshop

Mac OS 10.X is pretty clever about generating previews of graphic files all on its own. Depending on the file format, you can generally get a preview of a graphic file, no matter what the thumbnail saving settings were. Select an image in the Finder and press ⌘+I to access the Get Info command. Twirl down the arrow next to the word Preview to view a miniature version of the image, as pictured in Figure 3.8. You also can open and view PSD files through Apple's own Preview application

FIGURE 3.8

The Get Info command in Mac OS X can show previews of many different graphic file types.

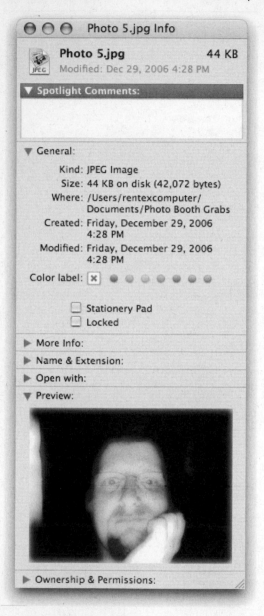

The Open dialog box isn't the only place where you can preview an image before you open it. To preview an image file directly in Windows Explorer under Windows XP or 2000, simply navigate to the folder in which the image is located and click the file to highlight it. A section on the left side of the folder window, labeled Details under Windows XP, displays a high-quality image preview, provided a preview was saved along with the image. Alternatively, you can view thumbnail previews for an entire folder of images by choosing View ⇨ Thumbnails from the menu bar at the top of the folder window.

Opening elusive files in Windows

The scrolling list in the Open dialog box contains the names of the documents that Photoshop recognizes it can open. If you can't find a desired document on your PC, it may be because the Files of Type pop-up menu is set to the wrong file format. To view all supported formats, either select All Formats from the Files of Type pop-up or type *.* in the File Name option box and press Enter.

If a file lacks an extension, the Open dialog box won't be able to identify it. This unusual situation may arise in one of two ways. On rare occasions, a file transmitted electronically (through the Internet, for example) loses its extension en route. But more likely, the file comes from a Macintosh computer. The Mac doesn't need file extensions—the file type identification resides in the resource fork—so many Mac users never give a thought to three-character extensions.

You can solve this problem by renaming the file and adding the proper extension or by choosing File ⇨ Open As (Ctrl+Alt+O). If you choose Open As, Photoshop shows you all documents in a directory, whether or not it supports them. Just click the extension-less file and select the correct file format from the Open As pop-up menu. Provided that the image conforms to the selected format option, Photoshop opens the image when you press Enter. If Photoshop gives you an error message instead, you need to select a different format or try to open the document in a different application.

Opening elusive files on a Mac

If you can't find a document in the Open dialog box on your Mac, it may be because Photoshop doesn't recognize the document's four-character type code. The type code for a document created or last edited on a Macintosh computer corresponds to the file format under which the image was saved (as explained in the upcoming section on file formats).

For example, TIFF is the type code for a TIFF image, JPEG is the code for a JPEG image, GIF is the code for a GIF image, and so on. However, if you transferred a document from another platform, such as a Windows machine or a Unix workstation, it probably lacks a type code. In the absence of a type code, Photoshop looks for a three-character extension at the end of the file name, such as *.tif* or *.jpg* or *.gif*. But if the extension is as much as a character off—*.tff* or *.jpe* or *.jif*, for example—Photoshop won't know what to do.

To see *all* documents regardless of their type code or extension, select All Documents from the Show pop-up menu in the Open dialog box, as shown in Figure 3.9. When you click a document in the scrolling list, the Format option displays the format that Photoshop thinks the file was saved in—if it has any thoughts to offer. If you disagree, click the Format option and select the correct file format from the pop-up menu. As long as the image conforms to the selected format option, Photoshop opens the image when you press Return. If you get an error message instead, either select a different format or try to open the document in a different application.

Finding lost files on a Mac

If you know the name of a file — or at least part of the name — but you can't remember where you put it, click the Find button, type some text in the resulting option box, and press Return. Photoshop searches the disk in a fairly random fashion and takes you to the first file name that contains the exact characters you typed.

If the first file name isn't the one you're looking for, click the Find button again to find the next file name that contains your text. If you want to search for a different string of characters, click Find and type some different text.

FIGURE 3.9

Select the All Documents option to access any document regardless of its four-character type code.

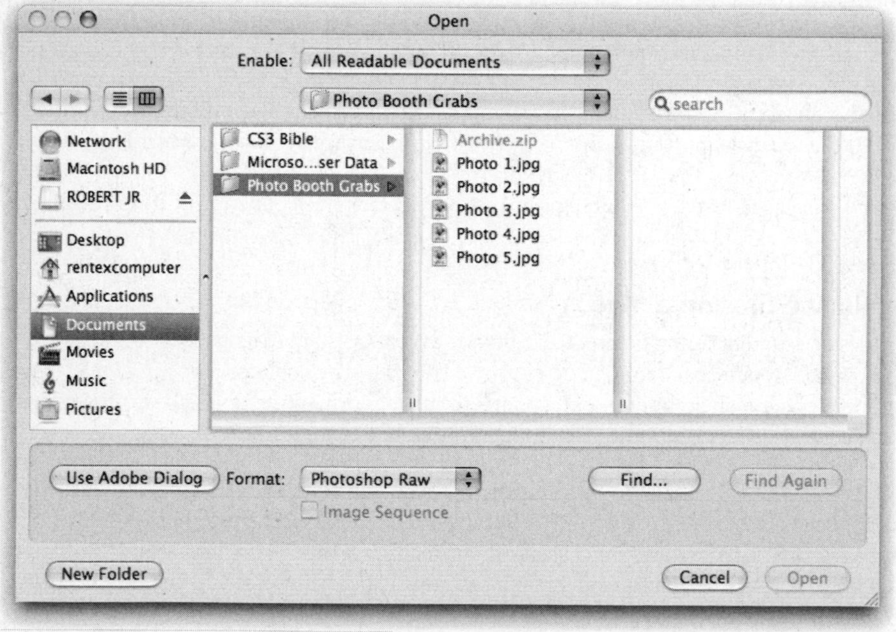

Using the Bridge

The Bridge, introduced with Photoshop CS2 and enhanced for CS3, replaces the File Browser for accessing, organizing, and storing data about your images. To call the Bridge a feature seems like a gross understatement. The Bridge is really an application unto itself — it has its own workspace, menus, and tools, and it opens as a separate application in terms of how the operating system (Windows or Mac) sees it.

You can access the Bridge without opening Photoshop at all, or you can use any one of these methods for opening it from within Photoshop:

- **The Go to Bridge button:** Click this button, shown in Figure 3.10, found to the left of the palette dock. The Bridge opens in its own window shortly thereafter.

FIGURE 3.10

Click this button to access the Bridge. Photoshop remains open, and the Bridge opens in its own window.

- **Choose File ⇨ Browse:** This opens the Bridge in its own window.
- **Choose File ⇨ Close and Go to Bridge:** This closes the active image and opens the Bridge in its own window. You would do this when you're finished with an image and ready to go find another one, using the Bridge tools for accessing images. The Bridge interface appears in Figure 3.11.

FIGURE 3.11

The Bridge workspace provides a menu bar, tabbed panels on the left and right, a large viewing area for looking at your files and folders, and navigational tools for moving around in the workspace. It's kind of like the old File Browser on steroids.

A typical Bridge session

The sequence of events that takes you to and through the Bridge might go something like this: You remember that you need to find a particular photo, but you're not sure of the file name. Or, you want to check whether you have all the photos you should have stored in a particular folder or on a particular CD. The Open dialog box doesn't show you all your photos at once, and hopping out to the Finder (Mac) or Explorer (Windows) to look at thumbnails is too time-consuming. What to do? Fire up the Bridge.

Meta-what?

What the heck is metadata? The Metadata panel (upper-right side of the Bridge window) lets you view and edit more information about your images than you ever thought possible. By default, it's divided into three sections: File Properties, IPTC, and Camera Data (EXIF). The Exchangeable Image File format (EXIF) is a standard for appending non-pixel information — known as *metadata* — to an image file. EXIF is most widely used by digital cameras to describe a photograph's history, including the date and time it was shot, the make and model of the camera, the flash setting, and the focal length. In the Camera Data (EXIF) section of the Metadata panel, you may be able to find out all kinds of wonderful information about digital photographs that you shot and edited years ago. You also see a new section containing DICOM data, which as you can see by the labels for the information that can be stored in that section, pertains to medical imaging. As this is so very industry-specific, DICOM is not covered in any detail in this book.

Using any of the aforementioned methods — clicking the Go to Bridge button or using the File ⇨ Browse command — you open the Bridge and begin looking for or at your photos. If you know where the photo is stored and just want to see all the images in a particular folder or on a specific disk, you can use the Folders panel on the left side of the workspace. Figure 3.12 shows the Folders panel, with a folder selected, its contents displayed as thumbnails in the main viewing area of the Bridge workspace.

> **TIP** You can resize the different parts of the Bridge workspace by clicking and dragging the walls of the various panels. Drag to the right to widen the panel of tabs on the left; drag up and down on the dividers between the Favorites/Folders, Content, and Metadata/Keyword panel areas. By resizing different areas of the workspace, you can rob space from information that you don't care about to make more room for the stuff you need to see more clearly or in its uncluttered entirety.

Assuming that you're now looking at an array of thumbnails of the subfolders and images within the folder, drive, or disk you've chosen from the tree, you can click an individual photo and view its data (see the Metadata panel in the upper right, shown in Figure 3.13) or change your view to Details — by choosing View ⇨ As Details — so that you can see the name, size, and date/time the file was last modified.

FIGURE 3.12

Default view gives you information about the files and a preview of the selected image, and it reminds you which folder you're in.

Folders and Favorites   Name of current folder appears in these two places   Preview panel

Filter panel   Thumbnails   Selected image   Metadata panel

Opening images from the Bridge

If you want to open a particular file, just double-click it. If Photoshop was not already open, it opens in its own window (the Bridge remains open, too), with the selected file open in its own image window. If Photoshop was already open, it becomes the active application and displays the selected file in its own image window — so the final outcome is the same, whether the Bridge tells Photoshop to open and show you your image, or if you had Photoshop open, ready, and waiting.

You also can select multiple images, too — just click them and press Shift to select a series of files, or Ctrl (Windows) or ⌘ (Mac) to select random files from the same folder. After they're all selected, you can drag them to a different folder or to a disk as represented in the Folders panel on the left. You also can rate the images or turn them into Favorites, which you can then access as a separate group through the Favorites panel (sharing a panel with Folders) on the left side of the Bridge workspace.

FIGURE 3.13

In Metadata Focus view, you see more information than images.

Panels reflect more data about the images.

Metadata placard   Selected image   Thumbnail size slider   View buttons

> **TIP**
> If you want to open or move everything but the file or files you have selected, choose Edit ➪ Invert Selection. The Edit menu also houses commands for selecting everything in the open folder (Select All), deselecting (Deselect All), and viewing only certain files — such as only those files that are labeled. Find out about applying labels later in this section on the Bridge.

> **NEW FEATURE**
> The Bridge in CS3 now has a Stacks menu, which should not be confused with Stack Mode in Photoshop (see Chapter 14). You can stack a group of photos [select them with the Shift or Ctrl (⌘) keys], and choose Stack ➪ Group as Stack and then open them all together in Photoshop. The menu also contains an unstacking command and the ability to Expand and Collapse stacks. Not terribly exciting, but there you go.

Your Bridge view options

The whole point of the Bridge is to give you a powerful, yet simple way to view your images and access information about them. Of course, being able to open the files after viewing them is important, too, but you can do that through Photoshop itself. No, the big plus to the Bridge are the image viewing options, each accessible through the View menu (big surprise, eh?). You also can use the view buttons in the lower-right corner of the workspace.

In the View menu, you have these choices:

■ **Compact Mode:** Choose this, and the Bridge workspace is reduced to a small window, without a menu, as shown in Figure 3.14, and it moves to the lower right of your desktop. You can resize it with your mouse, but the idea is for it to be small and out of the way. Double-click the title bar (or click the Maximize/Restore button) to return it to its original size.

FIGURE 3.14

Compact Mode is just that—compact. It keeps the Bridge open and onscreen, but smaller and out of your way.

■ **Slide show:** Choose View ➪ Slideshow, or press Ctrl+L (⌘+L on the Mac) to see a one-image-at-a-time view of the images in a particular folder or on a particular disc. After the show is over (press Esc to stop the show at any time), you return to whichever view you were in when you invoked the show. A slide show in progress appears in Figure 3.15.

TIP   The next command after Slideshow is Slideshow Options. Choose this to change how your slideshow looks and works. As shown in Figure 3.16, you can customize the Display, the way the slides run (and how the whole show runs, including choosing how long individual slides stay onscreen), and how the slides transition from one to the next.

FIGURE 3.15

Want to have your images shown to you one at a time? Choose View ➪ Slideshow. Your images take up the full screen, for maximum preview power.

FIGURE 3.16

View and edit the settings for your slideshow.

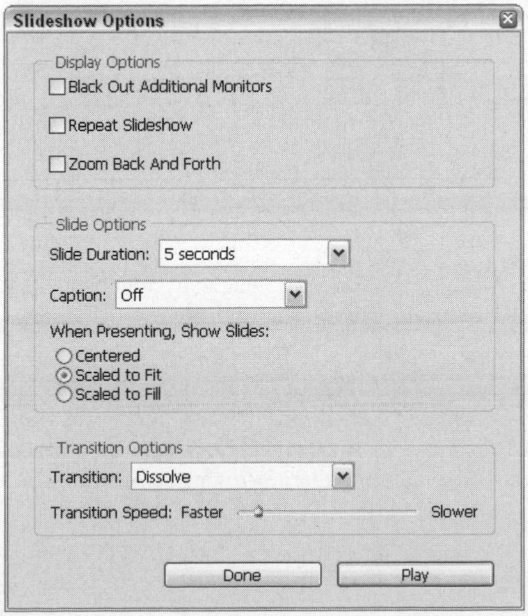

Slideshow Options

Display Options
- ☐ Black Out Additional Monitors
- ☐ Repeat Slideshow
- ☐ Zoom Back And Forth

Slide Options
Slide Duration: 5 seconds
Caption: Off
When Presenting, Show Slides:
- ○ Centered
- ⦿ Scaled to Fit
- ○ Scaled to Fill

Transition Options
Transition: Dissolve
Transition Speed: Faster ——⊐———— Slower

[Done] [Play]

That's it in the View menu, in terms of choices for how your images display in the Bridge. Now let's look at the numbered buttons in the lower-right corner of the Bridge workspace. By default, you see three buttons — 1, 2, and 3 — and if you click any one of them and hold the mouse (or click the tiny triangle in the lower-right corner of the button), the pop-up menu shown in Figure 3.17 appears. These eight viewing options offer something for everyone:

FIGURE 3.17

A quick pop-up gives you your view options from these numbered buttons in the lower right of the Bridge window.

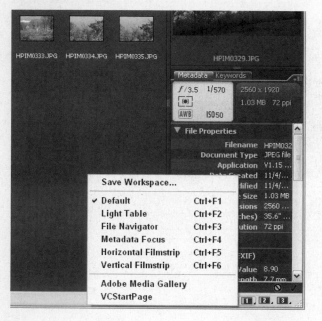

- **Default:** That's the view we first showed you, with Content in the middle, Folders/Favorites in the upper left, Filter information in the lower left, and Metadata/Keywords on the right. You can see this view back in Figure 3.12.

- **Light Table:** This view shows you just your images, in thumbnails that you can resize with the slider in the lower right, next to the numbered view buttons.

- **File Navigator:** Choose this view if finding files is your big issue — maybe you don't know where the one you want is hiding, or you need to get a better sense of your overall file storage system — assuming you have one, that is! Figure 3.18 shows this view, with thumbnails taking up the entire right 2/3rds of the Bridge, and navigational tools — Favorites and Folders broken out into their own separate panels — on the left.

FIGURE 3.18

File Navigator view helps you find your files quickly and doesn't waste space on information that's not key to finding your images.

- **Metadata Focus:** This view is the opposite of File Navigator, in that on the left, instead of Folders and Favorites, you see the Metadata and Keywords tabs broken out into two panels, and the rest of the window is your image thumbnails. This view assumes you know where your files are, but want to look at and edit the information stored about them.

- **Horizontal and Vertical Filmstrips:** These two views give you just what you'd expect — a strip of images, running either horizontally or vertically, in sizes that you can control with the slider on the lower right, next to the numbered view buttons. As shown in Figure 3.19 (Horizontal Filmstrip view only, but you get the idea), a strip of images appears along the bottom, and a larger thumbnail appears singly, above the strip. To see a large version of any image in the scrollable strip, click the thumbnail in the strip, and the large image appears in the Preview area. The left panels are Favorites and Filter in this view.

- **VCStart Page:** Again, you have a very simple view, this time with only Favorites and Folders tabs on the left and resizable thumbnails in the remaining majority of the window.

FIGURE 3.19

View your images one at a time, selecting them from a filmstrip that either runs along the bottom (as shown here) or down the right side of the window (Vertical Filmstrip, not shown).

> **NOTE**   You can move and resize the panels on the left side of the Bridge workspace much like you can move and resize the palettes in Photoshop. Click the panel's tab itself and drag it up or down to regroup the tabs within the right-hand panel. You can group the palettes in any configuration you want—for example, you can drag them all so that they share a single box so less vertical space is taken up in the left-hand panel. To determine which tabs are displayed, use the View menu to select and deselect them by name. A check mark indicates that the panel is currently displayed.

Selecting images

You can select images—choosing from those displayed in the main viewing area—by clicking them with your mouse, as shown in Figure 3.20, or by making selection command choices from the Edit menu. You also can select images by searching for them (see coverage of the Find dialog box later in this section of this chapter). Once found, the images meeting your Find dialog box criteria can be selected en masse or by clicking the one that you really wanted to find.

To select images with your mouse, click once on the single image you want, or to gather more images, press Shift to select a series — as shown in Figure 3.20 — or press Ctrl (⌘ on the Mac) to select random images. Once selected, the images can be moved to a new folder (drag them to the target folder on the Folder panel on the left side of the workspace) or opened in Photoshop — just press Enter (Return) while they're selected.

FIGURE 3.20

Select a contiguous group of images with the Shift key, or use Ctrl (⌘ on the Mac) to collect non-contiguous images from those currently displayed as thumbnails.

Control your selections from the Edit menu.

These images were selected with the Shift key, clicking the first and the last in the series.

This image was added to the selection with the Ctrl (⌘ on the Mac) key.

CAUTION If yours is not the latest and greatest computer with lots of memory, you may want to avoid opening several images at once. Start small: Open one or two images, and if things don't slow down too much, you can open additional images until you notice the application becoming a bit clumsy. You may be prompted that your virtual memory setting is too low, and if you're a Windows user, Windows beefs up the memory allocation to meet your needs at the time.

Rotating images

In Photoshop, you can rotate the image canvas, turning an image that was scanned lengthwise or upside down that you want to see turned around. The change made through the Image ➪ Rotate Canvas command is actually applied to the image itself. In the Bridge, you can rotate images, but only for the purpose of viewing them within the Bridge. The change in the rotation of an image within the Bridge is not made a part of the file itself; the image rotation will not be changed if you open the image in Photoshop.

As shown in Figure 3.21, you can select an image and then choose Edit ➪ Rotate 180, 90 Clockwise, or 90 Counterclockwise. The display changes for the selected images (you can select more than one before issuing the command).

FIGURE 3.21

Rotate an image thumbnail for easier viewing, without actually rotating the image itself.

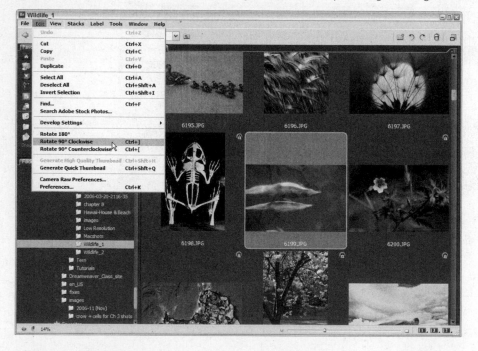

TIP   In the upper-right corner of the workspace is a series of buttons — New Folder, and then the two rotation buttons: Rotate 90 Clockwise and Rotate 90 Counterclockwise. You can use these on whichever image is selected at the time — or use them to rotate multiple selected images all at once. There's also a trash can button for deleting images, and the last one gives you quick access to Compact Mode.

Adding an image to Favorites

Like the sites you've added to your Favorites (or Bookmarks) in your Web browser, images that you want to be able to come back to quickly and easily (and frequently) also can be turned into Favorites, accessible through the Favorites panel on the left side of the Bridge workspace. Figure 3.22 shows the Favorites list, which includes locations on the computer, folders, and images.

FIGURE 3.22

Are there images you use often and navigating to them via the Open dialog box is a pain? Add them to the Bridge Favorites list, and they're always right where you need them.

TIP

If you're not a big Bridge user and want your oft-used images to be easily accessible, increase the number of files that can be included in the File ➪ Open Recent submenu (in Photoshop). Choose Edit ➪ Preferences ➪ File Handling (Photoshop ➪ Preferences ➪ File Handling on the Mac) and increase the Recent file list contains setting to 30. If 30 is way more than you need for this list, choose some lower number that makes it possible for the file(s) you want to see in the list to remain there even with the other files you'll open and use throughout the day or week, which could potentially push your desired files off the list.

To add an image to Favorites, just right-click (Control-click on the Mac) and choose Add to Favorites from the pop-up menu. You also can choose File ➪ Add to Favorites. Once added to Favorites, you can remove an image from favor by right-clicking (Control-clicking on the Mac) the image in the Favorites list and choosing Remove from Favorites from the pop-up menu. Note that if you only want to add a single image to the Favorites, be sure that only that image is selected when you right-click it; if you have multiple files selected, even if you right-click (Control-click on the Mac) that one file, all of the selected files become Favorites.

TIP   When you click an image in the Favorites list, the Bridge assumes you want to open it in Photoshop, so don't click the image in the list unless you want that to happen.

Labeling and rating images

Humans' affinity for ranking and rating things is obvious — there are entire books of top-ten lists, and a popular late-night talk host compiles a funny top-ten list for each show. Applying value, even if it's totally subjective, is something most of us can't resist. The Bridge, being aware of this, gives you the ability to rate and label your images — ranking them with stars (from one star to five stars) and applying color-coded labels. As shown in Figure 3.23, the Label menu offers five ratings and five color labels, plus the ability to incrementally increase and decrease the existing rating for any image. You also can right-click (Control-click on the Mac) an image and use the Image command in the pop-up menu to access the Label color options.

FIGURE 3.23

Here, the selected image to the right of the Label menu already has a two-star rating and a "Second" label; from the Label menu, the rating is about to be increased.

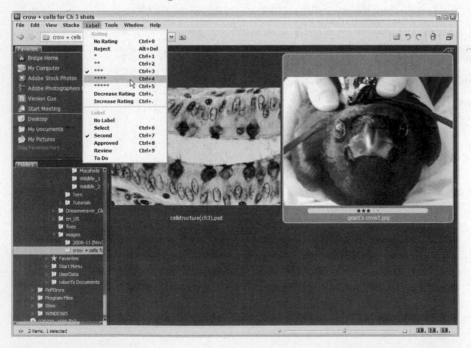

Viewing and using metadata

Metadata, as described earlier in this chapter, is a cornucopia of file information, divided into three sections. You can scroll through them in the Metadata panel, shown in Figure 3.24. You can look at File Properties (the most commonly used and therefore visible without scrolling), IPTC Core data, and Camera Data (EXIF). As stated earlier, in CS3, there's also DICOM data, for medical imaging (storing patient's name, gender, etc.).

For many of your files, the vast majority of these bits of data will be blank; clicking the little pencil icon next to any currently blank or editable fields opens a text box into which you can type the appropriate information. Actually, for many users, this area may be entirely ignored, because either the file name or one glance at the image itself tells you all you need to know. On the other hand, if you need to keep track of things like when the picture was taken, how big a file it is, what its width and height are, and its pixel depth, the File Properties section is there for you, ready to house that sort of thing.

FIGURE 3.24

"Intellectual Genre"? Okay, maybe somebody needs that field, but information about the photographer and the date the picture was taken are the fields most of us will use.

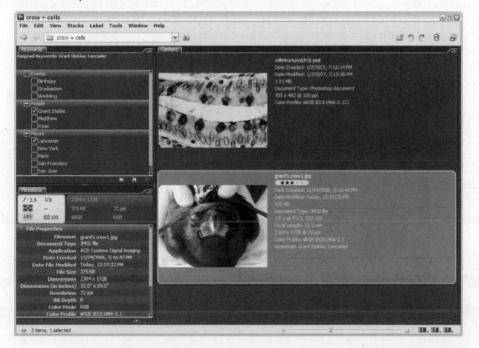

The IPTC Core data houses even more information that you may or may not care about — usually stuff that pertains to other people's images — so if you typically work with other artists' images, you'll find plenty of places to keep their facts straight. Camera Data is just that — data about the camera used to take the image, which is right there and filled in if you took the picture with a digital camera. If you (or someone else) took the picture the old-fashioned way, the camera data will have to be entered manually.

Whether or not you use some or all of the data in these categories in the Metadata panel, you may have need of what little is there. The Bridge makes it easy to use the data, as desired, and one of the ways you can do so is through the Metadata panel's options menu button (triangle button on the top right of the panel's tab), where you're presented with the following commands/options:

- **Find:** This command opens the Find dialog box (now there's a surprise), through which you can search for files based on various criteria and locations, and you can customize the results you want to see included. You set up your search from the top of the dialog box, shown in Figure 3.25, starting with Look In, where you can choose from all the folders and drives to which you have access on and through your computer. You also can click Browse at the foot of that folder to open a navigation window that makes it easier to search for the drive/folders in which you want to search.

  Next, enter your search Criteria through the three fields in that section. You can select the field to look in (a list of the fields in the Metadata section of the Bridge window appears), choose the standard (contains, does not contain, exists, does not exist), and then type the text that should be compared to your criteria. Click the plus sign to add multiple criteria levels [such as Date Created is greater than (after) 03/01/2005 AND Filename contains "Beach"]. You can have up to 13 criteria levels (use the minus sign to remove extra criteria levels from your search), and for each type of criteria, the appropriate choices for matching records and entering in your values change, helping you fill things in a way that'll make sense to the software.

FIGURE 3.25

Use the Find dialog box to locate a file based on any of the stored information about the file.

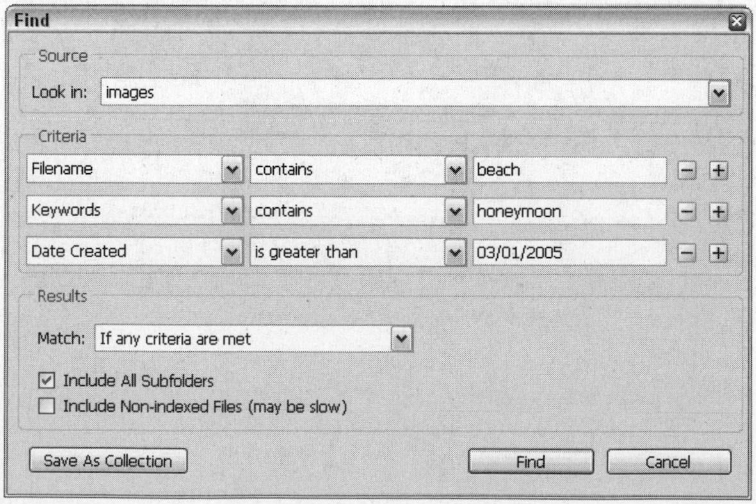

After you have your search set up, use the Results section to fine-tune your results. Include Subfolders is a good one to turn on, and of course the Match setting allows you to decide how stringently your criteria settings are followed (if *any* criteria are met versus if *all* criteria are met). Click Find to send the Bridge sniffing for your files, or click Cancel to scrap the whole enterprise.

- **Increase Font Size** and **Decrease Font Size:** These commands change the display font size for the data in the Metadata panel.

- **Preferences:** This opens the Preferences dialog box, shown in Figure 3.26, through which you can customize the Bridge. You can customize the settings for nine different areas of the Bridge, including General (basic Bridge settings) to Thumbnails (how they look) to Labels (what the colors mean) to File Type Associations (which applications fire up automatically for which file types).

FIGURE 3.26

Click General, Metadata, Labels, or any of the other Bridge areas listed on the left to display those preferences options in the main dialog box.

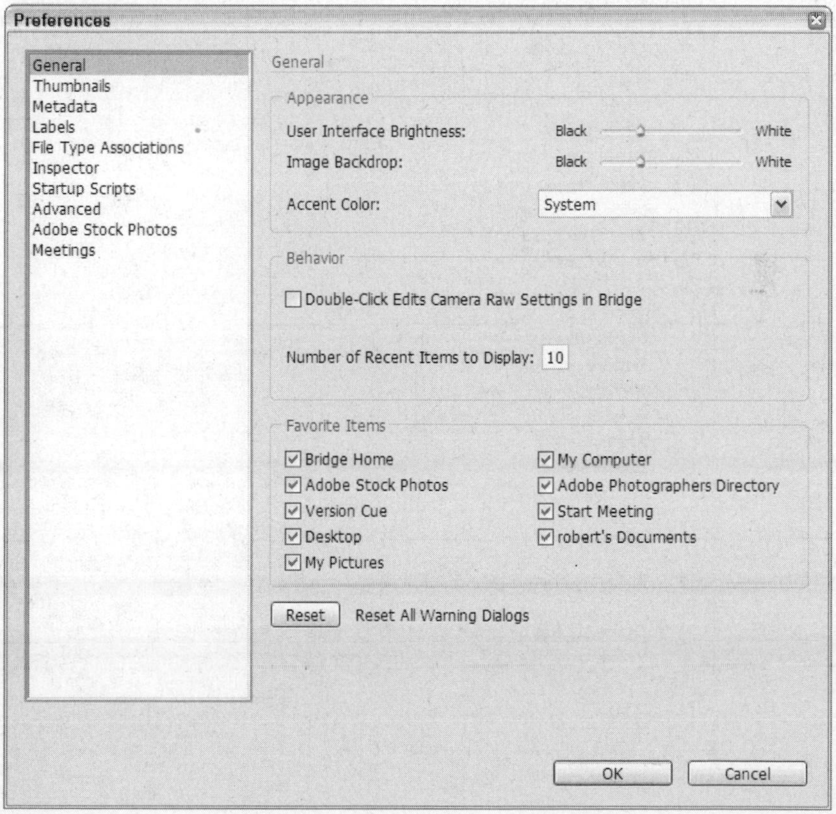

■ **Show Metadata Placard:** You know that little graphic on the upper left of the Metadata panel, with a gray background (it's shown in any view of the Metadata panel)? Well here's your chance to say sayonara to that little item if you find it bothersome. Maybe it takes up too much room, or maybe you don't care about the data it displays (camera settings). Whatever your reason, you can turn the placard on and off through this command.

■ **Create Metadata template:** Choose this if you want to pick and choose the fields that show in the Metadata panel and save your own set of fields as a template. For any fields where you want something to always appear, enter those values into the boxes on the right of the individual fields. After you've done this, the following two commands become available, and their submenus list your saved templates. Figure 3.27 shows the IPTC Core data list of fields.

Pick the IPTC data you want to see, and give your template a name.

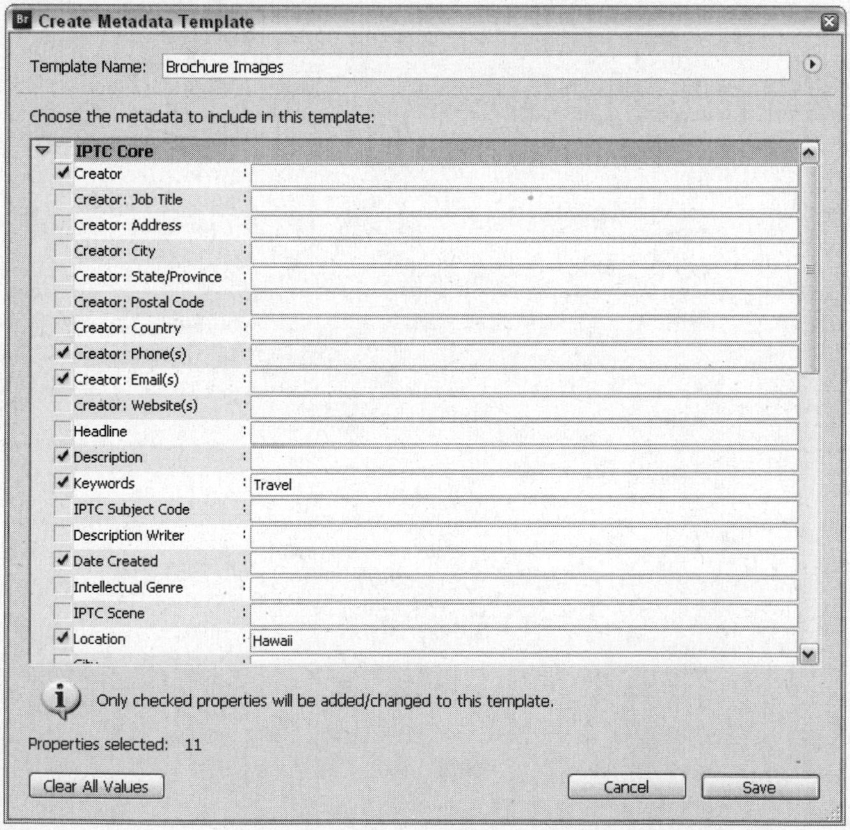

- **Append Metadata:** Using preset templates, you can establish new data that will be stored about individual files.

- **Replace Metadata:** Instead of adding to the metadata, this command allows you to choose from data templates that replace the metadata that appears by default.

Viewing and adding Keywords

Next to the Metadata panel tab is the Keywords panel tab, shown in Figure 3.28. Keywords are searchable text that is associated with individual images and stored with the file's data to help you locate files easily. Keywords are one of the Criteria you can set in the Find dialog box used to search for files. For example, if you're looking for all your wedding photos, you can tell Photoshop to find all files with "Wedding" in the Keyword list.

To view the Keywords for any file, click the file in the main display area and then click the Keywords tab on the left. A list of words — names, places, and categories such as "Birthday" and "Graduation" — appears with check boxes next to them. Boxes with check marks indicate an association with that keyword.

To add your own keywords to the list, click within the Keyword Set you want to add a keyword to and click the Keywords panel options menu button (that triangle again). Choose New Keyword, and an "Untitled Key" entry appears in the list (see the menu and the resulting Untitled Key in Figure 3.28) and becomes highlighted; you can type a new keyword to replace the sample text. In this case, a new keyword is being added to the Events Keyword Set.

To set up a new category, click the Options button and choose New Keyword Set. As shown in Figure 3.29, an Untitled Set appears, and you can again replace the sample text with a set name of your choice. After making a new set, you need to use the New Keywords command to create keywords for the set. For example, if you create a set called "Family," you can create keywords for individual people ("Mom" or "Uncle Emil") and/or you can create keywords for family events, like "Christmas" or "Bar Mitzvahs."

After you've created your own keywords and sets, additional commands become available in the Keywords panel options menu. The Rename and Delete commands appear, and you can use them to do just what you'd expect — rename a selected keyword or set, or delete a keyword or set you no longer need.

NOTE The Find command appears in the Keywords options menu, just as it does in the Metadata menu. The resulting dialog box is the same as the one described earlier in our discussion of the Metadata options menu commands.

FIGURE 3.28

Add a new keyword to any of the Keyword Sets.

To apply a keyword to an individual image, select the image and then place check marks in the boxes next to one or more of the words in the Keywords panel. You can check as many boxes as you want, and if you think of any other words that you might want to use in searching for the selected image in the future, use the New Keyword command to create them.

Choosing Suite Color Settings

The Creative Suite (referenced by the "CS" in Photoshop CS3) is a group of Adobe applications that are typically used — if not at the same time — together in terms of sharing files. The movie clips edited in Adobe Premiere may end up edited as still shots in Photoshop, for example, or the still photos you edit in Photoshop might end up in a Dreamweaver Web site or used for page layout with InDesign. You get the idea.

FIGURE 3.29

Choose to create a new Keyword Set to give yourself even more ways to categorize and organize your images — for your use and to simplify things for other people who use your images, too.

What assists the suite in operating as a cohesive unit is the synchronization of color settings. Through the Bridge, you can make sure that Photoshop holds up its end of the bargain, working with the dialog box shown in Figure 3.30. To display and work with this dialog box, choose Edit ⇨ Creative Suite Color Settings. You can play around with 13 different settings — from Monitor Color, which works with most video settings, to settings for North America, Europe, and Japan. There are prepress, general-purpose, and Web settings for each region, and default settings for prepress and Web graphics, too.

FIGURE 3.30

Check the available color settings for the Creative Suite.

To synchronize the settings, you can select one from within the dialog box. This sets up the suite applications — as many as you have installed on your computer from the same version of the suite — to work together with the same color settings.

TIP To access the settings files, click the Show Saved Color Settings Files button, which opens an Explorer window with a folder tree on the left and the settings files on the right. If the right side of the window is empty, you have no saved color settings files.

Setting Camera Raw preferences

Camera Raw, a file format supported by Photoshop, is discussed later in this chapter and elsewhere in this book (see Chapter 18). You can set your Camera Raw preferences through the Bridge, using the Edit menu (or the Bridge CS3 menu if you're on a Mac). After the Camera Raw Preferences dialog box, shown in Figure 3.31, is open, you can choose how image settings are saved (pick a format; Sidecar ".xmp" files is the default), choose how sharpening is applied, set the Default Image Settings, and set up the Camera Raw cache, which includes deciding where the cache file is saved (find out more about cache later in this chapter) and how much space to allocate to cache files. You also can choose how CS3 deals with DNG files. After you like your settings, click OK.

FIGURE 3.31

Customize where and how Camera Raw preferences are applied.

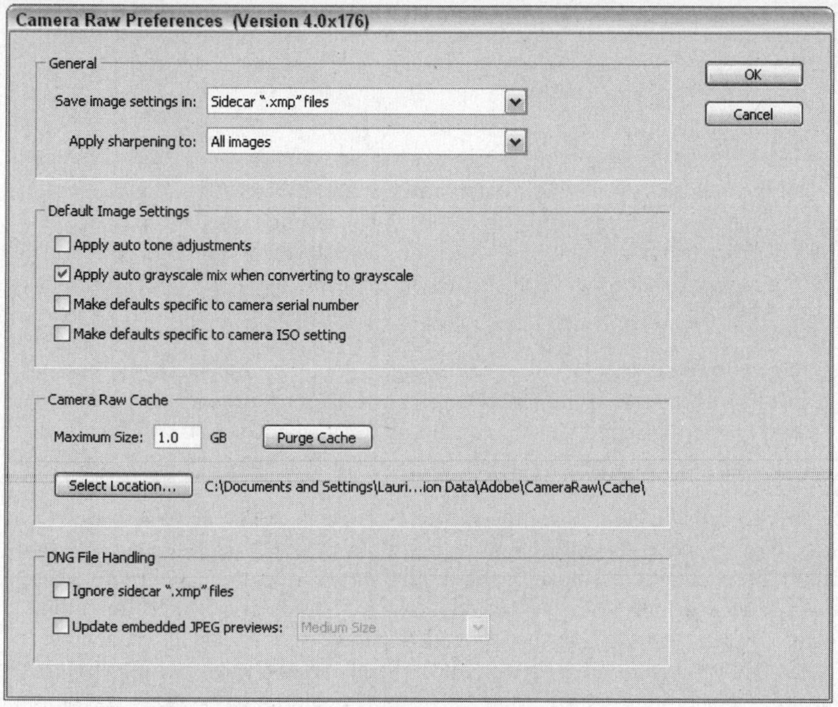

Camera Raw Preferences (Version 4.0x176)

General

Save image settings in: Sidecar ".xmp" files

Apply sharpening to: All images

OK

Cancel

Default Image Settings

☐ Apply auto tone adjustments

☑ Apply auto grayscale mix when converting to grayscale

☐ Make defaults specific to camera serial number

☐ Make defaults specific to camera ISO setting

Camera Raw Cache

Maximum Size: 1.0 GB   [Purge Cache]

[Select Location...] C:\Documents and Settings\Lauri...ion Data\Adobe\CameraRaw\Cache\

DNG File Handling

☐ Ignore sidecar ".xmp" files

☐ Update embedded JPEG previews: Medium Size

Selecting and saving a Bridge workspace

The old saying "A place for everything, and everything in its place" is a philosophy that many tidy people live by. It's also a good motto for Photoshop users, because productivity hinges on easy access to the tools you need. Keyboard shortcuts can help put things at your fingertips (literally), but they don't always help enough when it comes to using palettes, tools, and so forth. Photoshop is sensitive to this and gives you the Window ⇨ Workspace ⇨ Save Workspace command. The Bridge is similarly helpful, offering a Window ⇨ Workspace ⇨ Save Workspace command of its own.

When you choose this command, the Save Workspace dialog box appears, giving you the chance to apply a relevant name to the workspace and to choose a keyboard shortcut (Ctrl + any of the function keys from F6 through F12, except F10, for Windows users, cmd + the F1 through F6 keys if you're on the Mac) that invokes the saved workspace configuration. You also have an option to Save Window Location as Part of Workspace — meaning if you have the Bridge window sized and positioned the way you want it, you can save that position, too.

NOTE "What about preset workspaces?" you may ask. Good question. If you choose Window ⇨ Workspace, you can choose from different workspaces, including Light Table, File Navigator, Metadata Focus, and the two Filmstrip options (Horizontal and Vertical). Each workspace caters to a different perspective on your images — looking at particular images in specific folders. You'll find that you may choose different views/workspaces depending on your needs within the Bridge at any given time.

Managing the cache

You may spend several minutes generating previews, rotating thumbnails, and ranking images inside the Bridge. Because not a single one of these functions or their impact on the image display in the Bridge is saved with the image file, you might wonder how Photoshop prevents you from losing your work. It does this by saving a cache file that records all changes made to an entire folder full of images.

This all happens in the background without any assistance from you, but problems can crop up, and if Photoshop didn't have some sort of plan in the works, you'd lose your work if anything went wrong while you were trying to juggle multiple open images, view new images on a CD, share files over a network, or any other combination of common, often concurrent activities.

It can't be that you have to lose all your work at the slightest change in display or other settings, nor can it be that you have to spend all your time worrying about this caching process. There is, in fact, a backup plan, in the form of two commands that can help ease the burden and prevent the loss of your work — just choose Tools ⇨ Cache ⇨ Build Cache for Subfolders, or if you tend to spend days and nights combing through a seemingly endless parade of images, your cache files can grow fairly quickly. Luckily, you can delete, or *purge*, the cache just as easily as you can export it. From the Bridge Tools menu, choose Cache ⇨ Purge Cache for "Folder name" — where "Folder name" is the active folder at the time.

Renaming files

To rename a handful of specific files, click and Shift-click their thumbnails to select them. To rename all files in a folder, choose Select All or Deselect All from the Edit menu. Then right-click (Control-click on the Mac) and choose Batch Rename (or choose Tools ⇨ Batch Rename from the Bridge menu bar) to display the dialog box pictured in Figure 3.32.

You have the option of renaming files in the folder where they currently reside (the most common choice) or moving them to a different folder. If you click Move to New Folder, the File Browser asks you to select a destination. Note that *moving* means just that — Photoshop relocates the files as opposed to copying them to the new location.

You can specify up to six File Naming variables, though two or three are usually sufficient. The three Document Name options retain or change the case of the name currently assigned to the file. Alternatively, you can type your own name in an option box.

FIGURE 3.32

Use the Batch Rename command to rename multiple files in a single operation. You can select naming options from a pop-up menu or type your own name.

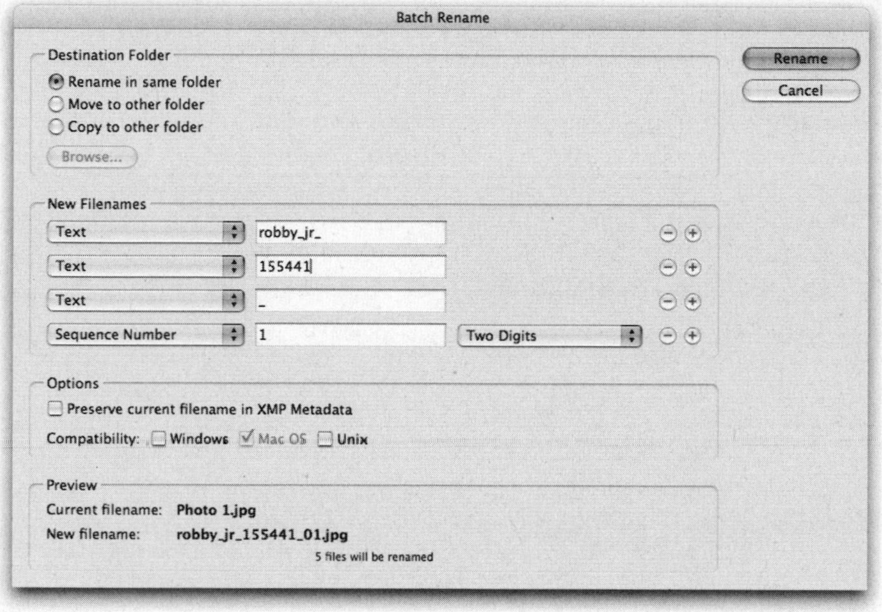

CAUTION To ensure that your images are named so that they'll work on any computer, select all three Compatibility options. (Either Windows or Mac OS is already selected, depending on your platform.) Then click OK to apply your changes. Note that, as with other File Browser operations, renaming is not undoable. So be sure that all settings are correct before you click OK. If you have any doubt about how the command works, experiment on a few trial images before renaming important files.

Using the File Info command

As we've seen, an image file can contain much more information than the image data. On top of pixels, alpha channels, color profiles, and all the other image data you can cram into your image files, you can add a variety of reference information — where you shot the picture, who owns the image copyright, your thoughts on the photo, potential uses for the prints, and so on.

Despite the abundance of data already available to you through the Bridge Metadata panel, sometimes you need to be able to edit and access more information than a little panel can hold. That's when you should choose File ➪ File Info from the File Browser's menu bar or press Ctrl+Alt+Shift+I (Shift+Cmd+Option+I on the Mac) to display the File Info dialog box, shown in Figure 3.33. You can also right-click (Ctrl+click on the Mac) the image for which you want File Info. Select File Info from the resulting pop-up menu.

FIGURE 3.33

Store all sorts of useful information about your images in the File Info dialog box.

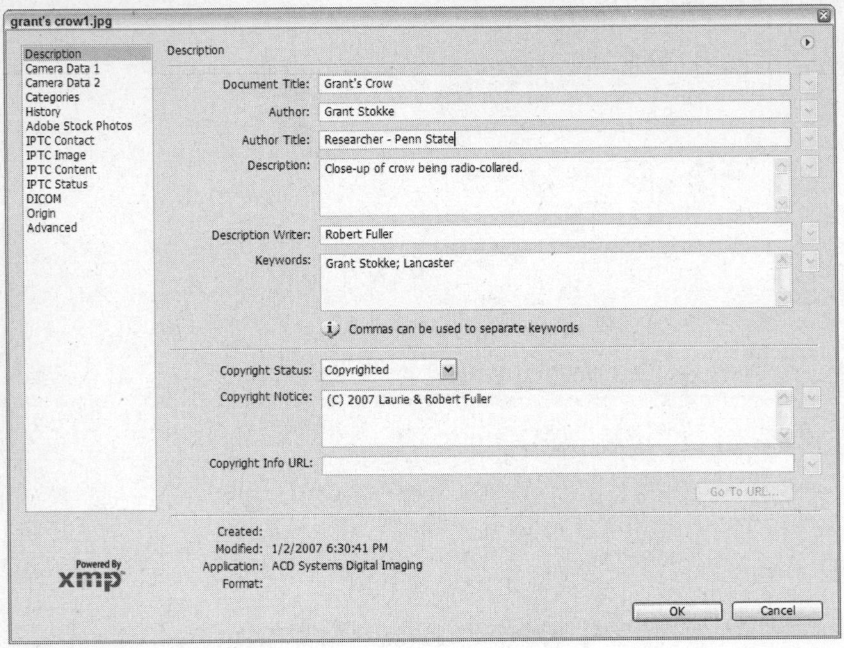

To switch from one File Info area to another, press Ctrl+1 through Ctrl+8 (⌘+1 through ⌘+9 on the Mac) or select the panel name from the list on the left side of the window. On the PC, Alt+N and Alt+P navigate you to the next and previous panel, respectively. Here's a brief overview of the options on each panel:

- **Description:** The options in this panel are fairly straightforward. For example, if you want to create a caption, type it in the Description option box, which can hold up to 2,000 characters. If you select Description in the Output section of the Print dialog box, the caption appears below the image when you print it from Photoshop. You also can add a copyright notice to your image. If you choose Copyrighted Work from the Copyright Status pop-up menu, a copyright symbol (©) appears in the image window title bar and in the information box at the bottom of the screen on the PC or at the bottom of the image window on the Mac. This symbol tells people viewing the image that they can go to the Description panel to get more information about the owner of the image copyright. Choose Public Domain if you want to make it clear that the work isn't copyrighted (an Unmarked image might actually be a neglected copyrighted one).

  You also can include the URL for your Web site, if you have one. Then, when people have your image open in Photoshop, they can come to this panel and click Go to URL to launch their Web browser and jump to the URL.

TIP Click the down arrow to the right of an option to reveal a pop-up menu containing information that you've previously entered for the option in other images. For example, if you've listed yourself as the author of another image you recently worked on, you can click the arrow next to the Author option and select your name.

NOTE Because only people who open your image in Photoshop have access to the information in the File Info dialog box, you may want to embed a digital watermark in your image as well. Many watermarking programs exist, ranging from simple tools that merely imprint copyright data to those that build in protection features designed to prevent illegal downloading and reproduction of images. Photoshop provides a watermarking utility from Digimarc as a plug-in on the Filters menu; before using the plug-in, visit the Digimarc Web site (`www.digimarc.com`) to find out which, if any, of the Digimarc watermarking schemes best suits the type of work you do.

- **Camera Data:** Following the Description options you'll find two panels of Camera Data values. This is where the EXIF information discussed earlier in the chapter is displayed. EXIF data is written by the digital camera, not the user, so these fields cannot be altered.

- **Categories:** The Categories panel may seem foreign to anyone who hasn't worked with a news service. Many large news services use a system of three-character categories to file and organize stories and photographs. If you're familiar with this system, you can type the three-character code in the Category option box and even throw in a few supplemental categories up to 32 characters long.

- **History:** If you've selected the History Log option in the General panel of the Preferences dialog box, this panel displays the history data for the image. Otherwise, it's blank. (For complete details on setting up the History Log, see Chapter 2.)

- **Origin:** This panel provides more option boxes for entering specific information about how the image came to be, including the date, the location, and a headline. Click the Today button to automatically enter the current date and time in the Date Created field. You can use the Urgency pop-up menu to indicate the editorial timeliness of the photo.

- **Advanced:** The Advanced panel displays all the information you've set for the image in metadata's XMP format. On a PC, file information is saved only in image file formats that support saving extra data with the file. This includes the native Photoshop (*.psd*) format, EPS, PDF, JPEG, and TIFF. On a Mac, file information is saved with an image regardless of the format you use. Photoshop merely tacks the text onto the image's resource fork. If you need the metadata of an image to travel with the image file, regardless of platform, application, or operating system, saving an XMP file is the way to go. XMP, which stands for *eXtensible Metadata Platform,* is essentially a text file containing metadata that can be assigned to an image and read by many applications. The Advanced panel lets you save this type of file with the metadata you're currently viewing. From this panel, you also can open an XMP file and use it in place of your current metadata, as well as add the information from an XMP file on top of your image's metadata. Selecting any of the categories of metadata in the Advanced panel and clicking Delete clears that specific data from your image file.

Perhaps the most useful metadata-related feature in Photoshop is the capability to create metadata templates. If you have a collection of images with the same author or origin information, you don't want to have to go through the task of opening the File Info dialog box and manually entering metadata (or importing an XMP file) for each and every one. Photoshop can take care of this for you. Creating a metadata template is simple: Just open the File Info dialog box for any one of the images, and enter the common characteristics of the group. Next, click the right-pointing arrowhead in the upper-right corner of the dialog box, and choose Save Metadata Template. You'll be asked to type a name but not a location (Photoshop does that for you). Click Save, and you're finished. Photoshop automatically adds the metadata template to the pop-up menu in the File Info dialog box, so you can easily access it.

You can assign your saved metadata templates to multiple files at once in the File Browser. Simply select the files to which you want to assign the metadata and choose Edit ➪ Replace Metadata to display a submenu that contains all the templates you've saved. If you want to add metadata from a saved template but keep the original characteristics of your image (such as name, description, or source), choose Edit ➪ Append Metadata instead and select a template. One of the advantages of appending versus replacing metadata in an image is that appending adds any keywords saved in the template to the existing keywords in the image.

Duplicating an image

Have you ever wanted to try an effect without permanently damaging an image? Photoshop offers multiple undos, and you'll get a kick out of using the History palette to see before and after views of your image (as explained in Chapter 7). But what if you want to apply a series of effects to an image independently and compare them side by side? And save the variations as separate files? Or perhaps even merge them? This is a job for image duplication.

To create a new window with an independent version of the foreground image, choose Edit ➪ Duplicate. A new copy of your selected image appears with the word "copy" added to the filename. You can then rename it and do whatever you had in mind with it or with the original, depending on which file — the original or the duplicate — you intended to serve as backup.

Saving an Image to Disk

The first rule of image editing — and of working on computers in general — is to save the file frequently. If your computer or Photoshop crashes while you're working on an image, all edits made during the current editing session are lost.

To save an image for the first time, choose File ➪ Save or press Ctrl+S (⌘+S on the Mac) to display the Save dialog box. Name the image, select the drive and folder where you want to store the image file, select a file format, and press Enter or Return.

After you save the image once, choosing the Save command updates the file without bringing up the Save dialog box. To save the image with a different name, location, or format, choose File ➪ Save As.

You also can execute the Save As command by pressing Ctrl+Shift+S (⌘+Shift+S on the Mac). As for the Save a Copy command found in some earlier versions of Photoshop, that function is provided through the As a Copy option in the Save As dialog box.

> **TIP** To speed the save process, you may want to save an image in Photoshop's native format until you've finished working on it. Then, when the file is all ready to go, you can choose File ➪ Save As and save the image in whatever compressed format is needed. This way, you compress each image only once during the time you work on it.

If you have multiple files open, you can close them in one step by choosing File ➪ Close All. Or better yet, press Ctrl+Shift+W (⌘+Option+W on the Mac). Photoshop prompts you to save any images that haven't yet been saved and closes the others automatically.

Adding an extension to Mac files

On the Mac, the Preferences dialog box includes an option that lets you append a three-character file extension to your files. Again, this option is located in the File Handling panel, so press ⌘+K, ⌘+3 to get to it. There are two general recommendations for this option: First, leave the Use Lower Case option selected, because it ensures fewer conflicts if and when you post your images on the Web; second, go ahead and append extensions to your file names.

Why add PC file extensions on a Mac? Obviously, it makes life easier when sharing images with Windows users, and for Mac users, if you're working with an application that uses file extensions to indicate the source application (such as iPhoto, for example), you'll find it to be very helpful. More importantly, it's another form of insurance. If you're a Mac person and you ever find yourself using a PC, you're going to have tons and tons of old Macintosh image files that you'd like to open and reuse. With file extensions, you'll have no problem. Without them, good luck. The file extension is the only way a Windows application has to identify the file format. If there's no file extension, you have to tell the application which format to use. Although I don't question the basic record-keeping capabilities of your brain, you probably have better things to remember than what file format you used five years ago.

> **TIP** As mentioned in Chapter 2, you can automatically append an extension from the Save dialog box regardless of your preference settings. Press Option, choose an option from the Format pop-up menu, and there it is.

Choosing other save options

Certain save options that once upon a time were available only through the Save a Copy command now appear in the Save dialog box all the time. You also get access to these options when you choose Save As or press its keyboard shortcut, Ctrl+Shift+S (⌘+Shift+S on the Mac). Figure 3.34 shows the dialog box.

FIGURE 3.34

Here's a look at the default Save As dialog box, which incorporates the Save a Copy command (previously a separate File menu command) as a save option.

There's a Use Adobe Dialog button in the Save As dialog box, which opens the Adobe Save dialog box — just like there's an Open dialog box in Adobe format, as described earlier in this chapter. After you click the Use Adobe Dialog button, the dialog box changes and you see the version shown in Figure 3.35. Note that the dialog box has a Use OS Dialog button that you can click to go back to the default Save As dialog box.

FIGURE 3.35

Should you use the Adobe Save As dialog box? Sure, why not? Its layout is a little different, and you may prefer it to the OS Dialog box, especially if you have to work in both Mac and Windows versions of Photoshop.

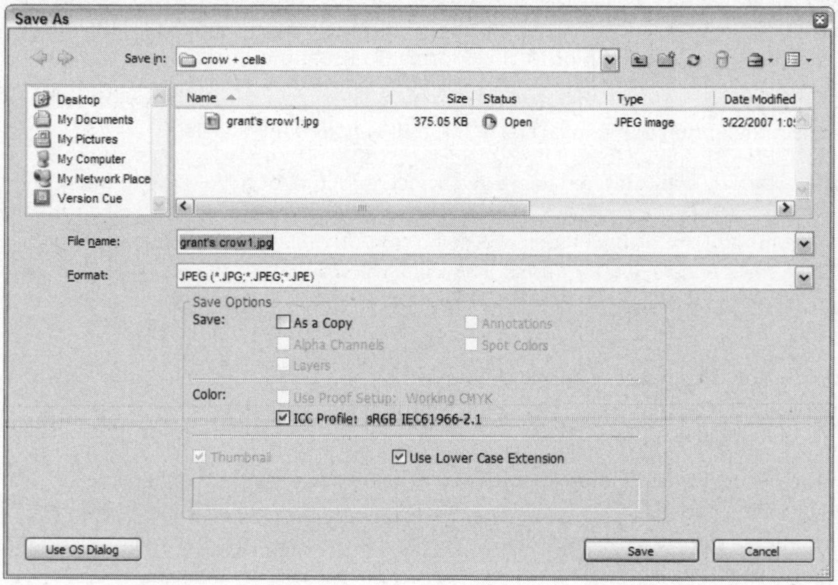

Note that the options you can select vary depending on the image file and the selected file format. If an option is dimmed, it either doesn't apply to your image or isn't supported by the file format you chose. And if your image includes features that won't be saved if you go forward with the current dialog box settings, Photoshop gives you the heads up by displaying a warning message at the bottom of the dialog box.

- **As a Copy:** Select this option to save a copy of the image while leaving the original open and unchanged — in other words, to do what the Save a Copy command did in Photoshop 5.5 and earlier. The result is the same as duplicating an image, saving it, and closing the duplicate all in one step.

  The whole point of this option is to enable you to save a flattened version of a layered image or to dump other extraneous data, such as masks. Just select the file format you want to use, and let Photoshop do the rest for you.

- **Annotations:** Select this option to include any annotations that you created using the notes and audio annotation tools. You can find out how to annotate your images in the section "Adding Annotations" later in this chapter.

■ **Alpha Channels:** If your image contains an alpha channel — Photoshop's techy name for an extra channel, such as a mask (discussed in Chapter 9) — select the Alpha option to retain the channel. Only a few formats — notably Photoshop, PDF, PICT, PICT Resource, TIFF, and DCS 2.0 — support extra channels.

■ **Spot Colors:** Did you create an image that incorporates spot colors? If so, select this option to retain the spot-color channels in the saved image file. You must save the file in the native Photoshop, PDF, TIFF, or DCS 2.0 format to use this option.

■ **Layers:** TIFF and PDF can retain independent image layers, as can the native Photoshop format. Select the option to retain layers; deselect it to flatten the image.

> **CAUTION** If you're working with a layered image and select a file format that doesn't support layers, a cautionary message appears at the bottom of the dialog box. However, Photoshop doesn't prevent you from going through with the save, so be careful. All layers are automatically merged when you save the file in a nonlayer format. However, when you close the file, Photoshop reminds you that you haven't saved a version of the image that retains all data and gives you the opportunity to do so.

■ **Use Proof Setup:** This option relates to Photoshop's color profile options. If the current view's proof setup is a "convert to" proof, Photoshop converts the image to the selected proofing space when saving.

■ **ICC Profile (Win)/Embed Color Profile (Mac):** If you're saving your image in a file format that supports embedded ICC profiles, selecting this option embeds the profile. The current profile appears next to the option name. See Chapter 17 for advice about working with color profiles.

The Save for Web & Devices dialog box

If your image is bound for the Web, you want to use the File ➪ Save for Web & Devices command rather than simply choosing File ➪ Save or Save As. Although you can access the two Web-preferred formats, JPEG and GIF, through the Save As dialog box, the Save for Web & Devices dialog box, shown in Figure 3.36, does much more than just save your image — it provides the following abilities and information:

■ **View side-by-side versions of the image:** On the left, as shown in Figure 3.36, is the original; on the right (in the 2-up view), the optimized version. This enables you to see whether the optimization process has degraded the file at all.

■ **Preview File Sizes and Load Times:** Under the optimized view, the current file format, the file size, and how long that file would take to load for a site visitor using a 28.8 Kbps modem are displayed. The quality setting chosen on the upper-right side of the dialog box also appears in this area. Note that if you're using Windows, Preset options appear in a drop-down list, and on the Mac, they appear in a pop-up menu.

- **Choose the right format for the file:** GIF, JPG, or PNG? Although these options are discussed later in this chapter, you can make your pick through the Preset options in the Save for Web dialog box. From GIF 128 Dithered to PNG-8 128 Dithered (with 10 options in between), you can choose from any Web-safe format, in any configuration.

- **Set the file quality or color density:** If you've opted to save the file as a JPEG (which you should if it's a photo), there's a Quality slider. If you chose GIF (for line art or drawings with solid colors), you have a Colors option that allows you to set the image to display from 2 to 256 colors.

- **Customize the image:** Using options that vary depending on which Preset you chose, you can totally customize the quality and display behavior of the file. Choose the Transparency, Dither, Lossy, and Matte settings (for GIF images), or choose to make your JPEG appear in Progressive fashion, with or without Blur.

- **Animate your GIF images:** If the image is already saved as a GIF file, you can use the buttons along the bottom-right side of the dialog box (in the Color Table tab) to animate the image, layer by layer. You can create animated GIF images from simple on-off affairs to more elaborate movie-like graphics. Read more about this in Chapter 20.

FIGURE 3.36

The Save for Web & Devices dialog box provides one-stop shopping for images that you'll be using online. Choose from the right formats for Web use, tweak their settings to make them load as fast as possible, and customize their appearance for maximum effectiveness on the Web.

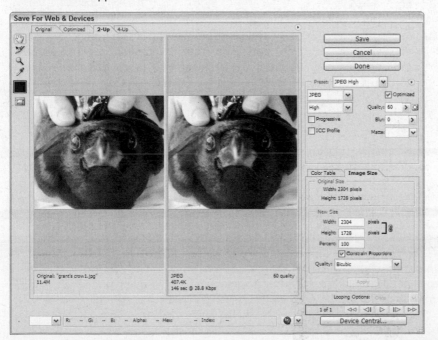

After making your choices in the Save for Web dialog box, all you have to do is click Save, which opens a Save dialog box through which you can name and choose a location for your file. By default, if the file is already saved in PSD or another format (prior to your opening the Save for Web dialog box), Photoshop attempts to give the file that same name — with the extension for the format you chose for the Web-bound file. If the file name you gave it previously is not Web-friendly — bearing capital letters and punctuation other than dashes — edit the name accordingly.

And speaking of file formats, in the next section you learn more about different formats supported by Photoshop, their uses, benefits, and possible drawbacks.

File Format Roundup

Photoshop CS3 supports more than 25 file formats from inside both the OS and Adobe versions of the Open and Save dialog boxes. It can support even more through the addition of plug-in modules that attach commands to the File ⇨ Save As, File ⇨ Import, and File ⇨ Export submenus.

File formats represent different ways to save a file to disk. Some formats provide unique image-compression schemes that save an image in a manner that consumes less space on a hard drive. Other formats enable Photoshop to trade images with different applications running under Windows, the Mac, or some other platform.

The native format

Like most programs, Photoshop offers its own native format — that is, a format optimized for Photoshop's particular capabilities and functions. This PSD format saves every attribute that you can apply in Photoshop — including layers, extra channels, file info, and so on — and is compatible with versions 3 and later of the program. Of course, when you open files in earlier versions of Photoshop, you lose file attributes related to later versions, such as annotations, color proof options, and so on.

NOTE   Photoshop isn't the only application that uses PSD as its native format; PSD also is the native format for the "lite" version of Photoshop, called Photoshop Elements.

TIP   Perhaps not surprisingly, Photoshop can open and save more quickly in its native format than in any other format. The native format also offers image compression. Like TIFF's LZW compression, the Photoshop compression scheme does not result in any loss of data. But Photoshop can compress and decompress its native format much more quickly than it can TIFF, and the compression scheme is better able to minimize the size of mask channels (as explained in Chapter 9).

The downside of the Photoshop format is that relatively few applications other than Photoshop support it, and those that do don't always do a great job. Some applications, such as Corel Photo-Paint and Adobe After Effects, can open a layered Photoshop image and interpret each layer independently. But most of the others limit their support to flat Photoshop files. To accommodate these programs, you can either deselect the Layers option in the Save dialog box to save a flattened version of the image or set the Maximize PSD File Compatibility option in the Preferences dialog box to Ask or Always.

There's another way to look at this, however. Photoshop's native format was never intended to be an inter-application standard. It's not like a DOC or RTF file created by Microsoft Word, which is meant to be compatible with any other word processor. You can save your Photoshop creation in a variety of formats, making it possible to work with other programs, but the PSD format isn't so transferable. It's actually easier to set the Maximize PSD File Compatibility to Never, which you can read about in Chapter 2. If you need to share an image you've created or edited in Photoshop with someone who doesn't have Photoshop, just save it in a format that person can use — like TIFF or JPEG. And always keep a PSD version for yourself, so that flattening the file for someone else doesn't rob you of future editing capabilities in Photoshop.

Special-purpose formats

With so many file formats from which to choose, you can imagine that most are not the kinds you'll be using on a regular basis. In fact, apart from the native Photoshop format, you'll probably want to stick with TIFF, JPEG, and GIF for Web images and EPS when preparing images for placement in InDesign, QuarkXPress, and other layout programs.

Many of the other formats are provided simply so that you can open an image created on another platform, saved from some antiquated paint program, or downloaded from the Web. These formats are covered in other places in the book — Chapter 20 for Web-safe formats, for example. Moving forward here, you learn about the more robust formats — from BMP to TGA, and lots of other alphabet soup in between.

Microsoft Paint's BMP

BMP (*Windows Bitmap*) is the native format for Microsoft Paint (included with Windows) and is supported by a variety of Windows and DOS applications. Photoshop supports BMP images with up to 16 million colors. You also can use RLE (*Run-Length Encoding*), a lossless compression scheme specifically applicable to the BMP format.

> **NOTE** The term *lossless* refers to compression schemes that conserve disk space without sacrificing any data in the image, such as BMP's RLE and GIF's LZW (*Lempel-Ziv-Welch*). The only reasons not to use lossless compression are that it slows down the open and save operations, although this isn't as much of an issue on newer machines, and it may prevent less-sophisticated applications from opening an image. (Lossy compression routines, such as JPEG, sacrifice a user-defined amount of data to conserve even more space, as explained later.)

The most common use for BMP is to create images for use in help files and Windows wallpaper. In fact, designing your own Windows wallpaper can be a fun way to share your Photoshop skills with coworkers, family, and with yourself, too. For the best results, make sure you set your image to exactly the same pixel dimensions as your screen (which you can check from the Settings panel in the Display control panel). To conserve memory, you may want to reduce the number of colors in your wallpaper image to 256 using Image ➪ Mode ➪ Indexed Color.

When you save the wallpaper image, Photoshop displays the options shown in Figure 3.37. Generally, you'll want to select the Windows and Compress (RLE) options, but it really doesn't matter when creating wallpaper. Don't mess with the Depth options. Either you reduced the bit depth using the Indexed Color command as directed previously, or you didn't. There's no sense in changing the colors during the save process.

Want to save an image for use as your desktop? Choose Bitmap as your file format, and respond to this dialog box.

To load the wallpaper onto your Windows desktop, right-click anywhere on the desktop and choose the Properties command. This brings up the Display Properties dialog box. Go to the Background tab, and click Browse to locate your BMP image on disk. After you find it, double-click it to select it, and then click Apply to see how the image looks. You can tweak its appearance on the desktop by choosing from the three Picture Display options — Stretch, Center, or Tile.

Camera Raw

When opening images from a digital camera, Photoshop gives you the ability to work with Camera Raw files. These are the untouched, pristine files generated by mid-level to high-end digital cameras before the images are run through various in-camera compression and color-correction passes. Think of Camera Raw as the digital equivalent of a film negative. Camera Raw files are proprietary, meaning that cameras manufactured by Canon, Fuji, Minolta, and others produce different types of files. Luckily, Photoshop supports a variety of Camera Raw file formats. When you open a supported Camera Raw file, it appears in a special Camera Raw dialog box, where you can make minute adjustments to colors, brightness levels, and other values in your image with virtually no loss in quality. You can find more information on the Camera Raw dialog box in Chapter 18.

Cineon

Cineon is a film- and video-related format supported by Photoshop. Developed by Kodak and used for years as the standard for transferring computer-based images to film, Cineon is a robust, high-quality format and one of the few capable of saving images in 16-bit mode. When Cineon files are used with the Cineon Digital Film System, they can be output to film with absolutely no loss in image quality.

CompuServe's GIF

In the old days, the CompuServe online service championed GIF (short for *Graphics Interchange Format*) as a means of compressing files so you could quickly transfer photographs over your modem. Like TIFF, GIF uses LZW compression, but unlike TIFF, GIF is limited to just 256 colors.

Over the years the GIF format has grown slightly more sophisticated. You can save an image with or without transparency by choosing File ➪ Save and then choosing CompuServe GIF from the Format pop-up menu. When you index (reduce) the image to 256 colors — which you can do either before or during the file save process — select the Transparency option in the Indexed Color dialog box if you want any transparent areas of the image to remain transparent when you view the image file in a Web browser.

TIP GIF files can be animated through the Save for Web dialog box. Save the file in GIF format through Photoshop's Save As dialog box, and then open the Save for Web dialog box to access animation tools that turn image layers into components that can be made to move or blink on and off for one loop or an endless series of repeating actions.

PC Paintbrush's PCX

PCX doesn't stand for anything. Rather, it's the extension PC Paintbrush assigns to images saved in its native file format. Although the format is losing favor, many PCX images are still in use today, largely because PC Paintbrush is the oldest painting program for DOS. Photoshop supports PCX images with up to 16 million colors. You can find an enormous amount of art, usually clip art, in this format. However, don't save files to PCX unless a client specifically demands it. Other formats are better.

Adobe's paperless PDF

PDF (*Portable Document Format*) is a variation on the PostScript printing language that enables you to view electronically produced documents onscreen. This means that you can create a publication in QuarkXPress or InDesign, export it to PDF, and distribute it without worrying about color separations, binding, and other printing costs. Using a program called Adobe Reader, you can open PDF documents, zoom in and out of them, and follow hypertext links by clicking highlighted words. Adobe distributes Mac, Windows, and Unix versions of the Adobe Reader for free, so almost anyone with a computer can view your stuff in full, natural color. Mac OS X users will also enjoy the fact that PDF files can be displayed in virtually any Mac application (written for use in OS X), and that in many Mac applications' Print dialog boxes, a Save as PDF option appears, making the creation of PDF files quite simple.

PDF files come in two flavors: those that contain just a single image and those that contain multiple pages and images. You can only save single-page PDF files using the File ➪ Save command. To save multi-page PDF files, you must use the new PDF Presentation command, discussed in Chapter 20. When opening either a single-image or multi-page PDF file, Photoshop always rasterizes the contents of the file.

You open PDF files in different ways depending on what elements of the file you want to access:

■ Use File ⇨ Open to open a particular page in a multi-page PDF file. After selecting the page you want to view, you can set the image size and resolution of the rasterized file. You also can choose File ⇨ Place to add a page as a new layer to an open image; in this case, you can't control the size and resolution before adding the page. However, you can scale the page after the fact as you can any layer.

■ Choose File ⇨ Import ⇨ PDF Image to bring up a dialog box that enables you to open a particular image in the PDF file.

■ Choose File ⇨ Automate ⇨ Multi-Page PDF to PSD to turn each page in the PDF file into a separate Photoshop image file.

The real question, however, is why would you *want* to open or place a PDF file in Photoshop instead of viewing it in Adobe Reader, which provides you with a full range of document-viewing tools not found in Photoshop? Furthermore, because you can save only single-page PDF files, why on earth would you save to PDF in Photoshop?

There are really only two scenarios where Photoshop's PDF functions may be of use:

■ You want to see how images in a PDF document will look when printed on a high-resolution printer. Open the PDF file using File ⇨ Open, set the resolution to match that of the output device, and eyeball those images onscreen. This "soft-proofing" technique enables you to spot defects that may not be noticeable in draft proofs that you output on a low-res printer.

■ You need a convenient way to distribute images for approval or input. You can save an image as a PDF file and send it to clients and colleagues, who can view the image in Acrobat or Adobe Reader if they don't have Photoshop. You can even add text or voice annotations to your PDF file. In addition to annotations, Photoshop PDF supports layers, transparency, embedded color profiles, spot colors, duotones, and more. This enables you to route an image for approval without having to flatten the image or otherwise strip it of its Photoshop features. Of course, features not supported by Adobe Reader aren't accessible to the viewer.

When you save to PDF in Photoshop, you have a choice of two encoding options, as shown in Figure 3.38. Choose ZIP only for images that feature large expanses of a single color; otherwise, opt for JPEG. Keep the Quality option set to Maximum to maintain the best print quality, just as you do for regular JPEG files.

NOTE   If you select JPEG encoding, you need a PostScript Level 2 or later printer to output your PDF file. Also be aware that separating files into individual plates can be problematic if you're working in a Windows environment.

FIGURE 3.38

Click any one of the five items listed on the left to display a new set of options. Here, the Compression options are displayed.

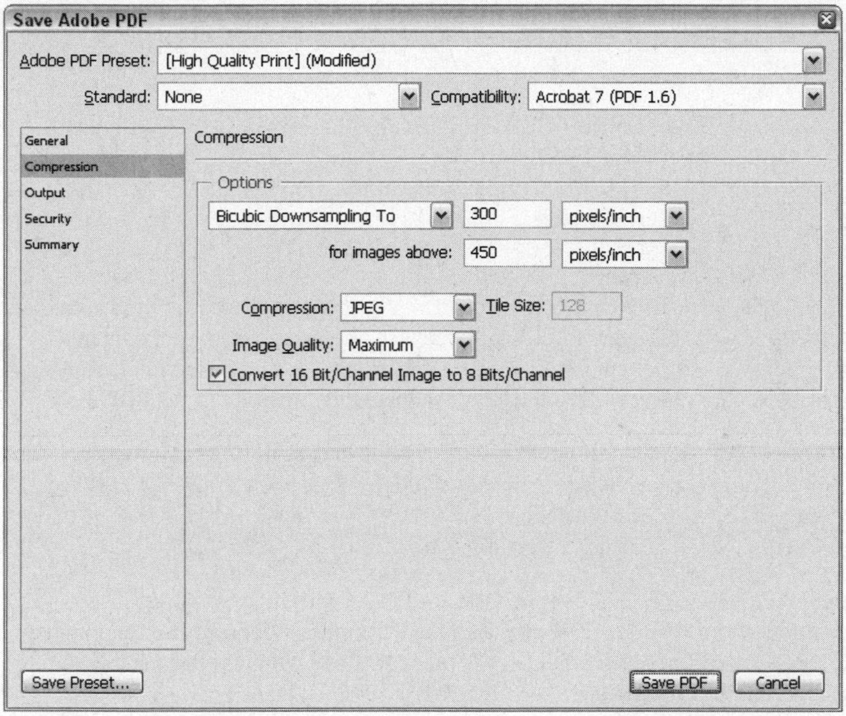

When saving to PDF, you also encounter several other options:

- **Save Transparency:** If your image has transparency and you're saving it as a PDF without layers, the Save Transparency option determines whether or not the transparency is maintained.

- **Image Interpolation:** Selecting this option enables other programs to interpolate the image when resampling to another size.

- **Downgrade Color Profile:** Here's an option you'll probably never use. PDF doesn't support version 4 ICC profiles. Selecting this option converts them to version 2 profiles so that they'll work in PDF. The thing is, you probably don't have a version 4 ICC profile anyway, in which case this option is dimmed. For more on ICC profiles, see Chapter 17.

- **PDF Security:** This option allows you to assign passwords to PDF documents — if users don't know the password, they can't open the document. To set the security information, select the PDF Security option and click Security Settings. You can set the user password here, along with a master password, which can prevent others from changing the user password. The Encryption Level options take effect only when the document is being opened with Adobe Acrobat; you can choose the version of Acrobat and determine whether options such as saving changes and printing are allowed.

- **Include Vector Data** and **Embed Fonts:** Select these two options to retain any vector graphics and font data, respectively. Alternatively, you can select Use Outlines for Text to save text as character outlines that are editable in the PDF file.

Apple's PICT

PICT (*Macintosh Picture*) was the native graphics format for Mac OS 9. (Mac OS X has adopted PDF as its standard graphics file format.) Based on the QuickDraw display language that the system software uses to convey images onscreen, PICT handles object-oriented artwork and bitmapped images with equal aplomb. It supports images in any bit depth, size, or resolution. PICT even supports 32-bit images, so you can save a fourth masking channel when working in the RGB mode.

If you've installed QuickTime on the Mac, you can subject PICT images to JPEG compression. But although PICT's compression options may look similar to JPEG's, they are actually significantly inferior. The differences become especially noticeable if you open an image, make a change, and again save it to disk, effectively reapplying the compression.

In most cases, you'll want to use the JPEG format instead of PICT when compressing images. JPEG images are compatible with the Web; PICT images are not. Also, more Windows applications recognize JPEG than PICT, and it's extremely difficult to find a Windows program that can handle PICT files with QuickTime compression.

In fact, the only reason to use PICT is low-end compatibility. If you're trying to save an image in a format that your mom can open on her ancient Mac, for example, PICT may be a better choice than JPEG. Heck, you can open PICT files inside a word processor, including everything from SimpleText to Microsoft Word. Just be sure mom has QuickTime loaded on her machine.

When you save a PICT image, Photoshop also lets you set the bit depth. You should always stick with the default option, which is the highest setting available for the particular image. Don't mess around with these options; they apply automatic pattern dithering, which is a bad thing.

If you're using a PC, you may need to open a PICT file a Mac friend sends you. Photoshop can do this, but one thing may trip you up: On the Mac, you have the option of saving PICT files with a variety of JPEG compressions supplied by Apple's QuickTime. Unless you have QuickTime installed on your PC or if you've installed iTunes for your iPod (which installs QuickTime automatically) — you won't be able to open compressed PICT images.

PICT resource

PICT resources were the images contained in the resource fork of a Mac file in OS 9. (Windows programs can't recognize resource forks, so this section is relevant only to Mac users.) The only reason you would want to save a PICT resource is if you are creating an OS 9 startup screen, and the most likely reason to open one is to extract images from the OS 9 Scrapbook. However, because Photoshop CS3 (and its predecessors, CS and CS2) no longer runs under OS 9, you can be fairly confident that you won't be using this format. For the time being, however, Photoshop continues to support the format.

Pixar workstations

Pixar has created some of the most memorable computer-animated short films and features in recent memory. Pixar works its 3-D magic using extremely expensive proprietary workstations. Photoshop enables you to open a still image created on a Pixar machine or to save an image to the Pixar format so you can integrate it into a 3-D rendering. The Pixar format supports grayscale and RGB images.

PNG for the Web

The PNG (pronounced *ping*) format enables you to save 16-million color images without compression for use on the Web. Although PNG has been generally supported by Netscape Navigator and Microsoft Internet Explorer since 1997, these main two browsers still can't be counted on to fully support all the features of PNG. Couple that info with the obvious fact that you can't count on the general public to have anywhere near the most recent version of any software application, and using PNG might seem like a dicey proposition. It's a great format, though, offering full-color images without the pesky visual compression artifacts you get with JPEG.

Large Document Format (PSB)

Recently, many applications have adopted the capability to work with and save files more than 2GB in size. If you're editing nonlinear video, the need to use gigantic files makes perfect sense. Image-editing applications like Photoshop have been slower to adopt support for such huge files, but Photoshop has leapt into the fray with its new Large Document Format (PSB). Finally, you won't need to figure out a work-around when designing that billboard for the surface of the moon.

Photoshop is capable of opening and saving existing PSB files by default, but if you want to create a Large Document Format file from scratch, you need to select the Enable Large Document Format (.psb) option in the File Handling panel of the Preferences dialog box (that's Ctrl+K, Ctrl+3 on the PC and ⌘+K, ⌘+3 on the Mac). Keep in mind that images saved in PSB format cannot be opened in other applications or versions of Photoshop prior to CS2.

> **NOTE** Another format that you can use for storing enormous files is Photoshop Raw, but it's not nearly as capable as PSB. Most important, the image needs to be flattened, meaning you can kiss your layers goodbye. Photoshop Raw can be useful for other purposes, though, as is explained shortly.

Scitex image processors

Some high-end commercial printers use Scitex printing devices to generate color separations of images and other documents. Photoshop can open images digitized with Scitex scanners and save the edited images to the *Scitex CT* (*Continuous Tone*) format. Because you need special hardware to transfer images from the PC to a Scitex drive, you'll probably want to consult with your local Scitex service bureau technician before saving to the CT format. The technician may prefer that you submit images in the native Photoshop, TIFF, or JPEG format. The Scitex CT format supports grayscale, RGB, and CMYK images.

TrueVision's TGA

TrueVision's Targa and NuVista video boards enable you to overlay computer graphics and animation onto live video. The effect is called *chroma keying* because, typically, a key color is set aside to let the live video show through. TrueVision designed the TGA (*Targa*) format to support 32-bit images that include 8-bit alpha channels capable of displaying the live video. Support for TGA is widely implemented among professional-level color and video applications on the PC.

Acrobat TouchUp Image

If your preferences are set correctly in Adobe Acrobat, you can select any image file in a PDF document, right-click it (Control-click on the Mac), and choose to edit the image externally in Photoshop. Acrobat creates a temporary file with a long, indecipherable name, called a TouchUp Image, and opens Photoshop. After you save the file and return to Acrobat, the changes you made are incorporated automatically. A quick tip: Make sure you don't alter the dimensions of an image you're touching up — doing so alters the layout of the PDF file — and remember to flatten any layers you may have created before you return to Acrobat.

Wireless Bitmap

Hey, those crude little graphics found on handheld wireless devices have to come from somewhere, right? Why not Photoshop? Photoshop can open and save in WBMP (*Wireless Bitmap*) format, an up-and-coming standard for cell phones and personal digital assistants. To save an image to the Wireless Bitmap format, the image must be in Bitmap mode, with only black and white pixels.

Inter-application formats

In the name of inter-application harmony, Photoshop supports a few software-specific formats that permit you to trade files with popular object-oriented programs, such as Illustrator and QuarkXPress. Every one of these formats is a variation on EPS (*Encapsulated PostScript*), which is based in turn on Adobe's industry-standard PostScript printing language.

Rasterizing an Illustrator or FreeHand file

Photoshop supports object-oriented files saved in the EPS format. EPS is specifically designed to save object-oriented graphics that you intend to print to a PostScript output device. Just about every drawing and page-layout program on the planet (and a few on Mars) can save EPS documents.

Prior to version 4, Photoshop could interpret only a small subset of EPS operations supported by Illustrator (including the native *.ai* format). But then Photoshop 4 came along and offered a full-blown EPS translation engine, capable of interpreting EPS illustrations created in FreeHand, CorelDraw, and more. You can even open EPS drawings that contain imported images, something else version 3 could not do. When you open an EPS or native Illustrator document, Photoshop *rasterizes* (or *renders*) the artwork — that is, it converts the artwork from a collection of objects to a bitmapped image.

Photoshop renders the illustration to a single layer against a transparent background. Before you can save the rasterized image to a format other than native Photoshop, you must eliminate the transparency by choosing Layer ➪ Flatten Image. Or save a flattened version of the image to a separate file by choosing the As a Copy option in the Save dialog box.

TIP Rendering an EPS illustration is an extremely useful technique for resolving printing problems. If you regularly work in Illustrator or FreeHand, you no doubt have encountered *limitcheck errors*, which occur when an illustration is too complex for an imagesetter or other high-end output device to print. If you're frustrated with the printer and tired of wasting your evening trying to figure out what's wrong (sound familiar?), use Photoshop to render the illustration at 300 ppi and print it. Nine times out of 10, this technique works flawlessly.

If Photoshop can't *parse* the EPS file — a techy way of saying Photoshop can't break down the individual objects — it attempts to open a TIFF preview. This exercise is usually futile, but occasionally you may want to take a quick look at an illustration to, say, match the placement of elements in an image to those in the drawing.

Placing an EPS illustration

If you want to introduce an EPS graphic into the foreground image rather than render it into a new image window of its own, choose File ➪ Place. Unlike other File menu commands, Place supports only EPS illustrations and PDF files.

After you import the EPS graphic, it appears inside a box — which Photoshop calls a *bounding box* — with a great, big X across it. You can move, scale, and rotate the illustration into position before rasterizing it to pixels. Click and drag a corner handle to resize the image; drag outside the image to rotate it. You also can nudge the graphic into position by pressing the arrow keys. When everything is the way you want it, press Enter (Return on the Mac) or double-click inside the box to rasterize the illustration. If the placement isn't perfect, don't worry. The graphic appears on a separate layer, so you can move it with complete freedom. To cancel the Place operation, press Esc instead of Enter or Return.

Saving an EPS image

When preparing an image for placement in a drawing or page-layout document that will be printed to a PostScript output device, many artists prefer to save the image in the EPS format. Converting the image to PostScript up front prevents the drawing or page-layout program from doing the work. The result is an image that prints more quickly and with less chance of problems. (Note that an image does not *look* any different when saved in EPS. The idea that the EPS format somehow blesses an image with better resolution is pure nonsense.)

A second point in the EPS format's favor is clipping paths. As explained graphically at the end of Chapter 8, a clipping path defines a free-form boundary around an image. When you place the image into an object-oriented program, everything outside the clipping path becomes transparent. While some programs — notably InDesign and PageMaker — recognize clipping paths saved with a TIFF image, many programs acknowledge a clipping path only when saved in the EPS format.

Third, although Illustrator has remedied the problems it had importing TIFF images, it still likes EPS best, especially where screen display is concerned. Thanks to the EPS file's fixed preview, Illustrator can display an EPS image onscreen very quickly compared with other file formats. And Illustrator can display an EPS image both in the preview mode and in the super-fast artwork mode.

So if you want to import an image into Illustrator, QuarkXPress, or another object-oriented program, your best bet is EPS. On the downside, EPS is an inefficient format for saving images thanks to the laborious way that it describes pixels. An EPS image may be three to four times larger than the same image saved to the TIFF format with LZW compression. But this is the price we pay for reliable printing.

CAUTION   Absolutely avoid the EPS format if you're a Windows user and you plan on printing your final pages to a non-PostScript printer. This defeats the entire purpose of EPS, which is meant to avoid printing problems, not cause them. When printing without PostScript, use TIFF or JPEG.

To save an image in the EPS format, choose Photoshop EPS from the Format pop-up menu in the Save dialog box. After you press Enter or Return, Photoshop displays the dialog box shown in Figure 3.39. The options in this dialog box work as follows:

- **Preview:** Technically, an EPS document comprises two parts: a pure PostScript-language description of the graphic for the printer and a bitmapped preview so you can see the graphic onscreen. On a PC, select the TIFF (8 bits/pixel) option from the Preview pop-up menu to save a 256-color TIFF preview of the image. On a Mac, select the Macintosh (8 bits/pixel) option from the Preview pop-up menu to save a 256-color PICT preview of the image for users of Mac OS9 and earlier (they won't be using CS3, obviously). Or select the Macintosh (JPEG) option for a 24-bit preview (which in most cases takes up less room on disk, thanks to the JPEG compression). If you plan on passing off the image to a Windows colleague, select TIFF (8 bits/pixel). The 1-bit option provides a black-and-white preview only, which is useful if you want to save a little room on disk. Select None to include no preview and save even more disk space.

- **Encoding:** If you're saving an image for import into Illustrator, QuarkXPress, or some other established program, select the Binary encoding option (also known as *Huffman encoding*), which compresses an EPS document by substituting shorter codes for frequently used characters. The letter *a*, for example, receives the 3-bit code 010, rather than its standard 8-bit ASCII code, 01100001 (the binary equivalent of what we humans call 97).

  Sadly, some programs and printers don't recognize Huffman encoding, in which case you must select one of the less efficient ASCII options. ASCII stands for *American Standard Code for Information Interchange*, which is fancy jargon for text-only. In other words, you can open and edit an ASCII EPS document in a word processor, provided you know how to read and write PostScript.

138

FIGURE 3.39

When you save an image in the EPS format, you can specify the type of preview and tack on some printing attributes.

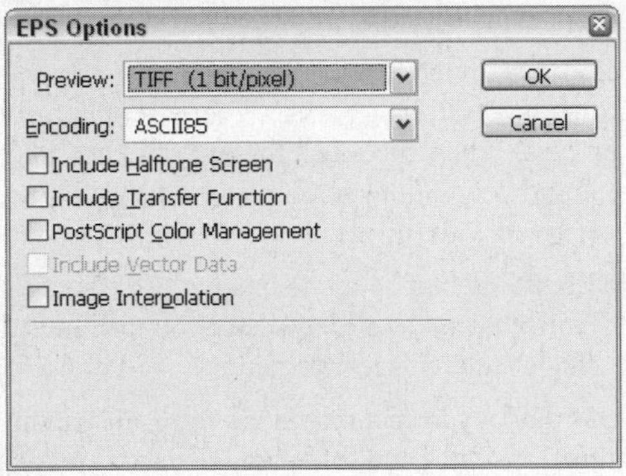

TIP Actually, this can be a useful technique if you have a Mac file that won't open on a PC, especially if the file was sent to you electronically. Chances are that a Mac-specific header got into the works. Open the file in a word processor and look at the beginning. You should see the four characters *%!PS*. Anything that comes before this line is the Macintosh header. Delete the gobbledygook before *%!PS*, save the file in text format, and try again to open the file in Photoshop.

CAUTION The remaining Encoding options are JPEG settings. JPEG compression not only results in smaller files on disk but also degrades the quality of the image. Select JPEG (Maximum Quality) to invoke the least degradation. Better yet, avoid the JPEG settings altogether. These options work only if you plan to print your final artwork to a PostScript Level 2 or Level 3 device. Earlier PostScript printers do not support EPS artwork with JPEG compression and will choke on the code.

So to recap, ASCII results in really big files that work with virtually any printer or application. Binary creates smaller files that work with most mainstream applications but may choke some older-model printers. And the JPEG settings are compatible exclusively with Level 2 and later PostScript printers.

- **Include Halftone Screen:** Another advantage of EPS over other formats is that it can retain printing attributes. If you specified a custom halftone screen using the Screens button in the Page Setup dialog box, you can save this setting with the EPS document by selecting the Include Halftone Screen option. But be careful; you can just as easily ruin your image as help it. Read Chapter 20 before you select this option.

- **Include Transfer Function:** As described in Chapter 20, you can change the brightness and contrast of a printed image using the Transfer button in the Page Setup dialog box. To save these settings with the EPS document, select the Include Transfer Function option. Again, this option can be dangerous when used casually.

- **PostScript Color Management:** Like JPEG compression, this option is compatible with Level 2 and Level 3 printers only. It embeds a color profile, which helps the printer to massage the image during the printing cycle to generate more accurate colors. Unless you plan on printing to a Level 2 or later device, leave the option deselected. (For more information about color profiles, read Chapter 17.)

- **Include Vector Data:** Select this option if your file contains vector objects, including shapes, non-bitmap text, and layer clipping paths. Otherwise, Photoshop rasterizes the objects during the save process. When you select the option, Photoshop displays a warning in the dialog box to remind you that if you reopen the file in Photoshop, you rasterize any vector objects that you saved with the file.

- **Transparent Whites:** When saving bitmap mode images as EPS files in Photoshop, the four options previously discussed drop away, replaced by Transparent Whites. Select this option to make all white pixels in the image transparent.

  Although Photoshop EPS is the only format that offers the Transparent Whites option, many programs — including Illustrator and InDesign — treat white pixels in black-and-white TIFF images as transparent as well.

- **Image Interpolation:** Select this option if you want another program to be able to interpolate the image when resampling it to another size. For example, suppose you import an EPS image into InDesign and scale it to 400 percent. If Image Interpolation is deselected, InDesign just makes pixels in the image four times larger, as if you had used the nearest neighbor interpolation in Photoshop. If you select Image Interpolation, however, InDesign applies bicubic interpolation to generate new pixels. (For details on nearest neighbor and bicubic interpolation, see Chapter 2.) Unless you have a reason for doing otherwise, select this option.

QuarkXPress DCS

Quark developed a variation on the EPS format called DCS (*Desktop Color Separation*). When you work in QuarkXPress, PageMaker, and other programs that support the format, DCS facilitates the printing of color separations. Before you can use DCS, you have to convert your image to the CMYK color space using Image ➪ Mode ➪ CMYK Color. (DCS 2.0 also supports grayscale images with spot-color channels.) Then open the Save As dialog box and select Photoshop DCS 1.0 or 2.0 from the Format pop-up menu.

If you add a Pantone channel to an image, DCS 2.0 is the only PostScript format that you can use. If your image doesn't contain any extra channels beyond the basic four required for CMYK, DCS 1.0 is the safer and simpler option.

After you press Enter or Return, Photoshop displays the DCS Options dialog box, the contents of which varies depending on whether you've selected DCS 1.0 or 2.0, as shown in Figure 3.40. The DCS 1.0 format invariably saves a total of five files: one master document (which is the file that you import into QuarkXPress) plus one file each for the cyan, magenta, yellow, and black color channels (which are the files that get printed). The DCS 2.0 format can be expressed as a single file (tidier) or five separate files (better compatibility).

Either way, the DCS pop-up menu gives you the option of saving a 72-ppi PostScript composite of the image inside the master document. Independent from the bitmapped preview — which you specify as usual by selecting a Preview option — the PostScript composite makes it possible to print a low-resolution version of a DCS image to a consumer-quality printer. If you're using a black-and-white printer, select the 72-pixel/inch grayscale option; if you're using a color printer, select the final option. Be forewarned, however, that the composite image significantly increases the size of the master document on disk. The two options at the bottom of the options dialog boxes for DCS 1.0 and 2.0, Include Vector Data and Image Interpolation, work just as described earlier for the Photoshop EPS format.

FIGURE 3.40

The DCS Options dialog box allows you to prepare your image for use in QuarkXPress.

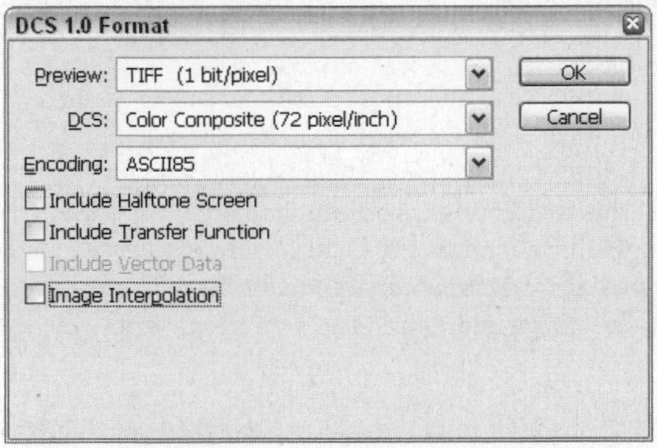

Premiere Filmstrip

Adobe Premiere Pro is a popular video-editing application for the PC. The program is a wonder when it comes to fades, frame merges, and special effects, but it offers no frame-by-frame roto-scope-style animating capabilities. For example, you can neither draw a mustache on a person in the movie nor can you make brightly colored brushstrokes swirl about in the background — at least, not in Premiere.

You can export the movie to the Filmstrip format, though, which is a file-swapping option exclusive to Photoshop and Premiere. A Filmstrip document organizes frames in a long vertical strip. A gray bar separates each frame from the next. The number of each frame appears on the right; the SMPTE (Society of Motion Picture and Television Engineers) time code appears on the left. The structure of the three-number time code is minutes:seconds:frames, with 30 frames per second.

CAUTION If you change the size of a Filmstrip document inside Photoshop in any way, you cannot save the image back to the Filmstrip format. Feel free to paint and apply effects, but stay the heck away from the Image Size and Canvas Size commands.

While you won't really find much coverage of the Filmstrip format anywhere else in this book, it's useful to pass along a few quick Filmstrip tips:

- First, you can scroll up and down exactly one frame at a time by pressing Shift+Page Up or Shift+Page Down, respectively.

- Second, you can move a selection exactly one frame up or down by pressing Ctrl+Shift+up arrow (⌘+Shift+up arrow on the Mac) or Ctrl+Shift+down arrow (⌘+Shift+down arrow on the Mac).

- If you want to clone the selection as you move it, press Ctrl+Shift+Alt+up arrow (⌘+Shift+Option+up arrow on the Mac) or Ctrl+Shift+Alt+down arrow (⌘+Shift+Option+down arrow on the Mac).

CROSS-REF   **Although we don't get into any particular video-editing software in this book, we do delve further into editing video frames and working with video through Photoshop, because CS3 has added lots of functionality in this area. To find out more, check out Chapter 19.**

The process of editing individual frames as just described is sometimes called *rotoscoping*, named after the traditional technique of using live-action film as a source when creating animated sequences. You also can try out some scratch-and-doodle techniques, which is where an artist scratches and draws directly on frames of film. If this isn't enough, you can emulate *xerography*, in which an animator makes Xerox copies of photographs, enhances the copies using markers or whatever else is convenient, and shoots the finished artwork, frame by frame, on film. In a nutshell, Photoshop extends Premiere's functionality by adding animation to its standard supply of video-editing capabilities.

CROSS-REF   **Rotoscoping is something Photoshop CS3 is built to do, thanks to enhanced capabilities discussed in Chapter 19.**

You can save an image in the Filmstrip format through the Save As dialog box. But remember, you can save in this format only if you opened the image as a Filmstrip document and did not change the size of the image.

The mainstream formats

The formats discussed so far are all very interesting and they fulfill their own niche purposes. But two formats — JPEG and TIFF — are the all-stars of digital imagery. You'll probably use these formats the most because of their outstanding compression capabilities and almost universal support among graphics applications.

JPEG

The JPEG format is named after the people who designed it, the Joint Photographic Experts Group. JPEG is the most efficient and essential compression format currently available and is likely to be the compression standard for years to come. JPEG is a lossy compression scheme, which means it sacrifices image quality to conserve space on disk. You can control how much data is lost during the save operation, however.

When you save an image in the JPEG format, you're greeted with the JPEG Options dialog box, as shown in Figure 3.41. The most vital option in this dialog box is the Quality setting, which determines how much compression Photoshop applies to your image.

The JPEG Options dialog box provides a total of 13 compression settings, ranging from 0 (heaviest compression) to 12 (best quality).

Select an option from the Quality pop-up menu or click and drag the slider from 0 to 12 to specify the quality setting. Of the named options, Low takes the least space on disk but distorts the image rather severely; Maximum retains the highest amount of image quality but consumes more disk space. Of the numbered options, 0 is the most severe compressor and 12 does the least damage.

NOTE JPEG evaluates an image in 8×8-pixel blocks, using a technique called *Adaptive Discrete Cosine Transform,* or ADCT. It averages the 24-bit value of every pixel in the block (or the 8-bit value of every pixel, in the case of a grayscale image). ADCT then stores the average color in the upper-left pixel in the block and assigns the remaining 63 pixels smaller values relative to the average.

Next, JPEG divides the block by an 8×8 block of its own called the *quantization matrix*, which homogenizes the pixels' values by changing as many as possible to zero. This process saves the majority of disk space but loses data. When Photoshop opens a JPEG image, it can't recover the original distinction between the zero pixels, so the pixels become the same, or similar, colors. Finally, JPEG applies lossless Huffman encoding to translate repeating values to a single symbol.

In most instances, using JPEG only at the Maximum Quality setting (10 or higher) is a good idea, at least until you gain some experience with it. The smallest amount of JPEG compression saves more space than any non-JPEG compression format and still retains the most essential detail from the original image.

CROSS-REF Check the coverage of the Save for Web dialog box earlier in this chapter, and see Chapter 20 for more information on the JPEG format and its use for images that will be displayed online.

CAUTION   JPEG is a *cumulative compression scheme*, meaning that Photoshop recompresses an image every time you save it in the JPEG format. There's no disadvantage to saving an image to disk repeatedly during a single session, because JPEG always works from the onscreen version. But if you close an image, reopen it, and save it in the JPEG format, you inflict a small amount of damage. Use JPEG sparingly. In the best of all possible worlds, you should save to the JPEG format only after you finish all work on an image. Even in a pinch, you should apply all filtering effects before saving to JPEG, because these have a habit of exacerbating imperfections in image quality.

JPEG is best used when compressing continuous-tone images (images in which the distinction between immediately neighboring pixels is slight). Any image that includes gradual color transitions, as in a photograph, qualifies for JPEG compression. JPEG is not the best choice for saving screen shots, line drawings (especially those converted from EPS graphics), and other high-contrast images. These are better served by GIF if you want to post them on the Web or by a lossless compression scheme, such as TIFF with LZW. The JPEG format is available when you are saving grayscale, RGB, and CMYK images.

Occupying the bottom half of the JPEG Options dialog box are three radio buttons, designed primarily to optimize JPEG images for the Web. If your image is destined for print, just select the first option, Baseline ("Standard"), and be done with it. For Web graphics, select the Baseline Optimized option to make images display onscreen line by line or select the Progressive option to make images display in multiple passes.

TIFF

Developed by Aldus in the early days of the Mac to standardize an ever-growing population of scanned images, TIFF (*Tagged Image File Format*) is the most widely supported image-printing format across both the Macintosh and PC platforms. Unlike EPS, it can't handle object-oriented artwork, but otherwise it's unrestricted. In fact, TIFF offers a few tricks of its own that make it very special.

In Photoshop, TIFF supports up to 24 channels, the maximum number permitted in any image. In fact, TIFF is the only system other than DCS 2.0, "raw," and the native Photoshop format that can save more than four channels. To save a TIFF file without extra mask channels, deselect the Alpha option in the Save As dialog box. (For an introduction to channels, read Chapter 4.) Even more impressive, TIFF supports multiple layers. If you want layers to remain independent when you save the file, you can select the Layers option in the Save As dialog box.

When you save an image as a TIFF file, Photoshop displays the TIFF Options dialog box, shown in Figure 3.42, which offers the following controls:

- **Image Compression:** You can choose among three different types of compression: LZW (which stands for Lempel-Ziv-Welch, in case you're ever on a game show and ask the host, "File Format Trivia for $200, Alex!"), ZIP, or JPEG. Here are the major differences:

  - **LZW:** Like Huffman encoding (previously described in the section "Saving an EPS image"), LZW digs into the computer code that describes an image and substitutes frequently used codes with shorter equivalents. But instead of substituting characters, as Huffman does, LZW substitutes strings of data. Because LZW doesn't so much as touch a pixel in your image, it's entirely lossless. Most image editors and desktop-publishing applications—including Illustrator, FreeHand, InDesign, PageMaker, and QuarkXPress— import LZW-compressed TIFF images, but a few still have yet to catch on.

■ **ZIP:** The problem with LZW (from a programming perspective) is that it's regulated by a patent. And whenever a bit of technology costs money to use, you can bet somebody out there is trying to come up with a free equivalent. Hence ZIP, a competing lossless compression scheme used in PDF documents. Why use it? Theoretically, it's a bit smarter than LZW and can on occasion deliver smaller image files. On the other hand, Photoshop is currently one of the few programs to support ZIP compression in a TIFF file. So unless you discover big savings when using ZIP, you should stick with LZW until ZIP support becomes more widespread.

■ **JPEG:** If two lossless compression schemes aren't enough options, the TIFF format also permits you to apply lossy JPEG compression. Long-time Photoshop users may balk at JPEG compression inside TIFF options. After all, one of the major benefits of TIFF is that it ensures optimum image quality; by applying JPEG compression, which results in loss of image data, you defeat the purpose. But now that TIFF supports layers, JPEG inside TIFF permits you a unique opportunity to cut the size of your layered image files in half. Experience shows that JPEG in TIFF results in only a modest loss of data. And because JPEG does not affect the transparency mask — which defines the outlines of the layers — the layers continue to exhibit nice, sharp edges.

FIGURE 3.42

Photoshop offers a myriad of compression schemes for TIFF files.

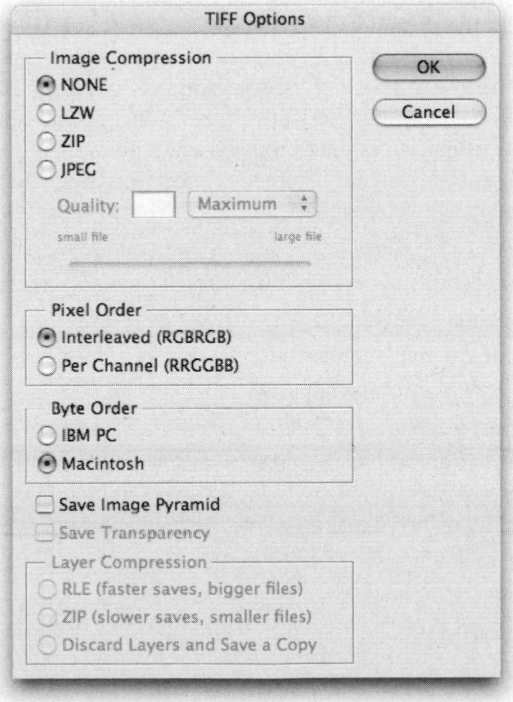

NOTE   If names such as Huffman, LZW, and ZIP ring a faint bell, it may be because these are the same compression schemes used by StuffIt, PKzip, WinZIP, and other file compression utilities. For this reason, using an additional utility to compress a TIFF image that you've already compressed using LZW, ZIP, or JPEG makes no sense. Neither do you want to compress a standard JPEG image, because JPEG takes advantage of Huffman encoding. You may shave off a few K, but this isn't enough space to make it worth your time and effort.

CAUTION   Also be aware that some programs may gag on compressed TIFF files, regardless of which compression scheme you apply. If an application balks at opening your Photoshop TIFF file, try resaving the file with no compression.

- **Pixel Order:** These two options allow you to choose how pixels will be organized — note the symbolic use of "RGBRGB" and "RRGGBB" (respectively) next to the options. The default (Interleaved) is your best bet because not all TIFF-reading applications will be able to support Per Channel pixel order.

- **Byte Order:** Every once in a while, Photoshop chooses to name a straightforward option in the most confusing way possible. Byte Order is a prime example, and it relates to the two variations of TIFF, one for the PC and the other for the Mac. This probably has something to do with the arrangement of 8-bit chunks of data, but do you care? Probably not. More likely, you're sure about your choice of either wanting to use a PC or a Mac, regardless of TIFF variations.

- **Save Image Pyramid:** Select this option to save *tiled* TIFF files. This variation of the standard TIFF file-saving algorithm divides your image into tiles and then stacks the tiles in a pyramid. Each level of the pyramid represents your image at a different resolution, with the highest-resolution version serving as the base of the pyramid. The idea is that an application can use the low-resolution tiles to perform certain image-processing tasks and dig down to the high-resolution version only when absolutely necessary. When you're working with very large image files, this approach not only speeds up certain editing tasks but also puts less strain on your computer's resources. (If you're familiar with the FlashPix format, the concept is the same.)

  Unless you're saving your image for use in a program that you know supports tiled TIFF images, however, deselect this option. Photoshop itself can't take advantage of the tiled technology, and many applications can't open tiled images at all.

- **Save Transparency:** If the image contains transparent areas, select this option to retain the transparency. Otherwise, transparent areas become white.

- **Layer Compression:** Not only can you decide whether you want to use lossless or lossy image compression, but Photoshop lets you specify how you want to save the layers themselves. The choices speak for themselves; RLE saves more quickly but makes bigger files, and the reverse is true for ZIP. Alternatively, you can choose to discard the layers altogether and save a flattened copy of your file.

Formatting Outcasts

Nope, the discussion of formats is not quite complete. There are two more, the odd men out. Why are they formatting pariahs? One format has a purpose so specific that Photoshop can open files saved in the format but it can't save to the format. The other is not so much a format but a manual file can opener that may come in handy for prying open a file from an unknown source.

Photo CD YCC images

Photoshop can open Eastman Kodak's Photo CD and Pro Photo CD formats directly. A Photo CD contains compressed versions of every image in each of the five scan sizes provided on Photo CDs — from 128×192 pixels (72K) to 2,048×3,072 pixels (18MB).

The Pro Photo CD format can accommodate each of the five sizes included in the regular Photo CD format, plus one additional size — 4,096×6,144 pixels (72MB) — that's four times as large as the largest image on a regular Photo CD. As a result, Pro Photo CDs hold only 25 scans; standard Photo CDs hold 100. Like their standard Photo CD counterparts, Pro Photo CD scanners can accommodate 35mm film and slides. But they also can handle 70mm film and 4-x-5-inch negatives and transparencies. The cost can be an issue, as scanning an image to a standard Photo CD costs between $1 and $2, but scanning it to a Pro Photo CD costs about $10. Your budget will determine which path makes the most sense for you.

Both Photo CD and Pro Photo CD use the YCC color model, a variation on the CIE color space, which is discussed in Chapter 4. YCC provides a broader range of color — theoretically, every color your eye can see. By opening Photo CD files directly, you can translate the YCC images directly to Photoshop's Lab color mode, another variation on the CIE color space that ensures no color loss.

When you open a Photo CD image, a Photo CD dialog box appears divided into three main sections: Image Info, Source Image, and Destination Image. The Image Info section simply tells you the type of film on which the image was shot and the type of scanner used to scan the image to CD. Selections that you make in the Source and Destination areas tell Photoshop how you want it to open the image.

Photoshop cannot save to the Photo CD format. And frankly, there's little reason you'd want to do so. Photo CD is strictly a means for transferring slides and film negatives onto the world's most ubiquitous and indestructible storage medium, the CD-ROM.

NOTE Kodak also offers a product called Picture CD, which is quite different from Photo CD: Don't get the two confused. With Picture CD, consumers can drop off rolls of undeveloped film and receive both traditional prints and a CD containing scanned versions of their pictures. Picture CD images are provided in the JPEG format, so none of the Photo CD file-opening features discussed here apply. You open Picture CD images like any other JPEG file.

Opening raw documents

A *raw document* is a plain binary file stripped of all extraneous information. It contains no compression scheme, specifies no bit depth or image size, and offers no color mode. Each byte of data indicates a brightness value on a single color channel, and that's it. Photoshop offers this function specifically so you can open images created in undocumented formats, such as those created on mainframe computers.

To open an image of unknown origin on a PC, choose File ➪ Open As. On a Mac, choose File ➪ Open and select All Readable Documents from the Enable pop-up menu. Then select the desired image from the scrolling list and choose Photoshop Raw (*.RAW) from the Open As pop-up menu (Format pop-up menu on the Mac). After you press Enter or Return, the Raw Options dialog box appears, featuring these options:

- **Width, Height:** If you know the dimensions of the image in pixels, type the values in these option boxes.

- **Swap:** Click this button to swap the Width value with the Height value.

- **Count:** Type the number of color channels in this option box. If the document is an RGB image, type 3; if it is a CMYK image, type 4.

- **Interleaved:** Select this value if the color values are stored sequentially by pixels. In an RGB image, the first byte represents the red value for the first pixel, the second byte represents the green value for that pixel, the third the blue value, and so on. If you deselect this option, the first byte represents the red value for the first pixel, the second value represents the red value for the second pixel, and so on. When Photoshop finishes describing the Red channel, it describes the Green channel and then the Blue channel.

- **Depth:** Select the number of bits per color channel. Most images contain 8 bits per channel, but scientific scans from mainframe computers may contain 16.

- **Byte Order:** Though not the issue it once was before the recent changes in Mac's move to the Intel processor, if you specify 16 bits per channel, you may want to tell Photoshop whether the image comes from a Mac or a PC.

- **Header:** This value tells Photoshop how many bytes of data at the beginning of the file consist of header information it can ignore.

- **Retain When Saving:** If the Header value is greater than zero, you can instruct Photoshop to retain this data when you save the image in a different format.

- **Guess:** If you know the Width and Height values, but you don't know the number of bytes in the header — or vice versa — you can ask Photoshop for help. Fill in either the Dimensions or Header information, and then click Guess to ask Photoshop to take a stab at the unknown value. Photoshop estimates all this information when the Raw Options dialog box first appears. Generally speaking, if it doesn't estimate correctly the first time around, you're on your own. But hey, the Guess button is worth a shot.

TIP   If a raw document is a CMYK image, it opens as an RGB image with an extra masking channel. To display the image correctly, choose Image ➪ Mode ➪ Multichannel to free the four channels from their incorrect relationship. Then recombine them by choosing Image ➪ Mode ➪ CMYK Color.

NOTE Don't confuse Photoshop Raw with Camera Raw, which is the untreated image created by a digital camera before processing. Camera Raw is as impressive as Photoshop Raw is bland. You take a closer look at Camera Raw in Chapter 18.

Saving a raw document

Photoshop also lets you save to the raw document format. This capability is useful when you create files you want to transfer to mainframe systems or output to devices that don't support other formats, such as the Kodak XL7700.

CAUTION Do not save 256-color indexed images to the raw format, or you will lose the color lookup table and, therefore, all color information. Be sure to convert such images first to RGB or one of the other full-color modes before saving.

When you save an image in the raw document format, Photoshop presents the dialog box shown in Figure 3.43. The dialog box options work as follows:

- **File Type:** This option is only pertinent to Mac users. (Under Windows, the option is always dimmed. Feel free to ignore it.) Type the four-character file type code (TIFF, PICT, and so on) in this option box. (You should check the documentation for the application you plan to use to open the raw document.) If you plan to use this file on a computer other than a Mac, you can type any four characters you like; only Macs use this code.

FIGURE 3.43

When saving a raw document on a Mac, enter the file type and creator codes and specify the order of data in the file.

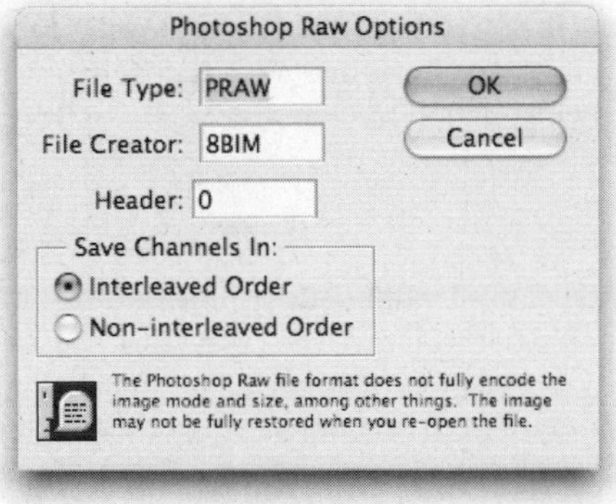

- **File Creator:** Again, this option is relevant only on a Mac. Type the four-character creator code, which tells the system software which application created the file. By default, the creator code is 8BIM, Photoshop's code. Ignore this option unless you have a specific reason for changing it — for example, to open the image in a particular Macintosh application. (You won't hurt anything by changing the code, but you will prevent Photoshop from opening the image when you double-click the document icon at the Finder desktop.) On Windows machines, the 8BIM default code is selected for you and the option is dimmed.

- ■ **Header:** Type the size of the header in bytes. If you type any value but 0, you must fill in the header using a data editor, such as Norton Disk Editor.

- ■ **Save Channels In:** Select the Interleaved Order option to arrange data sequentially by pixels, as described earlier. To group data by color channel, select the Non-interleaved Order option.

Still can't get that file open?

File format specs are continually evolving, so programs that provide support for a particular format may not support the specific version of the format used to save the file you're trying to open. For example, JPEG is notorious for causing problems because there were several private implementations in the early days. As a result, some JPEG files can be read only by the originating application.

If you can't open a file in Photoshop, you may have another program that can read and write the problem format. Try the problem file in every program you have, and hope you get lucky.

> **TIP** You also may want to try a program such as GraphicConverter from Lemke Software, or HiJaak, TransverterPro, DeBabelizer Toolbox, or DeBabelizer Pro from Equilibrium.

Adding Annotations

Adobe PDF has become the "it" file format for sharing and reviewing documents, but you don't need to export to PDF to add comments to your images. Borrowing from Adobe Acrobat, Photoshop offers tools that let you attach written notes and audio clips that you can view and play right from the image window. The following section has the details.

Making a note of it

Photoshop enables you to slap the digital equivalent of a sticky note onto your image. The notes can be viewed in Adobe Acrobat (assuming that you save the image as a PDF) as well as in Photoshop. You can jot down ideas that you want to remember later, for example. Or, if you're routing an image for approval, you can ask questions about a certain image element — or, more likely, explain why a part of the picture looks the way it does and why changing it would be a mistake of life-altering proportions.

The Photoshop Notes tool works like its counterpart in Adobe Acrobat: Click in the image window to display a blank note or drag to create a custom-sized note. If you don't want to use the name that appears in the note's title bar (it defaults to the name you typed when you installed Photoshop), type the desired name in the Author box in the Options bar. Next, type your comments — all the standard text-editing techniques apply — and then click the Close box in the upper-left corner of the note window. Your note shrinks to a little note icon, as shown in Figure 3.44. Double-click the icon to redisplay the note text, as shown in the figure.

When you save your image, be sure to save in the native Photoshop format or PDF and select the Annotations option in the Save dialog box. Otherwise, you lose all your notes. For information on how to delete individual notes in an open image and how to customize and import notes, see the section "Managing annotations."

FIGURE 3.44

After adding text-based notes or audio comments to an image, save the file in PDF so that others can access the annotations when viewing the image in Adobe Reader.

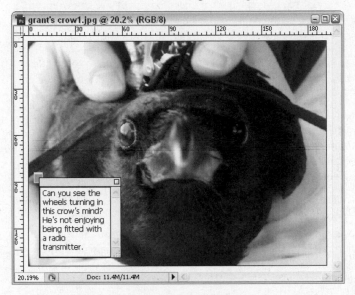

Speaking your mind

If you like to speak your mind rather than put your thoughts in writing, check out the Audio Annotation tool. This tool works like the Notes tool except that it inserts an audio recording of your voice rather than a text message into the file. Of course, you need a microphone, speakers, and a sound card installed in your computer to use this feature, and so does the intended recipient of the file — if you'll be sharing the file with a coworker or other associate. Photoshop retains audio annotations only when you save the image file using the Photoshop native format or PDF, as with text notes. Be aware, too, that audio files increase file size significantly — which probably will make e-mailing the file out of the question.

The Audio Annotation tool shares a button with the Notes tool in the Toolbox. Press N to toggle between the two tools (or Shift+N, depending on your preference setting for switching tools). Click in your image at the spot where you want the icon representing your message to appear. When the Audio Annotation dialog box appears, click Start to begin your recording and then talk into the microphone. Click Stop when you've said all you have to say.

Photoshop represents your audio message with a little speaker icon in the image window. Double-click the icon to play the message.

Managing annotations

If you're a solo artist and the only approval of your work you need is your own, you may not have much reason to use the Notes or Audio Annotation tools. Then again, even if you do work alone, you may be forgetful or so busy that real notes or even thoughts just get lost in the shuffle. Whatever the reason you want to commit ideas and so forth to memory, annotations are a terrific way to remind yourself exactly what you're trying to accomplish in an image. And why not store a recording of your baby's first words with a picture of the kid? If someone wants to look at the picture in the first place, chances are good that this feature will be entertaining. Whether you're using annotations for fun or profit, employ the following strategies to manage audio and text annotations:

- Use the Font and Size controls in the Options bar to change the font and type size in an open note.

- Click the Color icon to change the color of the icon and title bar for any new note you create. This option comes in handy if several people will be reviewing the image and contributing their thoughts and ideas. You can assign a different color to each author. To change the color of an existing note, open the note and click the Color icon. This time, you affect only the open note — other notes by the same author don't change.

- You can move and copy annotations between image windows. Just click the icon and use the Cut, Copy, and Paste commands as you do to move and copy any selection.

- If an icon blocks your view of the image, you can click and drag it out of the way. However, when you open the note, its window appears in the icon's original location. Click and drag the size box in the lower-right corner of an open note to shrink the window if necessary. You also can drag the title bar of a note to reposition it onscreen.

- Choose View ➪ Show ➪ Annotations to toggle the display of annotation icons on and off. Alternatively, choose View ➪ Show ➪ All and View ➪ Show ➪ None to display and hide icons and other interface elements, such as selection marquees, guides, and so on.

- To delete a single annotation, click its icon and press Delete. Or right-click (Control-click on the Mac) the icon and choose Delete Note or Delete Audio Annotation. If you want to delete all annotations, choose Delete All Annotations or click the Clear All button in the Options bar.

TIP If you send out several copies of the same image for approval, you don't have to open each copy individually to read the annotations. Instead, open just one copy and then import the annotations from the other files. Choose File ➪ Import ➪ Annotations, select the files containing the annotations, and click Open. Photoshop gathers up all the annotations and dumps them into your open image.

CAUTION Remember to save your image as a PDF or a TIFF or in the native Photoshop file format to retain annotations in a file. And if you're sending an annotated file to other people for viewing, tell them that they need to use Adobe Acrobat 4.0 or higher to access the annotations.

Resampling and Cropping

After you bring up an image — whether you created it from scratch or opened an existing image stored in one of the formats from the seemingly endless list discussed in the preceding pages — its size and resolution are established. Neither size nor resolution is carved in stone, however. Photoshop provides two methods for changing the number of pixels in an image: resampling and cropping.

Resizing versus resampling

Typically, when people talk about *resizing* an image, they mean enlarging or reducing it without changing the number of pixels in the image, as demonstrated back in Figure 3.1. By contrast, *resampling* an image means scaling it so the image contains a larger or smaller number of pixels. With resizing, an inverse relationship exists between size and resolution: Size increases when resolution decreases, and vice versa. But resampling affects either size or resolution independently. The resampled and original images have identical resolutions, but the resized image has twice the resolution of its companions.

Resizing an image

To resize an image, use one of the techniques discussed near the beginning of this chapter. To recap briefly, the best method is to choose Image ⇨ Image Size, deselect the Resample Image option, and type a value into the Resolution option box. Refer to Figure 3.2 to refresh your memory.

Resampling an image

You also use Image ⇨ Image Size to resample an image. The difference is that you leave the Resample Image option selected, as shown in Figure 3.45. As its name implies, the Resample Image option is the key to resampling.

FIGURE 3.45

With the Resample Image option selected, you can modify the number of pixels in your image.

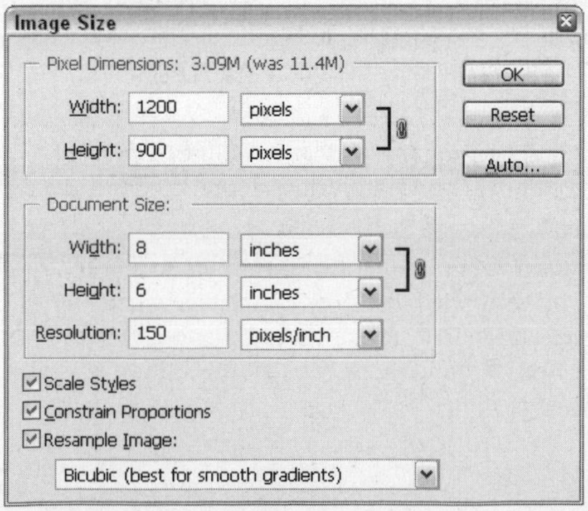

When Resample Image is selected, the Resolution value is independent of both sets of Width and Height values. (The only difference between the two sets of options is that the top options work in pixels and the bottom options work in relative units of measure, such as percent and inches.) You can increase the number of pixels in an image by increasing any of the five values in the dialog box; you can decrease the number of pixels by decreasing any value. Photoshop stretches or shrinks the image according to the new size specifications.

At all times, you can see the new number of pixels Photoshop will assign to the image, as well as the increased or decreased file size. In Figure 3.45, for example, the first Width value has been changed to 1200 pixels. The Pixel Dimensions value at the top of the dialog box reflects the change by reading *3.09M (was 11.4M)*, which shows that the file size has decreased.

To calculate the pixels in the resampled image, Photoshop must use its powers of interpolation, as explained in Chapter 2. The interpolation setting defaults to the one chosen in the Preferences dialog box, but you also can change the setting right inside the Image Size dialog box. Simply select the desired method from the Resample Image pop-up menu. Bicubic generally results in the smoothest effects, as does Bicubic Smoother; it does its best to reinterpret your image with the smoothest pixel transitions possible. Bicubic Sharper is recommended for preserving the sharpness of an image that you're reducing or downsampling. Bilinear is faster than any of the other options, but doesn't provide the smoothest results. Nearest Neighbor turns off interpolation, so Photoshop merely throws away the pixels it doesn't need or duplicates pixels to resample up.

Here are a few more random items you should know about resampling with the Image Size dialog box:

- This may sound wrong, but you generally want to avoid adding pixels. When you resample up, you're asking Photoshop to make up details from thin air, and the program isn't that smart. Simply put, an enlarged image almost never looks better than the original; it merely takes up more disk space and prints slower.

> **TIP**   Resampling down, on the other hand, is a useful technique. It enables you to smooth away photo grain, halftone patterns, and other scanning artifacts. One of the most tried-and-true rules is to scan at the maximum resolution permitted by your scanner and then resample the scan down to, say, 72 or 46 percent (with the interpolation set to Bicubic Sharper, naturally). By selecting a round value other than 50 percent, you force Photoshop to jumble the pixels into a regular, homogenous soup. You're left with fewer pixels, but these remaining pixels are better. And you have the added benefit that the image takes up less space on disk.

- To make an image tall and thin or short and fat, you must first turn off the Constrain Proportions option. This enables you to edit the two Width values entirely independently of the two Height values.

- Layer styles in Photoshop are dynamic, meaning you never lose the ability to edit their values. Accordingly, the look of a style you've applied to a layer can change when you resample an image. Select the Scale Styles option to avoid unwanted changes in your image's layer styles when you resample. Keep in mind, however, that this option is available only if Constrain Proportions is also selected.

TIP   You can resample an image to match precisely the size and resolution of any other open image. While the Image Size dialog box is open, choose the name of the image you want to match from the Window menu.

If you ever get confused inside the Image Size dialog box and want to return to the original size and resolution settings, press Alt (Option on the Mac) to change the Cancel button to Reset. Then click Reset to start from the beginning.

CAUTION   Photoshop remembers the setting of the Resample Image option and uses this same setting the next time you open the Image Size dialog box. This can trip you up if you record an action in the Actions palette that uses the Image Size command. Suppose that you create an action to resize images, deselecting the Resample Image option. If you later resample an image — selecting Resample Image — the option stays selected when you close the dialog box. The next time you run the action, you end up resampling instead of resizing. Always check the status of the option before you apply the Image Size command or run any actions containing the command.

NEW FEATURE   The Resample Image options include parenthetical information about which method works best in various situations and images. For example, the default Bicubic is accompanied by the advice that it's best for smooth gradients, while Bicubic Smoother is said to be best for enlargements. This assistance, new to CS3, is a nice addition.

Cropping

Another way to change the number of pixels in an image is to *crop* it, which means to clip away pixels around the edges of an image without harming the remaining pixels. (The one exception occurs when you rotate a cropped image or use the perspective crop feature, in which case Photoshop has to interpolate pixels to account for the rotation.)

Cropping enables you to focus on an element in your image. For example, the top image in Figure 3.46 shows an image with some unwanted content in the periphery — visual distractions that aren't necessary. By cropping down to the content seen at the bottom, a real portrait is created.

Photoshop offers several cropping options, including the capability to crop nonrectangular selections, automatically trim away transparent areas from the borders of an image, correct perspective effects while cropping, and crop and straighten crooked scans. You can read about all these features in the upcoming sections.

Changing the canvas size

One way to crop an image is to choose Image ⇨ Canvas Size, which displays the Canvas Size dialog box shown in Figure 3.47. The options in this dialog box enable you to scale the imaginary canvas on which the image rests separately from the image itself.

FIGURE 3.46

Focus your viewer's eyes on the really important part of the picture by cropping away all distractions. Of course, what's important is entirely subjective, as the beautiful beach background disappears in favor of the happy couple.

The Canvas Extension Color pop-up menu lets you specify a color when you increase the canvas area in your image. You can choose the current Background or Foreground color, Black, White, or Gray, or Other to select a color using Photoshop's Color Picker dialog box. Keep in mind that you can select a color only when you're working with an image that contains a background layer. Otherwise, Photoshop fills the newly expanded canvas area with transparent pixels. Either way, if you reduce the canvas, you crop the image. Just type the new desired pixel dimensions in the Width and Height boxes.

FIGURE 3.47

Choose Image ⇨ Canvas Size to crop an image or to add empty space around the perimeter of an image.

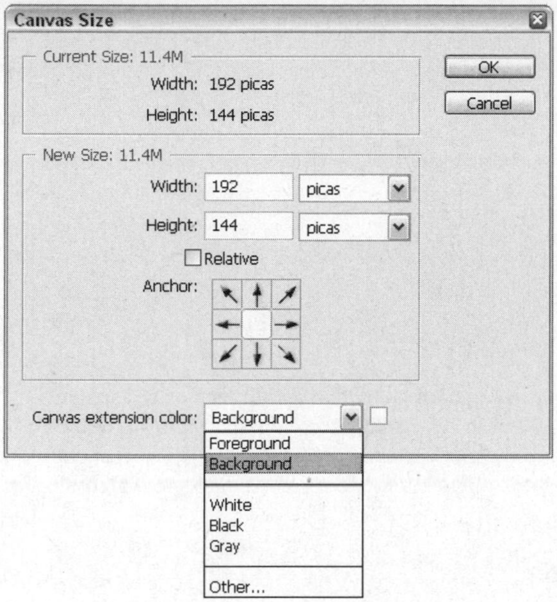

Selecting the Relative option allows you to change the height or width (or both the height and the width) of the canvas by a specific pixel amount. For example, type 2 in each option box to change a 100-×-100-pixel image into a 102-×-102-pixel image; type –2 to crop it down to a 98-×-98-pixel image. Not only can this save you from having to do a little math, but it can really be quite useful when you want to add the same number of pixels to a batch of different-sized files.

Click inside the Anchor grid to specify the placement of the image on the new canvas. For example, if you want to add space to the bottom of an image, enlarge the canvas size and then click the upper-middle square. If you want to crop away the upper-left corner of an image, create a smaller canvas size and then click the lower-right square. The Anchor grid offers little arrows to show how the canvas will shrink or grow.

To shrink the canvas so that it exactly fits the image, try the Image ⇨ Trim command. With the Trim command, you can automatically clip away empty canvas areas on the outskirts of your image, using the dialog box shown in Figure 3.48. To snip away empty canvas, select the Transparent Pixels option. Then specify which edges of the canvas you want to slice off by using the four Trim Away options. Alternatively, you can tell Photoshop to trim the image based on the pixel color in the top-left corner of the image or the bottom-right corner; just click the appropriate Based On radio button. For example, if you have a blue stripe running down the left edge of your image and you select the Top Left Pixel Color option, Photoshop clips away the stripe. No trimming occurs unless the entire edge of the image is bounded by the selected color.

FIGURE 3.48

To quickly snip away transparent areas from the edges of an image, use the Image ⇨ Trim command.

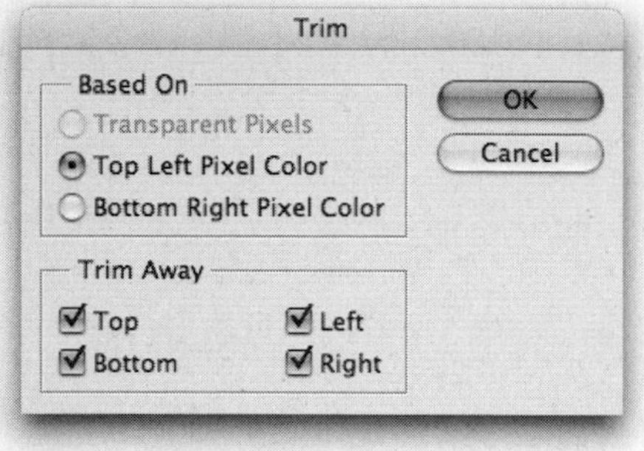

> **Trim**
>
> ┌─ Based On ──────────────
> ○ Transparent Pixels
> ⊙ Top Left Pixel Color
> ○ Bottom Right Pixel Color
>
> ┌─ Trim Away ─────────────
> ☑ Top   ☑ Left
> ☑ Bottom   ☑ Right
>
> OK
> Cancel

> **TIP**   When you want to enlarge the canvas but aren't concerned with making it a specific size, try this timesaving trick: Click and drag with the Crop tool to create a crop marquee and then enlarge the crop marquee beyond the boundaries of the image (see the next section if you need help). When you press Enter or Return to apply the crop, the canvas grows to match the size of the crop marquee.

Using the Crop tool

In general, the Canvas Size command is most useful for enlarging the canvas or shaving a few pixels off the edge of an image. If you want to crop away a large portion of an image, the Crop tool is a better choice — if only because you can actually see what you're doing and see the crop as it happens.

Press C or click the crop icon in the Toolbox to activate the tool, and then click and drag to create a rectangular marquee that surrounds the portion of the image you want to retain. You can see what will be cropped away if you proceed, because the content outside the box you've created is now darker than what's inside the box: It's an overlay, which you can choose not to see if you don't want to, as you'll discover in these cropping tips:

- To help you distinguish the borders of the crop marquee, Photoshop displays a colored, translucent overlay on the area outside the crop box — similar to the way it indicates masked versus unmasked areas when you work in the Quick Mask mode. If you hate the overlay, deselect the Shield option in the Options bar. You also can click the neighboring color box to change the overlay color and set the overlay opacity through the Opacity pop-up menu. Note that these controls don't appear in the Options bar until after you create your initial crop marquee.

- You have the option of permanently discarding the pixels you crop or simply hiding them from view. Before you drag with the Crop tool, click the Delete or Hide option in the Options bar to signify your preference. If you choose Hide, you can bring the hidden regions back into view by enlarging the canvas or by using the Image ⇨ Reveal All command.

As you drag, you can press the spacebar to move the crop boundary temporarily on the fly. To stop moving the boundary and return to resizing it, release the spacebar.

If you don't get the crop marquee right the first time, you can move, scale, or rotate it at will. Here's what you do:

- Click and drag inside the crop marquee to move it.

- Drag one of the square handles to resize the marquee. You can Shift-drag a handle to scale the marquee proportionally (the same percentage vertically and horizontally). You also can drag the sides of the marquee to resize it.

- Drag outside the crop marquee to rotate it, as explained in the next section. This may strike you as weird at first, but it works wonderfully.

- Drag the origin point, labeled in Figure 3.49, to change the center of a rotation.

FIGURE 3.49

When rotating a crop boundary, you can "eye it up," or align the marquee with an obvious axis in your image to determine the proper angle. It all depends on your desired result.

Crop tool   Point of origin   Rotate cursor

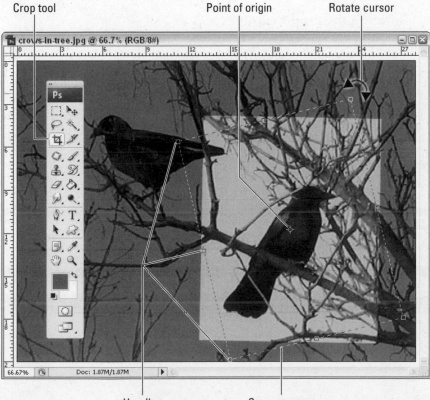

Handles   Crop marquee

■ Select the Perspective option in the Options bar, and you can click and drag corner handles to distort the image. This corrects any convergence problems that occur when shooting images at an angle. For example, let's say you have a billboard in perspective, so that it declines toward the horizon. Using the Perspective option, you can crop the billboard and remove its perspective so it appears flat.

Although Perspective is a solid feature, it can prove confusing. For one thing, you can't preview the results of your changes before applying the crop. Also, in an attempt to conserve important detail, Photoshop tends to stretch the image after applying the perspective. This is actually a good thing — better to stretch an image than trash data — but it requires you to reverse the stretch in a second operation. If this bothers you, you may be better off tackling perspective problems using the Free Transform command, covered in Chapter 12, and do your cropping afterward.

When the marquee surrounds the exact portion of the image you want to keep, apply the crop by pressing Enter (Return on the Mac) or double-clicking inside the marquee. You also can click the OK (check mark) button at the right end of the Options bar.

If you change your mind about cropping, you can cancel the crop marquee by pressing Esc or clicking the Cancel button, the universal "no" symbol next to the check mark in the Options bar.

Rotating the crop marquee

As stated earlier, you can rotate an image by clicking and dragging outside the crop marquee. Straightening a crooked image, however, can be a little tricky. Rarely, if ever, does your first (or sometimes second) attempt to straighten an image by rotating it manually (in Free Transform mode) work the way you want it. Either you rotate it too far or not far enough. If your rotation fails to give you the straightening effect you want, choose Edit ⇨ Undo (Ctrl+Z or ⌘+Z) and try again. Do not try using the tool a second time to rotate the already rotated image. If you do, Photoshop sets about interpolating between already interpolated pixels, resulting in more lost data. Every rotation gets farther away from the original image.

A better solution is to do it right the first time. Locate a line or general axis in your image that should be straight up and down. Rotate the crop marquee so it aligns exactly with this axis. In Figure 3.50, the crop marquee was rotated so one edge bisected the vertical content on the right. After you arrive at the correct angle for the marquee, drag the handles to size and position the boundary properly. As long as you don't drag outside the marquee, its angle remains fixed throughout.

Yet another solution is to use the Measure tool. Just click and drag with the tool along the axis you want to make vertical. Choose Image ⇨ Rotate Canvas ⇨ Arbitrary, and the angle of rotation you just sampled with the Measure tool is automatically added to the Rotate Canvas dialog box. Just click OK, and the transformation is complete.

FIGURE 3.50

The Crop and Straighten Photos command in Photoshop takes the pain out of separating and straightening multiple photos in a single scanned image.

Cropping an image to match another

You can crop an image so it matches the size and resolution of another image in two ways:

- Bring the image you want to crop forward, and choose Image ⇨ Canvas Size. Then, while inside the Canvas Size dialog box, select the name of the image you want to match from the Window menu. Of course, the image you want to match has to be open, so that it can be selected from the Window menu (look at the very bottom of the menu).

 **TIP**   This method doesn't give you much control when cropping an image, but it's a great way to enlarge the canvas and add empty space around an image.

■ Better yet, use the Crop tool in its fixed-size mode. First, bring the image you want to match to the front. Then select the Crop tool, and click the Front Image button in the Options bar. The Width, Height, and Resolution options automatically update to show the size and resolution of the front image.

Now bring the image you want to crop to the front, and drag with the Crop tool as normal. Photoshop constrains the crop marquee to the proportions of the targeted image. After you press Enter or Return, Photoshop crops, resamples, and rotates the image as necessary.

NOTE The next time you select the Crop tool, it starts out in fixed-size mode. To return the tool to normal, click the Clear button in the Options bar.

Cropping a selection

Another way to crop an image is to create a selection and then choose Image ➪ Crop. One advantage of the Crop command is that you needn't select the Crop tool if the Marquee tool is already active. One tool is all you need to select and crop. As with the Crop tool, you can press the spacebar while you draw a marquee to move it on the fly. It's quite simple to get the placement and size exactly right: The only thing you can't do is rotate.

Another advantage of the Crop command is flexibility. After drawing a selection, you can switch windows, apply commands, and generally use any function you like prior to choosing Image ➪ Crop. The Crop tool, by contrast, is much more limiting. After drawing a cropping marquee, you can't do anything but adjust the marquee until you press Enter or Return to accept the crop or Esc to dismiss it.

And finally, you can use the Crop command on selections of any shape, even feathered selections and multiple noncontiguous selections. Of course, your image canvas remains rectangular no matter what the selection shape. Photoshop simply crops the canvas to the smallest size that can hold all selected areas.

Cropping and straightening crooked scans

When it comes to scanning images, you have two basic options: Scan each and every image in a separate pass, which can be hopelessly time-consuming, or scan a group of images together. In the past, if you scanned your images as a group, you had to go at them with the Marquee tool, slice them up, separate them into layers, duplicate the layers into new images, rinse and repeat. It was arduous and soul-numbing to say the least, not to mention the fact that you then needed to rotate every new image to compensate for slightly skewed scanning. With the release of Photoshop CS, however, Adobe streamlined all these steps into one simple command, and this ability remains in CS3.

Naturally, you need to begin with a one-layer scanned image consisting of the photos you want to crop out, such as the one on the left side of Figure 3.50. Then choose File ➪ Automate ➪ Crop and Straighten Photos. As if by magic, Photoshop detects each of the photos in your master scanned image, straightens them according to their borders, copies them to the Clipboard, and pastes them into new image windows (refer to the right side of Figure 3.49).

NOTE It's important to note, however, that the Crop and Straighten Photos command only fixes images that were scanned crookedly, not photos that were taken with a shaky hand. For a quick trick that makes correcting crooked photos a snap, see Chapter 13.

If you want to crop out and straighten only certain images from your scan, draw a selection border around the area you want to isolate and carry on as you normally would. If the command repeatedly splits one scanned image into two, select that particular scanned image, press and hold Alt (Option on the Mac), and repeat the process. This tells Photoshop that the selected area represents only one scanned image. Keep in mind that the Crop and Straighten Photos command doesn't even need real photos to work its wonders. For example, suppose you have a sheet full of drawings that you want to divide into separate images. You can simply draw a clear border around each drawing and scan in the page. Because Photoshop is now intelligent enough to detect the borders inside of a multi-image scan, you're one leap closer to a collection of mini-masterpieces.

Using the Analysis Menu Tools

New in Photoshop CS3, the Analysis menu provides measurement tools that you can customize for your own purposes, meeting the need to mark, scale, and measure various points in your images, simply and accurately. The menu consists of the following commands:

- **Set Measurement Scale:** This offers two options, Default and Custom. If you choose Custom, you can use the Measurement Scale dialog box, shown in Figure 3.51, to choose from preset measurement scales, set the pixel and logical length, and save your own presets. Whenever this dialog box is open, the Ruler tool is activated, so you can use it to set the scale within your image while the dialog box is onscreen. Be sure to press and hold the Shift key as you drag the distance with the Ruler tool, so that you know your line is straight. For example, if you want 150 pixels to be equal to 1 pixel in terms of scale, you can drag 150 pixels within your image (you may have to drag the dialog box aside) and you can see your new scale set in the dialog box as a result. Of course, if your dragging doesn't allow for an exact measurement or you know exactly what scale you want to set, you can type it in manually.

FIGURE 3.51

Like establishing that 1 inch equals a mile on a map, you can set the scale for your image.

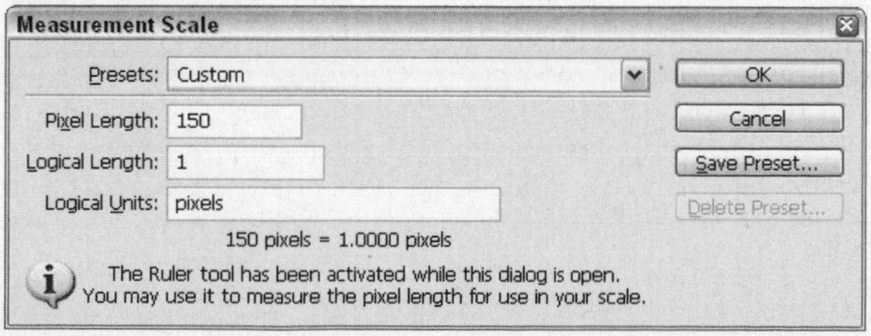

■ **Select Data Points:** This command has only one submenu option: Custom. Choosing this opens the Select Data Points dialog box, shown in Figure 3.52, through which you can choose which pieces of information are stored about each of the points you click on when using the Record Measurements command (that's the next one we talk about here). By default, all the data points in four categories are on: Common (things like Label, Date and Time, Document, Source, and so on), Selections, Ruler tool, and Count tool. You can turn any of these on and off as you please, and if you want to save the data point selections you've made, use the Save Preset button to save your selections for future use.

FIGURE 3.52

Decide how much or how little you want to know about each of the data points you record with the Record Measurements tool.

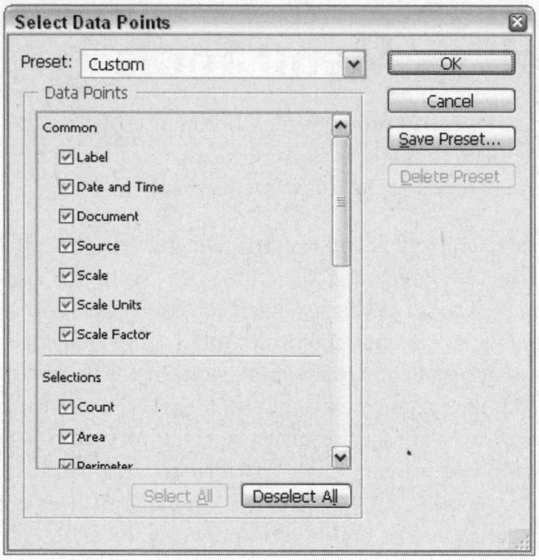

■ **Record Measurements:** This does just what you'd expect it to do — record your measurements. Wouldn't it be awful if we just stopped our explanation there? Just kidding. The use of this command opens a new palette, called Measurement Log, shown in Figure 3.53. This palette, sharing its home with the Animation palette (and its Timeline version, covered in Chapter 19), shows the measurements you've made with the Ruler, recorded each time you chose the Record Measurements command (or clicked the Record Measurements button in the Measurement Log palette itself). You see a column in the palette for each Data Point you chose in the Select Data Points dialog box, and you also have four buttons for selecting, deselecting, exporting, and deleting your recorded measurements. You can see these buttons in the upper-right corner of the palette, as shown in Figure 3.53.

FIGURE 3.53

Record any number of lengths within your image—the length of items within the image, the size of sections of the image itself, or any span from point A to point B, where A and B are locations you choose.

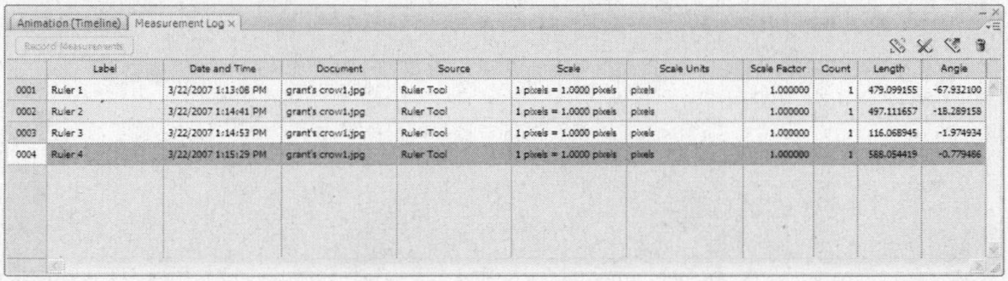

- **Ruler Tool:** This command simply activates the Ruler tool, which you also can do by pressing the letter I on your keyboard (keep pressing it to toggle through Ruler, Count, Eyedropper, and Color Sampler, too). Once active, the Ruler tool, discussed at greater length shortly, allows you to measure lengths you drag with your mouse. Pretty simple. The data about the lengths you've measured appears in the Info dialog box, covered in Chapter 2.

- **Count Tool:** Again, this command simply activates a tool you also can activate from the Toolbox or by pressing the letter I on your keyboard. While the Count tool is active, you can click in various spots in your image to mark places that you want to edit or that you simply think are important to look at, such as the spots in Figure 3.54. Both automatic counting and manual counting are covered in greater detail later in this section.

- **Place Scale Markers:** This command fires up the Measurement Scale Marker dialog box, shown in Figure 3.55. Through this dialog box, you can set the appearance of the scale marker—a graphic that appears as a key or legend within your image, defining the scale you've established for your image. When the scale marker appears in your image, it also appears as a new layer (with two sub-layers), represented in the Layers palette. As shown in Figure 3.56, the scale marker can be black or white, can be any length you set, and can appear either at the top or bottom of the image. The figure also shows the Layers palette, which you can use to hide or display the marker, set the font and font size, and even apply blend modes to the text. If you attempt to add more scale markers when there are already some in place, the prompt appearing in Figure 3.56 pops up, allowing you to Remove or Keep the existing markers. This is handy if you want to come back and add another marker (Keep) or if you want to start from scratch (Remove).

FIGURE 3.54

Count and mark special items in your image — for editing later or just so you don't forget to study them in greater detail later.

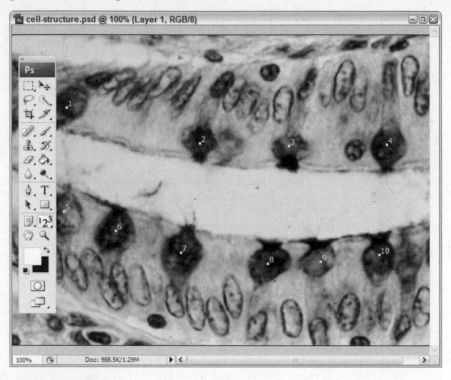

FIGURE 3.55

Decide how you want your scale markers to look, and then work with them through the layers palette.

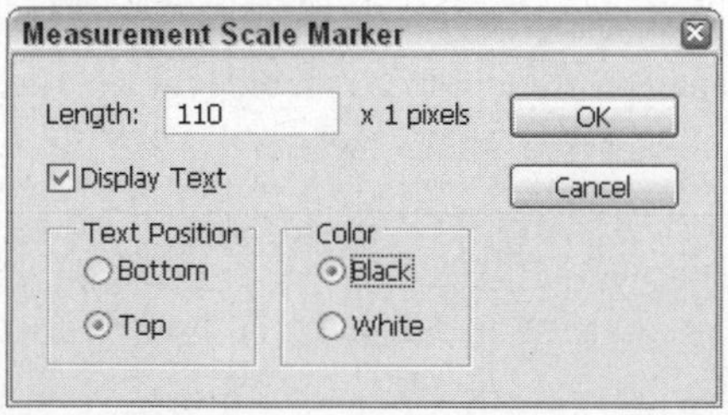

FIGURE 3.56

Remove or Keep your existing scale markers, through a prompt that reminds you that you already have a marker in place.

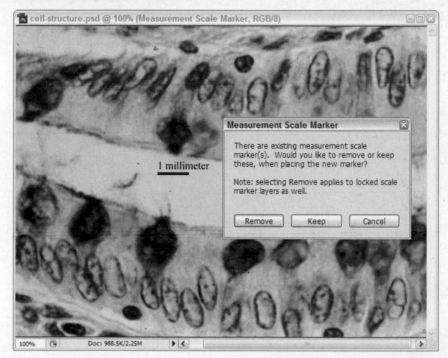

TIP Quickly resize the text part of your scale marker by pressing Ctrl+T (⌘+T on the Mac) to enter Transform mode. Once there, you can move, resize, or even rotate your scale marker text using the handles that appear around the layer. The marker itself (the line representing your scale) also can be transformed, but in so doing, you might eliminate usefulness within the image; if it's supposed to represent 100 pixels, it should be only 100 pixels long. Of course, if the layers (the text and the line) aren't meant to be to scale, go ahead and make them as big or as small as you want.

Measuring with the Ruler tool

The Ruler tool is painfully simple to use. Simply click and drag, as shown in Figure 3.57, to mark the distance between two points. The data about that span appears in the Info palette which also appears in the figure and also on the Options bar for the Ruler tool.

You also can measure angles, creating two lengths of line and connecting them at the end of the first and the beginning of the second. To do this, drag the first line, being sure to release the mouse and end the first line. Then, press Alt (Option on the Mac), and click at the end of the first line, dragging a new line, as shown in Figure 3.58. The resulting data — the length of the two lines (L1 and L2) and the angle between the two lines (A) — appears in the Info palette and on the Options bar.

167

FIGURE 3.57

Measure any part of your image with the Ruler tool.

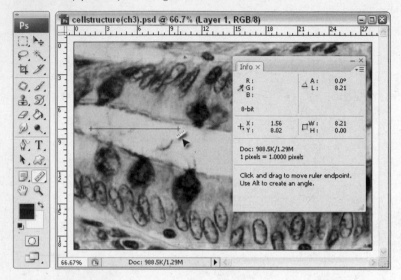

FIGURE 3.58

Draw two connected lines, and observe their length and the angle created.

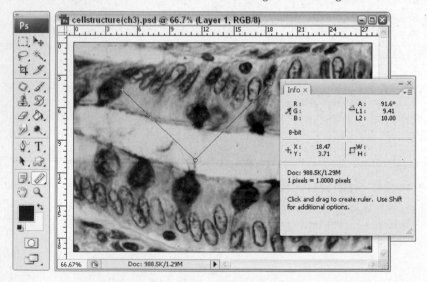

You can draw only one line or one set of two lines. Subsequent clicks of the mouse while the Ruler tool is active wipe out existing measurements in favor of whatever you do next with the tool.

Counting within your image

The Count tool, which you can access from the Toolbox (it shares a button with the Eyedropper, Color Sampler, and Ruler tools) or by choosing Analysis ➪ Count Tool, allows you to click and place counting markers on your image, the locations of which appear in your Info palette as you click to place another count marker (the data does not accumulate).

On the Options bar, shown in Figure 3.59, you can see the total count of Count tool markers placed, and the markers themselves are quite obvious. You can click the Color button to open the Color Picker and set a new color for your markers, choosing a color that will stand out against your image colors.

FIGURE 3.59

Need to count the occurrences of something in your image? Use the Count tool to mark each one and keep track of the total items counted.

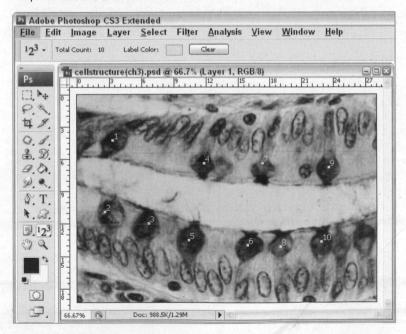

CAUTION The counts you create with the Count tool do not remain in place after you close an image — even if you save it after having used the Count tool.

Creating Custom Actions

Photoshop provides a ridiculous number of shortcuts. To be perfectly honest, it provides more shortcuts than you'll ever need. For example, you may never meet anyone who regularly links layers by Ctrl+Shift+Alt-right-clicking (⌘+Shift+Option+Control-clicking) on elements in the image window. But it *is* possible. And by choosing Edit ➪ Keyboard Shortcuts, Photoshop gives you the unprecedented ability to assign your own keyboard shortcuts to such important but hitherto-shortcut-challenged commands as Unsharp Mask, Variations, and Color Range.

But sometimes a simple keyboard shortcut isn't enough. You may find yourself performing certain sequences of commands in the same order each time. Maybe you have a series of very similar images shot with a digital camera, and they all need the same saturation adjustment via Hue/Saturation, the same gamma tweak via Levels, and the same sharpening via Unsharp Mask. Even hitting three shortcuts in a row for each image in a large group can get pretty tiresome.

Photoshop's answer is the Actions palette, which lets you record an entire sequence of commands and other operations as a single *action*, and then apply those operations to an open image or an entire folder of files while you take a much-needed break. Much better than a keyboard shortcut that can only open a command, actions can actually use the command to change your image, close that file, and move on to the next one. If you spend lots of your time performing repetitive tasks, actions can help you automate your workaday routine so you can devote your creative energies to something more important, such as a nap.

How actions work

Choose Window ➪ Actions or press Alt+F9 (Option+F9 on the Mac) to view the Actions palette. The icons along the bottom of the palette, labeled in Figure 3.60, enable you to record operations and manage your recorded actions. An action may include just a single command, or you can record many operations in a row.

As with layers, you can organize actions into sets. But although sets are optional with layers, they're essential with actions. Sets are the only method for saving actions so that you can use them on another machine, transfer them to an upgraded version of Photoshop, or keep them safe in case of a crash.

With that in mind, here is how you go about recording your own custom action.

FIGURE 3.60

The Actions palette lets you record a sequence of operations and assign a keyboard shortcut.

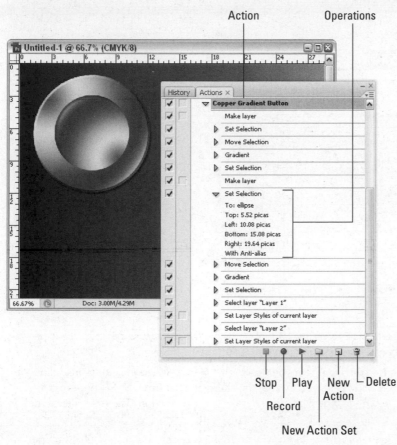

Action · Operations

Stop | Play | New Action — Delete

Record

New Action Set

Steps: Recording an Action

1. **Select a set in which to store your new action.** Just click the set that makes sense. Or create a new set by clicking the little folder icon at the bottom of the Actions palette. Sets are useful for organizing similar actions, but you don't absolutely have to create a set for any action unless you want to or feel you'll be creating similar actions or actions that are somehow related to each other.

TIP Naturally, Photoshop asks you to name the set. If you don't want Photoshop to bother you with such trivialities, Alt+click (Option+click on the Mac) the folder icon to bypass the New Set dialog box. You can likewise Alt+click other icons to skip other dialog boxes, but it's not really a good idea; when recording actions, it always pays to stay as organized as possible.

2. **Create a new action.** This is very important. Much as you might like to click the record button and go, you have to first make an action to hold the recorded operations. Click the new action icon — the one that looks like a little page at the bottom of the Actions palette. Photoshop responds with the New Action dialog box, shown in Figure 3.61.

FIGURE 3.61

When creating a new action, you can assign a name, shortcut, and color. The shortcut must involve a function key. The color shows up in the Actions palette's button mode.

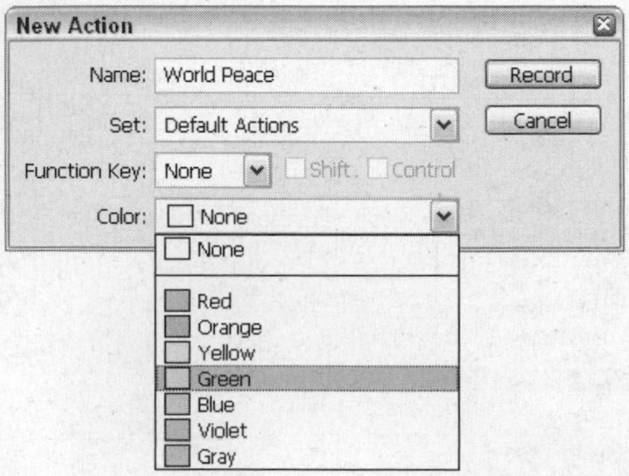

If you accidentally start recording and immediately decide against it, press Ctrl+Z (⌘+Z on the Mac) before initiating an operation to kill the new action.

3. **Enter a name for your action.** If you decide that your new action belongs in a different set than you originally imagined, choose the alternative set from the Set pop-up menu. Strange as it may sound, you also can assign a color to an action. The color affects the appearance of the action in the Actions palette's button mode, as discussed later.

4. **Assign a keyboard shortcut.** Photoshop prohibits you from assigning alphanumeric shortcuts, instead limiting you to function keys in combination with Shift and/or Ctrl (⌘ on the Mac). This is particularly debilitating on the PC, where Windows reserves Ctrl+F4, Ctrl+F6, and all combinations of F1, and reduces your maximum number of possible shortcuts to a scant 42, a small fraction of the quantity otherwise supplied by Photoshop. Things are slightly better on the Mac. F1 is fair game, and on some keyboards, function keys go as high as F16 with F8 through F12 defaulting to Spaces, Exposé, and Dashboard. These defaults can be turned off through System Preferences, however, increasing your maximum number of shortcuts to 60.

5. **Press Enter or Return to start recording.** The circular record icon at the bottom of the Actions palette turns red to show you that Photoshop is now observing your every action.

6. **Perform the desired operations.** If you want to record a sequence of operations, work through the sequence as you normally would.

Selective recording

Photoshop does not necessarily record your every action. Operations that do not affect layers or selections, such as zooms, scrolls, and commands under the View or Window menu, go ignored. (To force Photoshop to record a command under the View or Window menu, see "Editing an action.") Perhaps the most important thing to remember is that Photoshop doesn't record the Undo command in actions, meaning that if you make a mistake as you're recording an action and then undo, the action contains your goof but not your correction. If you have any concerns, keep an eye on the Actions palette. By the time you begin an operation, the previous operation has appeared as an item inside the palette. If it fails to appear, it wasn't recorded. Switching palettes is not recorded, so you can return to the Actions palette and to your bearings anytime you like.

But whatever you do, relax. There's no hurry and no pressure to perform. Photoshop is not recording your actions in real time, and nobody's watching you. Failed attempts to make a selection, pulling down the wrong menu: These things can happen during your recording and they don't matter. You can start to choose a command and then change your mind. You can even open a dialog box and cancel out of it. Even if you mess up, just keep going. Photoshop lets you insert, delete, and reorder operations after you've finished recording an action.

7. **When you're finished, click the stop button.** That's the square icon at the bottom of the Actions palette. Or just press the Escape key. Congratulations, you've now successfully recorded an action.

> **TIP** Photoshop not only records your operations in the Actions palette, but it also applies them to whatever image or images you have open. If you switch to a different image window or open an image while recording, Photoshop adds the operation to the action. For this reason, it's usually a good idea to have a dummy image open. When you're finished recording, you can choose File ⇨ Revert (or if you're using Windows, press F12, if you haven't reassigned it) to restore the original, unaltered image. Also, if you want to include a Save operation, be sure to choose File ⇨ Save As. This way, the original file remains intact.

Editing an action

If you take it slow and easy, you have a good chance of recording your action right the first time. But it's no problem if you flub it. Photoshop offers the following options to help you get it exactly right:

■ **Adding more operations:** To add more operations at the end of an action, select the action and click the round record icon. Then start applying the operations you want to record. When you finish, click the stop icon. Photoshop automatically adds the new operations to the end of the action. To add operations at a specific point, twirl open the action, select the operation name after which you want to begin recording, and click record.

■ **Moving an operation:** To change the order of an operation, drag the operation up or down in the list. You can even drag an operation from one action into another if you like.

■ **Copying an operation:** To make a copy of an operation, press Alt (Option on the Mac) and drag it to a different position in the action.

■ **Investigating an operation:** If you can't remember what settings you entered in a dialog box or you don't recognize what an operation name such as Set Current Layer means, click the triangle in front of the operation name to expand it. Figure 3.62 shows an example of the operations Set Selection, Move Selection, and Gradient (only part of this last one's operations are visible) expanded to show the recorded settings.

FIGURE 3.62

Triangles twirl and expand an operation to reveal settings. The check marks turn on whole sets, actions, or independent operations. Click in the second column to force the display of a dialog box.

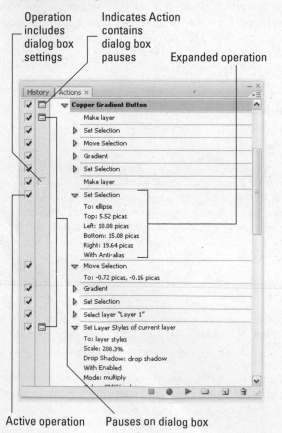

- **Changing a setting:** If an operation name includes an empty square to the left of it (as it does next to one of the steps in Figure 3.62), it includes dialog box settings. When you expand the operation, Photoshop lists those settings. To modify the settings, double-click the operation name, revise the options in the dialog box, and click OK.

TIP As when you record an action, Photoshop applies the settings to your current image. If this is a problem, press Ctrl+Z (⌘+Z) to undo the operation. This reverses the settings applied to the image, but has no effect on the changed settings in the action. The Actions palette ignores Edit ➪ Undo, which can be a double-edged sword. When editing a setting, it's handy to be able to undo without affecting the action itself. But don't forget that Undo is ignored while recording actions.

- **Leaving a setting open:** Not all images are alike, and not all images need the same settings applied to them. If you want to enter your own settings as the action plays, click inside the empty square in front of the operation name. A little dialog box icon appears to show you that you must be on hand when the action is played. In Figure 3.62, for example, a dialog box icon appears next to Make layer. When the action is played, Photoshop leaves the "Save Changes?" alert message onscreen until you confirm your decision. Then the action continues playing until it reaches the next dialog box icon or the end of the action.

TIP Press Alt (Option on the Mac) and click the square in front of an operation name to display a dialog box icon for that one operation and hide all others. To bring up dialog boxes for everybody, Alt-click (Option-click on the Mac) the same dialog box icon again or click the red dialog box icon in front of the action name.

- **Forcing Photoshop to record a command:** If Photoshop seems unable or unwilling to record a command, choose Insert Menu Item from the Actions palette menu, shown in Figure 3.63. Photoshop displays a dialog box that asks you to choose a command. Go ahead and do it; the dialog box won't interfere with your progress.

TIP Insert Menu Item also turns out to be the only way to record a dialog box with no settings whatsoever. This means that you can capture commands such as Image Size and Canvas Size with no predetermined changes. Insert Menu Item also recalls filters such as Unsharp Mask and Gaussian Blur with the last-applied settings.

- **Inserting a stop:** A *stop* is a pause that permits you to convey a message to the user of an action. The user can't do anything during the stop except read your message and then opt to continue or cancel. But it's a great way to identify a complex action so you remember its purpose and how it works later on.

TIP Right at the outset of a big action, choose Insert Stop from the Actions palette menu. Then enter a message that explains the action. (Select the Allow Continue check box to enable the user to continue the action after reading the message.) After you record the action and get all the bugs ironed out, deactivate the stop by turning off its check in the left-hand column of the palette. This way, it's there when you need it. What do you do two years later when you forget what the action does? Turn on the stop, play the action, and read your message.

FIGURE 3.63

Use the Actions palette menu to insert menu items and stops and to set your playback options.

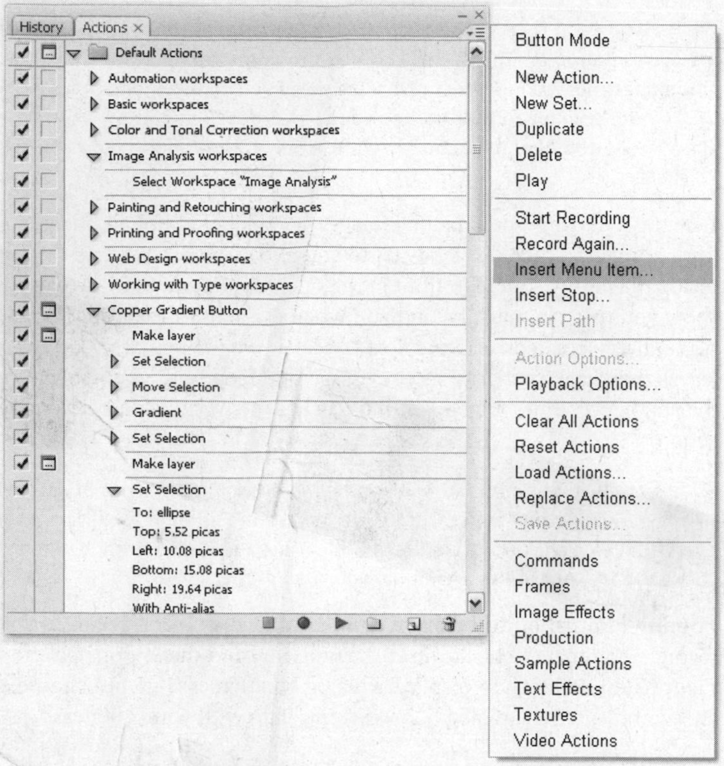

- **Changing the name and function key:** Renaming an action works just like it does in the Layers palette: Double-click the name to highlight it, and then enter a new one. To change the shortcut or color assigned to an action, press Alt (Option on the Mac) and double-click the action name. Note that function keys assigned to other actions appear dimmed and unavailable.

- **Deleting an operation:** To delete an operation, drag it to the trash icon at the bottom of the Actions palette, or select the operation and Alt-click (Option-click on the Mac) the trash can icon. If you use the latter technique, a warning appears, giving you the chance to rethink your deletion.

Playing actions and operations

When it comes time to play your action, you can play all of it or just a single operation. The simplest way to play back an entire action is to press the function key you assigned to it. If you can't remember the function key or didn't assign one, you may prefer to switch to the button mode. To do so, choose the Button Mode command from the Actions palette menu, as shown in Figure 3.64. You can now see the colors you assigned to the actions, as well as the function keys. Just click the button for the action you want to play.

But the button mode has its drawbacks. All you can do is click buttons. You can't edit actions, you can't change the order of actions, you can't assign new function keys, and you can't play individual operations. This is a great mode if you want to protect your actions from less adept users, but it's an awful mode if you want to modify your actions and create new ones.

FIGURE 3.64

Choose the Button Mode command to view each action as an independent button. You can resize the palette to view buttons in a single column (bottom) or as multiple columns (top).

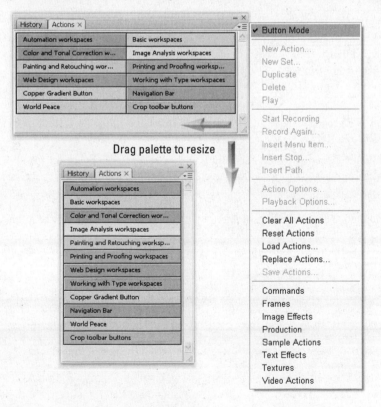

Drag palette to resize

To return to the standard Actions palette, choose the Button Mode command again. Then try some of these less-restrictive action-playing techniques:

- To play a selected action, click the play icon at the bottom of the palette. You also can play an action by Ctrl-double-clicking an action name. (On the Mac, ⌘-double-click the action name.)

- To play an action from a certain operation on, select that operation name in the palette and click the play icon.

TIP To play a single operation and no more, Ctrl-double-click (⌘-double-click on the Mac) the operation name.

- You can tell Photoshop which operations to play and which to skip using the check marks in the on/off column (the leftmost column, labeled back in Figure 3.62). Click a check mark to turn off the corresponding operation. Alt-click (Option-click on the Mac) the check mark in front of an operation to turn that one operation on and the rest off. To turn all operations on again, Alt-click (Option-click on the Mac) the check mark again or click the red check mark by the action name.

TIP If an action makes a mess of your image, it's generally not a problem thanks to Photoshop's multiple undos. To restore your image to its previous appearance, switch to the History palette and click the state in the list that comes directly before the first operation in your action. If you're at all concerned that an action may do irreparable damage — say, it contains more than 20 undoable steps — then record yourself saving a snapshot at the very beginning of the action. As long as the image remains open, the snapshot remains available. For complete information on the History palette, see Chapter 3.

Saving and loading sets

Photoshop requires you to put every action inside a set. But that doesn't mean the set automatically gets saved. It's true that Photoshop saves sets and actions to a special preferences file, *but only when you quit the program*. If you crash, any actions recorded during this session are lost.

Anytime you record an action, go ahead and take a moment to save or update its set. To do so, click the set name in the Actions palette, and then choose Save Actions from the palette menu. Actions are 100 percent cross-platform. But to work on any platform, the file name must include the three-character extension *.atn*.

You also can load sets of actions. By default, Photoshop displays only the Default Actions, a set of a dozen actions from Adobe. To open other predefined Adobe sets, choose one of the commands at the end of the Actions palette menu. To load some other set, choose the Load Actions command.

TIP Turns out, you can add your own custom sets to the presets at the end of the Actions palette menu. Quit Photoshop. Then copy the action set (*.atn*) files to the Photoshop Actions folder inside the Presets folder that's inside the same folder as the Photoshop application. Then relaunch Photoshop and check out the Actions palette menu. Note that Photoshop doesn't automatically load the custom set; you have to choose the command to do that.

Summary

In this chapter, you learned to resize an image for the printer and for the screen, keeping in mind the needs of your image and your goals for its use. In addition, core skills for opening and saving images were covered, along with techniques for searching for and viewing images, and managing image data with the Bridge. You also learned about pixel depth, dimensions, and resolution, resampling an image, and cropping images to rid them of unnecessary edge content.

File formats were covered, too; you explored JPEG, GIF, PDF, and many other file formats and learned about rendering object-oriented EPS images. Using Photoshop's less-often-used but very important tools for annotating and adding voice commentary to images, you learned to extend the editing process beyond the image itself.

This chapter also introduced you to the new Analysis menu and its tools for scaling, scale-marking, and measuring your image and its contents. You also learned about the Count tool, and the creation, editing, and use of actions was covered — enabling you to record your steps in oft-performed tasks or to automate complex operations for repeated use.

Part II

Painting and Retouching

Chapter 4

Defining Colors

From cell phones that take pictures to Web sites that let you print and share your latest batch of vacation photos, color images have never been more prevalent and universally accessible. Even someone on a meager budget can afford a low-end digital camera, an inkjet printer, and some photo paper — thus making the taking and printing of color photos something just about anyone can do. This also puts the use of color images for commercial use — brochures, ads — within the reach of more organizations, resulting in their producing more color themselves or expecting the graphic artists they employ to do the same. For those who still find the color brochure to be too expensive, a full-color Web site is entirely doable and can be updated at any time, which allows for timely information to be maintained continuously and for marketing efforts to be both proactive and responsive.

Photoshop, of course, is not typically the domain of the family photographer or the small business. At least in the past it hasn't been, due to its price tag, and it's still a more serious tool for more serious photographers and graphic artists. If you own Photoshop and are reading this book, don't be put off or think anyone's telling you that you're in over your head, because you're not. Anyone who can use a computer can use Photoshop, but it has always been considered a higher-end application for very specific uses and users.

> **NOTE** Photoshop's "lite" cousin, Elements, brings much of Photoshop's power to the home and small-business user, and that makes color photos and their capture and manipulation even more commonplace.

In the meantime, check out Photoshop's color tools. With color, color everywhere, you need to know how to use Photoshop's tools to select colors, edit them, apply them, and tinker with them.And you need to know how Photoshop looks at and interprets color and how you can enhance its ability to give you the color results you're looking for. So let's get started.

IN THIS CHAPTER

Controlling colors through the Toolbox

Selecting and defining colors with the Color Picker

Understanding the RGB, HSB, CMYK, Lab color, and HDR modes

Converting an image bit-per-channel setting

Creating grayscale and black-and-white images

Getting to know the Trumatch and Pantone color standards

Working with the Color palette, Eyedropper, and color sampler

Understanding how color channels work

Using channel editing commands in the Channels palette

Cleaning up after a bad scanner

Specifying Colors

To begin your journey into the world of color, Photoshop provides four color controls in the Toolbox, as shown in Figure 4.1. These icons work as follows:

- **Foreground color:** The foreground color icon indicates the color you apply when you use the Paint Bucket, Pencil, Brush, or one of the type tools, and also if you Alt-drag (Option-drag on the Mac) with the Smudge tool. The foreground color also begins any gradation created with the Gradient tool in its default state. Photoshop uses the current foreground color to fill any shape you create with the shape tools, and if you make a selection and then click inside it with the Paint Bucket or use the Edit ⇨ Fill command, the foreground color fills it up. Remember that you also can apply the foreground color to a standard selection by pressing Alt+Backspace (Option-Delete on the Mac).

  To change the foreground color, click the foreground color icon to display the Color Picker dialog box. Then select a new color in the Color palette, or click anywhere in an open image window with the Eyedropper tool. You also can set the foreground color by clicking a swatch in the Swatches palette. (All are explained later in this chapter.)

FIGURE 4.1

Photoshop's color selection tools include Foreground color, Background color, and tools for going back to the default colors and swapping foreground for background colors. You also can see the Eyedropper in this figure.

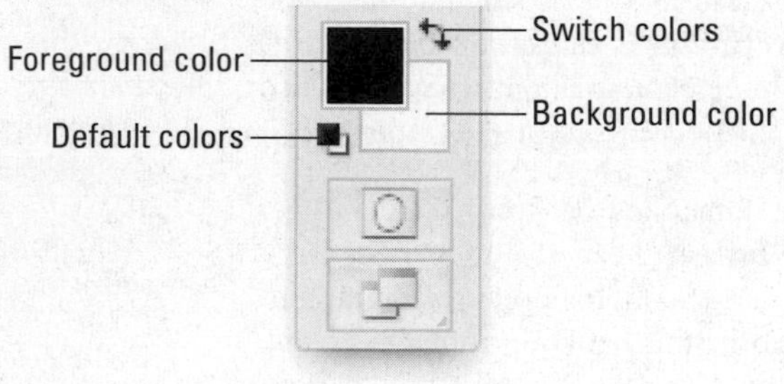

- **Background color:** The active background color indicates the color you apply with the Eraser tool when you're working on the background layer. By default, the background color also ends any custom gradation created with the Gradient tool. To change the background color, click the background color icon to display the Color Picker dialog box. Or define the color by using the Color palette, clicking a swatch in the Swatches palette, or Alt-clicking (Option-clicking on the Mac) any open image window with the Eyedropper tool.

  You can apply the background color to a selection by pressing Backspace or Delete, or by choosing Background Color from the Use list in the Fill dialog box opened by choosing Edit ⇨ Fill. Note that if the selection is floating or exists on any layer except the background layer, pressing Backspace or Delete actually deletes the selection instead of filling it. For complete safety, use Ctrl+Backspace (⌘-Delete on the Mac) to fill a selection with the background color.

■ **Switch colors:** Click this icon (or press X) to swap the current foreground and background colors.

■ **Default colors:** Click this icon (or press D) to make the foreground color black and the background color white, according to their factory default settings. If you're editing a layer mask or an adjustment layer, the default colors are reversed, as explained in Chapters 9 and 18.

Using the Color Picker

When you click the foreground or background color icon in the Toolbox or the Color palette, Photoshop displays the Color Picker dialog box, which is shown in Figure 4.2. The assumption is that you're also looking at the Adobe Color Picker, and if you're saying "As opposed to what?", we refer you now to Chapter 2. You'll find that you can use an OS-based version of the Color Picker. If you aren't sure which picker you've selected, or if you'd like to pick a different picker (try saying *that* five times fast), check the General panel of the Preferences dialog box.

All tongue-twisters aside, you are now presented with the many elements and options offered by the Color Picker dialog box:

■ **Color slider:** Use the color slider to home in on the color you want to select. Click and drag up or down on either of the slider triangles to select a color from within the range. You also can click directly on any color in the slider. The colors represented inside the slider correspond to the selected radio button. For example, if you select the H (Hue) radio button, which is the default setting, the slider colors represent the full 8-bit range of hues. If you select S (Saturation), the slider shows the current hue at full saturation at the top of the slider, down to no saturation — or gray — at the bottom of the slider. If you select B (Brightness), the slider shows the 8-bit range of brightness values, from solid color at the top of the slider to absolute black at the bottom. You also can select R (Red), G (Green), or B (Blue), in which case the top of the slider shows you what the current color looks like when subjected to full-intensity red, green, or blue (respectively), and the bottom of the slider shows every bit of red, green, or blue subtracted.

■ **Color field:** The color field shows a 16-bit range of variations on the current slider color. Click inside it to move the color selection marker and select a new color. The field plots colors against the two remaining attributes not represented by the color slider. For example, if you select the H (Hue) radio button, the field displays colors according to brightness vertically and saturation horizontally.

NOTE   Slider and field always work together to represent a range of over 16-million-colors. The slider displays 256 colors, and the field displays 65,536 variations on the slider color; 256 times 65,536 is 16,777,216. No matter which radio button you select, you have access to the same colors; only your means of accessing them changes.

■ **Current color:** The color currently selected from the color field appears in the top rectangle immediately to the right of the color slider. Click OK or press Enter or Return to make this the current foreground or background color (depending on which color control icon in the Toolbox you originally clicked to display the Color Picker dialog box).

FIGURE 4.2

Use the Color Picker dialog box to specify a new foreground or background color from the 16-million-color range.

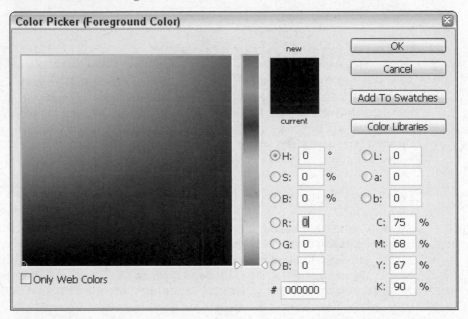

■ **Previous color:** The bottom rectangle to the right of the color slider shows how the foreground or background color whichever one you are in the process of editing — looked before you displayed the Color Picker dialog box. Click Cancel or press Esc to leave this color intact.

■ **Alert triangle:** The alert triangle appears when you select a color that Photoshop can't print using standard process colors. The box below the triangle shows the closest CMYK equivalent, invariably a duller version of the color. Click either the triangle or the box to bring the color into the printable range. Pressing Ctrl+Shift+Y (⌘-Shift-Y on the Mac) or choosing View ➪ Gamut Warning automatically grays out any colors not allowed in the CMYK spectrum.

- **Web-safe alert cube:** This little cube appears if you select a color that's not included in the so-called Web-safe palette, a 216-color spectrum that's supposedly ideal for creating Web graphics — "supposedly" refers to the fact that it's been a long time since any computer was limited to displaying only 216 colors. If you click either the cube or the swatch below it, Photoshop selects the closest Web-safe equivalent to the color you originally selected.

- **Only Web Colors:** This option changes the display in the Color Field so that it displays delineated sections of Web-safe colors. The rest of the options in the dialog box work the same way when you're in Only Web Colors mode.

- **Add to Swatches:** This button, new in Photoshop CS3, does just what you'd imagine. It allows you to add the new color (see the top half of the new/current box) to the Swatches palette, where it will be available for you to select with the Eyedropper while you're working in your image. When you click this button, a dialog box opens, asking you to name your new color; do so, and then click OK.

- **Color Libraries:** This button opens the Color Libraries dialog box, through which you can choose from colors in various commercial color sets — Pantone, Focoltone, Trumatch — just to name a few. You find out more about these options and how to use this dialog box later in this chapter.

Typing Numeric Color Values

In addition to selecting colors using the slider and color field, you can type specific color values in the option boxes in the lower-right region of the Color Picker dialog box. Novices and intermediates may find these options less satisfying to use than the slider and field. These options, however, enable artists and print professionals to specify exact color values, whether to make controlled adjustments to a color already in use, or whether to match a color used in another document. The options fall into one of four camps:

- **HSB:** These options stand for hue, saturation, and brightness. Hue is measured on a 360-degree circle. Saturation and brightness are measured from 0 to 100 percent. These options permit access to more than 3 million color variations.

- **RGB:** You can change the amount of the primary colors red, green, and blue by specifying the brightness value of each color from 0 to 255. These options enable access to more than 16 million color variations.

- **Lab:** This acronym stands for luminosity, measured from 0 to 100 percent, and two arbitrarily named color axes, *a* and *b*, whose brightness values range from −120 to 120. These options enable access to more than 6 million color variations.

- **CMYK:** These options display the amount of cyan, magenta, yellow, and black ink required to print the current color, using percentages from 0 to 100. When you click the alert triangle, these are the only values that don't change, because they make up the closest CMYK equivalent.

At the bottom of the dialog box, the value next to the pound sign (#) shows you the hexadecimal value for the chosen color (refer to Figure 4.2). This value comes into play only if you're creating Web graphics — and maybe not even then.

When creating graphics for use on a Web page, you may want to make sure that the Only Web Colors option is selected, so that you can easily select only those colors deemed "Web-safe" for older computers' monitors. Every color in the 216-color Web-safe palette has a numeric value based on the hexadecimal numbering system. Each value includes a total of three pairs of numbers or letters, one pair each for the R, G, and B values. When you create a color tag in HTML code, you type the hexadecimal value for the color you want to use. Fortunately, you can create a Web page without having to write your own HTML code; page-creation programs like GoLive and Macromedia Dreamweaver do the work for you. But if you prefer to do your own coding or if you have been given a hexadecimal number and told to use that color in your design (say, by a client who already has Web content that you have to work with or enhance), make note of the hexadecimal value in the Color Picker dialog box.

> **TIP**   The hexadecimal number can be useful if you want to precisely match a color on an existing Web page and don't have a client telling you what color that is. Just look at the HTML coding for the page (in Internet Explorer, for example, choose View ➪ Source), note the hexadecimal value in the appropriate color tag, and type that value in the Color Picker dialog box.

You may find the numerical range of your various color options somewhat confusing. For example, the CMYK options enable you to create 100 million unique colors, whereas the RGB options enable the standard 16 million variations, and the Lab options enable a measly 6 million. Despite this deficit, Lab is the largest color space, theoretically encompassing all colors from both CMYK and RGB. The printing standard CMYK provides by far the fewest colors, the opposite of what you might expect. Huh? These statistics seem misleading and unrelated to what we think of as the reality of displayed and printed color. To find out more about color models and how they really work, read on.

Working in Different Color Modes

The four sets of option boxes in the Color Picker dialog box represent color models — or, if you prefer, color modes, which more closely matches the Image ➪ Mode command terminology, wherein you choose a mode for your image. *Color models* are different ways to define colors on both the screen and the printed page.

Outside the Color Picker dialog box, you can work in any one of these color models by choosing a command from the Image ➪ Mode submenu. In doing so, you generally change the colors in your image by dumping a few hundred, or even thousand, colors with no equivalents in the new color model. The only exception is Lab, which in theory encompasses every unique color your eyes can detect.

Rather than discuss the color models in the order in which they occur in the Mode submenu, let's talk about them in logical order, starting with the most common and widely accepted color model, RGB. The Multichannel mode, meanwhile, is not even a color model. Rather, Image ➪ Mode ➪ Multichannel enables you to separate an image into independent channels, which you then can swap around and splice back together to create special effects. For more information, see the section "Using multichannel techniques" later in this chapter.

CROSS-REF Duotone mode is not covered here. The Image ➪ Mode ➪ Duotone command represents an alternative method for printing grayscale images, so it is discussed in Chapter 20.

RGB

RGB is the color model of light. RGB comprises three primary colors — red, green, and blue — each of which can vary between 256 levels of intensity, called brightness values. The RGB model is also called the *additive primary model* because a color becomes lighter as you add higher levels of red, green, and blue light. All monitors, projection devices, and other items that transmit or filter light — including televisions, movie projectors, colored stage lights, and even stained glass — rely on the additive primary model. This, in case you were wondering, is why RGB is the color mode for Web graphics.

Red, green, and blue light mix as follows:

- **Red and green:** Full-intensity red and green mix to form yellow. Subtract some red to make chartreuse; subtract some green to make orange. All these colors assume a complete lack of blue.

- **Green and blue:** Full-intensity green and blue with no red mix to form cyan. If you try hard enough, you can come up with 65,000 colors in the turquoise/jade/sky-blue/sea-green range.

- **Blue and red:** Full-intensity blue and red mix to form magenta. Subtract some blue to make rose; subtract some red to make purple. All these colors assume a complete lack of green.

- **Red, green, and blue:** Full-intensity red, green, and blue mix to form white, the absolute brightest color in the visible spectrum.

- **No light:** Low intensities of red, green, and blue plunge a color into blackness.

As far as image editing is concerned, the RGB color model is ideal for editing images onscreen because it provides access to the entire range of 24-bit screen colors. Furthermore, you can save an RGB image in every file format supported by Photoshop except GIF and the two DCS formats. As shown in Table 4.1, grayscale is also compatible with a wide range of file formats.

TABLE 4.1

File-Format Support for Photoshop CS3 Color Models

	Bitmap	Grayscale	Duotone	Indexed	RGB	CMYK	Lab
Photoshop	Yes	Yes	Yes	Yes	Yes	Yes	Yes
BMP	Yes	Yes	No	Yes	Yes	No	No
DCS 1.0	No	No	No	No	No	Yes	No
DCS 2.0	Yes	Yes	Yes*	No	No	Yes	No
EPS	Yes	Yes	Yes	Yes	Yes	Yes	Yes
GIF	Yes	Yes	No	Yes	No	No	No
JPEG	No	Yes	No	No	Yes	Yes	No
PCX	Yes	Yes	No	Yes	Yes	No	No
PDF	Yes	Yes	No	Yes	Yes	Yes	Yes
PICT	Yes	Yes	No	Yes	Yes	No	No
PNG	Yes**	Yes	No	Yes	Yes	No	No
Scitex CT	No	Yes	No	No	Yes	Yes	No
TIFF	Yes	Yes	No	Yes	Yes	Yes	Yes

* You can save a duotone in DCS 2.0 only after first converting the image to the Multichannel mode. For more information, consult Chapter 20.

** PNG supports bitmap mode only on the Mac.

NOTE   Table 4.1 lists color models in the order in which they appear in the Image ⇨ Mode submenu. Again, the Multichannel mode is skipped because it is not a true color model.

On the negative side, the RGB color model provides access to a wider range of colors than you can print. If you are designing an image for full-color printing, therefore, you can expect to lose many of the brightest and most vivid colors in your image. The only way to avoid any color loss whatsoever is to have a professional scan your image to CMYK and then edit it in the CMYK mode. Colors can get clipped when you apply special effects, and the editing process can be exceptionally slow. The better solution is to scan your images to RGB and edit them in the Lab mode, as explained in the section "CIE's Lab."

HSB

Way back in Photoshop 2, the Modes submenu provided access to the HSB—hue, saturation, brightness—color model, now relegated to the Color Picker dialog box and the Color palette (discussed later in this chapter). *Hue* is pure color, the stuff rainbows are made of, measured on a 360-degree circle. Red is located at 0 degrees, yellow at 60 degrees, green at 120 degrees, cyan at 180 degrees (midway around the circle), blue at 240 degrees, and magenta at 300 degrees. This is basically a pie-shaped version of the RGB model at full intensity and is the basis of the color wheel you often see offered as a tool for selecting complementary and opposite colors; colors' relationships (what goes with what) can be demonstrated on that wheel.

Saturation represents the purity of the color. A zero saturation value equals gray. White, black, and any other colors you can express in a grayscale image have no saturation. Full saturation produces the purest version of a hue.

Brightness is the lightness or darkness of a color. A zero brightness value equals black. Full brightness combined with full saturation results in the most vivid version of any hue.

CMYK

In nature, our eyes perceive pigments according to the *subtractive color model*. Sunlight contains every visible color found on Earth. When sunlight is projected on an object, the object absorbs (subtracts) some of the light and reflects the rest. The reflected light is the color you see. For example, a fire engine is bright red because it absorbs all the light that is not red — meaning all blue and green — from the white-light spectrum.

Pigments on a sheet of paper work the same way. You can even mix pigments to create other colors. Suppose you paint a red brushstroke, which absorbs green and blue light, over a blue brushstroke, which absorbs green and red light. You get a blackish mess with only a modicum of blue and red light left, along with a smidgen of green because the colors weren't absolutely pure.

But wait! Every child knows red and blue mix to form purple. So what gives? What gives is that what you learned in elementary school is only a clumsy approximation of the truth. Did you ever try mixing a vivid red with a canary yellow only to produce an ugly orange-brown glop? The reason you didn't achieve the bright orange you wanted is because red starts out darker than bright orange, which means you must add a great deal of yellow before you arrive at orange. And even then, the yellow had better be an incredibly bright lemon yellow, not some deep canary yellow with lots of red in it.

Commercial subtractive primaries

The subtractive primary colors used by commercial printers — cyan, magenta, and yellow — are for the most part very light. Cyan absorbs only red light, magenta absorbs only green light, and yellow absorbs only blue light. On their own, these colors unfortunately don't do a good job of producing dark colors. In fact, at full intensities, cyan, magenta, and yellow all mixed together don't get much beyond a muddy brown. That's where black comes in. Black helps to accentuate shadows, deepen dark colors, and, of course, print real blacks.

In case you're wondering how colors mix in the CMYK model, it's basically the opposite of the RGB model. Because pigments are not as pure as primary colors in the additive model, though, some differences exist:

- **Cyan and magenta:** Full-intensity cyan and magenta mix to form a deep blue with a little violet. Subtract some cyan to make purple; subtract some magenta to make a dull medium blue. All these colors assume a complete lack of yellow.

- **Magenta and yellow:** Full-intensity magenta and yellow mix to form a brilliant red. Subtract some magenta to make vivid orange; subtract some yellow to make rose. All these colors assume a complete lack of cyan.

- **Yellow and cyan:** Full-intensity yellow and cyan mix to form a bright green with a hint of blue. Subtract some yellow to make a deep teal; subtract some cyan to make chartreuse. All these colors assume a complete lack of magenta.

- **Cyan, magenta, and yellow:** Full-intensity cyan, magenta, and yellow mix to form a muddy brown.

- **Black:** Black pigmentation added to any other pigment darkens the color.

- **No pigment:** No pigmentation results in white (assuming white is the color of the paper).

Editing in CMYK

If you're used to editing RGB images, editing in the CMYK mode can require some new approaches, especially when editing individual color channels. When you view a single color channel in the RGB mode (as discussed later in this chapter), white indicates high-intensity color and black indicates low-intensity color. It's the opposite in CMYK. When you view an individual color channel, black means high-intensity color and white means low-intensity color.

This doesn't mean RGB and CMYK color channels look like inverted versions of each other. In fact, because the color theory is inverted, they look much the same. But if you're trying to achieve the full-intensity colors mentioned in the preceding section, you should apply black to the individual color channels, not white as you would in the RGB mode.

Should I edit in CMYK?

RGB doesn't accurately represent the colors you get when you print an image because the RGB color space contains many colors—particularly very bright colors—that CMYK can't touch. This is why when you switch from RGB to CMYK, the colors appear somewhat dull.

For this reason, many people advocate working exclusively in the CMYK mode, but you may want to reconsider just blindly following this advice. Although working in CMYK eliminates color disappointments, it also is much slower because Photoshop must convert CMYK values to your RGB screen on the fly.

Furthermore, your scanner and monitor are RGB devices. No matter how you work, a translation from RGB to CMYK color space must occur at some time. If you pay extra to purchase a commercial drum scan, for example, you simply make the translation at the beginning of the process—Scitex has no option but to use RGB sensors internally—rather than at the end. In fact, nearly every color device on earth is RGB except the printer.

You should wait to convert to the CMYK mode until right before you print. After your artwork is finalized, choose Image ➪ Mode ➪ CMYK Color and make whatever edits you deem necessary. For example, you may want to introduce a few color corrections, apply some sharpening, and even retouch a few details by hand. Photoshop applies your changes more slowly in the CMYK mode, but at least you're slowed down only at the end of the job, not throughout the entire process.

CROSS-REF Before converting an image to the CMYK color space, make certain Photoshop is aware of the monitor you're using and the printer you intend to use. These two items can have a pronounced effect on how Photoshop generates a CMYK image. You learn how to set up your personal RGB and CMYK color spaces in Chapter 17.

NOTE The advice about converting to CMYK before printing applies only to professional printing situations. If you're just in your home office printing to your inkjet printer, you should leave your image in RGB mode when you print. Your printer and the printer driver installed to run it will handle the CMYK conversion, with no effort required from you.

Previewing the CMYK color space

While you're editing in RGB mode, you can *soft proof* your image — display a rough approximation of what the image will look like when converted to CMYK and printed. To display colors in the CMYK color space, choose View ➪ Proof Colors. You also can press Ctrl+Y (⌘-Y on the Mac). This command is a toggle, so you also can use the menu or keyboard shortcut to turn this preview off.

Before you proof your colors, however, you should select the output you want to preview from the View ➪ Proof Setup submenu. Photoshop creates the proof display based on your selection. You can preview the image using the current CMYK working space, choose Custom to specify a particular output device, or preview the individual cyan, magenta, yellow, and black plates. The plates appear as grayscale images unless you colorize them by selecting the Color Channels in Color option in the Display & Cursors panel of the Preferences dialog box (that's Ctrl+K or Ctrl+3 on the PC and ⌘-K or ⌘-3 on the Mac). If you work with an older-model color inkjet printer that prints using just cyan, magenta, and yellow, you can choose the Working CMY Plates option to see what your image will look like when printed without black ink.

View ➪ Gamut Warning (Ctrl+Shift+Y on the PC or ⌘-Shift-Y on the Mac) is a companion to Photoshop's CMYK preview commands that covers so-called out-of-gamut colors — RGB colors with no CMYK equivalents — with gray. You may find this command less useful because it demonstrates a problem without suggesting a solution. You can desaturate the grayed colors with the Sponge tool (which is explained in Chapter 5), but this doesn't accomplish anything that Photoshop won't do automatically. A CMYK preview is much more serviceable and representative of the final CMYK image.

CIE's Lab

RGB isn't the only mode that responds quickly and provides a bountiful range of colors. Photoshop's Lab color space comprises all the colors from RGB and CMYK and is every bit as fast as RGB. Many high-end users prefer to work in this mode, and even if you don't consider yourself "high end," give it a shot to see if you like it.

Whereas the RGB mode is the color model of your luminescent computer screen and the CMYK mode is the color model of the reflective page, Lab is independent of light or pigment. Perhaps you've already heard the bit about how, in 1931, an international color organization called the Commission Internationale d'Eclairage (CIE) developed a color model that, in theory, contains every single color the human eye can see. Then, in 1976, the CIE came up with two additional color systems. One of those systems was Lab, and the other was either a big secret or somebody lost the minutes to the meeting where the systems were devised, because we don't know what the other one was.

The beauty of the Lab color model is it fills in gaps in both the RGB and CMYK models. RGB, for example, provides an overabundance of colors in the blue-to-green range but is stingy on yellows, oranges, and other colors in the green-to-red range. Meanwhile, the colors missing from CMYK are as numerous as the holes in the Albert Hall. Lab gets everything right.

Understanding Lab anatomy

The Lab mode features three color channels, one for luminosity and two others for color ranges, known simply by the initials *a* and *b*. Upon hearing luminosity, you might think, "Of course, just like HSL," but that's not entirely so. To make things confusing (weren't they already?), Lab's *luminosity* is like HSB's brightness. White indicates full-intensity color.

Meanwhile, the *a* channel contains colors ranging from deep green (low-brightness values) to gray (medium-brightness values) to vivid pink (high-brightness values). The *b* channel ranges from bright blue (low-brightness values) to gray to burnt yellow (high-brightness values). As in the RGB model, these colors mix together to produce lighter colors. Only the brightness values in the luminosity channel darken the colors. So you can think of Lab as a two-channel RGB with brightness thrown on top. Now it's clear why in elementary school, you learn that red and blue make purple — can you imagine the reaction of an average five-year-old if you read him or her the beginning of this paragraph? "Pass me the crayons and shut up!"

Using Lab

Because the Lab mode is device independent, you can use it to edit any image. Editing in the Lab mode is as fast as editing in the RGB mode and several times faster than editing in the CMYK mode. If you plan on printing your image to color separations, you may want to experiment with using the Lab mode instead of RGB, because Lab ensures that no colors are altered when you convert the image to CMYK, except to change colors that fall outside the CMYK range. In fact, anytime you convert an image from RGB to CMYK, Photoshop automatically converts the image to the Lab mode as an intermediate step.

> **TIP**   If you work with photo CDs often, open the scans directly from the Photo CD format as Lab images. Kodak's proprietary YCC color model is nearly identical to Lab, so you can expect an absolute minimum of data loss; some people claim that no loss whatsoever occurs.

Indexed Color

Choose Image ➪ Mode ➪ Indexed Color to display the dialog box shown in Figure 4.3. This command permits you to strip an image of all but its most essential colors. Photoshop then generates a color look-up table (LUT) that describes the few remaining colors in the image. The LUT serves as an index, which is why the process is called *indexing*.

> **TIP** Before the advent of the Save for Web dialog box, which was added to Photoshop in version 5, you needed to use the Indexed Color dialog box to prepare images for the Web — especially GIF images. However, with the Save for Web dialog box (accessed by choosing File ➪ Save for Web, or pressing the very finger-intensive Alt+Shift+Ctrl+S, or Option+Shift+⌘+S on the Mac), you have the ability to both strip out colors and preview your results.

Photoshop doesn't let you apply the Indexed Color command to Lab or CMYK images. And although you can apply Indexed Color to a grayscale image, you don't get any control over the indexing process; Photoshop doesn't let you reduce the image to fewer than 256 colors, for example. So if you want to index a Lab or CMYK image or custom-prepare a grayscale image, choose Image ➪ Mode ➪ RGB to convert the image to the RGB mode and then choose Image ➪ Mode ➪ Indexed Color. You also cannot index an image that you've converted to the 16 Bits/Channel mode, which is discussed shortly. If you want to index such an image, you must first choose Image ➪ Mode ➪ 8 Bits/Channel.

FIGURE 4.3

Use the Palette option to select the kinds of colors that remain in the image. Use the Colors option to specify how many colors remain.

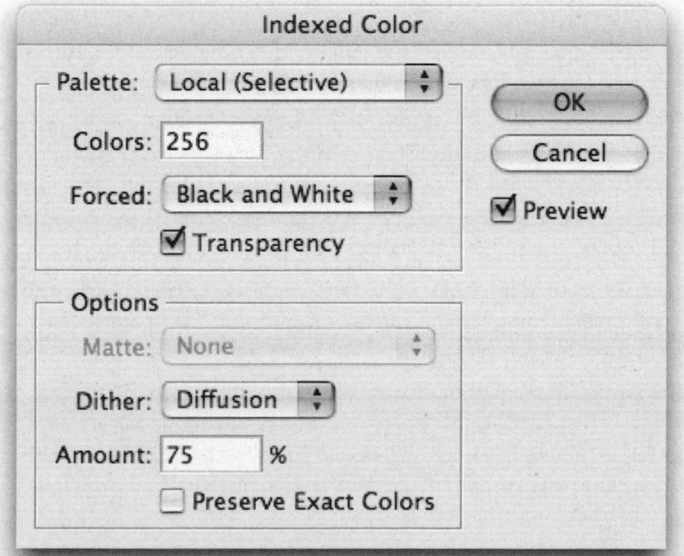

CAUTION   Don't expect to be able to edit your image after indexing it. Most of Photoshop's functions — including the Gradient tool, all the edit tools, and the filters — will refuse to work. Others, such as Feathering and the Brush tool, produce undesirable effects. If you plan on editing an 8-bit image much in Photoshop, convert it to the RGB mode, edit it as desired, and then switch back to the Indexed Color mode when you finish.

Now that you have all the warnings and special advice, the following list provides a brief rundown of the options inside the Indexed Color dialog box, along with some recommended settings for Web graphics:

- **Palette:** This pop-up menu tells Photoshop how to compute the colors in the look-up table. You have lots of options here, but only a handful are really useful. If your image already contains fewer than 256 colors, the Exact option appears by default, in which case you should just press Enter or Return and let the command do its stuff. The Web option converts your image to the 216 so-called "Web-safe" colors. The Adaptive option selects the most frequently used colors in your image, which typically delivers the best possible results. The Perceptual and Selective options are variations on Adaptive. But where Adaptive maintains the most popular colors, Perceptual is more intelligent, sampling the colors that produce the best transitions. The Selective option tries to maintain key colors, including those in the Web-safe palette. The Adaptive, Perceptual, and Selective options each come in two flavors: Local and Master. Choose Local if you want Photoshop to consider the colors in only the current image. If you have several images open and want to create a palette based on all the images, choose Master.

TIP   Select Perceptual for images in which smooth transitions are more important than color values. Use Selective when an image contains bright colors or sharp, graphic transitions. And if an image contains relatively few colors and you want to maintain those colors as exactly as possible, go for Adaptive.

- **Colors:** You can specify the number of colors in the palette by typing a number in this option box. As you can guess, fewer colors result in smaller files. For GIF images, you might start with 64 colors. If the image looks okay, try going even lower.

- **Forced:** This option enables you to lock in important colors so that they don't change. Black and White locks in black and white. Primaries protects 8 colors — white, red, green, blue, cyan, magenta, yellow, and black. And Web protects the 216 colors in the Web-safe palette. If you choose Custom, you can select the colors that you want to lock in.

- **Transparency:** If an image is set on a layer against a transparent background, selecting this option maintains that transparency. Bear in mind, however, that transparency in a GIF file is either on or off; there are no soft transitions as in a Photoshop layer.

- **Matte:** The Matte option works in collaboration with the Transparency option. (If an image has no transparency — that is, all layers cover one another to create a seamless opacity — the Matte option is dimmed.) When you select Transparency, the specified Matte color fills the translucent pixels in the image. When Transparency is deselected, the Matte color fills all translucent and transparent areas.

- **Dither:** This option controls how Photoshop mimics the colors that you asked it to remove from an image. The None setting maps each color in the image to its closest equivalent in the look-up table, pixel for pixel. This results in the harshest color transitions, but it is frequently the preferable option. Diffusion dithers colors randomly to create a naturalistic effect. Pattern dithers colors in a geometric pattern, which is altogether ugly. Noise mixes pixels throughout the image, not merely in areas of transition.

- **Amount:** When you choose Diffusion as the dithering mode, you can modify the amount of dithering by raising or lowering this value. Lower values produce harsher color transitions but decrease the file size. It's a trade-off. Keep an eye on the image window to see how low you can go.

- **Preserve Exact Colors:** This option is available only when the Diffusion option is selected from the Dither pop-up menu. When selected, this option turns off dithering inside areas of flat color that exactly match a color in the active palette. As mentioned before, you may often get better-looking images if you apply no dithering. But if you decide to dither, select the Preserve Exact Colors option. Even if you can't see a difference on your screen, it may show up on another screen.

Grayscale

Grayscale is pretty neat because it frees you from all the problems and potential expense of working with color and provides access to every bit of Photoshop's power and functionality. Anyone who says you can't do as much with grayscale as you can with color probably *likes* what Ted Turner did to great old movies like *It's a Wonderful Life*. Let's not even talk about that; it's too depressing. Anyway, you can print grayscale images to any laser printer, reproduce them in any publication, and edit them on nearly any machine. In addition to being universally printable and displayable, they look great, they remind you of classic movies (before Ted got his hands on 'em), and they make a humongous book, such as this one, affordable. What could be better?

Beyond discussing how neat grayscale is, however, there isn't a whole lot to say about it. You can convert an image to the grayscale mode regardless of its current mode, and you can convert from grayscale to any other mode just as easily. In fact, choosing Image ➪ Mode ➪ Grayscale is a necessary step in converting a color image to a duotone or black-and-white bitmap. (You also can use the Channel Mixer command to create a custom grayscale version of a color image, as you learn near the end of this chapter.)

Search your channels before converting

When you convert an image from one of the color modes to the grayscale mode, Photoshop normally weights the values of each color channel in a way that retains the apparent brightness of the overall image. For example, when you convert an image from RGB, Photoshop weights red more heavily than blue when computing dark values. This is because red is a darker-looking color than blue (much as that may seem contrary to popular belief).

TIP If you choose Image ⇨ Mode ⇨ Grayscale while viewing a single color channel, Photoshop retains all brightness values in that channel only and abandons the data in the other channels. This can be an especially useful technique for rescuing a grayscale image from a bad RGB scan.

So before switching to the grayscale mode, be sure to look at the individual color channels — particularly the red and green channels (the blue channel frequently contains substandard detail) — to see how each channel might look on its own. To browse the channels, use the following shortcuts (on the Mac, substitute ⌘ for Ctrl): Press Ctrl+1 for red, Ctrl+2 for green, and Ctrl+3 for blue. Or Ctrl+1 for cyan, Ctrl+2 for magenta, Ctrl+3 for yellow, and Ctrl+4 for black. Or even Ctrl+1 for luminosity, Ctrl+2 for *a*, and Ctrl+3 for *b*. You read about color channels in more detail later in this chapter.

16 and 32 bits per channel

The potential number of colors that an image can contain depends on the image's bit depth. A pixel 2 bits long can be one of four colors, and each additional bit doubles the number of colors available to the pixel. A typical RGB image contains 8 bits per channel, or a total of 24 bits (3 channels × 8 bits = 24 bits), which translates to 2^{24} = 16.8 million colors. You can increase the bit depth of an image by choosing Image ⇨ Mode ⇨ 16 Bits/Channel to convert the image to 16-bit mode, which gives you 2^{48} = 281.5 trillion colors. If you choose 32 Bits/Channel, you're looking at 2^{96}, which is equal to — well, a heck of a lot of colors.

NOTE When your images are in 32 Bits/Channel mode, they're considered HDR — High Dynamic Range — images, which are typically used in 3D rendering and advanced special effects software for animation. Photoshop's support for these images has increased with recent versions of the software, and you can choose View ⇨ 32-bit Preview Options to choose the Method (Exposure and Gamma or Highlight Compression), and if you select the former, use the sliders to set the Exposure and Gamma levels for the preview.

TIP Want to make your image a 32 Bits/Channel image? The command is dimmed until you raise your RGB image to 16 bits/channel. After you increase the bits per channel in the image to 16, you can increase it again to 32 and take advantage of HDR viewing options.

When you consider that even the largest images don't contain more than a couple million pixels, and each pixel can display only one color, 281.5 trillion colors may seem like overkill. In most cases it probably is, but 16-bit mode, and certainly 32-bit mode, does offer one big advantage: You can apply multiple color adjustments without noticeably damaging your image. And now that most of Photoshop's features are applicable to images in 16-bit mode (fewer are applicable in 32-bit mode) — prior to version CS, many commonly used features, such as layers, text, and paint tools, were unavailable — it's more practical for everyday image editing.

But Photoshop's 16-bit and 32-bit modes have their drawbacks. Most significantly, when you double the bit depth of an image, you double the size of the file in memory, which can make for some very large and unwieldy files. You have a limited choice of file formats, including TIFF and PSD, but not JPEG, and most of the commands on the Filter menu are unavailable to images in 16-bit or

32-bit mode. Also note that the 16 Bits/Channel command is applicable to RGB, CMYK, Lab, and grayscale images but not indexed or black-and-white files, and only RGB images can be set to 32-bits/channel.

Black and white (bitmap)

Choose Image ⇨ Mode ⇨ Bitmap to convert a flattened grayscale image to exclusively black-and-white pixels. This may sound like a boring option, but it can prove useful for gaining complete control over the printing of grayscale images. After all, output devices such as laser printers and imagesetters render grayscale images as a series of tiny dots. Using the Bitmap command, you can specify the size, shape, and angle of those dots.

When you choose Image ⇨ Mode ⇨ Bitmap, Photoshop displays the Bitmap dialog box, shown in Figure 4.4. Here you specify the resolution of the black-and-white image and select a conversion process. The options work as follows:

- **Output:** Specify the resolution of the black-and-white file. If you want control over every single pixel available to your printer, raise this value to match your printer's resolution. As a general rule, try setting the Output value somewhere between 200 to 250 percent of the Input value.

FIGURE 4.4

The Bitmap dialog box converts images from grayscale to black and white.

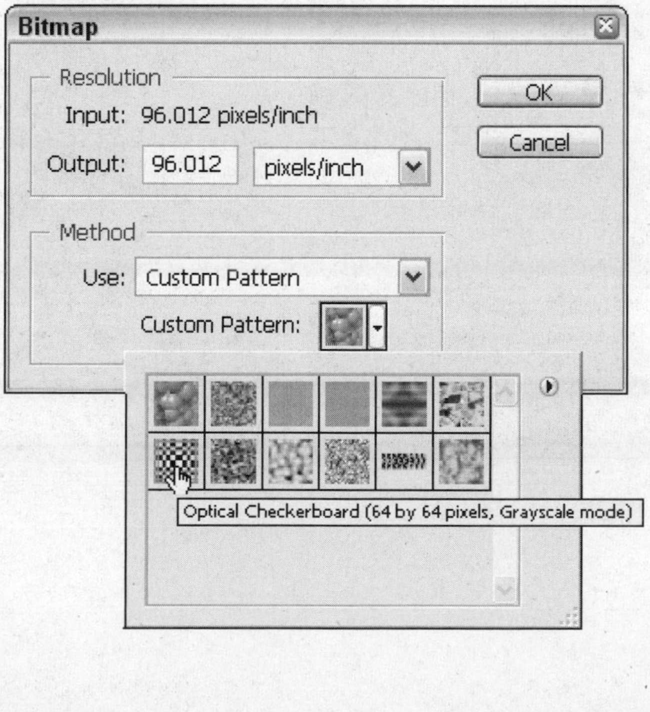

■ **50% Threshold:** Select this option from the Use pop-up menu to change every pixel that is darker than 50 percent gray to black and every pixel that is 50 percent gray or lighter to white. Unless you are working toward some special effect — for example, overlaying a black-and-white version of an image over the original grayscale image — this option most likely isn't for you. (And if you're working toward a special effect, Image ➪ Adjustments ➪ Threshold is the better alternative.)

■ **Pattern Dither:** To *dither* pixels is to mix them up to emulate different colors. In this case, Photoshop mixes up black and white pixels to produce shades of gray. The Pattern Dither option (in the Use pop-up menu) dithers an image using a geometric pattern. Unfortunately, the results are pretty ugly, as demonstrated in the left example in Figure 4.5. And the space between dots has a tendency to fill in, especially when you output to a laser printer.

FIGURE 4.5

Compare the results of selecting the Pattern Dither option (the choppy-looking one on the left) to the Diffusion Dither option (the smoother one on the right).

200

- **Diffusion Dither:** Select this option from the Use pop-up menu to create a mezzotint-like effect, as demonstrated in the right example in Figure 4.5. Again, because this option converts an image into thousands of stray pixels, you can expect your image to darken dramatically when it is output to a low-resolution laser printer and reproduced. So be sure to lighten the image with something like the Levels command (as described in Chapter 18) before selecting this option.

- **Halftone Screen:** When you select this option from the Use pop-up menu and press Enter or Return, Photoshop displays the dialog box shown in Figure 4.6. These options enable you to apply a dot pattern to the image, as demonstrated in Figure 4.7. Type the number of dots per inch in the Frequency option box and the angle of the dots in the Angle option box. Then select a dot shape from the Shape pop-up menu. Figure 4.7 shows examples of three dot patterns applied to a photo of a zebra, each with a frequency of 24 lines per inch.

CROSS-REF You can learn all about screen patterns and frequency settings in Chapter 20.

FIGURE 4.6

This dialog box appears when you select the Halftone Screen option in the Bitmap dialog box.

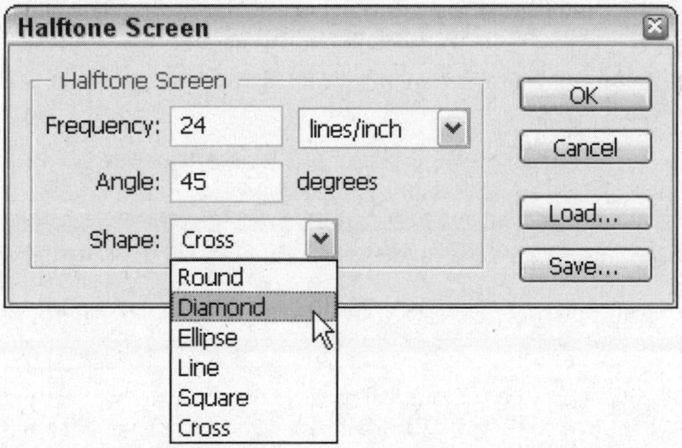

FIGURE 4.7

Three examples of halftone cell shapes (from left to right): Diamond, Line, and Cross. In all cases, the Frequency value was set to 24.

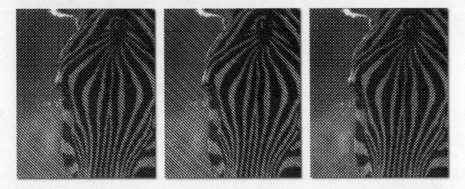

- **Custom Pattern:** To use a custom dither pattern, select this option from the Use pop-up menu and open the Custom Pattern palette, as shown in Figure 4.8. The palette includes a number of predefined patterns that ship with Photoshop as well as any custom preset patterns that you may have defined using Edit ➪ Define Pattern. Simply click the icon for the pattern you want to use — the smaller or more intricate the pattern, the more detail you retain in the image. If you use a large-scale pattern, you may not recognize anything in the photo — which can be a good thing, if that's the effect you're looking for. Figure 4.8 also shows two examples of predefined patterns (Gravel and Woven) used as custom halftoning patterns.

TIP To access additional preset patterns, choose Load Patterns from the palette menu (click the right-pointing triangle in the upper-right corner of the palette to display the menu). You can find the patterns in the Patterns folder, which lives inside the Presets folder. To delete a pattern from the palette, click its icon and choose Delete Pattern from the palette menu.

CROSS-REF For a complete guide to creating and defining patterns in Photoshop, see Chapter 6.

CAUTION Photoshop lets you edit individual pixels in the so-called bitmap mode, but that's about the extent of it. After you go to black-and-white, you can neither perform any serious editing nor expect to return to the grayscale mode and restore your original pixels. So be sure to finish your image editing before choosing Image ➪ Mode ➪ Bitmap. Even more important, make certain to save your image before converting it to black and white, and maybe save a backup copy of the image to go back to in case you discover problems after converting it to bitmap mode. I would say that saving is always good idea prior to performing any color conversion, and when making any kind change that limits the use of Photoshop's tools for editing an image, making a backup copy of the image is a smart thing to do.

FIGURE 4.8

Two examples of employing repeating patterns as custom halftoning patterns — you can still make out the zebra's head, but he's become a design unto himself, thanks to the patterns' effects.

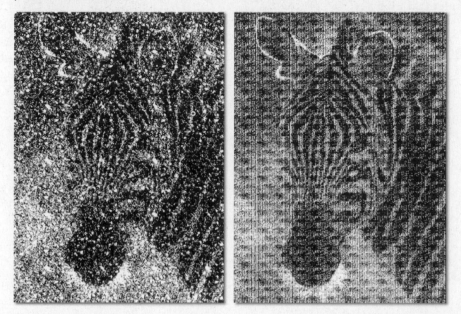

Using Color Libraries

In addition to the Color Picker dialog box, Photoshop provides a handful of additional techniques for selecting colors. The next several sections explain how to use the Color Libraries dialog box, the Color palette, and the Eyedropper tool. When you've finished reading it, words like *Pantone* and *sampling* will become allegedly valuable additions to your vocabulary, and you can use them to dazzle your friends — at least the ones who don't know anything about Photoshop or commercial printing.

Predefined colors

If you click the Color Libraries button in the Color Picker dialog box, Photoshop displays the Color Libraries dialog box shown in Figure 4.9. In this dialog box, you can select from a variety of predefined colors by choosing the color family from the Book pop-up menu, moving the slider triangles up and down the color slider to specify a general range of colors, and ultimately, selecting a color from the color list on the left. If you own the swatchbook for a color family, you can locate a specific color by typing its number on the keyboard.

FIGURE 4.9

The Color Libraries dialog box enables you to select predefined colors from brand-name libraries such as Pantone, Focoltone, and Trumatch.

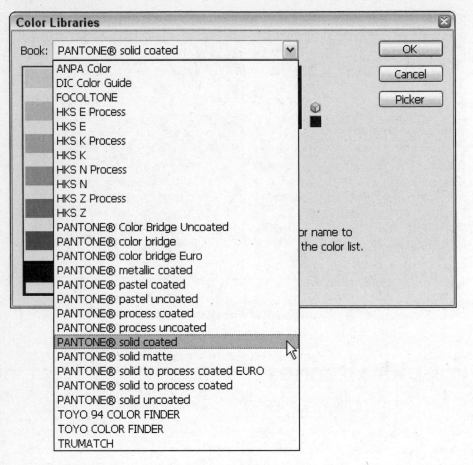

The color families represented in the Book pop-up menu fall into seven brands: ANPA (now actually NAA, as explained shortly), DIC, Focoltone, HKS, Pantone, Toyo, and Trumatch. At the risk of offending a few of these companies, you're likely to find certain brands more useful than others. The following sections briefly introduce the brands in order of their impact, from smallest to greatest, on the American market — with apologies to readers in other parts of the world, of course.

> **TIP**   The most popular use for predefined colors in Photoshop is in the creation of duotones, tritones, and quadtones (described in Chapter 20). You also can use predefined colors to match the colors in a logo or some other important element in an image to a commercial standard. And you can add an independent channel for a predefined color and print it to a separate plate, as discussed later in this chapter.

Focoltone, DIC, Toyo, and HKS

Focoltone, Dianippon Ink and Chemical (DIC), Toyo, and HKS have a very small impact on the market and are foreign color standards with followings abroad. Focoltone is a British company, and DIC and Toyo are popular in the Japanese market, but have very few subscribers outside Japan. HKS formerly was provided only in the German and French versions of Photoshop, but enough people asked for it to be included in other languages that it now is available in all versions of the program.

Newspaper Association of America

American Newspaper Publishers Association (ANPA) is now part of NAA, which stands for Newspaper Association of America, and has updated its color catalog. NAA provides a small sampling of 45 process colors (mixes of cyan, magenta, yellow, and black ink) plus five spot colors (colors produced by printing a single ink). The idea behind the NAA colors is to isolate the color combinations that reproduce most successfully on inexpensive newsprint and to provide advertisers with a solid range of colors from which to choose, without allowing the color choices to get out of hand.

Trumatch

Designed entirely using a desktop system and created especially with desktop publishers in mind, the Trumatch Colorfinder swatchbook features more than 2,000 process colors, organized according to hue, saturation, and brightness. Each hue is broken down into 40 tints and shades. Reducing the saturation in 15 percent increments creates tints; adding black ink in 6 percent increments creates shades. The result is a guide that shows you exactly which colors you can attain using a desktop system. If you're wondering what a CMYK blend will look like when printed, you need look no further than the Trumatch Colorfinder.

As if the Colorfinder weren't enough, Trumatch provides the ColorPrinter Software utility, which automatically prints the entire 2,000-color library to any PostScript-compatible output device. The utility integrates EfiColor and PostScript Level 2, thereby enabling design firms and commercial printers to test the entire range of capabilities available to their hardware. Companies can provide select clients with swatches of colors created on their own printers, guaranteeing that what you see is darn well what you'll get.

Pantone

On the heels of Trumatch, Pantone released a 3,006-color Process Color System Guide (labeled Pantone Process in the Book pop-up menu) priced at around $85. Pantone also produces the foremost spot-color swatchbook, the Color Formula Guide. Then there's the Solid to Process Guide, which enables you to figure out quickly if you can closely match a Pantone spot color using a process-color blend or if you ought to give it up and stick with the spot color.

Pantone spot colors are ideal for creating duotones and adding custom colors to an image for logos and the like, both discussed in Chapter 20. Furthermore, Pantone is supported by every computer application that aspires to the color prepress market. As long as the company retains the old competitive spirit, you can, most likely, expect Pantone to remain the primary color-printing standard for years to come.

The Color palette

Another means of selecting colors in Photoshop is to use the Color palette, shown in Figure 4.10. The Color palette is convenient, it's always there, and it doesn't take up lots of your screen like the Color Picker dialog box does.

FIGURE 4.10

The Color palette as it appears normally (top) and with the Web Color Sliders option selected (bottom)

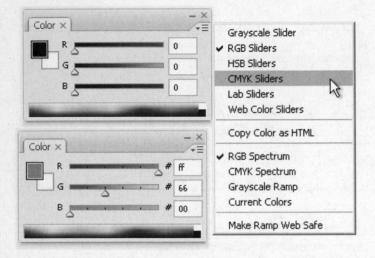

The Color palette is a default palette in the default workspace, found in a group with the Swatches and Styles palettes. If it's not showing, however, you can display it by choosing Window ➪ Color or by pressing F6. After the palette's visible, you use the elements and options in the palette as follows:

- **Foreground color** or **background color:** Click the foreground or background color icon in the Color palette to specify the color you want to edit. If you click the foreground or background color icon when it's already highlighted — as indicated by a double-line frame — Photoshop displays the Color Picker dialog box.

- **Sliders:** Click and drag the triangles in the slider controls to edit the highlighted color. By default, the sliders represent the red, green, and blue primary colors when a color image is open. You can change the slider bars by choosing a different color model from the palette menu.

- **Option boxes:** Alternatively, you can type numerical values in the option boxes to the right of the sliders. Press Tab to advance from one option box to the next; press Shift+Tab to go to the previous option.

■ **Alert triangle** and **cube:** Photoshop displays the alert triangle when a color falls outside the CMYK color gamut. The color swatch to the right of the triangle shows the closest CMYK equivalent. Click the triangle or the color swatch to replace the current color with the CMYK equivalent.

If you select the Web Color Sliders option from the palette menu, the alert cube appears to indicate colors that aren't included in the Web-safe palette. The palette also displays the hexadecimal values for the color, as shown in Figure 4.10. And as you drag the sliders, they automatically snap to Web-safe hues. To limit the palette so that it displays only Web-safe colors, choose Make Ramp Web Safe from the palette menu.

TIP If you're writing your own HTML code to set up a Web page, you can use the Color palette to help you grab the hexadecimal number for any color you're using on the page. After you define a Web color, choose Copy Color as HTML from the palette menu to save the hexadecimal code for the color to the Clipboard. You can then paste the code into an HTML file by choosing Edit ➪ Paste in the Web application.

■ **Color bar:** The bar along the bottom of the Color palette displays all colors in the CMYK spectrum. Click or drag inside the color bar (your mouse pointer turns to an eyedropper when you're pointing in or on the bar) to make the color you choose the current foreground or background color. Which color it becomes depends on whether the foreground or background icon is selected. The sliders update as you drag. Alt-click (Option-click on the Mac) or drag to lift the background color if the foreground icon is selected or the foreground color if the background color is selected.

You needn't accept the CMYK spectrum in the color bar, however. To change to a different spectrum, just choose the spectrum from the palette menu. Or Shift-click the color bar to cycle through the available spectrums. You can opt for the RGB spectrum, a black-to-white gradation (Grayscale Ramp), or a gradation from the current foreground color to the current background color (Current Colors). The color bar continuously updates to represent the newest foreground and background colors.

Notice the black and white squares at the right end of the color bar? You can click them to set a color to absolute black or white. But if all you want to do is set the foreground color to black, don't bother with the Color palette — just press D. For white, press D and then X. The first shortcut restores the foreground and background colors to black and white, respectively; pressing X swaps the colors to make white the foreground color and black the background color.

The Swatches palette

Another of the default workspace palettes, the Swatches palette should be hanging out in a group with Color and Styles. If you're in a custom workspace or have turned this palette off, however, you can bring it back by choosing Window ➪ Swatches. This palette, shown in Figure 4.11, lets you collect colors for future use, sort of like a list of favorites. You also can use the palette to set the foreground and background colors.

FIGURE 4.11

You can create custom swatch collections in the Swatches palette.

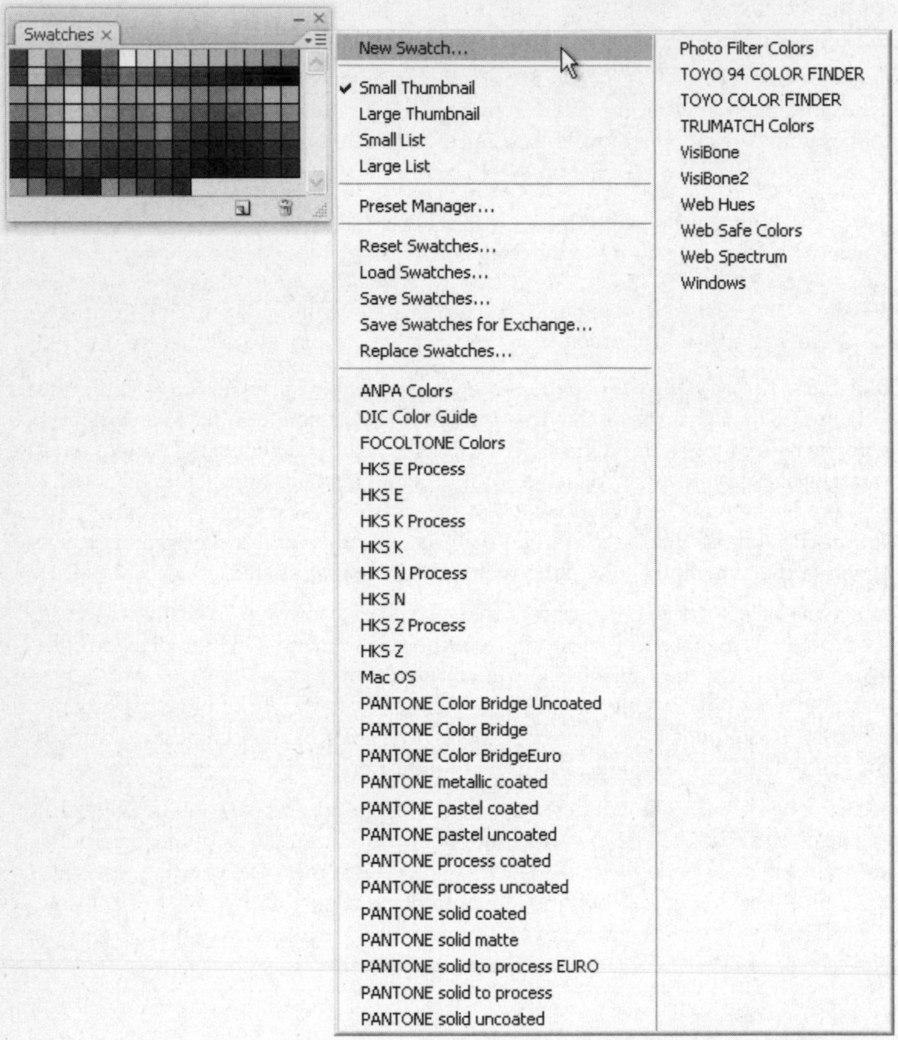

Swatches ×	New Swatch...	Photo Filter Colors
	✓ Small Thumbnail	TOYO 94 COLOR FINDER
	Large Thumbnail	TOYO COLOR FINDER
	Small List	TRUMATCH Colors
	Large List	VisiBone
	Preset Manager...	VisiBone2
		Web Hues
	Reset Swatches...	Web Safe Colors
	Load Swatches...	Web Spectrum
	Save Swatches...	Windows
	Save Swatches for Exchange...	
	Replace Swatches...	
	ANPA Colors	
	DIC Color Guide	
	FOCOLTONE Colors	
	HKS E Process	
	HKS E	
	HKS K Process	
	HKS K	
	HKS N Process	
	HKS N	
	HKS Z Process	
	HKS Z	
	Mac OS	
	PANTONE Color Bridge Uncoated	
	PANTONE Color Bridge	
	PANTONE Color BridgeEuro	
	PANTONE metallic coated	
	PANTONE pastel coated	
	PANTONE pastel uncoated	
	PANTONE process coated	
	PANTONE process uncoated	
	PANTONE solid coated	
	PANTONE solid matte	
	PANTONE solid to process EURO	
	PANTONE solid to process	
	PANTONE solid uncoated	

Here's how to take advantage of the Swatches palette:

■ Click a color swatch to make that color the foreground color. Ctrl-click (⌘-click on the Mac) to set the background color.

■ To add the current foreground color to the reservoir, Shift-click an existing color swatch to replace the old color or click an empty swatch to append the new color. In either case, your cursor temporarily changes to a Paint Bucket. After you click, you're asked to give the swatch a name. Type the name, and click OK. If you later want to change the name, just double-click the swatch to redisplay the name dialog box.

> **TIP** You can bypass the dialog box and add an unnamed color to the palette by Alt-clicking (Option-clicking on the Mac) an empty space in the palette.

■ To delete a color from the palette, Alt-click (Option-click on the Mac) a color swatch. Your cursor changes to a pair of scissors and cuts the color away.

■ The Swatches palette includes a New icon (it's the one that looks like a page) and a Trash icon, similar to those you find in the Layers palette. The icons provide alternative methods of adding and deleting colors: Click the New icon to add a new swatch in the current foreground color; Alt-click (Option-click on the Mac) to display the Name dialog box and then add the color. Drag a swatch to the Trash icon to delete it from the palette.

You also can save and load color palettes on disk using options in the palette menu. Load Swatches appends swatches stored in a swatches file to the current set of swatches; Replace Swatches replaces the current swatches with the ones in the file. Save Swatches lets you create a new swatch collection and save it to disk.

The Presets folder, located inside the main Photoshop folder, contains folders for all available preset items: Tool presets (see Chapter 2) and color swatches are only two of them. The Photoshop Only folder, found inside the Color Swatches folder of the Presets folder, contains palettes for the major color libraries from Pantone, Trumatch, and others. You can load these palettes by simply selecting them from the palette pop-up menu. You're then given the choice of appending the swatches to the existing swatches or replacing the current swatches altogether. Custom swatch sets that you create also appear on the palette menu, but only after you close and restart Photoshop.

> **TIP** When a color library palette is loaded, positioning your cursor over a color swatch displays a tool tip showing the name of that color. If you prefer to select colors by using the color names, select Small List from the palette menu. Now you see a scrolling list of colors instead of just the swatches.

Swatches presets

You also can create and manage swatch collections using the Preset Manager dialog box. Choose Preset Manager from the Swatches palette menu, choose Edit ➪ Preset Manager, and then choose Swatches from the Preset Type pop-up menu, or choose Edit ➪ Preset Manager, and then press Ctrl+2 (⌘-2 on the Mac) to display the Swatches presets panel, shown in Figure 4.12. The presets panel shows the current swatch set.

FIGURE 4.12

To easily create a new swatch collection using just some colors from an existing collection, head for the Preset Manager.

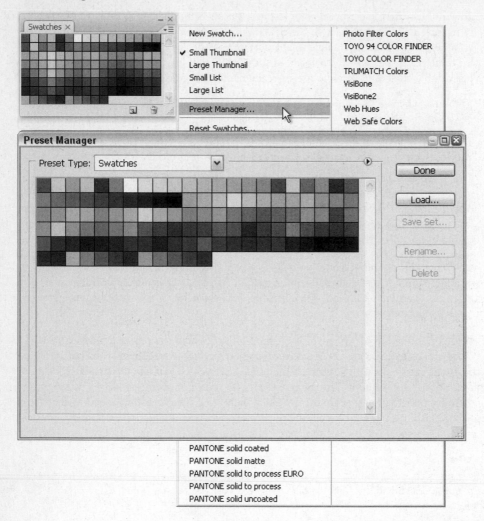

Many functions in the Swatches panel of the Preset Manager duplicate those offered by the Swatches palette. If you click the arrow to the upper left of the Done button (refer to Figure 4.12), a pop-up menu appears that's nearly identical to the Swatches palette menu. You can choose the

Replace Swatches command on the pop-up menu to replace the current swatch collection with another or choose Reset Swatches to return to the default swatch collection. To append a collection, click Load. Alternatively, click a collection name in the pop-up menu, in which case you have the choice of appending or replacing the current collection with the new one. To create a new swatch collection comprised of colors from an existing set, Shift-click the swatches you want to include, click Save Set, and then name the collection and store it in the Color Swatches folder.

CROSS-REF For complete details on using the Preset Manager, see Chapter 2.

The Eyedropper tool

The Eyedropper tool — which you can select by pressing I at any time or by pressing the Alt (Option) key while you're using a painting tool — provides the most convenient and straightforward means of selecting colors in Photoshop. The process is so straightforward, in fact, that you may be surprised that there is so much to say about it — but there is, so please read on:

- **Selecting a foreground color:** To select a new foreground color, click the desired color inside any open image window with the Eyedropper tool. (This assumes the foreground icon in the Color palette is selected, which it is by default, unless you've tinkered with the palette. If the background icon is selected, Alt-click or Option-click with the Eyedropper tool to lift the foreground color.) You can even click inside the image window of an open, yet inactive image to lift a color without bringing that window to the foreground.

TIP To select a color on your computer screen that isn't contained in one of Photoshop's image windows, click inside an image window with the Eyedropper, and then drag the tool outside the window. This means that you can select a color found on the Photoshop workspace (in any open image window, or in various palettes), or on your desktop, should the Photoshop window not be obscuring the desktop beneath it. As you drag the Eyedropper, you'll see it pick up all the colors you pass — to select one of the colors as you drag over it, just release the mouse and see that color appear in the Foreground Color block (or the Background Color block, if that's what you have selected in the Color palette).

- **Selecting a background color:** To select a new background color, Alt-click (Option-click on the Mac) the desired color with the Eyedropper tool. (Again, this assumes that the foreground icon is selected in the Color palette. If the background icon is selected, click with the Eyedropper to lift the background color.)

- **Skating over the color spectrum:** You can animate the foreground color icon by clicking and dragging with the Eyedropper tool. As soon as you achieve the desired color, release the mouse button. To animate the background color icon, Alt-drag (Option-drag on the Mac) with the Eyedropper tool. The icon color changes as you move the Eyedropper tool. Again, swap these procedures if the background color icon is selected in the Color palette.

- **Sampling multiple pixels:** Normally, the Eyedropper tool selects the color from the single pixel you click, because it's set to Point Sample by default. If you prefer to average the colors of several neighboring pixels, however, select any of the other choices from the Sample Size drop list on the options bar. You can pick 3 by 3, 5 by 5, 11 by 11, 31 by 31, 51 by 51 or 101 by 101 Average, or right-click (Control-click on the Mac) with the Eyedropper to display a pop-up menu of sampling options near the cursor. In this case, you get one additional option, Copy Color as HTML, which works just as it does when you select it from the Color palette pop-up menu. Photoshop determines the hexadecimal code for the color and sends the code to the Clipboard so that you can use Edit ➪ Paste to dump the code into an HTML file.

  Obviously, the larger the Sample Size that you choose, the wider the variety of pixels that is considered part of the sample. Unless that entire field of pixels, say in an 11 by 11 sample, is made up of identically colored pixels, the Eyedropper is going to give you a color that's a combination of the colors found within that sample area — thus the term "Average," for the sample size you chose.

> **TIP** To access the Eyedropper tool temporarily (and set a new Foreground color) when using the Paint Bucket, Gradient, Line, Pencil, or Brush tool, press and hold Alt (Option on the Mac). The Eyedropper cursor remains in force for as long as Alt or Option is pressed, and then when you release the key, you return to the tool that you were using before activating the Eyedropper. To set the Background color, switch to the Eyedropper tool by pressing I and then Alt-click (Option-click on the Mac) in an image window.

The Color Sampler tool

Found in the same Toolbox flyout as the Eyedropper, the Color Sampler tool looks like the Eyedropper with a little cross-hair target. Unlike the Eyedropper, however, which lifts foreground and background colors, the Color Sampler merely measures the colors of pixels so that you can monitor how the pixels react to various color changes.

To use the tool, select the Color Sampler and click somewhere inside the image window. By default, the tool is set to Point Sample (see the Options bar's Sample Size), and Photoshop adds a cross-hair target to indicate the point you clicked. You also can switch to the same 3 by 3, 5 by 5, 11 by 11, 31 by 31, 51 by 51, or 101 by 101 Average options found in the Eyedropper's Options bar, enabling you to sample groups of pixels instead.

When you begin using the Color Sampler, Photoshop opens the Info palette (or brings it to the top of its palette group it is grouped by default with the Navigator and Histogram palettes — if it was already open) and adds a new color measurement item labeled #1. This item corresponds to the target in the image, which is also labeled #1. Click again, and you add a second target and a corresponding item #2 in the Info palette. You can add up to four targets to an image, as demonstrated in Figure 4.13, which also shows the Info palette and four targets' worth of information.

FIGURE 4.13

The Color Sampler tool lets you click on and measure the colors of four points in your image. You can also measure a fifth point by merely moving the cursor around, without clicking.

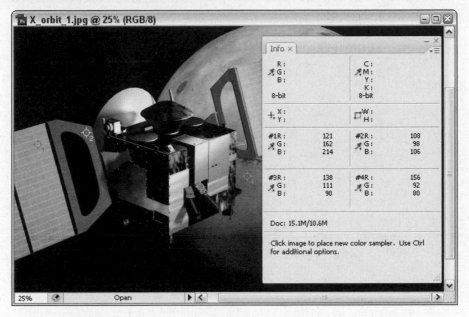

CROSS-REF The Color Sampler is intended primarily for printers and technicians who want to monitor the effects of color corrections on specific points in an image. If you apply Image ➪ Adjustments ➪ Levels, for example, Photoshop constantly updates the items in the Info palette to reflect your changes (for more detail, see Chapter 18). But you also can sample points in an image to monitor the effects of filters (see Chapters 10 and 11), blend modes (Chapter 14), and edit tools, such as Dodge and Burn (Chapter 5). The Color Sampler is just another way to monitor changes to an image.

Here are a few more techniques of interest when color sampling:

- Photoshop limits you to four color targets. If you try to create a fifth one, the program generates an error message. If you want to measure a different point in the image, you can either position your cursor over the point and note the top set of color values in the Info palette (as in Figure 4.13), or you can move one of the existing targets to the spot you now want to sample.

- To move a target inside the image window, click and drag it with the Color Sampler tool. You also can move a target by pressing Ctrl (Win) or ⌘ (Mac) and dragging the target with the Eyedropper tool. Press and hold Shift to constrain the drag to a 45-degree angle.

- To delete a target, Alt-click (Win) or Option-click (Mac) it. To delete all targets, click the Clear button in the Options bar.

- The Info palette grows to more than twice its normal size when you start clicking with the Color Sampler. To hide the sampler information without deleting targets, click the Info palette's collapse box or choose Color Samplers from the palette menu. If you go the second route, you have to choose Color Samplers again to bring the samples back.

- By default, the sampler items in the Info palette measure colors in the active color space. If you want to track a target in a different color space, click the item's Eyedropper icon in the Info palette or right-click (Control-click on the Mac) the target in the image window. Either way, you get a pop-up menu of color-space alternatives, including Grayscale, RGB, and several others that you may recall from previous explanations in this chapter.

> **TIP**   To select the Color Sampler, press I when the Eyedropper is active or Alt-click (Option-click on the Mac) the Eyedropper icon. Or press I repeatedly to cycle between the Eyedropper, Color Sampler, and Measure tool (add Shift if you selected the Use Shift Key for Tool Switch option in the Preferences dialog box). You can temporarily access the Color Sampler anytime the Eyedropper is active by pressing Shift. You also can use this convenient trigger when a color correction dialog box such as Levels or Curves is open, as explained in Chapter 18.

Introducing Color Channels

It may surprise you, especially in a chapter devoted to color, to read that Photoshop approaches a full-color image not as a single collection of 24-bit pixels but as three or four bands of 8-bit (grayscale) pixels. This is because Photoshop is really a grayscale editor, even though it offers tools for applying, tweaking, printing, and displaying color. How does this work in a color image? An RGB file contains a band of red, a band of green, and a band of blue, each of which functions as a separate grayscale image. A Lab image likewise contains three bands, one corresponding to luminosity and the others to the variables a and b. A CMYK file contains four bands, one for each of the process-color inks. These bands are known as *channels*.

Channels frequently correspond to the structure of an input or output device. Each channel in a CMYK image, for example, corresponds to a different printer's plate when the document goes to press. The cyan plate is inked with cyan, the magenta plate is inked with magenta, and so on. Each channel in an RGB image corresponds to a pass of the red, green, or blue scanner sensor over the original photograph or artwork. Only the Lab mode is device independent, so its channels don't correspond to any piece of hardware.

For those of you who just said "So?"

You're not alone in thinking that channels are something you don't really need to think about. Like many people, you use Photoshop to edit the way a photo looks and prints, and isolating one of the aforementioned channels is something you've never had to do in the past (assuming you've used Photoshop before, even momentarily), and your photos look just fine, thank you.

But what would you do if your client is self-publishing a book about bird-watching and wants you to use what turn out to be some really below-average photos? Given that many bird sightings are fleeting, irreproducible events, you can't say, "Man, these are awful. Can you go out again and get a new shot of this yellow-bellied sapsucker?" No, you have to go with what he's given you, and that's it. So you're faced with tinkering endlessly with Photoshop's commands found in the Image ⇨ Adjustments submenu, and maybe some filters, and that fails to fix up these really abysmal images. Then, suddenly, it hits you that you've never really looked at that Channels palette. Maybe it can help you, maybe there's something there. You choose Window ⇨ Channels, and before you stand four bands in the palette, one labeled RGB, one labeled Red, another Green, and finally Blue (this is an RGB image in this dream sequence). You click the different bands (much like activating layers in the Layers palette), and you look at the channels in your image.

How channels work

So now that we've sold you on the value of channels, how do you use them? First, let's do some math, which will show you how this all works:

For a typical full-color image, Photoshop devotes 8 bits of data to each pixel in each channel, thus permitting 256 brightness values, from 0 (black) to 255 (white). Therefore, each channel is actually an independent grayscale image. At first, this may throw you off. If an RGB image is made up of Red, Green, and Blue channels, why do all the channels look gray?

Photoshop provides an option in the Display & Cursors panel of the Preferences dialog box (that's Ctrl+K and then Ctrl+2 on the PC or ⌘-K and ⌘-2 on the Mac) called Show Channels in Color. When selected, this function displays each channel in its corresponding primary color. But although this feature can be reassuring — particularly to novices — it's equally counterproductive.

When you view an 8-bit image composed exclusively of shades of red, for example, it's easy to miss subtle variations in detail that may appear obvious when you print the image. You may have problems accurately gauging the effect of filters and tonal adjustments. So leave the Show Channels in Color option deselected (it's off by default for good reason) and temporarily suspend your understandable desire for onscreen color. With a little experience, you can better monitor your adjustments and predict the outcome of your edits in plain old grayscale.

CROSS-REF You can add channels above and beyond those required to represent a color or grayscale image for the purpose of storing masks, as described in Chapter 9. But even then, each channel is typically limited to 8 bits of data per pixel — meaning that it's just another grayscale image. Mask channels do not affect the appearance of an image onscreen or when it is printed. Rather, they serve to save selection outlines, as Chapter 9 explains.

Switching and viewing channels

The Channels palette is part of the default workspace, docked in a group with the Layers and Paths palettes, so it may well be on the screen right now. If it's not, though, you can redisplay it by choosing Window ⇨ Channels. Every channel in the image appears in the palette — including any mask channels — as shown in Figure 4.14. Photoshop even shows a thumbnail view of each channel so that you can see what it looks like.

To switch to a different channel, click a channel name in the Channels palette. The channel name becomes selected—like the Blue channel in Figure 4.14—showing that you can now edit it independently of other channels in the image.

> **TIP** To edit more than one channel at a time, click one channel name, and then Shift-click another. You also can Shift-click an active channel to deactivate it independently of any others.

When you select a single channel, Photoshop displays that one channel's content in the active image window. However, you can view additional channels beyond those that you want to edit. To specify which channels appear and which remain invisible, click in the boxes in the far-left column of the Channels palette. Click the Visibility icon (an eye, as appears in the Layers palette, also used there to hide and display) to make the eye disappear and therefore hide that channel. Click where there is no eye and an eye appears, thus displaying the channel.

FIGURE 4.14

Photoshop displays tiny thumbnails of each color channel in the Channels palette.

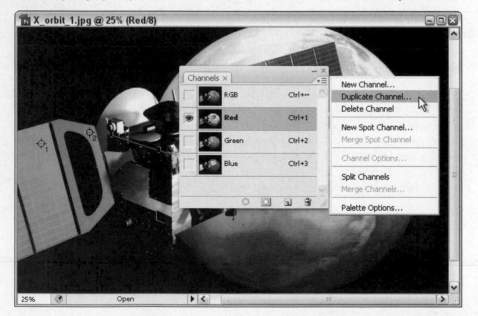

When only one channel is visible, that channel appears as a grayscale picture in the image window (possibly colorized in accordance with the Color Channels in Color option in the Preferences dialog box, should you have ignored the advice to leave this option in its default off state). However, when more than one channel is visible, you always see color. If both the Blue and Green channels are visible, for example, the image appears blue-green. If the Red and Green channels are visible, the image has a yellow cast, and so on.

In addition to the individual channels, Photoshop provides access to a *composite view* that displays all colors in an RGB, a CMYK, or a Lab image at once. (The composite view does not show mask channels; you have to specify their display separately.) The composite view is listed first in the Channels palette and is displayed by default. Notice that when you select the composite view, the names of all individual color channels in the Channels palette become highlighted along with the composite channel. This shows that all the channels are active. The composite view is the default in which you will perform the majority of your image editing.

Press Ctrl (⌘ on the Mac) plus a number key to switch between color channels. Depending on the color mode you're working in, Ctrl+1 (⌘-1 on the Mac) takes you to the Red (RGB), Cyan (CMYK), or Luminosity (Lab) channel — the first band in the palette; Ctrl+2 takes you to the Green, Magenta, or *a* channel; and Ctrl+3 takes you to the Blue, Yellow, or *b* channel. In CMYK mode, Ctrl+4 displays the Black channel. Other Ctrl-key equivalents — up to Ctrl+9 — take you to mask or spot-color channels (if there are any). To go to the composite view, press Ctrl+~ (tilde) (⌘-~ on the Mac). Tilde, in case you aren't familiar with it, is typically the Shift value of the key to the left of 1, or on some keyboards, to the right of the spacebar.

NOTE You do not need to press Shift to execute a keyboard shortcut that includes the tilde character or any other Shift value character.

The shortcuts are slightly different when you're working on a grayscale image. You access the image itself by pressing Ctrl+1 (⌘-1 on the Mac). Ctrl+2 (⌘-2 on the Mac) and higher take you to extra spot-color and mask channels.

TIP When editing a single channel, you may find it helpful to monitor the results in both grayscale and full-color views. Choose Window ➪ Arrange ➪ New Window to create a new window for the image, and then press Ctrl+~ (tilde) to set it to the color composite view. Then return to the first window and edit away on the individual channel. One of the amazing benefits of creating multiple views in Photoshop is that the views may show entirely different channels, layers, and other image elements — so create as many new windows of the image in progress as you need.

Trying Channels on for Size

Of course, if you're like most people, you need to see or use something to understand it. Luckily, channels are something you can both see and use, and the following sections show you exactly how to use channels for each of the major image color modes and how to control what's seen in the Channels palette.

RGB channels

Suppose that the Alaskan seal is an RGB image. Figure 4.15 compares a grayscale composite of this same image (created by choosing Image ➪ Mode ➪ Grayscale) with the contents of the Red, Green, and Blue color channels from the original color image. The Green channel is closest to the grayscale composite because green is such a dominant color in the image. The Red channel differs the most from the grayscale composite, simply because the image doesn't have much red. The overall darkness of the Red channel bears this out. The pixels in the Blue channel are lightest in the water because — you guessed it — the water is rich with blue (and in this case, oil, but that's another story).

As you look at Figure 4.15, you probably notice that each of the channel versions of the image has its own unique and interesting qualities. For example, the Red channel is darker overall, and the oily water looks more dense and, well, oily. You can feel the weight of the water and the ripples around the seal look less like clean, clear water. The Blue channel looks more washed out overall, and you focus more on the seal and the name of the ship in the background. Both versions of the image make a similar statement but in different ways. The Green channel, being closest to the grayscale composite of the image, doesn't say anything that the image as a whole doesn't say on its own.

The point? If you see that one of your channels, when viewed on its own, creates an interesting version that you might like to keep, remember that when converting a color image to grayscale, you have the option of retaining the image exactly as it appears in one of the channels. You also can calculate a grayscale composite by choosing Image ⇨ Mode ⇨ Grayscale when viewing all colors in the image in the composite view. To retain a single channel only, switch to that channel and then choose Image ⇨ Mode ⇨ Grayscale. Instead of the usual *Discard color information?* message, Photoshop displays the message *Discard other channels?* If you click OK, Photoshop throws out the other channels in favor of the interesting single channel you've elected to keep. Of course, you may want to save a backup copy of the image before doing any of this, so that you can go back to the color, multichannel image at any time.

CAUTION When the Warning dialog box appears, carefully consider the impact of selecting the Do Not Show Again option. It can be tempting to select this, especially if you think you don't want Photoshop to ask for permission to dump color information or channels when you convert to grayscale in the future — but turning this prompt off is risky. Without the warning, you may not realize that you have a single channel selected and end up tossing the other channels when all you meant to do was convert to grayscale. Of course, if you decide to ignore the warning here, and you later realize you should have listened, click Reset All Warning Dialogs on the General panel of the Preferences dialog box.

CMYK channels

If only to show you the interesting single-channel versions of this photo in CMYK and Lab modes, Figures 4.16 and 4.17 (respectively) show the channels from the image after it was converted to these two color modes. In Figure 4.16, the image has been converted to the CMYK mode with each of the individual channels captured. Because this color mode relies on pigments rather than light, as explained in the section "CMYK," dark areas in the channels represent high color intensity.

The CMY channels have more contrast than their RGB pals, but the basic brightness distribution is the same. Here's another graphic demonstration of color theory. You would think that the CMY channels would be very similar to the RGB channels — one color model would simply be the other turned on its head, with cyan pairing up with blue, magenta with red, and yellow with green. But they don't — and as a result, Photoshop has to boost the contrast of the CMY channels and throw in black to punch up those shadows.

FIGURE 4.15

A grayscale composite of an image from the Exxon Valdez oil spill, with views of the same photo's Red, Green, and Blue color channels

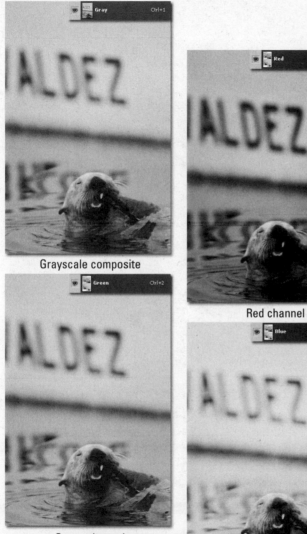

Grayscale composite

Red channel

Green channel

Blue channel

FIGURE 4.16

The contents of the cyan, magenta, yellow, and black channels from the image first seen in Figure 4.15

Cyan channel

Magenta channel

Yellow channel

Black channel

Lab channels

To create Figure 4.17, the original image was converted to the Lab mode. The image in the luminosity channel looks similar to the grayscale composite in Figure 4.15 because it contains the lightness and darkness values for the image. The *a* channel maps the greens and magentas, while the *b* channel maps the yellows and blues, so both channels are working hard to provide color information for this photograph. Certainly there are differences — the seal is much darker in the *a* channel, and there is a dark halo around the seal's head and the letters on the side of the ship in the *b* channel — but the two channels carry roughly equivalent amounts of color information.

FIGURE 4.17

The contents of the luminosity channel and the *a* and *b* color channels after converting the original image to Lab mode

  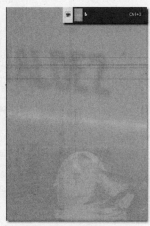

Lightness channel
(luminosity)

"a" channel
(greens are darkest)

"b" channel
(blues are darkest)

Other Channel Functions

In addition to viewing and editing channels using any of the techniques discussed in future chapters of this book, you can choose commands from the Channels palette menu and select icons along the bottom of the palette (refer to Figure 4.14). The following items explain how the commands and icons work:

 **CROSS-REF** Channels are discussed in Chapters 9 and 14, so after have the basics under your belt with this chapter, you can flip ahead and check out these subsequent discussions.

- **Palette Options:** Even though this is the last command in the menu, it's the easiest, so you can start with it. When you choose Palette Options, Photoshop displays four Thumbnail Size radio buttons, enabling you to change the size of the thumbnail previews that appear along the left side of the Channels palette. Why might you want to change the thumbnail size? Most likely so that you can see the image and see the differences between the individual channels' views from within the palette — large gives you the best view, and None, of course, gives you, well, None. The default is small, and for the terminally wishy-washy, there's medium.

TIP   Have you ever wondered what those thumbnail icons in the Palette Options dialog box are supposed to show? No? Well, shame on you for not being more inquisitive. Whether you want to know or not, you're gonna find out. They're silhouettes of tiny Merlins (wizards) on a painter's palette. Want proof? Switch to the Layers palette and choose Palette Options, and you see them in color. But how do I know they're specifically Merlins? Press Alt (Option on the Mac) when choosing Palette Options to see the magician up close. This is a real "Easter egg" here — going back to Photoshop 2.5.

- **New Channel:** Choose this command to add a mask channel to the current image. The Channel Options dialog box appears, requesting that you name the channel. You also can specify the color and translucency that Photoshop applies to the channel when you view it with other channels. We explain how these options work in Chapter 9.

TIP   You also can create a new channel by clicking the Create New Channel icon at the bottom of the Channels palette (it's the one that looks like a little page with a dog-eared corner). Photoshop creates the channel without displaying the dialog box. To force the dialog box to appear, Alt-click (Option-click on the Mac) the page icon.

NOTE   How many channels can one image contain? The answer used to be 24, but as of the release of Photoshop CS, you can have up to 56 total channels, regardless of color mode — and of course in Photoshop CS3 you can still have all 56 of 'em.

- **Duplicate Channel:** Choose this command to create a duplicate of the selected channel, either inside the same document or as part of a new document. (If the composite view is active, the Duplicate Channel command is dimmed because you can duplicate only one channel at a time.) The most common reason to use this command is to convert a channel into a mask. Again, you can find real-life applications in Chapter 9.

TIP   You also can duplicate a channel by dragging the channel name onto the new channel icon. No dialog box appears; Photoshop merely names the channel automatically. To copy a channel to a different document, drag the channel name and drop it into an open image window. Photoshop automatically creates a new channel for the duplicate.

- **Delete Channel:** To delete a channel from an image, click the channel name in the palette and choose this command. You can delete only one channel at a time. The Delete Channel command is dimmed when any essential color channel is active or when more than one channel is selected.

TIP If you're all tuckered out and choosing a command is too much effort, just drag the channel onto the delete channel icon (the little trash icon in the lower-right corner of the Channels palette). You also can click the trash icon, in which case Photoshop asks you if you really want to delete the channel — a nice little reminder and your last chance to rethink. Of course, if you are absolutely sure and don't want Photoshop questioning your intentions, you can bypass this warning by Alt-clicking (Option-clicking on the Mac) the trash icon.

■ **New Spot Channel:** Photoshop lets you add spot-color channels to an image. Each spot-color channel prints to a separate plate, just like spot colors in Illustrator or QuarkXPress. When you choose the New Spot Channel command, Photoshop asks you to specify a color and a Solidity, as shown in Figure 4.18. Click the color square to display the Color Picker and then as needed, click the Color Libraries button to bring up the Color Libraries dialog box, from which you can select a Pantone or other spot color. The Solidity option in the New Spot Channel dialog box lets you set the opacity of the ink, perfect for special effects inks like Day-Glo fluorescents and metallics.

TIP To create a spot-color channel without choosing a command, Ctrl-click (⌘-click on the Mac) the page icon at the bottom of the Channels palette. For more information on spot-color channels, see Chapter 18.

FIGURE 4.18

Create a spot channel, and then specify its color and density. The more solid the color, the more the ink in the new channel obscures the other inks in the image.

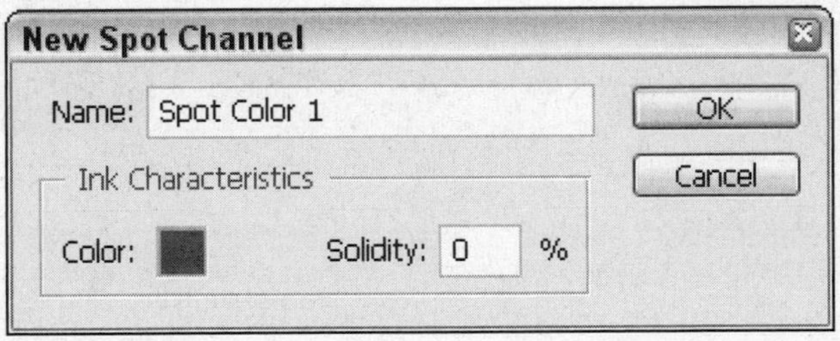

New Spot Channel

Name: Spot Color 1   OK

Ink Characteristics   Cancel

Color: [ ]   Solidity: 0 %

■ **Merge Spot Channel:** Select a spot-color channel, and choose this command to merge the spot color with the RGB, Lab, or CMYK colors in the image. Most spot colors don't have precise RGB or CMYK equivalents, so you lose some color fidelity in the merge. Adobe includes this command to enable you to proof an image to a typical midrange color printer.

■ **Channel Options:** Choose this command or double-click the channel name in the palette's scrolling list to change the settings assigned to a spot-color or mask channel. The Channel Options command is dimmed when a regular, everyday color channel is active.

■ **Split Channels:** When you choose this command, Photoshop splits off each channel in an image to its own independent grayscale image window with the channel color appended to the end of the window name. The Split Channels command is useful as a first step in redistributing channels in an image before choosing Merge Channels, which is demonstrated later in this chapter.

■ **Merge Channels:** Choose this command to merge several images into a single multichannel image. The images you want to merge must be open, grayscale, and absolutely equal in size — the same number of pixels horizontally and vertically — so be sure to verify these common attributes before proceeding. When you choose Merge Channels, Photoshop displays the Merge Channels dialog box, shown in Figure 4.19. It then assigns a color mode for the new image based on the number of open grayscale images that contain the same number of pixels as the foreground image.

FIGURE 4.19

The two dialog boxes that appear after you choose Merge Channels enable you to select a color mode for the merged image (top) and associate images with color channels (bottom).

You can override Photoshop's choice by selecting a different option from the Mode pop-up menu. (Generally, you won't want to change the value in the Channels option box because doing so causes Photoshop to automatically select Multichannel from the Mode pop-up menu. You find out more about multichannel images in the section "Using multichannel techniques.")

After you press Enter or Return, Photoshop displays a second dialog box, which also appears in Figure 4.19. In this dialog box, you can specify which grayscale image goes with which channel by choosing options from pop-up menus. When working from an image split with the Split Channels command, Photoshop automatically organizes each window into a pop-up menu according to the color appended to the window's name.

TIP   If the thumbnails for the channels aren't big enough for you, choose Palette Options from the menu and choose a larger thumbnail size from the three choices offered. You also can choose None if you don't want any thumbnails at all.

Color Channel Effects

Now that you know how to navigate among channels and apply commands, it's time to talk about *why* you'd do these things. There are lots of reasons for tinkering with channels in an image, but one of the most pragmatic applications for channel effects involve the restoration of bad color scans. If you use a color scanner, you know what is meant by "bad color scans," of course. Everyone has ended up with scans that look like all the people in the photo were terminally embarrassed, nauseated, or under water. The excess red, green/yellow, or blue can be eliminated with some of the Image ⇨ Adjustment submenu tools, of course, but with channels, you can target the specific problems with color and also improve clarity and clean edges within the image.

Improving the appearance of color scans

The following are a few channel-editing techniques that you can use to improve the appearance of poorly scanned full-color images. Keep in mind that these techniques don't work miracles, but they can make a big difference.

NOTE Don't forget that you can choose Window ⇨ Arrange ⇨ New Window to maintain a constant composite view. Or you can click the Visibility icon (the eye) in front of the composite view in the Channels palette to view the full-color image, even when editing a single channel.

- **Aligning channels:** Every so often, a scan may appear out of focus even after you use Photoshop's sharpening commands to try to correct the problem, as discussed in Chapter 10. If, on closer inspection, you can see slight shadows or halos around colored areas, one of the color channels probably is out of alignment. To remedy the problem, switch to the color channel that corresponds to the color of the halos. Then select the move tool (by pressing V), and use the arrow keys to nudge the contents of the channel into alignment. Use the separate composite view (created by choosing Window ⇨ Arrange ⇨ New Window) or click the eyeball in front of the composite channel to monitor your changes.

- **Channel focusing:** If all channels seem to be in alignment (or, at least, as aligned as they're going to get), one of your channels may be poorly focused. View each individual channel (using the visibility icon on the Channels palette), and when you find out which one's the culprit, use the Unsharp Mask filter to sharpen it as desired. You also may find it helpful to blur a channel, to eliminate moiré patterns in a scanned halftone, for example. To find out more about these and other corrective filters, check out Chapter 10.

- **Bad channels:** In your color channel tour, if you discover that a channel is not so much poorly focused as simply rotten to the core — complete with harsh transitions, jagged edges, and random brightness variations — you may be able to improve the appearance of the channel by mixing other channels with it.

  For an example of how this might be done, imagine that in your image, the blue channel is awful, but the red and green channels are in fairly decent shape. The Channel Mixer command lets you mix channels together, whether to repair a bad channel or achieve an interesting effect. Choose Image ⇨ Adjustments ⇨ Channel Mixer and press Ctrl+3 (⌘-3 on the Mac) to switch to the blue channel. Then raise the Red and Green values and lower the Blue value to mix the three channels together to create a better blue. To maintain consistent brightness levels, use a combination of Red, Green, and Blue values that add up to 100 percent, as in Figure 4.20. If you can live with the inevitable color changes—and you may not be able to, in which case a channel mask is required—the appearance of the image should improve dramatically.

NOTE   You also can try the new Preset option, which appears at the top of the Channel Mixer dialog box. Select from some these combinations of black and white with a color filter— blue, green, orange, red, or yellow. Applied to a particular layer, this can be useful in improving an image if the offending content can be (or is) isolated on a single layer. After a preset is chosen, you can change its effects by dragging the Source Channels' sliders. If you like a particular setup—through the presets or with the Preset option set to None and you've simply dragged the Source Channel sliders to a desirable set of percentages—save those settings with the button to the right of the Preset drop-down list. Choose Save Preset, and then use the resulting dialog box to name the settings for future loading (see the Load Preset command available through the same button). Of course, choosing a name that describes the situation where the given preset would be most useful is a good idea.

FIGURE 4.20

Here the Channel Mixer command is used to repair the blue channel by mixing percentages of the red and green channels. The red and green channels themselves remain unaffected.

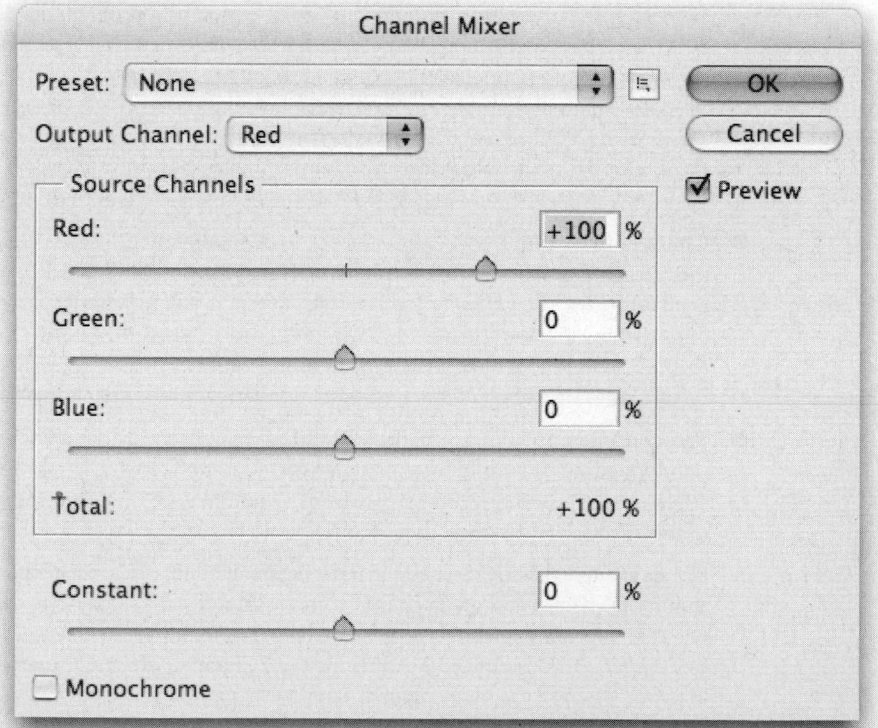

Note that Channel Mixer is also a great command for creating custom grayscale images. Rather than choosing Image ⇨ Mode ⇨ Grayscale and taking what Photoshop gives you, you can choose the Channel Mixer command and select the Monochrome option. Then adjust the Red, Green, and Blue values to mix your own grayscale variation. With the new Preset option, as soon as you choose one of the Black & White with X Filter (where X is a color), the Monochrome option is automatically checked.

Incidentally, the Constant slider simply brightens or darkens the image across the board. Usually, you want to leave it set to 0, but if you're having problems getting the color balance right, give it a nudge with your mouse or the arrow keys.

If at any point you hate the effects you're seeing through the Preview, click Reset to go back to the way things were before you opened the dialog box in the first place.

Using multichannel techniques

The one channel function not looked at so far is Image ⇨ Mode ⇨ Multichannel. When you choose this command, Photoshop changes your image so that channels no longer have a specific relationship to one another. They don't mix to create a full-color image; instead, they exist independently within the confines of a single image. The multichannel mode is generally an intermediary step for converting between different color modes without recalculating the contents of the channels. Multichannel is also the only Mode option if you use the Merge Channels command and have only two images open; the other modes are dimmed.

In terms of multichannel's use in converting between different color modes, when you normally convert between the RGB and CMYK modes, Photoshop maps RGB colors to the CMYK color model, changing the contents of each channel as demonstrated back in Figures 4.15 and 4.16. But suppose, just as an experiment, that you want to bypass the color mapping and instead transfer the exact contents of the red channel to the cyan channel, the contents of the green channel to the magenta channel, and so on. You convert from RGB to the multichannel mode and then from multichannel to CMYK as described in the following procedure.

STEPS: Using Multichannel mode as an intermediary step

1. **Open an RGB image.** If the image is already open, make sure that it is saved to disk.

2. **Choose Image ⇨ Mode ⇨ Multichannel.** This eliminates any relationship between the formerly Red, Green, and Blue color channels.

3. **Click the new channel icon at the bottom of the Channels palette.** Or choose the New Channel command from the palette menu, and press Enter or Return to accept the default settings. Either way, you add a mask channel to the image. This empty channel serves as the black channel in the CMYK image. (Photoshop won't let you convert from the multichannel mode to CMYK with less than four channels.)

4. **Press Ctrl+I (⌘-I on the Mac).** Unfortunately, the new channel comes up black, which would make the entire image black. To change the channel to white, press Ctrl+I (⌘-I on the Mac) or choose Image ⇨ Adjustments ⇨ Invert.

5. **Choose Image ⇨ Mode ⇨ CMYK Color.** The image looks washed out and a tad dark compared to its original RGB counterpart, but the overall color scheme of the image remains more or less intact. This is because the Red, Green, and Blue color channels each have a respective opposite in the cyan, magenta, and yellow channels.

6. **Press Ctrl+Shift+L (⌘-Shift-L on the Mac).** Or choose Image ⇨ Adjustments ⇨ Auto Levels. This punches up the color a bit by automatically correcting the brightness and contrast.

7. **Convert the image to RGB and then back to CMYK.** The problem with the image is that it lacks any information in the black channel. So although it may look okay onscreen, it will lose much of its definition when printed. To fill in the black channel, choose Image ⇨ Mode ⇨ RGB Color and then choose Image ⇨ Mode ⇨ CMYK Color. Photoshop automatically generates an image in the black channel in keeping with the standards of color separations (as explained in Chapter 20).

Keep in mind that these steps are by no means a recommended procedure for converting an RGB image to a CMYK image. Rather, they merely suggest one way to experiment with channel conversions to create a halfway decent image. Likewise, you can experiment with converting between the Lab, multichannel, and RGB modes, or Lab, multichannel, and CMYK.

> **TIP**   If you want to really manipulate the colors in an RGB or a CMYK image, there's nothing like replacing one color channel with another to produce spectacular (or at least quite interesting) effects — and the Channel Mixer is your manipulation tool of choice. You can try swapping the Red and Blue channels in an RGB image, setting red to 0 and blue to 100, then flip that around, setting red to 100 and blue to 0. You can mix and match your CMYK image channels, too, tinkering with the sliders until you get bored.

Summary

In this chapter, you learned about using the color controls in the Toolbox, selecting and defining colors in the Color Picker dialog box, and all about the RGB, HSB, CMYK, Lab color, and HDR modes. You learned how to convert images to 16 and 32 bits per channel and how to create grayscale and black-and-white images.

You learned to apply colors using the Color palette, Eyedropper, and color sampler, and you found out how color channels work. You also learned to use channel editing commands in the Channels palette and how to improve the appearance of poorly scanned images.

Chapter 5

Painting and Brushes

Over the years, quite a few applications have offered both PC and Mac users the ability to paint and draw — using their mouse, or in more recent years, a pen and tablet. Most of these applications have faded into obscurity, and for good reason. Frankly, there isn't that much painting going on, and the tools for manipulating the brush tools are either skimpy or hard to work with.

Of course, Photoshop's great painting tools and the plentiful options for completely customizing them have helped nail the coffins shut for many of these alleged painting programs. While Photoshop was originally designed to be (and remains) an image-editing program, it has always had painting tools, and it turned out that most people wanted to edit images rather than paint them from scratch. Of course, you can in fact paint or draw an image from scratch in Photoshop, but strangely, scores of the artistically challenged who would rate themselves unable to draw a stick figure with pencil and paper become quite adventurous with a computerized painting program. Professional photographers and graphic artists are among Photoshop's painting tool fans, too — for the tools' ability to add and change image content on a large or small scale.

As for Photoshop CS3, the tradition of great painting tools continues, with improved access to brush options, two new brush modes, and for those of you who've used Photoshop before, all the great core painting features, right where you left them. If you're new to Photoshop, get ready to unleash your inner artiste.

Getting to Know the Painting and Editing Tools

Photoshop provides two basic varieties of brush tools. There are paint tools, which allow you to apply colors to an image, and there are edit tools, which modify existing colors in an image. Both types of tools work the same way — you activate the tool and drag your cursor within the image window, much like you drag a brush across a canvas or a sheet of paper.

Now, don't think that these tools require any sort of artistic ability, because they don't. If you can drag a mouse or a tablet's pen, you can paint and edit with Photoshop. The tools are designed to cater to users of all levels, and they provide simple ways to apply straight, curved, and free-form strokes to an image as well as more complex tool options that make it possible for true visionaries with great eye-hand coordination to create serious works of art.

So what are these tools? Photoshop CS3 provides the big two that you'll find in any fledgling or accomplished artist's studio: the Brush and the Pencil. You also get seven editing tools: Blur, Sharpen, Smudge, Dodge, Burn, Sponge, and — housed with the Brush and Pencil — Color Replacement, which debuted with Photoshop CS2. Figure 5.1 shows all the tools along with the keyboard shortcuts for selecting them.

FIGURE 5.1

Sharing three spots in the Toolbox, you find all nine of Photoshop's painting and editing tools.

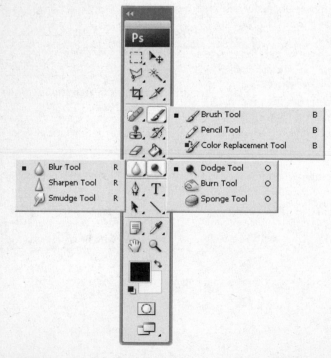

You'll know when a button in the Toolbox represents multiple tools—a small triangle appears in the lower-right corner of the button. When you see that triangle, you can click and hold the button to display a flyout menu of tools (refer to Figure 5.1). Of course, unlike that illustration, you can't activate three different tools and show their flyout menus simultaneously—you can activate only one button (and its flyout menu) at a time.

> **TIP** Did you know the Eraser tool offers nearly all the same tool options and settings that the Brush does? That's right. You can select from the same brush presets and apply the same brush dynamics to the Eraser that you can with the Brush. Of course, the Eraser removes content from your image rather than applying it, but because it works just like the Brush in so many ways, many people consider it a painting *and* editing tool. You'll find out more about the Eraser's other features in Chapter 9, and you can get to know more about the basic Eraser in Chapter 2.

To activate any tool, you can select it from the Toolbox and click it in the flyout menu, or you can skip using your mouse entirely and just press the keyboard shortcut. When more than one tool shares a single shortcut, you can simply press Shift along with the shortcut key (B, for example, to select the Brush or Pencil) and the tool you want appears in the Toolbox and on the Options bar at the top of the workspace. If you want to avoid having to press two keys, you can deselect the Use Shift Key for Tool Switch option in the General Preferences dialog box, and then all you have to do is keep pressing the single keyboard shortcut key to cycle through the tools associated with that key until the tool you want is selected.

The paint tools

The paint tools apply strokes of color. In most cases, you'll be painting with the foreground color, though you also can create multicolored brushstrokes using the Color Dynamics options in the Brushes palette, as you'll see later. Here's how the paint tools work:

- **Brush:** This tool paints a line of any thickness that you specify, using the Options bar or the Brushes palette. You can make the line sharp or blurry, but it's always slightly soft— that is to say, the edges of the brushstroke blend to some extent with the background. Known as *anti-aliasing*, this softness produces halftone dots when printing, ensuring smooth transitions between a brushstroke and its surroundings. If the stroke doesn't look soft to you when you make it, try zooming in a bit—you'll see those smooth transitions, even on lines that look quite crisp at lower-level magnification.

  Normally, the Brush tool applies a continuous stream of color and stops applying paint whenever you stop dragging. However, if you activate the Airbrush function by clicking the Airbrush icon next to the Flow setting in the Options bar, the color continues to build as long as you press the mouse button, even when holding the cursor in a stationary position. This pooling of paint, shown in Figure 5.2, is the most obvious impact of the airbrush option. Also shown in this figure are similar strokes made with a hard and a soft brush of the same dimension.

> **TIP** To invoke the Airbrush function from the keyboard, press Shift+Alt+P (Shift+Option+P on the Mac). Pressing Shift+Alt+P again turns the function off. If you think remembering the P will be difficult, it won't be—P stands for Paint.

FIGURE 5.2

Three lines are painted in black — the first two with the Brush, the third with the Pencil. Note the extra paint that holding the brush in place at the end of the stroke created in the middle example.

Brush   Airbrush   Pencil

■ **Pencil:** Like the Brush tool, the Pencil paints a line of any thickness, in the current foreground color. However, whereas Brush tool lines are always soft, Pencil lines are always hard edged, with no interaction between the Pencil line and background colors. At high resolutions, Pencil lines appear sharp. At low resolutions, Pencil lines have jagged edges. Again, zooming in on your pencil strokes helps you see this if it's not obvious at your current zoom.

When you select the Pencil tool, a unique check box, Auto Erase, appears in the Options bar. When selected, this option instructs Photoshop to paint with the background color — thereby erasing — whenever you begin painting on an area already colored with the foreground color.

TIP As when painting in real life, one of the keys to painting in Photoshop is choosing the color you'll apply with your brush. The Colors palette is handy and is certainly more convenient than opening the Color Picker to change colors, but if you need color quickly, and see it there in front of you, try the Eyedropper. The Eyedropper lets you sample (and simultaneously select as your Foreground color) any color in any open Photoshop image window, the Color palette, or the Swatches palette, and if you're on a Mac, anywhere on the desktop or the visible areas of any other running application. To activate the Eyedropper, click it in the Toolbox, press the letter I, or if you're using the Brush or Pencil, just press the Alt key (Option key on the Mac) and then click the color you want to sample. You'll know you've activated the Eyedropper because your mouse pointer changes to an actual dropper icon, waiting to sip up some color from anywhere onscreen.

The edit tools

Rather than applying color, the edit tools influence existing colors in an image. Figure 5.3 shows the effect of dragging with each of the edit tools, except the Sponge and Color Replacement tools, both of which work best with color images (and whose effects would therefore be lost in a black and white image here). Future sections cover these tools in more detail, but here's a brief introduction:

■ **Blur:** The first of the two focus tools, the Blur tool blurs an image by reducing the amount of color contrast between neighboring pixels.

■ **Sharpen:** The second focus tool selectively sharpens by increasing the contrast between neighboring pixels.

■ **Smudge:** The Smudge tool smears colors in an image. The effect is rather like dragging your finger across wet paint. Although simple, this tool can be effective for smoothing out colors and textures. See the section "Painting with the Smudge tool" for more information.

■ **Dodge:** The first of three toning tools, the Dodge tool lets you lighten a portion of an image by dragging across it. Named after a traditional darkroom technique, the Dodge tool is supposed to look like a little paddle. Before computers, a technician would wave such a paddle (or anything, really) over photographic paper to prevent light from hitting the paper, thereby leaving areas less exposed.

■ **Burn:** The Burn tool is the Dodge tool's opposite, darkening an area as you drag over it. Again referencing old darkroom techniques, technicians would create a mask over the developing print, using their hands or a piece of paper with a hole cut in it. The mask would protect areas of photographic paper that had already been exposed and darken the area inside the hole. Photoshop's metaphor for this is found in the Burn tool's button, which depicts a hand in the shape of an O.

■ **Sponge:** The Sponge tool has two modes — Saturate and Desaturate. In Desaturate mode, the Sponge tool robs an image of color when working inside a color image, or contrast when working in grayscale. If you switch to Saturate mode, the Sponge tool adds more color (in color images), or contrast in grayscale images.

■ **Color Replacement:** At its most basic level, the Color Replacement tool provides a great way to get rid of any color in favor of a preferred shade. Through the tool's Options bar, you can pick which color goes and which color replaces it. The intricacies of the tool's use are covered in detail later.

FIGURE 5.3

This figure shows the effects of dragging with five of Photoshop's edit tools. The boundaries of each line are highlighted so you can clearly see the distinctions between line and background.

Blur   Sharpen   Smudge   Dodge   Burn

Tools versus Filters

As you work with Photoshop's Filters, you'll notice that there also are Blur and Sharpen filters, and you may wonder how these differ (or if they differ) from the Blur and Sharpen tools. It's a matter of opinion, of course, but I find that the Blur tool, while it requires scrubbing with the mouse, is more effective and controllable than the Blur filter. There are other Blur filters, such as Gaussian, Motion, Smart, Radial, Box, Shape, and Surface, which provide very effective and dramatic results — but the plain old Blur filter would not be a first choice for blurring edges or background content. The Sharpen filter, on the other hand, is a bit better than the Sharpen tool, in that it provides an effective, yet subtle effect. You may find that the Sharpen tool usually ends up creating a mess of randomly colored pixels, even at a low Strength setting, and more often than not, you'll end up regretting its use and using Undo.

TIP Some tools are often used together — not at the same time, of course, but you'll find yourself hopping from one to the other and wishing you could do so more quickly. The Sharpen and Blur tools are an example of this, because you often need to soften one area and add more focus to another, all in the same image. To access the Sharpen tool temporarily when the Blur tool is selected, press and hold Alt or Option while using the tool. The Sharpen tool remains available only as long as you press Alt (Option on the Mac). Likewise, you can press Alt (Option on the Mac) to access the Blur tool when the Sharpen tool is selected. You can use the same Alt/Option technique with other likely pairs such as the Dodge and Burn tools.

Basic Techniques

Even if you're one of the people who think they can't draw at all (and I'd argue with you, because most people can draw much better than they think), Photoshop makes it possible for anyone to paint and draw. In this section, we hope you'll feel freed to unleash your creativity and let that artist within you loose — with Photoshop's painting and editing tools as the means to that end. Don't say that "I can't even draw stick figures!" line — you have no idea what you can do until you try.

Painting a straight line

Let's start with the most basic of drawing skills, the straight line. With the Brush and Pencil tools, drawing straight lines is easy, because all you need is the tool (either one) and the Shift key. Pressing Shift while you drag the tool keeps the line straight and eliminates the little bumps and detours that occur when you try to create a freehand straight line. You can use the same technique with the Blur, Sharpen, Smudge, Dodge, and Burn tools, applying their editing effects in a straight line as you click and/or drag your mouse.

TIP If you find the Shift key technique to be too limiting, Photoshop also provides a Line tool (one of the Shape tool variants) that lets you draw straight lines. This surprisingly flexible tool permits you to draw vector-based layers or pixel-based lines, and you can even add arrowheads.

CROSS-REF   The Line tool and others like it are explained in greater detail in Chapter 15.

Click (don't drag) your mouse

To get started, try this Shift technique with the Brush and Pencil tools. First, using the Brush tool, click at one point in your image, and then press Shift and click at another point. Photoshop connects the start and endpoints with a straight stroke of paint. Try it again with the Pencil tool, and enhance your experiments by trying different Brush and Pencil presets to see the results. You also can create free-form polygons by continuing to Shift-click with the Brush or Pencil tool, creating a series of straight lines as shown in Figure 5.4. Figure 5.4 shows effects created by Shift-clicking with the Brush tool. Note that different brush sizes were used throughout the image and that at no point did I drag the mouse — every line shown was created by Shift-clicking with the Brush tool and then made more visually interesting with blending modes.

CROSS-REF   For more information on blending modes, see Chapter 14.

FIGURE 5.4

Look Ma! No dragging! Using the image on the left as our source, the image on the right is a simple tracing. This image was created entirely with the Brush tool, set to different colors, weights, and presets, and always using the Shift key to generate lines straight.

Click and drag your mouse

To create a line that runs parallel to either the top, bottom, or sides of your image — that is, a line that is either vertical or horizontal — with any of the paint or edit tools, Shift-drag with the tool. Unlike the click and click again method just discussed, which allows a straight line to be drawn at any angle, dragging with the Shift key allows you to draw a line of any length you want, running either horizontally or vertically — and that's it.

Of course, releasing the Shift key returns the line to free form, as illustrated in Figure 5.5, which shows a mix of straight, perpendicular, and free-form lines. For example, I started by pressing Shift to draw a vertical line — the spinal column. Then I moved the cursor out to where I wanted the first rib to end and released the Shift key to make the line hop out to that point. After that, I released the Shift key and the mouse so as not to draw anything, and returned the cursor to the spinal column — just a little further down from where the rib originally began. Then I Shift-clicked with the mouse to snap a slightly diagonal line back to the spinal column from the last point I drew anything. This gives a triangular appearance to the ribs.

After I finished the first side, I simply duplicated the layer, flipped it, and repositioned it to get the other side. The rest of the bones were accomplished using the Shift-click technique, and I free-handed the skull.

FIGURE 5.5

Periodically pressing and releasing the Shift key allowed me to define the ribs of my thin little friend.

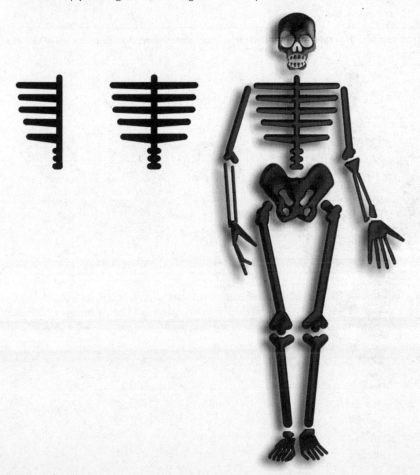

Remember one thing, however, as you create serial straight lines: When you press Shift to create a subsequent straight line, instead of a line going in the direction you want, you get a diagonal line connecting your last straight line with the starting point of your next one. You can avoid this by clicking once without the Shift key before clicking with the Shift key to make the next straight line. As long as you don't move the mouse on the non-Shift-accompanied click, the technique does not reveal itself in your resulting image. Photoshop's further tendency to snap to creating perpendicular lines is another potential problem, but you can use this to your advantage. For example, to create the lines shown in Figure 5.6, I dragged from right to left with the brush tool. I painted by intermittently pressing and releasing Shift as I dragged. In each case, pressing Shift snapped the line to the horizontal axis, the location of which was established by the beginning of the drag. After drawing the lines, I applied fill colors and then used the Watercolor filter to create a more visually interesting effect for this stylized still life.

CROSS-REF You can read more about applying fills in Chapter 6 and about Filters in Chapters 10, 11, and 12.

FIGURE 5.6

To create the lines shown here, I pressed and released Shift while dragging with the Brush tool. Fills and filters complete the finished effect.

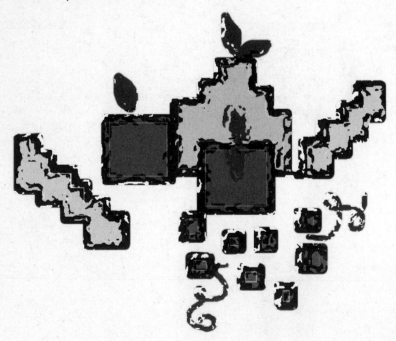

Painting with the Smudge tool

Many first-time Photoshop artists misuse the Smudge tool to soften color transitions, which is actually the purpose of the Blur tool. That's not to say that every tool in the Photoshop Toolbox has specific jobs and should never be used in new and different ways — feel free to experiment with non-traditional methods at any time. However, you should know that the Smudge tool is designed to smear colors by shoving them into each other. The process bears more resemblance to finger painting than to any traditional photographic-editing technique, especially if you have the tool set to a high Strength setting. At a low Strength, you can get subtle effects that may well allow you to do a little blending between areas of your image, especially if you zoom in tight on the area in question.

Returning to traditional use of the Smudge tool, in Photoshop, the performance of the Smudge tool depends in part on the settings of the Strength and Finger Painting controls in the Options bar. Here's what you need to know about these options:

- **Strength:** The Smudge tool works by stamping the image hundreds of times throughout the length of a brushstroke. The effect is that the color appears to get pushed across the length of the stroke. The Strength value determines the intensity of each stamping, so higher values push colors the farthest. A Strength setting of 100 percent equates to infinity, meaning the Smudge tool pushes a color from the beginning of your drag until you release your mouse button. Figure 5.7 shows three examples.

FIGURE 5.7

Three identical drags with the Smudge tool are subjected to different Strength settings: 35% (left), 50% (middle), and 65% (right). In each case, the smudge began at the same spot in the image and dragged for the same duration.

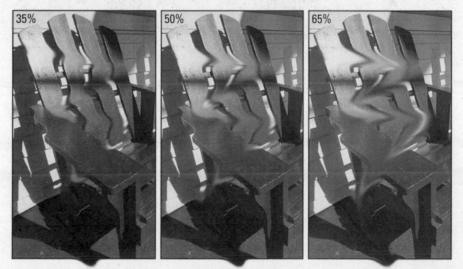

■ **Finger Painting:** In the distant Photoshop past, the people at Adobe called this effect *dipping*, which may accurately express the results of this option. When you select this option, the Smudge tool begins by applying a very small amount of the current foreground color, which it eventually blends in with the colors in the image. It's as if you dipped your finger in a color and then dragged it through an oil painting. Use the Strength setting to specify the amount of foreground color applied. If you turn on Finger Painting and set the Strength to 100 percent, the smudge tool behaves like the Brush tool. Figure 5.8 shows examples of Finger Painting with the Smudge tool when the foreground color is set to white.

FIGURE 5.8

This figure shows the same three drags pictured in Figure 5.7, but this time with the Finger Painting option turned on and the foreground color set to white.

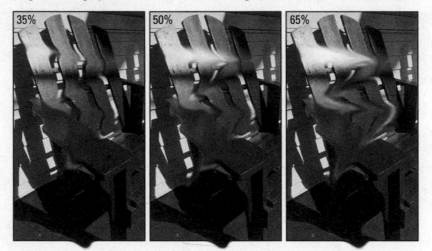

> **TIP** You can reverse the Finger Painting setting by pressing Alt (Option on the Mac) and dragging. If the option is off, Alt-dragging dips the tool into the foreground color. If Finger Painting is turned on, Alt-dragging smudges normally.

■ **Sample All Layers:** Selecting this option on the Options bar instructs the Smudge tool to grab colors in all visible layers and smudge them into the current layer. Whether the option is on or off, only the current layer is affected; the background and other layers remain intact. Figure 5.9 shows the effects this setting can produce. The "before image" image (left) features the Shift-click sketch of the Adirondack chair on the topmost layer, above the layer containing the original photograph. In the center panel, only the top layer's content is included in the smudging. The last panel shows how both layers get in on the act when the Sample All Layers option is checked.

FIGURE 5.9

See how colors from both layers get combined in the last frame.

Original two-layer image   Default smudge   Sample All Layers

Sponging color in and out

The Sponge tool is actually a really simple tool that works in one of two modes — Desaturate or Saturate. You choose the mode from the tool's Options bar, and then choose how much color the sponge removes or adds, respectively, by adjusting the Flow setting. When you pick one of the modes, this is what happens:

- **Desaturate:** When set to Desaturate, the Sponge tool reduces the saturation of the colors over which you drag. When you're editing a grayscale image, the tool reduces contrast.

- **Saturate:** If you select Saturate, the Sponge tool increases the saturation of the colors over which you drag or increases contrast in a grayscale image.

You can switch between the Desaturate and Saturate modes from the keyboard. Press Shift+Alt+D (Shift+Option+D on the Mac) to select the Desaturate option. Press Shift+Alt+S (Shift+Option+S on the Mac) for Saturate. No matter which mode you choose, higher Flow settings produce more dramatic results. Figure 5.10 shows an image that was both saturated and desaturated, with a Flow setting of 50.

> **TIP** You may find it helpful to turn on the Airbrush setting in the Options bar when using the Sponge tool (as well as the other toning tools, Dodge and Burn). This way, you can gradually build up effects. When you find a section of an image that needs more sponging than most, hold your cursor in place, watch Photoshop airbrush in the effect, and then move the cursor when you see that the desired effect has been achieved.

241

FIGURE 5.10

Sponge on, Sponge off. The Sponge applied to a rectangular selection on the left added color, and the Sponge applied to a rectangular selection on the right removed color.

Using the Color Replacement tool

The Color Replacement tool works by taking a color sample from the area in which you first click and then applying the foreground color to any area that matches the sample. For example, if you were trying to change the color of someone's clothing in a photo, you could use the Color Replacement tool to sample the unwanted color and then replace it with another color. This requires only that you set the Foreground color to the desired shade, and then activate the Color Replacement tool (found sharing a button with the Brush and Pencil tools) and drag it over the parts of your image where the offending color can be found. In Figure 5.12, a pair of blue jeans goes from denim blue to bright red (with an obvious stroke through the pant legs to make the change visible in black and white).

You control the behavior and sensitivity of the Color Replacement tool using the settings in the Options bar. Here's how they break down:

■ **Brush:** You don't get many brush choices when using the Color Replacement tool, as shown in Figure 5.11. You can set the Diameter, Hardness, and Spacing, and you can adjust the Angle and Roundness of the brush. You also can tinker with settings for your pen and tablet, if you're using one. You'll find these settings familiar if you've dabbled with the Brushes palette, specifically playing with Brush Presets. These options are covered later in this chapter.

FIGURE 5.11

You really need only a basic set of tools for establishing the size and shape of your Color Replacement tool brush.

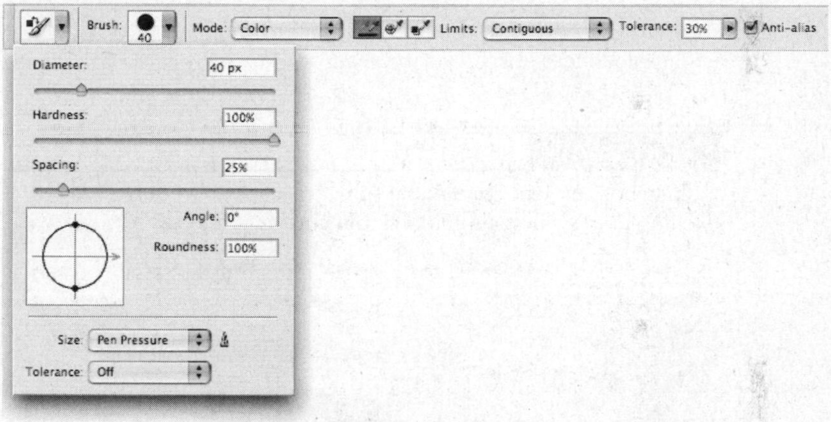

■ **Mode:** This setting tells the tool how to combine the newly painted pixels with the existing ones in your image. By default, the Mode option is set to Color, and you're generally going to want to leave it there. Because the Color mode affects hue and saturation, or the color values of an image, but doesn't affect luminance, or lightness values, it's generally the way to go. Your alternatives? Hue, Saturation, and Luminosity.

■ **Sampling:** The Sampling option lets you set how Photoshop decides what color you're replacing. The first (and default) option, Continuous, causes the tool to keep sampling colors, nonstop, for as long as you're using the tool.

Much more useful than Continuous is the second Sampling option, Once.. This sets the color on which you click when you begin your drag as the target of your replacement. This means that for as long as you continue dragging, only the original color is affected. The third and final Sampling setting is Background Swatch. Choosing this option tells the color replacement tool to alter only pixels in your image that share a color with the current background color. It can be a neat way of providing even more control over what the tool affects, but I still recommend you stick with the Once setting.

- **Limits:** The Limits option lets you set even more guidelines for determining which pixels the tool affects. Select Discontiguous to replace colors anywhere you drag with the tool. Select Contiguous to replace colors only in areas that are contiguous with, or connected by color to, the color currently under your cursor. The Find Edges option is designed to work the same way as Contiguous while better preserving edge details in the image.

- **Tolerance:** The Tolerance value determines how exact of a color match is required to deem a pixel suitable for replacement. Lower values replace colors similar to the sampled color, and higher values replace a broader range of colors. Most of your work with the Color Replacement tool lives or dies based on this setting, and getting it right can be a bit tricky. Keep in mind that a value that works for one section of color in an image may not be the correct setting to affect a lighter or darker section of the same color in the image.

- **Anti-alias:** This option lets you toggle anti-aliasing, or softening, on or off. It's almost certainly a good idea to keep it turned on.

FIGURE 5.12

In this photo by Terri Shadle, the subject's jeans go from blue to red. (Granted, it isn't as exciting in this grayscale printing, but you get the idea).

Undoing your damage

If you make a mistake in the course of painting an image, stop and choose Edit ➪ Undo or press Ctrl+Z (⌘+Z on the Mac). If this doesn't work, press Ctrl+Alt+Z (⌘+Option+Z on the Mac) to step back through a sequence of paint strokes.

CROSS-REF You also can undo a brushstroke by selecting a previous state in the History palette. As explained in Chapter 7, the History palette lists brushstrokes and other changes according to the tool you used to create them.

If you like the basic look of a brushstroke but you'd like to fade it back a bit, choose Edit ➪ Fade or press Ctrl+Shift+F (⌘+Shift+F on the Mac). The Fade command lets you reduce the Opacity or change the blend mode of the brushstroke you just finished painting. (If you have since clicked with another tool, the command may appear dimmed, indicating that you've lost your chance.) The Fade command is applicable to all paint and edit tools, as well as other operations in Photoshop, so you'll be seeing lots of it throughout this book.

Brush Size and Shape

Now that you have a feel for the purpose and basics of using the paint and edit tools, let's take a look at how you modify the performance of these tools. For example, every tool behaves differently according to the size and shape of your cursor, known in the case of the Brush tool, as the *brush tip*. Different styles of brush tips are known as *brush shapes*, or just plain *brushes* (not to be confused with the Brush tool, which people sometimes call "the brush" as well). The concept behind the brush shape is very simple. A big, round brush paints in broad strokes. A small, elliptical brush is useful for performing hairline adjustments. And if that's not enough — which it rarely is — there is a world of options in between these two extremes, plus an assortment of specialized brushes that come in handy in unique situations.

Selecting a brush shape

Provided that a paint or edit tool (other than the Color Replacement tool, which does not offer a full set of brushes from which to choose) is active, you can modify the brush shape in a number of ways in Photoshop:

- **Right-clicking:** Right-click anywhere in the image window (Control-click on the Mac) to display a small palette of preset brush shapes complete with a menu of additional options, as seen in Figure 5.13. Scroll through the list of brush shapes, click the one you want to use, and then press Enter or Return to hide the palette. You also can press Escape to hide the palette and leave the brush shape unchanged.

FIGURE 5.13

The Presets palette lets you select from a list of predefined brush shapes and load other ones from disk.

The Presets palette previews how the brush looks both when you click and when you drag. If your computer setup includes a pressure-sensitive drawing tablet, or if you've adjusted the Fade parameter in the brush's Shape Dynamics settings (as explained in the upcoming "Shape dynamics" section), the strokes appear to taper, as in the figure. Otherwise, they appear uniform. To dispense with the stroke previews, choose Large Thumbnail from the palette menu (displayed by clicking the right-pointing arrow button in the upper-right corner of the palette). To restore the stroke previews, choose Stroke Thumbnail.

- **Brushes palette:** Choose Window ➪ Brushes or press F5 to display the Brushes palette, or click the Brushes palette button on the dock, as shown in Figure 5.14. A Toggle the Brushes Palette button appears to the far right on the Options bar when any of the Brush tools are active.

   The palette displays a visual list of the default brush presets. The category list on the left provides an interface for changing the size, shape, and other brush attributes, such as angle roundness, scatter, and color dynamics.

To tinker with these settings, click the actual words, such as "Shape Dynamics," and the settings for that aspect of the brush settings appear on the right. To turn specific settings on (whether or not you tinker with them), place a check mark in the box to the right of the setting name.

TIP 　Simply mousing over the presets changes what appears in the preview pane at the bottom of the palette so you can quickly determine the result of a possible choice without necessarily committing to it first.

FIGURE 5.14

The Brushes palette appears as either a simple list of presets (shown on right side of palette) or with preset options (seen on the left) along *with* the presets. This combined view is known as Expanded View.

■ **Master Diameter:** With the Presets palette or Brushes palette onscreen, you can change the size of the brush by adjusting the Master Diameter value. Measured in pixels, this value represents the thickest stroke the brush will paint. (It can get thinner based on the Shape Dynamic settings, as I explain later in this chapter.) This means you're never locked into a preset brush diameter, even when painting with custom (nonround) brushes.

> **TIP**   Changing the brush diameter is so useful that you can do it from the keyboard. Press the left bracket key ([) to make the brush smaller. Press the right bracket key (]) to make the brush bigger. Keep an eye on the brush icon in the Options bar to see how much smaller or larger the brush diameter gets.

■ **Preset shortcuts:** You can cycle between presets even when no palette is visible. Press the comma (,) to toggle to the previous brush shape in the list. Press the period (.) to select the next brush shape. You also can press Shift+, (comma) to select the first brush shape in the list (1 pixel wide) and Shift+. (period) to select the last brush.

By default, your cursor outline reflects the active brush shape. If your cursor looks like a cross hair or tool icon instead, press Ctrl+K (⌘+K on the Mac) to open the Preferences dialog box, then press Ctrl+5 (⌘+5 on the Mac) for the Cursors panel, and select Brush Size from the Painting Cursors radio buttons. Now you can create a brush as big as 2,500 pixels in diameter and have your cursor grow accordingly.

> **TIP**   When you use a very small brush, four dots appear around the cursor perimeter, making the cursor easier to locate. If you need a little more help, press Caps Lock to access the more obvious cross-hair cursor.

Making your own brush shape

To create a custom brush shape, click Brush Tip Shape in the Brushes palette, which displays the options shown in Figure 5.15. Photoshop displays thumbnails for the predefined brushes on the right side of the palette, just above the settings for how the selected shape is applied. Select a brush to serve as a starting point for your custom creation, and then you can tweak the settings until you've created the brush you have in mind. These are the settings you can change:

■ **Diameter:** This option determines the width of the brush. If the brush shape is elliptical instead of circular, the Diameter value determines the longest dimension. You can type any value from 1 to 2,500 pixels.

> **CAUTION**   Brush shapes with diameters of 15 pixels or higher are too large to display accurately in the Options bar; the stroke preview at the bottom of the Brushes palette is accurate to no higher than 50 pixels. Therefore, you should essentially ignore the previews of such brushes, rather than assume that you've done something wrong with the setup.

■ **Flip X** and **Flip Y:** Select the Flip X option to flip the brush shape into a mirror image of itself. Select the Flip Y option to flip the brush shape upside-down. These options are most obvious when you're using one of the more detailed brushes or a brush preset you've created from an image.

FIGURE 5.15

To change the size, shape, and hardness of a brush, click Brush Tip Shape in the Brushes palette.

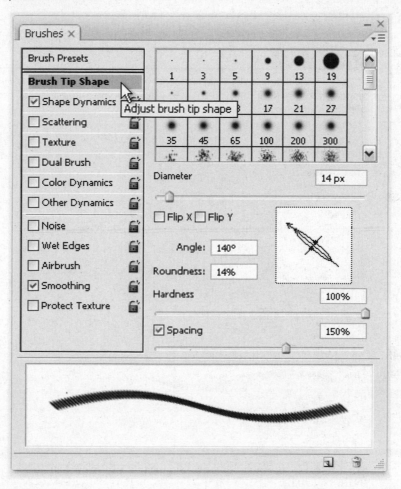

- **Angle:** This option pivots a brush shape on its axis. Unless the brush is elliptical, though, you won't see a difference. So it's best to first adjust the Roundness value and then adjust the Angle. You can use the Angle text box to enter a value, or as shown in Figure 5.16, you can drag the arrow on the ellipse in the box to the right of the Angle and Roundess settings.

- **Roundness:** Type a Roundness value of less than 100 percent to create an elliptical brush shape. The value modifies the height of the brush as a percentage of the Diameter value, so a Roundness of 50 percent results in a short, fat brush.

> **TIP** Not only can you adjust the Angle of the brush dynamically by dragging the gray arrow inside the box to the right of the Angle and Roundness options, but you can drag the handles on either side of the black circle to make the brush shape elliptical, as demonstrated in Figure 5.16. Drag the arrow tip to angle the brush, or click anywhere in the white box to move the arrow to that point.

FIGURE 5.16

Drag the black handles and gray arrow to change the roundness and angle of the brush, respectively. The Roundness and Angle values update automatically, as does the preview of the brushstroke at the bottom of the palette.

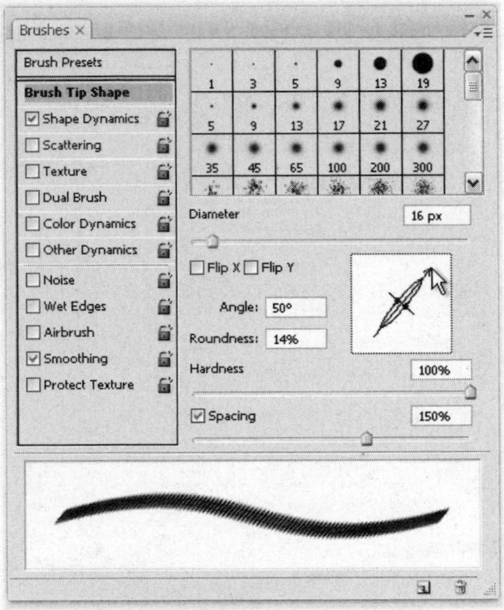

- **Hardness:** Except when using the Pencil tool, brushes are always anti-aliased. You can further soften the edges of a brush by dragging the Hardness slider bar away from 100 percent. The softest setting, 0 percent, gradually tapers the brush from a single solid-color pixel at its center to a ring of transparent pixels around the brush's perimeter. Figure 5.17 shows how low Hardness percentages expand the size of a 200-pixel brush beyond the Diameter value (as demonstrated by the examples in the bottom row). Even a 100-percent hard-brush shape expands slightly because it is anti-aliased. The Hardness setting is ignored when you use the Pencil tool.

> **TIP** Like Diameter, Hardness is one of those settings that you need regular access to. So the ever-helpful Photoshop lets you change the Hardness from the keyboard. Press Shift+[(Shift+left bracket) to make the brush softer; press Shift+] (Shift+right bracket) to make the brush harder. Both shortcuts work in 25-percent increments. For example, you have to press Shift+] four times to go from 0 percent Hardness to 100 percent.

FIGURE 5.17

A 200-pixel brush as it appears when set to each of four Hardness percentages. In the bottom row, the brushes are on a separate layer and a black fringe is added so you can see the effective diameter of each Hardness value.

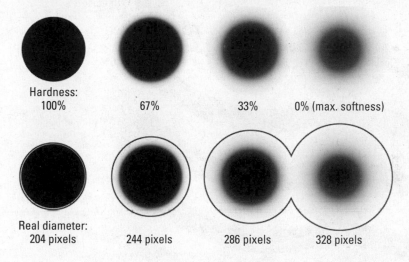

Hardness:
100%   67%   33%   0% (max. softness)

Real diameter:
204 pixels   244 pixels   286 pixels   328 pixels

- **Spacing:** As you paint in Photoshop, the brush blasts out a continuous stream of colored spots. The Spacing option controls how frequently the spots are emitted, measured as a percentage of the brush shape. For example, suppose the Diameter of a brush is 40 pixels and the Spacing is set to 25 percent (the default setting for all predefined brushes). For every 10 pixels (25 percent of 40) you drag with the Brush tool, Photoshop lays down a 40-pixel-wide spot of color. A Spacing of 1 percent provides the most coverage but also slows down the performance of the tool. If you deselect the Spacing option, the effect of the tool is wholly dependent on the speed at which you drag; this can be useful for creating splotchy or oscillating lines. Figure 5.18 shows examples.

TIP You may see ridges begin to appear at the default Spacing value of 25 percent, especially when painting with a mouse. If you notice lumps in your brush strokes, lower the Spacing to 15 percent, which ensures a good mix of speed and smoothness. When using a soft-edged brush, lower Spacing values result in a denser, fatter stroke, and higher values result in a lighter, thinner stroke. High Spacing values are great for creating dotted lines.

After you edit a brush, you can save the brush for later use by clicking the tiny page icon at the bottom of the palette; it's called Create New Brush, which displays as a screen tip if you hover your mouse over the button. In the resulting dialog box, Photoshop suggests a name, which you can then change to something that'll remind you of the brush's purpose and/or appearance. To save a brush without being asked to name it, Alt-click the Page icon (Option-click on the Mac). Whether or not you name it, Photoshop stores the brush with your program preferences so that it's preserved between editing sessions.

FIGURE 5.18

Examples of lines drawn with the Brush tool subject to different Spacing values. Values greater than 100 percent are useful for creating dotted-line effects.

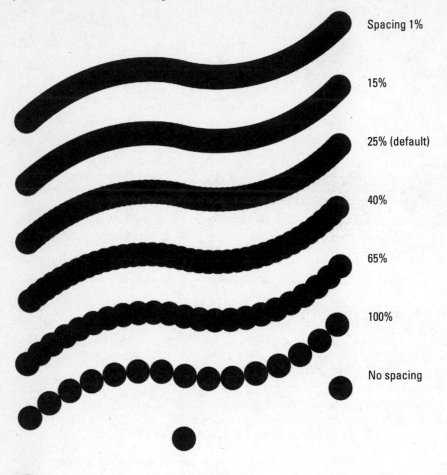

Spacing 1%

15%

25% (default)

40%

65%

100%

No spacing

CAUTION   If you delete the preferences file (as discussed in Chapter 2), you lose your custom brushes. To ensure that your custom brushes are saved in case you delete the preferences file or for use on another machine, choose Save Brushes from the Palette menu. See the section "Saving and loading brush sets" for more information.

To delete a brush from the list, switch back to the Brush Presets view and drag the brush to the trash icon at the bottom of the palette.

Creating your own specialized brushes

Photoshop allows you to not only modify the size and roundness of a brush, but define your own completely customized brushes as well. Start by making a new image and doodling a bit with your brush tip — just to test and experiment with the procedure. Doodle a bit with the brush, and don't worry about creating the perfect custom brush just yet. Next, use the rectangular marquee tool to select the doodle. You don't have to be particularly careful; just select the general area around the doodle, as shown in Figure 5.19. Photoshop is smart enough to distinguish the confines of the brush from its background.

CROSS-REF For more information on the Rectangular Marquee tool, see Chapter 8.

Next, choose the Define Brush Preset command from the Edit menu. Photoshop invites you to give your brush a name; if you're not feeling inspired, just press Enter or Return and accept the default name, Sampled Brush #1. A name is a good idea, though, if you can come up with one — "Sampled Brush #1" isn't going to mean much to you a week from now, and its thumbnail (which appears in the Brushes palette) may not tell the whole story as to why you created the preset, either.

FIGURE 5.19

After selecting a doodle against a white background, choose Edit ➪ Define Brush Preset and type a name to turn the doodle into a custom brush.

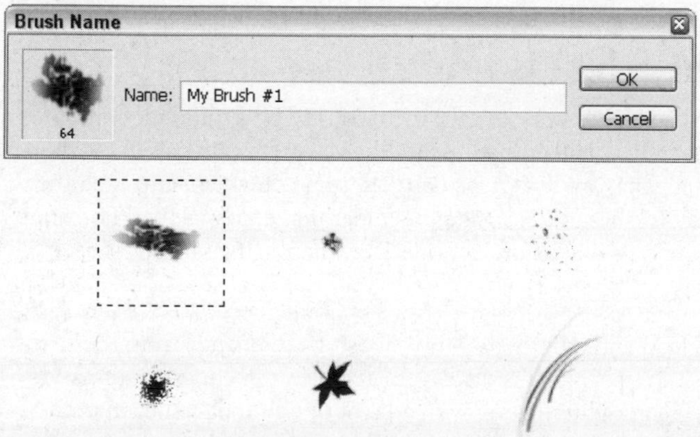

After you define a custom brush, you can tweak it just like any other brush inside the Brush Tip Shape panel of the Brushes palette. You can adjust the Diameter, Angle, and Roundness (height versus width) of your new brush. The only option that appears dimmed is Hardness; you have to accept the sharpness of the brush as it was originally defined (so if you want a very soft or very hard brush, start with one before you begin doodling). A custom brush even grows and shrinks according to stylus pressure if you're using a graphic tablet, or you can use the left and right bracket ([ ]) keys.

To restore any brush to its original size, click the Use Sample Size button on the Presets panel, shown in Figure 5.20.

FIGURE 5.20

The Use Sample Size button returns a brush to its original size settings.

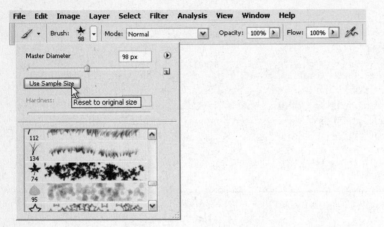

Saving and loading brush sets

After you define a handful of brushes, you may want to save them for use on a different computer or to avoid losing them in the event of any problem that might require you to reinstall Photoshop. Photoshop saves these brush groups in what are known as *libraries,* some of which ship with the software, and are found in the Presets/Brushes folder inside the folder that contains the Photoshop application. Brush libraries have the *.abr* file extension, as you'll see when you go to save one of your own.

You can save brush sets — as well as load and edit them — by choosing commands from the Brushes palette menu when the Brush Presets panel is displayed. You also can choose commands from the Presets palette that you get when right-clicking with a paint or edit tool (other than the Color Replacement tool) in the image window. You can manage libraries (those you've saved and those that ship with Photoshop) by choosing Edit ➪ Preset Manager, which is shown in Figure 5.21 with the Brushes panel at the forefront. If you're already working in the Preset Manager, press Ctrl+1 (⌘+1 on the Mac) to get to the Brushes panel.

Choose Edit ➪ Preset Manager to display the central headquarters for loading, saving, and editing brush sets.

By default, the Brushes palette displays a list of nearly 70 predefined brushes, including both elliptical and custom varieties. You can't delete this brush set, but you can prevent brushes you don't use from taking up space in the palette. You also can load or create a different set, combine two or more sets, and add or delete brushes from your custom brush sets. Here's the drill:

■ **Save a brush set:** To save all brushes currently displayed in the Brushes palette, choose Save Brushes from the palette menu. If you want to save only some of the brushes as a set, however, choose Edit ➪ Preset Manager. Shift-click the brushes you want to save (picking them from the displayed brushes in the Preset Manager dialog box), and then click the Save Set button. As it's likely that you'll want to grab brushes that don't happen to appear together in the displayed group of presets, you can make non-contiguous selections by holding the Ctrl key (Windows) or the ⌘ key (Mac) as you click the brushes you want to save.

Regardless of where you initiate the save, Photoshop takes you to the Save dialog box, where you can name your brush set. By default, brushes are saved in the Presets/Brushes folder. The next time you start Photoshop, your new brush set appears on the Brushes palette menu along with other available sets.

■ **Use a different brush set:** If you want to put the current brush set away and use a different set, choose Replace Brushes from the Brushes palette menu and select the brush set you want to use. Alternatively, click the arrowhead in the upper-right corner of the Preset Manager dialog box to display a similar menu, and then choose Replace Brushes from that menu.

■ **Load multiple brush sets:** You can keep multiple brush sets active if you want. After loading the first set, choose Load Brushes from the Brushes palette menu or click Load in the Preset Manager dialog box. Photoshop appends the second brush set onto the first. If you want to keep using the two sets together, you may want to save them as a new, custom brush set. If you're picking a brush set from the list that appears at the bottom of the palette menu (such as Dry Media Brushes or Faux Finish Brushes), you are asked if you want to replace the current set with the newly selected one or if you want to append the new set.

■ **Delete a brush:** To delete a brush from the current brush set, select it from the Brush Presets panel of the Brushes palette and click the trash icon. Or choose Delete Brush from the palette menu. This command (and the trash icon) are dimmed if the brush preset is one of the ones that came with Photoshop — it's only those you've made that can be deleted.

TIP   Want to give a bunch of brushes the axe? Cut them loose through the Preset Manager dialog box. Select the brushes you no longer want, and then click Delete.

■ **Restore default brushes:** To return to the default Photoshop brush set, choose Reset Brushes from the menu in the palette or the dialog box. You then have the option of either replacing the existing brushes with the default brushes or simply adding them to the end of the palette.

■ **Rename a brush:** If you want to rename a brush, select it in the Preset Manager dialog box and click Rename. Or, even easier, double-click the brushstroke in the Brush Presets panel of the Brushes palette — a dialog box appears, showing the current name, which you can replace by typing the new name.

CAUTION   If you want your new brush names to live in perpetuity, resave the brush set. Otherwise, the names revert to their previous labels when and if you replace the brush set.

Brush Dynamics

For a long time now, Photoshop has allowed you to vary the size, opacity, and color of paint according to input from a pressure-sensitive drawing tablet. Available from companies such as Wacom (www.wacom.com), pressure-sensitive drawing tablets respond to how hard you press on the stylus (the pen that is drawn across the surface of the tablet), as well as the angle of the stylus and other attributes.

Even if you don't have a tablet, Photoshop permits mouse users to enjoy much of the same flexibility as their stylus-wielding colleagues. Whether you use a stylus, a mouse, or even a finger on a notebook trackpad (and my hat's off to you if that's how you're drawing and painting), you can introduce an element of spontaneity into what seems at times like an absolute world of computer imaging.

Photoshop calls these imaginative options *brush dynamics*, and they open up lots of opportunities for faking pressure sensitivity. For example, you can make a brush shape twirl as you paint. You can add noise to the edges of a stroke. You can spray shapes, add texture, combine brushes, or even paint in rainbows. And most of the settings work every bit as well with, say, the Sponge tool as they do with the Brush tool. You may find this tinkering and experimenting with brush dynamics to be rather addictive — and the things you discover as you play will come back to you when you're editing or creating an image later, so it's time well spent.

Brush dynamic basics

To access Photoshop's brush dynamics when a paint or edit tool (other than the Color Replacement tool) is active, open the Brushes palette (press F5 if it's hidden) and be sure the Brush Tip Shape option is chosen. This displays the Shape Dynamics option, along with 10 additional options — Scattering, Texture, Dual Brush, Color Dynamics, Other Dynamics, and another group (below the horizontal divider) that apply special effects to the brush settings in place. As you click each option by name, settings for that option appear on the right side of the palette.

NOTE Note that all check boxes and options are available when using the Brush tool, but they come and go for the other paint and edit tools. For example, the Wet Edges option is unavailable when using the Pencil tool, Color Dynamics is dimmed when using the Dodge and Burn tools, and so on. And for the Eraser, which many users rightly consider to be a painting *and* editing tool, many of the brush options are available, making it quite powerful. Even with the lack of options for some tools, the sheer number of options available for even the most limited of the edit tools verges on fantastic, especially when compared with older versions of Photoshop. Also, each tool observes an independent set of defaults. So activating, say, Shape Dynamics, Texture, and Smoothing for the Brush tool does not turn them on for other tools. However, they will again be turned on the next time you return to the Brush tool.

If you want to save a group of brush dynamics for use with a variety of tools, click the Page icon along the bottom of the Brushes palette. Brush dynamics are considered part of a saved brush shape and transfer from one tool to another. To save a group of brush dynamics for use with a single tool, visit the Tool Presets palette (Window ⇨ Tool Presets) and choose Create New Tool Preset from the palette menu. It's equivalent to designing a custom tool that you can select from the Options bar, as discussed in Chapter 2.

TIP As you experiment with these options, don't forget to keep one eye on the big stroke preview at the bottom of the palette. It really is useful, especially when trying out settings that you haven't used before or combining options to achieve specific effects. Of course, there's no substitute for actually using the brush settings after you've set them, so be prepared to have to do some additional tinkering if you find that the brush settings, whether you've saved them or not, need some further adjustment.

Shape dynamics

Inside the Brushes palette, click the Shape Dynamics option — the name, not the check box — to display the panel of options illustrated in Figure 5.22. Notice that the panel is divided into three sections, which start with the words Size Jitter, Angle Jitter, and Roundness Jitter. These options permit you to vary the diameter, angle, and roundness, respectively, of the brush over the course of a single stroke. But the repetition of the word "Jitter" may be misleading. It implies (to many users) that each group of options is related to jittering — Photoshop's word for random brush shape fluctuations — when in fact jittering is a minor element of shape dynamics.

FIGURE 5.22

The Shape Dynamics panel, with a drawing made with the displayed brush settings

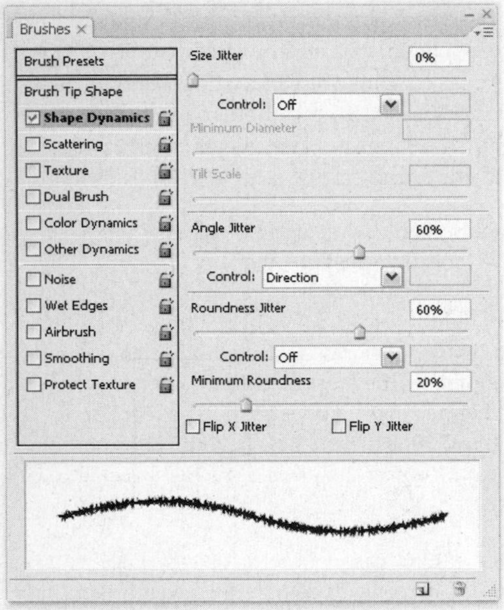

The diameter settings

The first group of options controls the thickness of the brushstroke. The most important of these is the Control pop-up menu, which links the diameter of the brush to one of several variables. If you own a pressure-sensitive tablet, the most obvious setting is Pen Pressure, which is the default. This turns the brush into a traditional, pressure-sensitive painting tool, growing when you bear down on the stylus and shrinking with you let up.

NOTE Three settings — Pen Pressure, Pen Tilt, and Stylus Wheel — require compatible hardware. If your only pointing device is a standard mouse, as is typical, selecting one of these options displays a triangular warning icon. This is Photoshop's way of telling you that, although you are welcome to select the option, it isn't really going to work. If you get the message in error — say, you get a warning for Pen Pressure even though you have a tablet installed — try clicking with the stylus on the Brushes palette. If that doesn't work, open the control panel or utility that manages the tablet to make sure the tablet is properly installed.

CROSS-REF As it turns out, you can take advantage of the Pen Pressure option even if you don't own a pressure-sensitive tablet. In Photoshop, you can simulate pressure by stroking a paint or edit tool along a path. For complete information, see Chapter 8.

In addition to Pen Pressure, the Control pop-up menu lets you select among the following options:

- **Off:** Select this option to turn off the capability to vary the thickness of the brushstroke. You can still add random variations to the thickness using the Size Jitter value.

- **Fade:** This option works every bit as well whether you use a mouse or tablet. Select Fade to reduce the size of the brush over the course of the drag, and then type a value in the option box on the right to specify the distance over which the fading should occur, enabling you to mimic painting with an actual paintbrush, which will run out of paint over the course of a stroke. This fading distance is measured in steps — that is, the number of spots of color the brush plops down before reducing the size of the brush to its minimum (defined by the Minimum Diameter setting). The default value is 25, which means 25 spots of color. Exactly how long such a stroke is in, say, inches, depends on the Diameter and the Spacing values in the Brush Tip Shape panel. In other words, be prepared to experiment.

  The Fade option can be most useful in the creation of a specular reflection, or in layman's terms, a sparkle. Figure 5.23 shows before and after versions of an image to which I applied a sparkle, or glow, using a series of strokes with a soft brush. The horizontal and vertical brush stroke settings use a diameter of 20 pixels and a Fade value of 100 steps. The diagonal brush stroke settings cut those values in half. To make each stroke, I clicked in the center and Shift-clicked farther out (creating a straight line).

FIGURE 5.23

Our subject gets his iris brightened (middle) and a twinkle added (right) using the Fade setting.

■ **Pen Tilt:** The tilt of a pen is its angle with respect to the tablet, as illustrated in Figure 5.24. Straight up and down, the pen communicates no tilt; at a severe angle, the pen communicates maximum tilt. When you set the Control option to Pen Tilt, you do two things. First, you vary the size of the brush according to pressure, just as you do when using Pen Pressure. Second, you add an element of vertical scaling so that the brush shape is oblong during a tilt. This scaling is defined by the Tilt Scale slider. All in all, it's an interesting idea, but for my money, Pen Tilt works more predictably when applied to roundness.

FIGURE 5.24

Most tablets are sensitive not only to the amount of pressure you apply to your stylus, but also to the angle of the stylus relative to the tablet.

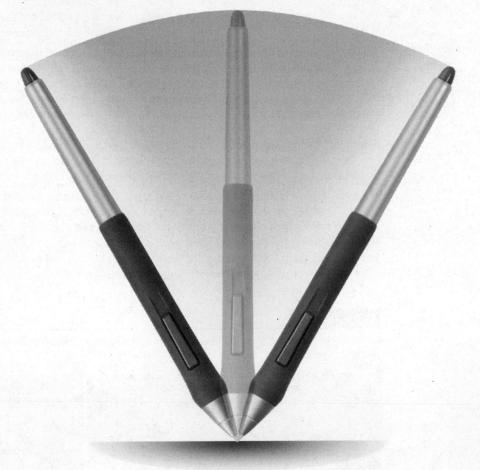

■ **Stylus Wheel:** If tablet owners account for 10 percent of Photoshop users, airbrush owners account for about 1 percent of tablet users. That's still enough people to populate a small town, so Photoshop might as well support them. Figure 5.25 shows Wacom's Intuos 3 airbrush, with stylus wheel. Unlike the scroll wheels included with many PC mice — which are exceptionally useful for scrolling Web pages and Word documents — the wheel on an airbrush locks into position. This means you can nudge it higher or lower and leave it there. Although typically associated with properties such as Flow (which you can set from the Other Dynamics panel), the airbrush wheel is surprisingly useful for diameter as well. Move the wheel up, and the brush gets thick and stays thick; move the wheel down, and you lock in a fine line, all in the middle of painting a brushstroke. This all sounds great, so is there a downside? Why, yes! A Wacom airbrush can cost upwards of $100, not including the tablet. So it's not a spur-of-the-moment gift for most of us.

FIGURE 5.25

The stylus wheel can be permanently set to increase or decrease the flow of 'paint,' mimicking a traditional airbrush.

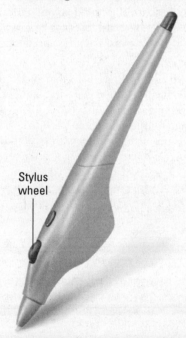

Stylus
wheel

Accompanying the Control pop-up menu are three slider bars:

■ **Minimum Diameter:** Use this option to determine the thinnest that a brushstroke can go. You can go as low as 1 percent.

■ **Tilt Scale:** Available only when you set the Control option to Pen Tilt, this setting stretches the height of the brush to make it elliptical when you tilt the stylus and attempts to mimic the way painting with a real brush feels. You can do this just as well with the roundness options, though, so you may not use this setting — then again, you may like it. It's up to you and your personal preferences.

■ **Size Jitter:** Use this slider to add an element of randomness to the thickness of a brush-stroke. It doesn't matter whether you use a mouse or a stylus; the brush jitters every bit as well either way. Higher values produce a wider range of jitter. Keep an eye on the preview at the bottom of the palette to get a sense of what different settings will do.

Angle and roundness

Now that you understand the diameter settings, the angle and roundness settings are pretty simple stuff. But to confirm your knowledge and make sure that we're all on the same page, here's how they work:

■ **Angle Control:** As with diameter, you can link the angle of the brush to such variables as Pen Pressure, Pen Tilt, and Stylus Wheel. More pressure or tilt equals more rotation of the brush. Naturally, the changes show up best with elliptical or asymmetrical brushes. You also can link the angle to Fade, which rotates the brush over the course of a specific number of steps, and then returns the brush to its normal angle (as specified in the Brush Tip Shape panel).

But this Control pop-up menu adds two more settings: Direction and Initial Direction. The first rotates the brush according to the direction of your drag. A horizontal drag is considered the normal angle; when dragging vertically, the brush rotates 90 degrees. For maximum effect, after setting this option to Direction, go to the Brush Tip Shape panel and set the Angle value to 90 degrees (or something close) with an elliptical brush. Then raise the Spacing value to something higher than 100 percent.

Meanwhile, the Initial Direction option rotates the brush according to the very start of your drag and then locks it into position. It's a nice idea, but the angle is locked down about 2 pixels into your drag, which means Photoshop is aware of your initial direction before you are.

■ **Angle Jitter:** This option rotates the brush randomly as you paint. As always, be sure to adjust the roundness of the brush so you can see the randomness at work.

■ **Roundness Control:** Set this option to Fade to reduce the roundness to its minimum over the course of a specified number of steps. You also can associate the roundness with Pen Pressure, Pen Tilt, or Stylus Wheel. Of these, Pen Tilt makes by far the most sense to me because that's what Pen Tilt does in real life.

■ **Minimum Roundness:** This value determines the minimum roundness or maximum flat-ness of the brush available to the Control and Jitter settings. If the Control option is set to Off and the Roundness Jitter is 0 percent, the Minimum Roundness slider is dimmed.

■ **Roundness Jitter:** Use this option to introduce random variations in roundness to your brushstroke.

- **Flip X Jitter** and **Flip Y Jitter:** Two check boxes at the bottom of the Shape Dynamics panel give you the ability to flip the jitter on its x-axis, y-axis, or both at once, much like you can flip the brush shape. Flipping the jitter on its axis may be more control than most of us will ever need, but it was nice of Photoshop's designers to make this option available.

Additional brush dynamics

For many, the Shape Dynamics settings are enough. They certainly permit you to achieve an enormous range of effects. But if you're feeling ambitious, you can venture much deeper. Fortunately, the other panels of options — Scattering, Texture, and so on — follow the same logic we've seen thus far, and you'll find they're quite simple to deal with, based on your having looked at the Shape Dynamics settings already.

Figure 5.26 demonstrates several dynamic permutations as applied to the Scattered Leaves predefined custom brush. Here's how these options work:

- **Scattering:** Highlight the Scattering option to spread the position of the spots of color around the brushstroke. When using a custom brush, such as Scattered Leaves in Figure 5.26, the effect is like spraying a pattern of images. Raise the Scatter value to increase the spread. Select Both Axes to scatter the brush spots along the stroke as well as perpendicularly to it. Use the Control pop-up menu to link it to stylus pressure or some other variable. Finally, use the Count options to increase the population of brush spots.

FIGURE 5.26

Several brush dynamics are applied to various Brush presets — Dune Grass, Scattered Maple Leaves, and Scattered Leaves. By varying the Scatter value, the preset's scattering effect can be heightened (bottom sample) or tightened (middle example).

Dune grass
Scatter 300%
Fade 10
Count 4
Count jitter 75%

Scattered maple leaves
Scatter 70%
Fade 50
Count 1
Count jitter 100%

Scattered leaves
Scatter 400%
Fade 200
Count 2
Count jitter 50%
Fade 8

■ **Texture:** Select this option to apply a texture to a brushstroke, useful for conveying a surface such as paper or canvas. After selecting a predefined texture, set the Scale and Depth values to determine the size and degree of texture applied. Use the Mode option to define how brush and texture mix. (You can find out more about modes in the "Brush Modes" section near the end of this chapter, but for now, just experiment with an eye on the preview.)

If you want to vary the depth of texture throughout a stroke, turn on the Texture Each Tip option. Then use the Control option to vary the depth according to, say, stylus pressure or add some random Depth Jitter.

■ **Dual Brush:** The Dual Brush panel lets you mix two brushes together. Select the second brush from the list of thumbnails, and use the Mode option to specify how the brushes intermix. You also can throw in settings such as Spacing, Scatter, and Count, all of which affect the second brush. Figure 5.27 shows another example, complete with settings in the Brushes palette. Notice how by mixing a standard round brush with one of Photoshop's predefined Dry Brush options, a complex brush that imparts its own texture is generated.

FIGURE 5.27

The look of chalk is achieved with a Brush. A larger-sized brush, with the Flow reduced, created the look of the blackboard having been erased before the drawing was done. Neat, huh?

- **Color Dynamics:** Use these options to vary the color of the stroke between the foreground and background colors depending on a fade or stylus pressure. You also can apply random changes to the hue, saturation, and brightness. The final slider bar, Purity, increases or decreases the saturation of colors throughout the brushstroke.

- **Other Dynamics:** The final set of brush dynamics permits you to associate the opacity, strength, flow, or exposure of the brush, depending on what tool you're using. You can find a discussion of each of these attributes in more detail in the section "Opacity and Strength, Flow and Exposure." If you happen to own an airbrush, settings such as the Flow and Exposure are what the wheel was originally designed for.

> **TIP** You'll notice that you have the ability to lock the settings you choose in the various brush dynamics panels. Click the Lock icon next to a panel name in the Brushes palette to toggle the lock option on or off. When a panel is locked, Photoshop retains the panel's settings even if you select a new brush preset that would normally contain different settings.

Noise, Wet Edges, and the rest

The list along the left side of the Brushes palette ends with five options that you can use to add highlights and constraints to your brushstrokes. Not all options work with all tools — none is compatible with the Smudge tool, for example — but when available, they're as effective as they are easy to use. And they work equally well with a mouse or a tablet.

- **Noise:** This option randomizes the pixels along the edge of a brushstroke. Because the option affects only the edge, softer brushes result in more noise. The middle line in Figure 5.28 shows an example.

- **Wet Edges:** When you select the Wet Edges option, the brush creates a translucent line with darkened edges, much as if you were painting with watercolors. Soft brush shapes produce more naturalistic effects. The final example in Figure 5.28 shows a brushstroke with wet edges, painted in black.

- **Airbrush:** This option duplicates the Airbrush icon in the Options bar. When turned on, paint builds up even when you hold the cursor in place, as if you were spraying color from a real airbrush. The Airbrush option is not available when using the pencil tool or any of the three focus tools (Blur, Sharpen, and Smudge).

- **Smoothing:** If you have difficulty drawing smooth lines and curves, turn this option on to even out the rough spots. It slows down Photoshop's tracking time a little, but it may be worth it in many cases. Adobe recommends this option when using a stylus, but I've found it most helpful when using optical mice, which are notoriously bad at tracking evenly on patterned surfaces, such as wood tabletops.

- **Protect Texture:** If you plan to paint lots of textured lines and you want your textures to match, select this option. It maintains a consistent pattern from one brushstroke to the next. The effect can be subtle, but I usually advise working with this option turned on.

FIGURE 5.28

Three lines are painted with the brush tool — the left without dynamics (soft), the middle with Noise, and the right with Wet Edges.

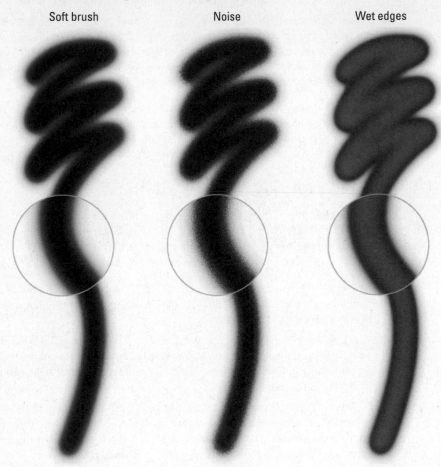

Soft brush   Noise   Wet edges

Undoing pressure-sensitive lines

In the old days, pressure-sensitive lines were a pain to undo. Because a stylus is so sensitive to gradual pressure, you can unwittingly let up and repress the stylus during what you perceive as a single drag. If, after doing so, you decide you don't like the line and press Ctrl+Z (⌘+Z on the Mac), Photoshop deletes only the last portion of the line because it detected a release midway.

This is why it's a good idea to get in the habit of using Ctrl+Alt+Z (⌘+Option+Z on the Mac). Each time you press this shortcut, you take another step back in the history of your image, permitting you to eliminate every bit of a line regardless of how many times you let up on the stylus.

CROSS-REF See Chapter 7 for complete information on Photoshop's multiple undos.

TIP Save time, aggravation, and your remaining hair by creating a new layer (by pressing Ctrl+Shift+N on the PC or ⌘+Shift+N on the Mac) before you paint with or without a stylus. This allows you to refine your lines and erase them without harming the original appearance of your image. (You can do this without layers using the history brush, explained in Chapter 7, but a relatively old-fashioned layer tends to be less trouble.)

Opacity and Strength, Flow and Exposure

Another way to change the performance of a paint or edit tool is to adjust the Opacity and Flow values, which also go by the terms Strength and Exposure, respectively, depending on the tool you're using. When available, these controls appear in the Options bar. Regardless of which setting you want to change, you click the triangle to display a slider bar, drag the slider to raise or lower the value, and then press Enter or Return. Alternatively, you can double-click the option box, type a value, and press Enter.

Here's a look at how these options work:

- **Opacity:** The Opacity value determines the translucency of colors applied with the Brush or Pencil tool. The option is available also when using the Gradient tool, Paint Bucket tool, History Brush tool, both stamp tools, and the Eraser tool, all of which I discuss in future chapters. At 100 percent, the applied colors appear opaque, completely covering the image behind them. (Exceptions occur when using the Brush tool with Wet Edges active, which produces a translucent stroke, and when applying Mode options, discussed in the "Brush Modes" section.) At lower settings, the applied colors mix with the existing colors in the image.

TIP You can change the opacity of brushstrokes or edits that you just applied by choosing Edit ➪ Fade or pressing Ctrl+Shift+F (⌘+Shift+F on the Mac). Then drag the Opacity slider in the Fade dialog box. While you're in the dialog box, you can apply one of Photoshop's brush modes to further change how the modified pixels blend with the original ones.

- **Strength:** When using the Blur or Sharpen tool, the Opacity option changes to Strength. The value determines the degree to which the tool changes the focus of the image; 1 percent is the minimum, and 100 percent is the maximum. Strength also appears when using the Smudge tool, in which case it governs the distance the tool drags colors in the image.

Another difference between Strength and Opacity is that the default Opacity value for each tool when you begin using Photoshop is 100 percent, but the default Strength value is 50 percent. Whether Strength is stronger than Opacity or these tools merely happen to know their own Strength is uncertain; but 50 percent is the baseline.

■ **Flow:** The Flow option appears when using the Brush, Sponge, and Eraser tools, both stamp tools, and the History Brush. Although it is always accompanied by the Airbrush icon, you can use Flow and Airbrush independently. The Flow value controls the opacity of each spot of color a tool delivers. So as a tool lays each spot of color onto the previous spot, the spots mix together and become more opaque. This means three things. First, a particular Flow setting produces a more opaque line than an equivalent Opacity setting. In Figure 5.29, for example, a Flow value of 50 percent comes in slightly darker than an Opacity value of 50 percent. Second, Flow results in a progressive effect that compounds as a brushstroke overlaps itself, also demonstrated in the figure. Third, because Flow works on a spot-by-spot basis, you can increase or decrease the opacity of a line further by lowering or raising, respectively, the Spacing value in the Brush Tip Shape panel.

When using the Brush, History Brush, Stamp, and Eraser tools, you can combine Opacity and Flow values to achieve unique effects. You also can add the Airbrush, which compounds Flow further by adding spots of color when you slow down a brushstroke or hold the cursor still.

■ **Exposure:** Available when using the Dodge or Burn tool, Exposure controls how much the tools lighten or darken the image, respectively. As with Flow, Exposure compounds when you corner or overlap a brushstroke, and it includes an airbrush variation. A setting of 100 percent applies the maximum amount of lightening or darkening, which is still far short of either absolute white or black. As with Strength, the default is 50 percent.

> **TIP**   You can change the Opacity, Strength, or Exposure setting for the active tool in 10 per-cent increments by pressing a number key on the keyboard or keypad. Press 1 to change the setting to 10 percent, press 2 for 20 percent, and so on, all the way up to 0 for 100 percent. If you want to change the Opacity, Strength, or Exposure setting in 1 percent increments, just press two keys in a row. Press 4 twice for 44 percent, 0 and 7 for 7 percent, and so on. This works whether or not the Options bar is visible. Get in the habit of using the number keys, and you'll thank yourself later.

Changing the Flow value on the fly is trickier but still possible. When the Sponge tool is active, Flow works just like Opacity: Type a number to change the value in 10 percent increments; type two numbers to enter a specific value. But what about the Brush tool and others that offer both Opacity and Flow? Typing a number changes the Opacity value *unless* the Airbrush icon is active, in which case typing a number changes Flow. If the Airbrush is turned off, press Shift plus a number key to change the Flow value. When the Airbrush is turned on, pressing Shift plus a number key changes the Opacity value.

FIGURE 5.29

Here you can see the difference between Opacity, which controls an entire brushstroke (left), and Flow, which affects individual spots of paint (middle). Tighter Spacing values also heighten the effect of Flow (right).

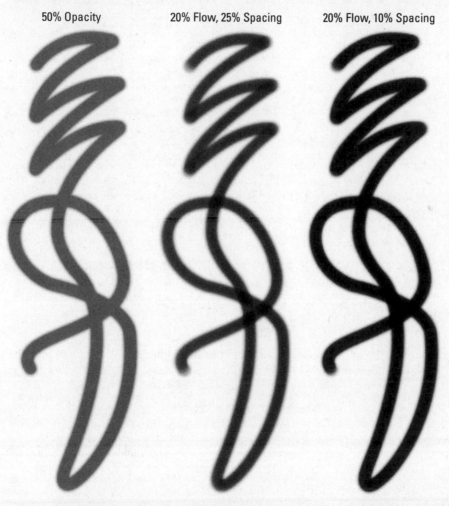

50% Opacity   20% Flow, 25% Spacing   20% Flow, 10% Spacing

Brush Modes

When certain painting or editing tools are active, the Options bar provides access to Photoshop's brush modes. The brush modes control how the colors applied by the tool mix with existing colors inside an image or layer. Figure 5.30 shows which brush modes are available when you select various tools.

With the exception of the specialized modes available for the Dodge, Burn, and Sponge tools, these brush modes are merely variations on the blend modes available in the Layers palette, which are discussed in Chapter 13. The difference is that the blend modes in the Layers palette mix colors between layers, but the brush modes in the Options bar mix colors inside a single layer. Because of this subtle distinction, the modes are covered twice, once in the following section and again in Chapter 13. The latter discussion is more detailed, so if you don't get all the info you need here, read Chapter 13 to find out more.

> **TIP** You can change brush modes from the keyboard by pressing Shift+plus (+) or Shift+minus (–). Shift+plus takes you to the next brush mode listed in the pop-up menu; Shift+minus selects the previous brush mode. It's a great way to cycle through the brush modes without losing your place in the image.

The 27 paint tool modes

Photoshop offers a total of 27 brush modes (two of them are new to Photoshop CS3) when you use the Brush, the Pencil, or any of the other tools shown in Figure 5.30. Of course, not all of them are available for each of the painting tools, but they all appear in the Mode drop list. Note that an additional mode, Threshold, is an alternative to Normal in certain color modes. The brush modes are organized into six groups, and the individual modes — what they do and how you might use them — are described here.

> **TIP** Just as you can cycle from one brush mode to the next from the keyboard, you can jump directly to a specific brush mode as well. Just press Shift+Alt (Win) or Shift+Option (Mac) and a letter key. For example, Shift+Alt+N (Shift+Option+N on the Mac) selects the Normal mode; Shift+Alt+C (Shift+Option+C on the Mac) selects the Color mode. The letter key for each brush mode is in parentheses along with its description.

- **Normal (N):** Choose this mode to paint or edit an image normally. A paint tool coats the image with the foreground color, and an edit tool manipulates the existing colors in an image according to the Opacity, Strength, Flow, and Exposure values.

   Two color modes prevent Photoshop from rendering soft or translucent edges. The Black-and-White and Indexed modes (Image ➪ Mode ➪ Bitmap and Image ➪ Mode ➪ Indexed Color) simply don't have enough colors to go around. When painting in such a low-color image, Photoshop replaces the Normal brush mode with Threshold (L), which results in harsh, jagged edges, just like a stroke painted with the Pencil tool. You can alternatively dither the soft edges by selecting the Dissolve mode.

- **Dissolve (I):** Dissolve scatters a random pattern of colors to simulate translucency. The pattern shows up along the edges of opaque brush strokes or inside translucent strokes, like those in Figure 5.31. Note that this mode and the two that follow are not applicable to the edit tools. To get something resembling Dissolve with, say, the Smudge tool, try applying the Noise setting in the Brushes palette.

FIGURE 5.30

The specific Mode settings in the Options bar vary depending on which tool is active. The Mode pop-up menu changes to Range when using the Dodge or Burn tool.

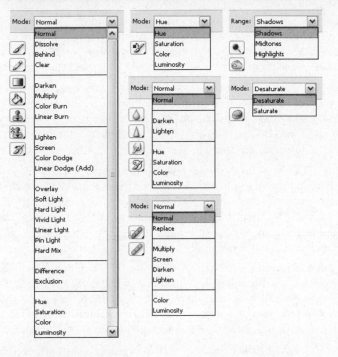

FIGURE 5.31

These lines were painted with the Normal (left) and Dissolve (middle) modes set to 50% opacity. Dissolve dithers colors to simulate transparency, as the magnified detail shows (right).

Normal (N), 50% opacity   Dissolve (I), 50% opacity   Dissolve, zoom 200%

- **Behind (Q):** This mode is applicable exclusively to layers with transparency. When Behind is selected, the paint tools apply color behind the image on the active layer, showing through only in the transparent and translucent areas.

- **Clear (R):** When working on a layer other than *Background*, the Clear mode turns the Brush, Pencil, or Paint Bucket into an erasing tool, clearing away pixels. Given that the Eraser tool already emulates the behavior of both the Brush and Pencil tools (as explained in Chapter 7), there's not much reason to use Clear mode with either of these tools. However, it creates a unique effect when combined with the Paint Bucket, as explained in Chapter 6.

- **Darken (K):** The first of the four darkening modes, Darken applies a new color to a pixel only if that color is darker than the pixel's present color. Otherwise, the pixel is left unchanged. The mode works on a channel-by-channel basis, so it may change a pixel in the green channel, for example, without changing the pixel in the red or blue channel. For more information on channels, see Chapter 4.

- **Multiply (M):** The Multiply mode combines the foreground color with an existing color in an image to create a third color, darker than the other two. Using the multiply analogy, cyan times magenta is blue, magenta times yellow is red, yellow times cyan is green, and so on. Discussed in Chapter 4, this is the subtractive (CMYK) color theory at work. The effect is almost exactly like drawing with felt-tip markers, except the colors don't bleed. The second example in Figure 5.32 shows the Multiply mode in action.

- **Color Burn (B)** and **Linear Burn (A):** The two Burn modes are designed to simulate colored versions of the Burn tool. Typically (though not always), Color Burn results in a darker, more colorful stroke than Multiply. Linear Burn is darker still and more muted, as shown in the last example in Figure 5.32. When combined with low Opacity values, the two modes can be interesting, but I wouldn't go so far as to call them particularly helpful.

- **Lighten (G):** Leading the lightening modes is the appropriately named Lighten, which ensures that Photoshop applies a new color to a pixel only if the color is lighter than the pixel's present color. The first panel in Figure 5.33 shows an example.

FIGURE 5.32

Here are examples of three of the four darkening modes applied to our Shift-click painting. In all cases, the opacity is set to 100%.

 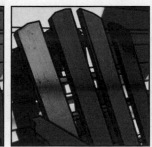 

Darken (K) Multiply (M) Linear Burn (A)

- **Screen (S):** The inverse of the Multiply mode, Screen combines the foreground color with each colored pixel you paint to create a third color, lighter than the other two. Red on green is yellow, green on blue is cyan, blue on red is magenta. In other words, Screen obeys the rules of the additive (RGB) color theory. You can see an example in the center panel in Figure 5.33.

- **Color Dodge (D)** and **Linear Dodge (W):** Intended to emulate the Dodge tool, these modes radically lighten an image. Check out the last panel in Figure 5.33 to see an example. Color Dodge produces the more colorful effect; Linear Dodge works out to be the lightest. As with the Color and Linear Burn modes, low Opacity values are likely to give you the best results.

FIGURE 5.33

These are three of the four lightening modes. As shown in the last panel here, Linear Dodge has a tendency to send light colors in images straight to white. This also is true of Color Dodge.

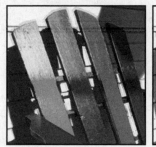
Lighten (G)

Screen (S)

Linear Dodge (W)

- **Overlay (O):** The seven modes starting with Overlay are cousins, each multiplying the dark pixels in an image and screening the light pixels. Of the seven, Overlay is the kindest and arguably the most useful. It enhances contrast and boosts the saturation of colors, rather like a colored version of the Sponge tool set to Saturate. The first pane in Figure 5.34 shows the overlay mode in action.

- **Soft Light (F)** and **Hard Light (H):** The Soft Light mode applies a subtle glazing of color to an image. Even black or white applied at 100 percent Opacity does no more than darken or lighten the image, but it does slightly diminish contrast.

- **Vivid Light (V)** and **Linear Light (J):** These two modes simultaneously burn the darkest colors in your image while dodging the lightest ones. Vivid Light works like a more colorful variation on the Hard Light mode, much like a Color Burn and Color Dodge effect combined. Linear Light produces an even higher contrast effect, as shown in the middle panel of Figure 5.34.

■ **Pin Light (Z):** This peculiar mode drops out all but the so-called "high-frequency" colors, which are the lightest, darkest, and most saturated color values, and in the last panel of Figure 5.34 has hardly any effect. It is almost never useful for brushing, though it can come in handy when applied to layers, as discussed in Chapter 13.

FIGURE 5.34

The medium Overlay and extreme Linear Light modes each mix brush strokes to darken the darkest colors while lightening the lightest colors in your image. Pin Light maintains only the high-frequency colors, turning less vividly colored brush strokes invisible.

Overlay (O)   Linear Light (J)   Pin Light (Z)

■ **Hard Mix (L):** This mode paints using the Vivid Light brush mode and then applies a threshold operation to each color channel. The result is a stark, high-contrast mix consisting of only eight primary colors: red, green, blue, cyan, magenta, yellow, white, and black. The chair, shown in the first example in Figure 5.35, is reduced to three colors — red, black, and white.

CROSS-REF   For more information on thresholds, see Chapter 18.

■ **Difference (E):** When a paint tool is set to the Difference mode, Photoshop subtracts the brightness value of the foreground color from the brightness value of the pixels in the image. If the result is a negative number, Photoshop simply makes it positive. The result of this complex-sounding operation is an inversion effect, as shown on the middle chair in Figure 5.35. Painting with black has no effect on an image; painting with white inverts it. In the case of our chair, red paint on top of the red image results in black.

TIP   Because the Difference mode inverts an image, it results in an outline around the brush-stroke. You can make this outline thicker by using a softer brush shape, which you get by pressing Shift+[(left bracket).

■ **Exclusion (X):** Exclusion, demonstrated in the last panel of Figure 5.35, inverts an image in much the same way as Difference, except colors in the middle of the spectrum mix to form lighter colors. As you can see in the example, painting the red on top of red resulting in a "photo negativistic" effect — a greening of the colors.

FIGURE 5.35

Hard Mix mode posterizes your brush strokes, while Difference and Exclusion give you color inversion effects.

  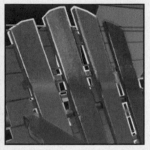

Hard Mix (L)   Difference (E)   Exclusion (X)

- **Hue (U):** Understanding this and the next few modes requires a color theory recap. Remember how the HSL color model calls for three color channels? One is for hue, the value that explains the colors in an image; the second is for saturation, which represents the intensity of the colors; and the third is for luminosity, which explains the lightness and darkness of colors. If you choose the Hue brush mode, therefore, Photoshop applies the hue from the foreground color without changing any saturation or luminosity values in the existing image, as in the first panel in Figure 5.36.

NOTE All HSL brush modes — Hue, Saturation, Color, and Luminosity — are exclusively applicable to color and are therefore unavailable when painting in grayscale images.

- **Saturation (T):** If you choose this mode, Photoshop changes the intensity of the colors in an image without changing the colors themselves or the lightness and darkness of individual pixels.

- **Color (C):** This mode combines Hue and Saturation to change the colors in an image and the intensity of those colors without changing the lightness and darkness of individual pixels.

TIP In concert with the Brush tool, the Color mode is most often used to colorize grayscale photographs. Here's how it works: Open a grayscale image and then choose Image ➪ Mode ➪ RGB Color to convert the image to the RGB mode. Then select the Brush tool — with or without the airbrush turned on — and set the Mode pop-up menu to Color. From that point on, you have only to select the colors you want to use and start painting.

- **Luminosity (Y):** The opposite of the Color mode, Luminosity changes the lightness and darkness of pixels, but leaves the Hue and Saturation values unaffected. The last panel in Figure 5.36 shows how Luminosity mode maintained the lines and shadows of the top layer without altering the color values of the underlying image.

- **Lighter Color:** Not to be confused with the aforementioned Lighten blend mode, which is applied to one channel at a time, the new Lighter Color mode applies to all channels at once. If you're blending two ore more colors with Lighter Color, guess which one is visible? That's right, the *lighter* one.

FIGURE 5.36

Hue mode mixes the hue values from the brush strokes with the saturation and luminosity values of the underlying image. Color is only slightly different, preserving the saturation values from the brush strokes also. Luminosity is Color's opposite, brushing in lights and darks but leaving colors unchanged.

Hue (U)   Color (C)   Luminosity (Y)

■ **Darker Color:** Much like it's pale partner, the new Darker Color mode applies to all the channels at one time. This, like Lighter Color and Lighten, can be confused with Darken, which applies to only one channel at a time. If you're blending two or more colors with Darker Color, the darker color is visible (big surprise, huh?). Figure 5.37 compares the results of the Normal, Lighter Color, and Darker Color modes.

FIGURE 5.37

Lighter Color pushes the lighter colors, while Darker Color preserves the darker ones.

  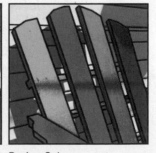

Normal, 100% opacity   Lighter Color   Darker Color

The three Dodge and Burn modes

The three modes available with the Dodge and Burn tools are accessed through the Range pop-up menu in the Options bar. As with other brush modes, you can select the Dodge and Burn modes from the keyboard. Just press Shift+Alt (Win) or Shift+Option (Mac) and the letter in parentheses as follows:

- **Midtones (M):** Selected by default, the Midtones mode applies the Dodge or Burn tool equally to all but the very lightest or darkest pixels in an image. Midtones enables you to adjust the brightness of colors without blowing out highlights or filling in shadows.

- **Shadows (S):** When you select this mode, the Dodge or Burn tool affects dark pixels in an image more dramatically than light pixels. As illustrated in Figure 5.38, medium values are likewise affected, so the Shadows option modifies a wider range of colors than Midtones.

- **Highlights (H):** This option lets you lighten or darken the midtones and lightest colors in an image.

FIGURE 5.38

The Dodge and Burn tools are applied at 100% Exposure settings, subject to each of the applicable brush modes.

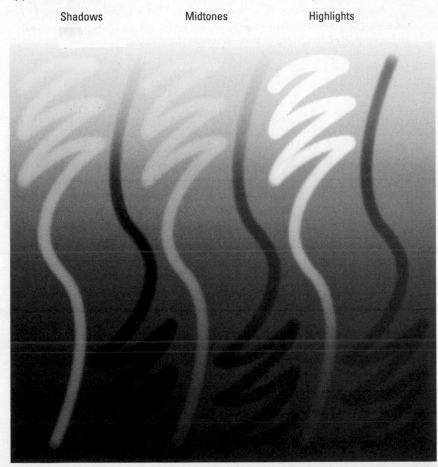

Shadows   Midtones   Highlights

Selecting Shadows when using the Dodge tool or Highlights when using the Burn tool has an equalizing effect on an image. For example, the first brushstroke in Figure 5.38 shows the Shadows option combined with the Dodge tool. As a result, Photoshop paints an almost consistent brightness value across the course of a white-to-black gradient. The same is true for the last brushstroke, which combines Highlights with the Burn tool.

Summary

In this chapter, you explored Photoshop's paint and edit tools, learned how to apply the airbrush control, and learned to paint straight and perpendicular lines. You also learned to use the Smudge and Sponge tools to play with your image colors and to use the Color Replacement tool.

In mastering all brush-based tools, you learned to change the brush size, shape, and hardness, to save and load custom brush sets, and to work with a pressure-sensitive drawing tablet.

Customizing brushes was discussed at length, and you learned to create lines that fade away or taper to a point, to use scatter, texture, and other dynamics that adjust opacity and flow, and finally, to work with brush modes.

Filling and Stroking

Before things go too far here, let's make sure everyone's clear on the terminology. To *fill* a selection or a layer is to put color inside it; to *stroke* a selection or a layer is to put color around it. You can *fill* a layer or a selection or shape; you place a *stroke* around that filled area. Of course, you may prefer the term *outline* to *stroke*, but an outline is typically a border, a line placed around something to encase it, like a fence or a wall, to delineate it from the stuff surrounding it. Outlines are solid, uniform, and one thinks of them as being straight lines with sharp corners. A stroke, on the other hand, is more like color and/or a texture (depending on the nature of the stroke) that envelopes content, conforming to its shape rather than confining it. Further, *stroke* is also the PostScript term, and given the history of graphics and desktop publishing and their ties to the PostScript world, *stroke* also became (and remains) the term Photoshop uses, so for clarity's sake, we'll use it.

This chapter will teach you to fill selections using keyboard shortcuts, how to create interesting framing effects, how to make the most of Photoshop's gradient options, and how to add an arrowhead to a curving line — all in addition to the really basic things every Photoshop user needs to know. Has that *filled* you with excitement? Then let's get started.

Filling Selections with Color or Patterns

Photoshop's fill and stroke functions are so straightforward that you may have long since forgotten about what to call them or how they actually work — they're just there, they work just fine, and you don't need to think about them too much. So how do you fill the layer, shape, or selection? Let us count the ways:

- **Paint Bucket tool:** Also known as the Fill tool, the Paint Bucket shares a flyout with the Gradient tool in the Toolbox. You can apply the foreground color or a repeating pattern to areas of related color in an image by clicking in the image window with the tool. For example, if you want to turn all pink pixels in an image into orange pixels, set the foreground color to orange and then click one of the pink pixels. As you learn later in this chapter, the tool has options for controlling how and where that fill is applied to the pink pixels, and it's worth noting that you can't use this tool on images that you converted to bitmap mode.

- **Fill command:** Choose Edit ➪ Fill to fill a selection with the foreground color, a repeating pattern, or any color you choose, because you can invoke the Color Picker from within the dialog box that results from the Edit ➪ Fill command. Bear in mind that you don't need to select a portion of the image to access the Fill command: If you choose the command while no selection is active, Photoshop fills the entire layer.

> **TIP** To choose the Fill command without even moving the mouse, press Shift+Backspace (Shift+Delete on the Mac).

- **Backspace (Win) and Delete (Mac) key techniques:** Keyboard shortcut fans will love this, and it gives you a chance to work with keys that are typically used only to edit a string of text. After selecting part of a single-layer image — or part of the background layer in a multilayered image — you can fill the selection with the background color by pressing Backspace (Win) or Delete (Mac). You also can fill any layer with the background color without a selection by pressing Ctrl+Backspace (Win) or ⌘-Delete (Mac). To fill with the foreground color, press Alt+Backspace (Win) or Option-Delete (Mac).

- **Gradient tool:** Drag across a layer or selection with a Gradient tool to fill it with a multi-color gradient in one of five gradient styles. You choose a gradient style by clicking an icon in the Options bar. Press G (or Shift+G, depending on your preferences setting for tool toggles) to toggle the Gradient and Paint Bucket tools, which occupy the same flyout menu in the Toolbox. In addition to the gradient styles, you also have scads of gradient presets that you can apply, in the style you choose. But more about that later.

- **Layer fills:** You can use Layer Style features to fill a layer with a solid color, gradient, pattern, or special effect fills.

The next sections explain the first four fill options.

> **CROSS-REF** To find out more about layer styles, turn to Chapter 15.

The Paint Bucket Tool

Unlike the very basic and limited paint bucket tools in other painting programs — heavy-handed devices that apply paint exclusively within outlined areas or areas of solid color — the Photoshop Paint Bucket is a more elegant tool, offering several useful and powerful adjustment options. When you activate the Paint Bucket tool, its Options bar appears, giving you access to those adjustment options.

 If you don't see the Options bar, press Enter or Return, double-click the paint bucket icon in the Toolbox, or choose Window ➪ Options.

In the Paint Bucket's Options bar, you can play with these controls:

■ **Source:** In this pop-up menu, you set the source for your fill. You can choose between Foreground (the default) and Pattern. If you choose the former, you fill with the current Foreground Color. If you choose the latter, you can use one of Photoshop's preset patterns (pick one from the adjacent option, which displays a pattern icon that displays a palette of pattern presets, as shown in Figure 6.1, when you click it) or one you create using Edit ➪ Define Pattern. The Define Pattern command is covered in Chapter 7. Note that Photoshop lets you create multiple patterns; you're not limited to one custom pattern, and after they're created, they can be applied in any image.

 You load, replace, edit, and create pattern presets just as you do tool and brush presets (see Chapters 2 and 5, respectively), working either in the Preset Manager dialog box or the Pattern palette menu.

FIGURE 6.1

The Paint Bucket's Options bar includes the opportunity to fill with a pattern, rather than the current foreground color. Click the Pattern field to apply a pattern and where you see the mouse pointer in the figure to access other pattern groups.

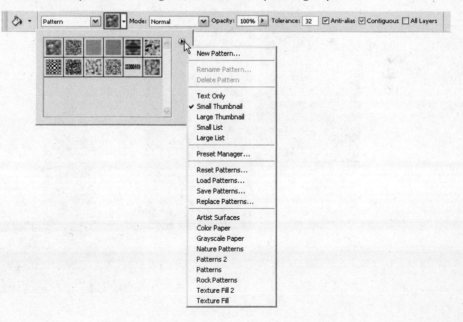

■ **Mode:** This menu offers a selection of blend modes (the same ones you read about in Chapter 5) that determine how and when color is applied, as demonstrated using a photo from our friend Terri Shadle, in Figure 6.2. The Clear mode creates a hole in the image, leaving transparency in its wake. The Soft Light mode (see the middle panel) effects are obvious, and Overlay does an interesting job of increasing contrast and boosting saturation. (Note that Clear is dimmed when working on a flat image or a Background layer.)

FIGURE 6.2

The results of selecting three of the many mode options available when using the Paint Bucket: Color Dodge severely lightens as it fills (top), Difference inverts colors as it fills (middle), and Clear deletes (bottom).

- **Opacity:** Type a new value or press a number key to change the translucency of a color applied with the Paint Bucket. (Press 0 for full opacity, 9 for 90 percent opacity, and so on.)

- **Tolerance:** Raise or lower the Tolerance value to increase or decrease the number of pixels affected by the Paint Bucket tool. The Tolerance value represents a range in brightness values, as measured from the pixel that you click with the Paint Bucket.

Immediately after you click a pixel, Photoshop reads the brightness value of that pixel from each color channel. Next the program calculates a color range based on the Tolerance value — which can vary from 0 to 255. The program adds the Tolerance to the brightness value of the pixel you clicked to determine the top of the range and subtracts the Tolerance from the pixel's brightness value to determine the bottom of the range. For example, if the pixel's brightness value is 100 and the Tolerance value is 32, the top of the range is 132 and the bottom is 68.

Figure 6.3 shows the result of clicking the same pixel three separate times, each time using a different Tolerance value — once set to a lower-than-default 20, once at 32 (the default), and once at 100. Because of the variety of colors in the background, it took a high Tolerance setting to fill the background. Of course, the tool's specificity is a good thing when you want to only fill areas based on very specific pixels — as you can see, when the Tolerance did its job and filled the background, nearly all of the flower and much of the butterfly was filled, too.

- **Anti-aliased:** Select this option to soften the effect of the Paint Bucket tool. As demonstrated in the middle example of Figure 6.4, Photoshop creates a border of translucent color between the filled pixels and their unaffected neighbors. If you don't want to soften the transition, deselect the Anti-aliased option. Photoshop then fills only those pixels that fall inside the Tolerance range, as demonstrated in the bottom example of the figure.

- **Contiguous:** When you select this option, Photoshop fills only contiguous pixels — that is, pixels that both fall inside the Tolerance range and touch another affected pixel. If you instead want to fill all pixels within the Tolerance range — regardless of where those pixels lie — deselect the check box. For what it's worth, the option was left selected when creating Figures 6.2 and 6.3.

- **All Layers:** Select this option to make the Paint Bucket see beyond the current layer. When the option is selected, the tool takes all visible layers into account when calculating the area to fill. Mind you, it fills only the active layer, but the way it fills an area is dictated by all layers.

FIGURE 6.3

In another photo by Terri Shadle, the wall in the background is only slightly filled by the gray foreground color when using a Tolerance of 32 (top), while a setting of 100 (middle) fills about half. A Tolerance of 160 (bottom) virtually obliterates the image.

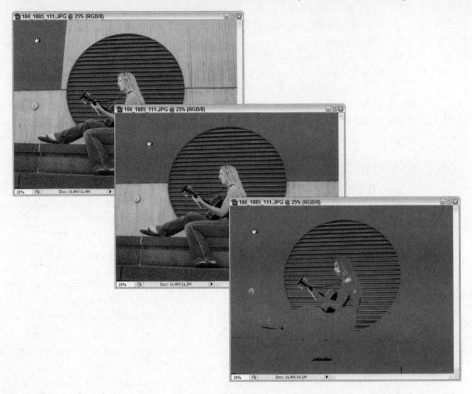

CROSS-REF   For a complete description of all the blend modes and their uses and effects, see Chapter 14.

In Figure 6.5, you can see the All Layers option in use. Layers were created for the chairs, so that fills could be added for each of them without harming our original Shift+click-created image from Chapter 5. To use the background layer as the source, the All Layers option is selected, and the Paint Bucket used as normal. As a result, Photoshop respected any outlines within the background when coloring the various layers, and we can deal with the fill on each layer separately.

FIGURE 6.4

The results of turning on (middle) and off (bottom) the Anti-aliased check box before using the paint bucket tool.

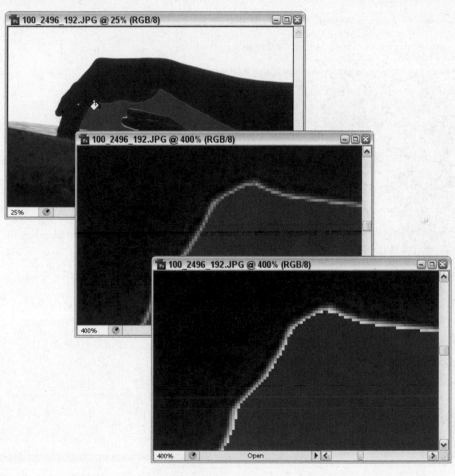

> TIP
> To limit the area affected by the Paint Bucket, select a portion of the image before using the tool. As when using a paint or edit tool, the region outside the selection outline is protected from the Paint Bucket.

When working on a layer, you can protect pixels by locking the layer's transparency in the Layers palette.

> CROSS-REF
> You can find out more about the locking options and every other exciting aspect of Layers in Chapter 13.

FIGURE 6.5

Despite each chair layer having no content to start with, the Use All Layers option is on, so the background image supplies the context for the Paint Bucket tool.

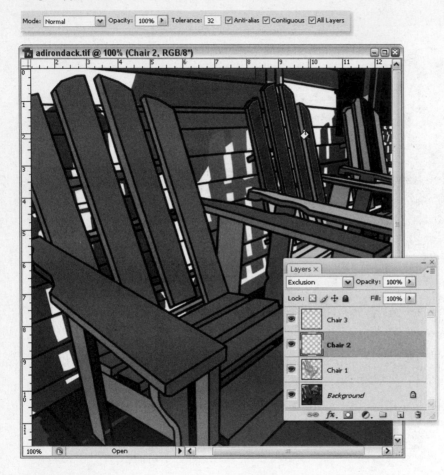

TIP   You can use the Paint Bucket to color the empty window area around your image. First, make your image window larger than your image so you can see some gray canvas area around the image. Now Shift+click with the Paint Bucket to fill the canvas area with the foreground color. This technique can come in handy if you're creating a presentation or you simply don't care for the default shade of gray.

The Fill Command

The one problem with the Paint Bucket tool is its lack of precision. Although the tool is undeniably convenient, the effects of the Tolerance value are so difficult to predict that you typically have to click with the tool, choose Edit ➪ Undo when you don't like the result, adjust the Tolerance value, and go through that process several times before you fill the image as desired.

A better option is to use one of Photoshop's selection tools to select the area to be filled and then choose Edit ➪ Fill. You also can press Shift+Backspace (Shift+Delete on the Mac, or if you prefer function keys, try Shift+F5). After issuing the command and choosing what kind of fill you want, your selected area is entirely filled with a color or pattern, whichever you chose from the Fill dialog box.

Why make a selection first? Well, instead of putting your faith in the Paint Bucket tool's Anti-aliased option (or the aforementioned Tolerance setting, which isn't always predictable in its results), you can draw a selection outline that feature's hard edges in one area, anti-aliased edges elsewhere, and downright blurry edges in between.

Of course, you don't have to make a selection first. For example, if you want to fill an entire layer, you don't need to create a selection outline before choosing Fill. The program assumes that you want to fill the whole layer if it doesn't see a selection outline.

CROSS-REF Dynamic fills and layer styles provide additional ways to fill a layer; see Chapter 15 for details on how these fills differ from those you create with the Fill command.

Selection outline or no, choosing the Fill command displays the dialog box shown in Figure 6.6. In this dialog box, you can apply a variety of fills, from the current Foreground color, to a color you choose (the Color Picker can be opened from within the dialog box), a pattern, black, white, or 50% gray. You also can apply a translucent color or pattern by typing a value in the Opacity option box. And you can choose a brush mode from the Mode pop-up menu, which offers the ubiquitous list modes we discussed in Chapter 5 and see again later in the book.

If you display the Use pop-up menu, you see a collection of fills that you can apply. Foreground Color and Pattern behave the same as they do for the Paint Bucket tool. When you select Pattern, the Custom Pattern option becomes available, as shown in Figure 6.6. Click the icon to display the Pattern drop-down palette (refer to Figure 6.6), which also works as described in the preceding section. Click an icon to select a pattern; click the right-pointing arrow to display the palette menu and load a different pattern preset.

CROSS-REF To find out how to load, save, edit, and create custom pattern presets, see Chapter 5. You use the same techniques for brush presets and pattern presets.

You also can fill a selection with the background color and such monochrome options as Black, White, and 50% Gray. Black and White are useful if the foreground and background colors have been changed from their defaults; 50% Gray fills the selection with the absolute medium color without having to mess around with the Color palette. History allows you to revert the selected area to a previous appearance, as you see in Chapter 7.

FIGURE 6.6

The Fill dialog box combines the opacity and brush mode options available for the Paint Bucket with an expanded collection of fill content options.

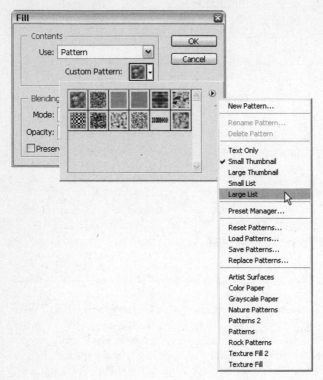

The Preserve Transparency option gives you the same result as locking the active layer's transparency in the Layers palette, which you can read about in Chapter 13. If you select Preserve Transparency, you can't fill transparent pixels in the active layer. Deselect Preserve Transparency, and you can fill the selection outline uniformly. (The option is dimmed when you're working on the background layer or if you already locked the layer's transparency in the Layers palette.)

Backspace and Delete Key Techniques

Of all the fill techniques, the Backspace key (Delete key on the Mac) is by far the most convenient and, in most respects, every bit as capable as the others. The key's only failing is that it can neither fill a selection with a repeating pattern nor revert a selection to a previous state. But with the exception of those two items, you can rely on the Backspace or Delete key for many of your fill needs.

Try these techniques for using Backspace (Win) or Delete (Mac):

- **Background color, method 1:** To fill a selection on the background layer with solid background color, press Backspace (Win) or Delete (Mac). The selection outline remains intact.

- **Background color, method 2:** Press Ctrl+Backspace (⌘+Delete on the Mac) instead. Ctrl+Backspace or ⌘+Delete fills the selection with the background color, no matter where (or on which layer) the selection is.

A word of caution here: A problem worth noting with pressing Backspace (Delete on the Mac) is that it's unreliable. If the selection is floating, as explained in Chapter 8, the Backspace (Delete on the Mac) key deletes it. The key also erases pixels on a layer. What to do? If you like the simplicity of using these keys for a quick fill, use method 2 above or the following options for controlling exactly how the fill is applied. These methods aren't single-key simple, but they are faster than Edit ⇨ Fill or grabbing the Paint Bucket and then clicking inside a selection.

- **Foreground color:** To fill a selection or a layer with solid foreground color, press Alt+Backspace (Win) or Option+Delete (Mac). This works when filling floating and non-floating selections alike.

- **Black or white:** To fill an area with black, press D to get the default foreground and background colors and then press Alt+Backspace (Option+Delete on the Mac). To fill an area with white, press D for the defaults and then Ctrl+Backspace (⌘+Delete on the Mac).

- **Preserve transparency:** You can fill only the opaque pixels in a layer — regardless of whether you locked the layer's transparency in the Layers palette — by pressing Shift. Press Shift+Alt+Backspace (Shift+Option+Delete on the Mac) to fill a selection with the foreground color while preserving transparency. Press Ctrl+Shift+Backspace (⌘+Shift+Delete on the Mac) to fill the opaque pixels with the background color.

CROSS-REF **Learn more about this technique for preserving transparency in Chapter 13.**

Applying Gradient Fills

Without demanding that you whip out a thesaurus to find a list of other words that you could substitute for "gradient," suffice to say it is a progression of colors that fade gradually into one another, as demonstrated in Figure 6.7. You specify a few key colors (or even just one, paired with transparency as the other "color") in the gradient, and Photoshop automatically generates the hundred or so colors in between to create a smooth transition.

NOTE **If you're accustomed to using gradients in a drawing program — such as Illustrator or FreeHand — you'll find that in many ways Photoshop is better. Because Photoshop is a pixel editor, it lets you blur and mix colors in a gradient if they start *banding* — that is, if you can see a hard edge between one color and the next when you print the image. And Photoshop's gradients never choke the printer or slow it down, no matter how many colors you add. In Illustrator, each band of color in an object-oriented gradient is expressed as a separate shape — so that one gradient can contain hundreds, or even thousands, of objects. Gradients in Photoshop are simply colored pixels, no more or less complicated than the pixels in any of the images we've looked at thus far in this book.**

FIGURE 6.7

A gradient dragged across a single selection and multiple selections. The distance dragged from starting point (upper left) to ending point (lower right) determines the span of the gradient from Foreground to Background color.

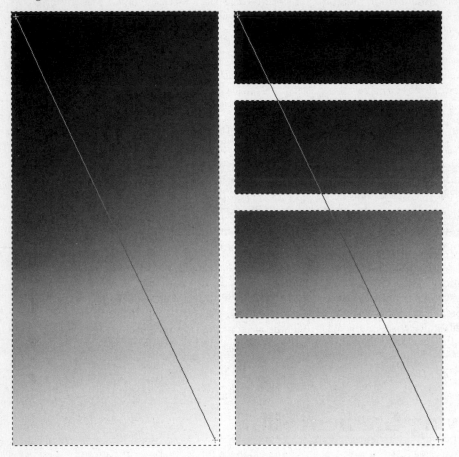

Using the Gradient tool

The Gradient and Paint Bucket tools share a Toolbox slot and a keyboard shortcut — press G to toggle between the two tools (or Shift+G, depending on whether you selected the Use Shift Key for Tool Switch option in the Preferences dialog box, as discussed in Chapter 2). But unlike the Paint Bucket, which fills areas of similar color according to the Tolerance setting, the Gradient tool affects all colors within a selection — or if you don't make a selection, it applies to an entire layer.

To use the tool and apply the default gradient, click the Gradient button in the Toolbox and drag inside the selection, as shown in Figure 6.7. The default gradient, which takes the foreground color and creates a gradient with the background color, is applied based on the point at which you begin dragging (the upper-left corner in the figure, in this case). This starting point defines the location of the first color in the gradient, and the point at which you release (the lower-right corner, as shown in the figure) defines the location of the last color. If multiple portions of the image are selected, the gradient fills all selections continuously. Photoshop doesn't stop and apply the gradient to the individual selections — it follows your mouse path across selections, skipping the intervening areas that are not within the selection.

Gradient options

As with other tools in Photoshop, the Gradient tool has its own Options bar, which you can see in Figure 6.8 (or on your own computer, if you're playing along). If you don't see the Options bar, press Enter or Return when the Gradient tool is active or double-click the tool icon in the Toolbox.

FIGURE 6.8

The Options bar gives you quick access to all Gradient tool options — including a list of gradient presets.

The following list explains how the controls in the Options bar work. In all cases, you must adjust the options before using the Gradient tool. They do not affect gradients you've already applied in the image:

- **Gradient preview:** The selected gradient appears in the gradient preview, the first option shown on the Options bar in Figure 6.10. Click the preview to open the Gradient Editor dialog box, discussed in the section "Creating custom gradients."

- **Gradient drop-down palette:** Click the triangle adjacent to the preview to display the Gradient palette, which contains icons representing gradients in the current gradient presets. Click the icon for the gradient you want.

NOTE In the default gradient preset, the first two gradients are dependent on the current foreground and background colors. The others contain specific colors bearing no relationship to the colors in the Toolbox.

You load gradient presets using the same techniques described in detail in the brush preset discussion in Chapter 5, but here's the short story:

- Click the triangle near the top of the drop-down palette to display the palette menu. The Photoshop collection of presets and any presets that you defined on your own appear at the bottom of the palette menu. Click a preset group by name to access those presets instead of or in addition to the default set of presets. The preset groups' names — like Metals and Pastels — are fairly revealing.

■ To append a preset from disk — such as when a coworker gives you a preset file — choose Load Gradients from the palette menu or click Load in the Preset Manager dialog box. If you want to replace the current preset instead, choose Replace Gradients from the palette menu or click Replace in the dialog box. To return to the default gradients, choose Reset Gradients from the palette menu, either from the Options bar palette or the one in the Preset Manager dialog box.

TIP   You can edit a gradient and perform the aforementioned preset manipulations from the Gradient Editor dialog box, too. The section "Creating custom gradients" covers this dialog box in detail.

■ **Gradient style:** Click an icon to select the gradient style. The section "Gradient styles" explains the five styles.

■ **Mode** and **Opacity:** These options work as they do for the paint and edit tools (as explained in Chapter 5), the Fill command, and every other tool or command that offers them as options. Select a different brush mode to change how colors are applied; lower the Opacity value to make a gradient translucent. Remember that you can change the Opacity value by pressing number keys as well as by using the Opacity control in the Options bar. Press 0 for 100 percent opacity, 9 for 90 percent opacity, and so on.

■ **Reverse:** When active, this option begins the gradient with the background color and ends it with the foreground color. Use this option when you want to start a radial or other style of gradient with white, but you want to keep the foreground and background colors set to their defaults.

■ **Dither:** Remember how we said that Photoshop doesn't give you *banding* when you print a gradient? Well, that's not totally true. In the old days, Photoshop drew its gradients one band at a time, and each band was filled with an incrementally different shade of color. The potential result, known as banding, made it so that you could clearly distinguish the transition between two or more bands of color. The Dither option helps to eliminate this problem by mixing up the pixels between bands (much as Photoshop dithers pixels when converting a grayscale image to black and white), smoothing the transitions between them. It's generally safe to deselect the Dither option if you're working on an image in 16-bit mode, as it's essentially unnecessary and banding won't occur anyway. If you're not working in 16-bit mode, you should leave this option turned on unless you want to use banding to create a special effect.

TIP   If you're not sure you're working in 16-bit mode, select the Image ➪ Mode submenu and note where the check mark is. If you're in 16-bit mode, it appears next to the 16 bits/channel mode.

■ **Transparency:** You can specify different levels of opacity throughout a gradient. For example, the Soft Stripes effect (available from the Gradient palette when the Special Effects preset is loaded) lays down a series of alternately black and transparent stripes. But you needn't use this transparency information. If you prefer to apply a series of black and white stripes instead, you can make all portions of the gradient equally opaque by deselecting the Transparency option.

For example, in Figure 6.9, the Soft Stripes effect is applied as a radial gradient in two separate swipes (first to a selection in the middle image, and again on the bottom image).

Both times, the Opacity setting is changed to 50 percent, so the eye is never completely obscured. (The Opacity setting works independently of the gradient's built-in transparency, providing you with additional flexibility.) In the top gradient (middle example), the Transparency option is selected, so the white stripes are completely transparent. In the bottom gradient, Transparency is turned off, so the white stripes become 50 percent opaque (as prescribed by the Opacity setting).

FIGURE 6.9

With the Opacity value set to 50 percent, the Soft Stripes gradient is applied to the middle and bottom eyes. Transparency is selected in the middle eye, so that you can see through what would otherwise be the white stripes. Transparency is deselected in the bottom eye, and the gradient is applied to a smaller elliptical marquee.

293

Gradient styles

You select the gradient style by clicking the gradient style icons in the Options bar; refer to Figure 6.8 to identify these icons. The five styles are illustrated in Figure 6.10:

- **Linear:** A linear gradient progresses in bands of color in a straight line between the beginning and end of your drag. The top two examples in Figure 6.10 show linear gradients created from black to white and from white to black. The point labeled "B" marks the beginning of the drag; "E" marks the end.

- **Radial:** A radial gradient progresses outward from a central point in concentric circles, as in the second row of examples in Figure 6.10. The point at which you begin dragging defines the center of the gradient, and the point at which you release defines the outermost circle. This means the first color in the gradient appears in the center of the fill. So to create the gradient on the right side of Figure 6.10, you must set the foreground color to white and the background color to black (or select the Reverse option in the Options bar).

- **Angle:** The angle gradient style creates a fountain of colors flowing in a counterclockwise direction with respect to your drag, as demonstrated by the third row of examples of Figure 6.10. This type of gradient is known more commonly as a *conical gradient* because it looks like the bird's-eye view of the top of a cone.

  Of course, a real cone doesn't have the sharp edge between black and white that you see in Photoshop's angle gradient. To eliminate this edge, create a custom gradient from black to white to black again, as explained in the "Adjusting colors in a solid gradient" section later in this chapter.

- **Reflected:** The fourth gradient style creates a linear gradient that reflects back on itself. Photoshop positions the foreground color at the beginning of your drag and the background color at the end, as when using the linear gradient style. But it also repeats the gradient in the opposite direction of your drag, as demonstrated in Figure 6.10. It's great for creating natural shadows or highlights that fade in two directions.

- **Diamond:** The last gradient style creates a series of concentric diamonds (if you drag at a 90-degree angle) or squares (if you drag at a 45-degree angle, as in Figure 6.10). Otherwise, it works exactly like the radial gradient style.

Creating custom gradients

Many users open this dialog box by accident. Attempting to display the Gradient presets (which display only if you click the triangle on the first Gradient option), they click the Gradient preview, and instead of a tidy array of potential gradients, they get this dialog box, as shown in Figure 6.11.

FIGURE 6.10

Examples of each of the five gradient styles created using the default foreground and background colors (left column) and with the foreground and background colors reversed (right column). B marks the beginning of the drag; E marks the end.

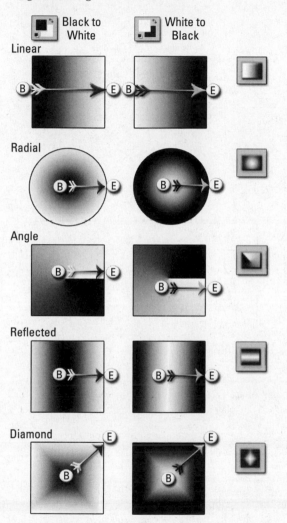

FIGURE 6.11

Click the gradient preview in the Options bar to display the Gradient Editor dialog box, which enables you to design custom gradients.

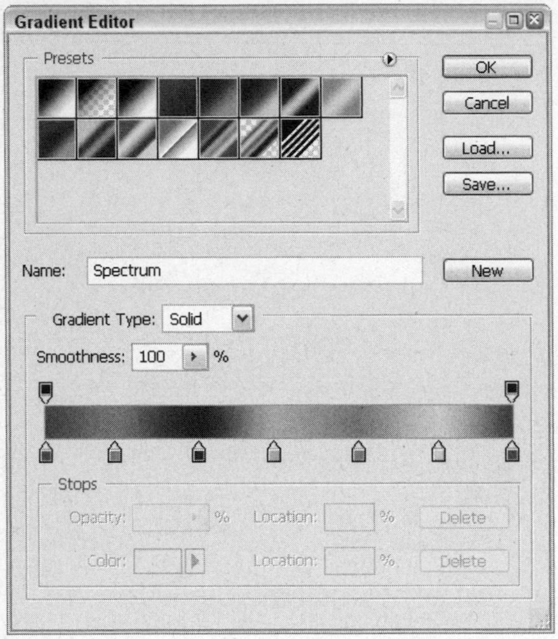

Here are some important points about the Gradient Editor:

- The scrolling list at the top of the dialog box mirrors the Gradient drop-down palette in the Options bar and the Gradients panel of the Preset Manager dialog box. If you click the triangle at the top of the scrolling list, you display a virtual duplicate of the palette menu.

 If you want to see gradient names instead of icons in the list, choose Text Only from the dialog box menu. Or choose Small List or Large List to see both the icon and the gradient name.

- To create a new gradient, find an existing gradient that's close to what you have in mind. Then type a name for the gradient in the Name option box and click New. The new gradient appears in the scrolling list, and you can edit the gradient as you see fit.

CAUTION Even though the gradient appears in the dialog box (as well as in the Gradient palette and the Preset Manager dialog box), it's vulnerable until you save it as part of a preset. If you make further edits to the gradient or replace the current gradient preset, the original gradient is lost. Deleting your main Photoshop preferences file also wipes out an unsaved gradient. See the section "Saving and managing gradients" for more details.

- You can create *noise gradients* as well as solid-color gradients. If you select Noise from the Gradient Type pop-up menu, Photoshop introduces random color information into the gradient, the result of which is a sort of special-effect gradient that would be difficult to create manually.

- The options at the bottom of the dialog box change depending on whether you select Solid or Noise from the Gradient Type pop-up. For solid gradients, Photoshop provides a Smoothness slider, which you can use to adjust how abrupt you want to make the color transitions in the gradient.

> **TIP** For greater control when creating or editing a gradient, make the dialog box wider by dragging the size box in the lower-right corner.

Editing solid gradients

If you select Solid from the Gradient Type pop-up menu, you use the options shown in Figure 6.12 to adjust the gradient. Note that this is a doctored screen shot — all the options are visible in the figure; normally, only some of the options associated with the active stops are available.

The *fade bar* (labeled in Figure 6.12) shows the active gradient. The starting color is represented by a *color stop* (see the triangle on top of a square) on the left; the ending color stop appears on the far right. The upside-down stop markers on the top of the fade bar are *opacity stops*. These stops determine where colors are opaque and where they fade into translucency or even transparency.

To select either type of stop, click it. The triangle portion of the stop appears black to indicate that it is active. After you select a stop, diamond-shaped *midpoint markers* appear between the stop and its immediate neighbors. On the color-stop side of the fade bar, the midpoint marker represents the spot where the two colors mix in exactly equal amounts. On the transparency side, a marker indicates the point where the opacity value is midway between the values that you set for the stops on either side of the marker.

You can change the location of any stop or marker by dragging it. Or you can click a stop or marker to select it and then type a value in the Location option box below the fade bar:

- When numerically positioning a stop, a value of 0 percent indicates the left end of the fade bar; 100 percent indicates the right end. Even if you add more stops to the gradient, the values represent absolute positions along the fade bar.

- When repositioning a midpoint marker, the initial setting of 50 percent is at equal points between two stops, 0 percent is all the way over to the left stop, and 100 percent is all the way over to the right. Midpoint values are, therefore, measured relative to stop positions. In fact, when you move a stop, Photoshop moves the midpoint marker along with it to maintain the same relative positioning. If you type a value below 5 percent or more than 95 percent, Photoshop politely ignores you.

> **TIP** Pressing Enter or Return after you type a value into the Location option box is tempting, but don't do it. Photoshop dumps you out of the Gradient Editor dialog box, which you may not be ready to leave just yet.

Use these controls to adjust the colors and transparency in a solid gradient.

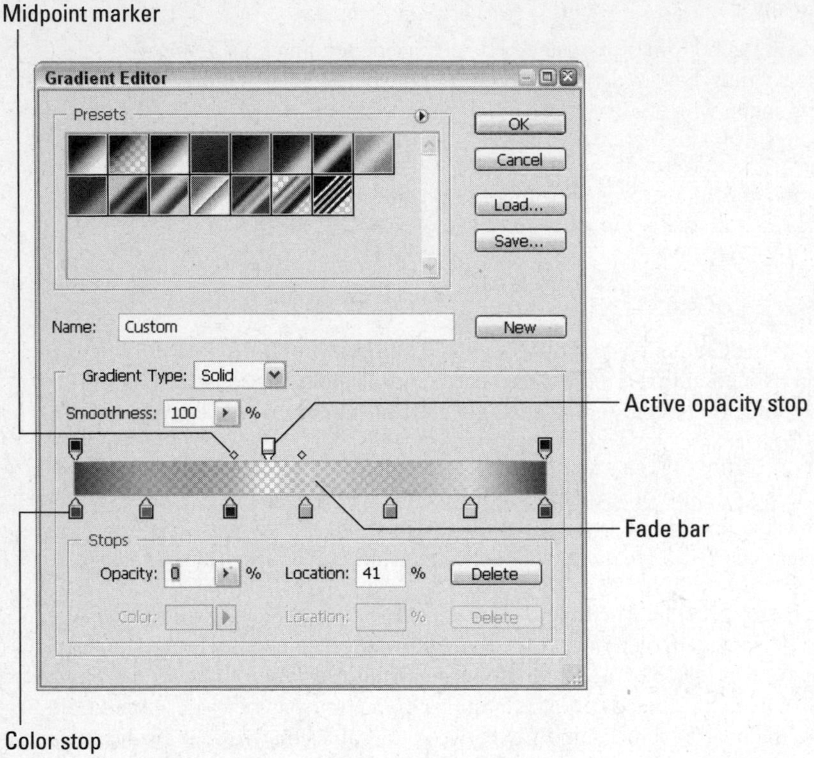

Midpoint marker

Active opacity stop

Fade bar

Color stop

Adjusting colors in a solid gradient

When editing a solid gradient, you can add colors, delete colors, change the position of the colors in the gradient, and control how two colors blend together. After clicking a color stop to select it, you can change its color in several ways:

- To change the color to the current foreground color, open the Color pop-up menu, as shown in Figure 6.13, and select Foreground. You also can select Background to use the background color instead.

  When you select Foreground or Background, the color stop becomes filled with a grayscale pattern instead of a solid color. If you squint real hard and put your nose to the screen, you can see that the pattern is actually a representation of the Foreground and Background color controls in the Toolbox. The little black square appears in the upper-left corner when the foreground color is active, as shown in the first stop on the fade bar in Figure 6.13.

A look at the color stop options in the Gradient Editor dialog box

Foreground color stop   Background color stop

Color midpoint marker

If you change the foreground or background color after closing the Gradient Editor dialog box, the gradient changes to reflect the new color. When you next open the Gradient Editor, you can revert the stop to the original foreground or background color by selecting User Color from the pop-up menu.

- To set the color stop to some other color, click the Color swatch or double-click the color stop to display the Color Picker and define the new color. Select your color and press Enter or Return.

TIP You may have noticed that when you open the Gradient Editor dialog box, Photoshop automatically selects the Eyedropper tool for you and displays that tool's controls in the Options bar. Why did it do that? Because you can click with the Eyedropper in an open image window to lift a color from the image and assign that color to the selected color stop. You also can sample a color from anywhere onscreen by first clicking with the Eyedropper in an image window and then dragging outside it.

To change the point at which two colors meet, drag the midpoint marker between the two stops. Or click the midpoint marker, and type a new value into the Location box. A value of 0 puts the midpoint marker flush against the left color stop; a value of 100 moves the stop all the way over to the right stop.

You add or delete stops as follows:

- To add a color stop, click anywhere along the bottom of the fade bar. A new stop appears where you click. Photoshop also adds a midpoint marker between the new color stop and those to its left and right. You can add as many color stops as your heart desires. To define the color of the stop, double-click the new color stop (double-click an existing stop if you want to change its color) and watch as the Color Picker dialog box opens. Make a selection, click OK, and voila! Your new color stop is created and its color is set.

TIP   If your goal is a gradient that features tons of random colors, you may be able to create the effect you want more easily by using the Noise gradient option. See the section "Creating noise gradients" for more information.

- To duplicate a color stop, Alt+drag (Option+drag on the Mac) it to a new location along the fade bar. One great use for this is to create a reflecting gradient.

  For example, select Foreground to Background from the scrolling list of gradients and click New to duplicate the gradient. After naming your new gradient — something like Foreground to Background to Foreground, for example — click the background color stop and change the Location value to 50. Then Alt+drag (Option+drag on the Mac) the foreground color stop all the way to the right. This new gradient is perfect for making true conical gradients with the angle gradient style, as demonstrated in Figure 6.14.

- To remove a color stop, drag the stop away from the fade bar. Or click the stop, and click Delete (the button in the dialog box or the key on your keyboard — Backspace, if you're on the Mac). The stop icon vanishes, and the fade bar automatically adjusts as defined by the remaining color stops.

FIGURE 6.14

A true "cone" is created (right). Two gradients have the angle gradient style applied, one using the standard Foreground to Background gradient (left) and the other with a reflected Foreground to Background to Foreground style (right).

Adjusting the transparency mask

If you like, you can include a *transparency mask* with each gradient. The mask determines the opacity of different colors along the gradient. You create and edit this mask independently of the colors in the gradient.

To create a transparency mask, you adjust the opacity stops across the top of the fade bar. When you click an opacity stop, the transparency options become available below the fade bar and the color options dim.

To add an opacity stop, click above the fade bar. By default, each new stop is 100 percent opaque. You can modify the transparency by selecting a stop and changing the Opacity value. The fade bar updates to reflect your changes. To reposition a stop, drag it or type a value in the Location option box.

Midpoint markers represent the spot where the opacity value is half the difference between the opacity values of a pair of opacity stops. In other words, if you set one opacity stop to 30 percent and another to 90 percent, the midpoint marker shows you where the gradient reaches 60 percent opacity. You can relocate the midpoint marker, and thus change the spot where the gradient reaches that midrange opacity value, by dragging the marker or typing a new value in the Location option box.

Creating noise gradients

Adobe describes a noise gradient as a gradient that "contains randomly distributed colors within the range of colors that you specify." This means that Photoshop adds random colors to the parameters that you set in the Gradient Editor dialog box. Figure 6.15 demonstrates examples of three noise gradients, which should help clarify what's going on. Of course, if you wanted the looks achieved here, you could create these same gradients using the regular Solid gradient controls, but it would take you forever to add all the color and midpoint stops required to produce the same effect. If you're willing to let Photoshop randomly apply the colors, you'll save lots of time and get generally as good an effect as if you'd set up each of the stops yourself.

FIGURE 6.15

Three Noise gradients — with 50% Roughness (top), 100% Roughness (middle), and finally, 100% Roughness plus Transparency (bottom)

To create a noise gradient, select Noise from the Gradient Type menu in the Gradient Editor dialog box, as shown in Figure 6.16. You can adjust the gradient as follows:

- Raise the Roughness value to create more distinct bands of color, as in the middle example in Figure 6.15. Lowering the Roughness value results in softer color transitions, as you can see from the top example, which are set at one-half the Roughness value of the middle example.

- Use the color sliders at the bottom of the dialog box to define the range of allowable colors in the gradient. You can work in one of three color modes: RGB, HSB, or Lab. Select the mode you want from the pop-up menu above the sliders.

FIGURE 6.16

Use the Noise gradient option to create gradients like the ones you see in Figure 6.17.

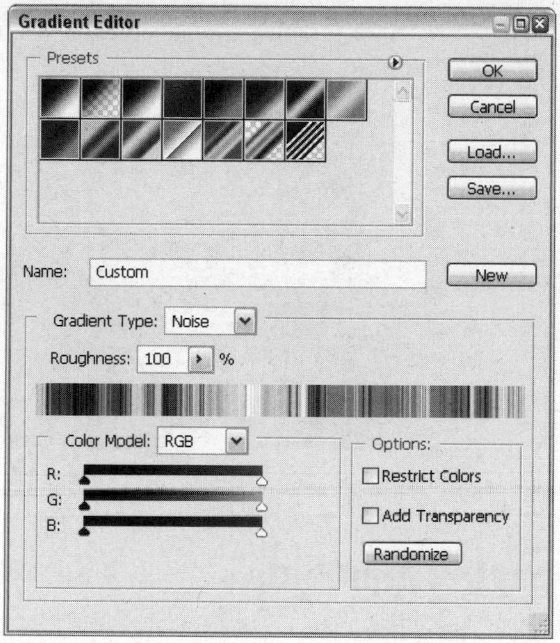

- The Restrict Colors option, when selected, adjusts the gradient so that you don't wind up with any oversaturated colors. Deselect the option for more vibrant hues.

- If you select Add Transparency, Photoshop adds random transparency information to the gradient, as if you had added many opacity stops to a regular gradient. In the bottom example of Figure 6.15, we started with the gradient from the middle example, selected the Add Transparency option, and left the Roughness value at 100.

- Click Randomize, and Photoshop shuffles all the gradient colors and transparency values to create another gradient. If you don't like what you see, just keep clicking Randomize until you're satisfied. Note that each click of Randomize produces a radically different gradient, so if you find a gradient that's close to what you're looking for, you may want to save it as a preset and continue tweaking it by hand.

TIP For some really cool effects, try applying special effects filters to a noise gradient. Figure 6.17 shows the results of applying the Gaussian Blur, Twirl, and Ripple filters on the original noise gradient shown in the left-most example. Find out how to apply these and other distorting filters in Chapter 11.

FIGURE 6.17

Four areas are selected along a rectangle, filled with a Noise Gradient. From left to right: Roughness set to 100%, Gaussian Blur filter set to 5 pixels, Twirl set at an angle of 300 degrees, and Ripple at 999% and set to Large. Experiment with other filters at various settings and see what cool results you get.

Saving and managing gradients

When you define a new gradient, its icon appears in the palette, the Preset Manager dialog box, and the Gradient Editor dialog box. But if you replace the current gradient set or edit the gradient, the originally applied gradient is deleted. You also lose the gradient if you delete your Photoshop CS3 preferences file because that's where the temporary gradient information is stored.

TIP   If you want to delete your preferences file, press Ctrl+Alt+Shift (⌘+Option+Shift on a Mac) as the application starts. A prompt asks if you really want to delete your preferences, and if you respond affirmatively, they're gone! Be sure to press the keys *before* you see the splash screen (the display that announces the software's name and developers) or you won't get the prompt.

If you want to preserve a gradient, you must save it as part of a *preset* — which is nothing more than a collection of gradients. Photoshop ships with several gradient presets stored in the Gradients folder, which resides inside the Presets folder in the main Photoshop program folder. You can create as many custom presets as you like. Gradient presets have the *.grd* file extension.

You can save all the gradients in the active preset — including any custom gradients that you define — by clicking Save in the Gradient Editor dialog box or by choosing Save Gradients from the Gradient palette pop-up menu. But if you want to save only some of the current gradients as a preset, choose Preset Manager from the Gradient palette pop-up menu and then display the Gradients panel, shown in Figure 6.18, by pressing Ctrl+3 (⌘+3 on the Mac) or by choosing Gradients from the Preset Type pop-up menu. Ctrl+click (Cmd+click on the Mac) the gradients you want to save, and then click Save Set. If you want to dump the selected gradients into an existing preset, select the preset file and press Enter or Return. Alternatively, you can type a new preset name to create a brand-new preset that contains only the selected gradients.

To select specific gradients and save them as a new preset, use the Preset Manager.

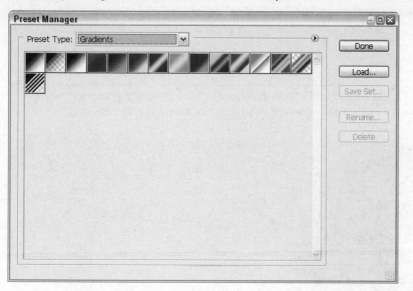

To delete a gradient, Alt+click (Option+click on the Mac) its icon in the palette, the Preset Manager, or the Gradient Editor dialog box. To delete multiple gradients, Ctrl+click (use Cmd+click on the Mac) the gradients in the Preset Manager and then click Delete. Save the preset immediately if you want the deleted gradients gone for good; otherwise, they remain an official part of the preset and reappear the next time you load the preset.

Gradients and brush modes

All standard brush modes, including the two new ones for CS3 (Lighter Color and Darker Color), are available when you apply gradients, and they make a tremendous impression on the performance of the gradient tool. This section examines one way to apply a brush mode in conjunction with the tool. Naturally, given the millions of combinations of gradients and modes, this section can't possibly do more than touch the surface of what's possible (otherwise, this would be a 5,000-page book), but it may inspire you to experiment and discover additional effects on your own.

To apply a mode when using a gradient, first select your gradient — using either the drop list of presets or setting up your own gradient through the Gradient Editor dialog box (access to this is described earlier in this section of the chapter). With your gradient chosen, use the Mode drop list to pick the mode you want used when the gradient is applied.

Next, click and drag your mouse to apply the gradient. As stated earlier, this can be done on a layer with no selection made (so the entire layer is affected) or to a selection within a layer. The gradient is applied, with the chosen mode's effect, as shown in Figure 6.19. You then can go back and apply different gradients or reapply the same one with different modes, creating interesting compound effects, or you can undo and start over with a different gradient, a different mode, or both.

FIGURE 6.19

The Dissolve mode is applied with a Foreground to Transparency gradient, creating a grainy fog over the surface of the image. The gradient was applied to an entire layer, rather than to a selection.

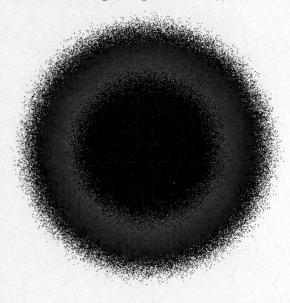

Applying Strokes and Arrowheads

Photoshop is nearly as adept at drawing lines and outlines as it is at filling selections — and like the fill tools and commands, Photoshop's tools for drawing lines and outlines are as varied. By "drawing lines" in this section, we don't mean the same lines we talk about in Chapter 5; the word "lines" here refers to what you'd call outlines and borders. The following sections discuss how to apply a border around a selection outline — which is practical, if not terribly exciting — and how to create arrowheads — which can yield more interesting results than you may think.

To further clarify what we mean by lines, bear in mind that we're talking about *raster* lines — that is, lines made of pixels that you create with the Line tool set to the Fill Pixels mode. To find out how to use the tool to produce vector lines and work paths, see Chapters 15 and 8, respectively. Some Line tool techniques discussed here apply to the Line tool also when it's set to vector mode or work path mode.

Stroking a selection outline

Strokes make great frames and outlines. Generally, you can apply a stroke to an image in Photoshop in four ways:

- **Stroke command:** Select the portion of the image that you want to stroke, and choose Edit ➪ Stroke to display the Stroke dialog box shown in Figure 6.20. Or, if you're working on a multilayered image, you can choose the Stroke command without making a selection; Photoshop then applies the stroke to the entire layer, unless the layer in question is the Background layer, which can only be stroked if it is unlocked and is no longer serving as the Background layer.

  In the Stroke dialog box, type the thickness of the stroke in the Width option box. The default unit of measurement here is pixels, but you can use inches and centimeters as well. Just type the value and then the unit abbreviation (*px* for pixels, *in* for inches, or *cm* for centimeters).

FIGURE 6.20

Use the options in the Stroke dialog box to specify the thickness of a stroke and its location with respect to the selection outline.

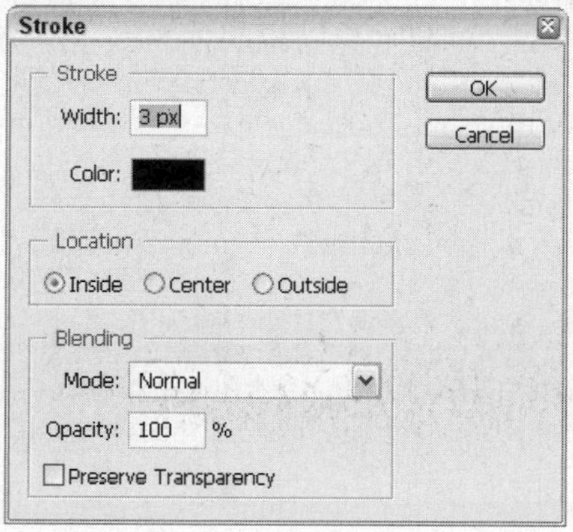

Stroke	☒
┌─ Stroke ────────────	
Width: 3 px	OK
Color: ▉	Cancel
┌─ Location ───────	
⊙ Inside ○ Center ○ Outside	
┌─ Blending ───────	
Mode: Normal ▾	
Opacity: 100 %	
☐ Preserve Transparency	

You also can set the stroke color from within the dialog box. Click the color swatch to select a color from the Color Picker — don't forget that you have full access to the Eyedropper tool (it is automatically activated simply by choosing Edit ➪ Stroke), so any color on your screen is fair game, too, and can be selected by clicking it while the Color Picker is open. Press Enter or Return to close the Color Picker and return to the Stroke dialog box after you've made your selection.

TIP Select a Location radio button to specify the position of the stroke with respect to the selection outline. When in doubt, select Inside from the Location radio buttons. This setting ensures that the stroke is entirely inside the selection outline in case you decide to move the selection. If you select Center or Outside, Photoshop applies part or all of the stroke to the deselected area around the selection outline — unless, of course, your selection extends to the edge of the canvas, in which case you wind up with no stroke at all for Outside and half a stroke inside the selection outline for Center.

The Stroke dialog box also includes Mode, Opacity, and Preserve Transparency options that work like those in the Fill dialog box.

- **Border command:** Select a portion of the image, and choose Select ⇨ Modify ⇨ Border to retain only the outline of the selection. Specify the size of the border by typing a value in pixels in the Width option box, and press Enter or Return. To fill the border with the background color, press Ctrl+Backspace (⌘+Delete on the Mac). To fill the border with the foreground color, press Alt+Backspace (Option+Delete on the Mac). To apply a repeating pattern to the border, choose Edit ⇨ Fill and select the Pattern option from the Use pop-up menu.

- **Layer Style effects:** If you want to stroke an entire layer, try the options provided by the Layer Style feature. Choose Layer ⇨ Layer Style ⇨ Stroke to display the Layer Style dialog box shown in Figure 6.21. At first glance, the options here appear to mirror those you find in the regular Stroke dialog box. They do, as long as you select Color from the Fill Type pop-up menu. If, on the other hand, you choose Gradient or Pattern, you can fill the stroke with (surprise!) a gradient or a pattern, or you can adjust the pattern and gradient on the fly and preview the results in the dialog box. For example, you can scale the gradient and change its angle — two things you can't do in the regular Gradient Editor dialog box, so the availability of these options courtesy of the pop-up menu is even more convenient. By using the settings shown in the figure, a plain, old black-to-white gradient has been adapted to produce the shadowed frame effect you see in the preview (the small block on the right side of the dialog box — just in case you were expecting an image preview).

CROSS-REF The Layer Style dialog box is covered in detail in Chapter 15, so if you have any questions about or problems with the stroke options, look there for help.

- **Canvas Size trick:** Okay, so this one is a bit unorthodox and probably was not intended for this purpose, but it works, so here you go. To create an outline around the entire image, choose Image ⇨ Canvas Size, select the Relative option, and type twice the desired border thickness in pixels in the Width and Height options.

  For example, to create a 1-pixel border all the way around, type 2 pixels for the Width value (1 for the left side and 1 for the right) and 2 pixels for the Height value (1 for the top and 1 for the bottom). (You also could deselect the Relative option and add 2 pixels to the existing Width and Height values if you're inordinately fond of doing math.) Leave the Anchor option set to the center tile so that the added canvas is applied on all sides of the image. Choose Other from the Canvas Extension Color pop-up menu to open the Color Picker dialog box. Select a color, and click OK to return to the Canvas Size dialog box. When you press Enter or Return, Photoshop enlarges the canvas size according to your specifications and fills the new pixels around the perimeter of the image with the color you chose. Simple, logical, and it works. Who could ask for more?

FIGURE 6.21

With the Stroke options in the Layer Style dialog box, you can stroke a layer with a solid color, gradient, or pattern. You also can adjust the angle and scale of gradients to create the effect shown in the preview.

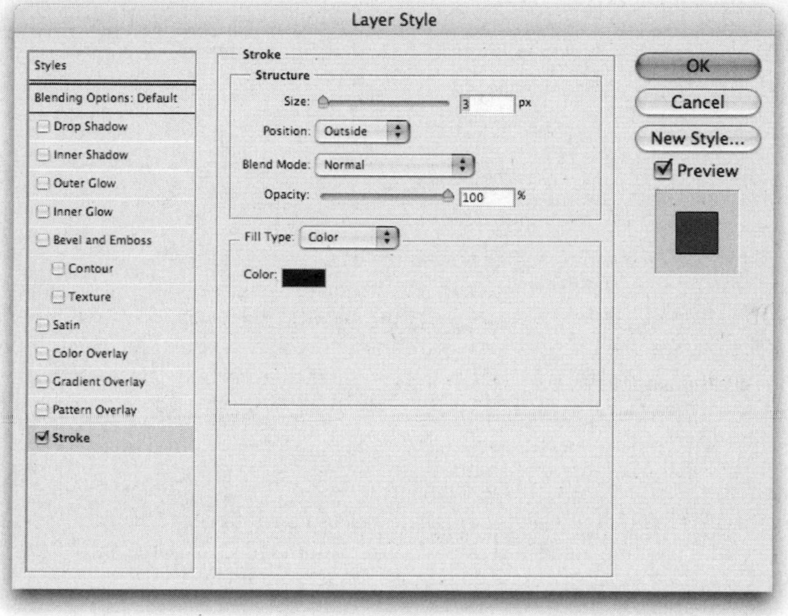

Applying arrowheads to straight lines

The one function missing from all the operations in the preceding list is applying arrowheads. This is not because we forgot to discuss it — rather, it's because, in Photoshop, you can apply arrowheads only to straight lines drawn with the Line tool.

The Line tool is grouped with the drawing tools — the tools you use for drawing shapes like rectangles, ellipses, polygons, and custom shapes. You can cycle among the tools by pressing U (or Shift+U, depending on your preferences setting for switching tools). The Line tool can create three kinds of shapes. You can paint raster lines — that is, lines made up of pixels — or you can draw vector-based lines on a new shape layer, as explained in Chapter 15. Finally, you can create a work path using the Line tool, which is discussed in Chapter 8.

You specify which type of line you want to create by clicking one of the three icons near the left end of the Options bar, which you can see labeled in Figure 6.22. If you don't see the Options bar, press Enter or Return, or double-click the Line tool icon in the Toolbox.

FIGURE 6.22

The arrowhead options appear in this drop-down palette.

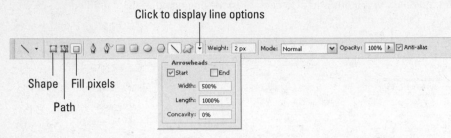

Click to display line options

Shape | Fill pixels

Path

TIP   When choosing the type of line you're going to create, remember that the Shape Layers option creates a...surprise!...shape layer (containing a vector shape, which you can later rasterize by right-clicking the layer and choosing Rasterize Shape from the pop-up menu), Paths creates a path from the line you draw, and Fill Pixels creates a raster line. If you choose Fill Pixels, the line you draw becomes part of the active layer (unless you're on a Shape or Type layer), so be careful to create a new layer for the raster line if your goals for further editing require the line to be on its own editable layer.

Regardless of which type of line you're creating, you set the width of the line by typing a value into the Weight box in the Options bar. Then you add arrowheads using the drop-down options palette shown in the figure. To display the options, click the triangle at the end of the strip of shape icons. Use the Arrowheads options as follows:

- **Start:** Select this option to add an arrowhead to the beginning of a line drawn with the Line tool.

- **End:** Select this option to add an arrowhead to the end of a line. This sounds like something you probably didn't need explained to you, but it's surprising how many people don't realize that the way the line is drawn, from where you begin to drag to where you stop dragging, determines the start and finish of the line and therefore which end is the pointy end of the arrow.

- **Width:** Type the width of the arrowhead in this option box. The width is measured as a percentage of the line weight, so if the Weight is set to 6 pixels and the Width value is 500 percent, the width of the arrowhead is 30 pixels. This opportunity to do some multiplication can be very exciting for you math fans out there.

- **Length:** Type the length of the arrowhead, measured from the base of the arrowhead to its tip, as a percentage of the line weight.

- **Concavity:** You can specify the shape of the arrowhead by typing a value between negative and positive 50 percent in the Concavity option box. Figure 6.23 shows examples of a few Concavity settings applied to an arrowhead 50 pixels wide and 100 pixels long, the top arrow at –50 percent and the bottom at 50 percent.

FIGURE 6.23

Various arrowhead concavity settings are in use on the left, and Outer Glow and Bevel blending modes were also applied to the arrows and the target.

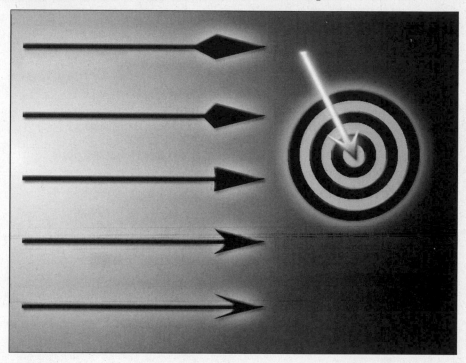

Summary

In this chapter, you learned to apply color with the Paint Bucket tool and Fill command, including the use of Fill tools and commands for filling a selection with custom patterns.

For interesting fills, you also learned about using the Gradient features, including the ability to design your own multicolor gradients and apply them with blend modes for interesting results. You also learned how to create outlines and borders and how to work with Stroke commands, including the ability to attach an arrowhead to any stroke.

Chapter 7

Retouching and Restoring

By now, assuming you're reading this book from cover to cover, you understand an extensive set of editing tools and methods — smearing and sponging, filling and stroking, and the art of painting. If you're not reading the chapters serially, which is fine, you can refer back to the chapters that precede this one for coverage of any unfamiliar tools referred to in this chapter.

The tools covered in this chapter — the stamps, healing and patching tools, Erasers, History Brushes, and red-eye removal tools — all enable you to repair damaged images, erase mistakes, and restore operations from your recent past. In short, they make it possible for you to perform the sorts of miracles that simply weren't possible in the days before computer imaging.

These sorts of miracles can be performed on both new, but poorly composed or developed photos and vintage photos showing decades of wear and tear. With Photoshop's restoration tools, you can bring new life to all your photos and scanned documents, all without the slightest fear of damaging the originals, whether they are electronic or printed. And, by scanning your originals — photos, documents, clippings, or even original artwork — you're helping to preserve those originals from further wear and exposure to sun and other damaging light sources. Put the originals away in a safe place, and enjoy the scanned versions without fear.

Using the Tools of the Trade

With these promises in mind, let's look at the tools we're talking about with this very brief but incisive tour:

- **Clone Stamp:** With its significant improvements in CS3, you can use the Clone Stamp tool to replicate pixels from up to five areas in an image to another. The added Clone Source palette (in conjunction with the tool's Options bar) makes it possible to clone from these multiple sources, as well as enabling you to fine-tune the clone source location, size, and opacity. The Clone Stamp, even before the beefing-up it received in this latest release of Photoshop, is ideally suited to removing dust, repairing minor defects, and eliminating distracting background elements. To fire up this tool, you can click the Clone Stamp icon on the Toolbox or press S. To open the Clone Source palette, choose Window ➪ Clone Source.

- **Pattern Stamp:** Sharing a button on the Toolbox with the Clone Stamp, you can activate the Pattern Stamp by Alt-clicking (Option-clicking on the Mac) the Clone Stamp icon in the Toolbox or pressing S or Shift+S to switch to the Pattern Stamp tool. This tool paints with a repeating image tile selected from Photoshop's library of predefined patterns or defined using Edit ➪ Define Pattern or Filter ➪ Pattern Maker.

- **Healing Brush, Spot Healing Brush,** and **Patch tools:** These three tools are in many ways variations on the Clone Stamp tool in that they take texture detail from one portion of an image and merge it with color and brightness values from another. This permits you more flexibility when retouching imperfections, particularly when repairing tricky defects, such as scratches and wrinkles. The Healing Brush uses a similar technique to that of the Clone Stamp, requiring you to establish a source point and then paint that source content over the rip, tear, or other defect. Unlike the Clone Stamp, however, the healing source content melds with the surrounding pixels to match the color, light, and textures in its new location. The Spot Healing Brush doesn't require sampling or setting a source first— instead, you just paint over the defect, and based on the surrounding pixels, Photoshop fixes the offending spot. Press J or Shift+J to switch to the Patch tool, which allows you to repair entire selections at a time.

- **Red Eye tool:** This tool, which shares a button with the Healing and Spot Healing Brushes and the Patch tool, removes red eye (or any unwanted glow in the eyes of the photo's subjects) through the use of two settings—Pupil Size and Darken Amount. Almost scarily simply, you can click a glowing pupil and darken it without creating that glass-eyed doll look that can often result from manually darkening a pupil or painting out the glow with the Brush tool or by using the Burn tool, the latter of which often results in a strangely colored pupil. Of course, for some red-eye situations, the manual approach with brush tools is the only way to get a flawless result—and this approach also is covered later in this chapter.

- **Eraser:** When used in a single-layer image or on the background layer, the Eraser tool paints in the background color. When applied to a layer, it erases pixels to reveal the layers below. The Eraser has three modes: Brush, Pencil, and Block. The former two offer the same brush options (on the Options bar) as the tools of the same name. In Block mode, a static-sized square "brush" is used to erase a single block of pixels (if you click) or a choppy, angular stroke of pixels (if you drag).

CROSS-REF The Eraser tool also includes two tool variations — the Background Eraser tool and Magic Eraser tool, shown in Figure 7-1 — which automatically extract background details from a layer. Because their specific purpose is to extract and they work only with layered images, they're discussed independently of the standard Eraser tool in Chapter 9.

FIGURE 7.1

The main tools for restoring, repairing, and retouching photos are found in four buttons in the Toolbox.

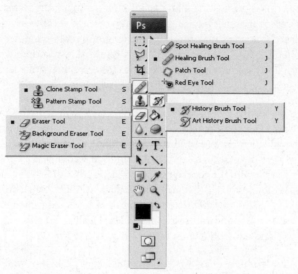

- **History Brush** and **Art History Brush:** The History Brush tool allows you to selectively revert to any of several states listed in the History palette. To select the *source state* that you want to paint with, click in the first column of the History palette, next to the state to which you'd like to go back. A brush icon identifies the source state, as illustrated by the Lasso item in Figure 7.1. If Photoshop displays a little "not-allowed" cursor when you try to use the History Brush tool, it means you can't paint from the selected state. Click another state in the History palette, and try again.

  Alt-click (Option-click on the Mac) the History Brush icon or press Y or Shift+Y to switch to the art History Brush tool, which lets you apply impressionistic effects based on the active source state in the History palette. It's not a terribly useful tool, but it can be lots of fun, allowing you to choose from different brush Style options, for long, short, or medium strokes.

Now, obviously, these are the very simplified introductions to Photoshop's restoring and retouching tools, but the goal at this point is to provide you with a general idea of how the tools work and why you'd use them — not to describe their use in complete detail. With this accomplished, you're ready to learn about the individual tools and how they work, how to get interesting effects from them, and how to manage their options for customized results.

Cloning and Healing

The Clone Stamp tool, which has been improved in Photoshop CS3, works by duplicating specified portions of an image and placing those cloned portions on top of existing content. Unlike a copy and paste that creates a new layer with the obscuring content, the Clone Stamp covers up things you don't want and places the obscuring content on the active layer. The process of using this tool is very simple (even with the new improvements) and has just a few options to keep in mind. The basic steps include selecting the tool — which you can do by pressing S and then Alt (Option on the Mac) — and Alt-click (Option-click on the Mac) in the image window to specify the portion of the image you want to clone. This is termed the *source point*. After sampling the source point, you can paint the cloned content onto any other part of the image — or even another image that's open at the same time. Read on to learn that you can control the Clone Stamp tool's effects by choosing a brush preset and Mode, and choosing how the cloned content is sampled as you drag your mouse to paint the clone over the image. You also can set up to five clone sources, on separate layers, and control their exact positions through the new Clone Source palette, which we discuss shortly.

Closely related to the Clone Stamp tool is the Healing Brush tool, which clones multiple attributes of an image at a time. Press J to select the tool, and then, as with the Clone Stamp, Alt-click (Option-click on the Mac) in the image to set the source of the clone. Note that the Clone Stamp and Healing Brush share a common source point, so setting the source for one tool sets it for both. To use the Healing Brush, drag with the tool to mix the texture from the source point with the highlights, shadows, and colors of pixels that are found adjacent to the brushstroke, and see them applied to the target location. This works differently than the Clone Stamp, which deposits the cloned material with its source lighting and color intact. The Healing Brush actually updates the cloned material so that it blends in with its new surroundings.

Of course, you can probably think of a few ways to use this. That pesky kid who makes faces in all family photos can now be replaced with whatever was behind him in the photo (or his smirk replaced with a normal expression, borrowed from a more mature sibling), that mud puddle in front of your house can be filled in with nice green grass, and those scratches, tears, and stains in your old and/or improperly stored photos can now be repaired, using clean content from elsewhere in the same image or from an image with compatible content. You also can use these tools artistically — not just as a repair mechanism — to improve by cloning and healing all sorts of interesting content from one place or image to another.

The Clone Stamp tool

Although easy to use, there are a few options that you can use to control the tool and achieve different results — and these require a little practice. CS3 also has a whole new palette, but you don't have to use the palette at all. If you've used the Clone Stamp in previous versions of Photoshop, you can continue to use it the "old way," ignoring the new capabilities. So, let's start with the basics, dealing only with the tool and its Options bar. We'll get to the new palette later.

First, if you just click the Clone Stamp and start dragging, Photoshop balks and throws a prompt in your face warning you that you must first define a source point. Do this by pressing Alt (Windows) or Option (Mac) and clicking the desired source point in the image. Of course, you'll want to have picked out your source point (and activated the layer on which the content resides) before clicking.

How cloning works

After you've established your source point, click or drag with the tool in some other region of the image to paint a cloned spot or line. Click if you want to place a single clone of the source point on some other place in the image, or drag if you want to create a series of clones in one continuous stretch. In Figure 7.2, for example, the bird was clicked with the Alt (Option) key pressed, and then the curved line shown to the right was painted. The stamp brush cursor shows the end of the drag: The clone source cross hair indicates the corresponding point in the original image.

FIGURE 7.2

The Clone Stamp tool is being dragged to paint with the image. To make things easier to see, the cloned content was applied to a white area.

Alt-click (Option-click) to set the source point…   and then paint away.

The Clone Stamp tool copies pixels from one location…   to another.

Clone source cross hair   Stamp brush cursor

It's worth noting that the Clone Stamp tool clones the image as it existed before you began using the tool and continues cloning for as long as you hold down the mouse button. Even when you drag over an area that contains a clone, the tool references the original appearance of the image. This means there may be a visual disconnect between what the Clone Stamp tool seems to be sourcing and what it paints. This is actually a good thing, however, because it avoids repetition of detail, a dead giveaway of poor retouching. This is illustrated in Figure 7.3, where the source cross hair is currently over a clone of the bird, yet the Stamp brush cursor is actually laying down more of the grass from the original image that the cloned bird is now concealing.

FIGURE 7.3

So that you don't end up creating more than a single clone in one drag, the Clone Stamp tool continues to clone from the image as it appears prior to your initial painting.

Throughout a drag, the clone tool copies from the original image.

 Photoshop lets you clone not only within the image in which you're working but from a separate image window as well. This technique makes it possible to merge two different images, as demonstrated in Figure 7.4. To achieve this effect, Alt-click (Option-click) to set a source point in one image, bring a second image to the foreground, and then drag with the Clone Stamp tool to copy from the first image. You also can clone between layers, assuming the layers are unlocked. Just Alt-click (Option-click) one layer and then switch to a different layer and drag.

FIGURE 7.4

The Clone Stamp tool allows us to merge our little bird with his #1 pal, the cheetah.

Cloning options

When the Clone Stamp tool is active, the Options bar gives you access to the standard Brush, Mode, and Opacity settings that you get when using the Brush tool. These options enable you to mix the cloned image with the original to get different effects, as explained in Chapter 5. You also get the Flow value and Airbrush icon, which make it possible for you to build up brushstrokes where they overlap and at points where you click without moving the cursor.

You'll also find the Sample option, which lets you clone from the Current Layer, the Current Layer and Below (the layer/s beneath the current layer), and All Layers. This sort of control is essential to using this tool effectively, especially when working with composite images where you may need to keep content on separate layers but want repairs to grab from all content, or where you want to clone only what's on one particular layer.

An option that you haven't seen before presents both a wrinkle and a real opportunity to get some interesting effects with the Clone Stamp tool. It's the Aligned option, which locks the relative source of a clone from one Alt-click or Option-click to the next. Huh? OK, try this. Think of the locations where you Alt-click (Option-click on the Mac) and begin dragging with the Clone Stamp tool to opposite ends of an imaginary straight line, as illustrated in Figure 7.5. When Aligned is selected, the length and angle of this imaginary line remains fixed until the next time you Alt-click. As you drag, Photoshop moves the line, cloning pixels from one end of the line and laying them down at the other. The benefit is that regardless of how many times you start and stop dragging with the stamp tool, all brushstrokes match up as seamlessly as pieces in a puzzle.

NOTE The glow around the cloned areas is added through blending modes (see Chapter 14) and was applied only to make it clearer to you where the cloning was applied.

If you want to clone from a single portion of an image repeatedly, deselect the Aligned option — note that this option was off in Figure 7.3, where the repeated pattern of feathers was desirable, yet total uniformity in terms of what was cloned was not desirable, as no two feathers are the same, even if they're growing in a uniform pattern. Figure 7.6 shows how, with the Aligned option selected, Photoshop clones from the same point every time you paint a new line with the Clone Stamp tool. As a result, each of the brushstrokes brings in some of the photo of the bird, but the strokes don't line up with each other as they did in Figure 7.4.

TIP If your image has adjustment layers (discussed in Chapter 18), you can ignore those layers by turning on the last option on the Clone Stamp's Options bar — whose screentip aptly states "Turn On to Ignore Adjustment Layers When Cloning." Told you this stuff was easy.

FIGURE 7.5

With the Aligned option selected, the cloned content stays in sync with the source points, a new one set each time you click and drag to place cloned content in target areas.

FIGURE 7.6

If you deselect the Aligned option, Photoshop clones only from the point at which you initially Alt-clicked or Option-clicked to set your source point.

The Clone Source Palette

New to Photoshop CS3, the Clone Source palette, which you can display by choosing Window ⇨ Clone Source, shares space on the dock with the Brushes palette. Therefore, if you've already displayed the Brushes palette at some point in your current session, you already have Clone Source onscreen, if minimized.

The palette, shown in Figure 7.7, contains four sections, each giving you different powers over different aspects of the Clone Stamp tool:

FIGURE 7.7

The Clone Source palette expands the Clone Stamp's power and your power over it.

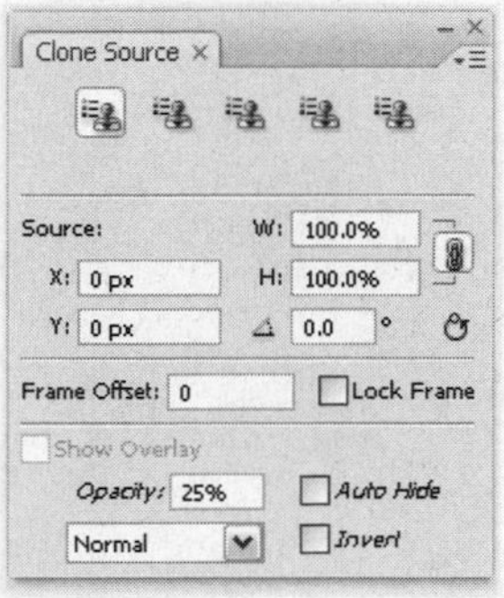

- **Clone Source:** The five icons in the top section each represent a source point in an image, on a particular layer. If you want to use them — if you plan to clone several parts of the image and want to establish them ahead of time — you can click the first Clone Source icon and then Alt-click (Option-click on the Mac) to set the source point. The icon then displays the name of the image and the active layer when the source point was established, below the icon itself. To set a second source, click the second button and set your source point. You can do this up to five times, and of course, you can replace any of the set sources with a new one, simply by clicking the button and using the Alt-click (or Option-click) method to resample a source point.

- **Transform:** The second set of options relate to the *offset*, or position, within the image for a clone source, as well as the *scale* of the source point and its *rotation*. You can use the first of these fields (X and Y) to determine the location of the cloned content, and then to the right of this are the W and H fields (for Width and Height), which you can use to set the horizontal (W) and vertical (H) scale of the clone you create. For example, you can set an offset of 50 pixels and a scale of 50 percent, and create a duplicate of the clone source content that's half the size of, and 50 pixels away from, the original content, as shown in Figure 7.8. If you create the clone on a new layer (by creating and switching to that layer before using the Clone Stamp and source), you can create duplicate content in varying sizes and positions for a variety of uses. Of course, you also can rotate the source point (enter a value in the field next to the rotation symbol) and reset the Transform information by clicking the last button in the lower left of this section of the palette.

TIP　When setting the scale, you can constrain the proportions so that any change to the W setting is reflected in the H setting, and vice versa. This setting is on by default (see the chain icon to the right of the fields), and clicking the chain turns it off — which you might choose to do if you want to adjust one scale setting without affecting the other at all.

FIGURE 7.8

Using another shot from our friend Terri Shadle, we've cloned from one layer to another, at 50 percent of the original size and rotated -45 degrees.

- **Frame:** Here you're dealing with the Frame Offset, which is used with video frames. This is discussed in Chapter 19. The Lock Frame option, also found in this section of the Clone Source palette, is discussed there, too.

- **Overlay:** In this last section of the Clone Source palette, you can display an overlay of your clone source layer — that is, all content from the layer from which you're cloning is displayed while you clone the content to another layer or elsewhere on the same layer. This option, which is particularly helpful if your clone source is not visible while you're cloning, is shown in Figure 7.9. If you turn on the Auto Hide option, the overlay is hidden while you're dragging the tool, but it appears while the Clone Stamp is active. The Invert option simply inverts the overlay color so that it's more visible if you're working in an image with lots of like colors. You can set the Opacity and choose a mode (Normal, Darken, Lighten, or Difference) for the overlay's visual quality. None of the overlay options affect the final image — they're just there to assist you in using your clone source.

TIP Keyboard shortcut fans will enjoy using Alt+Shift+Arrow (Option+Shift+Arrow for the Mac) to nudge the clone source when doing aligned cloning. You can use Alt+Shift+[or] to rotate the clone source (Option+Shift+[or] on the Mac) and use Alt+Shift+< or > (Option+Shift+< or > for the Mac) to scale the clone source.

FIGURE 7.9

Want to see your clone source while you're cloning? Here we have the Overlay option enabled, with the Opacity set to 50 percent and the Invert check box selected. Use the Overlay option to make it easy to clone specific content from your source and keep track of what you're cloning.

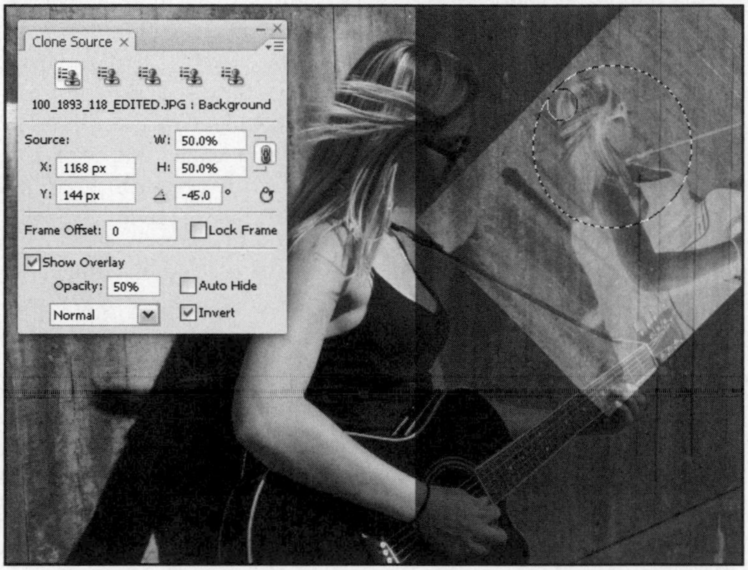

So, for non-video-related cloning, how would you use the Clone Source palette? The biggest new feature, and the feature to be of most use, is the ability to create those additional clone sources, and to use the buttons in the dialog box to go back to them as you're working in an image. You can click the buttons to tell Photoshop which source you're cloning from now, and use the Options bar to control how the cloning is applied. Then just click and/or drag the Clone Stamp tool to apply the cloned content to whichever open image (and layer within that image) you want. To switch to a different clone source from those you've already set in the palette, go to the palette, click the source (view the text underneath the button to make sure it's the one you want), return to the image, and begin cloning.

Of course, the ability to establish offset and scale options is great, too — with these settings, you can create exact duplicates of content, at the exact size you need, in the exact spot you need them. The Overlay option can help show you exactly what's being cloned, by referencing the source content, and with these three features in use, some of the "surprise" aspects of the Clone Stamp's effects are virtually eliminated.

TIP Like any other palette with fields into which you can enter values, you can establish your settings by typing numbers into the boxes, or select the current setting and use your up and down arrows to increase or decrease the values in small increments.

325

The Healing Brush tool

Way back in Photoshop 7, the nearly magical Healing Brush tool was presented to a grateful world of Photoshop users in need of help. Even now, its powers seem amazing, and almost too good to be true.

If you thought the Clone Stamp tool was the bee's knees (and you were right), get ready for the cat's pajamas. Open a photo that needs some work. For the example shown in Figure 7.10, a vintage photo with some serious scars on it is a great subject on which to demonstrate the tool. Because there are places that are unmarked, we can use them to cover the scars—but unlike the Clone Stamp, which can be used to take the clean content and duplicate it on top of the scars, the Healing Brush not only clones that clean content but also relights and colors it to meet the needs of its new surroundings. The Spot Healing Brush tool, which we discuss shortly, does the same thing, but with small troubled areas—thus the tool's name including the word "Spot."

Anyway, in Figure 7.10, see the before (left) and after (right) versions, wherein large scars—scuffs and scrapes with decades of dirt ground into them—are repaired with the Healing Brush tool.

FIGURE 7.10

Set the "way-back machine" to a time before this photo had been scuffed, scraped, and generally abused by storing it loose in a drawer full of other photos, pencils, rubber bands, and other bits and pieces that have no business bumping into a precious glimpse of relatives past.

To make the changes seen in Figure 7.10, select the Healing Brush tool by pressing J, which you can remember because it's the only letter missing from the words *heal*, *patch*, *mend*, *fix*, *knit*, *remedy*, *salvage*, *cobble*, and *requite*. Or, just click the tool with your mouse — it may be easier that way. Next, press Alt (Option) and click in the image to identify the texture that you want to match. Then paint over a spot, scratch, scar, or wrinkle, and watch as the Healing Brush lives up to its name.

How the healing works

In getting to know the Healing Brush tool, you quickly discover two things. When it works, it works incredibly well, better than any other retouching technique available in Photoshop. But when it doesn't work, it fails completely, in that it can bring in colors and shades that don't match their surroundings at all. What is the best way to avoid such a scenario and only have the Healing Brush make you happy? Take a little time to learn how the Healing Brush really works, and you'll learn not only how best to use it, but when to use the Clone Stamp tool instead.

Assuming that you're on board for the whole "take a little time" idea, let's take a moment and reveal some of the magic. The Healing Brush tool blends the pixels from the source point with the original pixels of your stroke made with the Healing Brush. In that respect, it works a little bit like the Clone Stamp tool combined with a brush mode — applying content from the source point, but at the same time changing colors and lighting as you paint. Instead of the rather simplistic technique of blending two pixels at a time as a brush mode does, the Healing Brush blends cloned pixels with those just outside the brushstroke, drawing information from those pixels to determine how to adjust the cloned content. The idea is that the pixels you're painting over are messed up, but the pixels just beyond the brushstroke are in good shape and should be emulated.

Figure 7.11 acts as a gross illustration of this concept. The Healing Brush tool has been used to clone portions of a photo onto a fabric background. The smooth image from the left is cloned onto the fabric, and the fabric's texture is smoothed away by the photo content applied by the Healing Brush. The lighting also is adjusted, achieved by Photoshop burning and dodging the healed content based on the source point. Bear in mind that it does all this according to the colors, highlights, and shadows that it encounters in tracing the very outer perimeter of the brushstroke, which is highlighted by the line drawn on the right side of Figure 7.11.

What can we deduce from this?

- First, the Healing Brush tool replaces the texture as you paint just as surely as if you were using the Clone Stamp tool. If you want to mix textures, you need to employ a brush mode, as explained in the next section.

- Second, the manner in which the color and shading are mixed is directly linked to the size and hardness of your brush. Bear in mind that Photoshop is looking at the outside edge of the brushstroke. As illustrated in Chapter 5 (on painting), the outer edge of the brush grows as the Hardness value shrinks. Therefore, you can count on soft brushes to cause the Healing Brush to factor in more surrounding colors and shading than hard brushes do.

FIGURE 7.11

The Healing Brush clones the content on the left side onto a textured background on the right. The line running down the ape's face on the left shows the path of the source point throughout the brushstroke. The line surrounding the brushstroke on the right shows that brushstroke's outer edge.

As with the Clone Stamp, press Alt-click (Option-click) to set the source point...

and then paint.

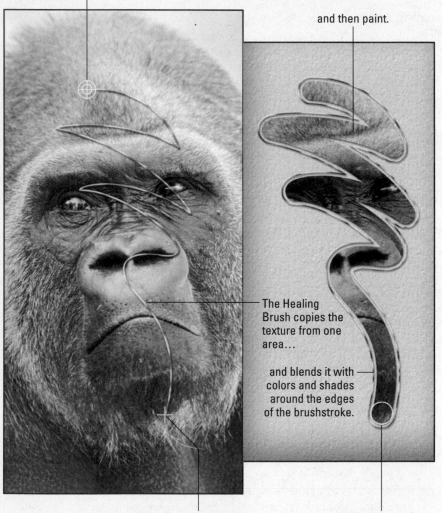

The Healing Brush copies the texture from one area...

and blends it with colors and shades around the edges of the brushstroke.

Clone source cross hair

Stamp brush cursor

So what if it all goes wrong and undesirable results appear where healing was expected? Just click Undo, or use the History palette to go back to before the healing began. Then tinker with your brush settings, changing the size and softness, until you get the results you are looking for. If all else fails, try the Clone Stamp tool — you may like the results. It could just be that the extra magic applied by the Healing Brush tool wasn't what was needed after all.

Healing options

Despite its powers and the intuitive way it applies content, you cannot customize the behavior of the Healing Brush tool in many ways. It permits you neither to use custom brushes nor to apply any of the settings in the Brushes palette. To modify a brush, click the Brush icon in the Options bar. This gives you access to Photoshop 6-style brush-tip settings along with a single dynamic that lets you link brush size to pen pressure or airbrush wheel.

You also have no control over Opacity or Flow. While this is a surprising omission, you can work around this problem by choosing Edit ⇨ Fade, as you discover later. The brush modes are limited to just eight, and in each case, the mode merges cloned and original pixels and then performs the additional healing blending. By way of example, Figure 7.12 shows four of the eight modes in use while the Healing Brush applied a single stroke (one stroke per Mode) to a gradient background. Thanks to the dodging and burning applied by the Healing Brush, dark modes such as Multiply and light modes such as Screen can be substantially compromised. In fact, most of the brush modes have little effect, as you can see in the figure — the strokes are not very different, and the differences you can see are subtle. This can either result in your finding the use of the modes to be a waste of time, or you may revel in their subtlety. Your choice.

The exception is Replace. Unique to the Healing Brush tool, the Replace mode clones pixels without any blending, just as if you were painting with the Clone Stamp tool set to Normal. The question is, why in the world would you want to do this, particularly when the Healing Brush set to Replace offers far fewer options than the highly customizable Clone Stamp tool? The answer is to test effects. Thanks to its blending routine, the Healing Brush sometimes takes several seconds to apply. But when set to Replace, it takes no time at all. You can test a brushstroke, make sure it's cloning the right area, undo it, switch back to Normal, and paint the real thing. Replace is so useful that it's worth remembering its shortcut, Shift+Alt+Z (Shift+Option+Z on the Mac). Press Shift+Alt+N (Shift+Option+N) to return to Normal.

Other options include the Source buttons, which determine whether the Healing Brush tool clones pixels (Sampled) or paints with a predefined texture (Pattern). You also have the Aligned option, which aligns multiple brushstrokes to a fixed source point, as described in the section "Cloning options." The Aligned options for the Healing Brush and Clone Stamp tools are linked, so selecting one selects the other as well.

FIGURE 7.12

Here are examples of the Healing Brush combined with four different Healing Brush modes across the same textured fabric as seen in Figure 7.10, with a light-to-dark gradient.

Source image

Healing brushstrokes

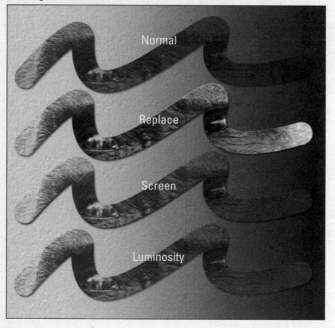

TIP   Don't forget the Healing Brush tool's Sample setting in the Options bar. Much like the similarly named option available to the Clone Stamp and Smudge tools (discussed in Chapter 5), selecting All Layers factors in information from every visible layer during the healing process. This can be a great asset because it allows you to create a new layer and perform all your pixel manipulation on it while retaining the original pixels on the layers below. Your other options, Current Layer and Current & Below, allow you to confine the healing effects to the active layer (Current) or that layer and those beneath it. Of course, you can shuffle layers before activating the tool if doing so facilitates the results you need — without bizarrely affecting the appearance of a composite image, that is.

The Spot Healing Brush

The Spot Healing Brush, which was introduced with Photoshop CS2, works very much like the Healing Brush tool in terms of its results, but the mechanism is a bit different when it comes to your role in the process. Instead of having to sample content and set a source point, all you have to do is click the tool on top of the offending spot—a small scratch, stain, blemish, or any other small area of unwanted content. If you attempt to sample by pressing Alt (Windows) or Option (Mac), you're prompted that if you want to manually set a source point, you should use the Healing Brush tool.

There are some drawbacks. As shown in Figure 7.13, Photoshop guesses which content to use in repairing the problem, and it can guess wrong. In the figure, you can see that the Proximity Match created a repair that is too light, and Create Texture created an unwanted texture (inset).

Of course, with a quick Undo, the bad results are reversed, and a click with the Spot Healing Brush tool on the other end of the scratch solves the problem, because there were more appropriate pixels nearby. Two more clicks along the scratch, and it is gone (see the "After" version on the right where the scratch is gone, although a problem created by the healing process remains). It's a great tool for a quick fix, but it does have its shortcomings. You also can try using a larger brush to do the repair in a single click, but you risk the area considered "proximity" including content that you don't want used in the healing process.

FIGURE 7.13

The Spot Healing Brush in Proximity Match mode works great when there is nothing but clear sailing next to the spot you're trying to heal. Here you can see its two healing types — Proximity Match and Create Texture — at work, and you also can see how the tool can sometimes go wrong.

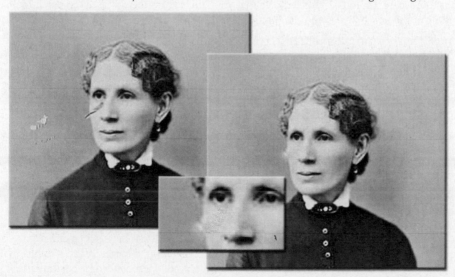

NOTE   This simple tool has options: You can go with the default Proximity Match, which heals the spot you click on using neighboring pixels; or you can click the Create Texture option, which heals and creates a texture based on nearby pixels. This can work well, or it can be a problem if the texture that Photoshop creates is visually effective. As shown in Figure 7.13, a texture on the face isn't a good thing—and its source is difficult to anticipate. The other option, Sample All Layers, enables Photoshop to draw its healing information from pixels on...well, you guessed it—all layers.

The Patch tool

If you prefer to heal a selected area all at once, choose the Patch tool from the Healing Brush flyout menu in the Toolbox. You also can press J—or if you did not deselect the Use Shift Key for Tool Switch option in the Preferences dialog box, press Shift+J instead.

You can use the Patch tool in two ways:

- **Define destination, drag onto source:** Assuming the Source option is selected in the Options bar, as it is by default, use the Patch tool to draw an outline around the portion of the image you want to heal. This creates a selection outline. In Figure 7.14, for example, the selection is shown in the top panel. Next, click and drag the selection outline to move it to a new location (the middle panel in Figure 7.14). The spot where you release the mouse button determines the source for the clone. When the selection is dropped (the bottom panel), Photoshop heals the content.

- **Define source, drag onto destination:** The former method seems a bit counterintuitive, or backward, to some people. If it seems backward to drag the offending content onto good content, then just swap things around. Choose Destination as the Patch method on the Options bar, and select an area to use as the patch. Then drag that onto the stuff you want to obscure. Of course, this requires that you either guess the shape of the patch by looking at the target area as you drag to select within the source area (where the good content is), or you can make the selection first, in the bad area, then move it to the good area, and *then* activate the Patch tool.

TIP   You can make a selection before using the Patch tool (in either Source or Destination mode) by using the Lasso or Marquee selection tools to draw the outline for the future patch. Then, activate the Patch tool and drag—either taking the selection to the place that needs healing or bringing healing content to the selection.

If you're wondering how the Patch tool's selection process works, it's just like the standard Lasso tool. You can add to a selection by Shift-dragging or delete by Alt-dragging (Option-dragging on the Mac), and you can soften a patch by using Select ➪ Feather or modify it in the Quick Mask mode, thus giving the Patch tool more room along the edge of the selection to sample colors and shades. For complete information on creating and editing selections, read Chapter 8.

The Patch tool lacks Opacity and brush mode controls, and you can't use it between layers or between different images. All work has to be performed on a single layer, which ultimately limits its potential. On the plus side, you can patch a selection with a predefined pattern by clicking the Use Pattern button in the Options bar.

FIGURE 7.14

Like cutting a swatch of fabric that's just a bit larger than the hole in your jeans, you can patch trouble spots with content from a clean spot on the photo. You can drag the patch to the problem, or drag the problem to the patch.

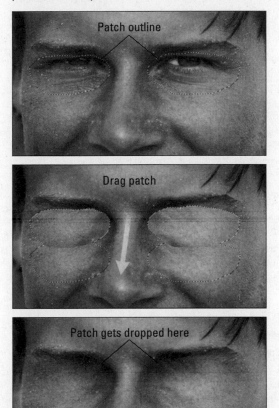

The Patch tool also gives you a preview of unaltered source pixels in your selected area while you're still dragging it around. This gives you a better idea of how the size and shape of the area from which you're pulling texture will fit when it combines with your original destination. You also have a Transparent option in the Options bar, which when selected enables the Patch tool to pull the texture but none of the color information from wherever you drag.

The Red Eye tool

Allegedly because of their large pupils, animals, especially those with some nocturnal vision capabilities, tend to become the most frequent victims of red eye in photos. Children are often victims, too, but that's often because one of them is either the adored subject and the photographer (mom or dad) gets too darn close when taking the picture, or the little darling moves in closer to the camera just as the picture's taken. The proximity of the lens and the flash also is a potential culprit, but with many cameras, you can't adjust this distance — the flash is atop the camera, and the lens is in a fixed position, too. Whatever the cause and whomever the victim, red eye is one of the most common problems faced by amateur photographers, especially the "home user" of cameras with a flash. As shown in Figure 7.15, you can get rid of it quickly with the Red Eye tool, a simple, fast tool for darkening and washing the glow right out of the demonically glowing pupil.

> **NOTE**   Red isn't always the color of the glow — sometimes, as shown in Figure 7.15, the glow is yellow (well, it appears light gray here, but take my word for it). In fact, rarely is the glow a single color — as you also see in this figure, where the glow is brightest in the center of the very large pupil. In the color version of this photo, it goes from canary yellow in the center to a burnt orange around the edges.

The Red Eye tool is bizarrely simple to use, and it's quite effective — to a point. It has two options — Pupil Size and Darken Amount, both set to 50% by default. You can drag the options' sliders to accommodate larger or smaller pupils and more or less of a glow in the subject's eyes. Remember to use different settings for each of the eyes if the subject was not facing the camera head-on — if the subject was at an angle, the eye farthest from the camera has a smaller pupil and may have less of a glow going on.

Now about that "to a point" comment: The tool works by washing out the color (as though you've used the Sponge tool in Desaturate mode), and it also darkens it (as if the Burn tool was used). In color photos, or in close-ups where the eye is quite visible in detail, this may not be a good thing, because having black or dark gray pupils in a color photo looks, well, weird. You may prefer to use the Burn tool yourself and use other color-adjustment tools to get rid of the red or yellow, essentially going back to one of the many manual methods of getting rid of red eye used in the past when this tool was not available. Figure 7.14 shows the almost grayscale-looking pupils, and as noted in the figure, shows the downside of not quite centering the tool when clicking the pupil — some of the iris has been relieved of its color as well, as seen in the left eye and shown in the zoomed inset.

FIGURE 7.15

Don't worry about selecting the pupil and painting or burning the glow away as you might have in previous versions of Photoshop. Instead, use the Red Eye tool to exorcise that glow and restore the look of sanity to your photos' subjects.

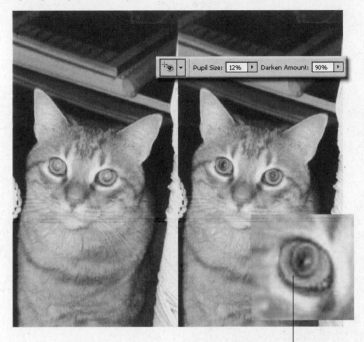

Be sure to center the tool, or you risk washing out the iris as well.

Retouching Photographs

Having seen how the Clone Stamp, Healing Brush, Spot Healing Brush, Patch, and Red Eye tools work, the following sections examine a few sample uses for the tools. For example, say you have a snapshot lying around, one that's really a good picture of someone you love, but it's in terrible shape, like the scanned photo shown in Figure 7.16. The problems are many — there are nicks and scratches in the photo's surface (damage from improper storage and rough handling of the print), and the photo is faded (age) and blurry (poor photographic and/or development). You probably don't need to *imagine* such a photo — you probably have many of them lying around the house, or if you're a professional photographer, your non-photographer relatives are creating these horrors on every holiday and vacation.

FIGURE 7.16

This is a very lovable shot of a child on a boat in 1965 at Cape Cod. The many problems shown in this zoomed-in view of the photo have Photoshop solutions.

Now, of course, there are some non-Photoshop solutions that you can try first. If you're scanning a printed photo, try cleaning your scanner's glass. Try tinkering with the scanner's settings for contrast and sharpness a bit (don't go wild, because these can cause more problems than they solve, depending on the scanner's software), and try increasing the resolution of your scan if lack of detail and color is a problem. Beyond that, you have what you have, and Photoshop is really your only solution.

So let's look at the solutions, some or all of which may be used depending on the photo, or perhaps only one of them will work—it really depends on the photo in question:

- **Dust & Scratches filter:** Try this if your image is sharp and clear but has lots of dust and scuffs on it—tiny, minor ones. This filter won't get rid of major scratches, but it will remove some of the "white noise" that can accumulate on a poorly stored or roughly handled photo.

- **Clone Stamp, Healing Brush, Spot Healing Brush,** and **Patch tools:** Yes, one or more of these, used to fix small and large problems, can be your salvation. They also can lead to backaches and headaches, because the more problems you have, the longer you'll spend fixing the photo flaws, bent over the monitor at a high, eye-scorching zoom. Figure 7.17 shows an "after" version of the photo in 7.16, where the Spot Healing Brush and Clone Stamp tools were used to clean up the bigger flaws, and the aforementioned Dust & Scratches filter was used on portions of the image — the sky, any place that didn't have too much detail to worry about losing — to do a general cleanup.

FIGURE 7.17

After a general sweep with the Dust & Scratches filter and some focused cleanup with the Clone Stamp and Spot Healing Brush tools, the photo looks much better — the stain in the sky behind the subject is gone and the tiny flaws have been softened and healed away.

As you discover in Chapter 10, the Dust & Scratches filter has one big downside — along with the dust, scratches, and tiny flaws that it miraculously removes, it also removes lots of your detail. Of course, you can tinker with the filter's settings to mitigate this a bit, or use it in selected areas only, perhaps restricting its use to the areas that are the most damaged, but if you let the filter work hard enough to really rid the photo of the tiny flaws, you lose the tiny details, too. Oh, well — Photoshop giveth, and Photoshop taketh away.

Because I don't like the loss of detail, in Figure 7.18, you can see the results of a final touch-up with the Smart Sharpen filter. This filter, also discussed in Chapter 10, goes over the image and adds back some of the detail lost to the Dust & Scratches filter. Of course, it can't re-create lost details, but it does add to the differences between adjacent pixels, eliminating that fuzzy, blurry look.

FIGURE 7.18

The final touch is to sharpen the image using the Smart Sharpen filter. The result is by no means perfect — Photoshop can't produce detail out of thin air — but the photo, one that I really love, is really suitable for framing now.

The lesson to draw from all this is that the Dust & Scratches filter may suffice for purging fibers and defects from a low-quality photo like this one, but it's hardly a professional-level tool. In most cases, the better alternative is to roll up your sleeves, get real with your image, and fix its flaws manually — not to mention lovingly — with the Healing Brush and Clone Stamp tools. You'll be glad you did.

Restoring an Old Photograph

Old photos present some unique problems. First, depending on their age, they may have been around for decades — maybe even a century — and even the most carefully stored photo of that vintage is going to show signs of its age. Add to that the fact that in the late nineteenth and early twentieth centuries, photos were printed on paper that doesn't hold up well: It was often textured, which can affect your scan adversely, and the paper dried out and crumbled, making what might have been an easily fixable fold or scrape into a huge scar that requires major restoration.

Figure 7.19 shows an old photo, one that was treated relatively well, but not stored in an environmentally controlled place. It was in a photo album since the 1960s, and before that, it was kept in a box. The photo was taken in 1887, and was scanned at 300 dpi as a color photo — despite it not really being "in color." Scanning it as a color photo brings in more information and allows the photo to be brought back to its sepia-tone glory with less loss of detail.

Despite the photo's rough condition, Photoshop's many restoration tools were able to restore it, as evidenced in Figure 7.20. After about an hour and a few hundred brushstrokes, the image was nearly back to its original state. If an hour sounds like a long time to fix a few rips and scrapes, bear in mind that photographic restoration is a labor-intensive activity that relies heavily on your talents and your mastery of Photoshop. The job of Photoshop's restoration tools is to make your edits believable, but they do little to automate the process. Retouching calls for a human touch, and that's where you come in.

The main trick in all this is to Alt-click (Option-click on the Mac) with the Clone Stamp or Healing Brush tools in an area that looks like it'd do a good job of covering up a blemish and then click or drag over the blemishes. For tiny spots where you aren't sure where to grab the cover-up material, use the Spot Healing Brush tool — just restrict its use to where there are clean pixels all around the spot — because that's where Photoshop will derive its content to cover the blemish you click on. Rather than take you back through a boring description of every click and drag we used to fix this image, here are some tips for ways to restore even the most damaged, faded, beat-up photo:

- **Toss the bad channels:** Most images in this kind of condition are in black and white. Scan them in color, and then look at the individual color channels, as shown in Figure 7.21, to see which grayscale version of the image looks best.
- **View actual pixels:** When possible, work at 100 percent view size or larger. It's difficult to judge scratches and other defects accurately at smaller zoom ratios, but if you must, stick with the "smooth views" — 50 percent and 25 percent.

■ **Keep an eye on the source:** Keep the original photo next to you as you work. What looks like a scratch onscreen may actually be a photographic element, and what looks like an element may be a scratch. Only by referring to the original image can you be sure.

TIP   Don't crop until you're finished retouching the image. You'd be surprised how useful that extra garbage around the perimeter is when it comes to covering up really big tears.

FIGURE 7.19

Portraits were serious business in the days when not everyone had access to a camera or a photographer. Smiling, even for a child, was virtually unheard of. Though treated reverentially over the years, it looks like this little guy knew how his photo would end up.

- **Vary the brush hardness:** Use hard brush shapes against sharp edges. But when working in general areas such as the shadow, the ground, and the wall, mix it up between soft and hard brushes using the shortcuts Shift+[and Shift+]. Staying random is the best way to avoid harsh transitions, repeating patterns, and other digital giveaways.

- **Keep it short:** Paint in short strokes. This helps keep things random, but it also means that you don't have to redraw a big, long brushstroke if you make a mistake.

TIP Use your History when you make a mistake. Don't automatically press Ctrl+Z (⌘+Z for you Mac people). In many cases, you'll be better off using the History Brush tool to paint back the image as it appeared before the last Healing Brush or Clone Stamp tool operation. You learn more about the History Brush later in this chapter.

FIGURE 7.20

Here's the same image after about an hour of work with the Clone Stamp, Spot Healing Brush, and the Healing Brush tools.

- **Deselect the Aligned option:** Another way to stay random is to change the source of your clone frequently. That means Alt-clicking (Option-clicking on the Mac) after every second or third brushstroke. And keep the Aligned option deselected. An aligned clone is not a random one.

FIGURE 7.21

When each channel is viewed separately, it's clear that the green channel looks best, with best contrast, fewest splotches, and crispest edges. Blue is way too dark and blotchy, and the red channel is nearly faded out to nothing.

Red   Green   Blue

- **Try out brush modes:** Feel free to experiment with the brush modes and, when using the Clone Stamp tool, the Opacity setting. You also can tinker with Mode settings for the Healing Brush tool, experimenting with lightening and darkening modes to see which one gives you the best results — of course, each picture and its individual flaws will dictate which one of the tools and which settings for it work best.

TIP   You also can try applying Edit ➪ Fade to change the opacity and brush mode of the pixels you just cloned. This little trick can be extremely useful when using the Healing Brush tool because it means you can introduce an Opacity value into the proceedings where none existed previously. Curious? After applying a Healing Brushstroke, choose Edit ➪ Fade or press Ctrl+Shift+F (⌘+Shift+F on the Mac). You get an Opacity value and no Mode option, exactly the opposite of what you see in the Options bar when using the tool.

- **Keep the grain:** Don't attempt to smooth out the general appearance of grain in the image. Grain is integral to an old photo, and hiding it usually makes the image look faked. If your image gets too smooth, or if your cloning results in irregular patterns, select the problem area and apply Filter ➪ Noise ➪ Add Noise. Enter very small Amount values (2 to 6 percent). Monochromatic noise tends to work best. If necessary, press Ctrl+F (⌘-F on the Mac) to reapply the filter one or more times.

Photoshop's History Brush gives you the sort of "do-over" freedom that you'll wish you had in real life. If you make a few mistakes in your restoration, let them go — and then go back and fix them all at once. After activating the History Brush, just click to the left of the state in the History palette that directly precedes the first state where things went wrong, and then drag with the History Brush. It's almost too easy. Of course, watch your History palette, and make sure you have enough states left to go back to — if the mistakes were made a long time ago in your current session with the image in question, you may have lost your window of opportunity.

Anyway, to paint back to the original scanned image, click in front of the very top item in the History palette — this brings things back to how they were before you did anything beyond opening or importing (scanning) the image. Again, there's more info to come on using the History palette, so stay tuned to this chapter.

Stepping Back through Time

One of the most annoying things about Photoshop — and there aren't that many truly annoying things, so given that this merits mentioning, you know it's really annoying — is that you can't undo more than your last step using the Edit ➪ Undo (Ctrl/⌘+Z) command. You can press Ctrl+Alt+Z (⌘+Option+Z on the Mac) to undo more than one thing, but the ubiquitous Ctrl/⌘+Z — the shortcut that allows multiple undos in every other piece of software under the sun — can't be used for more than one step backward. If you've ever seen or used Photoshop Elements, you know that you can undo several times in a row with Ctrl/⌘+Z in *that* application, so it's not like having multiple undos is something that's against the rules at Adobe.

With the release of Photoshop 5, the software gods at Adobe gave us the History palette, which is a great and powerful tool for going back in time and undoing many steps either serially or as a group. You learn a great deal more about it in the ensuing paragraphs, but it still is not as convenient as pressing Ctrl/⌘+Z repeatedly and watching your last several steps be undone. Sorry, I just had to say that.

No matter. The History palette is great, and this is the spot in the book where you're gonna learn all about it. Here are just a few of the marvelous things you can do with the History palette:

■ **Undo-independent stepping:** Step backward by pressing Ctrl+Alt+Z (⌘+Option+Z on the Mac); step forward by pressing Ctrl+Shift+Z (⌘+Shift+Z). Every program with multiple undos does this, but Photoshop's default keyboard equivalents are different. Why? Because you can backstep independently of the Undo command, so that even backstepping is undoable.

■ **Before and after:** Revert to a point in history to see a "before" view of your image and then fly forward to see the "after" view. From then on, Ctrl+Z (⌘+Z on the Mac) becomes a super-undo, toggling between the before and after views. The opportunities for comparing states and changing your mind are mind-boggling.

■ **Real time travel:** If before and after aren't enough, how about animated history? You can drag a control to slide dynamically forward and backward through operations. It's as if you recorded the operations to videotape, and now you're rewinding and fast-forwarding through them.

■ **Sweeping away mistakes:** Select a point in the history of your image and paint back to it using the History Brush. You can let the mistakes pile up and then brush them away. This brush isn't a paintbrush; it's a hand broom. Want even more variety? Use the Art History Brush to paint back to the image using various artistic styles.

■ **Take a picture, it'll last longer:** You can save any point in the History palette as a snapshot. That way, even several hundred operations after that point in history are long gone, you can revisit the snapshot.

■ **It was a very good year:** Each and every image has its own history. After performing a few hundred operations on Image A, you can still go back to Image B and backstep through operations you performed hours ago. The caveat is that the history remains available only as long as an image is open. Close the image, and its history goes away.

■ **Undo the Revert command:** Back in the days before Photoshop 5.5, you couldn't undo the Revert command. Now, the History palette tracks Revert. So if you don't like the image that was last saved to disk, you can undo the reversion and get back to where you were. Also notice that when you choose File ➪ Revert, Photoshop does not ask you to confirm the reversion. There's no reason for a warning because Revert is fully undoable.

The only thing you can't do through the History palette is travel forward into the future — say, to about three days from now when you've finished your grueling project, submitted it to your client, and received your big fat paycheck. Believe it or not, that's actually good news. The day Adobe can figure out how to do your work for you, your clients will hire Photoshop and stop hiring you.

Using the traditional undo functions

Before going any further with the History palette, let's make sure you're totally familiar with Photoshop's more traditional reversion functions. If you already know about this stuff, leaf ahead to the next section.

■ **Undo:** To restore an image to the way it looked before the last operation, choose Edit ➪ Undo or press Ctrl+Z (⌘+Z on the Mac). You can undo the effect of a paint or edit tool, a change made to a selection outline, or a special-effect or color-correction command. You can't undo disk operations, such as opening or saving. Photoshop does enable you to undo an edit after printing an image, though. You can test an effect, print the image, and then undo the effect if you think it looks awful. But to perform such an undo, you have to press Ctrl+Alt+Z (⌘+Option+Z on the Mac) to backstep through history.

■ **Revert:** Choose File ➪ Revert to reload an image from disk. In most programs, this is the last-resort function — the command you choose after everything else has failed. But in Photoshop, it's a very useful tool. Forget what the image looked like last time you saved it? Choose the Revert command. Don't like it? Press Ctrl+Z (⌘+Z on the Mac) to undo it. That's right, you can undo a reversion — what'll they think of next?

> **TIP** To restore the image to the way it looked when you originally opened it — which may precede the last-saved state — scroll to the top of the History palette and click the topmost item. (This assumes that you haven't deselected the Automatically Create First Snapshot option in the History Options dialog box.)

- **Selective reversion:** To revert a selected area to the way it appeared when it was first opened — or some other source state identified in the History palette — choose Edit ➪ Fill or press Shift+Backspace (Shift+Delete on the Mac). Then select History from the Use pop-up menu, and press Enter or Return.

> **TIP** Better yet, just press Ctrl+Alt+Backspace (⌘+Option+Delete on the Mac). This one keystroke combination fills the selection with the source state. With this or with Shift+Backspace, you set the source state for the reversion by clicking in the left column of the History palette, as explained in the next section.

- **The Erasers:** Click and drag in the background layer with the Eraser tool to paint in the background color. You're essentially erasing the image back to bare canvas. Or apply the Eraser to a layer to delete pixels and expose underlying layers.

> **TIP** You also can Alt-drag (Option-drag on the Mac) with the Eraser tool to revert to the targeted state in the History palette. Or select Erase to History in the Options bar, and just drag. But you're better off using the History Brush for this purpose. The History Brush offers more capabilities, including most notably brush modes.

Where warranted, these functions are explained in greater detail in the following sections. But first, the next few paragraphs look at the main office for reversion in Photoshop, the History palette.

The History palette

First, you want to actually see the History palette; if it's not onscreen now, choose Window ➪ History. This displays the History palette, which is shown in Figure 7.22. The History palette records each significant operation — everything other than settings and preferences (for example, selecting a new foreground color) — and adds it to a list. The oldest operations appear at the top of the list with the most recent operations at the bottom.

Each item in the list is called a *state*. Each item in the palette represents a step taken by you in the building and/or editing of the image, creating a condition at a moment in time — in other words, a state. Although it is similar in usage, don't confuse this type of state with the states in the Layer Comps palette. You learn all about the Layer Comps palette in Chapter 13.

Photoshop automatically names each item according to the tool, command, or operation used to arrive at the state — the nomenclature is pretty obvious, so it won't leave you wondering what was going on at a given point in time as displayed in the palette. The icon next to the name helps to identify the state further. But the best way to find out what a state is like is to click it. Photoshop instantaneously undoes all operations performed after that state and returns you to the state so that you can inspect it in detail. To redo all the operations you just undid in one fell swoop, press Ctrl+Z (⌘+Z on the Mac) or choose Edit ➪ Undo State Change.

That one action — clicking a state — is really the core of what you need to know to travel forward and backward through time in Photoshop. If that's all you ever learn, you'll find yourself working with greater speed, freedom, and security than is possible in virtually any other graphics application. But this represents only the first in a long list of the History palette's capabilities. Here's the rest of what you may want to know:

- **Changing the number of undos:** By default, Photoshop records the last 20 operations in the History palette. When you perform the 21st operation, the first state is shoved off the list. To change this behavior, choose Edit ➪ Preferences ➪ Performance (Photoshop ➪ Preferences ➪ Performance on the Mac) or press Ctrl+K (⌘+K on the Mac), and then click Preferences in the list on the left side of the dialog box. Either approach opens the Preferences dialog box to the Performance panel, and you can then type your preferred number of undoable operations in the History States option box. If you have plenty of RAM — say, 2 GB or more — feel free to increase the number of states. The History palette can hold up to 1,000 states, and while that's probably more than you want to use — after all, some states take up lots of memory when working on a single image, 100 states may be a good idea when, on rare occasions, you need that much flexibility.

FIGURE 7.22

The History palette records each significant event as an independent state. To return to a state, just click it.

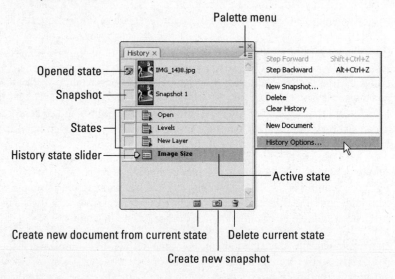

- **Undone states:** When you revert to a state by clicking it, every subsequent state is dimmed to show that it's been undone. You can redo a dimmed state simply by clicking it. But if you perform a new operation, all dimmed states disappear. You have one (count it, *one*) opportunity to bring them back by pressing Ctrl+Z (⌘+Z); if you perform another new operation, the once-dimmed states are gone for good. For an exception to this behavior, see the very next paragraph.

- **Working with nonsequential states:** If you don't like the idea of losing your undone states — every state is sacred, after all — choose the History Options command in the palette menu and select the Allow Non-Linear History option, as shown in Figure 7.23. Undone states no longer drop off the list when you perform a new operation. They remain available on the chance that you may want to revisit them. It's like having multiple possible time trails.

FIGURE 7.23

Choose History Options from the History palette menu, and select the Allow Non-Linear History option to permit Photoshop to keep states that you have undone.

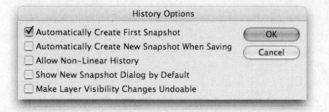

 Selecting the Allow Non-Linear History option does not permit you to undo a single state without affecting subsequent states. For example, let's say you paint with the Airbrush, smear with the Smudge tool, and then clone with the Clone Stamp tool. You can revert to the airbrush state and then apply other operations without losing the option of restoring the smudge and clone. But you can't undo the smudge and leave the clone intact. Operations can occur only in the sequence they were applied.

- **Stepping through states:** You can press Ctrl+Alt+Z (⌘+Option+Z) to undo the active step or Ctrl+Shift+Z (⌘+Shift+Z) to redo the next step in the list. Backstepping goes up the list of states in the History palette; forward-stepping goes down the list. So bear in mind that if the Allow Non-Linear History option is selected, backstepping may take you to a state that was previously inactive.

- **Flying through states:** Click and drag the right-pointing History State Slider (labeled in Figure 7.22) up and down the list to rewind and fast-forward, respectively, through time. If the screen image doesn't appear to change as you fly by certain states, it most likely means those states involve small brushstrokes or changes to selection outlines. Otherwise, the changes are quite apparent.

- **Taking a snapshot:** Every once in a while, a state comes along that's so great, you don't want it to fall by the wayside 20 operations from now. To set a state aside, choose New Snapshot or click the little camera icon at the bottom of the History palette (labeled in Figure 7.22). To rename a snapshot after you create it, just double-click its name at the top of the History palette and type a new one. Or you can name a snapshot as you create it by pressing Alt (Option on the Mac), clicking the little camera icon, and typing a name in the dialog box.

Photoshop lets you store as many snapshots as your computer's RAM permits. Also worth noting, the program automatically creates a snapshot of the image as it appears when it's first opened. If you don't like this opening snapshot, you can change this behavior by dese-lecting the Automatically Create First Snapshot option in the History Options dialog box — but this may not be wise, because having an opening state to go back to can really be a great thing if everything goes horribly awry and you just want to go back to square one. It doesn't really hurt anything to keep this one initial state hanging around, like it now or not.

- **Creating a snapshot upon saving the image:** Select the Automatically Create New Snapshot When Saving option in the History Options dialog box to create a new snap-shot every time you save your image. This is useful if you find yourself venturing down uncertain roads from one save to the next and you want the ability to backstep not only to the last saved state (which you can do by choosing File ⇨ Revert) but to the one before that and the one before that.

- **Saving the state permanently:** The problem with snapshots is that they last only as long as the current session. If you quit Photoshop or the program crashes, you lose the entire history list, snapshots included. To save a state so you can refer to it several days from now, choose the New Document command or click the leftmost icon at the bottom of the History palette. You also can drag and drop a state onto the icon. Either way, Photoshop duplicates the state to a new image window. Then you can save the state to the format of your choice.

- **Setting the source:** Click to the left of a state to identify it as the *source state*. The History Brush icon appears where you click. The source state affects the performance of the History Brush, Art History Brush, Fill command, and Eraser if you select Erase to History. The keystroke Ctrl+Alt+Backspace (⌘+Option+Delete on the Mac) fills a selection with the source state.

- **Trashing states:** If your machine is equipped with little RAM or you're working on a par-ticularly large image, Photoshop may slow down as the states accumulate. If it gets too slow, you may want to purge the History palette. To delete any state as well as those before it, drag the state to the trash icon at the bottom of the palette. Your image updates accordingly. If the Allow Non-Linear History option is selected, clicking the trash can deletes just the active state.

TIP   To clear all states from the History palette, choose the Clear History command from the palette menu. This doesn't immediately empty RAM, just in case you change your mind and decide you want to undo. Photoshop purges memory for real only after you perform another operation. If you want the memory emptied right away — and you're *positive* that you have no desire whatsoever to undo — press Alt (Option on the Mac) and choose the Clear History command. And if you're really hankering to purge, choose Edit ⇨ Purge ⇨ Histories, which gets rid of *all* states for *all* open documents.

Painting away the past

The History palette gives you a very simple, yet powerful way to step backward and forward in time. It's very linear (despite that Allow Non-Linear option), and it's very simple and reliable. But what if you want to step a little to the left or right? What if simply going back to before you selected and deleted something isn't enough for you?

As luck would have it, Photoshop offers three more liberating alternatives to the linear world of the History palette: the Eraser tool, the History Brush tool, and the Art History Brush tool. The Eraser tool washes away pixels to reveal underlying pixels or exposed canvas. The History Brush tool takes you back to a kinder, simpler state; the Art History Brush tool does the same but enables you to paint using special artistic effects. Although the functions of these tools overlap slightly, they each have a specific purpose, as becomes clear in the following sections.

CROSS-REF As you work with any of these tools, remember that you can use the Edit ➪ Fade command to blend the altered pixels with the originals, just as you can when applying a filter. You can adjust both the opacity and the blend mode of the erased or painted pixels. Chapter 18 explores the Fade command in detail.

The Eraser tool

When you work with the Eraser tool, you can select from three Eraser styles, all available from the Mode pop-up menu in the Options bar pictured in Figure 7.24. These are Brush, Pencil, and Block. Block is the ancient 16×16-pixel square Eraser that's great for hard-edged touch-ups. The other options work exactly like the tools for which they're named.

In addition to the Mode settings, the Options bar provides access to the Brush option, the Opacity and Flow values, and the Airbrush icon, all of which work as described in Chapter 5. All options are available when using the Brush-style Eraser, none is applicable to the Block style, and Flow and airbrush dim when painting with a Pencil-style Eraser.

FIGURE 7.24

When the Eraser tool is selected, the Mode pop-up menu offers a choice of Eraser styles rather than the brush modes available to the painting and editing tools.

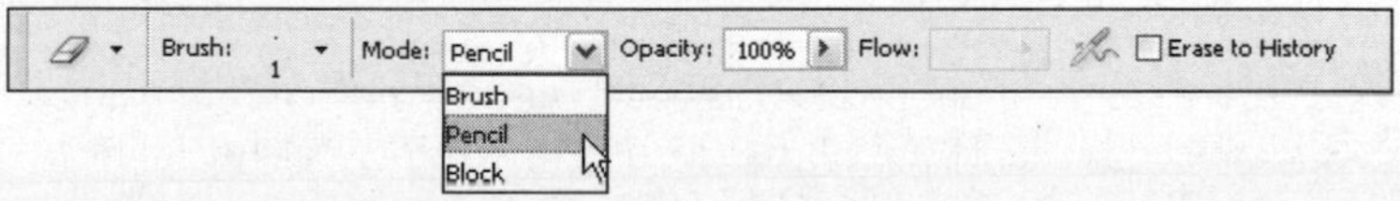

Although the Eraser tool is pretty straightforward, there's no sense in leaving any stone unturned. So here's everything you ever wanted to know about the art of erasing:

■ **Erasing on a layer:** When you're working on the Background layer, the Eraser merely paints in the background color. Not very exciting. What distinguishes the Eraser tool from the other brushes, though, is layers. If you click and drag on a layer and deselect the Lock buttons for transparency and image pixels in the Layers palette, the Eraser tool removes paint and exposes portions of the underlying image. The Eraser tool suddenly performs like that pink thing at the end of your pencil.

CROSS-REF   If you select the transparency Lock button in the Layers palette, Photoshop won't let the Eraser bore holes in the layer or alter areas that are already transparent. Instead, the Eraser paints opaque pixels in the background color. If you select the option for locking image pixels, you can't erase or paint any part of the layer. For more information on locking layers, see Chapter 13.

■ **Erasing lightly:** Change the Opacity setting in the Options bar to make portions of a layer translucent in inverse proportion to the Opacity value. For example, if you set the Opacity to 90 percent, you remove 90 percent of the opacity from the layer and, therefore, leave 10 percent of the opacity behind. The result is a nearly transparent stroke through the layer.

■ **Erasing versus using layer masks:** As described in Chapter 13, you also can erase holes in a layer using a layer mask. But unlike the Eraser — which eliminates pixels for good — a layer mask doesn't do any permanent damage. On the other hand, using the Eraser tool doesn't increase the size of your image as much as a layer mask does. Of course, you can argue that *any* operation — even a deletion — increases the size of the image in RAM because the History palette has to track it. But even so, the Eraser remains more memory-efficient than a layer mask. With the speed and power of most modern computers, this is hardly the issue that it once was.

■ **Erasing with the Pencil tool:** When you work with the Pencil tool — not the Eraser's Pencil mode but the actual Pencil tool — Photoshop presents you with an Auto Erase option in the Options bar. Turn it on to draw in the background color anytime you click or drag on a pixel that is already colored in the foreground color. This technique can be useful when you're drawing a line against a plain background. Set the foreground color to the color of the line; set the background color to the color of the background. Then use the Pencil tool to draw and erase the line until you get it just right.

NOTE   Unlike the Eraser tool, the Pencil tool always draws either in the foreground or background color, even when used on a layer.

■ **Erasing to history:** Press Alt (Option on the Mac) as you drag with the Eraser to paint with the source state identified by the History Brush icon in the History palette. It's like scraping away the paint laid down by the operations following the source state. Also, instead of pressing Alt, you can select the Erase to History option in the Options bar. In this case, dragging with the Eraser tool reverts and Alt-dragging (Option-dragging on the Mac) paints in the background color or erases the active layer.

In the old days, people used the term "Magic Eraser" to mean the Eraser tool set to the Revert mode. But when Photoshop 5.5 introduced the official Magic Eraser tool, which deletes a range of similarly colored pixels each time you click in the image window (see Chapter 9), this use of the term disappeared. So the old Magic Eraser is the modern History Eraser. Confused yet?

The History Brush tool

Painting with the History Brush tool — which you can select from the keyboard by pressing Y — is like painting with the Eraser tool when Erase to History is selected. Just click and drag with the History Brush to selectively revert to the source state targeted in the History palette. You also can vary the translucency of your strokes using the Opacity setting in the Options bar. But that's where the similarities end. Unlike the part-time history Eraser, the dedicated History Brush tool lets you take advantage of brush modes. By choosing a different brush mode from the Mode pop-up menu in the Options bar, you can mix pixels from the changed and saved images to achieve interesting, and sometimes surprising, effects.

TIP Using the History Brush tool instead of using the Eraser's Erase to History function is a good idea. Of course, with Pencil and Block, the Eraser offers more styles. But when weighed against brush modes, these styles aren't much of an advantage. The History Brush also is more intuitive because its icon matches the source state icon in the History palette.

As you play with the History Brush tool, keep in mind that you don't have to limit yourself to painting into the past. Just as the History palette lets you skip back and forth through time, the History Brush lets you paint to any point in time.

The Art History Brush tool

The Art History Brush tool lets you create impressionistic effects with the aid of the History palette. To get a sense of how it works, open any image, such as the one shown in Figure 7.25. Press D to get the default foreground and background colors, select the standard Brush tool, and paint wildly all over your image, as shown in Figure 7.26.

Select the Art History Brush tool, which shares a flyout menu and keyboard shortcut (Y) with the History Brush tool. Bring up the History palette, and make sure the first snapshot is identified as the source state (assuming that you haven't made any unauthorized changes to the image since you opened it). Now paint inside your black image. Each stroke reveals a bit of your original photograph in painterly detail, as illustrated in Figure 7.26.

FIGURE 7.25

A precious flower, soon to be defiled

FIGURE 7.26

After painting a random series of black brushstrokes all over the image (left), the Art History Brush is selected and used to paint in a rough translation of the original (right). Cool, no?

If you want to go even wilder, try applying various filters, maybe even an Artistic filter, so that you are painting with a painted or drawn filter — sort of trippy in terms of the irony. Anyway, you may end up with something like the now artistically filtered photo shown on the right in Figure 7.27.

Like the History Brush tool, the Art History Brush tool paints from the source state specified in the History palette. But it does so by painting tens or even hundreds of tiny brushstrokes at a time, swirling and gyrating according to settings you select in the Options bar. Many of these settings you've seen several times before. As shown in Figure 7.28, you have the standard Brush controls, a reduced Mode option, and the tried-and-true Opacity value. But starting with the Style option, the Art History Brush tool goes its own way:

FIGURE 7.27

The Displace filter is applied (left), and a texture added with the Texturizer filter (right). Now we have something suitable for any dentist's office waiting room!

FIGURE 7.28

Choose an option from the Style menu to change the type of strokes the Art History brush applies.

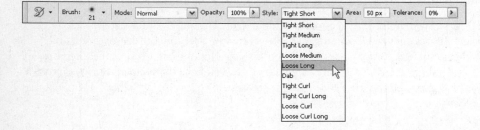

- ■ **Style:** The Art History Brush tool paints with randomly generated worms and corkscrews of color. You can decide the basic shapes of the creepy crawlies by selecting an option from the Style pop-up menu, displayed in Figure 7.28. Combine these options with different brush sizes to vary the detail conveyed by the impressionistic image. Tight styles and small brushes give you better detail; loose styles and big brushes produce less detail.

- **Area:** This value defines the area covered by a single spot of corkscrews. Larger values generally mean more corkscrews are laid down at a time, reducing the value for a sparser look. You can get some very interesting effects by raising the Area value to its maximum, 500 pixels, and clicking inside the image without moving the cursor. Watch those worms writhe.

- **Tolerance:** This value limits where the Art History Brush can paint. A value of 0 lets the brush paint anywhere; higher values let the brush paint only in areas where the current state and source state differ dramatically in color.

Source state limitations

Photoshop displays the Cancel cursor if you try to paint with the History Brush or Art History Brush using a source state that's a different width or height than the current image. One pixel of difference, and the source state is a dead issue. This same restriction applies to Edit ➪ Fill, Ctrl+Alt+Backspace (⌘+Option+Delete on the Mac), and any other history technique.

You also may see the Cancel cursor if the layer is locked or the source state lacks an equivalent layer. To find out exactly what the problem is, click the image with the Cancel cursor to display an explanatory alert message. If the problem relates to the source state, move the source state icon in the History palette to a point after you modified the width or the height of the image. The crop tool and the Image ➪ Image Size, Canvas Size, Rotate Canvas, and Crop commands can mix up the History Brush tool. If you applied one of these operations in the very last state, you have to back-step before that operation or find some alternative to the History Brush.

Summary

This chapter provided an overview of Photoshop's image restoration tools and showed you how to touch-up dust, hair, and other scanning artifacts, removing them from your images. You also learned to use the Healing Brush, Spot Healing Brush, and Patch tools, and to use these and other tools to restore damaged photographs.

In addition, this chapter showed you how to eliminate background elements from an image and to move backward through time with the History palette. You also learned to paint away mistakes with the Eraser and History Brush tools and how to get rid of red eye.

Part III

Selections, Masks, and Filters

Chapter 8

Selections and Paths

Selections, and your ability to make and edit them successfully, are key to your efficient and effective use of Photoshop. Why? Because a selection tells Photoshop what portion of your image or layer you want to address — that is, where it is you intend to make a deletion, change, or addition. It's like selecting text in a word processing document — dragging through some of the text tells that word processor which text you want bolded, indented, whatever. If you can't tell Photoshop which part of the image you're about to deal with, it assumes your next move should affect the entire active layer, and unless that's your goal, your ability to use all the tools that can be applied to a selection is compromised.

With that said, it also should be noted that no other program gives you as much control over the size and shape of selections as Photoshop. You can finesse selection outlines with unparalleled flexibility, alternatively adding to and subtracting from selected areas and moving and rotating selections independently of the pixels inside them. With the new Refine Edge dialog box, which accompanies all selection tools in Photoshop CS3, your abilities to control every selection down to the pixel are greatly increased, making Photoshop's selection tools even better than before.

> **TIP** You also can mix masks and selection outlines together, as covered in Chapter 9.

That's why this chapter and Chapter 9 are probably the most important chapters in this book — and you probably want to pay close attention to the fundamental concepts and approaches documented throughout this chapter. Although every technique couldn't be labeled "essential" — lots of artists get by without paying much attention to paths, for example, while other artists swear by them — a working knowledge of selection outlines is key to using Photoshop successfully.

Understanding How Selections Work

If you want to edit a portion of an image without fear that you might accidentally mess up another portion of the image, you must first *select* it, indicating the boundaries of the area you want to edit. To select part of an image in an image-editing program, you surround it with a selection outline or a marquee, which tells Photoshop where to apply your editing instructions. The selection outline appears as a moving pattern of dash marks, colloquially termed *marching ants*, as shown in Figure 8.1, by users who had probably been sitting in front of the computer screen for too long, looking at the marquee.

FIGURE 8.1

The dashed line, while static in this image, seems to dance around the selection in the image window, leaving no doubt as to which part of the picture is selected.

Visible selection outlines can be helpful sometimes, but they can just as readily impede your view of an image. If they do manage to annoy you, press Ctrl+H (⌘+H on the Mac) to get rid of them. Pressing Ctrl+H (Win) or ⌘+H (Mac) toggles the View ➪ Extras command, which hides and displays all onscreen aids so you also lose guides, the grid, note icons, slices, and target paths. If you want to hide just the selection "ants," choose View ➪ Show ➪ Selection Edges to toggle the command off.

Choose the command again to toggle the ants back on. You also can control which items disappear when you press Ctrl+H (⌘+H on the Mac) by choosing View ⇨ Show ⇨ Show Extras Options. In the resulting dialog box, select the items that you want Photoshop to display at all times.

As for creating selections, you have at your disposal a whole bunch of tools and options, all shown in Figure 8.2 and described briefly in the following list. You can access most of the tools by using keyboard shortcuts, which appear in parentheses. In-depth discussion of each of the selection tools follows, so don't think the quick descriptions you're about to read are "it"; rather, think of it as a fast guide that will help you decide which particular selection tool to focus on, or to give you a leg-up on playing around on your own to get a feel for one or more of the tools.

FIGURE 8.2

Selection tools abound in Photoshop. Add to this the Options bars that appear as each of these tools is selected (shown in later figures), and there's no limit to your selection potential.

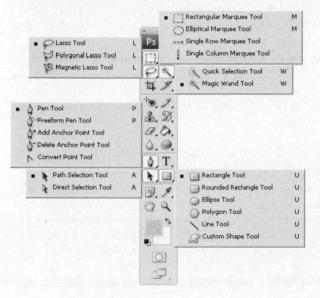

When multiple tools share the same shortcut, you press the key once to activate the tool that's visible in the Toolbox and press the key repeatedly to cycle through the other tools. This assumes that you have deselected the Use Shift Key for Tool Switch option in the Preferences dialog box. Otherwise, press Shift and the shortcut key to cycle through the following tools:

- **Rectangular Marquee (M):** Long a staple of painting programs, this tool enables you to select rectangular or square portions of an image.

- **Elliptical Marquee (M):** The Elliptical Marquee tool works like the Rectangular Marquee except it selects elliptical or circular portions of an image.

- **Single-Row** and **Single-Column:** The Single-Row and Single-Column tools enable you to select a single row or column of pixels that stretches the entire width or height of the image. These tools are used so rarely that Adobe didn't give them keyboard shortcuts.

- **Lasso (L):** Click and drag with the Lasso tool to select a free-form portion of an image. Unlike the lasso tools in most painting programs, which shrink selection outlines to disqualify pixels in the background color, Photoshop's Lasso tool selects the exact portion of the image you enclose in your drag.

- **Polygonal Lasso (L):** Click different points in your image to set corners in a straight-sided selection outline. This is a great way to select free-form areas if you're not good at controlling the mouse with the Lasso tool — your "sides" in the polygonal selection can be so small that in the end, the edges of the selection are as smooth and curvy as any Lasso-made selection. You can achieve the same effect by Alt-clicking or Option-clicking with the Lasso tool; you can learn more about this later in this chapter.

- **Magnetic Lasso (L):** Click with the Magnetic Lasso along the edge of an image element that you want to select independently from its background. Then move (you don't have to drag) the Magnetic Lasso around the edge of the element. It's a tricky tool to use, but its Options bar, which makes it easier, is discussed later in the chapter.

- **Magic Wand (W):** First introduced by Photoshop (not by any of its competitors), this tool lets you select a contiguous region of similarly colored pixels by clicking inside the region. For example, you might click inside the boundaries of a face to isolate it from the hair and background elements. You also can select all similarly colored pixels throughout an image, even if they're not contiguous — it can be a very powerful tool. As a result, novices tend to gravitate toward the Magic Wand because it seems like it performs selection miracles, but you may find that it can be the least predictable tool of the bunch.

- **Quick Selection Tool (W):** This is a selection tool that's been desired by users for a long time. Its ease of use, its ability to be sized and used like a brush, and its ability to sample from all layers or just one make it very powerful and sensitive. To use it, simply click and drag (after having chosen a brush size and decided on your layer-sampling option), and watch your selection grow as you drag the brush. The Auto Enhance option, along with the new Refine Edge button (present on the Options bar for all CS3 selection tools), might make this your favorite tool for both general and fine selections.

- **Pen (P):** The Pen tool is difficult to master, but it's the most accurate and versatile of the selection tools. You use the Pen tool to create a *path*, which is an object-oriented breed of selection outline. You click and drag to create individual points in the path. You can edit the path after the fact by moving, adding, and deleting points. You can even transfer a path by dragging and dropping between Photoshop, Illustrator, and FreeHand. For a discussion of the Pen tool, read the section "Drawing and Editing Paths."

- **Freeform Pen** and **Magnetic Pen (P):** If you hate setting points but you need to create a clipping path, the Freeform Pen is the tool for you. You just click and drag with the tool as if you were selecting with the Lasso tool and let Photoshop define the points automatically. Obviously, you can't expect the same level of accuracy that you get from the standard Pen tool, but it's very simple to use.

Selecting the Magnetic option in the Options bar transforms the Freeform Pen into the Magnetic Pen, which once upon a time was a tool in its own right. The Magnetic Pen is basically an object-oriented version of the Magnetic Lasso tool. Click to set the first point, and then move your mouse and watch Photoshop create the other points automatically. It's not a great tool, but it can prove handy when selecting image elements that stand out very clearly from their backgrounds.

■ **Shape tools (U):** To draw paths in simple geometric shapes, give the Shape tools a shot. First, put the tools in the path mode by clicking the Paths icon at the left end of the Options bar. Then simply click and drag to create the path. To find out more about working with these tools, visit Chapter 15.

■ **Path and shape selection tools:** Use the Path Selection tool (the black arrow) and the Direct Selection tool (the white arrow) to select and edit paths and vector shapes. You can read more about these tools later in the section "Drawing and Editing Paths."

CROSS-REF Photoshop's Horizontal Type Mask tool and Vertical Type Mask tool technically are selection tools because Photoshop converts each character of type to a selection outline. But type involves other issues that would merely confuse the contents of this chapter, so type and its uses as a selection tool are found in Chapter 16. Also, if your purpose for selecting an area is to separate it from its background, you should investigate the Extract command and the Magic Eraser and Background Eraser (covered in Chapter 9).

If this were all you needed to know to use the selection tools in Photoshop, the application would be on par with the average paint program. Part of what makes Photoshop exceptional, however, is that it provides literally hundreds of options, commands, and tricks to increase the functionality of every selection tool. Furthermore, all of Photoshop's selection tools work together in perfect harmony. You can exploit the specialized capabilities of multiple selection tools to create a single selection boundary, or maybe just tweak the way one selection tool works to achieve the desired effect. After you understand which tool best serves which purpose, you can isolate any element in an image, no matter how complex or how delicate its outline.

Geometric Selection Outlines

At the top of the Toolbox, just below the Move tool, you'll find the first of the three main selection tools. If your Toolbox is set to be two tools wide (rather than the default single vertical column), the selection tools begin in the top row, next to the Move tool. The selection tools are bundled, and like tools share single buttons (refer to Figure 8.2).

By default, in either configuration of the Toolbox, the Rectangular Marquee tool appears on the Toolbox button, and with good reason — it's probably the most often-used selection tool. You can select its alternates — the Elliptical, Single-Row, and Single-Column Marquee tools — from the flyout menu that appears when you click and drag from the Marquee tool icon.

TIP Press M to select the tool that's currently visible in the Toolbox. Press M again to toggle between the Rectangular and Elliptical Marquee tools. Alternatively, Alt-click (Win) or Option-click (Mac) the tool icon to toggle among all four marquee tools.

The marquee tools are more versatile than they may appear at first glance. You can adjust the performance of each tool as follows:

- **Constraining to a square or circle:** Press and hold Shift after beginning your drag to draw a perfect square with the Rectangular Marquee tool or a perfect circle with the Elliptical Marquee tool. (Pressing Shift before dragging also works if no other selection is active; otherwise, this adds to existing selection, as explained later in this chapter.)

- **Drawing a circular marquee:** Remember to press Shift after you begin to drag, and assuming you've selected the Elliptical Marquee tool to make the selection, the ellipse (which most people think of as an oval) becomes a circle. Pretty simple, huh?

- **Drawing out from the center:** Press and hold Alt (Option on the Mac) after you begin dragging to draw the marquee from the center outward instead of from corner to corner. (Again, pressing Alt or Option before dragging works if no selection outline is active; otherwise, this subtracts from the selection.) This technique is especially useful when you draw an elliptical marquee. Locating the center of the area you want to select is frequently easier than locating one of its corners — particularly because ellipses don't have corners.

- **Moving the marquee on the fly:** While drawing a marquee, press and hold the spacebar to move the marquee rather than resize it. When you get the marquee in place, release the spacebar and keep dragging to modify the size. The spacebar is most helpful when drawing elliptical selections or when drawing a marquee out from the center — this eliminates the guesswork, so you can position your marquees exactly on target.

- **Selecting a single-pixel line:** Use the Single-Row or Single-Column tools to select a single row or column (respectively) of pixels stretching across the width or length of your image. I use these tools to fix small mishaps, such as a missing line of pixels in a screen shot or to delete random pixels around the perimeter of an image. You also can use it to create perpendicular lines in a fixed space — giving you more control over the length of the line than you have if you use the Line tool (one of the Shape tool's variants).

- **Constraining the aspect ratio:** If you want to create an image that conforms to a certain aspect ratio, you can constrain either a rectangular or an elliptical marquee so that the ratio between height and width remains fixed, no matter how large or small a marquee you create. To accomplish this, select Fixed Ratio from the Style pop-up menu in the Options bar, as shown in Figure 8.3. Type the desired ratio values in the Width and Height option boxes.

FIGURE 8.3

Select Fixed Ratio from the Style pop-up menu in the Options bar to constrain the proportions of a rectangular selection outline.

TIP If you work with a digital camera, you may find this feature especially helpful. Many digital cameras produce images that fit the 4×3 aspect ratio used by computer screens and televisions. If you want to crop an image to a standard photo size — say, 6×4 inches — type 6 and 4, respectively, in the Width and Height option boxes. Then drag the marquee around to select the portion of the picture you want to retain, as shown in the figure, and choose Image ➪ Crop.

Remember that you're just establishing the image aspect ratio here, not setting the output width and height. So you could just as easily type 2 and 3 in the Width and Height option boxes. The size of the final, cropped image depends on how large you draw the marquee and the Resolution value you set in the Image Size dialog box.

■ **Sizing the marquee numerically:** If you're editing a screen shot or some other form of regular or schematic image, you may find it helpful to specify the size of the marquee numerically. To do so, select Fixed Size from the Style pop-up menu and type size values in the Width and Height option boxes. To match the selection to a 800×600-pixel screen, for example, change the Width and Height values to 800 and 600, respectively. Then click in the image to create the marquee.

NOTE You can set the marquee size in any unit of measurement you like. Just type the number followed by one of these units: px (pixels), in, mm, cm, pt (points), pica, or %.

■ **Drawing feathered selections:** A Feather option box is available in the Options bar when you use any of the marquee tools. To *feather* a selection is to blur its edges beyond the automatic anti-aliasing afforded by most tools. For more information on feathering, refer to the coverage of softening selections found later in this chapter.

■ **Creating jagged ellipses:** By default, elliptical selection outlines are anti-aliased. If you don't want anti-aliasing — you might prefer harsh edges when editing screen shots or designing screen interfaces — deselect the Anti-aliased option. (This option is dimmed when you use the Rectangular Marquee because anti-aliasing is always off for this tool.)

■ **Refine Edge:** This button, which appears on the Options bar for all of Photoshop CS3's selection tools, spawns a powerful dialog box that gives you several ways to do just what the button says — refine the edges of your selection. Because a selection is only as good as its accuracy in terms of including only the content you want, being able to fine-tune the edges of your selection is a really great addition to the software. The dialog box, shown in Figure 8.4, looks and works the same way for each selection tool, and a discussion of all its options appears later in this chapter.

CROSS-REF Photoshop novices often misunderstand the Rectangular and Elliptical Marquee tools and expect them to create filled and stroked shapes. For these tasks, Photoshop provides the shape tools, which can create filled vector and raster shapes. You can apply strokes and other effects to these shapes if you like. Chapter 15 takes you on a guided tour of the shape tools.

FIGURE 8.4

The Refine Edge dialog box accompanies all selection tools in CS3, and gives you even greater control over the scope of your selections.

Free-form Outlines

In comparison to the Rectangular and Elliptical Marquee tools, the Lasso tool provides a rather limited range of options. Generally speaking, you click and drag in a free-form path around the image you want to select. The few special considerations are as follows:

- **Feathering and anti-aliasing:** Just as you can feather rectangular and elliptical marquees, you can feather selections drawn with the Lasso tool by first selecting the Feather option in the Options bar. To soften the edges of a lasso outline, select the Anti-aliased option.

NOTE Although you can adjust the feathering of any selection after you draw it by choosing Select ⇨ Feather, you must specify anti-aliasing before you draw a selection. Unless you have a specific reason for doing otherwise, leave the Anti-aliased option deselected (as it is by default).

■ **Drawing polygons:** When you press and hold Alt (Option on the Mac), the Lasso tool functions like (and the icon even looks like) the Polygonal Lasso tool. (*Polygon*, incidentally, means a shape with multiple straight sides.) With the Alt or Option key pressed, click to specify corners in a free-form polygon. If you want to add curves to the selection outline, drag with the tool while still pressing Alt or Option. Photoshop closes the selection outline the moment you release both the mouse button and the Alt or Option key (see Figure 8.5).

FIGURE 8.5

We started with an original image by Krisha Martzall, and by combining single mouse clicks and the Alt (Option) key, we formed straight lines, as needed. When we wanted to select free-form lines, we simply dragged.

TIP You can extend a polygon selection outline to the absolute top, right, or bottom edges of an image. You also can Alt-click (Win) or Option-click (Mac) with the Lasso tool beyond the confines of the image window—clicking and creating a selection that exceeds the image window's dimensions. To prove that the selection shape you drew was retained, if you move the selection so that the portions that were outside of the window are now within it, you can see the corners and sides you drew.

■ **The Polygonal Lasso tool:** If you don't want to bother with pressing Alt (Win) or Option (Mac), select the Polygonal Lasso. When the Lasso is active, you can switch to the Polygonal Lasso by pressing L or Shift+L, depending on your Use Shift Key for Tool Switch setting in the Preferences dialog box. Or drag from the Lasso tool icon to display the Lasso flyout menu and select the Polygonal Lasso that way. Then click inside the image to set corners in the selection. Click the first point in the selection or double-click with the tool to complete the selection outline. To create free-form curves with the Polygonal Lasso tool, press Alt (or Option on the Mac) and drag.

TIP   If you make a mistake while creating a selection outline with the Polygonal Lasso, press Backspace (Delete on the Mac) to eliminate the last segment you drew. Keep pressing Backspace or Delete to eliminate more segments in the selection outline. This technique works until you close the selection outline and it turns into marching ants.

Adobe added the Polygonal Lasso for those times when Alt-clicking (Option-clicking on the Mac) isn't convenient. If no portion of the image is selected, it's no trick to Alt-click (Win) or Option-click (Mac) with the standard Lasso to draw a straight-sided selection. But if some area in the image is selected, pressing Alt or Option tells Photoshop that you want to subtract from the selection outline. For this reason, using the Polygonal Lasso is often easier — although you still can make it work by pressing Alt or Option after you click with the Lasso tool, as explained later in this chapter.

NOTE   The very same Refine Edge dialog box introduced earlier and explained later in this chapter allows you fine-tune your Lasso selections as well.

TIP   If you're using a tablet and pen instead of a mouse, you can click the Use Tablet Pressure to Change Pen Width button on the Options bar for any of the Lasso selection tools. If you click the button and turn this option on, pressing harder with your pen creates the effect of a thicker pen, much like you'd press harder with a pen on paper to make a more prominent line. This button is new to Photoshop CS3, although previous versions offered ways to use pen pressure to your advantage.

Magnetic Selections

In the old days of black-and-white painting programs, black pixels were considered foreground elements (the strokes you painted) and white pixels were the background (the electronic paper or canvas). To select a black element, you had only to vaguely drag around it with the lasso tool and the program would automatically omit the white pixels and "shrink" the selection around the black ones.

The Magnetic Lasso tool is Adobe's attempt to transfer shrinking into the world of color. Under ideal conditions a selection drawn with the Magnetic Lasso automatically shrinks around the foreground element and omits the background. Of course, it rarely works this well, but it does produce halfway decent selection outlines with very little effort — provided that you know how to tweak the tool's options in your favor.

Using the Magnetic Lasso tool

Typically, when people have a problem using the magnetic lasso tool, it's because they're trying to make the process too complex. Work less, and the tool works better. Here are the basic steps for using this unusual tool:

STEPS: Making Sense of the Magnetic Lasso Tool

1. **Select an image with very definite contrast between the foreground image and its background.** The content in Figure 8.6 is a good example of when you'd be compelled to use the Magnetic Lasso, because the central object stands out against the background and the tool will have no trouble discerning its edges. Here's something that Photoshop can really sink its teeth into.

FIGURE 8.6

Drag as long as you see the Magnetic Lasso doing its job—that is, following the edge of your desired content and creating a nice, tight selection up against that edge. When it wavers, click to keep the tool on track. You also can press Backspace to step back to the previous anchor point when the tool goes astray.

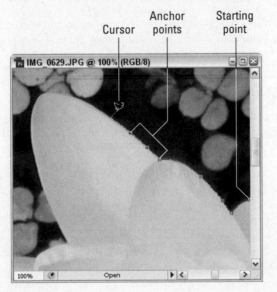

2. **Select the Magnetic Lasso.** If any tool but a Lasso tool is active, press L to grab the Lasso that's showing in the Toolbox. Then press L as necessary to cycle to the Magnetic Lasso.

3. **Click anywhere along the edge of the foreground element.** Note the starting point, labeled in Figure 8.6—of course, your image and its content may suggest another strategy.

4. **Move the cursor around the edge of the foreground element.** Just move the mouse, don't drag — that is, there's no need to press the mouse button. As your cursor passes over the image, Photoshop lays down a line along the edge of the element. The Magnetic Lasso also lays down anchor points at significant locations around the image. If you don't like where the program puts a point, press Backspace (Delete on the Mac). Each time you press Backspace or Delete, Photoshop deletes the most recent point along the line. To set your own anchor points, just click.

5. **When you make it all the way around to the beginning of the shape, click the first point in the outline to close the selection.** Photoshop makes it easy to spot this by displaying a tiny circle with your mouse pointer, just as you close in on the starting point of your selection. If you can't wait for that to appear or if you simply want to end things wherever you are in the selection process, just double-click in your current location to close with a straight edge back to the starting point.

TIP
To create a straight segment while working with the Magnetic Lasso tool, press Alt (Option on the Mac), click to set the start of the segment, and click again at the endpoint. The next time you click without holding down Alt or Option, the tool reverts to its normal magnetic self.

Modifying the Magnetic Lasso options

You modify the performance of the Magnetic Lasso tool by adjusting the values in the Options bar. The Feather and Anti-aliased options define the softness of the final selection outline, just as they do for the standard Lasso tool. The others control how the Magnetic Lasso positions lines and lays down points:

■ **Width:** This option determines how close to an edge you have to move the cursor for Photoshop to accurately see the image element. Large values are great for smooth elements that stand out clearly from their backgrounds. If you raise the Width to 20, for example, you can move the cursor 20 pixels away from the edges of the content you're trying to select and Photoshop still shrinks the selection tight around the content's edge. That gives even the shakiest mouse-users a pretty workable margin for error and makes your life easier. When you're selecting small areas or where there is little difference between what you want to select and the surrounding pixels, you need a low value to keep Photoshop from veering off to the wrong edge.

TIP
The great advantage to the Width value is that you can change it on the fly by pressing a bracket key. Press [(left bracket) to lower the Width value; press] (right bracket) to raise the value. Shift+[lowers the value to its minimum, 1, and Shift+] raises it to the maximum, 256.

If you have a pressure-sensitive tablet and select the Pen Pressure option, you can control the edge-tracking accuracy by adjusting how hard you press on the pen. Bear down to be careful; let up to be more casual about the selection's accuracy. Because this is the way you probably work naturally, you'll be able to adjust the width as needed without even thinking much about it.

■ **Contrast:** This is the simplest of the options. It tells Photoshop how much contrast there has to be between the element you're trying to select and its background to even be recognized. If the foreground element stands out clearly, you may want to raise the Edge Contrast value to avoid selecting random flack around the edges. If the contrast between foreground and background is subtle, lower the value.

■ **Frequency:** This option tells the Magnetic Lasso when to lay down points. As you drag with the tool, the line around the image changes to keep up with your movements. When some point in the line stays still for a few moments, Photoshop decides it must be on target and anchors it down with a point. If you want Photoshop to anchor points more frequently, raise the value. For less frequent anchoring, lower the option. High values tend to be better for rough edges; lower values are better for smooth edges.

Most of the time, you can rely on the bracket keys to adjust the Width and leave the Frequency and Edge Contrast values set to their defaults. When dealing with a low-contrast image, lower the Edge Contrast value to 5 percent or so. And when selecting unusually rough edges, raise the Frequency to 70 or more. But careful movements with the Magnetic Lasso tool go further than adjusting any of these settings. If you need the ability to further control the confines of your selection, click the Refine Edge button to open a dialog box that allows you to use a variety of settings to increase, decrease, soften, and view your selection in greater detail. Find out more about this button and its effects later in this chapter.

The Magic(al) Wand

Using the Magic Wand tool seems like — what's the word — magic, right? You just click with the tool, and it selects all colors that fall within a selected range. The problem, though, and where the magic can kind of wear off is in getting the wand to recognize the same range of colors that you see onscreen. For example, if you're editing a photo of a red flower amongst pink flowers, how do you tell the Magic Wand to select the red one and leave the pink ones alone?

For some users, adjusting the Wand seems too complicated, and it can be kind of frustrating to use. Other times, it seems like a gift from on high, in that it selects exactly what you want, without any difficulty. Its success as a selection tool depends on several factors, so try to resist the temptation to either write it off as too complex or really easy — because it's neither. Just read on, and then play with the tool and try it in different selection scenarios.

When the Magic Wand is active, you'll see the following four controls in the Options bar:

■ **Tolerance:** This option determines the range of colors the tool selects when you click with it in the image window.

■ **Anti-aliased:** This option softens the selection, just as it does for the Lasso tools.

■ **Contiguous:** When selected, this option tells Photoshop to select a contiguous region of pixels emanating from the pixel on which you click — this means that if you click a pixel in that hypothetical red flower, only the red pixels in that flower, touching the pixel you clicked (or touching one of the pixels that were touching the pixel you clicked) are selected. Red pixels in a flower on the other side of the image are not. To select all similarly colored pixels throughout the picture, deselect the option.

■ **Sample All Layers:** Select this option to take all visible layers into account when defining a selection.

You now know all you need to know about the Anti-aliased and Contiguous options; the next two sections explain Tolerance and Use All Layers.

Adjusting the tolerance

You may have heard the standard explanation for adjusting the Tolerance value: You can type any number from 0 to 255 in the Tolerance option box. Type a low number to select a small range of colors; increase the value to select a wider range of colors.

When you click a pixel with the Magic Wand tool, Photoshop first reads the brightness value that each color channel assigned to that pixel. If you're working with a grayscale image, Photoshop reads a single brightness value from the one channel only; if you're working with an RGB image, it reads three brightness values, one each from the red, green, and blue channels; and so on. Because each color channel permits 8 bits of data, brightness values range from 0 to 255.

Next, Photoshop applies the Tolerance value, or simply *tolerance*, to the pixel. The Tolerance describes a range that extends in both directions — lighter and darker — from each brightness value.

Suppose you're editing a standard RGB image. The Tolerance is set to 32 (as it is by default). You click with the Magic Wand on a turquoise pixel, whose brightness values are 40 red, 210 green, and 170 blue. Photoshop subtracts and adds 32 from each brightness value to calculate the Magic Wand range that, in this case, is 8 to 72 red, 178 to 242 green, and 138 to 202 blue. Photoshop selects any pixel that both falls in this range and, if the Contiguous option is turned on, can be traced back to the original pixel through an uninterrupted line of other pixels that also fall within the range.

From this information, you can draw the following basic conclusions about the Magic Wand tool:

■ **Clicking on midtones maintains a higher range:** Because the Tolerance range extends in two directions, you cut off the range when you click a light or dark pixel, as demonstrated in Figure 8.7. In all cases, the Contiguous option is selected, and in the top two boxes, a pixel with a brightness level of 150 was clicked. In the upper-right example, the Tolerance value is set to 75, and the range shrinks. But when a pixel with a brightness value of 10 is clicked, as in the bottom gradations (Tolerance set to 32 on the left, 75 on the right), the range shrinks to 0 to 70. Clicking on a medium-brightness pixel, therefore, permits the most generous range.

■ **Selecting brightness ranges:** Many people have the impression that the Magic Wand selects color ranges. The Magic Wand, in fact, selects brightness ranges within color channels. So if you want to select a flesh-colored region — regardless of shade — set against an orange or a red background that is roughly equivalent in terms of brightness values, you probably should use a different tool.

FIGURE 8.7

Note the results of clicking a pixel with a brightness value of 140 (top row) and a brightness value of 10 (bottom row) with the Tolerance set to the default of 32 and then at 75.

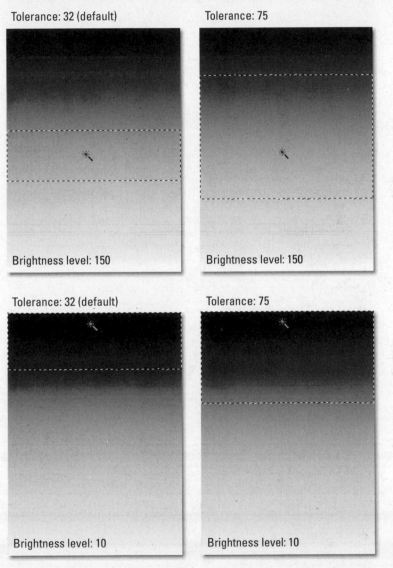

Tolerance: 32 (default)

Tolerance: 75

Brightness level: 150

Brightness level: 150

Tolerance: 32 (default)

Tolerance: 75

Brightness level: 10

Brightness level: 10

■ **Selecting from a single channel:** If the Magic Wand repeatedly fails to select a region of color that appears unique from its background, try isolating that region inside a single-color channel. You'll probably have the most luck isolating a color on the channel that least resembles it. For example, to select the background shown in Figure 8.8, each color channel was examined closely to see which provided the greatest contrast between the elements in the photo. In this case, the Red channel (top) won. Experiment with this technique, and it will prove even more useful over time.

FIGURE 8.8

Make your selection within the channel that provides the most difference in brightness — between your desired content and the rest of the image.

> **NOTE** Here's one more important twist in the Tolerance story: The Magic Wand is affected by the Sample Size option that you select for the Eyedropper tool. If you select Point Sample, the Wand bases its selection solely on the single pixel that you click. But if you select 3 by 3 Average or 5 by 5 Average, the Wand takes into account 9 or 25 pixels, respectively. As you can imagine, this obscure option can have a noticeable effect on the extent of the selection that you get from the Wand.

Making the Wand see beyond a single layer

The Use All Layers option enables you to create a selection based on pixels from different layers (see Chapter 13 for more about layers). With the image in use thus far (the crow) in mind, imagine that the crow is on its own layer, the flowers on another layer, and the sky behind them on yet a third layer. Without using the Sample All Layers option for the Magic Wand, one could only select a particular shade of gray in the crow's wings, and not that same shade as it appears in the flowers or the sky — at least not at the same time.

Mind you, while the Sample All Layers option enables the Wand to consider pixels on different layers when creating a selection, it does not permit the Wand to actually select content on two separate layers. Strange as this may sound, no selection tool is capable of that. Every one of the techniques explained in this chapter is applicable to only a single layer at a time. The Sample All Layers option merely allows the Wand to draw selection outlines that appear to encompass colors on many layers.

Well, if it's not actually sampling and selecting all the content on all the layers, what good is this? Well, imagine that you want to change all the blue in the image to purple — using any number of tools to tweak the blue and change its color. With the help of Sample All Layers, you can draw a selection outline that encompasses all the pixels that match the sampled pixel, and then you can hop between layers (with that same selection in place) and make the color changes to each individual layer. Of course, it would be easier if you could literally select content on multiple layers, but the ability to map out a selection that will work on all the individual layers will just have to do.

The Quick Selection Tool

This selection tool, new to Photoshop CS3 and sharing a button with the aforementioned Magic Wand, is a long-awaited addition to your selection arsenal. It's got a little bit of the wand's magic, a little bit of the magnetic lasso's "shrink" effect, and it's really simple to use.

First, let's look at the tool's Options bar. We begin with a variation on the buttons that allow you to add to, subtract from, and intersect with a selection, and three buttons are offered:

- **New Selection:** Make sure this button is on if you want each click of the mouse to start a new selection, ignoring whatever you'd selected with your previous stroke.

- **Add to Selection:** This is the default mode, and it allows you to continue sampling and selecting pixels as you drag, click, and drag some more.

- **Subtract from Selection:** Here, you can remove selected pixels by painting over previously selected pixels.

You cannot create a selection out of the intersection of existing and new selections, but that makes sense given how this tool works. To use it, click the tool to activate it, and then set your Brush size using the Options bar. If you click the triangle to the right of the current brush size, you'll see the set of options shown in Figure 8.9 — you can change the brush Diameter, Hardness, Spacing, Angle, and Roundness. These are much like the tools you can set in the Brushes palette, when you're in Expanded View of that palette and viewing the Brush Tip Shape settings (refer to Chapter 5). You can also choose at this point whether to use the Sample All Layers option, which does just what its name implies — it considers all the pixels at your starting point, regardless of the active layer, and establishes your selection based on that.

FIGURE 8.9

Want to control the Quick Selection by tweaking the size and shape of your selection brush? Use these settings to create the perfect brush for painting a selection from within your image.

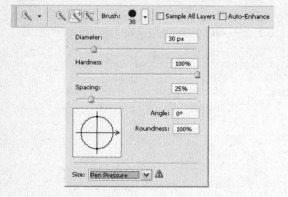

After setting your brush options (which you can change as you work, or deselect, reset, and start over), you can begin making your selection. Just click and drag, and watch as the Quick Selection tool selects an area around your brush, selecting those pixels that match the pixels you sampled by clicking to begin the selection. Of course, while this works much the way the Magic Wand does and also like the Magnetic Lasso: It shrinks around the pixels that it considers a "match" to the sampled ones; in other words, it allows you to keep selecting more and more pixels, widening the net, if you will, and increasing the amount of the layer that's selected.

You can hop between the three modes (New, Add to, Subtract from) between drags of the mouse, and after your selection is complete, you can use the Refine Edge dialog box (discussed in the following section) to gain more control than this very (intentionally) simple tool allows on its own.

TIP   The Auto-Enhance option increases the accuracy of the selection, based on the pixels you're encompassing with the tool as you paint to make a selection. With this option on (as it is by default), you're getting a more precise selection than you would if you turned the option off. Of course, as ever, you have a Refine Edge button, which opens the much-heralded Refine Edge dialog box, which we discuss in the next section.

Ways to Change Selection Outlines

If you don't draw a selection outline correctly the first time, you have two options. You can draw it again from scratch, which can be really tedious and time consuming, or you can change your botched selection outline, correcting the selection. Now, which one sounds more appealing? Assuming you chose the latter solution, it's time to talk about Photoshop's tools for changing the nature of selections — removing some or all of them, adding new stuff to them, resizing them, and changing their edges.

Quick changes

First, here are some fast and easy changes you can make. The following list explains how a few commands work. You'll find them all in the Select menu along with handy keyboard shortcuts you can use.

- **Deselect (Ctrl+D or ⌘+D):** You can deselect the selected portion of an image in three ways. You can select a different portion of the image; click anywhere in the image window with the Rectangular Marquee tool, the Elliptical Marquee tool, or the Lasso tool; or choose Select ⇨ Deselect. Remember, though, when no part of a layer is selected, the entire layer is susceptible to your changes. If you apply a filter, choose a color-correction command, or use a paint tool, you affect every pixel of the layer.

- **Reselect (Ctrl+Shift+D or ⌘+Shift+D):** If you accidentally deselect an image, you can retrieve the most recent selection outline by choosing Select ⇨ Reselect. It's a great function that operates entirely independent of the Undo command and History palette, and it works even after performing a long string of selection-unrelated operations. (You can restore older selections from the History palette, but that usually means undoing operations along the way.)

- **Inverse (Ctrl+Shift+I or ⌘+Shift+I):** Choose Select ⇨ Inverse to reverse the selection. Photoshop deselects the portion of the image that was previously selected and selects the portion of the image that was not selected. This way, you can begin a selection by outlining the portion of the image you want to protect, rather than the portion you want to affect, and then swap the two portions.

> **TIP** You also can access the Inverse and Deselect commands from a shortcut menu in the image window. Right-click (Control-click if you have a one-button mouse) to make the menu appear underneath your cursor.

Manually adding and subtracting

Imagine a portrait. How would you go about selecting both eyes and not selecting or otherwise affecting any other portion of the face? Well, if you're new to the selection tools, you might think that you'd have to select one eye and then do whatever you want to it, and then go select the other eye and repeat whatever was done to the first eye. This, however, is not tapping one of Photoshop's best set of options — found in the first group of four buttons on the Options bar for the Marquee, Lasso, Magic Wand, and even the Shape, Pen, and Path tools (though the buttons are not the first group on the Options bar for the last three tools listed).

With these buttons, Photoshop lets you add a bit more to a selection, whittle away at a selection, and create new selections out of overlapping areas within two or more selections. This makes it possible, too, to combine selection tools — starting out, for example, with the Marquee, and then tacking on a selection made with the Lasso or the Magic Wand. You can use the buttons shown in Figure 8.10, or you can use these handy-dandy keyboard shortcuts:

- **Adding to a selection outline:** To increase the area enclosed in an existing selection outline, Shift-drag with one of the marquee or lasso tools. You also can Shift-click with the Magic Wand tool or Shift-click with one of the marquee tools when the Fixed Size option is active (as described in the section "Geometric Selection Outlines" earlier in this chapter).

- **Subtracting from a selection outline:** To take a bite from an existing selection outline, press Alt (Win) or Option (Mac) while using one of the selection tools.

- **Intersecting one selection outline with another:** Another way to subtract from an existing selection outline is to Shift+Alt-drag (Shift+Option-drag on the Mac) around the selection with the Rectangular Marquee, Elliptical Marquee, or Lasso tool. You also can Shift+Alt-click (Shift+Option-click on the Mac) with the Magic Wand tool. Shift+Alt-dragging instructs Photoshop to retain only the portion of an existing selection that also falls inside the new selection outline.

If the keyboard shortcuts seem cumbersome, use the selection state buttons (labeled in Figure 8.10) at the left end of the Options bar to set your selection tool to the Add, Subtract, or Intersect mode. After clicking a button, simply drag to alter the selection outline. To toggle the tool back to the normal operating mode, click the first button in the bunch. Note that the keyboard techniques described in the preceding list work no matter what button you select in the Options bar. For example, if you click the Intersect button, Alt-dragging (Option-dragging on the Mac) still subtracts from the selection outline. Remember, too, that you can switch selection tools and then use the Add to, Subtract from, or Intersect with buttons, creating a selection that's created with a combination of tools.

FIGURE 8.10

You can use the selection state buttons as well as the Shift and Alt keys (Shift and Option keys on the Mac) when modifying a selection outline.

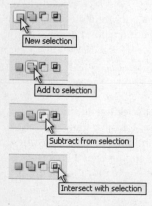

TIP   When you're working with the Magic Wand, you can right-click (Control-click on the Mac) to display a shortcut menu that contains the Add, Subtract, and Intersect mode options. Click the mode you want to use.

TIP   Photoshop displays special cursors to help you keep track of a tool's selection state. Suppose that you select part of an image and the Lasso tool is active. When you press Shift or click the Add button in the Options bar, Photoshop appends a little plus sign to the Lasso cursor to show you're about to add. A minus sign indicates that you're set to subtract from the selection outline; a multiply sign appears when you work in Intersect mode. If you're pressing keys to switch tool modes, Photoshop temporarily selects the corresponding selection state button in the Options bar as well.

Power-user tricks

The roles of the Shift and Alt keys (Shift and Option keys on the Mac) in adding, subtracting, and intersecting selection outlines can interfere with your ability to take advantage of other functions of the selection tools. For example, when no portion of an image is selected, you can Shift-drag with the Rectangular Marquee tool to draw a square. But after a selection is active, Shift-dragging adds a rectangle — not a square — to the selection outline.

This is one reason for the selection state buttons in the Options bar. After you click a button, the tool adds, subtracts, or intersects, with no additional keypresses on your part, depending on which button you click. But if you want to hide the Options bar or you just prefer pressing keys to clicking buttons, you can control the selection tools from the keyboard without giving up any selection flexibility.

The trick is to learn when to press Shift and Alt (Option on the Mac). Sometimes you have to press the key before you begin your drag; other times you must press the key after you begin the drag but before you release. For example, to add a square to a selection outline with the Rectangular Marquee tool, Shift-drag, release Shift while keeping the mouse button pressed, and press Shift again to snap the rectangle to a square. The same goes for adding a circle with the Elliptical Marquee tool.

The following list introduces you to a few other techniques. They may seem a little elaborate or complicated, but with a little practice, they will become second nature — really, they will. Before you try any of them, be sure to select Normal from the Style pop-up menu in the Options bar.

NOTE   To keep things visually simple in the text, the following list refers only to Windows users' keystrokes and commands. On a Mac, press Option instead of Alt.

- **Subtract a square or a circle from a selection.** Alt-drag, release Alt, press Shift, drag until you get it right, release the mouse button, and then release Shift.
- **Add a rectangle or an ellipse by drawing from the center outward.** Shift-drag, release Shift, press Alt, and hold Alt until after you release the mouse button. You can even press the spacebar during the drag to move the marquee around, if you like.

- **Subtract a marquee drawn from the center outward.** Alt-drag, release Alt, press Alt again, and hold the key down until after you release the mouse button.

- **Add a straight-sided area to an existing selection.** Shift-drag with the tool for a short distance. With the mouse button still down, release Shift and press Alt. Then click around as you normally would, while keeping the Alt key down.

- **Subtract a straight-sided area.** Alt-drag with the Lasso, release Alt, press Alt again, and click around with the tool.

The last two might be easier if you switch to the Polygonal Lasso instead of using the regular Lasso. In fact, one of the reasons Adobe provided the Polygonal Lasso tool was to accommodate people who don't want to have to press Alt or Option many times during the creation of a selection — so by all means, use the tool and make your life easier.

Adding and subtracting by command

Photoshop provides several commands under the Select menu that automatically increase or decrease the number of selected pixels in an image according to numeric specifications. The commands in the Select ⇨ Modify submenu work as follows:

- **Border:** This command selects an area of a specified thickness around the perimeter of the current selection outline and deselects the rest of the selection. For example, to select a 20-pixel-thick border around the current selection, choose Select ⇨ Modify ⇨ Border, type 20 in the Width option box, and press Enter or Return. But what's the point? After all, if you want to create an outline around a selection, you can accomplish this in fewer steps by choosing Edit ⇨ Stroke, right? The Border command, however, broadens your range of options. You can apply a special effect to the border, move the border to a new location, or even create a double-outline effect by first applying Select ⇨ Modify ⇨ Border and then applying Edit ⇨ Stroke.

- **Smooth:** This command rounds off the sharp corners and weird anomalies in the outline of a selection. When you choose Select ⇨ Modify ⇨ Smooth, the program asks you to type a Sample Radius value. Photoshop smoothes out corners by drawing little circles around them; the Sample Radius value determines the radius of these circles. Larger values result in smoother corners.

> **TIP** The Smooth command is especially useful in combination with the Magic Wand. After you make one of those weird, scraggly selection outlines with the Wand tool (or the Lasso, where eye-hand coordination deficits can be really obvious), use Select ⇨ Modify ⇨ Smooth to smooth out the rough edges. It's also helpful when you have used the Polygonal Lasso to make a more controlled selection along curvy edges; use the Smooth command to eliminate any of the angles you may inadvertently create as you click and move the mouse to make the selection.

■ **Expand** and **Contract:** Both of these commands do exactly what they say, either expanding or contracting the selected area by a specified amount. For example, if you want an elliptical selection to grow by 8 pixels, choose Select ➪ Modify ➪ Expand, type 8, and that's it.

> **TIP** Both Expand and Contract have a flattening effect on a selection. To round things off, apply the Smooth command with a Sample Radius value equal to the number you just typed in the Expand Selection or Contract Selection dialog box. This isn't the technique for making very precise selections, but that's the downside (and one that's usually worth it, for all the effort it saves you) of using automated commands. If the results are *almost* what you wanted but there are some areas where extra stuff was selected and you need to pare the selection down a bit, you can always zoom in very close and use one of the Lasso selection tools set to Subtract from Selection mode and whittle away at the selection as needed.

In addition to the Expand command, Photoshop provides two other commands — Grow and Similar — that increase the area covered by a selection outline. Both commands resemble the Magic Wand tool because they measure the range of eligible pixels by way of a Tolerance value. In fact, the commands rely on the same Tolerance value that you set for the Magic Wand (in the Options bar). So if you want to adjust the impact of either command, you must first select the Magic Wand and then apply the commands:

■ **Grow:** Choose Select ➪ Grow to select all pixels that both neighbor an existing selection and resemble the colors included in the selection, in accordance with the Tolerance value. In other words, Select ➪ Grow is the command equivalent of the Magic Wand tool. If you feel constrained because you can click only one pixel at a time with the Magic Wand tool, you may prefer to select a small group of representative pixels with a marquee tool and then choose Select ➪ Grow to initiate the Wand's magic.

■ **Similar:** Another member of the Select menu, Similar works like Grow, except the pixels needn't be adjacent. When you choose Select ➪ Similar, Photoshop selects any pixel that falls within the Tolerance range, regardless of the location of the pixel in the foreground image.

> **NOTE** Although both Grow and Similar respect the Magic Wand's Tolerance value, they pay no attention to the other Wand options — Contiguous, Sample All Layers, and Anti-alias. Grow always selects only contiguous regions; Similar selects noncontiguous areas. Neither can see beyond the active layer nor produce anti-aliased selection outlines.

One of the best applications for the Similar command is to isolate a complicated image set against a consistent background whose colors are significantly lighter or darker than the image. Figure 8.11, which features just such a scenario, contains some sample selections made to "train" Photoshop as to what the Similar command should look for when choosing pixels for selection.

FIGURE 8.11

Before choosing Select ⇨ Similar, select a few sample portions of the background for Photoshop to use as a basis for its selection range.

Softening selection outlines

Sometimes, you want to make sure that whatever you're selecting, or the hole left by deleting it, has a soft edge — for artistic reasons or simply to make the changes or deletion less jarring to the image, avoiding any hard, obvious edges. When you feel the need for such an effect, you can soften a selection in two ways. The first method is *anti-aliasing*, introduced in Chapter 5. Anti-aliasing is an intelligent and automatic softening algorithm that mimics the appearance of edges you'd expect to see in a sharply focused photograph.

NOTE   Where did the term *anti-alias* originate? Anytime you try to fit the digital equivalent of a square peg into a round hole — say, by printing a high-resolution image to a low-resolution printer — the data gets revised during the process. This revised data, called an *alias*, is frequently inaccurate and undesirable. Anti-aliasing is the act of revising the data ahead of time, essentially rounding off the square peg so it looks nice as it goes into the hole.

When you draw an anti-aliased selection outline in Photoshop, the program calculates the hard-edged selection at twice its actual size. The program then shrinks the selection in half using bicubic interpolation (described in Chapter 2). The result is a crisp image with no visible jagged edges.

The second softening method, *feathering*, is more dramatic. Feathering gradually dissipates the selection outline, giving it a blurry edge. Photoshop accommodates partially selected pixels; feathering fades the selection both inward and outward from the original edge.

You can specify the number of pixels affected either before or after drawing a selection. To feather a selection before you draw it with a Marquee or Lasso tool, type a value in the Feather option box, found in the Options bar — the option is set to 0 pixels by default. To feather a selection after drawing it, choose Select ⇨ Feather or press Ctrl+Alt+D (⌘+Option+D on the Mac). You also can right-click (Control-click on the Mac) in the image window and then choose Feather from the pop-up menu that appears next to your cursor.

The Feather Radius value (in the Feather Selection dialog box) determines the approximate distance over which Photoshop fades a selection, measured in pixels in both directions from the original selection outline. Figure 8.12 shows the effects of feathering a selection. In the first example, no feathering was used. In the second example, a 24-pixel feather was applied, and the resulting selection has a very soft edge. A pattern also was made from a selection on the stalk on which the bird is sitting, and this was used to fill the background — and then a Gaussian Blur was applied to it. If you missed it, creating patterns from selections within your image was covered in Chapter 6, and the Blur filters are covered in Chapter 10.

FIGURE 8.12

One with, one without. In the second image, the Feather was set to 10 pixels, creating this fuzzy frame around the selection.

The math behind the feather

In case you, like previous readers who've written to ask, might wonder why feathering blurs a selection outline more than the number of pixels stated in the Feather Radius value, here's how it works. A radius of 4 pixels actually affects a total of 20 pixels: 10 inward and 10 outward. The reason revolves around Photoshop's use of a mathematical routine called the *Gaussian bell curve*, which exaggerates the distance over which the selection outline is blurred.

TIP If exact space is an issue, you can count on the Feather command affecting about 2.7 times as many pixels as you type in the Feather Radius option box, both in and out from the selection. That's a total of 5.4 times as many pixels as the radius in all.

Putting feathering to use

You can use feathering to remove an element from an image while leaving the background intact, a process described in the following steps. The image in Figure 8.13 has some problem items in it — namely, a particular child who insists on making a crazy face every time a camera is pointed in his direction — but the one that can be removed without causing any family discord is the bright dot of light in the left side of the photo. A selection has been drawn around the offending spot.

FIGURE 8.13

Got something to hide? The smoother the edges of the patch you use to obscure it, the more convincing your cover up.

STEPS: Removing an Element from an Image

1. Draw a selection around the element using the selection tool that's most appropriate for the element you want to get rid of. As shown in Figure 8.13, the offending spot is encircled in an elliptical marquee selection, which is perfect for this unwanted "orb".

2. Drag the selection outline over a patch in the image. Now that you've specified the element you want to remove, you must find a patch — that is, some portion of the image to cover the element in a manner that matches the surroundings. In Figure 8.14, the best match was clearly from some of the wall to the right of the spot. To select this area, move the selection outline independently of the image merely by dragging it with the selection tool (the Marquee in this case). Dragging a selection with a selection tool moves the outline without affecting the pixels, unlike dragging a selection with the Move tool, which moves whatever's in the selection. Make certain you allow some space between the selection outline and the element you're trying to cover.

3. Choose Select ➪ Feather, or press Ctrl+Alt+D (⌘+Option+D on the Mac). Type a small value (8 or less) in the Feather Radius option box — just enough to make the edges fuzzy. Then press Enter or Return to initiate the operation.

4. Clone the patch onto the area you want to cover. Select the Move tool by pressing V. Then Alt-drag (Option-drag on the Mac) the feathered selection to clone the patch and position it over the element you want to cover, as shown in Figure 8.15. To align the patch correctly, choose Select ➪ Hide Extras or press Ctrl+H (⌘+H on the Mac) to hide the marching ants and then nudge the patch into position with the arrow keys.

FIGURE 8.14

After drawing a circle around the spot with the Marquee tool, the selection outline was moved to the right to select another portion of the wall. Feathering the selection is the next step.

FIGURE 8.15

Next, I used the Move tool to Alt-drag (Option-drag on the Mac) the feathered selection over the bright spot. As long as you have something to use in covering the offending content, this technique can mask just about anything, and often with fewer steps and better results than the Clone Stamp.

Refining Selection Edges

As mentioned throughout this chapter, each time the potential need to clean up or customize a selection is discussed, CS3 now offers a very handy and powerful feature — the Refine Edge dialog box. Opened by clicking the Refine Edge button on any selection tool's options bar or by choosing Refine Edge from the Select menu (the menu command is available whenever a selection is in place — even if none of the selection tools are active), the resulting dialog box appears in Figure 8.4 and here in Figure 8.16.

The dialog box is divided into four sections, four of which consist of tools for helping you change or view your selection to do a better job for you within the image at hand. You also can zoom in on the selection (use the Magnifying glass button) or pan around in the image (use the Hand button), and of course, you can preview the effects of the changes you're making by leaving the Preview option on.

FIGURE 8.16

Choose how to view your selection, and tweak its confines through the use of five different sliders.

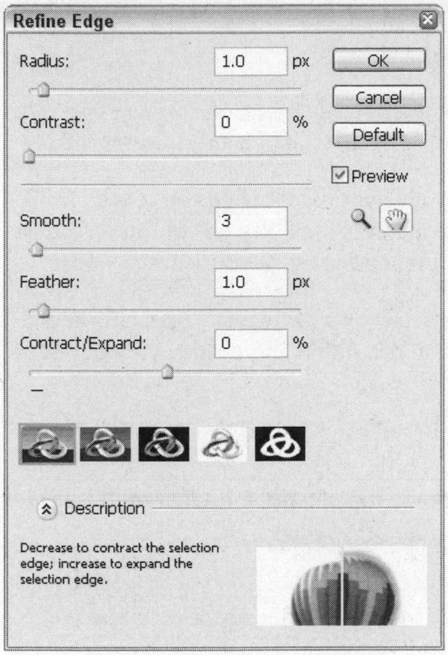

In terms of tweaking your selection, you have the ability to adjust the Radius and Contrast (see the top section of the dialog box) and to manipulate the Smooth, Feather, and Contract/Expand sliders to clean up, soften, and change the size of your selection (see the second section of the dialog box). Here's the skinny on each of these options:

- **Radius:** Use this slider to clean up a selection where fine or tiny details run along that selection's edges. The lower the number you set here, the crisper the edge of the selection.

- **Contrast:** To make a crisp, clean edge, drag this slider to the right. Using this refining method allows you to shear off the artifacts along the edges of an object in an image, clean up fuzzy contact points between elements in an image, and give your selection a nice, sharp edge.

- **Smooth:** Get rid of choppy, jagged edges in your selection with this slider. The higher the number, the smoother the edges of the selection, although without using Radius or Feather, the edges of the selection will not blur or soften the effects applied within the selection.

- **Feather:** If you want to blur or soften the edges of whatever's done to the area within (and directly outside of) your selection, use this slider, dragging it to the right for increased feathering.

- **Contract/Expand:** As the name implies, this slider allows you to reduce the size of your selection (drag to the left) or increase it (drag to the right).

> **TIP**   As you mouse over each slider, you can check the Description section for an explanation of each option's purpose, often accompanied by a visual to help you get the idea.

The last functional part of the dialog box consists of five View buttons, allowing you to take a different visual perspective on your selection. Note that you can press the F key on your keyboard to cycle through these views and choose the one that makes the most sense in your current image.

- **Standard:** You can choose the Standard view, which shows the regular "marching ants" edge on your selection, and displays the image content within and outside of your selection normally.

- **Quick Mask:** Pick this one if you want a rubylith (slightly see-through red wash) to cover all but your selected area/s.

- **Black Background:** This view puts your selection on top of a black background.

- **White Background:** Big surprise here, this one puts your selection on top of a white background.

- **Mask:** Choose this view to see your selection as a mask — a white shape on a black background.

The idea, of course, is to pick the view that gives you the best look at your selection so you can use the rest of the controls in the dialog box to make the necessary changes to the selection itself. If you're cleaning up the edges of a selection, for example, viewing it against a solid color (black or white) may be helpful. If you want to be able to see the rest of the image, but want your selection to stand out, Quick Mask might be better than Standard.

Moving and Duplicating Selections

In the preceding steps, you discovered that you can move the selected pixels or the empty selection outline to a new location, and with feathering the selection, make the moved content blend in with its new surroundings. Now it's time to examine these techniques in greater depth.

The role of the Move tool

To move selected pixels, you need the Move tool. This may seem rather obvious, but there are so many other ways to select and reposition content that you may not realize exactly what the Move tool does and how many other tools it can replace (in some situations) if you use it properly. When you want to use it, you can select the Move tool at any time by pressing V (for *mooV*). One of the chief advantages of using the Move tool is that there's no chance of deselecting an image or harming the selection outline. Drag inside the selected area to move the selection; drag outside the selection to move the entire layer, selection included. Layers are covered in more detail in Chapter 13.

> **TIP** To access the Move tool on a temporary basis, press and hold Ctrl (⌘ on the Mac). The Move tool remains active as long as you hold Ctrl or ⌘. This shortcut works when any tool except the Hand tool, the Direct Selection or Path Selection tool, or any Pen, Shape, or Slice tool is active. If you have any interest in keyboard shortcuts, it's worth committing this to memory. It will save you heaps of time, as you will probably spend lots of time Ctrl-dragging (⌘-dragging on the Mac) in Photoshop.

Making precise movements

Photoshop provides three methods for moving selections in prescribed increments. In each case, the Move tool is active, unless otherwise indicated:

- First, you can nudge a selection in 1-pixel increments by pressing an arrow key on the keyboard or nudge in 10-pixel increments by pressing Shift while pressing an arrow key. This technique is useful for making precise adjustments to the position of an image. Note that a series of consecutive nudges is recorded in the History palette (see Chapter 7) as only one history state, regardless of how far you move the selection. Choosing Undo takes the selection back to its original position in the image.

> **TIP** To nudge a selected area when the move tool is not active, press Ctrl (Win) or ⌘ (Mac) and an arrow key. Press Ctrl+Shift (Win) or ⌘+Shift (Mac) and an arrow key to move in 10-pixel increments. After the selection is floating — that is, after your first nudge — you can release the Ctrl or ⌘ key and use only the arrows (assuming a selection tool is active).

- Second, you can press Shift during a drag to constrain a move to a 45-degree direction — that is, horizontally, vertically, or diagonally.

- And third, you can use the Info palette to track your movements and to help locate a precise position in the image.

To display the Info palette, shown in Figure 8.17, choose Window ⇨ Info or press F8. The first section of the Info palette displays the color values of the image area beneath your cursor. When you move a selection, the other eight items in the palette monitor movement as follows:

- **X, Y:** These values show the coordinate position of your cursor. The distance is measured from the upper-left corner of the image in the current unit of measure. The unit of measure in Figure 8.16 is pixels.

- **$\Delta X, \Delta Y$:** These values indicate the distance of your move as measured horizontally and vertically.

- **A, D:** The A and D values reflect the angle and direct distance of your drag.

- **W, H:** These values reflect the width and height of your selection.

FIGURE 8.17

The Info palette provides a world of numerical feedback when you move a selection.

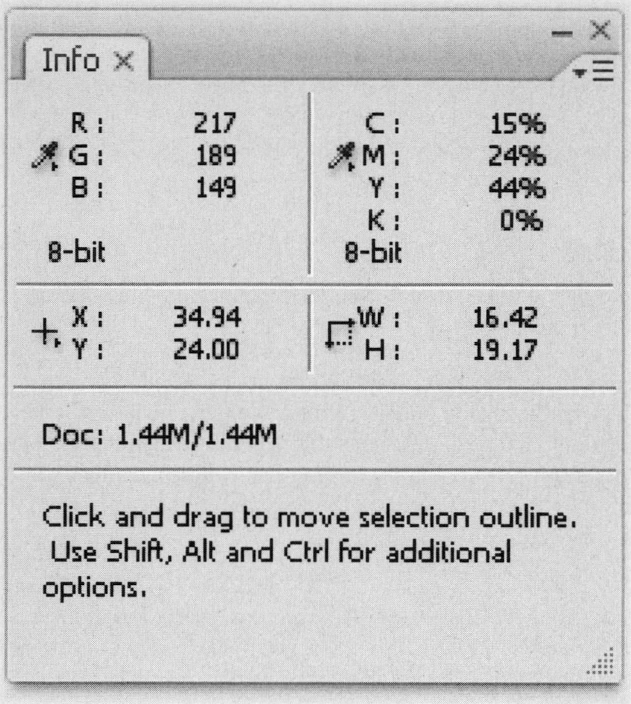

Cloning a selection

When you move a selection, you leave a hole in your image in the background color, as shown in the top half of Figure 8.18. If you prefer to leave the original in place during a move, you have to *clone* the selection — that is, create a copy of the selection without upsetting the contents of the Clipboard. Photoshop offers several ways to clone a selection:

- **Alt-dragging (Option-dragging on the Mac):** When the Move tool is active, press Alt (Option on the Mac) and drag a selection to clone it. Figure 8.18 shows a selection that was moved once and Alt-dragged three times.

- **Ctrl+Alt-dragging (⌘+Option-dragging on the Mac):** If some tool other than the Move tool is active, press Ctrl+Alt (⌘+Option on the Mac) and drag the selection to clone it. This is probably the technique you'll use most often.

FIGURE 8.18

When you move a selection, you leave a gaping hole in the selection's wake — and you can also see the edges where you may have missed some of the desired content (see edges of hole). When you clone an image, you leave a copy of the selection behind. To illustrate this point, the selection was moved once, and then duplicated three times.

- **Alt+arrowing (Option+arrowing on the Mac):** When the Move tool is active, press Alt (Win) or Option (Mac) and one of the arrow keys to clone the selection and nudge it one pixel away from the original. If you want to move the image multiple pixels, press Alt+arrow (Option+arrow on the Mac) the first time only. Then nudge the clone using the arrow key alone. Otherwise, you'll create a bunch of clones, which probably isn't what you want to do.

- **Ctrl+Alt+arrowing (⌘+Option+arrowing on the Mac):** If some other tool is active, press Ctrl and Alt (⌘ and Option on the Mac) and an arrow key. Again, press only Alt (Option on the Mac) the first time, unless you want to create a string of clones.

- **Drag-and-drop:** Like about every other program on the planet, Photoshop lets you clone a selection between documents by dragging it with the move tool from one open window and dropping it in another, as demonstrated in Figure 8.19. As long as you manage to drop into the second window, the original image remains intact and selected in the first window. Notice that the layer from the image on the right appears smaller in the left image where it was dropped because the image on the left was captured at a higher resolution.

 Don't worry about exact positioning during a drag-and-drop; first get the selection into the second window and then worry about placement.

 You can drag-and-drop multiple layers if you link the layers first. For more information on this subject, see Chapter 13.

FIGURE 8.19

Use the Move tool to drag a selection from one open window and drop it into another. This creates a clone of the selection in the target window.

■ **Shift-drop:** If the two images are exactly the same size — pixel for pixel — press Shift when dropping the selection to position it in the same spot that it occupied in the original image. This is called *registering* the selection.

 If an area is selected in the destination image, Shift-dropping positions the selection you're moving in the center of the selection in the destination image. This tip works regardless of whether the two images are the same size.

■ **Ctrl-drag-and-drop (⌘-drag-and-drop on the Mac):** Again, if some other tool than the Move tool is selected, you must press Ctrl (Win) or ⌘ (Mac) when you drag to move the selected pixels from one window to the other.

Moving a selection outline independently of its contents

After all this talk about the Move tool and the Ctrl key (⌘ key on the Mac), you may be wondering what happens if you drag a selection while the Marquee, Lasso, or Wand tool is active — right after you've used one or more of them to make the selection, presumably. The answer is, you move the selection outline independently of the image. This technique, which was used earlier in this chapter in the steps "Removing an Element from an Image," serves as yet another means to manipulate selection outlines. It also enables you to take a selection from one portion of an image to another portion of the image or to an entirely different image window — without bringing any image content with you.

> **TIP** You can nudge a selection outline independently of its contents by pressing an arrow key when a selection tool is active. Press Shift and an arrow key to move the outline in 10-pixel increments.

You also can drag and drop empty selection outlines between images. Again, the selection tool — the Marquee, Lasso, or Magic Wand — must be active. Just drag the outline from one image window and drop it into another. The difference is that only the selection outline gets cloned; the pixels remain behind. This is a great way to copy pixels back and forth between images. You can set up an exact selection outline in Image A, drag it into Image B with the Marquee tool, move it over the pixels you want to clone, and Ctrl-drag-and-drop (⌘-drag-and-drop on the Mac) the selection back into Image A. Add the use of the Feather option (to soften the selection edges, remember?) and you've got a seamless edit in Image A, and Image B won't even know what hit it.

So remember: The selection tools affect only the selection outline. The selection tools never affect the pixels themselves; that's the Move tool's job, as you'll see as you read on.

Scaling or rotating a selection outline

In case you were distracted while reading the last two sentences, here's the important thing to remember: Selection outlines stay independent — and entirely changeable — as long as a selection tool is active. In addition to moving a selection outline, you can transform it by choosing Select ⇨ Transform Selection.

When you select this command, Photoshop displays a transformation boundary framed by eight handles, as shown in Figure 8.20. This is known as a *bounding box*. You can drag the handles to adjust the outline as described in the upcoming list. In addition, the Options bar gives you access to a slew of mysterious option boxes, as shown at the top of the figure. You can type specific values to relocate, size, rotate, and skew the selection outline precisely.

FIGURE 8.20

Much like using the Transform and Free Transform commands on actual image content, after choosing Select ➪ Transform Selection, you can scale the selection outline (top) and rotate it (bottom), all without affecting the image in the slightest.

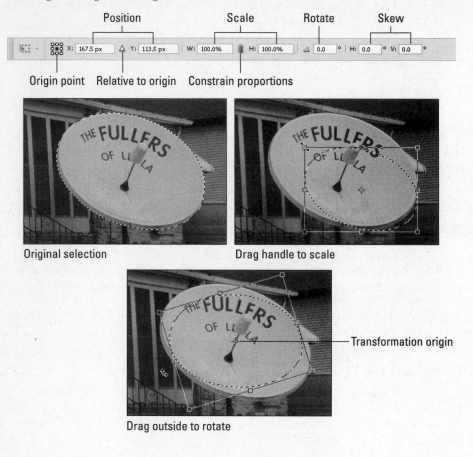

Original selection

Drag handle to scale

Drag outside to rotate

The handles and Options bar controls work just as they do for the Edit ➪ Free Transform command, which is covered in riveting detail in Chapter 13. To save you the backbreaking chore of flipping ahead five chapters, though, let's cut to the chase here:

- **Scale:** Drag any of the handles to scale the selection, as shown in Figure 8.20. Shift-drag to scale proportionally, Alt-drag (Option-drag on the Mac) to scale with respect to the origin (little cross hair/circle thing labeled in the figure). You can move the origin just by dragging it.

Alternatively, type a scale percentage in the W (width) and H (height) boxes in the Options bar. By default, Photoshop maintains the original proportions of the outline. If that doesn't suit you, click the Constrain Proportions button (it looks like a little chain) between the two boxes.

NOTE See that little replica of the transformation boundary near the left end of the Options bar? The black square represents the current origin. You can click the boxes to relocate the origin to one of the handles. Use the X and Y values to change the position of the origin numerically. Click the triangular delta symbol, labeled in Figure 8.20, to measure positioning relative to the transformation origin.

- **Rotate:** Type a value in the Rotate option box or drag outside the transformation boundary to rotate the selection, as in the second example in Figure 8.20. The rotation always occurs with respect to the origin.

TIP To rotate the outline by 90 or 180 degrees, right-click (Control-click on the Mac) the image window and choose the rotation amount you want from the resulting pop-up menu.

- **Flip:** You can flip a selection outline by dragging one handle past its opposite handle, but this is lots of work. The easier way is to right-click (Control-click on the Mac) inside the image window and choose Flip Horizontal or Flip Vertical from the pop-up menu.

- **Skew and distort:** To skew the selection outline, Ctrl-drag (⌘-drag on the Mac) a side, top, or bottom handle. Or type values in the H (horizontal) and V (vertical) skew boxes in the Options bar. To distort the selection, Ctrl-drag (Win) or ⌘-drag (Mac) a corner handle.

- **Warp:** Photoshop's Warp capabilities now extend to selections as well as image content. In Warp mode, you can distort the selection using the grid and additional handles shown in Figure 8.21. You can drag any of the grid intersections, the gray solid handles on the perimeter, the corner box handles, or points along any of the gridlines.

  You can click the Warp list (shown in Figure 8.21) and select a preset grid. The grid appears in the shape you choose, and the Bend, Height, and Width fields become available. The top image in Figure 8.18 shows the default Custom warp grid in place. The image on the bottom shows a warp in progress. When you drag from a handle once, additional handles appear to allow you to change the angle of the corner or slide in question. To commit to your warp changes, click the check mark button (shown in Figure 8.21), or press Return or Enter. Esc abandons the Warp and restores your selection to its prewarp state.

CROSS-REF Read more about warping image content in Chapter 13.

When you get the selection outline the way you want it, press Enter or Return or double-click inside the boundary. To cancel the transformation, press Escape. You also can click the check mark button near the right end of the Options bar to apply the transformation or click the "no" symbol button to cancel the operation.

FIGURE 8.21

Use the Warp mode grid to distort your selection; each gridline, grid intersection, and handle can be used by clicking and dragging with your mouse. After a handle has been dragged, new handles appear to let you change the angle of the distortion.

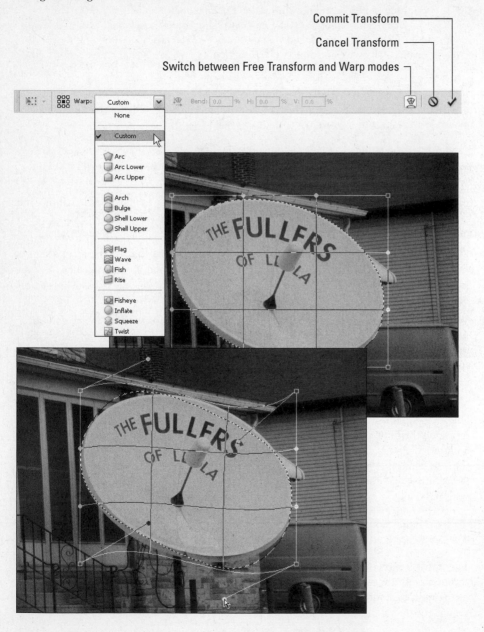

Drawing and Editing Paths

Now that you know all about the main, basic selection tools and how to manipulate their selections, it's time to move on to one of the more powerful, yet complex tools that can be used to create selections. Photoshop's path tools provide the most flexible and precise ways to define a selection short of masking, but they can be something of a mystery and a technical challenge to novices and intermediate-level users. Given that most people underestimate their knowledge of Photoshop (other than total novices, who know they have little or no experience), you may not know which level you're on — but don't worry. Most people take some time to grow comfortable with the Pen tool, for example, because it requires you to draw a selection outline one point at a time:

> **NOTE** If you're familiar with Illustrator's Pen tool and other path-editing functions, you'll find Photoshop's tools nearly identical. Users of other illustration programs, such as CorelDRAW, also will recognize many similarities with the Bézier tool, used to draw curved lines and shapes. Of course, Photoshop doesn't provide the breadth of options available in Illustrator and these other program's Pen/Bézier tools, but the basic techniques are the same. Photoshop also includes a set of path-drawing tools to help smooth out the learning curve — and the possibly undesirable paths you've drawn — for inexperienced users. You can use any of the shape tools — Rectangle, Rounded Rectangle, Line, Ellipse, Polygon, and Custom Shape — to draw a simple geometric path.

The following pages get you up and running with all the path features. You learn how to draw a path, edit it, convert it to a selection outline, and stroke it with a paint or edit tool. You'll be a path-drawing, editing, converting, painting maniac just a few pages from now.

Paths overview

You create and edit paths from scratch by using the various pen tools or shape tools. (Figure 8.2, earlier in this chapter, shows all the path-related tools along with their selection tool counterparts.) Path management options — which enable you to convert paths to selections, fill and stroke paths, and save and delete them — reside in the Paths palette, shown in Figure 8.22.

How paths work

Paths differ from normal selections because they exist on the equivalent of a distinct, object-oriented layer that sits in front of the bitmapped image. This setup enables you to edit a path with point-by-point precision with no fear that you'll accidentally make any change to the image, as you can when you edit ordinary selection outlines. After you get a path just so, one of the things you can do with it is convert it to a standard selection outline. This allows you to take advantage of the fine tools available for the creation and editing of a path, and then use that path as a regular selection to edit the contents of the image. Of course, you can do many other things with paths — and you'll find out about them as you read on in this and the following sections.

The following steps explain the basic process of drawing a selection outline with the path tools. The individual steps are explained in greater detail later in the chapter, but this procedure should enable you to sort of sneak up to the pool and dip your toe in — diving comes later.

FIGURE 8.22

To save and organize your paths, display the Paths palette by choosing Window ➪ Paths.

Fill   Make   New
path selection path

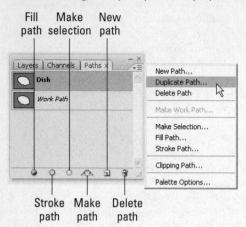

Stroke Make Delete
path   path   path

STEPS: Creating a Selection with the Path Tools

1. **Draw the path.** Make sure the Paths button is selected in the Options bar, and then use a Pen tool or a Shape tool to draw the outline of your prospective selection.

> **NOTE** If your goal is to select multiple areas of the image, draw outlines around all of them. A path can include as many separate segments as you like. Technically, the individual segments in a path are called *subpaths*.

2. **Edit the path.** If the path requires some adjustment, reshape it using the other path tools.

3. **Save the path.** When you get the path exactly as you want it, save the path by choosing the Save Path command from the Paths palette menu. Or double-click the *Work Path* item in the scrolling list.

4. **Convert the path to a selection.** You can make the path a selection outline by choosing the Make Selection command or by pressing Enter on the numeric keypad when a path or selection tool is active.

That's it. After you convert the path to a selection, it works like any of the selection outlines described earlier. You can feather a selection, move it, copy it, clone it, or apply one of the special effects described in future chapters. The path remains intact in case you want to do further editing or use it again.

Sorting through the path tools

Before you get into how you draw and edit paths, here's a quick introduction to the path tools. To start, take a look at the tools on the Pen tool flyout:

 Pen: Use the Pen tool to draw paths in Photoshop one point at a time. Click to create a corner in a path; click and drag to make a smooth point that results in a continuous arc. Fear not, this tool is explained *ad nauseam* in the section "Drawing paths with the Pen tool" later in this chapter. You can select the Pen tool by pressing P; press P again to toggle to the Freeform Pen, described next. (As always, the shortcuts assume that you have deselected the Use Shift Key for Tool Switch option in the Preferences dialog box.)

 Freeform Pen: Click and drag with this tool to create a path that automatically follows the twists and turns of your drag. Simplicity at its best; control at its lowest. Luckily, you can turn around and edit the path after you initially draw it, so the lack of control when drawing the path can be made up afterward as you edit it.

 Magnetic Pen: The Magnetic Pen doesn't actually appear in the Toolbox. But if you select the Freeform Pen and then select the Magnetic option in the Options bar, the Freeform Pen dashes into a phone booth and becomes the Magnetic Pen. Click the edge of the foreground element you want to select and then move the cursor along the edge of the shape. Photoshop automatically assigns points as it deems appropriate.

 Add Anchor Point: Click an existing path to add a point to it.

 Delete Anchor Point: Click an existing point in a path to delete the point without creating a break in the path's outline.

 Convert Point: Click or drag a point to convert it to a corner or smooth point. You also can drag a handle to convert the point. To access the Convert Point tool, press Alt (Win) or Option (Mac) when the Pen is active. Press Ctrl+Alt (⌘+Option on the Mac) when an Arrow tool (explained in the next section) is active. (The terms *anchor point*, *smooth point*, and others associated with drawing paths are explained in the upcoming section.)

You can use the Pen tool to add, delete, and convert points, too, providing that you select the Auto Add/Delete option in the Options bar. Pass the cursor over a segment in a selected path to toggle to the Add Anchor Point tool; move the cursor over a point to get the Delete Anchor Point tool. Press Alt (Option on the Mac) over a point to get the Convert Point tool.

If all you need is a simple, geometric path, you can save time by creating the path with the shape tools. The shape tools are covered in detail in Chapter 15, so there's no need to repeat everything here. Just know that after you select a shape tool, you shift it into Path-Drawing mode by clicking the Paths button in the Options bar, labeled in Figure 8.23. (The pen that appears on the button face serves as a reminder that you're in path country.) Photoshop sets the shape tools to that mode automatically if you select them while working on an existing path.

FIGURE 8.23

Click the Paths button in the Options bar to draw paths with the shape tools.

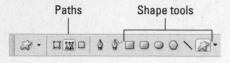

As you draw, Photoshop automatically adds whatever points are needed. You only need to worry about selecting a path overlap button, which determines how paths intersect and interact. See the next section to find out which button to choose when.

After you create a path, you can select it or edit it by using the two tools on the flyout directly above the pen tools flyout:

 Path Selection tool (black arrow): This tool selects an entire path. Just click inside the path to select it. If you created subpaths, the tool selects only the one under your cursor. You also use this tool to select vector objects, as explained in Chapter 14.

 Direct Selection tool (white arrow): This tool permits you to click and drag points and handles to reshape a path. You can access the tool when any other path tool is active by pressing and holding Ctrl (⌘ on the Mac). And you can Alt-click (Option-click on the Mac) inside a path to select the entire path without switching to the Path Selection (black arrow) tool.

NOTE From this point on, these two tools are referred to as the *black arrow* and *white arrow*. Why? Because Photoshop users are a visually oriented group, and it's a safe bet that you can find the right tool more quickly if you're told to "click with the black arrow" or "drag with the white arrow" than if you were to see the technical tool names in all references to the tools.

You can access the arrow tools from the keyboard by pressing A. You know the drill: Press A to switch to the tool that's currently active; press A again to toggle to the other tool. (Add Shift if you selected the Use Shift Key for Tool Switch option in the Preferences dialog box.)

Drawing paths with the Pen tool

When drawing with the regular Pen tool, you build a path by creating individual points. Photoshop automatically connects the points with segments, which are simply straight or curved lines. It will be hard not to drag (unless you're using the Freeform Pen), so be prepared to curse and start over a few times.

NOTE Adobe prefers the term *anchor points* rather than *points* because the points anchor the path into place. But most people just call them points. Given that *all* points associated with paths are anchor points, it's not like there's some potential for confusion, right? Right.

All paths in Photoshop are *Bézier* (pronounced bay-zee-ay) paths, meaning they rely on the same mathematical curve definitions that make up the core of the PostScript printer language. The Bézier curve model allows for zero, one, or two levers to be associated with each point in a path.

These levers, labeled in Figure 8.24, are called *Bézier control handles* or simply *handles*. You can move each handle in relation to a point, enabling you to bend and tug at a curved segment like it's a piece of soft wire.

FIGURE 8.24

Click and drag with the Pen tool to create a smooth point and then adjust the curve using Bézier control handles.

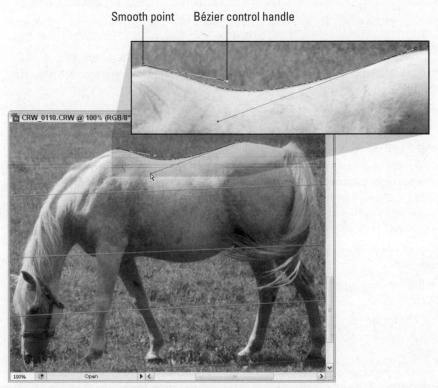

The following list summarizes how you can use the Pen tool to build paths in Photoshop:

- **Adding segments:** To build a path, create one point after another until the path is the desired length and shape. Photoshop automatically draws a segment between each new point and its predecessor. (The next section gets specific about how you use the tool to create points.)

- **Closing the path:** If you plan to convert the path to a selection outline, you need to complete the outline by clicking again on the first point in the path. Every point then has one segment entering it and another segment exiting it. Such a path is called a *closed path* because it completely encloses the desired area.

■ **Leaving the path open:** If you plan to apply the Stroke Path command (explained later), you may not want to close a path. To leave the path open, so it has a specific beginning and ending, deactivate the path by saving it (choose the Save Path command from the Paths palette menu).

■ **Extending an open path:** To reactivate an open path, click or drag one of its endpoints. Photoshop draws a segment between the endpoint and the next point you create.

■ **Joining two open subpaths:** To join one open subpath with another, click or drag an endpoint in the first subpath and then click or drag an endpoint in the second.

■ **Specifying path overlap:** You can set the path tools to one of four settings that control how Photoshop treats overlapping areas in a path when you convert the path to a selection.

To make your intentions known, click one of the buttons near the right end of the Options bar, identical to those seen back in Figure 8.10. The button you click remains in effect until you choose another button.

These buttons also appear when you draw paths with the shape tools. With either set of tools, your choices are as follows:

■ **Add to path area:** Select this button if you want all areas, overlapping or not, to be selected.

■ **Subtract from path area:** Select this button to draw a subpath that eats a hole in an existing path. Any areas that you enclose with the subpath are not selected. Note that if you select a path and the Make Selection command is dimmed in the Paths palette, it's probably because you drew the path with the Subtract option in force.

■ **Intersect path areas:** The opposite of Exclude, this option selects only overlapping areas.

■ **Exclude overlapping path areas:** Any overlapping regions are not included in the selection.

You can change the overlap setting for a subpath after you draw it if necessary. Select the paths with the black arrow tool, and then click the overlap button for the setting you want to use.

■ **Deactivating paths:** At any time, you can press Enter or Return to *dismiss* — deactivate — the path. When you do, Photoshop hides the path from view. To retrieve the path, click its name in the Paths palette. Be careful with this one, though: If you dismiss an unsaved path and then start drawing a new path, you can lose the dismissed one. For more details, see the section "Converting and saving paths" later in this chapter.

■ **Hiding paths:** If you merely want to hide paths from view, press Ctrl+H (⌘+H on the Mac), which hides selections, guides, and other screen elements as well. You also can press Ctrl+Shift+H (⌘+Shift+H on the Mac) or choose View ➪ Show ➪ Target Path to toggle the path display on and off. To select which items you want to hide with Ctrl+H (Win) or ⌘+H (Mac), choose View ➪ Show ➪ Show Extras Options.

To get a better sense of how the Pen tool works, click the arrow button at the right end of the row of path-drawing icons to access the Pen Options (or "Option," in this case). Here you can select the Rubber Band option. This tells Photoshop to draw an animated segment between the last point drawn and the cursor.

The anatomy of points and segments

Points in a Bézier path act like little road signs, each point steering the path by specifying how a segment enters it and how another segment exits it. You specify the identity of each little road sign by clicking, dragging, or Alt-dragging (Option-dragging on the Mac) with the Pen tool. The following items explain the specific kinds of points and segments you can create in Photoshop. See Figure 8.25 for examples.

- **Corner point:** Click with the Pen tool to create a corner point, which represents the corner between two straight segments in a path.

- **Straight segment:** Click at two different locations to create a straight segment between two corner points. Shift-click to draw a 45-degree-angle segment between the new corner point and its predecessor.

- **Smooth point:** Drag to create a smooth point with two symmetrical Bézier control handles. A smooth point ensures that one segment meets with another in a continuous arc.

FIGURE 8.25

This figure shows a path in progress, starting as a straight segment, containing two consecutive curved segments, and ending with a straight segment. Points where the curved segments meet straight segments have visible Bézier handles.

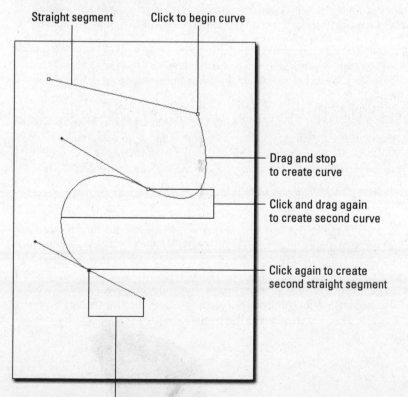

Straight segment   Click to begin curve

Drag and stop
to create curve

Click and drag again
to create second curve

Click again to create
second straight segment

Click on a point to activate Bézier handles

■ **Curved segment:** Drag at two different locations to create a curved segment between two smooth points.

■ **Straight segment followed by curved:** After drawing a straight segment, drag from the corner point you just created to add a Bézier control handle. Then drag again at a different location to append a curved segment to the end of the straight segment.

■ **Curved segment followed by straight:** After drawing a curved segment, Alt-click (Option-click on the Mac) the smooth point you just created to delete the forward Bézier control handle. This converts the smooth point to a corner point with one handle. Then click at a different location to append a straight segment to the end of the curved segment.

■ **Cusp point:** After drawing a curved segment, Alt-drag (Option-drag on the Mac) from the smooth point you just created to redirect the forward Bézier control handle, converting the smooth point to a corner point with two independent handles, sometimes known as a *cusp point*. Then click and drag again at a new location to append a curved segment that proceeds in a different direction than the previous curved segment.

Going freeform

If the Pen tool is still a little hard for you to use or for any reason seems like overkill, try the Freeform Pen tool. Just click the P key while you already have the standard Pen in use, and you're there. As you drag, Photoshop tracks the motion of the cursor with a continuous line. After you release the mouse button, the program automatically assigns and positions the points and segments needed to create the Bézier path, which you can then edit as though you drew it with the regular Pen.

TIP   Despite its popularity for drawing freeform, wavy paths, you can draw straight segments with the Freeform Pen: As you're dragging, press and hold Alt (Win) or Option (Mac). Then click around to create points. When you're finished drawing straight segments, drag again and release Alt (Option on the Mac).

Sometimes, even such a powerful tool (in the hands of such a capable artisan) can mess up. When the program finishes its calculations, a path may appear riddled with far too many points or equipped with too few. What to do? Fortunately, you can adjust the performance of the Freeform Pen to accommodate your personal drawing style using the Curve Fit control, which you can access by clicking the arrow at the end of the row of path-drawing tool icons in the Options bar. Set before you begin drawing (changing the setting won't affect existing paths), you can type any value between 0.5 and 10, which Photoshop interprets in screen pixels. The default value of 2, for example, instructs the program to ignore any jags in your mouse movements that do not exceed 2 pixels in length or width. Setting the value to 0.5 makes the Freeform Pen extremely sensitive; setting the value to 10 smoothes the roughest of gestures.

A Curve Fit from 2 to 4 is generally adequate for most people, but you should experiment to determine the best setting. Like the Magic Wand's Tolerance setting, you can't alter the Curve Fit value for a path after you've drawn it. Photoshop calculates the points for a path only once, after you release the mouse button.

Going magnetic

To use the Magnetic Pen tool, first select the Freeform Pen tool and then select the Magnetic option in the Options bar. The Magnetic Pen works like a combination of the Magnetic Lasso and the Freeform Pen. As with the Magnetic Lasso, you begin by clicking anywhere along the edge of the image element you want to select. (For a refresher on magnetism, go back and review Figure 8.6.) Then move the cursor — no need to drag — around the perimeter of the element, and watch Photoshop do its work. To set an anchor point, click. When you come full circle, click the point where you started to close the path.

You can create straight segments by Alt-clicking (Option-clicking on the Mac), just as you can when using the Freeform Pen without Magnetic selected. And the Curve Fit option, in the Freeform Pen Options drop-down palette shown in Figure 8.26, controls the smoothness of the path. Lower values trace the edges more carefully; higher values result in fewer points and smoother edges. The other options here give you access to the Width, Contrast, Frequency, and Pen Pressure, all of which should be familiar from your playing with the Lasso tool earlier in this chapter.

FIGURE 8.26

While the Freeform Pen is active, select the Magnetic option in the Options bar to access the Magnetic Pen. Click the arrow at the left of the check box to display additional options.

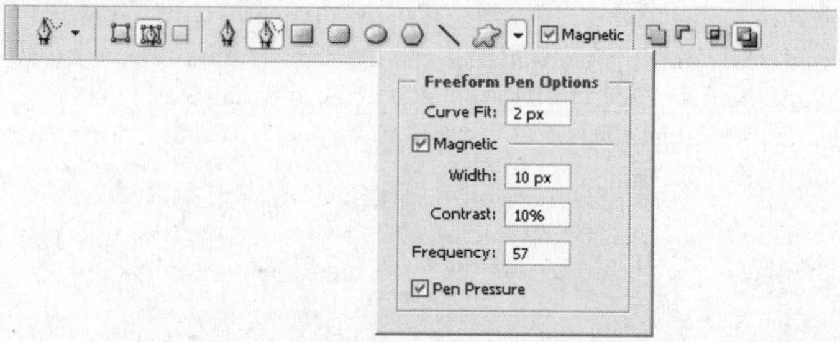

Editing paths

If you take time to master the default Pen tool, you'll find yourself drawing accurate paths more and more frequently. Even after mastering the tool's use and features, however, don't feel bad if you don't get it right 100 percent of the time — or even 50 percent of the time. When you rely on the Freeform or Magnetic Pen tools, the results are rarely, if ever, totally accurate – simply because your arm and hand are not robotic. From your first fledgling steps through to the point where you've developed into a maestro, you'll rely heavily on Photoshop's capability to reshape paths by moving points and handles, adding and deleting points, and converting points to change the curvature of segments. So don't worry too much if your path looks terrible. The path-editing tools provide all the correction capabilities you could ever want or need.

Reshaping paths

The white arrow tool — known officially as the Direct Selection tool — represents the foremost path-reshaping function in Photoshop. To select this tool from the keyboard, first press A to select the black arrow tool and then press A again to toggle to the white arrow. Or just Alt-click (Win) or Option-click (Mac) the black arrow tool in the Toolbox. You use the black arrow to select, relocate, and duplicate entire paths or subpaths, as explained in an upcoming section.

TIP   Press and hold Ctrl (Win) or ⌘ (Mac) to access the white arrow tool temporarily when one of the pen or path-editing tools is selected. When you release Ctrl or ⌘, the cursor returns to the selected tool. This is a great way to edit a path while you're drawing it.

However you choose to activate the white arrow, you can perform any of the following functions with it:

- **Select points:** Click a point to select it independently of other points in a path. Shift-click to select an additional point, even if the point belongs to a different subpath than other selected points. Alt-click (Win) or Option-click (Mac) a path to select all its points in one fell swoop. You can even select marquee points by dragging a rectangle around them. You cannot, however, apply commands from the Select menu, such as All or Deselect, to the selection of paths.

- **Drag selected points:** To move one or more points, select them and then drag one of the selected points. All selected points move the same distance and direction. When you move a point while a neighboring point remains stationary, the segment between the two points shrinks, stretches, and bends to accommodate the change in distance. Segments located between two selected or deselected points remain unchanged during a move.

TIP   You can move selected points in 1-pixel increments by pressing arrow keys. If both a portion of the image and points in a path are selected, the arrow keys move the points only. Because paths reside on a higher layer, they take precedence in all functions that might concern them.

- **Drag a straight segment:** You also can reshape a path by dragging its segments. When you drag a straight segment, the two corner points on either side of the segment move as well.

CAUTION   This technique works best with straight segments drawn with the default Pen tool. Segments created by Alt-clicking (Option-clicking on the Mac) with the Freeform or Magnetic Pen may include trace control handles that make Photoshop think that the segment is actually curved.

- **Drag a curved segment:** When you drag a curved segment, you stretch, shrink, or bend that segment.

TIP   When you drag a curved segment, drag from the middle of the segment, approximately equidistant from both its points. This method provides the best leverage and ensures that the segment doesn't go flying off in some weird direction you hadn't anticipated.

■ **Drag a Bézier control handle:** Select a point and drag either of its Bézier control handles to change the curvature of the corresponding segment without moving any of the points in the path. If the point is a smooth point, moving one handle moves both handles in the path. If you want to move a smooth handle independently of its partner, you must use the convert point tool, as discussed in the section "Converting points" later in this chapter.

Adding and deleting points and segments

The quantity of points and segments in a path is always subject to change. Whether a path is closed or open, you can reshape it by adding and deleting points, which, in turn, forces the addition or deletion of a segment:

■ **Appending a point to the end of an open path:** If a path is open, you can activate one of its endpoints by clicking or dragging it with the Pen tool, depending on the identity of the endpoint and whether you want the next segment to be straight or curved. Photoshop is then prepared to draw a segment between the endpoint and the next point you create.

■ **Closing an open path:** You also can use the technique just described to close an open path. Select one endpoint, click or drag it with the Pen tool to activate it, and then click or drag the opposite endpoint. Photoshop draws a segment between the two endpoints, closing the path and eliminating both endpoints by converting them to *interior points*, which simply means the points are bound on both sides by segments.

■ **Joining two open subpaths:** You can join two open subpaths to create one longer open path. To do so, activate an endpoint of the first subpath and then, using the Pen tool, click or drag an endpoint of the second subpath.

■ **Inserting a point in a segment:** Using the Add Point tool, click anywhere along an open or closed path to insert a point and divide the segment into two segments. Photoshop automatically inserts a corner or smooth point, depending on its reading of the path. If the point does not exactly meet your needs, use the Convert Point tool to change it. In addition to using the Add Point tool, you can select the Auto Add/Delete option in the Options bar. Then, whenever you pass the Pen tool cursor over a segment, you see the little plus sign next to your cursor, indicating that the Add Point tool is temporarily in the house. This trick works only if the path is selected, however.

■ **Deleting a point and breaking the path:** The simplest way to delete a point and break the path is to select it with the white arrow and press Delete or Clear. (You also can choose Edit ➪ Clear, though why you would want to expend so much effort is beyond me.) When you delete an interior point, you delete both segments associated with that point, resulting in a break in the path. If you delete an endpoint from an open path, you delete the single segment associated with the point.

■ **Removing a point without breaking the path:** Select the Delete Point tool and click a point in an open or closed path to delete the point and draw a new segment between the two points that neighbor it. The Delete Point tool ensures that no break occurs in a path.

TIP   To access the Delete Point tool when using the Pen tool, select the Auto Add/Delete option in the Options bar and then hover your cursor over a selected interior point in an existing path. You see the minus sign next to the cursor, indicating that the Delete Point tool is active. Click the point, and it goes away. Alternately, you can remove a point when the Add Point tool is active by Alt-clicking (Option-clicking on the Mac), and vice versa.

■ **Deleting a segment:** You can delete a single interior segment from a path without affecting any point. To do so, first click outside the path with the white arrow tool to deselect the path. Then click the segment you want to delete and press Delete. When you delete an interior segment, you create a break in your path.

Converting points

Photoshop lets you change the identity of an interior point. You can convert a corner point to a smooth point, and vice versa. You perform all point conversions using the convert point tool as follows:

■ **Smooth to corner:** Click an existing smooth point to convert it to a corner point with no Bézier control handle.

■ **Smooth to cusp:** Drag one of the handles of a smooth point to move it independently of the other, thus converting the smooth point to a cusp.

■ **Corner to smooth:** Drag from a corner point to convert it to a smooth point with two symmetrical Bézier control handles.

■ **Cusp to smooth:** Drag one of the handles of a cusp point to lock both handles back into alignment, thus converting the cusp to a smooth point.

TIP   Press Alt (Win) or Option (Mac) to access the Convert Point tool temporarily when one of the three pen tools is active and positioned over a selected point. To do the same when an arrow tool is active, press Ctrl+Alt (⌘+Option on the Mac).

Transforming paths

In addition to all the aforementioned path-altering techniques, you can scale, rotate, skew, and otherwise transform paths using the following techniques:

■ To transform all subpaths in a group—such as shown in the left example of Figure 8.27—select either arrow tool and click off a path to make sure all paths are deselected. Then choose Edit ➪ Free Transform Path.

■ To transform a single subpath independently of others in a group, click it with the black arrow and then select the Show Bounding Box option in the Options bar. Or click the path with the white arrow, and choose Edit ➪ Free Transform Path.

■ Photoshop even lets you transform some points independently of others inside a single path. Just use the white arrow to select the points you want to modify, and then choose Edit ➪ Free Transform Points.

FIGURE 8.27

To transform multiple paths at once, deselect all paths and press Ctrl+T (⌘+T on the Mac). If you don't want to transform your entire path, you can transform a portion thereof or a series of points by selecting them and pressing Ctrl+T (bottom).

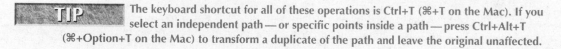

TIP The keyboard shortcut for all of these operations is Ctrl+T (⌘+T on the Mac). If you select an independent path — or specific points inside a path — press Ctrl+Alt+T (⌘+Option+T on the Mac) to transform a duplicate of the path and leave the original unaffected.

While the topic of transformation is found in one central location — in a major section of Chapter 13 — it's probably a good idea to repeat some of the concepts here. Read on for a brief rundown of your transformation options after you press Ctrl+T (⌘+T on the Mac):

■ **Scale:** To scale a path, drag one of the eight square handles that adorn the transformation boundary. Alt-drag (Win) or Option-drag (Mac) a handle to scale with respect to the origin point. You can move the origin by dragging it or by clicking one of the boxes in the little bounding box icon at the left end of the Options bar. To scale the path and maintain proportions, press the Shift key as you drag any of the corner handles.

■ **Rotate:** Drag outside the boundary to rotate the paths or points, as demonstrated in Figure 8.26.

■ **Flip:** Right-click (Control-click on the Mac) to access a pop-up menu of transformation options. Choose Flip Horizontal or Flip Vertical to create a mirror image of the path.

■ **Skew:** Ctrl-drag (Win) or ⌘-drag (Mac) one of the side handles to slant the paths. Press Shift along with Ctrl or ⌘ to constrain the slant along a consistent axis.

■ **Distort:** Ctrl-drag (Win) or ⌘-drag (Mac) one of the corner handles to distort the paths.

■ **Perspective:** Press Ctrl+Shift+Alt (⌘+Shift+Option on the Mac) and drag a corner handle to achieve a perspective effect.

NOTE   You can't take advantage of the distortion or perspective feature when individual points are selected. These techniques apply to whole paths only.

■ **Numerical transformations:** If you need to transform a path by a very specific amount, use the controls in the Options bar, which are the same ones you get when transforming a regular selection. Modify the values as desired and press Enter or Return.

■ **Warp:** Click the Warp button on the Options bar while you're in Transformation mode for your path. The same grid and preset warp options that were discussed earlier in this chapter (remember the section on transforming selections?) appear for your warping pleasure.

When you finish stretching and distorting your paths, press Enter or Return or double-click inside the boundary to apply the transformation. You also can click the check mark button at the right end of the Options bar. To undo the last transformation in the transform mode, press Ctrl+Z (⌘+Z on the Mac). Or bag the whole thing by pressing Esc.

TIP   To repeat the last transformation on another path, press Ctrl+Shift+T (⌘+Shift+T on the Mac).

Moving and cloning paths

You can relocate and duplicate paths as follows:

■ **Clone a path:** Click inside the path with the black arrow tool to select it. To select multiple subpaths, Shift-click them, or marquee-drag around them. Then Alt-drag (Option-drag on the Mac) to clone all selected paths.

■ **Move a path:** After selecting the path with the black arrow, drag the path to its new home.

■ **Align and distribute paths:** You can align two or more paths by selecting them with the black arrow and then clicking an alignment button in the Options bar. To space the paths evenly across the image, click one of the distribution buttons, which are shown in Figure 8.28. Press Enter or Return or click the check mark button in the Options bar to apply the transformation.

FIGURE 8.28

You can align and distribute multiple selected paths, just as you can layers and vector objects.

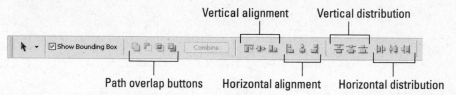

Vertical alignment   Vertical distribution

Path overlap buttons   Horizontal alignment   Horizontal distribution

Merging and deleting paths

When the black arrow is selected, the Options bar contains a Combine button (refer to Figure 8.28). Clicking this button merges all selected subpaths into one. When Photoshop combines the subpaths, it does so according to which path overlap options were active when you drew the subpaths. Remember, you can select a subpath with the black arrow to change its overlap setting if necessary. Just select the subpath, and then click the appropriate overlap button in the Options bar (refer to Figure 8.28). Refer to the section "Drawing paths with the Pen tool" for more information about overlap options.

To get rid of a path, click inside it with the black arrow or drag around it with the white arrow. Then press Delete. It's that simple!

Filling paths

After you finish drawing a path, you can convert it to a selection outline as described in the section "Converting paths to selections," or you can paint it. You can paint the interior of the path by choosing the Fill Path command from the Paths palette menu, or you can paint the outline of the path by choosing Stroke Path. In either case, Photoshop applies the fill on the active image layer.

The Fill Path command works much like Edit ⇨ Fill. After drawing a path, choose the Fill Path command or Alt-click (Option-click on the Mac) the fill path icon in the lower-left corner of the Paths palette. (The icon looks like a filled circle.) Photoshop displays a slight variation of the Fill dialog box discussed in Chapter 6; the only difference is the inclusion of two Rendering options. Type a value in the Feather Radius option box to blur the edges of the fill, as if the path were a selection with a feathered outline. Select the Anti-aliased option to slightly soften the outline of the filled area. If you simply click the fill path icon without pressing and holding a modifier key, the area within the path is automatically filled with the foreground color. The path, of course, is unaffected and can be moved to a new location and used again.

NOTE   If you select one or more subpaths, the Fill Path command changes to Fill Subpaths, enabling you to fill only the selected subpaths. The fill path icon also affects only the selected subpaths.

411

When applying the fill, Photoshop adheres to the overlap option you used when creating the path. Suppose that you draw two round paths, one fully inside the other. If you drew both circles with the Add overlap option active, both circles get filled. If you drew the interior circle with the Invert option active, Photoshop fills only the area between the two paths, resulting in the letter *O*.

If the Fill Path command fills only part or none of the path, the path probably falls outside a selection outline. Choose Select ➪ Deselect or press Ctrl+D (⌘+D on the Mac) to deselect the image, and then choose the Fill Path command again.

Painting along a path

Unlike the Fill Path command, which works much like the Edit ➪ Fill command, the Stroke Path command is altogether different from Edit ➪ Stroke. Edit ➪ Stroke creates outlines on an active selection, whereas the Stroke Path command enables you to paint a brushstroke along the contours of a path. This may not sound like such a big deal at first, but this feature enables you to combine all the flexible, artistic things about both the paint and edit tools with the structure and precision of a path.

To paint a path, choose the Stroke Path command from the Paths palette menu to display the Stroke Path dialog box shown in Figure 8.29. In this dialog box, you can choose the paint or edit tool with which you want to *stroke* the path (which only means to paint a brushstroke along a path). Photoshop drags the chosen tool along the exact route of the path, retaining any tool or brush shape settings that were in force when you chose the tool.

The Stroke Path dialog box includes a Simulate Pressure option, which is particularly useful for people who don't have a pressure-sensitive tablet. Provided you use appropriate settings in the Brushes palette, this option begins your stroke with a thin line, widens it as it reaches the middle, and then tapers it off as it reaches the end. The effect is similar to what you could achieve with a pressure-sensitive drawing tablet. Try experimenting with different settings in the Shape Dynamics dialog box (activated through the Brush Options bar), and tinker with pen pressure, pen shape, angle, and so forth. The more you play with this feature, the more you'll be able to anticipate the results of tweaking various settings and the more control you'll have over the tools in question — especially when they're applied to a path.

TIP You also can display the Stroke Path dialog box by Alt-clicking (Option-clicking on the Mac) the Stroke Path icon, the second icon at the bottom of the Paths palette. If you prefer to bypass the dialog box, select a paint or edit tool and then click the Stroke Path icon or simply press Enter or Return. Instead of displaying the dialog box, Photoshop assumes that you want to use the selected tool and strokes away. If any tool but a paint or edit tool is active, Photoshop strokes the path using the tool you previously selected in the Stroke Path dialog box.

NOTE If you select one or more subpaths, the Stroke Path command becomes a Stroke Subpath command. Photoshop then strokes only the selected path, rather than all paths saved under the current name.

FIGURE 8.29

Select the paint or edit tool that you want Photoshop to use to stroke the path.

Converting and saving paths

Photoshop provides two commands to switch between paths and selections, both of which are located in the Paths palette menu. The Make Selection command converts a path to a selection outline; the Make Work Path command converts a selection to a path. Regardless of how you create a path, you can save it with the current image, which enables you not only to reuse the path, but also to hide and display it as needed.

Converting paths to selections

When you choose the Make Selection command or Alt-click (Option-click on the Mac) the make selection icon, Photoshop displays the dialog box shown in Figure 8.30. You can specify whether to anti-alias or feather the selection and to what degree. You also can instruct Photoshop to combine the prospective selection outline with any existing selection in the image. The Operation options correspond to the keyboard functions discussed in the section "Manually adding and subtracting" earlier in this chapter.

FIGURE 8.30

When you choose the Make Selection command, you have the option of combining the path with an existing selection.

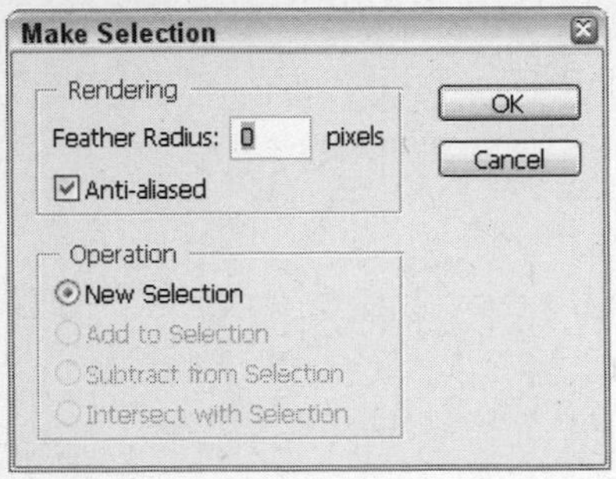

Photoshop offers several alternatives to convert a path to a selection outline, all of which are more convenient than the Make Selection command:

- **Press Ctrl+Enter (Win) or ⌘+Return (Mac).** As long as a path, shape, or selection tool is active, this keyboard shortcut converts the path to a selection.

- **Ctrl-click (Win) or ⌘-click (Mac) the path name.** If a tool other than a path, shape, or selection tool is active, you can Ctrl-click (Win) or ⌘-click (Mac) the name of a path in the Paths palette. The path needn't be active.

- **Ctrl+Shift+Enter or Ctrl+Shift-click (⌘+Shift+Return or ⌘+Shift-click on the Mac).** To add the path to an existing selection, press Shift with one of the previous techniques.

- **Alt+Enter or Ctrl+Alt-click (Option+Return or ⌘+Option-click on the Mac).** Naturally, if you can add, you can subtract.

- **Shift+Alt+Enter or Ctrl+Shift+Alt-click (Shift+Option+Return or ⌘+Shift+Option-click on the Mac).** Now we're starting to get into some obscure stuff, but what's possible is possible. You select the intersection of a path and a selection outline by pressing a whole mess of keys.

All these techniques offer the advantage of hiding the path when converting the path to a selection, giving you full, unobstructed access to your selection outline.

CAUTION   By contrast, the Make Selection command leaves the path onscreen in front of the converted selection. If you try to copy, cut, delete, or nudge the selection, you perform the operation on the path instead.

Converting selections to paths

You turn a selection into a path by choosing the Make Work Path command from the Paths palette. When you choose the command, Photoshop produces a dialog box containing a single option, Tolerance. Unlike the Tolerance options you've encountered so far, this one is accurate to $1/10$ pixel and has nothing to do with colors or brightness values. Rather, it works like the Curve Fit option for the Freeform Pen and Magnetic Pen. That is, it permits you to specify Photoshop's sensitivity to twists and turns in a selection outline. The value you type determines how far the path can vary from the original selection. The lowest possible value, 0.5, not only ensures that Photoshop retains every nuance of the selection, but also can result in overly complicated paths with an abundance of points. If you type the highest value, 10, Photoshop rounds the path and uses few points. If you plan on editing the path, you probably won't want to venture any lower than 2.0, the default setting.

To bypass the Make Work Path dialog box and turn your selection into a path using the current Tolerance settings, click the Make Path icon at the bottom of the Paths palette.

Saving paths with an image

As mentioned at the beginning of the paths discussion, saving a path is an integral step in the path-creation process. You can store every path you draw and keep it right where you need it in case you decide later to reselect an area. Because Photoshop defines paths as compact mathematical equations, they take up virtually no room when you save an image to disk — so you can make as many paths as you need in a given image and not worry about the impact on your hard drive.

You save one or more paths by choosing the Save Path command from the Paths palette menu or by simply double-clicking the italicized *Work Path* item in the scrolling list. After you perform the save operation, during which you name the path, the path name appears in non-italicized characters in the palette.

A path listed in the palette can include any number of separate paths. In fact, if you save a path and then set about drawing another one, Photoshop automatically adds the new path in with the saved path. To start a new path under a new name, you first must hide the existing path. Or click the new path icon — the little page at the bottom of the Paths palette — to establish an independent path. To hide paths, you can click the empty portion of the scrolling list below the last saved path name. You can even hide unsaved paths in this way. If you hide an unsaved path and then begin drawing a new one, however, the unsaved path is deleted, never to return again.

Importing and Exporting Paths

Paths are useful not only for working in Photoshop, but also for importing images into drawing programs, such as Illustrator and FreeHand, and into page-layout programs, such as InDesign and QuarkXPress. By saving a path as a clipping path, you can mask a region of an image so that it appears transparent when placed in other programs that support clipping paths.

In addition, you can swap paths directly with the most recent versions of Illustrator and FreeHand. That way, you can take advantage of the more advanced path-creation features found in those programs. You can even copy and paste paths into After Effects for use as masks or even motion paths.

The last few sections of this chapter explain some of these added uses for your Photoshop paths.

Swapping paths with Illustrator

You can exchange paths between Photoshop and Illustrator or FreeHand by using the Clipboard. This special cross-application compatibility feature expands and simplifies a variety of path-editing functions.

CAUTION   **To avoid having problems transferring data between Photoshop and Illustrator, go into Illustrator, choose Edit ⇨ Preferences ⇨ Files & Clipboards (Illustrator ⇨ Preferences ⇨ Files & Clipboards on the Mac), and select the AICB option. I also recommend that you select the Preserve Paths option when using Illustrator to alter Photoshop paths.**

Suppose that you want to scale and rotate a path. Select the path in Photoshop with the black arrow tool and copy it to the Clipboard by pressing Ctrl+C (⌘+C on the Mac). Then switch to Illustrator, paste the path, and edit as desired. About 95 percent of Illustrator's capabilities are devoted to the task of editing paths, so you have many more options at your disposal in Illustrator than in Photoshop. When you finish modifying the path, copy it again, switch to Photoshop, and paste.

When you paste an Illustrator path into Photoshop, the dialog box that opens gives you the option of rendering the path to pixels (just as you can render an Illustrator EPS document using File ⇨ Open), keeping the path information intact, or creating a new shape layer. Select the Paths option to add the copied paths to the selected item in the Paths palette. (If no item is selected, Photoshop creates a new *Work Path* item.) You can then use the path to create a selection outline or whatever you want.

NOTE   **You can copy paths from Photoshop and paste them into Illustrator or some other drawing program regardless of the setting of the Export Clipboard option in the Preferences dialog box. That option affects only pixels. Paths are so tiny that Photoshop always exports them.**

Exporting to Illustrator

If you don't have enough memory to run both Illustrator and Photoshop at the same time, you can export Photoshop paths to disk and then open them in Illustrator. To export all paths in the current image, choose File ⇨ Export ⇨ Paths to Illustrator. Photoshop saves the paths as a fully editable Illustrator document. This scheme enables you to trace images exactly with paths in Photoshop and then combine those paths as objects with the exported EPS version of the image in Illustrator. Whereas tracing an image in Illustrator can prove a little tricky because of resolution differences and other previewing limitations, you can trace images in Photoshop as accurately as you like.

NOTE   **Unfortunately, Illustrator provides no equivalent function to export paths for use in Photoshop, nor can Photoshop open Illustrator documents from disk and interpret them as paths. This means the Clipboard is the only way to take a path created or edited in Illustrator and use it in Photoshop.**

Retaining transparent areas in an image

Adobe's object-oriented design programs, InDesign 2 (or later) and Illustrator 10 (or later), can read transparency straight from a native Photoshop (PSD) file. However, in virtually every other program — including popular applications like QuarkXPress and FreeHand — any image file, whether it contains transparent pixels or not, comes in as a fully opaque rectangle. Even if the image appeared partially transparent in Photoshop — on a layer, for example — the pixels will be filled with white or some other color. In cases like this, you need to establish a *clipping path* to mask portions of an image that you want to appear transparent. Elements that lie inside the clipping path are opaque; elements outside the clipping path are transparent. Photoshop allows you to export an image in the EPS format with an object-oriented clipping path intact. When you import the image, it appears premasked with a perfectly smooth perimeter, as illustrated by the clipped image in Figure 8.31.

FIGURE 8.31

After defining the paths as clipping paths, the image was exported in EPS format, imported into Illustrator, and set against a gray background for contrast.

Summary

In this chapter, you learned about making selections in many ways. You learned special tricks that work with only the marquee tools, and found out how to gain greater control over your fine selections with the Polygonal and Magnetic Lasso tools, as well as the new Refine Edge dialog box, which is available with all of CS3's selection tools. You also learned to select based on pixels with the Magic Wand, and to create paths and selections with the Pen tool.

Because selections are often in need of a tweak, you learned manual and automatic methods for editing selection outlines, and how to use the Feather command. You also learned to move and clone selections and selection outlines, and to fill and stroke your selections and paths.

Chapter 9

Masks and Extractions

O ur communications with readers, students, and many graphic artists tells us that most Photoshop users don't use masks. It may be that masks seem complicated, or they may strike you as being more trouble than they're worth. It's quite likely that you've played with the basic selection tools—namely the marquee tools, the lassos, and the Magic Wand—and felt that these were good enough. On occasion, you may even resort to the Pen tools, which let you draw precise curves and convert them to selections or clipping paths, and maybe you're more likely to use paths after you've read Chapter 8 (you *did* read Chapter 8, didn't you?) You may, in fact, be so confident and content with these tools that you wonder what more a skilled Photoshop craftsman could possibly need.

Quite a bit, as it turns out. Every one of the tools just mentioned is only moderately suited to the task of selecting images. The lasso tools let you create free-form selections, but none of the tools—not even the Magnetic Lasso—can account for differences in focus levels. The Magic Wand selects areas of color, but it usually leaves important colors behind, and the edges of its selection outlines often appear ragged and ugly. Then there's the Pen tool, which is extremely precise, but it results in mechanical outlines that may appear incongruous with the natural imagery they contain.

Masks offer all the benefits of the other tools, but they give you much more—even *with* the new Refine Edge dialog box (available through any selection tool's options bar or via the Select menu) and its ability to enhance a selection. With masks, you can create free-form selections, select areas of color, and generate incredibly precise selections. But masks also address all the deficiencies associated with the selection tools. They can account for different levels of focus, they give you absolute control over the look of the edges, and they create selections every bit as natural as the image itself.

In fact, a mask *is* the image itself. Masks use pixels to select pixels. Masks are your way to make Photoshop see what you see using the data inherent in the photograph. Masks enable you to devote every one of Photoshop's powerful capabilities to the task of creating a selection outline. Masks are, without a doubt, the most accurate selection mechanism available in Photoshop.

If you're not entirely clear about what term *mask* means, then just continue reading. You'll be pleasantly surprised.

Technically, a mask is nothing more than a standard selection outline expressed as a grayscale image, and it has these properties:

- Selected areas appear white.

- Deselected areas appear black.

- Partially selected parts of the image appear gray. Feathered edges also are expressed in shades of gray, from light gray near the selected area to dark gray near the deselected area.

Figure 9.1 shows a selection outline and its equivalent mask. The image to the left shows a selection outline delineated by Photoshop's traditional marching ants and softened with the feather command (Select ➪ Feather). These little insects only show you the gross area of the selection. If you look to the right, you see the same selection expressed as a mask. The selected area is white (*unmasked*) and the deselected area is black (*masked*). You can't see the feathering effect in the selection outline — marching ants can't accurately express softened edges — but in the equivalent mask it's completely visible.

When you look at the Quick Mask view in Figure 9.1, you may wonder where the heck the image went. One of the wonderful things about masks is that you can view them independently of an image, as in Figure 9.1, or with an image, as in Figure 9.2. In the second figure, the mask is expressed as a color overlay. You can't tell here, but by default the color of the overlay is a translucent red, like a sheet of rubylith film used in printing. Areas covered with the rubylith are masked (deselected); areas that appear normal — without any red tint — are unmasked (selected). When you return to the standard marching ants mode, any changes you make to your image affect only the unmasked areas.

Now that you know roughly what masks are (the definition becomes progressively clearer throughout this chapter), the question remains, what good are they? Because a mask is essentially an independent grayscale image, you can edit the mask using paint and edit tools, filters, color-correction options, and almost every other Photoshop function. You can even use the selection tools, as discussed in Chapter 8. With all these features at your disposal, you can't help but create a more accurate selection outline in a shorter amount of time.

The outline of a feathered selection (left) and the physical mask itself (right)

FIGURE 9.2

In Quick Mask mode, you see how the mask actually affects the image.

Painting and Editing Inside Selections

Before diving into masking techniques, let's start with a warm-up topic: *selection masking*. What's that? Well, think of it this way. When you were a kid with a coloring book, grownups may have nagged you to color within the lines. While that was probably pretty destructive to your natural creativity (and hopefully, you didn't listen), those grownups would just love selection masking and how it can be used to confine a painting and fills.

In Photoshop, all selection outlines act as masks — hence the term *selection masking*. Regardless of which tool you use to create the selection — Marquee, Lasso, Magic Wand, or Pen — Photoshop permits you to paint or edit only the selected area. The paint can't enter the deselected (or protected) portions of the image, so you can't help but paint inside the lines. If you dread painting inside an image because you're afraid you'll screw it up, selection masking is the answer.

Figures 9.3 through 9.6 show a biology class skeleton subjected to some pretty free-and-easy use of the paint and edit tools. The following steps describe how these images were created using a selection mask.

STEPS: Painting and Editing Inside a Selection Mask

1. **Select the skeleton.** You can see the selection outline in the right example of Figure 9.3.

FIGURE 9.3

Starting with the image shown at left, a selection outline is drawn around the skeleton. The selection is then inversed, and the background, as you can see in the right-hand image, becomes the selection.

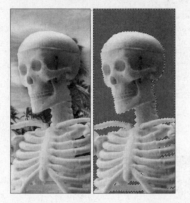

2. **Reverse the selection with the Inverse command.** You want to edit the area surrounding the head, so choose Select ⇨ Inverse (Ctrl+Shift+I under Windows or ⌘+Shift+I on the Mac) to reverse which areas are selected and which are not.

3. **Press Ctrl+Backspace (⌘+Delete on the Mac) to fill the selected area with the background color.** In this case, the background color is gray, as shown in the right half of Figure 9.3.

4. **Paint inside the selection mask.** But first choose View ⇨ Extras (Ctrl+H or ⌘+H). This toggles off those infernal marching ants, which enable you to paint without being distracted. (In fact, this is one of the most essential reasons for toggling the Extras command.)

5. **Select the Brush tool, and express yourself.** With the foreground color set to black, click and drag around the perimeter of the skeleton to set it apart from its gray background, and then rough in an outline around the black using white, as shown in Figure 9.4.

FIGURE 9.4

Painting inside the selection mask with a 150-pixel brush

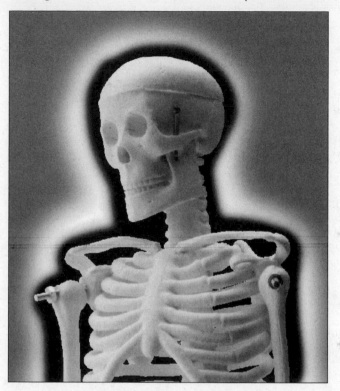

6. **Put the Smudge tool to work.** Set the tool's Strength value set to 80 percent by pressing 8. Then click and drag from inside the unselected area outward a few dozen times to create a series of curlicues. As shown in Figure 9.5, the Smudge tool can smear colors from inside the protected area, but it does not apply these colors until you go inside the selection. This is an important point to remember because it demonstrates that although the protected area is safe from all changes, the selected area may be influenced by colors from protected pixels.

FIGURE 9.5

Clicking and dragging with the Smudge tool smears colors from pixels outside the selection mask without changing the appearance of those pixels.

7. **Add some embellishments.** As you can see in Figure 9.6, the selection mask comes in handy when using the Burn tool to darken around the eye sockets and teeth. Out of a desire to create fabulous hair, the new hair layer was duplicated a few times, a handful of filters (Filter ➪ Distort ➪ Ocean Ripple, as well as Filter ➪ Pixelate ➪ Pointillize) were applied, and the layers were sandwiched using various blend modes (see Chapter 13).

 Want to know more about the filters used in this demonstration? Check out Chapters 10 and 11.

FIGURE 9.6

Is this Side Show Bob grabbing a live wire or a failed design for a Grateful Dead album cover? You decide.

Working in Quick Mask Mode

Selection masks give you an idea of what masks are all about, but they only scrape the surface of all that's possible with masking. The rest of this chapter revolves around using masks to define complex selection outlines.

The most straightforward environment for creating a mask is the *Quick Mask mode*. In the Quick Mask mode, a selection is expressed as a *rubylith* overlay. All deselected areas appear coated with red, and selected areas appear without red coating. You then can edit the mask as desired and exit the Quick Mask mode to return to the standard selection outline. The Quick Mask mode is — as its name implies — expeditious and convenient, with none of the trappings or permanence of more conventional masks.

What the heck is a *rubylith*? It's a term from printing and photo processing. Here's one definition, which sums it up pretty well: A rubylith is a separable two-layer acetate film of red or amber emulsion on a clear base. The film would protect some or all of an image, just as it does in Photoshop. The slightly opaque red wash shows you that you're in Quick Mask Mode, and the mask created remains in that color — showing you which parts of the image are protected, or masked, from any subsequent painting or filling.

How the Quick Mask mode works

Typically, you'll at least want to rough out a selection with the standard selection tools before entering the Quick Mask mode. Then you can concentrate on refining and modifying your selection inside the quick mask, rather than having to create the selection from scratch. You may want to experiment, however, with starting out with no selections in place — it's entirely up to you.

To enter the Quick Mask mode, click the Quick Mask mode icon in the Toolbox, as shown in Figure 9.7, or press Q. Starting with the same selection method used on the skeleton in the previous section (the selection was inverted so that the background was selected), Q was pressed and the image shown in Figure 9.7 resulted, this time with a wolf's face. The face receives the mask because it is not selected. (In Figure 9.7, the mask appears as a light gray coating; on your color screen, the mask appears in red.) The area outside the face looks the same as it always did because it's selected and, therefore, not masked.

Notice that the selection outline disappears when you enter the Quick Mask mode. This happens because the outline temporarily ceases to exist. Any operations you apply affect the mask itself and leave the underlying image untouched. When you toggle the Quick Mask mode button or press Q, Photoshop converts the mask back to a selection outline and again enables you to edit the image.

If you click the Quick Mask mode icon and nothing changes onscreen, your computer isn't broken; you simply didn't select anything before you entered the Quick Mask mode. When nothing is selected, Photoshop makes the entire image open for editing. In other words, everything's selected. (Only a smattering of commands under the Edit, Layer, and Select menus require something to be selected before they work.) If everything is selected, the mask is white; therefore, the quick mask overlay is transparent and you don't see any difference onscreen. This is another reason why it's better to select something before you enter the Quick Mask mode — you get an immediate sense that you're accomplishing something.

Also, Photoshop enables you to specify whether you want the red mask coating to cover selected areas or deselected areas. For information on how to change this setting, see the section "Changing the red coating."

FIGURE 9.7

You can see the marching ants-style selection in the upper image, indicating that the eyes and most of the head are selected. Clicking the Quick Mask mode icon instructs Photoshop to express the selection temporarily as a rubylith overlay (bottom).

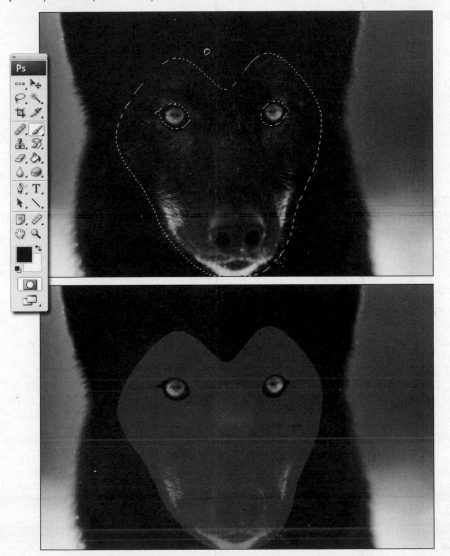

In the Quick Mask mode, you can edit the mask in these ways:

■ **Subtracting from a selection:** Paint with black to add a red coating and, thus, deselect areas of the image. This means you can selectively protect portions of your image by merely painting over them.

■ **Adding to a selection:** Paint with white to remove the red coating and, thus, add to the selection outline, as demonstrated in the top half of Figure 9.8. You can use the Eraser tool to whittle away at the masked area (assuming the background color is set to white). Or you can swap the foreground and background colors so you can paint in white with one of the painting tools.

■ **Adding feathered selections:** If you paint with a shade of gray, you add feathered selections. You also can feather an outline by painting with black or white with a soft brush shape, as shown in Figure 9.8. Here, a soft-edged brush is applying white paint, adding a nice feathered edge to the top of the selection. Then after reentering the world of the marching ants, a little more painting and smudging creates the image on the bottom of the figure.

■ **Cloning selection outlines:** If you have a selection outline that you want to repeat in several locations throughout the image, the Quick Mask is your friend. Select the transparent area with one of the standard selection tools, press and hold Ctrl+Alt (⌘+Option on the Mac), and drag the selection to a new location in the image, as shown in Figure 9.9. Although the Rectangular Marquee tool is used in the figure, the Magic Wand tool also works well for this purpose. To select an anti-aliased selection outline with the Wand tool, set the Tolerance value to about 10 and be sure the Anti-aliased option is selected. Then click inside the selection. It's that easy.

■ **Transforming selection outlines:** You can scale or rotate a selection independently of the image, just as you can with the Transform Selection command (covered in Chapter 8). Enter the Quick Mask mode, select the mask using one of the standard selection tools, and choose Edit ➪ Free Transform or press Ctrl+T (⌘+T on the Mac). (See Chapter 13 for more information on Free Transform and related commands.)

These are only a few of the unique effects you can achieve by editing a selection in the Quick Mask mode. Others involve tools and capabilities not yet discussed, such as filters and color corrections.

When you finish editing your selection outlines, click the Quick Mask mode icon again or press Q again to return to the marching ants mode. Your selection outlines again appear flanked by marching ants, and all tools and commands return to their normal image-editing functions.

TIP   The Quick Mask mode offers a splendid environment for feathering one selection outline while leaving another hard-edged or anti-aliased. Granted, because most selection tools offer built-in feathering options, you can accomplish this task without resorting to the Quick Mask mode. But the Quick Mask mode enables you to change feathering selectively after drawing selection outlines — something you can't accomplish with Select ➪ Feather. The Quick Mask mode also enables you to see exactly how your actions affect the selection — which is something the marching ants aren't capable of.

FIGURE 9.8

Painted in white with a soft-edged brush to enlarge the selected area (top). After switching out of the Quick Mask mode, the Brush and Smudge tools (bottom) have been used liberally.

FIGURE 9.9

To clone the eye selections, marquee around them. Then press Ctrl+Alt (⌘+Option on the Mac), and drag it into position below the original eye. This is done a second time and then repeated for the wolf's other eyeball (top). This makes it possible to switch out of Quick Mask mode and paint details into the new eye sockets (bottom).

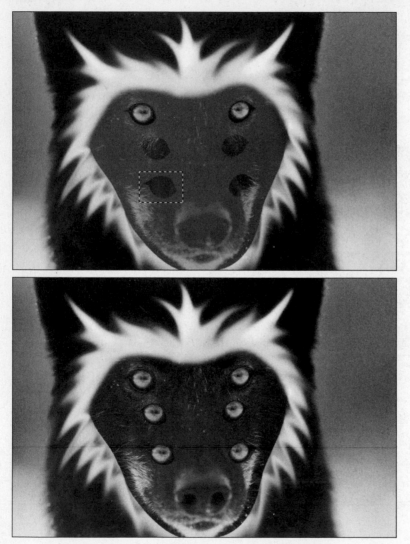

Changing the red coating

By default, the protected region of an image appears in translucent red in the Quick Mask mode, but if your image contains lots of red, the mask can be difficult to see. Luckily, you can change it to any color and any degree of opacity that you like. To do so, double-click the Quick Mask icon in the Toolbox (or double-click the Quick Mask item in the Channels palette) to display the dialog box shown in Figure 9.10.

■ **Color Indicates:** Choose Selected Areas to reverse the color coating so that the translucent red coating covers selected areas and deselected areas appear normally. Choose Masked Areas (the default setting) to cover deselected areas in color.

TIP You can reverse the color coating without ever entering the Quick Mask Options dialog box. Simply Alt-click (Win) or Option-click (Mac) the Quick Mask icon in the Toolbox to toggle between coating the masked or selected portions of the image. The icon itself changes to reflect your choice.

FIGURE 9.10

Double-click the Quick Mask mode icon to access the Quick Mask Options dialog box. You then can change the color and opacity of the protected or selected areas when viewed in the Quick Mask mode.

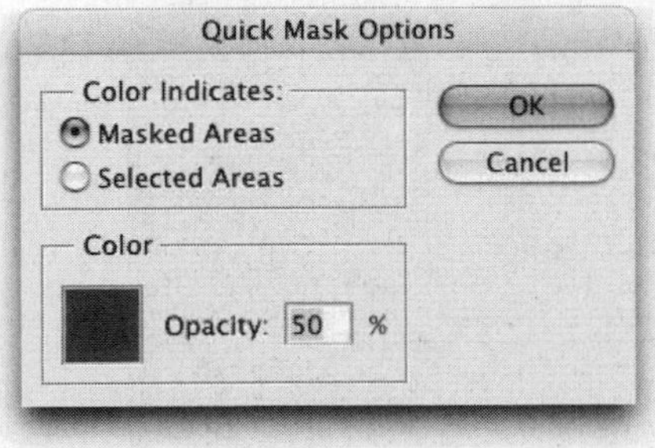

■ **Color:** Click the Color icon to display the Color Picker dialog box and select a different color coating. (If you don't know how to use this dialog box, see Chapter 4.) You can lift a color with the Eyedropper after the Color Picker dialog box appears; just keep in mind that you probably want to use a color that isn't in the image so that you can see the mask better.

■ **Opacity:** Type a value to change the opacity of the translucent color that coats the image. A value of 100 percent makes the coating absolutely opaque, which means you can't see through it — which is pointed out not because we think you don't know what opaque means, but so you realize that this can make it harder to edit the mask relative to the image content.

In the end, just be sure that if you change your coating, you set up a color coating that achieves the most acceptable balance between being able to view and edit your selection and being able to view your image.

Gradations as masks

If you think that the Feather command is the bee's knees when it comes to creating softened selection outlines, wait until you see the gradations in the Quick Mask mode. There's no better way to create fading effects than selecting an image with the Gradient tool and turning that gradient into a mask.

Fading an image

In the following example, you create a gradient mask to fade part of an image into nothingness. Figure 9.11 brings the handy biology class skeleton in the left half fading in from the ground up onto the stormy plain over on the right.

FIGURE 9.11

You can create a linear gradient in the Quick Mask mode to make the skeleton (left) rise from the stormy plain (right).

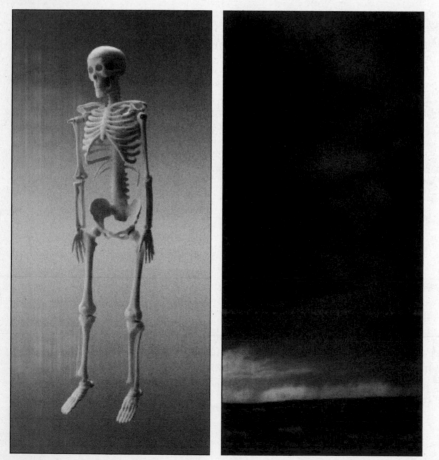

Here's how: Switch to the Quick Mask mode by pressing Q. Then use the Gradient tool to draw a linear gradation from black to white. (Chapter 6 explains exactly how to do so.) The white portion of the gradation represents the area you want to select. To select the top portion of the mask shown in Figure 9.12, draw the gradation as shown in the first example of the figure.

Banding can be a problem when you use a gradation as a mask. To eliminate the banding effect, apply the Add Noise filter at a low setting several times. To create the right example in Figure 9.12, apply Add Noise using an Amount value of 10 and the Uniform distribution option. To brush up on using filters, and specifically the Add Noise filter, check out Chapter 10.

FIGURE 9.12

After drawing a linear gradation in the Quick Mask mode over the bottom of the image (left), the image was hidden and the Add Noise filter applied with an Amount of 10 (right).

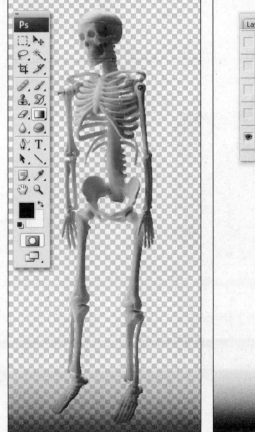
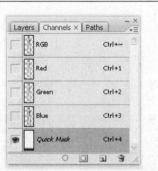

> **TIP** In the right example of Figure 9.12, the image is hidden so that only the gradient mask is visible. As the figure shows, the Channels palette lists the *Quick Mask* item in italics. This is because Photoshop regards the Quick Mask as a temporary channel. You can hide the image and view the gradient mask in black and white by clicking the eyeball in front of the color composite view, in this case RGB. Or just press tilde (~) to hide the image. Press tilde again to view the gradient mask and image together.

To apply the gradation as a selection, return to the marching ants mode by pressing Q. Then Ctrl-drag (⌘-drag on the Mac) the selected portion of the mask, and drop it onto the stormy plain, as seen in Figure 9.13. Then press Ctrl+T (⌘+T) to enter the Free Transform mode. Scale and Distort the image by Ctrl-dragging (⌘-dragging) the corner handles (see Chapter 13 for more information on transforming image content). Further enhancement is achieved by adding an outer glow and five little unfaded copies of the skeleton to stand in awe before the big guy.

> **TIP** Outer glow? How'd we do that? See Chapter 14 for everything you need to know about Blending Options.

FIGURE 9.13

This is the result of selecting the upper portion of the skeleton using a gradient mask and then Ctrl-dragging (⌘-dragging on the Mac) and dropping the selection onto the plain. Throw in a little more tweaking, and you've got a rather Bergman-esque tableau.

Applying special effects gradually

You also can use gradations in the Quick Mask mode to fade the outcomes of filters and other automated special effects. For example, you can apply a filter around the edges of the image that appears in Figure 9.14. Begin by deselecting everything in the image by pressing Ctrl+D (⌘+D on the Mac) and switching to the Quick Mask mode. Then select the Gradient tool, choose the linear gradient style icon in the Options bar, and select the Foreground to Transparent gradient from the Gradient drop-down palette. You also want to select the Transparency option in the Options bar.

Next, press D to make the foreground color black. Then drag with the Gradient tool from each of the four corners of the image inward to create a series of short gradations that trace around the focal point of the image, as shown in Figure 9.15. (The image is hidden here so that you see the mask in black and white.) Because the Foreground to Transparent option is selected, Photoshop adds each gradation to the previous gradation.

FIGURE 9.14

Surround the foreground image with a gradual filtering effect. Here, the darkness on the edges fades to light toward the lower center of the image.

To jumble the pixels in the mask (preventing banding), apply Filter ➪ Noise ➪ Add Noise (in this case, an Amount value of 10 was used). You see the effect in Figure 9.15.

> **TIP** Of course, as stated previously, white is selected and black is deselected. So now you need the edges to appear white and the inside to appear black — the opposite of what you see in Figure 9.15. No problem. All you do is press Ctrl+I (⌘+I on the Mac) to invert the image. Inverting inside the Quick Mask mode produces the same effect as applying Select ➪ Inverse to a selection.

FIGURE 9.15

Inside the Quick Mask mode, each of the four corners has been dragged with the Gradient tool (as indicated by the arrows).

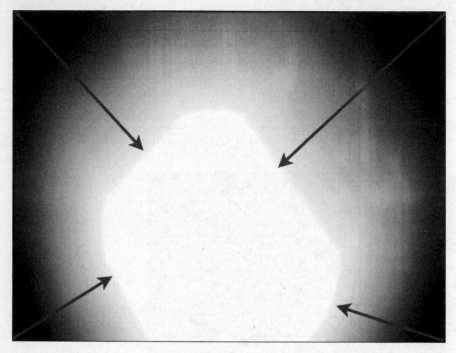

Finally, it's time to switch back to the marching ants mode by pressing Q. Apply Filter ➪ Render ➪ Difference Clouds to get the atmospheric effect you see in Figure 9.16. While somewhat less dynamic for the black and white version of the image shown here, when you try it, your color monitor will show the full effect.

TIP   The corners of the mask in Figure 9.15 are soft and rounded, but you can achieve all kinds of corner effects with the Gradient tool. For harsher corners, select the Foreground to Background gradient and select Lighten from the Mode pop-up menu in the Options bar. For some *really* unusual corner treatments, try the Difference and Exclusion brush modes.

FIGURE 9.16

For good measure, a little lightening was added to those clouds by nabbing such an image, adding it to a new layer, and using the selection to remove its center. Then the new layer's opacity was lowered to 50 percent.

Generating Masks Automatically

In addition to the Quick Mask mode and selection masking, Photoshop offers a few tools that automate the masking process — well, *some* parts of the process. You still need to provide some input to tell the program exactly what you're trying to mask. These tools are the Magic Eraser, Background Eraser, and Extract command. The standard Eraser tool is covered in Chapter 7, but in case you're skipping around, here's the rundown: The Eraser paints in the background color when used on the background layer. When applied to a layer, it erases pixels to reveal the layers below. The Magic Eraser works like the Fill tool, but in reverse. When you click with the Magic Eraser, you delete a range of similarly colored pixels. The Background Eraser, as its name implies, erases the background from an image and leaves the foreground intact — or at least that's what happens if you use the tool correctly. Otherwise, it just erases everything.

> **TIP**   You can cycle through the erasers by Alt-clicking (Option-clicking on the Mac) the eraser icon in the Toolbox or by pressing E (or Shift+E).

The Magic Eraser

As recently mentioned, the Magic Eraser, found on the same flyout as the regular Eraser, erases similarly colored pixels. If you're familiar with the Magic Wand, covered in Chapter 8, using the Magic Eraser is a cinch. The two tools operate virtually identically, except the Wand selects and the Magic Eraser erases.

When you click a pixel with the Magic Eraser, Photoshop identifies a range of similarly colored pixels, just as it does with the Magic Wand. But instead of selecting the pixels, the Magic Eraser makes them transparent, as demonstrated in Figure 9.17. Bear in mind that in Photoshop, transparency requires a separate layer. So if the image consists of only the background, Photoshop automatically converts the background into a layer with nothing underneath. As a result, you get the checkerboard pattern shown in the second example in the figure — transparency with nothing underneath.

> **NOTE**   The Lock buttons in the Layers palette affect the Magic Eraser. When you have no buttons selected, the Magic Eraser works as just described. But if you lock transparent pixels, the Magic Eraser paints opaque pixels in the background color and leaves transparent areas untouched. You can't use the Magic Eraser at all on a layer for which you've locked image pixels.

FIGURE 9.17

To delete a homogeneously colored background, such as the sky in this picture, click inside it with the Magic Eraser (bottom).

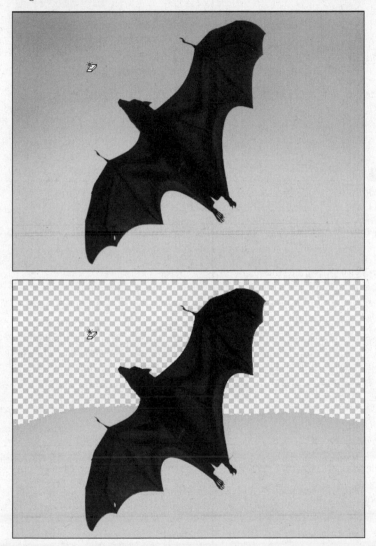

You can further alter the performance of the Magic Eraser through the controls in the Options bar, shown in Figure 9.18 and described in the following list. Except for the Opacity value, these options work the same way as the options for the Magic Wand:

- **Tolerance:** Just like the Magic Wand's Tolerance value, this one determines how similar a neighboring color has to be to the clicked color to be made transparent. A higher value affects more colors; a lower value affects fewer colors. (Remember, any change to the Tolerance value affects the *next* click you make; it does not affect the existing transparent area.)

- **Anti-aliased:** To create a soft fringe around the outline of your transparent area, leave this option selected. If you'd prefer a hard edge — as when using a very low Tolerance value, for example — deselect this option.

FIGURE 9.18

The Magic Eraser options are nearly identical to the options for the Magic Wand.

| ⌖ ▾ | Tolerance: 32 | ☑ Anti-alias | ☑ Contiguous | ☐ Sample All Layers | Opacity: 100% ▸ |

- **Contiguous:** Select this option, and the Magic Eraser deletes *contiguous* colors only — that is, similar colors that touch each other. If you prefer to delete all pixels of a certain color — such as the background pixels in Figure 9.17 that are divided from the rest of the sky by the bat — deselect the Contiguous option.

- **Sample All Layers:** When selected, this option tells Photoshop to factor in all visible layers when erasing pixels. The tool continues to erase pixels on only the active layer, but it erases them according to colors found across all layers.

- **Opacity:** Lower this value to make the erased pixels translucent instead of transparent. Low values result in more subtle effects than high ones.

The more magical Background Eraser

The Magic Eraser is as simple to use as a hammer, and every bit as indelicate. It pounds away pixels, but it leaves lots of color fringes and shredded edges in its wake. You might as well select an area with the Magic Wand and press Backspace (Win) or Delete (Mac). The effect is the same.

The more capable, more scrupulous tool is the Background Eraser. As demonstrated in Figure 9.19, the Background Eraser deletes background pixels as you drag over them. (Again, if the image consists only of a background, Photoshop converts the background into a new layer to accommodate the transparency.) The tool is intelligent enough to erase background pixels and retain foreground pixels provided that — and here's the clincher — you keep the cross in the center of the eraser cursor squarely centered on a background color pixel. Move the cross over a foreground pixel, and the background eraser deletes foreground pixels as well. As Figure 9.20 demonstrates, it's the position of the cross that counts.

NOTE As is the case when you work with the Magic Eraser, the Lock buttons in the Layers palette affect the Background Eraser. In this case, locking image pixels prevents you from using the Background Eraser. Be aware that if you drag over a selection that's already partially transparent, locking transparent pixels does not protect the selection from the Background Eraser.

FIGURE 9.19

Click and drag around the edge of an image with the Background Eraser to erase the background but leave the foreground intact.

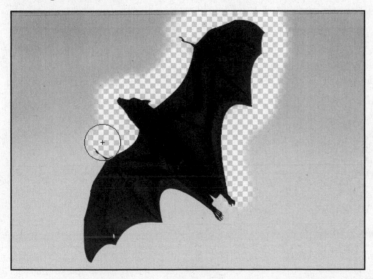

FIGURE 9.20

Keep the cross of the Background Eraser cursor over the background you want to erase (top). If you inadvertently move the cross over the foreground, the foreground gets erased (bottom).

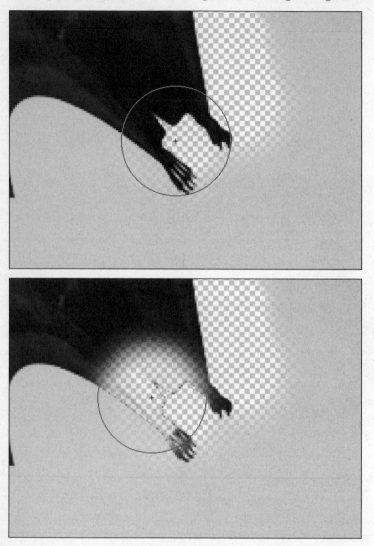

You also can modify the performance of the Background Eraser using the Options bar controls pictured in Figure 9.21. These options are a bit intimidating at first, but they're actually pretty easy to use:

FIGURE 9.21

The seemingly intimidating Background Eraser options are actually pretty intuitive.

- **Sampling: Continuous:** The first of three buttons (which replace the pop-up menu found in Photoshop CS2), lets you do just what the button's tool tip implies — continuously sample pixels as you drag. On by default, this first button tells the eraser to continuously reappraise which colors should be erased, which is quite handy, especially if your background is complex. Be careful, though, if the background has colors in it that are common to the parts of the image you're not trying to erase.

- **Sampling: Once:** The second of three buttons, this one is useful if your background is pretty homogenous — like an actual solid color, a cloudless blue sky, or something like that. Sampling: Once samples the background color when you first click and erases only that color throughout the drag — no matter where or how far from that starting point you drag. If you re-click, however, to start a new drag in another area of the background, the one-time sampling is repeated with that second click.

- **Sampling: Background Swatch:** Choose this third of three buttons to erase only the current background color (by default, white). Use the Color Picker to set a new Background Color, which then becomes the new color to erase.

- **Limits:** Choose Contiguous (the default) from this pop-up menu, and the background eraser deletes colors inside the cursor as long as they are contiguous with the color immediately under the cross. To erase all similarly colored pixels, whether contiguous or not, select Discontiguous. The third option, Find Edges, searches for edges as you brush and emphasizes them. Although interesting, Find Edges has a habit of producing halos and may prove to be less than useful. Feel free to experiment, though — one person's "not really useful" is another person's "Wow, this is great!"

- **Tolerance:** Raise the Tolerance value to erase more colors at a time; lower the value to erase fewer colors. Low Tolerance values are useful for erasing around tight and delicate details, such as hair.

- **Protect Foreground Color:** Select this option to prevent the current foreground color (by default, black) from ever being erased. Of course, you can use the Color Picker to set a new Foreground Color to protect.

- **Sampling:** This pop-up menu determines how the Background Eraser determines what it should and should not erase. The default setting, Continuous, tells the eraser to continuously reappraise which colors should be erased as you drag. If the background is pretty homogenous, you may prefer to use the Once option, which samples the background color when you first click and erases only that color throughout the drag. Select Background Swatch to erase only the current background color (by default, white).

The still more magical Extract command

Like the Magic Eraser and Background Eraser, the Extract command aims to separate — extract, if you will — an image element from its surroundings. After you draw a rough highlight around the subject you want to retain, Photoshop analyzes the situation and automatically deletes everything but the subject. Extract is only slightly more powerful than the background eraser and several times more complex. Some images respond very well to the command, others do not. That said, Extract can produce reasonably good results if you get the steps right. So take Extract for a test drive, as follows:

STEPS: Extracting Content from its Surroundings

1. **Choose Filter ➪ Extract, or press Ctrl+Alt+X (⌘+Option+X on the Mac).** Either way, Photoshop displays the large Extract dialog box shown in Figure 9.22.

FIGURE 9.22

The Extract dialog box serves as a miniature masking laboratory, complete with a Toolbox and options.

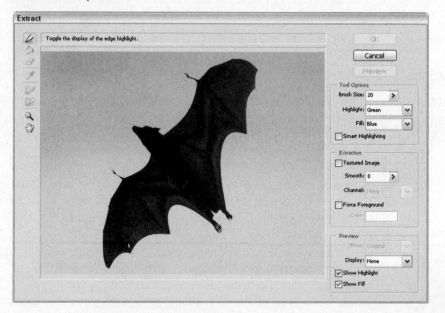

---

2. **Select the Edge Highlighter tool.** Most likely, this tool is already active, but if not, press B to select it.

3. **Outline the subject that you want to retain.** In this case, it would be the bat, as shown in Figure 9.23. Be sure to either completely encircle the subject or, if the subject is partially cropped, trace all the way up against the outer boundaries of the photograph.

FIGURE 9.23

After tracing around the portion of the image you want to retain, click inside the outline with the Fill tool.

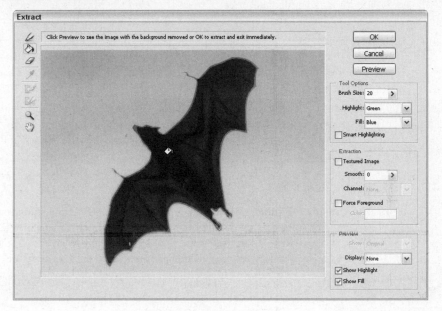

TIP · Often, Shift-clicking around the perimeter of an image is easier than dragging manually. Shift-clicking creates a straight highlight from one click point to the next. As long as you do a reasonably careful job, the performance of the Extract command won't be impaired.

TIP · Select the Smart Highlighting option in the Tool Options section of the Extract dialog box to get some assistance in drawing your outline. We used it in the example above. You can also just hold down your Ctrl key (⌘ key on the Mac) while dragging. Smart Highlighting seeks edges in the image and places the highlight along them. When you select Smart Highlighting, your cursor becomes a circle with four inward-pointing lines. Keep the center of the circle over the edge between the subject and the background as you drag. This feature works best when your subject has well-defined edges, of course. Note that you can't Shift-click with the tool to draw straight segments when Smart Highlighting is active.

TIP · Ctrl-drag (Win) or ⌘-drag (Mac) to temporarily turn off Smart Highlighting without deselecting the option. Or go the opposite direction: Deselect the option and then Ctrl-drag (Win) or ⌘-drag (Mac) to temporarily take advantage of Smart Highlighting.

4. **As you trace, use the bracket keys, [and], to make the brush larger or smaller.**
   When you work with brushes from 1 to 9 pixels in diameter, each press of [or] changes the brush size by 1 pixel. The increment of change gets larger as you increase the brush size.

445

> **TIP**   Small brush sizes result in sharper edges. Larger brush sizes are better for fragile, intricate detailing, such as hair, foliage, wispy fabric, bits of steel wool, thin pasta — you get the idea.

5. **If you make a mistake, press Ctrl+Z (⌘+Z on the Mac).** You get only one Undo level here — you can undo and redo only your last stroke with the Highlighter tool.

   If you want to erase more of the highlight, drag over the botched region with the Eraser tool (press E to access it from the keyboard) or press Alt (Option on the Mac) and drag with the Edge Highlighter tool. To delete the entire highlight and start over, press Alt+Backspace (Win) or Option+Delete (Mac).

6. **Navigate as needed.** If you can't see all of your image, you can access the Hand tool by pressing the spacebar or clicking the Hand tool icon. You also can zoom by pressing Ctrl+plus or Ctrl+minus (⌘+plus or ⌘+minus on the Mac) or by using the Zoom tool.

7. **Select the Fill tool.** It's the one that looks like a paint bucket. To select the Fill tool from the keyboard, press G as you do to select the paint bucket in the regular Photoshop Toolbox.

8. **Click inside the subject of the image.** The highlighted outline should fill with color. If the fill color spills outside the outline, your outline probably has a break. Press Ctrl+Z (⌘-Z on the Mac) to undo the fill and then scroll the image with the Hand tool to find the break. Patch it with the Edge Highlighter, and then click with the Fill tool again.

> **TIP**   You also can click inside a filled area with the Fill tool or Eraser to remove the fill.

9. **Click Preview.** Before you can apply your prospective mask, you need to preview it so you can gauge the finished effect, as in Figure 9.24.

> **TIP**   If you Shift-click with the Fill tool in Step 8, Photoshop fills the outline and processes the preview automatically, saving you the trouble of clicking Preview.

10. **Edit the mask as needed.** You have several tools at your disposal. These tools are labeled in Figure 9.24, and you can read about them in the list following these steps.

11. **Click OK to delete the masked portion of the image.** If the image consisted of only a background, Photoshop converts it into a separate layer. You then can use the Move tool to drag the layer against a different background. In Figure 9.25, the bat has been set against a New Zealand sky. The composite isn't perfect, but it's not half bad for 5 to 10 minutes of work.

12. **After you exit the Extract window, fix any problems using the Background Eraser and History Brush.** Use the Background Eraser to erase stray pixels that you wish the Extract command had deleted. Use the History Brush to restore details that you wish the Extract command hadn't deleted.

FIGURE 9.24

Click Preview to gauge the appearance of the final masked image.

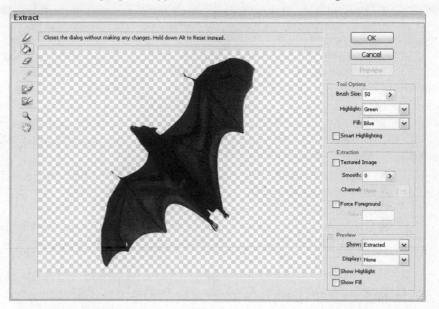

FIGURE 9.25

Is the fruit bat from South America? Not that it matters — it's cruising over New Zealand now.

Back in Step 10, it was stated that you can refine the mask in the Extract dialog box. You can use the following techniques to touch up the mask before clicking OK to create it:

- **Drag with the cleanup tool (C) to change the opacity of the mask.** Press the number keys to adjust the pressure of the tool and thus alter the amount of opacity that the tool subtracts. To erase to full transparency, press 0, as you do when working with the Eraser on a layer. Press 9 for 90 percent transparency, 8 for 80 percent, and so on. Alt-drag (Option-drag on the Mac) to add opacity.

- **Drag along the boundaries of the mask with the Edge Touchup tool (T) to sharpen the mask edges.** If the boundary between mask and subject isn't well defined, dragging with this tool adds opacity to the subject and removes it from the mask. In other words, it turns soft, feathery edges into crisp, clearly defined edges. Again, you can press the number keys to adjust the impact of the tool.

- **Raise the Smooth value to remove stray pixels from the mask.** A high value smoothes out the edges around the image and fills in holes. Basically, if your edges are a big mess, give this option a try.

- **Drag with the Edge Highlighter or Eraser Tool to edit the mask boundary.** When you select either tool, the original mask highlight reappears, and the tools work as they do when you initially draw the highlight. After you adjust the highlight, Shift-click inside it to redraw and preview the adjusted mask.

- **Choose an option from the Show pop-up menu to toggle between the original highlight and the extracted image preview.** You can press X to toggle between the two views without bothering with the pop-up menu.

That's 99 percent of what you need to know about the Extract command. For those of you who care to learn the other 1 percent, here's a quick rundown of the remaining options that appear along the right side of the Extract dialog box:

- **Highlight, Fill:** Use these pop-up menus to change the highlighter and fill colors. It doesn't matter what colors you use, as long as they show up well against the image.

- **Textured Image:** If your image is highly textured, try selecting this option. Much like the Smooth option, it helps smooth out jagged edges around the image.

- **Channel:** Advanced users may prefer to prepare the highlighter work by tracing around the image inside an independent mask channel, which you can create in the Channels palette before choosing the Extract command. Then load the mask by selecting it from the Channel pop-up menu. You can further modify the highlight using the Edge Highlighter and Eraser tools. One weirdness: When loading a mask, black in the mask channel represents the highlighted area and white represents the non-highlighted area. Strikes me as upside-down, but that's how it goes.

- **Force Foreground:** If the subject of your image is predominantly a single color, select Force Foreground and use the Eyedropper to sample the color in the image that you want to preserve. (Alternatively, you can define the color using the Color swatch, but it's much more work.) Then use the Edge Highlighter tool to paint over all occurrences of the foreground color. (Note that this option is an alternative to the Fill tool. When Force Foreground is selected, the Fill tool is dimmed.)

■ **Display:** You don't have to preview the image against the transparent checkerboard background. You also can view it against white (White Matte) or some other color. Or you can view it as a mask, where white represents the opaque area and black the transparent area. (Ironically, you can't export the extraction as a mask — go figure.)

> **TIP** Press F to select the next display mode in the menu; press Shift+F to switch to the previous mode in the menu.

■ **Show Highlight, Show Fill:** Use these options to hide and show the highlight and fill colors.

> **TIP** Before using the Extract command — or the Magic Eraser or Background eraser, for that matter — you may want to copy the image to a separate layer or take a snapshot of the image in the History palette. Either way, you have a backup in case things don't go exactly according to plan.

Using the Color Range command

Another convenient method for creating a mask is the Color Range command in the Select menu. This command enables you to generate selections based on color ranges. Use the familiar eyedropper cursor (it becomes your mouse/pen pointer the minute you open the dialog box) to specify colors that should be considered for selection and colors that you want to rule out. The Color Range command is much like the Magic Wand tool, except it enables you to select colors with more precision and to change the tolerance of the selection on the fly.

When you choose Select ➪ Color Range, Photoshop displays the Color Range dialog box shown in Figure 9.26. Like the Magic Wand with the Contiguous option deselected, Color Range selects areas of related color all across the image, whether or not the colors are immediate neighbors. Click in the image window to select and deselect colors, as you do with the Wand. But rather than adjusting a Tolerance value before you use the tool, you adjust a Fuzziness value anytime you like. Photoshop dynamically updates the selection according to the new value. Think of Color Range as the Magic Wand on steroids.

> **NOTE** So why didn't the people at Adobe merely enhance the functionality of the Magic Wand instead of adding this strange command? The Color Range dialog box offers a preview of the mask — something a selection tool can't really do within the limits of the interface — which is pretty essential for gauging the accuracy of your selection. And the Magic Wand is convenient, if nothing else. If Adobe were to combine the two functions, you would lose functionality and flexibility. And who'd want that?

When you move your cursor outside the Color Range dialog box, it changes to an eyedropper. Use it to click anywhere within your image to specify the color on which you want to base the selection, or click inside the preview, labeled in Figure 9.26. In either case, the preview updates to show the resulting mask.

FIGURE 9.26

The Color Range dialog box enables you to generate a mask by clicking and dragging with the Eyedropper tool and adjusting the Fuzziness value.

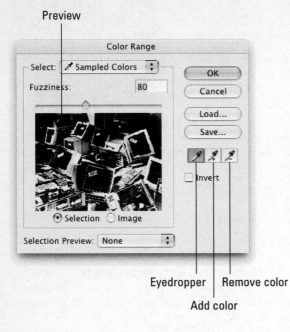

Preview

Eyedropper | Remove color

Add color

You also can do the following:

- **Add colors to the selection.** To add base colors to the selection, select the Add Color tool in the Color Range dialog box (in Figure 9.26, it's the little eyedropper with a plus sign next to it) and click inside the image window or preview. You also can access the tool while the standard Eyedropper is selected by Shift-clicking (just as you Shift-click with the Magic Wand to add colors to a selection). You can even Shift-drag with the Eyedropper to add multiple colors in a single pass, something you can't do with the Magic Wand.

- **Remove colors from the selection.** To remove base colors from the selection, click with the Remove Color tool (the little eyedropper with a minus sign as shown in Figure 9.26) or Alt-click (Option-click on the Mac) with the Eyedropper. You also can drag or Alt-drag (Option-drag on the Mac) to remove many colors at a time.

TIP   The Undo command works in the Color Range dialog box as well as out of it. If adding or removing a color sends your selection careening in the wrong direction, press Ctrl+Z (⌘+Z on the Mac).

■ **Adjust the Fuzziness value.** While this option appears sooner in the dialog box than the Add and Remove colors eyedroppers, I mention after them here because you can use the slider to tweak the results of using those tools. The Fuzziness option resembles the Magic Wand's Tolerance value because it determines the range of colors to be selected beyond the ones you click. Increase the Fuzziness value to expand the selected area; decrease the value to contract the selection. A value of 0 selects only the clicked color. Unlike changes to Tolerance, however, changing the Fuzziness value adjusts the selection on the fly; no repeat clicking is required, as it is with the Wand tool.

Fuzziness and Tolerance also differ in the kind of selection outlines they generate. Tolerance entirely selects all colors within the specified range and adds anti-aliased edges. If the selection were a mask, most of it would be white with a few gray pixels around the perimeter. By contrast, Fuzziness entirely selects only the colors you click and Shift-click, and it partially selects the other colors in the range. That's why most of the mask is expressed in shades of gray. The light grays in the mask represent the most similar colors; the dark grays represent the least similar pixels that still fall within the Fuzziness range. The result is a tapering, gradual selection, much more likely to produce natural results.

■ **Invert the selection.** Sometimes isolating the area you don't want to select is easier than isolating the area you do want to select. In that case, just select the Invert option to reverse the selection, changing black to white and white to black.

■ **Toggle the preview area.** Use the two radio buttons below the preview area to control the preview's contents. If you select the first option, Selection, you see the mask that will be generated when you press Enter (Win) or Return (Mac). If you select Image, the preview shows the image. The latter option is a little less telling in terms of what you can expect to be extracted when you click OK — so Selection is really the more effective option here.

> **TIP** Press and hold Ctrl (Win) or ⌘ (Mac) to toggle between the two previews. It's best to leave the option set to Selection and press Ctrl or ⌘ when you want to view the image.

■ **Control the contents of the image window.** The Selection Preview pop-up menu at the bottom of the dialog box enables you to change what you see in the image window. Leave the option set to None — the default setting — to view the image normally in the image window. Select Grayscale to see the mask on its own. Select Quick Mask to see the mask and image together. Select Black Matte or White Matte to see what the selection would look like against a black or white background.

Although they may sound weird, the Matte options enable you to get an accurate picture of how the selected image will mesh with a different background. Figure 9.27 includes two Matte views to help you see how this particular selection looks against two backgrounds as different as night and day. Use the Fuzziness value in combination with Black Matte or White Matte to come up with a softness setting that will ensure a smooth transition.

■ **Select by predefined colors.** Choose an option from the Select pop-up menu at the top of the dialog box to specify the means of selecting a base color. If you choose any option besides Sampled Colors, the Fuzziness value and Eyedropper tools become dimmed to show that they are no longer operable. Instead, Photoshop selects colors based on their relationship to a predefined color. For example, if you select Red, the program entirely selects red and partially selects other colors based on the amount of red they contain. Colors composed exclusively of blue and green are not selected.

The most useful option in this pop-up menu is Out of Gamut, which selects all the colors in an RGB or Lab image that fall outside the CMYK color space. You can use this option to select and modify the out-of-gamut colors before converting an image to CMYK.

FIGURE 9.27

The options in the Selection Preview pop-up menu change the way the Color Range command previews the selection in the image window.

None   Grayscale

Black Matte   White Matte

- **Load and save settings.** Click Save to save the current settings to disk. Click Load to open a saved settings file. To use a settings file on a PC, it must end in the *.axt* extension.

After you define the mask to your satisfaction, click OK or press Enter or Return to generate the selection outline. Although the Color Range command is more flexible than the Magic Wand, you can no more expect it to generate perfect selections than any other automated tool. After Photoshop draws the selection outline, therefore, you'll probably want to switch to the Quick Mask mode and paint and edit the mask to taste.

Even if you don't master every component of the Color Range dialog box right now (or ever), you'll do well to learn to use the Fuzziness value and the Eyedropper tools. Basically, you can approach these options in two ways. If you want to create a diffused selection with gradual edges, set a Fuzziness value — 60 or more — and click and Shift-click two or three times with the Eyedropper. To create a more precise selection, type a Fuzziness value of 40 or lower and Shift-drag and Alt-drag (Option-drag on the Mac) with the Eyedropper until you get the exact colors you want.

A few helpful Color Range hints

You can add to or subtract from an existing selection using the Color Range command. Press Shift when choosing Select ⇨ Color Range to add to a selection. Press Alt (Option on the Mac) when choosing Color Range to subtract from a selection.

> **TIP** You can limit the portion of an image that Select ⇨ Color Range affects by selecting part of the image before choosing the command. When a selection exists, the Color Range command masks only those pixels that fall inside it. Even the preview area reflects your selection.

If you get hopelessly lost when creating your selection and you can't figure out what to select and what to deselect, click with the Eyedropper tool to start over. This clears all the colors from the selection except the one you click. Or you can press Alt (Option on the Mac) to change the Cancel button to Reset, which returns the settings in the dialog box to those in force when you first chose Select ⇨ Color Range.

Creating an Independent Mask Channel

Masks generated through the Quick Mask mode and Color Range command are temporary. Once you let go of the selection, they're gone. Sometimes, this isn't a problem — you're only using the selection once, so what do you care? Other times, however, a selection is as much a work of art as the image you create with it is. You may need to work on it in stages; take a break, and come back to it when your brain isn't fried.

The simplest solution is to back up your selection, save your file, and then continue to work. In fact, anytime you spend 15 minutes or more on a selection, you should save it.

Saving a selection outline to a mask channel

The following steps describe how to back up a selection to an independent mask channel, which is any channel above and beyond those required to represent a grayscale or color image. Mask channels are saved along with the image itself, making them a safe and sturdy solution.

Transferring a Selection to an Independent Channel

First, you'll have to convert the selection to a mask channel. One way to do this is to choose Select ⇨ Save Selection or right-click (Control-click on the Mac) in the image window and choose Save Selection from the pop-up menu, which saves the selection as a mask. In most cases, you'll want to

453

save the mask to a separate channel inside the current image. To do so, make sure that the name of the current image appears in the Document pop-up menu. Then select New from the Channel pop-up menu, type any name for the channel that you like, and press Enter or Return.

If you have an old channel that you want to replace, select the channel's name from the Channel pop-up menu, shown in Figure 9.28. The radio buttons at the bottom of the dialog box become available, permitting you to add the mask to the channel, subtract it, or intersect it. These radio buttons work like the equivalent options that appear when you make a path into a selection outline (as discussed in Chapter 8), but they blend the masks together instead. The result is the same as if you were adding, subtracting, or intersecting selection outlines, except it's expressed as a mask.

FIGURE 9.28

The Save Selection dialog box enables you to convert your selection outline to a mask and save it to a new or existing channel.

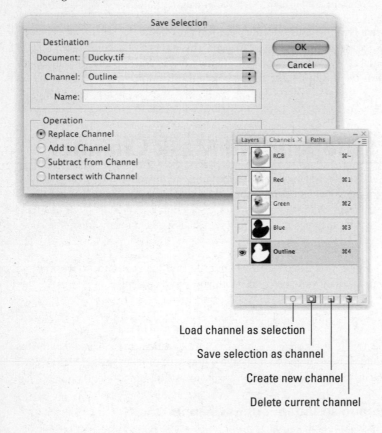

454

Alternatively, you can save the mask to a new multichannel document all its own. To do this, choose New from the Document pop-up menu and press Enter or Return.

> **TIP** If you want to simply save the selection to a new channel and be done with it, just click the make channel icon at the bottom of the Channels palette (labeled in Figure 9.28). Photoshop automatically creates a new channel, converts the selection to a mask, and places the mask in the channel.

Regardless of which of these many methods you choose, your selection outline remains intact.

Next, view the mask in the Channels palette. To do so, click the appropriate channel name in the Channels palette — automatically named *Alpha 1* unless you assigned a name of your own. In Figure 9.28, the contents of a channel called Existing Selection have been replaced, so this is where the mask now resides. Of course, this step isn't the least bit mandatory. It just lets you see your mask and generally familiarize yourself with how masks look. Remember, white represents selection, black is the deselected area, and gray is a partial selection.

> **TIP** If you didn't name your mask in Step 1 and want to name it now, double-click the Alpha 1 name in the Channels palette and type a new name.

At this point, you'll return to the standard image-editing mode by clicking the first channel name in the Channels palette. Better yet, press Ctrl+1 (⌘+1 on the Mac) if you're editing a grayscale image or Ctrl+tilde (⌘+tilde on the Mac) if the image is in color. You can save the image to disk to store the selection permanently as part of the file. A handful of formats — PICT, Pixar, PNG, TIFF, Targa, PDF, and native Photoshop — accommodate RGB images with an extra mask channel. But only TIFF, PDF, and the native Photoshop format can handle more than four channels, all saving up to a total of 56 channels.

Both the native Photoshop format and TIFF can compress masks so that they take up substantially less room on disk. The Photoshop format does this automatically. When saving a TIFF image, be sure to select the LZW Compression option. In both cases, this run-line compression is entirely safe. It does not change a single pixel in the image; it merely writes the code in a more efficient manner.

> **TIP** You also can save a quick mask to its own channel for later use. Here's how it works. When you enter the Quick Mask mode, the Channels palette displays an item called *Quick Mask*. The italic letters show that the channel is temporary and will not be saved with the image. (To clone it to a permanent channel, click and drag the Quick Mask item onto the page icon at the bottom of the Channels palette.) Now save the image to the TIFF or Photoshop format, and you're backed up.

Converting a mask to a selection

To retrieve your selection later, choose Select ➪ Load Selection. A dialog box nearly identical to the one shown in Figure 9.28 appears except for the addition of an Invert option. Select the document and channel that contain the mask you want to use. You can add the mask to a current selection, subtract it, or intersect it. Select the Invert option if you want to reverse the selected and deselected portions of the mask.

Want to avoid the Load Selection command? Ctrl-click (Win) or ⌘-click (Mac) the channel name in the Channels palette that contains the mask you want to use. If you Ctrl-click the Existing Mask item, Photoshop loads the equivalent selection outline into the image window.

But wait, there's more:

- You can press Ctrl+Alt (⌘+Option on the Mac) plus the channel number to convert the channel to a selection. For example, Ctrl+Alt+4 converts the Existing Mask channel shown in Figure 9.28.

- You also can select the channel and click the far-left mask selection icon at the bottom of the Channels palette. But you may find that's just too much effort.

- To add a mask to the current selection outline, Ctrl+Shift-click (⌘+Shift-click on the Mac) the channel name in the Channels palette.

- Ctrl+Alt-click (⌘+Option-click on the Mac) a channel name to subtract the mask from the selection.

- Ctrl+Shift+Alt-click (⌘+Shift+Option-click on the Mac) to find the intersection.

You can convert color channels to selections, too. For example, if you want to select the black pixels in a piece of scanned line art in grayscale mode, Ctrl-click (Win) or ⌘-click (Mac) the first item in the Channels palette. This selects the white pixels; press Ctrl+Shift+I (⌘+Shift+I on the Mac) or choose Select ⇨ Inverse to reverse the selection to the black pixels.

Viewing mask and image

Photoshop lets you view any mask channel along with an image, just as you can view the mask and image together in the Quick Mask mode. To do this, click in the first column of the Channels palette to toggle the display of the eyeball icon. An eyeball in front of a channel name indicates that you can see that channel. If you are currently viewing the full-color image, for example, click in front of the mask channel name to view the mask as a translucent color coating, again as in the Quick Mask mode. Or if the contents of the mask channel appear by themselves onscreen, click in front of the composite name (RGB, CMYK, or LAB) to display the image as well.

TIP   When the mask is active, you can likewise toggle the display of the image by pressing tilde (~). Few people know about this shortcut, but it's a good one to assign to memory. It works whether the Channels palette is open or not, and it permits you to focus on the mask without moving your mouse all over the screen.

Using a mask channel is different than using the Quick Mask mode in that you can edit either the image or the mask channel when viewing the two together. You can even edit two or more masks at once. To specify which channel you want to edit, click the channel name in the palette. To edit two channels at once, click one and Shift-click another. All active channel names appear highlighted.

You can change the color and opacity of each mask independently of other mask channels and the Quick Mask mode. Double-click the mask channel thumbnail, or choose the Channel Options command from the Channels palette menu. (This command is dimmed when editing a standard color channel, such as Red, Green, Blue, Cyan, Magenta, Yellow, or Black.) A dialog box appears, containing a Name option box so you can change the name of the mask channel. You can then edit the color overlay as described in the section "Changing the red coating" earlier in this chapter.

> **TIP** If you ever need to edit a selection outline inside the mask channel using the paint and edit tools, click the Quick Mask mode icon in the Toolbox. It may sound a little like a play within a play, but you can access the Quick Mask mode even when working in a mask channel. Make sure that the mask channel color is different from the quick mask color so you can tell what's happening.

> **NOTE** If all this talk of channels is confusing you, you can go back and review coverage of the topic in Chapter 4.

Summary

In this chapter, you learned about creating and using masks to control which parts of the image can be edited, how to separate content from its surroundings, and how to use Quick Mask mode to mask content and create standard selections using tools other than the standard selection tools. These new skills will help you make more effective use of Photoshop's painting, fill, and retouching tools.

Chapter 10

Corrective Filtering

In Photoshop, filters enable you to apply automated, yet customizable, special effects to an image. Although named after photographers' filters, which typically correct lighting fluctuations and perspective, Photoshop can help you accomplish much more. You can slightly increase the focus of an image, introduce random pixels, add depth to an image, break an image apart, or mimic a variety of artistic media, textures, natural and man-made substances, and distortions. Just about anything you can imagine doing to your photo can be achieved with one or more of the filters — and some of the most amazing results can be obtained through filter combinations, making for a nearly unlimited number of effects.

You may be approaching the whole concept of filters with some skepticism. If you're a veteran photographer or seasoned Photoshop user, you may want to write them off as little better than the layer styles discussed in Chapter 15, a bunch of "canned" effects that anyone can and will use. The thought of such conformity and standardization may be offending your creative sensibilities. If you're a new user, you may be either worried that the filters are hard to use or you may be thrilled at the prospect that they're so easy and you're going to head right for them, sure that they're the answer to your "but I don't have time to learn Photoshop!" blues.

In just about every one of those assumptions, you'd be...um...wrong. Filters are not cheats, they aren't "canned" effects, and they're not so uniform and conformist that your use of them will mark your photos as hopelessly pedestrian. With literally hundreds of combinations of individual filters' settings and combinations of filters that you can employ, uniformity is actually difficult to achieve — unless you're looking for that, say, between two of your photos that *should* look alike. And while they're easy to use, they're no substitute for learning Photoshop, nor will they let you off the hook easily — in fact, just using them may teach you a few things about Photoshop overall.

459

So, assuming you're willing and eager to give filters a try, let's get started. This chapter and the two following it are all about filters — and the creative and practical uses thereof. These three chapters explain exactly how filters in general work and, with a focus on the most important (or often used) filters, the way specific controls work. You also learn about how to figure out which filter to use in specific situations and get some good ideas for how to use them. Best of all: There's new functionality with regard to filters, in the form of Smart Filters, and you learn all about that, too — right here in this very chapter.

Looking at Filters

You access Photoshop's special-effects filters by choosing commands from the Filter menu. These commands fall into two general camps, although the submenus don't break them down that way. In any case, you can pretty much place all the filters into one of two groups: *corrective* and *destructive*.

Corrective filters

Corrective filters are tools that you use to modify scanned or otherwise captured images and to prepare an image for printing or screen display. In many cases, the effects are subtle enough that the viewer won't even notice that you applied a corrective filter. As demonstrated in Figure 10.1, these filters include those that change the focus of an image, enhance color transitions, and average the colors of neighboring pixels. You can find these filters in the Filter ➪ Blur, Noise, Sharpen, and Other submenus.

Many corrective filters have direct opposites. Blur is the opposite of Sharpen, Add Noise is the opposite of Median (but not Remove Noise, despite the names being polar opposites), and so on. This is not to say that one filter entirely removes the effect of the other; only reversion functions such as going back in time with the History palette provide that capability. Instead, two opposite filters produce contrasting effects — and you may want to use both of them together, despite their contrasting results.

Corrective filters are the subject of this chapter — the more artistic and "special effect" filters, also known as the *destructive* filters, are covered in Chapter 11. Although the corrective filters number fewer than their destructive counterparts, the coverage is extensive because they represent the functions you're most likely to use on a day-to-day basis.

Destructive filters

The destructive filters produce effects so dramatic that they can, if used improperly, completely overwhelm your artwork, making the filter more important than the image itself. Many of the destructive filters reside in the Filter ➪ Distort, Pixelate, Render, and Stylize submenus. A few examples of overwhelmed images appear in Figure 10.2.

FIGURE 10.1

Four corrective filters, including one each from the Sharpen, Blur, Other, and Noise submenus. Clockwise from upper left, they are Unsharp Mask, Gaussian Blur, Median, and High Pass.

Unsharp Mask   Gaussian Blur

Median   High Pass

Destructive filters produce very interesting effects, and many people gravitate toward them when first experimenting with Photoshop. These filters invariably destroy the original clarity and composition of the image (or the portion thereof to which you apply them), though, so that should be your goal before you apply them—unless you're just experimenting. Remember, as with anything you do to a photo and then regret, you can always use Undo or access the History palette to go back to a pre-destructive state.

FIGURE 10.2

These are the effects of applying four destructive filters, one each from the Distort, Pixelate, Stylize, and Render submenus (clockwise from upper left). Note that Lighting effects is applicable to color images only.

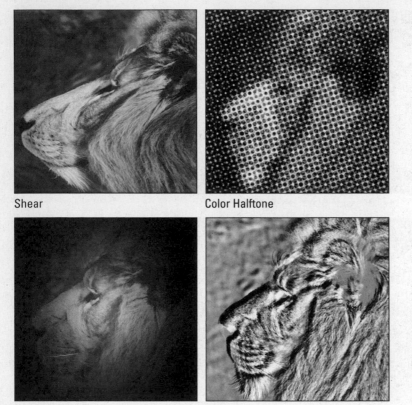

Shear

Color Halftone

Lighting Effects

Emboss

Effects filters

Photoshop also provides a subset of destructive filters called the *effects* filters. These filters are easily applied through the Filter Gallery, which debuted in Photoshop with version CS and has remained a welcome feature through CS2 and now CS3. In previous versions, each effect filter had to be applied separately, and there was no quick way of viewing how different effects would work with each other. All that changed with the introduction of the Filter Gallery, which lets you access all the effects filters in one convenient dialog box. Even more impressive, the Filter Gallery lets you stack as many of these filters as you want on top of one another to see how they interact. It's a great addition to the program, and one you explore in more detail in the next chapter.

In addition to the Filter Gallery dialog box, you can access most of the effects filters through the Filter ➪ Artistic, Brush Strokes, Sketch, and Texture submenus; see Figure 10.3 for some examples. A few have trickled out into other submenus, including Filter ➪ Distort ➪ Diffuse Glow, Glass, and Ocean Ripple and Filter ➪ Stylize ➪ Glowing Edges. You see these in Chapter 11, too.

FIGURE 10.3

Here you see the impact of one filter each from the Filter ➪ Artistic, Brush Strokes, Texture, and Sketch submenus (clockwise from upper left).

Plastic Wrap

Crosshatch

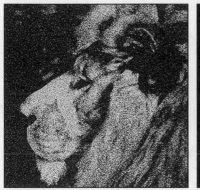
Reticulation

Stained Glass

Working with Smart Filters

While the Filter Gallery was a big breakthrough for filters back in Photoshop CS, it's got nothing on the addition of Smart Filters in CS3. Smart Filters are such a useful addition to Photoshop's already impressive filter features that they make you feel smart just for using them. How's that? Well, they enable you to apply a filter and have the filter's effects appear on a separate layer, much the way color or light corrections can reside on an adjustment layer — you can view or not view them, seeing the image enhanced with them or as it appeared before they were applied — all without having any direct effect on the original image content. You also can edit Smart Filters after applying them, by double-clicking an icon on the right end of the Smart Filters layer — at which point you can change the impact of the filter by tweaking its blending options and opacity. And you can drag and drop them to move or share them with other layers in your image. All this *and* you don't lose the filters' effects when you opt not to see them, as you would if your only way to not see a filter's impact was to Undo its application or use the History palette to go back to before the filter was applied. Of course, because Smart Filters work much like adjustment layers (in their ability to be seen or not seen and their impact on an image), they could have been called *filter layers*, but that wouldn't have made it clear how really brilliant they are.

How Smart Filters work

Before you can use a Smart Filter, you have to make the portion of the image to which they're applied — a layer, to be exact — into a Smart Object. After you've done that, you can apply filters (to some or all of the layer content) and see them do their stuff — correcting, destroying, or creating special effects in your image. But you also see the Smart Filters appear in the Layers palette, where you can click the visibility icon (the eye next to the layer) and turn them on and off. This means that you can apply a whole bunch of filters to a layer (or selection within a layer that's been turned into a Smart Object) and then view them individually or in combinations, just by turning Smart Filters layer visibility on and off, as shown in Figure 10.4.

When you're ready to apply a Smart Filter — not just apply a filter the "normal" way, where the filter's effects become part of the image, extricable only with Undo or the History Palette — click the layer on which you want to filter, and choose Filter ➪ Convert for Smart Filters. This displays a prompt, shown in Figure 10.5, that tells you that to make your filter smart, or to enable its re-editable-ness, the selected layer (including any content within it that you selected beforehand) must be converted to a *Smart Object*. Click OK to accept this, and note the change to the active layer in your Layers palette, shown in Figure 10.6.

FIGURE 10.4

The new Smart Filters feature in CS3 completely redefines Photoshop's filtering process.

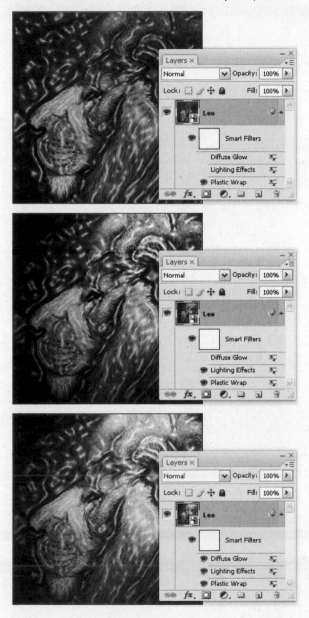

FIGURE 10.5

Photoshop CS3 warns you that you have to turn your layer into a Smart Object if a Smart Filter is going to want to play with it.

FIGURE 10.6

A layer that's been turned into a Smart Object has a tiny symbol in the layer's thumbnail. As soon as filters are applied, they'll appear below the active layer.

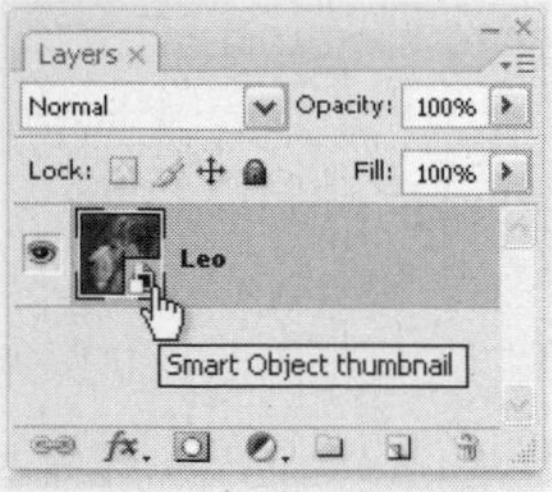

As shown in Figure 10.7, after a filter is applied, it appears on a new sub-layer of the Smart Object layer — and the name of the filter applied appears there, too. The eye icon controls the filter's visibility, and the icon on the far right allows you to edit the filter's blending options and opacity.

FIGURE 10.7

You can tell a Smart Filter because it has its own layer.

As stated, you can double-click the little icon at the far-right end of the Smart Filters layer and open the Blending Options dialog box (shown in Figure 10.8). Note that the dialog box title bar not only says "Blending Options," but it also states the name of the filter applied in the Smart Filters layer being edited. Here, you can choose from 25 different blend modes and also set the opacity of the filter's effects. While you're editing one filter, the others (even those still set to be visible) are not shown, as per the prompt included in Figure 10.8, which appears as soon as you double-click the icon and set about editing a Smart Filter's blending options.

FIGURE 10.8

Want more? How about being able to apply blend modes and adjust filter opacity? You've got it with Smart Filters.

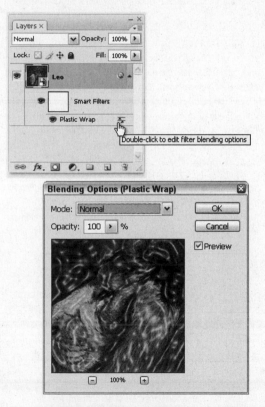

Move, copy, and rearrange Smart Filters

After a Smart Filter is applied (that's what you call any filter applied to a Smart Object), you can move and share it, or change its applied order in the current layer. Here's how:

■ To share your Smart Filter with another layer, first convert the target layer to a Smart Object (choose Filter ➪ Convert for Smart Filters, or right-click the layer and choose the same command from the pop-up menu), and then press the Alt key (or the Option key on the Mac) and drag the existing Smart Filters layer from its current layer to the target layer. It remains in effect on the current layer and is applied to the target layer, after a progress bar appears, informing you which Smart Filter is being applied.

■ To move your Smart Filter to another Smart Object (another layer that's been converted for Smart Filters), simply drag it. It leaves the layer it was applied to and is applied to the target layer — again, after a progress bar and notice of which Smart Filter is underway.

■ If you want to apply your Smart Filters in a different order with their current layer — say applying Add Noise *before* you apply Watercolor — drag the Smart Filters within their current stack underneath the layer to which they're applied. This is just like rearranging layers within an image.

> **NOTE** After you've made a layer into a Smart Object, certain filtering capabilities are unavailable. If you observe the Filter menu, you'll see that Extract, Liquify, Pattern Maker, and Vanishing Point are dimmed — because these are not compatible functionally with the ability to see or not see their results anytime you desire. If you want the best of both worlds — the ability to apply these filter features to your image *and* to employ Smart Filters, make a duplicate of the layer in question and turn one of them into a Smart Object. You can then hide the less intelligent one (and any Liquify or other non-smart-compatible filtering applied to it) and play with the Smart Object and its filters at will.

> **TIP** Can't tell whether a Smart Filter has been applied? Check the triangle on the far-right end of your layer. If it's pointing up, click it and it turns down, showing all related Smart Filters layers below the layer. This trick also works to display layer groups, where the group name appears but you can't see which layers are part of the group. If you're not clear on grouping layers (or all the little nuances of the Layers palette, for that matter), check out Chapter 13.

Using Smart Filters masks

As you saw in the preceding section, as soon as you apply a Smart Filter to a layer that's been converted to a Smart Object, you see an empty (white) mask thumbnail in the Layers palette, just beneath the Smart Object, labeled Smart Filters. By default, this mask displays the filter effect on the entire layer, and that white box represents the mask. Now, if you happened to make a selection on the Smart Object layer and then applied the Smart Filter, you see a mask in this thumbnail, as shown in Figure 10.9.

> **NOTE** Filter masks work much like layer masks in that they're stored as alpha channels (you can see them in the Channels palette) and you can turn the mask into a selection, just like you can with a Quick Mask.

FIGURE 10.9

The Smart Filters layer acts as a mask, which you can edit and use like virtually any other kind of mask.

Some important things to remember about Smart Filters masks:

- When you mask a Smart Filter, the masking applies to all Smart Filters, not just the one that was active when you created the mask.

- To adjust the mask by painting (it's just like any other mask), paint in black to hide content and paint in white to make other content visible through the mask. As expected, shades of gray also are used to mask in varying levels of transparency.

Masking Smart Filters

If you've read Chapter 9 on masks and extractions, this section will seem quite familiar, and with good reason — masks made from Smart Filters are created, edited, and deleted in much the same way as any other mask. As stated above, the use of painting tools and the application of black, white, and gray paint have the same effect on a Smart Filters mask. In addition, you can perform these actions:

- To see only the filter mask, Alt-click (Option-click on the Mac) the filter mask thumbnail in the Layers palette.

- To see the Smart Object layer again, Alt-click (Option-click on the Mac) the filter mask thumbnail again — it works like a toggle.

- To turn a Smart Filters mask off, disabling its effects, you can Shift-click the mask layer, or you can right-click the mask (Control-click on the Mac) and choose Disable Filter Mask from the pop-up menu. After you've disabled a Smart Filters mask, you see a red X on its thumbnail. To remove the red X (and re-enable the mask, of course), Shift-click the thumbnail.

- To get rid of a Smart Filters mask entirely, drag the Smart Filters layer to the trash (Delete) icon at the foot of the Layers palette.

> **TIP** Of course, after you've deleted a Smart Filters mask, you can add an empty mask to the Smart Object. If you right-click (Control-click on the Mac) the Smart Filters layer in the Layers palette, you can choose Add Filter Mask from the pop-up menu. If you made a selection first, this becomes part of the mask — otherwise, the mask encompasses the entire Smart Object layer.

Understanding How Filters Work

The remaining coverage of filters assumes that you're *not* applying them to Smart Objects. This is for two reasons — simplicity in describing their use and displaying the Photoshop interface as we discuss the filters themselves, and because you may not always apply a filter as a Smart Filter and may simply apply it to a selection or layer with no conversion of that layer to a Smart Object. Of course, all the filters we're about to demonstrate — in this chapter and the subsequent two chapters on filters — can be applied as Smart Filters, with the exception of Extract, Liquify, Pattern Maker, and Vanishing Point, which, as we've discussed, are dimmed in the Filter menu when a layer's been converted to a Smart Object.

When you choose a command from the Filter menu, Photoshop applies the filter to the selected portion of the image on the current layer. If no portion of the image is selected, Photoshop applies the filter to the entire layer. Therefore, if you want to filter every nook and cranny of the current layer, press Ctrl+D (⌘+D on the Mac) to cancel any existing selection outline and then choose the desired command.

> **TIP** Some filters are applied immediately upon making a selection from a Filter submenu, and others open a dialog box. You can tell which ones will spawn a dialog box by looking at the submenus — if the command is followed by an ellipsis (...), a dialog box will open. If not, the filter will be applied with no questions asked, based on built-in defaults. You may be thinking, "Yeah, I know about dialog boxes!," but it's worth remembering to check for that ellipsis; even seasoned users can forget which filters are applied with no dialog box to allow for customization and which ones just...happen.

External plug-ins

Some filters are built into the Photoshop application. Others are external modules that reside in the Plug-Ins folder. This enables you to add functionality to Photoshop by purchasing additional filters from third-party collections such as Eye Candy, from Alien Skin. You can search the Web for Photoshop plug-ins to find more.

If you open the Plug-Ins folder inside the Photoshop folder, you see that it contains several sub-folders. By default, Photoshop places the filters in the Filters and Effects subfolders, but you can place additional filters anywhere inside the Plug-Ins folder.

Previewing filters

For years, the biggest problem with Photoshop's filters was that none offered previews to help you predict the outcome of an effect. You just had to tweak the seemingly endless and often vaguely named settings and hope for the best. But today, life is much better. Photoshop 3 introduced previews, Version 4 made them commonly available to just about all the filters, and subsequent versions have maintained this vastly improved status quo.

Photoshop offers two previewing capabilities:

- **Dialog box previews:** Labeled in Figure 10.10, the 100-×-100-pixel preview box is now a common feature of all filter dialog boxes. Click and drag inside the preview box to scroll the portion of the image you want to preview. Move the cursor outside the dialog box to get the square preview cursor (labeled in the figure). Click with the cursor to center the contents of the preview box at the clicked position in the image.

   Click the zoom buttons (+ and –) to change the view of the image in the preview box. You can even take advantage of the standard Zoom tool by pressing Ctrl+spacebar or Alt+spacebar (⌘+spacebar or Option+-spacebar on the Mac), depending on whether you want to zoom in or out.

- **Image window previews:** Most corrective filters — as well as a few destructive ones such as Mosaic and Emboss — also preview effects in the full image window. Just select the Preview option to activate this function. While the effect is previewing, a blinking progress line appears under the Zoom value in the dialog box. If you're working on a slow computer, you'll probably want to deselect the Preview option to speed up the pace at which the filter functions.

NOTE   Incidentally, the Preview option has no effect on the contents of the preview box. The latter continually monitors the effects of your settings, whether or not you like it.

TIP   Use the Preview option to compare the before and after effects of a corrective filter in the image window. Select it to see the effect; deselect it to see the original image. You can compare the image in the preview box also by clicking in the box. Click to see the old image; release to see the filtered image.

FIGURE 10.10

Most filter dialog boxes let you preview the effects of the filter in both the dialog box and the image window — you may want to move the dialog box aside so you can see some or all of the image window at the same time.

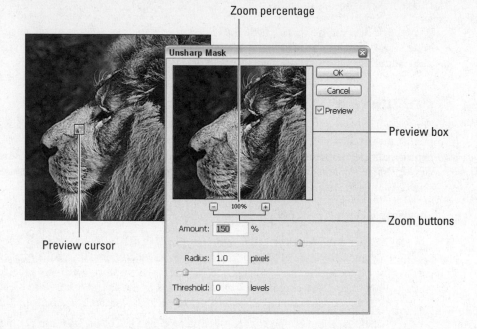

Zoom percentage

Preview box

Zoom buttons

Preview cursor

- Even though a dialog box is onscreen and active, you can zoom and scroll the contents of the image window. Ctrl+spacebar-click (⌘+spacebar-click on the Mac) to zoom in; Alt+spacebar-click (Option+spacebar-click on the Mac) to zoom out. Or you can zoom in and out by pressing Ctrl+plus and Ctrl+minus (⌘+plus and ⌘+minus on the Mac), respectively. Use spacebar+drag to scroll. You also can choose commands from the View and Window menus.

TIP One more tip: When you press Alt (Win) or Option (Mac), the Cancel button changes to Reset. Alt-click (Option-click on the Mac) this button to restore the settings that appeared when you first opened the dialog box. (These are not necessarily the factory default settings; they are the settings you last applied to an image.)

Six filters continue to offer no previews whatsoever: Radial Blur, Displace, Color Halftone, Extrude, Tiles, and De-Interlace. Of course, the filters that don't bring up dialog boxes at all don't need previews because there aren't any settings to adjust.

472

Reapplying the last filter

To reapply the last filter used in the current Photoshop session, choose the first command from the Filter menu or simply press Ctrl+F (⌘+F on the Mac). If you want to reapply the filter subject to different settings, press Alt (Option on the Mac) and choose the first Filter command or press Ctrl+Alt+F (⌘+Option+F on the Mac) to redisplay that filter's dialog box.

Both techniques work even if you undo the last application of a filter. However, if you cancel a filter in progress, pressing Ctrl+F or Ctrl+Alt+F (⌘+F or ⌘+Option+F on the Mac) applies the last uncanceled filter.

Nudging numerical values

In addition to typing specific numerical values in filter dialog boxes, you can nudge the values using the up-arrow and down-arrow keys. When working with percentage values, press an arrow key to raise or lower the value by 1. Press Shift+up arrow or Shift+down arrow to change the value in increments of 10. Note that with some destructive filters, you must use the arrow keys on the numeric keypad; the regular navigation arrow keys don't work.

If the value accommodates decimal values, it's probably more sensitive to the arrow key. Press an arrow for a 0.1 change; press Shift+arrow for 1.0.

Fading a Filter

In many cases, you apply filters to a selection or an image at full intensity — meaning that you can draw a marquee around an area using a selection tool (or not, if you want an entire layer to be affected), choose a filter command, type whatever settings you want if a dialog box appears, and then watch as the filter is applied.

This probably sounds pretty normal — a procedure not unlike any other editing command, such as applying Levels or Variations. But what if you want to reduce the intensity of the filter — and the level of reduction isn't something you can tweak through the filter's dialog box? You can reduce the intensity of the last filter applied by choosing Edit ⇨ Fade or by pressing Ctrl+Shift+F (⌘+Shift+F on the Mac). This command permits you to mix the filtered image with the original, unfiltered one.

As shown in Figure 10.11, the Fade dialog box provides you with the basic tools of image mixing — an Opacity value and a blend mode pop-up menu. To demonstrate the wonders of Edit ⇨ Fade, two particular destructive filters from the Filter gallery have been applied to our lion: Stylize ⇨ Glowing Edges and Sketch ⇨ Bas Relief. The right-hand images show the effects of pressing Ctrl+Shift+F (⌘+Shift+F on the Mac) and applying two blend modes, Screen and Vivid Light, with the Opacity values set to 100 and 65 percent, respectively.

FIGURE 10.11

The full-intensity versions of two filters are found on the left — Glowing Edges (upper left) and Bas Relief (lower left). When using Fade to apply them to the unfiltered original — reducing the intensity of the filters — you get the results seen on the right.

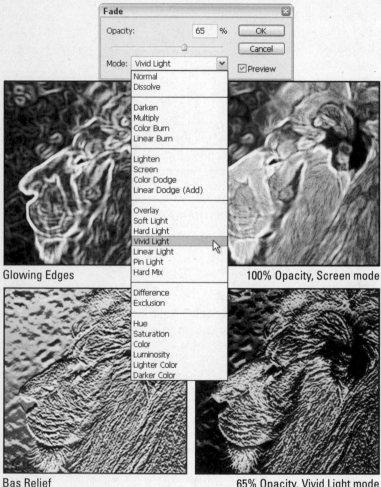

Glowing Edges

100% Opacity, Screen mode

Bas Relief

65% Opacity, Vivid Light mode

Creating layered effects

Due to the fleeting, sensitive nature of the Fade command, you may find it more helpful to copy a selection to a separate layer by pressing Ctrl+J (⌘+J on the Mac) before applying a filter. This way, you can perform other operations, and even apply many filters in a row, before mixing the filtered image with the underlying original.

CAUTION The drawback of the Fade command is that it's available only immediately after you apply a filter (or perform some other applicable edit). If you do anything after applying the filter — even something as benign as making a selection or saving the file — the Fade command dims and returns only when you apply the next filter.

Filtering inside a border

And here's another reason to layer before you filter: If your image has a border around it, like the ones shown in Figure 10.12, you don't want Photoshop to factor the border into the filtering operation. To avoid this, select the image inside the border and press Ctrl+J (Win) or ⌘+J (Mac) to layer it before applying the filter. The reason this works is that most filters take neighboring pixels into consideration even if they are not selected. By contrast, when a selection floats, it has no neighboring pixels, and therefore the filter affects the selected pixels only.

FIGURE 10.12

Layering your content prevents borders from affecting the performance of the filters.

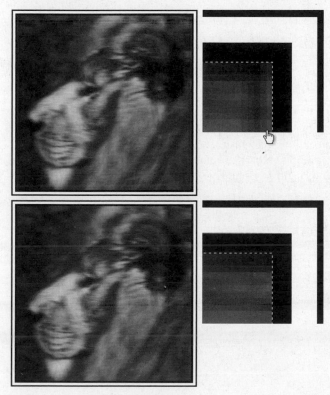

Figure 10.12 shows the results of applying the Motion Blur filter, both when the image is anchored in place and when it's layered. In both cases, the border itself was not selected when the filter was applied. The distortion created along the edge (top) vanishes when the filter is applied to a layered image (bottom).

Even if the area outside the selection is not a really a border — perhaps it's just a comparatively dark or light area that serves as a visual frame — layering comes in handy. You should always layer the selection unless you specifically want edge pixels to be calculated by the filter.

Undoing a sequence of filters

If you needed yet another reason to layer before you filter, consider this. Copying an image to a layer protects the underlying image. If you just want to experiment a little, pressing Ctrl+J (⌘+J on the Mac) is often more convenient than restoring a state in the History palette. After applying four or five effects to a layer, you can undo all that automated abuse by Alt-clicking (Win) or Option-clicking (Mac) the trash can icon at the bottom of the Layers palette, which deletes the layer. The underlying original remains unharmed.

Heightening Focus and Contrast

If you've experimented at all with Photoshop, no doubt you've had your way with many of the commands in the Filter ⇨ Sharpen submenu. By increasing the contrast between neighboring pixels, the sharpening filters enable you to compensate for image elements that were photographed or scanned slightly out of focus.

The Sharpen, Sharpen More, and Sharpen Edges commands are easy to use and immediate in their effect. However, you can achieve better results and widen your range of sharpening options if you learn how to use the Unsharp Mask and High Pass commands, which are discussed at length in the following pages.

Using the Unsharp Mask filter

The first thing you need to know about the Unsharp Mask filter is that it has a weird name. The filter has nothing to do with unsharpening, whatever that is, nor is it tied into Photoshop's masking capabilities. Unsharp Mask is named after a traditional film-compositing technique (which also is oddly named) that highlights the edges in an image by combining a blurred film negative with the original film positive.

That's all well and good, but the fact is that most Photoshop artists have never touched a stat cam-era (an expensive piece of machinery, roughly twice the size of a washing machine used by image editors of the late Jurassic, pre-Photoshop epoch). Even people who used to operate stat cameras professionally never had the time to delve into the world of unsharp masking. In addition — and much to the filter's credit — Unsharp Mask goes beyond traditional camera techniques.

To understand Unsharp Mask — or Photoshop's other sharpening filters, for that matter — you first need to understand some basic terminology. When you apply one of the sharpening filters, Photoshop increases the contrast between neighboring pixels. The effect is similar to what you see when you adjust a camera to bring a scene into sharper focus.

Two of Photoshop's sharpening filters, Sharpen and Sharpen More, affect whatever area of your image is selected. The Sharpen Edges filter, however, performs its sharpening operations only on the *edges between colors* in the image — those areas that feature the highest amount of contrast.

Unsharp Mask gives you both sharpening options. It can sharpen only the edges in an image, or it can sharpen any portion of an image according to your exact specifications, whether or not it finds an edge. It fulfills the same purposes as the Sharpen, Sharpen Edges, and Sharpen More com-mands, but it's much more versatile. Simply put, the Unsharp Mask tool is the only sharpening fil-ter you ever need.

When you choose Filter ➪ Sharpen ➪ Unsharp Mask, Photoshop displays the Unsharp Mask dialog box shown in Figure 10.13, which offers the following options:

- **Amount:** Type a value between 1 and 500 percent to specify the degree to which you want to sharpen the selected image. Higher values produce more pronounced effects.
- **Radius:** This option determines the thickness of the sharpened edge. Low values produce crisp edges. High values produce thicker edges with more contrast throughout the image.
- **Threshold:** Type a value between 0 and 255 to control how Photoshop recognizes edges in an image. The value indicates the numerical difference between the brightness values of two neighboring pixels that must occur if Photoshop is to sharpen those pixels. A low value sharpens lots of pixels; a high value excludes most pixels from the running.

The preview options offered by the Unsharp Mask dialog box are absolutely essential visual aids that you're likely to find tremendously useful throughout your Photoshop career. Just the same, you'll be better prepared to experiment with the Amount, Radius, and Threshold options and less surprised by the results if you read the following sections, which explain these options in detail and demonstrate the effects of each.

FIGURE 10.13

Despite any conclusions you may draw from its somewhat confusing name, the Unsharp Mask filter sharpens images according to your specifications in this dialog box.

Specifying the amount of sharpening

If Amount were the only Unsharp Mask option, no one would have any problems understanding this filter. If you want to sharpen an image ever so slightly, type a low percentage value. Values between 25 and 50 percent are ideal for producing subtle effects. If you want to sharpen an image beyond the point of good taste, type a value somewhere in the 300 to 500 percent range. And if you're looking for moderate sharpening, try out some value between 50 and 300 percent. Figure 10.14 shows the results of applying different Amount values while leaving the Radius and Threshold values at their default settings of 1.0 and 0, respectively.

If you're not sure how much you want to sharpen an image, try out a small value in the 25- to 50-percent range. Then reapply that setting repeatedly by pressing Ctrl+F (⌘+F on the Mac). As you can see in Figure 10.15, repeatedly applying the filter at a low setting produces a nearly identical result to applying the filter once at a higher setting.

FIGURE 10.14

The results of sharpening an image with the Unsharp Mask filter using eight different Amount values. The Radius and Threshold values used for all images were 1.0 and 0, respectively.

Original Amount: 25% Amount: 50%

Amount: 75% Amount: 100% Amount: 150%

Amount: 200% Amount: 350% Amount: 500%

The benefit of using small values is that they enable you to experiment with sharpening incrementally. As the figure demonstrates, you can add sharpening bit by bit to increase the focus of an image. You can't, however, reduce sharpening incrementally if you apply too high a value; you must press Ctrl+Z (Win) or ⌘+Z (Mac) and start again, unless you catch your error immediately after applying the too-intense sharpening. If you do catch it right away, you can use the Edit ⇨ Fade command to apply the last filter at reduced intensity.

FIGURE 10.15

Repeatedly applying the Unsharp Mask filter at 50 percent (top row) is nearly equivalent on a pixel-by-pixel basis to applying the filter once at higher settings (bottom row).

Amount: 50% × 2   Amount: 50% × 3   Amount: 50% × 4

Amount: 125%   Amount: 238%   Amount: 406%

CROSS-REF If you're a little foggy on how to access individual color channels, read Chapter 4.

Getting rid of halos

Photoshop applies filters to images one channel at a time, so when you apply the Unsharp Mask command to a full-color image, it actually applies the command in a separate pass to each of the color channels.

Therefore, the command always results in the color halos shown in Figure 10.16; however, sometimes the halos get mixed together, which can minimize the halo effect. To avoid any haloing whatsoever, convert the image to the Lab mode (Image ⇨ Mode ⇨ Lab Color) and apply Unsharp Mask to only the Lightness channel in the Channels palette. (Do not filter the *a* and *b* channels.) This sharpens the brightness values in the image and leaves the colors untouched.

FIGURE 10.16

Applying Unsharp Mask to a single channel or to a pair of channels creates predictable results, after you get the hang of it. For example, applying the filter to the red channel makes the edges appear red only where they're light and makes dark turquoise (the inverse of red) wherever the image is dark.

Red only

Red and Green

Green only

Green and Blue

Blue only

Blue and Red

481

Setting the thickness of the edges

The Unsharp Mask filter works by identifying edges and increasing the contrast around those edges. The Radius value tells Photoshop how thick you want your edges. Large values produce thicker edges than small values.

The ideal Radius value depends on the resolution of your image and the quality of its edges:

- When creating screen images — such as Web graphics — use a very low Radius value, such as 0.5. This results in terrific hairline edges that look so crisp, you'll think you washed your bifocals.

- If a low Radius value brings out strange imperfections — such as grain, scan lines, or JPEG compression artifacts — raise the value to 1.0 or higher. If that doesn't help, don't worry. You'll discover two very effective image-fixing techniques later in this chapter, one designed to sharpen grainy old photos and another that accommodates compressed images.

- When printing an image at a moderate resolution — anywhere from 120 to 180 ppi — use a Radius value of 1.0. The edges look a little thick onscreen, but they print fine.

- For high-resolution images — around 300 ppi — try a Radius of 2.0. Because Photoshop prints more pixels per inch, the edges have to be thicker to remain nice and visible.

TIP If you're looking for a simple formula, try 0.1 of Radius for every 15 ppi of final image resolution. That means 75 ppi warrants a Radius of 0.5, 120 ppi warrants 0.8, 180 ppi warrants 1.2, and so on. If you have a calculator, just divide the intended resolution by 150 to get the ideal Radius value.

You can, of course, type higher Radius values — as high as 250, in fact. Higher values produce heightened contrast effects, almost as if the image had been photocopied too many times, which is generally useful for producing special effects.

But don't take my word for it; you be the judge. Figure 10.17 demonstrates the results of specific Radius values. In each case, the Amount and Threshold values remain constant at 100 percent and 0, respectively.

Figure 10.18 shows the results of combining different Amount and Radius values. You can see that a large Amount value helps to offset the softening of a high Radius value. For example, when the Amount is set to 200 percent, as in the first row, the Radius value appears to mainly enhance contrast when raised from 0.5 to 2.0. However, when the Amount value is lowered to 50 percent, the higher Radius value does more to distribute the effect than to boost contrast.

FIGURE 10.17

These images show the results of applying eight different Radius values, ranging from precise edges to very soft. The upper-left image is the original, untouched by any filter.

Radius: 0.5 pixels

Radius: 1.0 pixel

Radius: 1.5 pixels

Radius: 2 pixels

Radius: 5 pixels

Radius: 10 pixels

Radius: 20 pixels

Radius: 50 pixels

Radius: 250 pixels

FIGURE 10.18

These images show the effects of combining different Amount and Radius settings. High Amount settings are countered by higher Radius levels, and as the Amount drops to 50 percent with a Radius of 10, the results are subtle, yet effective — sharpening all over, without a change in contrast. The Threshold value for each image was set to 0 (the default setting).

Amount: 75%, Radius 0.5

Amount: 75%, Radius 2.0

Amount: 75%, Radius 10.0

Amount: 150%, Radius 0.5

Amount: 150%, Radius 2.0

Amount: 150%, Radius 10.0

Amount: 300%, Radius 0.5

Amount: 300%, Radius 2.0

Amount: 300%, Radius 10.0

Recognizing edges

By default, the Unsharp Mask filter sharpens every edge in a selection. However, you can instruct the filter to sharpen only the edges in an image by raising the Threshold value from 0 to some other number. The Threshold value represents the difference between two neighboring pixels — as measured in brightness levels — that must occur for Photoshop to recognize them as an edge.

Suppose that the brightness values of neighboring pixels are 10 and 20. If you set the Threshold value to 5, Photoshop reads both pixels, notes that the difference between their brightness values is more than 5, and treats them as an edge. If you set the Threshold value to 20, however, Photoshop passes them by. A low Threshold value, therefore, causes the Unsharp Mask filter to affect a high number of pixels, and vice versa.

In the top row of images in Figure 10.19, the high Threshold values result in tiny slivers of sharpness that outline only the most substantial edges in the flower's petals. As the Threshold value is lowered incrementally in the second and third rows, the sharpening effect takes over more and more of the petals, ultimately sharpening all details uniformly in the lower-right example.

FIGURE 10.19

These images show the results of applying nine different Threshold values.

  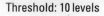

| Threshold: 80 levels | Threshold: 50 levels | Threshold: 30 levels |

| Threshold: 20 levels | Threshold: 15 levels | Threshold: 10 levels |

| Threshold: 5 levels | Threshold: 2 levels | Threshold: 0 levels |

Using the preset sharpening filters

So how do the Sharpen, Sharpen Edges, and Sharpen More commands compare with the Unsharp Mask filter? First, none of the preset commands permit you to vary the thickness of your edges, a function provided by Unsharp Mask's Radius option. Second, only the Sharpen Edges command can recognize high-contrast areas in an image. And third, all three commands are set in stone — you can't adjust their effects in any way (except, of course, to fade the filter after the fact). Figure 10.20 shows the effect of each preset command and the nearly equivalent effect created with the Unsharp Mask filter.

FIGURE 10.20

These images show the effects of the three preset sharpening filters (top row) compared with the Unsharp Mask equivalents (bottom row). Unsharp Mask values are listed in the following order: Amount, Radius, Threshold.

Sharpen	Sharpen Edges	Sharpen More
100%, 0.5, 0	100%, 0.5, 5	300%, 0.5, 0

Using the Smart Sharpen filter

The Smart Sharpen filter is found in Photoshop CS3's Filter ➪ Sharpen submenu. Using a dialog box with more bells and whistles than the average Filter dialog box, yet not as graphical and friendly as the Filter Gallery, the Smart Sharpen filter lets you tweak the Amount and Radius settings you're familiar with from the Unsharp Mask filter, but adds a Remove field, with a list of three of the Blur filters — Gaussian, Lens, and Motion — and enables you to counteract them.

Set to Advanced mode, the Smart Sharpen dialog box offers three tabs — Sharpen (shown in Figure 10.21), Shadow, and Highlight (shown in Figure 10.22), through which you can adjust the Sharpen and Fade Amount, Tonal Width, and Radius. Like most other filter dialog boxes, you can Preview your image in both the dialog box and the image window (thanks to the Preview option, which is selected by default), and unlike other filters, you can save your settings with the Save a Copy of the Current Settings icon, labeled in Figure 10.21. After settings have been saved, you can access them through the Settings drop-down list, which lists only "Default" until you've created settings of your own.

FIGURE 10.21

The Smart Sharpen filter uses familiar sharpening tools — Amount and Radius — plus a blur-fighting option in the Remove list, which defaults to Gaussian.

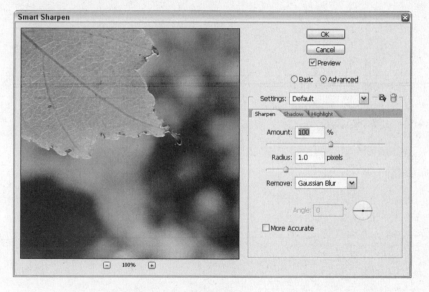

The additional fields in this unique dialog box offer the following features and are shown in Figure 10.22:

- **Fade Amount:** In both the Shadow and Highlight tabs, this option works much like the Fade command discussed earlier in this chapter. Instead of applying the filter at full intensity, it applies it in concert with the unfiltered layer for a more subtle result. The default is 16 percent for Shadows and 70 percent for Highlights.

- **Tonal Width:** This ranges from narrow (0) to broad (100) and determines the range of tones that are incorporated into the sharpening effect. Increasing the Tonal Width on the Shadows tab reduces contrast, and decreasing it on the Highlights tab increases contrast, deepening shadows and intensifying highlights.

FIGURE 10.22

The Shadow and Highlight tabs allow you to focus your sharpening attention on those aspects of the layer in question. Go for subtlety by increasing the Fade, and create more color diversity by expanding the Tonal Width.

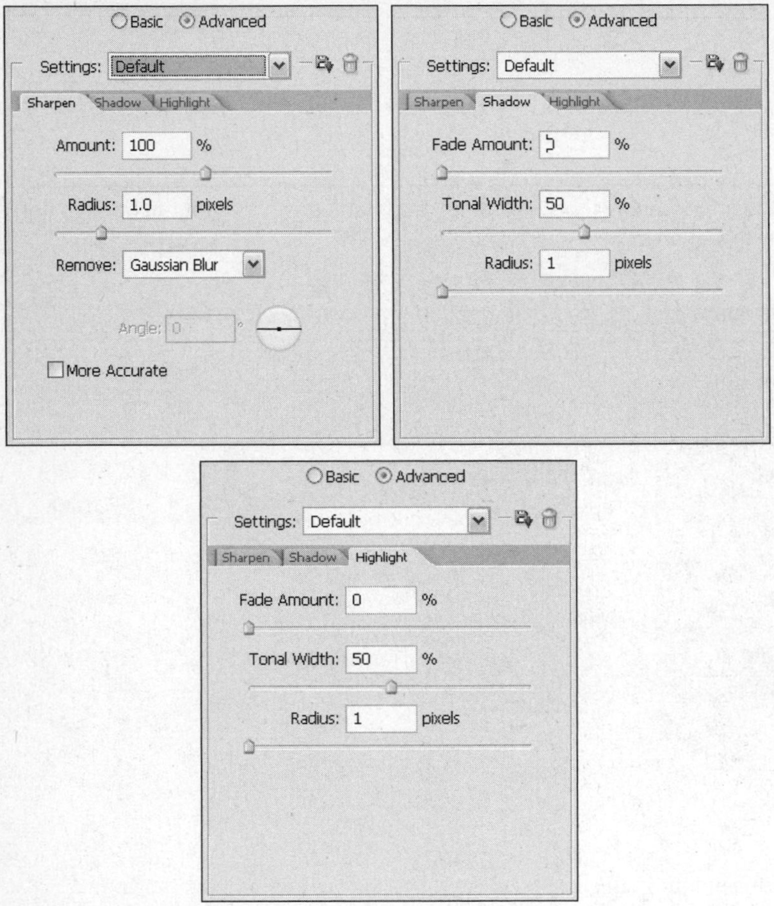

So how do you use this newfangled filter? Well, the "Smart" aspect is the key to its use. Instead of applying sharpening to all the pixels on the layer, and like the rest of the Sharpen filters (except Sharpen Edges), applying the sharpening with equal intensity to all the pixels, this filter lets you focus on pure sharpening (refer to the Sharpen tab in Figure 10.21) with a nod to the possible presence of blurring, either from the photo itself or from a Blur filter. The Shadow and Highlight tabs allow you to address the darkest and lightest pixels respectively, using a Fade setting to create less intense results in these two key areas of any photo.

In Figure 10.23, you see the different sharpening effects applied by switching among Gaussian Blur (left), Lens Blur (middle), and Motion Blur (right) in the Remove field of the Smart Sharpen dialog box. The three Remove options are displayed with identical Amount (300 percent) and Radius (5) settings. The More Accurate option also is selected. The Lens Blur gives the most grainy, artifact-filled sharpening effect, and Motion Blur is the least realistic — the cat's fur is strangely sharpened, as though he's been combed.

FIGURE 10.23

Depending on which type of blur you're trying to counteract, the Smart Sharpen filter targets different areas of the active layer. When Motion Blur is chosen from the Remove list, the Angle option activates, allowing you to counteract the direction of the motion's blur.

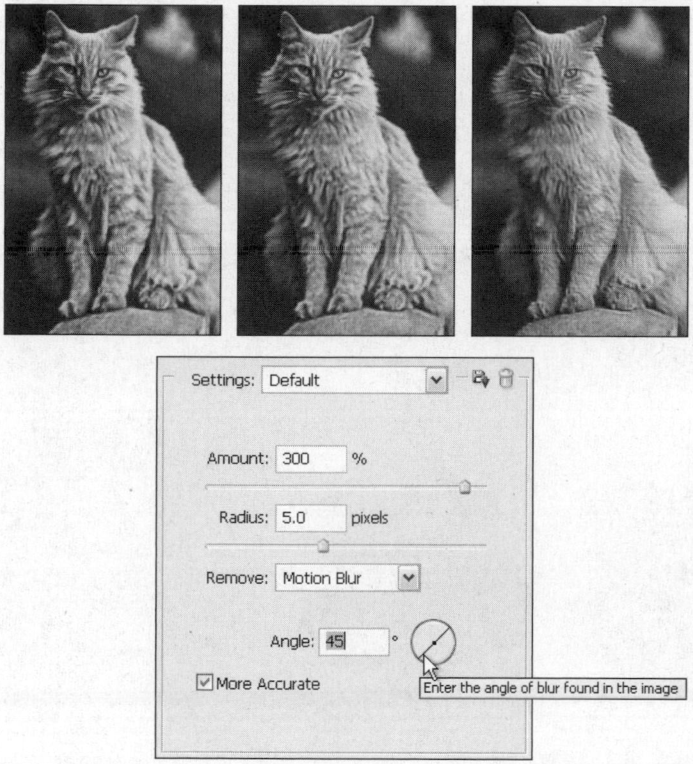

Using the High Pass filter

The High Pass filter falls more or less in the same camp as the sharpening filters but is not located under the Filter ➡ Sharpen submenu. This frequently overlooked filter enables you to isolate high-contrast image areas from their low-contrast counterparts.

When you choose Filter ➡ Other ➡ High Pass, Photoshop offers a single option: the familiar Radius value, which can vary from 0.1 to 250.0. As demonstrated in Figure 10.24, high Radius values distinguish areas of high and low contrast only slightly. Low values change all high-contrast areas to dark gray and low-contrast areas to a slightly lighter gray. A value of 0.1 (not shown) changes all pixels in an image to a single gray value and is therefore useless.

Converting an image into a line drawing

The High Pass filter is especially useful as a precursor to Image ⇨ Adjustments ⇨ Threshold (covered in Chapter 18), which converts all pixels in an image to black and white. As illustrated in Figure 10.25, the Threshold command produces entirely different effects on images before and after you alter them with the High Pass filter. In fact, applying the High Pass filter with a low Radius value and then issuing the Threshold command converts your image into a line drawing.

FIGURE 10.24

Going, going, gone. The results of separating high- and low-contrast areas in an image with the High Pass filter set at nine different Radius values.

100.0	50.0	35.0
20.0	10.0	5.0
3.5	2.0	1.0

In the second row of examples in Figure 10.25, Threshold was followed with Filter ➪ Blur ➪ Gaussian Blur (the subject of the next section). The Gaussian Blur Radius value was set to 1.0. Like the Threshold option in the Unsharp Mask dialog box, the Threshold command results in harsh transitions; Gaussian Blur softens them to produce a more natural effect.

Why change your image to a bunch of slightly different gray values and then apply a command such as Threshold? One reason is to create a mask, as discussed at length in Chapter 9. (In Chapter 9, Levels was used instead of Threshold, but both are variations on the same theme.)

FIGURE 10.25

This figure shows three different settings of the High Pass filter with low Radius values (top row), followed by the same images subject to Image ➪ Adjustments ➪ Threshold and Filter ➪ Blur ➪ Gaussian Blur (middle). Next, the second row was layered onto the first and modified with the Opacity and blend mode settings to create the third row.

5.0   2.5   1.0

Threshold & Gaussian Blur

Opacity: 45%, Overlay mode

You also may want to bolster the edges in an image. For example, to achieve the last row of examples in Figure 10.25, the images were layered before applying High Pass, Threshold, and Gaussian Blur. Next, the Opacity setting of 45% and the Overlay blend mode were applied to achieve an edge-tracing effect.

NOTE   It should be mentioned that Photoshop provides several automated edge-tracing filters — including Find Edges, Trace Contour, and the Gallery Effects acquisition, Glowing Edges. But High Pass affords more control than any of these commands and permits you to explore a wider range of alternatives. Also worth noting, several Gallery Effects filters — most obviously Filter ➪ Sketch ➪ Photocopy — lift much of their code directly from High Pass. Although it may seem at first glance a strange effect, High Pass is one of the seminal filters in Photoshop.

Blurring an Image

The commands under the Filter ➪ Blur submenu produce the opposite effects of their counterparts under the Filter ➪ Sharpen submenu. Rather than enhancing the amount of contrast between neighboring pixels, the Blur filters diminish contrast to create softening effects.

Applying the Gaussian Blur filter

The preeminent Blur filter, Gaussian Blur, blends a specified number of pixels incrementally, following a bell-shaped Gaussian distribution curve. When you choose Filter ➪ Blur ➪ Gaussian Blur, Photoshop produces a single Radius option box, into which you can enter any value from 0.1 to 250.0. As demonstrated in Figure 10.26, Radius values of 1.0 and smaller blur an image slightly; moderate values, between 1.0 and 5.0, turn an image into what might be seen if viewed through a dense fog; and higher values blur the image beyond recognition.

Using preset blurring filters

Neither of the two preset commands in the Filter ➪ Blur submenu, Blur and Blur More, can distribute its blurring effect over a bell-shaped Gaussian curve. For that reason, these two commands are less functional than the Gaussian Blur filter. However, just so you know where they stand in the grand Photoshop focusing scheme, Figure 10.27 shows the effect of each preset command and the nearly equivalent effect created with the Gaussian Blur filter.

FIGURE 10.26

The results of blurring an image with the Gaussian Blur filter using nine different Radius values, ranging from slightly out of focus to what the heck is that?

FIGURE 10.27

This figure shows the effects of the two preset blurring filters (top row) compared with their Gaussian Blur equivalents (bottom row), which are labeled according to Radius values.

Blur   Blur More

Gaussian Blur, Radius: 0.3   Gaussian Blur, Radius: 0.7

Anti-aliasing an image

If you have a particularly jagged image, such as found in a 256-color GIF file, there's a better way to soften the rough edges than applying the Gaussian Blur filter. The best solution is to anti-alias the image. How? As described in Chapter 8, Photoshop anti-aliases a brushstroke or selection outline at twice its normal size and then reduces it by 50 percent and applies bicubic interpolation. You can do the same thing with an image.

Choose Image ⇨ Image Size, and enlarge the image to 200 percent of its present size. Make sure that the Resample Image option is selected and set to Bicubic. (You also can experiment with Bilinear for a slightly different effect, but don't use Nearest Neighbor.) Next, choose Image ⇨ Image Size again, but this time shrink the image by 50 percent.

Figure 10.28 shows a hand-drawn (on paper) doodle, along with the Gaussian Blur applied to the top detail sample (in the hopes of smoothing the drawn lines), and then an example of anti-aliasing applied to the bottom sample. The image subjected to Gaussian Blur with a very low Radius value (0.5) has turned out fuzzy, instead of smoothed. After applying anti-aliasing, however, the lines in the drawing are smooth, not fuzzy.

Here's a doodle in need, indeed. Note the enlarged detail (top) showing the Gaussian Blur's results, compared with Anti-aliasing, which smoothes the lines without making them fuzzy (bottom). The secret? Bicubic interpolation, through the Images Size dialog box and the use of the Resample option.

Directional blurring

In addition to its everyday blurring functions, Photoshop provides two *directional blurring* filters: Motion Blur and Radial Blur. Instead of blurring pixels in feathered clusters like the Gaussian Blur filter, the Motion Blur filter blurs pixels in straight lines over a specified distance. The Radial Blur filter blurs pixels in varying degrees depending on their distance from the center of the blur. The following pages explain both filters in detail.

495

Motion blurring

The Motion Blur filter makes an image appear as if either the image or the camera was moving when you shot the photo. When you choose Filter ➪ Blur ➪ Motion Blur, Photoshop displays the dialog box shown in Figure 10.29. You type the angle of movement in the Angle option box. Alternatively, you can indicate the angle by clicking and dragging the straight line inside the circle to the right of the Angle option, as shown in the figure. (Notice that the arrow cursor actually appears outside the circle. After you begin dragging on the line, you can move the cursor anywhere you want and still affect the angle.)

FIGURE 10.29

Click and drag the line inside the circle to change the angle of the blur.

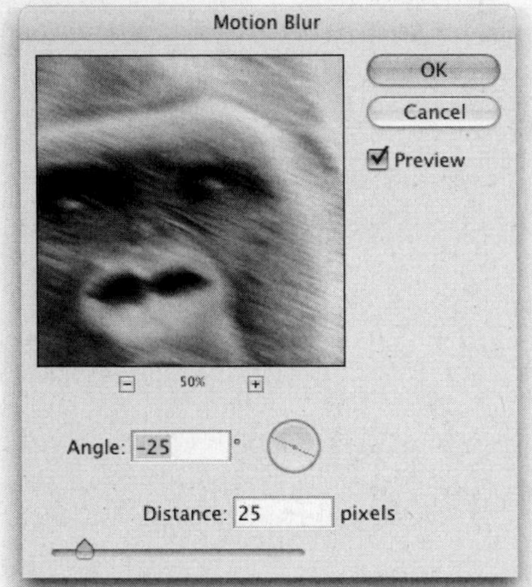

You then type the distance of the movement in the Distance option box. Photoshop permits any value between 1 and 999 pixels. The filter distributes the effect of the blur over the course of the Distance value, as illustrated by the examples in Figure 10.30.

NOTE Mathematically speaking, Motion Blur is one of Photoshop's simpler filters. Rather than distributing the effect over a Gaussian curve — which one might argue would produce a more believable effect — Photoshop creates a simple linear distribution, peaking in the center and fading at either end. It's as if the program took the value you specified in the Distance option, created that many clones of the image, offset half the clones in one direction and half the clones in the other — all spaced 1 pixel apart — and then varied the opacity of each.

FIGURE 10.30

Here's a single black rectangle followed by five different applications of the Motion Blur filter. Only the Distance value varied, as labeled. A 0-degree Angle value was used in all five examples.

Original

Motion Blur, Angle: 0 degrees, Distance: 50 pixels

Distance: 100 pixels

Distance: 250 pixels

Distance: 500 pixels

Distance: 999 pixels

Using the Wind filter

The problem with the Motion Blur filter is that it blurs pixels in two directions. If you want to distribute pixels in one absolute direction or the other, try the Wind filter, which you can use either on its own or with Motion Blur.

When you choose Filter ➪ Stylize ➪ Wind, Photoshop displays the Wind dialog box shown in Figure 10.31. You can select from three methods and two directions to distribute the selected pixels. Figure 10.32 compares the effect of the Motion Blur filter to each of the three methods offered by the Wind filter. Notice that the Wind filter does not blur pixels. Rather, it evaluates a selection in 1-pixel-tall horizontal strips and offsets the strips randomly inside the image.

FIGURE 10.31

Use the Wind filter to randomly distribute a selection in 1-pixel horizontal strips in one of two directions.

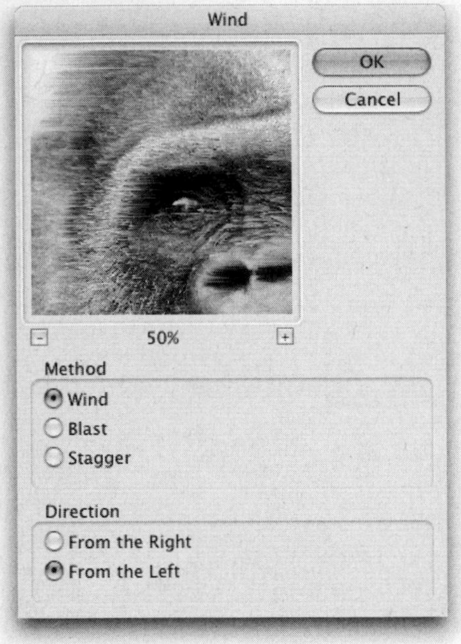

For interesting results, try combining the Motion Blur and Wind filters with a blending mode. For example, as shown in Figure 10.33, the entire image was cloned to a new layer and the Wind command was applied twice to the topmost layer, first with Stagger selected and then with Blast (top). Next, Motion Blur was applied with a 0-degree Angle and Distance value of 100 (second). After that, we changed the layer's blend mode to Lighten (third). And, to cap it all off and give those clothes an even more wind-swept feel, we duplicated the filter layer again, and skewed it to the left using Edit ➪ Transform ➪ Skew (bottom).

FIGURE 10.32

Here, you can see the difference between the effects of the Motion Blur filter (top) and the Wind filter (from top to bottom: Wind, Blast, and Stagger). In each case, From the Right was selected within the Direction section of the Wind filter dialog box.

Motion Blur, Distance: 30 pixels

Wind, Method: Wind

Wind, Method: Blast

Wind, Method: Stagger

FIGURE 10.33

Here, we combined the Wind filter (top) with Motion Blur (second) and the Lighten blend mode (third).

Wind, Stagger, and Blast

Motion Blur, Distance: 100 pixels

Lighten blend mode

Edit ⇨ Transform ⇨ Skew

Radial blurring

Choosing Filter ⇨ Blur ⇨ Radial Blur displays the Radial Blur dialog box shown in Figure 10.34. The dialog box offers two Blur Method options: Spin and Zoom.

Click and drag inside the Blur Center grid to change the point about which the Radial Blur filter spins or zooms the image.

If you select Spin, the image appears to be rotating about a central point. You specify that point by clicking and dragging in the grid inside the Blur Center box (as demonstrated in the figure). If you select Zoom, the image appears to rush away from you, as if you were zooming the camera while shooting the photograph. Again, you specify the central point of the Zoom by clicking and dragging in the Blur Center box. Figure 10.35 features examples of both settings.

After selecting a Blur Method option, you can type any value between 1 and 100 in the Amount option box to specify the maximum distance over which the filter blurs pixels. (You can type a value of 0, but doing so merely causes the filter to waste time without producing an effect.) Pixels farthest away from the center point move the most; pixels close to the center point barely move at all. Keep in mind that large values take more time to apply than small values.

TIP Select a Quality option to specify your favorite compromise between time and quality. The Good and Best Quality options ensure smooth results by respectively applying bilinear and bicubic interpolation (as explained in Chapter 2). However, they also prolong the amount of time the filter spends calculating pixels in your image. The Draft option *diffuses* an image, which leaves a trail of loose and randomized pixels but takes less time to complete.

FIGURE 10.35

Five examples of the Radial Blur filter, set to both Spin and Zoom, subject to different Quality settings. The Amount values were set to 10 pixels for each.

Original

Radial Blur, Spin, Amount: 10, Draft

Spin, Amount: 10, Good

Spin, Amount: 10, Best

Zoom, Amount: 10, Draft

Zoom, Amount: 10, Best

Blurring with a threshold

The purpose of Filter ➪ Blur ➪ Smart Blur is to blur the low-contrast portions of an image while retaining the edges. This way, you can downplay photo grain, blemishes, and artifacts without harming the real edges in the image. If you're familiar with Filter ➪ Pixelate ➪ Facet, it may help to know that Smart Blur is essentially a customizable version of that filter.

The two key options in the Smart Blur dialog box, shown in Figure 10.36, are the Radius and Threshold sliders. As with all Radius options, this one expands the number of pixels calculated at a time as you increase the value. Meanwhile, the Threshold value works just like the one in the Unsharp Mask dialog box, specifying how different two neighboring pixels must be to be considered an edge.

FIGURE 10.36

The Smart Blur filter lets you blur the low-contrast areas of an image without harming the edges.

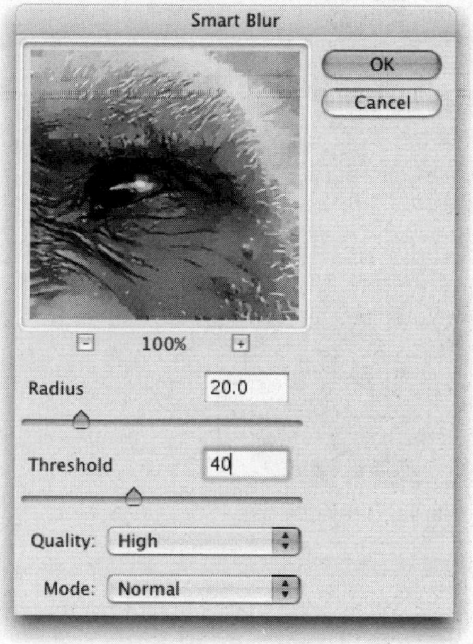

But the Threshold value has a peculiar and unexpected effect on the Radius. The Radius value actually produces more subtle effects if you raise the value beyond the Threshold. For example, take a look at Figure 10.37, where you see a grid of images subject to different Radius and Threshold values. (The first value below each image is the Radius.) In the top row of the figure, the 5.0 Radius value produces a more pronounced effect than its 20.0 and 60.0 cousins. This is because a value of 5.0 is less than the 10.0 Threshold, while 20.0 and 60.0 are more.

FIGURE 10.37

This figure shows combinations of different Radius and Threshold values. Notice that the most dramatic effects occur when the Radius is equal to about half the Threshold.

Radius: 5, Threshold: 10

Radius: 5, Threshold: 30

Radius: 5, Threshold: 80

Radius: 20, Threshold: 10

Radius: 20, Threshold: 30

Radius: 20, Threshold: 80

Radius: 60, Threshold: 10

Radius: 60, Threshold: 30

Radius: 60, Threshold: 80

The Quality settings control the smoothness of the edges. The High setting takes more time than Medium and Low, but it looks smoother as well; for the image shown in Figure 10.37, the value was set to High to create all the effects demonstrated. The two additional Mode options enable you to trace the edges defined by the Threshold value with white lines. Overlay Edge shows image and lines, and Edge Only shows just the traced lines. About the only practical purpose for these options is to monitor the precise effect of the Threshold setting in the preview box. Otherwise, the Edge options are clearly relegated to special effects.

Figure 10.38 shows how the masking technique compares with Smart Blur. In the first image, Unsharp Mask was applied with a Threshold of 20. Then Smart Blur was applied with a Radius of 2.0 and a Threshold of 20.0, matching the Unsharp Mask value.

FIGURE 10.38

This figure shows the difference between relying on Photoshop's automated Threshold capabilities (left) and sharpening and blurring with the aid of an edge mask (right). A little manual labor wins out over total automation.

Unsharp Mask +
Smart Blur, Threshold: 20

Unsharp Mask +
Gaussian Blur, Edge Mask

In the second image, an edge mask was created and an Unsharp Mask was applied with a Threshold of 0. Next, Ctrl+Shift+I (⌘+Shift+I on the Mac) was pressed to reverse the selection, and a Gaussian Blur was applied with a Radius of 2.0.

Using the Lens Blur filter

The Lens Blur filter is designed to simulate the type of optical blurring that occurs in the real world. For years, photographers have experimented with depth of field to determine the relative focus of foreground and background elements in their photos. Although a crisp, uniformly in-focus image is appropriate in many circumstances, sometimes a shallow depth of field (where one section is sharply in focus while others are blurred) can perfectly set the tone for an image. You can take pictures as crisp as you can manage and then perform the selective blurring later in Photoshop. Not content to simply be a compound blur effect, however, the Lens Blur filter also offers you a blissfully obsessive amount of control over Iris, Highlight, and Noise settings.

Choose Filter ➪ Blur ➪ Lens Blur to bring up the large Lens Blur dialog box, shown in Figure 10.39. On the left side of the dialog box is the image preview, which is scaled to fit entirely inside the dialog box by default. If you want to adjust the zoom ratio, use the plus and minus signs in the lower-left corner or click the right-pointing arrowhead and choose an option from the resulting pop-up menu. As usual, you can press and hold the spacebar and drag over your image to position it within the preview area. Next to the zoom options is the progress bar, which lets you know that Photoshop is still working hard during some of the slower, more complex Lens Blur calculations. The right side of the bulky Lens Blur dialog box contains the following options:

FIGURE 10.39

Bring your ideas into focus with the Lens Blur filter. Focus, blur — it works on many levels.

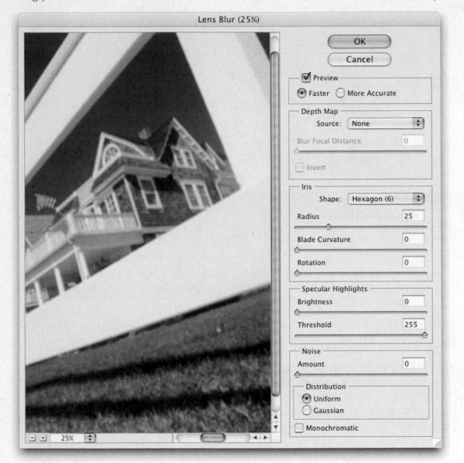

- **Preview:** When the Preview option is selected, the Lens Blur filter automatically updates the image preview every time you make an adjustment. For minute tweaking, this can be great, but sometimes this calculation-intense filter can take a while to give you a result, in which case you may want to deselect this option. Even better is the ability to choose between the Faster and More Accurate preview options. Generally, it's a safe bet to leave this set to Faster. Remember, these option are only for previewing. As soon as you click OK, Photoshop renders the best possible result it can.

- **Depth Map:** Here's where the wonders of the Lens Blur filter really shine. The Depth Map you specify contains information that assigns an imaginary position in space to every individual pixel in your image. By default, the Source pop-up menu offers three options: None, which performs blurring on each pixel in your image uniformly; Transparency, which determines what gets blurred in an image based on the transparency values of the pixels; and Layer Mask, which bases blur levels on the grayscale values in an image's layer mask. Under the default settings, the black areas of the mask are treated as though they are in the foreground and the white areas are treated as though they are in the background, though you can reverse this by selecting the Invert option or by adjusting these settings manually, as you'll see in a moment. If you've added an alpha channel to your layer, it too is available to choose as a Depth Map from the Source pop-up menu.

TIP The ability to create custom Depth Maps gives you the opportunity to individually tweak the blurriness of every single pixel in your image. You'll be astonished at the blurring power at your fingertips. Try this: Create a layer mask, and draw a black-to-white transparency gradient in your image. Then apply the Lens Blur filter with the Source set to Layer Mask. The result is an image that gradually increases in blurriness according to your gradient. Or add an alpha channel to your layer, and use the Brush tool to paint in random splotches of blacks and grays to emulate the random, selective focus that's so popular right now among music video directors and people with broken camera lenses. Why, the possibilities are endless, though blurry in the distance.

Figure 10.40 demonstrates a simple depth-of-field experiment. The foreground sphere is red, the sphere in the middle distance is green, and the one in the background happens to be blue — each on its own layer, created with the Elliptical Marquee tool and the Gradient tool set to Radial.

To apply the depth map, shown in the lower right, the appropriate alpha channel was loaded using the Source pop-up menu. Although dragging the Blur Focal Distance slider would have worked just as well to determine which part of the image needed to be in focus, the Lens Blur filter provides a quicker, more precise way to designate any portion of a layer as being in focus: Simply click any pixel in the preview window portion of the dialog box, and watch as the Blur Focal Distance slider snaps to attention. The Lens Blur filter takes the pixel you've chosen, looks at the corresponding grayscale level for that pixel in the Depth Map, and adjusts the focal distance accordingly. If you choose Invert, the portion of the image you click is set out of focus.

- **Iris:** The characteristics of genuine lens blur in a photograph can depend on the shape of the iris in the camera lens that captured the photo. (An *iris* is a diaphragm comprised of plates that expand and contract to determine the amount of light entering the lens.) Photoshop's Lens Blur filter gives you a number of options for simulating many different types of irises. From the Shape pop-up menu, you can select anything from a triangular iris to an octagonal one. Experiment with the various Shape options together with the Blade Curvature and Rotation settings to create different types of realistic details and imperfections in your lens blur effects. As the number of sides in the iris increases, along with the Blade Curvature, the blur highlights become smoother until they are virtually circular.

  The Radius setting is where you adjust the amount of blur applied to your image. You can think of it as the Photoshop counterpart to a camera's f-stop (which regulates depth of field in real life), though the fact that Photoshop doesn't know the focal length of the lens that captured the image prevents you from getting a direct, mathematical correlation.

- **Specular Highlights:** When you blur an image through one of the other blurring filters in Photoshop, colors can get averaged and bright whites can become shades of gray. Photographers are well aware of the fact that no matter how much a photo is optically blurred, whites remain bright white. The Lens Blur filter accounts for this with the

Specular Highlights section of the dialog box. Decrease the Threshold amount to add areas that are affected by the highlights and increase the Brightness level to blast the image with pools of white. In addition to being optically accurate, Specular Highlights also can add a nice, otherworldly quality to an image.

FIGURE 10.40

Here, a grayscale alpha channel was created for use as a Depth Map. Then, the Lens Blur filter was applied, and the Blur Focal Distance set by clicking each of the spheres in the image.

Focus on foreground sphere

Focus on middle sphere

Focus on background sphere

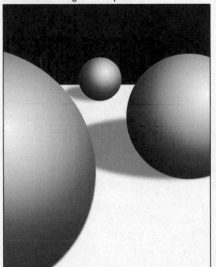

The Alpha channel used for the depth map

■ **Noise:** When you apply a drastic blur to sections of an image, it tends to smooth out detail and color values. But as you've seen, the name of Lens Blur's game is realism, and no matter how blurry a photograph is, it would look unnatural to lose film's inherent grain detail. Thankfully, the Noise options can help artificially pull this detail back in. Adjust the Amount slider until the noise in the blurred section matches the original photo's noise in the in-focus section. Below the slider, select either Uniform or Gaussian to set the type of noise (for my money, Gaussian is the way to go). Finally, you can make sure the noise you generate won't affect the color in your image by selecting the Monochromatic option.

Applying a Box Blur

The Box Blur works much like the Gaussian Blur, as you have only a Radius slider to adjust the effect, but the results are faster, and the filter works differently in terms of which pixels its using to make the blur happen. Figure 10.41 shows the Box Blur dialog box. The term "box" comes from the box-like direction that the pixel comparisons take. Each pixel is compared to the pixels directly above, below, and to the left and right — no diagonally positioned pixels are included. The true boxy-ness of this filter is most visible at high Radius settings.

FIGURE 10.41

Click and drag the Box Blur's Radius slider to adjust the intensity of the horizontal and vertical blurring effect.

Figure 10.42 shows the melding of two images — a sign post in an autumn shot by Terri Shadle, with a shallow depth of field, and the same sign post introduced into another shot of Terri's. The new background is then subjected to the Box Blur filter to reproduce the same depth-of-field origi-nally captured by the camera.

FIGURE 10.42

Want a quick blur effect? Box Blur may be your answer—unless you're blurring in the Radius range of 20 to 80 pixels. Higher than that, and the blur is so extensive that the boxy look disappears. Lower than 20, and the boxy look is negligible.

Using the Shape Blur

You know those shapes you can choose from when you use the Custom Shape drawing tool? Well, they come back to serve you again when you choose Filter ➪ Blur ➪ Shape Blur. The resulting dialog box, shown in Figure 10.43, offers you a preview of the image, the ubiquitous zoom controls, and the oft-seen Radius slider. Below that, you have a palette of shapes, with an options menu button that displays the menu also shown in Figure 10.43.

FIGURE 10.43

Pick a shape, or choose from different shape categories in the pop-up menu. Choose All to see the entire set of shapes with which you can blur your layer content.

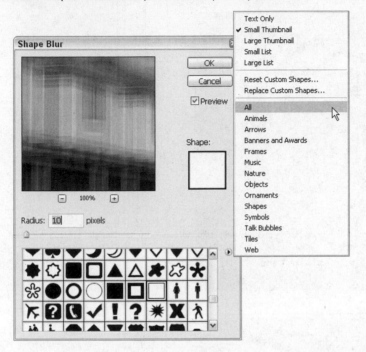

To blur with a shape — the shape dictating the sweep of the tool's comparisons of each pixel's neighbors — simply click a shape in the palette, and watch the results appear in the dialog box and in the image window (if you have selected the Preview option).

The results? Well, as shown in Figure 10.44, you can see that like the Box Blur (which is really a shape blur perpetually set to a box shape), the Radius setting determines whether the shape used is visible within the blur results. At low settings (below 10 pixels — and 5 is as low as you can go), you can't really tell the results from a Gaussian blur, which compares each pixel to all of its immediate neighbors, resulting in no discernable shape. At higher Radius settings — higher than 20, but less than 100 — you can really see that the blur effect is tweaked by the shape you chose. This isn't to say that you could tell which shape was used if you were handed a photo that was blurred, with say, the little dog paw shape, but you can tell it's not a uniform Gaussian blur, either.

TIP The simpler the shape — arrows, triangles, boxes, anything angular without too many sides, nooks, or crannies — the more obvious and identifiable the shape's impact is. If you're looking for a blur that's not the regular old Gaussian effect, this may be the one for you — you can even choose a shape that's similar to your photo's key subject.

FIGURE 10.44

In the top-most image, the Radius is set low and the blur is very Gaussian-like. On the bottom, the higher Radius setting shows the shape's effect.

Shape Blur, circle, Radius: 5 pixels

Radius: 30 pixels

Working with Surface Blur

The Surface Blur filter is intended for use in blurring images depicting shiny surfaces. It maintains luminosity while evening out underlying color tones, as can be seen in Figure 10.45. This as-yet unfried green tomato has a taut shiny surface. Notice that the skin is not a uniform green, but is speckled with flecks of varying green tones. (Okay, okay — we KNOW it's a grayscale image in your book! Just trust us on this one — those speckles are GREEN!) When the Surface Blur filter is applied, the shiny highlights are not diminished; however, the speckles virtually disappear.

If you don't want to lose detail in an image with shiny glass, chrome, or other glossy surfaces, select only those areas with a high shine that you need to tone down. Using low Radius and Threshold settings assures subtle results, and the Preview allows you to make sure that your Surface Blur doesn't make your highlights look dirty compared to the rest of the shiny content.

Understanding Noise Factors

Photoshop offers four loosely associated filters in its Filter ➪ Noise submenu. One filter adds random pixels, known as *noise,* to an image. The other three — Despeckle, Dust and Scratches, and Median — average the colors of neighboring pixels in ways that theoretically remove noise from poorly scanned images. But in fact, they function nearly as well at removing essential detail as they do at removing extraneous noise. In the following sections, you learn how the Noise filters work.

Adding noise

Noise adds grit and texture to an image. Noise makes an image look like you shot it in New York on the Lower East Side and were lucky to get the photo at all because someone was throwing sand in your face as you sped away in your chauffeur-driven, jet-black Maserati Bora, hammering away at the shutter release. In reality, of course, a guy over at Sears shot the photo for you, after which you tooled around in your minivan trying to find a store that sold day-old bread. But that's the beauty of Noise. It makes you look cool, even when you aren't.

FIGURE 10.45

The Surface Blur dialog box gives you two familiar sliders — Radius and Threshold — and here we see that when the photo isn't shiny or sparkly to begin with, you can achieve a cool, foggy result.

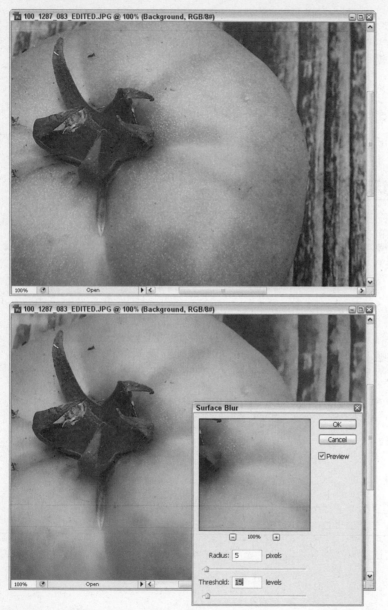

You add noise by choosing Filter ➪ Noise ➪ Add Noise. Shown in Figure 10.46, the Add Noise dialog box features the following options:

The Add Noise dialog box asks you to specify the amount and variety of noise you want to add to the selection.

- **Amount:** This value determines how far pixels in the image can stray from their current colors. The value represents a color range rather than a brightness range and is expressed as a percentage. You can type a value as high as 400 percent. The percentage is based on 256 brightness values per channel if you're working with a 24-bit image and 32,768 brightness values for 16-bit images. So with a 24-bit image (8-bit channels), the default value of 12.5 percent is equivalent to 32 brightness levels, which is 12.5 percent of 256.

  For example, if you type a value of 12.5 percent for a 24-bit image, Photoshop can apply any color that is 32 shades more or less red, more or less green, *and* more or less blue than the current color. If you type 400 percent, Photoshop theoretically can go 1,024 brightness values lighter or darker. But that results in colors that are out of range; therefore, they get clipped to black or white. The result is higher contrast inside the noise pixels.

- **Uniform:** Select this option to apply colors absolutely randomly within the specified range. Photoshop is no more likely to apply one color within the range than another, thus resulting in an even color distribution.

- **Gaussian:** When you select this option, you instruct Photoshop to prioritize colors along the Gaussian distribution curve. The effect is that most colors added by the filter either closely resemble the original colors or push the boundaries of the specified range. In other words, this option results in more light and dark pixels, thus producing a more pronounced effect.

- **Monochromatic:** When working on a full-color image, the Add Noise filter distributes pixels randomly throughout the different color channels. However, when you select the Monochrome option, Photoshop distributes the noise in the same manner in all channels. The result is grayscale noise. (This option does not affect grayscale images; the noise can't get any more grayscale than it already is.)

Figure 10.47 compares three applications of Gaussian noise to identical amounts of Uniform noise, the first of which produces higher contrast. The bottom row in the figure demonstrates Monochromatic noise, which tends to produce a more appealing effect.

Noise variations

Normally, the Add Noise filter adds both lighter and darker pixels to an image. If you prefer, however, you can limit the effect of the filter to strictly lighter or darker pixels. To do so, apply the Add Noise filter, apply the Fade command (Ctrl+Shift+F on the PC or ⌘+Shift+F on the Mac), and select the Lighten or Darken blend mode. Or you can copy the image to a new layer, apply the filter, and merge the filtered image with the underlying original.

Figure 10.48 shows sample applications of lighter and darker noise. After copying the image to a separate layer, the Add Noise filter was applied with an Amount value of 40 percent and Gaussian was selected. To create the top example in the figure, Lighten was selected from the blend mode pop-up menu. To create the bottom example, the Darken mode was selected. In each case, a layer of strictly lighter or darker noise was added while at the same time retaining the clarity of the original image.

FIGURE 10.47

The Gaussian option (middle row) produces more pronounced effects than the Uniform option (top) at identical Amount values. Select the Monochromatic check box to apply noise evenly to all channels (bottom).

Uniform, Amount: 6%

Uniform, 12%

Uniform, 25%

Gaussian, Amount: 6%

Gaussian, 12%

Gaussian, 25%

Monochromatic, Amount: 6%

Monochromatic, 12%

Monochromatic, 25%

FIGURE 10.48

You can limit the Add Noise filter to strictly lighter (top, 40 percent Add Noise, Lighten mode) or darker (bottom, 40 percent Add Noise, Darken mode) noise by applying the filter to a layered clone.

Add Noise, Amount: 40%, Lighten   ...Darken

Motion Blur, –30°, 30 pixels, Lighten   ...Darken

Chunky noise

You may find that your biggest frustration with the Add Noise filter is that you can't specify the size of individual specks of noise. No matter what you do, noise only comes in 1-pixel squares. It may occur to you that you can enlarge the noise dots in a layer by applying the Maximum or Minimum filter, but in practice, doing so simply fills in the image, because there isn't sufficient space between the noise pixels to accommodate the larger dot sizes.

Luckily, Photoshop provides several alternatives. One is the Pointillize filter, which adds variable-sized dots and then colors those dots in keeping with the original colors in the image. Though Pointillize lacks the random quality of the Add Noise filter, you can use it to add texture to an image.

To create the top-left image in Figure 10.49, Filter ➪ Pixelate ➪ Pointillize was used, with 5 in the Cell Size option box. After pressing Enter (Return on the Mac) to apply the filter, Ctrl+Shift+F (⌘+Shift+F on the Mac) was pressed to fade the filter, changing the Opacity value to 50 percemt. This effect is what we mean by "chunky noise." The top-right image is similar, but the Opacity is set to 100 percent and the Pin Light blend mode is applied instead.

The Gallery Effects filters provide a few noise alternatives. Filter ➪ Sketch ➪ Halftone Pattern adds your choice of dot patterns, as shown in the two middle examples in Figure 10.49. But like all filters in the Sketch submenu, it replaces the colors in your image with the foreground and background colors. Filter ➪ Texture ➪ Grain is a regular noise smörgåsbord, permitting you to select from ten different Grain Type options, each of which produces a different kind of noise. The bottom examples in Figure 10.49 show off two of the Grain options: Clumped and Stipple.

FIGURE 10.49

From top to bottom, noise was created with Pointillize, Halftone, and Grain. Experiment with different settings for each one on your own photos.

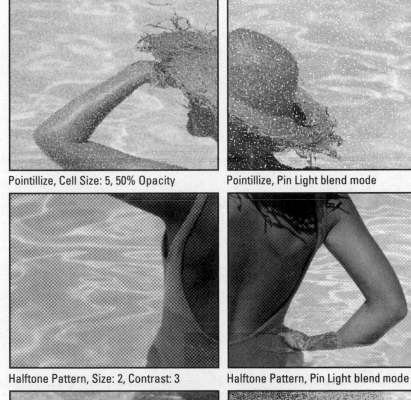

Pointillize, Cell Size: 5, 50% Opacity

Pointillize, Pin Light blend mode

Halftone Pattern, Size: 2, Contrast: 3

Halftone Pattern, Pin Light blend mode

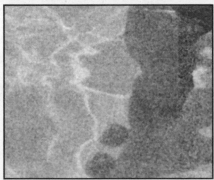
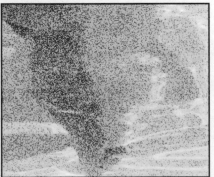

Grain, Intensity: 80, Contrast: 50, Clumped

Grain, Stipple, Soft Light blend mode

Getting rid of noise

"Getting rid of noise" may be an overstatement, but Photoshop's Reduce Noise filter does a pretty good job of removing noise from your images—whether it comes from a scanned original, JPEG *artifacts*, or just overall graininess from any number of sources. As shown in Figure 10.50, the dialog box offers more options for controlling the filter than you'll see in other Noise filter dialog boxes, and it comes in two flavors: Basic and Advanced.

FIGURE 10.50

Reduce noise a little bit or a whole lot—all while maintaining details within your image.

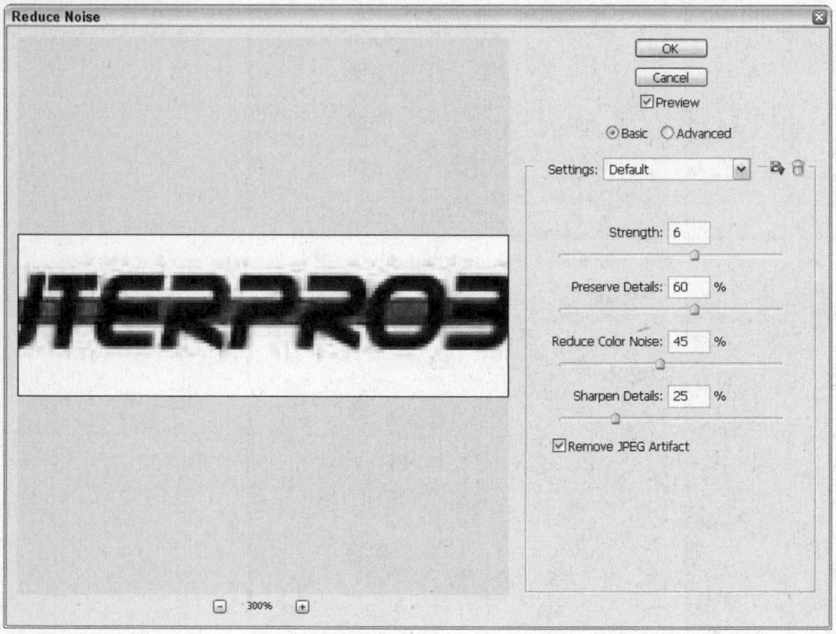

| TIP | What are *artifacts*? Stray pixels that stand out undesirably, created by saving files in a lossy format (like JPG, which is often used to make photos web-ready). The Reduce Noise filter can get rid of some of these pixels for you, changing their color to match the surrounding pixels more closely. If you want to review file formats, like JPG and others, check out Chapter 3. Terms like *lossy* and the specifics of web optimization are covered in Chapter 20. |

Like many filter dialog boxes, the Reduce Noise dialog box allows you to move and resize your image (the layer or selection being filtered) within the Preview window, using the Zoom buttons (+ and −) and with your mouse within the Preview itself (your mouse becomes a Hand by default). Using the sliders on the right, the Basic version of the dialog box allows you to tweak the following settings, until you like what you see on the left:

■ **Strength:** This setting controls luminance (light) noise. The higher the number, the more control you achieve, as the brightness of adjacent pixels is adjusted to create a more uniform appearance. You can leave this slider right where it is (6 is the default) if your noise isn't coming from light and dark pixels mixing inappropriately.

■ **Preserve Details:** Expressed as a percentage, this slider allows you to choose how much detail you keep as you smooth out the noisy pixels. The higher the percentage, however, the less noise you eliminate.

■ **Reduce Color Noise:** If your noise is color-based (rather than light-based), drag this slider toward the right, increasing the percentage of chromatic noise reduction achieved.

■ **Sharpen Details:** This would seem like a redundant setting with Preserve Details, but it's not. What this does is actually apply a sharpen filter to the image (or the active layer/selection) at the same time that whatever noise reduction you've established with the other settings is applied. The higher the percentage here, the more sharpening you get, which can actually create noise — so watch the preview closely to see if you're canceling out your noise reduction with too much sharpening.

■ **Remove JPEG Artifact:** This check box, unchecked by default, does just what it says it does — although not dramatically. The intention is to spot and get rid of artifacts (previously defined in this section) that occur through the application of the JPG format, but you may find that you don't see any appreciable change when you check this box.

> **TIP** Image noise comes in two flavors: luminance noise (graininess) and color noise (artifacts). Graininess typically can be isolated in the blue channel, and the Advanced mode of this filter has this little factoid in mind, so read on.

If you click the Advanced radio button at the top of the Reduce Noise dialog box, you see a change in the dialog box — it displays two tabs, Overall and Per Channel. The Overall tab offers the same settings as the Basic version of the dialog box. The Per Channel tab is the truly advanced part. Here you find what you see in Figure 10.51, which includes the following options:

■ **Channel:** Click the list, and pick your channel. The one you pick is the one you're adjusting, using the other two options in this version of the dialog box. Obviously, this is where you go when you want to reduce noise in that blue channel we were just talking about.

■ **Strength:** Like you found in the Basic version of the Reduce Noise dialog box, the Strength setting allows you to determine how much noise is removed, based on light levels between adjacent pixels.

■ **Preserve Details:** Again, just like in the Basic version of the dialog box, this percentage determines the amount of detail you keep as you remove noise. This time, however, the preservation of detail is per channel. This means you can remove more noise in one channel than another, perhaps allowing some detail to be lost in that channel so that more noise can be lost overall. If the remaining channels are less noisy and through them you still keep image clarity, you'll get the cleanup you needed without losing much of the specifics within your image. Note that this setting is dimmed unless the Strength setting is set to 1 or more.

The Advanced settings for noise reduction include the ability to reduce noise on a per-channel basis.

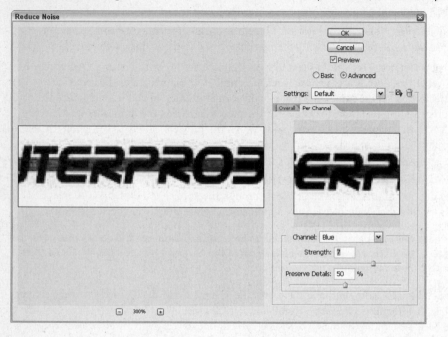

NOTE   You can save your settings in this filter dialog box by clicking the little Save button (it looks like a little disk) and giving the new filter settings a name. The trash can icon allows you to delete saved settings. To apply saved settings, click the Settings list and select them by name.

Removing noise with Despeckle

Strictly speaking, the Despeckle command probably belongs in the Filter ➪ Blur submenu, given that more than removing specks (or speckles), it blurs the image. Specifically, it blurs a selection while preserving its edges — the idea being that unwanted noise is most noticeable in the continuous regions of an image, rather than out along the perimeter. In practice, this filter is nearly the exact opposite of the Sharpen Edges filter — so it should be moved to Blur submenu, and called Blur Everything But The Edges.

How does it know where the edges are? The Despeckle command searches an image for edges using the equivalent of an Unsharp Mask Threshold value of 5. It then ignores the edges in the image and blurs everything else with the force of the Blur More filter, as shown in the upper-left image in Figure 10.52.

Here, you can see the effects of the Despeckle filter (upper left) and then the Median filter, the Radius values for which are noted in the images.

Despeckle

Median, Radius: 1 pixel

Radius: 3 pixels

Radius: 5 pixels

Radius: 8 pixels

Radius: 12 pixels

Averaging pixels with Median

Another command in the Filter ➪ Noise submenu, Median removes noise by averaging the colors in an image, one pixel at a time. When you choose Filter ➪ Noise ➪ Median, Photoshop produces a Radius option box. For every pixel in a selection, the filter averages the colors of the neighboring pixels that fall inside the specified radius — ignoring any pixels that are so different that they might skew the average — and applies the average color to the central pixel. You can type any value between 1 and 100. However, even at low settings like 16, significant blurring occurs, as you can see from the bottom-right example in Figure 10.53. At the maximum Radius value, you are left with a sort of soft, blurry gradient, with all image detail obliterated.

As with Gaussian Blur, you can achieve some interesting and useful effects by backing off the Median filter with the Fade command. But rather than creating a romantic, soft-yet-focused glow, Median clumps up details, giving an image a plastic, molded quality, as demonstrated by the examples in Figure 10.53. To create every one of these images, the Median filter was applied with a Radius of 5 pixels. For the second example, Ctrl+Shift+F (⌘+Shift+F on the Mac) was pressed to display the Fade dialog box, and the Opacity value was lowered to 65 percent. For the bottom-left image, Opacity was raised back up to 100 percent in the Fade dialog box, and the Darken blend mode was applied. And for the final example, the Opacity was brought back down to 80 percent, and the Linear Dodge mode was used.

Another difference between Gaussian Blur and Median is that Gaussian Blur destroys edges and Median invents new ones. This means that you can follow the Median filter with Unsharp Mask to achieve even more pronounced sculptural effects.

Cleaning up scanned halftones

Photoshop offers one additional filter in the Filter ➪ Noise submenu called Dust & Scratches. The purpose of this filter is to remove dust particles, hairs, scratches, and other imperfections that may accompany a scan. The filter offers two options: Radius and Threshold. As long as the offending imperfection is smaller or thinner than the Radius value and different enough from its neighbors to satisfy the Threshold value, the filter deletes the spot or line and interpolates between the pixels around the perimeter.

But like so many of Photoshop's older automated tools, Dust & Scratches works only when conditions are extremely favorable. It's not that you should never use it; in fact, you may always want to give it a shot at a dusty image. If it doesn't work, don't be surprised — just get to work and eliminate the imperfections manually using the Clone Stamp tool or Healing Brush, as discussed in Chapter 7.

Now, as stated, the Dust & Scratches filter was designed to get rid of the dirt from your scanner that ends up on your images. But another problem that the filter may be able to eliminate is moiré patterns. These patterns appear when scanning halftone images from books and magazines. The image shown in Figure 10.54 was scanned from a black-and-white newspaper image, and the original is really awful. It won't ever be a crisp, clean image, but it can be much better.

FIGURE 10.53

After applying the Median filter, the effect was reversed slightly using Edit ➪ Fade Median. The blend modes and Opacity values were varied, as indicated.

Gaussian Blur, Radius: 8 pixels

Normal, 65% Opacity

Darken, 100% Opacity

...plus Linear Dodge, 70% Opacity

CAUTION When scanning published photographs or artwork, take a moment to find out if what you're doing is legal. It's up to you to make sure that the image you scan is no longer protected by copyright — most, but not all, works more than 75 years old are considered fair game — or that your noncommercial application of the image falls under the fair-use umbrella of commentary, criticism, or parody. It's better to be extremely safe than even slightly sorry, so be careful and thorough in your copyright research.

The Dust & Scratches filter can be pretty useful for eliminating moirés, particularly if you reduce the Threshold value below 40. These halftone imperfections come from the halftone dots required to print images in books and magazines, which create periodic inconsistencies known as moiré patterns

In Figure 10.54, you see an image subjected to the Dust & Scratches filter (the original appears first, on the left) with a Radius of 2 and a Threshold value of 20. The moirés are for the most part gone, but the edges have all but disappeared as well. In the third version of the image (on the right), the Gaussian Blur, Median, and Unsharp Mask filters have been applied, and the result is an image with no moiré, and with a bit more contrast and a bit more detail — an improvement over the middle image, which was simply subjected to the Dust & Scratches filter.

 Always scan halftone images at the highest resolution available to your scanner. Then resample the scan down to the desired resolution using Image ➪ Image Size, as covered in Chapter 3. This step by itself goes a long way toward eliminating moirés.

FIGURE 10.54

The Dust & Scratches filter quickly eliminates the patterns (left image), but can result in loss of details and edges (middle image). Fix that with filters that blur and another that sharpens (right image).

Using the Average filter

Choosing Filter ➪ Blur ➪ Average will, on most color images, replace the image with a grayish wall of nothing. That gray void is what you usually end up with when you average all the varied color values in an image. Consequently, on its own, Average isn't really terribly useful. However, it does have some uses, when used with selections and blend modes.

When a portion of the image is selected, the Average filter makes calculations from and applies changes to only the selected area. Draw a marquee over a patch of grass, and the averaged area becomes a flat, solid green. Use the Magic Wand to grab a handful of sky, and Average makes it smooth and perfect. Of course, these averages may not be all that photographic or impressive on their own; when you begin to blend averaged sections of an image with the original underlying pixels, the filter proves its value.

You also can experiment with blend modes to achieve stylized results, as shown in Figure 10.55. First, select different areas of the image using Select ➪ Color Range, and apply the Average filter to each individually (top). Next, use a few blend modes and Opacity values on a copy of the image.

FIGURE 10.55

Three faces...with the original image on top, followed by a duplicate layer where the Average filter was applied to various selections. In the bottom image, a copy of the unfiltered chimp was placed on top of a copy of the Averaged image, and the top layer's Opacity was reduced to 90% with the Lighten mode applied. The underlying layer (with Average applied) was given a Gaussian Blur of 1 pixel.

Summary

In this chapter, you received an overview of corrective, destructive, and effects filters, and you learned about mixing a filtered image with the original. You also learned about the new Smart Filters feature in Photoshop CS3, which includes Smart Filters masks.

Through the Sharpen filters, you learned to fix the focus of an image with Unsharp Mask, to use the new Smart Sharpen filter, and to enhance a grainy photograph using a custom edge mask. You also learned about highlighting edges with the High Pass filter and creating glowing images with Gaussian Blur. You learned how to remove noise from photos with a variety of filters that help eliminate stray, unwanted bright, dark, or oddly colored pixels. Blur filters also were covered, as was the removal of unwanted patterns through combining blur and sharpen filters.

Chapter 11

Distortions and Effects

A s you discovered in Chapter 10, *corrective filters* enable you to eliminate image flaws and apply special effects that enhance the appearance of an image — generally without losing any details or changing the overall image content. These filters improve upon, rather than change, an image.

Destructive filters, on the other hand, are devoted solely to special effects. There are nearly twice as many destructive filters as corrective filters, perhaps because they simplify the creation of special effects, from simple artistic medium-mimicry to total distortion — things you could not easily do from scratch with any of Photoshop's tools or corrective commands and filters.

Now, some Photoshop veterans will tell you that destructive filters aren't useful or they aren't as important or effective as the corrective ones. That's an entirely subjective position, and one that isn't really worth defending or attacking. Suffice to say that many veteran designers love the destructive filters and would miss them terribly if they went away. Whether you're a veteran or a newbie, you'll probably find yourself loving some of the destructive filters and not seeing the need for or sense in others. That's why, as they say, "they make chocolate and vanilla" — there's something for everyone.

In this chapter, we make no attempt to cover each and every one of the destructive filters. First, for most of them, after you've mastered a few of the different controls that the filter dialog boxes offer, you don't need an explanation of the others. Second, you'd need a forklift to get this book from the shelf in your bookstore to the cashier (or you'd have to tip the mail carrier for lugging the book to your doorstep) if each one was covered.

Fear not: Even with the filters that have been skipped in this chapter, you're going to find yourself a master of destruction after reading the next 70-plus pages, and no filter's magic will elude you.

Creating Bizarre Effects

This list provides information about some of the more interesting special effects filters. Many of them may not seem immediately useful, but the more creative your work is, the more you'll find yourself making use of them:

- **Fragment:** Found in the Pixelate group of filters, this filter repeats an image four times in a square formation and lowers the opacity of each to give the illusion of the image being shaken — as though the photo was taken during an earthquake. Earthquake photography is not the technical purpose for this filter — it may not have a specific purpose at all — but it can be used alone or with other filters for interesting results, especially if you use it on a duplicate layer with reduced opacity. There are no options for controlling its effects, and it can make your eyes hurt if you stare at the photo for too long.

- **Lens Flare:** Found in the Render submenu, this filter adds sparkles and halos to an image to suggest light bouncing off the camera lens. Even though many photographers work hard to avoid these sorts of reflections, lens flares can have artistic merit and this filter lets you add them after the fact. You can select from one of three Lens Type options, adjust the Brightness slider between 10 and 300 percent (though somewhere between 100 and 150 is bound to deliver the best results), and move the center of the reflection by clicking and dragging a point around inside the Flare Center box. In addition, you can Alt-click (Win) or Option-click (Mac) inside the preview to position the center point numerically. By way of example, Figure 11.1 shows an Alpine landscape, and Figure 11.2 demonstrates the four Lens Type settings. In each case, the Brightness value was set to 140 percent.

> **TIP**   The Alt or Option key can be very helpful to you in the Lens Flare and many other filter dialog boxes: If you press and hold Alt or Option as you drag the slider, you can see the preview update on the fly.

If you want to add a flare to a grayscale image, first convert it to the RGB mode. Then apply the filter and convert the image back to grayscale. The Lens Flare filter is applicable only to RGB images and is dimmed in the menu if your image is in Grayscale mode.

FIGURE 11.1

Starting with this crisp mountain pool, the next figure shows you what the Lens Flare filter can do.

Before you write off Lens Flare as something too detail-obscuring or something you'd never need, consider this: Prior to choosing the filter, create a new layer, fill it with black, and apply the Screen blend mode by pressing Shift+Alt+S (Shift+Option+S on the Mac) with a nonpainting tool selected. Now apply Lens Flare. You get the same effect as you would otherwise, but the effect floats above the background image, protecting your original image from harm. You can even move the lens flare around and vary the Opacity value, giving you more control over the final effect.

TIP Want your lens flare to be an on-and-off affair? Turn your image layer into a Smart Object, using the Filter ➪ Convert for Smart Filter command, and then apply the Lens Flare as a Smart Filter. You can turn its visibility on and off depending on your print and display needs for the photo. Not sure you're clear on Smart Filters? Check back with Chapter 10 for all you need to know.

FIGURE 11.2

Here you see the four Lens Type settings available to you.

Lens Flare, 50-300mm Zoom

35mm Prime

105mm Prime

Movie Prime

- **Diffuse:** Located in the Stylize submenu — as are the three filters that follow — Diffuse dithers the edges of color, much like the Dissolve brush mode dithers the edges of a soft brush. The results are hard to describe in terms of "makes it look like this" or "mimics that," but the results are pretty neat.

- **Solarize:** This filter has no dialog box, so you can't control it. It serves mostly to distort your colors and may have a variety of creative purposes in the right situation — it's up to you. What it does is change all medium grays in the image to 50 percent gray, changes all blacks and whites to black, and remaps the other colors to shades in between. If you're familiar with the Curves command, the map for Solarize looks like a pyramid. What? You're not familiar with Curves? Go to Chapter 18.

- **Tiles:** This filter does its best to break an image up into a bunch of square, randomly spaced rectangular tiles. You specify how many tiles fit across the smaller of the image's width or height — a value of 10, for example, creates 100 tiles in a perfectly square image — and the maximum distance each tile can shift. You can fill the gaps between tiles with the foreground color, the background color, or an inverted or normal version of the original image. You can compare the Tiles filter to the Extrude filter (the next one discussed here) in Figure 11.3, where the original, untouched image appears on the far left, followed by two types of extrusions.

- **Extrude:** A functional cousin of the Tiles filter, Extrude breaks an image into tiles and forces them toward the viewer in three-dimensional space. The Pyramid option is lots of fun, turning an image into a collection of spikes. When using the Blocks option, you can select a Solid Front Faces option that renders the image as a true 3-D mosaic. The Mask Incomplete Blocks option simply leaves the image untouched around the perimeter of the selection where the filter can't draw complete tiles.

- **Diffuse Glow:** Filter ➪ Distort ➪ Diffuse Glow sprays a coat of dithered, background-colored pixels onto your image. It can be really helpful when you want the look of soft sunshine bathing your photo. Just set your Background color to an orangey-yellow, and it's dawn in springtime.

- **Custom:** The first of two custom effects filters in Photoshop, found under the Filter ➪ Other submenu, Custom enables you to design your own *convolution kernel*, a function that allows neighboring pixels to be mixed together. The kernel can be a variation on sharpening, blurring, embossing, or a half-dozen other effects. You create your filter by typing numerical values in a matrix of options, represented by little boxes, shown in Figure 11.4, although it's not a terribly illustrative dialog box. If this sounds interesting, check out Chapter 12, where this very powerful filter is given the coverage it richly deserves.

FIGURE 11.3

This figure shows two examples of the Extrude filter. Reminds you of one of those toys with the hundreds of little metal rods you can press parts of yourself into to create a relief, doesn't it? What the heck are those things called, anyway?

Original image   Blocks, Size: 6, Depth: 30   Pyramids, Size: 10, Depth: 20

FIGURE 11.4

Type numbers into these little boxes, and watch your photo's light, color, and clarity change — for better or worse — depending on the numbers you type, where you type them, and what you were hoping for. Again, Chapter 12 helps you make sense of this — and it's worth the trip!

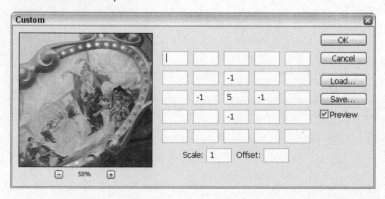

- **Displace:** Located in the Distort submenu, Displace is Photoshop's second custom effects filter, and it's also covered in detail in Chapter 12. It permits you to distort and add texture to an image by moving the colors of certain pixels in a selection. You specify the direction and distance that the Displace filter moves colors by creating a second image called a *displacement map,* or *dmap* (pronounced *dee-map*) for short. The brightness values in the displacement map tell Photoshop which pixels to affect and how far to move the colors of those pixels.

- **Artistic filters:** As a rule, the effects under the Filter ⇨ Artistic submenu add a hand-painted or drawn quality to your image. Colored Pencil, Rough Pastels, and Watercolor are examples of filters that successfully emulate traditional mediums. Other filters — Fresco, Palette Knife, and Smudge Stick — may produce results that don't immediately remind you of the mediums after which they're named, but they have their uses, alone or in combination with other filters. Figure 11.5 shows a photo broken into four blocks, each of which is filtered to look like a wet or dry artistic medium.

- **Brush Strokes filters:** The Brush Strokes filters could really have been packed into the Artistic group, because most of them mimic artistic tools such as pens, spray paint, and other methods for using ink. Some of them defy categorization (Accented Edges comes to mind here), but you'll find ways to use them regardless of where Adobe decided to store them.

- **Sketch filters:** Many of the Sketch filters replace the colors in your image with the current foreground and background colors, so be prepared to undo and then tinker with the Color settings before reapplying the filter for more pleasing results. If the foreground and background colors are black and white, the Sketch filter results in a grayscale image. Charcoal and Conté Crayon create artistic effects, Bas Relief and Note Paper add texture, and Photocopy and Stamp create extreme black-and-white results — not easy to imagine using every day, but... Figure 11.6 shows a group of Sketch filters (including Photocopy) in use.

TIP To retrieve some of the original colors from your image after applying a Sketch filter, press Ctrl+Shift+F (⌘+Shift+F on the Mac) to display the Fade dialog box and try out a few Mode settings. Overlay and Luminosity are particularly good choices.

- **Texture filters:** As a group, the commands in the Filter ⇨ Texture submenu are very useful effects filters. Craquelure, Mosaic Tiles, and Patchwork (think tiny tiles) apply interesting depth textures to an image. Texturizer provides access to several scalable textures and permits you to load your own (as long as the pattern is saved in the Photoshop format), as demonstrated in Figure 11.7. Stained Glass creates polygonal tiles like Photoshop's own Crystallize filter, only with black lines around the tiles — try applying this filter to a duplicate layer with reduced opacity for an interesting effect.

NOTE Adobe decided that 3D Transform and Texture Fill are somewhat dated and not terribly useful, so as of the release of Photoshop CS, they don't install automatically with the program. But if you want them, they're on the Photoshop CD/DVD, and you need to install them manually to access them.

 Learn more about patterns and textures and how filters can help you build them in Chapter 12.

FIGURE 11.5

A photo goes from reality (inset) to Watercolor, Colored Pencil, Rough Pastels, and Fresco (clockwise from upper left). Try them yourself on an otherwise boring photo to mask blemishes, unwanted details, or just plain ugliness.

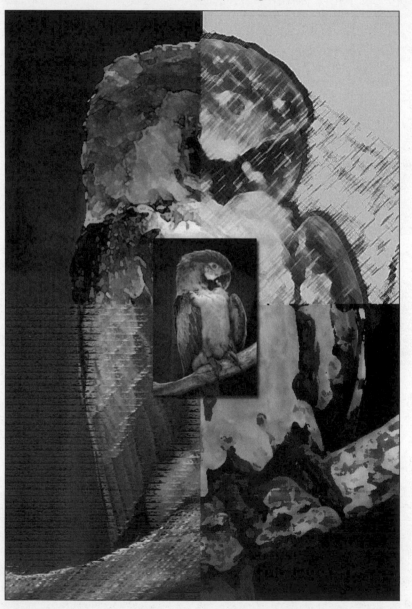

FIGURE 11.6

Clockwise from upper left, the parrot seen in Figure 11.5 has been Sketched with the Chalk & Charcoal, Bas Relief, Graphic Pen, and Photocopy filters.

FIGURE 11.7

Filter ➪ Texture ➪ Texturizer lets you select from four built-in patterns — from sandstone to brick, to canvas, to burlap (top to bottom).

What about the others?

Some filters don't belong in either the corrective or destructive camp. Take Filter ⇨ Video ⇨ NTSC Colors, for example, and Filter ⇨ Other ⇨ Offset. Both are examples of commands that probably don't belong in the Filter menu (maybe the Image ⇨ Adjustments menu would have been a better choice), and you may or may not be excited about their results.

The NTSC Colors filter modifies the colors in your RGB or Lab image for transfer to videotape. Vivid reds and blues that might otherwise prove very unstable and bleed into their neighbors are curtailed, as are pure white and black. The problem with this function is that it's not an independent color space; it's a dialog box-less filter (meaning you can't control it) that changes your colors and is finished with them. If you edit the colors after choosing the command, you may very well reintroduce colors that are incompatible with NTSC devices and therefore warrant a second application of the filter. Conversion to NTSC — another light-based system — isn't as risky as conversion to CMYK pigments, but you may wish you could have better results than this filter gives you.

The Offset command moves an image a specified number of pixels. Why wasn't it covered in Chapter 8 with the other movement options? Because the command moves the image inside the selection outline while keeping the selection outline itself stationary. It's as if you had pasted the entire image into the selection outline and were now moving it around. The command is a favorite among fans of channel operations, a topic covered in Chapter 4. You can duplicate an image, offset the entire duplicate by a few pixels, and then mix the duplicate and original to create highlight or shadow effects.

CROSS-REF Among the filters omitted in this chapter is Filter ⇨ Stylize ⇨ Wind, which is technically a destructive filter but is covered along with the Blur and Noise filters in Chapter 10.

As for the other filters in the Filter ⇨ Distort, Pixelate, Render, and Stylize submenus, keep reading this chapter to discover their details.

Having the right RAM and system resources

Why bring this up here, in a chapter on filters? Because RAM (and your other system resources) is a precious commodity when applying destructive filters. As mentioned in Chapter 2, scratch disk space typically enables you to edit larger images than your computer's RAM might permit. But all the filters in the Distort submenu and most of the commands in the Render submenu operate exclusively in memory. If they run out of physical RAM, they won't work.

Here's what Adobe states are the *minimum* requirements for Windows users. Next to some of these requirements are our suggestions (in italics) for more realistic performance expectations:

- Processor: Intel Xeon, Xeon Dual, Centrino, or Pentium 4
- System: Microsoft Windows XP with Service Pack 2 or higher, Vista
- RAM: 320 MB (384MB recommended). *1 GB is a better choice, and certainly anything less than 512 MB will result in very slow performance.*

- Hard-disk: 650MB
- Monitor: 1024×768 monitor resolution, 16-bit video card
- Video RAM: 64MB
- CD-ROM Drive: required
- Activation/Updater: Internet or phone connection required for product activation
- Browser: IE 6.0, Netscape 4.x, 6.1, 6.2 or 7.0, AOL 6.0 or 7.0, Opera 8.0+, Firefox 1.0.5+
- Multimedia: QuickTime 7 required for multimedia features

If you're on a Mac, here are the system requirements — again, at minimum:

- Processor: PowerPC G4 or G5, Intel-based Macs
- System: Mac OS X v. 10.3.X latest, 10.4. latest, Leopard (10.4.X)
- RAM: 320MB (384MB RAM recommended). In reality, anything less than 512 MB won't work, and new, Intel-based Macs ship with a 1 GB minimum RAM.
- Hard-disk: Estimated 1.5GB
- Monitor: 1024×768 monitor resolution, 16-bit video card
- Video RAM: 64MB
- CD-ROM Drive: required
- Activation/Updater: Internet or phone connection required for product activation
- Browser: IE 5.5+, Netscape 8.0+, AOL 5.0+, Safari 1.0+, Opera 8.0+, Firefox 1.0.5+
- Multimedia: QuickTime 7 required for multimedia features

These requirements aren't intended to raise the hardware bar so high that only the wealthy can afford the computer that'll run Photoshop. It's just that the software's capabilities require more "juice" from the hardware, so only a computer with adequate resources can run it properly. If you're serious about your photos and all the things you can do with Photoshop, you probably already have a computer that can handle Photoshop's system requirements. If not, you'll reap lots of other technological benefits by upgrading your system — enhanced experience on the Internet, viewing video, and running lots of other programs that run faster and better with more horsepower under the hood.

Using the Filter Gallery

Introduced to much applause in Photoshop CS, the Filter Gallery (shown in Figure 11.8) provides one-stop shopping for many of Photoshop's filters. To access the Filter Gallery, choose Filter ➪ Filter Gallery. Some of the filters open the Gallery as soon as you choose them from the various Filter submenus, and you'll get the hang of which ones do that and which ones don't. Avoid the surprise by opening the Gallery first and making your filter choices from within it.

One of the really nice things about the Filter Gallery is the ability to see that large preview of the image within the Gallery itself. As with the Lens Blur filter dialog box discussed in Chapter 10, you can adjust the zoom level of the preview using the plus and minus icons or the pop-up menu under the right-pointing arrowhead next to the zoom percentage. Whenever there is more to the image than fits in the preview window, you can use your mouse (its cursor appears as the Hand tool) to pan up, down, left, or right and to view other parts of the preview in the window. Also similar to the Lens Blur filter is the progress bar that appears next to the zoom controls during particularly time-consuming renders.

FIGURE 11.8

The Filter Gallery gives you access to a large preview of your image (without having to drag a filter dialog box aside to see your image window) and access to each filter's controls. Very handy.

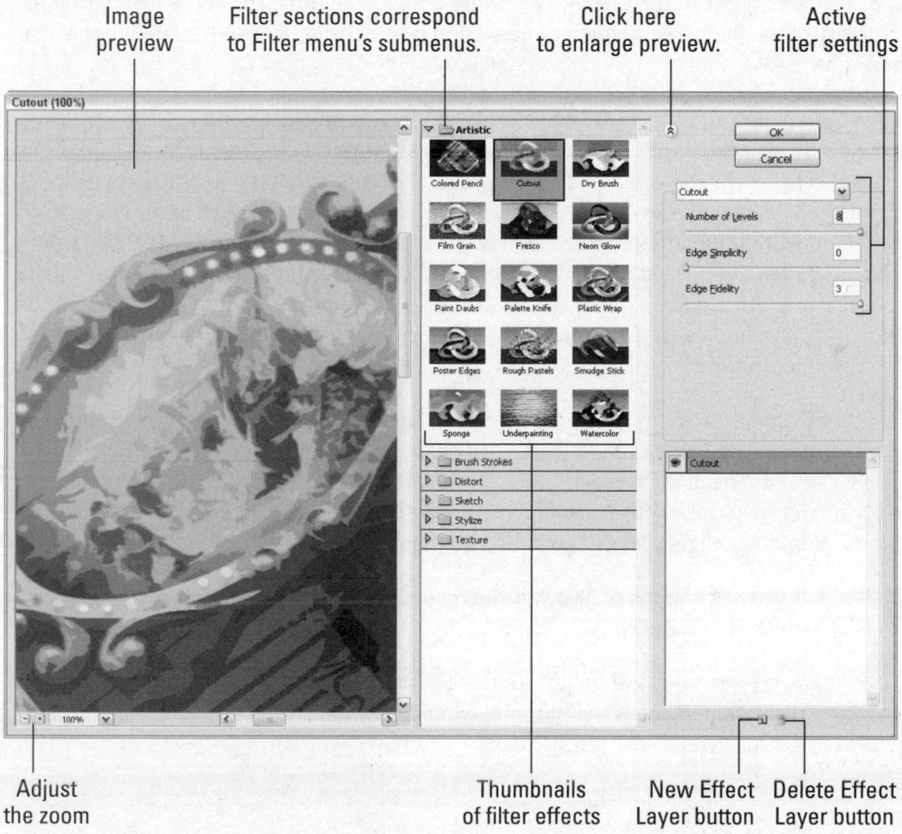

The middle vertical section of the Filter Gallery dialog box is where you access the filters themselves. The filters are organized in an assortment of sections that correspond to their respective submenus in the Filter menu. Click the triangles to the left of the section names (or simply click a section name) to reveal the thumbnails, each altered to represent the effect of applying a particular filter. Click any of the thumbnails to apply the effect to your image, bring up a preview in the left side of the dialog box, and display the filter's settings on the right side of the dialog box.

TIP Want to see all the Gallery's filters without having to navigate the sections? Click the down arrow next to the displayed filter name (above the active filter's settings on the right side of the dialog box) to see a list of all the Gallery's filters — regardless of section — displayed in one long list.

After you enable an effect, you can adjust its settings as you would any other filter. From here, you can more or less go wild — hop from section to section or filter to filter and play with the controls and watch the changes appear in the preview. Click the arrow icon to the left of the OK button to toggle the visibility of the filter area in the middle section of the dialog box and create more room for your image preview.

The real power of the Filter Gallery, however, is found in the bottom-right corner of the window (refer to Figure 11.8), where the applied filters are displayed in much the same manner as layers in the Layers palette. The filters also work in a similar fashion, if only because their stacking order plays a large role in determining how the final image looks. By default, you have only one layer of effects in the Filter Gallery, but adding more layers is as easy as clicking the New Layer Effect button (it's the little page) at the bottom of the dialog box and then selecting a different filter from the thumbnails. You also can press Alt (Option on the Mac) to apply another filter to your image and keep the filter/s you just applied in the Gallery in place. Figure 11.9 shows one of Krisha Martzall's images with three filters applied.

Additionally, you can stack the same filter on top of itself again and again, varying the settings to create some interesting effects. Click the eyeball icons next to the filter layers to toggle the visibility of any of the effects. Reordering the layers of filters in the Filter Gallery is as simple as clicking one and dragging it up or down the stack — just like restacking layers in the Layers palette. To remove any of the filters, simply highlight its layer and click the trash icon.

CROSS-REF With all these references to layers, if you're not clear on their use or how to manage them, check out Chapter 13.

Moving on, key filters are analyzed and demonstrated. Of course, as stated earlier, not all the filters in the whole Filters menu and submenus are discussed in detail, but most of them are and you'll find enough detail to enable you to use any filter successfully.

FIGURE 11.9

Apply as many filters as you need, and see them stack up here. Rearrange by dragging, and experiment with turning applied filters on and off by clicking the visibility eye.

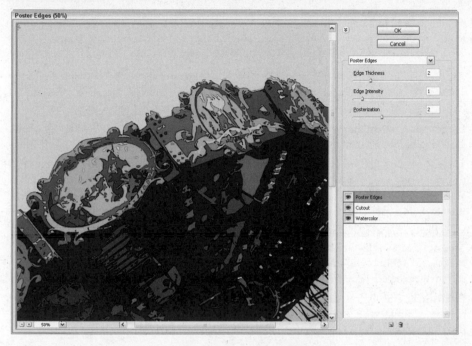

Playing with the Pixelate Filters

The Filter ⇨ Pixelate submenu features a handful of commands that rearrange your image into clumps of color:

- **Color Halftone:** This highly practical filter allows you to suggest the effect of a halftone pattern. You can't preview in the filter's dialog box, so if you don't like your results, just Undo and reopen the dialog box to tweak the settings and reapply. When applied to a CMYK image, Photoshop simulates a commercially reproduced color separation. Otherwise, the filter merely affects those channels that it can. For example, when working inside an RGB image, the Channel 4 value is ignored, because RGB images have no fourth channel. When working on a grayscale image or mask, the Screen Angles value for Channel 1 is the only angle that matters.

■ **Crystallize:** This filter organizes an image into irregularly shaped nuggets. You specify the size of the nuggets by typing a value from 3 to 300 pixels in the Cell Size option.

TIP   If your image is set to a very high resolution or is quite large in terms of print size, you'll want to back the zoom off a bit (using the plus and minus buttons) to see the overall effect on the image before clicking OK. This applies to just about all the filters that offer a preview in their dialog box — you want to zoom in to adjust the specific settings and their per-pixel impact on the image, but zoom out to see how it's going to affect things overall.

■ **Facet:** Facet fuses areas of similarly colored pixels to create a sort of hand-painted effect. There is no dialog box for this one, so if you don't see a big change, just repeat the filter a few times (Ctrl+F or ⌘+F, if you're on a Mac) until you can see an appreciable change.

■ **Fragment:** Another filter with no dialog box, this one shakes things up — literally. It creates the look of a photo taken by a camera sitting on a paint-shaker.

■ **Mezzotint:** This filter renders an image as a pattern of dots, lines, or strokes. See the section "Creating a mezzotint" for more information (it's coming right up after this section). You cannot adjust the zoom percentage for the Preview in the dialog box (or turn off the Preview), and your mouse has no panning ability in the dialog box. Just pick the Type of dots, lines, or strokes, and click OK to see what it does to your image.

■ **Mosaic:** The Mosaic filter blends pixels together into larger squares. You specify the height and width of the squares by typing a value in the Cell Size option box. Obviously, the smaller the cells are, the more recognizable your image details remain.

■ **Pointillize:** This filter is similar to Crystallize, except that it separates an image into disconnected nuggets set against the background color. As usual, you specify the size of the dots by changing the Cell Size value.

Creating a mezzotint

A *mezzotint* is a special halftone pattern that replaces dots with a random pattern of swirling lines and wormholes. Photoshop's Mezzotint filter is an attempt to emulate this effect. Although not entirely successful — true mezzotinting options can be properly implemented only as PostScript printing functions, not as filtering functions — they do lend themselves to some interesting interpretations.

The filter itself is straightforward. You choose Filter ➪ Pixelate ➪ Mezzotint, select an effect from the Type submenu, and press Enter or Return. A preview box enables you to see what each of the 10 Type options looks like. Figure 11.10 shows off four of the effects — dots, lines, and strokes — in fine, medium, and long varieties.

CROSS-REF   The Mezzotint line patterns are on par with the halftoning options offered when you select Mode ➪ Bitmap, as discussed in Chapter 4.

When applied to grayscale artwork, the Mezzotint filter always results in a black-and-white image. When applied to a color image, the filter automatically applies the selected effect independently to each of the color channels. Although all pixels in each channel are changed to either black or white, you can see a total of eight colors — black, red, green, blue, yellow, cyan, magenta, and white — in the RGB composite view.

FIGURE 11.10

This figure shows the results of applying the Mezzotint filter as Fine Dots (upper left), Coarse Dots (upper right), Medium Lines (lower left), and Long Strokes (lower right). In each case, the filter changes all pixels in each channel to black and white.

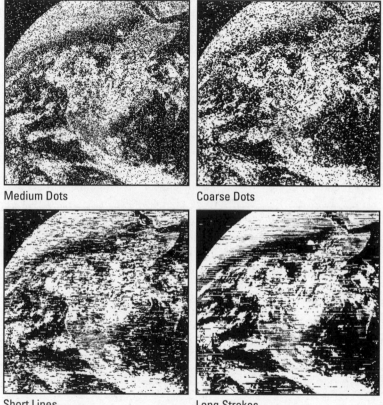

Medium Dots   Coarse Dots

Short Lines   Long Strokes

If the Mezzotint filter affects each channel independently, it follows that the color mode in which you work dramatically affects the performance of the filter. For example, if you apply Mezzotint in the Lab mode, you again whittle the colors down to eight, but a very different eight — black, cyan, magenta, green, red, two muddy blues, and a muddy rose. If you're looking for bright happy colors, don't apply Mezzotint in the Lab mode.

In CMYK, the filter produces roughly the same eight colors that you get in RGB — white, cyan, magenta, yellow, violet-blue, red, deep green, and black. However, the distribution of the colors is much different. The image appears lighter and more colorful than its RGB counterpart. This happens because the filter has lots of black to work with in the RGB mode but very little — just that in the black channel — in the CMYK mode.

Working with Edge-Enhancement Filters

The Filter ➪ Stylize submenu offers access to a triad of filters that enhance the edges in an image. The most popular of these undoubtedly is Emboss, which adds dimension to an image by making it look as if it were carved in relief. The other two — Find Edges and Trace Contour — may have fewer practical applications, but you'll find creative use for them, too.

Embossing an image

The Emboss filter works by searching for high-contrast edges (just like the Sharpen Edges and High Pass filters), highlighting the edges with black or white pixels, and then coloring the low-contrast portions with medium gray. When you choose Filter ➪ Stylize ➪ Emboss, Photoshop displays the Emboss dialog box shown in Figure 11.11.

FIGURE 11.11

The Emboss dialog box lets you control the depth of the filtered image (Height and Amount) and the Angle from which the image is lit.

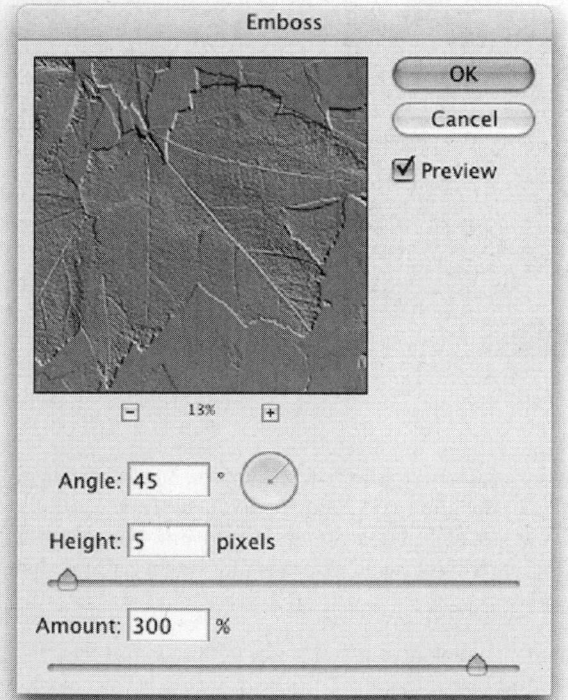

The dialog box offers three options:

■ **Angle:** The value in this option box determines the angle at which Photoshop lights the image in relief. For example, if you type a value of 90 degrees, you light the relief from the bottom straight upward. The white pixels therefore appear on the bottom sides of the edges, and the black pixels appear on the top sides. Figure 11.12 shows four reliefs lit from different angles and with different Height settings.

FIGURE 11.12

This relief demonstrates the effects of different Height and Angle settings. The Angles increment in multiples of 45 degrees — imagine a light source in the center, radiating out toward the four examples.

Angle: 135°, Height: 1 pixel

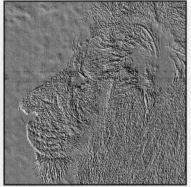
Angle: 45°, Height: 2 pixels

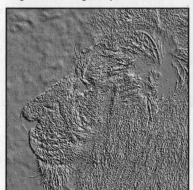
Angle: –135°, Height: 3 pixels

Angle: –45°, Height: 4 pixels

- **Height:** The Emboss filter accomplishes its highlighting effect by displacing one copy of an image relative to another. Using the Height option, you specify the distance between the copies, which can vary from 1 to 100 pixels. Lower values produce crisper effects, as demonstrated in Figure 11.12. Values above 4 work best if you also use a high Amount value. Together, the Height and Amount values determine the depth of the image in relief.

> **TIP** The Height value is analogous to the Radius value in the Unsharp Mask dialog box. You should therefore set the value according to the resolution of your image — 1 for 150 ppi, 2 for 300 ppi, and so on.

- **Amount:** Type a value between 1 and 500 percent to determine the amount of black and white assigned to pixels along the edges. Values of 50 percent and lower produce almost entirely gray images. Higher values produce sharper edges, as if the relief were carved more deeply.

> **TIP** To create a color-relief effect, apply the Emboss filter and then select the Luminosity option in the Fade dialog box. This retains the colors from the original image while applying the lightness and darkness of the pixels from the filtered selection. The effect looks something like an inked lithographic plate, with steel grays and vivid colors mixing together.

> **TIP** If you're not sure how you might use the Emboss filter (other than to create the illusion of a carving), think of Emboss as an extension of the High Pass filter. When considered this way, it takes on new meaning. You can use it to edit selection outlines in the Quick Mask mode, just as you might use the High Pass filter. You also can use it to draw out detail in an image.

Tracing around edges

Photoshop provides three filters that trace around pixels in your image and accentuate the edges. All three filters live in the Filter ⇨ Stylize submenu:

- **Find Edges:** This filter detects edges similarly to High Pass. Low-contrast areas become white, medium-contrast edges become gray, and high-contrast edges become black, as in the upper-right example in Figure 11.13. Hard edges become thin lines; soft edges become fat ones. The result is a thick, organic outline that you can overlay on an image to give it a waxy appearance. The original, unfiltered image appears in the inset in the upper-left corner of the figure.

- **Glowing Edges:** This Gallery Effects filter is a variation on Find Edges, with two important differences. Glowing Edges produces an inverted effect, changing low-contrast areas to black and edges to white, as shown in the upper-right and lower-left images in Figure 11.13. This filter also enables you to adjust the width, brightness, and smoothness of the traced edges by adjusting the Edge Width and Edge Brightness. The Smoothness setting reduces noise and heightens the intensity of the outline (the bottom-left example in Figure 11.13).

>  **TIP** If you want black lines against a white background, change the image to Grayscale mode, and press Ctrl+I (⌘+I on the Mac) to invert the image.

FIGURE 11.13

Find Edges and Glowing Edges have creative uses in their own right and also can be used to bring out the edges in a photo. The Trace Contour filter maps lines between light and dark pixels.

Original   Find Edges

Glowing Edges   Trace Edges

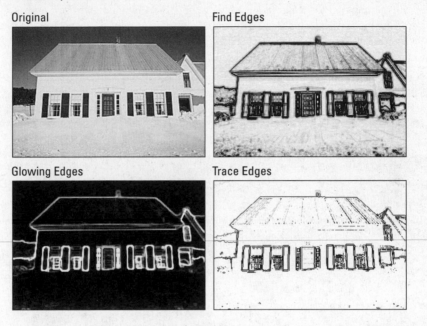

- **Trace Contour:** Illustrated in Figure 11.13, this filter traces a series of single-pixel lines along the border between light and dark pixels. Choosing the filter displays a dialog box containing two settings: Level and an Edge setting with two options, Upper and Lower. The Level value indicates the lightness value above which pixels are considered to be light and below which they are dark. For example, if you type 128 (medium gray), Trace Contour draws a line at every spot where an area of color lighter than medium gray meets an area of color darker than medium gray. The Upper and Lower options tell the filter where to position the line — inside the lighter color's territory (Upper) or inside the space occupied by the darker color (Lower).

Like Mezzotint, Trace Contour applies itself to each color channel independently and renders each channel as a 1-bit image. A collection of black lines surrounds the areas of color in each channel. The RGB, Lab, or CMYK composite view shows these lines in the colors associated with the channels. When you work in RGB, a cyan line indicates a black line in the Red channel (no red plus full-intensity green and blue becomes cyan). A yellow line indicates a black line in the Blue channel, and so on. You get a single black line when working in the Grayscale mode.

Creating a metallic coating

The edge-tracing filters are especially fun to use in combination with Edit ➪ Fade. If you want the look of a metal coating on your image, choose Filter ➪ Sketch ➪ Chrome, which turns your image (or a selection therein) to a melted pool of metallic slime. Chrome is best used with color images, and you may find that following it up with the Fade command gives you more subtle results that don't totally rob your image of any detail. Figure 11.14 shows Chrome applied normally (left) and with Fade at 75 percent Opacity used afterward (right).

FIGURE 11.14

Chrome can be very cool (left), but you may want to tone down its effects a bit with the Fade command (right). Here, the fine detail of the bird is retained, while on the left, the full chrome effect is distracting from the subject. The inset shows the original image.

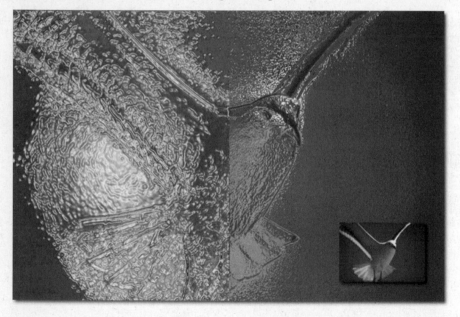

TIP   There's no end to the ways you can tweak one filter by combining it with another filter (or two) and various image adjustments. For example, while on the topic of metallic coatings and the gleaming highlights they promise, could there be another way to achieve that look without the problems that the Chrome filter can create? Absolutely — and the Find Edges filter can help. First, copy your image to a separate layer by pressing Ctrl+J (⌘+J on the Mac). Then apply the Gaussian Blur filter. A Radius value between 1.0 and 4.0 produces the best results, depending on how liquid you want the edges to look. Next, apply the Find Edges filter. If the resulting image is too light, you may want to darken it using Image ➪ Adjustments ➪ Levels (raise the first Input Levels value to 100 or so, as explained in Chapter 18).

Distortion Filters

For the most part, commands in the Distort submenu are related by the fact that they move colors in an image to achieve unusual stretching, swirling, and vibrating effects. They're rather like the transformation commands in the Edit menu in that they perform their magic by relocating and interpolating colors rather than by altering brightness and color values.

The distinction, of course, is that whereas the transformation commands let you scale and distort images by manipulating four control points, the Distort filters provide the equivalent of hundreds of control points, all of which you can use to affect different portions of an image. In some cases, you're projecting an image into a fun-house mirror; other times, it's a reflective pool. You can fan images, wiggle them, and change them in ways that have no correlation to real life, as illustrated in Figure 11.15.

FIGURE 11.15

This is your Daddy (left); this is your Daddy on Distortion filters (right) — six of them, in fact. Liquify was also used for the effects at the bottom of the image.

Regular Joe...?   ...or Tom Bombadil?

Distortion filters are powerful tools. Although they are easy to apply, they are extremely difficult to use well. Here are some rules to keep in mind:

- **Practice makes perfect:** Distortion filters are like complex vocabulary words. You don't want to use them without practicing a little first. Experiment with a distortion filter several times before trying to use it in a real project. You may even want to write down the steps you take so that you can remember how you created an effect.

- **Keep your eye on the clock:** Distortion filters are enormous time-wasters. Unless you know exactly how you want to proceed, you may want to avoid using them when time is short. The last thing you need when you're working under the gun is to get trapped trying to pull off a weird effect.

- **Apply selectively:** The effects of distortion filters are too severe to inflict all at once. You can achieve marvelous, subtle effects, however, by distorting feathered and layered selections. Although one would hardly call the image in Figure 11.15 subtle, no single effect was applied to the entire image.

- **Combine creatively:** Don't expect a single distortion to achieve the desired effect. If one application isn't enough, apply the filter again. Experiment with combining different distortions.

CAUTION   Distortion filters interpolate between pixels to create their fantastic effects. This means the quality of your filtered images depends on the setting of the Image Interpolation option in the General Preferences dialog box. If a filter produces jagged effects, the Nearest Neighbor option is probably selected. Try selecting the Bicubic or Bilinear option instead.

The fun-house mirror

Just about everyone has stood in front of a fun-house mirror and watched his or her face and/or body be squeezed, stretched, and otherwise twisted into a variety of shapes. Where it gets really weird is where your facial features are shrunken, as though your face was shrinking from the center, and where your face seems to expand from the center — making for a big nose and a receding brow-bone and chin. It's probably fun to play in front of such a mirror for the same reason kids dress up like scary characters for Halloween — when something's temporary and unreal, even something scary can be fun. In Figure 11.16, you'll see a photo turned into a fun-house mirror reflection, using the Pinch and Spherize filters to scrunch, stretch, and wrap what started out as a perfectly normal-looking face.

NOTE   A positive Amount value in the Pinch dialog box produces an effect similar to a negative value in the Spherize dialog box. There is a slight difference between the spatial curvature of the 3-D calculations: Pinch pokes the image inward or outward using a rounded cone — we're talking bell-shaped, much like a Gaussian model. Spherize wraps the image on the outside or inside of a true sphere. As a result, the two filters yield subtly different results. Pinch produces a soft transition around the perimeter of a selection; Spherize produces an abrupt transition. If this doesn't quite make sense to you, just play with one, try out the same effect with the other, and see which you like better.

FIGURE 11.16

Using Pinch and Spherize, you can create some amusing results. Notice how negative values can make Pinch spherize, and Spherize pinch?

Pinch, Amount: 50%

Spherize, Amount: 50%

Spherize, Amount: –50%

Pinch, Amount: –50%

Another difference between the two filters is that Spherize provides the additional options of enabling you to wrap an image on the inside or outside of a horizontal or vertical cylinder, as shown in the last sample in Figure 11.16, where Vertical Only was used. To try out these effects, select the Horizontal Only or Vertical Only options from the Mode pop-up menu at the bottom of the Spherize dialog box.

> **TIP**   Both filters can affect only elliptical regions. If a selection outline is not elliptical, Photoshop applies the filter to the largest ellipse that fits inside the selection. As a result, the filter may leave behind a noticeable elliptical boundary between the affected and unaffected portions of the selection. To avoid this effect, select the region you want to edit with the Elliptical Marquee tool and then feather the selection before filtering it. This softens the effect of the filter and provides a more gradual transition (even more so than Pinch already affords).

One of the more remarkable properties of the Pinch filter is that it lets you turn any image into a conical gradation. First, you may want to blur the image to eliminate any harsh edges between color transitions. Then apply the Pinch filter at full strength (100 percent). Reapply the filter several more times. Each time you press Ctrl+F (⌘+F on the Mac), the center portion of the image recedes farther and farther into the distance.

Twirling spirals

The Twirl filter rotates the center of a selection while leaving the sides fixed in place. The result is a spiral of colors that looks for all the world as if you poured the image into a blender set to a very slow speed.

When you choose Filter ➪ Distort ➪ Twirl, you can type a positive value from 1 to 999 degrees to spiral the image in a clockwise direction. Type a negative value to spiral the image in a counterclockwise direction. Figure 11.17 shows a 30-degree spiral (top left) and a 100-degree spiral (top right) in both positive and negative directions. As you are probably already aware, 360 degrees make a full circle, so the maximum 999-degree value equates to a spiral that circles around almost three times, as shown in the bottom example in Figure 11.17.

> **TIP**   The Twirl filter produces smoother effects when you use lower Angle values. Therefore, you're better off applying a 100-degree spiral 10 times rather than applying a 999-degree spiral once.

Zigging and zagging

When you hear ZigZag filter, you may picture lightening bolts or other back-and-forth patterns. When it comes to a Photoshop filter, however, you know it won't be that simple. The ZigZag filter does arrange colors into zigzag patterns, but it does so in a radial fashion, meaning that the zigzags emanate from the center of the image like spokes in a wheel. The result is a series of concentric ripples, as shown in Figure 11.18 (see original image in the center inset). If you want parallel zigzags, check out the Ripple and Wave filters, described in the next section. (The ZigZag filter creates ripples and the Ripple filter creates zigzags — don't ask.)

FIGURE 11.17

You can adjust the direction of the Twirl filter and also increase its intensity.

Twirl, Amount: 30°

Twirl, Amount: 100°

Twirl, Amount: –30°

Twirl, Amount: –100°

When you choose Filter ➪ Distort ➪ ZigZag, Photoshop displays a dialog box offering the following options:

- **Amount:** Type an amount between negative 99 and positive 100 in whole-number increments to specify the depth of the ripples. If you type a negative value, the ripples descend below the surface. If you type a positive value, the ripples protrude upward.

■ **Ridges:** This option box controls the number of ripples in the selected area and accepts any value from 0 to 20.

FIGURE 11.18

The ZigZag filter applied with Around Center, Amount -50, Ridges 5 (upper left), Out from Center, Amount 75, Ridges 10 (upper right), and Pond Ripples, Amount -50, Ridges 5 (lower left) Styles applied. The lower-right quadrant shows the Pond Ripples at the highest Amount (100) and Ridges (20) settings.

Around Center, Amount: –50, Ridges: 5   Out from Center, Amount: 75, Ridges: 10

Pond Ripples, Amount: –50, Ridges: 5   Pond Ripples, Amount: 100, Ridges: 20

- **Style:** The options in this pop-up menu determine how Photoshop moves pixels with respect to the center of the image or selection.

  - **Around Center:** Select this option to rotate pixels in alternating directions around the center without moving them outward. This is the only option that produces a true zigzag effect.

  - **Out From Center:** When you select this option, Photoshop moves pixels outward in rhythmic bursts according to the value in the Ridges option box.

  - **Pond Ripples:** This option is really a cross between the previous two. It moves pixels outward and rotates them around the center of the selection to create circular patterns.

Creating parallel ripples and waves

Photoshop provides four means to distort an image in parallel waves, as if the image were lying on the bottom of a shimmering or undulating pool. Of the four, the ripple filters — which include Ripple, Ocean Ripple, and Glass — are only moderately sophisticated, but they're also relatively easy to apply. The fourth filter, Wave, affords you greater control, but its options are among the most complex Photoshop has to offer.

The Ripple filter

To use the Ripple filter, choose Filter ➪ Distort ➪ Ripple. Photoshop displays the Ripple dialog box, giving you these options:

- **Amount:** Type an amount between negative 998 and positive 999 in whole-number increments to specify the width of the ripples from side to side. Negative and positive values change the direction of the ripples, but visually speaking, they produce identical effects. The ripples are measured as a ratio of the Size value and the dimensions of the selection — all of which translates to, "Experiment and see what happens." You can count on getting ragged effects from any value over 300, as illustrated in Figure 11.19.

- **Size:** Select one of the three options in the Size pop-up menu to change the length of the ripples. The Small option results in the shortest ripples and therefore the most ripples. Combining the Small option with a relatively high Amount value results in a textured-glass effect. The Large option results in the longest and fewest ripples. Figure 11.20 shows an example of each Size option.

TIP You can create a blistered effect by overlaying a negative ripple onto a positive ripple. Try this: First, copy the selection. Then apply the Ripple filter with a positive Amount value — say, 300. Next, paste the copied selection and apply the Ripple filter at the opposite Amount value, in this case, –300. Press 5 to change the Opacity value to 50 percent. The result is a series of diametrically opposed ripples that cross each other to create teardrop blisters.

FIGURE 11.19

This figure shows the effects of three different (increasing) Ripple filter Amount values. From the left, the Amount is set to 100 percent, then 300 percent in the middle, and finally 999 percent at the right.

Amount: 100%, Size: Medium   Amount: 300%, Size: Medium   Amount: 999%, Size: Medium

FIGURE 11.20

Here are the effects of the three different Ripple filter Size settings — Small (left), Medium (middle), and Large (right). In all three sections, an Amount of 300 percent was used.

Amount: 100%, Size: Small   Amount: 100%, Size: Medium   Amount: 100%, Size: Large

Ocean Ripple and Glass

Both of these filters emulate the effect of looking at an image through textured glass. These two distorters so closely resemble each other that they would be better merged into one. The Ocean Ripple filter's two parameters, Ripple Size and Ripple Magnitude, are illustrated in Figure 11.21. Compare the examples horizontally to observe an increase in Ripple Size values from 5 to the maximum of 15; compare vertically to observe an increase in Ripple Magnitude from 5 to the maximum of 20. As you can see, you can vary the Ripple Size value with impunity. But raise the Ripple Magnitude value, and you're looking through sculpted glass.

FIGURE 11.21

Raising the Ocean Ripple Size value spreads out the effect; raising the Ocean Ripple Magnitude adds more depth and contrast to the ripples.

Size: 5, Magnitude: 5   Size: 10, Magnitude: 5   Size: 15, Magnitude: 5

Size: 5, Magnitude: 10   Size: 10, Magnitude: 10   Size: 15, Magnitude: 10

 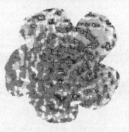 

Size: 5, Magnitude: 20   Size: 10, Magnitude: 20   Size: 15, Magnitude: 20

The principal difference between Glass and Ocean Ripple is that Ocean Ripple uses one preset distortion texture, and Glass gives you four to choose from, plus it lets you load your own (similar to Texturizer). You can invert the texture — high becomes low, low becomes high — and also scale it to change its size relative to the layer you're distorting. Figure 11.22 uses the Tiny Lens texture throughout and demonstrates how different the effect can be depending on the Distortion and Smoothness settings. Compare the examples in the figure horizontally for proof that Distortion is perhaps the best-named parameter in all of Photoshop. Smoothness, on the other hand, is sort of like an "anti-Ripple Magnitude" setting. High Smoothness settings in Glass are analogous to low Ripple Magnitude settings in Ocean Ripple.

FIGURE 11.22

Need to keep that nosy neighbor from peeking in the bathroom window? Select Glass windows with high Distortion, and low Smoothness.

Distortion: 3, Smoothness: 5   Distortion: 10, Smoothness: 5   Distortion: 20, Smoothness: 5

Distortion: 3, Smoothness: 12   Distortion: 10, Smoothness: 12   Distortion: 20, Smoothness: 12

The Wave filter

To go from baby ripples to serious water damage, choose Filter ⇨ Distort ⇨ Wave. This displays the Wave dialog box shown in Figure 11.23, which offers the following options:

The Wave dialog box lets you decide how high the tide will rise as it undulates over your image.

- **Number of Generators:** Think of Generators as rocks tossed into still water. The more rocks you throw (one at a time), the more pools of outward-flowing concentric waves you get. If the rocks are close to each other, the waves intersect and flow through and bounce off one another. As shown in Figure 11.24, the more rocks you throw in, the more extreme and complex the results. If you type a very high value in this field, however, be prepared to wait a few years for the preview to update. If you can't wait, press Esc, which turns off the preview until the next time you type a value in the dialog box.

- **Wavelength** and **Amplitude:** The Wave filter produces random results by varying the number and length of waves (Wavelength) as well as the height of the waves (Amplitude) between minimum and maximum values, which can range from 1 to 999. (The Wavelength and Amplitude options, therefore, correspond in theory to the Size and Amount options in the Ripple dialog box.) Figure 11.25 demonstrates an increase in Wavelength and Amplitude.

FIGURE 11.24

The only difference between the examples in this figure is in the Number of Generators. Adding generators increases random action by creating more intersecting waveforms.

One Generator

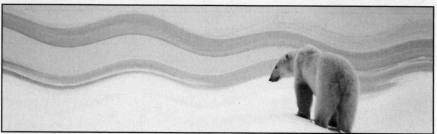

5 Generators

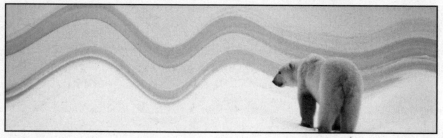

10 Generators

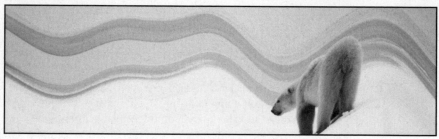

■ **Scale:** You can scale the effects of the Wave filter between 1 and 100 percent horizontally and vertically. Increasing Horizontal Scale makes the waves go back and forth as well as up and down.

■ **Type:** You can select from three kinds of waves. The Sine option produces standard sine waves that rise and fall smoothly in curves, just like real waves. The Triangle option creates zigzags that rise and fall in straight lines, like the edge of a piece of fabric cut with pinking shears. The Square option has nothing to do with waves at all, but rather organizes an image into a series of rectangular groupings, reminiscent of Cubism. You might think of this option as an extension of the Mosaic filter. All examples in Figure 11.26 utilize a Number of Generators setting of 1 and demonstrate the Sine, Triangle, and Square settings.

FIGURE 11.25

With all other parameters being equal (Generators: 1, Type: Sine, Horizontal Scale: 1%, and Vertical Scale 100%) — increasing your Wavelength value results in a larger distance between your peaks, while increased Amplitude make your peaks higher.

Max. Wavelength: 120, Max. Amplitude: 35

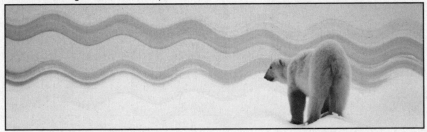

Max. Wavelength: 350, Max. Amplitude: 35

Max. Wavelength: 120, Max. Amplitude: 115

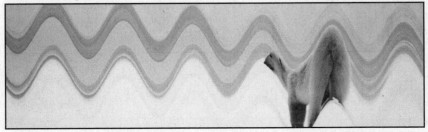

Max. Wavelength: 350, Max. Amplitude: 115

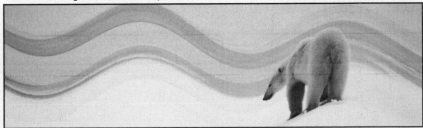

FIGURE 11.26

Here you see the effects of the Triangle and Square wave types. The top two samples use high Wavelength and low Amplitude values. The bottom two samples use the reverse.

Type: Triangle, Max. Wavelength: 120, Max. Amplitude: 35

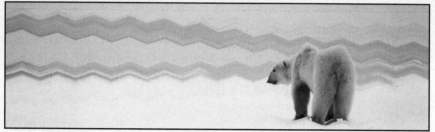

Type: Square, Max. Wavelength: 120, Max. Amplitude: 35

Type: Triangle, Max. Wavelength: 20, Max. Amplitude: 70

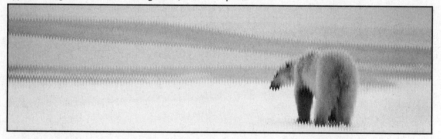

Type: Square, Max. Wavelength: 20, Max. Amplitude: 70

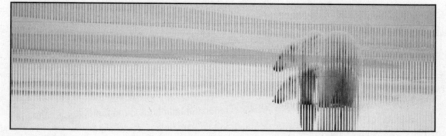

- **Randomize:** The Wave filter is random by nature. If you don't like the effect you see in the preview box, click Randomize (as illustrated in the bottom example in Figure 11.26) to stir things up a bit. You can keep clicking the button until you get an effect you like.

- **Undefined Areas:** The Wave filter distorts a selection to the extent that gaps may appear around the edges. You can fill those gaps by repeating pixels along the edge of the selection, as in the figures, or by wrapping pixels from the left side of the selection onto the right side and pixels from the top edge of the selection onto the bottom.

Distorting an image along a curve

The Distort command (Edit ⇨ Transform ⇨ Distort), which isn't discussed elsewhere in this book, creates four corner handles around an image. You click and drag each corner handle to distort the selected image in that direction. Unfortunately, you can't add other points around the edges to create additional distortions, which can be frustrating if you're trying to achieve a specific effect. If you can't achieve a certain kind of distortion using Edit ⇨ Free Transform, the Shear filter may be your answer.

Shear distorts an image or a selection along a path. When you choose Filter ⇨ Distort ⇨ Shear, you get the dialog box shown in Figure 11.27. Initially, a single line that has two points at either end appears in the grid at the top of the box. When you click and drag the points, you slant the image in the preview. This, plus the fact that the filter is named Shear leads many users to dismiss the filter as nothing more than a slanting tool. But in truth, it's more versatile than that.

FIGURE 11.27

Click the grid line in the left corner of the Shear dialog box to add points to the line. Click and drag these points to distort the image along the curve.

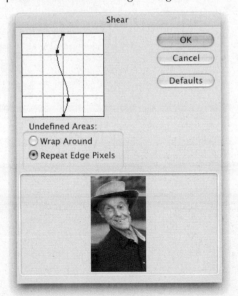

You can add points to the grid line simply by clicking it. A point springs up every time you click an empty space in the line. Drag the point to change the curvature of the line, and distort the image along the new curve. To delete a point, click and drag it off the left or right side of the grid. To delete all added points and return the line to its original vertical orientation, click Defaults.

The Undefined Areas options work just as they do in the Wave dialog box (described in the preceding section). You can either fill the gaps on one side of the image with pixels shoved off the opposite side by selecting the Wrap Around option or repeat pixels along the edge of the selection by selecting the Repeat Edge Pixels option.

TIP   Although Shear was conceived to create horizontal distortions, you may find that you need to create a vertically based distortion instead. If you can't change the filter, why not change the image? Simply rotating the image on its side (Image ⇨ Rotate Canvas ⇨ 90 degrees CW or CCW) allows you to give the desired slant to the image, as shown in Figure 11.28.

FIGURE 11.28

Don't like the effect that traditional shearing gives you? Turn it on its ear!

A standard horizontal shear   Rotate 90° CCW, Shear, Rotate 90° CW

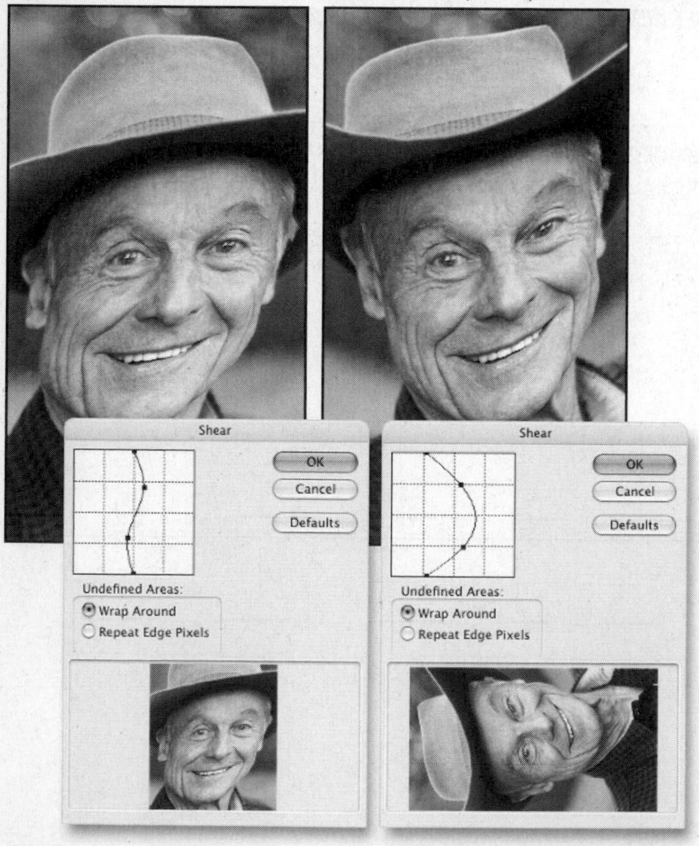

Changing to Polar Coordinates

The Polar Coordinates filter is another one of those gems that lots of people shy away from because it doesn't make much sense at first glance. When you choose Filter ⇨ Distort ⇨ Polar Coordinates, Photoshop presents a dialog box with two radio buttons, as shown in Figure 11.29. You can map an image from rectangular to polar coordinates or from polar to rectangular coordinates.

FIGURE 11.29

We've abused this guy in this chapter! Here he is in the Polar Coordinates dialog box, set to Rectangular to Polar.

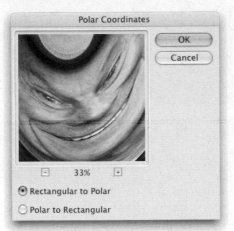

When you convert the image to Polar Coordinates (by selecting the Rectangular to Polar option in the Polar Coordinates dialog box), you look down on it from an extreme aerial view. This means that the entire length of the image becomes a single dot in the exact center of the polar projection. If you select the Polar to Rectangular option, the Polar Coordinates filter produces the opposite effect — instead of the entire image becoming a dot in the center of the project, the image flows from a polar center outward, in a rectangular shape. Figure 11.30 gives you a little food for thought.

TIP The Polar Coordinates filter is a great way to edit gradations. After drawing a linear gradation with the Gradient tool (as discussed in Chapter 6), try applying Filter ⇨ Distort ⇨ Polar Coordinates with the Polar to Rectangular option selected. (Rectangular to Polar just turns it into a radial gradation, sometimes with undesirable results.) You get a redrawn gradation with highlights at the bottom of the selection. Press Ctrl+F (⌘+F on the Mac) to reapply the filter to achieve another effect. You can keep repeating this technique until jagged edges start to appear. Then press Ctrl+Z (⌘+Z on the Mac) to go back to the last smooth effect.

FIGURE 11.30

Here you see the effects of converting some images from polar to rectangular coordinates. Go, Fishboy!

From 10 pinches and 7 twirls...

we get a series of waves.

A smiling face...

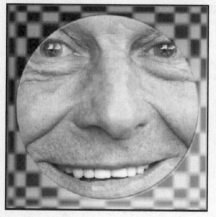

becomes the fish-faced boy.

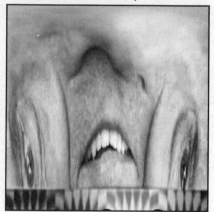

Working with Lens Correction

The Lens Correction filter opens a very large dialog box, shown in Figure 11.31. Your image appears in the Preview area, with a grid as an overlay. You can turn the Preview and the Grid off (hide them) using the check boxes just down and to the right of the preview — but you'd be better off keeping them on, at least while you're tinkering with the settings on the right side of the dialog box.

The tools on the left side of the dialog box allow you to use your mouse to adjust the Lens Correction settings — from top to bottom, the Remove Distortion tool, Straighten tool, Move Grid tool, Hand tool, and Zoom tool either correspond with a slider on the right or help you control the Preview area. For example, if you prefer a more hands-on approach to using this filter, use the Remove Distortion tool to drag on the Preview of the image instead of dragging the Remove Distortion slider. You can adjust the Angle setting by dragging to draw a line on the Preview with the Straighten tool.

FIGURE 11.31

The Lens Correction filter dialog box allows you to correct lens relative flaws in your images or introduce them for dramatic effect.

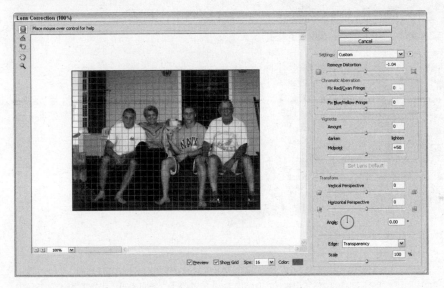

TIP If you can't see the grid (maybe it's the same color as the image — it's set to a medium gray by default), click the Color swatch and choose a color that stands out against your image.

Speaking of settings, your choices are as follows:

- **Remove Distortion:** This adjusts the default lens distortion to create a concave lens (drag to the right) or a convex lens (drag to the left). This feature exists to fill two functions: remove that fish-eye lens look or introduce it. Figure 11.32 shows a classic example of this problem — a shot taken with a Web cam.

FIGURE 11.32

Set the Remove Distortion level to correct concave or convex distortions.

- **Chromatic Aberration:** Chromatic aberration, or *color fringing* (shown in Figure 11.33), is the result of your lens focusing the various wavelengths of light onto different points on the camera's focal plane. This filter provides a Fix Red/Cyan Fringe and a Fix Blue/Yellow Fringe slider to correct for whichever type of color fringing your images is suffering from.

- **Vignette Amount:** A vignette is typically a distinct darkening around the edges of an image. This was seen often in vintage portraits, creating a dark, cloudy frame around the main subject. This option allows you to darken or lighten the edges of the image by dragging the slider. If you leave the slider in the middle, no vignette effect is added by the filter. Of course, if your image already has an unwanted vignette effect, like that seen in Figure 11.34, you can counter it by dragging the slider toward the opposite of your problem — most likely toward Lighten to counteract a traditional vignette.

FIGURE 11.33

Granted, trying to demonstrate a color-related issue with a grayscale image isn't easy, but we think you get the idea here. This mountaintop is suffering from some nasty color fringing (top), which is virtually eliminated with the help of the Chromatic Aberration sliders (bottom).

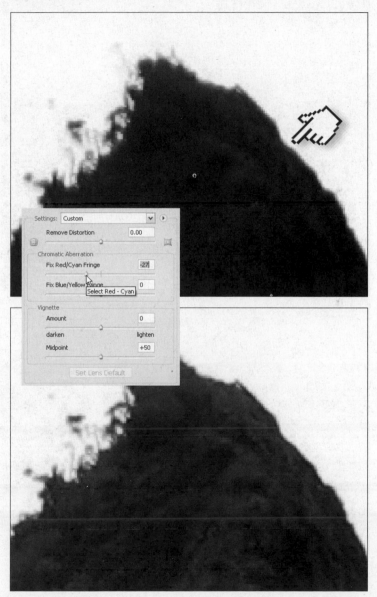

FIGURE 11.34

This image by Terri Shadle has a bit of darkened vignetting in the corners. But, with a little fiddling, we think we've got it under control.

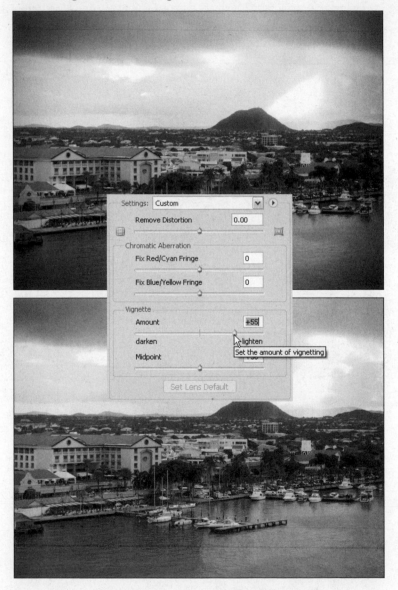

- **Vignette Midpoint:** Drag this slider to change the center of the vignette effect's origin.

- **Transform Vertical Perspective:** Drag this slider to tilt the image away from you at the top (drag to the right) or away from you at the bottom (drag to the left).

- **Transform Horizontal Perspective:** Drag this slider to swing the image like a door — a door opening away from you to the left by dragging the slider to the right, or a door swinging away from you to the right by dragging the slider to the left.

- **Transform Angle:** Rotate the image with this option, either by dragging within the circle, or by entering an angle of rotation into the box. Figure 11.35 shows an image in need of tinkering in both the Perspective and the Angle departments.

FIGURE 11.35

As you can see, no planes in this image were adhering to right angles. But, a Horizontal Perspective slider here and a little English on the Angle control and we're off to the right-angled races.

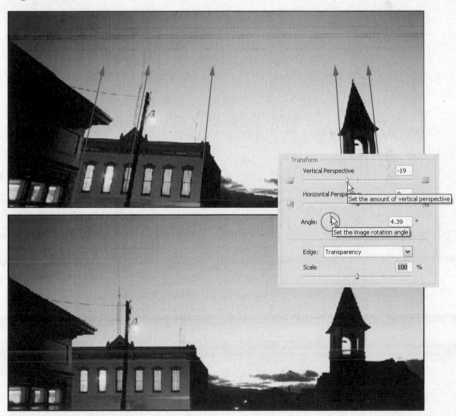

■ **Transform Edge:** Choose from Edge Extension, which (surprise) extends the ends of the image to the edges of the grid, Transparency (the default), which leaves the areas outside of the image yet within the grid transparent, and Background Color, which fills in around the image with the current background color. This option only becomes an issue when the lens has created space between the grid's edges and your image — through rotation, and perspective changes, or by dragging on the grid with your mouse to apply a lens effect to the image.

■ **Transform Scale:** This option simply sizes the image within the grid. Drag to the right to increase its size, or drag to the left to decrease it. If you're correcting a bulging image, increase the Scale to a level close to 100 plus the number shown in the Remove Distortion option — typically, this resolves any transparency or obvious expansion (if you have Edge Extension turned on for the Edge option).

Distorting with the Liquify command

The final essential distortion function isn't located under the Filter ➪ Distort submenu. In fact, in many respects, it's not a filter at all. The Liquify command is more of a separate distortion utility that just happens to run in Photoshop. It enables you to perform any number of distortions: You can warp, shift, twirl, expand, contract, and even copy pixels. It grants you multiple undos and redos before you apply the final effect. And unlike other distortion filters, which apply a uniform effect across a layer or selection, Liquify lets you modify pixels by pushing them around with a brush. Liquify is *not* applicable to Smart Objects; in fact, after you've converted a layer to a Smart Object, the Liquify command is dimmed. Actually, it'd be a little bit much to ask of Photoshop to make the effects of the Liquify dialog box something you could quickly turn off and on or re-order amongst other filters applied to the same layer.

Liquify is a distortion filter that also doubles as a powerful retouching tool. Consider the images in Figure 11.36. Thanks to the Liquify command, a calm and serene face was contorted into a mix of angered agitation — yet you could use it in subtler ways to widen eyes, soften lips, reduce a double chin, or raise cheekbones. Liquify could turn us all into supermodels.

NOTE English teachers and ex-spelling-bee champions may notice the habitual misspelling of the word "liquefy" throughout this and the following pages. Rather than referring to the strictly accurate "Liquefy command," which would not match your screen, or the condescending "Liquify [sic] command," which gets old fast, we have just stuck with Adobe's inexplicable spelling.

Liquify basics

To enter the world of Liquify, choose the Liquify command from the Filter menu or press the keyboard shortcut Ctrl+Shift+X (⌘+Shift+X on the Mac). Photoshop displays the immense Liquify image window shown in Figure 11.37, which tops even the Extract window (see Chapter 9) in its wealth of tools and options.

FIGURE 11.36

From content to contorted, all with the Liquify command's exciting set of tools

The miniature toolbox on the left side of the window contains seven tools for distorting your image. You drag or click with the tools as explained in the next section. (You can even select tools from the keyboard, as indicated by keys in parentheses.) But before you begin, here are a few basic facts:

- All tools respond to the Brush Size setting on the right side of the window. Press the right and left bracket keys ([and]) to raise and lower the brush size by 2 pixels. This is a bit of a departure from Photoshop's standard painting tools, where pressing [or] routinely changes the brush size by 10 pixels or more. To change the brush size in the Liquify window more rapidly, press and hold [or]. Throughout, your cursor reflects the approximate brush size. Note, however, that most distortions affect the pixels at the center of the cursor more quickly than those on the perimeter.

- The Brush Density setting determines how much feathering the edges of your cursor have while you are creating your distortions. A smaller Brush Density setting means that effects are more localized to the center of the brush.

- The Brush Pressure option controls the impact of the tools as you drag across your image; higher values produce more pronounced effects. If you work with a pressure-sensitive tablet, select the Stylus Pressure option to make Photoshop adjust the tool pressure based on the amount of pressure you put on the pen stylus.

- Available when you use the reconstruct, Twirl clockwise, Pucker, Bloat, and Turbulence tools, the Brush Rate option controls the strength of these tools when you click on a particular area but keep the cursor still. The higher the Brush Rate setting, the faster distortions are applied to the area.

FIGURE 11.37

Choose Filter ➪ Liquify to shove pixels around in your image by dragging them with a brush.

- You can use the standard shortcuts Ctrl+plus to zoom in and Ctrl+minus to zoom out (⌘+plus and minus on the Mac). Use the scroll bars to reposition the image, or press the spacebar to get the Hand tool and drag the image inside the window. The Liquify window also provides Zoom (Z) and Hand (H) tools for your navigation pleasure.

- If you select a portion of your image before choosing Filter ➪ Liquify, by default any deselected areas are considered *frozen*, which just means that they're unaffected by the distortion tools. You can freeze and then *thaw* — make available for editing — portions of the image as explained in the section "Freezing and thawing pixels." You can even create partially frozen or thawed areas, which further limits the impact of the distortion tools. With the release of Photoshop CS, Adobe introduced a number of new ways to control which pixels are frozen and which are thawed. In addition to a selection, you can freeze and thaw pixels based on a combination of the transparency information in the image and even through a layer mask.

You Really Must Mesh

As with other Save buttons found throughout Photoshop's myriad dialog boxes, the Save Mesh button may strike you as the kind of option that could prove useful every once in a while. Be that as it may, you should use it *every time you use the Liquify command*. Yes, *every time*. The last thing you should do, right before you click OK, is click Save Mesh. Why? Because Photoshop does not automatically keep track of your previous Liquify settings. So if you spend 15 minutes or so working in the Liquify window, click OK, and then decide that the distortion doesn't work exactly as you had hoped, you're left with two unpleasant options: Choose Liquify and try to tweak the image further, which can result in incremental damage to the detail, or undo the previous operation and start over. But if you saved the mesh, you always have that last distortion to come back to. And the beauty is, a mesh is purely mathematical until it's applied. So you can use one mesh as a jumping-off point for another without doing incremental damage. Pixels get involved only after you click OK. So don't forget to save your mesh. Got that?

- By default, frozen regions are covered with a red translucent coating, just like masked areas in the Quick Mask mode. You can change the appearance of the overlay by selecting a new color from the Mask Color pop-up menu at the bottom of the Liquify window. If you don't want to see the coating at all, deselect the Show Mask option.

- If your image contains layers, you see only the current layer against a transparent checker-board background when you enter the Liquify window. To see other layers, select the Show Backdrop option in the bottom-right corner of the window. You can view all layers or select a specific layer from the nearby pop-up menu. The Opacity option controls how well you can see the other layers.

- Use the Mode pop-up menu in the Show Backdrop settings to specify exactly how the layer you're currently distorting interacts with the other layers in the image. Regardless of what you see, Photoshop lets you edit only the active layer.

- Select the Show Mesh option to display gridlines on top of the image. You can use the gridlines as a guide if you want to apply very precise distortions. You can even apply your distortions while viewing only the grid by deselecting the Show Image option. Set the grid size and color by selecting options from the Mesh Size and Mesh Color pop-up menus.

- You can save a distortion for later use by clicking Save Mesh. To use the mesh on a Mac or PC, the file name needs to end with the *.msh* extension. Click Load Mesh to load a distortion stored on disk. Note that Photoshop is smart enough to scale the mesh to fit the current image, so a mesh specifically designed for one image may turn out to be useful for another.

The Liquify tools

Okay, so much for the basics. You're itching to start, so here's how the distortion tools along the left side of the Liquify window work:

Forward warp (W): Drag to shove the pixels under your cursor around the image. At first, it may feel like the Smudge tool. But instead of smearing pixels, you're incrementally moving points in the mesh that distort the image. The first example in Figure 11.38 shows a few large-scale changes made with a large brush and the default Pressure value. When used properly, the Forward Warp tool is the Liquify command's most practical tool. To create the second image, the Forward Warp tool was set to a smaller brush size. But the biggest difference was in the length of the strokes. Instead of dragging, say, 10 to 20 pixels at a time, the brush was dragged just 1 or 2 pixels. As you can see, making lots of little adjustments — in this case, somewhere in the neighborhood of 30 strokes — produces the best results.

FIGURE 11.38

Making big strokes with the Forward Warp tool produces wacky results (left); short, careful drags give you more control (right). But you have to be patient. It took 6 strokes to make the big changes on left and about 30 to make the subtle changes on right — broadening the nose, expanding the lips, raising the chin, and lifting the eyelids and brows.

Twirl clockwise (C): Click or drag to spin pixels under your cursor in a clockwise direction, or to the right.

This tool's companion, the Twirl counterclockwise tool, no longer owns a slot in the Liquify toolbox. But you can still access the Twirl counterclockwise tool by pressing Alt (Option on the Mac) when you drag with the Twirl clockwise tool. You can press and release Alt in mid-drag to switch the Twirl direction on the fly. Figure 11.39 shows the Twirl tool used with Alt (Option on the Mac) to change the Twirl direction.

FIGURE 11.39

Here the Twirl tool was used, twirling in two directions, thanks to the Alt (Option) key.

Pucker (S): Click and drag with this tool to move pixels toward the center of the brush cursor. The effect is similar to applying the Pinch filter with a positive Amount value. If you move your mouse down instead of dragging, Photoshop steadily increases the extent of the distortion until you release the mouse button.

Bloat (B): When you drag or move your mouse down with this tool, pixels underneath the cursor move outward. As is the case with the Pucker tool, the longer you hold down the mouse button, the more bloating you get.

TIP   Press Alt (Option on the Mac) to toggle between the Pucker and Bloat functions on the fly.

The Pucker and Bloat tools are particularly valuable for removing weight or adding bulk. For example, in the first image in Figure 11.40, the Pucker tool was used to contort the face and head shape.

Push Left (O): As you click and drag with this tool, pixels underneath the cursor move in a direction perpendicular to your drag. For example, if you drag down, pixels flow to the right. Drag straight up, and pixels move to the left. To reverse the direction of the pixels, press Alt (Option on the Mac).

At first, the Push Left tool may seem unwieldy, resulting in dramatic and sometimes unpredictable movements. But you can control it using two techniques. First, reduce the Brush Pressure value to 25 or lower. Figure 11.41 illustrates the difference between drags performed using Pressure settings of 50 and 20. Second, try using the Push Left tool in a straight line by clicking at one point and Shift-clicking at another, as you might with Photoshop's painting and editing tools. The result is a neat line, great for reducing flab along straight elements, such as arms and legs.

FIGURE 11.40

Armed with the Pucker tool, click and drag along the facial contours to reshape in ways a plastic surgeon can only imagine.

FIGURE 11.41

Pushing things around lets you totally revamp a face, body, or any photographic content.

Mirror (M): Clicking and dragging with this tool creates a reflection, albeit one you might see in a fun-house mirror. As you drag, Photoshop copies pixels from the area perpendicular to the direction you move the cursor. So if you drag up, you clone pixels to the right of the cursor into the area underneath the cursor; drag down to clone pixels from left to right, as shown in Figure 11.42. Press Alt (Option on the Mac) to reflect from another direction on the fly.

FIGURE 11.42

Using the Mirror tool, drag up on the left side and down on the right side. Pixels are reflected in a clockwise direction.

Turbulence (T): The Turbulence tool is a variation on the Forward Warp tool that distorts pixels in random directions as you drag. When you select this tool, Photoshop grants you access to a third Tool Options value labeled Turbulent Jitter. If the Brush Size value controls how many pixels are affected at a time and Brush Pressure controls the strength of the stroke, Turbulent Jitter specifies just how much random variation is permitted. The minimum value of 1 causes the Turbulence tool to behave much like the Forward Warp tool; a maximum value of 100 mixes pixels in all directions.

Figure 11.43 illustrates a few examples. For purposes of demonstration, all four images were created using a very large Brush Size (ranging from 100 to 200, throughout all the samples) and the maximum Pressure value, 100. For each image in the top row, the brush was held in place for 15 seconds. The random variations built up from one moment to the next. Not surprisingly, a higher Turbulent Jitter value produced a more dramatic effect than a lower one.

FIGURE 11.43

Four variations were created using the Turbulence tool, twice holding the mouse in place (top row) and twice dragging with the tool on the left and right sides of the face (bottom row).

After you drag with any of these tools, you can undo the effect by pressing Ctrl+Z (⌘+Z on the Mac). You also have the option of multiple undos. Press Ctrl+Alt+Z (⌘+Option+Z on the Mac) to backstep through your operations. Press Ctrl+Shift+Z (⌘+Shift+Z) to redo undone distortions. To learn how to go back in time nonsequentially and explore additional reversion options, read the section on reconstructing and reverting.

Freezing and thawing pixels

As mentioned earlier, if you make a selection in your image before choosing Filter ➪ Liquify, Photoshop automatically freezes unselected pixels when you enter the Liquify dialog box. Therefore, these unselected pixels are not affected by any distortions you apply. In previous versions of Photoshop (prior to CS), you couldn't thaw these pixels from within the Liquify window. But

Photoshop lets you thaw pixels, freeze new ones, and determine frozen pixels based on transparency and layer masks in ways never before possible.

To freeze a portion of your image from the Liquify window, you have two options:

 Freeze Mask (F): Press F to select the Freeze Mask tool, and then click and drag over areas that you want to protect. You can adjust the brush size and pressure as you can when working with the distortion tools. But in this case, the Brush Pressure setting determines how deeply frozen the pixels become. At anything less than 100 percent, the pixels become partially distorted when you drag over them with a distortion tool. If you set the pressure to 50 percent, the distortion is applied with half the pressure used in unfrozen areas. Likewise, the Brush Density setting controls how deeply pixels become frozen toward the outside of the brush. To freeze the entire image, click Mask All in the Mask Options settings.

 Thaw Mask (D): To thaw areas that you have frozen from the Liquify window, once again making them slaves to the distortion tools, paint over them with the Thaw Mask tool. The tool options affect this tool just as they do the Freeze Mask tool. To thaw the entire image, click None in the Mask Options settings.

> **TIP** Just as you can invert a selection outline or invert a mask in the Quick Mask mode, you can click Invert All to quickly freeze any unfrozen pixels and thaw any frozen ones.

Among the more complex features in the Liquify dialog box are the Mask Options settings, located below the Reconstruct Options. Above the None, Mask All, and Invert All buttons just mentioned, you're presented with five different buttons, each giving you a different option for interacting with the current mask. And each of those buttons has three options, when relevant; you can use information from the layer's current selection, transparency, or layer mask. From left to right, the options perform these functions:

- **Replace selection** replaces the current mask, completely wiping out any freezing or thawing you've done and replacing it with a mask drawn from the layer's current selection, transparency, or layer mask.

- **Add to selection** keeps all thawed areas in the current mask and also thaws other areas according to the layer's current selection, transparency, or layer mask.

- **Subtract from selection** keeps all frozen areas in the current mask and also freezes other areas according to the layer's current selection, transparency, or layer mask.

- **Intersect with selection** only allows an area to stay thawed if it is thawed both in the current mask *and* according to the layer's current selection, transparency, or layer mask.

- **Invert selection** takes the current mask and inverts it, but only within the thawed areas according to the layer's current selection, transparency, or layer mask.

Reconstructing and restoring

In the Reconstruct Options section of the Liquify window, you see a Mode pop-up menu plus two buttons, Reconstruct and Restore All. You can use these options not only to revert an image to the way it looked before you applied a distortion, but also to redo a distortion so that it affects the image differently.

The following list outlines reversion possibilities:

- **Undo:** The Liquify window doesn't give you a History palette, but Ctrl+Alt+Z and Ctrl+Shift+Z still let you undo and redo sequences of operations (⌘+Option+Z and ⌘+Shift+Z on the Mac).

- **Reset:** To return everything to the way it was the very first time you opened the Liquify window, press the Alt key (Win) or the Option key (Mac), which changes the Cancel button in the dialog box to Reset. Click the Reset button, and not only do you restore your original image, you restore the Liquify window's default settings.

TIP   Believe it or not, you can undo Reset and other reversion techniques. I know; it's too cool. Just press Ctrl+Z (⌘+Z on the Mac) to get your edits back.

- **Restore All:** To revert the image without resetting all values to their defaults, click Restore All. This affects frozen and thawed areas alike.

Liquify also offers a handful of reconstruction techniques that are more controlled and more complex than the reversion options. By selecting an option from the Mode menu and then clicking Reconstruct or clicking and dragging with the Reconstruct tool (R), you can reconstruct a distortion so that it extends from a frozen area into neighboring unfrozen pixels. The Reconstruct button affects all unfrozen areas, but dragging with the tool alters only pixels under your cursor, subject to the Brush Size and Pressure values.

All the reconstruction modes calculate the change to the image based on the warp mesh (grid). To get a better feel for how each mode works, deselect the Show Image option, select the Show Mesh option, and then apply a simple distortion across a portion of the grid. Freeze part of the distorted region and then keep an eye on the grid lines at the intersections between frozen and unfrozen regions as you try out each of these modes:

- **Revert:** The Revert mode restores unfrozen portions of the image to their original appearance, without regard to the borders between the frozen and unfrozen areas. Compare this to the Revert button, which restores frozen and unfrozen areas alike.

- **Rigid:** This mode extends the distortion only as needed to maintain right angles in the mesh where frozen and unfrozen areas meet. The result is unfrozen areas that look very much like they did originally but smoothly blend into the frozen areas.

- **Stiff:** Stiff interpolates the distortion so that the effect tapers away as you move farther from the boundary between the frozen and unfrozen areas.

- **Smooth** and **Loose:** These two modes extend the distortion applied to the frozen areas into the unfrozen areas. The Smooth setting tries to create smooth transitions between frozen and unfrozen areas. Loose shares more of the distortion from the frozen area with the unfrozen area. You'll achieve the most dramatic results when frozen and unfrozen areas have been distorted differently.

- **Displace**, **Amplitwist**, and **Affine:** The last three modes work exclusively with the reconstruct tool. Using these modes, you can apply one or more distortions that are in force at a specific reference point in the image. Click to set the reference point, and then drag through unfrozen areas to distort them. Use the Displace mode to move pixels to match the displacement of the reference point; select Amplitwist to match the displacement, rotation, and scaling at the reference point; and choose Affine to match all distortions at the reference point.

Although Liquify certainly gives you plenty of ways to reconstruct distortions, predicting the outcome of your drags with the Reconstruct tool can be nearly impossible. So be prepared to experiment. And if you don't get the results you want, remember that you can undo a reconstruction just as easily as you can any distortion.

Creating a vanishing point

The Vanishing Point filter, which really goes beyond what you expect from a filter, is used to manipulate image content to create the illusion of perspective. Of course, the Edit ⇨ Transform ⇨ Perspective command allows you to take the four corners of a layer and move them to create a new perspective, but that's nothing compared to what the Vanishing Point filter can do. Figure 11.44 shows the Vanishing Point dialog box, with tools on the left, preview in the middle, and controls across the top.

FIGURE 11.44

The Vanishing Point dialog box provides tools for creating and editing planes, cloning, stamping, sampling, panning, and zooming in on your image.

There are some new features of the Vanishing Point filter for Photoshop CS3:

- **You can bend selections across multiple surfaces.** When you drag a selection across two connected surfaces, the selection bends, following the orientation of both surfaces. The Brush tools behave the same way with the brush tip itself able to bend across multiple surfaces. This, along with the Brush tool's ability (within Vanishing Point) to bend as it moves across surfaces with different orientations, gives you great editing capability, in perspective.

- **You can rotate selections *and* bend them.** In the CS3 version of Vanishing Point, you could rotate selections, but now you can both rotate and bend them over more than one surface. You can wrap text around a building or packing box, or see a pattern fall down off the edge of a tablecloth (spread over the top and down the side of a table, for example).

- **Measurements can now be done in perspective.** To serve the needs of architects, landscape and interior designers, and a host of other users who need to be able to measure in perspective, Vanishing Point now provides tools for this purpose. You can draw a measurement within an image and tell Photoshop how long the measured length should be. This then affects all other measurements and grid spacing for that image.

- **Photoshop supports DXF (CAD format), with export of geometry and measurements.** Vanishing Point now takes 3-D sizes and positions on all surfaces and rebuilds them in DXF format. This enables you to take the measurement information from Vanishing Point-edited images and create CAD drawings. Press Ctrl+E (⌘+E on the Mac) to export the image in DXF format, as a two-layer file, consisting of the image and its measurements, respectively.

- **Photoshop supports 3DS (3d Studio), with export of geometry and textures.** This feature also will delight designers and architects, because it allows them to take what's edited in Vanishing Point and use it in a CAD, animation, or special effects application, with textures and other information gathered by the camera. Press Ctrl+Alt+E (⌘+Option+E on the Mac) to invoke this export.

> **TIP** To access the Show Edges and Show Measurement commands, click the menu button (a small right-pointing triangle just to the left of the Grid Size field) and make your selections there. These options are on by default. You'll find menu commands for the aforementioned exporting options (to DXF and 3DS) here, too.

To use the Vanishing Point filter, read the discussion below to find out about the main tools and techniques.

Vanishing Point basics

When you start with the Vanishing Point tool, you want to begin with a duplicate layer that contains the portions of the image you want to use in creating the vanishing point and the content-in-perspective.

STEPS: Creating a vanishing point

1. Create a duplicate layer of an image.

2. **Choose Filter ⇨ Vanishing Point.** The Vanishing Point dialog box opens (refer to Figure 11.44). The Create Plane tool is active as soon as the dialog box opens.

3. **Click and drag to create a four-sided plane, as shown in Figure 11.45.** If the resulting grid is yellow or red, you have not drawn a plane that follows a true perspective in your image.

The editing plane encompasses the front of the building. The window on the front of the building will be duplicated, in perspective, on the right side.

4. **Create a plane in the area of the image where you want to position content taken from the area within the first plane, as shown in Figure 11.46.**

5. Now clone the content from one plane to the next by clicking the Clone Stamp tool (within the Vanishing Point window, of course) to take content from the first plane into the second.

FIGURE 11.46

The second editing plane encompasses the side of the building and follows the intended vanishing point. Because the grid is blue (although it appears light gray in this black and white image), you know that the correct perspective is achieved.

TIP   If your grid is yellow or red, or if it's simply the wrong size, point to and drag the grid's side points to extend the edges of the grid to cover the area you wish to work in. If your resizing of the grid changes the perspective, the grid may change color, again indicating a problem with the perspective. Tinker with your grid until it's blue and the right size for your needs.

The cloning process is very much the same as it is when using the Clone Stamp tool in the Toolbox — use Alt (Option on the Mac) and click to set the source for the clone. You'll want to use the Heal option (it appears at the top of the dialog box as soon as you begin using the Clone tool). This ensures the colors and lighting in the cloned content match their new surroundings. You also can leave Aligned on so that you don't create any unwanted patterns if cloning a large area.

With the Clone tool active, drag your mouse over the target area to draw content from the source point. As shown in Figure 11.47, the window from the front of the garage is cloned to the right side of the building, and it appears in perfect perspective. You can save your modifications to the duplicate layer by clicking OK, which closes the Vanishing Point window and returns you to your image.

FIGURE 11.47

The green cross hair (gray here, over on the left) indicates the source point for the Clone Stamp. And with no need for a home construction how-to manual, a new window is placed on this building in just minutes.

Vanishing Panes and Planes

Another enhancement in Vanishing Point for Photoshop CS3 is the ability to adjust the angle between adjoining planes to an angle greater than or less than 90 degrees. You can now design around corners with greater flexibility, by selecting the surface and using the angle control in the Options bar, while either the Create Plane tool or the Edit Plane tool is active. You also can change the angle of any surface by pressing Alt (Option on the Mac) as you point to a node that's opposite to your intended rotation axis. If you add the Shift key as you rotate, you can constrain your angles in 15-degree increments.

TIP The Vanishing Point filter takes lots of practice, and you'll find that using images with buildings, roads, and other solid structures with lots of vertical and horizontal sides is your best bet for honing your Vanishing Point skills. With its new tools for exporting to other programs, and the ability to bend and rotate selections over multiple surfaces, your options for using this tool to design product packaging, buildings, rooms, and other designs is virtually unlimited.

Adding Clouds and Spotlights

The five filters in the Render submenu produce lighting effects. You can use Clouds and Difference Clouds to create a layer of haze over an image. Lens Flare creates light flashes and reflections (as shown earlier in the chapter). Lighting Effects lights an image as if it were hanging on a gallery wall. You also have the Fibers filter, which you may want to check out but then ignore — its results are a bit strange.

Creating clouds

The Clouds filter creates an abstract and random haze between the foreground and background colors. The Difference Clouds filter works exactly like layering the image, applying the Clouds filter, and selecting the Difference blend mode in the Layers palette.

Why would Difference Clouds make special provisions for a single blend mode? Because you can create cumulative effects. Try this: Select a sky blue as the foreground color, and then choose Filter ➪ Render ➪ Clouds. The results look like a nice, summer sky. Now choose Filter ➪ Render ➪ Difference Clouds. Not so nice and summery this time; instead, it's all blacks and oranges. Press Ctrl+F (⌘+F on the Mac) to repeat the filter; it's back to the blue sky. Keep pressing Ctrl+F (⌘+F on the Mac) over and over, and notice the results. A pink tone starts to seep into the blue sky; a green tone seeps into the orange one. Multiple applications of the Difference Clouds filter generate organic oil-on-water effects. Figure 11.48 shows an example of Clouds and Difference

Clouds — here in black and white, of course, but you can see the difference in the results — the one on the left could easily be added to fill in the sky on an outdoor photo, the one on the right might not be.

FIGURE 11.48

These are the effects of applying Clouds (left), followed by Difference Clouds (middle) and Difference Clouds repeated 20 times.

Clouds (FC: blue, BC: white) Difference Clouds (same) Difference Clouds × 20

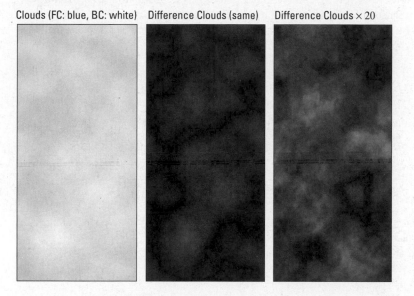

> **TIP**   To strengthen the colors created by the Clouds filter, press Shift when choosing the command. This same technique works when using the Difference Clouds filter as well. In fact, there may be no reason *not* to press Shift while choosing one of these commands, unless you have some specific need for washed-out effects.

Also, if you want to make a repeating texture using Clouds and Difference Clouds, make sure your image size is a square with pixel dimensions based on a power of two — something like 128×128 or 256×256 works well. Your cloudy image is seamlessly tiled, making it a perfect backdrop when you need something to fill in a large area.

> **TIP**   Tempted to use a Clouds filter-created image as your Web page background? Think again. First, background images are pretty passé for use on the Web, and second, even if a background image is appropriate in a table, frame, or layer (some smaller segment) of your Web pages, a background image that has any significant pattern or color diversity makes text hard to read and competes visually with any Web graphics placed on top of it.

Using the Fibers filter

Like the Clouds and Difference Clouds filters, the Fibers filter uses Perlin-based fractal noise to achieve a realistic randomness that, when stretched out in one direction, looks less like fluffy clouds and more like, well, fibers. This could be a problem for you if you don't want the fibers Photoshop gives you, because there is no way to vary the fibers greatly — you have two sliders (Variance and Strength) and one button (Randomize), and as you'll see, these don't do much more than change the appearance of the fibers — in the end, you still get fibers. If fibers are what you want, this is a great thing, but if you were hoping for a fibrous texture made from the content of your image, this is not what you're getting here. Programs such as Adobe's After Effects give you lots of options for tweaking and adjusting the noise this filter generates, but Photoshop's Fibers filter is rather limited in terms of its flexibility, and therefore its uses.

If you're still interested in using this filter — and you should be, if only to see for yourself how you might be able to use it — choose Filter ➪ Render ➪ Fibers. This opens the Fibers dialog box, shown in Figure 11.49. In the preview box, you can view the fibers generated by the filter based on the values of your foreground and background colors. Increase the Variance slider value to create shorter strands of fiber with more contrast between the colors. Ramp up the Strength slider value to make your fibers stringier. Click Randomize to call up a new random seed for the noise; it's a good way to mix it up a bit if the need arises. Also seen in Figure 11.49 are the results of the Fiber filter (in the visible image window) with more Strength, shorter strands (higher Variance), and Randomize turned on.

> **TIP**   Sadly, there's no way to change the angle of the fibers generated by the Fibers filter to create a woven effect, but you can cheat your way around this. Apply the Fibers filter to a layer, duplicate it, and then rotate the top layer 90 degrees. Set the top layer to the Darken blend mode, and you should wind up with a somewhat realistic interwoven pattern.

Lighting an image

The complex Lighting Effects filter enables you to shine lights on an image, color, position, and focus the lights, specify the reflectivity of the surface, and even create a surface map.

> **NOTE**   The Lighting Effects filter is applicable exclusively to RGB images.

When you choose Filter ➪ Render ➪ Lighting Effects, Photoshop displays one of its most complex dialog boxes, as shown in Figure 11.50. The dialog box has two halves: one in which you position light with respect to a thumbnail of the selected image and one that contains an intimidating number of options, many with rather confusing or vague names. Read on, because a valiant (and hopefully successful) attempt at making order and usefulness out of the confusion is made.

FIGURE 11.49

Here's the Fibers filter dialog box and a preview of its effect on...well, anything.

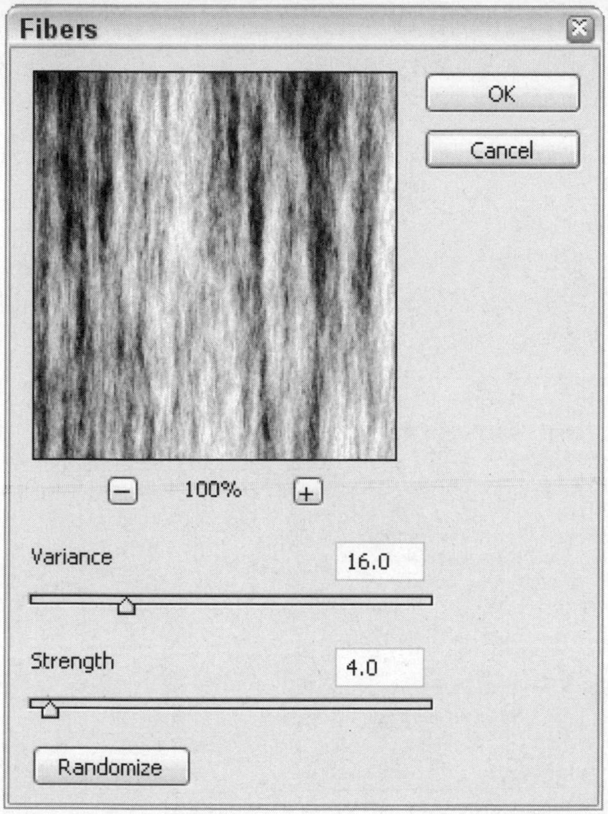

There's no way around it: This filter and its dialog box are complex. The easiest way to apply the filter is to choose one of the predefined lighting effects from the Style pop-up menu at the top of the right side of the dialog box, see how it looks in the preview area, and — if you like it — press Enter or Return to apply the effect.

If you want to create your own effects, you have to tinker with the settings a bit and risk some frustration. It can be worth it, though, for creating some striking lighting effects in your images. Here are the basic steps involved in creating a custom effect.

FIGURE 11.50

The Lighting Effects dialog box lets you light an image as if it were hanging in a gallery, lying on a floor, or perhaps resting too near a hot flame.

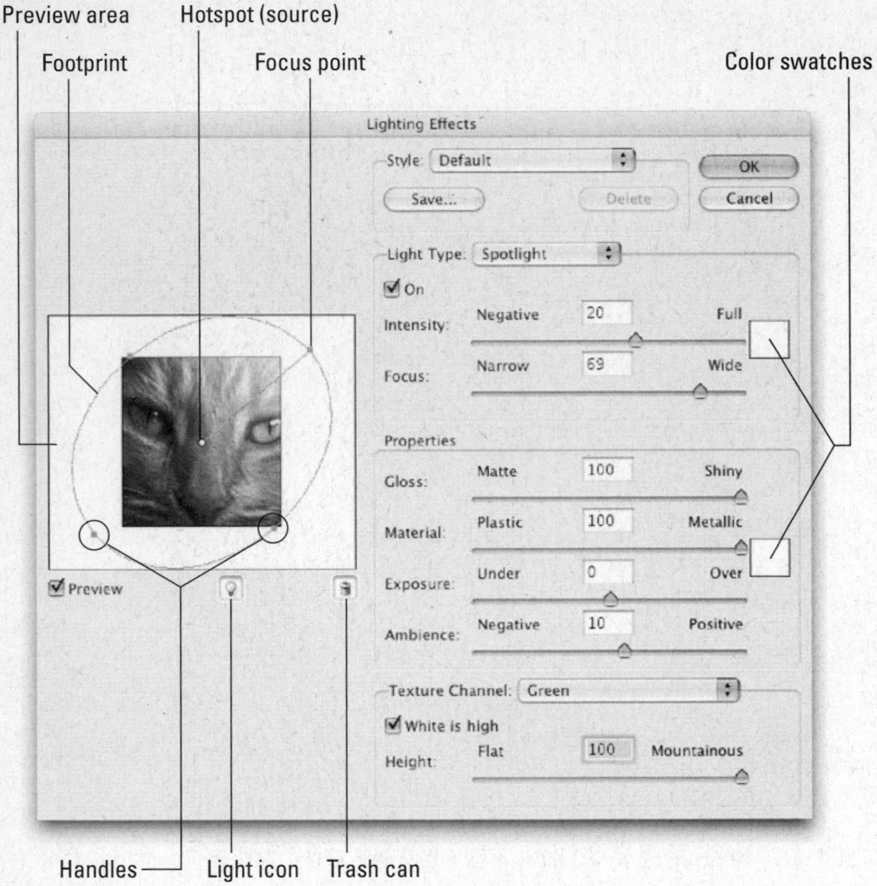

STEPS: Lighting an image

1. **Click and drag from the light icon at the bottom of the dialog box into the preview area to create a new light source.** Think of this area as the *stage* because it's as if the image is painted on the floor of a stage and the lights are hanging above it.

2. **Select the kind of light you want from the Light Type pop-up menu.** It's just below the Style pop-up menu. You can select from Directional, Omni, and Spotlight:

   ■ Directional works like the sun, producing a general, unfocused light that hits a target from an angle.

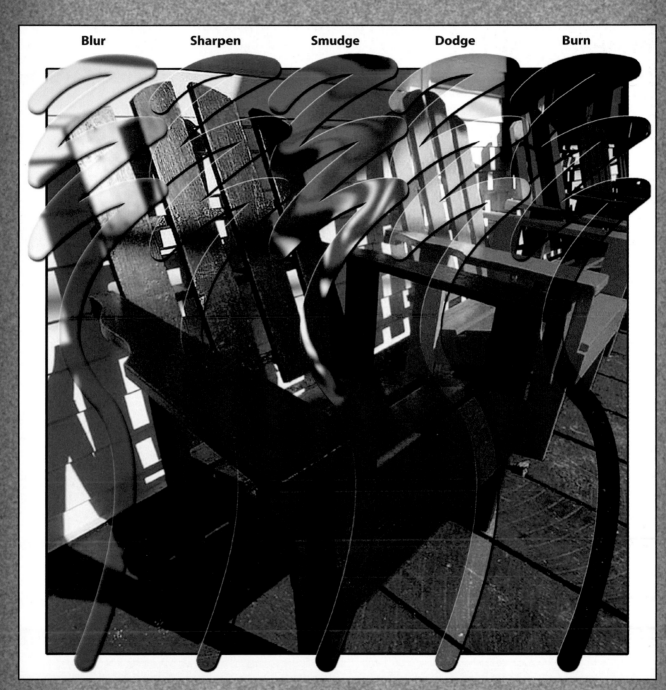

Blur   **Sharpen**   **Smudge**   **Dodge**   **Burn**

This figure shows the effects of dragging with five of Photoshop's edit tools. Rather than applying color, the edit tools influence existing colors in an image. The boundaries of each line are highlighted here so you can see clearly the distinctions between line and background. You can learn more about the edit tools in Chapter 5.

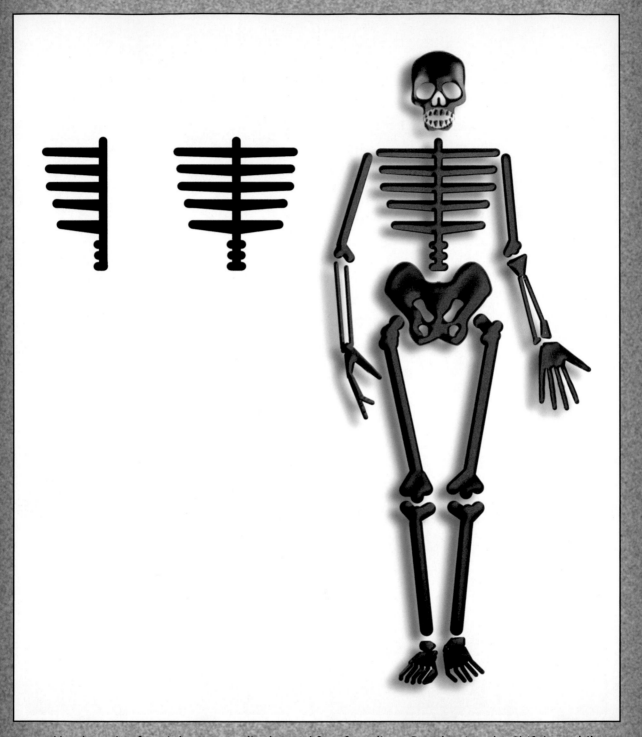

Here's a mix of straight, perpendicular, and free-form lines. By releasing the Shift key while dragging, the line returns to free form, as illustrated here with our skeletal pal. We started by pressing Shift to draw a vertical line — the spinal column. Then we moved the cursor out to where we wanted the first rib to end and released the Shift key to make the line hop out to that point. After that, we released the Shift key and the mouse so as not to draw anything, and returned the cursor to the spinal column — just a little further down from where the rib originally began. Read up on the Shift-click technique in Chapter 5.

Photoshop lets you clone from multiple image windows. This technique makes it possible to merge two different images, as demonstrated here. To achieve this effect, we Alt-clicked (Option-click on the Mac) to set a source point in one image. We then brought the cheetah image to the foreground and dragged with the Clone Stamp tool to copy from the first image. You also can clone between layers, assuming that the layers are unlocked. Just Alt-click (Option-click) one layer, and then switch to a different layer and drag. The Clone Stamp tool gets full coverage in Chapter 7.

The Healing Brush blends cloned pixels with those just outside the brushstroke, drawing in formation from those pixels to determine how to adjust the cloned content. The idea is that the pixels you're painting over are messed up, but the pixels just beyond the brushstroke are in good shape and should be emulated. This vintage photo has some serious scars, but because some places are unmarked, we can use them to cover up those scars. To learn more about the Healing Brush, check out Chapter 7.

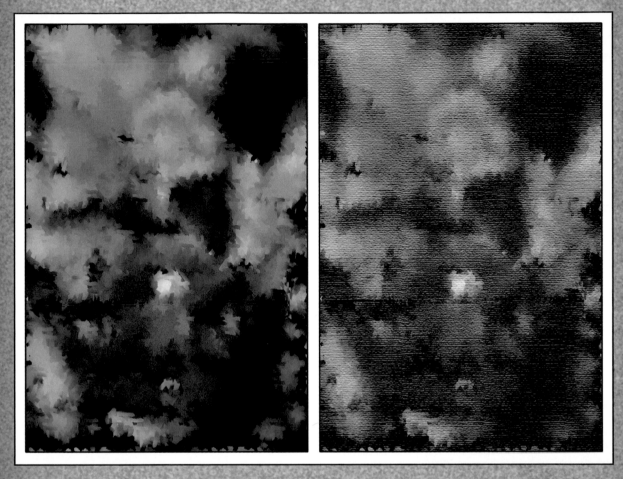

The Art History Brush tool lets you create impressionistic effects with the aid of the History palette. This tool paints from the source state specified in the History palette. But it does so by painting tens or even hundreds of tiny brush strokes at a time, swirling and gyrating according to settings you select in the Options bar. Try applying various filters, maybe even an Artistic filter, so that you'll be painting with a painted or drawn filter. You may end up with something like the now artistically filtered photo shown here. The Displace filter is applied (left), and a texture added with the Texturizer filter (right). You can learn more about these techniques in Chapter 7.

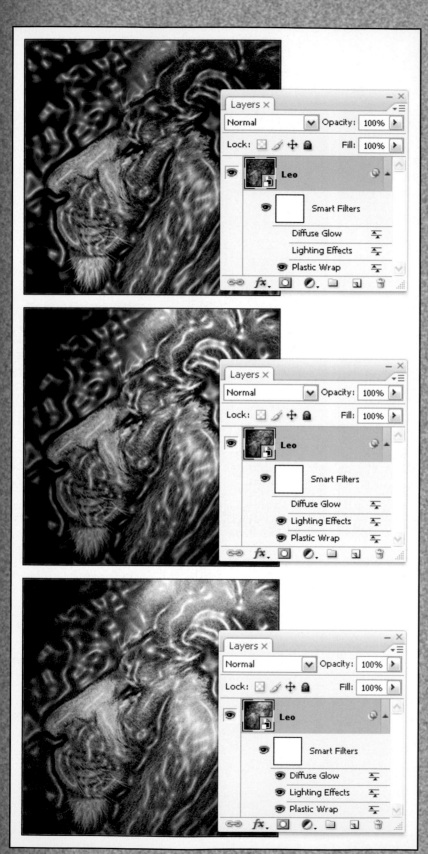

Here we see the cumulative effects of three Smart Filters applied to a Smart Object — first Plastic Wrap (top), then Lighting Effects (middle), and then Diffuse Glow (bottom). Smart Filters may be the greatest new feature in CS3. They enable you to apply a filter and have the filter's effects appear on a separate layer, thus they do not permanently alter the original image. Instead, view them (or not) as you would a normal layer, tweak their blending options and opacity, and copy or move them to new locations within the stack. Smart filters are covered in Chapter 10.

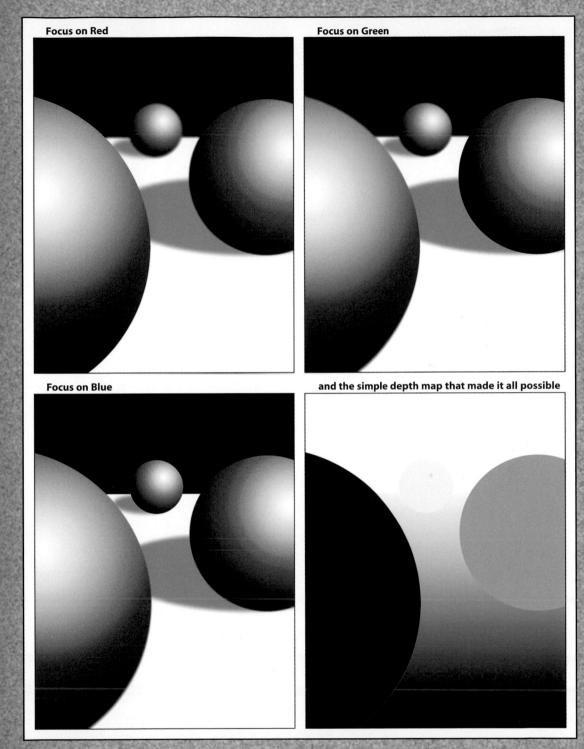

Focus on Red

Focus on Green

Focus on Blue

and the simple depth map that made it all possible

The ability to create custom Depth Maps gives you the opportunity to individually tweak the blurriness of every single pixel in your image. The Lens Blur filter takes the pixel you've chosen, looks at the corresponding grayscale level for that pixel in the Depth Map you've specified, and adjusts the focal distance accordingly. Here, a grayscale alpha channel was created for use as a Depth Map. Then the Lens Blur filter was applied, and the Blur Focal Distance set by clicking on each of the spheres in the image. The Lens Blur filter, and a whole lot more, is covered in Chapter 10.

Lens Flare, 50-300mm Zoom

35mm Prime

105mm Prime

Movie Prime

Lens Flare, found in the Render submenu (Filter ⇨ Render ⇨ Lens Flare), adds sparkles and halos to an image to suggest light bouncing off the camera lens. Here we see the four Lens Type settings. In each case, the Brightness value was set to 140%. See Chapter 11 for coverage of this and other filters.

The ZigZag filter arranges colors into zigzag patterns that emanate radially from the center of the image like spokes in a wheel. The result is a series of concentric ripples. We applied this filter to the center image, and the results are seen in the images around it. We used the following settings: In the upper left, Around Center, -50 Amount, Ridges 5; on the upper right, Out from Center, 75 Amount, Ridges 10; on the lower left, Pond Ripples, -50 Amount, Ridges 5; and the lower-right version shows the Pond Ripples at the highest Amount (100) and Ridges (20) settings. To learn more about this and other filters, see Chapters 10 and 11.

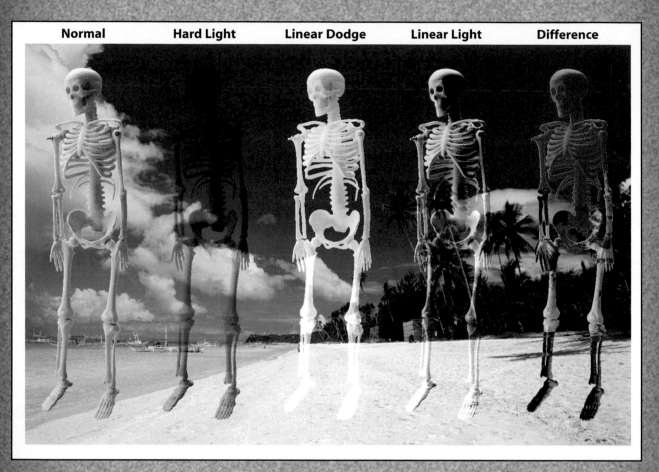

Normal   **Hard Light**   **Linear Dodge**   **Linear Light**   **Difference**

Blend modes permit you to mix the color of a pixel with that of every pixel in a straight line beneath it. A single blend mode can pack as much power as a mask, a filter, and a retouching tool combined. And, unlike some of those combined options, blend modes don't physically alter an image's pixels. Here you see several clones of our bony old pal. Each one has been mixed with the background using a random sampling of blend modes from Photoshop's Layers palette. The skeleton image itself never changes; each repeated layer contains the same collection of pixels. In all, there are six layers: five skeletons and the background, each skeleton layer subject to the blend mode labeled in the figure. You can read all about blend mode options in Chapter 14.

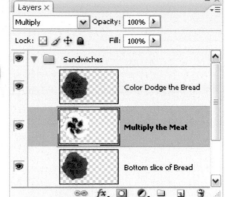

Color Dodge top layer, Multiply middle layer

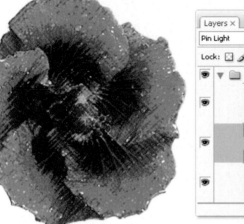

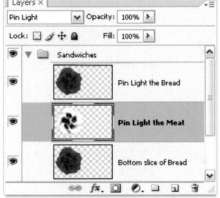

Pin Light both layers

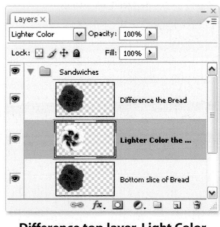

Difference top layer, Light Color middle layer

Layers and blend modes give you the flexibility to experiment as much as you want and for as long as you please. When you sandwich a filtered image between two originals, you can lessen the effect of the filter and achieve different effects by changing the blend modes. Here we cloned the original hibiscus layer and subjected it to the Charcoal filter. Charcoal absolutely destroys the detail in the image, replacing all brightness values with the foreground and background colors—in this case, black and white. Next, we sandwiched the filtered layer between two unfitered layers and applied different blend mode combinations to varying effect. To learn more about this sandwiching technique, read Chapter 14.

Looks like someone plucked a blossom and pinned it to a nice canvas matte, hung it on the wall, and lit it just so. Nope! It's all done in Photoshop. The flower was plucked from one image; its shadow was produced by duplicating it, filling it with black, fading the opacity, and then transforming it; and the background was produced with the Texturizer filter. If you'd like to view a tutorial that shows how this was done, see the CD-ROM—its contents are outlined in Appendix B.

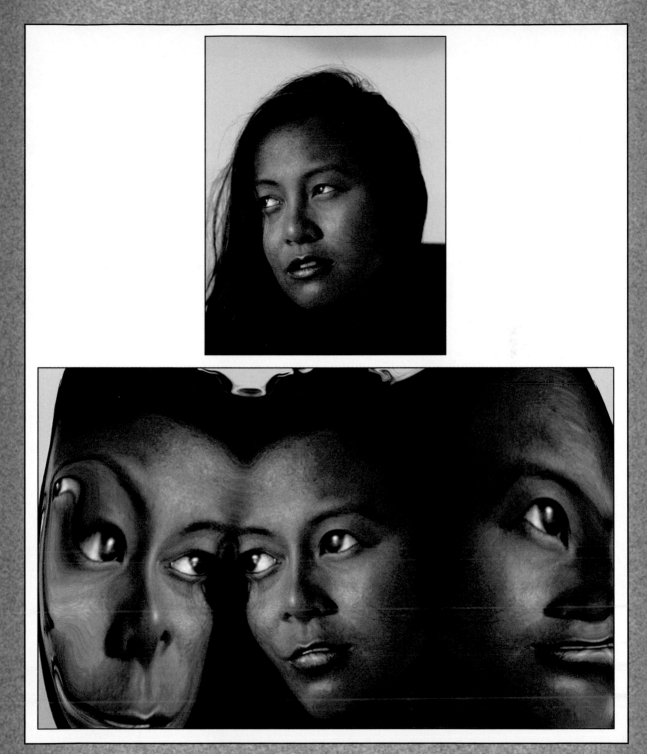

Up top, you see the original image; beneath it, we have an example of the Liquify filter. Using the mirror tool, we dragged down on the left side of the image and up on the right side. Consequently, the pixels are reflected in a clockwise direction. To learn more about this and other distortion effects, see Chapter 11.

www.lancastercrows.org

The crow in this image is an example of a knockout. Knockouts turn the contents of one layer into a floating hole that can bore through one or more layers behind it. Knockouts are governed by the Knockout drop-down menu, found in the middle of the Advanced Blending section of the Layer Styles dialog box. In this example, we have a crow image knocking a hole through the Escher-inspired layer behind it, revealing the black background layer beneath. You can find out more about knockouts in Chapter 14, and Layer Styles in Chapter 15.

Pointillize, Cell Size: 5, 50% Opacity

Pointillize, Pin Light blend mode

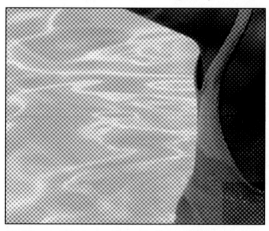

Halftone Pattern, Size: 2, Contrast: 3

Halftone Pattern, Pin Light blend mode

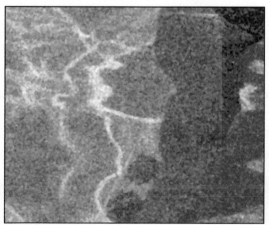

Grain, Intensity: 80, Contrast: 50, Clumped

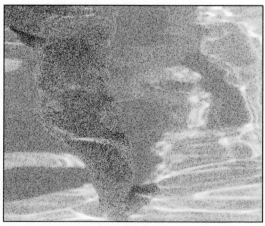

Grain, Stipple, Soft Light blend mode

The Pointillize, Halftone Pattern, and Grain filters offer hefty alternatives to the Add Noise filter, discussed in Chapter 10. Here you can see some examples of these filters coupled with a number of different blend modes. You can find out more about blend mode options in Chapter 14.

| Dirty Money | Auto Levels | Auto Contrast |

Time to launder the money. The original bill on the left has been around a bit, and the contrast isn't as sharp as it could be. We could hit the image with Auto Levels, which visits each channel in an RGB image and changes the darkest color to black and the lightest color to white, stretching the remaining shades of gray between these extremes. Enter Auto Contrast. This pumps up your lights and darks and bolsters contrast.

However, Auto Levels' greatest strength is also a weakness. While it can often correct a color cast in an image, it also can produce one (see the middle example). This is where Auto Contrast comes in. Auto Contrast doesn't mess around with the individual channels; instead, it works on the image as a whole. It fixes the contrast and reserves the color balance, as can be seen in the last example. You can find out more about color correction in Chapter 17.

■ Omni casts light like a bare light bulb hanging in the middle of the room, shining in all directions from a center point.

■ Spotlight is a focused beam that is brightest at the source and tapers off gradually.

3. **Specify the color of the light by clicking the top Color Swatch.** You also can tinker with the Intensity slider to control the brightness of the light. If Spotlight is selected, the Focus slider becomes available. Click and drag the slider toward Narrow to create a bright laser of light; drag toward Wide to diffuse the light and spread it over a larger area.

4. **Move the light source by clicking and dragging at the *focus point* (if you've chosen a color for your light, the focus point appears as a colored circle in the preview area).** When Directional or Spotlight is selected, the focus point represents the spot at which the light is pointing. When Omni is active, the focus point is the actual bulb.

5. **If Directional or Spotlight is active, you can change the angle of the light by clicking and dragging the hot spot.** The *hot spot* represents the location in the image that's likely to receive the most light. When you use a Directional light, the hot spot appears as a black square at the end of a line joined to the focus point. The same holds true when you edit a Spotlight; the confusing thing is that there are four black squares altogether. The light source is joined to the focus point by a line; the three *handles* are not.

TIP To make the light brighter, click and drag the hot spot closer to the focus point. Dragging the hot spot away from the focus point dims the light by increasing the distance that it has to travel. It's like having a flashlight in the living room when you're in the garage — the light gets dimmer as you move away from it.

6. **With Omni or Spotlight in force, you can edit the elliptical footprint of the light.** When Omni is in force, a circle surrounds the focus point. When editing a Spotlight, you see an ellipse. Either way, this shape represents the *footprint* of the light, which is the approximate area of the image affected by the light. You can change the size of the light by clicking and dragging the handles around the footprint. Enlarging the shape is like raising the light source. When the footprint is small, the light is close to the image so it's concentrated and very bright. When the footprint is large, the light is high above the image, so it's more generalized.

TIP When editing the footprint of a Spotlight, Shift-drag a handle to adjust the width or height of the ellipse without affecting the angle. To change the angle without affecting the size, Ctrl-drag (⌘-drag on the Mac) a handle.

7. Introduce more lights as you see fit.

TIP Duplicate a light in the stage by Alt-dragging (Option-dragging on the Mac) its focus point. To delete the active light, drag the focus point onto the Trash icon below the preview area.

8. **Change the Properties and Texture Channel options as you see fit.** This is explained in detail after the steps.

9. **If you want to save your settings for future use, click Save.** Photoshop invites you to name the setup, which then appears as an option in the Style pop-up menu. If you want to get rid of one of the presets, select it from the pop-up menu and click Delete.

10. **Press Enter or Return to apply your settings to the image.**

That's really about it; the only parts not yet discussed are the Properties and Texture Channel options. The Properties sliders control how light reflects off the surface of your image:

- **Gloss:** Is the surface dull or shiny? Click and drag the slider toward Matte to make the surface flat and non-reflective like dull enamel paint. Drag the slider toward Shiny to make it glossy, as if you had slapped on a coat of lacquer.

- **Material:** This option determines the color of the light that reflects off the image. According to the logic employed by this option, Plastic reflects the color of the light; Metallic reflects the color of the object itself.

- **Exposure:** Your options here are Under and Over — referring to exposure. This option controls the brightness of all lights like a dimmer switch. You can control a single selected light using the Intensity slider, but the Exposure slider offers the added control of changing all lights in the stage (preview) area and the ambient light (described next) together.

- **Ambience:** The last slider enables you to add *ambient light*, which is a general, diffused light that hits all surfaces evenly. First, select the color of the light by clicking the color swatch to the right. Then click and drag the slider to cast a subtle hue over the stage. Drag toward Positive to tint the image with the color in the swatch; drag toward Negative to tint the stage with the swatch's opposite. Keep the slider set to 0 — in the center — to cast no hue.

The Texture Channel options let you treat one channel in the image as a *texture map*, which is a grayscale surface in which white indicates peaks and black indicates valleys. (This is true as long as the White is High option is selected, that is; if you deselect that option, everything flips and black becomes the peak.) It's as if one channel has a surface to it. By selecting a channel from the pop-up menu, you create an embossed effect, much like that created with the Emboss filter except much better because you can light the surface from many angles at once and it's in color, too.

Choose a channel to serve as the embossed surface from the pop-up menu. Then change the Height slider to indicate more or less Flat terrain or huge Mountainous cliffs of surface texture.

Figure 11.51 shows a rather bland multi-layered image — a metallic faceplate layer in front of a textured background layer. To add a little depth, a texture channel can be created for the faceplate layer by first Ctrl-clicking (⌘-clicking on the Mac) to select the layer's transparency. Next, switch over to the Channels palette, and create a new Alpha channel, then fill the selection with white.

Now for the fun part! With the selection still in place, run the Gaussian Blur filter on it five times in a row using Radius values of 18, 9, 6, 3, and 1, in that order. What you've just created is a Depth map — the white area is the highest, and the fading edges are progressively lower, all the way down to the black zone (the lowest), as seen in Figure 11.52.

FIGURE 11.51

Nothing to write home about. But, just give us a sec...

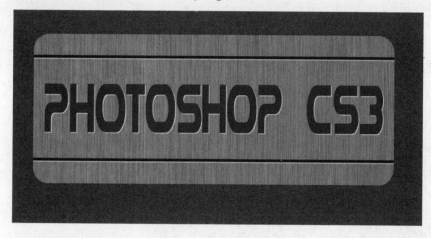

FIGURE 11.52

After selecting the faceplate layer transparency and then hopping to a new alpha channel, we create this new Texture Map by applying the Gaussian Blur filter to the white fill inside the selection.

Figure 11.53 shows what happens when we apply the Lighting Effects filter to the faceplate layer and assign the texture map using the Texture Channel pop-up menu.

FIGURE 11.53

Now the faceplate has nicely lit beveled edges — better than those you'd get with the Bevel and Emboss layer styles, too. FYI: Sometimes the best texture map for an image is the image itself. We ran the same Lighting Effects filter on the background layer, using the Blue channel as the texture map.

Summary

In this chapter, you learned about Photoshop's special effects filters, including those available exclusively through the Filter Gallery. We discussed the plusses and minuses of Photoshop's many special effects filters and followed with more specific coverage of the Pixelate and Mezzotint filters, the Edge-Enhancement filters, and the Distort filters. This included the new Lens Correction filter and the always-exciting Liquify filter.

You also learned to create metallic effects with Bas Relief, Plastic Wrap, and Chrome, and how to use the Fade command to reduce the sometimes over-the-top results these and other filters can give you.

Coverage of enhanced features continued with a section on the Vanishing Point filter, which enables you to build and modify structures and shapes in your photos like never before, and we discussed the Clouds and Lighting Effects filters.

Chapter 12

Custom Effects

H ere in this last chapter on filters, we'll cover three often-overlooked but important entries — Custom, Displace, and Pattern Maker — that enable you to create your own, custom-tailored special effects. Custom and Displace require some mathematical reasoning skills, and even then, you'll probably have occasional difficulty predicting the outcomes. It's not like other filters where you drag a slider and watch the Preview change, so you know when to stop or reverse your adjustments. With these first two filters, you're using numbers to make changes to the image, and you don't see the results until you've entered the numbers. Pattern Maker isn't quite so math-dependent.

Now, if math isn't your strong suit, or worse, if you simply hate dealing with any mathematical stuff, by all means don't put yourself through the torture; you can skip ahead to the Pattern Maker coverage at the end of this chapter. In defense of mathematical bravery, however, there are some cool results to be had by using these filters; but your life will remain rich and worth living, even if you choose to skip them.

If you'd like to read about some of the more math-free custom effects, skip all the mathematical background in this chapter and read the sections on applying custom values and using displacement maps, for some specific, visually exciting effects. As stated, you also find out about making your own patterns and textures with filters, something that should make you feel better if the whole math thing has you depressed.

Creating Homegrown Effects with the Custom Filter

The Custom filter enables you to design your own *convolution kernel*, which is a variety of filter in which neighboring pixels get mixed together. The kernel can be a variation on sharpening, blurring, embossing, or a half-dozen other effects. You create your filter by entering numerical values into a matrix of options.

When you choose Filter ➪ Other ➪ Custom, Photoshop displays the dialog box shown in Figure 12.1. It sports a 5×5 matrix of text boxes followed by two additional options, Scale and Offset. The matrix options can accept values from negative 999 to positive 999. The Scale value can range from 1 to 9,999, and the Offset value can range from negative 9,999 to positive 9,999. The dialog box includes Load and Save buttons so that you can load settings from disk and save the current settings for future use.

Like most of Photoshop's filters, the Custom filter also includes a constantly updating preview box, which you'll have lots of time to appreciate if you decide to try your hand at designing your own effects. Select the Preview check box to view the effect of the kernel in the image window as well.

FIGURE 12.1

The Custom dialog box lets you design your own convolution kernel by multiplying the brightness values of pixels.

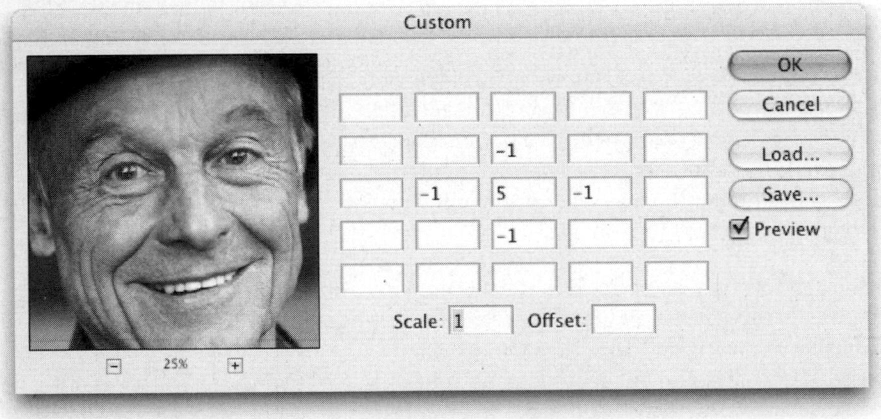

Here's how the filter works: When you press Enter or Return to apply the values in the Custom dialog box to a selection, the filter passes over every pixel in the selection, one at a time. For each pixel being evaluated — called the "PBE" from here on out, just to save ink and paper — the filter multiplies the PBE's current brightness value by the number in the center option box (the one that contains a 5 in Figure 12.1). To help keep things straight, this value is referred to as the CMV, for *central matrix value*.

The filter then multiplies the brightness values of the surrounding pixels by the surrounding values in the matrix. For example, Photoshop multiplies the value in the option box just above the CMV by the brightness value of the pixel just above the PBE. It ignores any empty matrix option boxes and the pixels they represent.

Finally, the filter totals the products of the multiplied pixels, divides the sum by the value in the Scale option, and then adds the Offset value to calculate the new brightness of the PBE. It then moves on to the next pixel in the selection and performs the calculation all over again. Figure 12.2 shows a schematic drawing of the process.

FIGURE 12.2

The Custom filter multiplies each matrix value by the brightness value of the corresponding pixel, adds the products together, divides the sum by the Scale value, adds the Offset value, and applies the result to the pixel being evaluated.

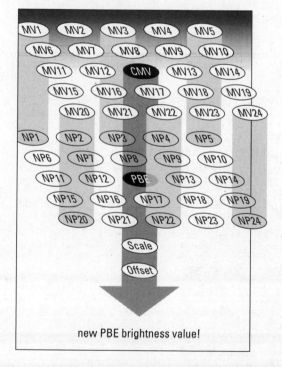

Perhaps seeing all this spelled out in an equation will help you understand the process; or, you may now know that you have absolutely no interest in using this filter and will be quickly flipping to the latter sections on displacement maps. Either way, here it is. Note that in the following equation, NP stands for *neighboring pixel* and MV stands for the corresponding matrix value in the Custom dialog box.

$$New\ brightness\ value = (\ (\ (PBE \times CMV) + (NP1 \times MV1) + (NP2 \times MV2) + \ldots) \div Scale) + Offset$$

601

Luckily, Photoshop calculates the equation without any help from you. All you have to do is punch in the values and see what happens.

Custom filter advice

Now obviously, if you go around multiplying the brightness value of a pixel too much, you end up making it white. And a filter that turns an image white is pretty much useless. The key, then, is to filter an image and at the same time maintain the original balance of brightness values. To achieve this, just be sure that the sum of all values in the matrix is 1. For example, the default values in the matrix shown back in Figure 12.1 are 5, −1, −1, −1, and −1, which add up to 1. If the sum is greater than 1, use the Scale value to divide the sum down to 1. Figures 12.3 and 12.4 show the results of increasing the CMV to 6, 7, and 8. This raises the sum of the values in the matrix to 2, then 3, and finally 4.

In Figure 12.3, the sum was entered into the Scale option to divide the sum back down to 1; any value divided by itself is 1, after all. The result is that Photoshop maintains the original color balance of the image while at the same time filtering it slightly differently. When the Scale value was not raised, the image became progressively lighter, as illustrated in Figure 12.4.

FIGURE 12.3

Raising the Scale value to reflect the sum of the values in the matrix maintains the color balance of the image.

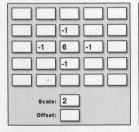

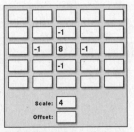

FIGURE 12.4

Raising the sum of the matrix values without counterbalancing it in the Scale option lightens the image.

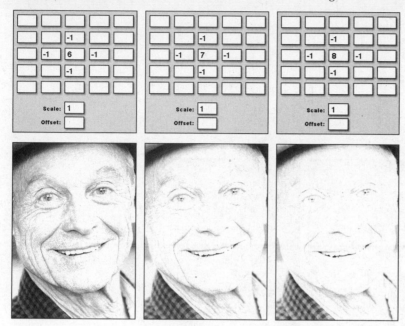

If the sum is less than 1, increase the CMV until the sum reaches the magic number. For example, in Figure 12.5, the values were lowered to the left of the CMV and then above and to the right of the CMV by 1 apiece to increase the sharpening effect. To ensure that the image did not darken, the CMV was also raised to compensate. When the CMV was not raised, the image turned black.

TIP Although a sum of 1 provides the safest and most predictable filtering effects, you can use different sums, such as 0 and 2, to try out more destructive filtering effects. If you do, be sure to raise or lower the Offset value to compensate. For some examples, see the "Non-1 variations" section later in this chapter.

Applying custom values

The following sections show you ways to sharpen, blur, and otherwise filter an image using specific matrix, Scale, and Offset values. We hope that, by the end of the Custom filter discussions, you not only know how to repeat the following examples, but also how to apply what you've learned to design special effects of your own.

FIGURE 12.5

Raising the CMV to compensate for the lowered values in the matrix maintains the color balance of the image.

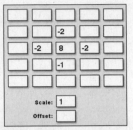

Symmetrical effects

Values that are symmetrical both horizontally and vertically surrounding the central matrix value produce sharpen and blur effects:

- **Sharpening:** A positive CMV surrounded by negative values sharpens an image, as demonstrated in the first example of Figure 12.6. Figures 12.3 through 12.5 also demonstrate varying degrees of sharpening effects.

- **Blurring:** A positive CMV surrounded by symmetrical positive numbers — balanced, of course, by a Scale value as explained in the preceding section — blurs an image, as demonstrated in the second example of Figure 12.6.

- **Blurring with edge detection:** A negative CMV surrounded by symmetrical positive values blurs an image and adds an element of edge detection, as illustrated in the last example of the figure. These effects are unlike anything provided by Photoshop's standard collection of filters.

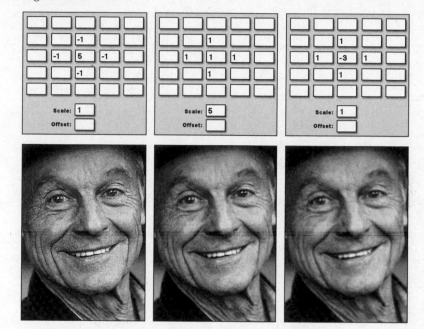

FIGURE 12.6

Symmetrical values can result in sharpening (left), blurring (middle), and edge detection (right) effects.

Sharpening

The Custom command provides as many variations on the sharpening theme as the Unsharp Mask filter. In a sense, it provides even more, for whereas the Unsharp Mask filter requires you to sharpen an image inside a Gaussian radius, you get to specify exactly which pixels are taken into account when you use the Custom filter.

To create Unsharp Mask–like effects — well, more like the Sharpen tool, actually — enter a large number in the CMV and small values in the surrounding option boxes, as demonstrated in the first two examples of Figure 12.7. To go beyond Unsharp Mask, you can violate the radius of the filter by entering values around the perimeter of the matrix and ignoring options closer to the CMV, as demonstrated in the last example of Figure 12.7.

FIGURE 12.7

To create severe sharpening effects, enter a CMV just large enough to compensate for the negative values in the matrix (first and second examples). To heighten the sharpening effect even further, shift the negative values closer to the perimeter of the matrix (last example).

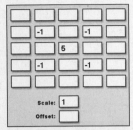 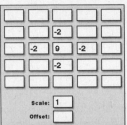 

You can sharpen an image using the Custom dialog box in two basic ways. First, you can enter lots of negative values into the neighboring options in the matrix and then enter a CMV just large enough to yield a sum of 1. This results in radical sharpening effects, as demonstrated in the examples in Figure 12.7.

Second, you can tone down the sharpening by raising the CMV and using the Scale value to divide the sum down to 1. Figure 12.8 shows the results of raising the CMV and Scale values to lessen the impact of sharpening effects typical of those performed in the first two examples of Figure 12.7. Figure 12.9 shows what happens when you apply slightly more adventurous values. Although the arithmetic is a little more involved, the values remain symmetrical and the sums remain 1.

FIGURE 12.8

To sharpen more subtly, increase the central matrix value and then enter the sum into the Scale value.

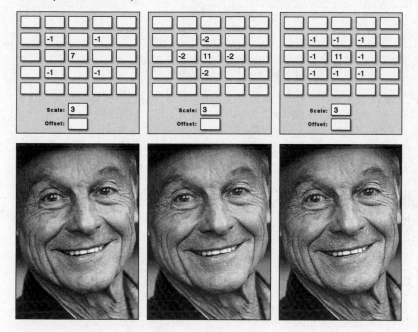

FIGURE 12.9

When you soften the effect of radical sharpening, you create a thicker, higher-contrast effect, much as when raising the Radius value in the Unsharp Mask dialog box.

Blurring

The philosophy behind blurring is very much the same as that behind sharpening. To produce extreme blurring effects, enter lots of values or high values into the neighboring options in the matrix, enter 1 into the CMV, and then enter the sum into the Scale option. Examples appear in Figure 12.10. To downplay the blurring, raise the CMV and the Scale value by equal amounts. In the last example of Figure 12.10, the same neighboring values were used as in the middle image, but the CMV and the Scale values were increased by 3.

FIGURE 12.10

To create severe blurring effects, enter 1 for the CMV and fill the neighboring options with 1s and 2s (first two images). To blur more subtly, increase the central matrix value and the Scale value by equal amounts (last image).

Edge detection

We hope that this is all beginning to make sense by now. However, in case you're still feeling a little confused, let's go through it one more time in the venue of edge detection. If you really want to see those edges, enter 1s and 2s into the neighboring options in the matrix, and then enter a CMV just *small* enough — it's a negative value, after all — to make the sum 1. The first two examples in Figure 12.11 illustrate.

To lighten the edges and bring out the blur, raise the CMV and enter the resulting sum into the Scale option box. The last example in Figure 12.11 pushes the boundaries between edge detection and a straight blur.

FIGURE 12.11

To create severe edge detection effects, enter a negative CMV just small enough to compensate for the positive values in the matrix (first two examples). To blur the edges, increase the central matrix value and then enter the sum into the Scale value (final example).

 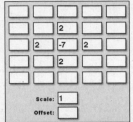 

Non-1 variations

Every image shown in Figures 12.6 through 12.11 is the result of manipulating matrix values and using the Scale option to produce a sum total of 1. Earlier in this chapter, you saw what can happen if you go below 1 (black images) or above 1 (white images). But you haven't seen how you can use non-1 totals to produce interesting, if somewhat washed-out, effects.

The key is to raise the Offset value, thereby adding a specified brightness value to each pixel in the image. By doing this, you can offset the lightening or darkening caused by the matrix values to create an image that has half a chance of printing well.

Lightening overly dark effects

The first image in Figure 12.12 uses nearly the same values used to create the extreme sharpening effect in the last image of Figure 12.7. The only difference is that the CMV is 1 lower (12, down from 13), which in turn lowers the sum total from 1 to 0.

The result is a dark image with hints of brightness at points of high contrast. The image reads well onscreen, but many of the details are likely to fill in during the printing process. To prevent the image from going too dark, lighten it using the Offset value. Photoshop adds the value to the brightness level of each selected pixel. A brightness value of 255 equals solid white, so you don't need to go too high. As illustrated by the last example in Figure 12.12, an Offset value of 100 is enough to raise most pixels in the image to a medium gray.

FIGURE 12.12

Here are three examples of a sharpening kernel with a sum total of 0. The only difference is that the second and third examples were lightened incrementally by entering positive values into the Offset option box.

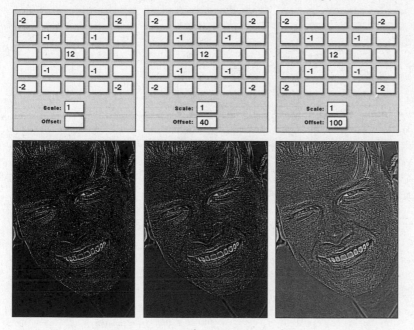

Darkening overly light effects

You also can use the Offset value to darken filtering effects with sum totals greater than 1. The images in Figures 12.13 and 12.14 show sharpening and edge detection effects whose matrix totals add up to 2. On their own, these filters produce effects that are too light. However, as demonstrated in the middle and right examples in the figures, you can darken the effects of the Custom filter to create high-contrast images by entering a negative value into the Offset option box.

FIGURE 12.13

Here are three examples of sharpening effects with sum totals of 2. You can darken images incrementally by entering negative values into the Offset option box.

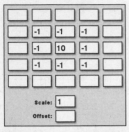

Using extreme offsets

If a brightness value of 255 produces solid white and a brightness value of 0 is solid black, why in the world does the Offset value permit any number between negative 9,999 and positive 9,999, a number 40 times greater than solid white? The answer lies in the fact that the matrix options can force the Custom filter to calculate brightness values much darker than black and much lighter than white. Therefore, you can use a very high or very low Offset value to boost the brightness of an image in which all pixels are well below black or diminish the brightness when all pixels are way beyond white.

FIGURE 12.14

These three examples show edge detection effects with sum totals of 2, darkened incrementally with progressively lower Offset values.

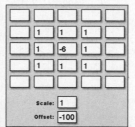

Figure 12.15 shows exaggerated versions of the sharpening, blurring, and edge detection effects. The sum totals of the matrices (when divided by the Scale values) are –42, 52, and 42, respectively. Without some help from the Offset value, each of these filters would turn every pixel in the image black (in the case of the sharpening effect) or white (blurring and edge detection). But as demonstrated in the figure, using enormous Offset numbers brings out those few brightness values that remain. The images are so polarized that there's little difference between the three effects, the first image being an inverted version of the last. The second row shows the results of choosing Edit ➪ Fade Custom immediately after applying the Custom filter and selecting the Luminosity blend mode.

FIGURE 12.15

You can create high-contrast effects by exaggerating all values in the matrix and then compensating with a very high or very low Offset value (top row). When you back off the effect using Edit ⇨ Fade (bottom row), these dramatic effects become interesting indeed.

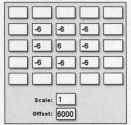

					600		60		600					
	-6	-6	-6			60	60	60			6	6	6	
	-6	6	-6		60	60	60	60	60		6	-6	6	
	-6	-6	-6			60	60	60			6	6	6	
					600		60		600					

Scale: 1   Scale: 60   Scale: 1
Offset: 6000   Offset: -7500   Offset: -6000

Edit ⇨ Fade Custom, Luminosity blend mode

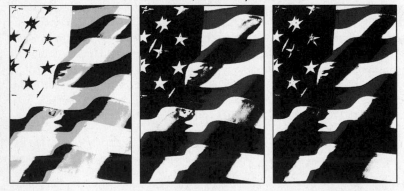

Other custom effects

By now, you may see what a very cool and flexible tool the Custom filter can be. At the very least, you now have a better idea of how it works, and if you tried any of the settings shown, you have seen it go to work on your images. In truth, another 20 or 30 pages easily could have been devoted to the myriad ways the Custom filter can be used, and even that wouldn't truly do the topic justice.

Given that the demonstrations thus far have been fairly tame—showing you how to use the Custom filter to achieve effects that also can be obtained through other filters, either alone or in combination—you may be wondering what happens if you just go absolutely berserk, in a crazed computer-geek sort of way, and start entering matrix values in random, arbitrary arrangements. The answer is that as long as you maintain a sum total of 1, you can achieve some pretty interesting and even usable effects. Many of these effects will be simple variations on blurring, sharpening, and edge detection, which are covered in upcoming sections of this chapter.

Directional blurs

Figure 12.16 shows examples of entering positive matrix values all in one row, all in a column, or in opposite quadrants. As you can see, as long as you maintain uniformly positive values, you get a blurring effect. However, by keeping the values lowest in the center and highest toward the edges and corners, you can create directional blurs. The first example resembles a slight horizontal motion blur, the second looks like a slight vertical motion blur, and the last example looks like it's vibrating horizontally and vertically.

FIGURE 12.16

Enter positive matrix values in a horizontal formation (left) or vertical formation (middle) to create slight motion blurs. By positioning positive values in opposite corners of the matrix, you create a subtle vibration effect (right) as the content is blurred in two directions, as though it's being shaken in place.

Embossing

So far, you aren't going very nuts, are you? Despite their unusual formations, the matrix values in Figures 12.16 still manage to maintain symmetry. Well, now it's time to lose the symmetry, which typically results in an embossing effect.

Figure 12.17 shows three variations on embossing, all of which involve positive and negative matrix values positioned on opposite sides of the CMV. (The CMV happens to be positive merely to maintain a sum total of 1.)

FIGURE 12.17

You can create embossing effects by distributing positive and negative values on opposite sides of the central matrix value.

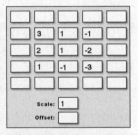

This type of embossing has no hard-and-fast light source, but you might imagine that the light comes from the general direction of the positive values. Therefore, when the positive and negative values are swapped throughout the matrix (all except the CMV), an underlighting effect is achieved, as demonstrated by the images in Figure 12.18.

FIGURE 12.18

Change the location of positive and negative matrix values to change the general direction of the light source.

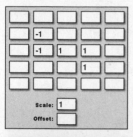

In truth, it's not so much a lighting difference as a difference in edge enhancement. White pixels collect on the side of an edge represented by positive values in the matrix; black pixels collect on the negative-value side. So when the locations of positive and negative values are swapped between Figures 12.17 and 12.18, the distribution of white and black pixels in the filtered images is changed as well.

Embossing is the loosest of the Custom filter effects. As long as you position positive and negative values on opposite sides of the CMV, you can distribute the values in almost any way you see fit. Figure 12.19 demonstrates three entirely arbitrary arrangements of values in the Custom matrix, downplayed by raising the CMV and entering the sum of the matrix values in the Scale option box. Notice, too, that unlike Filter ➪ Stylize ➪ Emboss, which sacrifices color and changes low-contrast areas to gray, the Custom filter preserves the natural colors in the image.

FIGURE 12.19

You can create whole libraries of embossing effects by experimenting with different combinations of positive and negative values. To emboss more subtly, increase the CMV (central matrix value) and the Scale values by equal amounts.

Displacing Pixels in an Image

Photoshop's second custom effects filter is Filter ➪ Distort ➪ Displace, which enables you to distort and add texture to an image by moving the colors of certain pixels in a selection. You specify the direction and distance that the Displace filter moves colors by creating a second image called a *displacement map,* or *dmap* (pronounced "dee-map") for short. The brightness values in the displacement map tell Photoshop which pixels to affect and how far to move the colors of those pixels:

- **Black:** The black areas of the displacement map move the colors of corresponding pixels in the selection a maximum prescribed distance to the right and/or down. Lighter values between black and medium gray move colors a shorter distance in the same direction.

- **White:** The white areas move the colors of corresponding pixels a maximum distance to the left and/or up. Darker values between white and medium gray move colors a shorter distance in the same direction.

- **Medium gray:** A 50-percent brightness value, such as medium gray, ensures that the colors of corresponding pixels remain unmoved.

Imagine that you start with the letter T pictured at the outset of Figure 12.20. Next, you create a new image window the same size as the letter T. Do this by choosing File ⇨ New and then choosing the letter T image from the bottom of the Window menu. This new image serves as the displacement map. Divide the image roughly into four quadrants, and as shown in the middle example of Figure 12.20, fill the upper-left quadrant with white, the lower-right quadrant with black, and the other two quadrants with medium gray. Note that the green arrows are not actually part of the dmap. They appear in the figure merely to indicate the direction in which the quadrants will move colors in the displaced image.

When finished, save the dmap image in the native Photoshop format (PSD) so that the Displace filter can access it. Then return to the original image, choose Filter ⇨ Distort ⇨ Displace, change both the Horizontal and Vertical Scale values to 40 percent each, and open the dmap from disk. The result is the image shown in the last example in Figure 12.20. In keeping with the distribution of brightness values in the dmap, the colors of the pixels in the upper-left quadrant of the carving image move up and to the left, the colors of the pixels in the lower-right quadrant move down and to the right, and the colors in the upper-right and lower-left quadrant remain intact.

FIGURE 12.20

The Displace filter moves colors in an image (left) according to the brightness values in a separate image, called the displacement map (middle). The green arrows indicate the direction that the dmap moves colors in the displaced image (right).

Original image   Displacement map   Displacement image (40%)

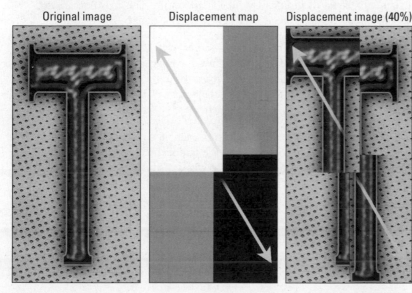

NOTE A dmap must be a grayscale or color image, and you must save the dmap as a flattened image in the native Photoshop file format. The Displace command does not recognize PICT, TIFF, or any of the other non-native file formats. It's an old filter, so it has its peculiarities.

At this point, you likely have two questions: How do you use the Displace filter, and why in the world would you possibly want to? The hows of the Displace filter are covered in the following section.

CROSS-REF To discover some whys — which should in turn help you dream up some whys of your own — read the "Using Displacement Maps" section later in this chapter.

Displacement theory

Like any custom filtering effect worth its weight in table salt, you need a certain degree of mathe-matical — or at least, geometric — reasoning skills to predict the outcome of the Displace filter. Don't be surprised if you're a bit befuddled by your first few experiments with this filter; you won't be alone in that, and your companions-in-befuddlement won't necessarily be the math-challenged. With some time and a reasonable amount of effort, you can learn to anticipate the approximate effects of this filter.

Direction of displacement

As mentioned just a paragraph or so ago, the black areas of a dmap move colors in an image to the right and/or down and the white areas move colors to the left and/or up. This may have caused you to wonder what all this "and/or" stuff is about, and rightly so. Is it right or is it down?

In fact, the direction of a displacement can go either way. It's up to you. Here's how it works: A dmap can contain one or more channels. If the dmap is a grayscale image with one color channel only, the Displace filter moves colors that correspond to black areas in the dmap both down *and* to the right, depending on your specifications in the Displace dialog box. The filter moves colors that correspond to white areas in the dmap both up and to the left.

Figure 12.21 shows two examples of an image displaced using a single-channel dmap, which appears on the left side of the figure. (To create this dmap, the middle image from Figure 12.20 was used, and the Filter ➪ Blur ➪ Gaussian Blur applied to it with a Radius value of 60 pixels.) The middle image was displaced both horizontally and vertically at 20 percent and the right image at 40 percent. Therefore, the colors in the right image travel twice the distance as those in the middle image, but all colors travel the same direction.

CROSS-REF The upcoming section "The Displace dialog box" explains exactly how the percentage values work.

FIGURE 12.21

After blurring the displacement map from the previous figure (left, with arrows added to show direction), this single-channel dmap was applied to the image at 20 percent (middle) and 40 percent (right).

Displacement map
(Gaussian Blur: 60 pixels)

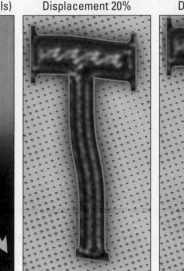

Displacement 20%

Displacement 40%

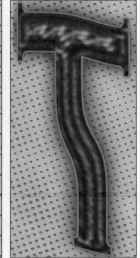

However, if the dmap contains more than one channel — whether it's a color image or a grayscale image with an independent mask channel — the first channel (red in the case of an RGB image) indicates horizontal displacement, and the second channel (green in RGB) indicates vertical displacement. All other channels are ignored. Therefore, the Displace filter moves colors that correspond to black areas in the first channel to the right and colors that correspond to white areas to the left. It then moves colors that correspond to the black areas in the second channel downward and colors that correspond to white areas upward.

Figure 12.22 examines an RGB image that contains a series of gradations. The first example shows the red channel, which transitions from gray to black to white to black and finally back to gray. The second example shows the green channel, which is filled with a white-to-black-to-white gradient. If the blue channel is filled with gray, the RGB dmap looks like the full-color image on right.

Figure 12.23 shows the effects of applying the RGB displacement map to a capital letter T. The first example shows a strictly horizontal displacement (again, set to 40 percent). The second example shows a vertical displacement. And the third shows both displacements calculated together.

FIGURE 12.22

Here you see the red (left) and green (middle) channels of a full-color displacement map (right). In a dmap, red shifts colors horizontally and green shifts them vertically.

Dmap, red channel   Same, green channel   Same, composite, RGB

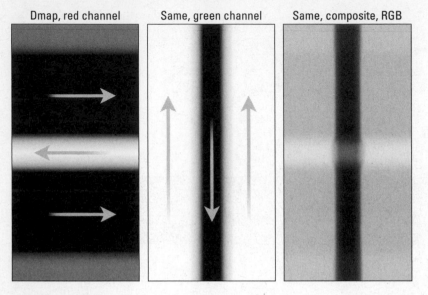

FIGURE 12.23

This figure shows the horizontal (left) and vertical (middle) results of applying the RGB dmap from the previous figure. The final image shows horizontal and vertical displacements combined. In all cases, the Scale values are 40 percent.

Displaced horizontally   Displaced vertically   Horizontally and vertically

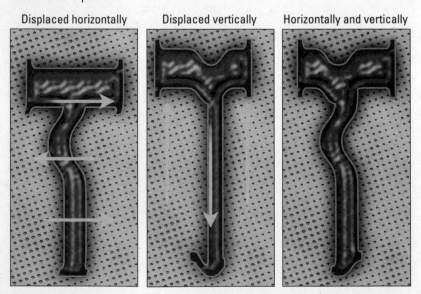

Brightness value transitions

If you look closely at the images in Figure 12.23, you'll notice stretching effects, most noticeable along the left edge of the image. Although very common with displacement maps, this is an effect you'll most likely want to avoid.

The cause of the stretching is twofold: First, the left and right edges of both channels in the dmap from Figure 12.22 are laced with black and white, which displace pixels around the perimeter of the image. This forces Photoshop to duplicate border pixels, hence the stretching. Second, neighboring brightness values in a gradient may be less similar than they appear. These differences are magnified when the gradient is expressed as a displacement map.

The Displace dialog box

When you choose Filter ➪ Distort ➪ Displace, Photoshop displays the Displace dialog box. Pictured in minimalist splendor in Figure 12.24, the Displace dialog box provides the following options:

FIGURE 12.24

Use these options to specify the degree of distortion, how the filter matches the displacement map to the image, and how it colors the pixels around the perimeter of the selection.

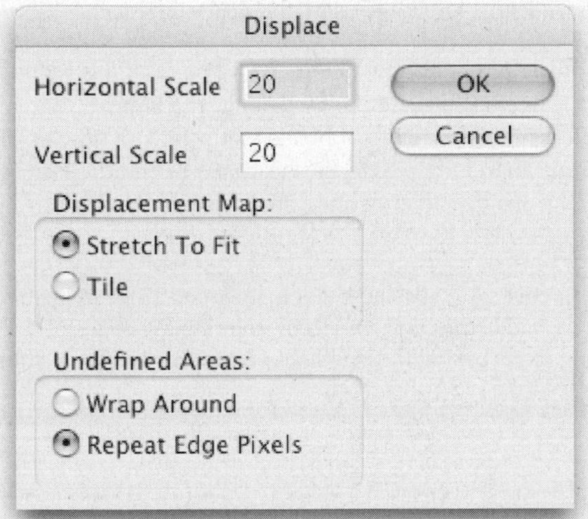

- **Scale:** You can specify the degree to which the Displace filter moves colors in an image by entering percentage values in the Horizontal Scale and Vertical Scale option boxes. At 100 percent, black and white areas in the dmap each have the effect of moving colors 128 pixels. That's 1 pixel per each brightness value over or under medium gray. You can isolate the effect of a single-channel dmap vertically or horizontally — or ignore the first or second channel of a two-channel dmap — by entering 0 percent into the Horizontal Scale or Vertical Scale option boxes, respectively.

  Figure 12.25 shows the effect of distorting an image exclusively horizontally (top row) and vertically (bottom row) using a variety of positive, negative, and even radical Scale values. In all cases, the single-channel dmap originally pictured in the first example in Figure 12.21 was used. Obviously, just as easily, a multi-channel map could have been applied. But this was already aptly demonstrated in Figure 12.23.

- **Displacement Map:** If the dmap contains fewer pixels than the image, you can either scale it to match the size of the selected image by selecting the Stretch To Fit radio button or repeat the dmap over and over within the image by selecting Tile. The first row of images in Figure 12.26 shows a single-channel dmap magnified to twice its normal size. It starts as a simple gradient stroked with gray and ends twirled to 999 degrees. The second row of images shows the T subjected to each of the dmaps above it with the Horizontal Scale and Vertical Scale values set to 25 percent and Stretch To Fit selected. The bottom row shows the same settings, except this time Tile was selected. The Displace command is unique in enabling you to distort an image using a repeating pattern.

- **Undefined Areas:** These radio buttons let you tell Photoshop how to color pixels around the outskirts of the selection that are otherwise undefined. By default, the Repeat Edge Pixels radio button is selected, which repeats the colors of pixels around the perimeter of the selection. This can result in extreme stretching effects, as shown in the middle example in Figure 12.27. To repeat the image inside the undefined areas instead, as demonstrated in the final example in the figure, select the Wrap Around option.

> **TIP** The Repeat Edge Pixels setting was active in all displacement map figures prior to Figure 12.28. As stated previously, you can avoid stretching effects by coloring the edges of the dmap with medium gray and gradually lightening or darkening the brightness values toward the center.

FIGURE 12.25

The results of applying the displacement map from Figure 12.21 to the letter T are shown here exclusively horizontally (top row) and vertically (bottom row) at each of several different percentage values. As illustrated by the right-hand examples, values over 100 percent can produce some surprising liquid image effects.

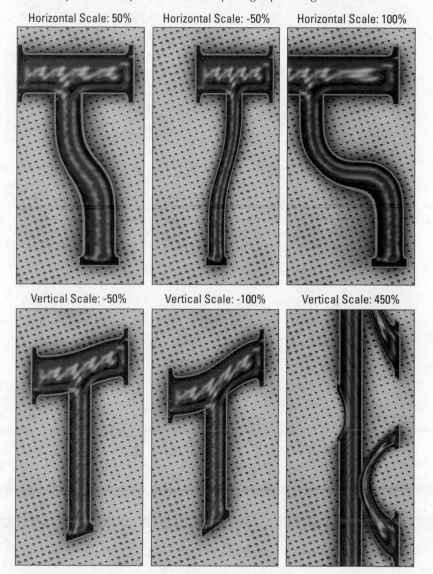

Horizontal Scale: 50%   Horizontal Scale: -50%   Horizontal Scale: 100%

Vertical Scale: -50%   Vertical Scale: -100%   Vertical Scale: 450%

FIGURE 12.26

Using a sequence of tiny dmaps, each measuring only a sixth the size of the letter (top row), dmap was alternately stretched to fit the image (middle row) and the dmap repeated using the Tile setting (bottom row).

Gradient & gray stroke   Gaussian Blur: Radius: 12   Twirl: 999%

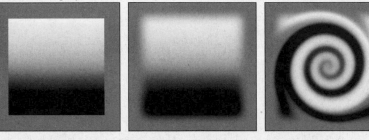

Displacement Map: Stretch to fit, Hscale & Vscale: 25%

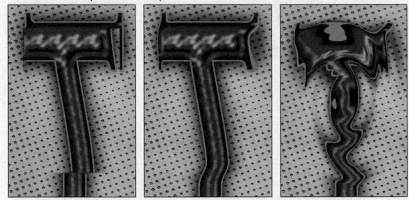

Displacement Map: Tile, same scale values

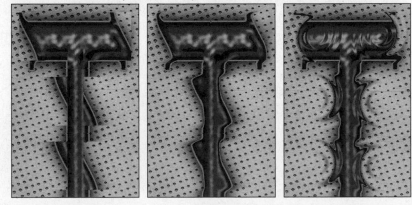

After you finish specifying options in the Displace dialog box, press Enter or Return to display the Open dialog box, which invites you to select the displacement map saved to disk. Only native Photoshop documents show up in the scrolling list.

FIGURE 12.27

After creating a straightforward, single-channel gradient dmap (left), the Displace filter was applied using two different Undefined Areas settings, Repeat Edge Pixels (middle) and Wrap Around (right).

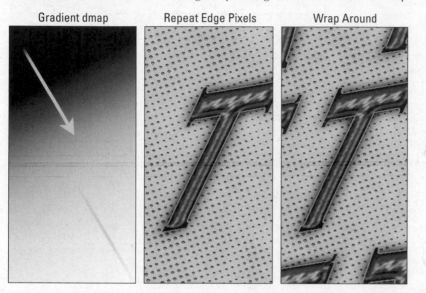

| Gradient dmap | Repeat Edge Pixels | Wrap Around |

Using Displacement Maps

So far, all the displacement maps demonstrated involve gradations of one form or another. Gradient dmaps distort the image over the contours of a fluid surface, like a reflection in a funhouse mirror. In this respect, the effects of the Displace filter closely resemble those of the Pinch and Spherize filters as well as the Free Transform command. But the Displace filter also offers its share of unique functions, including the ability to add texture to an image.

Applying predefined dmaps

Since the Displace filter was introduced in Photoshop 2.0, the program has shipped with a collection of predefined dmap files. These reside in the Displacement Maps folder that's inside the Plug-Ins folder, inside the folder that contains the Photoshop application file.

Figure 12.28 details four of the dozen images in the Displacement Maps folder. As you can see, the files contain sometimes independent information in the red and green channels. The blue channel is left white, hence the tendency of the colors toward blue, cyan, and magenta. In the final column of Figure 12.28, the blue channels are filled with 50 percent gray. This merely helps the colors to print better; because the Displace filter ignores the blue channel, it has no effect on the performance of the displacement map.

FIGURE 12.28

We're using four random files from the Displacement maps folder (typically a subfolder of the Plug-ins folder). Note that the red (left column) and green (middle column) channels often differ, thus conveying unique horizontal and vertical displacement information. The final column shows the full-color dmap, with the blue channel set to 50 percent gray.

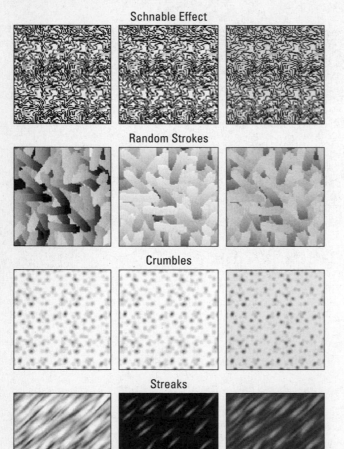

Schnable Effect

Random Strokes

Crumbles

Streaks

Figure 12.29 shows a sample image subjected to each of the four dmaps from Figure 12.28. The second and third columns in Figure 12.29 show the image displaced exclusively horizontally or vertically by the amounts described in the labels. Figure 12.30 shows the image displaced using a host of arbitrary Horizontal Scale and Vertical Scale values applied in tandem.

FIGURE 12.29

The stock photo from the Corbis image library (left) is displaced horizontally (middle) or vertically (right) using the dmaps featured in the previous figure.

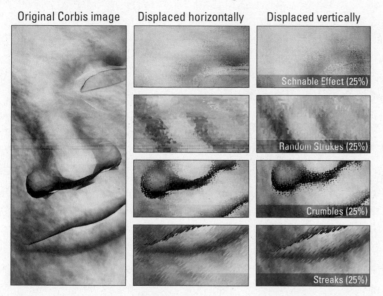

Original Corbis image · Displaced horizontally · Displaced vertically

Schnable Effect (25%)

Random Strokes (25%)

Crumbles (25%)

Streaks (25%)

You may notice that some of the dmap file names recommend a percentage amount for you to use, as in the case of Pentagons (10%). This happens to be the Scale value, Horizontal and Vertical, that precisely divides the image into solid blocks of color, as in the first example in Figure 12.31. In this regard, the Displace filter map may produce an effect similar to Filter ➪ Pixelate ➪ Crystallize; but armed with a custom dmap, you have the opportunity to design an infinite array of regularly repeating shapes. Of course, you shouldn't hesitate to experiment with values other than 10 percent. Figure 12.31 offers a few suggestions.

FIGURE 12.30

Here you see more applications of Photoshop's predefined dmaps, this time using independent Horizontal Scale and Vertical Scale values.

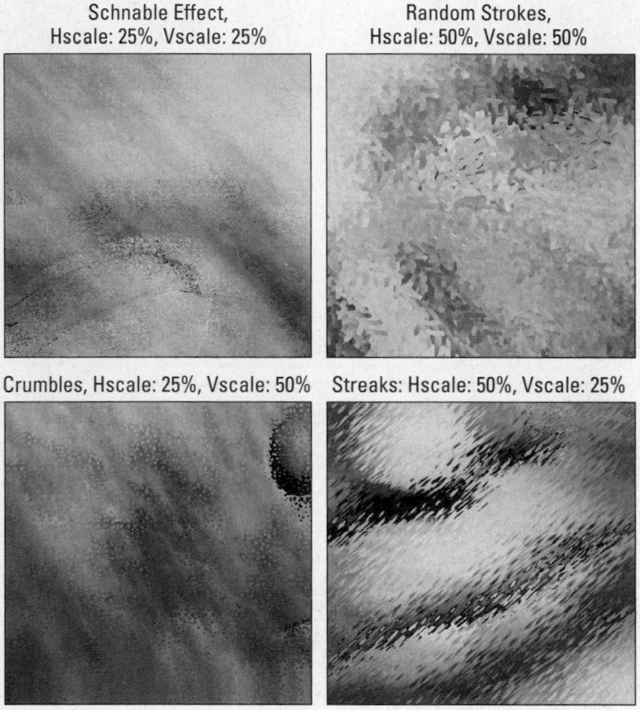

Schnable Effect,
Hscale: 25%, Vscale: 25%

Random Strokes,
Hscale: 50%, Vscale: 50%

Crumbles, Hscale: 25%, Vscale: 50%

Streaks: Hscale: 50%, Vscale: 25%

As illustrated in Figure 12.31, many of Photoshop's predefined dmaps produce the effect of viewing the image through textured glass — an effect known in the 3D realm as *glass refraction*. Those few patterns that contain too much contrast to pass off as textured glass — including Fragment Layers, Mezzo Effect, and Schnable Effect — can be employed to create images that appear as if they were printed on coarse paper or even textured metal. Note that the Fragment Layers dmap has nothing to do with Photoshop's layers; in fact, it was so named before Photoshop even had layers. Rather, it is intended to separate an image into multiple veins of fragmented color.

TIP   When using a repeating pattern — including any of the images inside the Displacement Maps folder — as a dmap, be sure to select the Tile radio button inside the Displace dialog box. This repeats the dmap rather than stretching it out of proportion.

FIGURE 12.31

Examples of an image displaced with the Pentagons dmap. By setting the Scale values to 10 percent apiece, you assign each pentagon its own solid color (top left). Other values result in glass-refraction effects.

Pentagons, Hscale: 10%, Vscale: 10%   Same, Hscale: 25%, Vscale: 25%

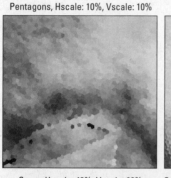

Same, Hscale: 48%, Vscale: 62%   One last time, Hscale: 120%, Vscale: 80%

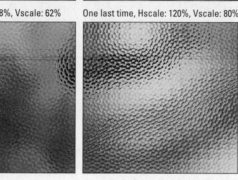

Customizing a dmap to an image

Want to get carried away? Then by all means, get carried away. Just as masking is the art of selecting an image using any tool inside Photoshop, displacing is the admittedly more arcane art of distorting an image using any tool inside Photoshop. The more fun you allow yourself to have with displacement maps, the more you'll come to understand how they work and the more likely you'll be to divine practical applications for them.

Case in point: In Figure 12.32, working in the standard composite RGB view, the Add Noise filter was applied three times in a row using the same 100-percent setting as before. Then Filter ➪ Pixelate ➪ Color Halftone was applied, with a Max. Radius value of 12 pixels, and the other values left set to their defaults. (Color Halftone automatically applies different settings to different channels, so there was no need to switch channels this time around.) Last, Filter ➪ Distort ➪ ZigZag was chosen, with an Amount value of 30 percent and a Ridges value set to 5. The Style was Pond Ripples. The first image in Figure 12.35 shows the finished dmap.

The second and third images in Figure 12.32 show displacements achieved using the Color Halftone dmap. Because the dmap texture is so busy, dramatic effects are produced using small Scale values. The results are ripple patterns that aren't possible using any filter but Displace.

631

FIGURE 12.32

A displacement map can be as wild as you want it to be. Here a colorful dmap is crafted using the Color Halftone and ZigZag filters (left) in which red and green channels are unique. Then the dmap was applied to the image using small Scale values (middle and right).

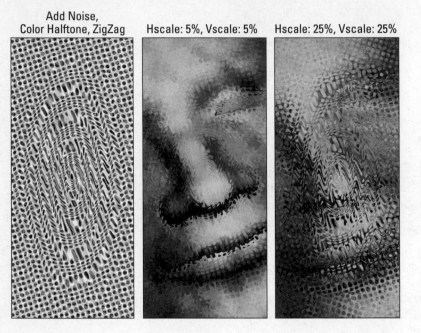

Add Noise,
Color Halftone, ZigZag   Hscale: 5%, Vscale: 5%   Hscale: 25%, Vscale: 25%

Using the Pattern Maker

Located under the Filter menu, the Pattern Maker is a repeating tile generator. It enables you to fill an entire image or layer with a repeating pattern — or even one massive texture — or save a pattern to Photoshop's presets for later use.

Unlike other patterning tools on the market, the Pattern Maker does not blur the edges of an image or create reflections to ensure seamless transitions. Rather, it chops an image into random clumps, pieces that clump together in random formation. It then makes a sort of chopped salad of the image to produce the randomness you see in the natural world. In most cases, the results are only marginally successful, and they often exhibit unacceptably defined edges. But every so often, you get something you can actually use. If that sounds like faint praise, bear in mind that the upside is that the Pattern Maker requires very little effort to use. It works like a free slot machine, so even though the odds are against you, you can take as many chances as you like. Just keep pulling the crank, and sooner or later you'll come up with a winner.

Generating a pattern

Start with an image that contains some basic texture like gravel or grass or something else that you'd want to repeat over a large image area. If you don't have such an image, you're in luck:

Photoshop has already given you some. Inside the folder that contains the Photoshop application, open the Presets folder, and then open the Textures folder. Inside you should find close to 30 images with names like Leafy Bush and Snake Skin. These are photographic textures provided specifically for use with the Pattern Maker filter.

When you get started on your own image, give yourself room to work:

STEPS: Creating a pattern

1. **Expand the canvas size by choosing Image ⇨ Canvas Size, select the Relative check box, and enter 200 for both the Width and Height options.** This way, you'll have space for your tile to repeat a few times, and you can see how it holds up as a pattern.

2. **Choose Filter ⇨ Pattern Maker.** This displays the commodious dialog box pictured in Figure 12.33. From here, creating a texture is the two-step process described in the figure.

FIGURE 12.33

Crafting a pattern with the Pattern Maker filter is a two-step process, provided that you regard repeatedly clicking the Generate button as a single step.

From within the image, select an area to serve as the source of the pattern.

Click the Generate button each time you select an area and wish to create a new pattern.

3. **Outline the portion of the image upon which you want to base the pattern.** (If you prefer, you can select the area before entering the Pattern Maker dialog box, or you can copy an image and select the Use Clipboard as Sample check box to base the pattern on that.)

4. **Click the Generate button to fill the image area with a random repeating pattern.** If that looks beautiful, you're in luck. But more likely, it won't look very good.

5. **Click Generate again.** And again. And again.

That's really the gist of it. Some might argue that there's more to using the Pattern Maker than clicking the Generate button like a couch potato searching for a good TV show, but of course they'd be wrong. Still, at the risk of overcomplicating the topic, here are a few things you might want to know:

- **Tweaking the settings:** If the filter consistently falls short of spawning a satisfactory effect, you can modify the Tile Generation options — Width, Height, Offset, and so on, all of which are discussed in the following section — and then click Generate Again to see what kind of difference your new settings make. You may want to click Generate Again two or three times before giving up on a setting and moving on.

- **History is now full:** The Pattern Maker saves your last 20 tiles to a temporary history buffer so that you can go back and compare them. After you generate your 20th tile, Photoshop warns you that the history buffer is full. After that point, an old tile drops off into the pit of pattern despair every time you generate a new one.

- **Managing your tiles:** Fortunately, you can manage the tiles in the history buffer, so you don't lose your best tiles. You do this using the Tile History options in the lower-right corner of the dialog box, magnified in Figure 12.34. So when you get the "History is now full" error message, go down to the Tile History options and browse through the tiles you've created so far by clicking the arrowhead icons. You also can click inside the tile number — 15 of 20, for example — and enter a different tile number. When you come across a bad pattern, click the trash can icon to delete it.

- **Saving a tile:** After you arrive at a tile that you deem satisfactory, don't just click the OK button. Instead, click the little disk icon in the Tile History area, labeled "Save pattern" in Figure 12.34. This saves the pattern to Photoshop's presets for later use. In fact, you may want to save several patterns, because they take up very little room.

When you're finished and you've saved the pattern or patterns you want to use, click Cancel. Yes, you read that right. Click Cancel. Clicking OK fills the entire image or active layer with the pattern, even if you have a selection active, which is almost never what you want. (The one exception occurs when using the Pattern Maker's exclusive Offset option, as explained in the next section.) With the pattern saved to the presets, you can apply it with more precision using the Pattern Stamp tool, History Brush, Fill command, or other function. So clicking Cancel opens up a wider world of options.

FIGURE 12.34

Once you've created a pattern you like, be sure to save it.

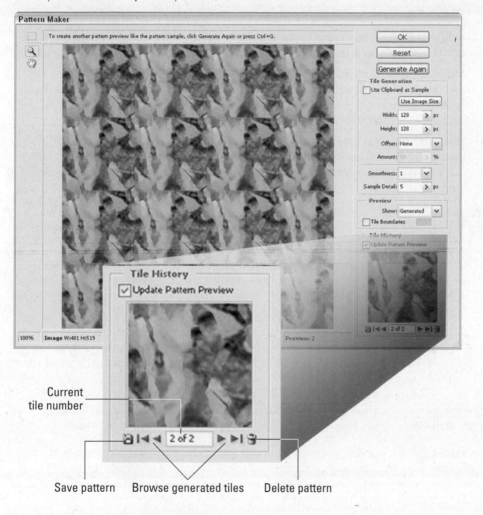

Current tile number

Save pattern   Browse generated tiles   Delete pattern

Tile Generation options

The options in the Tile Generation section of the dialog box allow you to change the size of the repeating tile and adjust other parameters that affect how the Pattern Maker calculates patterns. To make a modified setting take effect, you must click the Generate Again button. In order, here's how the options work:

- **Use Clipboard as Sample:** When selected, this check box generates the pattern from an image you copied to the Clipboard rather than the selected area in the image window.

- **Use Image Size:** Nothing says that you have to generate a repeating tile pattern: You can fill the image with one enormous texture. To do so, click the Use Image Size button to load the size of the foreground image into the Width and Height option boxes, and then click Generate Again. It takes several seconds to generate a very large tile, so be patient.

- **Width** and **Height:** By default, the Pattern Maker creates 128-×-128-pixel tiles, a common standard for background patterns inside your computer's operating system and on the Web. However, you can enter any values you like. And they can be different: Rectangular tiles are completely acceptable.

- **Offset** and **Amount:** Use the Offset option to offset rows or columns of tiles in the final pattern. The Horizontal setting offsets the rows; Vertical offsets the columns. Then use the Amount value to determine the amount of offset, measured as a percentage of the tile dimensions.

CAUTION   Note that the Offset values only work when you apply the pattern directly from the Pattern Maker by clicking the OK button. The Offset data is not saved with a pattern and cannot be accessed from other pattern functions inside Photoshop.

- **Smoothness:** If you keep seeing sharp edges inside your pattern, no matter how many times you regenerate it, try raising the Smoothness value. The value can only vary from 1 to 3, but higher values generally result in smoother transitions.

- **Sample Detail:** As mentioned earlier, the Pattern Maker works by chopping up an image and reassembling its parts. The size of those chopped up bits is determined by the Sample Detail value. Very small details result in faster pattern generation, with the potential for more cut lines and harsh transitions. A higher Sample Detail value creates a chunkier pattern, with better detail and more natural transitions, but it takes longer to generate as well. It's a good idea to try this value at its minimum and maximum settings, 3 and 21, to see if it makes much of a difference. If so, endure the delays and play with the value to get the desired results. If not, crank it down to 5 and focus on the other settings instead.

Bear in mind that, as you work on a pattern, you can zoom in and out of the preview area in the central portion of the dialog box to get a better idea of how the pattern will look. The Pattern Maker provides specific tools for this purpose, but it's generally easiest to rely on the keyboard shortcuts Ctrl+plus and Ctrl+minus (⌘+plus and ⌘+minus on the Mac).

Designing patterns with filters

The Pattern Maker is just the beginning of Photoshop's patterning capabilities. You also can create your own patterns, just as you'd expect from an accommodating program like Photoshop. And as luck would have it, you can do so without painting a single line. In fact, you can create a nearly infinite variety of background textures by applying several filters to a blank document. Figure 12.35 presents four examples. Note that none of these textures repeats seamlessly like the pattern tiles you've looked at so far; they're each intended to fill an entire background with very little effort.

FIGURE 12.35

A series of four different background textures is created using commands from the Filter menu, as noted. The background contains the Rusted Metal pattern fill, with the Crumble displacement map applied via the Filter ➪ Distort ➪ Displace command.

Add Noise, 100% X 3   Median, Radius: 2   Emboss, 45 degrees, 2, 100%

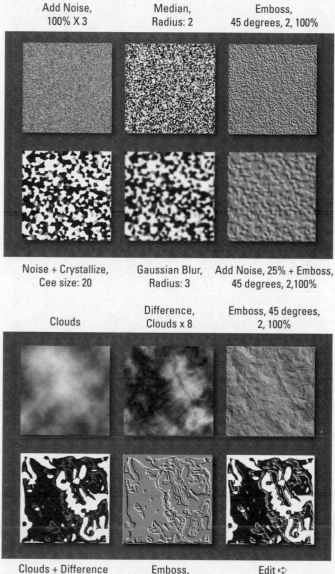

Noise + Crystallize, Cee size: 20   Gaussian Blur, Radius: 3   Add Noise, 25% + Emboss, 45 degrees, 2,100%

Clouds   Difference, Clouds x 8   Emboss, 45 degrees, 2, 100%

Clouds + Difference Clouds x 8 + Chrome 4.10   Emboss, 45 degrees, 2, 350%   Edit ➪ Fade + Pin Light

- **Using the Noise, Median, and Emboss filters:** To create the texture shown in the top row of the figure, start with a blank image. Then choose Filter ➪ Noise ➪ Add Noise, enter a value of 100 percent, and select the Monochromatic check box. After clicking OK, press Ctrl+F (⌘+F on the Mac) twice, each time repeating the filter, so that Add Noise is applied three times in a row. Next choose Filter ➪ Noise ➪ Median, and enter a value of 2 pixels, which averages the noise into clumps. Finally, choose Filter ➪ Stylize ➪ Emboss, and enter 45 degrees in the Angle option box, 2 pixels for the Height value, and 100 percent for the Amount. The result is a bumpy surface that looks a bit like stucco.

- **Using the Noise, Crystallize, Gaussian Blur, and Emboss filters:** To get the second row of effects in Figure 12.35, start at the point labeled "Add Noise (100%) × 3" in the first row, and apply Filter ➪ Pixelate ➪ Crystallize with a Cell Size of 20 pixels. Then blur the cells using Filter ➪ Blur ➪ Gaussian Blur and a Radius of 3 pixels. And finally, apply the Add Noise filter, this time at 25 percent, and the Emboss filter, using the same settings as before.

- **Using the Clouds, Difference Clouds, and Emboss filters:** To create the third row of textures, start with a blank image, and press the D key to make the foreground and background colors black and white. Choose Filter ➪ Render ➪ Clouds, and then apply Filter ➪ Render ➪ Difference Clouds, repeating the filter by pressing Ctrl+F (⌘+F) seven times in a row. In the last image, again apply the Emboss filter with an Amount value of 350 percent.

- **Using the Cloud Difference, Emboss, Fade, and Pin Light filters:** For the fourth row, take the second effect in the third row — the one labeled "Difference Clouds × 8" — and apply Filter ➪ Sketch ➪ Chrome with a Detail value of 4 and a Smoothness setting of 10. Next apply Emboss using the same Amount value of 350 percent as before. Finally, choose Edit ➪ Fade Emboss, and select Pin Light from the Mode pop-up menu. This blends the Chrome and Emboss effects into a frothy, plastery soup.

Summary

In this chapter, you learned about creating custom effects with the Custom filter; mastering the math behind that filter's ability to adjust light, color, blurring, sharpening; and a host of other effects. You also learned about displacement maps and how to make and use them, as well as creating displacement textures.

You learned to use the Pattern Maker to build custom patterns from images and selections, and you learned how to build textures and patterns with a variety of Photoshop's more specialized filters.

Part IV

Layers, Objects, and Text

Chapter 13

Working with Layers

Layers started out as little more than their name implies — sheets of pixels that you could edit and transform independently of each other. But since the feature was introduced in version 3, layers have become increasingly more sophisticated and complicated. Photoshop 4 introduced floating *adjustment layers* that let you correct colors without permanently affecting a single pixel (see Chapter 18). Photoshop 5 gave us layer effects, which included editable drop shadows, glows, and edge bevels (see Chapter 15). Photoshop 6 permitted you to bundle and color-code layers into logical clusters (this chapter), blend color channels independently of each other (see Chapter 14), and even add vector-based lines and shapes (see Chapter 15) and object-oriented text (see Chapter 16). Photoshop 7 gave you the ability to adjust the fill opacity and allowed for easier renaming of layers, but otherwise maintained the status quo. Photoshop CS dramatically improved the way you work with layers by introducing layer comps (covered later in this chapter).

With Photoshop CS2, to conclude our History of Photoshop Layers, we saw the biggest changes since version 4. Not necessarily improved so much as changed, the Layers Palette received a slight overhaul, as did the methods of linking, grouping, and merging layers. With CS3, these changes remain part of the palette, and we see the Layers palette on the dock (in the default workspace view, as described in Chapter 2). But not much else changed. Of course, the addition of Smart Filters, which you can read about in Chapter 10, has added something to the Layers palette, in that when Smart Filters are applied (to a Smart Object layer), the layer's status, along with all the filters applied to it as Smart Filters, are displayed as such in the palette.

For those of you who are new to Photoshop or for whom layers are some-thing of a conceptual enigma, let's back up and talk about what they are, what they do, and why you love them (you really do, you know).

The first and foremost benefit of layers is that they add versatility. Because each layer in a composition is completely independent, you can change your mind at a moment's notice. Consider Figure 13.1. This photo started out as a picture of the desert. The moon came from an entirely different image, and the two together are the result of layering.

Without layers you'd be hard-pressed to easily (just forget quickly) rearrange, resize, or remove anything from a photo. Because working with Photoshop means everything from the background to the smallest item in an image can be on its own layer, every aspect of an image is ultimately fluid and changeable.

FIGURE 13.1

Ah, the desert moon! Thanks to the inherent flexibility of layers, you can rearrange your image components, keeping them separate for easy editing, transformation, and removal.

Layering gives you freedom to try new things, make mistakes, make changes, and just generally expand your range of options. More than anything else, they permit you to restructure a composition and examine how it was put together after you assemble it. Layers can be very challenging or relatively simple to use: It depends on what you're doing with them and whether you've taken the time to get to know them, which is what you're about to do right now.

Sending a Selection to a Layer

To its credit, Photoshop lets you establish a new layer in roughly a billion ways. If you want to add a selected portion of one image to another image, the easiest method is to Ctrl-drag (Win) or ⌘-drag (Mac) the selection and drop it into its new home, as demonstrated in Figure 13.2. Photoshop creates the new layer from the selection, in one fell swoop.

CAUTION Be sure to Ctrl-drag (⌘-drag on the Mac) or use the Move tool. If you merely drag the selection with the Marquee, Lasso, or Wand, you drop an empty selection outline into the new image window. Also, be aware that pressing Ctrl (Win) or ⌘ (Mac) delivers the Move tool. But if the Pen, Arrow, or Shape tool is active, you get the Arrow tool instead, which won't work for you. Press V to get the Move tool, and then try dragging again.

When you drop the selection, the selection outline disappears. Not to worry, though. Now that the image resides on an independent layer, the selection outline is no longer needed. You can move the layer using the move tool, as you would move a selection. You can even paint inside what was once the selection by selecting the first of the Lock buttons in the Layers palette. Both the Move tool and the Lock buttons are covered in greater detail throughout this chapter.

If you want to clone a selection to a new layer inside the same image window — useful when performing complex filter routines and color corrections — choose Layer ➪ New ➪ Layer Via Copy, or simply press Ctrl+J (⌘+J on the Mac).

Other ways to make a layer

Those are only two of many ways to create a new layer in Photoshop. Here are a few others:

- Copy a selection (Ctrl+C or ⌘+C), and paste it into another image (Ctrl+V or ⌘+V). Photoshop pastes the selection as a new layer.

- If you want to relegate a selection exclusively to a new layer, choose Layer ➪ New ➪ Layer Via Cut or press Ctrl+Shift+J (⌘+Shift+J on the Mac). Rather than cloning the selection, Layer Via Cut removes the selection from the background image and places it on its own layer.

- To convert a floating selection to a new layer, press Ctrl+Shift+J (⌘+Shift+J on the Mac). The Shift key is very important. If you press Ctrl+J (Win) or ⌘+J (Mac) without Shift, Photoshop clones the selection (leaving the selected content behind on the layer of origin) at the same time that the new layer is created. *With* the Shift key, you get a new layer that consists of the content within your selection, and the content is removed from the layer of origin.

- To create an empty layer — to house, for example, a few brushstrokes without harming the original image — choose Layer ➪ New ➪ Layer or press Ctrl+Shift+N (⌘+Shift+N on the Mac). Or click the new layer icon at the bottom of the Layers palette (labeled in Figure 13.3).

- When you create a new layer, Photoshop positions it in front of the active layer. To create a new layer behind the active layer, Ctrl-click (Win) or ⌘-click (Mac) the new layer icon.

FIGURE 13.2

Ctrl-drag (⌘-drag on the Mac) a selected portion of an image, and drop it into a different image window to introduce the selection as a new layer. As you can see in the Layers palette, the moon is being moved into place as a new layer in front of the original background image.

Dropped selection
becomes new layer

Incidentally, you also can create a new layer by choosing New Layer from the Layers palette menu or the Layer menu's New submenu (choose Layer ➪ New ➪ Layer. But as you can see in Figure 13.3, nearly all the palette commands are duplicated in the Layer menu. Two unique palette commands are Dock to Palette Well, which sends the Layers palette tab to the Options bar, and Palette Options, which lets you change the size of the thumbnails in front of the layer names. As luck would have it, you can perform the latter technique more easily by right-clicking (Win) or Control-clicking (Mac) in the empty space below the layer names and choosing an option.

FIGURE 13.3

Nearly all the commands in the Layers palette menu are duplicated in the Layer menu — and supported by buttons at the bottom of the Layers palette itself.

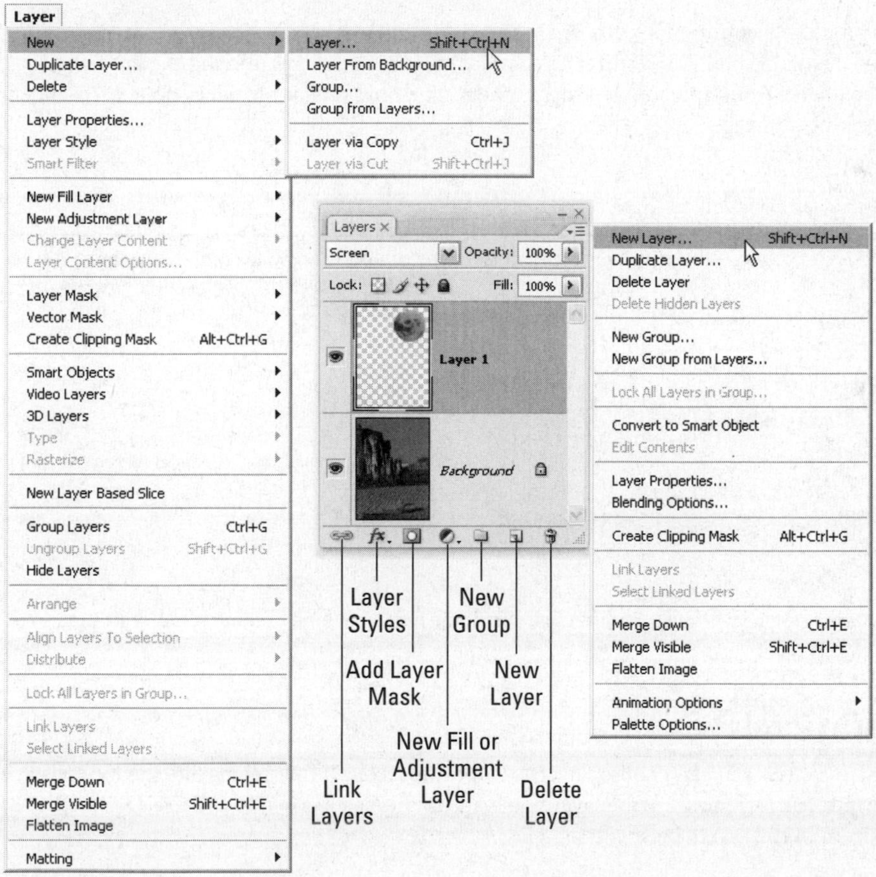

TIP

When you choose the Layer Via Copy or Layer Via Cut command or click the new layer icon, Photoshop automatically names the new layer for you. Unfortunately, the automatic names — Layer 1, Layer 2, and so on — are fairly meaningless and don't help to convey the contents of the layer.

If you want to specify a more meaningful name, add the Alt (Win) or Option (Mac) key. Press Ctrl+Alt+J (⌘+Option+J on the Mac) to clone the selection to a layer, press Ctrl+Shift+Alt+J (⌘+Shift+Option+J on the Mac) to cut the selection, or Alt-click (Option-click on the Mac) the new layer icon to create a blank layer. In any case, you see the dialog box shown in Figure 13.4. Type a name for the layer. If you like, you also can assign a color to the layer, which is helpful for identifying a layer name at a glance. Then press Enter or Return. For now, ignore the other options in this dialog box; you don't need to address them each time you use the dialog box, and anyway, you'll be getting to them later.

When creating a new layer from the keyboard, press Ctrl+Shift+Alt+N (⌘+Shift+Option+N on the Mac) to bypass the dialog box. Alt (Option on the Mac) works both ways, forcing the appearance of the dialog box some times and suppressing it others. The only time it produces no effect is when pasting or dropping an image.

FIGURE 13.4

Press Alt (Option on the Mac) to force the display of the New Layer dialog box, which lets you name the new layer.

TIP

To rename a layer, just double-click the name and type a new name directly in the Layers palette.

Duplicating a layer

To clone the active layer, you can choose Layer ➪ Duplicate Layer. If that seems like the long way 'round the barn to you, try dragging the layer you want to duplicate down to the Create New Layer icon at the bottom of the Layers palette.

To specify a name for the cloned layer or to copy the layer into another image, Alt-drag (Option-drag on the Mac) the layer onto the new layer icon. Always the thoughtful program, Photoshop displays the dialog box shown in Figure 13.5. You can name the cloned layer by typing something in the As option box. To apply the layer to some other open image, choose the image name from the Document pop-up menu. Or choose New, and type the name for an entirely different image in the Name option box, as the figure shows.

FIGURE 13.5

You can duplicate the layer into an entirely different image by Alt-dragging (Option-dragging on the Mac) the layer onto the new layer icon in the Layers palette. This dialog box helps you complete the process.

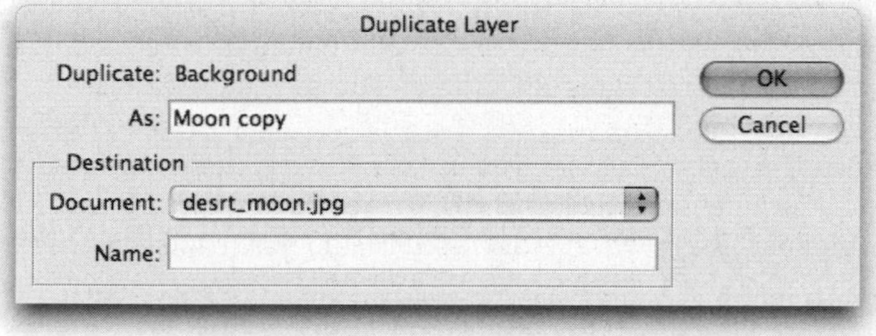

Duplicate Layer

Duplicate: Background

As: Moon copy

OK

Cancel

Destination

Document: desrt_moon.jpg

Name:

> **TIP** You can clone a layer by simply Ctrl+Alt-dragging (⌘+Option-dragging on the Mac) it inside the image window. This way, you clone the layer and reposition it in one operation. Just be sure not to begin your drag inside a selection outline; if you do, you create a floating selection.

Layer Basics

Regardless of how you create a new layer, Photoshop lists the layer along with a little thumbnail of its contents in the Layers palette. The new layer appears highlighted to show that it's active, and the layer's name appears in bold.

> **TIP** If the thumbnails aren't big enough for you, click the palette's option menu button. If you can't spot this menu button, look for the down-pointing triangle next to a stack of lines (which visually represents the menu you'e about to display), just above the Opacity setting. Once you've found it, click the button and choose Palette Options. In the resulting dialog box, you can choose from three sizes for the thumbnails (small is the default) and also choose to see either just the content of the layer (Layer Bounds) or Entire Document in the thumbnail.

Back in the Layers palette, to the left of the thumbnails is a column of eyeballs. These symbols invite you to hide and display layers temporarily. Click an eyeball to hide the layer; the eyeball disappears, and so does the layer's content within the image. Click where the eyeball previously was to bring it back and redisplay the layer. Whether hidden or displayed, all layers remain intact and ready for action, although some layer quality adjustments — such as the blending mode and Opacity — are dimmed if you click a hidden layer. To make such adjustments to the layer, redisplay it, tweak the desired settings, and then rehide the layer if you still don't need to see it in the image.

To view a single layer by itself, Alt-click (Win) or Option-click (Mac) the eyeball icon to hide all other layers. Alt-click (Win) or Option-click (Mac) the eyeball again to bring all the layers back into view.

Switching between layers

You can select a different layer by clicking its name in the Layers palette. The layer you click becomes active, enabling you to edit it. Here are some other layers palette tricks:

- **Click and activate multiple layers:** Just click the first layer you want to select, and then press and hold Shift to select additional consecutive layers (next to each other in the Layers palette, not necessarily in the image) or Ctrl (⌘ on the Mac) to select nonconsecutive layers. After the multiple layers are selected, you have limited abilities to do things to them; you can move them with the Move tool, and you can transform them as a unit. This is not the same as grouping them, which is discussed later in this chapter.

- **Link multiple layers and combine them into groups, as is explained later:** After they're linked, you have the same ability to move and transform the layers (press Ctrl+T [⌘+T] to enter Free Transform mode) as you do when you simply Shift-click or Ctrl-click (⌘-click) the layers to select them. You cannot, however, paint, draw, fill, or apply filters to the selected or linked layers. If you do want to formally merge the layers, you can do so by turning them into a single layer, which can then be treated like any other layer. We tell you more about that later, too.

- **Ctrl (⌘ on the Mac) gets you the Move tool:** If the Move tool is already selected, you don't have to press Ctrl or ⌘; Alt-right-clicking or Option+Control-clicking works just fine.

- **Right-clicking (Control-clicking on the Mac) alone brings up a shortcut menu:** When you right-click or Control-click with the Move tool — or Ctrl-right-click (⌘+Control-click on the Mac) with any other tool — Photoshop displays a pop-up menu that lists the layer that the image is on and any other layers in the image, as in Figure 13.6. (If a layer is completely transparent at the spot where you right-click or Control-click, that layer name doesn't appear in the pop-up menu.) Select the desired layer to go there.

TIP   If you'd prefer Photoshop to *always* go directly to the layer on which you click and avoid all these messy keyboard tricks, press V to select the Move tool. The first option in the Options bar is called Auto Select, and it's accompanied by a list. Select Layer, and then whenever you click a layer with the Move tool — or Ctrl-click (⌘-click on the Mac) with some other tool — Photoshop goes right to it, making it the active layer.

TIP   There also is an Auto Select: Groups option (using that Auto Select list again), which you may want to deselect — so that when you select a layer simply by clicking it, you don't necessarily select the entire group of which that layer may be a member. More about groups can be found later in this chapter.

FIGURE 13.6

Right-click (Control-click on the Mac) with the Move tool in an image to view a pop-up menu. The menu lists all the layers in the image that contain pixel data on the spot where you clicked.

Switching layers from the keyboard

You also can ascend and descend the layer stack from the keyboard:

- **Alt+] (Option+] on the Mac):** Press Alt+right bracket (Win) or Option+right bracket (Mac) to go to the next layer up in the stack. If you're already at the top layer, Photoshop takes you back around to the lowest one.

- **Alt+[(Option+[on the Mac):** Press Alt+left bracket (Win) or Option+left bracket (Mac) to go down a layer. If the Background layer is active (or the bottom-most layer in the image if there's no Background layer) Alt+[or Option+[takes you to the top layer.

- **Shift+Alt+] (Shift+Option+] on the Mac):** This takes you to the top layer in the image.

- **Shift+Alt+[(Shift+Option+[on the Mac):** This activates the background layer (or the lowest layer if no background exists).

NOTE These shortcuts work only with visible layers. Hidden layers are skipped.

NOTE While we haven't gotten into Layer Groups yet, it's important to note that Photoshop treats a closed group (a group whose layers are collapsed within the palette) in the Layers palette (a *layer group*) as if it were a layer unto itself. So every one of these tricks skips to or over the group in a single bound. For the complete lowdown on layer groups including support for nested layer groups, see the section on grouping layers found later in this chapter.

Selecting similar layers

If you right-click (Control-click on the Mac) any layer in the Layers palette, a pop-up menu (shown in Figure 13.7) appears. Among the pop-up menu's commands is an option called "Select Similar Layers." Similar? What does that mean? It means layers that have similar content in terms of size, shape, color, modes, and styles, so referring again to Figure 13-7, if the command were to be chosen in the image shown (with the "Moon copy 2" layer active), the Moon and Moon copy layers would also be selected automatically.

The Select Similar Layers command can be a great way to select several duplicate layers at once without having to hunt through (and possibly scroll through, if you have lots of layers) a long list of layers in the palette to find the ones you want to select for moving, resizing, linking, or dragging to another image in the workspace.

FIGURE 13.7

Choose Select Similar Layers to grab all the layers that have much in common.

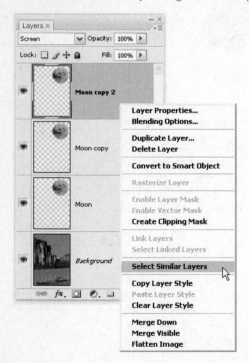

Understanding transparency

Although the selection outline disappears when you convert a selection to a layer, no information is lost. Photoshop retains every nuance of the original selection outline — whether it's a jagged border, a little bit of anti-aliasing, or a feathered edge. Anything that wasn't selected is now transparent. The data that defines the opacity and transparency of a layer is called the *transparency mask*.

To see this transparency in action, click the eyeball icon in front of the background item in the Layers palette. This hides the background layer and enables you to view the new layer by itself. In Figure 13.8, the background (the desert) is hidden (note the missing eyeball icon next to that layer) and only the moon layer is visible — and all of that layer except for the moon is transparent and filled with a checkerboard pattern. Opaque areas look like the standard image, and translucent areas, where they exist, appear as a mix of image and checkerboard — the visibility of the checkerboard, of course, dictated by the opacity of the content.

FIGURE 13.8

When you hide the background layer, you see a checkerboard pattern that represents the transparent portions of the layer.

TIP If the checkerboard pattern is hard to distinguish from the image, you can change the appearance of the pattern. Press Ctrl+K and then Ctrl+6 (⌘+K and then ⌘+6 on the Mac) to go to the Transparency & Gamut panel of the Preferences dialog box. Then edit the colors as you see fit (as explained in Chapter 2).

If you apply an effect to the layer while no portion of the layer is selected, Photoshop changes the opaque and translucent portions of the image but leaves the transparent region intact. For example, if you press Ctrl+I (⌘+I on the Mac) or choose Image ➪ Adjustments ➪ Invert, Photoshop inverts the image but doesn't change a single pixel in the checkerboard area. If you click in the left column in front of the background item to bring back the eyeball icon, you may notice a slight halo around the inverted image, but the edge pixels blend with the background image as well as they ever did. The only difference is that this selection is independent of its background. You can do anything you want to it without running the risk of harming the underlying background.

Only a few operations affect the transparent areas of a layer, and most of these are limited to tools. You can paint on transparent pixels to make them opaque. You can clone with the Clone Stamp or smear pixels with the edit tools. To send pixels back to transparency, paint with the Eraser. All these operations change both the contents of the layer and the composition of the transparency mask.

TIP   You also can fill all pixels by pressing Alt+Backspace (Option+Delete on the Mac) for the foreground color and Ctrl+Backspace (⌘+Delete on the Mac) for the background color. To fill the pixels in a layer without altering the transparency mask, toss in the Shift key. Shift+Alt+Backspace (Shift+Option+Delete on the Mac) fills the opaque pixels with the foreground color; Ctrl+Shift+Backspace (⌘+Shift+Delete on the Mac) fills them with the background color. In both cases, the transparent pixels remain every bit as transparent as they ever were.

When a portion of the layer is selected, pressing plain old Backspace (Win) or Delete (Mac) eliminates the selected pixels and makes them transparent, revealing the layers below. Note that this is not some display trick; you're actually clearing the pixels within the selection, so to get them back, you'll have to use Undo or use the History palette to go back in time to the pre-Clear state.

NOTE   Transparent pixels take up next to no space in memory, but opaque and translucent pixels do consume memory space. Thus, a layer containing 25 percent as many pixels as the background layer takes up roughly 25 percent as much space. Mind you, you shouldn't let this influence how you work in Photoshop, but it is something to keep in mind.

Modifying the background layer

At the bottom of the layer stack is the *Background layer*, the fully opaque layer that represents the base image. The background image is as low as you go. Nothing can be slipped under the background layer, and pixels in the background layer cannot be made transparent, unless you first convert the background to a floating layer. Blend modes and styles cannot be applied to the layer, nor can the background be changed in terms of its Opacity or Fill; these options become dimmed while the background layer is active.

To convert your Background layer to a floating layer, double-click the layer labeled Background in the Layers palette. A dialog box appears. Type a name for the new layer — Photoshop suggests Layer 0 — and press Enter or Return. You can now change the order of the layer or erase down to transparency.

TIP
To skip the dialog box and accept Layer 0 as the new layer name, press and hold Alt (Win) or Option (Mac) and double-click the Background item in the Layers palette.

In Figure 13.9, the background image has been converted to a layer. Had this particular image included a path that encircled the background layer's subject, or had the background content not completely filled the Background layer, you could Ctrl-click (⌘-click on the Mac) on the path to convert it to a selection outline and then press Ctrl+Shift+I (⌘+Shift+I on the Mac) to reverse the selection. This would select everything but the content on the layer, and that "everything but" could then be removed by pressing Delete. To demonstrate this in the image used thus far, the canvas size was increased to create white space around the image. This area then can be cleared, leaving transparency around the layer's actual content.

NOTE Although InDesign CS3 easily can handle layered Photoshop files complete with transparency, QuarkXPress 6.0 (and earlier versions) can't. As mentioned in Chapter 8, if you want to export transparency to Quark, you must use a clipping path.

FIGURE 13.9

After converting the Background layer to a floating layer, the white space around the content (canvas area) was selected and deleted, leaving transparency in its wake.

> **TIP** To convert the active layer to a background layer when there is currently no background layer, choose Layer ➪ New ➪ Background From Layer. It doesn't matter whether the active layer is at the top of the stack, the bottom, or someplace in between. Photoshop takes the layer and makes a new background out of it.

To establish a blank background, create an empty layer by pressing Ctrl+Shift+N (⌘+Shift+N on the Mac) and choosing Layer ➪ New ➪ Background From Layer. In Figure 13.10, a pattern fill (Wood, applied via the Edit ➪ Fill command and Fill dialog box) was used to create a texture, framing the image on the previous background, now called "main image." The main image layer was then selected, and Layer ➪ Layer Style ➪ Drop Shadow was chosen to add a drop shadow that makes the photo look like it's hovering over the textured paper backdrop.

> **CROSS-REF** Drop shadows and other layer styles are discussed in Chapter 15.

FIGURE 13.10

A new background layer is added below the main image layer (the former background) and a wood texture is added. Stroke and Drop Shadow layer styles were then added to the desert layer to give the composition a little false depth.

Photoshop permits only one background layer per image. If an image already contains a background layer, the command Layer ➪ New ➪ Background From Layer changes to Layer From Background, which converts the background layer to a floating layer, as when you double-click the Background item in the Layers palette.

Reordering layers

Layers would be rather limited in terms of enabling you to rearrange your image content if you couldn't change their stacking order. Luckily, Photoshop makes it easy to move layers up and down in the stack, making things overlap when they didn't before, preventing overlaps where you don't want them, and placing content behind other content so you can either see it (by reducing the opacity of the uppermost layer) or so you can't see some or all of the underlying layer. Rearranging the order of your layers also can have interesting effects on any blending modes previously applied to your layers.

You can reorder layers in two ways. First, you can click and drag a layer name up or down in the scrolling list to move it forward or backward in layering order (your mouse pointer turns from a pointing hand to a little determined fist while you're dragging). The only trick is to make sure that the black bar appears at the point where you want to move the layer before you release the mouse button, as illustrated in Figure 13.11.

The second way to reorder layers is to choose a command from the Layer ➪ Arrange submenu. For example, choose Layer ➪ Arrange ➪ Bring Forward to move the active layer up one level; choose Layer ➪ Arrange ➪ Send to Back to move the layer to just above the Background layer.

You can move faster if you remember the following keyboard shortcuts:

- **Ctrl+Shift+] (⌘+Shift+] on the Mac):** Press Ctrl+Shift+right bracket (Win) or ⌘+Shift+right bracket (Mac) to move the active layer to the top of the stack.
- **Ctrl+Shift+[(⌘+Shift+[on the Mac):** This shortcut moves the active layer to the bottom of the stack, just above the background layer.
- **Ctrl+] (⌘+] on the Mac):** This nudges the layer up one level.
- **Ctrl+[(⌘+[on the Mac):** This nudges the layer down one level.

NOTE   You can neither reorder the background layer nor move any other layer below the background layer until you first convert the background to a floating layer, as explained in the preceding section.

FIGURE 13.11

Here, one of the three layers containing versions of the moon is in transit, headed for the top of the stack. When restacking layers, consider not just their actual content, but any effects, such as blend modes or opacity, applied.

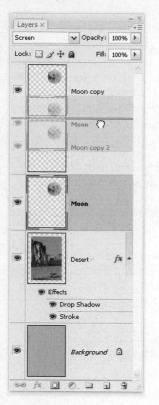

Displaying layer edges

When layer content is really tiny or is right next to, slightly behind, or mostly obscured by other content, it can be hard to spot and even harder to click it with your mouse to move it. To make your layers easier to see and click on, no matter how small, see-through, or camouflaged they may be, choose View ➪ Show ➪ Layer Edges.

To use the Layer Edges command feature, click the layer you want to see highlighted by an edge (use the Layers palette to click it). Then issue the View ➪ Show ➪ Layer Edges command to display the dark blue box that you see in Figure 13.12, where the moon layer is selected.

After you turn this option on, whichever layer you activate — be it by selecting the layer by clicking it in the Layers palette or by clicking the layer content directly with your mouse — is encompassed by the dark blue box. If you press Shift or Ctrl (⌘ on the Mac) to select multiple layers, each of the selected layers also is encompassed by its own box.

FIGURE 13.12

Turn on Layer Edges to display a helpful box that surrounds the active layer.

To stop seeing the boxes, you can either reselect the command to toggle it off or turn off the view of all Extras (guides, slice borders, and so on) with the View ➪ Extras command. This latter approach is rather radical, unless you want to eliminate all visual clutter in one sweeping command. To tweak which things to show and not show, use the View ➪ Show submenu to click on and off those features you want to see and not see.

Automated matting techniques

When you convert an anti-aliased selection to a layer, you sometimes take with you a few pixels from the selection's previous background. These *fringe pixels* can result in an unrealistic outline around your layer that really makes the selection-based layer stand out in its new location. Figure 13.13 shows this very problem in magnified detail from an early attempt to add the skeleton to the desert image. Although the selection outline is accurate — it was done at a high zoom, with great care — a few dark pixels from around the skeleton (he used to be on a busy background) came along with him.

FIGURE 13.13

This enlarged detail of a newly inserted skeleton layer demonstrates the extra, unwanted pixels that can accompany gross selections like those made with the Lassos or the Magic Wand.

You can instruct Photoshop to replace the fringe pixels with colors from neighboring pixels by choosing Layer ⇨ Matting ⇨ Defringe. Type the thickness of the perceived fringe in the Width option box to tell Photoshop which pixels you want to replace. To create the image shown in Figure 13.14, a value of 1 was used. But even at this low value, the effect is pretty significant, leaving gummy edges in its wake.

It's not that Defringe never works; sometimes the results are satisfactory. But keep in mind that it's not available when a selection is active or when the layer has a layer mask or vector mask.

FIGURE 13.14

Here the Defringe command was set to a Width value of 1 to replace the pixels around the edges of the skeleton layer with colors borrowed from neighboring pixels.

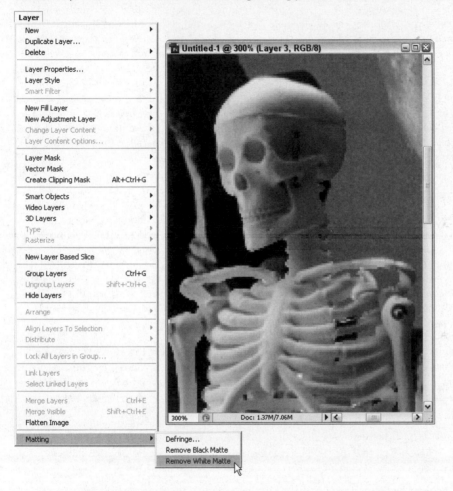

Photoshop provides two additional commands under the Layer ⇨ Matting submenu: Remove Black Matte and Remove White Matte. Frankly, it's unlikely that you'll have much call to use them, but here's their story:

- **Remove Black Matte:** This command removes the residue around the perimeter of a layer that was lifted from a black background.

- **Remove White Matte:** This command removes a white ring around a layer.

Adobe says that these commands were designed for compositing a scene rendered in a 3D drawing program against a black or white background. But for other purposes, they almost never work—unless your content did in fact come from a stark white or black background.

> **TIP**   If you encounter unrealistic edge pixels and the automatic matting commands don't solve your problem, you may be able to achieve better results by fixing the edges manually. First, switch to the layer that's making you crazy and Ctrl-click (Win) or ⌘-click (Mac) its thumbnail in the Layers palette. This creates a tight selection around the contents of the layer. Then choose Select ➪ Modify ➪ Contract, and type the width of the fringe in the Contract By option box. Next choose Select ➪ Feather or press Ctrl+Shift+D (⌘+Shift+D on the Mac), and type half of the Contract By value in the Feather Radius option box. Finally, press Ctrl+Shift+I (⌘+Shift+I on the Mac) to invert the selection, and press Backspace (Delete on the Mac) to eliminate the edge pixels. You also can use the Refine Edge dialog box, opened by clicking the Refine Edge button on the options bar (if a selection tool is active) or from the Select menu. This dialog box, discussed in detail in Chapter 8, allows you to clean up selection edges and preview your results at the same time.

Blending layers

Photoshop lets you blend layers like no other program available. In fact, Photoshop does such a great job that it takes almost all of Chapter 14 to explain these options in detail. This section serves as an introduction so that you're at least aware of the basics. If you have bigger questions, Chapter 14 is waiting to tell you the whole story.

The Layers palette provides four basic ways to blend pixels between layers, as shown in Figure 13.15. None of these techniques permanently changes as much as a pixel in any layer, so you can always return and reblend the layers at a later date.

- **Opacity value:** Type a value in the Opacity option box near the top of the Layers palette to change the opacity of the active layer or floating selection. If you reduce the Opacity value to 50 percent, for example, Photoshop makes the pixels on the active layer translucent, so the colors in the active layer mix evenly with the colors in the layers below.

> **TIP**   If any tool other than a paint or edit tool is active—including the selection and navigation tools—you can press a number key to change the Opacity value. Press 1 for 10 percent, 2 for 20 percent, up to 0 for 100 percent. Or you can enter a specific Opacity value by quickly pressing two number keys in a row. For example, press 3 and then 7 for 37 percent.

- **Fill value:** The Fill option lets you adjust the opacity of pixel information in the layer—anything painted, drawn, or typed—without affecting the opacity of any layer effects that might be applied. For example, if you have a text layer with the Drop Shadow layer effect applied, lowering the Fill slider to 0 fades out the text itself, leaving just the ghostly drop shadow behind. As with all other blending-related options, the Fill option is explained in excruciating detail in Chapter 14.

- **Blend mode pop-up menu:** Choose an option from the blend mode pop-up menu—open in Figure 13.15—to mix every pixel in the active layer with the pixels below it, according to one of several mathematical equations. For example, when you choose Multiply, Photoshop really does multiply the brightness values of the pixels and then divides the result by 255, the maximum brightness value. Blend modes use the same math as the brush modes covered in Chapter 5 (in fact, the two terms are sometimes used interchangeably). But you can accomplish much more with blend modes, which is why so much space is devoted to examining them in Chapter 14.

> **TIP** As with Opacity, you can select a blend mode from the keyboard when a selection or navigation tool is active. Press Shift+plus to advance incrementally down the list; press Shift+minus to inch back up. You also can press Shift+Alt (Win) or Shift+Option (Mac) and a letter key to select a specific mode. For example, Shift+Alt+M (Shift+Option+M on the Mac) selects the Multiply mode. Shift+Alt+N (Shift+Option+N on the Mac) restores the mode to Normal.

FIGURE 13.15

The blend mode pop-up menu and the Opacity and Fill option boxes enable you to mix layers without making any permanent changes to the pixels.

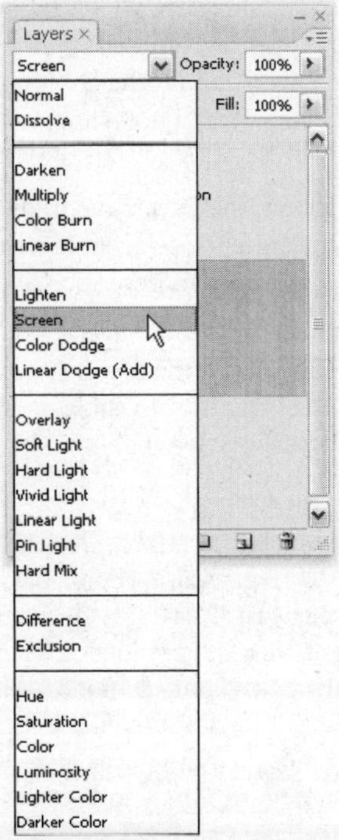

- **Blending Options:** Choose Layer ⇨ Layer Style ⇨ Blending Options, double-click a layer thumbnail, or choose Blending Options from the Layers palette options menu. Any of these methods open the Layer Style dialog box, in which you'll find the General Blending area provides access to a blend mode pop-up menu and an Opacity value, but it also offers a world of unique functions. As you learn in Chapter 14, you can hide one or more color channels, specify which colors are visible in the active layer, and force other colors to show through from the layers behind it. Select an item from the left-hand list to apply a layer style, as discussed in Chapter 15.

Fusing several layers

Although layers are wonderful and extremely helpful devices, they have their drawbacks. Of course, none of these negative aspects outweigh their usefulness. Layers do expand the size of an image in RAM and ultimately lead to slower performance, and as noted in Chapter 3, only four formats — PDF, TIFF, the new PSB, and native PSD — permit you to save layered compositions. You can use layers in the construction of any image. It's just that when you go to save it in any format other than those four, your layers are combined into a single layer, and further editing on an individual layer basis is impossible. Of course, you can save a PSD or TIFF version of the artwork, too, and that way you'll retain an editable, layer-laden copy.

With the size and performance-eating problem in mind, you may want to put your image on a diet of sorts. To slim down your image, Photoshop provides the following methods for merging layers:

- **Layer ➪ Merge Layers or Ctrl+E (⌘+E on the Mac):** Use this to merge two or more selected layers. This is a slight change from Photoshop CS, which had more merging options in terms of how the Merge commands appeared in the Layers menu. For example, if you had linked layers and went to the Layers menu, the command appeared as "Merge Linked." Now it appears as "Merge Layers," and Photoshop assumes you mean to merge the layers you have selected at the time.

- **Merge Down:** If you have only one layer selected, the Layers menu displays Merge Down instead of "Merge Layers." If you execute the merge, the selected layer merges with the layer directly beneath it. Note that the keyboard shortcut described above applies here, too — Ctrl + E (or ⌘+E on the Mac) merges the individual selected layer down.

- **Merge Visible (Ctrl+Shift+E or ⌘+Shift+E):** Choose the Merge Visible command to merge all visible layers into a single layer. If the layer is not visible — that is, if no eyeball icon appears in front of the layer name — Photoshop doesn't eliminate it; the layer remains independent.

TIP   To create a merged clone from two or more selected layers, press Alt when applying either the Layer ➪ Merge Layers or Layer ➪ Merge Visible commands. Pressing Alt (Win) or Option (Mac) and choosing Merge Layers — or pressing Ctrl+Alt+E (⌘+Option+E on the Mac) — clones the contents of the selected layer/s into the layer below it. Pressing Alt (Win) or Option (Mac) and choosing Merge Visible — or pressing Ctrl+Shift+Alt+E (⌘+Shift+Option+E on the Mac) — copies the contents of all visible layers to the active layer. The resulting layer in either case has the word "merged" in parentheses following the name of the top-most layer that was included in the merge. The History palette lists the action as Stamp Layers — something handy to know in case you want to go back and Undo this.

TIP   More useful is the ability to copy the merged contents of a selected area. To do so, choose Edit ➪ Copy Merged or press Ctrl+Shift+C (⌘+Shift+C on the Mac). You then can paste the selection into a layer or make it part of a different image.

- **Flatten Image:** This command merges all visible layers and throws away the invisible ones. The result is a single, opaque background layer. Photoshop does not give this command a keyboard shortcut because it's so dangerous. To take a safer, more conservative route, you may want to flatten an image incrementally using the two Merge commands — whittling away at the number of layers until you're ready to merge them all into one.

 Note that Photoshop asks whether you want to flatten an image when converting from one color mode to another. You can choose not to flatten the image (by pressing D or clicking Don't Flatten), but this may come at the expense of some of the brighter colors in your image. As discussed in Chapter 14, many of the blend modes perform differently in RGB than they do in CMYK.

Deleting layers

You also can throw a layer away. Drag the layer name onto the trash can icon at the bottom of the Layers palette, click the trash can icon to delete the active layer, or right-click (Control-click on the Mac) the layer to be deleted and choose Delete Layer from the pop-up menu. So many choices.

 When you click the trash can icon, Photoshop displays a message asking whether you really want to toss the layer. To give this message the slip in the future, Alt-click (Win) or Option-click (Mac) the trash can icon.

 Here's a good one for you: If the active layer is linked to one or more other layers (see the upcoming section "Linking and unlinking"), you can delete all linked layers in one fell swoop by Ctrl-clicking (Win) or ⌘-clicking (Mac) the trash can icon.

Saving a flattened version of an image

As already mentioned, only four file formats—PDF, TIFF, PSB, and the native Photoshop format—save images with layers. If you want to save a flattened version of your image—that is, with all layers fused into a single image—in some other file format, choose File ➪ Save As or press Ctrl+Shift+S (⌘+Shift+S on the Mac) and select the desired format from the Format pop-up menu. If you select a format that doesn't support layers—such as JPEG, GIF, or EPS—the Layers option is dimmed.

The Save As command does not affect the image in memory. All layers remain intact. So if you select the As a Copy option with the Layers option deselected—which is a good idea, really—Photoshop doesn't even change the name of the image in the title bar. It merely creates a flattened version of the image on disk. Nevertheless, be sure to save a layered version of the composition as well, just in case you want to edit it in the future.

Selecting the Contents of Layers

We mentioned a few sections back that every layer (except the background) includes a *transparency mask*. This mask tells Photoshop which pixels are opaque, which are translucent, and which are transparent. Like any mask, Photoshop lets you convert the transparency mask for any layer—active or not—to a selection outline. In fact, you use the same keyboard techniques you use to convert paths to selections (as explained in Chapter 8) and channels to selections (Chapter 9):

- Ctrl-click (Win) or ⌘-click (Mac) a layer's thumbnail in the Layers palette to convert the transparency mask for that layer to a selection outline.

- To add the transparency mask to an existing selection outline, Ctrl+Shift-click (Win) or ⌘+Shift-click (Mac) the layer thumbnail. The little selection cursor includes a plus sign to show you that you're about to add.

- To subtract the transparency mask, Ctrl+Alt-click (Win) or ⌘+Option-click (Mac) the layer thumbnail.

- To find the intersection of the transparency mask and the current selection outline, Ctrl+Shift+Alt-click (Win) or ⌘+Shift+Option-click (Mac) the layer thumbnail.

If you think you can't remember all these keyboard shortcuts, don't worry — you can use Select ➪ Load Selection instead. After choosing the command, select the Transparency item from the Channel pop-up menu. (You can even load a transparency mask from another open image if the image is exactly the same size as the one you're working on.) Then use the Operation radio buttons to merge the mask with an existing selection.

Selection outlines exist independently of layers, so you can use the transparency mask from one layer to select part of another layer. For example, to select the part of the background layer that exactly matches the contents of another layer, press Shift+Alt+[(Shift+Option+[on the Mac) to descend to the background layer and then Ctrl-click (Win) or ⌘-click (Mac) the thumbnail of the layer you want to match.

The most common reason to borrow a selection from one layer and apply it to another is to create manual shadow and lighting effects. After Ctrl-clicking (⌘-clicking on the Mac) a thumbnail, you can use this selection to create a drop shadow that precisely matches the contours of the layer itself. No messing with the Brush or the Lasso tool; Photoshop does the tough work for you.

Now, you might think that with Photoshop's extensive range of layer styles, manual drop shadows and the like would be a thing of the past. After all, you have only to choose Layer ➪ Layer Style ➪ Drop Shadow and, bang, the program adds a drop shadow. But the old, manual methods still have their advantages. You don't have to visit a complicated dialog box to edit a manual drop shadow, and you can reposition a manual shadow from the keyboard (or with your mouse, if you press Ctrl+T or ⌘+T) to enter transform mode, where you can scale, rotate, skew, and otherwise trans- form the shadow layer independently. The separate-layer approach gives you way more flexibility over the size, position, color, opacity, and edges of the shadow than you can get through the Layer Styles dialog box (discussed later in this chapter). Figure 13.16 shows the finished product of such a procedure — the main component, on its own layer, was duplicated, its opacity tweaked, and its shape transformed and repositioned; the result is a manually-created shadow that no Drop Shadow command could ever create.

On the other hand, the old ways aren't necessarily always better. A shadow created with the Drop Shadow command takes up less room in memory, it moves and rotates with a layer, and you can edit the softness of the shadow long after creating it. You also can set the shadow to employ Global Light, which means any other shadows in the image (drop shadows applied as Layer Styles, that is) will have the same angle, indicating light coming from the same direction. This can save time and effort if you have more than one item shadowed in an image.

FIGURE 13.16

Here's a truly happy penguin—his toes in the grass, the sun on his feathers, and a shadow cast behind him.

What you have are two equally powerful solutions, each with its own characteristic pros and cons. Luckily, you can easily master both, and then you'll be ready for any situation.

 For everything you ever wanted to know about the Layer Styles commands, read Chapter 15.

Moving, Linking, and Aligning Layers

You can move an entire layer or the selected portion of a layer by clicking and dragging in the image window with the Move tool. If you have a selection in place, drag inside the marching-ants outline to move only the selection; drag outside the selection to move the entire layer.

CAUTION If you have selected the Auto Select Layer option (it's a Move tool option) and forget that it's on, you may create a few stressful moments for yourself when attempting to move a layer that partially or completely overlaps another. You'll select the layer using the Layers palette or by right-clicking (Control-clicking on the Mac) the layer you want, and then when you click and drag to move the layer you *think* is active, you'll really grab the top-most layer and move *that* one instead. If you find that this happens, just forgo the potential convenience of Auto Select Layer and turn the darn thing off.

Speaking of the Move tool, as mentioned in Chapter 8, you can temporarily access the Move tool when some other tool is active by pressing Ctrl (Win) or ⌘ (Mac). To nudge a layer, press Ctrl or ⌘ with an arrow key. Press Ctrl+Shift (⌘+Shift on the Mac) to nudge in 10-pixel increments.

If part of the layer disappears beyond the edge of the window, no problem. Photoshop saves even the hidden pixels in the layer, enabling you to drag the rest of the layer into view later.

CAUTION If, while dragging a selection, you move your cursor outside the image window, Photoshop thinks you are trying to drag-and-drop pixels from one image to another and responds accordingly.

If you Ctrl-drag (⌘-drag on the Mac) the background image with no portion of it selected, you get an error message telling you that the layer is locked. If some portion of the layer is selected, however, you can drag that selected portion, and Photoshop fills in the hole with the background color.

TIP If you regularly work on huge images or your machine is old and kind of slow, Photoshop lets you speed the display of entire layers on the move. Press Ctrl+K and then Ctrl+3 (⌘+K and then ⌘+3 on the Mac) to display the Display & Cursors panel of the Preferences dialog box. Then select the Use Pixel Doubling option. From now on, Photoshop shows you a low-resolution proxy of a selection or a layer as you drag (or Ctrl-drag) it across the screen.

Linking and unlinking

With the release of Photoshop CS3, there were a few changes to the way you link and unlink layers. Of course, there's no big change in your overall capabilities in terms of layer linking and unlinking, but the procedure for linking layers (and then unlinking them later) has changed a bit for those of you whose most recent Photoshop experience was CS or version 7.

First, there is no longer any link check box or chain icon next to each layer. In Photoshop CS and its layer-supporting predecessors, in addition to the box where the eyeballs live, there was another column of boxes, which when clicked, would display a chain icon. This meant that the selected layers (you had to select them before clicking in the box) were linked. You could then unlink layers by clicking the chain icon and breaking the link.

Now, the Link Layers button is on the bottom of the palette, and you use it to link and unlink selected layers. Figure 13.17 shows two linked layers, and the Link Layers button is labeled.

NOTE Dragging inside a selection outline moves the selection independently of any linked layers. Dragging outside the selection moves all linked layers at once.

FIGURE 13.17

Select the layers you want to link, and then click the Link Layers button, found at the lower-left end of the Layers palette buttons.

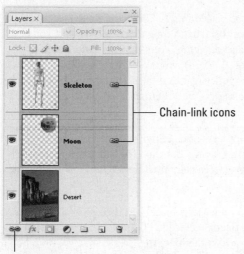

Chain-link icons

Link Layers button

You also can link layers with the shortcut menu. As you may recall from the section "Switching between layers" earlier in this chapter, you can bring up a pop-up menu listing the layers in an image by Ctrl-right-clicking (⌘+Control-clicking on the Mac) an image element with any tool. If you're a Windows user, add Shift while selecting a layer from the pop-up menu to link or unlink the layer rather than switch to it.

When you drag-and-drop linked layers from one image window into another, all linked layers move together and the layers retain their original order. If you want to move just one layer without its linked buddies, drag the layer name from the Layers palette and drop it into another open image window.

TIP If you press and hold Shift when dropping, Photoshop centers the layers in the document. If the document is exactly the same size as the one from which you dragged the layers, Shift-dropping lands the image elements in the same position they held in the original document. And finally, if something is selected in the document, the Shift-dropped layers are centered inside that selection.

When you have just two layers linked, unlinking is just as easy as previously stated: With the layers selected, click the Link Layers button and the link is broken. The chain icon leaves the layers, and the link is no more. But what if you have more than two layers linked? Is it an all-or-nothing proposition? Nope. If you have three, four, or more layers linked, to unlink them all, right-click (Control-click on the Mac) any one of the linked layers and choose Select Linked Layers from the pop-up menu. To unlink just one or two (or any number, just not all) of the linked layers, select just those that you want to unlink and click the Link Layers button. The layers you didn't select remain linked, but the selected layers are no longer part of the chain gang.

Organizing layers in groups

In versions of Photoshop prior to CS2, layers could be placed in *sets:* Using the Folder button at the foot of the Layers palette, you could create a set and click and drag layers into it, and you also could create nested sets by creating sets within sets and dragging layers into the nested sets. It all worked like file management in Windows (or even on the Mac), where you have folders and subfolders, and files can be stored in them to keep your work organized. Sets served the same purpose in Photoshop, enabling you to organize your layers and deal with them in large, well, groups. That may be why the name was changed, huh?

Anyway, now sets are called *groups,* and you call the process of creating them and placing layers in and taking layers out of them grouping and ungrouping layers. For those of you who are new to grouping layers, or if you're familiar with putting layers in the aforementioned sets, here's how the whole grouping/ungrouping thing works:

First, click the Create a New Group button (it's still a folder icon button) at the foot of the Layers palette. A generically named Group layer appears in the palette, called Group 1 (if it's your first in the current image). You also can Alt-click (Option-click on the Mac) the Create a New Group button and open the New Group dialog box shown in Figure 13.18. Through this dialog box, you can name your new group, choose a color for its display in the Layers palette, and choose a Mode and Opacity for it. You'll note that the default Mode is Pass Through, and that will be explained shortly.

FIGURE 13.18

Choose the Create a New Group command or Alt-click (Option-click on the Mac) the folder icon at the bottom of the Layers palette to create and name a new group.

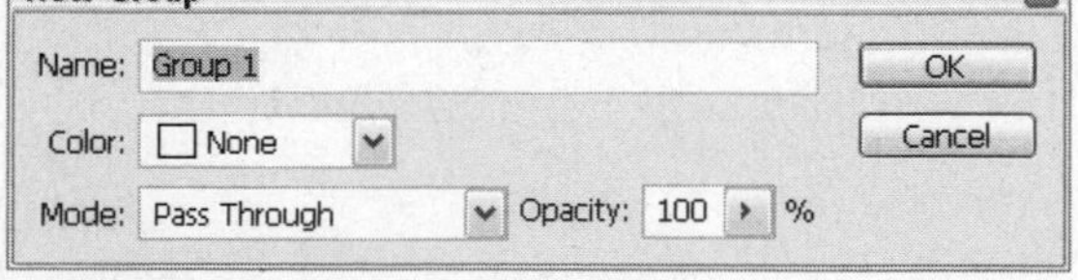

TIP The Pass Through Mode option tells Photoshop to respect the existing blend modes assigned to the individual layers in the group and keep them applied to those layers. By contrast, if you apply a different blend mode such as Multiply to the group, Photoshop overrides the existing blend modes of the layers in the group and applies Multiply to them all.

The group appears as a folder icon in the Layers palette scrolling list. There's also a little triangle next to the folder icon, which you'll use to display and collapse (not hide, as in not showing in the image) the list of grouped layers. The group's visibility as a whole is indicated by the eyeball icon to the left of the group's name.

To add a layer to the group, click and drag the layer name within the Layers palette and drop it on the folder icon. That little fist mouse pointer you saw in the coverage of restacking layers returns and follows you as you drag the layer up or down to the group in which it belongs. Figure 13.19 shows a new group in place (Lens Flare examples), with layers already in it, and an existing group (Callouts) with its layers collapsed.

Photoshop also lets you place groups inside of other groups, a process called *nesting*. Photoshop allows you to nest groups up to five levels deep. Nesting layer groups can be a great way to better organize your layers. To place one group inside another, simply drag-and-drop it onto the other group in the same manner you would a layer. As it does when you place a layer into a group, Photoshop applies the blend mode of the master group to every layer and nested group within it when the mode is not set to Pass Through.

FIGURE 13.19

A new group and its members — and a member being brought to its first meeting

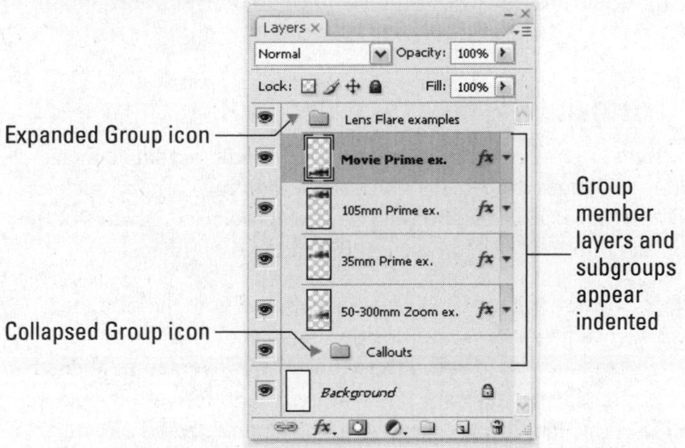

Expanded Group icon

Group member layers and subgroups appear indented

Collapsed Group icon

Here are some other ways to create and modify groups:

- Double-click a group name to rename it.
- Drag a group name up or down the palette to move it.
- When a group is expanded, you can drag a layer within the group, move a layer out of the group, or drop a layer into the group at a specific position.
- To duplicate a group, drag it onto the folder icon at the bottom of the Layers palette.

669

■ Hate dragging all those layers into a group? Select the layers before creating the group and choose Layer ⇨ Group Layers. The new group is created, and the selected layers are automatically its members. You can do this to create a nested group, too: Just select layers already in a group and issue the Layer ⇨ Group Layers command. A nested group, complete with members, is created.

■ In case you're wondering, "Can I link layers in different groups?," yes, you can. If you're wondering, "Can I link groups together?," yes, it's possible not only to link groups, but also to link individual layers to entire groups. Pretty snazzy, huh?

■ You know that you can click the triangle next to a folder icon to open or close the group and show or hide the layers and nested groups it contains. Alt-click (Option-click on the Mac) the triangle next to a folder icon to show or hide every element contained in the group, including nested groups and layer styles.

Anytime a group name is active in the Layers palette, you can move or transform all layers in the group as a unit, much as if they were linked. To move or transform a single layer in the group, just select that layer and go about your business as you normally would.

TIP   Hang on. What if you don't want a group anymore? You want the layers, but don't want them grouped. What to do? Right-click (Control-click on the Mac) the Group layer, and choose Ungroup Layers from the pop-up menu. The group disappears, but the layers that were in it remain, in place, maintaining their original modes, opacity settings, and stacking order. If you want to delete an entire group, members (layers) and all, right-click (Control-click on the Mac) and choose Delete Group.

Aligning layers automatically

New in Photoshop CS3, the Auto-Align Layers command aligns selected layers in a single image, based on any similar content — common edges or corners or actual overlapping content, such as would occur if you took a series of images to create a panorama, or if you took two pictures of the same scene, but with a different person or other object in the foreground in each image.

Through the command's dialog box, shown in Figure 13-20, you can choose how the alignment takes place, choosing from different special perspective and positioning effects. Before you begin the Auto-Align process, however, you can lock one of your layers (one of the layers to be aligned) and make it a reference point for the other layers you want Photoshop to align for you. By locking the layer, you establish a position against which the other layers will be aligned, based on your subsequent selection in the Auto-Align Layers dialog box. If you choose *not* to lock a layer and make it a reference, Photoshop makes its own decisions and selects one of your layers as the reference for the alignment of the other selected layers.

CAUTION   When selecting layers to be automatically aligned, don't include any vector layers, adjustment layers, or Smart Objects. These layers won't be properly interpreted by Photoshop in terms of their content, and cannot be aligned with this command.

To use the Auto-Align Layers feature, start by placing the layers you want to align in the same image. This can be done by copying content from other images into the target image or creating layers from content within the image you want to align. Once you have the layers in place, select them within the Layers palette, and then choose Edit ⇨ Auto-Align Layers.

The Auto-Align Layers dialog box lets you choose how your selected layers will line up.

- **Auto:** Photoshop looks at the selected layers and chooses to apply Perspective or Cylindrical alignment, based on which method creates the best result in terms of aligning the most common or similar content within the selected layers.

- **Perspective:** This method achieves alignment by establishing one of the selected layers (the one you locked, or if you didn't lock one, the middle layer) as the reference layer. The remaining layers are moved, resized, rotated, skewed — whatever's needed — to match up all overlapping edges across the selected layers.

- **Cylindrical:** Here you end up with a sort of "bow-tie" effect, similar to the Perspective method, but with the outer layers stretched vertically at their outer edges. This method is most effective when you're piecing a series of images together to create a panorama, and again, unless you've locked a particular layer before starting the process, the middle layer becomes the reference for the rest.

- **Reposition Only:** This is a safe method to use if you don't want any transformation (stretching, resizing, skewing) to occur. All that happens here is that overlapping or common content is matched up and aligned.

NOTE Auto-Align Layers isn't perfect, and you may want to tweak a few things in your image once the alignment is completed. You can, of course, transform your layers in Free Transform mode (Ctrl+T for Windows or Cmd+T on the Mac) to move, resize, rotate, or skew content a bit to make the aligned final image exactly what you had in mind.

TIP To build layers from multiple images, choose File ➪ Scripts ➪ Load Files into Stack. This creates individual layers from the files you choose from the Load Layers dialog box. Click the Browse button to navigate to and select the files, and once the files you want to use as layers appear in the dialog box, click OK to load them into the active image.

Creating and Using Smart Objects

Why would you turn your layers into a Smart Object? If you want to edit the content outside of Photoshop and then bring it back seamlessly later, Smart Objects are the way to go. Of course, you could copy the layers to a new image, save the image in a vector-friendly format (such as EPS, for example) and then open the new image in Illustrator, edit it there, and then bring it back to Photoshop, open it, copy its contents and the paste them back into their original Photoshop image, but that would be really taking the long way home — lots of steps and a large margin for error.

Another reason is that Smart Objects can be scaled, rotated, skewed, or warped losslessly — meaning that no details are lost to the process of pixels being edited and created to fill in as the image content changes size, position, shape, and so on. Essentially, turning content into a Smart Object protects it and makes it easier to move it back and forth between images and applications without the problems of loss of detail and wasted time and effort required in the past.

CROSS-REF If you've already read Chapter 10, you read about another benefit of Smart Objects — the ability to use Smart Filters. If you haven't read Chapter 10 yet, what are you waiting for?

Creating a new Smart Object

To turn content into a Smart Object, simply select the layer or layers from within any Photoshop image; it can be a PSD or TIFF file, or saved in any other format that supports the use of layers. With the layer(s) selected, right-click the layer names in the Layers palette (Control-click with a single button mouse on the Mac) and choose Convert to Smart Object. You also can choose Layer ➪ Smart Objects ➪ Convert to Smart Object from the menu bar. After a brief pause, your Smart Object appears as shown in Figure 13.21. This figure shows a Smart Object called "Foreground subjects," which consists of three former layers — "Moon," "Skeleton," and "Mountains." The three layers were combined into a single Smart Object, and the name of the top-most layer was automatically applied to the object — although in this case, the resulting Smart Object layer has been renamed. You can rename an object the same way you'd rename a layer: Just double-click the name in place and type a new one.

FIGURE 13.21

Select three layers (left), and turn them into a Smart Object (right). The Smart Object layer keeps the name of the uppermost layer you selected, which is why you can see us changing that name to something more appropriate here.

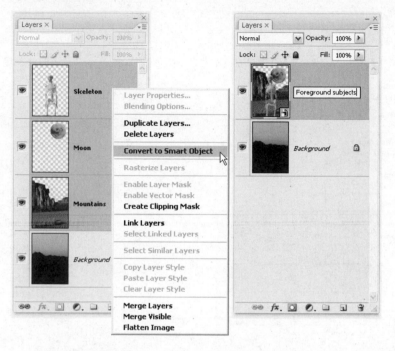

TIP You can use the Layers palette to create your Smart Objects, too. Select the layer(s) to be made into an object, and right-click (Control-click on the Mac) to display a pop-up menu. Choose Convert to Smart Object from the menu, and the object is created. The Layers ➪ Smart Objects submenu commands — New Smart Object Via Copy, Edit Contents, Export Contents, and Replace Contents — also are found in the pop-up menu.

Editing Smart Objects

So you've made a Smart Object. Now what do you do with it? You can double-click the object layer in the Layers palette or choose Layers ➪ Smart Objects ➪ Edit Contents. A large prompt window opens, shown in Figure 13.22, which gives you valuable instructions: After you finish your edits (you'll be working in a new image window with the object layers' content in it), choose File ➪ Save to keep your changes. If you don't do so, the changes won't be reflected in the original image. You also can save the changes to a new file — a new file name, format, and location — thus creating a new image from a Smart Object.

FIGURE 13.22

Take this good advice to make sure your edited Smart Object can return to the image from whence it came.

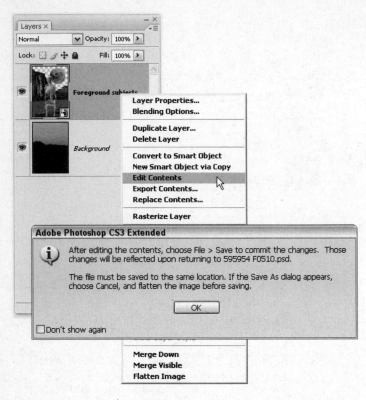

After clicking OK to acknowledge this great advice, you're presented with a new image window, titled with the same name as the original uppermost layer in the Smart Object. The format for the new image is PSB (large document format), and the image consists of the layer(s) you grouped into the Smart Object. Figure 13.23 shows the resulting main .psb file and its Layers palette.

You can edit the new PSB file as you would any Photoshop file using virtually any of the tools, commands, filters, and so forth that you want. You can use the Transform tools to rotate, skew, scale, and even warp the content, too (but you'll find Distort and Perspective dimmed). Warping, which also can be applied to transform the PSB file content, is discussed later in this chapter.

TIP Handling PSB files hogs lots of system resources. If you think you'll be creating and editing lots of Smart Objects, and you see that your system slows down to a crawl (or even gives you "scratch disks are full" prompts while you're editing them), consider increasing your RAM.

FIGURE 13.23

One Smart Object becomes a new image with three (in this case) layers.

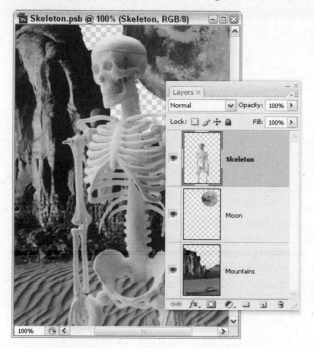

After you've finished your edits, you can use the File ➪ Save (Ctrl+S for Windows, ⌘+S on the Mac) command to save the object, and then return to your original image. The original image reflects any changes you made to the size, position, stacking order, and actual content of the object's layers (including new layers) while you edited it as a PSB file.

Exporting and replacing Smart Objects

To export a Smart Object, select Export Contents from the pop-up menu that appears when you right-click (Control-click) the object. A Save dialog box opens through which you can give your file a name (PSB is the default format, but you can pick another) and choose a location for the file. After you've saved the file, it can be opened in Illustrator as well as many other vector-based editing programs. You also can open it in Photoshop. After the edits are performed, you can save the image and reopen the original image in Photoshop — "original image" refers to the one from which the original layers that became the object came. The changes you made in the other program are reflected, and the content is rerasterized.

If you choose Replace Contents from the Layer ➪ Smart Objects submenu, a Place dialog box opens through which you can select another image — any Photoshop-recognized file — and use it to replace the Smart Object in your active image. The image you select literally replaces the Smart Object content and becomes a new layer in the image. You then can edit that layer, restack it to reveal original content beneath it, or apply any other Photoshop tool, command, or filter to the replacement content.

Working with image stacks

Speaking of stacking, another command you may have noticed in the Layer ➪ Smart Objects submenu is Stack Mode. While this doesn't refer directly to stacking layers as we've thought of it to this point (stacking them to determine their layered order in the image), stacking layers does have a significant purpose and can be used to create new images or improve the appearance of an existing one.

Understanding Stack Mode

So what is a stack, and what is Stack Mode? An image stack is a combination of images, represented by layers in an image file. It's created from multiple images and builds a single new image from the images in the stack. This is different from a simple composite image, where you manually drag content from multiple images into a target image, and it's different from blending (as discussed in Chapter 14), because the image your stack builds can be very different from the image/s used to build it. It might be in a different mode (set through the Image ➪ Mode command), a different pixel depth or resolution, or a different size than the images placed in the stack.

Making an image stack

To create an image stack, you take two or more images, convert them to layers in a single image file, and then convert those layers to a Smart Object (using techniques discussed previously in this chapter). You select all the layers and choose Layer ➪ Smart Objects ➪ Convert to Smart Object. With this done, you can then select the new Smart Object layer and choose Layer ➪ Smart Object ➪ Stack Mode, as shown in Figure 13.24.

Applying Stack Mode options

After the images have been combined into a new image as layers and those layers converted to a Smart Object, you can apply any one of 11 different Stack Modes to the image stack, or you can apply no specific mode and allow the combining of the image-based layers into a Smart Object stand on its own in terms of the impact the combined layers have on each other and their resulting single layer.

Figure 13.25 shows our sample figure of three spheres — red, green, and blue (yes, we KNOW it's grayscale, but check the color section!). Figure 13.26 shows the results of the 11 Stack Modes when applied to the image.

FIGURE 13.24

The Stack Mode submenu

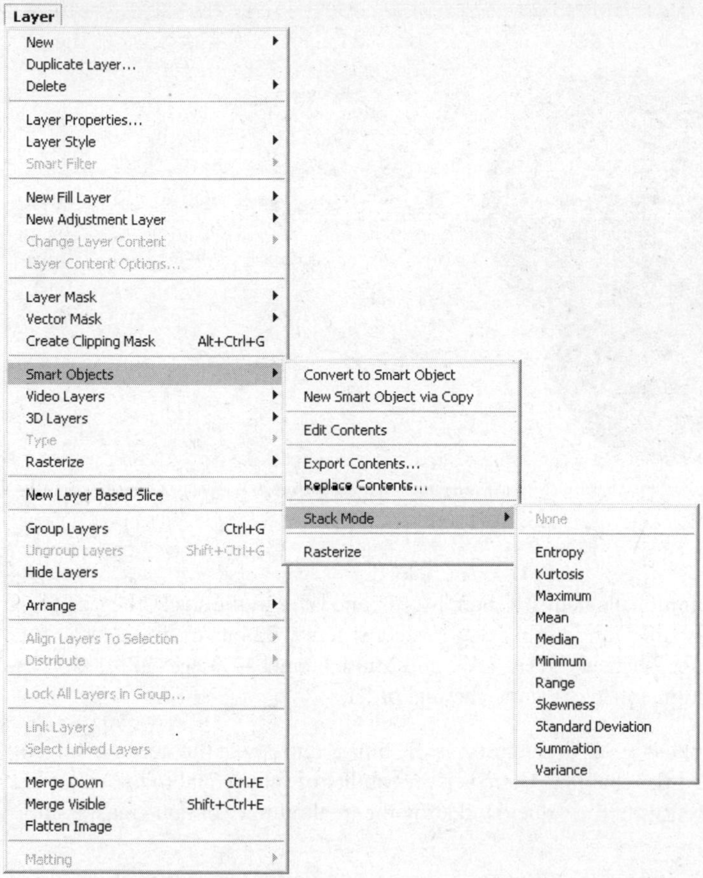

Layer		
New	▶	
Duplicate Layer...		
Delete	▶	
Layer Properties...		
Layer Style	▶	
Smart Filter	▶	
New Fill Layer	▶	
New Adjustment Layer	▶	
Change Layer Content	▶	
Layer Content Options...		
Layer Mask	▶	
Vector Mask	▶	
Create Clipping Mask	Alt+Ctrl+G	

Smart Objects ▶ — Convert to Smart Object / New Smart Object via Copy / Edit Contents / Export Contents... / Replace Contents... / Stack Mode ▶ / Rasterize

Stack Mode ▶: None / Entropy / Kurtosis / Maximum / Mean / Median / Minimum / Range / Skewness / Standard Deviation / Summation / Variance

Video Layers ▶
3D Layers ▶
Type ▶
Rasterize ▶

New Layer Based Slice

Group Layers — Ctrl+G
Ungroup Layers — Shift+Ctrl+G
Hide Layers

Arrange ▶

Align Layers To Selection ▶
Distribute ▶

Lock All Layers in Group...

Link Layers
Select Linked Layers

Merge Down — Ctrl+E
Merge Visible — Shift+Ctrl+E
Flatten Image

Matting ▶

If you choose to apply a Stack Mode, here are your options: Be forewarned that if you found the Custom filter's math daunting (see Chapter 12), these would blow your mind if we got into all the calculations that go into the application and execution of these modes. Here's the list, though, and you can experiment with each one, using your own images or those you'll find on this book's CD.

FIGURE 13.25

The "before" shot

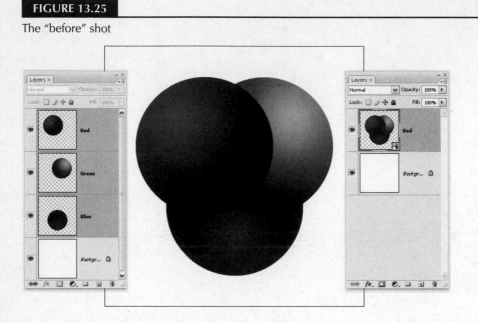

The first options have some common elements: If there is only one layer in the stack, the size of the original image stack is maintained, and output depth is consistently 32 bits/channel. As a result, some image modes change, such as CMYK, LAB, and Multichannel — images in these modes become RGB images and maintain the same channel order.

- **Entropy:** When this one is applied, the result is the binary entropy of the non-transparent pixel values, calculated per channel. There is a probability of value equal to the result of the number of occurrences of the value divided by the total number of non-transparent pixels.

- **Kurtosis:** Here, the result is the statistical kurtosis of the non-transparent pixel values, on a per-channel basis. Kurtosis is a measure of peakedness or flatness compared to a normal distribution. The kurtosis for a standard normal distribution is 3.0, and a Kurtosis of more than 3 is present in a peaked distribution, and kurtosis less than 3 means you have a flat distribution.

- **Maximum:** This one gives you the maximum of the non-transparent pixel values, on a per-channel basis. Figure 13.24 shows the results of this Stack Mode, with the original (unstacked) Smart Object shown on the left.

- **Mean:** Where the input stack is 8 or 16 bits/channel, the resulting image is 16 bits/channel. If the input stack is 32 bits/channel, the resulting image is, too. This Stack Mode results in an average of the non-transparent pixel values, calculated on a per-channel basis.

- **Median:** The median Stack Mode results in the median value of the non-transparent pixels, calculated per channel.

■ **Minimum:** Here, the result is the minimum of the non-transparent pixel values, per channel. Figure 13.26 shows the impact of this Stack Mode on a Smart Object. The original object appears on the left for comparison.

FIGURE 13.26

Here you see the results of applying Stack Modes to our original image.

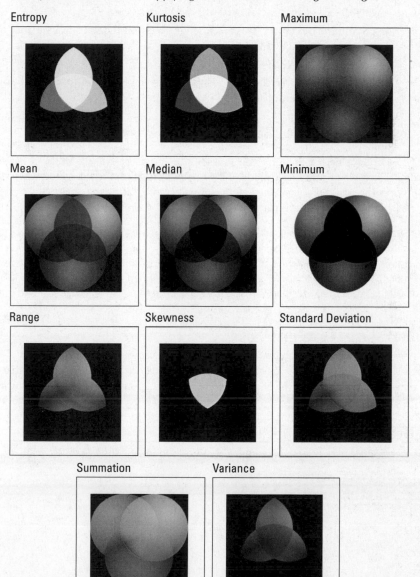

- **Range:** This gives you the maximum, minus the minimum, of the non-transparent pixel values, per channel.

- **Skewness:** In this case, the result is the statistical skewness of the non-transparent pixel values, again, on a per-channel basis. The skewness is a measure of symmetry or asymmetry around the statistical mean, relative to the non-transparent pixels. Positive skewness values are found when the distribution is skewed to the high side of the mean, and negative skewness values are found when the distribution is skewed to the low side of the mean.

- **Standard Deviation:** This Stack Mode gives you the statistical variance of the non-transparent pixel values, on a per-channel basis. The standard deviation is equal to the Square Root multiplied by the variance.

- **Summation:** Here, the stack displays the sum of the non-transparent pixel values, calculated on a per-channel basis.

- **Variance:** In this case, the result is the statistical variance of the non-transparent pixel values, again calculated per-channel.

These options have some things in common, too. First, these Stack Modes preserve the pixel depth, image size and image mode of the original images in the stack, and when there is only one layer in the stack (if you selected all the layers before creating the Smart Object, resulting in a single layer), the result is a duplicate of the input.

> **TIP**   If all the Stack Mode descriptions you just read have left your brain spinning or you gave up after the first few, don't despair. One of the ways you can use Stack Modes, without having to understand the math behind them, is to reduce noise in an image. Tinker with the modes — each one has a different impact on each different image you work with — to find the one that eliminates the pixels that are creating unpleasant blips of color, light, or darkness in your image.

Rasterizing a layer

As you may have discovered when trying to manipulate the style or fill of type, shape layers, vector masks, or Smart Objects, you can't use the Paint Brush or any Filter on layers that contain vector data. A prompt, such as the one shown in Figure 13.27, appears. What to do? Read on.

FIGURE 13.27

Stop right there. You can't apply many tools to vector-based image content, like type.

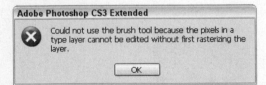

First, let's remind ourselves — what is vector data? Think (or refer directly) back to Chapter 1, where we talked about the difference between raster images and vector images. Vector images contain mathematical information, all of which combines to display content that's a certain size, filled with a certain color, bearing an outline of a certain width, and so on. Raster image are pixel-based, and the individual pixels can therefore be painted, filtered, and otherwise manipulated in ways that are impossible when the tool runs smack into a bunch of numbers and values.

To rasterize a layer, any layer, simple right-click (Control-click on the Mac) the layer, and choose Rasterize Layer from the pop-up menu. You also can select the layer in the Layers palette, choose Layer ⇨ Rasterize, and then choose the sort of layer you have — type, Smart Object, shape, and so on — from the resulting submenu shown in Figure 13.28.

FIGURE 13.28

Rasterize any type of layer, turning it from vector data to pixels that Photoshop can easily work with.

Locking layers

Just like a Smart Object can protect selected layers from loss of quality when transferred to and from an external editing program, the Layers palette can protect a layer from any kind of changes by allowing you to lock it. Photoshop also lets you lock only some attributes of a layer and leave other attributes unlocked, thus making this protection very flexible. Figure 13.29 labels the four Lock buttons available in the Layers palette. Here's how they work:

- **Lock transparency:** This button protects the transparency of a layer. When selected, you can paint inside a layer without harming the transparent pixels. This option is so useful that there is an entire section devoted to it (see "Preserving transparency" later in this chapter).

- **Lock pixels:** Select this button to prohibit further editing of the pixels in the active layer. Paint and edit tools will no longer function, nor will filters or other pixel-level commands. However, you'll still be able to move and transform the layer as you like. Note that selecting this button dims and selects the Lock Transparency button as well. After all, if you can't edit pixels, you can't edit pixels — whether they're opaque or transparent.

- **Lock position:** Select this button to prevent the layer from being moved or transformed. You can, however, edit the pixels.

- **Lock all:** To lock everything about a layer, select this button. You can't paint, edit, filter, move, transform, delete, or otherwise change a hair on the layer's head. About all you can do is duplicate the layer, move it up and down the stack, add it to a group, and merge it with one or more other layers. This button is applicable to layers and groups alike.

Photoshop shows you which layers are locked by displaying two kinds of lock icons in the Layers palette. As labeled in Figure 13.29, the hollow lock (white, as shown) means one attribute is locked; the filled lock (black) means all attributes are locked.

Using guides and Smart Guides

Photoshop's grids and guides allow you to move selections and layers into alignment. They're not the only tools that enable you to do this, of course, because you always have the Align and Distribute commands in the Layers menu, but when combined with the Move tool, guides and grids make it much easier to create rows and columns of image elements and even align layers by their centers. This capability, along with the enhanced alignment indicators known as Smart Guides (you'll read about them shortly), enables you to achieve a much greater control over your image elements, aligning and distributing your layers "by eye" with unexpected accuracy.

Adding guides

To create a guide, press Ctrl+R (⌘+R on the Mac) or choose View ➪ Rulers to display the horizontal and vertical rulers. Then point to the ruler with your mouse — the top ruler to create a horizontal guide, the left-side ruler to create a vertical guide — and click and drag a guideline onto your image. In Figure 13.30, we've dragged two guides to bisect our moon layer vertically and horizontally.

FIGURE 13.29

The Lock buttons at the top of the Layers palette let you protect certain layer attributes.

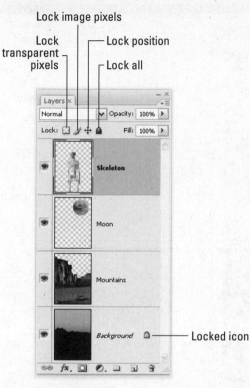

Lock image pixels

Lock
transparent
pixels

Lock position

Lock all

Locked icon

TIP You also can place a guide at a specific location horizontally or vertically, using the View ⇨ New Guide command and dialog box. Choose the direction the guide should go, and enter a specific measurement on the ruler (although the ruler need not be displayed at the time), and click OK to create the guide.

After you've created your guide or guides (drag as many as you need onto the image), you can use them to align and distribute your layers—against the guides, and against each other, using the guides to establish common vertical and horizontal planes.

To make sure your layers adhere to the guides, Ctrl-drag (Win) or ⌘-drag (Mac) as you move your layers and selections. In Figure 13.31, the moon, skeleton, and desert landscape are aligned by their left sides along a vertical guide on the left side of the image. Each item is on its own layer, and the layers snap into alignment at their centers.

FIGURE 13.30

Click and drag from one of the rulers to create a guide, and then Ctrl-drag (⌘-drag on the Mac) each layer or selection into position.

 Single-line text layers snap to horizontal guides a little differently than other kinds of layers. Rather than snapping by the top or bottom edge of the layer, Photoshop snaps a text guide by its baseline. It's just what you need when aligning type.

FIGURE 13.31

Pink lines flash when something lines up. In this example, we've dragged our moon so that its center is aligned to the top and right edges of the skeleton. Smart Guides are a big help when aligning both horizontally and vertically, with or without ruler-derived guides in use.

Showing, hiding, and controlling guides

Guides are straightforward creatures. A few minutes with the text below is all you need to master them:

- If you know the exact position where you want to put a guideline, choose View ⇨ New Guide. After selecting from a horizontal or vertical guide, type the location of the guide as measured from the ruler origin, by default in the upper-left corner of the image. For example, type "1 in" for 1 inch, "2.5 cm" for 2.5 centimeters, or "200 px" for 200 pixels.

- You can show and hide all guides by choosing View ➪ Show ➪ Guides. When the guides are hidden, layers and selections do not snap into alignment.

- You can hide or show guides also by pressing Ctrl+H (⌘+H on the Mac). But be aware that this turns on or off the visibility of other elements, including the grid, selection outlines, paths, and notes. To hide and show just the guides, press Ctrl+semicolon (;) under Windows (⌘+semicolon [;] on the Mac).

> **TIP** You can preselect which items are hidden and shown with the Show Extras command by selecting and deselecting the items in the View ➪ Show menu.

- You can turn a guide's snappiness on and off by choosing View ➪ Snap To ➪ Guides. You also can press Ctrl+Shift+semicolon (⌘+Shift+semicolon on the Mac). Again, this shortcut affects the snappiness of *everything*, including the grid, the perimeter of the image, and Web slices (read about slices in Chapter 20).

> **TIP** To turn off the snappiness in the middle of a brushstroke or layer movement, press Ctrl (Win) or ⌘ (Mac) in mid-drag. Release Ctrl or ⌘ to return to snappy land.

- As with all image elements in Photoshop, you can move a guide with the Move tool. If some other tool is active, Ctrl-dragging (Win) or ⌘-dragging (Mac) also works.

- To lock all guides so you can't accidentally move them while you're trying to Ctrl-drag or ⌘-drag something else, press Ctrl+Alt+semicolon (⌘+Option+semicolon on the Mac) or choose View ➪ Lock Guides. Press Ctrl+Alt+semicolon again to unlock all guides.

> **TIP** When moving a guide, press Shift to snap the guide to the nearest ruler tick mark.

- To convert a horizontal guide to a vertical guide, or vice versa, press Alt (Win) or Option (Mac) while pointing to or moving the guide.

- If you rotate your document in exact multiples of 90 degrees or flip the image horizontally or vertically, your guides also rotate unless they are locked.

> **TIP** You can position a guide outside the image if you want. To do so, make the image window larger than the image. Now you can drag a guide into the empty canvas surrounding the image. You then can snap a layer or selection into alignment with the guide.

- To edit the color of the guides, Ctrl-double-click (Win) or ⌘-double-click (Mac) a guide to display the Guides, Grid & Slices panel of the Preferences dialog box. You also can change the guides from solid lines to dashed. (This is only for screen purposes, by the way. Guides don't print.)

- On the Mac, guides are saved with any file format. But on the PC, the only formats that let you save guides are Photoshop (PSD), JPEG, TIFF, PDF, and EPS.

- If you don't need your guides anymore, choose View ➪ Clear Guides to delete them all at once.

Intelligent alignment with Smart Guides

Smart Guides, shown in action back in Figure 13.31, flash on the image when your layer-in-motion is lined up against the items above, below, and beside it. Depending on the Smart Guides that appear — straight lines pointing toward the items against which the active layer is being aligned — you know if your layer is where you need it to be.

Setting up the grid

For more control over the placement of layers in your image, Photoshop offers a grid, which is a regular series of snapping increments. Think of it like a ton of guides, positioned in uniform increments, and you don't have to drag each of them onto the image, because they all arrive at once when you choose View ➪ Show ➪ Grid. You can turn the snapping forces of the grid on and off by choosing View ➪ Snap To ➪ Grid.

You edit the grid in the Guides, Grid, Slices & Count panel of the Preferences dialog box, which you can get to by pressing Ctrl+K and then Ctrl+6 (⌘+K and then ⌘+6 on the Mac) or by Ctrl-double-clicking (Win) or ⌘-double-clicking (Mac) on a guide. You also can go at it the traditional way, by choosing Edit ➪ Preferences ➪ Guides, Grid, Slices & Count. The use of this dialog box is described in Chapter 2, but to save you leafing back right now, you type the major grid increments in the Gridline Every option box and type the minor increments in the Subdivisions option box, shown in Figure 13.32.

> **TIP** Don't want to see the grid anymore? Choose View ➪ Show ➪ Grid. The checked Grid command toggles off.

Using the Ruler tool

The final method for controlling movements in Photoshop is the Ruler tool. To activate it (it shares a button with the Eyedropper, Color Sampler, and Count tools), Alt-click (Option-click on the Mac) the Eyedropper tool a couple of times to select it, or press Shift+I twice (if the Eyedropper is displayed) to activate the tool.

When the tool's active, all you have to do is click and drag from one point to another point in the image window, and Photoshop itemizes the distance and angle between the two points in the Info palette. The Ruler tool is even smart enough to automatically display the Info palette if it's hidden.

From that point on, anytime you select the Ruler tool in the current image, Photoshop displays the original measurement line. This way, you can measure a distance, edit the image, and press I to refer back to the measurement. If you've switched to the Eyedropper or Color Sampler tool at any point in the interim, Shift+I brings back the Ruler tool.

To measure the distance and angle between two other points, you can draw a new line with the Ruler tool, or drag the endpoints of the existing measurement line.

FIGURE 13.32

With the grid in place — set by tweaking the Grid Preferences — you have a customizable network of guides you can snap to or not snap to, positioning your layers along the vertical and horizontal lines.

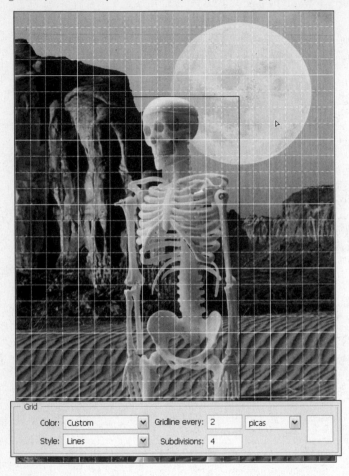

Photoshop accommodates only one measurement line per document. But you can break the line in two using what Adobe calls the "protractor" feature. Alt-drag (Win) or Option-drag (Mac) on one of the endpoints to draw forth a second segment. The Info palette then measures the angle between the two segments. As demonstrated in Figure 13.33, the L1 item in the Info palette lists the length of the first segment, L2 lists the length of the second segment, and A tells the angle between the segments.

The Ruler tool is great for straightening crooked layers. After drawing a line with the Ruler tool, choose Image ➪ Rotate Canvas ➪ Arbitrary. The Angle value automatically conforms to the A (angle) value listed in the Info palette. If you look closely, the two values may not exactly match. That's because Photoshop intelligently translates the value to between –45 and +45 degrees, which happens to be the simplest way to express any rotation. If you don't understand what I'm talking about, just trust in Photoshop. It does the math so you don't have to.

FIGURE 13.33

Here we have the distance from the center line of the skeleton to that of the moon and the 45-degree angle. The Info palette displays the data and serves as a guide as you drag; it updates as the Ruler tool's lines are drawn and adjusted.

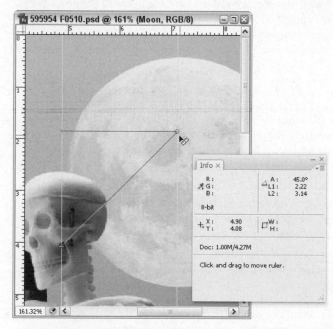

Applying Transformations

Photoshop treats some kinds of edits differently than others. Edits that affect the geometry of a selection or a layer are known collectively as *transformations*. These transformations include scaling (resizing), rotating, flipping, slanting, and distorting. Technically, moving is a transformation as well, but you just need to activate the Move tool to do that. Transformations are a special breed of edits in Photoshop because they can affect a selection, a layer, multiple layers, or an entire image at a time.

Transforming the entire image

Photoshop has two varieties of transformations. Transformation commands that affect the entire image — including all layers, paths, channels, and so on — are listed in the Image menu. Those that affect layers and selected portions of layers are in the Edit menu or, in the case of selection outlines, in the Select menu.

The following list explains how to apply transformations to every pixel in an image, regardless of whether or not the image is selected:

- **Scale:** To resize the image, choose Image ➪ Image Size. Because this command is one of the most essential low-level functions in the program, this is covered in Chapter 3.

- **Rotate:** To rotate the entire image, choose a command from the Image ➪ Rotate Canvas submenu. To rotate an image scanned on its side, choose the 90° CW or 90° CCW command. (That's clockwise and counterclockwise, respectively.) Choose 180° to spin the image on its head. To enter some other specific value, choose Image ➪ Rotate Canvas ➪ Arbitrary.

TIP To fix a crooked scanned image, for example, select the Ruler tool from the Eyedropper flyout in the Toolbox (press I or Shift+I, depending on your preference settings, three times). Drag along what should be a vertical or horizontal edge in the image. If you like, note the A value in the Info palette. Then choose Image ➪ Rotate Canvas ➪ Arbitrary. The angle value is preset to the angle you just measured, and all you have to do is press Enter or Return and the job's complete. Voila!

Whenever you apply the Arbitrary command, Photoshop has to expand the canvas size to avoid clipping any of your image. This results in background-colored wedges at each of the four corners of the image. You need to either clone with the Clone Stamp tool to fill in the wedges or clip them away with the Crop tool.

- **Flip:** Choose Image ➪ Rotate Canvas ➪ Flip Horizontal to flip the image so left is right and right is left. To flip the image upside down, choose Image ➪ Rotate Canvas ➪ Flip Vertical.

No command is specifically designed to slant or distort the entire image. In the unlikely event you're keen to do this, you'll have to link all layers and apply one of the commands under the Edit ➪ Transform submenu, as explained in the next section. Or, after linking your layers, you can use the Warp command and tools, discussed shortly.

Transforming layers and selected pixels

To transform a selection, a layer, or a collection of linked layers, you can apply one of the commands in the Edit ➪ Transform submenu. Nearly a dozen commands are here, all of which you can explore on your own. We're not skipping them arbitrarily or giving you less-than-extensive coverage. Rather, because you may not use many of them regularly, there are better ways to spend our time here. And it's not that there's anything wrong with the Transform submenu commands; they aren't bad, but one command — Free Transform — is infinitely better.

While you don't have the precision of entering specific measurements into the options bar that displays when you've picked one of the Transform submenu commands, with Free Transform, you can scale, flip, rotate, slant, distort, and move a selection or layer in one continuous operation. This one command lets you get all your transformations exactly right before pressing Enter or Return to apply the final changes. The command is demonstrated on the image shown in Figure 13.34. Each of the elements in this image resides on an independent layer. The blossom layer is active, and the shadow is linked to this layer. Therefore, both blossom and shadow will transform together.

FIGURE 13.34

This blossom and its shadow reside on separate layers. But because they are linked together, they will transform as one.

Here's how it works: To initiate the command, press Ctrl+T (⌘+T on the Mac) or choose Edit ➪ Free Transform. Photoshop surrounds the selection, layer, or linked layers with an eight-handle marquee. You are now in the Free Transform mode, which prevents you from doing anything except transforming the image or canceling the operation.

Here's how to work in the Free Transform mode:

- **Scale:** Drag one of the eight square handles to scale the image inside the marquee. To scale proportionally, Shift-drag a corner handle. To scale about the central *transformation origin* (labeled in Figure 13.35), Alt-drag (Option-drag) a corner handle.

> **TIP** By default, the origin is located in the center of the layer or selection. But you can move it to any place inside the image — even outside of the transformation box — by dragging it. The origin snaps to the grid and guides as well as to the center or any corner of the layer.

- **Flip:** You can flip the image by dragging one handle past its opposite handle. For example, dragging the left side handle past the right side handle flips the image horizontally.

> **TIP** If you want to perform a simple flip, it's generally easier to choose Edit ➪ Transform ➪ Flip Horizontal or Flip Vertical. Better yet, right-click (Control-click on the Mac) in the image window and choose one of the Flip commands from the shortcut menu. Quite surprisingly, you can choose any of the shortcut menu commands while working in the Free Transform mode.

- **Rotate:** To rotate the image, drag outside the marquee, as demonstrated in Figure 13.35. Shift-drag to rotate in 15-degree increments.

- **Skew:** Ctrl-drag (⌘-drag) a side handle (including the top or bottom handle) to slant the image. To constrain the slant, which is useful for producing perspective effects, Ctrl+Shift-drag (⌘+Shift-drag) a side handle.

- **Distort:** You can distort the image by Ctrl-dragging (⌘-dragging) a corner handle. You can tug the image to stretch it in any of four directions.

- **Perspective:** For a one-point perspective effect, Ctrl+Shift-drag (⌘+Shift-drag) a corner handle. To move two points in unison, Ctrl+Shift+Alt-drag (⌘+Shift+Option-drag) a corner handle.

- **Move:** Drag inside the marquee to move the image. This is useful when you're trying to align the selection or layer with a background image and you want to make sure the transformations match up properly.

- **Undo:** To undo the last modification without leaving the Free Transform mode altogether, press Ctrl+Z (⌘+Z on the Mac).

- **Zoom:** You can change the view size by choosing one of the commands in the View menu. You also can use the keyboard zoom shortcuts: Ctrl+spacebar-click, Alt+spacebar-click, Ctrl+plus, or Ctrl+minus (⌘+spacebar-click, Option+spacebar-click, ⌘+plus, or ⌘+minus on the Mac).

FIGURE 13.35

After pressing Ctrl+T (⌘+T on the Mac) to initiate the Free Transform command, drag outside the marquee to rotate the layer.

- **Apply:** Press Enter or Return to apply the final transformation and interpolate the new pixels. You also can double-click inside the marquee or click the check mark button in the Options bar.

- **Cancel:** To cancel the Free Transform operation, press Escape, click the "no" symbol button in the Options bar, or press Ctrl+period (⌘+period).

To tug two opposite corner handles in symmetrical directions, Ctrl+Alt-drag (⌘+Option-drag) either of the handles. The technique is applied to the blossom in Figure 13.36.

FIGURE 13.36

Press Ctrl and Alt (⌘ and Option) and drag a corner handle to move it and its opposite corner handle in symmetrical directions. The result is a free-form skew.

NOTE   If the finished effect looks jagged after you've applied the transformation, it's probably because you selected Nearest Neighbor from the Image Interpolation pop-up menu in the Preferences dialog box. To correct this problem, press Ctrl+Z (⌘+Z on the Mac) to undo the transformation and then press Ctrl+K (⌘+K). Selecting Bicubic from the Image Interpolation menu is your best all-around choice for a default. (This preference sets the default interpolation method in the Image Size dialog box, too.) Then press Ctrl+Shift+T (⌘+Shift+T) to reapply the transformation.

 To transform a clone of a layer or selected area, press Alt (Option) when choosing the Free Transform command or press Ctrl+Alt+T (⌘+Option+T).

If no part of the image is selected, you can transform multiple layers at a time by first linking them, as described in the "Linking and unlinking" section earlier in this chapter.

TIP To replay the last transformation on any layer or selection, choose Edit ➪ Transform ➪ Again or press Ctrl+Shift+T (⌘+Shift+T on the Mac). This technique is great to use if you forgot to link all the layers that you wanted to transform. You can even transform a path or selection outline to match a transformed layer. It's a handy feature. In fact, throw the Alt (Option) key in there, and the transformation can be repeated on a clone of the selected layer.

NOTE Neither Free Transform nor any of the commands in the Edit ➪ Transform submenu are available when a layer or linked layer is locked, either with the Lock Position or Lock All button. If a transformation command appears dimmed, therefore, the Lock buttons are very likely your culprits.

Warping layers

The Warp command allows you to totally disfigure (distort is too mild a term for what this feature does, and there's already a Transform ➪ Distort command, anyway). No, Warp lets you tug on, stretch, rip, and twist the content of a layer using a grid and bounding box to drag not just the sides and corners but the entire layer, in all different directions. Figure 13.37 demonstrates the process of warping on our previously abused blossom.

When you grab the edges where the gridlines meet the bounding box, dragging creates the sort of handles you see when drawing Bezier curves with the Pen tool. Also shown in Figure 13.37, these handles let you change the direction and curve of the stretched sides of the grid (and the layer within it, being dragged right along with the grid), pulling it up, down, in, and out.

After you've finished tormenting the layer, all you have to do is press Enter to commit to the transformation, or press Esc to abandon it and send the layer back to its pre-Warp state.

To really go to town on a layer and get some help in shaping the layer at the same time, you can click the Warp drop-down list, shown on the Options bar that appears when you activate the Warp command. Figure 13.38 shows the Options bar list. After a Warp preset has been applied, you can resize the Warp effect and click and drag from the single handle and flip the layer's content by dragging back through the layer itself.

FIGURE 13.37

Grab any grid intersection, corner, or bounding box handle, and pull, stretch, twist, and generally abuse the selected layer.

The Warp command's Options bar also offers numerical fields into which you can type the Bend (a percentage increase or decrease in it) or a Horizontal or Vertical percentage change, which changes the perspective of the preset Warp. For more about using such numerical transformation tools, keep reading — that's what the next section is all about.

FIGURE 13.38

Use the Warp tool's Options bar to apply a preset Warp to the layer, and then drag the lone grid handle to resize the layer and change the scale of the layer's distortion.

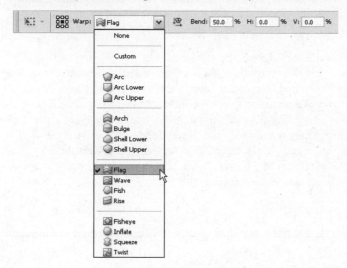

Numerical transformations

To track your transformations numerically, display the Info palette (F8) before you apply the Free Transform command. Even after you initiate Free Transform, you can access the Info palette by choosing Window ⇨ Info. You also can track and adjust the numerical equivalents of your mouse-driven transformations in the Options bar. Shown in Figure 13.39, the Options bar contains a series of numerical transformation controls anytime you enter the Free Transform mode. These values not only reflect the changes you've made so far, but also permit you to further transform the selection or layer by typing new values.

FIGURE 13.39

Normally, the options in the Options bar change only when you select a different tool, but choosing Free Transform adds a series of controls that permit you to transform a selection or layer numerically.

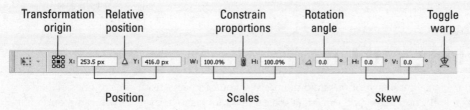

For the most part, the controls in the Options bar are straightforward. Click in the grid of nine squares to reposition the transformation origin. Use the X and Y values to change the location of the origin numerically. Click the triangular delta symbol to measure the movement relative to the transformation origin. Use the W and H values to scale the selection or layer. Click the link button to constrain the W and H values and resize the selection or layer proportionally. The angle value rotates; the H and V values skew.

Photoshop gives you the ability to control the values in the Options bar by "scrubbing," or dragging back and forth, over the icons or letters next to the editable values. When you see your mouse pointer turn to a two-headed arrow (at the tip of a pointing finger, labeled in Figure 13.40), you can drag over the position or scale values to increase or decrease them in increments of 1 pixel or 1 percentage point, respectively. Press and hold Alt (Option on the Mac) while scrubbing to change that to .1 pixel (or percentage point), and press and hold Shift to scrub the values in increments of 10. Scrubbing on the more sensitive angle and skew settings, however, raises or lowers them by .1 degree, and adding Shift changes the increment to 1 degree. By the way, at just about every location in Photoshop that you can find a numeric field, you can scrub.

FIGURE 13.40

Scrubbing values on the Options bar

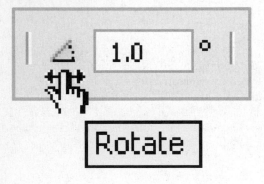

Probably, most people use the Options bar strictly for scaling and rotating: It's easy to picture the change that your entries into the Width, Height, and Set Rotation fields will do to the layer in question. You'd need the spatial awareness of a NASA navigation system to predict a numerical slant.

Masking and Layers

Layers offer special masking options unto themselves. You can paint inside the confines of a layer as if it were a selection mask; you can add a special mask for a single layer; or you can group multiple layers and have the bottom layer in the group serve as the mask. Although they're fairly complicated to use — you must be on your toes when you start juggling layer masks — these functions provide all sorts of image-editing and enhancement opportunities.

Preserving transparency

As you may recall, further discussion of the Lock Transparency button was promised when first mentioned in the section on locking layers. That further discussion begins here. Now, if you don't remember this, to refresh your memory, the Layers palette, with the Lock Transparency button labeled, appears in Figure 13.41.

FIGURE 13.41

The Lock Transparency button enables you to paint inside the layer's transparency mask without harming the transparent pixels.

Lock transparency

When selected, this button prevents you from painting inside the transparent portions of the layer. And although that may sound like a small thing, it is in fact the most useful Lock option of them all. Suppose you want to paint inside the moon shown in Figure 13.41. If this were a flat, non-layered image, you'd have to draw a selection outline carefully around the moon to isolate it from the other pixels in the image. With layers, however, there's no need to do this, because the moon lies on a different layer than its background, and a permanent selection outline exists because of this, telling Photoshop that there are both transparent and opaque pixels. Further, it tells Photoshop which pixels are which, and this creates the *transparency mask*.

The first example in Figure 13.42 shows the moon on its own with the background hidden. The transparent areas outside the mask appear in the checkerboard pattern. When the Lock Transparency button is deselected, you can paint anywhere you want inside the layer. Selecting the Lock Transparency button activates the transparency mask and places the checkerboard area off-limits.

The bottom image in Figure 13.42 shows what happens after the Lock Transparency button is selected and the Clone Stamp tool is used to paint in the other content. No matter how large the Clone Stamp was (it was much larger than the moon), the cloned content appears only within the moon's portion of the layer. The transparent areas are protected by the mask.

Some more useful information about Lock Transparency:

■ You can turn Lock Transparency on and off from the keyboard by pressing the standard slash character (/).

■ The Lock Transparency button is dimmed when the background layer is active because this layer is entirely opaque.

Creating layer-specific masks

In addition to the transparency mask that accompanies every layer (except the background), you can add a mask to a layer to make certain pixels in the layer transparent. Now, you might wonder if simply erasing portions of a layer wouldn't make those portions transparent—and you'd be right, it would. When you erase, however, you delete pixels permanently. By creating a layer mask, you make pixels temporarily transparent instead. You can return at any time in the future and bring those pixels back to life again simply by adjusting the mask. So layer masks add yet another level of flexibility.

To create a layer mask, select the layer you want to mask and choose Layer ➪ Add Layer Mask ➪ Reveal All. Or more simply, click the layer mask icon at the bottom of the Layers palette, as labeled in Figure 13.43. A second thumbnail preview appears to the left of the layer name, also labeled in the figure. A second outline around the preview shows the layer mask is active.

To edit the mask, simply paint in the image window. Paint with black to make pixels transparent. Because black represents deselected pixels in an image, it makes these pixels transparent in a layer. Paint with white to make pixels opaque.

Thankfully, Photoshop is smart enough to make the default foreground color in a layer mask white and the default background color black. This ensures that painting with the brush makes pixels opaque, whereas painting with the eraser makes them transparent, just as you would expect.

FIGURE 13.42

The layered moon as it appears on its own (top) and when content from another image has been clone stamped in with the Lock Transparency button turned on (bottom).

FIGURE 13.43

The layer mask thumbnail (to right of the moon's layer thumbnail) indicates the presence of a mask. The black areas in the mask translate to transparent pixels in the layer. The gradient to the moon selection makes it appear to fade out along its bottom-left side.

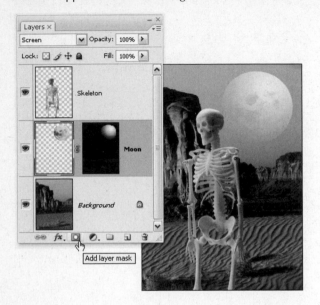

Photoshop offers lots of bells and whistles to make the function of layer masks both convenient and powerful. Here's everything you need to know:

- **Reveal the selection:** If you select some portion of your layer, Photoshop automatically converts the selection to a layer mask when you click the layer mask icon at the bottom of the palette. The area outside the selection becomes transparent. (The corresponding command is Layer ⇨ Add Layer Mask ⇨ Reveal Selection.)

- **Hide the selection:** You also can choose to reverse the prospective mask, making the area inside the selection transparent and the area outside opaque. To do this, choose Layer ⇨ Add Layer Mask ⇨ Hide Selection. Or better yet, Alt-click (Win) or Option-click (Mac) the layer mask icon in the Layers palette.

- **Hide everything:** To begin with a black mask that hides everything, choose Layer ⇨ Add Layer Mask ⇨ Hide All. Or press Ctrl+D (⌘+D on the Mac) to deselect everything and then Alt-click (Win) or Option-click (Mac) the layer mask icon.

- **View the mask:** Photoshop regards a layer mask as a layer-specific channel. You can actually see it listed in italics in the Channels palette. To view the mask on its own — as a black-and-white image — Alt-click (Win) or Option-click (Mac) the layer mask thumbnail in the Layers palette. Alt-click (Win) or Option-click (Mac) again to view the image instead.

- **Layer mask overlay:** To view the mask as a red overlay, Shift+Alt-click (Win) or Shift+Option-click (Mac) the layer mask icon. Or simply press backslash (\).

> **TIP** After you have both the layer and mask visible at once, you can hide the mask by pressing \, or you can hide the layer and view only the mask by pressing the tilde key (~). So many alternatives!

- **Change the overlay color:** Double-click the layer mask thumbnail to access the Layer Mask Display Options dialog box, which enables you to change the color and opacity of the overlay color.

- **Turn off the mask:** You can temporarily disable the mask by Shift-clicking the mask thumbnail. A red *X* covers the thumbnail when it's disabled, and all masked pixels in the layer appear opaque. Click the thumbnail to put the mask back in working order.

- **Switch between the layer and mask:** As you become more familiar with layer masks, you'll switch back and forth between the layer and mask quite frequently, editing the layer one minute and editing the mask the next. You can switch between the layer and mask by clicking their respective thumbnails.

> **TIP** You also can switch between the layer and mask from the keyboard. Press Ctrl+tilde (Win) or ⌘+tilde (Mac) to make the layer active. Press Ctrl+\ (Win) or ⌘+\ (Mac) to switch to the mask.

- **Link the layer and mask:** A little link icon appears between the layer and mask thumbnails in the Layers palette. When the link icon is visible, you can move or transform the mask and layer as one. If you click the link icon to turn it off, the layer and mask move independently. (You can always move a selected region of the mask or layer independently of the other.)

- **Convert the mask to a selection:** As with all masks, you can convert a layer mask to a selection. To do so, Ctrl-click (Win) or ⌘-click (Mac) the layer mask icon. Throw in the Shift and Alt (Win) or Option (Mac) keys if you want to add or subtract the layer mask with an existing selection outline.

- **Apply the mask to a group:** You also can apply a mask to a group of layers. Just select the group, and click the layer mask icon. The mask affects all layers in the group. If a layer in the group contains its own mask, no worries; Photoshop's smart enough to figure out how to mix them together. For another method of masking multiple layers, see the section "Masking groups of layers."

When and if you finish using the mask — you can leave it in force as long as you like — you can choose Layer ⇨ Remove Layer Mask. Or just drag the layer mask thumbnail to the trash can icon. Either way, an alert box asks whether you want to discard the mask or permanently apply it to the layer. Click the button that corresponds to your innermost desires.

Pasting inside a selection outline

One command, Edit ⇨ Paste Into (Ctrl+Shift+V or ⌘+Shift+V), creates a layer mask automatically. Choose the Paste Into command to paste the contents of the Clipboard into the current selection, so that the selection acts as a mask. Because Photoshop pastes to a new layer, it converts the selection to a layer mask. But here's the interesting part: By default, Photoshop turns off the link between the layer and the mask. This way, you can Ctrl-drag (⌘-drag on the Mac) the layer inside a fixed mask to position the pasted image.

> **TIP** Once upon a time in Photoshop, there was a command that made it possible to paste a copied image in back of a selection. Although the command is gone, its spirit lives on in — you'll be shocked — a keyboard shortcut. Just press Alt (Win) or Option (Mac) when choosing Edit ➪ Paste Into. Or just press Ctrl+Shift+Alt+V (⌘+Shift+Option+V on the Mac). Photoshop creates a new layer with an inverted layer mask, masking away the selected area.

Masking groups of layers

About now, you may be getting a little tired of the topic of layer masking. There's one more important facet of this very broad topic left to discuss, and then we'll move on. The facet? You can group multiple layers into something called a *clipping mask*, in which the lowest layer in the group masks the others. Where the lowest layer, or *base layer*, is transparent, the other layers are hidden; where the lowest layer is opaque, the contents of the other layers are visible.

> **NOTE** Despite the similarities in name, a clipping mask bears no relation to a clipping path. That is, a clipping mask doesn't allow you to prepare transparent areas for import into other applications. Nope, a clipping mask is used purely for controlling the editable parts of its layer pals, all of which are sitting on top of it. Quite a sport, that clipping mask.

You can create a clipping mask in three ways:

■ Alt-click (Win) or Option-click (Mac) the horizontal line between any two layers to group them into a single unit. Your cursor changes to the mask cursor, labeled in Figure 13.44, when you press Alt (Win) or Option (Mac); the horizontal line becomes broken after you click. To break the layers apart again, Alt-click (Win) or Option-click (Mac) the dotted line to make it solid.

■ Select the higher of the two layers you want to combine into a clipping mask. Then choose Layer ➪ Create Clipping Mask or press Ctrl+G (⌘+G on the Mac). To make the layers independent again, choose Layer ➪ Release Clipping Mask or press Ctrl+Shift+G (⌘+Shift+G on the Mac). In Figure 13.45, you see the results of the clipping mask. The effects applied to the clipping mask — the type — are also applied to the layer above it.

■ Select the layers you'd like to be part of the mask, and then choose Layers ➪ Create Clipping Mask. If you link your layers, the command is dimmed. You can, however, click the line between selected layers to create a clipping mask, as described earlier. Next, choose Layer ➪ Create Clipping Mask From Linked. Keep in mind that this works only if all the linked layers are next to each other in the stacking order.

> **NOTE** If you're familiar with Illustrator, you may recognize Photoshop's clipping mask as a relative of Illustrator's clipping mask, in which one object in the illustration acts as a mask for a collection of additional objects. In Illustrator, however, the topmost object in the group is the mask, not the bottom one. So much for consistency.

FIGURE 13.44

Alt-click (Win) or Option-click (Mac) the horizontal line between two layers to group them into a clipping mask.

FIGURE 13.45

Use one layer as a mask for another. The Layers palette shows you the relationship between the clipping mask and the rest of the image.

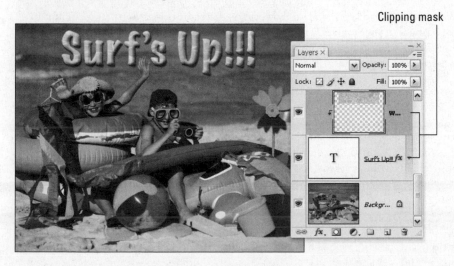

Working with Layer Comps

Photoshop's Layer Comps palette, shown in Figure 13.46, is designed to track certain aspects of an image and save their status at any given time. Essentially, it records snapshots of the Layers palette as individual states, or *layer comps*, which are saved with the image file on disk.

FIGURE 13.46

Time travel is finally a reality with the Layer Comps palette.

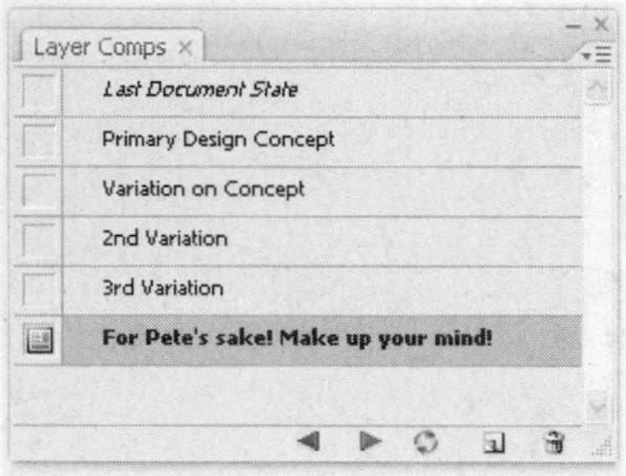

The key to successfully working with layer comps is to be extremely conscious of what they are and aren't capable of tracking. A saved layer comp can store and recall information about the visibility, opacity, and blend modes of the layers in an image, as well as the position of each layer. Layer comps also can record whether or not styles are applied to each layer and the settings of those styles. What you need to keep in mind, however, is that layer comps don't even attempt to track any pixel changes to your images. This applies to painting, creating gradients, using the Patch tool; any operation that alters the pixels (as well as text contents) of an image is not recorded in the Layer Comps palette. The palette turns the other way and pretends you've done nothing at all.

That said, layer comps can be a great and useful asset, especially when you're at the stage of assembling the final pieces into a composition. To save a layer comp, open the Layer Comps palette by choosing Window ⇨ Layer Comps or by clicking the Layer Comps tab in the Options bar's docking well (the palette is docked there by default). Next, click the new layer comp icon, labeled in Figure 13.46, to access the New Layer Comp dialog box, shown in Figure 13.47. Here, you set a name for your layer comp and any comments that might help you identify the state you're saving. This dialog box also is where you specify exactly what gets tracked by this layer comp. Three options are available to you:

- **Visibility:** Select this option to track the visibility of layers and layer masks.

- **Position:** This option tracks the position of each separate layer in relation to the others. Again, it's important to note that position changes within layers — say, if you marquee a section of a layer and drag it over to a corner — cannot be restored through layer comps.

- **Appearance (Layer Style):** This option saves all layer style attributes, including knockouts and effects, as well as the Opacity value and blend mode assigned to each layer.

The New Layer Comp dialog box lets you specify exactly what type of layer data you want to track.

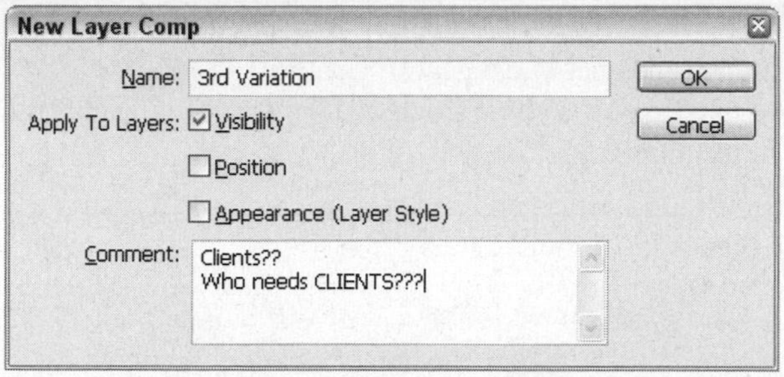

Click OK to confirm your settings and, presto, you've created a new layer comp. You can tell that you're looking at a saved state of your image because the little icon in the left column of the Layer Comps palette sits alongside your new layer comp, as shown in Figure 13.48. As soon as you make any layer-comp-friendly changes to your image, such as moving a layer or adjusting its opacity, the icon snaps back to the topmost layer comp, known as the Last Document State. This means that trackable changes have been made to the image since your last saved layer comp. You can save this new state as another layer comp, if you want, and continue working. To return to a saved state, simply click in the space to the left of the layer comp.

Nearly all the functions available to you in the Layer Comps palette menu can be accessed from icons in the palette.

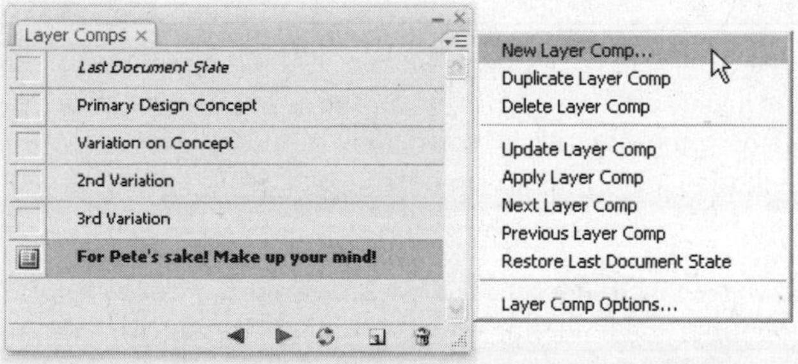

Working with the Layer Comps palette is pretty easy after you get used to it, but there are a few things you should know:

■ Use the left- and right-pointing arrows at the bottom of the palette to cycle through your various layer comps. Click the right-pointing arrow to view the next saved layer comp down the list, and click the left-pointing arrow to view the previous layer comp. To cycle through only specific comps, Ctrl-click (⌘-click on the Mac) or Shift-click to select them and then click the arrows.

- To the right of the arrow icons is the update layer comp icon (it's the one with two arrows that form a circle). Click this icon to assign changes to an existing selected layer comp. The icon in the left column of the palette leaps over to whatever layer comp you've selected, and the current state of the Layers palette is applied to this layer comp.

- To delete a layer comp, simply select it and click the trash can icon, just as you would to delete a layer in the Layers palette. Here, you also have the added benefit of being able to select and drag multiple layer comps to the trash icon at once.

- You can always return the image to its most recent unsaved layer state by clicking in the space next to the Last Document State item in the palette.

All these options also can be accessed from the Layer Comps palette menu, as shown in Figure 13.48. The palette menu also lets you duplicate any selected layer comp or access its options without having to double-click it.

CAUTION   Fragile creatures that they are, layer comps have a tendency to break down every once in a while. Luckily, though, they're pretty good at letting you know when they're unhappy. Whenever you make a change that will throw any of your layer comps out of whack—such as merging layers or converting a layer into a background—the affected comps display a little triangle with an exclamation point. You can either undo the destructive move or click one of the triangle icons, in which case you'll be presented with a warning explaining exactly how you've betrayed the layer comp. From this warning, you have the option of "clearing" the layer comp, which is a way of updating the comp to account for the changes you've made. Right-click (Control-click on the Mac) any of the triangles and choose Clear Layer Comp Warning to clear that particular layer comp, or choose Clear All Layer Comp Warnings to clear all the layer comps without having to wrangle with the warnings for each.

3D Image Editing

There's one last layer type to talk about — 3D layers. That's right, we said 3D (and no funny glasses are required). Okay, we're showing our age, and are sure anyone under the age of 21 who grew up on a steady diet of modern computer games probably isn't as blown away by this new set of features as we Baby Boomers are. More likely, the young 'uns are wondering what took so long — and now the wait is over.

In a nutshell, Photoshop now gives you the ability to import 3D models created in a vast array of formats, and manipulate the position, lighting, and rendering of these models. You also can edit any existing textures used in the model, as well as incorporate any and all of Photoshop's 2D features in your composites.

Photoshop CS3 supports the following 3D interchange formats:

- **3DS:** The native file format of Autodesk's 3ds Max, perhaps the most popular 3D animation application available on the Windows platform.

- **OBJ:** The open file format originally developed by Wavefront Technologies for its application, Advanced Visualizer. Many 3D graphics applications now have the ability to import and export to the OBJ format, including 3ds Max, Maya (another Autodesk application), and Lightwave, to name only a few.

- **U3D:** The Universal 3D format is the creation of Intel and the 3D Industry Forum (3DIF). It isn't so much a 3D editing file type, like OBJ, as it is a means for sharing 3D drawings both online and in common business applications such as Microsoft Office and Adobe Acrobat.

- **KMZ:** KMZ stands for Keyhole Markup Language-zipped. Keyhole was the original name of an application later bought out by Google and used in the creation of Google Earth files. You'd write the files in KML code (which is an XML application) and compress the files into .kmz zipped archive files. Don't panic — an understanding of KML is not required to open and work with these files in Photoshop (but obviously, it helps).

- **COLLADA:** This format is predominantly used in the creation of video game content. It began as the official format for Sony's PlayStation 3 and PSP platforms, and its specification is now jointly held by the Kronos Group (a member-funded consortium that focuses on creating open standards) and Sony. Many of the programs listed previously support COLLADA (3D Studio Max, Maya, Blender, and Google Earth, for example).

Working with 3D files

When you open a 3D file in Photoshop (File ➪ Open) you really aren't opening the file itself. Instead, you're importing the contents of the 3D file into a new Photoshop file. The first thing Photoshop asks for is dimension values, as you can see in the dialog box shown in Figure 13.49.

FIGURE 13.49

This figure shows an Image Size dialog box for importing an existing 3D image. Because we selected a .3ds file, the title bar for the dialog box repeats the type of content we're importing.

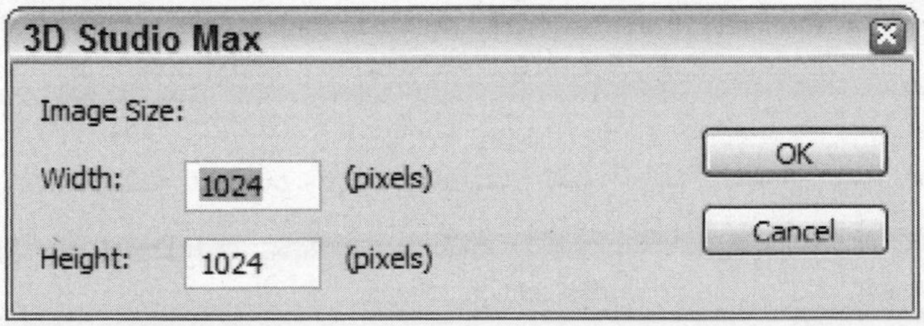

3D Studio Max

Image Size:

Width: 1024 (pixels)

Height: 1024 (pixels)

OK

Cancel

Once that's out of the way, the existing model is placed on its own layer within the file, as shown in Figure 13.50.

 When it comes to scaling, 3D file content is like vector art. You can scale it up or down without any loss of detail.

709

A 3D layer as seen in the Layers palette

If you already have a file open and want to import a 3D file in to a new layer, just choose Layer ⇨ 3D Layers ⇨ New Layer From 3D File from the menu, and the 3D content is placed on a new 3D layer above the last currently active layer in the stack. Instead of asking you what dimensions you'd like to use, the dimensions of the existing file govern the size of the new layer. You also can drag 3D layers from one open file to another. Any file you create that contains 3D layers can be saved in PSD, PSB, PDF, or TIFF format. Any setting changes you make to the model(s) in your image are incorporated upon saving.

Okay — so you have a 3D layer in your file. Now what? You can't do a whole lot with it at this point — it's just another layer in the stack, and Photoshop's 3D tools are hidden from view. Not a problem — give the layer icon a double-click and the 3D Options bar comes to life. Figure 13.51 shows the results.

The Options bar for an active 3D layer

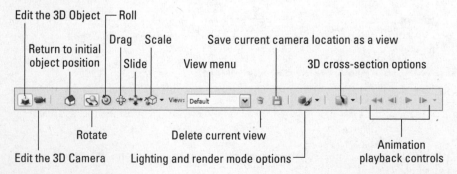

CAUTION While you're working with Photoshop's 3D tools, you can't access any of Photoshop's other features until you commit to or cancel any changes you've made to the 3D content.

It's important at this stage to understand what you can and can't do to 3D content in Photoshop. You can't edit the physical 3D model itself. For example, you can't turn a model of a banana into a beach ball. And, you can't create new textures and attach them to a model. If you need to do that, then it's back to a 3D authoring application you go. This doesn't mean you can't change various properties of the model. For example, you can modify its position, rotation, lighting, camera properties, and render modes. You also can view the models in cross section, and edit any existing textures the model possesses. And, of course, you can add anything to the composite image Photoshop is capable of — combining multiple 3D objects into a single image, adding 2D layers to the composition, and so forth.

TIP If your 3D model is animated, you can view the animation using the animation controls on the 3D Tools Options bar. These are the standard playback/fast-forward/rewind options we've been indoctrinated with since the days of the VCR. You can even scrub through an animated sequence by clicking the arrow next to the playback buttons. This opens a slider control you can drag to move forward or backward (called *scrubbing* in editing lingo) through the animation sequence.

Applying Transformations to a 3D model

Transforming a 3D model, for our purposes, means moving, rotating, or scaling. We're dealing with 3 dimensions as enacted within a 2-dimensional interface. There are the traditional left and right (the x-axis) and up and down (the y-axis), as well as a perceived front to back (the z-axis). It's the genius of 3D software that reconstructs the image each time we move something to create the illusion of looking out a window onto a 3-dimensional object, when in reality, we're just looking at colored pixels on the face of our monitor. These modifications are done using the six tools on the option bar to the left side of the View menu we showed in Figure 13.51. Simply double-click the 3D layer's icon in the Layers palette to activate the 3D tools Options bar, and then make sure the Edit 3D Object option button (the very first button on the Options bar) is selected. From here, it's just a matter of selecting a tool and modifying the object. Your options are:

 ■ **Rotate:** Dragging up or down rotates around the object's x-axis, while dragging side-to-side rotates around the y-axis.

 ■ **Roll:** Dragging side-to-side rotates the model around its z-axis.

 ■ **Drag:** This tool lives up to its name. Drag side-to-side to move the model horizontally, or up or down to move it vertically.

 ■ **Slide:** You typically use the Slide tool to position the object closer to you (dragging down) or farther away (by dragging up). If you drag left or right, the Slide tool simply mimics the Drag tool.

 ■ **Scale:** Drag up and the model gets bigger. Drag down and it gets smaller.

 ■ **Return to Initial Object Position:** This tool's icon looks like a house because when you click it you go back *home* — the initial position the object was in before you began the most recent round of transformations.

711

You also have a couple of toggles available when using these tools. Say, for example, you're rotating and want to roll the model a tad (or vice versa). Instead of swapping tools, just hold down your Options key (Mac) or Ctrl key (Win). You can use the same technique to toggle between Drag and Slide.

You also can use the Shift key to modify the way the Drag and Slide tools behave. Hold down the Shift key while dragging or sliding, and the tool moves only in the direction you're currently moving the cursor — left and right, or up and down.

If you need numeric accuracy in transforming an object, simply click the small drop arrow to the right of the Scale tool. This displays the Object Position pop-up, shown in Figure 13.52, where you can enter the desired values.

FIGURE 13.52

Enter numeric values for your transformations in the Object position pop-up.

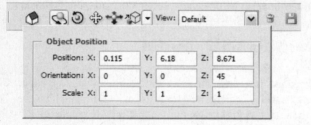

Modifying the position of the Camera

In the world of 3D imagery, you have the objects themselves, the "lights" that make them visible to us, and the "camera," which provides the view. When using the transformation tools discussed previously, the camera view remains fixed, but you can manipulate this imaginary camera just as you do the 3D objects. Just click the Edit the 3D Camera button on the Options bar to swap in the Camera Tools, and you're ready to go. The 3D Camera tools mirror the 3D Object tools, except now you're moving the camera around the object, as opposed to moving the object around in front of the camera. The tricky thing here is that everything looks pretty much the same — for example, what you see when you rotate the object is exactly what you see when you orbit the camera. It's up to you to pay attention to what tools you're using. With that said, your 3D Camera tools include:

 ■ **Orbit:** While the object stays fixed, you orbit the camera around the object's x (up or down) and y (left and right) axes.

 ■ **Roll:** Imagine the z-axis is shooting straight out the front of the lens (which it would be in a 3D universe). The Roll tool simply rotates the camera around that axis, as if you were pointing it at your subject and then flipping it around in your hand while your eye was pressed up to the view finder.

 ■ **Pan:** Panning simply means moving the camera left or right, up or down. Just drag in the direction you want to move the camera.

■ **Walk:** Walking means moving the camera closer to, or farther from the object. Drag up to walk toward the object, and down to walk back from the object. Side-to-side movement just pans.

 ■ **Zoom:** We're all familiar with zooming. Drag up to zoom in, and down to zoom out. The camera's maximum field of view is 180 degrees.

 ■ **Return to Initial Camera Position:** If you guessed that this button returns the camera to the position it was in before you began the most recent round of changes, you were right.

Just as shown earlier, you can set exact numeric values by clicking the small drop arrow, this time to the right of the Zoom tool. A similar pop-up appears (called 3D Camera Settings), and you can enter your desired values, as shown in Figure 13.53.

FIGURE 13.53

The 3D Camera Settings pop-up. The Orthographic View check box displays the 3D model in accurate scale view while removing perspective distortion.

3D Camera Settings		
Position: X: -40.74	Y: -10.73	Z: 17.45
Orientation: X: -101.25	Y: 0	Z: -112.5
Field of View: 30	degrees vertical	
☐ Orthographic View Scale: 1/ 24		

> **TIP** The same toggling features exist for the camera tools as for the object tools. The Ctrl (Win) and Option (Mac) keys let you toggle between Orbit and Roll, and Pan and Walk. The Shift key has the same constraining effects here too.

Creating Camera Views

What's a camera view? You simply move the camera into a new location/orientation with respect to the object, and save that position. The 3D Camera tools already have some preset camera views: Default (the original position of the camera set in the 3D authoring application), and the standard isometric views: Left, Right, Top, Bottom, Back, and Front.

> **NOTE** The same view options are available from the View drop menu when in Edit 3D Object mode, but of course those options move the object around in front of the camera instead of moving the camera around the object. And, you can't create and save 3D Object views.

To add a custom camera view, use the 3D Camera tools to position the camera where you'd like, and simply click the Save button (which uses a floppy disk for its icon) found to the right of the View drop menu. This opens the the New 3D View dialog box, where you can enter a name for your view, as shown in Figure 13.54.

Your new view option now appears at the bottom of the View drop menu, in both 3D Object and 3D Camera modes (Figure 13.55).

FIGURE 13.54

Saving a new view to the View drop menu

FIGURE 13.55

Once saved, your view options are available in both 3D Camera and 3D Objects modes.

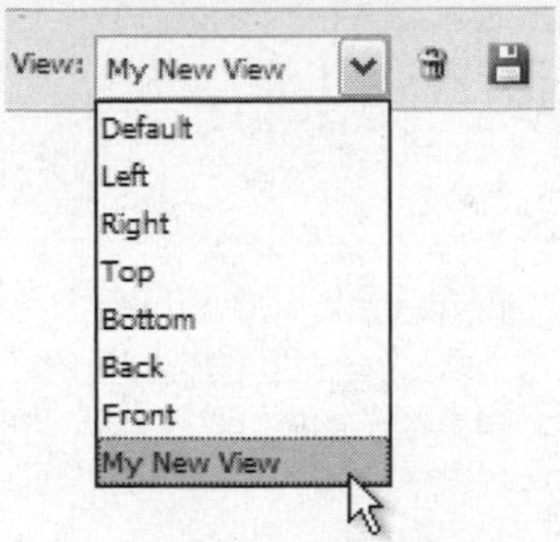

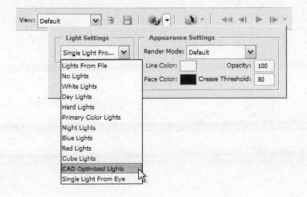

Working with Lighting and Rendering Effects

We mentioned lighting a little while back. In 3D authoring programs, it's the lighting that makes the objects visible. Otherwise, the camera view simply displays black silhouetted objects. Photoshop allows you to change the light settings for the object, giving you a choice of the default lighting created in the 3D authoring program, or a series of presets.

To change the current light settings, first click the Light and Render Mode Options button. This pops up the Light and Appearance settings. From here, click the drop menu under Lighting settings and choose from the list of available presets, as shown in Figure 13.56.

FIGURE 13.56

The Lights from File option use the lighting effects created in the original authoring program.

You can change the method by which the 3D model is rendered using the Appearance pop-up. When you import the 3D model, its default rendering is solid. To change the render mode, simply select a different option from the Render Mode drop menu. For example, in Figure 13.57 we've changed the rendering mode from Solid to Shaded Wireframe. You then can set Line Color, Face Color, Opacity, and Crease Threshold values, as applicable.

Working with Cross Section Views

The 3D layer tools allow you to slice and dice models in your 3D layers along each of the three axes, as shown in Figure 13.58. With the 3D tools active on the Options bar, click the Cross Section Settings button to display the corresponding pop-up palette. From here, you need to select the Enable Cross Section check box to activate the rest of the tools there.

FIGURE 13.57

You have seven possible options on the Render Mode drop menu.

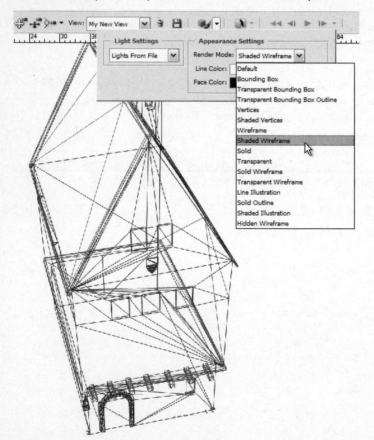

FIGURE 13.58

You can modify the Alignment, Position, and Orientation of your cross section.

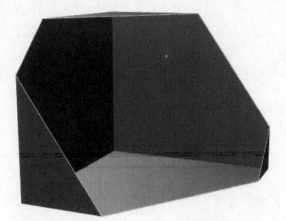

The following options are at your disposal:

■ **Alignment:** When you choose an axis, you're specifying which of the three axes (x, y, or z) perpendicular to which you want the intersecting plane aligned. For example, if you choose the y axis, the intersecting plane cuts across the x axis.

■ **Position and Orientation:** Here you have access to the Offset and two tilt settings. The Offset value moves the intersecting plane along the axis perpendicular to the axis you chose previously. For example, a value of zero places the intersecting plane in the middle of the object along the chosen axis. You can set positive or negative values to cut off more or less of the object. The tilt settings allow you to rotate the intersecting plane 360 degrees around the two axes not chosen in the Alignment settings. So, if you chose to align the intersecting plane perpendicular to the x axis, your Tilt 1 slider would rotate the plane around the y axis, and Tilt 2 would rotate it around the z axis.

■ **Flip:** Swaps the area of the model displayed on screen to the other side of your intersecting plane.

Editing Textures in 3D models

Many 3D objects are textured, meaning they've had 2D images applied to their surfaces to provide realism. When you import a 3D model that contains textures, those texture files are displayed in the Layers palette, indented beneath the 3D layer to which they are attached, as shown in Figure 13.59.

While you can't create and attach new textures to a 3D model, you certainly can use every tool in Photoshop's arsenal to edit the existing textures. Just double-click a texture layer in the Layers palette to open the associated text image in a separate document window. Now you can do anything you like to it. Once you've finished, simply save the file and the texture is updated in the 3D model.

FIGURE 13.59

As with other layer types, textures appear with the traditional Eye icons beside them. Use these to hide or display the textures in your image.

Summary

In this chapter, you learned all about layers—from creating and cloning them to floating the background layer, to reordering layers, to merging layers and converting layers to selections. You also learned about combining layers using links, grouping layers, and moving, scaling, rotating, and aligning layers, too. You learned to rasterize layers with vector content, and the use of Smart Guides was also covered, making much of the other layer-related activity lots easier.

To make further use of layers, this chapter also showed you how to make drop shadows, halos, and spotlights, and to work with the new Smart Objects. You also learned to apply Stack Modes to your Smart Objects for some interesting, if mathematically enigmatic, results. You learned to use the Ruler tool, to select the Lock Transparency option, and to work with layer masks and the Layer Comps palette, and last but not least, you learned how Photoshop CS3 allows you to work with 3D content. You learned about importing and manipulating 3D models—their position, lighting, textures, and the use of Photoshop's 2D features in the resulting composites.

Chapter 14

The Wonders of Blend Modes

Blend modes permit you to mix the color of a pixel with that of every pixel in a straight line beneath it. A single blend mode can pack as much power as a mask, a filter, and a retouching tool combined. And, unlike some of those combined options, blend modes don't physically alter an image's pixels — they're temporary. As long as one image remains layered in front of another, you can replace one calculation with another as easily as you change a letter of text in a word processor.

To appreciate the most rudimentary power of blend modes, consider Figure 14.1. Here you see several clones of our bony old pal. Each one has been mixed with the background using a random sampling of blend modes from Photoshop's Layers palette. The skeleton image itself never changes; each repeated layer contains the same collection of pixels. In all, there are six layers: five skeletons and the background, each skeleton layer subject to the blend mode labeled in the figure.

Now, don't worry — you'll delve into the specifics of every one of these blend modes later in this chapter. However, before you get ahead of yourself, a few basics are in order.

In this chapter, you investigate three fundamental ways to mix pixels:

- **The Layers palette:** You can combine the active layer with underlying pixels using the Opacity and Fill values, along with the blend mode pop-up menu, all members of the Layers palette, as seen in Figure 14.2. Opacity and Fill options are examined in detail in the next section. Blend modes are covered in the section after that.

721

FIGURE 14.1

Five identical layers mixed in a variety of ways with the background image using a different blend mode option

| Normal | Hard Light | Linear Dodge | Linear Light | Difference |

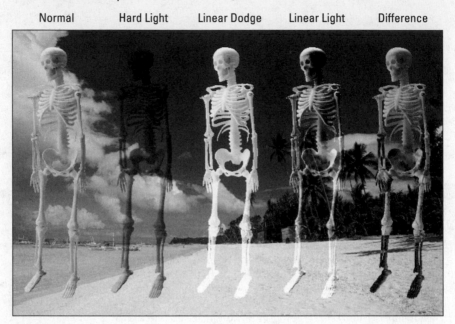

- **Blending options:** Right-click a thumbnail in the Layers palette (Control-click on the Mac) and choose Blending Options to display the Blending Options panel of the extensive Layer Style dialog box. Along with the Blend Mode, Opacity, and Fill Opacity options, you get an assortment of advanced blending options, including the Knockout pop-up menu and Blend If sliders. The Knockout options let you use one layer to cut a floating hole into one or more layers below it. Using the Blend If sliders, you can drop colors out of the active layer and force colors to show through from layers below. For more information about these and other options, read the section "Advanced Blending Options."

- **Channel operations:** The so-called channel operations permit you to combine two open images of identical size, or one image with itself. Photoshop offers two commands for this purpose: Image ➪ Apply Image and Image ➪ Calculations. Largely archaic and completely lacking in sizing and placement functions, these commands are unique in that they provide access to two otherwise hidden blend modes: Add and Subtract. Simply put, unless a technique involves the Add or Subtract mode, or you want to clone two images into a third image window, you can mix images with greater ease, flexibility, and feedback using the Layers palette. For more on this lively topic, see the section "Whole Image Calculations."

FIGURE 14.2

The blend mode menu and the Opacity and Fill sliders are located on Photoshop's Layers palette.

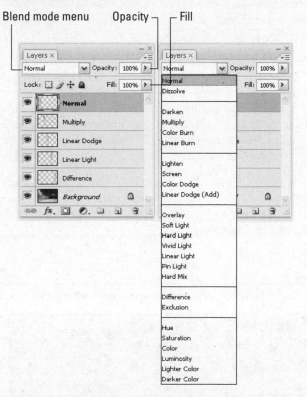

Blend modes are not Photoshop's most straightforward feature. There may even come a time when you utter the words, "Blend modes are stupid." They demand a generous supply of experimentation, and even then they'll try to fool you. The key is to combine a basic understanding of how blend modes and other compositing features work with your natural willingness to experiment, grow, and bond with pixels. Sometime when you don't have a deadline looming, take a multilayered composition you have lying around and hit it with a few calculations. Even if the result is a disaster that you wouldn't share with your best friend, let alone a client, you can consider it time well spent.

Opacity and Fill

The Opacity value permits you to mix the active layer with the layers beneath it in prescribed portions. By way of example, consider Figure 14.3. The left side of the image shows a grouping of the skeletons at full opacity. In the example on the right, the Opacity setting was reduced, thereby transforming the group of skeletons into mere ghosts of their former selves.

The option directly below Opacity in the Layers palette is the field for controlling Fill opacity. Where Opacity controls the translucency of everything associated with a layer, Fill adjusts the opacity of the filled areas of a layer independently of any layer effects you add to it. Take a gander at Figure 14.4, where a drop shadow and outer bevel have been added to each of the skeleton layers. (You can add a layer effect to a layer by choosing an option from the cursive *f* icon at the bottom of the Layers palette, as discussed in Chapter 13.) Opacity affects pixels and layer effects alike; Fill affects pixels and leaves effects unchanged.

Fill also is more flexible than Opacity. While you can take Opacity and Fill all the way down to 0%, when you reduce Opacity to zero, the content disappears. When you reduce Fill to zero, the content disappears, but you leave the effects intact. Figure 14.5 shows the results of lowering the Fill value to 20 percent and then 0 percent.

FIGURE 14.3

Skeletons at 100% Opacity (left) and faded by 50% (right) directly beneath the Opacity field

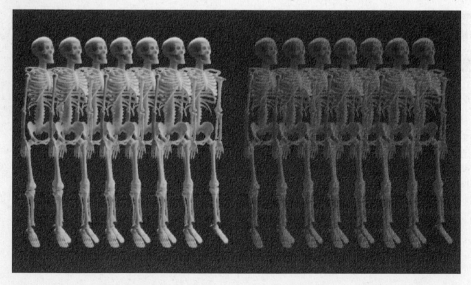

724

FIGURE 14.4

By adding a layer effect or two, the difference between Opacity and Fill becomes obvious: 50% Opacity makes layer and effects translucent (left); 50% Fill alters the layer independently of its effects (right).

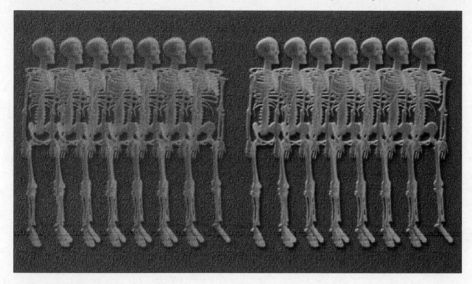

FIGURE 14.5

Using the Fill value, you can subordinate a layer to its effect (20% Fill left) or fade the layer away entirely (0% Fill right).

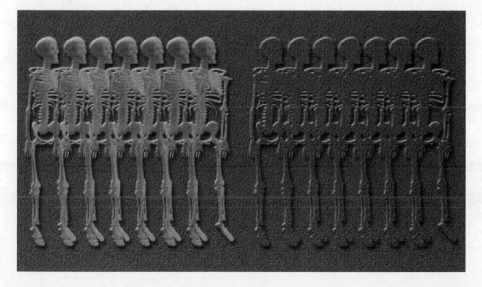

TIP   When a selection or navigation tool is active, you can change the Opacity setting for a layer from the keyboard. Press a single number key to change the Opacity in 10 percent increments. That's 1 for 10 percent, 2 for 20 percent, up to 0 for 100 percent, in order along the top of your keyboard. If you have the urge to be more precise, press two keys in a row quickly to specify an exact two-digit Opacity value.

Hankering to change the Fill just as easily? Then press Shift. Shift+1 changes the Fill value to 10 percent; Shift+0 makes it 100 percent. Shift plus two numbers enters a two-digit value.

You also can change the setting by clicking and dragging the Opacity or Fill slider in the Layers palette (labeled back in Figure 14.2). Click the arrowhead to the right of the option to display the slider, and then drag the triangle to change the value. Or press the up and down arrows to nudge the triangle along; press Shift with the arrow key to nudge the value in 10 percent increments. Want yet *another* way? Point to the word Opacity or Fill on the palette, and when your mouse turns to a pointing figure with a two-headed arrow, you can "scrub" to the left to reduce the value for that field, or to the right to increase it. However you choose to change the setting, you can press Enter or Return to confirm the slider setting (or simply click onto another part of the workspace), or press Escape to restore the previous setting.

NOTE   Incidentally, both the Opacity and Fill options are dimmed when working on the background layer or in a single-layer image. There's nothing underneath, so there's nothing to mix. Naturally, this goes double when editing a black-and-white image, an indexed image, a single channel, or a mask, because none of these circumstances supports layers.

Blend Modes

Photoshop offers a total of 25 blend modes, starting with Normal and ending with Luminosity. If you've been reading the chapters sequentially, you'll notice this isn't the first time blend modes have been touched upon. In fact, given that the blend modes mimic the brush modes described in Chapter 5 both in name and in function, we're covering some familiar territory. But you'll soon find that there's a big difference between laying down a color or pattern with a brush and merging the myriad colors that inhabit a single layer. This difference is the stuff of the following pages.

To demonstrate the effects of Photoshop's blend modes, we'll be compositing the series of images shown in Figure 14.6, in more or less the order shown. The background layer (being a true background layer) can have no blend mode applied to it. Also note that the flower includes a drop shadow layer effect, fading off to the right.

TIP   You can apply every one of the blend modes to a layer from the keyboard by pressing Shift+Alt (Shift+Option on the Mac) plus a letter, provided that the active tool doesn't offer its own brush mode options. (If the tool supports brush modes — as in the case of the Brush tool, Pencil, Clone Stamp, Healing Brush, and others — the shortcuts set the mode for the tool and not the layer.)

FIGURE 14.6

The default order of the images is the order pictured here: the hibiscus blossom on top, followed by the Confetti pattern (one of the predefined patterns included with Photoshop), then the gradient, and then at the bottom, a lovely view along Waiamanalo Beach. Sometimes we'll push the pattern and gradient layers around, if it better suits the discussion.

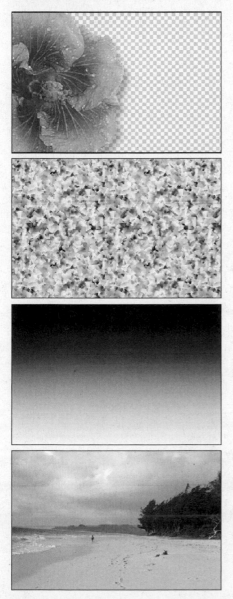

Here are Photoshop's 25 blend modes, in order of appearance:

- **Normal (N):** In combination with Opacity and Fill settings of 100 percent, this option displays every pixel in the active layer normally, regardless of the colors in the underlying layers. When you use opacity values (whether Opacity or Fill) of less than 100 percent, the color of each pixel in the active layer is averaged with the composite pixel in the layers behind it. Figure 14.7 shows examples applied to the flower layer on its own.

  Composite pixel refers to the pixel color that results from all the mixing that's going on beneath the active layer. For example, your document may contain hordes of layers with all sorts of blend modes in effect, but as long as you're working on, say, Layer 23, Photoshop treats the image formed by Layers 1 through 22 as if it were one flattened image filled with a bunch of static composite pixels.

FIGURE 14.7

The Hibiscus layer set to the Normal mode when combined with Opacity values of 100 percent (top) and 60 percent (bottom)

Normal blend mode

60% Opacity

When it comes to groups of layers (read about how to create them in Chapter 13), groups have no blending properties of their own. When you apply a blending mode to a group, you change the order of the image elements, with the layers within the group combined first, resulting in the composite group being treated like a single image and then blended with the rest of the image, based on the blending mode applied. So — if you use a blend mode other than Pass Through for a group, any adjustment layers or layer blending modes inside the group will not apply to layers outside the group.

- **Dissolve (I):** This option affects feathered or softened edges. If the active layer is entirely opaque with hard edges, Dissolve has no effect. But when the edges of the layer fade into view, as seen in Figure 14.8, Dissolve randomizes, or dithers, the pixels. If you look closely, you'll see that Dissolve does not dither pixels in the drop shadow; as discussed in Chapter 13, layer effects are governed by their own, independent blend modes. Things change, however, when you drop the Opacity value below 100 percent, in which case Dissolve dithers all pixels, as demonstrated in the second example in the figure.

- **Darken (K):** The first of the four darkening modes, Darken applies colors in the active layer only if they are darker than the corresponding pixels below. Keep in mind that Photoshop compares the brightness levels of pixels in a full-color image on a channel-by-channel basis. So although the blue component of a pixel in the active layer may be darker than the blue component of the underlying composite pixel, the red and green components may be lighter. In this case, Photoshop would assign the blue component but not the red or green, thereby subtracting blue and shifting the pixel toward yellow. Darken is most useful for covering up light portions of an image while letting dark areas show through.

  To illustrate Darken and the other darkening modes, a light background was established by setting the pattern layer on top of the background and lowering its Opacity to 25 percent. Then the gradient layer was placed on top of that and set to the Screen mode, which left the white portion of the gradient visible and dropped out the black portion. The hibiscus (flower) layer was then added and set to the Darken mode, as shown at the bottom of the figure. The result, shown in Figure 14.9, is a flower that appears smooth in both the midtones and the shadows and patterned in the light areas, with relatively sharp transitions between the two.

- **Multiply (M):** Multiply is one of the rare blend modes that emulate a real-world scenario. Imagine that the active layer and the underlying composite are both photos on transparent slides. The Multiply mode produces the same effect as holding these slides up to the light, one slide in front of the other. Because the light has to travel through two slides, the outcome invariably combines the darkest elements from both images. So unlike Darken, Multiply universally darkens, resulting in smooth transitions that are ideal for preserving contours and shadows, as shown in Figure 14.10.

FIGURE 14.8

Here the Dissolve mode has been applied to the hibiscus layer at an Opacity setting of 100 percent (top) and 60 percent (bottom). Instead of creating translucent pixels, Dissolve turns pixels on and off to simulate transparency.

Dissolve blend mode

60% Opacity

> **TIP**
>
> If the Multiply mode produces too dark an effect, reduce the Opacity or Fill value. If it isn't dark enough, clone the layer by pressing Ctrl+J (⌘+J on the Mac). This technique holds true throughout Photoshop: Provided that two layers share a common blend mode, you can merge the layers and preserve the effect.

FIGURE 14.9

This time we've got the Confetti layer turned on, set to 25% Opacity. With the flower layer set to Darken mode, only those pixels that are darker than the pixels in the in the Confetti remain visible.

Darken blend mode

FIGURE 14.10

For this version of the hibiscus, the Multiply blend mode produces the same effect as holding two overlapping transparencies up to the light.

Multiply blend mode

■ **Color Burn (B)** and **Linear Burn (A):** Where the Multiply mode darkens your images, the two Burn modes can literally char them. They both use colors in the active layer to reduce brightness values, resulting in radical color transformations. As demonstrated in Figure 14.11, Color Burn results in crisp, often colorful, toasted edges; Linear Burn creates a smoother, less vibrant effect. Both modes have an uncanny ability to draw colors from background layers.

FIGURE 14.11

After applying the Screen blend mode to the confetti pattern and the gradient layers, Color Burn (top) and Linear Burn (bottom) blend modes are applied to the flower layer. For high-contrast stamping effects, these are the blend modes to use.

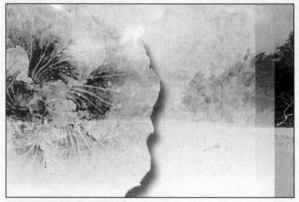

Color Burn blend mode

Linear Burn blend mode

■ **Lighten (G):** The next four options use the active layer to lighten those below it. If you select Lighten, for example, Photoshop applies colors in the active layer only if they are lighter than the corresponding pixels in the underlying image. As with Darken, Photoshop compares the brightness levels of all channels in a full-color image.

To set the stage for the lightening figures, the background layers were modified, restoring the pattern layer to Normal and switching the gradient layer to Multiply. As a result, Photoshop dropped out the whites in the gradient and kept the blacks. The Lighten blend mode was then assigned to the face. The drop shadow also was modified — which would have otherwise remained black — by changing its color to white and its blend mode to Screen. The result, shown in Figure 14.12, is a drop glow, as described in Chapter 13.

FIGURE 14.12

We've swapped the gradient layer (Opacity 80%) and the pattern layer (Opacity 50%), and we'll holler when we switch 'em back. The gradient layer is set to Multiply, and then Lighten was applied to the Hibiscus layer.

Lighten blend mode

■ **Screen (S):** From a creative standpoint, Screen is the opposite of Multiply. Rather than creating a darker image, as you do with Multiply, you create a lighter image, as demonstrated in Figure 14.13.

You can use the Screen blend mode to emulate film that has been exposed multiple times. However, you should apply Screen only when working with images that are sufficiently dark so that you avoid over-lightening. Screen is equally useful for creating glows, retaining just the light colors in a gradient, and creating light noise effects such as snow and stars.

FIGURE 14.13

The Screen mode produces the same effect as shining two projectors at the same screen. In this case, one projector contains the background layers, and the other contains the hibiscus (top).

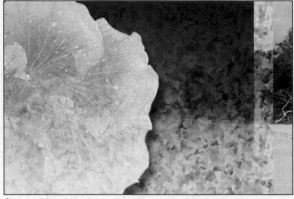

Screen blend mode

- **Color Dodge (D)** and **Linear Dodge (W):** When you apply one of the two Dodge modes, each color in the layer becomes a brightness-value multiplier. Light colors such as white produce the greatest effect, and black drops away. As a result, the Dodge modes are Photoshop's most dramatic whitening agents. Imagine mounting your image on a gel and projecting it from a spotlight. Of the two, Color Dodge produces the sharper, rougher effect; Linear Dodge smoothes out the transitions, as shown in Figure 14.14. Because they send so much of an image to white, the Dodge modes are most useful for simulating hot spots and other intensely bright effects.

- **Overlay (O), Soft Light (F),** and **Hard Light (H):** Photoshop's six Light modes darken the darkest colors and lighten the lightest colors, thereby allowing the midtones to inter-mix, so that foreground and background remain independently identifiable. Of the six, the first three — Overlay, Soft Light, and Hard Light — are the oldest and arguably the most useful, so the discussion begins with them.

  Each of these three modes alternatively multiplies the blacks and screens the whites, but to different degrees. For example, where Overlay favors the background layers, Hard Light emphasizes the active layer. In fact, the two are direct opposites: Layer A set to Overlay in front of Layer B produces the same effect as Layer B set to Hard Light in front of Layer A. Meanwhile, Soft Light is a modified version of Hard Light that results in a more subtle effect than either Hard Light or Overlay.

FIGURE 14.14

Color Dodge (top) and Linear Dodge (bottom) are never subtle. Both modes simultaneously bleach the image and draw out some of the dark outlines from the Confetti pattern.

Color Dodge blend mode

Linear Dodge blend mode

When experimenting with these modes, always start with Overlay. If Overlay produces too strong an effect, reduce the Opacity or Fill value to favor the composite pixels.

Alternatively, you can switch from Overlay to Soft Light, as was done in the bottom example of Figure 14.15. On first glance, the examples in the figure — one showing Overlay at 50 percent and the other Soft Light at full opacity — look almost identical. But on closer inspection, you notice that where the balance of lights and darks is roughly equivalent, their distribution is quite different. The Overlay example favors the details in the flower; the Soft Light example favors the edges of the Confetti pattern.

FIGURE 14.15

With the pattern layer in front of the flower, the Overlay mode (top) was applied, and its Opacity setting changed to 50%. Next we set the pattern layer to Soft Light mode with an Opacity of 100%.

Overlay blend mode

Soft Light blend mode

If the Overlay mode at 100 percent seems too subtle, consider switching to the Hard Light mode, shown in Figure 14.16, which provides the best marriage of emphasis on the flower and balance with the background.

FIGURE 14.16

Here we've turned off the pattern layer, set the gradient to 50% Screen and the flower to Hard Light.

Hard Light blend mode

- **Vivid Light (V)** and **Linear Light (J):** Where Overlay and family combine Multiply and Screen, the next two Light modes combine Dodge and Burn. Vivid Light combines Color Dodge and Color Burn, where Linear Light combines Linear Dodge and Linear Burn. Figure 14.17 shows examples.

The pattern layer is still in front, at 50 percent Opacity and set to Soft Light. The gradient layer is set to 50 percent Opacity and set to Normal. Sandwiched between them is the flower, set to Vivid Light (top) and Linear Light (bottom).

FIGURE 14.17

Here you see the effect of setting the flower to the Vivid Light (top) and Linear Light (bottom) modes. Because the effects are so intense, the flower was sandwiched between a Soft Light pattern layer and a Screen gradient layer, each with Opacity settings of 50%.

Vivid Light blend mode

Linear Light blend mode

- **Pin Light (Z):** Pin Light is as simple as it gets. This mode keeps the darkest blacks and the lightest whites, and then makes everything else invisible, which makes it a natural for modifying edge filters.

  In Figure 14.18, we've gone back to the original stacking order and created a "Multiply on Pin Light" sandwich. The flower is set to Pin Light, as is the gradient layer. Both of these layers are set to 100 percent Opacity. Stuck in the middle is the pattern layer, set to 50 percent Opacity.

FIGURE 14.18

Pin Light, Multiply, Pin Light is the name of the game here. The Pin Light mode was applied to keep just the lightest and darkest pixels.

Pin Light blend mode

- **Hard Mix (L):** The Hard Mix blend mode combines the pixels in your layers using the Vivid Light blend mode and then performs a color threshold operation on them. The results that Hard Mix produces don't fit a standard definition of "pretty," as shown in Figure 14.19. Hard Mix mixes two layers and pushes the colors to their absolute extreme. All in all, Hard Mixed pixels come in only eight colors: black, white, red, green, blue, cyan, magenta, and yellow. The end result is quite similar to the Posterize command (Image ⇨ Adjustments ⇨ Posterize).

  Believe it or not, a color threshold created with the Hard Mix blend mode has its uses, rare as they may be. For a closer look at some effects you might be able to pull from thresholds, check out Chapter 18.

- **Difference (E)** and **Exclusion (X):** Difference inverts lower layers according to the brightness values in the active layer. White inverts the composite pixels absolutely, black inverts them not at all, and the other brightness values invert them to some degree in between. In the first example of Figure 14.20, the Difference mode was applied to the flower layer, which is set against the gradient layer, also set to Difference.

  Exclusion works just like Difference except for one small difference. Illustrated in the second example in Figure 14.20, Exclusion sends midtones to gray — much as Pin Light sends midtones to transparent — creating a lower-contrast, often smoother effect.

FIGURE 14.19

The flower layer set to Hard Mix, the pattern and gradient layers set to Normal, 50% Opacity: Hey, we warned you it wasn't going to be pretty.

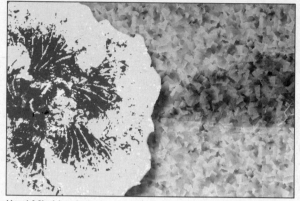

Hard Mix blend mode

- **Hue (U):** Hue and the remaining four blend modes make use of the HSL color model to mix colors between the active layer and the underlying composite. When you select Hue, Photoshop retains the hue values from the active layer and mixes them with the saturation and luminosity values from the underlying image.

> **NOTE**   Hue, Saturation, Color, and Luminosity blend modes affect only color images, so trying to demonstrate their effects here in grayscale would be a little pointless. In fact, if you tried to use any of these options in a grayscale document, you'd find them dimmed.

- **Saturation (T):** When you select this option, Photoshop retains the saturation values from the active layer and mixes them with the hue and luminosity values from the underlying image. Saturation produces such subtle effects that you'll typically want to apply it in combination with other blend modes. For example, after applying a random blend mode to a layer, you might duplicate the layer and then apply the Saturation mode to either boost or downplay the colors, much like printing a gloss or matte coating over an image.

- **Color (C):** This option combines hue and saturation. Photoshop retains both the hue and saturation values from the active layer and mixes them with the luminosity values from the underlying layers. Because the saturation ingredient of the Color mode produces such a slight effect, Color frequently produces a very similar effect to Hue.

- **Luminosity (Y):** The Luminosity blend mode retains the lightness values from the active layer and mixes them with the hue and saturation values from the composite pixels below. So just as the Color mode uses the layer to colorize its background, the Luminosity mode uses the background to colorize the layer.

FIGURE 14.20

The pattern layer was turned off, and the flower and gradient layers set to Difference (top) and Exclusion (bottom).

Difference blend mode

Exclusion blend mode

- **Lighter Color:** Not to be confused with the aforementioned Lighten blend mode, which is applied to one channel at a time, the new Lighter Color mode applies to all channels at once. If you're blending two ore more colors with Lighter Color, guess which one is visible? That's right, the *lighter* one.

- **Darker Color:** Much like its pale partner, the new Darker Color mode applies to all of the channels at one time. This, like Lighter Color and Lighten, can be confused with Darken, which applies to only one channel at a time. If you're blending two or more colors with Darker Color, the darker color is visible (big surprise, huh?).

The hierarchy of blend modes

Blend modes are amazing. They permit you to try out so many permutations that you can lose yourself for hours. Predicting the outcome of these permutations might require a brain on par with Einstein's, but let's leave prediction to Nostradamus. Experimenting with Photoshop's different blend mode settings requires no intelligence at all, just the willingness to begin the experimentation in the first place — and that's where this book comes in.

An excellent technique to incorporate into your scientific method is *sandwiching*. This refers to the process of placing a heavily filtered version of an image between two originals. This technique is based on the principal that more than half the blend modes — including Normal, Dissolve, Color Dodge and Burn, the seven Light modes, and the four HSL modes — change depending on which of two images is on top.

For example, Figure 14.21 shows two layers, A and B, and the result of blending them with the Overlay mode. When the moon is on top, as in the third example, the Overlay mode favors the man; but when the man is on top, Overlay favors the moon.

FIGURE 14.21

After establishing two layers, moon and man, the moon was placed on top and Overlay applied to get the third image. Then the order of the layers was switched, and Overlay was applied to the man to get the last image.

Layer A
(The face of the moon)

Layer B
(The face of the man)

Overlay: A over B
(Spotlight on the man)

Overlay: B over A
(The man in the moon)

Overlay just happens to be balanced by its opposite, the Hard Light blend mode, which favors the layer to which it's applied. So you could have achieved the exact effect shown in the last example in Figure 14.21 by placing the man under the moon and setting the moon to Hard Light.

Therefore, you see that the order in which you stack your layers is as important as the blend mode you select. Even modes that have no stacking opposites — Color Dodge, Linear Light, and others — produce different effects depending on which layer is on top.

NOTE Like Overlay, Color Dodge favors the composite pixels below the active layer. This holds true for Color Burn as well. Meanwhile, Linear Light, Pin Light, and all the other modes with Light in their name favor the active layer. Modes that do not change based on layering order — Multiply, Screen, Difference, and the like — favor neither front nor rear layer.

Sandwiching a filtered image

When you sandwich a filtered image between two originals you can lessen the effect of the filter and achieve different effects than those discussed in Chapters 10 and 11. Layers and blend modes give you the flexibility to experiment as much as you want and for as long as you please.

Returning to our hibiscus again in Figure 14.22, it was copied to a new layer and then Filter ➪ Sketch ➪ Charcoal was applied with the foreground and background colors set to their defaults, black and white.

FIGURE 14.22

The ingredients for our blend mode sandwich include the original image layer (left) and a cloned version on an independent layer subject to the Charcoal filter (right).

Control layer (unfiltered)   Filter ➪ Sketch ➪ Charcoal (5, 5, 80)

Like most filters under the Sketch submenu, Charcoal absolutely destroys the detail in the image, replacing all brightness values with the foreground and background colors — in this case, black and white. Fortunately, because Charcoal was applied to a clone of the image, a blend mode to restore some of the detail can be used. Figure 14.23 shows two of the many possibilities that exist — one using the Multiply mode, which kept the blacks in the Charcoal effect and threw away the whites, and the other using Pin Light, which allowed colors from the original image to show through the gray areas of the Charcoal rendering.

FIGURE 14.23

Each of two blend modes applied to the filtered layer in front of the original image

Charcoal layer over Control layer, Multiply   Same, Pin Light

So that's an open-faced sandwich. Let's get three layers involved. Let's sandwich the filtered layer between two of the unfiltered layers by cloning the background layer and moving it to the top of the stack. Now you can really increase your opportunity for blend mode variations. Check out Figure 14.24 to get an idea of what's on the menu.

Creating a Difference sandwich

Check out the middle example in Figure 14.24 and you'll see a purist's sandwich, Pin Light on the cheese and Pin Light on the bread. In Photoshop, that's one of the best, most reliable sandwich combinations you can create. If blend modes were condiments, Pin Light would be mustard — it works for everything.

> **TIP** When it comes to things that "work for everything," you just can't forget the Difference mode. By applying Difference to both the filtered layer and the cloned original on top, you do a double-invert, first inverting the filter into the original image and then reinverting the original into the composite. The result is a subtler and utterly unique combination.

FIGURE 14.24

Here you see three layers, each with a different blend mode.

Color Dodge top layer,
Multiply middle layer

Pin Light both layers

Difference top layer,
Lighter Color middle layer

Advanced Blending Options

To display the Advanced Blending options, you have three options: First, you can double-click the layer thumbnail. Second, if you want to modify the Advanced Blending options for a specialty layer — such as type or an adjustment layer — right-click the layer name or thumbnail (Control-click on the Mac) and choose the Blending Options command. You also can right-click in the image window with one of the selection tools and access Blending Options that way. Third, you can press Alt (Option), and double-click the layer name. So you decide.

In any case, you'll see the vast and stately Layer Style dialog box. This one multi-paneled window holds controls for adding layer effects, changing the opacity and blend mode of a layer, and achieving some special blending tricks, which are discussed here. By default, you should see the Blending Options panel, pictured in Figure 14.25. If you're working in some other area of the dialog box, click the Blending Options item at the top of the list on the left side of the dialog box.

You already know how the two General Blending options — Blend Mode and Opacity — work. The same goes for the Fill Opacity slider (though as you'll see, it takes on broader meaning in this dialog box). These are the same options found in the Layers palette and discussed in the first half of this chapter. The next few sections explain the Advanced Blending options, spotlighted in Figure 14.25. Like so many aspects of blend modes, these options can be perplexing at first. But after you get the hang of them, they enable you to gain a degree of control over your layers unrivaled by any other image editor.

CROSS-REF Many of the Advanced Blending options affect the performance of layer effects, such as drop shadows, glows, bevels, and so on. These effects fall into the broader category of layer styles, which are discussed at length in Chapter 15.

Blending interior layer effects

It should be said at the outset that the Fill Opacity value behaves exactly like the Fill option in the Layers palette. Type a value in one option and it appears in the other as well. They are as one. The same goes for the Blend Mode setting in the dialog box and the selected mode in the Layers palette. However, you're about to discover a few ways to modify the performance of the Fill Opacity and Blend Mode options that are possible only from the Advanced Blending options.

As you may recall, the Opacity value controls the translucency of all aspects of a layer, including pixels and layer effects alike. This is a fact of life, regardless of any other settings that may be in place. Meanwhile, the Blend Mode and Fill Opacity settings modify the interaction of pixels independently of most or all layer effects. This caveat "most or all" is where things get interesting.

You see, Photoshop divides layer effects into two groups that you can control independently of each other. *Interior effects* fall inside the boundaries of the filled areas of a layer and consist of the Inner Shadow, Inner Glow, Satin, and three Overlay effects. *Exterior effects* fall either outside or both inside and outside the boundaries of a layer. These consist of the Drop Shadow, Outer Glow, Bevel, Emboss, and Stroke effects.

FIGURE 14.25

Using the Advanced Blending options, you can turn a layer into a floating hole, make specific color ranges invisible, and more.

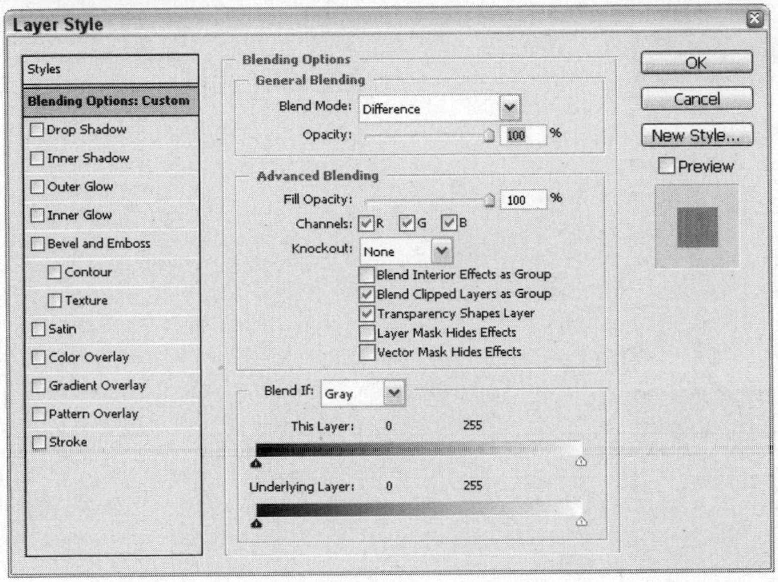

Using blend modes and Fill Opacity, Photoshop permits you the option of modifying interior effects independently from exterior effects. The catalyst at the heart of this behavior is the Blend Interior Effects as Group option. When deselected, as by default, blend modes and Fill Opacity affect the pixels on a layer only. But if you select this option, Photoshop applies the blend mode and Fill Opacity to the interior layer effects as well; only the exterior effects remain unchanged.

Figures 14.26 and 14.27 show examples. In Figure 14.26, you see a layer to which a red Inner Glow as been assigned as well as two exterior effects — Drop Shadow and Stroke. When the Fill Opacity is lowered to 60 percent, the pixels that make up the yacht within the circle drop away, but the layer effects remain unchanged. However, if you also select the Blend Interior Effects as Group option, Photoshop reduces the opacity of the Inner Glow effects as well.

Note, however, that neither Fill Opacity nor blend mode affects the exterior layer effects — even when those exterior effects actually fall inside the boundaries of the layer. The Stroke effect, for example, is set to trace the inside of the layer. In fact, the only effect that truly exists outside the layer is the drop shadow. However, as far as Photoshop is concerned, an exterior effect is an exterior effect, regardless of where it happens to fall.

FIGURE 14.26

Here you see the results of taking a layer subject (the yacht) to an interior effect and two exterior effects (top), reducing the Fill Opacity value to 60 percent (middle), and then selecting the Blend Interior Effects as Group option (bottom).

FIGURE 14.27

This figure shows the default image (top) and the effect of the Difference blend mode when applied to the yacht layer with the Blend Interior Effects as Group option deselected (middle) and selected (bottom).

TIP   Found just beneath the Blend Interior Effects as Group option, the Blend Clipped Layers as Group option controls whether the upper layers in a clipping mask blend along with the base layer or remain unchanged. By default, this option is selected, blending all layers in a clipping mask as a single unit. To adjust the blending of the base layer in a clipping mask by itself, simply deselect the option. Then only the Opacity slider affects the other layers in the group.

Masking and unmasking effects

The Transparency Shapes Layers, Layer Mask Hides Effects, and Vector Mask Hides Effects options permit you to manage the boundaries of interior and exterior effects alike. Here's how:

- **Transparency Shapes Layer:** Deselecting this option deactivates the transparency mask that is normally associated with a layer, permitting layer effects and clipped layers to spill outside the boundaries of a layer to fill the entire image window. If the layer includes a layer mask, effects and clipped layers fill the mask instead. So it serves two purposes: First, you can fill an image or clipping mask with a Color Overlay or other interior effect associated with a layer. And second, you can substitute a transparency mask with a layer or vector mask. You'll see both of these in the following pages.

- **Layer Mask Hides Effects:** When selected, this option uses the layer mask to mask both the pixels in the layer and the layer effects. When deselected, as by default, the layer mask defines the boundary of the layer, and the effect traces around this boundary just as it traces around other transparent portions of the layer.

- **Vector Mask Hides Effects:** Photoshop's shape tools allow you to draw vector-based shapes that you can fill with flat colors, gradients, patterns, or even layered images. When working inside a layer inside a shape, you can use the Vector Mask Hides Effects option to specify whether the shape defines the outline of the layer (selected) or clips layer effects just as it clips pixels (deselected). For complete information on defining a layer mask, see Chapter 13.

Typically, you use these options to change Photoshop's default behaviors because something has gone wrong and you want to correct it. Don't like how your layer effects look? Select or deselect one of these options and see whether it makes a difference. Of course, it helps to have a little experience with these options before you start randomly hitting switches, so let's work through an example.

Take a look at Figure 14.28. Here, the basic elements of the previous two figures are thrown in with a few items for a quaint little postcard effect. A head shot of a woman eating watermelon has been clipped to the circular layer of the yacht on the beach (which now becomes her backdrop), and a color Overlay layer effect was included, set to a blending mode of Saturation and an Opacity of 60 percent to punch up the colors of the clipped layers. The circular layer's blending options have both the Blend Interior Effects as Group and Blend Clipped Layers as Group options deselected.

Now let's say you want to add a layer mask to the circular layer. Nothing fancy, just a gradient from black at the bottom of the image to white near the middle, as shown in the second example in Figure 14.28. Naturally, this makes the layer transparent at the bottom and opaque toward the middle, but it has an unexpected consequence. Rather than fading into view, that red Inner Glow effect begins meshing at the point where the layer becomes fully opaque. At first glance, you might say, "Gee, I guess I can't combine this type of layer mask here." Not at all; simply consult your Advanced Blending options and make some adjustments.

FIGURE 14.28

Beginning with the woman masked inside the circle (top), a layer mask was added to the circle layer using the Gradient tool (middle). But instead of fading the effects, the mask shoved the Inner Glow so far upward the effects began to obscure the face (bottom).

In the first image in Figure 14.29, the problem was fixed by simply selecting the Layer Mask Hides Effects option. This way, rather than constraining the effects, the layer mask fades them out just like a good gradient mask is supposed to do.

FIGURE 14.29

After fading out the Inner Glow and Stroke effects by selecting the Layer Mask Hides Effects option (top), the Transparency Shapes Layer option was deselected (middle). A vector mask was added, and the Vector Mask Hides Effects option was deselected (bottom).

The second example of Figure 14.29 shows what happens when the Transparency Shapes Layer option is deselected (it's selected by default). Suddenly, the layer effects are no longer constrained by the boundaries of the circular layer and grow to fill the entire layer mask. Edge-dependent effects, such as Inner Glow, Drop Shadow, and Stroke disappear.

Next, a vector mask was added to the circular layer. To do this, the Ctrl key (⌘ on the Mac) was pressed and the layer mask icon at the bottom of the Layers palette was clicked. After selecting the Custom Shape tool and selecting a shape from the menu in the Options bar, the plus key (+) was pressed to make sure the Add to Path Area button was active and the shape was drawn. Photoshop automatically traced the Drop Shadow, Inner Glow, and Stroke effects around the shape. However, if for some reason this weren't to occur, you would only have to visit the Advanced Blending options and deselect the Vector Mask Hides Effects option.

Dumping whole color channels

That takes care of the most complex of the options. All that remain are the Channels options. Located directly below the Fill Opacity slider in the Layer Style dialog box, the Channels options let you hide the layer inside one or more color channels. For example, deselecting R makes the layer invisible in the Red channel, sending colors careening toward vivid red or turquoise (all red or no red, respectively), depending on the colors in the layers underneath.

Some opinion/advice here: You may find the Channels options useless. There are exceptions, of course — in a CMYK image, it can prove helpful to drop a layer inside, say, the Black channel — but for general RGB image editing, they just don't offer much. This is a shame, because if slightly retooled, they could. For example, it might be nice to be able to control the translucency of a layer on a channel-by-channel basis, but instead you have only on or off controls. Maybe in a future version of Photoshop....

Making knockouts

Nestled in the middle of the Advanced Blending section of the Layer Style dialog box sits the Knockout pop-up menu, shown in Figure 14.30. Knockouts turn the contents of the active layer into a floating hole that can bore through one or more layers behind it. It's like a layer mask, except that you can use it to mask multiple layers and any associated layer effects simultaneously. You also can apply layer effects to the knockout, making them extremely flexible.

FIGURE 14.30

Selecting Shallow or Deep from the Knockout pop-up menu determines how deep a hole you're going to punch through the layers of your image.

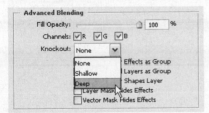

To create a knockout, you specify how deep the hole goes using the Knockout pop-up menu. Then use the Fill Opacity or Blend Mode option to define the translucency of the hole. The Knockout pop-up menu provides the following three options:

- **None:** This default setting turns the knockout function off. The layer is treated as a standard layer, not a hole.

- **Shallow:** Choose this option to cut a hole through a group of layers and expose the layer immediately below the set. In a clipping mask where the Blend Clipped Layers as Group option is deselected, Shallow burrows down to the layer directly below the base layer of the group. When the Blend Clipped Layers as Group option is selected, the knockout layer burrows down to the base layer in the group. If the layer resides inside neither a set nor a clipping mask, the Shallow option typically cuts a hole down to the background layer.

- **Deep:** The final setting bores as far down as the background layer, even if the knockout layer resides in a group. A notable exception occurs when working inside a clipping mask. If the Blend Clipped Layers as Group option is selected, Deep burrows down to the base of the clipping mask, just like Shallow.

Those are your Knockout options, but making one has less to do with what option you choose and more to do with your Fill Opacity settings, your layer order, and any groups you have in place.

Figure 14.31 shows the basic ingredients used to create a knockout. In the example, there's a ratty scan of a crow from the local paper as the top — and eventual knockout — layer (the crow is surrounded by transparency, represented by Photoshop's checkerboard pattern), followed by an Ode-to-Escher pattern beneath that. These two layers are placed in a group. Next down in the layer stack is a gradient that reflects the colors in the pattern. All these layers ride above a black background layer.

With the crow and pattern placed in a layer group, you then can use the two knockout options to punch through to either the gradient layer (Knockout: Shallow) or through to the background layer (Knockout: Deep). Figure 14.32 shows the first option.

Not satisfied with the results, the crow's knockout option was pushed to Deep — knocking all the way through to the background layer — and included a gradient Stroke layer effect, reversing the colors used in the gradient layer. Last, the URL for the site for which this crow would serve as a logo was thrown in, as shown in Figure 14.33.

FIGURE 14.31

Using this collection of layers and layer groups, you can punch through to either the gradient layer or the black background layer — depending on the knockout option you use.

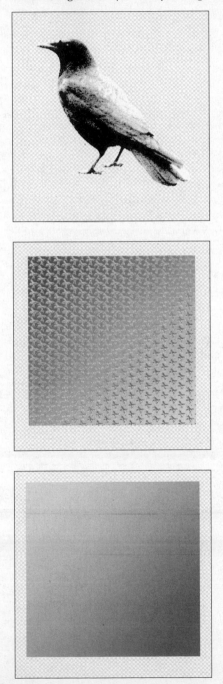

FIGURE 14.32

With the knockout option for the crow layer set to Shallow and its Fill Opacity set to 0 percent, the layer only punches through to the very next layer beneath the layer group — the gradient layer.

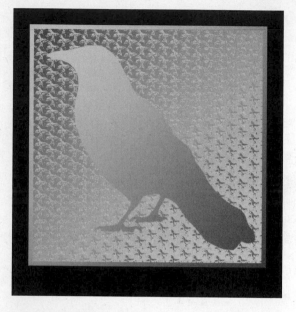

FIGURE 14.33

The final product has the crow layer's knockout option set to Deep and a gradient Stroke layer effect.

www.lancastercrows.org

Dropping Out and Forcing Through

Found at the bottom of the Blending Options panel of the Layer Style dialog box, the Blend If sliders are among Photoshop's oldest and most powerful compositing features. Pictured in Figure 14.34, these sliders permit you to drop out pixels in the active layer and force through pixels from lower layers according to their brightness values. You can even use them in combination with the Knockout option. For example, if you set the Knockout to Deep, you force through pixels from the background layer instead of from the layer immediately below the active layer.

FIGURE 14.34

Use the This Layer sliders to drop pixels out of the active layer, and use the Underlying Layer sliders to force pixels through from lower layers.

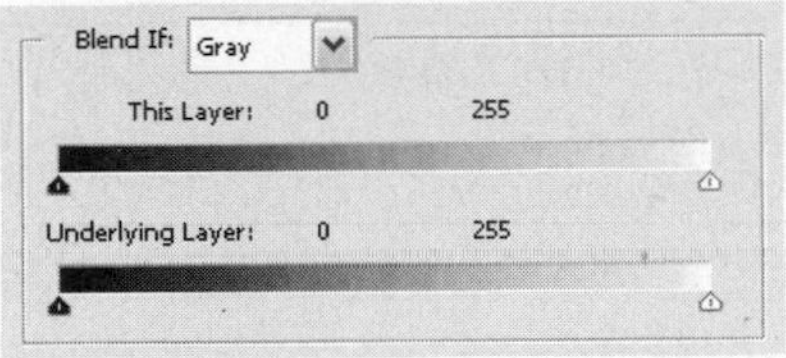

Here's how the Blend If options work:

- **Blend If:** Select a color channel from the Blend If pop-up menu to apply the effects of the sliders according to the contents of a single color channel. If you choose Gray, as by default, Photoshop bases the changes on the grayscale composite. Each time you select a different Blend If option, the slider triangles change to the positions at which you last set them for that color channel. Regardless of how you set the sliders, Photoshop applies your changes evenly to all channels in the image; the selected channel is merely used for the calculation.

- **This Layer:** This slider lets you exclude ranges of colors according to brightness values in the active layer. You exclude dark colors by clicking and dragging the black triangle to the right; you exclude light colors by clicking and dragging the white triangle to the left. In either case, the excluded colors disappear from view.

- **Underlying Layer:** The second slider forces colors from the underlying layers to poke through the active layer. Any colors outside the range set by the black and white triangles are not covered and are therefore visible regardless of the colors in the active layer.

- **Preview:** Don't forget to select the Preview option on the right side of the Layer Style dialog box so you can see the effects of your modifications in the image window every time you adjust a setting.

These options are far too complicated to fully explain in a bulleted list. You'll probably want to read the following sections, if only to make the authors feel better for having taken the time to write them.

Color range sliders

The first Blend If slider, This Layer, hides pixels in the active layer according to their brightness values. You can abandon dark pixels by clicking and dragging the left slider triangle and abandon light pixels by clicking and dragging the right triangle. To demonstrate the Blend If options, we'll use the composite image first introduced in Figure 14.6.

In Figure 14.35, the top example has the blend mode for the hibiscus layer set to Multiply. Then the black slider triangle was dragged until the value immediately to the right of the words This Layer is set to 130. This hides all dark pixels whose brightness values are 130 or lower. In the bottom example we've set the blend mode to Pin Light, returned the black slider to 0, and pulled the white slider down to 175, thus tuning out any pixels with a brightness value higher than that.

FIGURE 14.35

Examples of modifying the blend mode and This Layer settings in the Layer Style dialog box

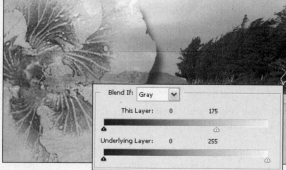

Let's move down a slider. You use that Underlying Layer slider to force pixels in the underlying layers to show through, again according to their brightness values. To force dark pixels in the underlying image to show through, drag the black slider triangle; to force light pixels to show through, drag the white slider triangle. Figure 14.36 gives you an idea of what happens when you repeat the same values and procedure using this slider.

FIGURE 14.36

The top example has the blend mode set to Overlay, and the black slider has been cranked up to 150. The bottom example uses Vivid Light, with the white slider toned down to 150.

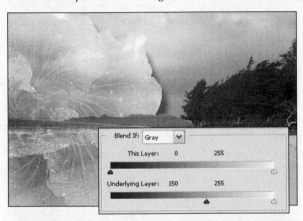

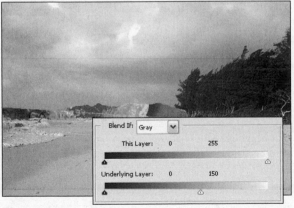

Bear in mind, like every other adjustment made in the Layer Style dialog box, changes made to the Blend If slider bars are temporary. These options hide pixels; they don't delete them. As long as the layer remains intact, you can revisit the Blend If sliders and restore hidden pixels or hide new ones.

Fuzziness

The problem with hiding and forcing colors with the sliders is that you achieve some pretty harsh color transitions. But wait — there's a solution to this problem! If you take a close look at those sliders we've been mucking with, you'll notice they have a little line down the middle. This is Photoshop's tiny visual cue that they can be split in half. By doing so, you create a fuzziness range, not unlike the Fuzziness value in the Color Range dialog box. This feature allows you to soften the color transitions by dropping and forcing pixels gradually, leaving some pixels opaque and tapering others off into transparency.

To taper the opacity of pixels in either the active layer or the underlying image, press Alt (Option on the Mac) and drag one of the triangles in the appropriate slider. The triangle splits in half, and the corresponding value above the slider bar splits into two values separated by a slash.

The left triangle half represents the beginning of the fuzziness range — that is, the brightness values at which the pixels begin to fade into or out of view. The right half represents the end of the range, or the point at which the pixels are fully visible or invisible. Take a look at Figure 14.37.

Here's what we've done: We used the same blend modes as in Figure 14.35 (Multiply up top, and Pin Light on the bottom). In the upper example, we split the black This Layer slider and covered a range that sets that original 130 value in the middle. We've set the left half of the slider to 100 and the right half to 160. As a result, colors with a brightness value of 100 or darker turn transparent, fade into view from 101 to 159, and become opaque from 160 on up.

In the bottom example, both halves of the black triangle are restored to 0. Then we split the white slider. The left half is set to 150 and the right half to 200, just 25 points either side of 175. Those few pixels with brightness values from 0 to 150 are opaque, the pixels from 151 to 199 become gradually translucent, and pixels of 200 and brighter are transparent.

Now let's turn our attention to the Underlying Layer slider. This one works best when you're trying to force through very bright or dark details, like highlights or shadows. It also helps to work with a foreground layer that has lots of flat areas of color for the background to show through. Keeping this in mind, take a look at Figure 14.38.

FIGURE 14.37

Alt-drag (Option-drag on the Mac) a slider triangle to split it in half. You then can specify a range over which brightness values will fade into transparency.

In the top image, we've used the Linear Dodge mode. We've split the black slider and set a fuzziness range from 135 to 215. This fades the dark regions of the surf and shoreline through the hibiscus layer where their brightness values fall between these two values. In the bottom example, we've change the bland mode to Linear Light, split the white slider, and set them to a zone of 105 to 155. As you can see, the hibiscus is now only visible in the surf and shoreline.

FIGURE 14.38

Setting a fuzziness range using the Underlying Layer sliders

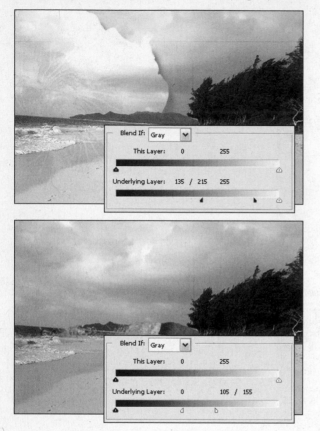

Whole Image Calculations

Image ➪ Apply Image and Image ➪ Calculations provide access to Photoshop's *channel operations*, which composite one or more channels with others according to predefined mathematical calculations. Once considered Photoshop's most powerful capabilities, channel operations have been eclipsed by the standard and more accessible functions available from the Layers and Channels palettes. Of course, there may come a day when Adobe decides to get rid of Apply Image and Calculations, but for now, they're part of the program, so you should at least read about them here.

Based on that encouraging and enthusiastic introduction to the Apply Image and Calculations commands, you'll no doubt be excited to learn what they do. The Apply Image and Calculations commands allow you to merge one or two identically sized images using 18 of the 23 blend modes discussed earlier plus two additional modes, Add and Subtract. In a nutshell, the commands duplicate the process of dragging and dropping one image onto another (or cloning an image onto a new layer) and then using the blend mode and the Opacity settings in the Layers palette to mix the two images together.

Although Apply Image and Calculations are more similar than different, each command fulfills a specific — if not entirely unique — function:

- **Apply Image:** This command takes an open image and merges it with the foreground image (or takes the foreground image and composites it onto itself). You can apply the command to either the full-color image or one or more of the individual channels.

- **Calculations:** The Calculations command works on individual channels only. It takes a channel from one image, mixes it with a channel from another (or the same) image, and puts the result inside an open image or in a new image window.

The primary advantage of these commands over other, more straightforward compositing methods is that they allow you to access and composite the contents of individual color channels without lots of selecting, copying and pasting, cloning, floating, and layering. You also get two extra blend modes, Add and Subtract, which may prove useful.

The Apply Image and Calculations commands provide previewing options, so you can see how an effect will look in the image window. But thanks to the sheer quantity of unfriendly options offered by the two commands, it's probably a good idea to use them only occasionally, if at all. The Calculations command can be a useful way to combine masks and layer transparencies to create precise selection outlines. Apply Image offers the unique capability to composite images in different color models. For example, you could mix a layer or channel from an RGB image with another image in the CMYK mode.

However, if your time is limited and you want to concentrate your efforts on learning Photoshop's most essential features, feel free to skip Apply Image and Calculations. No one will know if you skip right on to the next chapter.

The Apply Image command

Channel operations work by taking one or more channels from an image, called the *source*, and duplicating them to another image, called the *target*. When you use the Apply Image command, the foreground image is always the target, and you can select only one source image. Photoshop then takes the source and target, mixes them together, and puts the result in the target image. Therefore, the target image is the only image that the command actually changes. The source image remains unaffected.

When you choose Image ➪ Apply Image, Photoshop displays the dialog box shown in Figure 14.39. Notice that you can select from a pop-up menu of images to specify the Source, but the Target item — listed just above the Blending option — is fixed. This is the active layer in the foreground image.

If this sounds a little complicated, think of it this way: The source image is the floating selection and the target is the underlying original. Meanwhile, the Blending options are the blend modes pop-up menu and the Opacity value in the Layers palette.

FIGURE 14.39

The Apply Image dialog box lets you mix one source image with a target image and make the result the new target.

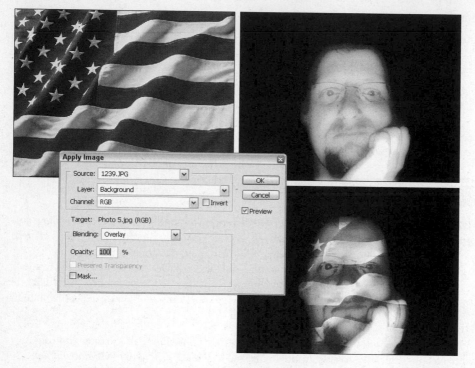

Using the Apply Image command is a five-step process. You can always simply choose the command and hope for the best, but you'll get the most use out of it if you do the following:

STEPS: Applying the Apply Image command

1. **Open the two images that you want to mix.** If you want to mix the image with itself to create some effect, just open the one image.

2. **Make sure that the two images are exactly the same size, down to the last pixel.** Use the Crop tool and Image Size command as necessary. (You don't have to worry about this step when mixing an image with itself.)

3. **Inside the target image, switch to the channel and layer that you want to edit.** If you want to edit all channels, press Ctrl+tilde (⌘+tilde on the Mac) to remain in the composite view.

TIP   If you're thinking of editing a single channel, you should display all channels onscreen. For example, after pressing Ctrl+1 (⌘+1) to switch to the Red channel, click in front of the RGB item in the Channels palette to display the eyeball icon and show all channels. Only one channel is active, but all are visible. This way, you can see how your edits inside the Apply Image dialog box affect the entire image, not just the one channel.

4. **Select the portion of the target image that you want to edit.** If you want to affect the entire image, don't select anything.

5. **Choose Image ➪ Apply Image.**

Obviously, that last step is a little more difficult than the concise instructions let on. In fact, it takes an entire section to explain all the details you'll need to know, and that section begins now.

The Apply Image options

The following list explains how to use each and every option in the Apply Image dialog box:

■ **Source:** The Source pop-up menu contains the name of the foreground image as well as any other images that are both open and exactly the same size as the foreground image. If the image you want to merge is not available, you must not have been paying much attention to Step 2. Press Esc to cancel, resize and crop as needed, choose Image ➪ Apply Image, and try again.

■ **Layer:** This pop-up menu lists all layers in the selected source image. If the image doesn't have any layers, Background is your only option. Otherwise, select the layer that contains the prospective source image. Select Merged to mix all visible layers in the source image with the target image.

■ **Channel:** Select the channels that you want to mix from this pop-up menu. Both composite views and individual color and mask channels are included. Keep in mind that you'll be mixing these channels with the channels that you made available in the target image before choosing the command.

For example, if the target image is an RGB image shown in the full-color composite view, and you choose RGB from the Channel pop-up menu in the Apply Image dialog box, Photoshop mixes the Red, Green, and Blue channels in the source image with the corresponding Red, Green, and Blue channels in the target image. However, if you switched to the Red channel before choosing Apply Image and then selected the RGB option, the program mixes a composite grayscale version of the RGB source image with the Red channel in the target and leaves the other target channels unaffected.

■ **Selection, Transparency,** and **Layer Mask:** If a portion of the source image is selected, the Channel pop-up menu offers a Selection option, which lets you apply the selection outline as if it were a grayscale image, just like a selection viewed in the Quick Mask mode. If you selected a specific layer from the Layer pop-up menu, you'll find a Transparency option that represents the transparency mask. If the layer includes its own layer mask, a Layer Mask option also appears.

None of the three options is particularly useful when you work in the composite view of the target image; you'll usually want to apply the Selection, Transparency, or Layer Mask option only to a single channel, as described in the section "The Calculations command."

■ **Invert:** Select this option to invert the contents of the source image before compositing it with the target image.

■ **Target:** You can't change this item. It merely shows which image, which channels, and which layers are being affected by the command.

- **Blending:** This pop-up menu offers access to 18 of the blend modes discussed in the section "Blend Modes" earlier in this chapter. The Dissolve, Hue, Saturation, Color, and Luminosity options are missing. Two additional options, Add and Subtract, are discussed in the section on the Add and Subtract options later in this chapter.

- **Opacity:** By now, you're well aware of how this one works. If you're not, stop now and go back and reread the book

- **Preserve Transparency:** When you're editing a layer in the target image — that is, you activated a specific layer before choosing Image ➪ Apply Image — the Preserve Transparency option becomes available. Select it to protect transparent portions of the layer from any compositing, much as if the transparent portions were not selected and are therefore masked.

- **Mask:** Select this option to mask off a portion of the source image. As stated previously, you can specify the exact portion of the target image you want to edit by selecting that portion before choosing the Apply Image command. You also can control which portion of the source image is composited on top of the target through the use of a mask. When you select the Mask option, three new pop-up menus and an Invert option appear at the bottom of the Apply Image dialog box. For complete information on these options, see the next section.

Compositing with a mask

The Mask option in the Apply Image dialog box provides a method for you to import only a selected portion of the source image into the target image. Select the Mask option and choose the image that contains the mask from the pop-up menu on the immediate right. As with the Source pop-up menu, the Mask menu lists only those images that are open and happen to be the exact size as the target image. If necessary, select the layer on which the mask appears from the Layer pop-up menu. Then select the specific mask channel from the final pop-up menu. This doesn't have to be a mask channel; you can use any color channel as a mask.

After you select all the necessary options, the mask works as follows:

- Where the mask is white, the source image shows through and mixes in with the target image, just as if it were a selected portion of the floating image.

- Where the mask is black, the source image is absent. Gray values in the mask mix the source and target with progressive emphasis on the target as the grays darken.

If you prefer to swap the masked and unmasked areas of the source image, select the Invert option at the bottom of the dialog box. Now, where the mask is black, you see the source image; where the mask is white, you don't.

TIP You can even use a selection outline or layer as a mask. If you select some portion of the source image before switching to the target image and choosing Image ➪ Apply Image, you can access the selection by choosing Selection from the Channel pop-up menu at the very bottom of the dialog box. Those pixels from the source image that fall inside the selection remain visible; those that do not are transparent. Use the Invert option to create an inverse of the selection. To use the boundaries of a layer selected from the Layer pop-up menu as a mask, choose the Transparency option from the Channel menu. Where the layer is opaque, the source image is opaque (assuming that the Opacity option is set to 100 percent, of course); where the layer is transparent, so too is the source image.

Add and Subtract

The Add and Subtract blend modes found in the Apply Image dialog box (and also in the Calculations dialog box) add and subtract the brightness values of pixels in different channels. The Add option adds the brightness value of each pixel in the source image to that of its corresponding pixel in the target image. The Subtract option takes the brightness value of each pixel in the target image and subtracts the brightness value of its corresponding pixel in the source image. When you select either Add or Subtract, the Apply Image dialog box offers two additional option boxes, Scale and Offset. Photoshop divides the sum or difference of the Add or Subtract mode, respectively, by the Scale value (from 1.000 to 2.000) and then adds the Offset value (from negative to positive 255).

Perhaps an equation will help. Here's the equation for the Add blend mode:

Resulting brightness value = ((Target + Source) ÷ Scale) + Offset

And here's the equation for the Subtract mode:

Resulting brightness value = ((Target – Source) ÷ Scale) + Offset

Okay, so maybe that didn't help. Anyway, if equations only confuse you, just remember this: The Add option results in a destination image that is lighter than either source; the Subtract option results in a destination image that is darker than either source. If you want to darken the image further, raise the Scale value. To darken each pixel in the target image by a constant amount, which is useful when applying the Add option, use a negative Offset value. If you want to lighten each pixel, as when applying the Subtract option, use a positive Offset value.

Applying the Add command

The best way to demonstrate how the Add and Subtract commands work is to offer examples. To create the effects shown in Figures 14.40 and 14.41, use the hibiscus and the Waiamanalo background we started with way back in Figure 14.6. The only difference is, for purposes of the Apply Image command, both images have been separated out so they're now in independent images in their own windows.

After switching to the background image and choosing Image ⇨ Apply Image, the hibiscus image was selected from the Source pop-up menu. We selected the Add option from the Blending pop-up menu and accepted the default Scale and Offset values of 1 and 0, respectively, to achieve the first example. The flower goes blindingly bright, much lighter than it would under any other blend mode, even the Dodge modes. To improve the quality and detail of the image, the Scale value was changed to 1.2 to slightly downplay the brightness values, and an Offset value of –60 was used to darken the colors uniformly. The result of this operation is the more satisfactory image shown in the second example of the figure.

For the sake of comparison, the final example shows what happens when introducing the background image into the face layer using the Add mode, with a Scale of 1.2 and an Offset of –60. Note that Add automatically respects the transparency mask of the hibiscus layer, regardless of whether you select the Preserve Transparency option.

Applying the Subtract command

To create the first example in Figure 14.41, the Subtract option was selected from the Blending pop-up menu, again accepting the default Scale and Offset values of 1 and 0, respectively. This time, the hibiscus turns extremely dark (were you surprised?) because the light values of the flower are subtracted from the light values in the background image, leaving no brightness value at all.

The result seems too dark, so it was lightened by raising the Scale and Offset values. To create the second image in the figure, the Offset value was raised to 100, thus adding 100 points of brightness value to each pixel. This second image is more likely to survive reproduction with all detail intact.

Subtracting the other direction — that is, applying the Subtract mode inside the face image — produces a radically different effect, as verified by the final example of Figure 14.41. Portions of the background are generally quite dark, so they have little effect when subtracted from the flower.

The Calculations command

The Calculations command performs a different function than Apply Image, although its options are nearly identical. Rather than compositing a source image on top of the current target image, Image ➪ Calculations combines two source channels and puts the result in a target channel. You can use a single image for both sources, a source and the target, or all three (both sources and the target). Although Photoshop previews the effect in the foreground image window, the target doesn't have to be the foreground image. The target can even be a new image. But the biggest difference is that instead of affecting an entire full-color image, as is the case with Apply Image, the Calculations command affects individual color channels. Only one channel changes as a result of this command.

Choosing Image ➪ Calculations displays the dialog box shown in Figure 14.42. When you open the dialog box, you select your source images from the Source 1 and Source 2 pop-up menus. As with Apply Image, the images have to be exactly the same size. You can composite individual layers using the Layer menus. Select the channels you want to mix together from the Channel options. In place of the full-color options — RGB, Lab, CMYK — each Channel menu offers a Gray option, which represents the grayscale composite of all channels in an image.

The Blending pop-up menu offers the same 20 blend modes — including Add and Subtract — found in the Apply Image dialog box. However, it's important to keep in mind how the Calculations dialog box organizes the source images when working with blend modes. The Source 1 image is equivalent to the source when using the Apply Image command (or the floating selection when compositing conventionally). The Source 2 image is equivalent to the target (or the underlying original). Therefore, choosing the Normal blend mode displays the Source 1 image. The Subtract command subtracts the Source 1 image from the Source 2 image.

Half of the blend modes perform identically regardless of which of the two images is Source 1 and which is Source 2. The other half — including Normal, Overlay, Soft Light, and Hard Light — produces different results based on the image you assign to each spot. Sound confusing? Don't worry. As long as you keep in mind that Source 1 is the floater, you'll be fine.

FIGURE 14.40

Here you see two applications of the Add blend mode from inside the background image (top and middle), each subjected to different Scale and Offset values. When adding an image into an independent layer, Add always preserves transparency (bottom).

FIGURE 14.41

The Subtract command was used on the background image: The top image shows Scale and Offset values of 1 and 0, and the middle shows values of 1.2 and 100. When subtracting into the flower layer, Subtract not only respects the transparency mask but also delivers a very different result (bottom).

TIP The only mode that can throw you off is Subtract, because you see Source 1 at the top of the dialog box and naturally assume that Photoshop subtracts Source 2, which is underneath it. Wouldn't you know it, though, this is exactly opposite to the way it really works? If you find yourself similarly confused and set up the equation backward, you can reverse it by selecting both Invert options. Source 2 minus Source 1 results in the same effect as an inverted Source 1 minus an inverted Source 2. After all, the equation (255 – Source 1) – (255 – Source 2), which represents an inverted Source 1 minus an inverted Source 2, simplifies down to Source 2 – Source 1. Are your eyes spinning like a cartoon character's yet?

As in the Apply Image dialog box, you can specify a mask using the Mask options in the Calculations dialog box. The difference here is that the mask applies to the first source image and protects the second one. So where the mask is white, the two sources mix together normally. Where the mask is black, you see only the second source image.

The Result option determines the target for the composited channels. If you select New Document from the Result pop-up menu, as in Figure 14.43, Photoshop creates a new single-channel image. Alternatively, you can stick the result of the composited channels in any channel inside any image that is the same size as the source images.

Combining masks

As described for the Apply Image command, the Channel pop-up menus may offer Selection, Transparency, and Layer Mask as options. Here, however, they serve a greater purpose. You can composite layer masks to form selection outlines, you can composite selection outlines to form masks, and you can make all sorts of other pragmatic combinations.

Figure 14.43 shows how the Calculations command sees selected areas. You see two selections, one for the penguin with his wings outstretched and one for penguins behind him that he directly overlaps. Whether you're working with masks, selection outlines, transparency masks, or layer masks, the Calculations command sees the area as a grayscale image. So in Figure 14.43, white represents selected or opaque areas, and black represents deselected or transparent areas.

Assuming that you've chosen Image ⇨ Calculations and selected the images using the Source 1 and Source 2 options, the only remaining step is to select the proper blend mode from the Blending pop-up menu. Screen, Multiply, and Difference are the best solutions. Figure 14.44 shows the common methods for combining selection outlines. In the first example, the two have been added together using the Screen mode, just as in the preceding steps. In fact, screening masks and adding selection outlines are equivalent operations. To subtract the Source 1 selection from Source 2, the former was inverted (by selecting the Invert option in the Source 1 area) and the Multiply blend mode was applied. To find the intersection of the two masks, Multiply was applied without inverting.

FIGURE 14.42

Use the Calculations command to mix two source channels and place them in a new or an existing target channel.

The Calculations command doesn't stop at the standard three — add, subtract, and intersect. Figure 14.45 shows three methods of combining selection outlines that are not possible using single keystroke operations. For example, if you invert the Source 1 mask and combine it with the Screen mode, it's like inverting the first selection and adding it to the second. The Difference mode adds the selections but subtracts the area where they overlap, an operation known as exclusion. And inverting Source 1 and then applying Difference retains the intersection, subtracts the areas that do not intersect, and selects the area outside the penguin — which is equivalent to excluding two selections and then inverting the result. You may not use these options every day, but they are extremely powerful if you can manage to wrap your brain around them.

FIGURE 14.43

Here's our original photo, followed by two selections expressed as grayscale images (also known as masks). The joyous, skyward-looking penguin serves as the first source; the penguins behind him are the second source.

FIGURE 14.44

Here the penguin masks are combined using the Calculations command in concert with the Screen and Multiply modes, simulating the effects of adding, subtracting, and finding the intersection of two selection outlines.

Screen
(same as add)

Invert + Multiple
(same as subtract)

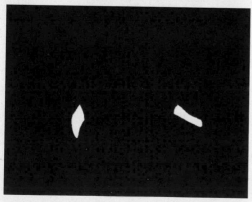

Multiply
(same as intersect)

FIGURE 14.45

Three nontraditional ways to combine selection outlines, all greatly facilitated by the Calculations command

Summary

In this chapter, you learned to modify the Opacity and Fill values for image content, and you discovered how these settings affect both layer content and the blend modes applied to your layers. You also learned more about blend modes and how to use them to mix an active layer with those layers beneath it.

The use of filters and the sandwiching of heavily filtered images between unfiltered originals also were covered, along with the use of advanced blending options. You also discovered the need for and how to create knockouts, preserving transparency within an image. To further your ability to control visibility through your image layers, you learned to fade pixels according to brightness values using the Blend If sliders, and when and how to use the Add and Subtract blend modes.

In addition, you learned about mixing same-sized images with the Apply Image command and how to modify selection outlines and masks using the Calculations command.

Chapter 15

Shapes and Styles

Adobe is famous for its art-producing and creative product line. We have Photoshop for pixel-based images, Illustrator for vector images, and applications like Premiere and AfterEffects for motion graphics and special video effects. Photoshop's tools and features have certainly grown over the last few versions, and some "overlap" has resulted between what people can use Photoshop to do and what would typically have been solely the domain of Illustrator or AfterEffects.

How's that? Well, consider, if we stick just to the topics relevant to this chapter, Photoshop's shape tools (all six of them). With the addition, back in version CS, of the ability to draw crisp, sharp shapes and lines and have them appear as separate shape layers (rather than the user just filling selections to achieve similar, yet more limited results), Photoshop enables you to create totally original artwork. No longer is photo editing the sum total of what you can do, and much of the artwork you can create in Photoshop finds its way into print, onto the Web, and in video and animation.

In addition to these shapes, you'll find that layer styles, which promise (among other things) quick and easy drop shadows and glows, help make Photoshop even more of an artist's tool. Of course, to purists, or those who simply believe that quick and simple can't *possibly* be good, this sort of "just add water" approach might sound like a cheap trick. However, nothing could be farther from the truth.

Layer styles, whether used for quick effects such as shadows and glows or for loftier artistic goals, have proven to be an invaluable addition. Layer styles give you painstaking control over drop shadows, glows, and bevels, and you can coat layers with gradients, patterns, and contoured wave patterns, as well as trace outlines around layers. When combined with the advanced blending options introduced in Chapter 14, layer styles blossom into a powerful special-effects laboratory, one of the most far-reaching and flexible Adobe has ever delivered. Furthermore, you can save the effects and reapply them to future layers.

These features may not be the reason you set out to learn Photoshop in the first place, and there's no question that they'll take time and patience to fully understand. But you'll be rewarded with greater proficiency and versatility in the long run — and you'll be that much farther down the road to mastery when Adobe finally releases the application that does absolutely everything for absolutely everyone.

Drawing Polygons, Lines, and Custom Shapes

Photoshop provides six *shape tools* that allow you to draw geometric and predefined shapes and lines. By default, the shapes are separated into independent *shape layers*, which are a mix of objects and pixels. The vector-based outlines of the shapes print at the maximum resolution of your printer, while the interiors may consist of solid colors, gradients, or pixel-based patterns and images — all based on your choices either before or after the shape has been drawn.

The pros and cons of shapes

Why should you love shapes? Let us count the ways:

- **Shapes are editable.** Unlike the shapes you create by filling a selection, you can change a shape by moving points and control handles. Likewise, you can scale, rotate, skew, or distort shapes, or even transform specific points and segments inside shapes. Nothing is ever set in stone, and nothing weird happens when you resize or reshape. This cannot be said of the pixels that make up a filled selection.

- **Shapes help to disguise low-resolution images.** Sharply defined edges can add clarity to a printed image, and those sharply defined edges are achieved through the use of vector-based outlines. You get the line-art look without having to use a program like Illustrator or CorelDraw to get it.

- **You can color a shape with a layer style.** As shown later in this chapter, layer effects such as drop shadows and beveled edges, are equally applicable to shape layers as they are to standard image layers.

- **You can preview clipping paths directly in Photoshop.** Before object-oriented shapes, you were never quite sure if you traced an image properly with a clipping path until you imported it into InDesign, QuarkXPress, or some other application. Now you can preview exactly what your clipping path will look like directly in Photoshop.

■ **Shapes expand with an image.** In Chapter 3, you were advised against using Image ⇨ Image Size to resample an image upward on the grounds that it adds pixels without adding to the image quality. But you can enlarge shapes as much as you want. Because the shape is mathematically defined, it remains crystal clear no matter how big or small you make it. Layer styles likewise resize without a problem. Figure 15.1 shows a shape with a layer style applied (see exciting fill), resized (smaller original appears in upper left) with no loss of clarity or crispness to the edge.

FIGURE 15.1

Resizing doesn't require the addition of pixels to make up the difference, so making a shape layer's content larger doesn't result in a choppy edge or a muddied fill. Compare the shape on the upper left (the small original shape) with its resized copy in the lower right.

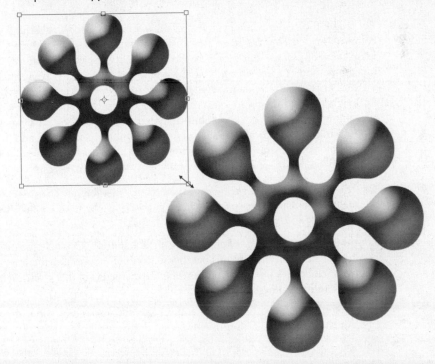

Now, of course this list of vector-based delights begs the question: If vectors are so great, why not forsake pixels and start drawing entirely with shape layers instead? Well, a shape can clip a continuous-tone photograph, but it can't replace one. Although there have been all kinds of experiments using objects and fractals, pixels are still the most viable medium for representing digital photographs. Because Photoshop's primary job is photo editing, pixels are (for the foreseeable future) the program's primary commodity.

CAUTION One downside to shape layers is compatibility. Photoshop has stretched TIFF and PDF files to accommodate any kind of layer — shape layers included, but that doesn't mean other programs have any idea what Photoshop is doing. Of all the formats, PDF is the most likely to work with other programs. Just be sure to proof the document on a laser printer before taking it to a commercial printer.

The shape tools

There's much to know and love about the shape tools. Now that you've read the list of Shape tool affirmations, it's time to get to know the tools and begin the getting-acquainted process. We'll start by looking at the Shape tool and its flyout of alternate tools shown in Figure 15.2. You can click and hold the default Rectangle tool so that the flyout of six shape tools displays, or you can press U to select the Rectangle tool and then press U again (or Shift+U) to switch from one tool to the next. Each of the tools, no matter how you access it, works as follows:

■ **Rectangle tool:** At one time, you had to draw a rectangular marquee and then fill it with color or a pattern in order to create a filled rectangle. This wasn't difficult, but it certainly wasn't very efficient or flexible. With the advent of the Shape tool, however, this anti-quated method of shape creation has been replaced (although you can still use this method, if you so desire), and all you have to do to draw a rectangle is activate the Rectangle tool and then from one corner of the desired area (the area you'd like to see containing a shape) to the other, Shift-drag to draw a square, or Alt-drag (Win) or Option-drag (Mac) to draw the shape outward from the center. Oh, and if you want to set the fill color beforehand, set can your foreground color with the Color Picker, or use the Color box on the options bar to the color you want filling your shape. That's it.

TIP While drawing a rectangle or any other shape, press the spacebar to reposition the shape. Then release the spacebar and continue dragging to resize the shape as you normally do.

■ **Rounded Rectangle tool:** When you select the Rounded Rectangle tool, a Radius value becomes available in the Options bar. If you think of each rounded corner as a quarter of a circle, the Radius value is the radius (half the diameter) of that circle. Bigger values result in more roundness.

■ **Ellipse tool:** The Ellipse tool draws ellipses (big surprise there!). Shift-drag to draw circles; Alt-drag (Win) or Option-drag (Mac) to draw the ellipse outward from the center.

■ **Polygon tool:** This tool draws regular polygons, which are straight-sided shapes with radial symmetry. Examples include equilateral triangles (3 sides), squares (4 sides), pentagons (5 sides), hexagons (6 sides), heptagons (7 sides), octagons (8 sides), decagons (10 sides), dodecagons (12 sides), and a bunch of other shapes with so many sides that they're virtually indistinguishable from circles. Type a Sides value in the Options bar to set the number of sides in the next polygon you draw. Or better yet, press the bracket keys, [and], to decrease or increase the Sides value from the keyboard. You also can draw stars and rounded shapes, as explained in the next section.

FIGURE 15.2

There are six — count 'em — six shape tools. Click the tiny triangle in the corner of the Rectangle tool to display them en masse, or press U or Shift+U to switch between tools.

- **Line tool:** Wait a minute; how is a line a shape? Well, technically, the lines created with the Line tool *are* shapes — they're just very skinny rectangles, drawn at whatever angle you drag them. When you activate the Line tool, you get the chance to type a Weight value into the Options bar, which defines the thickness of the so-called "line." Next, just drag from point A to point B (assuming the line is intended to point to something or span a particular distance). The Options bar also allows you to apply arrowheads (true pointing jobs, or other shapes created by adjusting the width, length, and concavity of the heads) to one or both ends of your line. Snazzy.

- **Custom Shape tool:** The Custom Shape tool makes up for the fact that it's very hard (if not impossible) to do more than draw simple polygons with the other shape tools. If you opt to see all the available Custom Shape tool shapes, you're presented with more than 250 shapes — everything from stars to paw prints to flowers to things that look like the symbols in the Zapf Dingbats or Monotype Sorts font libraries.

Drawing the shape

The act of drawing a shape can be as simple as clicking and dragging with a tool. How that shape manifests itself, however, depends primarily on which of the first three Options bar buttons pictured in Figure 15.3 is clicked. The first option creates a new shape layer when you draw with the Shape tool. The second option creates a work path, available for inspection in the Paths palette. And the final option creates a pixel-based shape. In this latter scenario, Photoshop doesn't add a new layer; it merely recolors the pixels on the active layer. Although simple in theory, the program offers you a wealth of additional controls.

First, you want to select the shape tool you want to use. Remember, U is the keyboard shortcut for the shape tools, and you can use it or simply click one of the shape tools buttons when you display the flyout of all six buttons. You also can pick a different shape from the Shape tool Options bar, changing from, say, the Rectangle to the Custom Shape tool.

Next, you can specify the color. This is done from the Options bar, by clicking the Color button on the Options bar, which opens the Color picker. If you want to fill the shape with a gradient, a pattern, or an image, you can do that after you finish drawing the shape, as explained in the section entitled "Beauty on the inside," later in this chapter.

With the type of shape and color out of the way, you can specify how you want to draw the shape. Pictured in Figure 15.3, the first three buttons in the Options bar determine what the Shape tool draws. Remember that to draw shape layer, you'll want to make sure that the first button is selected; otherwise, you'll be drawing a path or just some filled pixels, the same thing you'd get by clicking with the Paint Bucket inside a Marquee or Lasso selection.

Before you draw the shape, if you want to control the geometric aspects of the shape — such as drawing the shape in a fixed size, changing the number of sides in a polygon, determining the thickness of your line — you need to click the Geometry Options button labeled in Figure 15.3.

Click the down-pointing triangle to the right of the tool buttons in the Options bar (to see a pop-up palette of options geared to the selected shape tool), and make your changes and selections.

NOTE   When you're drawing rectangles and rounded-corner rectangles, the one unusual option in the Geometry Options palette is Snap to Pixels. Object-oriented shapes don't have any resolution, so their sides and corners can land in the middle of pixels. To prevent potential anti-aliasing in rectangles, select the Snap to Pixels option to precisely align them with the pixels in the image.

TIP   When drawing a custom shape, click the Shape button to display a pop-up palette of presets, as shown in Figure 15.3. You can load more shapes by choosing the Load Shapes command or by choosing a predefined presets (.csh) file from the presets palette menu. (The triangle that opens this menu is labeled in Figure 15.3, too.)

FIGURE 15.3

Use the options in the Options bar to specify the appearance of a shape *before* you draw it.

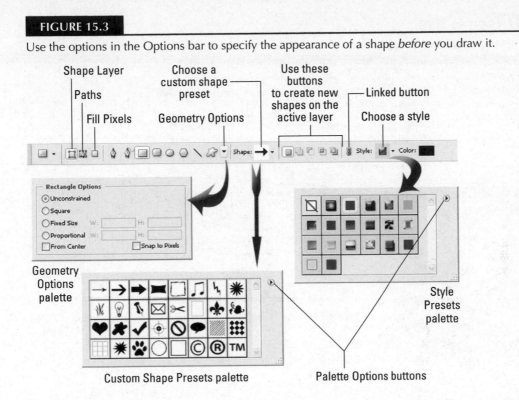

The last thing you'll do before drawing the shape is to choose a layer style. This can be none, if you want a solid color fill based on what's chosen in the Color button, or you can pick from a seemingly endless selection of styles. The palette is shown in Figure 15.3.

TIP   When drawing a shape layer, you can assign a layer style to your shape before drawing it or after the fact — which is sometimes the better approach, because some fills don't translate very well in certain shapes. The Layer Style pop-up palette (refer to Figure 15.3) offers all presets available in the Styles palette, as discussed at the end of this chapter.

Finally, you're ready to draw the shape. Because you've already chosen a shape (by clicking the appropriate button, as shown in Figure 15.3) to draw a shape layer, Photoshop automatically creates a new layer as soon as you draw the shape and release the mouse. As shown in Figure 15.4, the Layers palette shows a colored fill (labeled "Layer contents" in the figure) with a clipping path — or *vector mask* in Photoshop parlance — to the right of it, masking the fill. If you assigned a layer style, a list of one or more effects appears under the layer name.

FIGURE 15.4

A shape layer is actually a vector mask that masks a color or other contents directly in Photoshop. Here you also see the polygon's options and the settings for drawing a star.

By default, Photoshop creates a new shape layer for each new shape that you draw. This can have lots of benefits, and at other times, you'll find that having a layer for each and every shape is a little confusing. The choice as to whether to have them all on their own layers or sharing a single layer is up to you, and the decision will vary by the image. If you prefer to keep adding to the same shape layer so that all shapes share the same fill, click the Add to Shape Area button in the Options bar (labeled in Figures 15.3 and 15.5). Then draw a new shape.

NOTE If you press Enter, Return, or Esc, the current shape layer is deactivated, signifying that you no longer want to add shapes to that layer. This change is visible in the Layers palette; notice that the vector mask thumbnail no longer has a selection border around it. To reactivate the layer, simply click the thumbnail.

You now have one or more shape layers that you can use as you please. From this point, it's a matter of editing the shape, as explained in the following sections.

Combining and editing shapes

So you've drawn your shape. Now what? Well, if you don't like a segment, you can change it. Don't like a point? Move it. Hate the entire shape? Delete it. Here's how:

- **Using compound path options:** As explained in the preceding section, you can draw multiple shapes on a single layer. Because they all share a single fill, Photoshop thinks of the shapes as being bits and pieces of a single, complex path. In drawing parlance, such a path is called a *compound path*. This presents Photoshop with a dilemma when the bits and pieces overlap. Because the pieces of the compound path share a fill, they could just merge together. Or perhaps you'd rather use one shape to cut a hole in the other. Or maybe you'd like the intersection to be transparent. You have to tell Photoshop which of these possible outcomes you prefer.

  You specify your preference by selecting one of the last four compound path buttons, shown in Figure 15.5. (As mentioned previously, the first button, which is on by default, makes Photoshop create every shape on its own shape layer.) Click the second button or press the plus key (+) to add the new shape to the others, or press Shift as you draw shape after shape, adding each one to the active shape layer. Click the third button or press the minus key (–) to subtract the new shape from the others. The fourth button retains the intersection, while the fifth makes the intersection transparent.

FIGURE 15.5

The five compound path buttons; the last four are available when editing or adding to an existing shape layer.

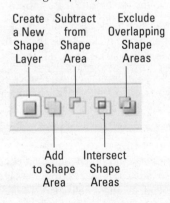

- **Selecting shapes:** You have access to all but the first compound path button when selecting shapes with the arrow tool. Press A to get the black arrow tool — if you get the white arrow instead, press A again (or Shift+A if the Use Shift Key for Tool Switch option is selected) — and then click a shape to select it. Or Ctrl-click (⌘-click on the Mac) a shape when using a shape tool.

- **Moving and transforming:** Click and drag a selected shape to move it. Select the Show Bounding Box option in the Options bar to access the transformation controls. Or press Ctrl+T (⌘-T on the Mac) to enter the free transform mode. Then click and drag a handle to scale, drag outside the bounding box to rotate, and Ctrl-drag (Win) or ⌘-drag (Mac) a handle to skew or distort. If you need a transformation refresher, see Chapter 13.

- **Arranging and combining shapes:** After selecting a shape with the arrow tool, you can apply any of the four available compound path buttons. As you do, bear in mind that the topmost shape takes precedence, and the stacking order is entirely dependent on the order in which you draw the shapes — with more recent shapes in front. (The Layer ➪ Arrange commands affect whole layers; they can't be used to reorder shapes.) After you get the effect you're looking for, the relationship created by selecting two or more paths and clicking the Combine button in the Options bar causes Photoshop to fuse the selected paths into one.

CAUTION Technically, you can combine multiple shapes that don't overlap, but it's not advisable. At first, the shapes behave as if they're grouped together. But try to combine other paths with them, and your results may not be what you expected.

- **Selecting points and segments:** Press A (or Shift+A) to get the white arrow tool, which selects individual points and segments. Move individually selected points by dragging them; transform such points by pressing Ctrl+T (Win) or ⌘+T (Mac). To select an entire shape, Alt-click (Win) or Option-click (Mac) it.

- **Adding and deleting points:** The best tool for reshaping a shape is the Pen tool. First select part of the shape with one of the arrow tools. Then click a segment to insert a point; drag on a segment to add a smooth point; click a point to remove it. You also can use the Convert Point tool, as well as any other technique that's applicable to paths.

- **Disabling a vector mask:** Shift-click the vector mask thumbnail in the Layers palette to turn it off (a red X appears on the thumbnail) and make visible the entire contents of the layer. Shift-click the thumbnail again to turn the vector mask on.

- **Duplicating a vector mask:** As far as Photoshop is concerned, shapes are just another kind of path. So it's not surprising that you can access the paths in an active shape layer from the Paths palette. Drag the *Vector Mask* item onto the tiny page icon at the bottom of the Paths palette to duplicate the shapes so you can use them elsewhere as standard paths (as discussed in Chapter 8).

- **Deleting a vector mask:** Click the vector mask thumbnail and then click the trash can icon at the bottom of the Layers palette to delete the shapes from the layer. You also can just drag the thumbnail to the trash can icon. To add a new shape to the layer, first choose Layer ➪ Add Vector Mask ➪ Hide All. Then draw shapes in the layer to expose portions of the layer's contents.

- **Defining your own custom shape:** If you create a shape that you think you might want to repeat in the future, select the shape with either arrow tool and choose Edit ⇨ Define Custom Shape. Then name the shape, and press Enter or Return. Photoshop adds the shape to the presets so you can draw it with the Custom Shape tool. If you want to keep it around, save the shape with the Preset Manager, as discussed in Chapter 2.

The moral of the story is this: Shapes work much like paths, bearing many of the accuracy-maintaining and change-supporting attributes that you may have grown to love. If you're forgetting exactly what it is that you're supposed to love about paths, go back to Chapter 8 and get reacquainted.

Beauty on the Inside

When it comes to shapes, all they have is their insides. Of course, you can apply a stroke to a shape, but that's discussed later, and it's only a veneer anyway. So with the knowledge that a shape is only as good as what's inside it, here are a few ways to modify the color and general appearance of shape layers:

- **Change the color:** To change the color of a shape layer, double-click the layer contents thumbnail in the Layers palette. Then select a new color from the Color Picker dialog box. Or better yet, change the foreground color and then press Alt+Backspace (Option+Delete on the Mac).

- **Change the blending options:** You can change the blend mode and Opacity value for a shape layer using the standard controls in the Layers palette. Or double-click anywhere on the layer (except the layer name, layer contents thumbnail, vector mask thumbnail, or the link icon) to display the Blending Options section of the Layer Style dialog box. As discussed in Chapter 13, these options work the same for shape layers as they do for normal layers. You also can apply or modify layer effects, as is explained later in this chapter.

- **Change the layer style:** Another way to apply or switch out layer effects is to apply a predefined style from the Styles palette. Just click a preset in the Styles palette and Photoshop automatically applies it to the active layer. After that, you can edit an effect by double-clicking its name in the Layers palette.

  The Linked button, labeled back in Figure 15.3, comes into play when you make a change to the layer style or color of a shape layer. If the button is selected, changes you make to the style or color are applied, or "linked," to the currently active shape layer. If the button isn't selected, the style or color change applies to the next shape layers you create.

- **Rename the shape layer:** Double-click the name of a shape layer to rename it. This works for renaming any kind of layer.

■ **Fill with a gradient or repeating pattern:** Is a solid color fill too boring for you? Don't limit yourself. To fill the active shape layer with a gradient, choose Layer ⇨ Change Layer Content ⇨ Gradient. Or choose Layer ⇨ Change Layer Content ⇨ Pattern to apply a repeating pattern. Figure 15.6 shows the dialog boxes for these commands. Most of the options are familiar from the Gradient tool discussion in Chapter 6. The only new options are in the Pattern Fill dialog box. Scale lets you resize the pattern inside the shape; Link with Layer makes sure the shape and pattern move together; and Snap to Origin snaps the pattern into alignment with the origin.

After applying a gradient or pattern, you can edit it just by double-clicking the layer contents thumbnail in the Layers palette. Photoshop calls these kinds of editable contents *dynamic fills.*

FIGURE 15.6

Gradients and patterns inside a shape layer are considered dynamic fills, which means you can edit them simply by double-clicking the layer contents thumbnail and editing the options shown here.

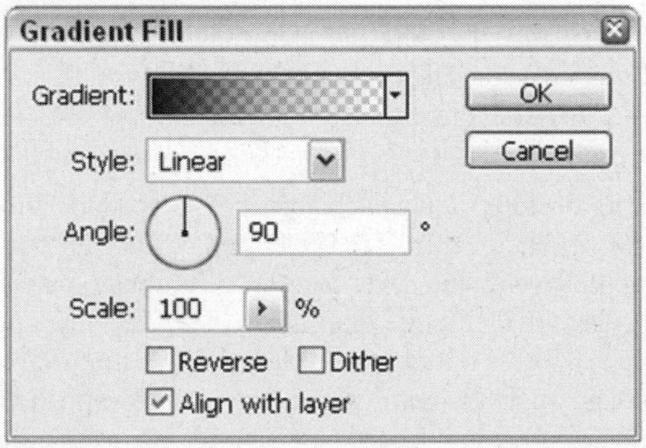

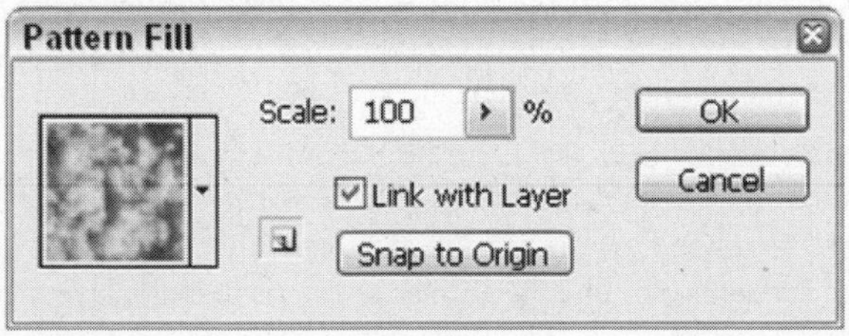

TIP You can reposition a gradient or pattern inside a shape just by dragging anywhere inside the image window while the dialog box is onscreen.

- **Make a color adjustment shape:** Where layer content is concerned, shape layers have unlimited potential. You can even fill a shape with a color adjustment. Just choose Levels, Curves, Hue/Saturation, or any of the other color-correction classics from the Layer ⇨ Change Layer Content submenu. Read Chapter 18 for complete information.

- **Paint inside a shape layer:** Wish you could paint or edit the contents of a shape layer? Well, thanks to subtle genetic alterations to Photoshop's core subroutines, you can. Assuming the shape is filled with a solid color, gradient, or pattern (this technique is not applicable to adjustment layers), choose Layer ⇨ Rasterize ⇨ Fill Content. From this point on, the fill is no longer dynamic. This means you can't double-click its thumbnail to edit it. However, you can edit it like any other layer full of pixels — paint, clone with the Stamp tool, blur, sharpen, dodge, burn, whatever your heart desires.

- **Fill a vector mask with an image:** Applying a vector mask to an image is a more delicate operation. Draw a shape — not as a new shape layer but rather as a working path (see coverage of the shape drawing process earlier in this chapter). Then select the layer that you want to mask (it must be a floating layer, not the background) and choose Layer ⇨ Add Vector Mask ⇨ Current Path.

TIP After establishing a work path, Ctrl-click (Win) or ⌘-click (Mac) the add layer mask icon at the bottom of the Layers palette to make the path clip the active image layer.

- **Go from clipping mask to vector mask:** What if you've already made a shape layer, and you want to fill that shape with an image? Again, you can use several approaches, but the easiest is to paste the image onto a layer in front of the shape layer. Then press Ctrl+G (Win) or ⌘+G (Mac) to group it with the shape layer.

- **Fuse image and shape layer:** That's enough to create the same visual effect as a shape masking an image, but it involves two layers instead of one. If, for any reason, you want to fuse the two layers together, you have to take a special approach. First, select the shape layer and choose Layer ⇨ Rasterize ⇨ Fill Content to convert the dynamic fill to pixels. Then select the image layer and press Ctrl+E (Win) or ⌘+E (Mac) to merge it with the shape layer below.

Have a (Masked) Ball

Still not dazzled by all these ways to perform near feats of magic with shape layers? Jeez — how jaded *are* you? Don't answer that. Instead, consider that you also can add a layer mask to a shape layer. Dazzled yet? That's right; Photoshop lets you combine pixel masking and vector masking on one layer, as shown in this figure.

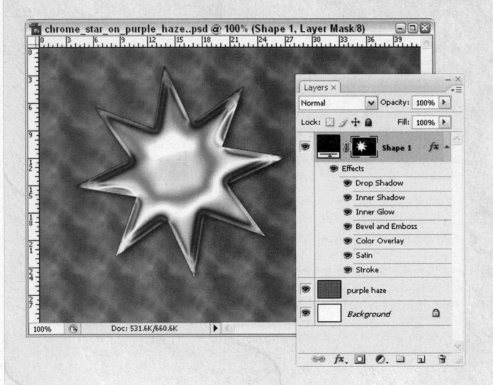

Why would you do such a thing? The combination permits you to have soft and razor-sharp edges all in the same layer. For example, to achieve the results shown in the figure, you would Ctrl-click (⌘-click on the Mac) the vector mask and then load that as a layer mask by clicking the add layer mask icon at the bottom of the Layers palette. In other words, the layer mask is identical to the vector mask. So what does that do for you? As shown in the next figure, you could then apply, say, the Gaussian Blur to the layer mask and then apply the Crystallize filter (or virtually any other filter that strikes your fancy). This results in soft filtered edges along the inside of the vector shape but then a hard edge after that. The layer mask masks the layer, and then the vector mask masks that. Cool, no?

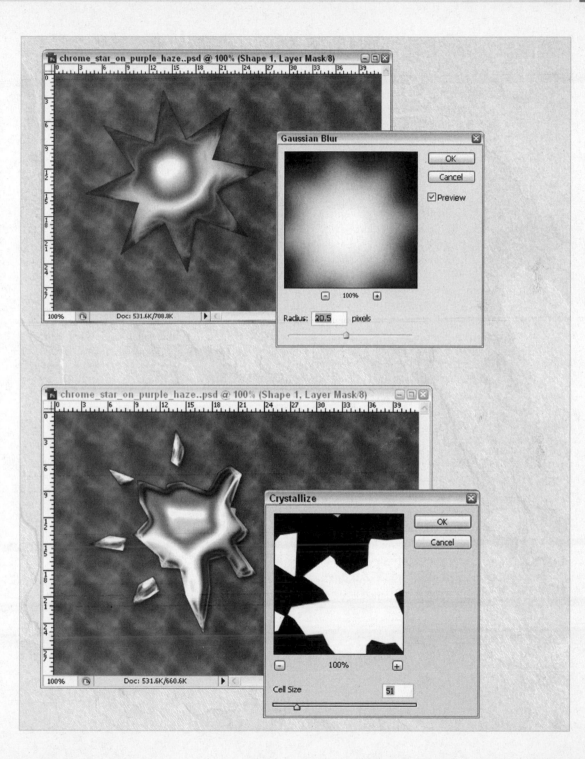

Beauty on the Outside

Way back in Photoshop 5, Adobe introduced a series of *layer effects* that automated the creation of shadows, glows, and beveled edges, applicable to individual layers in an image. Version 6 took those rudimentary tools several steps further, dramatically improving the quality of the existing effects and adding effects that overlay colors, stroke outlines, and create textures and contours. It also let you define exactly how effects are blended with background layers and permitted you to save them as preset *layer styles* for later use. Not much has changed since then, but why mess with a good thing, right? Photoshop's layer styles save you tons of time, make it easy to apply consistent effects throughout one or more images, and allow you to customize effects for a totally unique look.

To apply a layer effect, start with content on an independent layer, such as shown in the image in Figure 15.7. You can use any kind of layer, including a text layer (see Chapter 16) or a shape layer. After activating the layer in question, click the add layer style icon at the bottom of the Layers palette — the one that looks like a florin (cursive *f*) — and choose any of the commands following Blending Options. Or double-click anywhere on the layer other than the layer name to display the Layer Style dialog box, and then select an effect from the left-hand list. Or you can right-click (Control-click on the Mac) and choose Blending Options from the resulting pop-up menu. In the resulting dialog box, select or deselect the check box to turn the effect on and off; you also can highlight the effect name to edit its settings. Figures 15.8 and 15.9 show inner shadows and inner and outer glows. You can select from the following effects to apply similar effects to your images:

- **Drop Shadow:** The Drop Shadow command applies a common, everyday drop shadow, as seen in the first example of Figure 15.8. You can go with the default setting for the size, shape, and color of the shadow, or you can tweak it, specifying your own color, opacity, blend mode, position, size, and contour for the shadow. Photoshop makes it pretty — and pretty easy.

- **Inner Shadow:** This command applies a drop shadow inside the layer, as demonstrated in the second example in Figure 15.8. The command simulates the kind of shadow you'd get if you were looking through a piece of fabric that was cut through — casting a shadow through the cutout onto the paper beneath it.

- **Outer Glow:** The Outer Glow command creates a traditional halo, as seen in the first example in Figure 15.9. You can adjust the color, size, and other aspects of the glow, to meet your illumination needs.

- **Inner Glow:** This command creates a glow from within — applying the effect inside the layer rather than outside, as demonstrated in the second example in Figure 15.9.

FIGURE 15.7

Select a layer (here a Shape layer — a puzzle piece), click the add layer style icon at the bottom of the Layers palette, and choose an effect from the menu shown at the top here. Then, as needed, adjust the settings in the very comprehensive Layer Style dialog box.

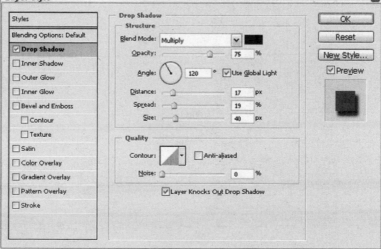

FIGURE 15.8

A 3D look, with a shadow cast beneath the layer (top) or simulating a shadow seen through the layer (bottom) can be created easily with the Drop Shadow or Inner Shadow effects.

FIGURE 15.9

Choose an Inner Glow or Outer Glow, or both; these effects can be applied in combination, too. Here, an Outer Glow emanates from the edges of the content (top), and an Inner Glow shows a light within (bottom).

To create a glow around the perimeter of a layer, apply both the Outer Glow and Inner Glow commands. Figure 15.10 shows an example of this (top right), as well as other effects that you can obtain by mixing and matching shadows and glows.

- **Bevel and Emboss:** The Bevel and Emboss option produces one of five distinct edge effects, as defined using the Style pop-up menu. The first four appear in Figure 15.11; the fifth one is exclusively applicable to stroked layers and requires the Stroke effect to be turned on. You can add a three-dimensional beveled edge around the outside of the layer, as in the first example in the figure. The Inner Bevel effect produces a beveled edge inside the layer. The Emboss effect combines inner and outer bevels. The Pillow Emboss effect reverses the inner bevel so the image appears to sink in and then rise back up along the edge of the layer. By tweaking the settings for a bevel, you can achieve a soft effect or a hard, chiseled look. The depth and intensity of the beveled effect is also adjustable.

- **Contour** and **Texture:** The Contour and Texture options aren't actual effects unto themselves. Instead, you use them to modify the Bevel and Emboss effect. The Contour settings create waves in the surface of the layer that result in rippling lighting effects. Texture stamps a pattern into the surface of the layer, creating a texture effect. Figure 15.12 illustrates these two options. On the top is an example of an Inner Bevel with the Contour set to Ring and a Range of 30 percent. On the bottom is another example of Inner Bevel, this time with the Contour set to Ring, a Range of 30 percent, and Texture set to Pattern (River Rocks Inverted).

- **Satin:** This option creates waves of color, as in Figure 15.13. You define the appearance of the waves using the Contour options. One of the stranger effects, Satin can be difficult to predict. As long as you keep the Preview option selected, though, you can experiment and play with settings for all the styles you're applying until you see a desirable result.

- **Color Overlay, Gradient Overlay,** and **Pattern Overlay:** These three options fill the layer with a coating of solid color, gradient, or repeating pattern, respectively. They work almost identically to the three dynamic fills available to shape layers, as discussed earlier in this chapter. All three can be quite useful when defining your own style presets. Figure 15.14 shows the Gradient Overlay and Pattern Overlay effects, applied with a drop shadow, too.

- **Stroke:** Use this option to trace a colored outline around a layer, as shown in Figure 15.15. The default stroke is rarely, if ever, useful: It's red and quite thick. You can change the color and thin it out as needed, and you also can choose to apply it to the inside or outside of the layer's edge. The Stroke effect is often preferable to Edit ➪ Stroke because you can edit it long after creating it. By comparison, Edit ➪ Stroke is a permanent effect.

FIGURE 15.10

Combining two or more layer styles gives you virtually unlimited options — especially when you factor in all the options for each style. Clockwise from the upper left, these are: Drop Shadow and Inner Shadow, Outer Glow and Inner Glow, Inner Shadow and Outer Glow, and Drop Shadow and Inner Glow.

FIGURE 15.11

Choose Layer ⇨ Layer Style ⇨ Bevel and Emboss to select one of several beveling options. Here, all four types of bevels are applied, clockwise from the upper left: Outer Bevel, Inner Bevel, Pillow Emboss, and Emboss.

FIGURE 15.12

Create even more interesting effects by adding Contour and/or Texture options to your beveled layer.

FIGURE 15.13

Satin, all by itself (top), looks ... satiny ... but may not create a very distinct effect without a bevel to go with it. On the bottom, the satin effect is confined and its edges sharpened by adding a contoured Inner Bevel.

FIGURE 15.14

Gradient (top) and Pattern (middle) overlays are relatively interesting, but they really pop when combined with other styles, such as bevels and contours (bottom). A shadow appears in all three shapes to make them stand out against the background.

FIGURE 15.15

At the top, a 10-pixel outside stroke is applied, in black, with a Normal blend mode. The bottom shape has a 10-pixel inside stroke, also in black, set to 65% Opacity, with a Dissolve blend mode, No shadow or other layer style is in effect in either shape.

To apply a blending option and see its options at the same time, click the name of the effect: For example, click the words "Drop Shadow" and you see the settings for the shadow in place. If you only wanted to see the options and not apply the style, this might seem like a problem, but it's no big deal to turn the style off (deselect the check box to the left of the style name) if you don't want it and just wanted to look at the settings.

If you prefer keyboard shortcuts, try some of these to help you navigate the Layer Style dialog box, which truly is a vast labyrinth of options: To switch between effects without turning them on or off, press Ctrl (⌘ on the Mac) plus a number key. Ctrl+1 (⌘+1 on the Mac) highlights Drop Shadow, Ctrl+2 (⌘+2) highlights Inner Shadow, Ctrl+3 (⌘+3) highlights Outer Glow, and so on, all the way to Ctrl+0 (⌘+0) for Stroke. You cannot get to Blending Options, Contour, or Texture from the keyboard.

The advantages of layer effects

The quick and automatic, almost "canned," nature of the layer styles may cause some more advanced designers and photographers to turn up their noses. It seems so amateur, after all, to just click a button and have a drop shadow appear, or to create a glow or beveled edge without having to go through countless steps and use several tools — expertly, craftily, with great skill and creativity. Of course, new Photoshop users and people who don't consider themselves expert designers will love layer styles, and we can all learn from those users and their very reasonable response. Why sniff at something just because it's fast or easy? It would be harder and require more effort to push your car to the store than to drive it, but we all hop in and hit the gas rather than hoofing it to the mall. Why? Because the car was meant to make it fast and easy to get from place to place.

So hop in, hit the accelerator, and make use of layer styles with no guilt, no sense of taking the easy way out. Still feeling like a cheater? Consider these real benefits to using layer styles:

- They stick to the layer. Move or transform the layer and the effect tags along with it.
- The effect is temporary. As long as you save the image in one of the three layered formats — native Photoshop (PSD), TIFF, or PDF — you can edit the shadows, glows, bevels, overlays, and strokes long into the future.
- Layer effects are equally applicable to standard layers, shape layers, and editable text. This is unusual because both shape layers and editable text prohibit many kinds of changes.
- Thanks to the Contour presets, layer effects enable you to create effects that would prove otherwise exceedingly difficult or even impossible.
- You can combine multiple effects on a single layer.
- You can copy an effect from one layer and paste it onto another.
- You can save groups of effects for later use in the Styles palette.
- The effects show up as items in the Layers palette. You can expand and collapse a list of effects, as well as temporarily disable and enable effects by clicking the familiar eyeball icons.
- Layer effect strokes print as vector output, so they're guaranteed to be smooth.

That's it. How many good reasons do you need? Just accept that layer styles are great, use them, and just get over it.

Inside the Layer Style dialog box

The Layer Style dialog box offers 13 panels containing more than 100 options. The first panel, Blending Options, was discussed in Chapter 14. The remaining 12 panels are devoted to layer effects. Select the desired effect from the list on the left; use the check box to turn the effect on and off.

Although there are tons of options, most are self-explanatory. For example, you select a blend mode from the Blend Mode pop-up menu. (For explanations of these, see Chapter 14.) Next, you make the effect translucent by typing a value in the Opacity option box. Easy enough?

Other options appear multiple times throughout the dialog box. All the options that appear in the Inner Shadow panel also appear in the Drop Shadow panel; the options in the Outer Glow panel appear in the Inner Glow panel; and so on. After you've played with the settings for an Outer Glow or a Drop Shadow, tweaking the settings for the Bevel or Stroke styles won't present any mystery. Figure 15.16 shows the Bevel and Emboss settings, which include most of the settings you'll encounter for any of the other effects — adjusting angles, contours, depth, size, spread, and opacity, as well as choosing where in the layer to place the effect in question.

FIGURE 15.16

The Bevel and Emboss settings are pretty representative of the other effects' settings. Master these and you're ready to tackle anything the Layer Style dialog box throws at you.

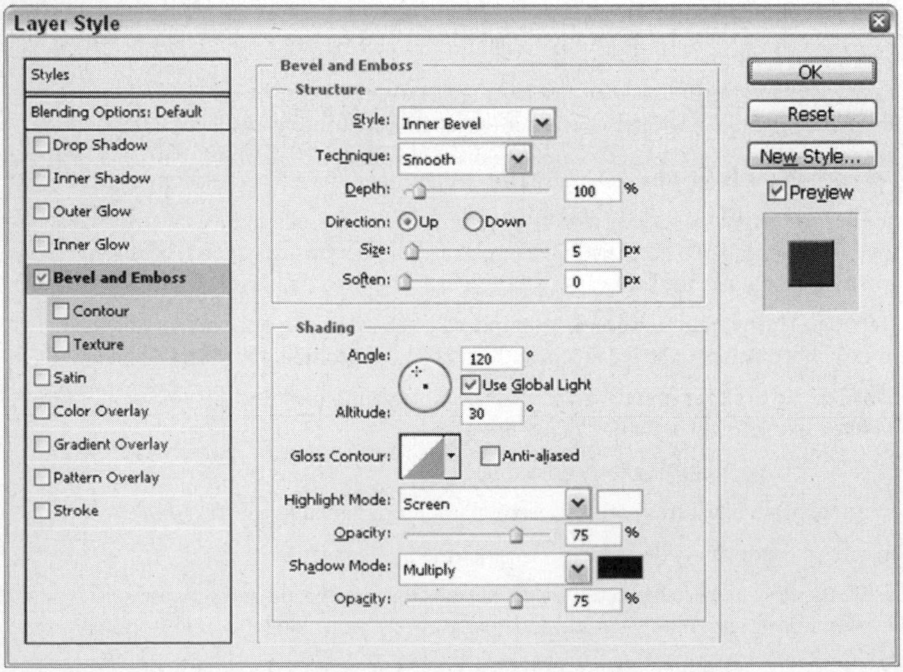

This list explains the options in the order in which they appear throughout the panels. Each option is explained only once, so if an option appears in multiple panels (or versions of the dialog box, for different styles, to put it another way), check this list for more information or clarification:

■ **Blend Mode:** This pop-up menu controls the blend mode. So much for the obvious. But did you know that the Blend Mode menu can let you turn an effect upside-down, select a light color and apply the Screen mode to change a drop shadow into a directional halo, or use a dark color with Multiply to change an outer glow into a shadow that evenly traces the edge of the layer? Don't be constrained by the traditional or allegedly intended uses of shadows and glows. Layer effects can be anything.

■ **Color swatch:** To change the color of the shadow, glow, or beveled edge, click the color swatch. When the Color Picker is open, click with the eyedropper cursor in the image window to select a color from the layered composition. When editing a glow, you can apply a gradient in place of a solid color. Click the gradient preview to create a custom gradation or select a preset from the pop-up palette.

■ **Opacity:** Use this option to make the effect translucent. Remember, a little bit of effect goes a long way. When in doubt, reduce the Opacity value for more subtle results.

■ **Angle:** Associated with shadows, bevels, the Satin effect, and gradients, this value controls the direction of the effect. In the case of shadows and bevels, the option controls the angle of the perceived light source. With Satin, it controls the angle at which contour patterns overlap. And with a gradient, the Angle value represents the direction of the gradient.

TIP You can avoid the numerical Angle option by clicking and dragging inside the little compass or clock-looking device in the dialog box or simply by dragging inside the image window. When the Drop Shadow or Inner Shadow panel is visible, click and drag inside the image window to move the shadow with respect to the layer. You also can drag the Contour effect when working in the Satin panel. Other draggable effects include Gradient Overlay and Pattern Overlay, although dragging affects positioning, not angle.

■ **Use Global Light:** In the real world, the sun casts all shadows in the same direction. By selecting the Use Global Light option, you tell Photoshop to cast *all* direction-dependent effects — drop shadows, inner shadows, and the five kinds of bevels — in the same direction. If you change the angle of a drop shadow applied to Layer 1, Photoshop rotates the sun in its digital heaven and so changes the angle of the pillow emboss applied to Layer 9, thus preventing you from applying conflicting shadows and other light-direction-dependent effects to different parts of the image.

Conversely, if you deselect the option, you tell Photoshop that physics and the laws of nature be damned, and you're going to dictate where the sun is on each layer and there may be conflicts, but who cares? You can change an Angle value in any which way you like, and none of the other layers will care — or at least they won't let on if they do.

TIP If you have established a consistent universe, you can edit the angle of the sun by choosing Layer ➪ Layer Style ➪ Global Light. Change the Angle value and all shadows and bevels created with the Use Global Light turned option selection will move in unison. You also can set the Altitude for bevels.

- **Distance:** The Drop Shadow, Inner Shadow, and Satin panels feature a Distance value that determines the distance between the farthest edge of the effect and the corresponding edge of the layer. Like Angle, this value is affected when you click and drag in the image window.

- **Spread** and **Choke:** Associated with the Drop Shadow and Outer Glow panels, the Spread option expands the point at which the effect begins outward from the perimeter of the layer. If you were creating the effect manually (as discussed in Chapter 14), this would be similar to applying Select ➪ Modify ➪ Expand. Spread changes to Choke in the Inner Shadow and Inner Glow panels, in which case it contracts the point at which the effect begins. Note that both Spread and Choke are measured as percentages of the Size value, explained next.

- **Size:** One of the most ubiquitous settings, the Size value determines how far an effect expands or contracts from the perimeter of the layer. In the case of shadows and glows, the portion of the Size that is not devoted to Spread or Choke is given over to blurring. For example, if you set the Spread for Drop Shadow to 0 percent and the Size to 30 pixels, Photoshop blurs the shadow across 100 percent of the 30-pixel size. If you set the Spread to 100 percent, 0 percent is left for blurring. The shadow expands 30 pixels out from the perimeter of the layer and has a sharp edge. This makes the effect seem larger, but only the opaque portion of the effect has grown.

  Size and Depth observe a similar relationship in the Bevel and Emboss panel, with Depth taking the place of Spread or Choke. When adjusting a Satin effect, Size affects the length of the contoured wave pattern. And in Stroke, Size controls the thickness of the outline.

- **Contour:** Photoshop creates most effects — namely shadows, glows, bevel, and the Satin effect — by fading a color from a specified Opacity value to transparent. The rate at which the fade occurs is determined by the Contour option. Click the down-pointing arrowhead to select from a palette of preset Contours; click the Contour preview to design your own. If you think of the Contour preview as a graph, the top of the graph represents opacity and the bottom represents transparency. So a straight line from top to bottom shows a consistent fade. A spike in the graph shows the color hitting opacity and then fading away again. Figure 15.17 shows two examples applied to individual layers.

  The most challenging contours are associated with Bevel and Emboss. The Gloss Contour option controls how colors fade in and out inside the beveled edge, as if the edge were reflecting other colors around it. The indented Contour effect — below Bevel and Emboss in the Layer Style list — wrinkles the edge of the layer so that it casts different highlights and shadows.

TIP You can make your own Contours, too. Instead of clicking the drop-list to choose from preset Contours, click the Contour icon itself. A Mapping graph displays, with a curved line and nodes along its length, representing the current contour's effects. You can drag the line and nodes to change the impact of that contour on the image, and watch the impact of your changes in the image, just as you watch any other style preview. You can save new presets, using the New button, which gives you dialog box through which you can name your new Contour for future use.

- **Anti-aliased:** If a Contour setting consists of sharp corners, you can soften them by selecting this option. Most presets have rounded corners, making anti-aliasing unnecessary.

- **Noise:** Associated strictly with shadows and glows, the Noise value randomizes the transparency of pixels. It's like using the Dissolve blend mode, except that you have control over how much randomization to apply. The Noise value does not change the color of pixels; that is the job of an option called Jitter.

- **Layer Knocks Out Drop Shadow:** In the real world, if an object is translucent, you can see through it to its own shadow. However, this turns out to be an unpopular law of nature with most image editors. So when creating a drop shadow, Photoshop gives us the Layer Knocks Out Drop Shadow option, which when selected makes the drop shadow invisible directly behind the layer. Deselect the option for a more natural effect.

- **Technique:** Moving out of the Shadow panels and into Outer Glow, the first unique option is the Technique pop-up menu. Also available when creating bevel effects, Technique controls how the contours of the effect are calculated. When a glow is set to Softer, Photoshop applies a modified Gaussian Blur to ensure optimal transitions between the glow and background elements. Your other option is Precise, which calculates the effect without the Gaussian adjustment. Of course, the effect may remain blurry, but strictly as a function of the Spread and Contour settings. Precise may work better in tight corners, common around type and shape layers. Otherwise, stick with Softer.

  The Bevel and Emboss panel doesn't provide the same kind of blurring functions that you get with shadow and glow effects, so the Technique option works a bit differently. The default setting, Smooth, averages and blurs pixels to achieve soft, rounded edges. The two Chisel settings remove the averaging to create sawtooth abrasions into the sides of the layer. Chisel Hard results in thick cut marks; Chisel Soft averages the perimeter of the layer to create finer cuts. Increase the Soften value (described shortly) to blur the abrasions.

- **Source:** When working in the Inner Glow panel, Photoshop wants to know where the glow starts. It can glow inward from the perimeter of the layer (Edge, as seen in the topmost example in Figure 15.18) or outward from the middle (Center, as seen on the bottom in Figure 15.18).

FIGURE 15.17

Two different Contour presets (Ring at the top, Double Ring at the bottom). Both are set to 90% Opacity, with a 60% Spread. The Noise is set to 65%, and the glow is set to 30 pixels in Size. The Range for the Contour is 70%. When used with an Outer Glow style, the Contour setting controls how the halo drops from opacity to transparency and back again (as in the case of ring and other peaked contours).

FIGURE 15.18

The two options — Edge and Center — for the Source setting in the Inner Glow panel are applied to these two shapes. A heart was cut out of each puzzle piece, to enhance the effect's visibility.

Inner Glow
Source: Edge
Size: 25 px
Choke: 7%
Contour: Ring
Range: 50%
Jitter: 20%

Inner Glow
Source: Center
Size: 15 px
Choke: 35%
Contour: Rolling Slope Descending
Range: 15%
Jitter: 20%

- **Range:** The two Glow panels and the Contour panel (subordinate to Bevel and Emboss) use Range values to modify the Contour settings. This value sets the midpoint of the contour with respect to the middle of the size. Figure 15.19 shows the two extremes — values less than 50 percent and greater than 50 percent — and their impact on the results.
- **Jitter:** Where the Noise value randomizes the transparency of pixels, Jitter randomizes the colors. This option is operable only when creating gradient glows in which the gradation contains two or more colors (not a color and transparency).

FIGURE 15.19

Here an Outer Glow is added to the shapes from Figure 15.18, with a Linear Contour and the Size set to 70 pixels in both shapes; the only difference is Range — 75% at the top and just 15% on the bottom. Less really *is* more!

- **Depth:** The first unique Bevel and Emboss setting is Depth, which makes the sides of a bevel steeper or shallower. In most cases, this translates to increased contrast between highlights and shadows as you raise the Depth value.

  The Texture panel includes its own Depth setting. Here, Photoshop renders the pattern as a texture map, lighting the white areas of the pattern as high and the black areas as low. The Depth value determines the depth of the texture. The difference is that you can type a negative value, which inverts the texture. Meanwhile, you also have an additional Invert option, which, when selected, reverses the lights and darks in the pattern. So a positive Depth value with Invert selected produces the same effect as a negative Depth value with Invert deselected.

- **Direction:** When working in the Bevel and Emboss panel, you see two radio buttons: Up and Down. If the Angle value indicates the direction of the sun, Up, when selected, positions the highlight along the edge near the sun and the shadow along the opposite edge. Down, when selected, reverses things, so the shadow is near the light source. Presumably, this means the layer sinks into its background rather than protrudes from it. But, in practice, the layer usually appears merely as though it's lit differently.

- **Soften:** This value sets the amount of blur applied to the beveled highlights and shadows. Small changes make a big difference when Technique is set to one of the Chisel options.

- **Altitude:** The Bevel and Emboss panel includes two lighting controls, Angle and Altitude. The Angle value is just that: the angle of the sun with respect to the layer. Altitude measures the height in the "sky" of the light source. A maximum value of 90 degrees puts the sun directly overhead (noon); 0 degrees puts it on the horizon (sunrise). Values in the medium range — 30 to 60 degrees — generally produce the best results. If you find the effect to be too sharp, you can temper it with the Soften setting.

- **Scale:** The Texture and Pattern Overlay panels include Scale values, which scale the pattern tiles inside the layer. Values greater than 100 percent swell the pattern; values lower than 100 percent shrink it.

- **Link/Align with Layer:** When selected, this option centers a gradient inside a layer. If you want to draw a gradient across many layers, deselect the option to center the gradient inside the canvas. When editing a pattern, this option links the pattern to the layer so the two move together.

- **Position:** The final Layer Style option appears in the Stroke panel. The Position pop-up menu defines how the width of the stroke aligns with the perimeter of the layer. Photoshop can draw the stroke outside the edge of the layer, draw the stroke inside the edge, or center the stroke exactly on the edge.

Modifying and Saving Effects

After you apply a layer effect, Photoshop stamps the layer with a florin symbol (ƒ), accompanied by a small x, as shown in Figure 15.20. Clicking a triangular toggle switch lets you expand and collapse the displayed list of applied effects to permit more room for layers in the palette. If the triangle points up, it indicates the effects are displayed; if the triangle points down, the effects are hidden. From that point on, you can edit an effect by double-clicking its name in the Layers palette. Or double-click the florin symbol to display the Blending Options panel of the Layer Style dialog box.

FIGURE 15.20

The florin symbol (ƒ) with a small x indicates that one or more layer effects have been applied to the layer. Here one layer's effects are collapsed, and the others are expanded.

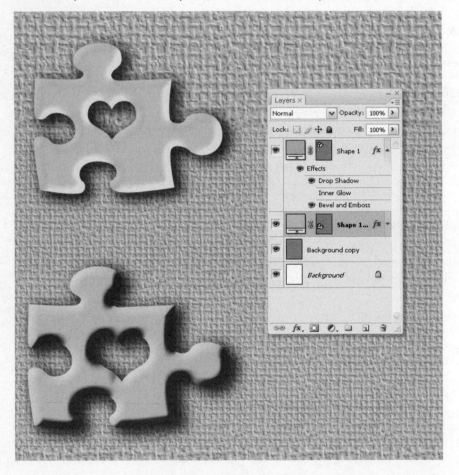

Disabling effects

To temporarily disable all effects applied to a layer, choose Layer ⇨ Layer Style ⇨ Hide All Effects. Or just click the eyeball in front of the word "Effects" in the Layers palette. Click the eyeball spot again to show the effects. You likewise can hide and show individual effects — without permanently disabling them — by clicking eyeballs. Photoshop even goes so far as to save hidden effects. This makes it easy to bring an effect back to life later without reentering settings.

To permanently delete an effect, click and drag it to the trash icon at the bottom of the Layers palette. To delete all effects, drag the word "Effects" to the trash.

> **TIP** Right-click (Control-click on the Mac) the florin symbol (or anywhere other than the layer thumbnails, or the link and eye icons) to display a pop-up menu from which you can choose Clear Layer Style. This deletes all effects on the layer in question.

Duplicating effects

After you apply an effect to a layer, the effect becomes an element that you can copy and apply to other layers. Select the layer with the effects you want to duplicate, and choose Layer ⇨ Layer Style ⇨ Copy Layer Style. Or right-click (Control-click on the Mac) anywhere other than the layer thumbnails or the link or eye icons in the Layers palette, and choose Copy Layer Style from the shortcut menu. Then select another layer, right-click (Win) or Control-click (Mac) it, and choose Paste Layer Style. To paste a copied effect onto multiple layers at a time, link them together (as explained in Chapter 14) and choose the Paste Layer Style to Linked command. To copy a layer style between layers, you can also use the Alt key (or Option on the Mac) and drag a layer style from one layer to another.

> **NOTE** The Copy and Paste Layer Style commands bypass the Clipboard. This means that you can copy an image and then copy an effect without displacing the image.

> **TIP** The Paste Layer Style command duplicates all effects associated with one layer onto another. But what if you want to duplicate only a single effect? Just click and drag the effect name from one layer, and drop it below another in the Layers palette. Be sure that you see a bar below the layer name when dropping the effect; otherwise, it won't take.

Scattering effects to the four winds

When you apply an effect, Photoshop is actually doing all the manual layer work for you in the background. But if Photoshop doesn't seem to be generating the precise effect you want, you can take over and edit the layers to your satisfaction. Choose Layer ⇨ Layer Style ⇨ Create Layers to resolve the automated effect into a series of layers and clipping masks. In some cases, a warning appears telling you that one or more attributes of an effect cannot be represented with layers. Go ahead and give it a try; you can always undo. If you like what you see, inspect it and edit at will.

CAUTION   After choosing Create Layers, you're on your own. From that point on, you lose the ability to edit the effects from the Layer Style dialog box (unless, of course, you decide to go back in time with the History palette).

NOTE   If you like layer effects (and you should, you really should), there's no doubt you'll eventually find yourself experiencing a curious phenomenon. After you've gone and applied a bunch of different effects — particularly Color Overlays, Gradient Overlays, and Pattern Overlays — your layer may no longer respond to blend modes.

Saving effects as styles

Photoshop lets you save layer effects and blending options for later use by creating layer styles, which appear as items in the Styles palette. You can create a style in the following ways:

- **Click the new style icon.** When working in the Styles palette, click the new style icon to display the options shown at the bottom of Figure 15.21. Name your style, and then select the check boxes to decide which settings in the Layer Style dialog box are preserved. The first check box saves the effects covered in this chapter; the second saves the blending options discussed in the previous chapter.

FIGURE 15.21

Click in the Styles palette (top) to display the New Style dialog box (bottom).

■ **Click in the Styles palette.** Choose Window ➪ Styles to view the Styles palette. Then point within the palette, right-click (⌘-click on the Mac), and choose New Style from the pop-up. Photoshop responds by showing you the New Style dialog box (refer to Figure 15.21). Set the options as described previously.

After you press Enter or Return, Photoshop saves the style as a new preset. As with any preset, you can apply it to future images during future Photoshop sessions if you use the Preset Manager to save it — otherwise, it will only live on during the current session. In any case, just click a style to apply it to the active layer, or drag the style and drop it on any layer name (active or not) in the Layers palette. Have you forgotten how to access and use the Preset Manager? See Chapter 2.

Don't forget that Photoshop ships with a big bunch of preset styles that you can explore at your leisure. Load a set of styles from the Styles palette menu, apply one to your favorite layer, and take a look at how it's put together in the Layer Style dialog box. This sort of play — testing, trying things on for size — is a really effective way to get a feel for the amazing variety of effects that are possible in Photoshop.

> **TIP** A style may include blending options, layer effects, or both. Applying a new style to a layer replaces all blending options and effects associated with that style. If you would rather add the blending options and effects from a style to the existing blending options and effects associated with a layer, Shift-click an item in the Styles palette.

> **NOTE** Sadly, there is no way to update a style — and even if you could, the style and layer are not linked, so updating the style would have no effect on the layer. Photoshop lets you create new styles, rename existing styles, and delete old ones — but that's about it.

Summary

In this chapter, you learned about object-oriented shapes and how to create them. Tricks for setting up your polygon, line, and custom shape options were covered, along with techniques for combining shapes into compound paths. You also learned about defining custom shapes and filling shapes with gradients, patterns, and images.

Because shapes reside on their own layers, you also learned about creating and modifying automatic layer effects and how to apply layer-based styles through the Layer Style dialog box. This included must-have information on duplicating effects and saving effects and blending options as styles for future use.

Chapter 16

Fully Editable Text

All things considered, Photoshop's handling of type has come a long way. The journey has taken us from a Type tool that was about as forgiving and friendly as trying to write with a broken pencil while riding in an old truck on a bumpy road to the very efficient, useful, and powerful tool we have today. If you weren't there for those bumpy rides, consider yourself lucky.

The lack of layers before version 3 was the biggest problem; after you typed the text, it was part of your image, no editing, no taking it back or saying, "Hey, how does it look *without* the type?" There also was no spell-check, so if you weren't a spelling bee champion or the most accurate typist, it was very frustrating. To say the least.

With the release of version 5 came something new and welcome — editable bitmapped type. Suddenly, you could type your text and then go back and edit it. Imagine that! You could adjust the font, size, and color of the type, responding to the ubiquitous need for changes after first creating an image and adding type to it. You could adjust kerning and leading, giving you the ability to essentially typeset your images and not just rely on the defaults. Photoshop 5.5 expanded the type possibilities further, but with version 6, type finally evolved — into a graceful, intelligent part of the application. Here are some of the advances that users of Photoshop 5.5 and above can count on:

- Scale text as large as you want, without any repercussions, just as you could with any vector object — because the text is vector text.

- Create and edit text by typing directly on the image canvas — no more side trips to the Type tool dialog box required.

- Create text inside a frame and then apply paragraph formatting to control hyphenation, justification, indents, alignment, and paragraph spacing. You can even create lists that use hanging punctuation and control word and character spacing in justified text, as you can in QuarkXPress, Adobe PageMaker, and InDesign.

- Make per-character adjustments to color, width, height, spacing, and baseline shift.

- Bend, twist, and otherwise distort text using a simple Warp Text dialog box instead of wrestling with the Wave filter or other distortion filters.

- Convert characters to shapes that you can then edit, fill, and stroke just as you do objects you create with the shape tools (which are explored in Chapter 15). Alternatively, you can convert text to a work path.

- Rasterize text so that you can apply any filters or tools applicable to ordinary image layers.

Photoshop 7 introduced a few useful type features, such as the type mask tools and the Check Spelling command, but you still couldn't put type on a drawn path, a feature by now standard to most illustration and layout programs. The closest Photoshop got was the Warp Text command, which is nice but fairly limited.

That limitation disappeared in Photoshop CS. Photoshop CS2 didn't really offer any major changes in the Type tool, but with Photoshop CS3, we see what may seem like a small change, but it's a huge one: We can now change the size of the font previews. If you've ever been nearly pressing your nose to the monitor, trying to see the font samples on the right side of the Font drop-down list (on the Type tool's Options bar and in the Character palette), you can certainly appreciate the excitement at being able to view those samples in Large and Extra Large.

Of course, even if you think the aforementioned improvement is so minor it's hardly worth mentioning, you have to admit that Photoshop continues to offer great features with regard to creating and editing type. In addition to supporting text on a path, Photoshop also can create and modify text around and even inside shape layers and paths. Finally, Photoshop's text features are fully in line with those found in page-layout, illustration, and even advanced word-processing programs. You should be able to make them a regular part of your text routine in no time.

NEW FEATURE   Woo hoo! You can stop squinting now. Choose Preferences ⇨ Type and in the Type Preferences dialog box, choose Large or Extra Large from the list of Font Preview Size options. The default is Medium, and unless you have superhuman vision or your screen resolution is set to some unbelievably screen-wasting size, you will find that Medium is too darn small. Large is nice, Extra Large is nicer — almost decadently so.

NOTE   This book doesn't cover the options for formatting Chinese, Korean, and Japanese text, which become available when you select the Show Asian Text Options check box on the General panel of the Preferences dialog box. Like the rest of Photoshop's type controls, these options should be familiar to you if you work regularly with type in these languages. But if you're not sure what each control does, check the Photoshop online help system for details.

The Five Flavors of Text

Photoshop's Type tool produces vector type. But that's not all. You also can create a text-based selection outline or work path, convert each character to a separate vector object, or create a bitmap version of your text. Here's a rundown of your type choices:

- To create regular text, select the Type tool (also known as the Horizontal Type tool, which is the default Type tool), click in the image window, and begin typing. Or, to create paragraph text, click and drag with the Type tool to create a text frame that's roughly the size you want the paragraph/s to take up in the image and then type your text in the frame. You then can choose from a smorgasbord of type-formatting options, apply layer effects, and more. There are a few things you can't do, at least while the type is still considered type, such as apply the commands in the Filter menu or use the standard selection tools. You can apply these features if you rasterize the type, but that's covered later on.

TIP The process of selecting text can be somewhat enigmatic, but after you know how it's done, it's no big deal. You can use the Type tool to drag through and select existing text (note that the I-beam cursor changes from being in a small box to just being the I-beam when you get right next to existing type), and then just like you use your mouse to select text in a word processor, you can drag through the type, selecting as much or as little of it as you need. You also can use your mouse to select portions of the type on a given layer, without dragging — double-click to select a single word, triple-click to select a single line, quadruple-click to select an entire paragraph, or quintuple-click to select everything on the active Type layer. If "quintuple-click" sounds like you might end up short-circuiting your mouse, you can also select all the text on a given Type layer by double-clicking the T icon on the type layer. Easy as pie.

- To produce a text-based selection outline, select the Horizontal or Vertical Type Mask tool from the Type tool flyout menu, shown in Figure 16.5 later in this chapter, and create your text. Photoshop covers your image with a translucent overlay, just like when you work in the Quick Mask mode, and your text appears transparent. You can apply all the same formatting options that are available when you work with ordinary text. When you commit the text (by clicking another tool or clicking the green checkmark at the far right end of the Type tool's Options bar), the overlay disappears and your selection outline appears.

TIP You also can create type masks using the regular Type tool. Simply type and format your text as usual. Then Ctrl-click (⌘-click on the Mac) the type layer in the Layers palette to generate the selection outlines. What's the advantage of this approach? It's simple: Type on a layer is forever editable; a type mask is not. Therefore, it is hard to see any real advantage to using the Type Mask tools at all.

- After creating text, choose Layer ➪ Type ➪ Convert to Shape to turn each character into an individual vector shape that works just like those you create with the shape tools (covered in Chapter 15). You then can edit the shape of individual characters, an option explored in the section "Editing text as shapes" later in this chapter.

- Choose Layer ➪ Type ➪ Create Work Path to generate a work path from text. One reason to use this option is to create a clipping path based on your text.

- Finally, you can convert text to bitmapped type by choosing Layer ➪ Rasterize ➪ Type. After rasterizing the text, you can apply Photoshop's filters and other pixel-based features to it.

> **CAUTION**   After you rasterize text or convert it to a shape or work path, you can't go back and run the spell-checker or change the text formatting as you can while working with vector text or type masks. So be sure that you're happy with the spelling, capitalization, and font before you convert it. And here's a tip embedded right here in this caution: You can save a copy of the vector text in a new layer so that you can get it back if needed.

When you save images in the PSD, PDF, TIFF, or PSB format, you must select the Layers option to retain the vector properties of your text—assuming you still have un-rasterized Type layers in your image. If you deselect this option or save in a format that doesn't support vectors, Photoshop rasterizes your text. Saving a backup copy of the image in the native Photoshop format is a good idea.

Text as Art

Before diving into the nuts and bolts of creating text, it would probably be useful and inspiring for you to see some examples of out-of-the-ordinary ways to use type in your images. By combining the powers of the Type tool with the program's effects, filters, paint, and edit tools, and layering features, and you can create an almost unlimited array of text effects; you can even produce text that stands alone as a powerful image in its own right. Here goes:

- **Create translucent type.** Because Photoshop automatically creates type on a new layer, you can change the translucency of type simply by adjusting the Opacity value for the type layer in the Layers palette. Using this technique, you can merge type and images to create subtle overlay effects, as illustrated in Figure 16.1.

- **Use type as a selection.** By creating a type mask, you can use type to select a portion of an image, and then move, copy, or transform it. To create Figure 16.2, for example, we used the text from Figure 16.1. Two selections were copied (including the background, grabbed with the text selection) and pasted into a new image window. Further enhancements came through new type, a photo on its own layer, and another independent text layer, overlapping the selection-based "type" from Figure 16.1.

- **Apply layer effects.** Photoshop's layer effects are fully applicable to type. In Figure 16.3, a type object is again pasted into an image (the sky photo again), but a layer style was applied by right-clicking on the layer and choosing Blending Options from the pop-up menu. The Magic Wand tool was then used to select some of the clouds. That selection was copied and pasted it into a new layer, which was then subjected to the same pillow embossing applied to the type layer. A follow-up blurring with a Blur filter was the final touch.

FIGURE 16.1

Not only are some of the type layers translucent due to reduced opacity, the type layers were easily duplicated and resized to create a graphic statement that enhances the meaning of the type itself.

FIGURE 16.2

The word "CROWS" and a Web address were turned into selections in Figure 16.1 and then copied into this image, bringing their background with it. An additional type layer was created and placed on top of the selections and a new photo layer.

■ **Edit type as part of the image.** After rasterizing text (by choosing Layer ➪ Rasterize ➪ Type), you can paint type, erase it, smear it, apply a filter or two, or do anything else that you can do to pixels. In Figure 16.4, the Chrome filter was applied, and then the Edit ➪ Transform ➪ Distort command was used to make the type look like it's coming at the viewer. One little tip: The Image ➪ Adjustments ➪ Variations command was used to darken the sky layer a bit so that the type would stand out on top of it.

FIGURE 16.3

Text from Figure 16.1 has had a variety of layer styles applied to it. The less-opaque word "Crows" has an outer glow, and the black text layers have a soft chisel emboss.

FIGURE 16.4

Here the type has been rasterized, and the Chrome layer style applied. The type, now an elaborate shape, also has been transformed, the layer stretched to provide visual interest using the Skew and Warp commands under Edit ⇨ Transform.

Using the Type Tool

So now that you've had a taste of just some of what's possible with Photoshop's Type tool and the things Photoshop will let you do to and with type, let's look at how to create a type layer in the first place.

Building text in Photoshop

First, of course, you want to select the Type tool by clicking its icon in the Toolbox or pressing T. Photoshop activates the Type tool, displays the I-beam cursor in the image window, and displays type controls in the Options bar. You can access additional formatting options by displaying the Character and Paragraph palettes shown in Figure 16.5.

FIGURE 16.5

Choose Window ➪ Character or Window ➪ Paragraph to display the text palettes. The rest of the type tools and features appear automatically when you click to activate the Type tool.

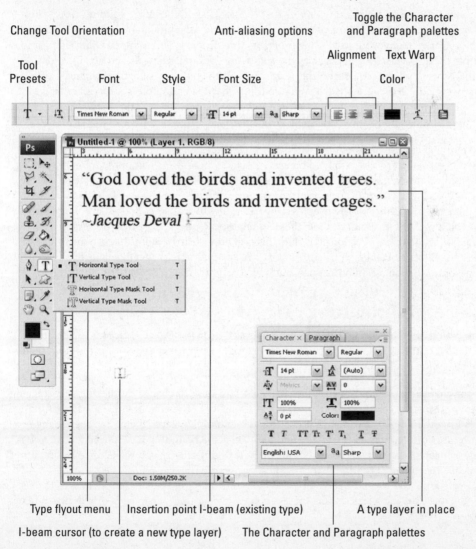

Change Tool Orientation   Anti-aliasing options   Toggle the Character and Paragraph palettes

Tool Presets   Font   Style   Font Size   Alignment   Text Warp   Color

Type flyout menu   Insertion point I-beam (existing type)   A type layer in place

I-beam cursor (to create a new type layer)   The Character and Paragraph palettes

> **TIP**   You can toggle the Character and Paragraph palettes on and off with either the little palette button at the end of the Options bar, or the vertical strip of palette buttons on the left side of the dock: A opens the Character palette, and the paragraph symbol (looks like a backwards "P," also known as a "pilcrow") opens the Paragraph palette.

Before you begin typing, you can select the font, type size, and other formatting attributes from the Options bar and palettes. These are identified in Figure 16.5 and are quite easy to use. You'll also want to check the Color button on the Type Options bar and make sure it's set to the color you want to type in. That's not to say that you can't change it after you've typed the text (in fact, you probably will), but if you have a white background and are set to type in white and don't realize it, you'll sit there wondering why you can't see your type.

At this point, you're ready to begin typing, so just click or drag in the image window. If you click, Photoshop places the first character you type at the location of the blinking insertion marker, the same way it works in any word processing program. You can press Shift+Enter or Shift+Return to insert a line break, or just keep typing and the text string goes on as long as you do. Of course, you're likely to run off the edge of the image window, but the type is visible if you increase the Canvas size enough to accommodate it. You also can go back later and press Shift+Enter or Shift+Return at various points to force line breaks where you need them. Adobe calls this process of clicking on a single point and then typing *point text*.

Alternatively, you can create paragraph text by clicking and dragging with the Type tool to draw a frame — called a *bounding box* — to hold the text. Now your text flows within the frame, wrapping to the next line automatically when you reach the edge of the bounding box. If you create your text this way, you can apply standard paragraph-formatting attributes, such as justification, paragraph spacing, and so on. In other words, everything works pretty much like it does in every other program in which you create text in a frame. Pressing Enter or Return starts a new paragraph in the bounding box. Note that if you don't type like this — if you use the point text method to insert your text, not all of the Paragraph palette options will be applicable — you'll be able to adjust alignment, but not justification or margins, and hyphenation won't apply either.

Editing and formatting

As you're typing, if you make a mistake, press Backspace (Win) or Delete (Mac) to delete the character to the left of the insertion marker. To remove the character to the right of the insertion point, press Delete (Windows) or Del (Mac).

To alter the character formatting, select the characters you want to change by clicking and dragging over them or using the selection shortcuts listed in Table 16.1. Then choose the new formatting attributes from the Options bar, Character palette, or Paragraph palette. If you don't select any text, paragraph formatting affects all text in the bounding box (the bounding box appears only if you're working with paragraph text). If you're editing point text, any change you make to your formatting options while the cursor (insertion point) is still active within the text (but while no text is selected) will apply to new text that you type at the insertion point only. To make changes to existing text, the text must be selected. This enables you to change single characters or words to a new font, size, or color.

You also can choose the Check Spelling command to spell-check your text, as well as use the Find and Replace Text feature to search for words in large chunks of text.

After your text is typed, you can click the OK button (the check mark at the end of the Type Options bar) to commit the text. You also can simply click another tool, such as the Move tool, to let Photoshop know you've finished dealing with the type layer for now. If you want to keep the Type tool active, use the OK button. Oh—and don't worry—"committing the text" simply takes you out of text-editing mode. As long as you don't convert the text to a regular image layer, work path, or shape, you can edit it at any time.

TIP If the Options bar is hidden or you just don't like reaching to click the button, you can commit text by selecting any other tool, clicking any palette but the Character or Paragraph palette, or pressing Ctrl+Enter (⌘+Return on the Mac).

NOTE While you're in text-editing mode, most menu commands are unavailable. You must commit the text or cancel the current type operation to regain access to them. To abandon your type operation, click the Cancel button—the "no" symbol at the right end of the Options bar—or press Esc.

Type layers

When you create the first bit of type in an image, Photoshop creates a new layer to hold the text— you'll see the layer created as soon as you began typing changes from "Layer 1" (or whatever generic layer number you're up to in the image at hand) to a layer named using the first 30 characters of the text you've typed.

After you commit the type, clicking or dragging with the Type tool has one of two outcomes. If Photoshop finds any text near the spot where you click or drag, it assumes that you want to edit that text and, therefore, selects the text layer and puts the Type tool into Edit mode. For paragraph text, the paragraph is selected as well. If no text is in the vicinity of the spot you click, the program decides that you must want to create a brand-new text layer and responds accordingly. You can force Photoshop to take this second route by Shift-clicking or Shift-dragging with the Type tool, which comes in handy if you want to create one block of text on top of another.

TIP If you don't like the type layer being named for the text you've typed, you can double-click the name in the Layers palette and type something new.

Creating vertical type

The Vertical Type tool is entirely dedicated to creating vertically oriented text. To get this tool, press T (or Shift+T) when the regular Type tool is active. In truth, the Vertical Type tool is nothing more than the standard Type tool lifted from the Japanese version of Photoshop. As shown in the first example of Figure 16.6, it creates vertical columns of type that read top to bottom, and right to left, as in Japan. If you want to make columns of type that read left to right, you have to create each column as an independent text block.

> **TIP**   If you want to do what I do (and hey, who doesn't), type the text with the Horizontal Type tool, and then rotate it with the Edit ➪ Transform ➪ Rotate command, or press Ctrl+T (⌘+T for Mac users) to enter Transform mode. In order to access these tools, however, you cannot be using the Type tool at the time; be sure to commit to your type and/or switch to the Move tool (which commits your type) before trying to do any kind of transformation. Then point to a corner handle, and when your mouse pointer turns to a curved arrow, click and drag to rotate the text. You can refer to the Options bar to see if you've achieved the desired angle of rotation.

FIGURE 16.6

By default, vertical type reads right to left, as shown in the first example. If you deselect the Standard Vertical Roman Alignment option in the Character palette menu, your characters appear like those on the right.

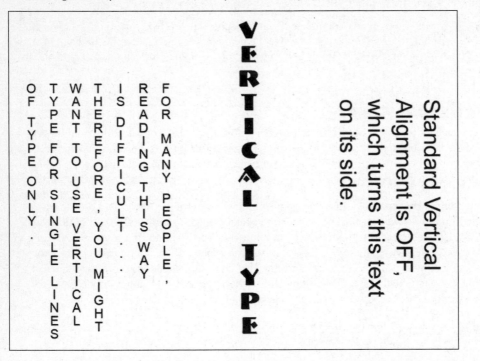

After you click the image, you have access to the Standard Vertical Roman Alignment command in the Character palette menu. (If the palette isn't open, click the Display/Hide palettes button at the right end of the Options bar. It's labeled in Figure 16.5.) By default, the option is selected, which gives you upright characters such as those on the left side of Figure 16.6. Choose the command again to rotate the text 90 degrees clockwise and flip characters on their side, as shown in the right side of the figure. You also can deselect this feature before typing, which can be easier on the eyes if you're not from a country that typically reads right to left.

You also can choose Layer ➪ Type ➪ Horizontal and Layer ➪ Type ➪ Vertical to change vertically oriented type to horizontally oriented type, and vice versa.

Creating and Manipulating Text in a Frame

If you click and drag the Type tool within your image window, Photoshop draws a bounding box to hold your text, as shown in Figure 16.7. If you want to create a bounding box that's a specific size, Alt-click (Win) or Option-click (Mac) with the Type tool instead of dragging. Photoshop displays the Paragraph Text Size dialog box, in which you can specify the width and height of the box. Press Enter or Return, and Photoshop creates the bounding box, placing the top-left corner of the box at the spot you clicked.

FIGURE 16.7

Click and drag the box handles to transform the frame alone or the frame and text together.

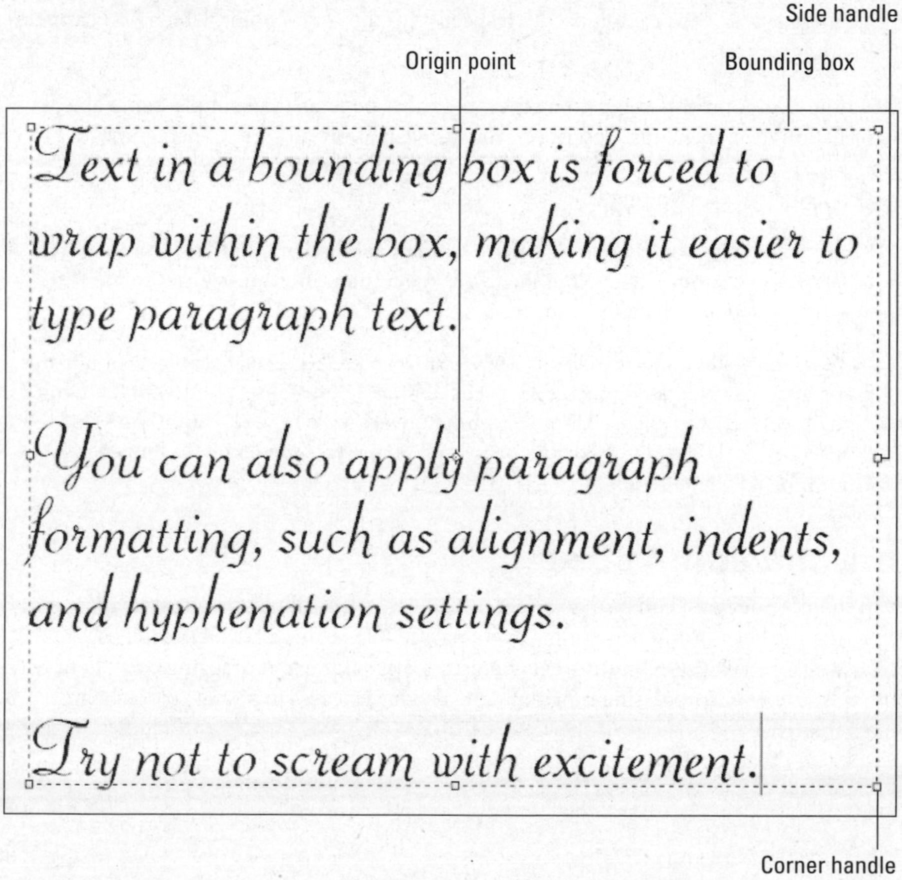

Text in a bounding box is forced to wrap within the box, making it easier to type paragraph text.

You can also apply paragraph formatting, such as alignment, indents, and hyphenation settings.

Try not to scream with excitement.

The bounding box looks just like the one that appears when you choose Edit ⇨ Free Transform (and you can do this to point text as well), and some of its functions are the same with regard to paragraph text:

- Click and drag a corner handle to resize the box. Shift-drag to retain the original proportions of the box. The text reflows to fit the new dimensions of the box.

- Ctrl-drag (Win) or ⌘-drag (Mac) a corner handle to scale the text and box together. Ctrl+Shift-drag (⌘+Shift-drag on the Mac) to scale proportionally. To scale text alone, use the character formatting controls in the Options bar or in the Character palette. Either way, you can scale up or down as much as you want without degrading the text quality, thanks to the vector nature of the Type tool.

- To rotate both box and text, move the cursor outside the box and drag, just as you do when transforming selections, crop boundaries, and layers. Shift-drag to rotate in 15-degree increments. The rotation occurs respective to the origin point, which you can relocate by dragging, as usual.

Using the bounding-box approach to type, however, has more benefits than simply being able to use the transformation techniques just described. You also can apply all sorts of paragraph-formatting options to control how the text flows within the bounding box, as described in the section "Applying paragraph formatting."

NOTE Keep in mind that you also can scale, skew, rotate, and otherwise transform the text layer after you commit the text to the layer. In addition, you can size and rotate text using the options in the Character palette.

TIP If you ever decide that you'd like to work with your text as regular text instead of paragraph text, cancel text-editing mode by clicking the OK or Cancel button in the Options bar. Then select the text layer, and choose Layer ⇨ Type ⇨ Convert to Point Text. Photoshop splits the paragraph text into individual lines. To go back to paragraph text, select the text layer and choose Layer ⇨ Type ⇨ Convert to Paragraph Text.

Selecting and editing text

Before you can modify any type, you have to select it. You can select all text on a text layer by simply double-clicking the layer thumbnail in the Layers palette. (This automatically switches you to the Type tool as well.) You can select individual characters by clicking and dragging over them with the Type tool, as in any word-processing program. You also have access to a range of keyboard tricks listed in Table 16.1.

TABLE 16.1

Using the Mouse and Keyboard to Select Text

Text Selection	Keystrokes
Select character to left or right	Shift+left or right arrow
Select entire word	Double-click the word
Select entire line	Triple-click the line
Select entire paragraph	Quadruple-click the paragraph
Move left or right one word	Ctrl+left or right arrow (⌘+left or right arrow)
Select word to left or right	Ctrl+Shift+left or right arrow (⌘+Shift+left or right arrow)
Select to end of line	Shift+End
Select to beginning of line	Shift+Home
Select one line up or down	Shift+up or down arrow
Select range of characters	Click at one point, Shift-click at another
Select all text	Ctrl+A (⌘+A)

After selecting type, you can replace it by typing new text — no need to delete and then type the replacement text. You also can cut, copy, or paste text (perhaps a paragraph you already have in a document) by pressing the standard keyboard shortcuts (Ctrl/⌘+X, C, or V) or by choosing commands from the Edit menu. You can undo a text modification by pressing Ctrl+Z (⌘+Z on the Mac) or choosing Edit ➪ Undo. However, if you type a few characters and then choose Undo, you wipe out all the new characters, not just the most recently typed one. If things go terribly wrong, press Esc or click the Cancel button in the Options bar to cancel the current type operation.

TIP Selected text appears highlighted onscreen, as is the convention. If the highlight gets in your way, press Ctrl+H (Win) or ⌘+H (Mac) to hide it. This shortcut hides all onscreen helpers, including guides.

Applying Character Formatting

The Options bar gives you easy access to the collection of formatting controls shown in Figure 16.8. The Character palette and its palette menu, also shown in the figure, offer some of these same controls plus a few additional options. If you use Adobe InDesign, the palette should look familiar to you — with a few exceptions, it's a virtual twin of the InDesign Character palette.

To open the palette and its partner, the Paragraph palette, click the Toggle the Character and Paragraph Palettes button in the Options bar. Alternatively, you can choose Window ➪ Character or press Ctrl+T (⌘+T on the Mac) when in text-editing mode.

FIGURE 16.8

Photoshop provides many character-formatting controls in the Options bar and the Character palette, including increased support for OpenType features.

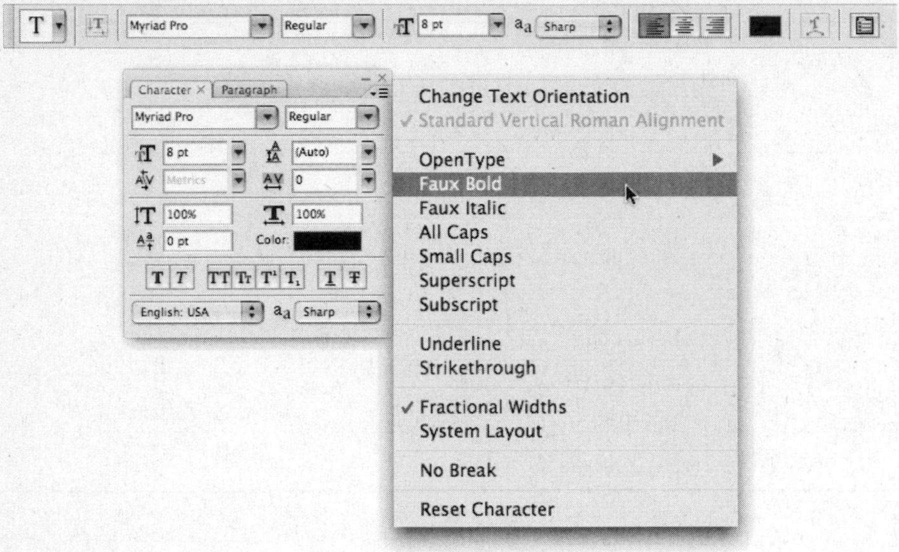

You can apply formatting on a per-character basis. For example, you can type one letter, change the font color, and then type the next letter in the new color. You can even change fonts from letter to letter, either as you type or by selecting existing text character by character.

The next several sections explain the character-formatting options. All apply to both paragraph and point text. You can specify formatting before you type or reformat existing type by selecting it first.

If you ever want to return the settings in the Character palette to the defaults, make sure that no type is selected. Then choose Reset Character from the bottom of the palette menu.

Font

Select the font (typeface) and type style you want to use from the Font and Style lists. Photoshop offers a full list of designer-style options. For example, whereas Times is limited to Bold and Italic, the Helvetica family may yield such stylistic variations as Oblique, Light, Black, Condensed, Insert, and Ultra Compressed. The fonts that are available through Photoshop are dependent on the fonts that are installed on your computer. In general, if you have access to a font in your word processor, you'll find it in the Font list in Photoshop.

TIP If you're working with multiple linked text layers, you can quickly change the font or type style on all linked layers in one fell swoop by pressing Shift while choosing an option from the Font or Style list.

The Character palette menu contains a whole lot of additional style options, which you can see in Figures 16.5 and 16.8. Click these options in the menu to toggle them on and off. A check mark next to the style name means that it's active; clicking it again turns it off.

Many of the style options in the palette menu also are available in the row of buttons near the bottom of the palette. They include the following (in order from left to right on the palette itself and top to bottom in the palette menu):

- Faux Bold and Faux Italic enable you to apply bold and italic effects to the letters when the font designer doesn't include them as a type style. Use these options *only* if the Style pop-up menu doesn't offer bold and italic settings. You get better-looking type by applying the font designer's own bold and italic versions of the characters.

- Choose All Caps and Small Caps to convert the case of the type. Small Caps works only on text that was typed using the Shift key to capitalize the first letter in words, SUCH AS THIS TEXT HERE. The Small Caps effect makes all the letters capital, but the ones typed with the Shift key are taller.

TIP Pressing Ctrl+Shift+K (Win) or ⌘+Shift+K (Mac) toggles selected text from uppercase to lowercase, or to its original case if there was a mixture of cases to begin with (such as text with the first letters capitalized). Remember that this shortcut works only when text is selected. If you're working with the Type tool and haven't selected text, the shortcut affects any new text that you create after the insertion marker; with any other tool, it brings up the Color Settings dialog box.

- Superscript and Subscript shrink the selected characters and move them above or below the text baseline, respectively, as you might want to do when typing mathematical equations or chemical formulas. If Superscript and Subscript don't position characters as you want them, use the Baseline option to control them, as explained in the section "Baseline."

TIP You also can "cheat" and type the tiny character in its own type layer and then use the Move tool to place it right where you need it — just above or just below the text (on another layer) to which it relates.

- Underline Left and Underline Right apply to vertical type only and enable you to add a line to the left or right of the selected characters, respectively. When you work with horizontal type, the option changes to Underline and does just what its name implies. Strikethrough draws a line that slices right through the middle of your letters.

NOTE It's a bit confusing when working with vertical type to have two Underline options available in the menu — left and right — but only one Underline button on the palette itself. Activating the button turns on whichever type of underlining you used last; it's probably safer to ignore the Underline button when using vertical text and just use the palette menu.

TIP   Keep in mind that you can always produce these styles manually by using the Pencil or Brush tool — a choice that enables you to control the thickness, color, and opacity of the line and even play with blend modes. Just click to set a starting point, and then Shift-click to draw a straight line with these tools.

Although version 7 included support for a few OpenType font features, such as Old Style and Ligatures, Photoshop CS greatly expanded its OpenType support — and this support continues in CS3. Longtime favorites of designers and layout artists, OpenType fonts contain information for up to thousands of extra or alternate characters. The OpenType options are available only in the Character and Paragraph palettes' menu, and they appear dimmed unless an OpenType font is selected. Among the options added in recent releases of Photoshop is Ordinals, which lets you automatically create those little letter combinations that are often coupled with ordered numbers, such as 1st, 2nd, 3rd, and so on. Swash gives you those pretty, swooping letters that often extend below the baseline and out under the other letters in the word.

One of the more useful OpenType options is Ligatures. A ligature is a special character that produces a stylized version of a pair of characters, such as *a* and *e*, tying the two characters together with no space between, like so: æ. The rest of the OpenType options are specialized, and you're more likely to use them in a layout program such as Adobe InDesign. As with the Asian fonts, if you're going to be working with them, you probably already know what they do. If you're still curious, check the manual for a description of each option. The expanded OpenType support is an improvement that most Photoshop users won't need, but it gives you some great new options nonetheless.

Size

You can measure type in Photoshop in points, pixels, or millimeters. To make your selection, press Ctrl+K and then Ctrl+6 (⌘+K and then ⌘+6 on the Mac) to open the Units and Rulers panel of the Preferences dialog box. (You must exit the Text mode to do so.) Select the unit you want to use from the Type pop-up menu. Of course, for the traditionalists among us, you can always choose Edit ➪ Preferences ➪ Units and Rulers (or Photoshop ➪ Preferences ➪ Units and Rulers, if you're on the Mac) if you're not good at remembering countless keyboard procedures.

TIP   You can type values in any of the acceptable units of measurement, and Photoshop automatically converts the value to the unit you select in the Preferences dialog box. For example, if you've set the units to pixels but want to type a point value when selecting a size, leave the units setting alone (don't reset the preference, in other words) and type the size plus "pt," and Photoshop changes the size and displays the pixel equivalent of the point size you typed in the Size field.

CROSS-REF   See Chapter 2 for more information about measurement units in Photoshop and how to choose the measurement units that are right for you and your individual projects.

If the resolution of your image is 72 ppi, points and pixels are equal. There are 72 points in an inch, so 72 ppi means only 1 pixel per point. If the resolution is higher, however, a single point may include many pixels. Therefore, you want to select the point option when you want to scale text according to image resolution and select pixels when you want to map text to an exact number of pixels in an image. (If you prefer, you can use millimeters instead of points; 1 millimeter equals

0.039 inch, which means 25.64 mm equals 72 points—not easy to remember, perhaps, but if you're working with other metric measurements in a project, it's good to know.)

Whatever unit of measure you choose, type is measured from the top of its *ascenders*—letters such as *b*, *d*, and *h* that rise above the level of most lowercase characters—to the bottom of its *descenders*—letters such as *g*, *p*, and *q* that dip below the baseline. That's the way it's supposed to work, anyway. But throughout history, designers have played pretty loose and free with type size. To illustrate, Figure 16.9 shows four fonts, including a display font (Tekton) and a script font (Brush Script). Each line is set to a type size of 180 pixels, and then placed between two solid lines exactly 180 pixels apart. The dotted horizontal lines indicate the baselines. As you can see, the only font that comes close to measuring the full 180 pixels is Tekton. The Brush Script sample is relatively minuscule, and neither Times New Roman or Arial comes close to spanning the entire 180-pixel height of the space between the two lines. So if you're looking to fill a specific space, be prepared to experiment; if you have your heart set on a particular font, you may end up applying a much larger font size than you expected in order for the type to take up the desired space in your design.

FIGURE 16.9

These four samples of 180-pixel type set inside 180-pixel boxes are, from top to bottom, Tekton, Times New Roman, Brush Script, and Arial. As you can see, type size is an art, not a science.

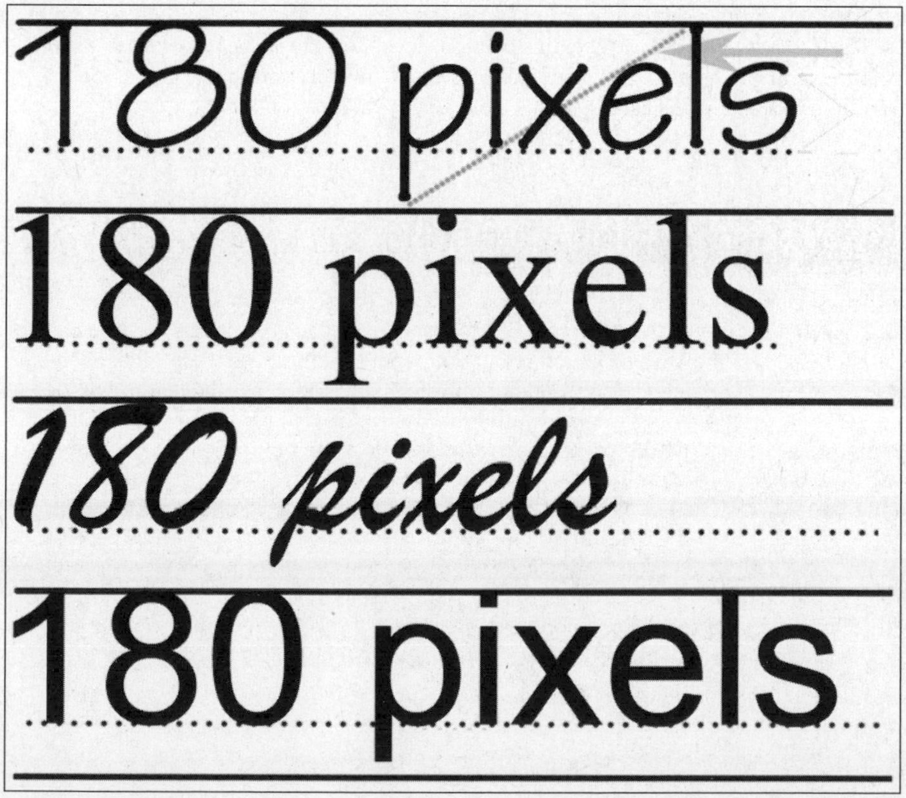

> **TIP** You can change the type size by selecting a size from the Size pop-up menu or double-clicking the Size value, typing a new size, and pressing Enter or Return. But the quickest option is to use the following keyboard shortcuts: To increase the type size in 2-point (or pixel) increments, press Ctrl+Shift+> (⌘+Shift+> on the Mac). To similarly decrease the size, press Ctrl+Shift+< (⌘+Shift+< on the Mac). Add Alt (Option on the Mac) to raise or lower the type size in 10-point (or pixel) increments. If you select millimeters as your unit of measurement, Photoshop raises or lowers the type size by 0.71 mm, which is equivalent to 2 points.

Leading

Also called line spacing, *leading* in Photoshop is the vertical distance between the baseline of one line of type and the baseline of the next line of type, as illustrated in Figure 16.10. Note that in manual typesetting, *leading*, which was named for the placement of strips of lead between lines of type on a printing press, is the distance between the top line's descenders (the tail on the y, for example) an the bottom line's ascenders (the vertical part of the lowercase b, for example). As stated, however, Photoshop simplifies it and separates the lines by their baselines, and you set leading using the Leading pop-up menu in the Character palette, labeled in Figure 16.8. Again, either select one of the menu options or double-click the current value, type a new value, and press Enter or Return. Leading is measured in the unit you select from the Type pop-up menu in the Preferences dialog box.

If you choose the Auto setting, Photoshop automatically applies a leading equal to 120 percent of the type size. The 120 percent value isn't set in stone, however. To change the value, open the Paragraph palette menu and choose Justification to display the Justification dialog box. Type the value you want to use in the Auto Leading option box, and press Enter or Return.

Leading Shortcuts

There are easier ways to adjust leading that allow you to tweak the settings in small increments and make your adjustments "by eye," tweaking until it looks the way you want it to. First, you can select the lines (or characters, in the case of kerning) that you want to adjust, and then click in the Leading field box in the Character palette. Now, use your up-arrow key to increase the leading or the down arrow to decrease it. Keep pressing the key/s until the desired spacing is achieved. Another technique: When adjusting the leading between a pair of lines, select the bottom of the two. Then press Alt+up arrow (Option+up arrow on the Mac) to decrease the leading in 2-point (pixel) increments and move the lines closer together. Press Alt+down arrow (Option+down arrow on the Mac) to increase the leading and spread the lines apart. To work in 10-point (pixel) increments, press Ctrl+Alt+up or down arrow (⌘+Option+up or down arrow on the Mac). Again, if you work in millimeters, the leading value changes by 0.71 mm and 3.53 mm — the equivalent of 2 points and 10 points, respectively. Obviously, the second method is going to be a thrill for those of you who love keyboard shortcuts, and the first one is more low-tech, but just as effective. Choose the one that's right for you.

FIGURE 16.10

Here you can see three examples of 100-pixel type, each with a different leading. The top example is leading of 80, the middle is 100, and the bottom is 120.

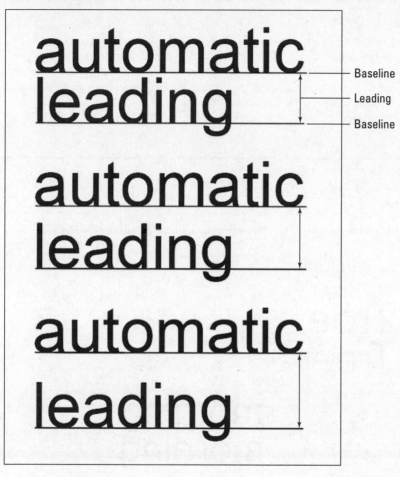

Kerning

Technically, *kern* is the predetermined amount of space that surrounds each character of type and separates it from its immediate neighbors. (Some type-heads also call it *side bearing*.) Therefore, *kerning* became the verb based on that term — to adjust the kern around characters, thus changing the space between them. You establish kerning using the Kerning pop-up menu in the Character palette. Select 0 to use the amount of side bearing indicated by the specifications in the font file on your hard drive.

Some character combinations, however, don't look right when subjected to the default kern. The spacing that separates a *T* and an *h* doesn't look so good when you scrap the *h* and insert an *r*.

Another pair that can look funky in certain fonts is an *r* and an *n*, which may look like an *m*. You may have your own pet pairs that look wrong to you in some or all fonts. You can select Metrics from the Kerning pop-up menu and ask Photoshop to look further into the font specifications and pull out a list of special-needs letter pairs. After it has done that, it applies a prescribed amount of spacing compensation.

Figure 16.11 shows a few ways to fix the awkward spacing that default kerning can create. The first word pair shows the before and after uses the Optical kern to create enough spacing between the *r*'s. The second pair shows the before and after of using Metrics (auto kerning) on the *T* and the *r*. Finally, the third pair shows how to avoid having your *r* and *n* combination from looking like an *m* by using Manual kerning to create a slight separation.

FIGURE 16.11

Examples of some problematic pairs and their adjusted versions

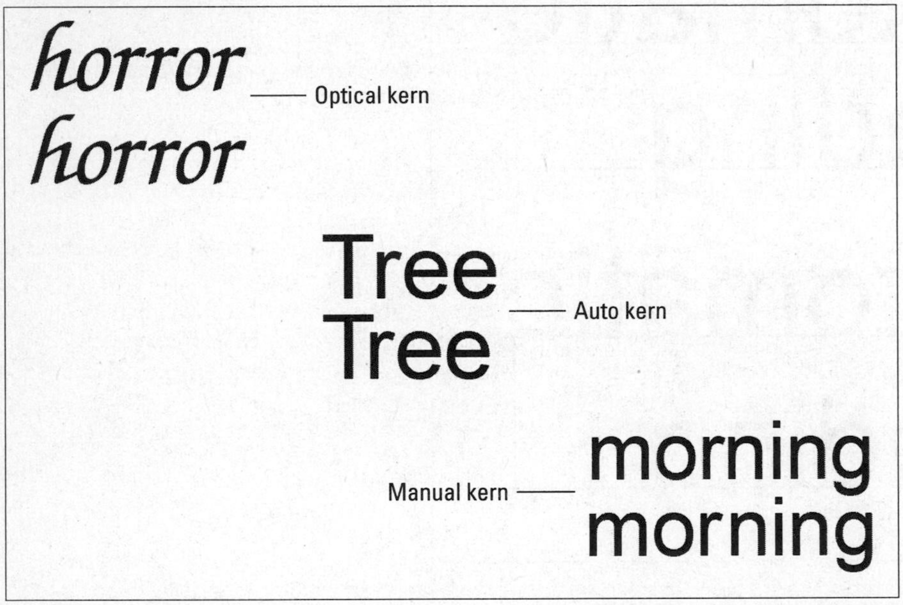

NOTE   In most cases, you'll want to select Metrics or the Optical option (which was new in Photoshop CS), which relies on Photoshop's built-in artificial intelligence to examine the shapes of letters and determine the proper spacing. One advantage of Optical kerning is that it provides professional results with even the most nonprofessional custom fonts.

Still, there may be times when the prescribed kerning isn't really pleasing to the eye — even if it's only to *your* eye. To establish your own kerning, click between two badly spaced characters of type. Then select any value other than 0 from the Kerning pop-up menu. Or double-click the current kerning value, type a value (in whole numbers from −1000 to 1000), and press Enter or

Return. Type a negative value to shift the letters closer together. Type a positive value to kern them farther apart. The last line in Figure 16.11 shows examples of tighter manual kerns.

TIP To decrease the Kerning value (and thereby tighten the spacing) in increments of 20, press Alt+left arrow (Option+left arrow on the Mac). To increase the Kerning value by 20, press Alt+right arrow (Option+right arrow on the Mac). You also can modify the kerning in increments of 100 by pressing Ctrl+Alt+left or right arrow (⌘+Option+left or right arrow on the Mac). You also can just click in the Kerning field and use the up and down arrows on your keyboard to adjust the spacing until you like what you see. Of course, select the pair of improperly kerned characters first, so Photoshop knows which ones you want to adjust.

Incidentally, the Kerning and Tracking values (explained shortly) are measured in $1/1000$ em, where an *em* (or *em space*) is the width of the letter *m* in the current font at the current size. This may sound weird, but it's actually very helpful. Working in ems ensures that your character spacing automatically updates to accommodate changes in font and type size.

Fractional Widths and System Layout

If kerning is too annoying for you, try turning off Fractional Widths, found in the Character palette menu. (Click the option name to toggle the feature on and off.) When type gets very small, the spacing between letters may vary by fractions of a single pixel. Photoshop has to split the difference in favor of one pixel or the other, and 50 percent of the time the visual effect is wrong. It's better, in most cases, to turn the feature off and avoid the problem entirely.

However, turning off Fractional Widths isn't always a complete solution. A better choice when using small type for onscreen display — for example, in a graphic that will be used in a Web page — is to turn on the System Layout option in the Character palette menu. Doing so turns off anti-aliasing — in fact, choosing System Layout when you have an active text layer makes Photoshop automatically perform three tasks, the first of them setting anti-aliasing to None. This anti-aliasing method is the best option for small onscreen type and a particularly good choice when you need to match the type used in onscreen interface elements.

Tracking

The Tracking value, which you set using the pop-up menu to the right of the Kerning pop-up, is almost identical to Kerning. It affects character spacing, as measured in em spaces. The Tracking value even reacts to the same keyboard shortcuts. The only differences are that you can apply Tracking to multiple characters at a time, and Photoshop permits you to apply a Tracking value on top of either automatic (as in Metrics or Optical) or manual kerning. Tracking is usually applied to body text, such as paragraphs, whereas kerning is typically used in single lines of text, such as headlines or character pairs.

Horizontal and vertical scaling

Using the two scaling options, you can scale the width and height of letters individually. A value of 100 percent equals no change to the width and height. Type a value larger than 100 percent, and you make the characters larger. If you type a value lower than 100 percent, the characters shrink.

Photoshop applies horizontal and vertical scaling with respect to the baseline. If you're creating vertical type, the Vertical value affects the width of the column of letters and the Horizontal value changes the height of each character.

You also can distort text after you create it by applying the Edit ➪ Free Transform command to the text layer. If you want to keep the proportions of the letters — not stretching them in any one direction but simply enlarging or reducing them — press and hold Shift as you click and drag from a corner handle. You also can distort the text entirely by stretching it up, down, or totally out of whack with the Ctrl key (⌘ on the Mac) as you click and drag, making the text lean forward or backward. You also can distort the bounding box by skewing the sides, and the characters will reshape as a group to fit the new shape of the bounding box. This applies to point text and paragraph text, both of which are contained in a bounding box while you're in Free Transform mode. Now, if you apply the Free Transform approach to type resizing and then decide that you want the letters back at their original proportions, just open the Character palette and type scaling values of 100 percent to reapply the size last set through the Character palette or Type Options bar.

CROSS-REF   See Chapter 13 for more information on the uses of Free Transform, most of which can be applied to type.

 **TIP**   By converting text to shapes, you can reshape characters with even more flexibility, clicking and dragging points and line segments as you do when reshaping paths and objects created with the shape tools.

Baseline

The Baseline value, which you set using the bottom-left option box in the Character palette (refer to Figure 16.8), raises or lowers selected text with respect to the baseline. In the lingo of the typesetting world, this is called *baseline shift*. Raising type above the baseline results in a superscript. Lowering type results in a subscript.

Typically, when type is raised or lowered relative to the baseline, the shifted type also is shrunken — and both superscript and subscript formatting, when applied through any word processor, automatically includes a size reduction in the process. The baseline shift value in the Character palette doesn't shrink the type for you, though, so if you're trying to create the look of scientific notation, a chemical formula, or a footnote, you'll want to reduce the font size on your own. You can do that with the Size value or by using the Superscript or Subscript style buttons at the foot of the Character palette instead of adjusting the baseline shift. By using these two buttons, you get both a shift and a size reduction — but no control over the amount of either. Examples of both superscript and subscript (with font size reductions also applied) appear in Figure 16.12.

The top example shows the 3 raised with the Superscript Style button on the Character palette. The asterisk was lowered with the Baseline Shift value, which also is in the Character palette. Its size was not changed. In the middle example, the 2s were reduced in size and then the baseline shift was adjusted to −30. Finally the bottom example creates a fraction by reducing the size of both numbers and adjusting their baseline shift. Then the size of the slash was increased so its top lines up with the top of the first number and its bottom lines up with the bottom of the second number.

FIGURE 16.12

Here we have scientific notation and a chemical formula. The last example is a fraction, and both numbers are reduced in size as well as shifted relative to the baseline.

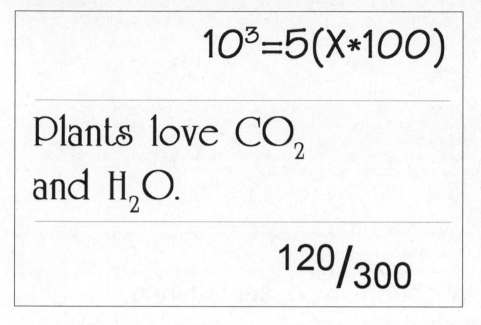

You also can raise type to create a built fraction, as shown in Figure 16.12. Select the number before the slash (the *numerator*), and type a positive value into the Baseline option box. Reduce the type size of the number (the denominator) after the slash, but leave the Baseline value set to 0.

> **TIP** Press Shift+Alt+up arrow (Shift+Option+up arrow on the Mac) to raise the Baseline value by 2 or Shift+Alt+down arrow (Shift+Option+down arrow on the Mac) to lower the value by 2. To change the value in increments of 10, add in the Ctrl key (⌘ key on the Mac).

Color

Click the Color swatch in the Options bar or in the Character palette to display the Color Picker dialog box. You can apply color on a per-character basis. The color you select affects the next character you type and any selected text. Your best results come from setting the color first and then typing, at least in cases where all the type in the type layer will be the same color. By default, when you activate the Type tool, the current Foreground color is used and appears on the Options bar, which may or may not be convenient at the time. If it's not convenient, then use the Color swatch to open the Color Picker and choose another color.

> **TIP** When applying color to selected text, you can't preview the new color accurately because the selection highlight interferes with the display. Press Ctrl+H (⌘+H on the Mac) to toggle the selection highlight (as well as all other onscreen guides) on and off so that you can better judge your color choice.

Anti-aliasing

The Anti-alias pop-up menu, found both in the Character palette and in the Options bar, offers five choices: None, Sharp, Crisp, Strong, and Smooth. Although all of those things are nice (well, except "None"), type can be only one of them at a time, and whichever option you choose, the entire layer gets the effect. You can't apply anti-aliasing to individual characters on a layer, as you can other character formatting options.

In Figure 16.13, you can see several examples of various anti-aliasing settings. Choose None from the pop-up menu, as in the first line, to turn off anti-aliasing (softening, for those of you who've forgotten what anti-aliasing does) and give characters hard, choppy edges, which is good for very small type. Sharp, in the second line, applies a slight amount of anti-aliasing, creating sharp contrast. Crisp is similar to Sharp but a little bit softer, as in the third line. If anti-aliasing seems to rob the text of its weight, you can thicken it up a bit with the Strong setting as in the fourth line. If you notice jagged edges, try applying the Smooth setting as in the last line. Sharp, Crisp, Strong, and Smooth produce more dramatic effects at small type sizes.

FIGURE 16.13

The differences can be subtle and are most obvious on the smaller type. If you're not sure which one you need, try 'em all and see which one looks best on a case-by-case basis.

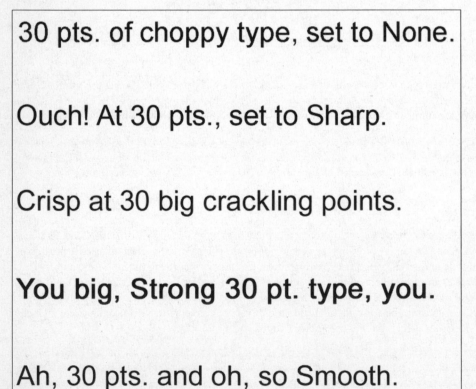

30 pts. of choppy type, set to None.

Ouch! At 30 pts., set to Sharp.

Crisp at 30 big crackling points.

You big, Strong 30 pt. type, you.

Ah, 30 pts. and oh, so Smooth.

Applying Paragraph Formatting

Photoshop offers a comprehensive set of paragraph-formatting options, including ways to set your justification, alignment, hyphenation, line spacing, and indents. With the exception of the alignment, all these controls appear only in the Paragraph palette and affect text that you create inside a bounding box. (See the section "Creating and Manipulating Text in a Frame" for information about this method of adding text.) Point text, not typed into a bounding box, can be aligned, but the other paragraph formatting cannot be applied to it.

Figure 16.14 shows you the lay of the land in the Paragraph palette and also shows the palette menu, which offers additional paragraph formatting choices.

FIGURE 16.14

You can control the flow and position of text created in a bounding box by using the options in the Paragraph palette.

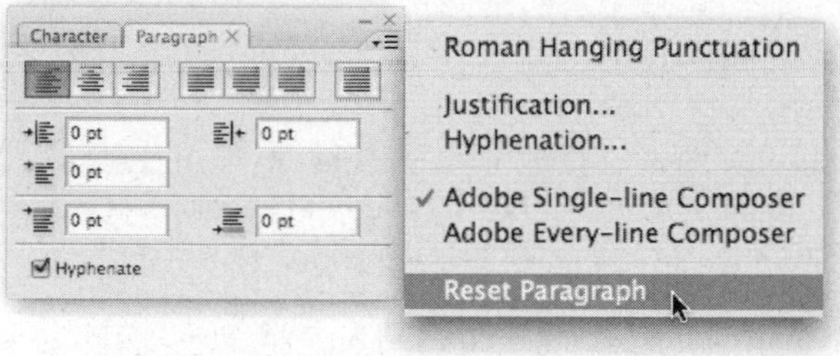

> **NOTE** If your bounding box contains more than one paragraph, you can apply formatting to individual paragraphs. Click with the Type tool inside a paragraph to alter the formatting of that paragraph only, or click and drag through the paragraph to select it, being careful not to select the blank lines above or below it. To format multiple paragraphs, you must click and drag over them. If you want to format all paragraphs in the bounding box, double-click the type layer thumbnail in the Layers palette, which selects every word, space, and blank line in the bounding box. You also can click the type and then press Ctrl+A (Win) or ⌘+A (Mac) to select everything in the box.

> **TIP** When no text is selected, you can restore the palette's default paragraph settings by choosing Reset Paragraph from the Paragraph palette menu.

Alignment

The alignment options, found both in the Paragraph palette and in the Type tool's Options bar, let you control how lines of type align with each other. This is close to what's occurring in a word processor when you use alignment tools there, but in the case of a word processor, you're also aligning relative to the page. As there is no page in Photoshop, the type is aligned to itself. If you're using the Horizontal Type tool, Photoshop lets you left-align, center, or right-align text. The lines on the alignment buttons indicate what each option does, and they change depending on whether

843

you're formatting vertical or horizontal type. If you're using the Vertical Type tool, the lines run up and down, but align to the top (right alignment), bottom (left alignment), or vertical center (center alignment) of the button.

If you create paragraph text (in a bounding box), Photoshop aligns text with respect to the boundaries of the box. For example, if you draw a bounding box with the right alignment option selected, the text cursor appears at the right edge of the box and moves to the left as you type. For vertical type, the right-align and left-align options align text to the bottom and top of the bounding box, respectively. You must choose a different alignment option to relocate the cursor; you can't simply click at another spot in the bounding box.

When you create point text (that is, by simply clicking in the image window instead of drawing a bounding box), the alignment occurs with respect to the first spot you click and affects all lines on the current text layer.

> **TIP** You can change the alignment using standard keyboard tricks. Press Ctrl+Shift+L (⌘+Shift+L on the Mac) to align selected lines to the left. Ctrl+Shift+C (⌘+Shift+C on the Mac) centers text, and Ctrl+Shift+R (⌘+Shift+R on the Mac) aligns it to the right.

Roman Hanging Punctuation

One additional alignment option controls the alignment of punctuation marks. You can choose to have punctuation marks fall outside the bounding box so that the first and last characters in all lines of type are letters or numbers. This setup can create a cleaner looking block of text and approximates the look of full justification in a word processor. Choose Roman Hanging Punctuation from the Paragraph palette menu to toggle the option on and off.

Justification

Speaking of justification, the justification options (second set of three buttons across the top of the Paragraph palette) adjust text so that it stretches from one edge of the bounding box to another. The different options, labeled in Figure 16.15, affect the way Photoshop deals with the last line in a paragraph.

Assuming that you're using the Horizontal Type tool, choose Justify left to align the line to the left edge of the box; Justify right to align to the right edge; and center to align the type exactly between the left and right edges. With Force justify, Photoshop adjusts the spacing of the last line of text so that it, too, fills the entire width of the bounding box. This option typically produces unsightly results, especially with very short lines, because you wind up with huge gaps between words. However, if you want to space a word evenly across an area of your image, you can use Force justify to your advantage. Click and drag the bounding box to match the size of the area you want to cover, type the word, and then choose the Force justify option. If you later change the size of the bounding box, the text shifts accordingly.

FIGURE 16.15

The Justification Options dialog box lets you control how Photoshop adjusts your paragraph text when you use the Justify tools in the Paragraph palette.

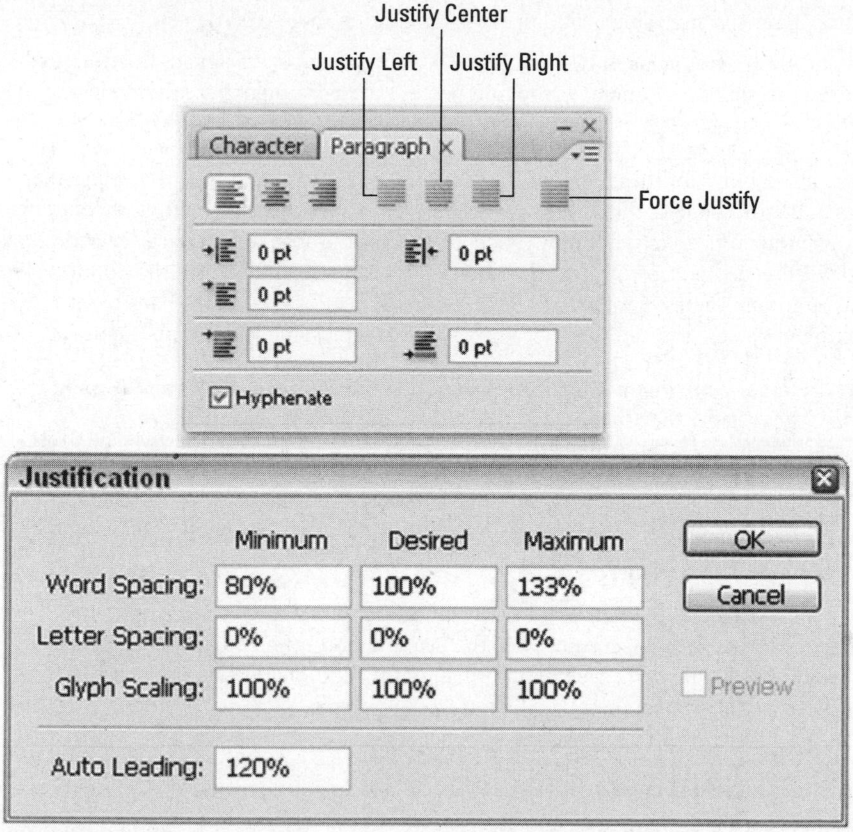

Justify Center

Justify Left   Justify Right

Force Justify

Photoshop lets you apply a couple of the justification options from the keyboard: Press Ctrl+Shift+J (⌘+Shift+J on the Mac) to left-align the last line; press Ctrl+Shift+F (⌘+Shift+F on the Mac) to Force justify the last line.

You can further control how Photoshop justifies text by using the spacing options in the Justification dialog box, also shown in Figure 16.15. To open the dialog box, choose Justification from the Paragraph palette menu. You can adjust the amount of space allowed between words and characters, and you can specify whether you want to alter the width (scaling) of *glyphs* — a fancy word meaning the individual characters in a font. Here's what you need to know:

- The values reflect a percentage of default spacing. The default word spacing is 100 percent, which gives you a normal space character between words. You can increase word spacing to 1000 percent of the norm or reduce it to 0 percent.

- The default letter spacing is 0 percent, which means no space between characters. The maximum letter spacing value is 500 percent; the minimum is −100 percent.

- For glyphs, the default value is 100 percent, which leaves the characters at their original width. You can stretch the characters to 200 percent of their original width or squeeze them to 50 percent.

To establish your ideal settings for these options, use the Desired column and type the values there. Whenever possible, Photoshop uses these values — when it can't accommodate you, it refers to the Minimum and Maximum options to tell it how much it can alter the spacing or character width when justifying text. If you wind up with text that looks like sardines jammed into the bounding box, increase the Minimum values. Similarly, if the text looks spacey and becomes hard to read, decrease the Maximum values. You can type negative values to set a value lower than 0 percent.

NOTE   You can't type a Minimum value that's larger than the Desired value or a Maximum value that's smaller than the Desired value; nor can you type a Desired value that's larger than Maximum or smaller than Minimum.

TIP   If you want a specific character width used consistently throughout your text, use the Horizontal scale option in the Character palette rather than the Glyph spacing option. You can apply Horizontal scaling to regular text as well as paragraph text.

As for the Auto Leading option at the bottom of the Justification dialog box, it determines the amount of leading used when you select Auto from the Leading pop-up menu in the Character palette. As luck would have it, if you're seeking information on additional paragraph spacing controls, the next sections pertain to just that.

Indents and paragraph spacing

The five option boxes in the Paragraph palette control the amount of space between individual paragraphs in the same bounding box (like the space before and space after settings control paragraph spacing in a word processor) and between the text and the edges of the bounding box (like adjusting margins, if you think of the bounding box as though it's a tiny page). Photoshop's indent options work the same as their counterparts in just about any word processing or graphics program that supports the use of type, so there shouldn't be any surprises there either. Here are the details:

- Type values in the top two option boxes to indent the entire paragraph from the left edge or right edge of the box.

- To indent only the first line of the paragraph, type a value into the first-line indent option box, the second of three boxes on the right. Type a positive value to shove the first line to the right; Type a negative value to push it to the left, so that it extends beyond the left edge of the other lines in the paragraph, which creates a hanging indent.

- Use the bottom option boxes to increase the space before a paragraph (left box) and after a paragraph (right box).

NOTE In all cases, you must press Enter or Return to apply the change. To set the unit of measurement for these options, use the Type pop-up menu in the Units & Rulers panel of the Preferences dialog box; you can choose from pixels, points, and millimeters. As is the case with options in the Character palette, however, you can type the value using a unit of measurement other than that which is currently the preferred unit by typing the value followed by the desired unit's abbreviation ("in" for inches, for example, while pixels, points, or millimeters is the current unit). When you press Enter or Return, Photoshop converts the value to the unit you selected in the Preferences dialog box. (See Chapter 2 to find out more about setting preferences for units.)

Hyphenation

In most cases, you probably won't be typing text that requires hyphenation in an image. If you need to type that much text, you're better off doing it in your page-layout program (such as PageMaker, InDesign, or QuarkXPress), and then importing the image into that layout.

Even knowing that most images won't or shouldn't contain so much text that hyphenation is needed, Photoshop still offers the Hyphenate option in the Paragraph palette. When you select this option, the program automatically hyphenates your text using the limits set in the Hyphenation dialog box, shown in Figure 16.16. Choose Hyphenation from the Paragraph palette menu to display the dialog box and make any changes. If you move the dialog box so that you can see your text, the Preview option (on by default) can help you adjust the settings so that they meet the needs of your text and you won't have to close and reopen the dialog box in order to find the right settings.

FIGURE 16.16

If you want to hyphenate text in a bounding box, set the hyphenation controls here.

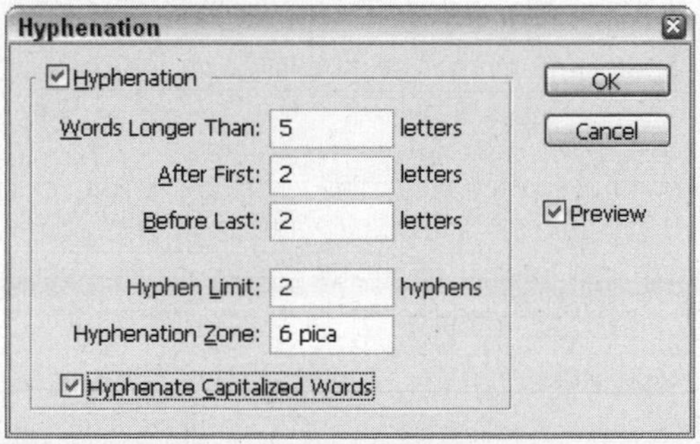

Hyphenation			☒
☑ Hyphenation			
Words Longer Than:	5	letters	OK
After First:	2	letters	Cancel
Before Last:	2	letters	☑ Preview
Hyphen Limit:	2	hyphens	
Hyphenation Zone:	6 pica		
☑ Hyphenate Capitalized Words			

This dialog box controls work as follows:

■ Type a value in the Words Longer Than option box to specify the number of characters required before Photoshop can hyphenate a word.

■ Use the After First and Before Last options to control the minimum number of characters before a hyphen and after a hyphen, respectively.

- Type a number in the Hyphen Limit option box to tell Photoshop how many consecutive lines can contain hyphens.

- Finally, specify how far from the edge of the bounding box Photoshop can place a hyphen by typing a value in the Hyphenation Zone box.

- Deselect the Hyphenate Capitalized Words option if you want Photoshop to keep its mitts off words that start with an uppercase letter.

Line breaks and composition methods

When you create paragraph text that includes several lines, you may not like the way Photoshop breaks text from line to line. Maybe you feel it's jumping the gun when it gets close to the right edge of the bounding box, or maybe you wish it were more conservative and didn't cram things so close to the sides of the box. Whatever your complaint is, you may be able to get some resolution by changing the equation that Photoshop uses to determine where lines break.

If you choose Adobe Every-line Composer from the Paragraph palette (available only if you have an active type layer with text in a bounding box), the program evaluates the lines of text in the active bounding box as a group and figures out the best place to break lines. In doing so, Photoshop takes into account the Hyphenation and Justification settings that are in place at the time. Typically, this option results in more evenly spaced text and fewer hyphens. That's a good thing most of the time: If bounding boxes are small and you use lots of long words, such as medical or legal terminology, your right edge (if your type is left-aligned) can end up with so many hyphens that it looks fringed.

Adobe Single-line Composer takes a line-by-line approach to your text, using a few basic rules to determine the best spot to break a line. The program first attempts to fit all words on the line by adjusting word spacing, opting for reduced spacing over expanded spacing where possible. If the spacing adjustments don't work for the given type, Photoshop hyphenates the last word on the line and breaks the line after the hyphen.

Remember, these options may not be an issue very often because most people don't create long blocks of text in Photoshop. If you want to control line breaks for a few lines of text, you can just create your text using the regular, point text method instead of putting the text in a bounding box. Then you can just press Enter or Return at the spot where you want the line to break, adding a hyphen to the end of the line if needed.

Checking your spelling

Found in the Edit menu, the Check Spelling command compares the words in your document with the words in Photoshop's built-in dictionary. If you've typed a word not found in the dictionary, Photoshop brings this to your attention by displaying the Check Spelling dialog box, shown in Figure 16.17.

FIGURE 16.17

The Check Spelling dialog box offers helpful suggestions for replacing words it doesn't recognize. Here you can see that it doesn't recognize itself. Hmmmm....

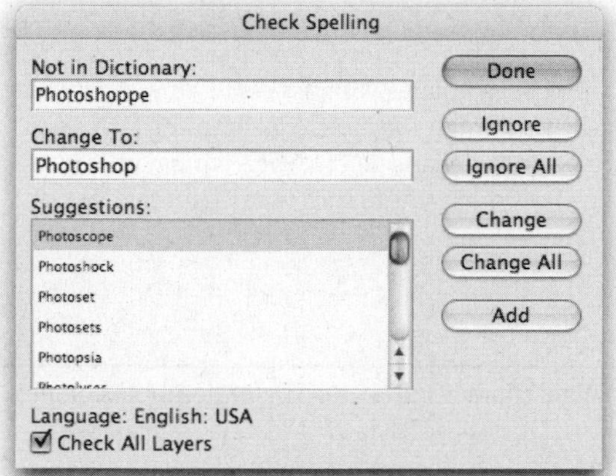

The unrecognized word appears in the Not in Dictionary option box, and Photoshop offers you its favorite replacement word in the Change To option box. Other choices can be found in the Suggestions list. If you have made an error but none of Photoshop's suggested words is correct, you can type the correct word in the Change To option box. After you have the appropriate replacement word in the Change To option box, click Change. If you've made the same mistake throughout the rest of the text, click Change All. If the highlighted word is correct but simply isn't in Photoshop's vocabulary, you can click Ignore to tell it to ignore the word, or click Ignore All to tell it to ignore that and all other instances of the word. If you will be using the word often in the future, click Add to add the word to the dictionary — be sure it's spelled correctly, though, before doing so. After you finish making corrections, click Done to exit the dialog box.

If you're in text-editing mode — defined as when there's an insertion marker blinking away in your text — Photoshop performs the spell-check only on the currently active layer and only on the text that follows the placement of the insertion marker. In other words, if you want to check the entire text layer, make sure the insertion marker is at the beginning of the text block. Better yet, you can check spelling on all text layers at once. Just make sure that no active insertion marker appears in any text layer when you choose Edit ➪ Check Spelling, and make sure the Check All Layers option is selected in the Check Spelling dialog box.

NOTE You can specify the dictionary used by the Check Spelling command by choosing Window ➪ Character and selecting a language from the pop-up menu in the bottom-left corner of the Character palette. The language you choose also is used to determine proper hyphenation when words need to be broken over two lines.

Finding and Replacing Text

In the unlikely event that you find yourself entering tons and tons of text into an image in Photoshop, you can choose Edit ⇨ Find and Replace Text to display the dialog box shown in Figure 16.18. As you may have guessed, this dialog box lets you search for specific words in your text and replace them with other text. In reality, you don't have to have a ton of text for this to be useful — even in an image with just a few type layers, it can be easy to miss something like a name, date, or even a symbol. Using Find and Replace can be a handy way to check for things you tend to do, such as pressing the percent (%) sign instead of the dollar sign ($) when typing, or forgetting to capitalize certain names or words. You can click Find Next to skip to the next instance of the content you are looking for.

FIGURE 16.18

Find one or all instances of a particular word, phrase, or single character and insert more desirable content.

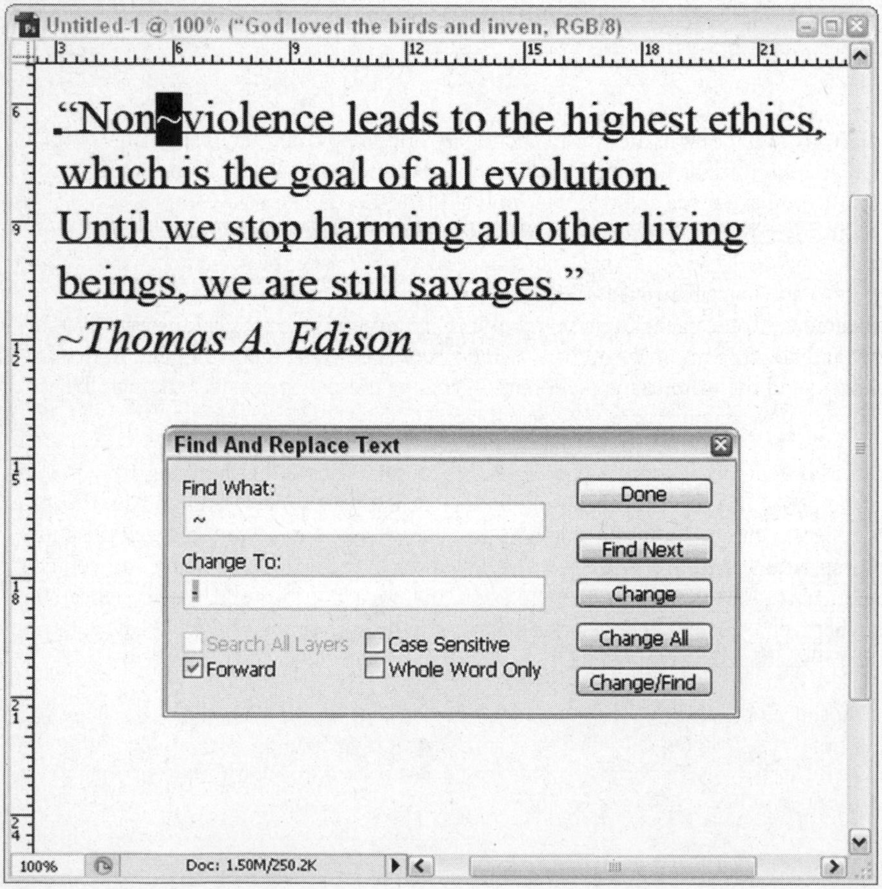

If you've ever used a similar command in a word-processing program, there are no big surprises here. Type the word, phrase, or symbol you're looking for in the Find What option box. If you want to replace that word with another, type the new word in the Change To option box. Click Find Next to locate the next instance of your word relative to the placement of the insertion marker; click Change to replace the word; click Change All to replace all instances of the word; and click Change/Find to replace the current instance and highlight the next. The remaining options are common in Find/Replace commands found in word processors. The one quirky thing about Photoshop's version of the command is that if you start your search in the middle of a text block, Photoshop doesn't wrap around when it reaches the end of the text and start looking at the beginning. That's the main use for the Forward option; leave it selected and Photoshop searches forward from the text insertion marker; deselect it and Photoshop looks backward.

Fitting Type on a Path

Photoshop CS introduced the ability to place text on a path, and this long-overdue feature remains in CS3; who'd have had the nerve to remove such an essential feature? Even if you're not sure why this was considered long overdue or why tears would be shed if it were removed from Photoshop, this one little addition opens up a boatload of possibilities for the creation and placement of Photoshop text. Imagine not being able to draw text both around and inside paths you create with the shape tools. Imagine if all you had was the very limited Warp Text tool that gives you the ability to type text in an arc or along a wave. Yawn. In Photoshop CS3, not only can you place text along a path, you can even place two different pieces of text on the same side of the same path and keep them entirely independent of each other. Try *that* with the Warp Text option.

Perhaps the most impressive thing about Photoshop's new text-on-a-path capability is how easy it is to use. Instead of adding a new tool for creating path text or for creating the text path itself, Photoshop lets you use the regular Type tool to create path text, and you can drop text of any font, size, or formatting onto any path in your image.

Creating text on a path

To begin, you need to tell Photoshop which path it is you want the type to follow. The type doesn't exist at this time, but that comes later. To tell Photoshop where the path is, draw one by pressing P to select the Pen tool and click to set a few points to form an open path in your image. If you create a path with a few smooth curves using the Bézier handles discussed in Chapter 8, you'll provide a better line for the type. You can add text to any path you draw, but hard edges (corners, spikes, very sharp curves) cause harsh character jumps, and they're usually quite undesirable.

Now, you can add the type, by pressing T to select the Type tool and then position your cursor over the path you just drew. You'll notice that your cursor changes from the normal I-beam to one with a little diagonal line crossing through the bottom of it — a subtle change, but a change nonetheless. When you see it, click once to make the path active, and then type; it's that easy.

After the text is typed, you can work with it as you would any other type. You can format your text to any font, size, type style, and so on that you like. From here on, any formatting changes work just as they do when you're working with regular text, as shown in Figure 16.19. You can change the font, adjust the size of characters, increase the tracking to spread them out over the course of the path, and even alter the baseline for a specific character or word. Manual kerning comes in handy here, because Photoshop's Optical and Metrics options may not be able to accommodate the fine-tuning you require along certain paths and with certain words and fonts.

NOTE   When you create text on a path, the letters orient themselves according to the direction in which the path was originally drawn. For example, if you draw a path from left to right and then add text to it, the text appears as it normally does. But if you draw the path from right to left, no matter where on the path you click with the Type tool, the text appears upside-down and headed in the "wrong" direction — which you may find useful if you want the type to literally follow the underside of a path.

TIP   Very fancy fonts may not be legible when placed on an intricate path. You'll see the problem right away if you inadvertently create it by choosing an ornate font and placing it on a very curvy path, but it's a good idea to keep this in mind before you go to the trouble of selecting a font. If you see that your text is hard to read in the font you've chosen, try another one, using the Type Options bar or the Character palette.

Press A to select the Arrow tool. Position the cursor over a path with text on it until your pointer changes to an I-beam cursor with a black arrow protruding from one side. This protruding arrow tells you that you can now use the tool to slide the text along on the path. If you accidentally typed your text upside-down, drag the text all the way to the end of the path and continue dragging to pull the text back up to the correct side. You also can use the Arrow tool to move the path around your image. To do so, move the cursor away from the path until you again see the standard Arrow tool cursor. Then click and drag to reposition the text and path in unison.

TIP   The point at which you originally click on a path with the Type tool is designated as the start point of your text. By default, an endpoint is set at the far end of your line. You can click and drag this point with the Arrow tool back toward the start point to remove letters from the end of your text. Any letters that fall beyond your end point will get clipped and disappear.

By now, you're probably sitting on the edge of your chair, one hand clasped over your mouth, which fell open as you read about dragging your text along a path. Well, close your mouth and use that hand to keep turning pages — in the following section, you learn to add text inside a closed path, and you wouldn't want to miss that, would you? Quoth the raven, "No way, man!"

FIGURE 16.19

This literary quote takes a new turn as it follows the path of its subject. A slight drop shadow has been added to the text, and some spacing along the text's path was required for legibility. The font is Black Adder.

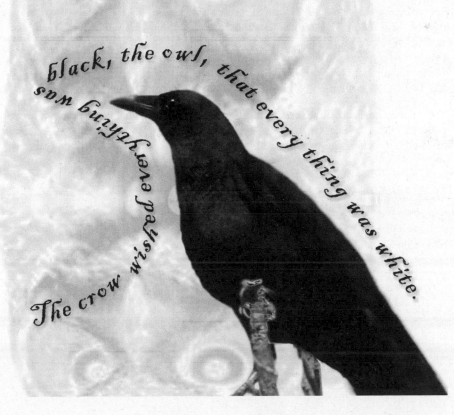

Adding text inside a path

The process of adding text inside of, rather than along, a path is quite simple — and very much like the one we just discussed in the preceding section. Here, though, the examples involve using a shape-based path and not a path drawn with the Pen tool.

You want to start with the Paths button selected in the Shape tool's Options bar and then draw a shape. Press U (or Shift+U) to select the desired shape tool, and click the Paths button in the Options bar. Click and drag to draw a shape in the image. You can play it safe your first time out and draw a circle or a square, but you also can try something more interesting, such as the shape you see in Figure 16.20. When choosing a path, remember that sharp or tight corners can be difficult for the type to follow without losing legibility. If you're emotionally tied to a very complex shape, be prepared to use the Pen tool's variants to add and remove anchor points along the path, smoothing out any undesirable twists and turns. Don't remember how to do that? Go back to Chapter 8. No, really. We'll wait.

After your shape path is drawn, select the Type tool and position your cursor at the center of the shape. As you hover, the cursor should look like an I-beam with parentheses around it — again, a slight variation on the standard Type cursor, just to let you know something different is going on. Click once and begin to type your text. As you type, notice that the text appears inside the shape, like the text inside the arrowhead shape in Figure 16.20. The shape essentially functions as a bounding box for the text, thus molding the text to its shape. When you finish typing text, click the OK button in the Options bar or click another tool in the Toolbox.

TIP To use the same path and have text to run along it, choose Window ⇨ Paths to bring up the Paths palette. You should see the path you created with the shape tool, as well as an identical path that Photoshop created when you typed the text. This is just Photoshop's way of keeping track of how text has been typed on a path. Next, click the top Work Path item, and then click somewhere else in the shape with the Type tool, or Shift-click if necessary to force Photoshop to create a new text layer. Then type some new text.

NOTE Just because you've fit type to a path doesn't mean that the shape of the path is set in stone. On the contrary, you can reshape a path freely with the Convert Point tool; any text fitted to the path bends and moves according to your edits.

FIGURE 16.20

You can place text inside a shape to confine it to a thematically appropriate space. Here a right-pointing arrowhead shape was used to confine the type to a shape that conveys the concept of movement.

"Be
like the bird
that, pausing in
her flight awhile on
boughs too slight, feels them
give way beneath her, and yet
sings, knowing that she
hath wings."
~Victor Hugo,
1802-1885

Warping Text

Prior to the addition of Photoshop's tools for fitting text to a path, the Warp Text feature was the only way to make editable text bend in a circle, an arc, or a wave. With the Warp Text tool, you also can control the nature of the warp, adjusting its horizontal and vertical distortion. You can choose from 15 different warp shapes and choose to curve type, distort it, or both.

TIP You can warp paragraph text or regular text, but the warp affects all existing text on the layer, making it a little difficult to use on paragraph text and sometimes tricky to use on a long string of point text. If you want to reshape just a part of a line of text — for example, to make the last few letters in a word bend upward — put that bit of text on its own layer and position the two layers so that the text looks continuous.

NOTE You can't warp type to which you've applied the faux bold style (applied through the Character palette), nor can you warp bitmap fonts or fonts for which the designer hasn't provided the paths, or outlines, that make up the font characters.

To warp text, select the text layer, click the text warp button in the Options bar, labeled in Figure 16.21, or choose Layer ➪ Type ➪ Warp Text. Photoshop displays the Warp Text dialog box, shown in the figure.

After choosing a warp style from the Style pop-up menu, set the orientation of the warp by selecting the Horizontal or Vertical radio button. Then adjust the Bend, Horizontal Distortion, and Vertical Distortion sliders until you get an effect that fits your needs. You can preview your changes in the image window.

NOTE You can warp text that you create on a path, but you basically lose all ability to perform any more path-related adjustments with the text.

Some tips for making effective use of the Warp tool:

- When you select the Horizontal radio button, the warp occurs as the shape in the Style pop-up menu suggests. If you choose Vertical, the warp is applied as if you turned the shape on its side.

- Use the Bend value to change the direction of the curve. A positive Bend value curves the text upward, and a negative value curves the text downward.

- You can use the Horizontal and Vertical Distortion options to create perspective effects. Horizontal Distortion puts the origin point of the perspective to the left if you type a positive value and to the right if you type a negative value.

- Vertical Distortion places the origin point above the text if you type a positive value and below the text if you type a negative value.

- If you edit warped text, Photoshop reapplies the warp to the layer after you finish editing the text.

FIGURE 16.21

Use the controls in the Warp Text dialog box to bend, stretch, and curve type.

warped

Warp Text

Style: 〰 Flag ▼

OK

Reset

⦿ Horizontal ○ Vertical

Bend: +50 %

Horizontal Distortion: 0 %

Vertical Distortion: 0 %

really warped

way warped

TIP   The effects of a warp can be enhanced by tweaking the tracking, kerning, and other character-spacing and scaling formatting. If you have trouble achieving the distortion or perspective effect you're after, try choosing Edit ⇨ Free Transform to manipulate the text layer. Remember that you must get out of text-editing mode to access the Free Transform command.

Editing Text as Shapes

As stated earlier in this chapter, you can convert each letter in a text layer to individual shapes by choosing Layer ⇨ Type ⇨ Convert to Shape. The command converts all text on a layer, so if you want to turn only some of your text to shapes, put that text on its own layer and leave the text that must remain editable on its own layer, too. If the Convert to Shape command is dimmed, that means you're in text-editing mode; to leave that mode and make the command accessible, click the OK (check mark) or Cancel ("no" symbol) button in the Options bar to exit the editing mode.

After you make the conversion to a shape, each character works just like a shape that you create with the shape tools. Photoshop creates points and line segments as it sees fit for each letter, as shown in Figure 16.22. This enables you to fool with the shape of each letter by clicking and dragging points and segments, as you can see in Figure 16.22. You also can apply all the same effects to your new text shapes as you can to any shape.

CROSS-REF   See Chapter 15 for a complete list of your options.

CAUTION   Before you convert text to shapes, make sure that you don't need to make further changes to character or paragraph formatting or do any editing. Photoshop sees your text purely as shapes after the conversion, so you can't edit the text using the Type tool anymore. For safety's sake, you should save the text to a new layer or image before choosing Convert to Shape; you can hide the backup layer and only use it if you find that your converted text needs editing.

TIP   Like regular shapes, type shapes appear jagged around the edges because of the tiny outline that Photoshop displays around the shape. To hide the outline and smooth the onscreen appearance of the text, press Ctrl+H (⌘+H on the Mac). Of course, this command also hides the marching ants, guides, and other onscreen aids. The View ⇨ Show ⇨ Target Path command enables you to toggle just the shape outlines.

FIGURE 16.22

Sure, you can make editable text look cool, but can you reshape the individual letters? Not without converting them to shapes first. Here, text has been converted to shapes, the shapes have been pushed, pulled, and stretched like mad, and some interesting background elements have been added to pull the image together.

Summary

After a short retrospective on the use of text in Photoshop, this chapter showed you how to insert text, to edit existing text, and several ways to use text artistically — including the creation of vector type, text-based selection outlines, and rasterized text. You learned how to create paragraph text in a bounding box, and to build vertical text, as well as how to use the Character and Paragraph palettes to customize the appearance of your individual type characters and the flow of your text within its own layer.

To make sure text is not only beautiful but also correct, you learned to use the Check Spelling, and Find and Replace commands, and finally, to take your type to a whole new level, you learned to fit your text to a path and to warp your text using a variety of preset shapes.

Part V

Color and Output

Chapter 17

Essential Color Management

Most artists react very warmly to the word "color" and a bit more coolly to the word "management." One's reaction is normally a matter of temperament, and you may be able to empathize. Put the two words together, though, and you can clear a room in seconds. The term *color management* has been known to simultaneously frighten and bore the most steadfast of graphic artists, photographers, and computer users.

It's no exaggeration to say that color management is the least understood topic in all of computer imaging. Most people, if they think about it at all, expect to calibrate their monitors and achieve reliable if not perfect color. But in point of fact, there's no such thing as perfect color. So-called *device-dependent color* — synthetic color produced by a piece of hardware — is a moving target. The best that Photoshop or any other piece of software can do is to convert from one target to the next.

For what it's worth, most consumer monitors (and video boards, for that matter) are beyond calibration, in the strict sense of the word. You can try using a hardware calibrator (one of those devices where you plop a little suction cup onto your screen), but calibrators often have less to do with changing screen colors than identifying them. Even if your monitor permits prepress-quality calibration — as in the case of $3,000-plus devices sold by different vendors over the years, including Radius, Mitsubishi, and LaCic — it's not enough to simply correct the colors onscreen; you also have to tell Photoshop what you've done.

Therefore, color management is first and foremost about identifying your monitor. You have to explain your screen's weaknesses to Photoshop so it can make every attempt to accommodate them. In days gone by, Photoshop used the screen data to calculate CMYK conversions and that was it. These days,

Photoshop embeds a *profile* that identifies the source of the image and uses this information to translate colors from one monitor to another. Photoshop also permits you to work in multiple profile-specific color spaces at the same time, which is great for artists who alternatively create images for print and for the Web. Photoshop also permits you to specify exactly what to do with images that lack profiles.

The Color Settings command is that interesting combination of wonderful and bewildering. It can just as easily mess up colors as fix them, but if you read this chapter, you and your colors should be able to ride the currents safely from one digital destination to the next. And best of all, color management in Photoshop is consistent with color management in recent versions of Illustrator and other Adobe applications, so you can learn one, and then the others make much more sense.

A Typical Color-Matching Scenario

For Windows users, Photoshop CS3 devotes three features to color management; Mac users have only two. Formerly a standard component of Photoshop on both platforms (prior to version CS), the Adobe Gamma control panel, which characterizes your monitor, is now a Windows-only utility accessible in the Control Panel. Mac users can use the built-in Display Calibrator Assistant, available from the Color section of the Displays system preferences.

The second color management feature, common to both platforms, is the Color Settings command, found under the Edit menu for Windows users and under the Photoshop menu on the Mac. Choose the command or press Ctrl+Shift+K (⌘+Shift+K on the Mac) to display the Color Settings dialog box, which lets you edit device-dependent color spaces and decide what to do with profile mismatches. Finally, choose File ⇨ Save As and use the resulting Save As dialog box to decide whether to embed a profile into a saved image or include no profile at all.

Now, we could just explain each of these color-management features — each on its own — and hope you can put it all together, but that might prevent you from seeing the bigger picture and understanding the concepts as a whole. Therefore, we begin our tour of color management by showing the various control panels, commands, and options in action. In this introductory scenario, an RGB image has been created on the Mac and opened on a Windows system. The Mac is equipped with a high-end monitor, and the PC is hooked up to relatively low-end monitor, so we're covering two extremes and allowing for the many users whose monitors fall somewhere in between.

Despite the change of platforms and the even more dramatic change in monitors, Photoshop maintains a high degree of consistency, so the image looks the same at both ends of the spectrum. The specifics of setting up your system obviously will vary, but this tour should give you an idea of how color management in Photoshop works.

Setting up the source monitor

If you own a monitor with calibration capabilities, start by calibrating it. You can use OS 10.X's built-in Display Calibrator Assistant. You can access this feature by clicking the Calibrate button in the Color panel of the Displays system preferences, as shown in Figure 17.1. The Display Calibrator Assistant utilizes ColorSync, which is Apple's system-wide color management system.

FIGURE 17.1

On the Mac, clicking the Calibrate button on the Color panel of the Displays system preferences launches the Display Calibrator Assistant.

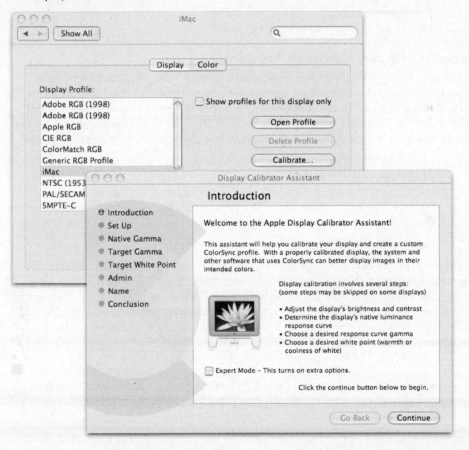

Gimme Some Gamma

The term *gamma* refers to the amount of correction required to convert the color signal generated in the monitor (let's call it *x*) to the color display that you see onscreen (*y*). Imagine a simple graph with the input signal *x* along the bottom and the output *y* along the side. A gamma of 1.0 would result in a diagonal line from the lower-left to the upper-right corner. A higher gamma value tugs at the center of that line and curves it upward. As you tug, more and more of the curve is taken up by darker values, resulting in a darker display. So a typical Mac screen with a default gamma of 1.8 is lighter than a typical PC screen with a default gamma of 2.2. For a real-time display of gamma in action, see Chapter 18 for a discussion of the Curves dialog box.

The Macintosh Display Calibrator Assistant

If you feel particularly confident (and even if you don't), go ahead and select the Expert Mode option. That gives you access to a few more options, but you also may find that you can't access every option in the Display Calibrator Assistant (or for that matter of the Adobe Gamma control panel on the PC). Some monitors, particularly LCDs, don't allow for every adjustment. Again, your situation may vary from the one depicted and described here, but the overall concept is the same.

The Adobe Gamma control panel

For the Windows/PC users, Photoshop ships with the Adobe Gamma control panel. Under Windows XP and Vista, the Control Panel is available immediately under the Start menu. After the Control Panel window appears, double-click the Adobe Gamma icon. (Make sure you're viewing all Control Panel options.)

If you don't see the Adobe Gamma icon in the Control Panel window, select the Appearance and Themes option, and then double-click the Adobe Gamma icon. (If the Control Panel displays a warning that your video card doesn't support systemwide color management, don't lose any sleep over it — many video cards don't.) Select the Step By Step (Wizard) option and click Next to walk through the setup process one step at a time. If you don't want to take it step by step, you can choose the Control Panel option and use the dialog box shown in Figure 17.2. If that dialog box scares you, click the Wizard button to go back to the step-by-step process.

If you do choose to use the Adobe Gamma Wizard, all you have to do is answer questions and click Next to advance from one screen to another. For example, after adjusting the contrast and brightness settings, Gamma asks you to specify the nature of your screen's red, green, and blue phosphors. If you own a Trinitron or Diamondtron monitor — which you'll know because you paid more for it — select the Trinitron settings. Or select Custom, and type values according to your monitor's documentation. If the documentation does not suggest settings, ignore this screen and click Next to move on. This isn't a big problem, so don't worry if you don't know or can't find all of your monitor's specs and suggested settings.

This Control Panel Adobe Gamma dialog box lets you set the Brightness and Contrast, Phosphors, Gamma, and White Point for your monitor.

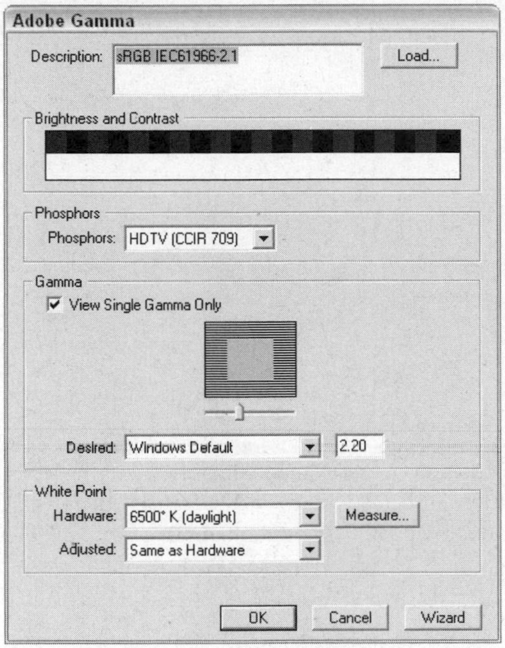

As with the Native Gamma section of the Mac Display Calibrator Assistant, the next screen, pictured in Figure 17.3, is the most important. It asks you to balance the red, green, and blue display functions of your monitor. But to do so, you need to deselect the View Single Gamma Only option; this presents you with separate controls over each of the three monitor channels. Then use the sliders to make the inner squares match the outer borders. You are in essence calibrating the monitor according to your unique perceptions of it, making this particular brand of characterization a highly personal one.

The next screen asks you to set the white point, which defines the general colorcast of your screen from 5,000 degrees Kelvin for slightly red to 9,300 degrees for slightly blue. A medium value of 6,500 degrees is a happy "daylight" medium. To find the best setting for your monitor, click Measure. Then click the gray box that appears the most neutral—neither too warm nor too cool—until you get dumped back into the Gamma Wizard. Click Next.

After you click Finish, the Gamma utility asks you to name your new monitor profile and save it to disk. Name it whatever you want, but don't change the location because the profile has to stay in the default location to be made available to Photoshop and other applications.

FIGURE 17.3

Deselect the View Single Gamma Only option to modify each of the three color channels independently.

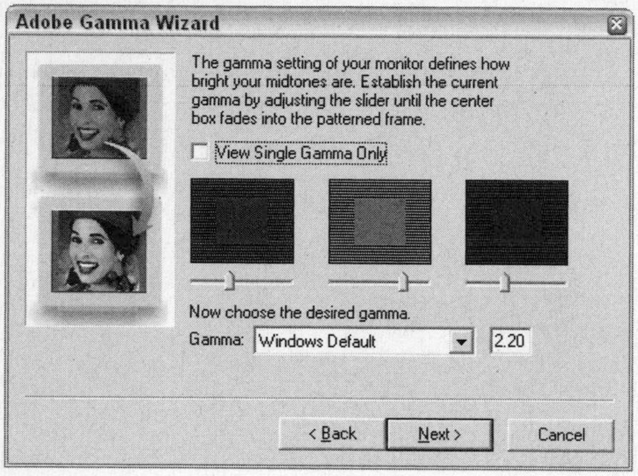

Adobe Gamma generates a custom monitor profile and automatically alerts Photoshop to the change. Your screen may not look any different than it did before you opened Gamma, but you can rest assured that Photoshop is now officially aware of its capabilities and limitations.

Selecting the ideal working space

Now that you've identified your monitor, it's time to select an RGB *working environment*, which is a color space other than the one identified for the monitor. This is the strangest step, but it's one of the most important as well. Fortunately, all it requires is a bit of imagination to understand fully.

On the Mac, switch to Photoshop and choose Photoshop ➪ Color Settings (Windows users choose Edit ➪ Color Settings). Photoshop displays the dialog box shown in Figure 17.4. You're immediately faced with a dizzying array of options — think of it like being shoved off the diving board when being taught to swim — but Photoshop does make a small attempt to simplify the process. The program offers several collections of predefined settings under the Settings pop-up menu. Among the settings are Color Management Off, which deactivates Photoshop's color management entirely; ColorSync Workflow, which is useful in all-Macintosh environments; and Emulate Photoshop 4, which both turns color management off and mimics version 4's screen display. With the release of Photoshop CS (and maintained in CS3), there are a few new settings, but mostly these let you assign a working space that's standard for Adobe products in Europe, Japan, and North America.

Each of these options has its relative advantages in certain settings, but most people gravitate toward two other options. If you create most of your images for the Web, select the Web Graphics Defaults option. This directs Photoshop's color functions so that they're most amenable to screen display. On the other hand, if most of your artwork finds its way into print, and if you live in the United States or a country that supports U.S. printing standards, select North America Prepress 2.

If you develop images for both print and Web use and aren't sure if you should commit to settings for one over the other, select North America Prepress 2, as shown in Figure 17.4. Why? Among its other attractions, the North America Prepress 2 option sets the working RGB color space to Adobe RGB (1998), arguably the best environment for viewing 24-bit images onscreen.

Adobe RGB includes a wide range of theoretical RGB colors, whether or not they can truly be displayed on a monitor. You may see some *clipping*, which is when two or more color spaces appear as one, onscreen, but Photoshop has greater latitude when interpolating and calculating colors.

After selecting North America Prepress 2, click OK. The source environment is fully prepared, and you can now save an image and send it on its way.

FIGURE 17.4

Select the North America Prepress 2 option to access the Adobe RGB (1998) color space, which affords a large theoretical RGB spectrum.

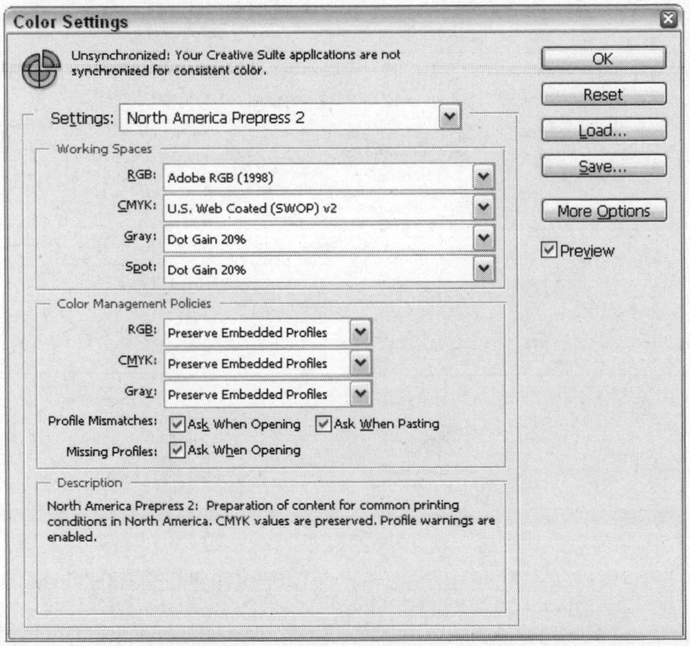

Embedding the profile

The final step on the Mac side in this scenario is to *embed* the Adobe RGB profile into a test image. (Embed simply means that Photoshop adds a little bit of code to the file stating where it was last edited.) For this, choose File ➪ Save As, which displays the dialog box in Figure 17.5. After naming the file and specifying a location on disk, select the Embed Color Profile option, which embeds the Adobe RGB color profile into the test image. Then click Save to save the file.

FIGURE 17.5

Select the Embed Color Profile option to append the Adobe RGB profile to the image saved on the Mac.

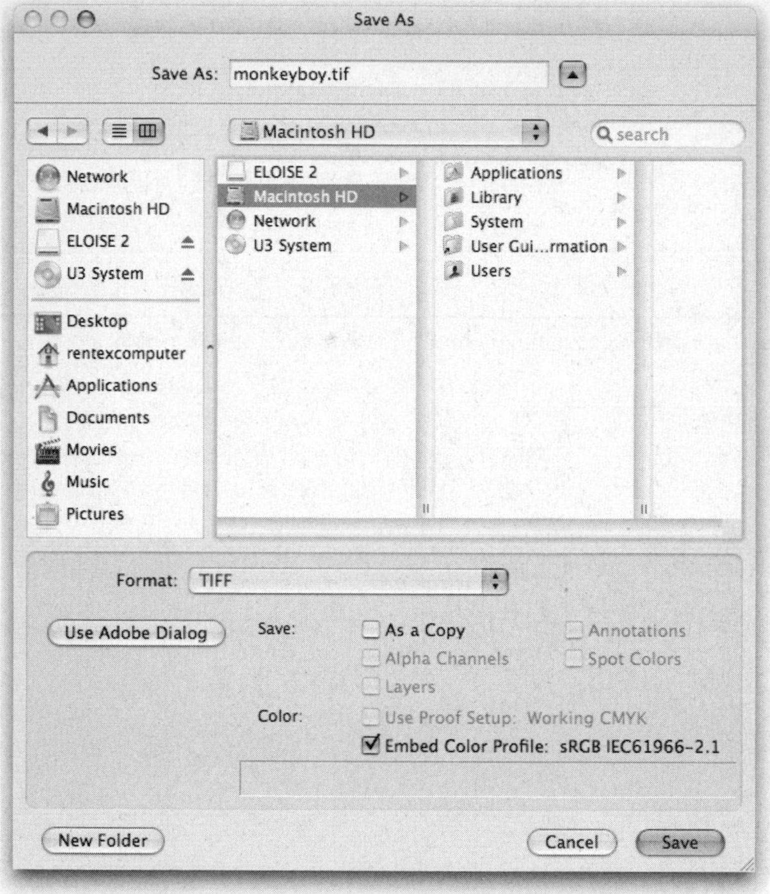

CAUTION To save a profile with an image, you have to select a file format that supports profiles. This includes the native Photoshop (PSD) format, TIFF, JPEG, EPS, PSB, and PICT. The two DCS formats also save profiles, but because DCS supports only CMYK images, it converts the RGB image to CMYK and saves a CMYK profile. If you select another format — GIF, PNG, BMP, or the like — the Embed Color Profile option becomes dimmed.

NOTE The Embed Color Profile option always embeds the device-independent profile defined in the Color Settings dialog box. This is very important: It does *not* embed the monitor profile. Photoshop handles the conversion from monitor space to RGB space internally without the help of either the Color Settings or Save As commands. This permits Photoshop to accommodate a world of different monitors from a single RGB working space.

Setting up the destination space

After saving the test image with the embedded Adobe RGB profile, you can transfer the file from your Mac to your PC. You can do this by e-mailing the file to yourself (if you have two computers, one Mac and one PC), or by sending it to a network folder that you can access from the PC (if you're on a network). With either transfer method — or if you want to bring the file over on a flash drive or CD — no translation occurs; this is a simple file copy from one computer to another. Before you can open the image and display it properly on the PC, you have to set up the RGB colors. Start by characterizing the monitor using the Adobe Gamma Wizard, as discussed earlier in this chapter.

After you finish with Adobe Gamma, go into Photoshop and choose Edit ➪ Color Settings or press Ctrl+Shift+K. If you really want to the two systems to match, select North America Prepress 2 from the Color Settings pop-up menu, just as you did (if you took my sage advice) on the Mac. For the purpose of educational experimentation, however, you can try forcing Photoshop to perform a conversion, so choose Web Graphics Defaults from the Settings option, as shown in Figure 17.6. This sets the RGB Working Spaces pop-up menu to the utterly indecipherable sRGB IEC61966-2.1.

The truncated name for this working space is *sRGB*, short for *standard RGB*, the ubiquitous monitor space touted by Hewlett-Packard, Microsoft, and a host of others. Although much smaller and drabber than Adobe RGB, the sRGB space is perfect for Web graphics because it represents the colors projected by a run-of-the-mill PC monitor. It also happens to be Photoshop's default setting. Given that many users will never visit this dialog box, sRGB is fast becoming a cross-platform standard.

Defining color management policies

The Color Settings command determines not only how Photoshop projects images onscreen but also how it reads embedded profiles. The three Color Management Policies' pop-up menus control how Photoshop reacts when it tries to open an image whose embedded profiles don't match the active color settings. When Web Graphics Defaults is active, the RGB pop-up menu is set to Off, which tells Photoshop to resist managing colors when it opens an RGB image. Disabling color management entirely is probably not a good move, especially when it threatens to ruin your color-conversion scenario. Instead, set the option to Convert to Working RGB, as shown in Figure 17.6.

FIGURE 17.6

On the Windows side, select North America Web/Internet to set the working environment to sRGB. This forces Photoshop to make a conversion. The setting also may appear as Web Graphics Defaults.

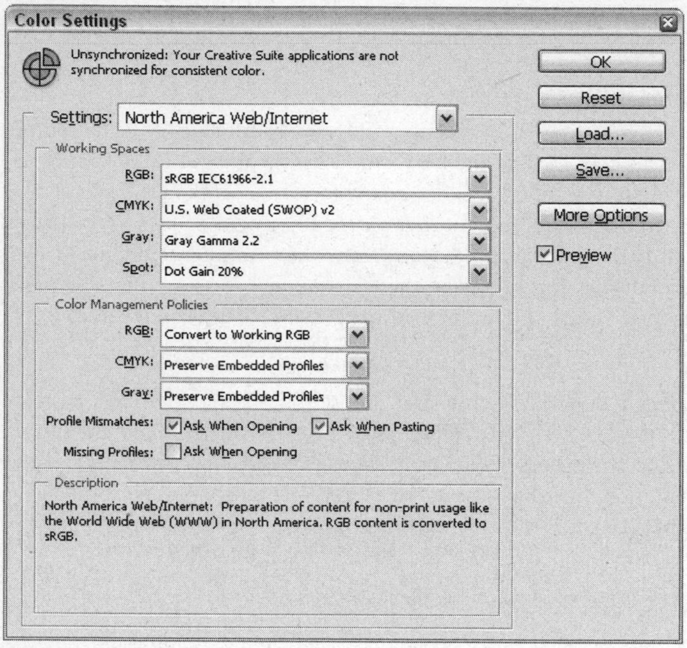

Finally, Photoshop wants to know how it should behave when it encounters an image with a profile other than sRGB. Should it convert all colors in the image to the sRGB environment? Or should it ask permission before proceeding? If you want to be able to make this choice on a case-by-case basis, select the Ask When Opening option from the Profile Mismatches options, as shown in Figure 17.7.

Converting the color space

When you're ready to open the test image (assuming you're working along here; if not, you can refer to these pages when you're doing this "for real"), choose File ⇨ Open. As Photoshop opens the test image, it detects the embedded Adobe RGB profile and determines that it does not match the active sRGB profile. Slightly flipped out by this development, Photoshop displays the alert box shown in Figure 17.8. You can select from three conversion options:

FIGURE 17.7

Set the first of the Color Management Policies to Convert to Working RGB to convert the image from the Adobe RGB working space to the sRGB space.

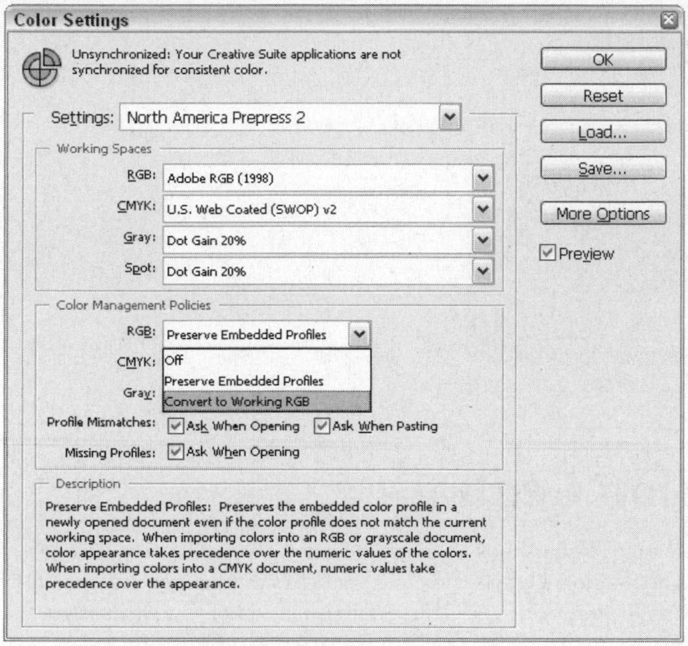

- **Use the embedded profile:** Photoshop is perfectly capable of displaying multiple images at a time, each in a different color space. Select this option to tell Photoshop to use the Adobe RGB space instead of sRGB to display the image it's about to open. No colors are converted in the process.

- **Convert document's colors to the working space:** This option converts the colors from the Adobe RGB space to sRGB. Because Convert to Working RGB was selected in the preceding section, this option is selected by default. Had the Ask When Opening option not been activated, Photoshop would have performed the conversion without asking you.

- **Discard the embedded profile:** Select this option to ignore the embedded profile and to display the image in the sRGB space without any color manipulations. Thanks to the low saturation inherent in sRGB, the result would be a significantly grayer, gloomier image.

Select the Convert document's colors to the working space option, and click OK. Photoshop spends a few seconds converting all pixels in the image from Adobe RGB to the smaller sRGB and then displays the converted image onscreen. The result is an almost perfect match — much better than the sort of results you could achieve without profile-based color management.

FIGURE 17.8

The alert box gives you the option of converting the colors from the foreign image or opening the image as is.

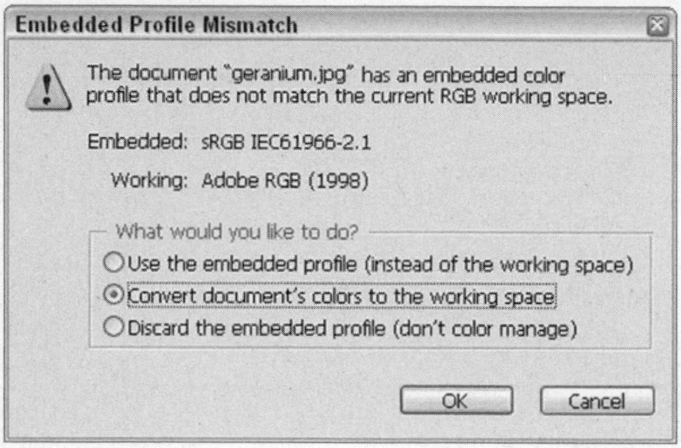

Embedded Profile Mismatch

The document "geranium.jpg" has an embedded color profile that does not match the current RGB working space.

Embedded: sRGB IEC61966-2.1

Working: Adobe RGB (1998)

What would you like to do?

○ Use the embedded profile (instead of the working space)
◉ Convert document's colors to the working space
○ Discard the embedded profile (don't color manage)

[OK]   [Cancel]

Color Conversion Central

Color Settings is the command that puts Photoshop's color conversion functions in play. It defines the color space parameters and at the same time makes the color conversions happen. This section explains the specific options as they're grouped in the Color Settings dialog box. You'll also find some suggestions for using particular settings, in case you're interested in a little advice.

Description

This portion of the Color Settings dialog box comes last, but it's also the most important. It tells you what every one of the Color Settings options does. Just position the cursor over an option to see a detailed description. To see how an option in a pop-up menu works, select the option and then position your cursor over it. With help like this, what do you need us for?

No, seriously, what *do* you need us for? Before we take the rest of the chapter off — there's laundry to do, after all — we will tell you that if you save your own color settings, you can type a description that shows up in the Description section when you load your settings.

Working spaces

Because every color model except Lab varies according to the hardware — the screen or the printer — Photoshop has to tweak the color space to meet your specific needs. There's no such thing as a single, true CMYK color model, for example. Instead, there are lots of printer-specific CMYK color models. These color models inside color models are called *working spaces*. You define the default working spaces that Photoshop uses when opening unprofiled images, creating new ones, or converting mismatched images using the four Working Spaces pop-up menus:

- **RGB:** The RGB environment defines what you see onscreen. Rather than limiting yourself to the circumscribed range of colors that your particular brand of monitor can display — known as the monitor's *gamut* — you can work in a larger, richer color environment, filled with theoretical color options that will serve your image well when projected on other monitors and output from commercial presses. Unless you work strictly on the Web and never create artwork for print, select the Adobe RGB (1998) option. If you're working with images destined for After Effects, Adobe recommends that you choose the Monitor RGB working space. Notice that your monitor space also appears in the pop-up menu; this shows that your monitor was correctly tagged with Adobe Gamma or the Display Calibrator Assistant.

TIP If you're a Web artist and want to preview how an image will look on a different kind of monitor, choose View ⇨ Proof Setup after closing the Color Settings dialog box. For example, choose View ⇨ Proof Setup ⇨ Windows RGB to see how the image looks on a typical PC monitor. Choose Macintosh RGB for a typical Mac monitor or Monitor RGB to turn off the RGB working space and see the image as it appears without conversion. Then use Ctrl+Y (Win) or ⌘+Y (Mac) to turn the preview on and off.

- **CMYK:** Use this option to specify the kind of printer you intend to use to print your final CMYK document. This option defines how Photoshop converts an image to the CMYK color space when you choose Image ⇨ Mode ⇨ CMYK Color. It also governs the performance of the CMYK preview (View ⇨ Proof Setup ⇨ Working CMYK). Finally, it decides how the colors in a CMYK image are converted for display on your RGB monitor. So anytime you open a CMYK image, the RGB working space becomes dormant and this option kicks into gear. For more information about characterizing a CMYK device, see the section "Custom CMYK Setup."

- **Grayscale:** This command defines how Photoshop displays a grayscale image (created using Image ⇨ Mode ⇨ Grayscale). You can adjust the gray values in the image to account for a typical Macintosh or PC display (Gray Gamma 1.8 or Gray Gamma 2.2, respectively). Or preview the image according to how it will print, complete with any of several Dot Gain values. (*Dot gain* is the factor by which halftone dots grow when absorbed into paper, as discussed in the section "Custom CMYK Setup.") My preferred setting is Gray Gamma 2.2. It's dark enough to account for dot gains of more than 25 percent, so it accurately reflects the printing conditions typical of grayscale work. Plus it predicts how grays display on a typical PC monitor. Everybody wins.

- **Spot:** From a printing perspective, a spot-color separation behaves like an extra grayscale print. Specify the dot gain value that correlates to your commercial printer. If you don't know that value, Dot Gain 20% is a safe bet.

If the Assign Profile command leaves pixels unchanged so that they appear to change onscreen, there must be a command that converts pixels so that they appear consistent onscreen. That command is Edit ⇨ Convert to Profile, which displays the dialog box pictured in Figure 17.9. The options in the lower half of the dialog box — Engine, Intent, and so on — also appear in the Color Settings dialog box when you enter the advanced mode, so you'll be hearing more about them later. For now, just select the color space to which you want to convert the image from the Destination Space pop-up menu, and press Enter or Return.

FIGURE 17.9

Convert to Profile is the complement to Assign Profile. Choose it to switch an open image to a different color space and convert the pixels. The result is an image that looks the same onscreen as it did before.

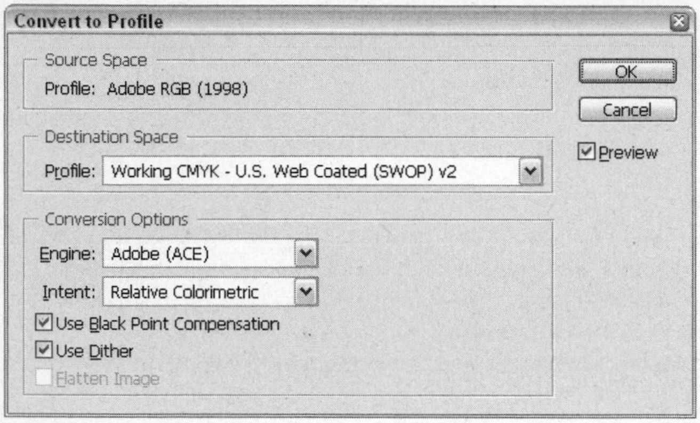

Assigning a Profile

An open profiled image remains in its working space regardless of how you change the settings in the Color Settings dialog box. Suppose that you open an image in sRGB and then change the working space to Adobe RGB. The open image remains unchanged onscreen, safe in its sRGB space. If you prefer the image to change to the new space, choose Edit ➪ Assign Profile. Then select the Working RGB option. The figure here shows the Assign Profile dialog box. Because Assign Profile leaves the color values of all pixels unchanged, Photoshop merely displays the old pixels in the new space, which permits the colors to shift onscreen. So perhaps perversely, not converting pixels results in a visible color shift, whereas converting pixels does not.

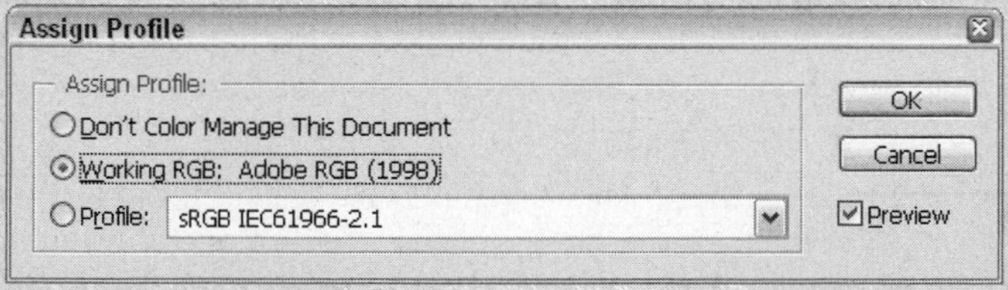

To permit the image to change on the fly according to the active working space, choose Edit ➪ Assign Profile and select the Don't Color Manage This Document option. A pound, or number, symbol (#) appears in the title bar to show that the image is no longer tagged with a color profile. Now, whenever you change the image's working space in the Color Settings dialog box, the image is updated in kind. Select the Preview option to view changes without exiting the dialog box.

TIP At first glance, the Destination Space pop-up menu may seem complicated, offering RGB, CMYK, and grayscale working spaces, and even allowing you to create your own. Surprisingly, this vast array of options may result in less work for you. The Destination Space option permits you to switch color modes. For example, if you open an RGB image, choose the Convert to Profile command, and select a CMYK space such as U.S. Web Coated (SWOP), Photoshop remaps the colors and converts the RGB channels to CMYK. Convert to Profile has an edge over Image ⇨ Mode ⇨ CMYK Color: You can switch color modes and nail a specific working space in one operation.

Color management policies

Highlighted in Figure 17.10, the next set of options controls how Photoshop reacts when opening an image that either lacks a profile or contains a profile that doesn't match the specified Working Spaces options previously listed. These are the options that are most likely to cause confusion because they're responsible for the error messages that Photoshop delivers when opening images. The trick is to keep the error messages to a minimum while keeping control to a maximum. Here are some suggestions for each option accompanied by what is hopefully enough explanation for you to make your own educated decisions:

■ **RGB:** The first three pop-up menus establish default policies that Photoshop suggests or implements according to the options that follow. For example, when opening an untagged RGB image, tag it with the working RGB profile, which in my case is Adobe RGB. Select Convert to Working RGB, and deselect the Missing Profiles option. This way, when no profile is evident, Photoshop assigns the Adobe RGB profile without any further fanfare. However, if the image contains a profile, you could go either way. An image tagged with an sRGB profile is probably a Web image, so you could go ahead and open it in the sRGB space without conversion. However, if you have an image tagged with the Apple RGB profile — intended to match a typical Apple Macintosh screen — you may want to convert it to Adobe RGB. Therefore, set Profile Mismatches to Ask When Opening. This way, Photoshop asks you what you want to do every time you open an image with a non-matching RGB profile. It will suggest that you convert the image to Adobe RGB, but permit you to override it if you prefer.

■ **CMYK:** Whereas RGB color is a function of your monitor and the RGB working space, accurate CMYK is all about matching colors to a specific output device. Therefore, if you're accepting CMYK images from clients and colleagues, you probably want to be very careful about making arbitrary conversions. By setting CMYK to Preserve Embedded Profiles, you tell Photoshop to open a tagged CMYK image in its own color space and override the default CMYK space specified in the Working Spaces option mentioned previously. Again, setting Profile Mismatches to Ask When Opening gives you the option to change your mind and convert the image to your working CMYK space if it seems appropriate. If the image has no profile, Photoshop leaves it untagged, giving you the option of testing multiple CMYK working spaces and assigning the one that fits best. This is case-by-case decision making at its best.

FIGURE 17.10

Here are the settings recommended for the five Color Management Policies options. They tell Photoshop to ask you when opening images with mismatches, but otherwise proceed automatically.

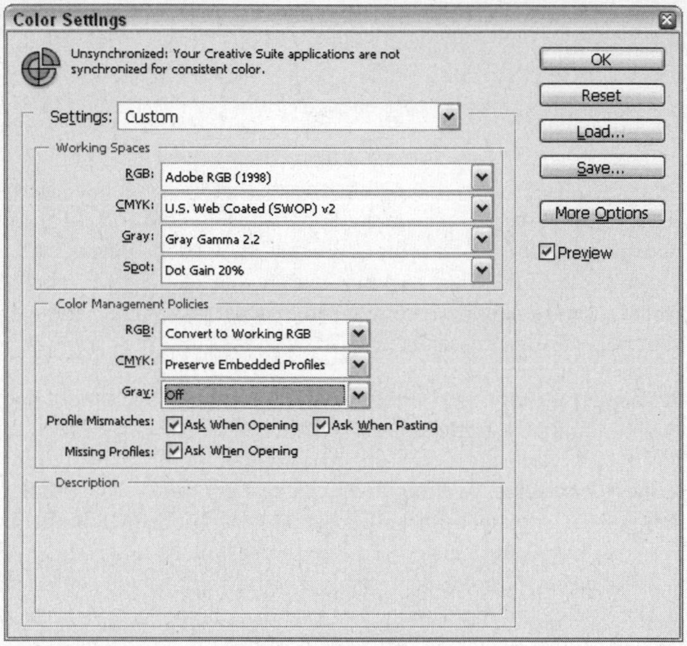

- **Gray:** Making automatic color manipulations to color images is all very well and good, but clipping is bound to occur, and with millions of theoretical colors at your disposal, the clipping is unlikely to do any visible harm. Grayscale images are another story. Blessed with just 256 brightness values, they are significantly more fragile than color images, and few grayscale images are tagged properly, which makes Photoshop's automatic adjustments less than reliable. You, therefore, would be well served to correct grayscale images manually (as explained in Chapter 18) and keep Photoshop out of the process. Set the Gray option to Off.

- **Profile Mismatches:** These two options tell Photoshop how to behave when opening an image whose profile does not match the working color space. If you select Ask When Opening, Photoshop asks your permission to perform the conversion suggested in the previous pop-up menus. This prompt also gives you the option of opening the image in its native color space or leaving the image untagged. Back in the Color Settings dialog box, select the Ask When Pasting option to tell Photoshop to warn you when you copy an image from one working space and paste it into another. As for the Ask When Pasting option, deselect that, too, and let Photoshop do its work unhindered.

■ **Missing Profiles:** When you open an image that lacks an embedded profile, Photoshop likes to ask you whether you want to manage the colors. I say deselect the Ask When Opening option — enough alert messages already! — and let Photoshop take its cues from the RGB, CMYK, and Gray pop-up menus. According to Figure 17.10, this means Photoshop tags most unprofiled RGB images with an Adobe RGB profile and leave unprofiled CMYK and grayscale images alone. An exception occurs when opening newer unprofiled images. If you save an image without a profile using version 5 or later, Photoshop inserts a tag that explicitly states, "I have no profile." In this case, the file opens untagged and Photoshop resists color managing the image until you tell it to do otherwise.

The Color Management Policies options are particularly dense, so no one will blame you if you find yourself reading and rereading the text trying to make sense of it. If you can't for the life of you make heads or tails of it, try this instead: Set your options to match the ones suggested in Figure 17.10. Then work in Photoshop for a few days or weeks and see how it feels. The good news about suggestions is that they're just that, and the settings they affect can be reset as needed. In the suggested positions, they won't hurt your images, even if you don't know what you're doing. With a little time and practice, you'll get a feel for how the settings work. Then come back, read the text again, and see if it makes more sense.

More options

Up to this point, admiration for Photoshop's color management tools has outweighed frustration with its complexity. But the moment More Options is clicked patience evaporates. Suddenly, this really is too much. The next portion of the Color Settings dialog box that is covered is the stuff that appears when you click More Options. This button brings with it many frustrations, and it's tempting to just skip it. But that's not something a bible can do — skip entire sections of pivotal dialog boxes — so here you go.

Think of More Options as the key to the color management underworld. When you click it, you unleash two categories of demonic preference settings: Conversion Options and Advanced Controls. Shown in Figure 17.11, each set of options possesses its own special brand of loathsome and horrible power. Save yourself now, dear reader — run while you still can.

Wait — you're still here? Brave soul. Oh, well, as long as you're here, we may as well go over it. Here goes:

■ **Engine:** The first of the Advanced Mode options is Engine, and it does just what it sounds like it does. The force behind the color management process is the engine. If you don't like one engine, you can trade it for another. If you work in a Macintosh-centric environment, for example, you may want to select Apple ColorSync. You should probably stick with the Adobe Color Engine, or ACE. Not only is ACE a great engine, it ensures compatibility with Illustrator, InDesign, and other Adobe applications.

FIGURE 17.11

Click More Options to display the Conversion Options and Advanced Controls, as well as define your own CMYK working space. The button changes to Fewer Options, and that will seem like a good idea.

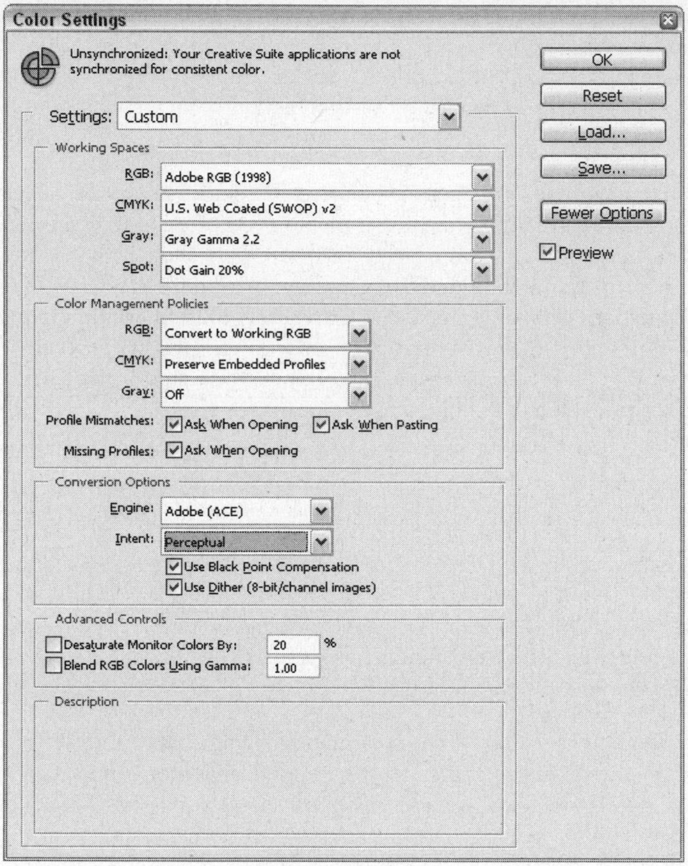

- **Intent:** Whenever you remap colors, a little something gets lost in the translation. The trick is to lose as little as possible, and that's the point of Intent. In previous versions of Photoshop, the option was set by default to Relative Colorimetric, which converts every color in the source profile to its closest equivalent in the destination profile. Although such a direct transfer of colors may sound attractive, it can create rifts in the image. The closest equivalent for two similar colors in the source profile might be a single color in the destination, or they might be two very different colors. As a result, gradual transitions may become flat or choppy. Wisely, Adobe has now set Perceptual as the default, which sacrifices specific colors in favor of retaining the gradual transitions between colors, so important to the success of continuous-tone photographs.

TIP Is Perceptual *really* better? Well, we think so, but don't take our word for it. Instead, position your cursor over the word Perceptual and read the Description text (refer to Figure 17.11), which tells you that Perceptual "requests a visually pleasing rendering, preserving the visual relationships between source colors." The truth is that most people at Adobe believe Perceptual to be the better choice. Who are we to disagree?

- **Use Black Point Compensation:** Like any other colors, Photoshop wants to convert black and white to new values. Whites are compensated naturally by the Intent setting, which may in many cases map white to a different color in the name of smoother transitions. But if you let black map to a lighter color, you can end up with wimpy gray shadows. To keep your blacks their blackest, select this option.

- **Use Dither (8-bit/channel images):** Just so we're all on the same page, a 24-bit image contains 8 bits per channel. So don't think we're talking about 8-bit GIF images here; this option uses *dithering* (random patterns of pixels) to smooth out what otherwise might be harsh color transitions. Ostensibly, it can result in higher file sizes when saving an image in the native PSD format or TIFF with LZW compression. But the effect is usually minimal. Leave this option selected.

- **Desaturate Monitor Colors By:** The Adobe RGB space in particular has a habit of rendering such vivid colors that the brightest areas in the image flatten out onscreen. Because they may or may not have a direct outcome on the appearance of the final image, whether in print or on the Web, such flat areas can be a bit misleading. To better see details in bright areas of color, select the Desaturate Monitor Colors option. Note that this option affects only the screen view; the colors continue to print as vividly as ever. Use this option only for running previews in the Color Settings dialog box. Leaving this option selected for extended periods of time can be more deceiving than deselecting it.

- **Blend RGB Colors Using Gamma:** When this option is deselected, as by default, Photoshop blends layers according to the gamma of the working color space. For example, the gamma of Adobe RGB is 2.2, the same as a typical PC screen and a few shades darker than a typical Macintosh screen. On occasion, however, this may result in incongruous highlights around the edges of layers. If you encounter this, try selecting this option. Photoshop recalculates all blends using a theoretically more desirable gamma value.

Custom CMYK Setup

To prepare an image for reproduction on a commercial offset or web press, you first need to specify how you want Photoshop to convert the image from the RGB to CMYK color space. This step also affects the conversion from CMYK to RGB, which in turn defines how CMYK images appear onscreen.

You specify the CMYK space by choosing Edit ⇨ Color Settings. Then select the color profile you want to use from the CMYK pop-up menu in the Working Spaces section of the dialog box. You can select a predefined color profile, or you can define a custom CMYK conversion setup by choosing Custom CMYK from the CMYK pop-up menu. When you choose Custom, Photoshop displays the Custom CMYK dialog box shown in Figure 17.12.

FIGURE 17.12

Use the options in the Custom CMYK dialog box to prepare an image for printing on a commercial offset or web press.

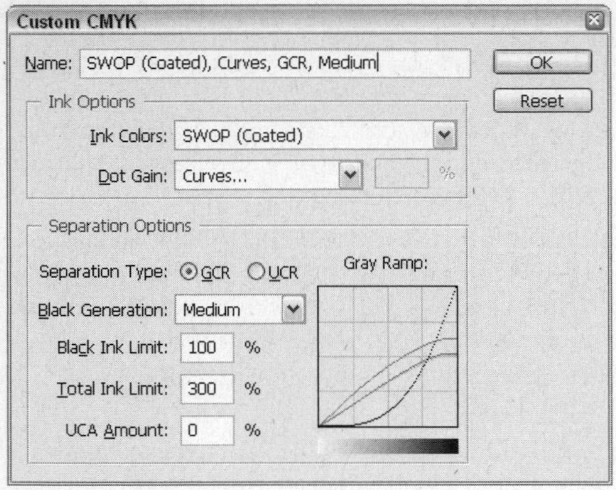

The following list explains each and every option in the Custom CMYK dialog box. If you're not a print professional, some of these descriptions may seem a little abstruse. After reading this section, you may want to talk with your commercial printer and find out what options, if any, he or she recommends.

- **Name:** Okay, so this one's not so abstruse after all. Type a name for your custom CMYK settings here.

- **Ink Colors:** This pop-up menu offers access to a handful of common press inks and paper stocks. Select the option that most closely matches your printing environment. (Your commercial printer can easily help you with this one.) The default setting, SWOP (Coated), represents the most common press type and paper stock used in the United States for magazine and high-end display work. Regardless of which setting you choose, Photoshop automatically changes the Dot Gain value to the most suitable setting.

- **Dot Gain:** Type a value from −10 to 40 percent to specify the amount by which you can expect halftone cells to shrink or expand during the printing process, a variable known as *dot gain*. When printing to uncoated stock, for example, you can expect halftone cells to bleed into the page and expand by about 25 to 30 percent. For newsprint, it varies from 30 to 40 percent. In any case, Photoshop automatically adjusts the brightness of CMYK colors to compensate, lightening the image for high values and darkening it for low values.

- **Separation Type:** When the densities of cyan, magenta, and yellow inks reach a certain level, they mix to form a muddy brown. The GCR (*gray component replacement*) option avoids this unpleasant effect by overprinting these colors with black to the extent specified with the Black Generation option. If you select the UCR (*under color removal*) option, Photoshop removes cyan, magenta, and yellow inks where they overlap black ink. GCR is almost always the setting of choice except when printing on newsprint.

Curve Control

For more control, select Curves from the Dot Gain pop-up menu. As shown in the figure, this brings up the Dot Gain Curves dialog box, which permits you to specify how much the halftone dots expand on a separation-by-separation basis. If the All Same option is selected, deselect it. Then use the Cyan, Magenta, Yellow, and Black radio buttons in the lower-right corner of the dialog box to switch among the four separations and modify their output independently. To do this, locate the lone point in the center of the curved line in the graph on the left side of the dialog box. Drag this point up to add dot gain, which in turn darkens the display of CMYK colors onscreen; drag the point down to lighten the display. If you need more control, you can add points to the graph by clicking on the curved line. Points added to the left side of the curve affect the display of light colors; points added to the right side of the curve affect dark colors.

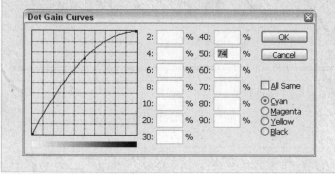

- **Black Generation:** Available only when the GCR option is active, the Black Generation pop-up menu determines how dark the cyan, magenta, and yellow concentrations must be before Photoshop adds black ink. Select Light to use black ink sparingly; select Heavy to apply it liberally. The None option prints no black ink whatsoever, and the Maximum option prints black ink over everything. You may want to use the UCA Amount option to restore cyan, magenta, and yellow ink if you select the Heavy or Maximum option.

- **Black Ink Limit:** Type the maximum amount of black ink that can be applied to the page. By default, this value is 100 percent, which is solid ink coverage. If you raise the UCA Amount value, you'll probably want to lower this value by a similar percentage to prevent the image from over darkening.

- **Total Ink Limit:** This value represents the maximum amount of all four inks permitted on the page. For example, assuming you use the default Black Ink Limit and Total Ink Limit values of 100 and 300 percent, respectively, the darkest printable color contains 100 percent black ink. The sum total of cyan, magenta, and yellow inks, therefore, is the difference between these values: 200 percent. A typical *saturated black*—a mix of inks that results in an absolute pitch-black pigment—is 70 percent cyan, 63 percent magenta, 67 percent yellow, and 100 percent black. And 70 + 63 + 67 + 100 =, you guessed it, 300.

- **UCA Amount:** The opposite of UCR, UCA stands for *under color addition*, which enables you to add cyan, magenta, and yellow inks to areas where the concentration of black ink is highest. For example, a value of 20 percent raises the amount of cyan, magenta, and yellow inks applied with black concentrations between 80 and 100 percent. This option is dimmed when the UCR option is selected.

- **Gray Ramp:** The Gray Ramp graph on the right side of the Custom CMYK dialog box shows the effects of your changes. Four lines — one in each color — represent the four inks. Although you can't edit the colored lines in this graph by clicking and dragging them, you can observe the lines to gauge the results of your settings. If you have an urge to grab a curve and yank it, choose Custom from the Black Generation pop-up menu. The ensuing dialog box lets you edit the black curve directly while you preview its effect on the C, M, and Y curves in the background.

TIP To see how your changes affect an open CMYK image in Photoshop, do this: Before choosing the Color Settings command, choose Edit ⇨ Assign Profile and select the Don't Color Manage This Document option. Then choose Edit ⇨ Color Settings and select the Preview option. From then on, the image is updated every time you press Enter or Return to accept changes from the Custom CMYK dialog box.

Saving and loading color settings

As we've seen, it can be a painstaking process of trial and error to arrive at the perfect color settings. Furthermore, the perfect settings for one job may be highly imperfect for another. Clearly, there's a pressing need for a way to save and load color settings; and just as clearly, Photoshop is the sort of obliging application to provide a way to do it.

You might logically surmise that the Load and Save buttons on the right side of the Color Settings box will come into play here — and you'd be correct. After you have your settings just the way you want them, click Save. You'll be prompted to save your settings in a Settings folder located deep within the bowels of your hard drive. (Should you ever need to find it again, here's the path: Under Windows, it's Program Files\Common Files\Adobe\Color\Settings. On the Mac, it's located in your User folder at Library/Application Support/Adobe/Color/Settings.) Clicking Load takes you to the same folder, where you can choose the saved settings that you want to load.

And that's not all. Not only can you save and load individual CMYK Working Spaces settings, but with the dreaded Advanced Mode option activated, you can save Working Spaces files for RGB, Grayscale, and Spot color settings as well. You'll find the load and save commands under the individual pop-up menus for each space.

Creating a profile that appears in the CMYK pop-up menu

What if you work with multiple commercial prepress houses? Wouldn't it be nice to be able to select different custom working spaces from the CMYK pop-up menu without having to constantly open setup files using the Load CMYK option? Yes, it would, and here's how you do it.

STEPS: Creating a CMYK profile

1. **In the Color Settings dialog box, choose Save CMYK from the CMYK pop-up menu, and give the file a name ending in the** *.icm* **extension to create an ICM file.** Other than the extension, the name you give it here isn't really that important; the original name you assigned when you first created the settings with the Custom CMYK command is the name you'll see when you actually load the settings.

2. **Save the ICM file to the Recommended folder.** For Photoshop to see the CMYK profile, you have to save it to a specific folder. On the PC, the path for that folder is C:\Program Files\Common Files\Adobe\Color\Profiles\Recommended. On the Mac, start with the Library folder at the root level of your hard drive, and then go to Application Support/Adobe/Color/Profiles/Recommended. When you finally arrive inside the Recommended folder, save the ICM file.

3. **Quit Photoshop.** Regardless of which version of Photoshop you're using, quit it by choosing File ➪ Exit (Photoshop ➪ Quit on the Mac).

4. **Launch Photoshop.** By starting (or restarting) Photoshop, you force the program to load the ICM profile.

5. **Confirm that the profile has loaded.** Press Ctrl+Shift+K (⌘+Shift+K on the Mac) to display the Color Settings dialog box, and then click the CMYK pop-up menu in the Working Spaces area. You should see the profile you saved in the menu.

> **TIP** Because the ICM file created in the preceding steps resides in the Recommended folder, it appears in the CMYK pop-up menu even when More Options has not been clicked. Any ICM files saved in the Profiles folder but outside the Recommended folder appear only when Advanced Mode is turned on.

Synchronizing Bridge Color Settings

As discussed in Chapters 3 and 20, Photoshop CS3's Bridge feature enables you to both organize your images and use them in creative ways that go beyond the Save for Web & Print commands in the main Photoshop workspace. You can use the Bridge to scan images or to capture images from a digital camera or video phone, as well as other sources.

So what's all this synchronizing business? It's simple, actually — unbelievably so, considering all the dialog boxes and steps and settings you have to deal with in Photoshop — choosing color settings, embedding them, dealing with those dreaded More Options. When you work with images in the Bridge, though, assuming you want to make sure you've got the same color settings in place as you do in the main Photoshop workspace, all you have to do is choose Edit ➪ Creative Suite Color Settings. The resulting dialog box appears in Figure 17.13. You also can open this dialog box by pressing Ctrl+Shift+K.

FIGURE 17.13

The Suite Color Settings dialog box offers 13 color management choices, including Color Management Off. Choose the one that matches your Photoshop settings so you're in synch with the Bridge.

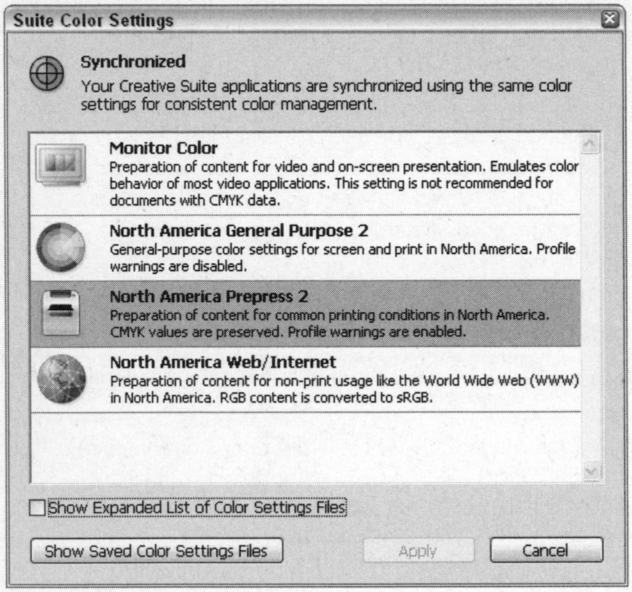

So anyway, you want to synchronize your color settings. You may not have *known* that is what you want to do, but you do. Synchronization is something you want to maintain because, as the dialog box itself tells you, it provides "consistent color management." What's life without consistency? Interesting, you say? Well, yes. But in Photoshop, consistency is a good thing.

After the Suite Color Settings dialog box is open, you can scroll through the 13 options, reading the short blurb about each one, and then you can make a selection by clicking the setting you want to use, the one that matches your Photoshop color settings choice. If you click the Show Expanded List of Color Settings Files option and then click Apply, the list expands (what a surprise) to show 18 additional settings, the last of which is Web Graphics Defaults, so if you're a Web artist and have your Photoshop color settings set for the Web, you may want to expand the list and choose this one. The expanded list, showing the tail end of the 18 additional settings, appears in Figure 17.14.

> **TIP** The Show Saved Color Settings Files option takes you to Windows Explorer (it opens a new Windows Explorer window, even if you have such a window open already) and shows you the location of the settings files — a handy tool if you can't remember the exact path (C:\Documents and Settings\Default\Application Data\Adobe\Color\Settings).

FIGURE 17.14

More, more, more: You have 18 more color settings to choose from, including North America Prepress 2 and North America Web/Internet.

After you click the setting you want to use, click Apply, and the dialog box closes. That's all there is to it. You can reset the selection as needed, matching your Photoshop settings for individual images or for groups of photos that need different handling—images bound for a Web Gallery rather than a printed Contact Sheet, for example. Luckily, all the hard work is done on the Photoshop side, and all you have to do in the Bridge is match the main color management method, and you're good to go.

Summary

In this chapter, you learned about controlling how Photoshop displays and uses color. This included everything from testing the way your image will appear on different monitors to embedding a color profile to making sure that your color settings in Photoshop follow your images to the Bridge and beyond.

Chapter 18

Mapping and Adjusting Colors

olor mapping is a term that doesn't really explain itself. Both of the words make sense, but paired up, what to do they mean? Maybe *color converting* might be a better term, or perhaps *color organization* or *assignment*. Anyway, we're stuck with *color mapping*, at least in a technical sense, and the term simply refers to the process of shuffling colors around, taking them from where they are now to where you want or need them to be. For example, to map Color A to Color B simply means to take all the A-colored pixels and convert them to B-colored pixels. Photoshop provides several commands that enable you to map entire ranges of colors based on their hues, saturation levels, and most frequently, brightness values. They've even added a new one — Black and White — that we'll delve into later in the chapter.

Color Effects and Adjustments

You may want to change colors in your photos and other artwork for lots of reasons. Perhaps you want to achieve some special effect or improve the clarity of an image or make some portion of the image stand out more so than it does under its current color scheme. In Figure 18.1, the image at the bottom is greatly improved by color mapping that was applied to the original version of the same image at the top: The colors stand out, edges are crisper and cleaner, and detail is much more evident. Of course, this is a black and white book (except for the Color Section), so the only things you can see here are the "crisper and cleaner" and the increase in detail. But believe it, the colors are the culprits, both in the original and the re-mapped version. The image in the middle shows the sort of "special" effects you also can achieve when tinkering with color settings.

889

While some mapping is done to create special — sometimes psychedelic — effects, most of the time the sort of correction or improvement shown in the bottom image in Figure 18.1 is the goal. You're making straightforward repairs, alternatively known as *color adjustments* and *corrections*. The reasons to need or want to make such adjustments or corrections are plentiful. Scans are never perfect, no matter how much money you spend on a scanning device or a service bureau. They can always benefit from tweaking and subtle adjustments, if not outright overhauls, in the color department. And, of course, digital cameras, and certainly lower-end traditional film cameras and their development methods can create images with colors that leave much to be desired.

Of course, Photoshop's color adjustment functions can't make something from nothing. In creating the illusion of more and better colors, most of the color adjustment operations that you perform actually take some small amount of color *away* from the image. Somewhere in your image, two pixels that were two different colors before you started the correction change to the same color. The image may look ten times better, but it will in fact be less colorful than when you started.

Remembering this principle is important because it demonstrates that color mapping is really a balancing act. The first several operations you perform may make an image look progressively better, but the tenth may send it into decline — the perfect example of less being more, or knowing when to quit. This knowledge, however, of when to quit or when correction has become corruption is a matter of experience and developing a good "eye" for when that line has been crossed. Of course there's no magic formula; the amount of color mapping you need to apply varies from image to image. But if you follow basic principles — use the commands in moderation, know when to stop, and save your image to disk before doing anything drastic — you should be happy with your results the majority of the time.

> **NOTE**   Many of the commands discussed in the following sections also can be applied as *adjustment layers*. An adjustment layer is an extremely flexible tool, giving you all the advantages of the color correction commands without the drawback of having your original image permanently altered. Adjustment layers are discussed in full at the end of this chapter, but you should know they're "out there" from the beginning of any discussion of color mapping and image correction; this knowledge can help you put all the techniques covered between now and then in better perspective, evaluating the differences between techniques, weighing pros and cons, and so on. So there, now you know.

FIGURE 18.1

From bad to bizarre to better, color adjustments can serve many different purposes. The top image (original) is faded and blurry, and a gradient map makes it interesting — but not clearer or crisper, as it appears in the bottom image after some corrections were made to light and color levels.

Colors in Need of Adjustment

Photoshop stores all its color mapping commands under the Image ⟐ Adjustments submenu. (The one exception is Photoshop CS3's Camera Raw dialog box, which can be accessed only by opening a Camera Raw file, which is covered later in the chapter.) Basically, these commands fall into three categories:

- **Color mapping:** Commands such as Invert and Threshold are quick-and-dirty color mappers, swapping, for example, the original colors for their color opposites (Invert). They don't correct images, but they can be useful for creating special effects and adjusting masks.

- **Easy color corrections:** Brightness/Contrast and Color Balance are true color-correction commands, but you may feel that they sacrifice functionality for ease of use. By ease of use, we mean that the corrections are achieved through a few simple sliders, as shown in Figure 18.2. By sacrifice functionality, we also mean that the corrections are achieved through a few simple sliders. Too few. But you will end up using them from time to time, even if you think they're painfully simple and wish they offered more or more nuanced controls.

  One thing that is improved in Brightness/Contrast in Photoshop CS3 is the addition of the Use Legacy checkbox. By turning this on, you can elect to clip extreme highlight and shadow detail. It's off by default, but when you turn it on, changes to brightness and contrast are made on a non-linear basis — mid-tones are effected to a greater extent than highlights or shadows — unlike the CS2 and previous versions of this tool, which affected highlights, midtones, and shadows to the same degree as you dragged the slider/s.

- **Expert color corrections:** The third, more complicated variety of color-correction commands provides better control, but they take a fair amount of effort to learn. Levels, Curves, Hue/Saturation, and Shadows/Highlights are examples of color correcting at both its best and most complicated.

This chapter contains little information about the second category of commands for the simple reason that so little information is required. You issue a command from the Image ⟐ Adjustments submenu, and either the automatic adjustment takes place with no interaction required from you, or a dialog box opens, you drag a slider, you see if you like the previewed change, and if so, you click OK. If not, you close the dialog box without making any changes, and that's it.

Now, it's important to state up front that some of the quick and automatic adjustment tools aren't going to wow you, even when you consider their incredible speed and ease of use. Some exceptions: Auto Color, which usually does a pretty good job of adjusting an image's midtones and removing color casts; Auto Levels and Auto Contrast, which are decent quick fixers; and Variations, which offers deceptively straightforward sophistication; this last one's not really that automatic compared with the others, in that you have several choices of color and lighting adjustments that you can make and you can confine the adjustments to specific ranges of color.

No matter how you end up feeling about the individual commands and the three types of adjustments that can be made, you're about to master them — so grab a really dysfunctional photo and let the color therapy begin.

FIGURE 18.2

These two simple dialog boxes can make big changes in an image, but they're rather blunt tools when you need subtle changes.

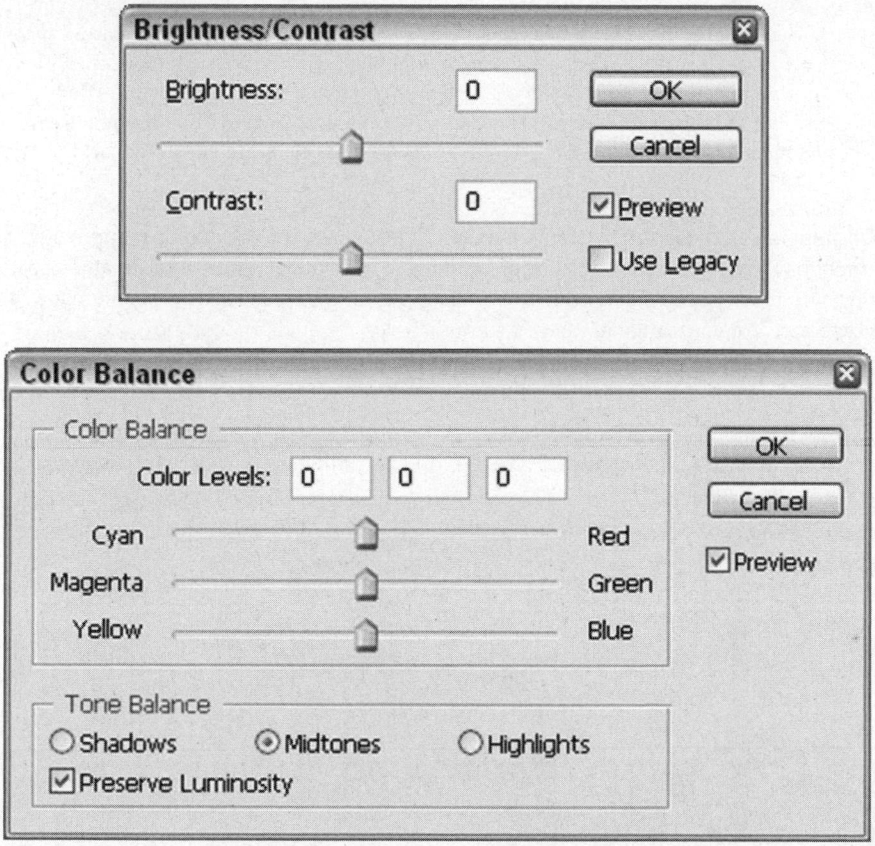

Brightness/Contrast

Brightness: 0   OK

Cancel

Contrast: 0   ☑ Preview

☐ Use Legacy

Color Balance

Color Balance

Color Levels: 0   0   0   OK

Cancel

Cyan — Red   ☑ Preview

Magenta — Green

Yellow — Blue

Tone Balance

○ Shadows   ⦿ Midtones   ○ Highlights

☑ Preserve Luminosity

Quick and Automatic Color Effects

The first category of commands, the color mapping tools, all occupy one of the lower sections in the Image ⇨ Adjustments submenu. These commands — Invert, Equalize, Threshold, and Posterize — produce immediate effects that are difficult or require too much effort to duplicate with the more full-featured commands.

Invert

When you choose Image ⇨ Adjustments ⇨ Invert or press Ctrl+I (⌘+I on the Mac), Photoshop converts every color in your image to its exact opposite, as in a photographic negative. As shown in Figure 18.3, you can take some or all of a photo and swap every color — black becomes white,

white becomes black, yellow becomes blue, red becomes green, and so on. The brightness value of every primary color component changes to 255 minus the original brightness value, if you want to get all technical about it.

Now, you might have already thought, "Hey, this means I can scan a negative and convert it to a positive image with this command!" Well, not really, at least not that simply. By itself, the Invert command is not sufficient to convert a scanned color photographic negative to a positive. Negative film produces an orange cast that the Invert command does not address. After inverting, you can use the Variations command to remove the colorcast. Or avoid Invert altogether, and use the Levels command to invert the image. Both Variations and Levels are explained later in this chapter.

One really good thing about the Invert command is that it's just about the only color-mapping command that retains the rich diversity of color in an image. (The Hue/Saturation command also retains color diversity under specific conditions.) For example, if you apply the Invert command twice in a row, you arrive at your original image without any loss in quality. Cool, no?

FIGURE 18.3

You can turn some or all of your image to its negative. Here the top half of the image has been inverted, showing you the before and after in one image.

Of course, bear in mind that when you're working on a full-color image, the Invert command simply inverts the contents of each color channel. This means the command produces very different results when applied to RGB, Lab, and especially CMYK images. Typically, the Invert command changes most pixels in a CMYK image to black. Except in rare instances—such as in night scenes—the black channel contains lots of light shades and few dark shades. So when you invert the channel, it becomes extremely dark.

NOTE Just so you know, when we discuss applying color corrections in the CMYK mode, we assume that you're applying them after choosing Image ➪ Mode ➪ CMYK Color. Applying corrections in the RGB mode when View ➪ Proof Setup ➪ Working CMYK is active produces the same effect as when Working CMYK is not selected. The only difference is that the onscreen colors are limited slightly to fit inside the CMYK color space. You're still editing inside the same old Red, Green, and Blue color channels, so the effects are the same.

TIP As mentioned in Chapter 9, inverting the contents of the mask channel is the same as applying Select ➪ Inverse to a selection outline in the marching ants mode. In fact, this is one of the most useful applications of the filter.

Equalize

When you invoke the Equalize command, Photoshop searches for the lightest and darkest color values in a selection and then maps the lightest color in all the color channels to white, maps the darkest color in the channels to black, and distributes the remaining colors to other brightness levels in an effort to evenly distribute pixels over the entire brightness spectrum. This doesn't mean that any one pixel actually appears white or black after you apply Equalize, however. Instead, one pixel in at least one channel is white and another pixel in at least one channel is black. In an RGB image, for example, the red, green, or blue component of one pixel would be white, but the other two components of that same pixel might be black. The result is a higher contrast image with white and black pixels scattered throughout the color channels.

If no portion of the image is selected when you choose Image ➪ Adjustments ➪ Equalize, Photoshop automatically maps the entire image across the brightness spectrum. If you select a portion of the image before choosing the Equalize command, Photoshop displays a dialog box containing these two radio buttons:

- **Equalize Selected Area Only:** Select this option to apply the Equalize command strictly within the confines of the selection. The lightest pixel in the selection becomes white, the darkest pixel becomes black, and the others remap to shades in between. Figure 18.4, at the top, shows an image that's been Equalized in only one selected area.

- **Equalize Entire Image Based on Selected Area:** If you select the second radio button, which is the default setting, Photoshop applies the Equalize command to the entire image based on the lightest and darkest colors in the selection. All colors in the image that are lighter than the lightest color in the selection become white, and all colors darker than the darkest color in the selection become black. The bottom image in Figure 18.4 shows the same image with the Equalize command applied to the entire image based on the same selection.

FIGURE 18.4

Equalize this! Equalize a selection or the whole image based on a selection.

What you may find with the Equalize command is that it can rely too heavily on the automation of its procedure to be of much use as a color-correction tool. You simply don't have enough control over the equalization process, or the equation it's using to distribute colors over the entire spectrum of light to dark. You can create some interesting special effects, though, and sometimes it can be a helpful command, depending on the photo in question, its problems, and your goals for it.

> **TIP** If you really want to automatically adjust the colors in an image from black to white regardless of the color mode and composition of the individual channels, choose Image ➪ Adjustments ➪ Auto Levels or press Ctrl+Shift+L (⌘+Shift+L on the Mac). If you want to adjust the tonal balance manually and therefore with a higher degree of accuracy, the Levels and Curves commands are really great. They're all explained at length later in this chapter.

Threshold

The Threshold command converts all colors to either black or white, based on their brightness values. When you choose Image ➪ Adjustments ➪ Threshold, Photoshop displays the Threshold dialog box shown in Figure 18.5. The dialog box offers a single Threshold Level option box and a slider bar, either of which you can use to specify the medium brightness value in the image. Photoshop changes any color lighter than the value in the Threshold option box to white and changes any color darker than the value to black.

FIGURE 18.5

The histogram in the Threshold dialog box shows the distribution of brightness values in the selection. The weird mountain-range silhouette thing is what's known as a *histogram*.

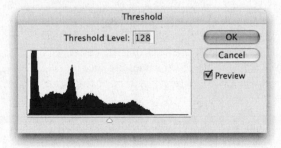

The dialog box also includes a graph of all the colors in the image, even if only a portion of the image is selected. This graph is called a *histogram*. The width of the histogram represents all 256 possible brightness values, starting at black on the left and progressing to white on the right. The height of each vertical line in the graph demonstrates the number of pixels currently associated with that brightness value. Therefore, you can use the histogram to gauge the distribution of lights and darks in your image. You may have trouble imagining that looking at the histogram in a dialog box could ever translate to a useful tool for perceiving and adjusting color, but with enough experience, the histogram becomes an invaluable tool, permitting you to greatly improve the colors that you see onscreen. You may even get excited enough about histograms to spend some time using the Histogram palette, discussed later in this chapter.

Generally speaking, you achieve the best effects if you change an equal number of pixels to black as you change to white (and vice versa). So rather than moving the slider bar to 128, which is the medium brightness value, move it to the point at which the area of the vertical lines to the left of the slider triangle looks roughly equivalent to the area of the vertical lines to the right of the slider triangle. The example at the top in Figure 18.6 shows the result of applying the Threshold command with a Threshold Level value of 128 (right smack in the middle of the slider), while the image at the bottom shows a lower Threshold level of 70.

> **TIP** If you want to achieve a colorful Threshold effect, try applying the Threshold command independently to each color channel. In an RGB image, for example, press Ctrl+1 (⌘+1 on the Mac) and then choose Image ⇨ Adjustments ⇨ Threshold. Then press Ctrl+2 (⌘+2 on the Mac) and repeat the command, and press Ctrl+3 (⌘+3 on the Mac) and do it again. Alternatively, you can make Photoshop perform this process for you by using the new Hard Mix blend mode, discussed in Chapter 14. Don't forget that you also can apply the same effect to two channels at once by selecting one channel and Shift-clicking the second.

Posterize

Where Threshold boils down an image into only two colors, Posterize can retain as many colors as you like. Of course, you can't control how colors are mapped, as you can when you use Threshold; the Posterize dialog box provides neither a histogram nor a slider bar. Instead, Posterize automatically divides the full range of 256 brightness values into a specified number of equal increments.

To use this command, choose Image ⇨ Adjustments ⇨ Posterize and type a value in the Levels option box. The Levels value represents the number of brightness values that the Posterize command retains. Higher values result in subtle color adjustments; lower values produce more dramatic effects, as shown in Figure 18.7, where just two levels and then a near normal-looking 16 levels are applied.

Like Threshold, the Posterize command is something you can play with in conjunction with filters to get some really interesting results. You can apply it before a filter or after it — or along with more than one filter. By reducing the number of levels and thus simplifying the color palette in the image, the Posterize command makes various filters perform differently than they would on a photo with millions of colors.

FIGURE 18.6

Use the histogram and your own eyes — trained on the preview — to determine when the Threshold command is delivering interesting or simply destructive results.

FIGURE 18.7

On the top, Posterize was applied at two levels. On the bottom, 16 levels were applied, which makes the image look almost "normal," like the original photo with millions of colors. Note that the sky is one of the giveaway areas: Bands of colors are visible there more than in the busier areas of the image.

Quick and Automatic Corrections

Photoshop offers four quick, automatic correctors under the Image ⇨ Adjustments submenu. Introduced in Photoshop 7, the Auto Color command is the most useful of them. Desaturate removes all color from a selection, leaving it looking like a grayscale image, and the Auto Levels and Auto Contrast commands automatically adjust the contrast of an image according to what Photoshop deems to be ideal brightness values. Auto Levels examines each color channel independently; Auto Contrast examines the image as a whole. Note that Auto Color, which works only with RGB images, looks at the entire image as it attempts to automatically correct the image's midtones and remove colorcasts.

Gray areas

The Desaturate command is quite useful for removing color from selected areas or from independent layers. You can use it to reduce or remove color from an entire image, but for that you'd probably be better off using the Image ⇨ Mode ⇨ Grayscale command. Using the Mode command also disposes of the extra channels that would otherwise consume room in memory and on disk. Now, there are reasons to circumvent this alleged benefit. You might want to use the Desaturate command to get rid of color in an entire photo for the following reasons:

- You want to retain the option of applying RGB-only filters, such as Lens Flare and Lighting Effects. You'd lose these options if you convert to Grayscale.

- You intend to downsize the colors using Image ⇨ Mode ⇨ Indexed Colors and save the final image as a GIF file for use on the Web.

TIP You can use Edit ⇨ Fade (Ctrl+Shift+F or ⌘+Shift+F) to reduce the effects of Desaturate or any other command under the Image ⇨ Adjustments submenu. As always, the Fade command is available immediately after you apply the color correction; if you alter a selection outline, Fade becomes unavailable.

NOTE Desaturate isn't the only way to remove colors from an image. You also can invert the colors and mix them with their original counterparts to achieve a slightly different effect. Just press Ctrl+I (⌘+I on the Mac) to invert the area you want to desaturate. Then press Ctrl+Shift+F (⌘+Shift+F on the Mac), change the Opacity setting to 50 percent, and — here's the important part — select Color from the Mode pop-up menu. You can get a close approximation of converting an image to the Grayscale mode simply by creating a new layer, filling it with black, and switching the blend mode to Color. You also can use the Channel Mixer, which gives you the most exacting control over converting to grayscale. For details, see Chapter 4.

The Auto Levels command

Image ⇨ Adjustments ⇨ Auto Levels (Ctrl+Shift+L or ⌘+Shift+L) goes through each color channel and changes the lightest pixel to white, changes the darkest pixel to black, and stretches all the shades of gray to fill out the spectrum. In Figure 18.8, you see a very dull gray image on the left, and a more dynamic version of the same image on the right. The right-hand image was improved through the Auto Levels command because Photoshop increased the lights and darks, which increased the contrast. You might get better results by applying Levels and dragging the sliders by hand, as you can see from this example; this very quick, automated tool is not too shabby.

FIGURE 18.8

After the use of the Auto Levels command, you see more contrast, more discernable detail, more interest.

You may be thinking that Auto Levels is a whole lot like Equalize, and you'd be right — except that unlike the Equalize command, which considers all color channels as a whole, Auto Levels looks at each channel independently. This results in more dynamic, profound results, based on the color mode for the photo. Like Invert, Equalize, and other automatic color mapping commands, Auto Levels is designed for use in the RGB mode. If you use it in CMYK, you may not like the results.

By default, the Auto Levels command produces the same effect as the Auto button in the Levels dialog box, as discussed later in this chapter.

The Auto Contrast command

If you find that Image ➪ Adjustments ➪ Auto Levels (which modifies values on a channel-by-channel basis) results in an unpleasant skewing of the balance of colors in an image, you can use Image ➪ Adjustments ➪ Auto Contrast (Ctrl+Shift+Alt+L or ⌘+Shift+Option+L). The Auto Contrast command adjusts the composite levels, which preserves the colors.

Not sure which one to use? If a low-contrast image suffers from a colorcast that you want to correct, try Auto Levels. If the image is washed out but the colors are okay, try Auto Contrast. If you're working on a grayscale image, the two commands work the same, so choose whichever is more convenient. Given that neither command is perfect, you may want to make additional Levels and Variations adjustments (these commands are covered in detail later in this chapter) — or try Auto Color, which is up next.

The Auto Color command

The Auto Color command is such a smart and useful tool that it serves as the exception to the rule that one must be somewhat reserved in praise for or use of any command that starts with the word "Auto." Auto Color is great at tweaking skin tones and making other subtle changes — something you'll notice right away, especially in photos where the Auto Levels and Auto Contrast commands don't seem to make much, if any, difference in the image.

Choose Image ➪ Adjustments ➪ Auto Color or press Ctrl+Shift+B (⌘+Shift+B on the Mac) to apply the Auto Color command. To get a sense of how the command works, and how it compares with Auto Levels in particular, take a look at Figure 18.9, which shows the two commands applied to the same image.

Auto Color is different from Auto Levels in that rather than setting the darks to black and the lights to white, Auto Color neutralizes an image's highlights, midtones, and shadows, thereby restoring balance to other colors in the image. That's the plan, anyway. If you don't see the results that this command promises, you can always customize it using the Levels and Curves commands — a process discussed later in this chapter.

FIGURE 18.9

Auto Levels (middle) didn't do much of anything to the original (top), but Auto Color made a more significant difference, as shown in the bottom copy of the image.

Adjusting Hues and Colorizing Images

In this section, you're looking at the commands that change the distribution of colors in an image. You can move the hues across the color spectrum, change the saturation of colors, adjust highlights and shadows, and even tint an image. Four of these commands — Hue/Saturation, Selective Color, Photo Filter, and Match Color — are applicable only to color images. The other two — Replace Color and Variations — can be applied to grayscale images, too. You may find that they're better suited to color images, but it depends on the photo as to whether these commands are the most effective choice for a grayscale image. If you're more interested in editing grayscale photographs, you can check out the Levels, Curves, and new Shadow/Highlight commands, all of which are covered toward the end of the chapter. For those of you who want to correct colors, however, read on.

TIP Remember how Ctrl+Alt+F (⌘+Option+F on the Mac) redisplays the last filter dialog box so that you can tweak the effect? Well, a similar shortcut is available when you apply color corrections. Press Alt (Option on the Mac) when choosing any of the commands described throughout the rest of this chapter to display that command's dialog box with the settings last applied to the image. If the command has a keyboard equivalent, just add Alt (Option on the Mac) to restore the last settings. Pressing Ctrl+Alt+U (⌘+Option+U on the Mac), for example, brings up the Hue/Saturation dialog box with the settings you last used.

Using the Hue/Saturation command

The Hue/Saturation command provides two functions. First, it enables you to adjust colors in an image according to their hues and saturation levels. You can apply the changes to specific ranges of colors or modify all colors equally across the spectrum. And second, the command lets you colorize images by applying new hue and saturation values while retaining the core brightness information from the original image.

This command is perfect for colorizing grayscale images. You can give your images the Ted Turner treatment with just a little effort. Just scan and change the Hue value to 140 degrees.

When you choose Image ⇨ Adjustments ⇨ Hue/Saturation or press Ctrl+U (⌘+U on the Mac), Photoshop displays the Hue/Saturation dialog box, shown in Figure 18.10. Before you look at how to use this dialog box to produce specific effects, we introduce the options, starting with the three option boxes:

- **Hue:** The Hue slider bar measures colors on the 360-degree color circle, as explained in the section of Chapter 4 that discusses the HSB model. You can adjust the Hue value from _180 to +180 degrees. As you do, Photoshop rotates the colors around the Hue wheel. Consider the example of flesh tones. A Hue value of +30 moves the flesh into the orange range; a value of +100 makes it green. Going in the other direction, a Hue of −30 makes the flesh red and −100 makes it purple.

NOTE When the Colorize option is selected, Hue becomes an absolute value measured from 0 to 360 degrees. A Hue value of 0 is red, 30 is orange, and so on, as described in Chapter 4.

The Hue/Saturation dialog box as it appears when editing all colors in a layer (top) or just a specific range of colors (bottom)

- **Saturation:** The Saturation value changes the intensity of the colors. Normally, the Saturation value varies from –100 for gray to +100 for incredibly vivid hues. The only exception occurs when the Colorize option is selected, in which case saturation becomes an absolute value, measured from 0 for gray to 100 for maximum saturation.

- **Lightness:** You can darken or lighten an image by varying the Lightness value from –100 to +100.

CAUTION Because this value invariably changes *all* brightness levels in an image to an equal extent — whether or not Colorize is selected — it permanently dulls highlights and shadows. We advise that you avoid this option at virtually all costs and rely instead on the Levels or Curves commands to edit brightness and contrast.

Like many sliders and settings in the program, Photoshop now lets you "scrub" to adjust the values. Position your cursor over the name of one of the sliders (such as Hue) until you get a hand cursor with two arrows protruding from it. Drag left to decrease the value of the slider, drag right to increase it. Shift-drag to change the value in increments of 10.

- **Edit:** The Edit pop-up menu controls which colors in the active selection or layer are affected by the Hue/Saturation command. If you select the Master option, as by default, Hue/Saturation adjusts all colors equally. If you prefer to adjust some colors in the layer differently than others, choose one of the other Edit options or press the keyboard equivalent — Ctrl+1 (Win) or ⌘+1 (Mac) for Reds, Ctrl+2 (Win) or ⌘+2 (Mac) for Yellows, and so on.

  Each Edit option isolates a predefined range of colors in the image. For example, the Reds option selects the range measured from 345 to 15 degrees on the Hue wheel. Naturally, if you were to modify just the red pixels and left all non-red pixels unchanged, you'd end up with some jagged transitions in your image. So Photoshop softens the edges with 30 degrees of fuzziness at either end of the red spectrum (the same kind of fuzziness as described in Chapter 9).

You can apply different Hue, Saturation, and Lightness settings for every one of the color ranges. For example, to change all reds in an image to green and all cyans to gray, choose the Reds option and change the Hue value to +50 and then choose Cyans and change the Saturation value to –100.

- **Color ramps:** You can track changes made to colors in the Hue/Saturation dialog box in two ways. One way is to select the Preview option and keep an eye on the changes in the image window. The second way is to observe the color ramps at the bottom of the dialog box. The first ramp shows the 360-degree color spectrum; the second ramp shows what the color ramp looks like after your edits.

- **Color range controls:** You also can use the color ramps to broaden or narrow the range of colors affected by Hue/Saturation. When you choose any option other than Master from the Edit pop-up menu, a collection of color range controls appears between the color ramps. The range bar identifies the selected colors and also permits you to edit them.

  Figure 18.11 shows the color range controls up close and personal. Here's how they work:

  - Drag the central range bar to move the entire color range.

  - Drag one of the two lighter-colored fuzziness bars to broaden or narrow the color range without affecting the fuzziness.

  - Drag the range control to change the range while leaving the fuzziness points fixed in place. The result is that you expand the range and condense the fuzziness, or vice versa.

  - Drag the triangular fuzziness control to lengthen or contract the fuzziness independently of the color range.

By default, red is the central color in the color ramps, with blue at either side. This is great when the range is red or some other warm color. But if you're working with a blue range, the controls get split between the two ends. To move a different color to the central position, Ctrl-drag (Win) or ⌘-drag (Mac) in the color ramp. The spectrum revolves around the ramp as you drag.

■ **Eyedroppers:** To lift a color range from the image window, click inside the image window with the Eyedropper cursor. The cursor automatically changes to an eyedropper when you move it outside the Hue/Saturation dialog box, and then when you click on a color, Photoshop centers the range on the exact color you click.

> **TIP**   To expand the range to include more colors, Shift-click or drag in the image window. To remove colors from the range, Alt-click (Option-click on the Mac) or drag in the image. You also can use the alternative plus and minus Eyedropper tools, but Shift and Alt (Shift and Option on the Mac) work well, too.

■ **Load/Save:** You can load and save settings to disk in case you want to reapply the options to other images using the Load/Save options. These options are especially useful if you find a magic combination of color-correction settings that accounts for most of the color mistakes produced by your scanner.

FIGURE 18.11

Choose which range you want to edit, and then use the color range controls — the eyedroppers and spectrum sliders — to modify the range or the fuzziness.

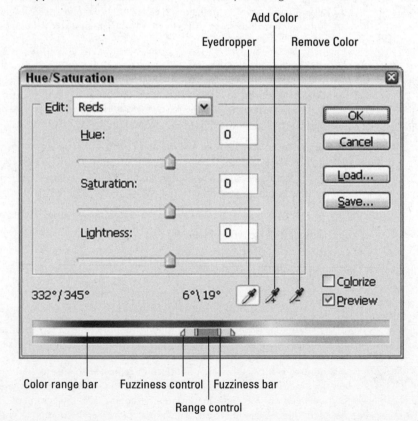

908

- **Colorize:** Select this option to apply a single hue and a single saturation level to the entire selection or layer, regardless of how it was previously colored. All brightness levels remain intact, although you can adjust them incrementally using the Lightness slider bar (a practice that should be avoided, as mentioned earlier).

  Color ranges are not permitted when colorizing. The moment you select the Colorize option, Photoshop dims the Edit pop-up menu and sets it to Master.

- **Restore:** Wait — there's no Restore button in this dialog box. Or is there? If you Alt-click (Windows) or Option-click (Mac) the Cancel button, it becomes a Restore button. While in Restore mode, you can restore the options in the Hue/Saturation, Levels, and Curves dialog boxes to their original settings by clicking Restore. You also can press Option+Escape on the Mac to achieve the same result.

To track the behavior of specific colors when using Hue/Saturation or any of Photoshop's other powerful color adjustment commands, display the Info palette (press F8) before choosing the Hue/Saturation command. Then move the cursor inside the image window. As shown in Figure 18.12, the Info palette tracks the individual RGB and CMYK values of the pixel beneath the cursor. The number before the slash is the value before the color adjustment; the number after the slash is the value after the adjustment. Note that the Info palette shows these before and after numbers only while the adjustment dialog box is open; if you're just sampling pixels with the Eyedropper, there is only one value shown in the palette — the color values for the pixel you're sampling at the time.

NOTE Photoshop's Histogram palette also updates continuously as you work in the Hue/Saturation dialog box or with any of the other color adjustment commands. The Histogram palette is discussed a little later in this chapter.

Remember that you don't have to settle for just one color readout. Shift-click in the image window to add up to four fixed color samples, just like those created with the color sampler tool, described in Chapter 4. To move a color sample after you've set it in place, Shift-drag it.

In the case of the Hue/Saturation dialog box, you can set color sample points only when the Edit pop-up menu is set to Master. After you set the samples, select some other options from the pop-up menu to modify a specific range. As long as you select only the Master option and edit only the Hue value, Photoshop retains all colors in an image. In other words, after shifting the hues in an image +60 degrees, you can later choose Hue/Saturation and shift the hues –60 degrees to restore the original colors.

NOTE Just as the Saturation option works like the Color control on a television, the Hue value serves the same purpose as the Tint control, and the Lightness value works like the Brightness control. Note that increasing the Saturation has the effect of heightening the contrast of the color channels, so display the Channels palette before opening the Hue/Saturation dialog box and display just one channel. Watch as you drag the Saturation slider, and then switch channels to see the impact on each one individually. You have to close the dialog box to switch channels though.

 **TIP** The Saturation option is especially useful for toning down images captured with low-end scanners and digital cameras, which have a tendency to exaggerate certain colors.

FIGURE 18.12

When you move the Eyedropper outside a color adjustment dialog box and into the image window, the Info palette lists the color values of the pixel beneath the cursor before and after the adjustment.

Before adjustments

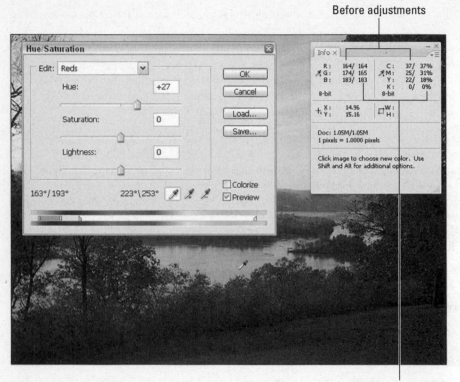

After adjustments

Correcting out-of-gamut colors

Another common use for the Saturation option is to prepare RGB images for process-color printing. As explained in Chapter 4, many colors in the RGB spectrum are considered out-of-gamut, meaning that they fall outside the smaller CMYK color space. Photoshop provides a means for recognizing such colors while remaining inside the RGB color space. Choose View ⇨ Gamut Warning or press Ctrl+Shift+Y (⌘+Shift+Y on the Mac) to color all out-of-gamut colors with gray (or some other color that you specify using the Preferences command). The pixels don't actually change to gray; they just appear gray onscreen as long as the command is active. To toggle View ⇨ Gamut Warning off, choose the command again.

How do you eliminate these out-of-gamut colors? Consider these options:

- Let Photoshop take care of the problem automatically when you convert the image by choosing Image ⇨ Mode ⇨ CMYK Color. This tactic can be a bit risky because Photoshop simply cuts off colors outside the gamut and converts them to their nearest CMYK equivalents, and this can result in flattened hues. Choosing View ⇨ Proof Setup ⇨ Working CMYK gives you an idea of how dramatic the flattening might be while permitting you to continue working in the RGB color space. Sometimes the effect is hardly noticeable, in which case no additional attention may be warranted.

- Another method is to scrub with the Sponge tool. Although it theoretically offers selective control — you just scrub at areas that need attention until the gray pixels created by the Gamut Warning command disappear — the process leaves too much to chance and can do more damage than simply choosing Image ⇨ Mode ⇨ CMYK Color. If you want to try this method, be ready to go back in History if you don't like the results.

- The third and best solution involves the Saturation option in the Hue/Saturation dialog box.

If you're surprised to read the last item (and wondering why it's listed last if it's the best bet), don't be; read on for a procedure you can try to bring your colors back into the CMYK color space.

STEPS: Eliminating out-of-gamut colors

1. **Create a duplicate of your image to serve as a CMYK preview.** Choose Image ⇨ Duplicate to create a copy of your image. Then choose View ⇨ Proof Setup ⇨ Working CMYK. Alternatively, you can press Ctrl+Y (⌘+Y on the Mac) to invoke color proofing. By default, Photoshop selects the working CMYK space. This image represents what Photoshop does with your image if you don't make any corrections. It's good to have around for comparison.

2. **Return to your original image, and choose Select ⇨ Color Range.** Then select the Out Of Gamut option from the Select pop-up menu, and press Enter (Win) or Return (Mac). You have now selected all anti-gamut pixels throughout your image.

3. **To monitor your progress, choose View ⇨ Gamut Warning to display the gray pixels.** Don't forget to press Ctrl+H (⌘+H on the Mac) to get rid of the marching ants.

4. **Press Ctrl+U (⌘+U on the Mac) to display the Hue/Saturation dialog box.**

5. **Lower the saturation of individual color ranges.** Don't change any settings while Master is selected; it's not exacting enough. Instead, experiment with specifying your own color ranges and lowering the Saturation value. Every time you see one of the pixels change from gray to color, it means that another pixel has now left the "out of gamut" ranks and is officially within the CMYK color space.

6. **When only a few hundred sporadic gray spots remain onscreen, click OK to return to the image window.** Choose Image ⇨ Mode ⇨ CMYK Color, and watch as Photoshop forces them into the gamut.

Bear in mind that the differences between your duplicate image and the one you manually forced into gamut may be very subtle and you may not really notice any immediate improvement. When the image is printed, however, the difference is more obvious and produces a better-looking image with a more dynamic range of colors.

Avoiding gamut-correction edges

The one problem with the previous procedure is that the Color Range command selects only out-of-gamut pixels without even partially selecting their neighbors. As a result, you desaturate out-of-gamut colors while leaving similar colors fully saturated, an effect that may result in jagged and unnatural edges.

One solution is to insert a step between Steps 2 and 3 in which you do the following: Select the Magic Wand tool, and change the Tolerance value in the Options bar to 12, for example (feel free to tinker). Next, choose Select ➪ Similar, which expands the selected area to incorporate all pixels that fall within the Tolerance range. Finally, choose Select ➪ Feather, and type a Feather Radius value that's about half the Tolerance. In this case, you'd set the Feather Radius to 6 because the Tolerance setting is at 12.

This solution isn't perfect — ideally, the Color Range option box wouldn't dim the Fuzziness slider when you choose Out Of Gamut — but it does succeed in partially selecting a few neighboring pixels without sacrificing too many of the out-of-gamut pixels, and makes for a smoother result.

Colorizing images

When you select the Colorize option in the Hue/Saturation dialog box, the options perform differently. Every pixel in the selection receives the same hue and the same level of saturation, and only the brightness values remain intact to ensure that the image remains recognizable. In most cases, you'll want to colorize only grayscale images or bad color scans. After all, colorizing ruins the original color composition of an image. For the best results, you'll want to set the Saturation values to somewhere in the neighborhood of 25 to 75.

> **TIP**   To touch up the edges of a colorized selection, change the foreground color to match the Hue and Saturation values you used in the Hue/Saturation dialog box. You can do this by choosing the HSB Sliders command from the Color palette menu and typing the values in the H and S option boxes. Set the B (Brightness) value to 100 percent. Next, select the Brush tool and change the Brush mode to Color by pressing Shift+Alt+C (Shift+Option+C on the Mac).

Shifting selected hues

The Replace Color command allows you to select an area of related colors and adjust the hue and saturation of that area. When you select Image ➪ Adjustments ➪ Replace Color, you get the dialog box shown in Figure 18.13. The Replace Color dialog box bears a strong resemblance to the Color Range dialog box; in fact, it varies in only a few respects. It's missing the Select and Selection Preview pop-up menus, and it offers three slider bars, just like the ones in the Hue/Saturation dialog box.

For further comfort or confusion (however the similarities with other tools strike you), this dialog box works the same as selecting a portion of an image using Select ➪ Color Range and editing it with the Hue/Saturation command, as done previously. You don't have as many options to work with, but the outcome is the same. The Replace Color and Color Range dialog boxes even share the same default settings. If you change the Fuzziness value in one, the default Fuzziness value of the other changes as well.

So given that the Replace Color command's dialog box looks and acts like two other tools, why does it even exist? Because it allows you to change the selection outline and apply different colors without affecting the image. Just select the Preview option to see the results of your changes onscreen, and you can play with the settings and click OK only when you like what you see.

CROSS-REF If you're not clear on how to use all the options in the Replace Color dialog box, read the section in Chapter 9 on using the Color Range command. The content there tells you all about the Eyedropper tools and the Fuzziness option so you'll have a better idea of how they work.

FIGURE 18.13

The Replace Color dialog box works like the Color Range dialog box described in Chapter 9, with the Hue/Saturation sliders thrown in.

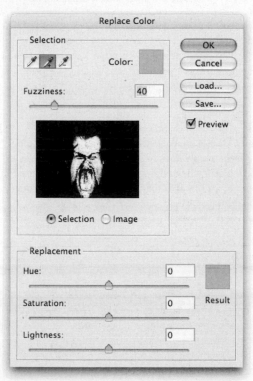

Shifting predefined colors

The Selective Color command permits you to adjust the colors in CMYK images. Although you can use Selective Color also when working on RGB or Lab images, it makes more sense in the CMYK color space because it permits you to adjust the levels of cyan, magenta, yellow, and black inks.

NOTE You may find that the Variations command provides better control and more intuitive options than the Selective Color command. Adobe created the Selective Color command to accommodate traditional press managers who prefer to have direct control over ink levels rather than monkeying around with hue, saturation, and other observational color controls. If Selective Color works for you, great. But don't get hung up on it if it never quite gels. You can accomplish all that Selective Color provides and more with the Variations command, described in the next section.

Choosing Image ⇨ Adjustments ⇨ Selective Color brings up the dialog box shown in Figure 18.14. To use the dialog box, choose the predefined color that you want to edit from the Colors pop-up menu and then adjust the four process-color slider bars to change the predefined color. When you select the Relative option, you add or subtract color, much as if you were moving the color around like musical chairs using the Hue slider bar. When you select Absolute, you change the predefined color to the exact value entered in the Cyan, Magenta, Yellow, and Black option boxes. The Absolute option is therefore very much like the Colorize option in the Hue/Saturation dialog box.

If you examine the Selective Color dialog box closely, you'll notice that it is very much like the Hue/Saturation dialog box. You have access to predefined colors in the form of a pop-up menu instead of radio buttons, and you can adjust slider bars to alter the color. The two key differences are that the pop-up menu lets you adjust whites, medium grays (Neutrals), and blacks — options missing from Hue/Saturation — and that the slider bars are always measured in the CMYK color space.

TIP As mentioned at the outset, the Selective Color command produces the most predictable results when you're working on a CMYK image. When you drag the Cyan slider to the right, for example, you're actually transferring brightness values to the cyan channel. However, you have to keep an eye out for a few anomalies, particularly when editing black. In the CMYK mode, areas of your image that appear black include not only black but also shades of cyan, magenta, and yellow, resulting in what printers call a *rich black* (or *saturated black*). Therefore, to change black to white, you have to set the Black slider to –100 percent and also set the Cyan, Magenta, and Yellow sliders to the same value.

Filtering colors

Since the dawn of color film, photographers have used different filters and balanced film stocks to correct the color balance in their photos. Different types of light sources produce a variety of *color temperatures*: Natural daylight generally takes on a bluish cast, or a higher color temperature, whereas artificial light often produces more shades of reds and yellows, or a lower color temperature. When not shooting on film that has been prebalanced to account for these casts, photographers often place a color filter over the lens to compensate — adding blue to an indoor scene to counteract the yellows, for example. It's similar to how folks who work in video need to set the white balance on their cameras before they shoot.

FIGURE 18.14

Select a predefined color from the Colors pop-up menu, and adjust the slider bars to change that color.

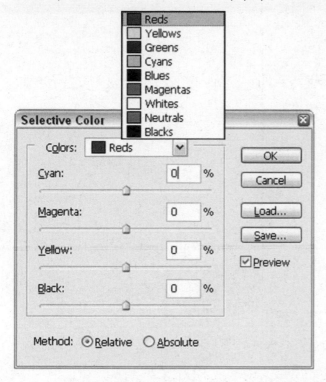

Although it has long let you correct the colorcast of an image through Variations (which is discussed next), Photoshop also offers a handy tool through the Photo Filter command. Choose Image ➪ Adjustments ➪ Photo Filter to display the Photo Filter dialog box, as shown in Figure 18.15. You are presented with the following options:

■ **Filter:** The Filter pop-up menu includes six specific filter options followed by a list of colors you can use to fix various colorcasts on your image. The first three options, Warming Filter (85), Warming Filter (LBA) and Warming Filter (81), simulate filters that a photographer would use when the color temperature is too cool, or bluish. Warming Filter (85) produces an orange colorcast, and Warming Filter (81) adds more of a tan tint to your image. Conversely, Cooling Filter (80), Cooling Filter (LBB) and Cooling Filter (82) add to your image a dark and rich cast of blue or a light cast of blue, respectively, to account for the yellows of artificial light. The rest of the options in the pop-up menu are different color presets that let you achieve photographic effects similar to those provided by some real-life filters.

FIGURE 18.15

You can use Photoshop's Photo Filter dialog box to simulate various lens filters and correct the overall colorcasts of your images.

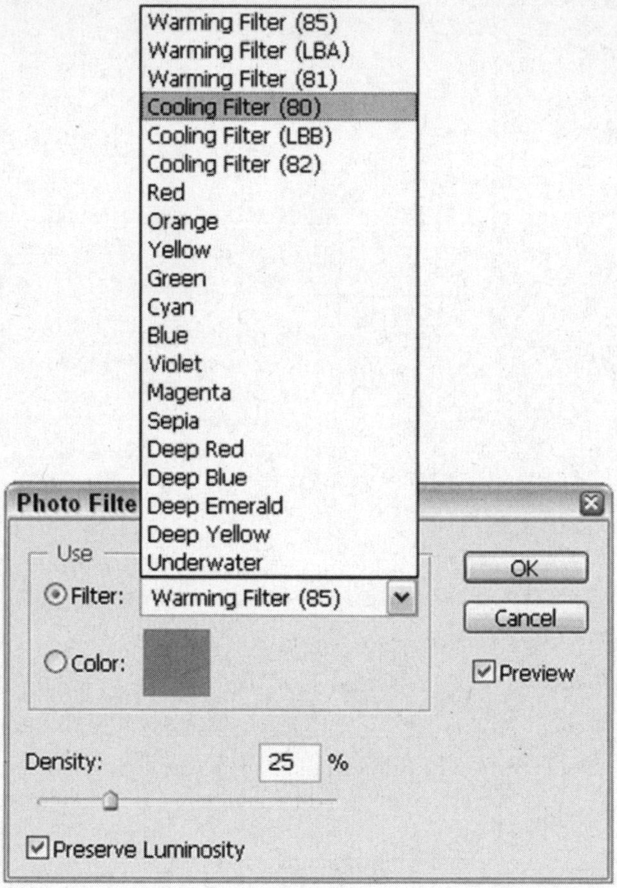

- **Color:** You also can specify any color and use it as though it were a filter. This is a great way to compensate for an unusual colorcast, such as a color light source in a scene that you'd like to neutralize. Click the color swatch to open the Color Picker, and select a color. Alternatively, after the Color Picker is open, you can click anywhere in your image to choose a particular color.

- **Density:** The Density slider adjusts the amount of color correction that the Photo Filter command will apply. You also can manually type a value in the option box above the slider. Remember that you can always adjust the amount of correction after you click OK by choosing Edit ➪ Fade Photo Filter and changing the Opacity value.

- **Preserve Luminosity:** Select this option to ensure that the brightness values are not darkened by your color adjustments.

You also can apply the Photo Filter command as an adjustment layer, ensuring that none of the changes you make is permanent. You'll take a look at adjustment layers later in this chapter.

Using the Variations command

The Variations command is Photoshop's most essential color-correction function *and* its most un-Photoshop-ish in that it's amazingly simple and highly effective all at the same time. Typically, control comes with complexity, but not so here.

When it comes to control and effectiveness, you can adjust hues and luminosity levels based on the brightness values of the pixels, something Hue/Saturation cannot do. You also can see what you're doing by clicking little thumbnail previews, shown in Figure 18.16, which takes much of the guesswork out of the correction process. This is where the "alarmingly simple" description comes in.

On the other hand, the Variations dialog box takes over your screen and prevents you from previewing corrections in the image window — not a big deal, but if you're used to seeing a preview in the image window, this can be jarring. Another problem (equally slight, really) is that you can't see the area outside a selection, which can be disconcerting when making color adjustments to just part of your image. You won't know until you click OK if the adjustment you made to the selection works in context, but you can slide the dialog box aside to see the entire original image. Just click the title bar of the dialog box and drag it.

The Variations command is really great for correcting an image in its entirety, although it can be useful for adjusting selections (with the previously mentioned issues kept in mind). Whether you like it for the whole image or just part of it, here's how it works: To infuse color into the image, click one of the thumbnails in the central portion of the dialog box. The thumbnail labeled More Cyan, for example, shifts the colors toward cyan. The thumbnail even shows how the additional cyan will look when added to the image. You can also use the Lighter and/or Darker thumbnails to adjust the overall light levels in your image or a selected portion thereof.

Notice that each of the color thumbnails is positioned directly opposite its complementary color, with the Current Pick between them. More Cyan is across from More Red, More Blue is across from More Yellow, and so on. In fact, clicking a thumbnail shifts colors not only toward the named color but also away from the opposite color. For example, if you click More Cyan and then click its opposite, More Red, you arrive at the original image.

NOTE Although this isn't exactly how the colors in the additive and subtractive worlds work — cyan is not the empirical opposite of red — the colors are theoretical opposites, and the Variations command makes the theory a practicality. After all, you haven't yet applied the color to the image, so the dialog box can calculate its adjustments in a pure and perfect world. Cyan and red ought to be opposites, so for the moment, they are.

To control the amount of color shifting that occurs when you click a thumbnail, move the slider in the upper-right corner of the dialog box. Fine produces minute changes; Coarse creates massive changes. Just to give you an idea of the difference between the two, you have to click a thumbnail about 40 times when the slider is set to Fine to equal one click when it's set to Coarse.

FIGURE 18.16

Click the "More" thumbnails to add more of one color or another to your image. Refer to the Current Pick to see your results before okaying them. Start over by clicking the Original thumbnail, and use the radio buttons to choose which aspect of the image to change. The slider adjusts sensitivity.

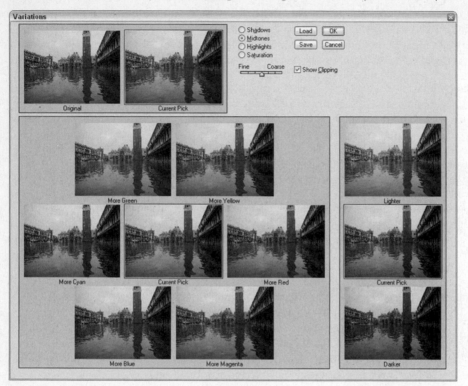

The radio buttons at the top control which colors in the image are affected. Select Shadows to change the darkest colors, Highlights to change the lightest colors, and Midtones to change everything in between.

NOTE In fact, if you're familiar with the Levels dialog box, you may have noticed that the first three radio buttons have direct counterparts in the sliders in the Levels dialog box. For example, when you click the Lighter thumbnail while the Highlights option is selected in the Variations dialog box, you perform the same action as moving the white slider in the Levels dialog box to the left — that is, you make the lightest colors in the image even lighter.

Selecting the Saturation option lets you increase or decrease the saturation of colors in an image. Only one thumbnail appears on each side of the Current Pick image: one that decreases the saturation and another that increases it. The Variations command modifies saturation differently than

Hue/Saturation. Hue/Saturation pushes the saturation of a color as far as it will go, but Variations attempts to modify the saturation without changing overall brightness values. As a result, an image saturated with Hue/Saturation looks lighter than one saturated with Variations.

As you click the options — particularly when modifying saturation — you may notice that unexpected colors spring up in the thumbnails. These brightly colored pixels are gamut warnings, highlighting colors that exceed the boundaries of the current color space. For example, if you're working in the RGB mode, these colors extend beyond the RGB gamut. Although the colors won't actually appear inverted as they do in the dialog box, don't exceed the color space because it results in areas of flat color, just as when you convert between the RGB and CMYK spaces. To view the thumbnails without the weirdly colored pixels, deselect the Show Clipping option.

Using the Match Color command

With Adobe's introduction of the Match Color command in Photoshop CS, the Photoshop user community wondered if Adobe had really added a true color-matching tool. Well, even with the release of Photoshop CS2 and now CS3, the answer was and is no, and the wait continues: The Match Color command has nothing to do with emulating the color of a match. It does, however, adjust the colorcast of one image to match that of another, which can still be pretty useful.

In case you were wondering how such a tool might be useful, imagine that you have a series of photos taken outdoors, on a day when the sun was coming in and out over the course of your shoot and the lighting was really different in several of the shots. Or you were taking photos of people indoors, and in the later afternoon, when the room got hotter, people started to look a bit flushed, or the sunlight coming into the room was starting to change and it no longer drowned out the fluorescent lighting from overhead in the room. Any of these scenarios would present you with the need to change a colorcast, making one photo's cast match another's. Brighten the cloudy photos, smooth out the ruddy cheeks, soften the pasty fluorescent glow.

You begin by opening both the image you want to adjust and the image whose color you want to match. If you want Match Color to base its analysis on a particular part of the image, such as skin tones, select the colors you want to isolate in both the source and destination images. Make sure the destination image is in the active image window and choose Image ➪ Adjustments ➪ Match Color to display the dialog box shown in Figure 18.17.

The following list explains the options available to you in the Match Color dialog box:

- **Target:** The Target is automatically set as whatever image was active when you chose the command, and you can't change this. If your destination image contains a selection, the Ignore Selection when Applying Adjustment option is available. If you don't select this option, the effect applies only to the selected area in your image, which may not be the desired result. If you've made a selection in your destination image and you don't want to confine the effect to that selection, select the option.

FIGURE 18.17

The Match Color command in Photoshop lets you adjust the colorcast of one image to match another.

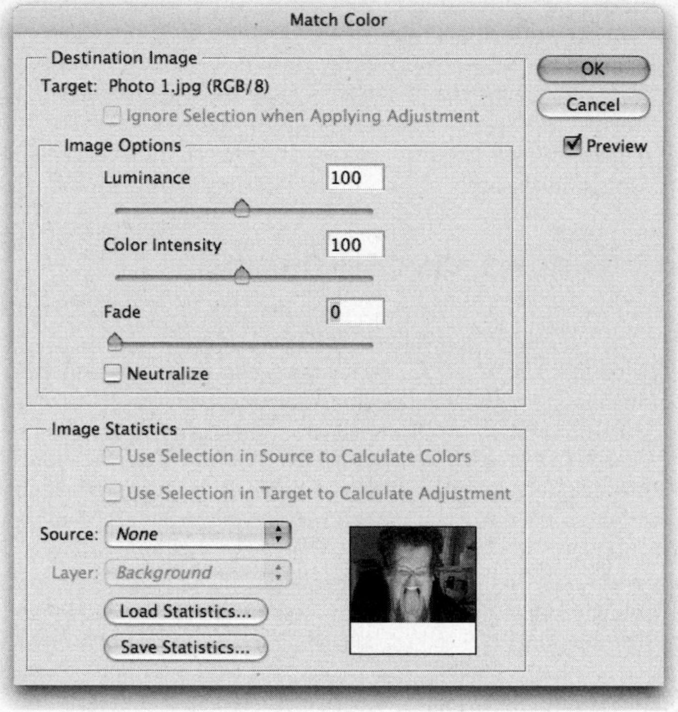

- **Image Options:** The Image Options let you make adjustments to the lightness, saturation, and strength of the Match Color command. The Luminance slider defaults to a value of 100 and lets you increase or decrease the brightness of your destination image. Color Intensity works much like the Saturation slider in the Hue/Saturation command. The Fade slider saves you the step of applying Match Color and then choosing Edit ⇨ Fade Match Color. Increase this value to gradually bring in color elements from your unaltered destination image. A value of 100 exactly matches your pre-Match Color image.

TIP   Select the Neutralize option to tell Photoshop to examine the destination image, without factoring in any values from the source image, and attempt to remove any colorcast that it finds. You may find that sometimes it works really well and sometimes it just dulls your image. If you don't get the results you want, try using the Photo Filter command or the Variations dialog box, discussed earlier in this chapter, to manually target and correct a colorcast.

- **Image Statistics:** These options let you specify a source image and determine how it is interpreted. The source can be any other open image, or even a layer within the destination image itself. The latter is particularly useful if, for example, you're trying to composite a person from another photo on a separate layer into your destination image. If your source image contains a selection, select the Use Selection in Source to Calculate Colors option to only analyze the statistics, or characteristics, of the selected region. When this option is deselected, Match Color determines the statistics of the source by looking at all the pixels in the image. Similarly, selecting the Use Selection in Target to Calculate Adjustment option makes changes to the target image using colors found in only the selected area of that image. If you selected similarly colored areas in both your target and source images, leave both of these options selected.

Use the Source pop-up menu to choose the source image from among all open images. If you select None, you still have access to the Neutralize option and other Image Options settings. If you select a source with more than one layer, you can specify the layer from which you're culling statistics in the Layer pop-up menu. You also have the option of choosing a merged composite of all the layers in the source image.

Finally, the Match Color dialog box offers you the option of both saving and then loading the statistics it has calculated from a source image. This can be useful in a couple of ways. First, it means you don't need to have a source image open when applying the Match Color command. It also means that you can save the statistics of an image and use them to adjust an unlimited number of other images, on other machines, long after the original source image is out of the picture.

> **NOTE** The Match Color command works only with images in the RGB mode.

Enhancing colors in a compressed image

Now that you know several methods for adjusting hues and saturation levels with Photoshop, we want to discuss some of the possible challenges you may face in using them. The danger of rotating colors or increasing the saturation of an image is that you can bring out some unstable colors. Adjusting the hues can switch ratty pixels from colors that your eyes aren't very sensitive to — particularly blue — into colors your eyes see very well, such as reds and greens. Drab color also can hide poor detail, which becomes painfully obvious when you make the colors bright and vivid; all the problems in the image will come screaming out at you after you've heightened the colors.

Unstable colors may be the result of JPEG compression, as in the case of the digital photo. Or you may be able to blame bad scanning or poor lighting; the potential causes are abundant, and we've all been victims. No matter what's caused your color problems, you can correct the problem using the Median and Gaussian Blur commands, explained in the following procedure. Grab a particularly color-challenged digital photo and try the following:

STEPS: Boosting the saturation of digital photos

1. **Select the entire image, and copy it to a new layer.** You can speed this process along with the keyboard shortcuts Ctrl+A and Ctrl+J (⌘+A and ⌘+J on the Mac).

2. **Press Ctrl+U (⌘+U on the Mac) to display the Hue/Saturation dialog box.** Then raise the Saturation value to whatever setting you desire. Don't worry if your image starts to fall apart: That's the whole point of these steps. Pay attention to the color and don't worry about the rest.

3. **Choose Filter ⇨ Noise ⇨ Median.** Median is a great tool for fixing JPEG color problems, and a Radius value of 4 or 5 pixels works well for most images. You can take it even higher when working with resolutions of 200 ppi or more. This destroys the detail, but that's not important in this exercise, because you're only concerned with color right now.

4. **Choose Filter ⇨ Blur ⇨ Gaussian Blur.** As always, the Median filter introduces its own edges, and because you don't want strong edges here, you can be fairly aggressive with the Gaussian Blur settings.

5. **Select Color from the blend mode pop-up menu in the Layers palette.** Photoshop mixes the blurry color with the crisp detail underneath.

If your image is still a little soft, flatten the image and sharpen it until you like the results.

CROSS-REF Take a little refresher on those Blur, Sharpen, and Noise filters in Chapter 10.

Making Custom Brightness Adjustments

You may find the Lighter and Darker options in the Variations dialog box to be more effective and controllable than the Lightness slider in the Hue/Saturation dialog box because you can specify whether to edit the darkest, lightest, or medium colors in an image. Focusing on these areas gives you the ability to target trouble spots, which is handy if not all of your pixels are in need of lighting adjustment. If your needs are even more specific, you may find that neither command is adequate for making very precise adjustments to the brightness and contrast of an image. If this is the case, Photoshop provides three expert-level commands for adjusting the brightness levels in both grayscale and color images:

■ **Levels:** This command is great for most color corrections. It lets you adjust the darkest values, lightest values, and midrange colors with a minimum of complexity and a maximum amount of control.

■ **Curves:** This command is great for creating special effects and correcting images beyond the help of the Levels command. Levels didn't really do it all? Using the Curves command, you can map every brightness value in every color channel to an entirely different brightness value. Hop from channel to channel, and let Curves work its magic until you're happy with the results.

- **Shadow/Highlight:** This command is great for altering the brightness levels of certain sections of an image without harming other sections. It provides for a different approach than the Levels command and is particularly good at fixing backlighting problems in images.

The Histogram palette

As discussed earlier in the section on the Threshold command, a histogram is a graph depicting the intensity of different values in your image. While the histogram in the Threshold command displays only brightness values, the Histogram palette is capable of showing not only the brightness values but the combined color values and the individual color values in an image as well. Keep the palette onscreen, and you're never more than a quick look away from knowing the distribution of levels in your image at any given time.

Choose Window ➪ Histogram to display the Histogram palette. While at first it may seem like there's not much to the palette, give it a chance. It saves you the trouble of choosing the Levels command, but you don't have access to any other information or the ability to select different channels. Or do you? Click Expanded View in the palette menu, and you'll gain access to Channels. The basic, not terribly illuminating view as well as the Expanded View are shown in Figure 18.18.

The expanded view is where you can explore the real power of the Histogram palette. It contains the following options:

- **Channel:** The Channel pop-up menu lets you determine the types of values displayed by the Histogram palette. By default, it's set to the color mode in which you're working. If you're editing an image in either the Grayscale or Indexed Color modes, this menu is unavailable.

  From the Channel menu, you can choose to display the default combined tonal levels or any of the color channels individually. Choose Show Channels in Color from the palette menu to display the individual channels in the colors they represent. Any additional channels you have created also can be selected from the Channel pop-up menu. Choose Luminosity to display a histogram of only the brightness levels in your image. Finally, you can call up an overlapping composite graph of all the color channels by choosing Colors.

FIGURE 18.18

The Histogram palette's Expanded View (on the right) gives you an impressive amount of information about the intensity levels of your pixels.

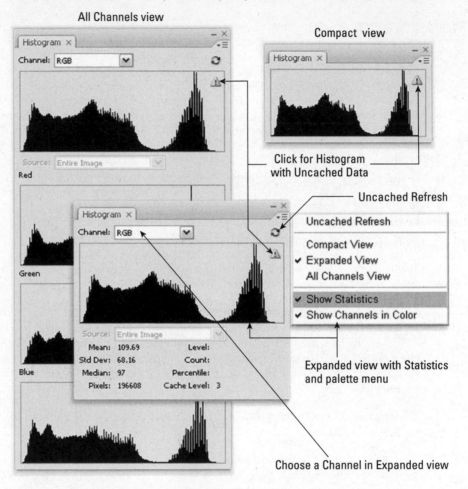

All Channels view

Compact view

Click for Histogram
with Uncached Data

Uncached Refresh

Uncached Refresh

Compact View
✔ Expanded View
All Channels View

✔ Show Statistics
✔ Show Channels in Color

Expanded view with Statistics
and palette menu

Source: Entire Image
Mean: 109.69   Level:
Std Dev: 68.16   Count:
Median: 97   Percentile:
Pixels: 196608   Cache Level: 3

Choose a Channel in Expanded view

- **Uncached Refresh:** Whenever you make an adjustment to an image that affects its brightness or color intensity levels, the histogram redraws itself to compensate. It saves time doing this by analyzing the already existing cache of the image and guessing how the change you've made will affect the graph. The Preferences setting that enables the Levels command to use the image cache is covered in Chapter 2.

Regardless of how you've set your preferences, the Histogram palette automatically regenerates based on the image cache unless you click Uncached Refresh (labeled in Figure 18.18), which tells the palette to redraw the graph based on the current image.

Photoshop provides a number of other ways to refresh the histogram. You also can click the cached data warning icon (labeled in Figure 18.18) that appears in the top-right corner of the histogram whenever you're viewing a graph created from the cache. Additionally, you can accomplish the same thing by doubling-clicking the histogram itself. Finally, you can choose the Uncached Refresh option from the palette menu.

■ **Source:** In a multilayered image, you can tell the Histogram palette to display values for either the Entire Image or just the Selected Layer from the Source pop-up menu. If the image contains any adjustment layers, select one of them and choose Adjustment Composite from the Source pop-up menu to display a histogram of the adjustment layer and any visible layers below it.

Below the Source menu in the expanded view, you'll find statistical information about the image or layer, which you can toggle on or off by choosing Show Statistics from the palette menu. The statistics give you some useful information about the intensity values in your image, plus you can find out about the intensity Level at the spot under your cursor. You also can view the Count, which tells you the total number of pixels in the image that match a particular intensity.

One of the great strengths of the Histogram palette is the fact that it updates on the fly even while you're working in one of the color adjustments dialog boxes (but only if you have selected the Preview option). Even better, the palette doesn't simply replace the original histogram with the new one; it keeps the original histogram visible behind the adjusted histogram in a grayed-out version.

TIP   When you select a portion of an image, the Histogram palette displays intensity levels and statistics for only the selected area.

Although many of the other palettes become frozen when you're working in a dialog box, you never lose access to the options in the Histogram palette — given that it is used in conjunction with so many of them. One exception? You can't access the Histogram palette options when the Filter Gallery window is open.

Oh, and don't panic if you go to the palette and see a circle with a line through it where the histogram should be: This is simply what's displayed when there is no image open in the Photoshop workspace.

The Levels command

When you choose Image ➪ Adjustments ➪ Levels or press Ctrl+L (⌘+L on the Mac), Photoshop displays the Levels dialog box shown in Figure 18.19. The dialog box offers a histogram, matching the combined tonal histogram found in the Histogram palette, as well as two sets of slider bars with corresponding option boxes and a three automated Eyedropper options in the lower-right corner. You can compress and expand the range of brightness values in an image by manipulating the Input Levels options (drag the sliders). Then you can map the original brightness values to new brightness values by adjusting the Output Levels options.

FIGURE 18.19

Use the Levels dialog box to map brightness values in the image (Input Levels) to new brightness values (Output Levels).

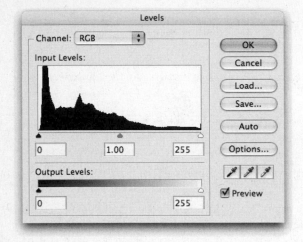

The options in the Levels dialog box work as follows:

- **Channel:** Select the color channel that you want to edit from this pop-up menu. You can apply different Input Levels and Output Levels values to each color channel.

- **Input Levels:** Use these options to modify the contrast of the image by darkening the darkest colors and lightening the lightest ones. The Input Levels option boxes correspond to the slider immediately below the histogram. You map pixels to black (or the darkest Output Levels value) by typing a number from 0 to 255 in the first option box or by dragging the black slider. For example, if you raise the value to 50, all colors with brightness values of 50 or less in the original image become black, darkening the image as shown in the first example of Figure 18.20.

  You can map pixels at the opposite end of the brightness scale to white (or the lightest Output Levels value) by typing a number from 0 to 255 in the last option box or by dragging the white slider. If you lower the value to 200, all colors with brightness values of 200 or greater become white, lightening the image, as shown in the second example of Figure 18.20. In the last example of the figure, the first value was raised and the last value lowered, thereby increasing the amount of contrast in the image.

 The Input Levels value is to select the numeric field and then press the up-arrow or down-arrow key. Each press of an arrow key raises or lowers the value by 1. Press Shift with an arrow key to change the value in increments of 10.

 If you press and hold Alt (Option on the Mac) while dragging the black and white Input Levels sliders, you can watch where the first shadows appear and where the first highlight detail begins in your RGB image.

FIGURE 18.20

Here you see the results of raising the first Input Levels value to 50 (left), lowering the last value to 200 (right), and combining the two (bottom).

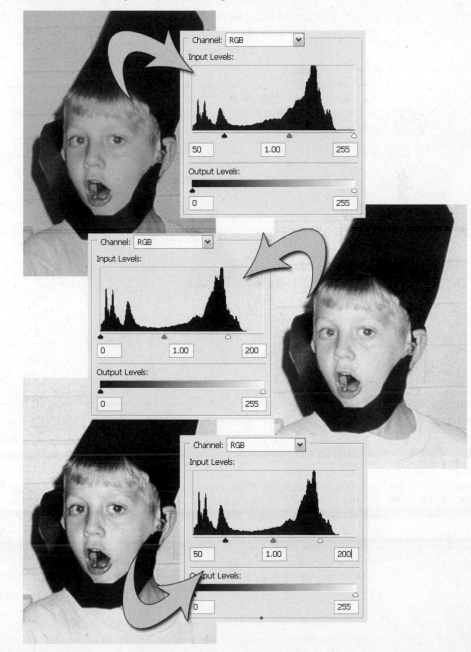

■ **Gamma:** The middle Input Levels option box and the corresponding gray triangle in the slider bar (shown in Figure 18.21) represent the midtone, or *gamma value*, which is the brightness level of the medium-gray value in the image. The gamma value can range from 0.10 to 9.99, with 1.00 being dead-on medium gray. Increase the gamma value or drag the gray slider to the left to lighten the medium grays (also called *midtones*). Lower the gamma value or drag the gray slider to the right to darken the medium grays.

FIGURE 18.21

The middle slider under the Histogram controls midtones. Drag it to adjust the middle box, or type a new number in the middle of the three Input Levels boxes and see the slider move to indicate the new midtone level.

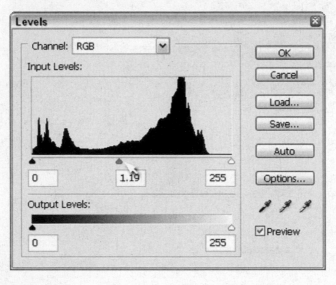

TIP You also can edit the gamma value by pressing the up-arrow and down-arrow keys. Pressing an arrow key changes the value by 0.01; pressing Shift+arrow changes the value by 0.10.

■ **Output Levels:** Use these options to curtail the range of brightness levels in an image by lightening the darkest pixels and darkening the lightest pixels. You adjust the brightness of the darkest pixels — those that correspond to the black Input Levels slider — by typing a number from 0 to 255 in the first option box or by dragging the black slider. For example, if you raise the value to 100, no color can be darker than that brightness level (roughly 60 percent black), which lightens the image. You adjust the brightness of the lightest pixels — those that correspond to the white Input Levels slider — by typing a number from 0 to 255 in the second option box or by dragging the white slider. If you lower the value to 175, no color can be lighter than that brightness level (roughly 30 percent black), darkening the image. If you raise the first value and lower the second value, you dramatically decrease the amount of contrast in the image. Note that any change to the Output Levels values decreases the contrast of the image. Figure 18.22 shows two halves of the same image: The left half has darks made lighter, and the right half has lights made darker.

TIP   You can fully or partially invert an image using the Output Levels slider triangles. Just drag the black slider to the right and drag the white slider to the left past the black slider. The colors flip, whites mapping to dark colors and blacks mapping to light colors.

- **Load** and **Save:** You can load settings to disk and save settings to disk using these buttons.

- **Auto:** You might assume that the Auto button in the Levels dialog box performs the same function as the Auto Levels command, discussed earlier in this chapter. And if you were working in a version of the program before Photoshop 7, you'd be right. Photoshop 7, however, added the Options button into the mix. Since then, the effect of clicking Auto in the Levels dialog box (as well as in the Curves dialog box) has depended on the settings in the Auto Color Correction Options dialog box, described next.

- **Options:** Clicking Options in the Levels (or Curves) dialog box brings up the Auto Color Correction Options dialog box, shown in Figure 18.23. The top section, Algorithms, determines the type of correction you want to apply. Instead of the long, somewhat confusing names, these three choices could be labeled Auto Contrast, Auto Levels, and Auto Color, because that's what the choices are equivalent to. In fact, you can rest your cursor over each name to see an informative tool tip telling you just this. Select the Snap Neutral Midtones option, and you'll apply Auto Color's automatic gamma correction as well. If you select the Save as Defaults option, your settings are remembered the next time you click Auto in the Levels and Curves dialog boxes.

The Target Colors & Clipping settings come into play not only when you click Auto in the Levels and Curves dialog boxes but also when you choose the Auto Levels and Auto Contrast commands in the Adjustments submenu. (This is assuming that Save as defaults check box is selected.) Here you can choose colors to assign to the target values for the highlights, midtones, and shadows in your image. You also have access to the Clip values for the highlights and shadows. Type higher values to increase the number of pixels mapped to black and white; decrease the values to lessen the effect. Figure 18.24 compares the effect of the default 0.50 percent values to higher values of 5.00 and 9.99 percent (the highest setting the field accepts). As you can see, raising the Clip value produces higher contrast effects.

FIGURE 18.22

Lighten your darks and darken your lights, and you'll get something like these results of raising the first Output Levels value to 100 (left) and lowering the second value to 175.

FIGURE 18.23

Customizing the settings in the Auto Color Correction Options dialog box lets you take the "auto" out of Photoshop's auto correction commands.

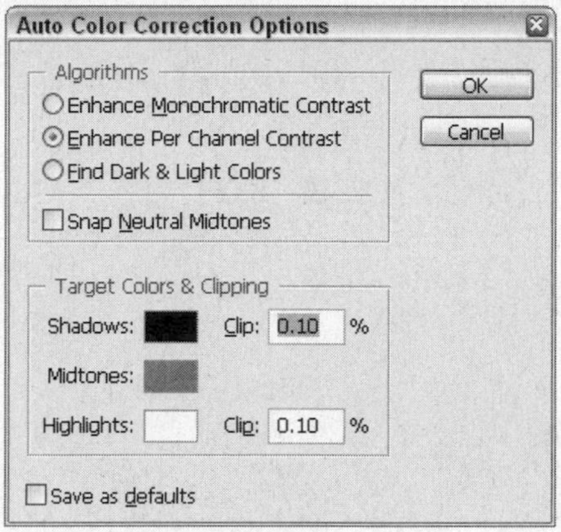

NOTE The Clip settings have an effect only on Auto Levels and Contrast, not Auto Color. The reason is that Auto Color seeks to neutralize shadows and highlights, as opposed to clipping away the darkest and lightest colors.

TIP You can combine the Auto Color Correction Options with the Auto Color command to create a truly useful tool. If you have a batch of photos you need to correct that share similar problems — maybe you've scanned an overexposed roll of film from a recent holiday — make adjustments to the first photo with the Target Colors & Clipping settings and make sure you select the Save as defaults option. Now when you open subsequent photos, you can simply choose Image ➪ Adjustments ➪ Auto Color — or press Ctrl+Shift+B (⌘+Shift+B on the Mac) — to instantly apply the same color correction.

- **Eyedroppers:** Select one of the Eyedropper tools in the Levels dialog box and click a pixel in the image window to automatically adjust the color of that pixel. If you click a pixel with the black Eyedropper tool (the first of the three), Photoshop maps the color of the pixel and all darker colors to black. If you click a pixel with the white Eyedropper tool (the last of the three), Photoshop maps it and all lighter colors to white. Use the gray Eyedropper tool (middle) to change the color you clicked to medium gray and adjust all other colors accordingly.

TIP One way to use the Eyedropper tools is to color-correct scans without lots of messing around. Include a neutral swatch of gray with the photograph you want to scan. (For those who own a Pantone swatch book, Cool Gray 5 or 6 is your best bet.) After opening the scan in Photoshop, choose the Levels command, select the gray Eyedropper tool, and click the neutral gray swatch in the image window. This technique doesn't perform miracles, but it helps you distribute lights and darks in the image more evenly. You then can fine-tune the image using the Input Levels and Output Levels options.

FIGURE 18.24

This figure shows the effect of the default Clip values in the Auto Color Correction Options dialog box (.50% on the left) and the effect after raising the values (5.00% in the middle and 9.99% on the right).

TIP By default, the Eyedroppers map to white, gray, and black. But you can change that. Double-click any one of the three Eyedroppers to display the Color Picker dialog box. For example, suppose you double-click the white Eyedropper, set the color values to C:2, M:3, Y:5, K:0, and then click a pixel in the image window. Instead of making the pixel white, Photoshop changes the clicked color—and all colors lighter than it—to C:2, M:3, Y:5, K:0, which is great for avoiding hot highlights and ragged edges.

The Curves command

If you want to be able to map any brightness value in an image to absolutely any other brightness value, the Curves command is what you need. When you choose Image ➪ Adjustments ➪ Curves or press Ctrl+M (⌘+M on the Mac), Photoshop displays the Curves dialog box, shown in Figure 18.25, which offers access to the most complex and powerful color-correction options on the planet.

Here's a quick sketch of how the Curves dialog box options work:

- **Channel:** The concept of channels isn't new, certainly, and the use of channels within an adjustment dialog box is nothing new in the case of Curves either. You select the color channel that you want to edit from this pop-up menu, and then apply different mapping functions to different channels by drawing in the graph below the pop-up menu. Of course, as always, the options along the right side of the dialog box affect all colors in the selected portion of an image regardless of which Channel option is active.

- **Brightness graph:** The brightness graph is where you map brightness values in the original image to new brightness values. The horizontal axis of the graph represents input levels; the vertical axis represents output levels. The *brightness curve* charts the relationship between input and output levels. The lower-left corner is the origin of the graph (the point at which both input and output values are 0). Move right in the graph for higher input values and up for higher output values. The brightness graph is the core of this dialog box, so upcoming sections explain it in more detail.

TIP By default, a grid of horizontal and vertical dotted lines crisscrosses the brightness graph, subdividing it into quarters. For added precision, you can divide the graph into horizontal and vertical tenths by Alt-clicking (Win) or Option-clicking (Mac) in the graph to toggle between tenths and quarters.

- **Brightness bar:** The horizontal brightness bar shows the direction of light and dark values in the graph. When the dark end of the brightness bar appears on the left—as by default when editing an RGB image—colors are measured in terms of brightness values. The colors in the graph proceed from black on the left to white on the right, as demonstrated in the left example of Figure 18.26. Therefore, higher values produce lighter colors. This setting measures colors in the same direction as the Levels dialog box.

  This dialog box has seen some changes in CS3. In previous versions of Photoshop, you clicked the brightness bar to toggle the view between brightness values and ink coverage. Adobe has extended the interface here, so this option is a little more obvious. The bottom portion of the dialog box now presents the Curve Display Options button. By clicking this, you gain access to radio buttons that toggle the view between Light and Pigment/Ink. You also have check boxes that allow you to show the channel overlays, histogram, baseline, and intersection lines. If you select Pigment/Ink, white and black switch places on the brightness bar, as shown in the second example of the figure, and the dialog box then measures the colors in terms of ink coverage, from 0 to 100 percent of the primary color. Higher values now produce darker colors. This is the default setting for grayscale and CMYK images.

FIGURE 18.25

Click the curved line in the Curves dialog box, and drag the line up or down, from one or more points on the line. The brightness in the active photo is thereby adjusted.

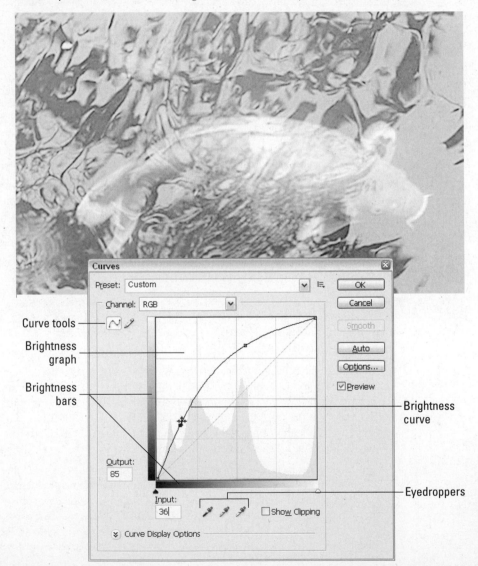

FIGURE 18.26

Click the brightness bar to change the way in which the graph measures color: by brightness values (left) or by ink coverage (right).

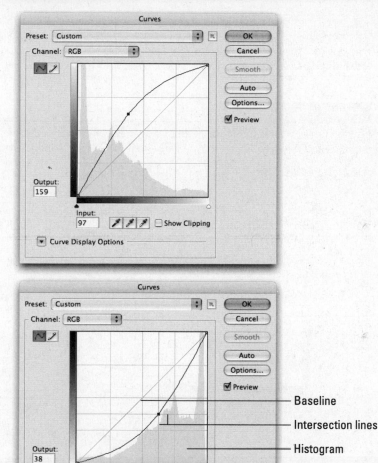

- **Curve tools:** Use the Curve tools to draw the curve in the brightness graph. The Point tool (labeled in Figure 18.27) is selected by default. Click in the graph with this tool to add a point to the curve. Drag a point to move it. To delete a point, Ctrl-click (Win) or ⌘-click (Mac) it.

  The Pencil tool lets you draw free-form curves simply by dragging in the graph, as illustrated in Figure 18.27. This pencil works much like Photoshop's standard Pencil tool, in that you can draw straight lines by clicking one location in the graph and Shift-clicking a different point.

FIGURE 18.27

Use the Curves dialog box Pencil tool to draw free-form lines in the brightness graph. If the lines end up jagged or spiky, you can soften them by clicking Smooth.

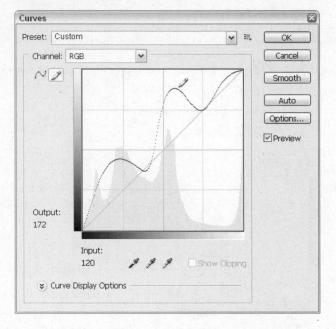

- **Input and Output values:** The Input and Output values monitor the location of your cursor in the graph according to brightness values or ink coverage, depending on the setting of the brightness bar. You can modify the Input and Output values when working with the Point tool. Just click the point on the graph that you want to adjust and then type new values. The Input number represents the brightness or ink value of the point before you entered the Curves dialog box; the Output number represents the new brightness or ink value.

When editing multiple graph points from the keyboard, you may want to activate the points from the keyboard. To advance from one point to the next, press Ctrl+Tab (Control+Tab on the Mac). To select the previous point, press Ctrl+Shift+Tab (Control+Shift+Tab on the Mac). To deselect all points, press Ctrl+D (⌘+D on the Mac).

 You also can change the Output value by using the up-arrow and down-arrow keys. Click the point you want to modify, and then press the up-arrow or down-arrow key to raise or lower, respectively, the Output value in increments of 1. Press Shift+up arrow or down arrow to change the Output value in increments of 10. Note that these techniques — and the ones that follow — work only when the Point tool is active because you can't change points with the Pencil tool.

- **Load** and **Save:** Use these buttons to load and save curve settings to disk, respectively.

- **Smooth:** Click Smooth to smooth out curves drawn with the Pencil tool. Doing so leads to smoother color transitions in the image window. This button is dimmed unless the Pencil tool is active.

- **Auto:** This button is identical to the Auto button available in the Levels dialog box: It allows you to apply, automatically, the settings you can establish in the Options dialog box (opened by clicking Options, discussed in the next paragraph) when Auto is clicked. For more details on this concept, see the section "The Levels command" earlier in this chapter; the Levels dialog box has an Auto button too.

- **Options:** Identical to the Options button in the Levels dialog box, this opens the Auto Color Correction dialog box, wherein you can set the Target Colors & Clipping settings discussed in the Levels command coverage earlier in this chapter. Whatever you set in this dialog box is applied by the aforementioned Auto button.

- **Eyedroppers:** If you move the cursor out of the dialog box and into the image window, you get the standard eyedropper cursor. Click a pixel in the image to locate the brightness value of that pixel in the graph. A circle appears in the graph, and the Input and Output numbers list the value for as long as you hold down the mouse button, as shown in the first example in Figure 18.28.

  The other eyedroppers work as they do in the Levels dialog box, mapping pixels to black, medium gray, or white (or other colors if you double-click the eyedropper icons, which opens the Color Picker). For example, the White Point Eyedropper tool changes to white whichever pixel you click.

NOTE Bear in mind that Photoshop maps the value to each color channel independently. So when editing a full-color image in the Curves dialog box, you need to switch channels to see the results of clicking with the eyedropper. You can further adjust the brightness value of that pixel by dragging the corresponding point in the graph, as demonstrated in the last example of the figure.

TIP Remember to keep an eye on the Histogram palette to view dynamic, constantly updating results while working in the Curves dialog box.

FIGURE 18.28

Use the standard eyedropper cursor (the first of the three buttons) to locate a color in the brightness graph. Click with one of the Eyedropper tools from the Curves dialog box to map the color of that pixel in the graph. You then can edit the location of the point in the graph by dragging it.

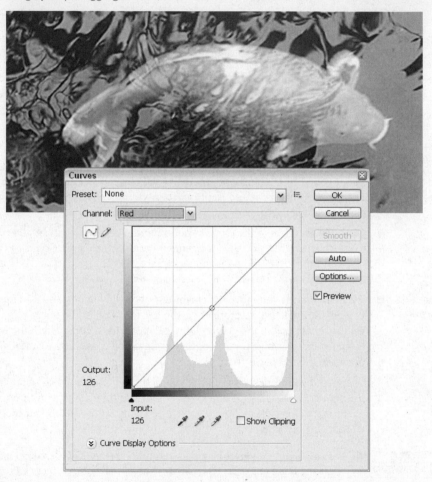

Tricks for Curves

The eyedropper tools aren't the only way to add points to a curve from the image window. Photoshop offers two more keyboard tricks that greatly simplify the process of pinpointing and adjusting colors in the Curves dialog box. Bear in mind, both techniques work only when the Point tool is active.

- To add a color as a point along the Curves graph, Ctrl-click (⌘-click on the Mac) a pixel in the image window. Photoshop adds the point to the channel displayed in the dialog box. For example, if the RGB composite channel is visible, the point is added to the RGB composite curve. If the Red channel is visible, Photoshop adds the point to the red graph and leaves the green and blue graphs unchanged.

- To add a color to all graphs, regardless of which channel is visible in the Curves dialog box, Ctrl+Shift-click (⌘+Shift-click on the Mac) a pixel in the image window. In the case of an RGB image, Photoshop maps the red, green, and blue brightness values for that pixel to each of the red, green, and blue graphs in the Curves dialog box. The RGB composite graph shows no change; switch to the individual channels to see the new point.

Gradient maps

The Gradient Map command permits you to apply a gradation as a Curves map. In other words, you can use a gradient map to adjust the brightness values of an image so that they match the values in a custom gradient. Just choose Image ⇨ Adjustments ⇨ Gradient Map to display the dialog box pictured in Figure 18.29. Make sure the Preview option is selected. Then click the button to the right of the gradient preview to display the familiar gradient drop-down palette, and select a gradient from the palette.

FIGURE 18.29

Choose the Gradient Map command to apply a preset gradient as a Curves map.

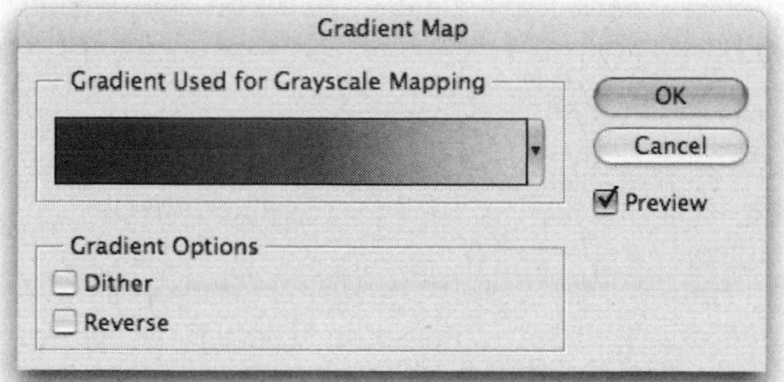

How does this work? Well, any gradient can be expressed as a Curves graph, progressing through a variety of brightness values in each of the three (RGB) or four (CMYK) color channels. When applied as a gradient map, the beginning of the gradient maps black and the end of the gradient maps white. If you apply the Violet, Orange preset, for example, the dark colors in the image map to violet and the light colors map to orange. Noise-type gradients (introduced in Chapter 6) produce especially interesting effects.

When drawing arbitrary curves, you may find the Pencil tool to be more flexible than the Point tool — although you will probably want to follow the Pencil tool with a click of the Smooth button so that any unwanted zigs, zags, or jags in the line can be ironed out in favor of smooth waves.

The Shadow/Highlight command

Sometimes it seems that the camera, be it digital or film, sees more than we do with our eyes. This is normally an observation made when a photo exposes some detail that no one noticed had the scene in question not been captured in a still photo, where every little object could be studied. In truth, the lens on any camera, but especially a digital camera, can't hold a candle to the human eye in terms of capturing light and color.

Modern cameras try their best to keep up with complicated and varied lighting situations, but unlike your eyes, which can probably adjust and absorb the next scene after just one blink, when it comes to a camera, you're often stuck having to choose between sacrificing the darker areas of an image or overexposing the lighter areas because the camera just can't keep up. For example, how many times have you photographed someone against the sky, only to find the sky perfectly exposed and your subject so dark you can barely make out his or her features?

Thanks to Photoshop's Shadow/Highlight command, the camera's limitations can be accommodated. It's a great tool for both the too-bright and the too-dark photo (or portions thereof), pulling detail out of the shadows and shielding your eyes from blinding highlights. You may find that that you're happier with its results on images with dark shadows, however, but you'll be glad to have it in your arsenal for a variety of lighting problems.

To use the command, choose Image ⇨ Adjustments ⇨ Shadow/Highlight and select the Show More Options check box to view the dialog box shown in Figure 18.30. As soon as you choose the command, you'll see a change take place in your image, as the command does a little bit of its job right away. You can further the effects by adjusting the three areas of the dialog box — Shadows, Highlights, and Adjustments — and the sliders within them.

The Shadow/Highlight command examines the image and, according to your settings, deems certain spots to be "shadows" and others "highlights." From there, you adjust the sliders to tell Photoshop just how much brightening or darkening it should perform on those areas. It's a smart feature that's deceptively easy to master. The first two sections of the dialog box, Shadows and Highlights, contain identically named sliders. Naturally, the Shadows section controls the lightening of shadows in an image, and the Highlights section controls the darkening of brighter areas. Here's a list of the options available in both sections:

- **Amount:** In the Shadows section, the Amount slider lets you specify the degree to which the shadows in an image will be lightened. In the Highlights section, the slider controls how much the highlights will be darkened. A value of 0 percent yields no change in the image; a value of 100 percent results in maximum lightening of the shadows (in the Shadows section) or darkening of the highlights (in the Highlights section). The default Shadows Amount setting of 50 percent is a safe place to start when lightening shadows in an image.

FIGURE 18.30

The Shadow/Highlight dialog box lets you correct exposure problems in specific areas of an image without harming other areas.

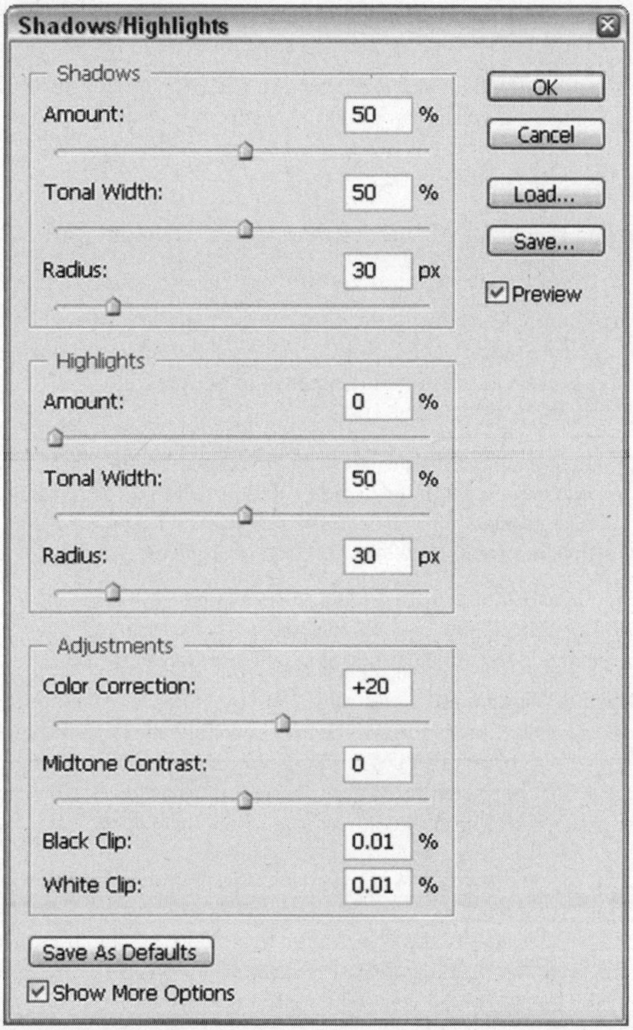

- **Tonal Width:** This setting adjusts the range of the pixels that get modified by the command. In the Shadows section, higher values increase the range of shadow areas that gets lightened and lower values concentrate on only the darker regions of the image. In the Highlights section, higher values increase the range of light areas that gets darkened and lower values restrict the adjustment to only the lighter regions. The default Tonal Width value in both sections is 50 percent. If you find that the command is lightening too much of an image, lower the value in the Shadows section to correct it.

- **Radius:** The Shadow/Highlight command determines which areas are shadows and which are highlights by examining each pixel compared to the pixels that surround it. This prevents every stray dark pixel from being classified as a shadow and subsequently lightened, for example. Adjust the Radius sliders to determine the size of each pixel's neighborhood or, in other words, the number of surrounding pixels that are taken into account when each pixel is categorized as shadow or highlight.

  Radius is the setting you'll most likely need to adjust on an image-by-image basis. The default setting of 30 pixels is a good place to start, but keep in mind that by increasing the Radius value you apply a less exacting change to the image, and by decreasing the value you lose some of the contrast.

Below the Shadows and Highlights sections is a third area labeled Adjustments. It contains the following options:

- **Color Correction:** Occasionally, the Shadow/Highlight command can make the colors in an image a little less vivid. The Color Correction slider lets you adjust the saturation of the color in the affected portion of the image. In grayscale images, this option is replaced with a general Brightness setting.

TIP   You can achieve an interesting effect by increasing the Amount value in the Shadows section and ramping down the Color Correction setting. The result is an image in which all pixels formerly in the shadowed areas become grayscale. In addition to producing an interesting effect, it also lets you glimpse exactly which pixels are being affected.

- **Midtone Contrast:** This setting is fairly self-explanatory. It increases or decreases the contrast of the midtone pixels in the image. Generally speaking, higher values mean a darker image and lower values produce a lighter, more even result.

- **Black Clip** and **White Clip:** These values let you adjust the maximum settings for how dark the adjusted shadow pixels will be and how light the adjusted highlight pixels will be. While the limit for both values is 50 percent, it is advisable to never even approach that high a value. On the contrary, keep these settings as low as you can to provide for smooth transitions and healthy contrast levels in your images.

The Shadow/Highlight dialog box lets you save your settings and then load them later using the Save and Load buttons on the right. If you want to designate your current settings as the default for the command, click Save As Defaults at the bottom of the dialog box. Finally, select the Show More Options check box to toggle between the default reduced view, which gives you access only to the two Amount sliders, and the expanded view, which presents you with all the options just discussed.

TIP   Okay, this has been mentioned before, but it's worth repeating: The Histogram palette is a great way to keep track of brightness and tonal changes to an image. It keeps up with you expertly while you're working in the Shadow/Highlight dialog box.

Figure 18.31 shows a photo of a stand of trees at Susquehannock State Park in autumn. The details of the branches and leaves are lost to the shadows, however, and need to be revealed so that the image looks more the way it did to the eye, live, in the park. In the second image, you can see the settings that worked for this image. Your results and settings will vary, depending on your image and its problems.

FIGURE 18.31

The Shadow/Highlight command reveals details that would otherwise be lost to intense shadows, while leaving the correctly exposed portions of the image just as they were. The original photo is on the top.

Correcting exposure

It may seem like the Shadow/Highlight command is all you need for a photo that's too dark or too light, with detail-smothering shadows and blinding, eye-piercing highlights. For some photos, that's true — Shadow/Highlight and its extensive set of tools are all you need. On the other hand, if all-over exposure is the problem and one shadowy or glaring area isn't what you're trying to fix, the Exposure command, which was introduced in Photoshop CS2, is your answer. As shown in Figure 18.32, the dialog box is very simple — three sliders and three eyedroppers for setting black, gray, and white points. There's also a Preview option, so you can see your adjustments take effect in the image window, as you make them.

FIGURE 18.32

Adjust your photo's overall Exposure with three simple sliders. Used alone or with the help of other Adjustment submenu commands, the Exposure tools can fix underexposed or overexposed photos quickly.

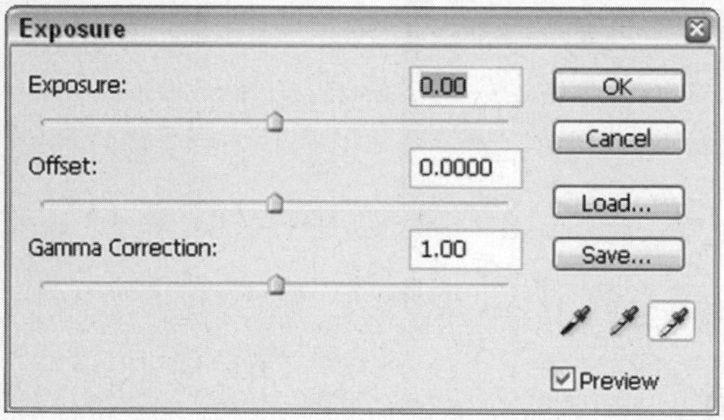

Here are some details about your options in the Exposure dialog box:

- **Exposure:** This slider does just what you'd expect: It increases or decreases exposure, depending on how far you drag it to the left or right. Drag to the right, and the image brightens; drag to the left and it darkens. Sometimes, this is the only slider you need to use, depending on the nature of the problems caused by the exposure of the original image. If the colors look fine after just a slight increase in the exposure (brightening an underexposed image, for example), you won't need to tinker with the other two sliders at all. On the other hand, if sliding the Exposure setting in either direction creates colorful havoc, the Offset and Gamma sliders (to be explained next) may need a tweak.

- **Offset:** Set to 0.00 by default, increasing it both decreases contrast and brings all the pixels closer to gray. Decreasing the Offset increases contrast and brings all pixels closer to black.

- **Gamma:** This setting adjusts the brightness of the midtone values. Set to a default of 1.00, an increase in Gamma brightens the colors, eventually shifting the entire image to white. Drag the other way, and the colors are darkened.

- **Eyedroppers:** Click the Set Black Point button (the first of three eyedropper buttons), and then click the pixel in your image that's closest to black. The image exposure adjusts as soon as you click the pixel. The middle button, Set Gray Point, establishes a midpoint for your photo's pixel range, and the Set White Point button is used to establish the white or lightest pixel in the photo. In the photo in Figure 18.33, the black point could be any of the shadows on the trees or the shadowed ground, a midpoint or gray pixel could be on the tree's bark or the ground, where the sun has illuminated it slightly, and a white point would be in the sky, or where sunlight is illuminating a particular leaf. Figure 18.33 shows an original photo with exposure problems — the same one used to demonstrate Shadow/Highlight, to show that two different tools can be used to attack the same problem — and includes the "after" version and the Exposure dialog box so you can see the settings that fixed the photo.

Adjusting Black and White per channel

New in Photoshop CS3, the Black and White dialog box is the first step in a more long-term goal for Adobe — to offer a complete tone-adjustment solution for black and white and duotone images. For a first step, it's not too shabby, as you've got 10 presets that meet lots of needs, and six sliders, one per RGB and CMY (well, no K) channel. As shown in Figure 18-34, you also have a Tint section, which if turned on, allows you to create duotones of any shade in the rainbow.

Now, it won't be terribly dramatic here in black and white (we can't show you a "before" in color and an "after" in black and white), but suffice to say that this dialog box replaces or betters several other tools that people traditionally use for going grayscale. It's better than switching to Grayscale mode, and it's better than Desaturate or the Sponge tool. (Yes, some people will scrub over an image with the Sponge tool set to Desaturate, to remove color — not because we told them to, but they just feel compelled to do so.)

To use this fantastic dialog box, after opening your image (and perhaps selecting a single layer or making a selection), choose Image ➪ Adjustments ➪ Black and White. Your image (or the layer or selection therein) is automatically turned to a black and white image, as shown in Figure 18.35. This is based on the "None" preset, which is code for "Defaults." You can choose a preset, selecting various channel-based filters (Blue Filter, Green Filter, Red Filter, Yellow Filter), High Contrast presets, Infared, Maximum Black, Maximum White, or Neutral Density. As you make a selection from the presets, the sliders are automatically adjusted to show the settings required to achieve the results of that preset, and you can then tweak them further. Figure 18.35 shows a series of the presets and their impact on an image.

FIGURE 18.33

Here are the before (top) and after (bottom) images. The underexposure resulting in darks that hide details can be remedied by increasing the exposure and increasing Offset and Gamma just a tiny bit.

FIGURE 18.34

Quickly turn a color photo to black and white or a duotone, using any one of the presets and/or the channel sliders.

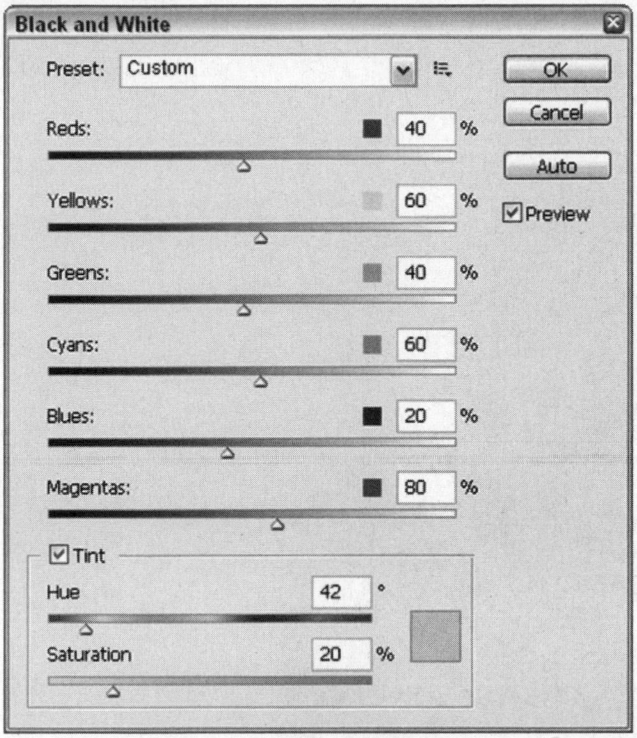

Interestingly, even if you've used the Channels filter prior to opening the dialog box — say displaying only the Red or Green channel and *then* opening the Black and White dialog box — the results of the dialog box's opening and application of default settings are unaltered. The changes that you can make through the dialog box, of course, are all channel-based, but don't waste your time tinkering with the Channels palette beforehand, unless you want to change something about the photo in general, using the Channels and another correction tool along with them before the image is converted to black and white.

Overall, the results of the dialog box are quite impressive, and the flatness one typically sees when color is simply drained out of an image is not seen here. A very convenient feature is the Tint option, which allows you to create duotones, using the Hue and Saturation sliders. They work like the sliders in the dialog box of the same name, but of course, you're only getting the addition of a single color as you drag the sliders, and you're starting with a black and white photo (or one that's become a black and white photo, actually).

FIGURE 18.35

None, Maximum Black, and the Red Filter are shown here, from top to bottom. We'd show you the color original, but in a black and white book, what would be the point?

Adjustment Layers

Every one of the commands discussed in this chapter is applicable to a single layer at a time. If you want to correct the colors in multiple layers, you have to create a special kind of layer called an *adjustment layer*. Adjustment layers are layers that contain mathematical color correction information. The layer applies its corrections to all layers beneath it, without affecting any layers above.

You can create an adjustment layer in one of two ways:

■ Choose Layer ⇨ New Adjustment Layer. This displays a submenu of color adjustment commands, ranging from Levels and Curves to Invert, Threshold, and Posterize. The menu appears in Figure 18.36.

■ Click the button that looks like a black and white cookie (the New Fill or Adjustment Layer button) at the bottom of the Layers palette, also shown in Figure 18.36. The first three options — Solid Color, Gradient, and Pattern — are dynamic fill layers, as discussed in Chapter 15. Choose any one of the remaining options to make a new adjustment layer.

FIGURE 18.36

The Fill and Adjustment Layer menu offers three Fill options and 14 Adjustment Layer choices.

Create New Fill or Adjustment Layer

If you choose a command from the Layer ➪ New Adjustment Layer submenu, Photoshop displays the New Layer dialog box, which permits you to name the layer, assign a color, and set the blend mode, as shown in Figure 18.37. If you choose an option from the Create New Fill or Adjustment Layer button in the Layers palette (labeled in Figure 18.36), Photoshop bypasses the New Layer dialog box and targets the selected correction. Choosing Curves, for example, displays the Curves dialog box. Invert is the only option that produces no dialog box. Change the settings as desired, and press Enter or Return as you normally would. If you press and hold Alt or Option while clicking the adjustment layer icon in the Layers palette, you'll get the New Layer dialog box just as if you'd chosen from the menu commands.

Regardless of the color adjustment you select, it appears as a new layer in the Layers palette, as shown in Figure 18.37. Photoshop marks adjustment layers with special icons that look like miniature versions of their respective dialog boxes. This way, you can readily tell them apart from image layers. You can double-click these icons to reopen the dialog box used to make the adjustment in the first place.

FIGURE 18.37

The New Layer dialog box appears if you start the Adjustment Layer process from the menu; name your layer, and choose its Color and Mode. The Layers palette is shown after two Adjustment Layers have been added; the name of the layer is determined by the choice made from the submenu of adjustments that can be made.

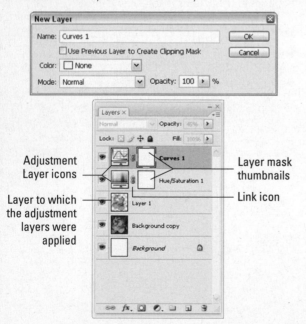

The Advantages of Layer-Based Corrections

The whole concept of using Adjustment Layers to apply corrections to multiple layers may not seem so revolutionary, given that there are other ways to make your adjustments affect multiple layers. Before you write off everything said so far about Adjustment Layers as some sort of hype, though, consider these points:

- **They're forever editable.** As long as the adjustment layer remains intact, stored in one of the four formats that support layers (native Photoshop PSD, TIFF, PDF, and PSB), you can edit the color correction over and over again without damaging the underlying pixels. Unlike standard color corrections that alter selected pixels directly, adjustment layers have no permanent effect on the pixels.

CAUTION When editing the settings for an adjustment layer, be sure to double-click the first icon that precedes the layer name (labeled "Adjustment layer icon" in Figure 18.37). Double-clicking elsewhere displays the Layer Mask Display Options or the Layer Style dialog box, or it allows you to rename the layer.

- **They offer versatile layer masking.** You also can adjust the affected area to your heart's content. Unless it's grouped with another layer, an adjustment layer covers the entire image like a tight-fitting blanket. An adjustment layer doesn't contain pixels, so painting inside the layer changes its layer mask. Paint with black to remove the correction from an area; use white to paint the correction back in.

TIP In fact, if a selection is active when you create a new adjustment layer, Photoshop automatically creates a layer mask according to the selection outline.

- **You can reorder your corrections.** As with any layers, you can shuffle adjustment layers up and down in the stacking order. For example, if you decide you don't want the correction to affect a specific layer, just drag the adjustment layer to a level in the Layers palette below the layer you want to exclude. If you're juggling multiple adjustment layers, you can shuffle the adjustment layers to change the order in which they're applied. This includes the standard reordering keyboard shortcuts, Ctrl+[and Ctrl+] (⌘+[and ⌘+] on the Mac).

- **You can Fade corrections.** As you know, you can use the Edit ➪ Fade command on a standard color correction right after you apply the correction. With an adjustment layer, however, you can use the Fade command on a correction.

- **You can correct using blend modes without ballooning file sizes.** Some people prefer to correct overly light or dark images using blend modes. For example, such a person might take an image, copy it to a new layer, and apply the Multiply mode to darken the layer or Screen to lighten it. The problem with this approach is that it increases the size of the image in memory. Duplicating the image to a new layer requires Photoshop to double the size of the image in RAM. If you darken or lighten through an adjustment layer, no such size increase or memory hogging occurs.

> **TIP** Adjustment layers permit you to apply this same technique without adding pixels to RAM. Create a new adjustment layer with the Levels option selected, and after the Levels dialog box appears, press Enter or Return to ignore it. Next, select Multiply or Screen from the blend mode pop-up menu in the Layers palette. The adjustment layer serves as a surrogate duplicate of the layers below it, mimicking every merged pixel. It does all this without any significant file size increase.

- **You can change one adjustment to another.** After applying one kind of adjustment layer, you can convert it to another kind of adjustment layer. For example, you could swap an existing Levels adjustment for a Curves adjustment. To do so, choose the desired color adjustment from the Layer ⇨ Change Layer Content submenu. Photoshop doesn't try to preserve the prior color adjustment when making the conversion — in other words, it can't convert the Levels information into Curves data — but it does preserve the layer mask, the blend mode, and other layer attributes.

Correcting Camera Raw Images

The images produced by modern digital cameras can be nothing short of breathtaking. Yet by the time a photo leaves a digital camera and enters an image-editing program like Photoshop, even a noncompressed TIFF can be many steps removed from what the CCD or CMOS (the camera's "eye") saw. That's because the camera itself takes that input from the sensor and performs a slew of processes meant to make the image more presentable. These can include white-balance adjustments, color and brightness correction, and sharpening and compression passes over an image. It's almost as if there was a tiny little person inside your camera, using a tiny little computer running a tiny little version of Photoshop, and that little guy is trying to make your photos look better.

Although many people would welcome the help of the tiny guy — after all, the picture generally looks brighter, more balanced, and sharper by the time it's opened — the real digital photo pro knows that almost any improvement comes at a cost. In truth, lots of the original information captured by the camera has been lost by the corrections. And who is that suspicious little guy inside the camera anyway? Why should we trust him to correct our images willy-nilly? He may know a few things about image editing, but there's certainly no way he could have a big helpful book like this one inside the camera for reference. For professional digital photographers and graphic designers, every last pixel counts, and there's no way those big-leaguers are going to trust the judgment of some little guy who lives in a camera over their own judgment. "Eliminate the little middle man!" is the professional's rallying cry.

Luckily, all hope is not lost. Some midrange and high-end digital cameras now offer the option of saving images as Camera Raw files, which skip all that post processing and save a perfect, pristine representation of the exact image as originally captured. It's very much akin to a digital negative. Between the releases of Photoshop 7 and Photoshop CS, Adobe quietly introduced a plug-in for the program that was capable of opening and making adjustments to certain Camera Raw files. The current phenomenally expanded version of the Camera Raw plug-in gives you access to better image detail and a wider range of colors than would be available otherwise. In many cases, raw format images offer more than 24 bits of information in a full-color file; some cameras provide up to 30 or 36 bits, meaning you have billions and billions of potential colors to work with. For professionals who need to get the absolute most out of their digital images, getting access to this raw data is nothing short of a godsend. Camera Raw lets you *be* the little guy in the camera, taking the raw pixels captured by the camera's sensor and manipulating them *yourself* before you open the image up in Photoshop proper.

It's important to know that Camera Raw files are proprietary, meaning that each and every manufacturer adheres to a different and unique format. At this time, Photoshop supports Camera Raw files created by several different cameras from Canon, Fujifilm, Leaf, Minolta, Nikon, and Olympus. Additionally, Adobe has pledged to continue expanding support to more manufacturers and models over the life of the product. Check `www.adobe.com/products/photoshop/cameraraw.html` to see if your camera has been added to the list.

Instead of the gigantic, unmanageable files you might expect them to be, Camera Raw files are very efficiently compressed, and Adobe's Camera Raw dialog box can make adjustments at an impressive speed. Instead of displaying the image, Photoshop first brings up the massive Camera Raw dialog box, as shown in Figure 18.38.

FIGURE 18.38

Think of the Camera Raw dialog box as your first stop along the road to correcting raw images with Photoshop. Here an image captured with Canon Powershot Pro1 digital camera is adjusted.

TIP Before delving into the intricacies of Camera Raw settings, here's a little-known tip: Holding down the Shift key bypasses the Camera Raw dialog box altogether and immediately opens the image inside Photoshop. If you've used Camera Raw on the image before, the last settings you used are automatically applied as the image opens. If you've never opened the image before, Camera Raw's default settings for your camera are used instead.

At the bottom of the Camera Raw dialog box, you'll see a link that describes the file's current workflow options. Click the link to open the Workflow Options dialog box, shown in Figure 18.39.

FIGURE 18.39

The Workflow Options dialog box

Workflow Options	
Space: Adobe RGB (1998)	OK
Depth: 8 Bits/Channel	Cancel
Size: 2448 by 3264 (8.0 MP)	
Resolution: 240 pixels/inch	
☐ Open in Photoshop as Smart Objects	

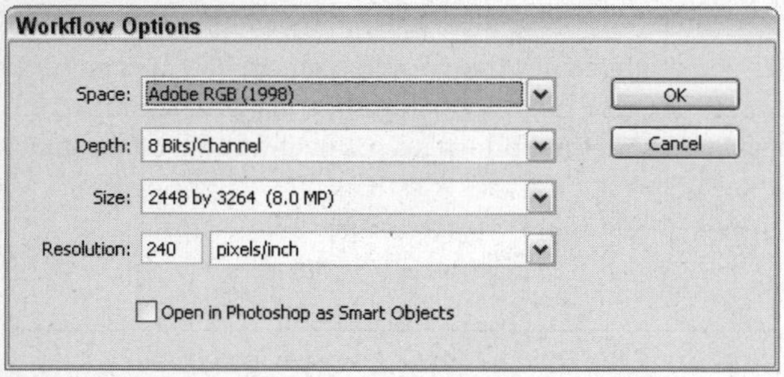

You can set the target color space of the image (probably the same as the color settings you're currently using), the number of bits per channel desired, even the size and printing resolution of the image.

- **Space:** Use this list to select your target color space profile. You'd typically set this to the same color space in Photoshop in which you're working (Adobe RGB). The source image usually has the native color space of the camera embedded in it, and if you want to use a color space that isn't on the list, choose ProPhoto RGB. You then can convert to the working space of your choice after you're finished in the Camera Raw dialog box and open the image in the Photoshop workspace.

- **Depth:** Here you'd set the bits-per-channel that you want the image to open with — either 8-bit or 16-bit.

- **Size:** By default, the image opens in the Camera Raw dialog box at whatever dimensions the camera took the shot at. If you want to resample the image to different dimensions, you'd use the values on this drop-down menu to specify an alternative.

  Camera Raw uses slightly different interpolation methods than Image Size, but the results are very good. And if you're going to downsample anyway, it probably will save you some Camera Raw processing time if you go ahead and downsample now. If your camera uses nonsquare pixels, the default Size amount is automatically set to try to maintain the same approximate number of pixels when the image is converted to square pixels in Photoshop. To achieve this, one dimension (width or height) is upsampled and the other downsampled. Setting Size to the next highest choice causes the pixel count to be maintained along the high-resolution dimension of the image; the low-resolution dimension is upsampled to achieve square pixels (almost certainly a better choice for nonsquare pixel images).

- **Resolution:** This is where you set the print resolution the image should use. You can easily change this later with the Image ⇨ Image Size command in the Photoshop workspace.

Making color adjustments

As you can see in Figure 18.38, the Basic panel in the Camera Raw dialog box is composed of three sections: settings for adjusting white balance, settings for adjusting the tonal qualities, and a section for converting the image to grayscale. *White balance* is a process where something white (like a sheet of paper) is typically used to calibrate the camera; with many cameras, this information is recorded at the time an image is shot and saved as metadata in the Camera Raw file. When available, the Camera Raw dialog box uses this white balance information as the default when it opens an image; hence the As Shot setting in the White Balance pop-up menu. If Camera Raw can't read white balance info from your camera, it makes a decent guess. In this case, As Shot is the equivalent of the Auto setting. The pop-up menu also contains several other options that reflect various lighting conditions that may have been present when the image was first shot. The options contain different presets for the Temperature and Tint sliders below. The White Balance pop-up menu is a good place to start when adjusting white balance. It's quite possible you'll be happy with one of the preset options. If not, you can tweak the two sliders below the pop-up menu by hand:

- **Temperature:** This setting lets you modify the color temperature of an image. Increase the Temperature value (which is measured in Kelvin) to bring out the more yellow colors in the image, as seen in the middle example in Figure 18.40. The right example shows a decrease in Temperature to cool the image into the realm of blue.

FIGURE 18.40

Similar to the Photo Filter command, Camera Raw's Temperature slider takes an image (left) and lets you warm up (right) or cool down (bottom) the color temperature.

Temperature: 5550

Temperature: 6600

Temperature: 4600

■ **Tint:** The Tint slider adjusts and compensates for different color tints that the image may contain. Drag the slider to the left to increase the amount of green in the image, and drag it to the right to remove green and add in magenta values.

> **TIP**   You also can set the white balance manually by selecting the White Balance tool (it's the eyedropper located in the top-left corner of the dialog box) and clicking at a spot in the image that you'd like to assign as neutral, either white or gray. The White Balance settings in the Adjust panel snap into a position that adjusts the selected pixel to white and the other pixels in the image accordingly.

Below the White Balance settings are five sliders that let you make adjustments to the tonal qualities of an image. Generally, you should adjust these controls in the order they're presented:

■ **Exposure:** Quite simply, the Exposure setting adjusts the brightness of the image. But if you look a couple of sliders down, you see one labeled Brightness, so now you may quite rightly be wondering, "What gives?" The Exposure slider is based on the f-stop of a camera (a setting of +1.00 is the equivalent of opening the lens one stop wider), and adjusts in much larger increments than the Brightness setting. In fact, adjust this value more than a little, and you're bound to encounter some clipping, which occurs when pixels are pushed to pure white or black and lose all detail. It's best to adjust this setting until it begins to clip, ramp it back a smidge, and then do your finer brightness adjustments with the Brightness slider.

■ **Shadows:** Increase this value, and watch as more and more pixels get sucked into darkness and, eventually, pure black. It may appear as though the Shadows slider is just upping the contrast in the image, but it's really performing a function that's more in line with the black point slider in the Input Levels section of the Levels command, discussed in the preceding chapter.

Alt+drag (Option+drag on the Mac) the Exposure or Shadows slider triangles to see a dynamic depiction of any and all clipping pixels in the image. Different colors mean there is clipping only in one or two color channels. For Exposure, black means no clipping for highlights; contrariwise, white means no clipping for shadows. Figure 18.41 shows the clipping display for the Exposure slider.

■ **Brightness:** As mentioned previously, this setting makes gentle adjustments to the general brightness levels of the image.

■ **Contrast:** This setting increases (higher values) or decreases (lower values) the contrast in the midtone colors of the image.

■ **Saturation:** This is the basic saturation option that you've encountered a number of times before. Decrease the value to −100 to remove all colors from an image; increase the value to +100 to get colors so vibrant you may need to close your eyes.

FIGURE 18.41

Holding down Alt (Option on the Mac) while using the Exposure slider (see this slider in Figure 18.38) brings up a graphic display of which pixels are being clipped to pure white (right). In this case, the brightest clouds are clipping.

Sharpening and smoothing

Click the Detail tab to access options you can use to adjust the sharpness and smoothness of a Camera Raw image. The Detail panel contains the following three settings:

- **Sharpness:** The Sharpness slider works in much the same way as the Unsharp Mask filter, which is discussed in Chapter 10. The biggest difference lies in the fact that the Camera Raw dialog box does not give you controls for Radius or Threshold. This is because Camera Raw calculates these factors for you using information based on the camera model and the ISO (or light sensitivity) for the image.

- **Luminance Smoothing:** This slider adjusts the amount of blurring that the Camera Raw dialog box applies in an attempt to reduce grayscale noise in an image. Depending on the ISO and general quality of the camera, a little bit of noise — those random speckles that lower the quality of an image — is a common occurrence. Increase this setting to smooth out some of the noise, but don't go overboard: Too much smoothing, and you'll lose valuable detail in the image.

NOTE The Camera Raw dialog box fully supports multiple undos through the usual keyboard shortcut, Ctrl+Alt+Z (⌘+Option+Z on the Mac), so don't be afraid to experiment.

- **Color Noise Reduction:** This slider performs the same function as Luminance Smoothing, except it works toward decreasing the amount of colored noise artifacts in the image.

Correcting for the camera lens

A camera lens is an imperfect thing. As a result of lens imperfections, which are generally more prevalent in less expensive lenses, many times an image looks terrific in the center, but subtle problems start to creep in toward the edges and in the corners. Clicking the Lens Correction button in the Camera Raw dialog box gives you access to two additional panels full of settings. The first of these, Lens, compensates for the imperfections of a camera lens.

- **Chromatic Aberration Fix Red/Cyan Fringe:** One of the problems that lenses can intro-duce into an image is *color fringing*, where sharp edges seem to have a fringe of pixels run-ning along them. This happens when the color channels are slightly different sizes, creating a sort of *misregistration* like a bad printing job of the Sunday funnies. Commonly, this fringe runs red on the side of the edge toward the center of the image and cyan along the other side. The Chromatic Aberration Red/Cyan slider, shown in Figure 18.42, fixes this by slightly scaling the size of the red channel in relation to the green.

FIGURE 18.42

Adjust the Chromatic Aberration sliders to shift your colors and resolve the color fring-ing that can occur in digital images.

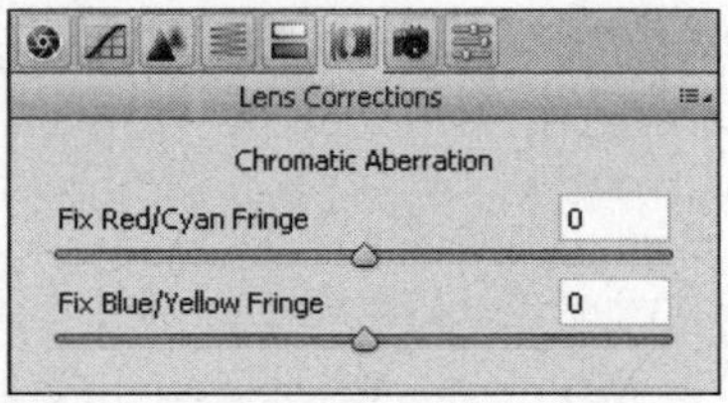

- **Chromatic Aberration Fix Blue/Yellow Fringe:** Similar to the Chromatic Aberration Red/Cyan slider, this control can eliminate a blue/yellow fringing problem on high-con-trast edges found along the sides and in the corners of images by slightly scaling the blue channel in relation to the green.

> **TIP**   If your image has both kinds of fringing, hold down the Alt key (Option on the Mac) as you adjust one slider to temporarily turn off the effects of the other slider. And remem-ber that these sliders do nothing to the center of an image. This type of chromatic aberration occurs only along the sides and in the corners of images.

- **Vignetting Amount:** As shown in the top image in Figure 18.43, imperfections in lenses also can cause the edges and corners of an image to be darker than the center, creating a sort of vignette that frames the image. Drag the Vignetting Amount slider triangle to the right to lighten the edges of the image, which helps to eliminate the problem. And should you *want* this type of vignetting, drag the Vignetting Amount slider triangle to the left.

- **Vignetting Midpoint:** This controls the vignetting transition from dark to light. Drag to the left to increase the range of the vignetting compensation; drag to the right to decrease it.

FIGURE 18.43

The top image shows typical vignetting, where the edges of the image are darker than the center. Adjusting the Vignetting Amount and Vignetting Midpoint sliders can fix the problem handily, as shown in the bottom image.

Tweaking the profile

If you're using Camera Raw, it's safe to assume that Photoshop has a profile based on the model of your camera. But it's possible that your particular camera might not exactly match the one Adobe used when they created the profile for your model. If your camera has a repeatable, predictable problem that you always need to compensate for, you may want to use the controls available in the Calibrate tab of the Advanced Camera Raw settings. The first option, Shadow Tint, lets you fix a color cast lurking in the dark areas of the image. As with the Exposure and Shadows sliders in the Adjust tab, holding down the Alt key (Option on the Mac) gives you a look at any clipping that might occur as a result of your adjustments.

The remaining six sliders exist so you can give your Camera Raw settings a little extra tweak. Each color channel has both a hue and a saturation slider, enabling you to account for slight differences between your actual camera and the model of your camera that Adobe used to build its Camera Raw profile. There's no right or wrong way to use these sliders. The whole idea is to adjust things until they look right to you. If, after tweaking all the controls in the Adjust, Detail, and Lens tabs, those skin tones still don't look quite right, this is your chance to fix them.

Opening and saving Camera Raw images

If you feel you've thoroughly botched things with the Camera Raw dialog box, just hold down the Alt key (Option on the Mac) and, as with many Photoshop dialog boxes, the Cancel button changes to a Reset button. Click it, and the image is restored to its state when you first began this session of Camera Raw adjustments. You also may notice that the OK button changes to an Update button; clicking this updates the associated Camera Raw settings to reflect your changes and closes the Camera Raw window, but it doesn't open the image in Photoshop. And holding down the Shift key makes the OK button turn into a Skip button, in case you want to open an image with its default settings (disregarding any changes you may have already made).

After you are happy with your Camera Raw settings, click the OK button, and Photoshop proceeds to apply your adjustments and open the image. Note that you can't save the image back to the Camera Raw format. Just to thoroughly confuse things, there *is* a Photoshop Raw format available when you choose Save As, but that's a different format useful at times for saving images you plan to transfer between different computer systems. Photoshop is incapable of writing the raw format used by your digital camera. After you adjust the Camera Raw settings, Photoshop essentially opens a copy of your image, leaving the original file untouched.

Yet, here's an odd thing: The original file is untouched, but you probably will notice that the Bridge preview of your Camera Raw image has changed to reflect the adjustments you made. How can this be? Well, the changes you make with Camera Raw get saved in one of two places. By default, the changes are stored in the Camera Raw database, located on the Macintosh in the Preferences folder of the user, and under Windows in the user's Application Data folder. When the Bridge displays a RAW format image, it draws the preview both from the image and from the settings for that image in the database. The problem with this is that your Camera Raw settings will fail to travel with your images to another computer. Adobe's solution can be found in the Camera Raw Preferences dialog box, which you can access by selecting the Advanced radio button, clicking the right-pointing arrowhead next to the Settings pop-up menu, and choosing Preferences. Choosing Sidecar ".xmp" Files from the Save image settings in pop-up menu instructs Photoshop to store the Camera Raw settings for an image not in the default database, but rather in a small file located in the same folder as the image. The data file shares the same base name as the image. For example, the image "water-melon.orf" would have its settings stored in a file called "watermelon.xmp." Keep these sidecar files along with the main image files when you move images or burn CDs, and your Camera Raw settings will travel with you.

> **NOTE** These XMP files can be the same as those mentioned earlier in the chapter in the section "Using the File Info Command." In fact, when Camera Raw opens an image, it stores the settings in the XMP metadata. With File Info, you can export this metadata into an external XMP file and then load it back into Camera Raw.

Saving your Camera Raw settings

Whether you decide to have your image's Camera Raw settings saved in the main Camera Raw database or in an individual XMP file, it's a darned good thing you *can* save them, isn't it? It would be a drag to have to try to recreate those Camera Raw settings from scratch if you should decide to open the image from the original raw file. But when you think about it, lots of the image problems you compensated for exist not just in that image, but in every image you take with that camera. Wouldn't it be great if you could save the settings from that image and apply them to other images? Apparently, Adobe figured you'd say, "Yes!," because Camera Raw lets you do just that.

When you open an image in the Camera Raw dialog box, by default the Settings pop-up menu is set to Camera Default, meaning that the default Camera Raw settings for your camera are being applied. Choosing Selected Image means that if you've ever opened that image with Camera Raw before, your last settings are automatically applied. Previous Conversion uses the settings from the last opened raw format image that came from the same camera. To save your current settings so that they can be used by other images, click the right-pointing arrowhead next to the Settings pop-up menu and choose Save Settings. You can name the settings anything you like, but make sure you save them inside the suggested Camera Raw folder (which is inside the Presets folder in the application folder on your hard drive, in case you're curious). From then on, the settings are available in the Settings pop-up menu. If for some reason you ignore the advice and choose to save the settings somewhere else, you'll need to use the Load Settings command (available in the same pop-up menu as the Save Settings command) to access them in the future.

When the Advanced mode is activated, it's also possible to save just a subset of settings. Maybe your camera consistently introduces chromatic aberration and vignetting to images, so you always want to apply those settings to images from that camera, but you'd rather tweak the other settings on an image-by-image basis. Click the right-pointing arrowhead next to the Settings pop-up menu, and choose Save Settings Subset. You'll be presented with a column of check boxes, enabling you to specify which settings you want included in the subset. The Subset pop-up menu contains a few preset options, designed to save you from having to click a bunch of check boxes. From there, click the Save button, and save your subset in the Camera Raw folder. If you want to delete settings you previously saved, choose them from the Settings pop-up menu, click the ever-popular right-pointing arrowhead, and choose Delete Current Settings.

It's also possible to override Camera Raw's default settings for your camera model by choosing Set Camera Default from the pop-up menu that appears when you click the right-pointing arrowhead. Thereafter, the Camera Default option in the Settings pop-up menu will load your current settings. To restore Camera Raw's default settings for your camera, choose Reset Camera Default.

Applying your saved Camera Raw settings

Applying saved Camera Raw settings to a raw image before opening it in Photoshop is pretty straightforward. Start by double-clicking the raw image to open it in the Camera Raw dialog box. If you saved your settings in the Camera Raw folder as Photoshop suggested (see the preceding section), the settings appear at the bottom of the Settings pop-up menu. Just choose the settings, click OK, and go to work inside Photoshop.

But remember what happens to the OK button when you hold down the Alt key (Option on the Mac) inside the Camera Raw dialog box? It turns into an Update button, and clicking that button updates the Camera Raw settings for that image by changing the data saved in either the Camera Raw database or the image's XMP sidecar file. You then can see the change evident in the thumbnail and preview within the Bridge. (It's important to remember that Camera Raw never actually changes a single pixel of the raw format file. It can only change the data applied to that file which is saved in the database or the XMP file, and then open a copy of the image in Photoshop with that data applied. But you can't save back to your camera's raw format from Photoshop, so the original raw file — reflecting exactly what your camera's sensors saw — is always there on your hard drive.)

Because Photoshop is such a flexible tool, it should come as no surprise that you can actually update raw images with new Camera Raw settings without even opening the images. With one or more raw format images selected in the Bridge, either choose Edit ➪ Apply Camera Raw Settings from the Bridge menu bar or just right-click (Control-click on the Mac) one of the images and choose Apply Camera Raw Settings. You're presented with the small Apply Camera Raw Settings dialog box, where you can select an option from the Apply Settings From pop-up menu. (If you have more than one image selected in the Bridge, the standard Selected Image option instead appears as First Selected Image.) Click Update, and the Camera Raw data for the selected raw file or files is updated without opening the images.

And in case that seems all too simple for a complicated feature like Camera Raw, you're exactly right. Clicking the Advanced radio button opens what is basically the Camera Raw dialog box without preview but with the Save Settings Subset dialog box. You can load saved settings, modify them, apply them, and save them as new settings or as just a subset of settings. Seriously, go nuts. Just click Update when you're finished, and the data for the selected image or images automatically updates to show the fruits of your labor.

And if that wasn't enough of an automated way to end this chapter on file management and automation, let me point out that Camera Raw works beautifully with actions and the Batch command. Just start recording an action, open a raw image, set the Settings pop-up menu to Selected Image so the action draws on each image's saved Camera Raw data, perform your action, and click the stop button in the Actions palette. You can then apply that action to a whole batch of raw images with the Batch command. And really, however cool it may be, don't just sit there watching the batch processing. Go away and read a book or something. Photoshop finds you distracting.

Summary

In this chapter, you learned about mapping colors with Invert, Equalize, Threshold, and Posterize, and tweaking colors with the Hue/Saturation dialog box. You learned how to raise and lower saturation levels, how to colorize grayscale images, and conversely, how to take a color photo and give it depth and detail as a black and white photo with the aptly-named Black and White dialog box.

You also learned about correcting colors with Replace Color, Selective Color, Variations, Photo Filter, and Match Color commands, and to use the Histogram palette. The process of boosting brightness and contrast levels, editing specific color values with Curves, and using the Shadow/Highlight command were also covered, along with techniques for fixing exposure problems and correcting multiple layers at once with adjustment layers. Finally, Photoshop's support for Camera Raw was covered, including techniques for correcting Camera Raw images.

Animating and Working with Video

Well, the time has come. Everything Photoshop could ever do (virtually) to a static image can now be done to motion graphics. That's right — got a video clip of your hated Uncle Harry making a fool of himself at Thanksgiving? Open it up in Photoshop and paint horns and Groucho glasses on him! Mom will get a kick out of it!

Photoshop used to be limited to animated GIF's, courtesy of the old add-on application ImageReady. If you wanted to make a little Web animation, that was where you went — you fired up ImageReady from within Photoshop, and you could optimize images for online use and create rollovers, animated GIFs, anything graphical for the Web. Over the next few releases, however, some of ImageReady's features moved over to Photoshop: The Save for Web dialog box is a major example. CS2 users may recall that with CS2, ImageReady was still a separate application, but that more and more of ImageReady's capabilities had been integrated into Photoshop (an Animation palette was added, for example), and we all heard that ImageReady would be gone with the release of Photoshop CS3.

Adobe kept that promise, and with CS3, the absorption of ImageReady is complete: There is no more ImageReady, and Photoshop can now do everything you used to do with it — and then some. In addition to being the home of all of ImageReady's Web-related image features, Photoshop can now manipulate video files and is no longer limited just to the Web animation that it pulled out of ImageReady. Considering how Photoshop essentially sucked the life out of and eventually killed ImageReady, this begs the question, "Will Photoshop now begin to suck the tools out of After Effects? Premiere? When will it end? When finally there are no individual Adobe programs?? Just one Colossal Adobe Everything CS-megaplex?!?! "

But let's not get carried away. We've moved beyond simple Web animations, and now with CS3, you can import video and image sequences for manipulation, create images to use in your video work, and create both Web-based and video animations. The one caveat is QuickTime: You must have at least QuickTime 7 installed on your machine because virtually all of CS3's new multimedia features are dependent on the QuickTime engine.

> **TIP**   QuickTime is available as a free download from the Apple Computer Web site.

Working with Video, Image Sequences, and Animation

So it's true. Photoshop is now getting closer to offering the sort of one-stop shopping for all things image-related that Microsoft Word brought to the corporate office: You have one application; it can do letters and reports, it can do basic tables and calculations, it can format text and pictures in just about any way an office employee might desire, and it offers the ability to save documents as Web pages (not well, but it does offer the ability). It "does it all," so to speak.

Photoshop is following that path, but it's running miles ahead and doing a better job. It didn't just mimic what you could do with ImageReady for Web graphics; it does it just as well or better. It didn't just offer a slap-dash Web-animation tool; it has an entire palette and fleet of tools at the ready. And now, for video, it offers an armada of tools that enable you to create and edit video and apply special effects, and it works with common video file formats:

- **MOV:** MOV is a video container or "wrapper" format developed by Apple. It's used to store video encoded in any of a variety of codecs. You can use MOV in both the Macintosh and Windows platforms.

- **AVI:** AVI is Microsoft's wrapper format. It uses less compression than similar formats such as .MPEG/MPG and .MOV.

- **MPEG/MPG:** MPEG is more routinely seen as MPG as a file extension. It's a video format standardized by the Moving Picture Experts Group (thus the initials). MPG is used for creating movies that are distributed over the Internet.

Photoshop CS3's video features also support Image Sequence formats:

- **BMP:** BMP (*Windows Bitmap*) is the native format for Microsoft Paint (included with Windows) and is supported by a variety of Windows and DOS applications. Photoshop supports BMP images with up to 16 million colors. You also can use RLE (*Run-Length Encoding*), a lossless compression scheme specifically applicable to the BMP format.

- **Cineon:** Cineon is a film and video format supported by Photoshop. Developed by Kodak and used for years as the standard for transferring computer-based images to film, Cineon is a robust, high-quality format and one of the few capable of saving images in 16-bit mode. When Cineon files are used with the Cineon Digital Film System, they can be output to film with absolutely no loss in image quality.

- **JPEG** and **JPEG 2000:** The JPEG format is named after the people who designed it, the Joint Photographic Experts Group. JPEG is the most efficient and essential compression format currently available and is likely to be the compression standard for years to come. JPEG is a lossy compression scheme, which means it sacrifices image quality to conserve space on disk. This can introduce *artifacts* (visible imperfections), but because you can control how much data is lost during the save operation, you can compensate for this.

- **OpenEXR:** OpenEXR is a high dynamic-range (HDR) image file format developed by Industrial Light & Magic as a computer-imaging application. The first projects to utilize OpenEXR were *Harry Potter and the Sorcerer's Stone, Men in Black II, Gangs of New York,* and *Signs.* Since that time, OpenEXR has become Industrial Light & Magic's primary image file format.

- **PNG:** The Portable Network Graphics format (pronounced *ping*) is an open format initially created to replace the proprietary GIF format. Like GIF, PNG's compression is lossless, and actually better than GIF by anywhere from 5 to 25 percent. Unlike GIF, which has only a bit depth of 8 bits, PNG supports up to 48-bit truecolor or 16-bit grayscale, which means it even beats JPEG's 24 bits. (However, when transmitting a finished image over a network, JPEG is still the better choice, because it can compress a 24-bit image more than the lossless PNG compression can — therefore images are smaller and faster images.) PNG also supports alpha channels, which provide for variable transparency, and also supports cross-platform gamma correction.

- **PSD:** This format, created by Adobe for Photoshop, supports image layers, adjustment layers, layer masks, annotation notes, file information, keywords, and other Photoshop-specific elements. A PSD file can be in Large Document Format (PSB), RGB, CMYK, grayscale, monochrome, duotone, indexed color, Lab color, and multi-channel color modes.

- **SGI:** This is the native image format used by Silicon Graphics workstations; similar to a .RGB file. It runs in either a Mac or Windows environment, but is not widely used (other than with the aforementioned workstations).

- **Targa/TGA:** TrueVision designed the TGA (Targa) format to support 32-bit images that include 8-bit alpha channels capable of displaying the live video. It's a Bitmap image format with new extensions that accommodate the creation of thumbnails, including file date and time information, authoring information, gamma values, pixel aspect ratio, and Alpha channels. TGA files also are used for storing texture files utilized by 3D video games.

■ **TIFF:** Developed by Aldus in the early days of the Mac to standardize an ever-growing population of scanned images, TIFF (*Tagged Image File Format*) is the most widely supported image-printing format across both the Macintosh and PC platforms. TIFF supports up to 24 channels, the maximum number permitted in any image. Even more impressive, TIFF supports multiple layers.

NOTE   When you bring video into Photoshop, you are working with the images only, not the audio.

Understanding video layers

When you open a video file or image sequence in Photoshop (using the File ⇨ Open command), you end up with a file containing frames within a video layer. The video layer refers to the original video and image sequence files, and any editing you perform on the video layer affects only that layer — it doesn't change the original video and image sequence files at all. Editable video layers can contain files in grayscale, RGB, CMYK, and Lab modes, and can have bit depths of 8, 16, or 32 bits per channel.

To move through a series of frames, use the controls in the Timeline palette, as shown in Figure 19.1. You can work with video layers just as you would layers in any image — adjusting the blending mode, opacity, position, and layer style, layer by layer. You also can organize video layers in the Layers palette by grouping them, and by adding adjustment layers, you can apply color and light adjustments without making any permanent changes to the actual layers themselves.

CROSS-REF   If you're forgetting how adjustment layers work, you can go back and review Chapter 18 to get reacquainted.

FIGURE 19.1

The Timeline palette is an alternate view of the Animation palette. It provides all the tools you need for controlling the order and content of your video frames and layers.

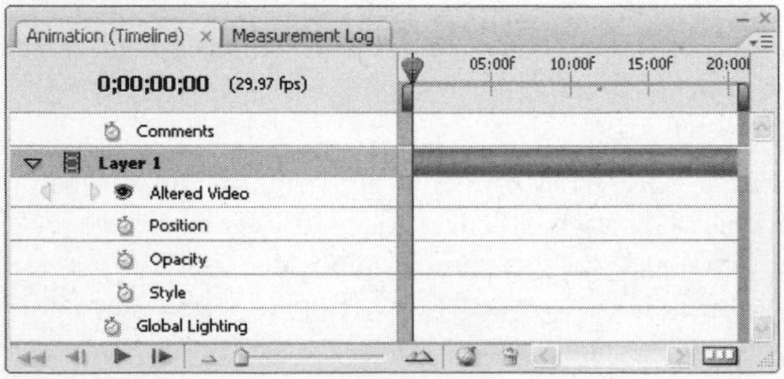

What, you don't see Timeline in the Window menu? Isn't that where all the palettes are listed? Well, yes, but the Timeline palette isn't really a palette unto itself; it's part of the Animation palette, and it is opened by choosing Window ⇨ Animation. Then, after the Animation palette is displayed, click the Convert to Timeline Animation button in the lower-right corner of the palette.

The Timeline palette and Layers ⇨ Video Layers submenu both provide a wealth of tools for managing your video layers while you've got them on the operating table in Photoshop CS3. You can add layers, add frames, rearrange your layers, delete and duplicate layers — just about anything you can imagine doing to administer your video files.

Remember these important things:

- **Connections can be broken, especially on Windows machines.** Whenever you move, rename, — or, obviously — delete a video source file, you break the link between it and its video layer. You'll see an icon in the Layers palette to inform you of this severed connection, at which point you can reconnect the two by clicking the Replace Footage command by choosing Layer ⇨ Video Layers ⇨ Replace Footage. After opening the Replace Footage dialog box, select the file to which you want to reconnect your layer and click OK. The connection is restored. On the Mac, the link won't break unless you move the source file to a different volume.

- **Adding video layers is easy.** Just choose File ⇨ Open, then select a video file, and click Open. Next choose Layer ⇨ Video Layers ⇨ Add Video Layer, choose a video or image sequence file, and click Open.

- **Blank video layers allow you to add new content.** To add one, choose Layer ⇨ Video Layers ⇨ Add Blank Video Layer. This enables you to keep your frame edits on a separate layer, so that, for example, you can use the Clone Stamp (sampling from all layers) on that blank layer, making your cloned content live on that layer — rather than on the layers from which cloned content is being taken. Figure 19.2 shows the creation of a new blank video layer.

TIP Another great use for blank video layers is to house drawn content; you can place animations that you've created with the brush, pencil, and pen tools (as well as the Shape tool) in these blank video layers.

The Timeline palette

The Timeline palette, which as we've said is really a part or variation of the Animation palette, makes it possible for you to view the length of animation properties established for any Photoshop-supported file containing an image sequence, video, or animation. Using the palette's controls (refer to Figure 19.1), you can move through the frames of video or an image sequence. You also can use *keyframes* to animate layer features and to establish the duration and sequence of layers in an animation.

FIGURE 19.2

Create blank video layers to give your new or edited content a home of its own.

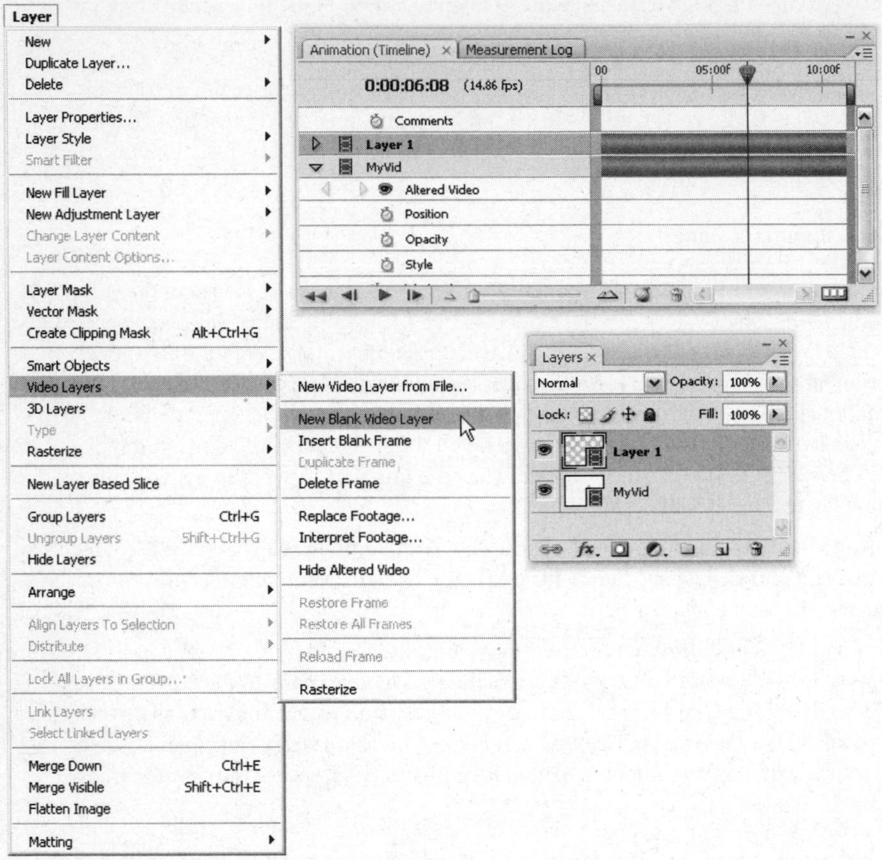

As shown in Figure 19.3, each layer in a Photoshop document appears in the Timeline palette — well, all but the Background layer, which is visible in the Layers palette instead. Further parallels between these two palettes include the fact that whenever you add, delete, rename, group, delete, or change the properties of a layer in the Timeline palette, the changes are reflected in the Layers palette.

NOTE   If you group animation layers as a Smart Object, the information from the Timeline palette is stored in the Smart Object. The fact that the layers are Smart Objects is reflected in the Layers palette, and related Photoshop features — such as Smart Filters — are then applicable to the layers.

FIGURE 19.3

The Timeline palette and the Layers palette have quite a bit in common in terms of how they store and display in formation about your video layers.

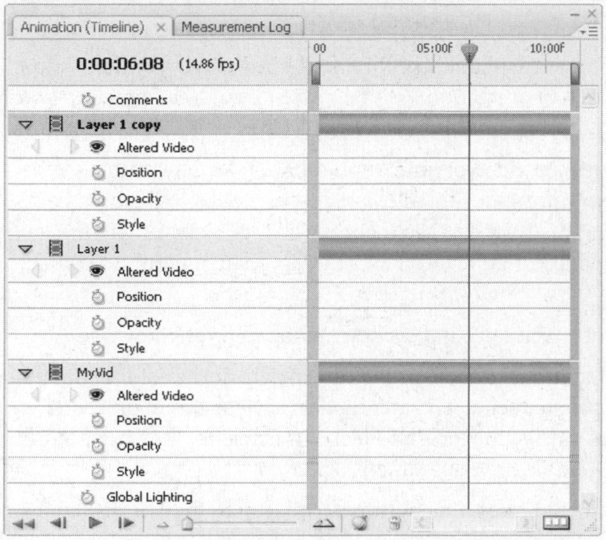

Timeline palette controls and features

As shown in Figures 19.1 and 19.3, the Timeline palette has several buttons that you don't see elsewhere in Photoshop palettes. These controls allow you to control your video's timing and the order of its frames, and they let you apply features that help you keep an eye on time in the movie overall and movement within and between the frames themselves. Look for these buttons:

- **Altered frame indicator:** This icon tells you that a frame has been retouched.

- **Current time display:** You can display the current time and drag its display to move through the frames of the video or animation.

- **Current-time indicator:** This establishes the current frame in the video or animation, and displays it in the document window. Look for the light blue triangle on the Timeline ruler; as shown in previous figures, a vertical line runs from the current-time indicator down to the bottom of the time ruler, and as you drag the indicator, the current-time indicator changes to reflect the indicator's current position in time.

- **Delete keyframes:** You can delete keyframes in three ways. You can click a keyframe and then click the Trash icon. You can drag the keyframe to the trash. Or you can click the keyframe and then press the Delete (Win) / Del (Mac) key.

- **Keyframe navigators:** Use these controls to reposition the current-time indicator to the previous or next keyframe.

- **Layer duration bar:** This bar indicates the portion of time within a video or animation that is taken up by a layer's content. You can drag the moving In and Out points to trim the duration of any layer.

- **Next/previous altered video:** These controls move forward and backward between and among retouched frames.

- **Playback controls:** These buttons, which look like VCR and DVD-player controls, allow you to run a preview of your video or animation. As you move through the preview, note that the current-time indicator adjusts according to where you are.

- **Time ruler:** This device measures the video or animation duration serially, with a counting method you establish in your settings for the file's properties. Observe the tick marks (calibrations) and numbers along the ruler and see that they change according to the level of detail at which you view the video or animation. You can Zoom in and out, of course, using the Zoom slider.

- **Time vary stopwatch:** This tool enables or disables keyframing in layer animation.

- **Timeline options:** Click the ubiquitous triangle in the upper-right corner of the Timeline palette to display the Timeline palette menu. The menu offers several commands, including those that control keyframes, layers, the look and feel of the palette, the use of onion skins, and general settings for your video or animation file.

- **Toggle onion skins:** As the name indicates, this button allows you to hide or display onion skins in the document window.

- **Work area bar:** This bar indicates the span within the animation or video that you want to preview or export to another file.

- **Work area start and end brackets:** These controls allow you to determine the span of the video or animation that will be previewed, rendered, or exported.

- **Zoom controls:** Also known as the Zoom slider, these controls (two buttons and a slider between them) allow you to see more or less detail in the timeline, zooming in on the scale of the ruler.

Customizing the Timeline palette

Like any other Photoshop palette, you can change the way the palette looks and works through the palette menu. You can open the Timeline palette menu by clicking the triangle in the upper-right corner of the palette. The resulting menu is shown in Figure 19.4.

TIP Want to make your palette thumbnails bigger or smaller? From the Palette menu, choose Options, and then choose small, medium, or large thumbnails. You also can decide whether you want to see Timeline Units, including Frame Number (off by default) and Timecode (on by default) in the palette. After you've made all the desired changes, click OK.

FIGURE 19.4

The Timeline options menu lets you customize the way the Timeline palette looks and works.

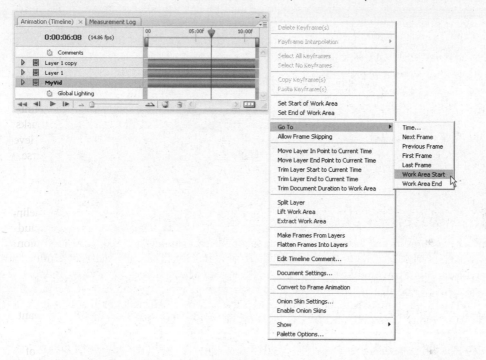

The aforementioned options aren't the only changes you can make in how the Timeline palette looks and works. Here are some other things you can do:

- **Display the current time.** To do this, drag the current-time indicator and click in the time ruler where you want the current-time indicator to appear. Next, drag the current time display into position. You also can make the current time display by using the playback controls, or whenever you zoom in or out with the Zoom slider, which runs across the bottom of the palette. You'll note that this looks just like the slider in the Navigator palette, which controls your zoom on an image window.

- **Change the Timeline view.** Again, you can use the Zoom slider, shown in Figure 19.5, or click the Zoom In or Zoom Out buttons (at either end of the slider). Choosing to hide or display layer properties (using the triangles to the far left on each layer) also changes the Timeline palette's view, by making more room to see individual layers within the vertical space in the palette. To see those layers that are currently not showing, drag the scrollbar on the right side of the palette.

FIGURE 19.5

Drag the Zoom slider to zoom in on your timings. Just like zooming in on a photo lets you edit down to the pixel, zooming in on the Timeline lets you edit frames and control time in greater detail.

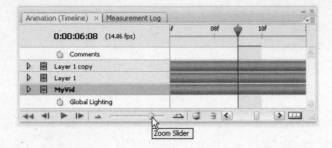

Editing duration and frame rate settings

You can set the duration and frame rate for a Photoshop file that contains video or animation content. *Duration*, obviously, is the overall length of video or animation. The *frame rate* is determined by the type of output you produce — for example, NTSC video has a frame rate of 29.97 frames per second (fps), PAL video has a frame rate of 25 fps, and motion picture film has a frame rate of 24 fps. DVD video may have the same frame rate as NTSC video or PAL video, or a frame rate of 23.976 (NTSC Film). Video intended for CD-ROM or the Web is often 10 to 15 fps.

What can you do with all this information? Well not much just by reading it, but you'll find practical applications for it when you begin producing or editing your own video and animations. As soon as you start a new video or animation file in Photoshop CS3, default timeline settings are in place. These include a duration of 10 seconds and a frame rate of 30 fps. Using the Timeline palette menu, you can choose Document Timeline Settings and, in the resulting dialog box, enter your own settings for these values, as shown in Figure 19.6.

FIGURE 19.6

Set the duration and frame rate for your video or animation with the Document Timeline Settings dialog box.

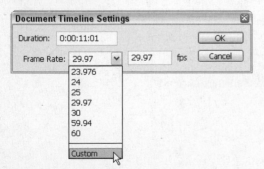

Creating video images

After you've set up the basics for your video or animation — its duration and frame rate (which you can change later, so don't worry that you've carved anything in stone) — you're ready to start building your video. This, of course, assumes that while you're in Photoshop, and perhaps *because* you're in Photoshop, this includes the creation and insertion of images for use in the video.

Before you dig in, consider these issues:

- **Adobe Premiere, and other video-editing applications to which you might export the finished file, do not support 16-bits-per-channel images.**

- **If your video has more than one layer, you may be able to export just one of the layers to another video-editing application.** So don't restrict yourself to a single layer if your eventual goal is to export only one layer; you can develop with multiple layers in place and then export only one of them, or merge the layers before export.

- **Check the ability of the video-editing application to preserve transparency.** Going to lots of trouble to include transparency in your video or animation is a wasted effort if the application won't support it. Programs like Final Cut and Adobe Premiere have no problem with transparency, fortunately.

- **Make a flattened copy of your file in PSD (Photoshop Document) format** so you've got backward compatibility issues covered. While files that include layer masks or multiple layers may not have to be flattened to be used in some applications, it could happen. With your flattened PSD file on hand, you'll be able export your Photoshop file successfully into video-editing applications such as Adobe Premiere.

- **Actions aren't just for still photos.** Photoshop also offers a bunch of video actions that automate various tasks for dealing with video files. The use of these actions is covered later in this chapter.

Add existing images to your video file

When you're ready to start building the video file, you can start adding images to your file's frames. You can insert those images by dragging layers (shape layers, rasterized type layers, drawn content) from other images, copying and pasting from other images, or use the File ➪ Place command to open the Place File dialog box and select an image. The dialog box, shown in Figure 19.7, allows you to navigate to the image file you want to use and to preview it either within the dialog box controls or through changing your view to Thumbnails view (for Windows users), and a click of the Place button gets that image into your new video file.

When you add content, using any of the aforementioned methods, Photoshop automatically converts and scales the image to the pixel aspect ratio of the video file, also known as a *nonsquare pixel document*. This applies to vector files, such as Adobe Illustrator images, too.

FIGURE 19.7

The File ➪ Place command does just that — it places a file in your new video file.

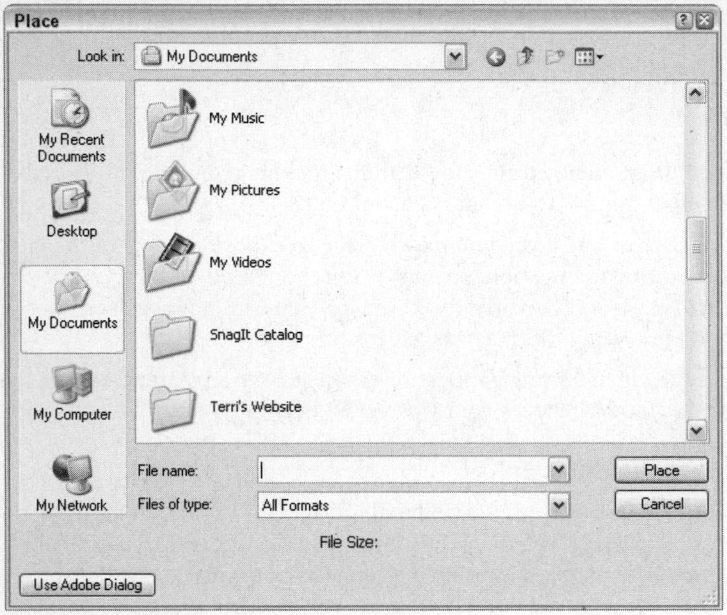

Creating new images for video

The process of creating a new video file is pretty straightforward: Choose File ➪ New, and in the resulting New dialog box, shown in Figure 19.8, pick a Preset for the video system that you believe is likely the one in which your video will be viewed. You can click the Advanced button to pick a color profile and choose your pixel aspect ratio, or use the View ➪ Pixel Aspect Ratio Correction command to eliminate scaling correction in the image if it's ever shown on a square pixel display. As shown in Figure 19.9, this choice regarding Pixel Aspect Ratio Correction can have significant impact on your video's visual quality.

TIP Nonsquare pixel files open by default with Pixel Aspect Ratio Correction turned on, which scales the image for a nonsquare pixel display device, such as a video monitor. If you know that this will be the only type of monitor used to view your video, feel free to leave this default in the on position. If you have an HD monitor, it may already have square pixels, and do the conversion itself.

FIGURE 19.8

Use these handy Video preset file size guides to start your video file off on the right foot.

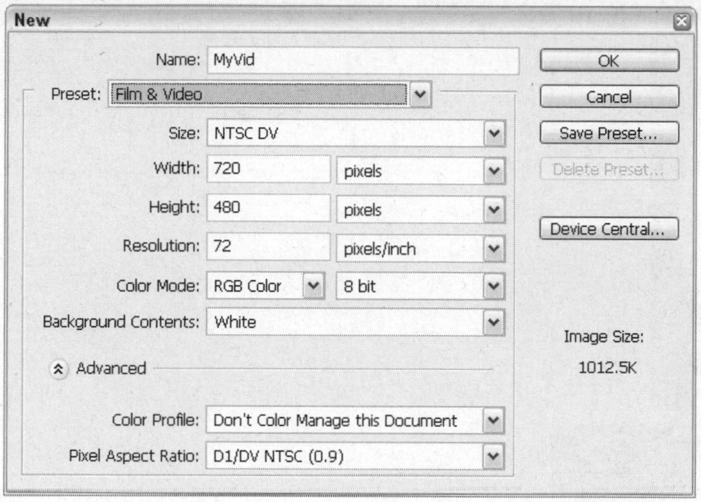

Of course, you may want more proof than just our say-so. Toward that end, Photoshop offers the Window ⇨ Arrange ⇨ New Window command so that you can view your file with Pixel Aspect Ratio turned on and off (one way per window). You also can preview your file on a likely monitor, if you have one handy, connecting your test monitor to your computer through a FireWire or similar connection device. Use the File ⇨ Export ⇨ Video Preview command, and send the preview to the connected monitor. If you don't care about tinkering with output options, choose File ⇨ Export ⇨ Send Video Preview To Device.

Setting the right pixel aspect ratio

In addition to turning this feature on or off at the time you create a new video document, you have another chance to change this setting later on — using the Image ⇨ Pixel Aspect Ratio command. Pick one of the submenu's options, shown in Figure 19.10, and you're good to go. If you want to customize things a bit, you can choose Custom Pixel Aspect Ratio from that same submenu and enter values into the dialog box fields — Name (to give your custom setting a relevant moniker) and Factor (which is the ratio itself). Click OK, and your custom setting is applied, and it will be available the next time you use the New dialog box and want to choose a preset aspect ratio for a new video file.

FIGURE 19.9

Compare the circle in a NTSC DV 720×480 file when viewed on a computer monitor (square pixel) with Pixel Aspect Ratio Correction turned on (top) and Pixel Aspect Ratio Correction turned off (bottom).

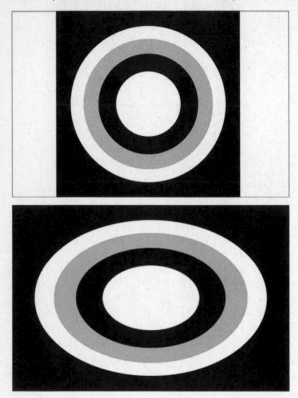

What to do with an unwanted custom pixel aspect ratio? If you just can't stand seeing one that you've created in that Preset list any longer, you can kill off the unwanted ratio by choosing Image ⇨ Pixel Aspect Ratio ⇨ Delete Pixel Aspect Ratio. Not much of a surprise there, eh?

When the resulting Delete Pixel Aspect Ratio dialog box opens, pick the preset you want to kill and click the Delete button. If all you wanted to do was change an existing preset, take a slightly different path: This time, instead of Delete Pixel Aspect Ratio, choose Reset Pixel Aspect Ratios from the Image ⇨ Pixel Aspect Ratio submenu, and tinker with the Append field, which allows you to restore a previously deleted default ratio value and also keep your custom settings. If you skip the Append option and just click OK, all defaults are restored and anything custom is gone. Seems a bit rash, so handle this with care.

FIGURE 19.10

Choose your Pixel Aspect Ratio from this Image command submenu — including the ability set your own parameters with the Custom Pixel Aspect Ratio option.

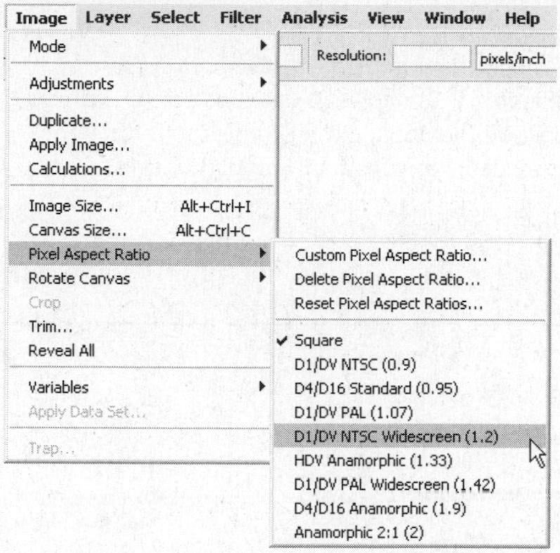

Working with video actions

Actions, as you read in Chapter 3, automate frequently used features and/or complex tasks so that you can perform them quickly, uniformly, and conveniently over and over again. Photoshop's video actions bring this convenience and power to the video "side" of the application, and you'll find them very useful in creating and editing images and video.

With these actions, you can automate tasks that help your images work within the confines of display standards, to convert images for DVD, to set various aspect ratios, and to build layers and set up special effects. Virtually anything that can cause unique problems for video-bound images can be resolved with the use of actions, as you automate the process of invoking a series of Photoshop commands, tools, and features.

Of course, the process of creating actions for video is no different than creating actions that create or edit images bound for print or still images headed for the Web: You'll be using the same Actions palette, and the rules and techniques for building an action are the same as those that you read in Chapter 3. Where things differ is in the use of video-related actions that you can load, use, and edit for your needs. Here's how to install them:

STEPS: Creating an action

1. Display the Actions palette by choosing Window ➪ Actions.
2. Click the palette menu button.

3. Select Load Actions from the menu.

4. In the resulting Load dialog box, locate the Photoshop Actions folder and select the Video Actions.atn file.

5. Click Load.

The video-related actions are loaded, and you can access them from within the Actions palette, playing them just as you would any other action. Figure 19.11 shows the Actions palette with the video actions added. If you display the action's steps (by clicking the triangle next to the action's name), you can turn various steps on and off, activate dialog box pauses, and play with all the other controls you learned in Chapter 3.

FIGURE 19.11

Add actions that help you prepare your video files for a variety of display situations.

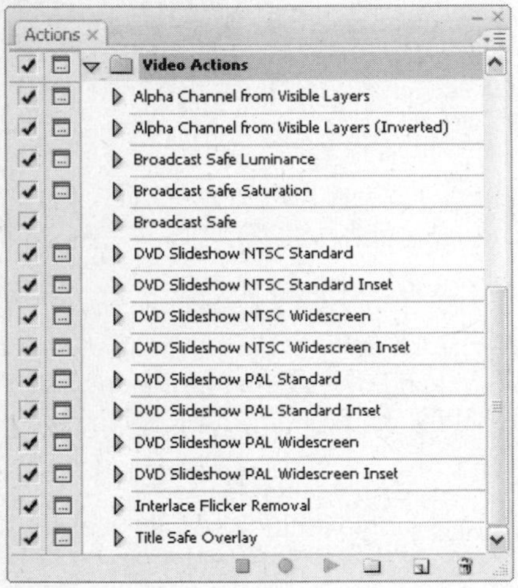

> **TIP**   If you can't find the actions files through the Load dialog box, you can do one of two things: (1) Use your operating system's search tools and look for files with an .atn extension, or (2) go to the Photoshop CS3 folder, check inside the Presets subfolder, and look for an Actions folder. Depending on your computer and your specific installation of CS3, these locations may vary.

> **CROSS-REF**   What? You skipped that section in Chapter 3? Well, go back and read it now so you can make full use of actions with Photoshop's video tools.

Working with Adobe After Effects

Of course, because it's an Adobe product, compatibility between Photoshop and After Effects is built in: You can build images in Photoshop, and use them in After Effects to create motion graphics. This means that your Photoshop PSD files can be imported into After Effects, where layers, styles, and transparency are preserved.

With all this compatibility, however, you need to keep these things in mind as you build Photoshop images that you intend to use later in After Effects (or if you are giving them to someone else for use in that application):

- **Give your layers unique names, and make sure they're well organized.** Why? This prevents lots of changes being needed later on, and if you don't do this organization until after you've imported the file into After Effects, the layers won't synchronize between the two applications, and After Effects' Project window will list the layers that you've renamed or moved as being missing. Unique names are important for your layers because any layers with duplicate names (like two layers called "cloned content") will create footage update issues.

- **Always maximize your PSD file compatibility.** This option, accessed through the File Handling version of the Preferences dialog box, improves inter-application compatibility for your files. Some people turn this off to create smaller image files for print and Web use, especially if they're fairly certain everything will remain in Photoshop throughout its development life, but if you're working in video and know you'll be porting out to other applications, leave this option set to Always.

- **Don't use a custom New File preset.** When you intend to export your Photoshop image file to After Effects, things go much better if you've used a file size preset for the image file than if you started out with a custom set of dimensions.

Importing video and image sequences

Speaking of importing, files can go the other way, too — from another application into Photoshop. To open a video file in Photoshop, you can choose File ⇨ Open and then use the Layer menu to add a New Video Layer. You also can use the Bridge to open a file, choosing File ⇨ Open With ⇨ Photoshop CS3. Figure 19.12 shows a video file in the Bridge thumbnails area, with its metadata listed in the panel of the same name.

Of course, bringing in image sequence files isn't really any different than bringing in a video file. The only difference is that the image sequences are typically imported in a folder, and each image sequence in that folder becomes a frame in a single video layer, in a single video image file.

For the import (or opening) to work, you want to be sure that the image sequence files are in one folder, and the folder only have image sequences in it; otherwise, Photoshop may become confused as to what to do with other content. Bear in mind that the video file you end up with is more visually appealing if all the supplemental files have the same pixel dimensions (set to the right aspect ratio for the output method that you'll be using to view the final video), and the whole thing runs properly if your frames are named so as to be alphabetically or numerically ordered in the folder from whence they came. Otherwise, you'll have to rearrange them after the file is open, and that can get messy.

FIGURE 19.12

Cross the Bridge from any other application where video was prepared and edit it frame by frame in Photoshop. Here, the Bridge gives you access to a likely suspect.

TIP   Lucky for you, Photoshop is pretty intuitive. If you used the New Video Layer command to import the image sequence, click Open, and note that the Image Sequence option is already on — *unless* you select multiple files or folders.

Inserting video and image sequences

After you've opened an existing or started a new video image, you may want to add another video file to it, or add image sequences to expand or enrich the video. This is just like bringing in other photos to make a composite image with still content.

To add video and image sequences, just use the Place command, which transforms video as you import it into a video file. After they are placed in the file, video frames are contained within a Smart Object, which means you can move through the frames using the Timeline palette.

Choose File ➪ Place to open the Place dialog box, and navigate to the file/sequence that you want to add and click the Place button. Photoshop does the rest, and then you can go to work integrating the added content into the video.

TIP   Again, if you're placing image sequences, be sure the individual files (in a single folder) are ordered by their file name so that they become frames in the right order within the resulting video layer.

Working with alpha channels and mattes

The color data in your video files is stored, just like it is in still images, in three channels: red, blue, and green. Also like your still images, a video image can contain an alpha channel, which as you learned in Chapter 9, is an invisible channel that stores transparency data and makes it possible for the effects of the alpha channel to operate without affecting the color channels in the image.

As shown in Figure 19.13, which includes the Channels palette (with an alpha channel in place), the alpha channel appears in black and white — white representing 100 percent opacity, and black representing 100 percent transparency. Obviously, any shades of gray represent areas that are less than 100 percent opaque, but more than 100 percent transparent.

FIGURE 19.13

An alpha channel applies and controls transparency within areas of a video image layer.

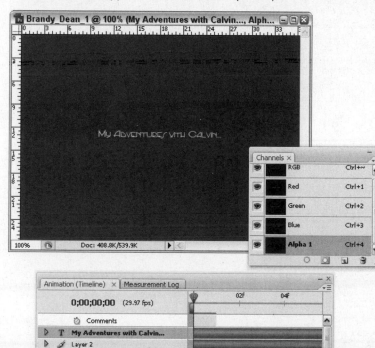

As if all the information about channels in Chapters 4 and 9 wasn't enough to confuse you, now let's talk about two other types of channels that represent the types of alpha channels you'll find in video:

- **Premultiplied alpha channels** allow an image to be composited on top of a background image or solid background color fill. This creates a totally opaque layer, and transparency data is stored in both the alpha and color channels.

- **Straight alpha channels** store transparency only in the alpha channel, and the color channels are not affected.

> **NOTE** Related to alpha channels in terms of their role in the image, a matte is a layer that establishes the transparency of a layer or another layer. The white and black areas work the same way, and the matte itself may be created through an alpha channel.

Using the Interpret Footage command

All the features we've discussed thus far—alpha channels, frame rates, sequence order—can be controlled by the Interpret Footage command, found in the Layer ➪ Video Layers submenu. As shown in Figure 19.14, the resulting dialog box allows you to choose how all these elements of a video image are applied. You don't have to run this command for every video image or layer, but if you have issues with any of these parts of your image, it can be a big help.

FIGURE 19.14

Use the Interpret Footage command to control channels and frame rate settings and how Photoshop applies them to an image.

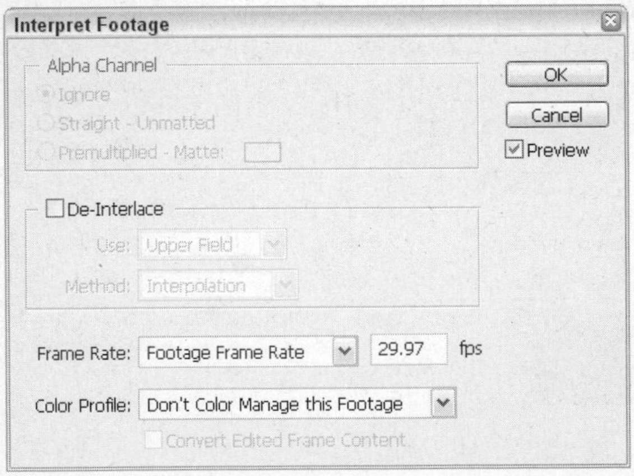

Interpolate to Animate

What the heck is "interpolation"? Interpolation is a mathematical method of filling in missing data. You've seen the concept before in Photoshop: In the Image Size dialog box, you have to choose how to resample the image for enlargement or reduction, and this resampling is a form of interpolation. Typically, interpolation generates a new pixel by using the average of the value of the two pixels on either side of the one to be created, and as Photoshop does this to an entire layer or channel, all the pixels considered as new pixels are added.

When it comes to digital video, interpolation means generating new values between two keyframes. Photoshop interpolates the frames between the two selected and creates the intervening frames and their content. You'll see this demonstrated in our upcoming discussion of creating animated GIFs on the Animation palette, wherein this interpolation is called *tweening* (as in creating frames be*tween*) existing frames. In video and animations, the new frames can create movement — changes in color, light, or styles. Opacity may change between frames, as can the visibility of various layers within the image. Photoshop supports both linear and hold interpolation, the former building a structured change as keyframes move forward, with clean stops and starts between each keyframe pair. The latter method is more progressive and works well for flashing effects or whenever you want the content of a frame to appear quickly, rather than building over a series of frames.

To change your interpolation method, in the Timeline palette, select one or more keyframes and then right-click to display a pop-up menu from which you can choose an interpolation method. Then open the Timeline palette menu, and choose either Interpolation ➪ Linear or Interpolation ➪ Hold.

From within the Interpret Footage dialog box, you can do these things:

- **Choose how the alpha channel in the video layer is interpreted** by selecting the Alpha Channel option. Of course, the footage must have an alpha channel for this option to be available, and if Premultiplied - Matted is selected, you can choose the matte color against which the image channels is premultiplied.

- **Choose the Frame Rate.** This option is unavailable for image sequence-based layers.

- **Choose the dominant field for interlaced video** from the De-Interlace section, choosing a field from the Use drop-down list and a Method for interpolation. If your video is headed for progressive-scan monitors, turn De-Interlace on, which activates the fields within that section of the dialog box.

- **Choose a Color Profile for your frames and video layers.**

Understanding interlaced and non-interlaced video

As we move through discussions of the different "flavors" of things when it comes to video — different types of alpha channels, different video output settings, etc. — it's time for another set of video-related flavors: interlaced and non-interlaced video. These are the only two types of video, and they serve different purposes and meet different needs. Read on to find out more.

Interlaced video

When it comes to interlaced video, it is so named because of how the horizontal lines in the frames line up. Interlaced video frames consist of two fields, and each one stores half the number of horizontal lines in the frame. The upper field (or Field 1) stores all the odd-numbered lines, and the lower field (or Field 2) stores all the even-numbered lines. An interlaced video monitor, therefore, displays the video by showing each frame, first drawing all the lines in one field and then drawing all the lines in the other field, one after the other. The order of the fields determines which one is drawn onscreen first, and in NTSC video, fields are drawn to the screen approximately 60 times per second, working out perfectly with a frame rate for the same format of approximately 30 frames per second.

> **TIP** Most broadcast video is interlaced, including the new high-definition television standards, which have interlaced (such as 1080i) and non-interlaced variants (such as 1080p).

Non-interlaced video

Conversely, non-interlaced video frames are not separated into fields and work well on a progressive-scan monitor, which can display these frames by drawing all the horizontal lines, from top to bottom, in one pass. Nearly all computer monitors are progressive-scan monitors, and most video designed for use on computer screens — video for the Web, that is — is non-interlaced.

Creating Animations

Not to be confused with the process of creating simple layer-based animations with the Animation palette (*not* in Timeline mode), this discussion pertains to an animation made up of a sequence of images, or frames, displayed over time and built through the Timeline palette. In such an animation, much like the "simpler" variety coming up later in this chapter, each frame has different content, and layers are in different positions, opacities, and styles — and the result is the illusion of movement and change over time.

To create a Timeline-based animation, you build your image content, layer by layer, and then establish keyframes as you move the current-time indicator forward. At each keyframe, you modify the position, opacity, or style of the layer content, so that whatever movement and change you have in mind is physically achieved by the progression of frames. You can ask Photoshop to automatically modify (through interpolation) the content of intervening frames, or you can do it manually, inserting frames and tinkering with content on your own.

Keyframes defined

Keyframes are used to create and control animation, effects, and many other kinds of change that occur over time. A keyframe marks the point in time where you specify a value, such as spatial position, opacity, or layer style. Values between keyframes are interpolated. When you use keyframes to create a change over time, you must use at least two keyframes — one for the state at the beginning of the change and one for the new state at the end of the change.

Use keyframes to animate layer properties. Using keyframes, you can animate different layer properties, such as position, opacity, and style. Each change can occur independently of, or simultaneously with, other changes. If you want to animate different objects independently, you should create them on separate layers.

Here are some examples of how you can animate layer properties:

- You can animate position by adding a keyframe to the Position property, and then moving the current-time indicator and dragging the layer in the document window.

- You can animate a layer's opacity by adding a keyframe to the Opacity property, and then moving the current-time indicator and changing the layer's opacity in the Layers palette.

To animate a property using keyframes, you must set at least two keyframes for that property. Otherwise, changes that you make to the layer property remain in effect for the duration of the layer.

Each layer property has a time-vary stopwatch icon that you click to begin the process of animating with keyframes. After the stopwatch is active for a specific property, Photoshop automatically sets new keyframes whenever you change the current time and the property value. When the stopwatch is inactive for a property, the property has no keyframes. If you type a value for a layer property while the stopwatch is inactive, the value remains in effect for the duration of the layer. If you deselect the stopwatch, any existing keyframes for that layer property disappear, so don't deselect the stopwatch unless you're sure that you want to permanently delete all the keyframes for that property.

Working with keyframe icons

Because keyframes are so ... well, pardon the expression, "key" ... to the use and understanding of the Timeline palette, let's look at how to work with them, how to identify their markers in the palette, and later on, how to connect them to the current-time indicator and time within the span of your video.

Of course, in the Timeline palette, the appearance of a keyframe relies upon the interpolation method that you select for the interval between keyframes. Here are the two icons you'll see:

 The diamond icon appears for a linear keyframe, which as discussed previously means that the frame moves in a very structured, paced way. Animations utilizing linear interpolation result in an animation that changes evenly over the span of keyframes (from the previous one to the next one).

 The half-diamond/half-rectangle icon appears in the presence of a hold keyframe. As discussed previously, hold interpolation allows for random and sudden changes within the video. This apparent randomness is the result of allowing a keyframe to change only when the current-time indicator is positioned directly on a hold keyframe.

Associating keyframes with the current time

Now, as soon as you've set up a keyframe for a property, the keyframe navigator can be used to move through the keyframes, as well as to set new and remove unwanted keyframes. When the keyframe navigator box is active, the current-time indicator is positioned on the selected keyframe; on the other hand, if the navigator is inactive, the current-time indicator is between keyframes. Again, we see the impact of interpolation, in terms of linear and hold keyframes and the relative position of the current-time indicator.

Repositioning the keyframe navigator and selecting keyframes

To navigate with the keyframe navigator, use the navigator arrows. The left arrow moves the current-time indicator to the previous keyframe (big surprise there), and the right arrow moves the current-time indicator to the next keyframe. Just as you'd expect, right? Sometimes, things work sensibly, believe it or not!

As simple as it is to move around within keyframes, you can select them just as easily. You can do any of the following to select one or more keyframes:

- Click the keyframe icon to select a single keyframe.

- Click the layer property name next to the stopwatch icon to select all the keyframes for a given property.

- Shift-click on multiple keyframes. This allows you to select a series of contiguous keyframes.

- Drag with your mouse to draw a marquee around the keyframes you want to select. This is much like selecting a group of thumbnails on the Bridge or icons on your Windows or Mac desktop.

Moving, copying, and pasting keyframes

After you've selected one or more keyframes, you'll probably want to move, cut, copy, or paste them — the motivations behind selecting them in the first place. To move keyframes, drag them from their current location to any desired time. If you're moving more than one keyframe, all the selected frames come with you as you drag, and they keep their relative timings (the length of time the keyframe is displayed). You can copy keyframes in the same layer or between layers for the same property (such as Position) fusing the Timeline palette menu by clicking the menu button and choosing Copy Keyframes. Figure 19.15 show a series of selected keyframes and the palette menu, awaiting the user's selection.

When you're at the spot along the timeline where the copied keyframes belong, click there to select that spot and then select the target layer. After those two preparatory steps are taken, click the Timeline palette menu again and choose Paste Keyframes.

To delete a keyframe or keyframes, select one (or more) and display the Timeline palette menu. From the menu, choose Delete Keyframes. You also can simply right-click (Ctrl-click on the Mac) and choose Delete from the pop-up menu.

FIGURE 19.15

Select the keyframes you want to move, and then use the Copy Keyframes command to move them. For a short distance, dragging works, too; but for a long-range move, copying and pasting is your best bet.

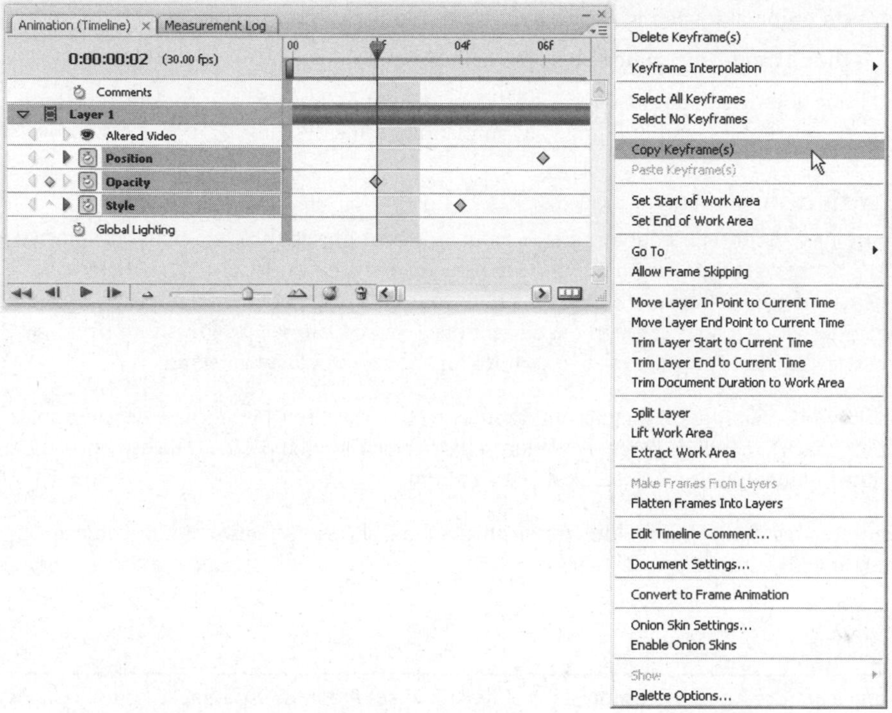

Building an animation with drawing tools

Animations that consist of drawn content — painted lines and curves, shapes, filled selections, and other original artwork — can be created easily using blank video layers and Photoshop's drawing tools. The drawn content can already exist in a standard PSD or other format image file, or you can build it while the Timeline palette is open and the video is in progress.

To build an animation, using existing content, follow these steps:

STEPS: Building an animation

1. **Start a new document, using the File ⇨ New command.**
2. **Insert a blank video layer, by choosing Layer ⇨ Video Layers ⇨ New Blank Video Layer.**

3. **Add your content.** You can drag it, from the Layers palette, from existing images, or as needed, utilize the brush, pencil, pen, shape, and paint bucket tools to build original art content. Be sure that content that has to move or operate independently is on a separate layer from other content; repeat Step 2 for each such element.

4. **Turn on onion skins using the Toggle Onion Skins button.**

5. **Drag the current-time indicator to the next frame.**

6. **Continue adding content, using the directions in Step 3, dragging the current-time indicator to new frames, and building your animation, frame by frame.**

Working with onion skins

Onion skins are named for their counterparts in nature — the thin, see-through, paper cover that protects onions as they grow underground and are handled after the gardener plucks them from the earth. The use of onion skins in video production takes advantage of that see-through nature and lets you see previous frames through the current ones, so you can see progressive movement, position, and size changes, and plan your next move for the frames you're working on.

Onion skins show the painting on the current frame as well as the painting on the adjacent frames, appearing at an opacity that you set. To use onion skins in the Timeline palette, click to open the Timeline palette menu and select Onion Skin Settings from the menu.

While you're in the resulting Onion Skin Options dialog box, shown in Figure 19.16, you can establish the following settings:

FIGURE 19.16

Choose how many frames are displayed via onion skins at any time, set the frame spacing, and the opacity of the skins themselves. You can even apply a blend mode!

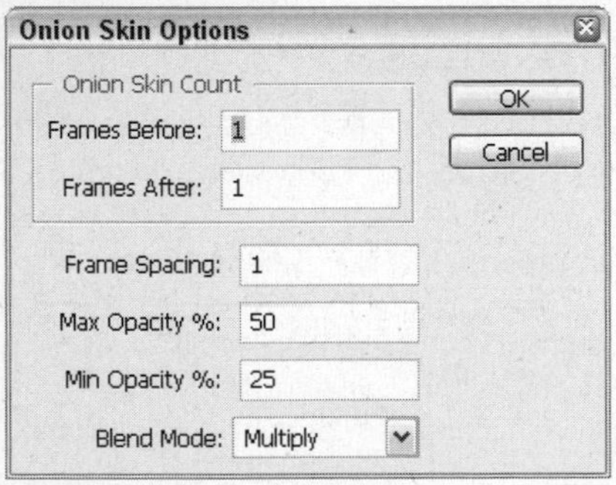

- **Onion Skin Count:** This setting determines how many previous and forward frames are displayed as onion skins as you work. Fill in values in the Before (previous frames) and After (forward frames) fields.

- **Frame Spacing:** This determines the number of frames displayed between the strokes painted on your frames. To help you get the idea, imagine that you have a value of 1 entered into this field. This means that every single frame is displayed, while a value of 2 displays every other frame.

- **Opacity:** How thick should the skins be? The opacity setting determines how see-through they are.

- **Blend Mode:** This option, which offers four familiar blend modes (Normal, Multiply, Screen, and Difference), determines how the overlapping parts of the frames are displayed. If you forget what these particular blend modes do to content, check out Chapter 14.

Turning layers on and off

Unlike hiding or displaying layers in a still image, which requires a simple click of the eyeball icon in the Layers palette, turning video layers on and off is a bit more complex. You can turn layers on and off and on again over the duration of a video or animation, or you can turn one or more layers off entirely — perhaps showing them in one version of a video and not in another, the versions kept separate by different file names assigned through individual rendering/naming operations.

Deciding when and where a layer appears in a video or animation can be performed in two ways: (1) You can hide frames at the beginning or end of a layer, which changes the layer's beginning ("In") point and ending ("Out") point, or (2) you can drag the entire layer duration bar to a specific span of the timeline.

> **NOTE** To prepare your video layers for operations that require rasterized content, you can use the Layer ➪ Rasterize ➪ Video command. This can be applied to one or more video layers at a time. As soon as you do this, though, note that the current frame displayed in the image window is set as the layer's raster image, so although you can rasterize more than one video layer simultaneously, the current frame is the top layer in the stack that you're rasterizing.

Previewing video and animations

You'd never want to export your video or animation to another application — or worse — give it to someone else to play until you've tested it yourself. The preview is your chance to do just that, making sure that the frames are in the right order, that the animation proceeds as desired and expected, and that your effects and content look just like you want them. Of course, further enhancements and special effects can be applied in an application such as Adobe After Effects, or your video can be put together with other content through Adobe Premiere or Final Cut, but for the part you're taking care of in Photoshop, the preview is your big chance to find errors, set about fixing them, and make sure everything looks right before you move on to the next step in your video production.

To begin, you'll want to determine which area of your video or animation you want to preview. This entails dragging the work area bar through the section you want to preview or dragging work area markers into place (at the beginning and end of the area you want to preview) to set the span of your preview. After you've done this, you can watch the preview, using the playback buttons on the Timeline palette.

Of course, a Web browser window gives you a great preview, too, if your creation is an animation bound for the Web. The browser's Stop button (typically a red X or stop sign symbol) and Reload button (two arrows in a circle, typically) serve for stop and play, respectively. To bring your video up in a browser window, choose File ⇨ Save for Web & Devices, and click the Preview in Browser button within the resulting dialog box. To review the rest of the Save for Web & Devices dialog box and look into Web graphics and still content more thoroughly from a Web perspective, check out Chapter 20.

> **TIP** You also can press the spacebar to play or stop the playback.

Previewing video display

Photoshop's Video Preview plug-in enables you to use FireWire or any other video display device to preview your video and animations. This also gives you a chance to tweak your aspect ratio settings for your intended display device/s and to make sure color is right in your file. Toward that end, note that the Video Preview plug-in supports RGB, grayscale, and indexed images, in either 8 or 16 bits per channel. If you have a 16-bit image, it's converted to 8-bits-per-channel. If you have an alpha channel in place, it's disregarded, and any pixels set to be transparent appear as black. This can be quite a shock if you don't remember this limitation.

This set of steps explains how to set up and do your video display.

STEPS: Setting up video display

1. **Be sure that your video file is open, and in the active image window.** If it's not, choose File ⇨ Open and select the file by name. Click the Open button to open the file, and proceed with your display setup.

2. **Connect a display device, such as a video monitor, to your computer via FireWire.**

3. **Choose File ⇨ Export ⇨ Send Video Preview To Device.** You can skip the rest of the steps in this procedure. This step is essential if you don't want to set output options for viewing your document on a device,

4. **Choose File ⇨ Export ⇨ Video Preview.** This allows you to establish output options before you view your document on the display device. This also opens the Video Preview dialog box, shown in Figure 19.17. If your document's pixel aspect ratio doesn't match the aspect ratio settings of the display device, an alert appears to let you know.

FIGURE 19.17

Set your Video Preview settings, and check to see if your aspect ratio is set properly for your designated device.

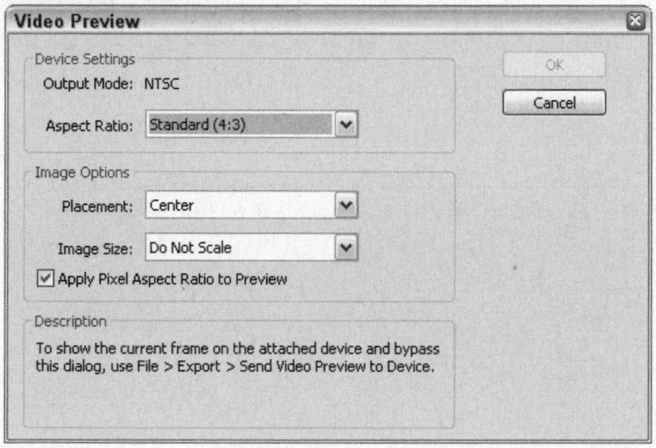

```
┌─────────────────────────────────────────────────────┐
│ Video Preview                                    [×] │
│ ┌─ Device Settings ──────────────┐  ┌──────────┐    │
│ │  Output Mode:  NTSC            │  │    OK    │    │
│ │                               │  └──────────┘    │
│ │  Aspect Ratio: │Standard (4:3)│▼│ ┌──────────┐    │
│ │                               │  │  Cancel  │    │
│ │                               │  └──────────┘    │
│ ├─ Image Options ───────────────┤                  │
│ │  Placement:  │Center        │▼│                  │
│ │                               │                  │
│ │  Image Size: │Do Not Scale  │▼│                  │
│ │  ☑ Apply Pixel Aspect Ratio to Preview           │
│ ├─ Description ─────────────────┤                  │
│ │  To show the current frame on the attached device │
│ │  and bypass this dialog, use File > Export > Send │
│ │  Video Preview to Device.                         │
│ └───────────────────────────────┘                  │
└─────────────────────────────────────────────────────┘
```

CAUTION   Whatever you set through the Video Preview dialog box is maintained by the Send Video Preview To Device command.

Within the Video Preview dialog box, you can set the following:

- **In the Device Settings section**, you can set the Aspect Ratio for your file, choosing between Standard and Widescreen. The Output Mode is already set, and can't be changed; it was determined by the device to which you're connected.

NOTE   For Mac users, choosing an output mode gives you two choices: NTSC and PAL.

- **In the Image Options section**, you can set the Placement, choosing from the following:
  - **Center:** This setting positions the center of the image in the center of the screen, cropping the portions that are beyond the display edges of the video preview device.
  - **Crop to 4:3:** This setting displays a 16:9 image on a 4:3 display with the center of the image at the center of the screen. There is no distortion through cropping from the left and right edges of the frame that are beyond the display edges of the video preview device.
  - **Letterbox:** This setting scales a 16:9 image to fit on a 4:3 display, and gray bands are displayed on the top and bottom of the image. This is caused by the difference in aspect ratio between the 16:9 image and the 4:3 display. There is no cropping or distortion.
  - **Crop to 14:9/Letterbox:** Here, you get a widescreen image cropped to a 14:9 aspect ratio with black bands appearing at the top and bottom of the image. There is no distortion.

Saving your video and animations

Videos and animations can be saved as QuickTime movies or PSD files. Additionally, you can save animations as GIFs for viewing on the Web. To save in a video format, you need to use the File ➪ Export ➪ Render Video command. This gives you the Render Video dialog box, shown in Figure 19.18, which allows you to choose how your video is rendered, or prepared for preview and/or used in another video application and final display.

FIGURE 19.18

The Render Video dialog box lets you pick where to store your video file, how to export it relative to QuickTime and Image Sequences, which frames to render, and how to handle alpha channels and frame rates. It does it all!

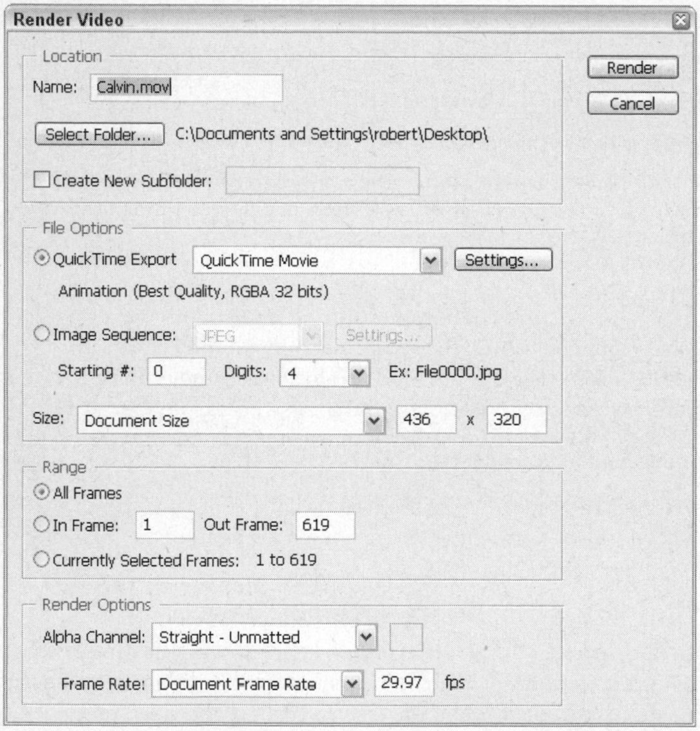

When you're ready to export your video or image sequence, follow these steps.

STEPS: Rendering your video and image sequences

1. **Choose File ⇨ Export ⇨ Render Video.** This opens the Render Video dialog box.

2. **In the Render Video dialog box, enter a name for the video or image sequence.** You also can click the Select Folder button, choose a place to store your video, and click Choose to pick that location.

3. **Under File Options, select either QuickTime Export, or Image Sequence.** You can specify settings and options for the video or image sequence using the drop-menus to the right of these options.

4. Under Range, select one of the following:

   ■ **All Frames** renders all the frames in the file.

   ■ **In Frame** allows you to choose which frames to render.

   ■ **Currently Selected Frames** restricts the rendering to only those frames selected through the work area bar in the Timeline palette.

5. As desired, you can establish Render Options:

   ■ **Alpha Channel** lets you choose how your alpha channels are rendered — straight or pre-multiplied, in a variety of ways for each possibility.

   ■ **Frame Rate** determines the frames-per-second setting for the video when it plays after rendering.

Creating Animated GIF Images

We've all seen them — little "movies," very cartoon-like, in Web pages. They can be short and sweet like a smiley face winking or a stick-figure digging with a shovel, up and down, to show that a Web page is under construction. These animations, while often overused in amateur and personal Web sites, can be useful — demonstrating a concept or conveying a message through a series of images or symbols.

The animations you create in Photoshop, using the Animation palette (rather than the Timeline palette, discussed earlier in this chapter) are saved in GIF format, a format that allows the movement and changes between animation frames to be saved as part of the file. When viewed through a browser, the GIF file that contains these frames plays, based on the information also included in the file as to the duration and repetition of the frames' playback.

You can loop an animation indefinitely or have it play through just once (or any other specific number you choose). You can choose how long each frame remains onscreen, and you can force Photoshop to build frames for you — *tweening* the intervening frames so that what appears in frame 1 slowly morphs or evolves into what's currently in frame 2. If you tell Photoshop to take five frames to make the transition from frame 1 to frame 2, frame 2 becomes frame 7 in the post-tween process.

Creating an animated GIF requires no special skills — at least nothing that you haven't already learned in the previous 18 chapters. You build an image, using layers to house individual image elements that you create with painting, drawing, and Type tools. You apply blend modes and layer styles — all the things you'd do to a still image. The difference? Each layer becomes a frame in the animation.

STEPS: Creating an animation

1. **Create an image in which each layer acts as an individual frame of the finished animation.**

2. **Access the Animation palette by choosing Window ⇨ Animation.** The first frame is already waiting, displaying whatever layers you currently have active in the Layers palette.

3. **Click the New Frame button, labeled in Figure 19.19, to insert the next frame, and make any necessary changes to the visibility of your various layers to advance the action in your animation.**

FIGURE 19.19

A simple animation, showing the Layers and Animation palettes

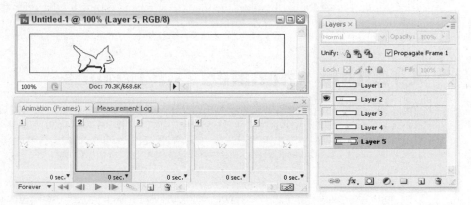

4. **Increase or decrease the amount of time a frame stays onscreen using the pop-up menu located directly beneath the frame on the Animation palette.**

5. **If your animation simply requires moving an object from point A to point B, create only a single layer.** Place the object in its starting position in frame 1, click the New Frame button in the Animation palette, and go back to your layer and reposition the object in its final location. From here, click the Animation palette's Tween button (meaning to create the frames "in between," as shown in Figure 19.20) to have Photoshop create all the frames in between. The Tween dialog box provides fields to specify how many frames Photoshop should place between your two starting frames, as well as which direction the tween should go (tweening between the selected frame and the frame before it or after it, depending upon which frame you have selected at the time).

FIGURE 19.20

The Tween dialog box allows you to specify how many frames Photoshop should place between your two starting frames, as well as which direction the "tween" should go.

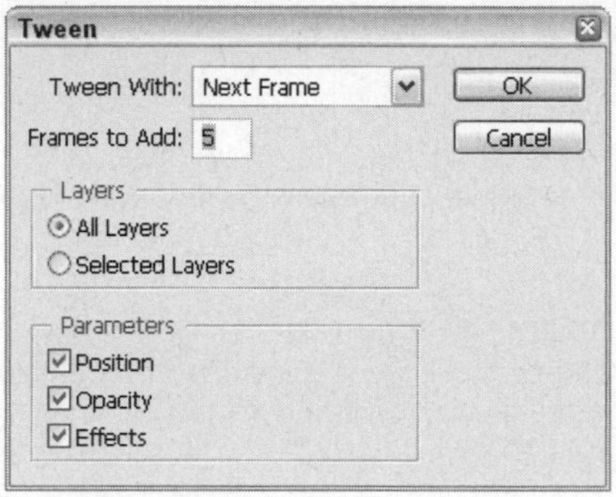

Tween	⊠

Tween With: Next Frame ▾   [OK]

Frames to Add: 5   [Cancel]

— Layers —
◉ All Layers
○ Selected Layers

— Parameters —
☑ Position
☑ Opacity
☑ Effects

Rotoscoping

What is *rotoscoping*? It's painting in video layers, turning video content into drawings, which historically meant tracing actual live-action film, frame by frame, and creating animation from them. Current advertising campaigns have made this quite popular — using live-action video and turning it into a realistic-looking animation.

Photoshop CS3's video tools allow you to create an animation from live-action video, applying painting tools to video frames. The process is rather simple, and it begins with your selecting a video layer in the Timeline palette and moving the current-time indicator to the frame within that layer that you want to paint. Next you choose Layers ➪ Video Layers ➪ Add Blank Video Layer, to create a place for your painting if you want it to be on a separate layer, thus leaving your original layer content intact. It's a matter of choice.

At this point, you can begin painting, cloning, and otherwise drawing on the layer, using the tools you read about in Chapters 5 and 6. You also can apply filters, mimicking various artistic mediums. To prepare, thumb through Chapters 10 and 11 for ideas as to which filters will give you the effects you want.

NOTE   Much of your success will rely on selections made on the original layer and then applied to the blank layer, if you've opted to paint on a separate layer. Remember, as you read in Chapter 8, that you can make a selection in one layer, and then switch to a different layer, keeping the selection intact, where you can apply the fill or paint within the selection.

Summary

In this chapter, you learned about the Timeline palette and all its tools for editing and creating video and animations. You learned which video and animation formats Photoshop CS3 supports and discovered how to open, manipulate, and save those files in Photoshop, including how to export them in any number of still image formats for print and Web use.

You also learned to create animated GIF files, using the Animation palette, and to prepare animations for use on the Web — from setting up a layered image to creating frames within the animation and testing the file before saving it.

Finally, you learned about 3D image editing, a new feature in CS3, as well as Rotoscoping, which also is a new feature in this release of Photoshop. Between the video, the animation, and the ability to render 3D images and rotoscope video frames, Photoshop CS3 has taken great strides toward becoming a significant video development and editing tool.

Chapter 20

Printing and Publishing with Photoshop

Conceptually, printing is a pretty straightforward process. You choose the Print command, press Enter or Return, wait for something to come out of your printer, and then you admire yet another piece of forest that you've destroyed. Of course, printing can be an unbelievably complicated subject too, involving things like *dot-gain compensation*, hardware *calibration*, *under-color* removal, toxic processor chemicals, *separation table* generation, infinitesimal color parameters, and then factor in the publishing requirements for graphics bound for the Web and you're liable to spend a whole lot of your otherwise valuable time trying to figure out what the heck's going on — or pulling your hair out. At the very least, you're going to feel some anxiety at some point.

This chapter is intended to help you avoid that anxiety — or maybe lessen it — and to help you make sense of it all. By the time you finish this chapter, you should be able to figure your way out of any printing dilemma, or at least know how to avoid them by taking the proper preparatory steps before embarking on an important print job — be it one you're doing yourself on your own printer or one you're taking to a "professional" for specialized results.

Although the chapter is *not* intended to cover every possible facet of printing and publishing digitized images, it does take you through the process of preparing and printing the four major categories of output: composites, color separations, duotones, and Web graphics. By the end of the chapter, you'll be familiar with all of Photoshop's printing and publishing options for both paper and Web production. You'll also be prepared to communicate with professionals at your service bureau or at a commercial printer, if need be, and to learn from their input and expertise.

Understanding Printing Terminology

While not a glossary in the traditional sense, the following is a general list of the printing and publishing terms that you'll encounter as you work with commercial printers, your own printer, and your Web master or host. Ready? Here you go:

- **Service bureau:** A *service bureau* is a shop often filled with young graphic artists, printer operators, and about a billion dollars worth of hardware. A small service bureau is usually outfitted with a few laser printers, photocopiers, and self-service computers. Big service bureaus offer scanners, imagesetters, film recorders, and other varieties of professional-quality input and output equipment.

  Service bureaus once relied exclusively on the Macintosh. This has changed, but a substantial number of Mac-based service bureaus remain. Most service bureaus are equally ready to help Photoshop users on both Windows and Mac platforms, but many will take your Windows Photoshop file and run it through a Mac. There's nothing wrong with this — Photoshop is nearly identical on the two platforms — but cross-platform problems may crop up. If you're a PC user, try to be sure that your service bureau knows how to address cross-platform incompatibilities and has a general working knowledge of Windows. How can you be sure? Ask.

- **Commercial printer:** Generally speaking, a *commercial printer* takes up where the service bureau leaves off. Commercial printers reproduce black-and-white and color pages using offset presses, Web presses, and a whole bunch of other age-old technology. The process is less expensive than photocopying when you're dealing with large quantities, say, more than 100 copies, and it delivers professional-quality reproductions.

- **Web host:** This sounds like the Internet version of a game-show host, but in truth, your Web host is simply the company (or maybe it's just a person) who has a Web server, and who sells or rents you space on that server for your Web site. The impact this entity (the host) has on your Photoshop use relates to your creation of Web graphics. If you try, for example, to load an image that's not in a Web-friendly format onto you Web page, it may well be your host (or one of his or her customer service staff) who has to explain to you that the type of file you tried to use won't work on the Web. So knowing the file formats that the Web *does* like is a good thing to have under your informational belt. Between Chapter 3 and its "File Format Roundup" and this chapter's coverage of Web-related issues, you'll be ready to take on your Web host and know exactly what kind of images you can and cannot use online.

- **Output device:** This is just another way to say *printer*. *Output devices* include printers, imagesetters, film recorders, and a whole bunch of other machines.

- **Laser printers:** A *laser printer* works much like a photocopier, and comes in both black and white-only and color laser varieties. First, it applies an electric charge to a cylinder, called a *drum*, inside the printer. The charged areas, which correspond to the black portions of the image being printed, attract fine, petroleum-based dust particles called *toner*. The drum transfers the toner to the page, and a heating mechanism fixes the toner in place. Most laser printers have resolutions of at least 300 dots (or *printer pixels*) per inch. The newer printers offer higher resolutions, such as 600 and 1200 dots per inch (*dpi*), and as prices come down, color laser printing is now within more people's reach.

- **Color printers:** *Color printers* fall into three categories. Generally speaking, inkjet and thermal-wax printers are at the low end, and dye-sublimation printers occupy the high end. *Inkjet printers* deliver colored dots from disposable ink cartridges. *Thermal-wax* printers, which aren't much in vogue these days, apply wax-based pigments to a page in multiple passes. Both kinds of printers mix cyan, magenta, yellow, and, depending on the specific printer, black dots to produce full-color output. Inkjet output quality can be quite good, but if you want truly photographic quality prints, you must migrate up the price ladder to *dye-sublimation printers*. Dye-sub inks permeate the surface of the paper, literally dying it different colors. Furthermore, the cyan, magenta, yellow, and black pigments mix in varying opacities from one dot to the next, resulting in a continuous-tone image that appears nearly as smooth on the page as it does onscreen.

- **Imagesetter:** A typesetter equipped with a graphics page-description language (most often PostScript) is called an *imagesetter*. Unlike a laser printer, an imagesetter prints photo-sensitive paper or film by exposing the portions of the paper or film that correspond to the black areas of the image. The process is like exposing film with a camera, but an imagesetter knows only two colors: black and white. The exposed paper or film collects in a lightproof canister. In a separate step, the printer operator develops the film in a processor. Developed paper looks like a typical glossy black-and-white page. Developed film is black where the image is white and transparent where the image is black. Imagesetters typically offer resolutions between 1200 and 3600 dpi. But the real beauty of imageset pages is that blacks are absolutely black (or transparent), as opposed to the irregular gray you get with many laser-printed pages.

- **Film recorder:** A *film recorder* transfers images to full-color 35mm and 4-×-5-inch slides, perfect for professional presentations. Slides also can be useful to provide images to pub-lications and commercial printers. Many publications can scan from slides, and commer-cial printers can use slides to create color separations. So, if you're nervous that a color separation printed from Photoshop won't turn out well, ask your service bureau to output the image to a 35mm slide. Then have your commercial printer reproduce the image from the slide.

- **PostScript:** The *PostScript* page-description language was the first product developed by Adobe — the same people who bring you Photoshop — and is now a staple of hundreds of brands of laser printers, imagesetters, and film recorders. A *page-description language* is a programming language for defining text and graphics on a page. PostScript specifies the locations of points, draws line segments between them, and fills in areas with solid blacks or *halftone cells* (dot patterns that simulate grays). Some newer printers instead use *sto-chastic screens* that simulate grays and colors using almost-random patterns.

- **Spooling:** Printer *spooling* allows you to work on an image while another image prints. Rather than communicating directly with the output device, Photoshop describes the image to the system software. In Windows (XP and Vista), you set spooling options using the Control Panel. In Windows XP, you can select Printers and Faxes from the Start menu, or choose the same icon within the Control Panel window (choose Control Panel from the Start menu). In Windows Vista, you choose Control Panel from the Start menu, and then choose Hardware and Sound from the resulting Control Panel window. Then, choose Printers. Once you're looking at the Printers icons, right-click the icon for your specific printer, and choose Properties from the pop-up menu. In the printer's Properties dialog box, switch to the Details panel and click the Spool Settings button. When Photoshop finishes describing the image — a relatively quick process — you are free to resume working while the system software prints the image in the background. This isn't an issue anymore under Mac OS 10.X, which has spooling turned on at all times.

- **Calibration:** Traditionally, *calibrating* a system means synchronizing the machinery. In the context of Photoshop, however, calibrating means to adjust or compensate for the color displays of the scanner, monitor, and printer so what you scan is what you see onscreen, which in turn is what you get from the printer. Colors match from one device to the next. Technically, this is impossible; a yellow image in a photograph won't look exactly like the onscreen yellow or the yellow printed from a set of color separations. But calibrating is designed to make the images look as much alike as possible, taking into account the fundamental differences in hardware technology. Expensive hardware calibration solutions seek to change the configuration of scanners, monitors, and printers. Less expensive software solutions, including those provided by Photoshop, manipulate the image to account for the differences between devices.

- **Brightness values** and **shades:** As described in Chapter 4, there's a fundamental difference between the way your screen and printer create gray values and colors. Your monitor shows colors by lightening an otherwise black screen; the printed page shows colors by darkening an otherwise white piece of paper. Onscreen colors, therefore, are measured in terms of *brightness values*. High values equate to light colors; low values equate to dark colors. On the printed page, colors are measured in percentage values called *shades* or, if you prefer, *tints*. High-percentage values result in dark colors, and low-percentage values result in light colors.

- **Composite:** A *composite* is a page that shows an image in its entirety. A black-and-white composite printed from a standard laser printer or imagesetter translates all colors in an image to gray values. A color composite printed from a color printer or film recorder shows the colors as they actually appear. Composites are useful any time you want to proof an image or print a final grayscale image from an imagesetter, an overhead projection from a color printer, or a full-color image from a film recorder.

- **Proofing:** To *proof* an image is to see how it looks on paper before the final printing. Consumer proofing devices include laser printers and color inkjet printers, which provide quality and resolution sufficient only to vaguely predict the appearance of your final output. Professional-level proofing devices include the Rainbow dye-sublimation printer and Matchprint laser proofer, both developed by Imation; DuPont's toner-based Cromalin; and Creo's Iris, the latter of which uses a special variety of inkjet technology.

- **Bleeds:** Simply put, a *bleed* is an area that can be printed outside the perimeter of a page. You use a bleed to reproduce an image all the way to the edge of a page, as in a slick magazine ad. For example, this book includes bleeds. Most of the pages — such as the page you're reading — are encircled by a uniform 2-pica margin of white space. This margin keeps the text and figures from spilling off into oblivion. A few pages, however — including the parts pages and the color plates — print all the way to the edges. In fact, the original artwork goes 2 picas beyond the edges of the paper. This ensures that if the paper shifts when printing — as it invariably does — you won't see any thin white edges around the artwork. This 2 picas of extra artwork is the bleed. In Photoshop, you create a bleed by clicking the Bleed button in the Print dialog box.

■ **Color separations:** To output color reproductions, commercial printers require *color separations* (or slides, which they can convert to color separations for a fee). A color-separated image comprises four printouts, one each for the cyan, magenta, yellow, and black primary printing colors. The commercial printer transfers each printout to a *plate*, which is used in the actual reproduction process.

■ **Duotone:** An 8-bit grayscale image in Photoshop can contain as many as 256 brightness values, from white on up to black. A 16-bit grayscale image can contain thousands of brightness levels. Most printers can convey significantly fewer shades. A laser printer, for example, provides anywhere from 26 to 65 shades. An imagesetter provides from 150 to 200 shades, depending on resolution and screen frequency. And this assumes perfect printing conditions. You can count on at least 30 percent of those shades getting lost in the reproduction process. A *duotone* helps to retain the depth and clarity of detail in a grayscale image by printing with two inks. The number of shades available to you suddenly jumps from 150 to a few thousand. Photoshop also lets you create *tritones* (three inks) and *quadtones* (four inks). Note that using more inks translates to higher printing costs.

■ **Spot color:** Most color images are printed as a combination of four *process color* inks — cyan, magenta, yellow, and black. But Photoshop also lets you add premixed inks called *spot colors*. As mentioned in Chapter 4, the most popular purveyor of spot colors in the United States is Pantone, which provides a library with hundreds of mixings. But many large corporations use custom spot colors for logos and other proprietary emblems. Most spot colors fall outside the CMYK gamut and thus increase the number of colors available to you. In addition to using spot colors in duotones, Photoshop lets you add a spot color channel to any image.

CROSS-REF But what about the Web? This chapter's title and introduction give the impression that Web publishing is covered, and it is. Look to the latter sections on the Save For Web & Devices dialog box (also covered in Chapter 3), and for tips on animating Web graphics in Chapter 18. Slicing images for use on the Web is covered later in this chapter. And the Bridge and its commands for creating Web-based output from one or more of your Photoshop creations is covered in nearly excruciating detail in Chapter 3 — and also later on in this chapter.

Printing Composites

Now that you're armed with a bit of printing jargon, you're ready to learn how to put it all together. This section explores the labyrinth of options available for printing composite images. Later in this chapter, you'll learn about color separations and duotones.

Like any Windows or Macintosh application, Photoshop can print composite images to nearly any output device you can hook up to your computer. Assuming that your printer is turned on, properly attached, and in working order, printing a composite image from Photoshop is a five-step process, as outlined next. The sections that follow describe each of these steps in detail.

Printing a composite image

Perhaps not surprisingly, you start this process by choosing your printer. You can use the Printers control panel on your PC (in Windows XP, Printers and Faxes is in your Start menu, in Vista, go to Hardware and Sound, and then Printers via the Control Panel) or the Print & Fax System Preferences utility on the Mac to select the output device to which you want to print. If your computer is not part of a network, you probably rely on a single output device, in which case you can skip this issue and go right to the process of sending the print job to the printer to which you're directly connected.

Next, with the image you want to print open and in the active image window (it can be minimized, however), choose File ⇨ Print or press Ctrl+ P (⌘+P on the Mac). This command displays the Print dialog box, which incorporates previous versions of Photoshop's Print with Preview command and the Print command. Now, in CS3, selecting plain 'ol Print from the File menu gives you a dialog box with all the printing options, *plus* a preview of your print job, whether or not you want it. Figure 20.1 shows you the default view of the Print dialog box — with your Color Management settings in view, along with a preview of an image to be printed.

FIGURE 20.1

The Print with Preview dialog box enables you to precisely position and scale the image, and to handle almost all other print setup chores. Here you see the Color Management version of the lower half of the dialog box, plus the Output version too.

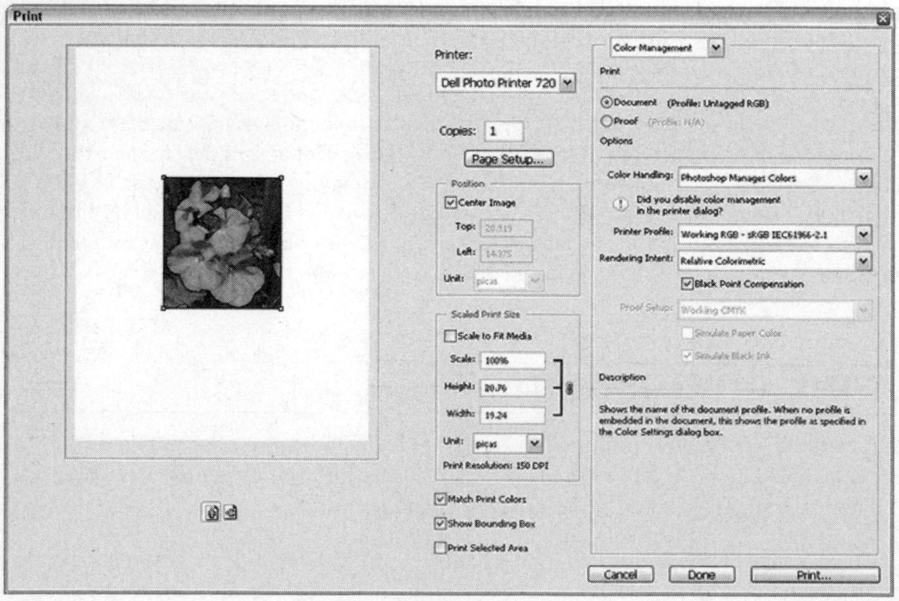

Basic print setup

Within the preview area of the Print dialog box, you can position the image on the page, scale the print size of the image, and select a few other options, as discussed later in this chapter. Before you select those settings, however, you can click Page Setup to specify the page size and orientation of the image on the page — through a dialog box that varies based on your printer, as the interface offers tools for customizing your specific printer's settings with respect to this particular print job. After making your choices, click OK to apply them, and you're returned to the Print dialog box to continue setting up the print job.

Color management

On the right side of the Print dialog box (refer to Figure 20.1), the list at the top gives you two choices: Output or Color Management. The rest of the contents of the right side of the Print dialog box hinge on which one you choose, and for many print jobs, you need to dabble in both sets of options. Dealing with Color Management first, this version of the right side of the Print dialog box offers options for whether you're printing a document or a proof, if you've got your printer set up to color-manage your output, selecting a printer profile, choosing your Rendering Intent (this is explained later), and setting up a proof (if that's what you're printing). Much of the time, you won't have to tinker much with these options. If you've already set up how Photoshop handles color issues, and if you have it set up to have your printer bow to Photoshop's desires on that score, you shouldn't have much else to deal with here.

Output

If you choose Output from that list at the top of the right side of the Print dialog box, your options change, as we said, and this different right side of the Print dialog box is shown in Figure 20.2. You get a list of check boxes, things you can choose to include in the print job, such as calibration and registration marks, crop marks, and labels. You also can click any of a series of five buttons at the bottom of the dialog box to affect how backgrounds, borders, screening, bleeds, and transfer are handled. You can turn on Interpolation, and choose whether to include vector data with the printout. Here's more about these options (and there's more information on them later in the chapter too):

- **Background:** Click Background to pick a color for your printout's background. The Color Picker opens when you click the Background button, and you can use it just as you would at any other time. Of course, don't pick a color that's going to make the content of your image invisible, so keep your image content in mind.

- **Border:** Click Border to determine how thick a border you want added around the print job. Pretty straightforward.

- **Bleed:** Click Bleed to determine the width of the bleed (extra ink or toner applied around the edge of an image or sections thereof to make sure the content goes fully to the edges of the print area). You can express this in millimeters (mm, the default), inches, or points.

- **Screen:** The Screen button opens a dialog box through which you can change the size, angle, and shape of the halftone screen dots. This step is purely optional and useful mostly for creating special effects.

- **Transfer:** Click Transfer to map brightness values in an image to different shades when printed. This step also is optional, though frequently useful.

When you're ready to send your print job to your printer, click Print. This opens the printer-based Print dialog box, which varies depending on your operating system (Windows or Mac), your printer, and any accessories you have on your printer. After you've tweaked all relevant print settings, click Print to send the image to the printer.

FIGURE 20.2

Switch to Output mode in the Print dialog box to control what's included in your print job.

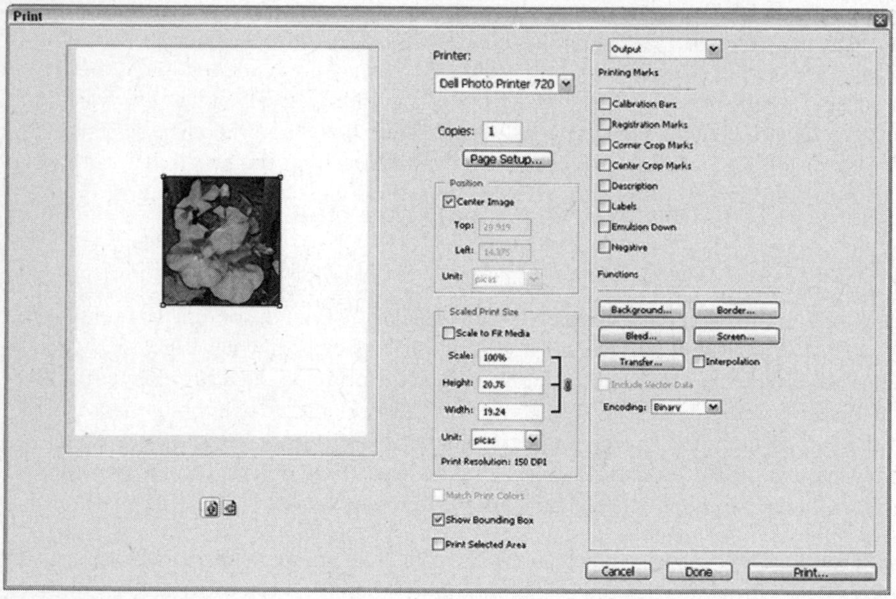

> **TIP** Just want to send one copy of your image to the printer, no questions asked? Choose File ➪ Print One Copy. Voila!

Setting up the page

The Page Setup dialog box varies depending on what kind of printer you use and based on how you open it. If you click the Page Set up button in the Print dialog box, you get a printer-specific dialog box that allows you to communicate directly with your printer, using an interface designed by your printer manufacturer. Figure 20.3, for example, shows the Page Setup dialog box for a Dell 720 printer. If you choose File ➪ Page Setup, on the other hand, from outside of the Print dialog box, you get a more generic dialog box, one that's operating-system-based. Figure 20.4 shows the Mac OS X (bottom) and Windows XP (top) Page Setup dialog boxes that appear when you use the menu route to the dialog box.

FIGURE 20.3

Your mileage (and dialog box) may vary, depending on who made your printer.

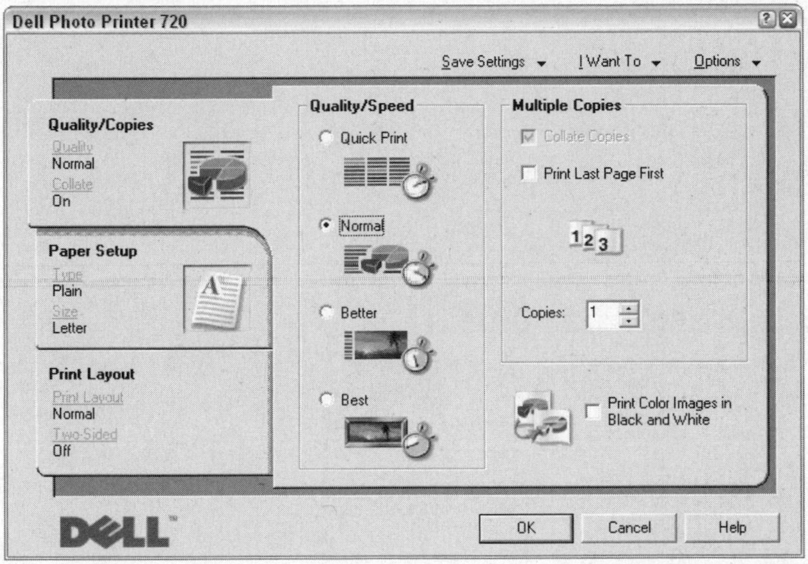

Even though the Page Setup dialog box offers different options for different printers, you should always have access to the following (or their equivalents):

- **Paper size:** Select the size of the paper loaded into your printer's paper tray. The paper size you select determines the *imageable area* of a page — that is, the amount of the page that Photoshop can use to print the current image. For example, the Letter option calls for a page that measures 8.5×11 inches, but only about 7.5×10 inches are imageable.

- **Source (Windows only):** Virtually all printers include paper cartridges, but some permit you to manually feed pages or switch between cartridges. Use this option to decide where your paper is coming from.

- **Orientation:** You can specify whether an image prints upright on a page (Portrait) or on its side (Landscape) by selecting the corresponding Orientation option. Use the Landscape setting when an image is wider than it is tall.

FIGURE 20.4

Use the File ➪ Page Setup dialog box to choose the page size and image orientation.

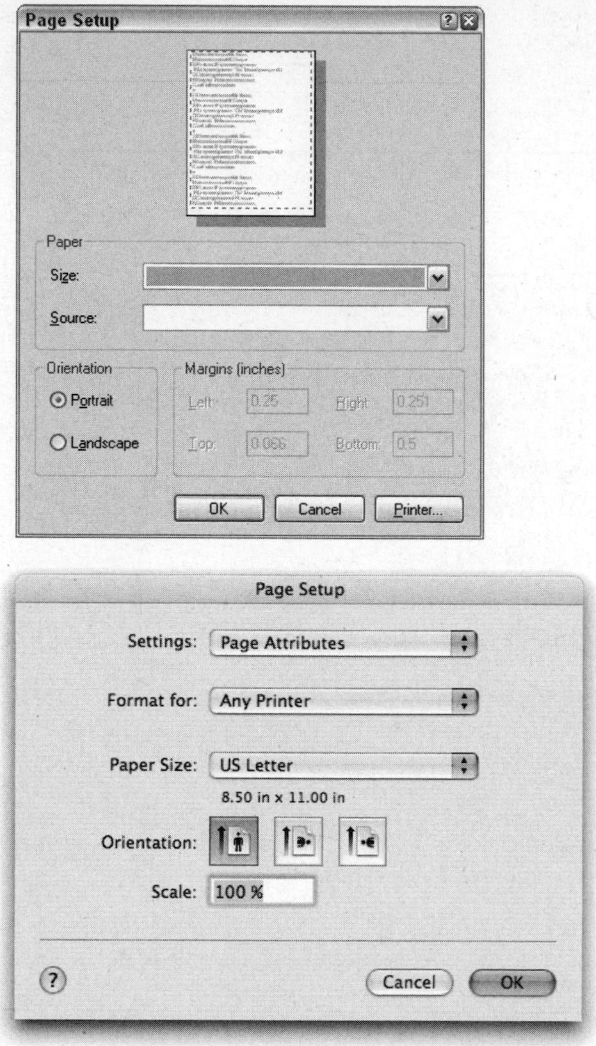

Position and scaling options

All the options described so far are constant regardless of what application you're using. However, the settings in the Print dialog box (refer to Figure 20.1) are unique to Photoshop. These settings enable you to position the image on the page and perform a few other handy printing adjustments:

■ **Position:** If you want the image to print in the middle of the page, leave the Center Image option selected. Otherwise, deselect the Center Image option and type values in the Top and Left option boxes to position the image with respect to the top-left corner of the page. You can select from five different measurement units for these options. If you're not overly concerned about placing the image exactly at a certain spot, deselect the Center Image option and then just click and drag the image in the preview on the left side of the dialog box. The Unit option is available only if Center Image is unchecked, and then you can pick how the position is measured — in picas, points, inches, centimeters, or millimeters. The preview updates to show you the current image position.

■ **Scaled Print Size:** If you want to adjust the image size for only the current print job, use these controls. They have no effect on the actual image file; they merely scale the image for printing. You can type a scale percentage; values greater than 100 percent enlarge the image, and values less than 100 percent reduce the image. Or type a specific size in the Height and Width option boxes. If you want Photoshop to adjust the image automatically to fit the page size, select the Scale to Fit Media option. You also can set the Unit (again, same as with the Position version of this field, picas, points, inches, centimeters, or millimeters) and verify (but not change) the current print resolution as would have been set through the Image Size dialog box.

■ **Show Bounding Box:** This option, when selected, displays handles at the corners of the preview image. For faster scaling, you can drag the handles until the image is the approximate print size you want.

■ **Match Print Colors:** This option, off by default, allows you to do a soft-proof of the colors in your image, within the preview area.

■ **Print Selected Area:** If you've made a selection in your image prior to opening the Print dialog box, this option is available and simply allows you to print only what's within the selection.

> **TIP** Photoshop prints only visible layers and channels, so you can print select layers or channels in an image by hiding all the other layers or channels. (To hide and display layers and channels, click the eyeball icon next to the layer or channel name in the Layers or Channels palette, respectively.) To print a single layer or channel, Alt-click (Win) or Option-click (Mac) the eyeball.

Output options in depth

To display the special print options shown in Figure 20.2, choose Output from the drop-down list at the top of the Print dialog box, as stated earlier. The five most important Output buttons work as follows:

■ **Background:** To assign a color to the area around the printed image, click this button and select a color from the Color Picker dialog box, described in Chapter 4. This button and the one that follows (Border) are designed specifically to accommodate slides printed from a film recorder. If you select either of these options, Photoshop updates the preview to show them.

- **Border:** To print a border around the current image, click this button and type the thickness of the border in the Width option box. The border automatically appears in black.

- **Bleed:** This button lets you print outside the imageable area of the page when outputting to an imagesetter. (Imagesetters print to huge rolls of paper or film, so you can print far outside the confines of standard page sizes. Most other printers use regular old sheets of paper; any bleed — were the printer to acknowledge it — would print off the edge of the page.) Click Bleed and type the thickness of the bleed in the Width option box. Two picas (24 points) is generally a good bet. (Bleeds are defined in the section "Understanding Printing Terminology" at the beginning of this chapter.)

- **Screen:** Click this button to enter a dialog box that enables you to change the size, angle, and shape of the printed halftone cells, as described in the upcoming section "Changing the halftone screen."

- **Transfer:** The dialog box that appears when you click this button enables you to redistribute shades in the printed image, as explained in an upcoming section.

Most of the Output options — all except Negative, Emulsion Down, Interpolation, and Include Vector Data — append special labels and printer marks to the printed version of the image. Except for Interpolation and Include Vector Data, Photoshop shows the result of selecting the option in the image preview.

- **Interpolation:** If you own an output device equipped with PostScript Level 2 or later, you can instruct Photoshop to anti-alias the printed appearance of a low-resolution image by selecting this option (the check box with the five buttons, just above "Include Vector Data"). The output device resamples the image up to 200 percent and then reduces the image to its original size using bicubic interpolation (as described in Chapter 2), thereby creating a less-jagged image. This option has no effect on older-model PostScript devices.

- **Calibration Bars:** A *calibration bar* is a 10-step grayscale gradation beginning at 10 percent black and ending at 100 percent black. The function of the calibration bar is to ensure that all shades are distinct and on target. If not, the output device isn't properly calibrated, which just means that the printer's colors are out of whack and need realignment. When you print color separations, the Calibration Bars option instructs Photoshop to print a gradient tint bar and a progressive color bar, also useful to printing professionals.

- **Registration Marks:** Select this option to print eight cross hairs and two star targets near the four corners of the image. Registration marks are imperative when you print color separations; they provide the only reliable means to ensure exact registration of the cyan, magenta, yellow, and black printing plates. When printing a composite image, however, you can ignore this option.

- **Corner Crop Marks:** Select this option to print eight hairline crop marks — two in each of the image's four corners — that indicate how to trim the image in case you anticipate engaging in a little traditional paste-up work.

- **Center Crop Marks:** Select this option to print four pairs of hairlines that mark the center of the image. Each pair forms a cross. Two pairs are located on the sides of the image, the third pair is above it, and the fourth pair is below the image.

- **Description:** To print a description below the image, select this option. Then press Enter or Return to exit the dialog box, choose File ⇨ File Info, and type a caption in the Description field of the Description section of the File Info dialog box. The description prints in 9-point Helvetica. This is strictly an image-annotation feature, something to help you 17 years down the road, when your brain starts to deteriorate and you can't remember why you printed the image in the first place. You may also use the description to keep images straight in a busy office where hundreds of people have access to the same images.

- **Labels:** When you select this option, Photoshop prints the name of the image and the name of the printed color channel in 9-point Helvetica. If you process many images, you'll find this option extremely useful for associating printouts with documents on disk.

- **Emulsion Down:** The emulsion is the side of a piece of film on which an image is printed. When the Emulsion Down option is deselected, film prints from an imagesetter emulsion side up. When the option is selected, Photoshop flips the image so the emulsion side is down. Like the Negative option, discussed next, this option is useful only when you print film from an imagesetter, and this option should be set in accordance with the preferences of your commercial printer.

- **Negative:** When you select this option, Photoshop prints all blacks as white and all whites as black. In-between colors switch accordingly. For example, 20 percent black becomes 80 percent black. Imagesetter operators use this option to print composites and color separations to film negatives.

- **Include Vector Data:** If your image contains any vector objects or type for which outline data is available (not outline or protected fonts), select this option to send the actual vector data to a PostScript printer. If your image has no vector objects, the option is dimmed. Your vector objects then can be scaled to any size without degrading the quality. Including the vector data increases the image file size, which can slow printing and cause other printing problems. But if you deselect the option, everything in the image is sent to the printer as raster data. This reduces the file size, but you no longer can scale the vector objects or type with impunity. They're subject to the same quality loss that occurs when you enlarge any pixel-based image.

- **Encoding:** Select an option from this pop-up menu to control the encoding method used to send the image file to the printer. In normal printing situations, leave the option set to the default, Binary. If your network doesn't support binary encoding (highly unlikely) or your printer is attached through the local parallel printer port instead of the network, select the ASCII option to transfer PostScript data in the text-only format. The printing process takes much longer to complete, but at least it's possible. If your printer supports PostScript Level 2 or later, you also can choose to use JPEG compression to reduce the amount of data sent to the printer. (This option is applicable only to PostScript printers.)

Color management options in depth

If you choose Color Management from the list at the top of the Print dialog box (refer to Figure 20.1), you can adjust settings that enable you to convert the image color space for printing only. You may want to do this to print a proof of the image on a printer other than the printer you'll use for final output. To convert the color space of the actual image file, you need to use the techniques discussed in Chapter 17.

First, you can select from two Print options: Document and Proof. These options tell Photoshop whether you want to print the image according to the color profile officially assigned to the image file or according to the Proof Setup profile (the so-called "soft proofing" profile). Document uses the actual color profile; Proof uses the profile currently selected in the View ⇨ Proof Setup submenu.

The Printer Profile options (available only if Color Handling is set to give Photoshop control), determine whether Photoshop converts the image to a different profile during the printing process. To convert to a different profile, select the profile from the drop-down menu. You then can specify the rendering method by selecting it from the Rendering Intent pop-up menu.

> **TIP** As you're working in the Print dialog box later, perhaps without this trusty book by your side, note that there's a big "Description" section at the bottom of the right side of the dialog box. This area displays an explanation of each area of the dialog box, changing as you mouse over different options, menus, lists, and so forth.

You can convert to any color space offered by Photoshop, Kodak's ICC CMS (Win), or Apple's ColorSync (Mac). Ideally, you want to select the specific profile for your brand of printer. If you can't find such a profile, you'll probably want to stick with the RGB color space (specified in the Color Settings dialog box). Another option is to choose Working CMYK, which prints the image just as if you had converted it to the CMYK color space. Unfortunately, most consumer-grade printers are designed to accommodate RGB images and fare pretty badly when printing artwork converted to CMYK.

> **CROSS-REF** Again, if you're unfamiliar with any of these terms or just don't know which options are best for your printing situation, review Chapter 17, where color management is discussed in detail.

Changing the halftone screen

Before discussing the Screen option, available when you select Output from the pop-up menu in the Print with Preview dialog box, you should learn a bit more about how printing works. To keep costs down, commercial printers use as few inks as possible to create the appearance of a wide variety of colors. Suppose you want to print an image of a pink flamingo wearing a red bow tie. Your commercial printer could print the flamingo in one pass using pink ink, let that color dry, and then load the red ink and print the bow tie. But why go to all this trouble? After all, pink is only a lighter shade of red. Why not imitate the pink by lightening the red ink?

Unfortunately, with the exception of dye-sublimation printers, high-end inkjets, and film recorders, output devices can't print lighter shades of colors. They recognize only solid ink and the absence of ink. So how do you print the lighter shade of red necessary to represent pink?

The answer is *halftoning*. The output device organizes printer pixels into spots called *halftone cells*. Because the cells are so small, your eyes cannot quite focus on them. Instead, the cells appear to blend with the white background of the page to create a lighter shade of an ink.

The cells grow and shrink to emulate different shades of color. Large cells result in dark shades; small cells result in light shades. Cell size is measured in printer pixels. The maximum size of any cell is a function of the number of cells in an inch, called the *screen frequency*.

For example, suppose the default frequency of your printer is 60 halftone cells per linear inch and the resolution is 300 printer pixels per linear inch. Each halftone cell must, therefore, measure 5 pixels wide by 5 pixels tall ($300 \div 60 = 5$), for a total of 25 (5^2) pixels per cell. When all pixels in a cell are turned off, the cell appears white; when all pixels are turned on, you get solid ink. By turning on different numbers of pixels — from 0 to 25 — the printer can create a total of 26 shades.

Photoshop enables you to change the size, angle, and shape of the individual halftone cells used to represent an image on the printed page. To do so, click Screen in the Print with Preview dialog box (after clicking More Options and choosing Output from the pop-up menu). The Halftone Screen dialog box shown in Figure 20.5 appears.

FIGURE 20.5

Use the Halftone Screen dialog box to edit the size, angle, and shape of the halftone cells for any one ink.

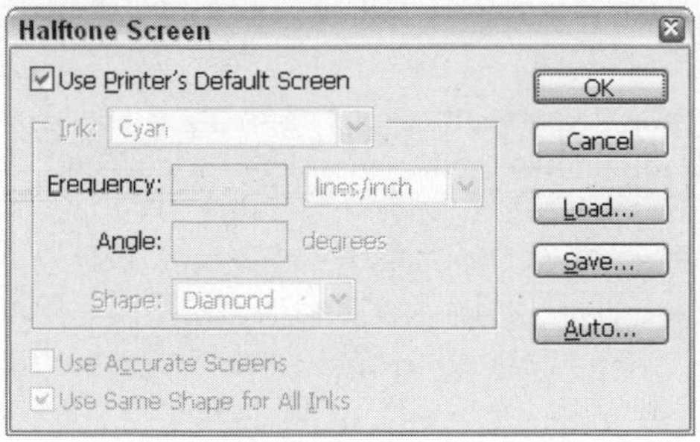

In the dialog box, you can manipulate the following options:

- **Use Printer's Default Screen:** Select this option to accept the default size, angle, and shape settings built into your printer's ROM. All other options in the Halftone Screen dialog box automatically become dimmed to show that they are no longer in force.

- **Ink:** If the current image is in color, you can select the specific ink you want to adjust from the Ink pop-up menu. When you work with a grayscale image, no pop-up menu is available.

- **Frequency:** Type a new value in this option box to change the number of halftone cells that print per linear inch. A higher value translates to a larger quantity of smaller cells; a smaller value creates fewer, larger cells. Frequency is traditionally measured in *lpi*, or *lines per inch* (as in lines of halftone cells), but you can change the measurement to lines per centimeter by selecting Lines/cm from the pop-up menu to the right of the option box.

TIP Higher screen frequencies result in smoother looking printouts. Raising the Frequency value, however, also decreases the number of shades an output device can print because it decreases the size of each halftone cell and, likewise, decreases the number of printer pixels per cell. Fewer printer pixels mean fewer shades. You can calculate the precise number of printable shades using the following formula:

```
Number of shades = (printer resolution ÷ frequency)² + 1
```

- **Angle:** To change the orientation of the lines of halftone cells, type a new value in the Angle option box. In the name of accuracy, Photoshop accepts any value between negative and positive 180 degrees.

CAUTION   When printing color composites to inkjet and thermal-wax printers, and when printing color separations, Photoshop calculates the optimum Frequency and Angle values required to print seamless colors. In such a case, you should change these values only if you know exactly what you're doing. Otherwise, your printout may exhibit weird patterning effects. When printing grayscale images, though, you can edit these values to your heart's content.

- **Shape:** By default, most PostScript printers rely on roundish halftone cells. You can change the appearance of all cells for an ink by selecting one of six alternate shapes from the Shape pop-up menu. If you know how to write PostScript code, you can select the Custom option to display a text-entry dialog box and code away.

- **Use Accurate Screens:** If your output device is equipped with PostScript Level 2 or later, select this option to subscribe to the updated screen angles for full-color output. Otherwise, don't worry about this option.

- **Use Same Shape for All Inks:** Select this option if you want to apply a single set of size, angle, and shape options to the halftone cells for all inks used to represent the current image. Unless you want to create some sort of special effect, leave this option deselected. The option is unavailable when you are printing a grayscale image.

- **Auto:** Click this button to display the Auto Screens dialog box, which automates the halftone editing process. Type the resolution of your output device in the Printer option box. Then type the screen frequency you want to use in the Screen option box. After you press Enter or Return to confirm your change, Photoshop automatically calculates the optimum screen frequencies for all inks. This technique is most useful when you print full-color images; because Photoshop does the work for you, you can't make a mess of things.

- **Load** and **Save:** You can load and save settings to disk in case you want to reapply the options to other images. These buttons are useful if you find a magic combination of halftone settings that results in a really spectacular printout.

TIP   You can change the default size, angle, and shape settings that Photoshop applies to all future images by Alt-clicking (Win) or Option-clicking (Mac) Save. When you press Alt (Win) or Option (Mac), the Save button changes to read ->Default. To restore the default screen settings at any time, Alt-click (Win) or Option-click (Mac) Load (<-Default).

CROSS-REF   The Halftone Screens dialog box settings don't apply to printing images only directly from Photoshop. You can export these settings along with the image for placement in QuarkXPress or some other application by saving the image in the Photoshop EPS format. Make sure you select the Include Halftone Screen option in the EPS Format dialog box, as discussed in Chapter 3. This also applies to transfer function settings, explained in the following section.

CAUTION   If you decide to include the halftone screen information with your EPS file, be sure the settings are compatible with your intended output device. You don't want to specify a low Frequency value such as 60 lpi when printing to a state-of-the-art 3600-dpi imagesetter, for example. If you have any questions, be sure to call your service bureau or commercial printer before saving the image.

Specifying a transfer function

A *transfer function* enables you to change the way onscreen brightness values translate — or *map* — to printed shades. By default, brightness values print to their nearest shade percentages. A 30 percent gray pixel onscreen (which equates to a brightness value of roughly 180) prints as a 30 percent gray value.

Problems arise, however, when your output device prints lighter or darker than it should. Depending on your printer, you might compensate for this overdarkening effect by clicking Transfer in the Print with Preview dialog box after clicking More Options and choosing Output from the pop-up menu. The resulting Transfer Functions dialog box, shown in Figure 20.6, can be a big help in fixing printer problems.

FIGURE 20.6

The Transfer Functions curve enables you to map onscreen brightness values to specific shades on paper.

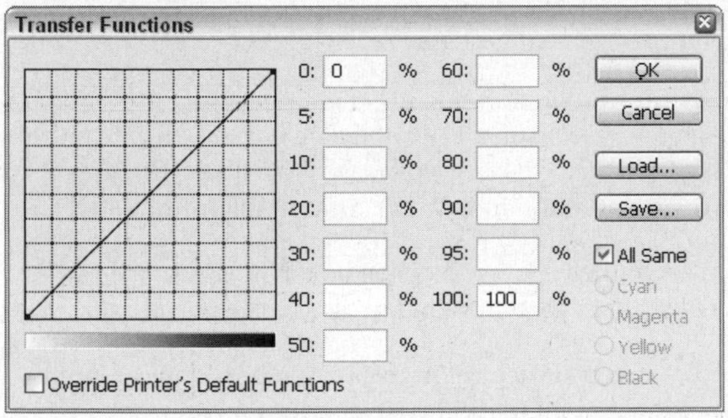

The options in the Transfer Functions dialog box work as follows:

- **Transfer graph:** The *transfer graph* is where you map onscreen brightness values to their printed equivalents. The horizontal axis of the graph represents onscreen brightness values; the vertical axis represents printed shades. The *transfer curve* charts the relationship between onscreen and printed colors. The lower-left corner is the origin of the graph — the point at which both the onscreen brightness value and the printed shade are white. Move to the right in the graph for darker onscreen values; move up for darker printed shades. Click in the graph to add points to the line. Click and drag up on a point to darken the output; drag down to lighten the output.

CROSS-REF For a more comprehensive explanation of how to graph colors on a curve, read about the incredibly powerful Curves command in Chapter 18.

- **Percentage option boxes:** The option boxes are labeled according to the onscreen brightness values. To lighten or darken the printed brightness values, type higher or lower percentage values in the option boxes. There is a direct correlation between changes made to the transfer graph and the option boxes. For example, if you type a value in the 50 percent option box, a new point appears along the middle line of the graph.

- **Override Printer's Default Functions:** As an effect of printer calibration, some printers have custom transfer functions built into their read-only memory (ROM). If you have problems making your settings take effect, select this option to instruct Photoshop to apply the transfer function you specify, regardless of the output device's built-in transfer function.

- **Load** and **Save:** Use these buttons to load settings to disk and save settings to disk, respectively. Alt-click (Win) or Option-click (Mac) the buttons to retrieve and save default settings.

- **Ink controls:** When you print a full-color image, five options appear in the lower-right corner of the Transfer Functions dialog box. These options enable you to apply different transfer functions to different inks. Select the All Same option to apply a single transfer function to all inks. To apply a different function to each ink, deselect the option, and then select one of the radio buttons and edit the points in the transfer graph as desired.

Printing pages

When you finish slogging your way through the Page Setup and Print dialog boxes, you can initiate the printing process by clicking Print in the Print dialog box. A secondary Print dialog box appears, this time operating system-based, shown in its Mac and Windows XP forms in Figure 20.7.

Several options in this dialog box also appear in the Page Setup dialog box, both discussed earlier in this chapter. The few remaining options you need to understand work as follows:

- **Copies:** Type the number of copies you want to print in this option box. You can print up to 999 copies of a single image if you want to. Will you want to? Probably not.

- **Print Range (Pages on the Mac):** No such thing as a multipage document exists in Photoshop, so you can ignore these options for the most part. If you selected an image area with the rectangular marquee tool, you can print just the selected area by choosing the Selection radio button (Win) or the Print Selected Area check box (Mac), if available. Alternatively, you can select the Print Selected Area option in the Print with Preview dialog box. You may want to use this option to divide an image into pieces when it's too large to fit on a single page.

- **PDF:** This option lets you save a PostScript-language version of the file on disk rather than printing it directly to your printer. Under Windows, deselect the Print to File option to print the image to an output device as usual. Select Print to File to write a PostScript-language version of the image to disk. To save a PostScript file to disk on the Mac, choose Save PDF as Postscript from the pop-up menu that appears when you click the PDF button in the lower left of the dialog box.

> **TIP**   Because Photoshop offers its own EPS option in the Save dialog box, you'll probably want to ignore this option. In fact, the only reason to select Print to File is to capture printer's marks, as shown back in Figure 20.4. If you do, a second dialog box appears, asking where you want to save the PostScript file. You can navigate just as in the Open and Save dialog boxes. For the best results, select the Binary radio button.

FIGURE 20.7

FIGURE 20.7

The Print dialog box as it appears on the Mac (bottom) and in Windows XP (top)

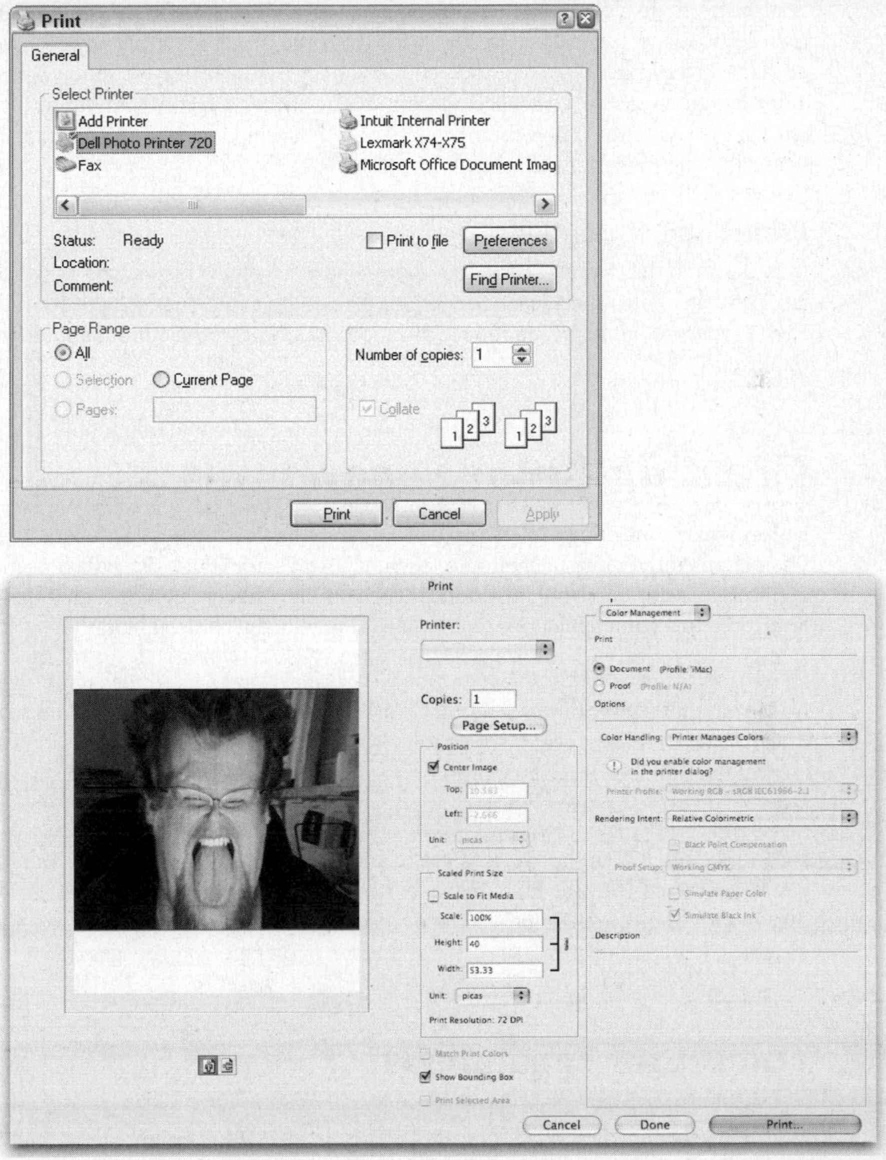

NOTE Mac OS 10.x offers a handy Preview button at the bottom of the Print dialog box; click it to generate a PDF file of the image and display it in Adobe Reader (if you have Reader installed). To save the image to Adobe PDF without opening it in Adobe Reader, click Save As PDF.

Press Enter or Return in the Print dialog box to start the printing process on its merry way. To cancel a print in progress, click Cancel. If you neglect to cancel before Photoshop spools the print job, don't worry because you can still cancel. On the PC, choose Settings ⇨ Printers from the Windows Start menu to display the Printers dialog box. Right-click the icon for the printer you're using and then select Open. Or you can double-click that tiny printer icon that appears on the far-right side of the taskbar. Either way, Windows shows you a window listing the current print jobs in progress. You can pause or cancel the selected print job by choosing a command from the Document menu. On the Mac, you can cancel the print job from the Print Utility, which appears in the Dock automatically when you start printing.

Printer-specific options

In addition to the options in the Page Setup and Print dialog boxes, you may be able to control certain print attributes specific to the selected printer. To explore these options in the Print dialog box, click Properties on the PC or choose the appropriate command from the middle pop-up menu on the Mac.

Creating Color Separations

Unless you're a printing professional, you'll rarely have to print color separations directly from Photoshop. You'll more likely import the image to QuarkXPress, PageMaker, InDesign, or a similar application before printing separations. It's even more likely that you'll take the image or page-layout file to a commercial printer and have a qualified technician take care of it.

So why discuss this process? Two reasons. First, it's always a good idea to at least peripherally understand all phases of the computer imaging process, even if you have no intention of becoming directly involved. This way, if something goes wrong on the printer's end, you can decipher the crux of the problem and either propose a solution or strike a compromise that still works in your favor.

Second, before you import your image to another program or submit it to a commercial printer, you'll want to convert the RGB image to the CMYK color space. (You don't absolutely *have* to do this — with Photoshop's improved color-matching functions, you can exchange RGB images with greater confidence — but it's always a good idea to prepare your images down to the last detail, and CMYK is invariably the final destination for printed imagery.)

Outputting separations

Accurately converting to CMYK is the trickiest part of printing color separations; the other steps require barely any effort at all, but for simplicity's sake, we're enumerating them here so you can follow them anytime you need to and to help make the whole process clearer.

STEPS: Printing color separations

1. **Calibrate your monitor, and specify the desired RGB environment.** Use the techniques discussed in the sections in Chapter 18 that pertain to the Gamma control panel, the Macintosh Display Calibrator Assistant, and selecting the ideal working space.

2. **Identify the final output device.** If you're lucky, your commercial printer may provide a CMYK table that you can load. Otherwise, you have to grapple with some weird settings. The good news is that you need to complete this step only once each time you switch hardware. If you always use the same commercial printer, you can set it up and forget about it.

3. **Convert the image to the CMYK color space.** Choose Image ➪ Mode ➪ CMYK Color to convert the image from its present color mode to CMYK.

4. **Adjust the individual color channels.** Switching color modes can dramatically affect the colors in an image. To compensate for color and focus loss, you can edit the individual color channels as described in the section on color channel effects in Chapter 4.

5. **Trap your image, if necessary.** If your image features many high-contrast elements and you're concerned that your printer may not do the best job of registering the cyan, magenta, yellow, and black color plates, you can apply Image ➪ Trap to prevent your final printout from looking like the comics in the Sunday paper. When working with typical "continuous-tone" photographs, you can skip this step.

6. **Choose your printer.** Select the printer you want to use, as described earlier in this chapter.

7. **Turn on a few essential printer marks.** Choose File ➪ Page Setup or press Ctrl+Shift+P (⌘+Shift+P on the Mac) to specify the size of the pages and the size and orientation of the image on the pages, as described in the section on the Page Setup dialog box, earlier in this chapter. In the Print with Preview dialog box, also introduced earlier, be sure to select the Calibration Bars, Registration Marks, and Labels options at the very least. (You need to select the Show More Options check box and then select Output from the pop-up menu to display these options.)

8. **Adjust the halftone and transfer functions as needed.** Click Screen and Transfer in the Print with Preview dialog box to modify the halftone screen dots and map brightness values for each of the CMYK color channels, as described earlier in this chapter. This step is entirely optional.

9. **Send the job to the printer.** In the Print with Preview dialog box, make sure the Show More Options check box is selected and choose Color Management from the pop-up menu. Then choose Separations from the Profile pop-up menu in the Print Space section of the dialog box. This tells Photoshop to print each color channel to a separate piece of paper or film. Finally, click Print to open the Print dialog box and initiate the print job.

 You also can create color separations by importing an image to a page-layout or drawing program. Instead of choosing your printer in Step 6, save the image in the DCS format, as described in Chapter 3.

Steps 1 through 4 were covered at length in Chapters 4 and 17. Steps 6 through 9 are repeats of concepts explained in previous sections of this chapter. This leaves Step 5, trapping, which is explained in the following section.

Color trapping

If color separations misalign slightly during the reproduction process (a problem called *misregistration*), the final image can exhibit slight gaps between colors. Suppose an image features a 100 percent cyan shape against a 100 percent magenta background. If the cyan and magenta plates don't line up exactly, you're left with a shape that has a white halo partially around it. Not good.

A *trap* is an extra bit of color that fills in the gap. For example, if you choose Image ⇨ Trap and type 4 in the Width option box, Photoshop outlines the shape with an extra 4 pixels of cyan and the background with an extra 4 pixels of magenta. Now the registration can be off by a full 8 pixels without any halo showing.

Continuous-tone images, such as photographs and natural-media painting, don't need trapping because no harsh color transitions occur. In fact, trapping actually harms such images by thickening up the borders and edges, smudging detail, and generally dulling the focus.

One of the primary reasons to use the Trap command, therefore, is to trap rasterized drawings from Illustrator or FreeHand. Some state-of-the-art prepress systems trap documents by first rasterizing them to pixels and then modifying the pixels. Together, Photoshop and Illustrator (or FreeHand) constitute a more rudimentary but, nonetheless, functional trapping system. When you open an illustration in Photoshop, the program converts it into an image according to your size and resolution specifications, as described in Chapter 3. After the illustration is rasterized, you can apply Image ⇨ Trap to the image as a whole. Despite the command's simplicity, it handles nearly all trapping scenarios, even going so far as to reduce the width of the trap incrementally as the colors of neighboring areas grow more similar.

CAUTION If you plan on having a service bureau trap your files for you, do not apply Photoshop's Trap command. You don't want to see what happens when someone traps an image that's already been trapped. If you're paying the extra bucks for professional trapping, leave it to the pros.

Printing Duotones

It's been a few pages since the printing terminology section of this chapter, so here's a quick recap: A *duotone* is a grayscale image printed with two inks. This technique expands the depth of the image by allowing additional shades for highlights, shadows, and midtones. If you've seen a glossy magazine ad for perfume, designer clothing, a car, or just about any other overpriced commodity, you've seen a duotone. Words like *rich*, *luxurious*, and *palpable* come to mind. Photoshop also enables you to add a third ink to create a tritone and a fourth ink to create a quadtone, so you can create those glossy, rich, luxurious photos.

Creating a duotone

To convert a grayscale image to a duotone, tritone, or quadtone, choose Image ➪ Mode ➪ Duotone. Photoshop displays the Duotone Options dialog box shown in Figure 20.8. By default, Monotone is the active Type option, and the Ink 2, Ink 3, and Ink 4 options are dimmed. To access the Ink 2, Ink 3, and Ink 4 options, select Duotone, Tritone, or Quadtone, respectively, from the Type pop-up menu.

Specify the color of each ink that you want to use by clicking the color swatch associated with the desired ink option. You can define colors with the Color Picker or with the Custom Colors dialog box. You can switch back and forth between the two by clicking the Custom button or the Picker button, depending on which dialog box you currently are using.

FIGURE 20.8

The Duotone Options dialog box enables you to apply multiple inks to a grayscale image. If you click the Ink 1, Ink 2, Ink 3, or Ink 4 curve, the Duotone Curve dialog box opens (bottom image).

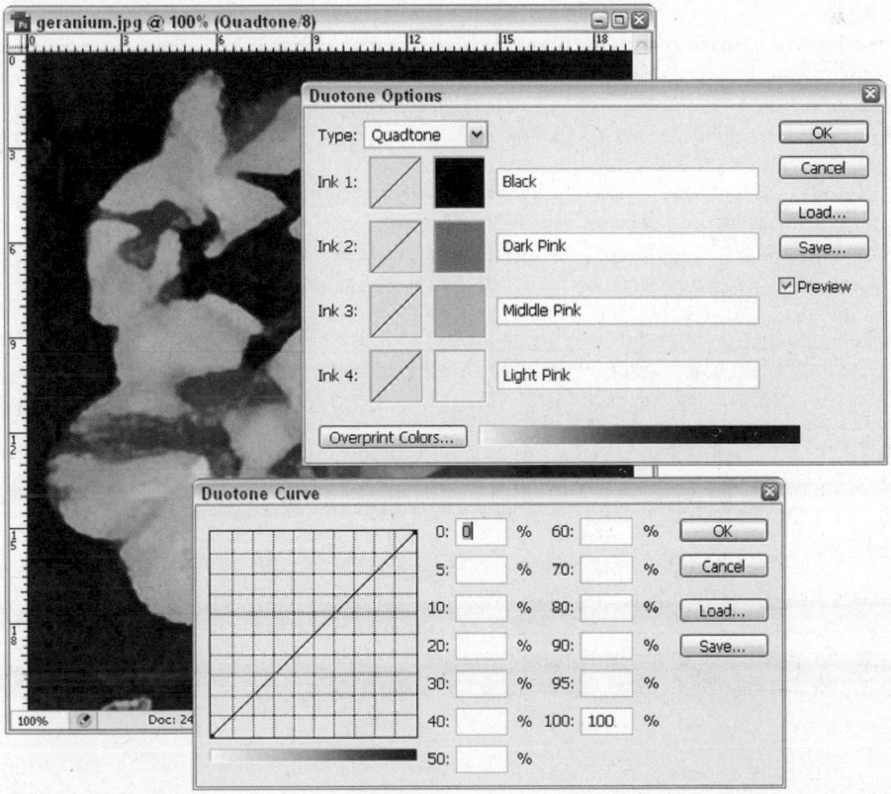

Photoshop takes the guesswork out of creating a duotone by previewing your settings in the image window when the Preview option is selected. Keep in mind that the preview may not exactly match your output when using certain Pantone inks. (This is a common problem when previewing Pantone inks in any program, but it's always a good idea to keep in mind, particularly because Photoshop mixes inks to create its duotone effects.) The next time you create a duotone, Photoshop displays the same colors you defined in your last visit to the Duotone Options dialog box.

When creating duotones, tritones, and quadtones, prioritize your inks in order — from darkest at the top to lightest at the bottom — when you specify them in the Duotone Options dialog box. Because Photoshop prints inks in the order in which they appear in the dialog box, the inks will print from darkest to lightest. This ensures rich highlights and shadows and a uniform color range.

After selecting a color, you can use either of two methods to specify how the differently colored inks blend. The first and more dependable way is to click the curve box associated with the desired ink option. Photoshop then displays the Duotone Curve dialog box (refer to Figure 20.8), which works just like the Transfer Functions dialog box described in the section "Specifying a transfer function." This method permits you to emphasize specific inks in different portions of the image according to brightness values.

The second method for controlling the blending of colors is to click Overprint Colors. An Overprint Colors dialog box appears showing how each pair of colors will mix when printed. Other color swatches show how three and four colors mix, if applicable. To change the color swatch, click it to display the Color Picker dialog box.

The problem with this second method is that it complicates the editing process. Photoshop doesn't actually change the ink colors or curve settings in keeping with your new specifications; it just applies the new overprint colors without any logical basis. And you lose all changes made with the Overprint Colors dialog box when you adjust any of the ink colors or any of the curves.

To return and change the colors or curves, choose Image ➪ Mode ➪ Duotone again. Instead of reconverting the image, the command now lets you edit the existing duotone, tritone, or quadtone.

CROSS-REF   You also can use the new Black and White dialog box, opened by choosing Image ➪ Adjustments ➪ Black and White. This option for producing duotones does *not* require changing the image mode and allows you to create a duotone of any shade desired, using the Tint section of the Black and White dialog box and dragging the Hue and Saturation sliders. This coverage can be found in Chapter 18.

If you want a commercial printer to reproduce a duotone, tritone, or quadtone, you must print the image to color separations, just like a CMYK image. Because you already specified which inks to use and how much of each ink to apply, however, you needn't mess around with all those commands in the Color Settings dialog box. Just follow these simple steps:

STEPS: Reproducing a duotone (or tritone or quadtone)

1. **Choose the printer you want to use.** Select a printer as described previously in this chapter.

2. **Set the page size, orientation, and printer marks options.** In the Page Setup dialog box (Ctrl+Shift+P or ⌘+Shift+P), specify the size of the pages and the size and orientation of the image on the pages, as described in the section "Setting up the page." Then, with Output chosen from the list in the upper-right side of the Print dialog box, select the Registration Marks option. As you know, you can use Ctrl+ P or ⌘+P (Mac) to access the Print dialog box.

3. **Adjust the halftone screens, if desired.** If you're feeling inventive, click Screen to change the size, angle, and shape of the halftone screen dots for the individual color plates, as described in the section "Changing the halftone screen."

4. **Specify output to color separations.** Still in the Print with Preview dialog box, choose Color Management from the pop-up menu. Then choose the Separations option from the Profile pop-up menu in the Print Space section of the dialog box to print each ink to a separate sheet of paper or film.

To prepare a duotone to be imported to QuarkXPress, Illustrator, or some other application, save the image in the EPS format, as described in Chapter 3. As listed in Table 4.1 of Chapter 4, EPS is the only file format other than the native Photoshop format that supports duotones, tritones, and quadtones.

Editing individual duotone plates

If you'll be printing your duotone using CMYK colors and you can't quite get the effect you want in the Duotone Options dialog box, you can convert the duotone to the CMYK mode by choosing Image ➪ Mode ➪ CMYK Color. Not only do all the duotone shades remain intact, but you also have the added advantage of being able to tweak and add colors using Photoshop's standard color correction commands and editing tools. You can even edit individual color channels, as described in Chapter 4.

If your duotone includes Pantone or other spot colors, converting to CMYK is not an option. But you can still access and edit the individual color channels. To separate the duotone inks into channels, choose Image ➪ Mode ➪ Multichannel. Each ink appears as a separate spot color in the Channels palette, as shown in Figure 20.9. You can experiment with different color combinations by turning eyeball icons on and off. You can even switch out one spot color for another by double-clicking the channel name and then clicking the color swatch.

To save a duotone converted to the multichannel mode, you have just two options: native Photoshop (as always) and DCS 2.0. For complete information on the latter, see Chapter 3.

Image ⇨ Mode ⇨ Multichannel was chosen to separate a quadtone into four independent spot-color channels, and then the Deep Red channel was double-clicked to access the Spot Channel Options dialog box.

Optimizing Images for Web Publication

Audio and video content may be cooler, and text-based content, databases, and hyperlinks are the main stock and trade of the Internet, but bitmapped graphics rule the Web. They make the Web intelligible and invite us to come back for more. From the moment the <img> tag was added, enabling embedded graphics in HTML documents, those graphics have brought the masses to the Web. Because Photoshop is the world's number one image editor, it's no surprise that Photoshop has become as inextricably linked to the Web as Internet Explorer, Firefox, Mozilla, Macromedia Flash, Apple QuickTime, and a hundred other programs.

Choosing the Right Web Graphic Format

The Web provides a highly satisfying outlet for creative expression. How else can you get your work in front of hundreds of thousands of viewers without running up the world's largest postage debt or television advertising fee? But as is the case with just about everything in life, success on the Web depends not just upon your artistic prowess, but also upon your understanding of the right and wrong ways to prepare your images.

If you have any experience with the Web, you know that small images are speedy images. Physically small images are flexible, because they can coexist with text and other elements on a page displayed on a low-resolution screen. Meanwhile, disk size affects speed. A 20K image that fills your screen takes less time to download and display than a 50K file no larger than a sticky note. It's the act of getting the data through the network lines, routers, cables, and modems that takes the time. Even in a time when more and more Web visitors have broadband connections to the Web — cable modems, DSL, and so on — small, speedy files are still your goal if you're designing graphics for the Web.

So, in a nutshell, optimizing an image for use on the Web is a process of reducing that image to its smallest possible file size (to facilitate quick downloading), while maintaining the highest level of clarity and fidelity.

At the time of this writing, Web browsers support three graphic file types: Graphics Interchange Format (GIF), Joint Photographic Experts Group (JPEG) format, and Portable Network Graphics format (PNG). The trick is to know which format to use for the type of image you've created. What follows is a rundown of the strengths and weaknesses of these three Web file formats.

Graphic Interchange Format (GIF)

When talking about image formats, we have to talk about bits. A bits is the smallest unit of data that computers work with, and the number of bits that a format can devote to each pixel determines the maximum number of colors the format can display. Now it's time for some new terms:

- **Bit depth:** This is the total number of bits a file format is capable of devoting to each pixel. This stat determines the total number of colors that a format can display in a single image, which is our next term.

- **Color depth:** This is the total number of colors that a format can display in a single image. For example, GIF files can display a total of 256 colors in a single image, therefore GIF files have a color depth of 256. Pretty simple so far, yes?

A format's color depth is calculated this way: We begin by taking the number of states a bit has — which is two (one state being on, the other being off) — and raise that number to the power indicated by the format's bit depth.

GIF is an 8-bit format, meaning it can devote 8 bits of data to each pixel. So, using our handy little equation, this makes its color depth 2^8 — or 2x2x2x2x2x2x2x2 — which totals 256. This is the first of GIF's strengths: A low color depth helps ensure a low file size.

GIF's next major strength is how it compresses file data. GIF uses a compression method called LZW, after its creators Lempel, Ziv, and Welch. If you've been creating TIFF files for ages, then you've already seen this option in the TIFF Options dialog box. When turning an image into a GIF file, this compression method exploits inefficiencies in the file's data structure, effectively removing unused space within the file. Consequently, no additional information is removed from the image. In techno-babble, LZW compression is called a "lossless" compression method because no image data is lost in the process.

If GIF supports only a maximum of 256 colors in an image, then it follows that you wouldn't try to optimize an image with thousands of colors into this format. GIF is best suited for images with a limited number of total colors, preferable with a high degree of contrast where the edges at which two colors meet are sharply defined. Figure 20.10 shows a prime candidate for GIF optimization.

Granted, Figure 20.10 is produced as a grayscale image here, but regardless, it has only a handful of colors. Furthermore, those colors aren't jumbled together along a continuous tone gradient. The image is divided into distinct regions of solid color. GIF loves these — unlike its cousin JPEG, which you'll examine in a just a second and which has a nasty habit of introducing pixilated noise (called artifacts) into regions of solid color.

Another of GIF's strengths is its support for transparency. Sadly, GIF doesn't support multiple levels of transparency. GIF supports binary transparency, meaning a pixel is either transparent or it's not, unlike the Portable Network Graphics format, discussed momentarily. GIF also is capable of animation (the bane of the early Web), and we'll grudgingly look at this feature later in the chapter.

FIGURE 20.10

LZW compression favors images with large zones of solid colors, straight, clean lines, and text. This logo for an online bakery Web site (www.wendyjos.com) is a perfect example.

GIF's major strengths — a limited number of total colors per image, a lossless compression method, and a liking for regions of solid color — also are the format's major weaknesses. After all, what do you do if your image has millions of colors that fade from one to the next all over the place? For example, how do you deal with the average color photograph? We thought you'd never ask.

JPEG file interchange format

Members of the Joint Photographic Experts Group represent a wide variety of companies and academic institutions throughout the world who meet to discuss and create the standards for still-image compression. The standards they developed for continuous-tone images — images with an unlimited range of color or shades of gray — were used by C-Cube Microsystems to create the JPEG File Interchange Format.

JPEG has a bit depth of 24, giving it a color depth of 2^{24} or 16,777,215 colors. Its method of compression reduces file size by removing "unessential" data from the image. What is this unessential data? The JPEG format takes advantage of certain limitations inherent in the human eye. You see (no pun intended), our eyes perceive minute changes in brightness better than they perceive equally minute changes in color. JPEG's compression method favors changes in brightness, discarding colors the eye won't necessarily miss, while still reproducing up to 16,777,215 million colors. When viewing the image on a 72 dpi monitor, we humans perceive an image we consider highly detailed.

Because JPEG compression removes data, it is referred to as a "lossy" compression method. The degree of compression is adjustable, allowing you to choose how much data is lost. The more you compress the file, the smaller its size. The less you compress it, the better the image quality.

The type of images best optimized in the JPEG format can be deduced from the name: photographs and photo-realistic images — in other words, images with millions of colors or shades of gray, heavy degrees of gradation, where large zones of single colors are few. Figure 20.11 shows a good candidate for the JPEG format (top), with the results of trying to optimize Figure 20.10 as a JPEG (bottom).

Portable Network Graphics (PNG) format

The PNG format has an interesting history. When Unisys, the owner of the patent on LZW compression, began demanding royalty payments eight years after the format's introduction, some confusion erupted and there were those who thought the royalties would be levied against anyone who so much as used a GIF image in a Web site. This confusion turned out to be a boon for graphics artists when the Internet Engineering Task Force produced its answer to GIF: PNG, a format that used a lossless compression method AND came in 8-bit and 24-bit flavors, effectively combining the best aspects of both GIF and JPEG.

Used in its 8-bit version, PNG and GIF are fairly even in their abilities to produce quality images with low file sizes. PNG tends to produce slightly larger files, but only by a kilobyte or two, and is fine for optimizing the same sort of images GIF should be used for.

The 24-bit version of PNG does not, however, compare with JPEG. Because the compression method is lossless (removing no additional data from the image), files optimized in this format tend to be double in size than when optimized in the JPEG format. Of course, you'll find that as a trade-off for this larger file size, PNG images are often cleaner-looking than JPEG files, with no artifacts and no deterioration over the course of subsequent edits and re-saves of the image files.

As mentioned earlier, PNG supports transparency. It offers binary transparency equivalent to GIF's. It also has a more impressive version, called *alpha transparency*, which gives the format something Photoshop users can wrap their brains around — a *mask channel*. In total, PNG supports 256 levels of transparency from fully opaque to completely transparent, with 254 stops in between. Most current browsers support PNG's transparency, but to be safe, test your Web graphics locally, using at least two different browsers, before publishing them to the Web.

FIGURE 20.11

While best for photos, avoid using JPEG to optimize images with large zones of a solid color, type, and any edges that you'd like to keep clean, especially against a drastically different color. JPEG compression introduces distortions (called *artifacts*) when attempting to render them (bottom).

The Save For Web & Devices dialog box

In the mid 1990s, Adobe received a fair number of complaints regarding Photoshop's relatively paltry collection of Web-savvy features. Adobe explained to Web designers that they were missing the point: Photoshop was for print graphics, and a separate program Adobe had acquired, ImageReady, was for the Web. But most Web designers ignored this advice and continued to grouse, so Adobe eventually caved, and started to do the right thing, bringing ImageReady into the fold, distributing it with Photoshop. The two programs, ImageReady and Photoshop, continued to be sold as a package deal until CS3, in which ImageReady is finally gone, its capabilities rolled completely into Photoshop. We saw the final throes of ImageReady's independence in CS2, but even with the release of that last version, we all heard it was ImageReady's swansong, and to look for CS3 to be all-inclusive, which it is — at least with regard to the Web tools that used to live in ImageReady.

Part of Photoshop since CS, the Save for Web dialog box is now the Save For Web & Devices dialog box in CS3, and it appears in Figure 20.12. Why "& Devices"? Because graphic artists also are designing images for use on handheld devices — phones, i-whatevers, and PDAs. Through the dialog box, you preview your optimized image, selecting the format, compression, and color options. To display the Save For Web & Devices dialog box, choose File ⇨ Save For Web & Devices, or press Alt+Ctrl+Shift+S (⌘+Option+Shift+S on the Mac), if you like to tangle up your fingers.

In the Save For Web & Devices dialog box, you compare your original image with the optimized results, deciding which optimization settings prove best for your image. The annotation area beneath the original image displays the file name and file size. Beneath the optimized image, the current optimization settings, file size, and estimated download time are shown.

The download time is based on the dialog box's currently selected Internet access speed. To change the selected Internet access speed, click the small arrow to the right of the optimized image to display the Preview pop-up menu, shown in Figure 20.13, and select the access speed of your choice.

The Save For Web & Devices dialog box also allows you to view the differences in gamma correction between platforms. Gamma measures the intensity to voltage response of a signal sent to a computer system's monitor. The Windows and Macintosh platforms, for example, use significantly different gamma correction methods. Macintosh systems have partial gamma correction integrated into their hardware. Windows systems have no such gamma correction, though some graphics card manufacturers do provide this functionality. Because Macintosh has gamma correction, images created on Windows PCs look washed out on Macintosh systems. Conversely, images created on Macintosh systems look darker to Windows users.

FIGURE 20.12

The Save For Web & Devices dialog box

Toolbox   Original image   Settings for selected file format

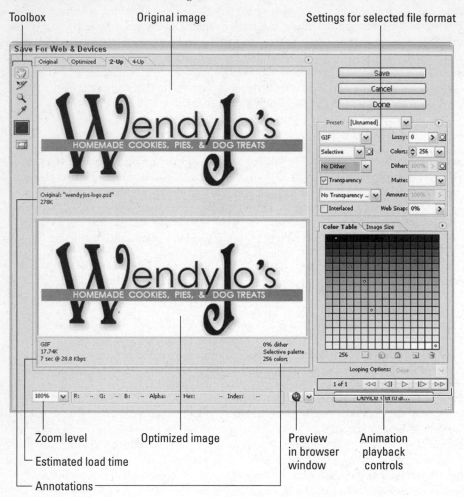

Zoom level   Optimized image   Preview   Animation
                                                  in browser   playback
Estimated load time   window   controls

Annotations

FIGURE 20.13

The Preview pop-up menu allows you to choose among multiple modem, ISDN, cable, or DSL speeds.

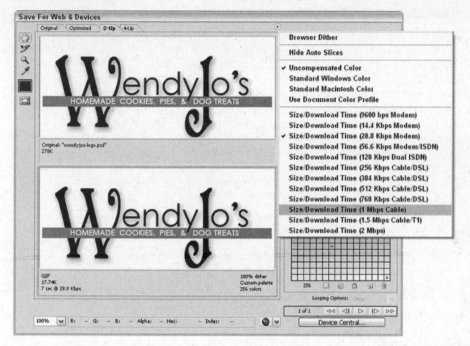

To preview differences in gamma correction, access the Preview pop-up menu by clicking the small arrow to the right of the optimized image, and choose one of the following display options:

- **Uncompensated Color:** This default option displays the image with no color adjustment.

- **Standard Windows Color:** This option displays the image with the color adjusted to simulate the gamma of a standard Windows monitor.

- **Standard Macintosh Color:** This option displays the image with color adjusted to simulate the gamma of a standard Macintosh monitor.

- **Use Document Color Profile:** This option displays the image with its current color profile if it has one.

These options only adjust the color display in the Save For Web & Devices dialog box alone. The original and optimized images are not physically modified in any way. Windows users should view their images in Standard Macintosh Color, and Mac users in Standard Windows color to see the differences. If the change is too great, the typical remedy is for Macintosh users to slightly lighten their images and for Windows users to slightly darken their images.

Device Central

What's that Device Central button in the Save for Web & Devices dialog box all about? You can test your graphics to see how they'll look on a handheld device, making sure they look as you'd expected (or hoped). You can choose the type of device and adjust the backlighting, gamma, and contrast of the display; scale and stretch the display for the screen in question; and adjust the horizontal and vertical alignment. As you drag the sliders in each of the five main areas on the right side of the dialog box, you can see the changes reflected in the Preview in the center of the dialog box. The devices to which your computer is or has been attached (in terms of there being some setup information for the device installed on your computer) will restrict the list of Available Devices, although a good assortment of generic display presets are stored for your use. To see specs for the devices to which you're are or have been attached (along with the generic device presets), click on a device in the list on the left, and then click the Device Profiles tab to see pictures of the model/s for that device and lists of features and capabilities. The figure shows the Device Central window with the Emulator tab displayed.

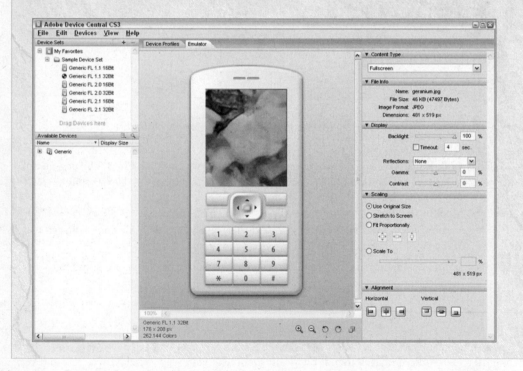

Optimizing Images into GIF and PNG-8 Formats

GIF and PNG are both indexed color formats. When images are optimized into either format, Photoshop indexes the colors used, storing them in a *color lookup table* (CLUT). Limiting the color palette in this way helps to reduce file size while preserving image quality.

To reiterate, GIF and PNG-8 are best suited to images with a limited range of colors to begin with (under 256), where zones of color are crisply defined. Optimization settings are adjusted in the Settings area of the Save For Web & Devices dialog box, shown in detail in Figure 20.14.

Optimization presets

The Optimization preset menu provides seven GIF and one PNG-8 preset:

- GIF 128 Dithered
- GIF 128 No Dither
- GIF 32 Dithered
- GIF 32 No Dither
- GIF 64 Dithered
- GIF 64 No Dither
- GIF Web Palette
- PNG-8 128 Dithered

The numbers 128, 64, and 32 represent total number of colors Photoshop maintains in the image. The Web Palette preset pushes each color in the image to its closest corresponding value in the Web-safe color palette — the palette of 216 colors identical to all browsers, operating systems, and monitors when running in 8-bit, 256-color mode.

In the color indexing process common to GIF and PNG, choosing Dithered or No Dither indicates whether some colors lost by optimization are simulated by alternating pixels in a checkerboard-like pattern using colors left within the CLUT.

Custom GIF and PNG-8 optimization settings

Custom optimization settings are adjusted using the remaining menus, pop-ups, and sliders in the Settings area.

To specify your chosen file format, select GIF or PNG-8 from the File Format menu. Next choose a method for establishing the CLUT of the image by making a selection from the Color Reduction Algorithm menu.

In Photoshop, CLUTs fall into three categories: Dynamic options, Fixed options, and Custom options.

FIGURE 20.14

The options in the Settings area change based on the file format you choose. GIF and PNG-8 have identical Settings options.

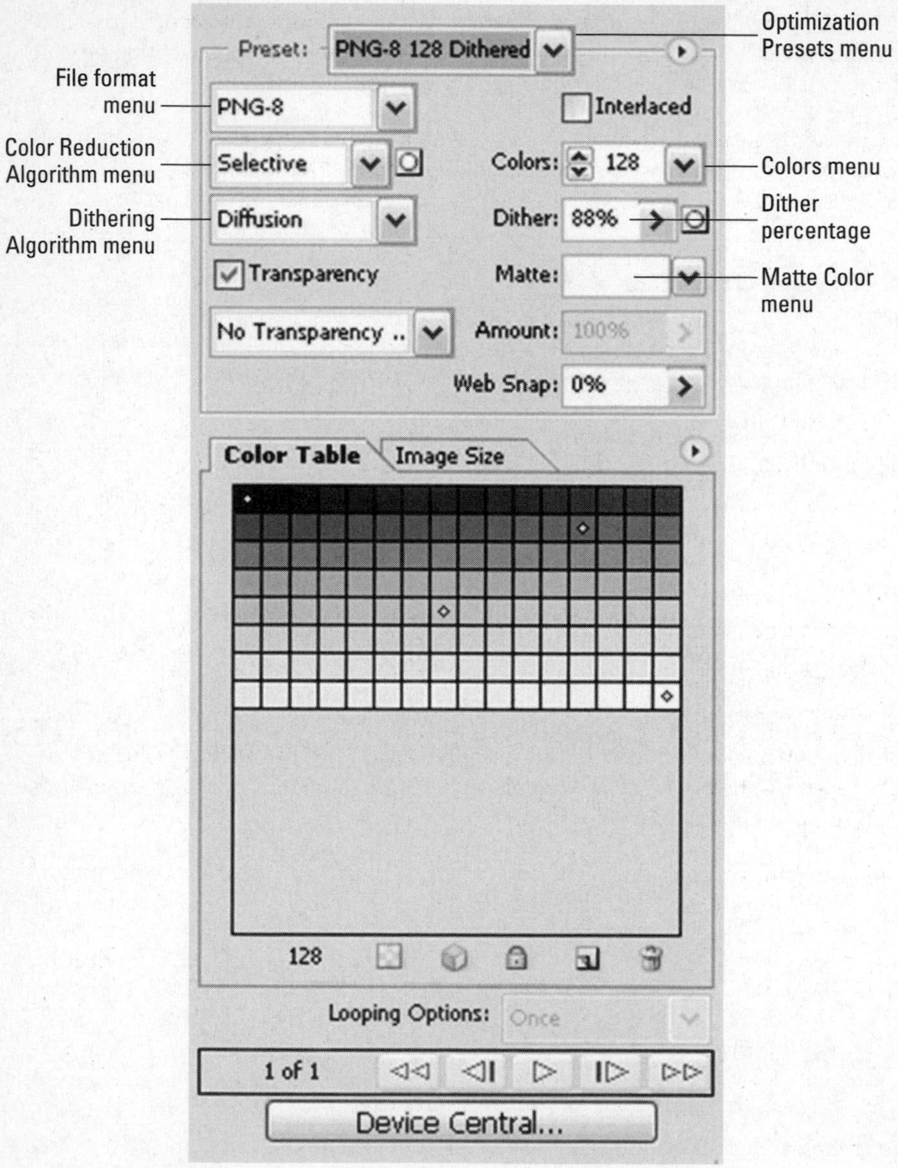

Dynamic Color palette options

Using Photoshop's dynamic options, CLUTs are based on colors present in the image and the number of colors chosen from the Colors menu.

These are the Color Reduction Algorithm menu's dynamic options:

- **Perceptual:** The perpetual palette creates a customized CLUT using colors in the image to which human eyes are more sensitive.

- **Selective:** The selective palette — similar to the perceptual palette in its inclination toward colors favored by human visual response — creates a table that is more sensitive to areas of single flat colors. This algorithm prevents such colors from being merged with other colors in the image and preserves any existing Web-safe colors. This palette tends to be the best for Web graphics.

- **Adaptive:** The adaptive palette creates a CLUT by sampling the predominant colors within the image. For example, if the image you're optimizing has a preponderance of yellows and greens, choosing the adaptive palette creates a CLUT slanted to those two colors.

Fixed Color palette options

Instead of using colors present in the image as the basis from which the CLUT is derived, Photoshop's fixed options use predefined palettes from which to build the CLUT.

These are the fixed options:

- **Web:** The Web palette consists of 216 colors common to Windows, Macintosh, Netscape Navigator, and Internet Explorer out of the 256 colors available in 8-bit mode. Choosing this option pushes the image's existing colors to their closest Web palette equivalent.

- **Mac OS:** Choosing this palette pushes existing colors to their closest equivalents in the default 256 system colors of the Macintosh operating system's 8-bit color mode.

- **Windows:** Choosing this palette pushes existing colors to their closest equivalents in the default 256 system colors of the Windows operating system's in 8-bit color mode.

Custom Color palette options

When you select Custom from the Color Reduction Algorithm menu, this maintains your current color table as a fixed palette that doesn't update with changes to the image.

After the Color reduction algorithm is selected, choose the maximum number of colors you want the image to contain using the Colors pop-up menu. The maximum number of colors available is 256, because you're creating an indexed color file when optimizing as GIF or PNG-8. The fewest colors possible are two.

If you chose either Web or Custom for the Color Reduction Algorithm, you can choose Auto in the Colors menu, which tells Photoshop to decide the optimal number of colors in the color table based on the frequency of colors in the image.

Applying dither settings

Dithering creates the illusion of different colors and shades by varying a pattern of pixels using colors within the image's existing palette. For example, Figure 20.15 shows how a simple checkerboard pattern of black and white pixels can appear gray.

FIGURE 20.15

The image appears gray, but on closer examination we see it is actually made up of alternating black and white pixels.

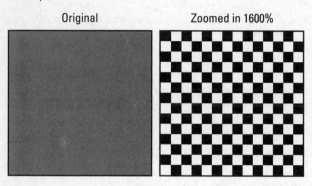

Original   Zoomed in 1600%

Dithering can happen in one of two ways: through Photoshop's optimization process (application dither), or through the Web browser if the user has his or her system set to 8-bit color mode (browser dither). The likelihood, however, that contemporary computer users have their system set to 8-bit color mode when the typical graphics card is capable of 24-bit or 32-bit color is slim. Application dither, then, is your primary concern.

The reason to apply dither is to prevent colors from *banding,* a situation in which the chosen color reduction method has eliminated any continuous tone, leaving nothing but solid bands of color, as shown in Figure 20.16.

To dither an image in the Save For Web & Devices dialog box, simply make a selection from the Dithering Algorithm menu. These are your options:

- **Diffusion:** The Diffusion algorithm, instead of using an obvious checkerboard-like pattern, diffuses the pattern of dithered pixels. This algorithm works in conjunction with the Dither percentage slider. The higher the dither percentage, the more latent colors you simulate, increasing the overall file size.

- **Pattern:** The Pattern algorithm dithers pixels in a clear, linear pattern.

- **Noise:** The Noise algorithm creates a randomized pattern of dithered pixels.

Figure 20.17 shows a close-up of the differences between Diffuse, Pattern, and Noise.

FIGURE 20.16

The original image on the left contains a gradient that, when optimized without dither, creates the banded results on the right.

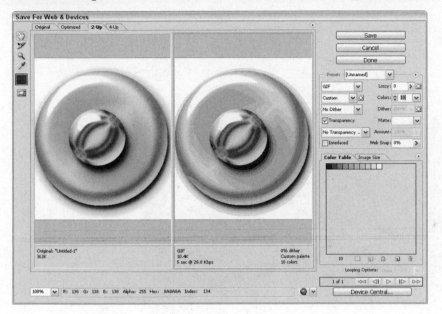

GIF and PNG-8 Transparency and Matte settings

Unlike native Photoshop files, whose layers can have varying degrees of opacity, in a GIF or PNG-8 file a pixel is either opaque or transparent. This presents a dilemma when Photoshop needs to optimize a drop-shadow or anti-aliased edge. Here Photoshop translates any pixels of partial transparency into a fully opaque pixel, calculating the appropriate color based on that of the original semi-opaque color and the color you choose for the matte.

To preserve transparent regions when optimizing images in GIF or PNG-8 formats, simply select the Transparency option. Any completely transparent pixels remain so, while semi-transparent pixels are blended with your chosen matte color (typically, the intended Web page's background color) to simulate a gradual transition.

FIGURE 20.17

Where Diffuse creates a more random dither, Pattern creates a noticeable checkerboard-like effect. Noise generates a randomized pattern.

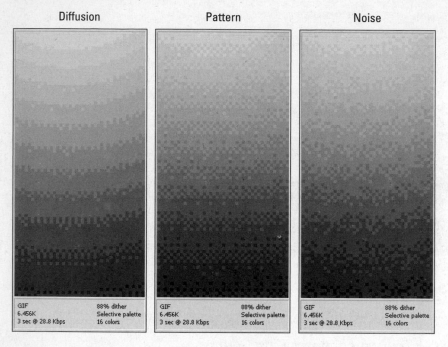

The matte color is selected using the Matte Color menu. The Matte Color menu provides the following options:

- **None:** This option disables matte color. Pixels of less than 50 percent transparency are made entirely opaque, while pixels of more than 50 percent transparency are made completely transparent.

- **Eyedropper Color:** This option uses the color last selected with the Save For Web & Devices dialog box's eyedropper, shown beneath the Eyedropper tool on the left side of the dialog box. Clicking this color swatch also invokes the Photoshop Color Picker from which to make a selection.

- **Black:** This option sets the matte color to black.

- **White:** This option sets the matte color to white.

- **Other:** This option invokes the Photoshop Color Picker from which to make a selection.

The Photoshop Color Picker also can be invoked by clicking the Matte Color menu's text field directly.

Interlacing graphics

To interlace an image, select the Interlace option in the Settings area. When an optimized image is interlaced, browsers start by displaying it at a lower resolution and bring it up to full resolution over seven progressive scans. The purpose of this is to get something to the site visitor's screen ASAP so there are no blank areas on the screen while the visitor waits for the entire page to download.

In the days of 14.4 and 28.8 Kbps modems, interlacing graphics was a common practice. While it resulted in insignificant increases in file size, at least the visitor wasn't staring at text with a bunch of square holes punched in it waiting for something to appear. With contemporary Internet connection speeds being light years faster than this, interlacing images isn't really necessary, and doing so can even hurt performance because imposing seven scans may take longer than simply allowing the image to download unencumbered.

Optimizing Images into JPEG and PNG-24 Formats

JPEG and PNG-24 are meant for optimizing continuous-tone images. This is facilitated by their 24-bit color depth, supporting 16,777,215 colors. The JPEG format uses a *lossy* compression method that removes color data, while PNG-24 (like PNG-8 and GIF) uses *lossless* compression that results in significantly larger file sizes than JPEG, but often with greater color fidelity.

Figure 20.18 shows the Save For Web & Devices dialog box's Settings area options for JPEG and PNG.

FIGURE 20.18

JPEG settings are shown on the bottom and PNG-24 settings at the top.

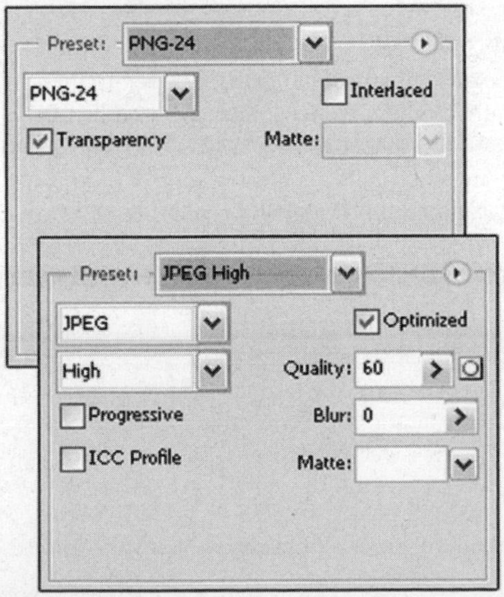

Optimization presets

Photoshop offers three presets for JPEG and one for PNG-24:

- JPEG Low
- JPEG Medium
- JPEG High
- PNG-24

In Photoshop, JPEG compression is represented by a scale of 0 to 100. The three presets of Low, Medium, and High represent compressions of 10, 30, and 60, respectively. The higher the number, the greater the degree of compression — which decreases the overall image quality. Your mission is to achieve a balance between image quality and file size.

Custom JPEG and PNG-24 optimization settings

The JPEG Quality Level menu offers one setting not provided by the presets — Maximum — which equals a compression value of 80. The Quality slider manually adjusts the compression value to any point on the 0-100 scale.

The Optimized option available for JPEG optimization should always be selected. It improves color optimization and produces smaller files.

NOTE   If you opt to save as JPEG without going through the Save for Web & Devices dialog box, once you've chosen JPEG as the file format in the Save As dialog box and click Save, the JPEG Options dialog box offers a Quality setting that ranges from 1 to 12, 12 being Maximum (commensurate with the same quality through the Save for Web & Devices dialog box) and includes a slider that allows you to choose between a small and large resulting file size. On the right side of the dialog box, a size estimate appears, based on the selected Quality setting.

JPEG and PNG-24 Transparency and Matte settings

Unlike GIF and PNG-8, JPEG lacks transparency support, so a matte color must be used to fill such zones created in the original image. The JPEG Matte menu is identical to those used by GIF and PNG-8, described earlier in the chapter.

PNG-24 supports up to 256 levels of transparency by selecting the Transparency option, and consequently doesn't need a Matte option. Most current browsers, such as Mozilla Firefox, do support this option. As always, test your Web graphics locally, using at least two browsers, before you publish your images to the Web.

Progressive JPEG and interlaced PNG-24

Like GIF and PNG-8, PNG-24 provides an interlacing option, and the same rules apply. JPEG provides similar functionality with a feature referred to as Progressive JPEG.

Where interlacing GIF and PNG files increases their overall file size, using the progressive option results in smaller JPEG files. But again, forcing the image into a series of progressive scans can actually make the download take longer.

Resizing Images

Beneath the Save For Web & Devices dialog box's Settings area sits the Image Size area, shown in Figure 20.19, which allows you to adjust an image's dimensions without going back to the Photoshop workspace.

> **TIP** Don't use the resizing features of the Save For Web & Devices dialog box for radically altering an image's dimensions. Knocking an image 5 pixels one way or the other (provided that such a number doesn't account for 50 percent of an image's initial width or height) is fine. But, if you're starting with a high-resolution image that's over 300 dpi, with dimension values in the thousands of pixels, do your reducing out in the main Photoshop interface where you have the rest of the program's tools at your disposal to maintain sharpness and clarity.

FIGURE 20.19

The Image Size area resembles the Pixel Dimensions area of the Image Size dialog box.

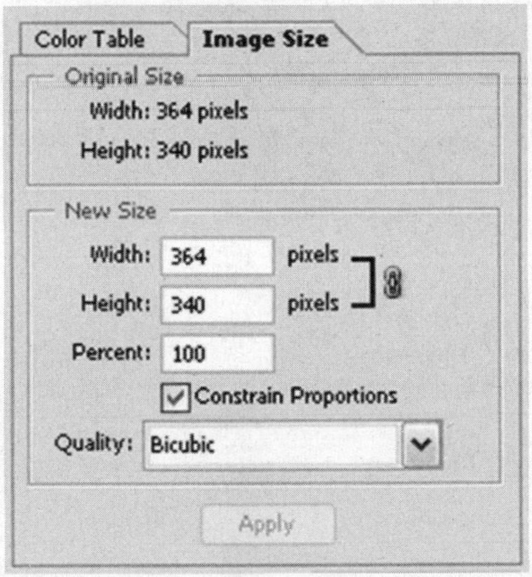

The image's original dimensions are shown in the Original Size area, with the New Size area beneath, where you can type new values. Adjust the image's dimensions proportionally by selecting the Constrain Proportions option, which also activates the Percent field.

Slicing and Dicing an Image

Some Web designers who come from a graphic arts background like to rough out their pages in Photoshop, which allows them to assemble all the buttons, special text, and other elements the way that they want them to appear on the final Web page. Then they can cut the elements apart and save them out to later assemble in HTML.

Consider the image in Figure 20.20. This image contains a text layer whose position in the finished Web page actually will be occupied by physical page text typed into the HTML code. The simplest way to combine text blocks and graphics on a Web page is to create an HTML table. And Photoshop's slicing feature can divvy up your image and generate the required HTML table code for you all in one sitting.

FIGURE 20.20

Here's a mock-up of an image destined for Web use. The Layers palette, obviously, is not part of the Web-bound image, but you get the idea.

Illustrated in Figure 20.21, *slices* are rectangular containers that permit you to add structure to a Web page design. The slices in the figure act like children's blocks, each of which contains just enough of the graphic to fit together into a seamless whole. The blocks marked in blue (appearing in dark gray here) are the *user slices*, the ones that the designer drew. They indicate the boundaries of the text. The remaining blocks are *auto slices*, which Photoshop creates automatically to fill in the gaps. In the figure, a total of six auto slices are needed to keep all slices exactly rectangular.

FIGURE 20.21

Use the Slice tool (right) to subdivide a Web page design into rectangular blocks. Photoshop later assembles the blocks into an HTML table, which adds structure to the otherwise free-flowing arrangement of elements on a Web page.

Creating slices

Photoshop provides two Slice tools, one for drawing slices and one for editing them. Press K to select the Slice tool (highlighted in Figure 20.21), which lets you draw slices. That tool shares a flyout with the Slice Select tool, which you use to move and scale slices.

Draw a rectangle around the portion of the image that you want to slice into an independent image; Shift-drag to constrain the shape of the slice to a square. For each slice that you create, a number appears in the upper-left corner of the slice, also as shown in Figure 20.20. Here are a few other things you should know:

- As you draw your user slices, Photoshop automatically fills in the auto slices, which it differentiates using dotted outlines. The program also numbers the slices from left to right and then top to bottom. User slice numbers appear in blue; auto slice numbers appear in gray.

- Simple tables are reliable tables. This means you want to draw as few slices as absolutely possible. In Figure 20.21, just one slice has been drawn around the text block. Avoid overlapping slices and avoid having two slices that almost, but don't quite, touch, because both result in Photoshop having to draw extra auto slices.

> **TIP** If you need help aligning your slices, choose View ➪ Snap To ➪ Slices to snap one user slice into agreement with another. Although this option is deselected by default, there is no good reason not to always have it selected.

> **TIP** You also can align slices on the fly. While drawing a slice, press and hold the spacebar to move the slice as you drag. Release the spacebar to put the slice down and return to sizing it.

- To create a slice that surrounds everything on a particular layer, select the layer in the Layers palette and then choose Layer ➪ New Layer Based Slice. If you later change the layer's contents, Photoshop redraws the slice boundary as necessary to include the new pixels.

> **TIP** Use this technique when saving slices that contain layer effects, such as drop shadows. This way, you can edit the effect without having to worry about redrawing the slice manually if the new effect takes up more space.

- Photoshop also can make slices from guides. First, drag one or more guidelines from the horizontal and vertical rulers (View ➪ Rulers) to establish divisions inside your image. Then select the slice tool, and click the Slices From Guides button in the Options bar.

- To hide and show the slice boundaries, press Ctrl+H (⌘+H on the Mac). By default, this hides all onscreen aids, including selection outlines and guides. (If it doesn't, choose View ➪ Show ➪ Show Extras Options, and then select the Slices option and try again.) To toggle the slice boundaries on and off independently, choose View ➪ Show ➪ Slices.

- After you get your slices just so, choose View ➪ Lock Slices to fix them in place. That way, you won't accidentally alter a slice boundary. To delete all slices, choose View ➪ Clear Slices.

Editing slices

Need to change a slice boundary? Grab the Slice Select tool (Shift+K), and click a slice to select it. You also can Shift-click and drag in the image window to select multiple slices. Then edit the slice or slices as described in the following list.

> **TIP** To temporarily access the Slice Select tool while the Slice tool is active, press and hold Ctrl (⌘ on the Mac). This means you can Ctrl-click (⌘-click) on a slice with the Slice tool to select it. Conversely, if the Slice Select tool is active, holding Ctrl (⌘) gets you the slice tool.

- A selected user slice displays corner handles. Click and drag a handle to change the size and shape of the slice. You also can drag inside a selected slice to change its location. Press Backspace (or Delete) to delete it.

- To duplicate a slice, press Alt (or Option) and drag the slice.

- When the Slice Select tool is active, you can promote an auto slice to a user slice. Click the auto slice, and then click the Promote to User Slice button in the Options bar. Then adjust the boundaries of the slice as desired. If the Slice tool is active, right-click an auto slice (Control-click on the Mac) and choose Promote to User Slice.

> **TIP** To change a user slice to an auto slice, simply select and delete the user slice. Photoshop has to fill the vacated space, and does so with an auto slice.

Setting slice options

Double-click a selected slice with the Slice Select tool to display the Slice Options dialog box, shown in Figure 20.22, which lets you assign a name to the slice image file, add a link, and set other slice attributes described in the following list. You also can access a version of this dialog box with slightly different options (as you'll see) by double-clicking a slice inside the Save For Web window.

- **Slice Type:** You can fill a slice with either an image or text. To keep the slice an image, leave this option unchanged. If you would prefer to fill the slice with text, select No Image.

  To convey your text to the HTML document, select the text using the Type tool and copy it to the Clipboard by pressing Ctrl+C (⌘+C on the Mac). Then switch to the Slice tool, double-click the slice, and switch the Slice Type to No Image. Photoshop gives you a text-entry box into which you can place text. Simply click inside it, and press Ctrl+V (⌘+V) to paste the text, as shown in Figure 20.23. Although Photoshop cannot preview this text correctly inside the standard image window, it saves the text when you choose File ➪ Save As. Then open the resulting HTML page in your favorite browser.

- **Name:** Photoshop automatically names the slices after the saved image name followed by an underscore and number. If you want to override the automatic naming convention, type your preferred slice name here. (Note that this option and the four that follow apply only when you select Image as the Slice Type.)

- **URL:** To turn the slice into a button, type the appropriate pathname to the page to which you want to link.

- **Target:** If you need to target your link — for example, if your site is frames-based — type the appropriate frame name or reserved HTML target value (_blank, _parent, etc.) in this option box.

FIGURE 20.22

Double-click a slice with the Slice tool to name the slice file that Photoshop eventually saves to disk, assign a hyperlink, and insert a status bar message.

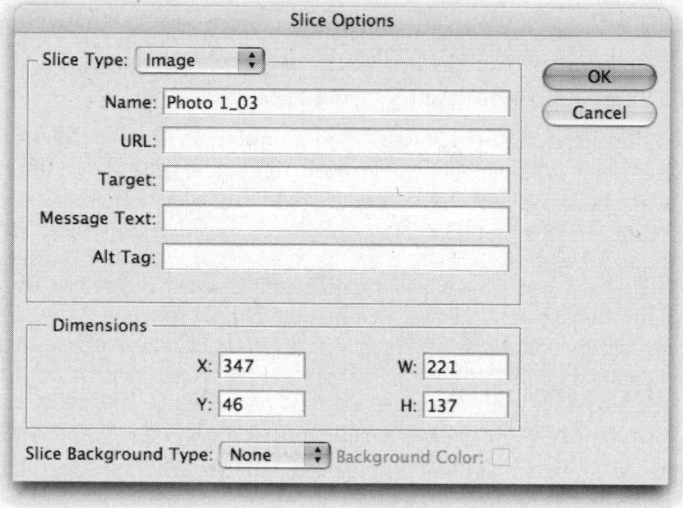

Slice Options		

Slice Type: Image

Name: Photo 1_03
URL:
Target:
Message Text:
Alt Tag:

OK
Cancel

Dimensions

X: 347   W: 221
Y: 46   H: 137

Slice Background Type: None   Background Color:

FIGURE 20.23

Select the No Image option to fill a slice with text and HTML tags.

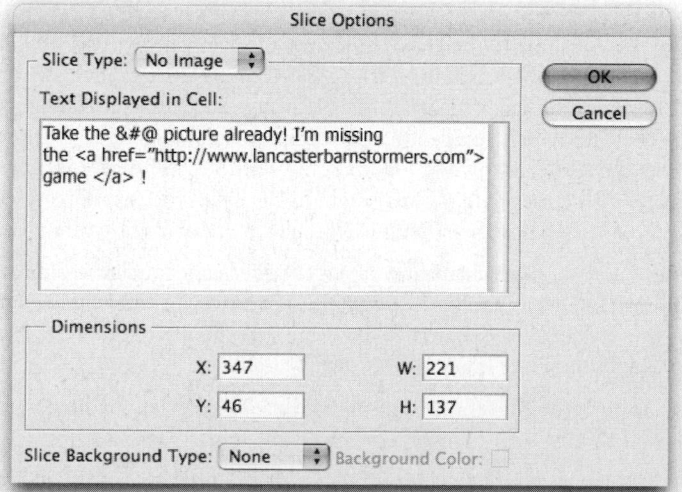

Slice Options

Slice Type: No Image

Text Displayed in Cell:

Take the &#@ picture already! I'm missing
the <a href="http://www.lancasterbarnstormers.com">
game </a> !

OK
Cancel

Dimensions

X: 347   W: 221
Y: 46   H: 137

Slice Background Type: None   Background Color:

■ **Message Text:** Type a message to appear in the status bar at the bottom of the browser window when a visitor hovers the cursor over the slice. For those familiar with JavaScript, Photoshop handles this using an *onMouseOver="window.status"* event handler.

■ **Alt Tag:** To provide a text alternate for a button, type the text into this option box.

■ **Dimensions:** To specify the exact placement and size of a slice boundary, type the pixel coordinates into the X and Y options and the dimensions into the W and H options. This can be useful when trying to delete auto slices by getting the user slices into exact alignment.

■ **Slice Background Type:** If your image contains transparent areas, you can fill them with a color selected from this pop-up menu. The Matte option uses the matte color specified in the Save For Web optimization settings. Choose Other to select a color from the Color Picker. Note that you can't preview this background color in Photoshop; you must use a browser.

TIP   You can likewise insert HTML tags into the text-entry area, but if you do, things get a bit trickier. In Figure 20.22, an *<a href>* tag has been added (colorized for emphasis) around the word *game*. This should turn the word into a hyperlink, but instead, the Web page merely ends up displaying the tags as text. The solution is to visit the Save For Web & Devices dialog box, double-click the slice, and select an option not otherwise found in Photoshop — Text is HTML. Highlighted in Figure 20.24, this option correctly interprets HTML tags and once selected, remains selected as long as you work on the image.

FIGURE 20.24

Available only inside the Save For Web & Devices dialog box, select the Text is HTML option to properly interpret HTML tags in the text-entry area.

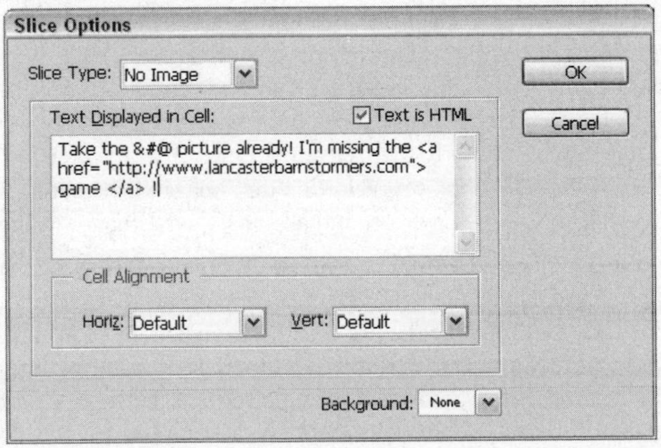

Slice Options

Slice Type: No Image

Text Displayed in Cell: ☑ Text is HTML

Take the &#@ picture already! I'm missing the <a href="http://www.lancasterbarnstormers.com"> game </a> !

OK

Cancel

Cell Alignment

Horiz: Default   Vert: Default

Background: None

Saving slices

After you create and edit your slices to absolute perfection, you'll want to perform both of the following kinds of saves:

- **Save the image itself.** To save your original image with all slice information, layers, and other doodads intact, choose File ➪ Save As and select either the Photoshop (PSD) or TIFF format. (Depending on your platform, other formats also may store slices, but PSD and TIFF are the safest.) When you reopen the image, choose the slice tool to redisplay the slice boundaries and make any further changes.

- **Save the HTML table and slice files.** To output the image in Web-ready form, choose File ➪ Save For Web. This command enables you to save all the slices as individual image files and create the HTML page that will reassemble the slices in the Web browser.

Publishing from the Bridge

So far in this chapter, you've looked at the various printing options that Photoshop provides. Next, the many automated methods of publishing images for presentation in print or for use on the Web are up for discussion.

If you're going to print and publish from within Photoshop, the commands reside in the File ➪ Automate submenu. If you're in the Bridge, you'll find the same commands there, in the Tools ➪ Photoshop submenu. Despite the virtually accurate statement that both environments offer the same commands in their respective menus, there are a few differences between these two submenus:

- **The Bridge offers an Image Processor command.** This opens the dialog box shown in Figure 20.25. Through this dialog box, you can send images from the Bridge to Photoshop for "processing." This is meant to be used for images coming from your digital camera primarily; "processing" means saving in a particular format (you pick this through the File Type section of the dialog box), and running actions and inserting copyright information. You can save the files in up to three formats: JPEG, PSD, and TIFF. If you're not sure of what other settings to use, select the Open first image to apply settings option, and the Camera Raw dialog box opens for the first image in the batch. You can use the dialog box to set things up for the first and all subsequent images in the batch.

- **Photoshop offers a Create Droplet command.** This opens a dialog box through which you can create an executable file (.exe extension, for Windows users, no extension appears for Mac droplets) for automating the use of Photoshop actions. You can create droplets, store them as icons (say, on your Desktop), and then click and drag images (or folders thereof for batch processing) onto the icons, and the specified actions are performed on the image(s). You also can swap droplets between Mac and Windows, if you so desire; a Windows droplet much be dropped onto the Photoshop icon on the Mac desktop, at which point Photoshop accommodates the platform changes and automatically runs it, stopping, as needed to prompt you for any required settings, commands, or file names.

FIGURE 20.25

The Image Processor is available only through the Bridge, and for good reason — it sends images selected on the Bridge to Photoshop.

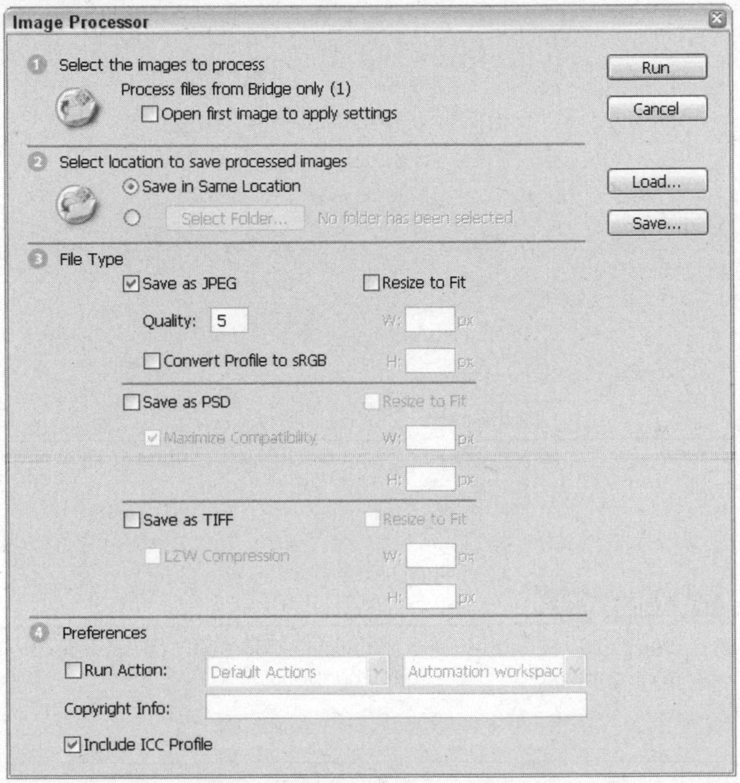

- **Photoshop has a Conditional Mode Change command.** Choose File ↪ Automate Conditional Mode Change, and it produces the dialog box shown in Figure 20.26. This dialog box lets you take all the open images (open in image windows in Photoshop) and convert them to a particular mode, selected from the dialog box. Using the Source Mode section of the dialog box, select the check boxes next to the current modes represented by your open images, and then choose the Target Mode from the list. Click OK, and the images' modes are changed. If you're not sure which mode to choose, or wonder if your open images can even be changed to the mode you're about to select as the target, read Chapter 4.

- **The Fit Image command is available.** This offers the dialog box shown in Figure 20.27. This can be a handy procedure to run an image through before printing, as it constrains the image to a particular width and height, measured in pixels. If your image is bound for the Web — and you haven't fired up the Save For Web & Devices dialog box yet — you can resize it with this dialog box first, and then go about the optimization process described earlier in this chapter and also in Chapter 3.

FIGURE 20.26

Need to change all your open images to a different mode in one fell swoop? Choose
Conditional Mode Change from the File ⇨ Automate submenu.

Conditional Mode Change

Source Mode

☐ Bitmap ☑ RGB Color

☐ Grayscale ☐ CMYK Color

☐ Duotone ☐ Lab Color

☐ Indexed Color ☐ Multichannel

[All] [None]

Target Mode

Mode: [CMYK Color ▼]

Bitmap
Grayscale
Duotone
Indexed Color
RGB Color
CMYK Color
Lab Color
Multichannel

[OK] [Cancel]

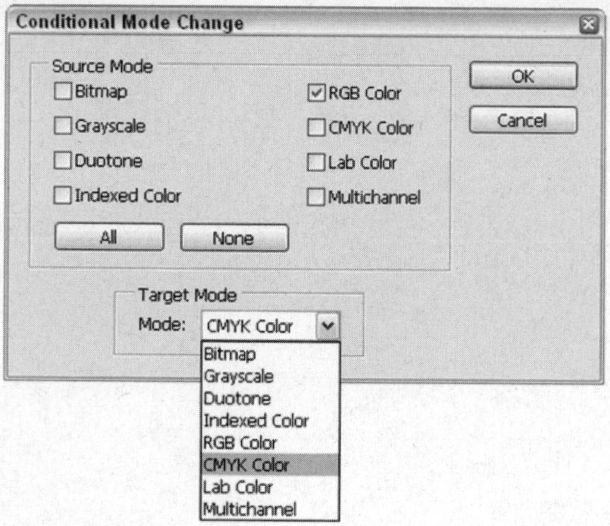

FIGURE 20.27

Need an image to be this wide by this tall? Choose Fit Image from the File ⇨ Automate
submenu and enter your desired dimensions there.

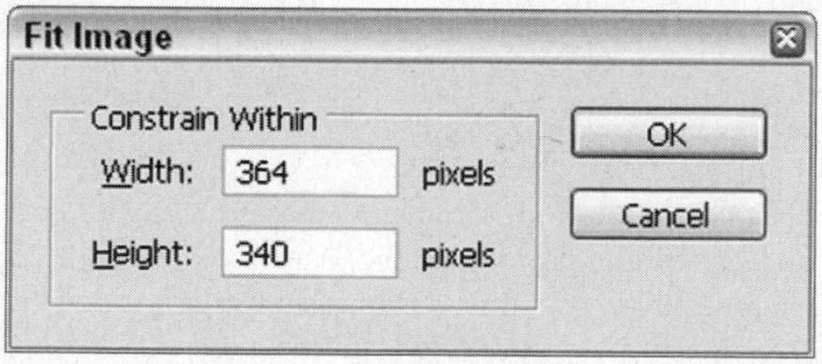

Fit Image

Constrain Within

Width: [364] pixels

Height: [340] pixels

[OK] [Cancel]

So you can print and publish your images, singly or in groups, from either the Bridge or from right
within Photoshop. For the next several sections of this chapter, you'll learn how to combine multiple images into printable and Web-displayable creations for business, personal, and artistic use.

Printing contact sheets

Choose File ➪ Automate ➪ Contact Sheet II to display the dialog box shown in Figure 20.28. The options here permit you to take a folder of images and arrange them as thumbnails on a page, greatly expediting the creation of image catalogs. You specify the location of the folder, the number of columns and rows in the grid, and the color mode, and Photoshop does the rest. You also have the ability to look into folders in the specified folder (very useful) and label image thumbnails according to their file names (even more useful). You can even select the typeface and type size for the labels from the Font and Font Size lists.

Figure 20.29 shows a contact sheet. You can add your own content later — additional captions, shapes, drawings, even layers from other images — and jazz the sheet up as desired. Right out of the box, however, it's a pretty cool way to print out a bunch of photos to be reviewed for use elsewhere or just to share them all on one page.

FIGURE 20.28

The Contact Sheet II dialog box lets you label thumbnails with their corresponding file names.

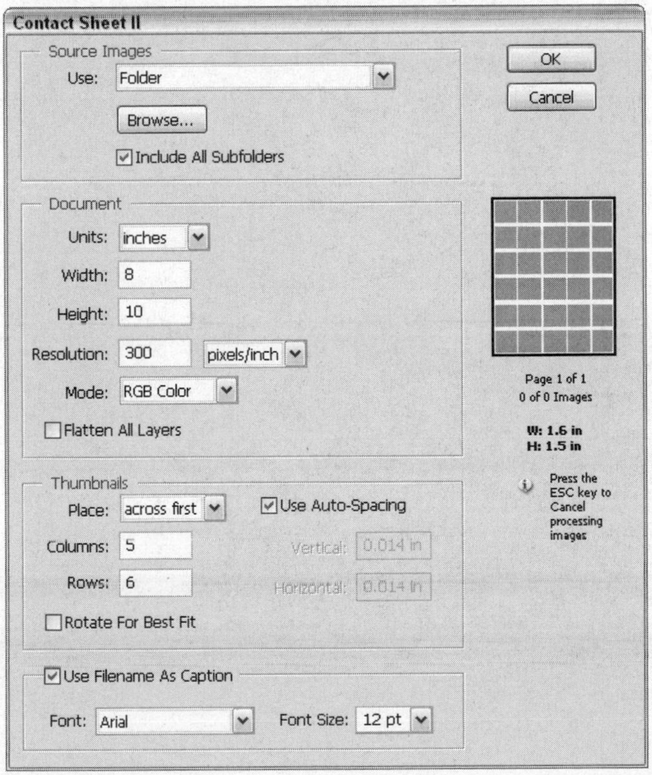

FIGURE 20.29

Each image in the contact sheet is on its own layer. The configuration of the images is dictated by your choices in the Contact Sheet II dialog box.

american_crow.jpg

autumn trees.jpg

byodo-koi.jpg

cat on blue chair.jpg

hibiscus1.jpg

reading pagoda.jpg

Creating a picture package

In addition to Contact Sheet II, Photoshop offers two other commands under the File ⇨ Automate submenu that organize multiple images onto a single page. You also can access them both from the Bridge through the Tools ⇨ Photoshop submenu. The first of these is called Picture Package. Originally designed for printing multiple copies of an image in different sizes on one page (a lot like the selection of photos you get with your kid's school pictures, everything from 5×7 to 4×6 to "wallet size"), the Picture Package command can now fill a page with multiple copies of multiple images scaled to common print sizes. If you're a photographer, or you simply want to print some pictures of the kids for Grandma, this command does it all. After choosing a layout from the Layout menu, you can replace any image in the layout with a different one by clicking the image thumbnail in the preview to bring up the Select an Image File dialog box. You also can replace any image by clicking and dragging it in from your desktop and dropping it on top of another image.

The Label section of the Picture Package dialog box, shown in Figure 20.30, lets you add text to your image. The options are pretty self-explanatory, but it's worth pointing out that the Custom Text option box keeps you from having to quit the Picture Package command to jump over to File ⇨ File Info just so you can type a caption.

FIGURE 20.30

Save a tree: Print a Picture Package. By tiling several images on a single sheet of paper — how about photo paper? — you can share one image in several sizes or multiple images in a variety of layouts.

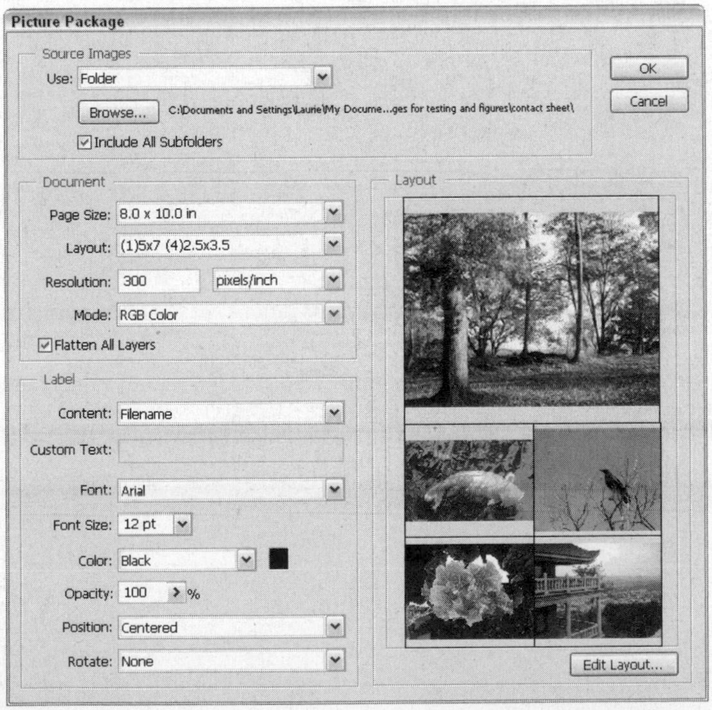

You can create and edit custom layouts for the Picture Package command. Click Edit Layout (refer to Figure 20.30) to display the Picture Package Edit Layout dialog box, shown in Figure 20.31. From the Layout section of this dialog box, you can create a template that sets a custom Name, Page Size, Width, and Height for the picture package. But the real power of the Edit Layout command is the ability to completely rearrange or even create from scratch a template that sets the actual positions and sizes of the images in your picture package.

By default, the Picture Package Edit Layout dialog box opens with the most recently selected layout template displayed. The dialog box also displays just one of your images, even if you clicked the individual tiles in the main dialog box and selected alternate images. Pay this no mind; just arrange the images without respect to what's in them, and your package in the end reflects the images you chose in the main Picture Package dialog box.

FIGURE 20.31

Photoshop gives you total control over the scale and position of the images in a picture package.

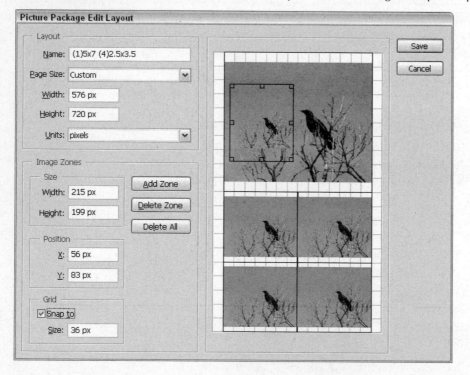

To alter the layout, just click one of the instances of the image, or "image zones" as Photoshop calls them, and drag it around the window. As soon as an image zone is selected, you gain access to handles that let you scale it. You also can manually type the Size and Position values for each individual zone in the Width, Height, X, and Y option boxes. The buttons in the Image Zone section of the dialog box let you add and remove zones at will. You can even place image zones on top of each other. Finally, the Grid section is where you specify whether the image zones snap to a grid and, if so, the size of the boxes within the grid. Click Save to save your new layout template as a text file or overwrite an existing template.

Creating a Web Photo Gallery

Again geared toward professional and aspiring photographers, the Web Photo Gallery command assembles a folder or selected group of images into a Web page, complete with HTML pages and JPEG images. In the Web Photo Gallery dialog box, shown in Figure 20.32, first select a page style from the Styles pop-up menu. The preview on the right side of the dialog box shows a sample page created using that style. You also can type an e-mail contact. You can make further design choices by selecting the various items in the Options pop-up menu. For each item, you get a different set of accompanying design options:

- **General:** Choose between *.htm* and *.html* extensions. Additionally, you can choose to preserve the images' metadata when they're converted to JPEG files. You also can elect to use UTF 8 encoding, which enables older operating systems to view the generated Web pages.

- **Banner:** Name your page and add the photographer's name, contact info, and the date. You also can select the font and type size for these items.

- **Large Images:** Add a border around your images, resize images, add titles, and apply JPEG compression.

- **Thumbnails:** Specify the thumbnail size and the number of columns and rows of thumbnails. You also can add borders around the thumbnails, add captions based either on the image file name or the description info typed in the File Info dialog box, and specify a font and type size.

- **Custom Colors:** Set the colors for the page background, banner, text, and links.

- **Security:** Create a text message that will be embedded into each image, making people much less likely to steal the images from your Web site for their own nefarious purposes. You can type custom text, use the File Info description or the name of the file, choose the placement of the text, and choose whether you want the text to be rotated at an angle on the image.

  The Source Images options let you choose either a folder of images or a group of selected images in the File Browser for use in your Web Photo Gallery, allow you to determine whether to include folders nestled in a specified folder, and also choose where the resulting files should finally end up. Figure 20.32 shows a Web page created with the settings from Figure 20.33.

1055

The Web Photo Gallery assembles your images for display on a Web page.

Web pages created using the Web Photo Gallery command aren't going to win any design awards, but the command is easy to navigate and it gets the job done. And if you know a little HTML, you can use the pages as a jumping-off point for a more sophisticated site.

The Web Photo Gallery includes styles that let a visitor or client submit feedback about your images directly from the Web page. Choose one of the three Styles that contain the word Feedback, and Photoshop includes a live tab in the finished Web Photo Gallery in which a visitor can type text or click a check box to mark the currently selected image as "approved." The Feedback styles can even program the generated Web page to e-mail visitor comments back to you by automatically opening the local mail program and generating a message instantly.

FIGURE 20.33

The visitor can click the thumbnails on the left to change the displayed large image on the right. It's a very basic page (using the Centered Frame 1 Info Only style here), but it's a clean design, and it's simple to navigate.

TIP Photoshop also lets you define custom Web Photo Gallery page styles. Using an HTML editor, you can create a batch of HTML files that contain the instructions for formatting the various elements of the page. To get an idea of how to build a custom style, take a look at the HTML files provided for the Photoshop default styles, found in the Presets\Web Photo Gallery folder. After creating your custom pages, store them together in a new styles folder in the Web Photo Gallery folder.

Creating a PDF presentation

In addition to letting you create an HTML-based slideshow using the Web Photo Gallery command, Photoshop lets you create PDF-based slideshows using the new PDF Presentation command. As you're probably aware by now, PDF is Adobe's increasingly widespread and immensely robust format for delivering digital information onscreen. While originally designed as a sleek, efficient format for text layout and vector-based shapes, recent PDF versions have added support for sound and even video clips embedded directly in PDF files. This means PDF is also a great way to transmit and distribute multipage files containing high-quality images, and the new PDF Presentation command lets you do this without leaving Photoshop.

Choose File ➪ Automate ➪ PDF Presentation to bring up the PDF Presentation dialog box, shown in Figure 20.34. Again, you also can access it through the Bridge and its Tools ➪ Photoshop menu. In the Source Files section, click Browse to display the Open dialog box and choose any images you'd like to include in the PDF file. If any images are currently open, you can select the Add Open Files option to add those to the list. Click and drag any of the listed files up or down the list to change the page order of the resulting PDF file. If you've opened this dialog box from the Tools ➪ Photoshop submenu in the Bridge, any selected files are included by default.

FIGURE 20.34

The PDF Presentation feature lets you create PDF slideshows and even set snazzy transitions between the images.

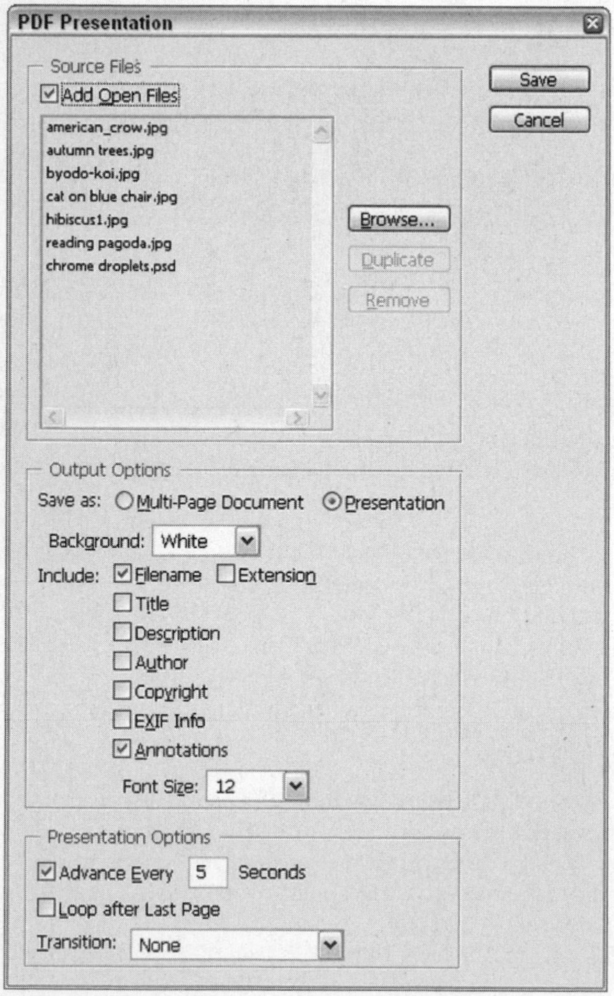

Below the Source Files section are the Output Options. Here, you can choose whether the PDF file will be a static, multi-page document or a slideshow, which Photoshop refers to as a Presentation. Choose Presentation and the Presentation Options at the bottom of the dialog box become available (refer to Figure 20.34) to you. Here you set the speed at which the slideshow advances, whether it loops continuously, and what type of transitions take viewers from one image to another while they watch it. You can experiment to see which transition you like best.

After you click Save, you can give the file a name (and choose a location and make some other choices) from the standard Save As dialog box, and then you're presented with the dialog box shown in Figure 20.35. Here you can customize the Adobe PDF settings for your file, selecting which version of Acrobat Reader to choose from the Compatibility list, make Security settings changes, and so on. It's the same dialog box you see when you save any Photoshop image in PDF format.

Figure 20.36 shows the PDF document window, and a panel of the images included, along with the main image that would appear in the individual slide during the show.

FIGURE 20.35

Customize your Adobe Acrobat/Reader settings for the new presentation.

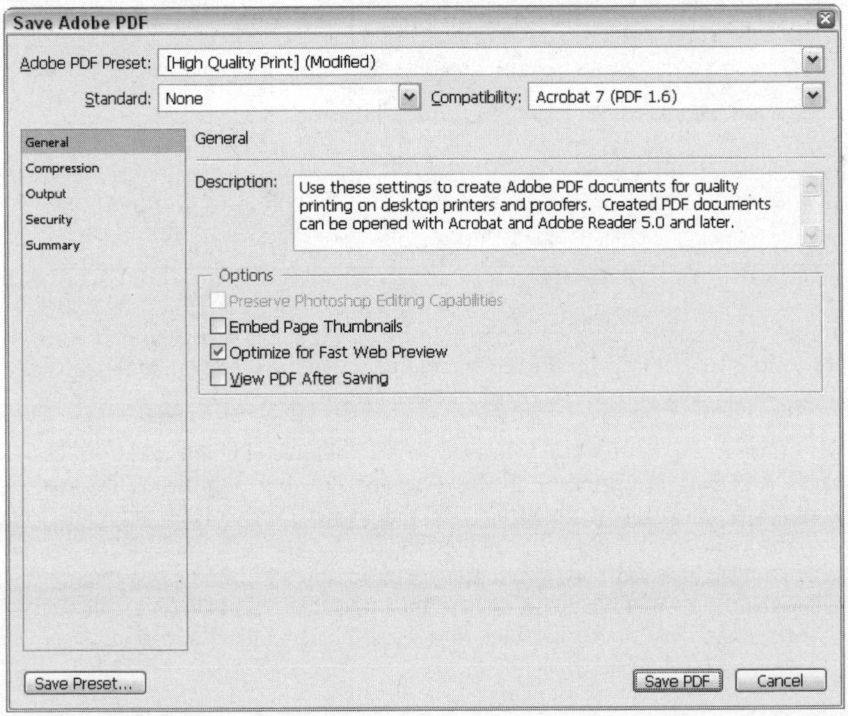

FIGURE 20.36

Open the PDF file, and watch the show; all you need is Adobe Reader.

When the show runs, the screen displays the images, full-screen, with a black background. Press Esc to end the show, and if you didn't set automatic timings (through the Presentation Options portion of the dialog box), you can press Enter to move from slide to slide.

There are a number of reasons to create a PDF slideshow instead of a Web Photo Gallery for distributing your images. A PDF file is just that — one file — as opposed to the numerous files that make up a Web Photo Gallery. Thus, you can burn a PDF file onto a CD or e-mail it to friends, family members, or coworkers to view onscreen using Adobe Reader software, available for free from www.adobe.com. PDF files also allow you to use your own fonts within the presentation without worrying that the recipient of the file won't have the same ones, and PDF files scale well — you don't have to worry about what monitor resolution is set at the file's final destination.

Combining Images with Merge to HDR

HDR stands for *High Dynamic Range*. The Merge to HDR command allows you to take multiple images and capture a full range of color and detail by merging them into a single image. Of course, the multiple images should be of identical content. The only differences between them, as shown in Figure 20.37, are in terms of their color and light values.

You can start with the Merge to HDR dialog box open (choose File ➪ Automate ➪ Merge to HDR to display the dialog box shown in Figure 20.38) and use that to Browse for the images you want to merge, or you can open the images first (File ➪ Open), open the Merge to HDR dialog box, and select Open Files from the Use drop-down list to indicate that your open images should be used for the merge.

FIGURE 20.37

The same flowers with detail-robbing light and too little contrast (left) and deeper shadows (right) can be merged to create a single improved image.

FIGURE 20.38

Click the Use list to choose between Files, Folder, or Open Files as the source for your images. You can click the Attempt to Automatically Align Source Images check box if your images are not exactly the same size and orientation.

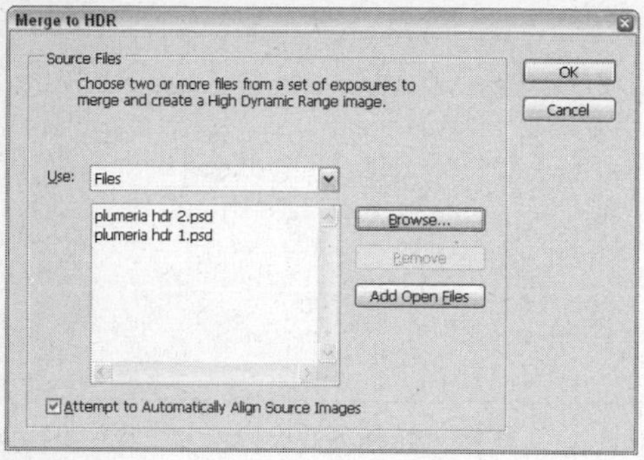

Next, click OK to begin the merge. Your computer pauses and creates a temporary merged version, along with a Manually Set EV dialog box, shown in Figure 20.39, that you can use to manually adjust the settings for the individual images. After you've used the Image < and > buttons to move through all the images to be merged, the OK button becomes available.

FIGURE 20.39

Make any manual adjustments before moving on to the final step, where your multiple images are merged into one HDR image.

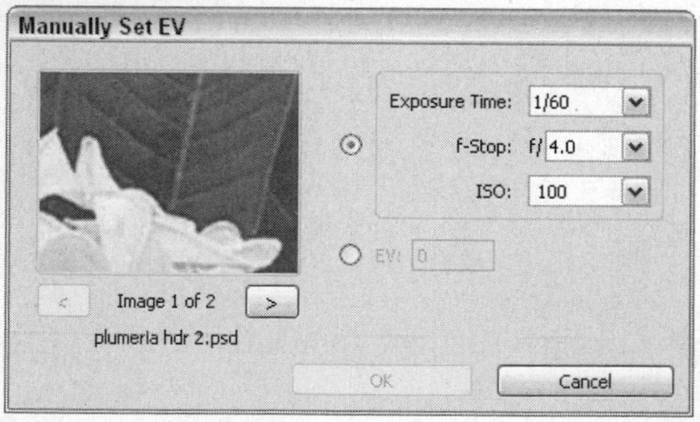

Now you can click OK in the Manually Set EV dialog box, and the Merge to HDR dialog box opens, as shown in Figure 20.40. Last, drag the slider to adjust the Set White Point Preview, and when you like the Merged Result image, click OK. This creates the final merged image, which you can then convert to an 8-bit or 16-bit image, using the Image ➪ Mode submenu.

FIGURE 20.40

See your images on the left, view the merged result in the middle, and use the slider to adjust the results before clicking OK to generate the new merged image.

Using Photomerge to create a panorama

Until the release of Photoshop CS, the ability to create a panoramic composite from a group of images was something you could only do with Photoshop Elements. With the release of CS, Photomerge was added to Photoshop, and with each subsequent release — CS2 and now CS3 — there's been a little bit more added to the functionality and successful creation of panorama images in Photoshop's Photomerge feature. Of course, despite its beginnings in what's often called "Photoshop Lite" (Elements), there's nothing pared down about the Photomerge feature, and it's quite effective at taking a series of images and merging them into a single, wide, panoramic shot. Of course, the only catch is that the images you plan to merge need to have been shot under specific circumstances — the same setting, the same size film, the same orientation of the camera. If you painstakingly stood there at the Grand Canyon, however, and took a series of shots of a very wide view and now you have each section of the view represented by two or more images, you're good to go with Photomerge.

To get started, choose File ➪ Automate ➪ Photomerge, or open the Bridge and choose Tools ➪ Photoshop ➪ Photomerge. The result is the Photomerge dialog box, as shown in Figure 20.41. Here you choose the images you want to merge into a single panorama, and you tell Photoshop how you want that done, choosing from five options on the left side of the dialog box. Which one to choose? Think about what you have in terms of the photos that will be pieced together, and what you want to end up with. Each of the five options meets a specific need, from simple, automatic matching up of left and right sides (Auto, if you want to end up with an image that's no wider than any one of your images, to Reposition Only, which lines all of them up into a long row) to the creation of the illusion of perspective or a curved panorama (Perspective and Cylindrical, respectively) to a merge that allows you to move the individual pieces (your contributing images) into place by eye, all by yourself. If you want to tinker with the panorama after the merge is performed, obviously you want to choose the last option, Interactive Layout.

You'll want to leave Advanced Blending on to take advantage of the improvements in this area added to CS3. With this feature turned on, the images are laced together more smoothly, allowing for a more natural-looking flow from image in the panorama to the next. After you click OK to perform your Photomerge, in the dialog box shown in Figure 20.42, a progress bar reminds you that it is blending the images "based on content."

After you've made your choice, either the merge is performed and gives you a file called "Untitled Panorama," or you see the dialog box shown in Figure 20.42, and this, as they say, is where the magic happens. Again, if you don't choose Interactive Layout, you just get the merged photos; you don't get the dialog box.

FIGURE 20.41

The Photomerge dialog box lets you choose the images that will make up your panorama.

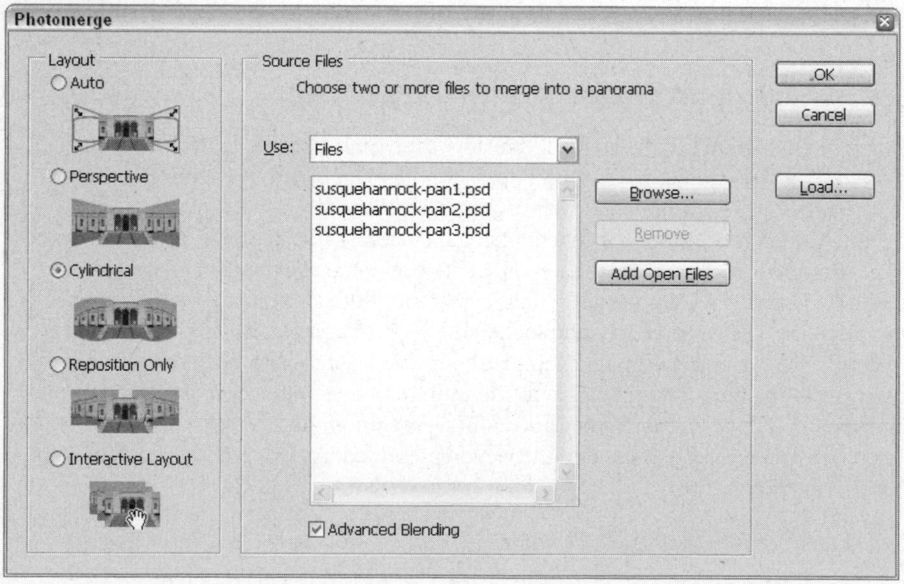

By default, Photomerge tries its best to make sense of the pixels in your images and match certain areas of one photo with similar areas of another. But it's something of a gamble; most of the time you'll see at least a few portions of your image that could use some fixing. You adjust the individual placement and rotation of the images in a panorama using the Select Image and Rotate Image tools available in the upper-left corner of the dialog box. The bottom two tools — the Zoom and Hand tools — work the same as they do everywhere else in the program. Between these two sets of tools is the Set Vanishing Point tool, which is covered in a moment.

> **TIP** If you adjust the settings without getting the results you want, try removing one of the images if the area it covers is already captured by the other images onscreen. To remove an image, simply select the arrow tool, click the image, and drag it to the Lightbox strip at the top of the screen, labeled in Figure 20.42. Giving the Photomerge command too much information about your scene can be a bad thing, and you may want to leave some of the images up in the Lightbox until you're ready to incorporate them. The Lightbox also is the all-purpose depository for any image that Photoshop cannot figure out how to fit within the panorama. If you'd like to reintroduce an image, simply click and drag it from the Lightbox and drop it back into the work area.

FIGURE 20.42

The very large Photomerge dialog box makes every attempt to create a panorama from a group of photographs, but you usually need to manually adjust the images to get the best results.

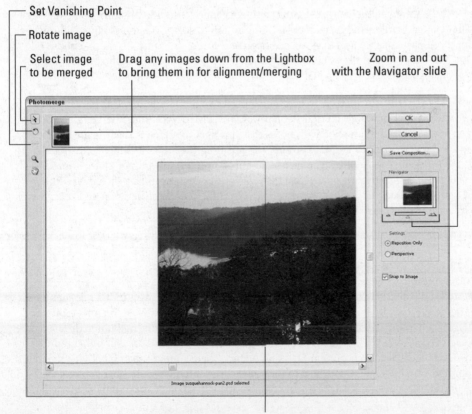

— Set Vanishing Point

— Rotate image

Select image to be merged

Drag any images down from the Lightbox to bring them in for alignment/merging

Zoom in and out with the Navigator slide

Red line around section indicates good alignment

By default, Photomerge assembles the images into a flat, jagged puzzle that rotates the images to fit each other but does not distort them in any way. If you'd like Photomerge to try bending and distorting the photos in an attempt to make them fit better, select the Perspective option (refer to Figure 20.42). When the Perspective option is selected, the command contorts the images and presents a more accurate, nearly 3D view of your scene. You can select the Set Vanishing Point tool and alter the perspective by clicking the different images in the composition. If you just want a straight panorama, leave the Reposition Only option selected.

The two options in the Composition Settings section of the Photomerge dialog box let you correct certain problems inherent in the Photomerge process. For example, the Perspective setting does a great job of distorting the images to ensure that they all fit together in the composition, but it also often results in a sort of "bowtie" shape for your final composition. The Cylindrical Mapping option, available only when the Perspective option is selected, corrects this by bending the more extreme corners of the composition back toward the center. Even more useful is the Advanced Blending option, which attempts to smooth over the common color and luminance shifts between images that can be dead giveaways of a computer-generated panorama. Both Composition Settings options make for pretty intense renders, so you may want to click the Preview button to see a lower-resolution preview while working in the dialog box.

If you've carefully arranged the images in your panorama and would like to return sometime later and continue adjusting the settings, click Save Composition to save a version of your Photomerge settings for these particular images that you can open and edit at any time. To do so, choose File ⇨ Automate ⇨ Photomerge, and then click Open Composition in the first dialog box that appears. This saves your panorama as a .PMG file.

As mentioned earlier, the way in which the original images were photographed is perhaps the most important factor in determining the results of a panorama created with Photomerge. The most crucial thing to keep in mind when shooting photos that you plan to merge is that the greater the consistency in focal length, camera angle, exposure, and position, the easier it is for Photoshop to merge the resulting images. Adobe recommends an image-to-image overlap of 15 to 40 percent and that you avoid using any sort of lens that distorts your images (such as a "fish-eye"). Finally, the use of a tripod or another stabilizing surface can mean the difference between an expert merge and an expressionist fiasco.

Batch Processing

Not to be confused with the Batch Rename command (found on the Bridge, in the File menu), the Batch command in Photoshop's Automate submenu allows you to run any action on a group of files, including renaming the resulting files and storing a log of any errors encountered. This makes it possible to do cool, timesaving things like creating thumbnails (record an action that reduces the images to a specified size and resolution first) and naming them so that the original file name plus a serial number (serially applied) is added to the names. Just about anything that you repeatedly do to a series of files can be done with the Batch command, augmented by the ability to ignore steps in your actions that might clash with the batch aspect of the procedure, such as Open and Save As commands that you don't want causing a pause and the display of a dialog box that's not needed when you're applying the action to a bunch of files.

You may want to have these things prepared before you embark on the Batch command:

- Have the action ready, recorded, running properly, and know which set it's in.

- Have all the files you want to handle as a batch either open within Photoshop already or stored in a single folder so that you can select them easily.

- Know your action so you know if Open and Save As commands need to be skipped.

- Know what you want to call the resulting files, if you do want to change the Destination for the files (renaming is not necessary, if what you're doing to the batch of files doesn't require that a new file be created for each file that's affected).

After you have all those ducks in a row, choose File ➪ Automate ➪ Batch. The dialog box shown in Figure 20.43 appears, and you're on your way.

FIGURE 20.43

The Batch Processing dialog box lets you pick an action, choose the files to apply it to, and rename batches of files, all in one fell swoop.

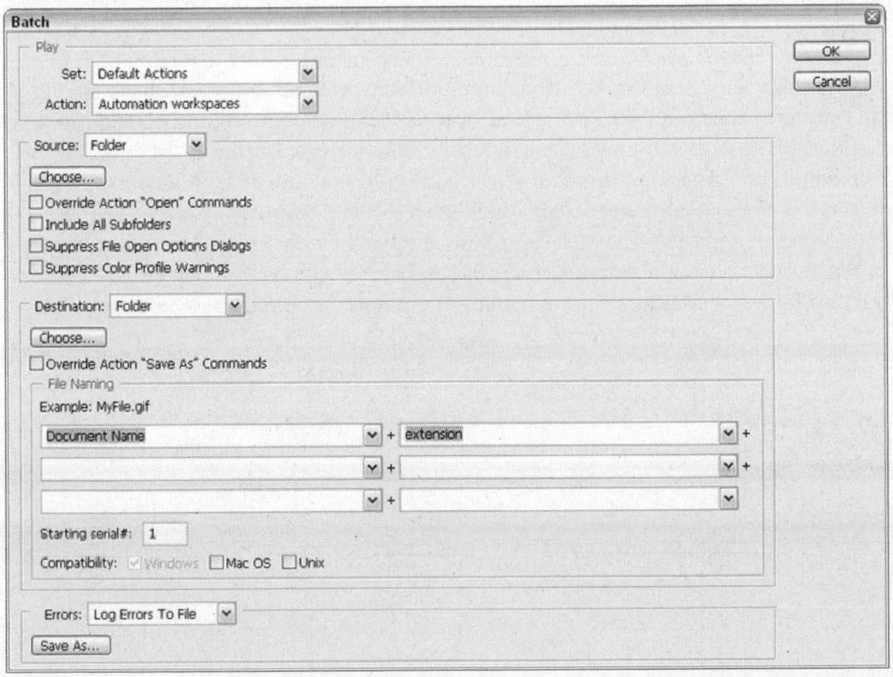

The dialog box has three main sections: Play, where you choose the action to run on the files; Source, where you choose the files that will be subjected to the action; and Destination, where you decide where new files created through the action will be stored. A small subsection entitled File Naming is where you set up the naming convention for the resulting files.

> **TIP** If things go awry, a file that logs the errors might come in handy. Choose Log to File from the Errors drop-down list, and click Save As to choose the name of the log file to create.

As you work through the dialog box, the Choose buttons allow you to pick the Source folder and Destination folders, respectively; the check boxes in the Source section allow you to turn action steps like Open off when the batch command is run, and to include subfolders or not. The other spot where you can tell Batch to skip an action step is in the Destination section. Mote the Override Action "Save As" Commands check box; turn this on if your action has such a command within it.

> **CAUTION** Whenever possible, you should make your Batch process create new files from the effects of whichever action you're applying. Why? Because if it goes wrong, you can just delete the deformed results of your efforts, and start over, tweaking the action and/or your Batch dialog box settings accordingly. If the only thing to go wrong is something in the naming process, use Batch Rename (again, from the Bridge) to fix things up name-wise.

Summary

In this chapter, you discovered terms to help you communicate with your commercial printer and learned how to print grayscale and color composites. You also learned about setting up and previewing your print job in Photoshop and how to assign transfer functions to distribute brightness values. Through a discussion of the color-separation process, you should now understand how to apply color trapping and know about adding spot-color highlights to a CMYK image. You also learned about publishing to paper and the Web, with Photoshop and via the new Bridge, and how to create Web graphics. Finally, you learned about processing files in batches, applying actions (discussed in Chapter 3) to whole folders of files for uniform naming and other mass-production activities.

Part VI

Appendixes

Appendix A

The Keyboard and Menus, and Making Photoshop Your Own

Maybe when you picture graphic artists or photographers using computers to create or edit their artwork, you imagine them using their mouse or a pen and tablet. If you imagine an accountant or a secretary using her computer, you probably picture them pounding away on the keyboard, not only entering data and text, but also issuing software commands.

While these images are probably accurate to some degree, the first one needs an adjustment. In truth, a Photoshop user can and should make much more use of the keyboard — borrowing a page from that accountant or secretary who can whip through menus and dialog box with efficient flair.

If you're using Photoshop, the keyboard, used to invoke the seemingly unlimited list of commands and features, is at least as important as the mouse or tablet to the creative process. Why? Because it's so much faster than taking your mouse and pointing to a menu or button. For example, if you just copied a picture or a portion thereof to the clipboard, you can make a new Photoshop image out if it with three keyboard shortcuts: one to open a new image window, one to paste the copied content, and one to save the file. Need to resize an image? Why stop, go to a menu, and choose a command when you can press a set of keys and see the appropriate dialog box open, which you also can spin through by typing values and then pressing Enter or Return to accept the new size settings?

In Photoshop CS3, the aforementioned reliance on the keyboard is taken a step further — with enhanced capabilities for customizing keyboard shortcuts, any discomfort with using and remembering the shortcuts is eliminated. For the things you'd rather do from the menus, there are new ways to customize their functioning and appearance as well, so if you're still not sold

IN THIS APPENDIX

Finding the hidden shortcuts and modifiers

Customizing keyboard shortcuts

Navigating Photoshop through all the shortcuts

on the keyboard as your primary way of "talking" to Photoshop, you still can customize things to make Photoshop work *your* way.

Photoshop's keyboard convenience comes in two varieties:

- **Shortcuts:** Some keystrokes (single keys) and keystroke combinations (two or more keys, pressed simultaneously) produce immediate effects. For example, pressing Ctrl+Backspace (⌘+Delete on the Mac) fills a selection with the current background color, while pressing M all by itself activates the Marquee tools, which you then can use to make a selection, which you might then fill. Pressing a single key also can activate a tool, enabling you to grab that mouse or pen and get right to work.

- **Modifiers:** Some keys change the behavior of a tool or command. Pressing Shift while dragging with the Lasso tool adds the lassoed area to the previous selection. Because they modify other keystrokes and combinations, the Shift, Alt, and Ctrl keys (also Shift, Control, Option, and ⌘ on the Mac) are known collectively as *modifiers*.

One of the goals of this Appendix is to help you become familiar with all that you can do with the keyboard in Photoshop. You may think of the keyboard only as some dry tool for typing text and numbers, but as you read on, you'll see that it's much, much more — it's what helps unleash the power of Photoshop's tools so that you can truly unleash your own imagination.

Hidden Shortcuts and Modifiers

Shortcuts permit you to initiate various Photoshop commands and features without having to stop what you're doing and click a Toolbox button or pull down a menu to make a selection. Some shortcuts are fairly obvious, and you'll find them easy to remember, either because the alpha characters used make sense or because the key combinations are ubiquitous, like Ctrl+S (⌘+S on the Mac) to Save a file — that one's both logical alphabetically *and* common to just about any software application out there.

Many of Photoshop's keyboard shortcuts are displayed in the form of tool tips, which are pop-ups that appear when you hover over a tool with your mouse. Some are listed in menus to let you know the keyboard equivalent of a given command. But many of Photoshop's shortcuts are hidden, and it's only in a book like this, or by digging through Photoshop's Help files, that you'll find out about them. What's weird is that the hidden shortcuts turn out to be some of the most important ones in the bunch.

Windows Alt-key combos

Under Windows, you can perform many operations using *hot keys*, which are the underlined letters you see in menus and dialog boxes. To access one of these functions, press Alt to display the hot keys and then press the underlined letter. This can be very useful when choosing commands that lack a Ctrl-key shortcut. For example, normally, you would choose Image ⇨ Adjustments ⇨ Channel Mixer to access the Channel Mixer, but with hot keys, you can press Alt+I, release the

Alt key and press A, and then press X. After the Channel Mixer dialog box appears, you can press Alt+G to select the Green value, Alt+B for Blue, and so on.

You can even access commands that have no underlines. To access the Unsharp Mask, you normally choose Filter ➪ Sharpen ➪ Unsharp Mask, but with hot keys, you can press Alt+T to bring up the Filter menu, S to highlight Sharpen, Enter to display the Sharpen submenu, and U to choose Unsharp Mask. For Filter ➪ Stylize ➪ Extrude, press Alt+T, S, S, S, Enter, E, E, Enter. I know, even as I'm writing this, I'm thinking that it sounds really cumbersome. But you may find you like it — and for procedures that you do frequently, you'll find you remember the shortcuts and save lots of time, despite it *sounding* like it would be hard to do.

For more mouse-less excitement, you also can zip through the menus with the arrow keys. After you press Alt plus the underlined letter to display a menu, use the up and down arrows to highlight commands in the menu. Use the left and right arrows to display neighboring menus. To choose a highlighted command, press Enter. To hide the menus and return focus to the image window, press Esc twice. Yeah, that's right — suddenly that keyboard is looking pretty useful.

> **TIP** Mac users can enjoy the same level of keyboard navigation power by turning on Full Keyboard Access through System Preferences.

The shortcut menu

One of the best and least documented tricks in Photoshop is right-clicking. For Mac users with a one-button mouse, control-clicking will net you the same shortcuts. Of course, if your Mac has a three-button mouse, you can right-click as well. It's not really a hidden concept if you use lots of other software, because right-clicking is fairly common in Windows and most Windows applications. For Mac users, Control-clicking isn't exactly a foreign concept, either.

When you right-click or Control-click the mouse button in the image window, Photoshop displays a shortcut menu of commands tailored to your current activity and/or the item you right-clicked/Control-clicked. For example, if you right-click or Control-click a layer in the Layers menu, you get the pop-up menu shown in Figure A.1. There are other ways to get at some of these commands, but this way is very quick and easy, especially if you're already using your mouse to paint or draw in the image window. You're already in the neighborhood, so why not right-click while you're there?

Shortcut menus are considered *context sensitive*, because they're triggered in and their commands relate to where you literally are in the program. Although some tools and onscreen elements have no shortcut menus associated with them, most do, and you'll find that simply seeing what the menu has to offer is educational unto itself.

> **TIP** As with the regular menus, you can press the up-arrow and down-arrow keys to highlight commands in the context-sensitive pop-up menus. To choose a command, press Enter. To hide the menu, press Esc.

FIGURE A.1

You're never really alone in Photoshop. Just about anywhere you wander, a right-click (or a Control-click) provides a list of commands relevant to the item you clicked.

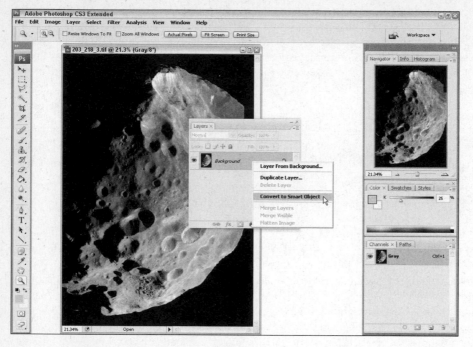

Toolbox shortcuts

Usability has always been one of Photoshop's great strengths, and the ability to activate Toolbox tools with a single keystroke is a perfect example of this. You can keep your dominant hand on the mouse and use the other hand to press the key (or use your mouse hand, if you prefer) — all without stopping to perform some digital gymnastics to reach two or three keys at the same time. The shortcuts also work even when the Toolbox is hidden. After you get used to the shortcuts, you may find that the only time you look at the Toolbox is to check which tool is selected.

Figure A.2 shows the Toolbox and all the keys that give you quick access to the tools. The way it works is simple, press the appropriate key, as shown in the figure; no Ctrl key, Option key, or other modifier key is required. Many of the shortcuts make sense. For example, M selects the Marquee tool, and L is for the Lasso tool. Some only make sense in a strange way — I for Eyedropper. But then there are the ones you have to wonder about, such as O for DOdge or R for BluR. Well, they *sort of* make sense — at least those letters are in the tool names, but they're not entirely memorable.

FIGURE A.2

Press these keys to select tools and activate controls. The bold letters indicate keys that they toggle between alternate tools or settings.

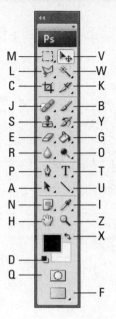

Note that when two or more buttons share a single slot on the Toolbox, the keyboard shortcut switches between those tools. For example, press G to access either the Gradient tool *or* the Fill Bucket. If you're on the Fill Bucket, pressing Shift+G switches to Gradient, and vice versa. If there are three or more tools sharing a slot, you can cycle through them all by continuing to press Shift plus the shortcut key.

You can eliminate the need for Shift by choosing Edit ➪ Preferences ➪ General (Ctrl+K) or Photoshop ➪ Preferences ➪ General (on the Mac) and deselecting the Use Shift Key for Tool Switch option, as explained in Chapter 2. This may make using these toggle-able keys easier, given that they make up the majority of the shortcuts.

> **TIP** One Toolbox shortcut doesn't require the Shift + combination. Represented on the Toolbox at the very bottom, the various workspace views can be accessed with the letter F. Cycle through all the view modes — Standard, Maximized, Full Screen with Menu Bar, and Full Screen — by continuing to press the F key.

Palette shortcuts

Photoshop also lets you access palette options from the keyboard, and a list of the palettes, their purpose, and shortcuts for access appears below. Note that each of the shortcuts works even when the palette is hidden:

- **Palette function keys:** Press F5 to show or hide the Brushes palette. Press F6, F7, F8, or Alt+F9 (Option+F9 on the Mac) to toggle the display of the Color, Layers, Info, or Actions palette, respectively. If for some weird reason the Options bar is hidden, press Enter or Return to bring it back. Note that if you're using a Mac, you may want to avoid the F8 key unless you've changed the default (Spaces) for that key. You can change this setting through your System Preferences.

- **Hide or show all palettes:** Press Tab to hide or show all palettes, including the Toolbox, Options bar, and the status bar. To hide or show the standard palettes only — that is, everything except the Toolbox, Options bar, and the status bar — press Shift+Tab.

- **Brush size:** Press left bracket ([) to decrease or right bracket (]) to increase the brush size when a paint or edit tool is active.

- **Brush hardness:** Press Shift with a bracket key to change the hardness of a brush. Shift+] gives the brush a sharper edge; Shift+[makes it softer. Again, a paint or edit tool must be active.

- **Brush preset:** Press comma (,) or period (.) to cycle between preset brushes. If this doesn't work for you, try pressing Shift+comma, which selects the first preset, the single-pixel brush. Then press period to move forward. Shift+period jumps to the last preset brush.

- **Gradient style:** Select the Gradient tool and press a bracket key, [or], to switch among the five gradient styles.

- **Gradient preset:** Press comma or period to step backward or forward, respectively, through the predefined gradients. Press Shift+comma or Shift+period to switch to the first or last gradient in the list.

- **Shape layer styles:** Select any of the shape tools and press comma (,) or period (.) to step backward or forward through the predefined layer styles. Press Shift+comma or Shift+period to jump to the first or last style in the list.

- **Shape attribute:** With the Rounded Rectangle tool active, press a bracket key, [or], to decrease or increase, respectively, the corner radius. Select the Polygon tool and press a bracket key, [or], to decrease or increase the number of sides in the next polygon or star you draw. For the Line tool, press a bracket key, [or], to decrease or increase the line weight.

- **Custom shape preset:** Select the Custom Shape tool, and press a bracket key, [or], to step backward or forward through the predefined shapes. Press Shift+[or Shift+] to switch to the first or last shape in the list.

- **Brush opacity:** When a paint or edit tool is active, press a number key to change the Opacity, Strength, or Exposure value in the Options bar. Press 1 to change the value to 10 percent, press 2 for 20 percent, and so on, up to 0 for 100 percent. Or use an exact value by typing two numbers in a row. For example, type 87 for 87 percent or 05 for 5 percent.

- **Airbrush:** If a tool offers an airbrush icon in the Options bar, press Shift+Alt+P (Shift+Option+P on the Mac) to toggle it on or off.

- **Airbrush flow:** If a tool offers the Airbrush, it includes both an Opacity value and a Flow value. When the Airbrush is turned off, press Shift with a number key to change the Flow value. When the Airbrush is on, press a number key to change the Flow value; press Shift with a number key to change the Opacity value.

- **Layer opacity:** When any tool other than a paint or edit tool is selected — that is, any tool in the first, third, or fourth group in the Toolbox — pressing a number key changes the Opacity value for the active layer. Again, press one number to modify the Opacity setting in 10 percent increments; press two numbers to specify an exact Opacity setting.

- **Fill opacity:** Press Shift with a number key to change the Fill value for the active layer, which modifies the opacity of the pixels in a layer without affecting the layer effects.

- **Brush mode:** When a paint or edit tool is active, you can cycle through brush modes by pressing Shift+plus (+) or Shift+minus (–). Shift+plus takes you down the brush mode pop-up menu, and Shift+minus takes you back up.

- **Blend mode:** When some other tool is selected, Shift+plus and Shift+minus affect the blend mode applied to the active layer. You also can access a particular blend mode by pressing Shift and Alt (or Option) with a letter key. For example, Shift+Alt+M selects the Multiply mode; Shift+Alt+S selects Screen; Shift+Alt+N takes you back to Normal.

- **Lock setting:** Press the forward slash (/) to toggle on and off the lock icon that controls transparency in the Layers palette. If one or more of the lock icons is already active, press / to turn off all four. Press / again to return the options to their former configuration. Layer locking can be extremely useful for protecting the contents of layers, as explained in Chapter 13.

- **Switch layer:** Press Alt+] to ascend through the layers. Press Alt+[to descend. Press Shift+Alt+] to activate the top layer in the composition. Press Shift+Alt+[to go all the way down to the bottom of the stack, usually the Background layer.

- **Arrange layer:** Press Ctrl+] (⌘+] on the Mac) to move the active layer one level forward in the stack; press Ctrl+[to move it back. Press Ctrl+Shift+] to move the layer to the top of the stack. Press Ctrl+Shift+[to move it to the bottom, usually just in front of the Background layer.

Customizing Keyboard Shortcuts

Photoshop CS gave us what many Photoshop users have been requesting for a very long time — the ability to edit keyboard shortcuts. Of course, CS2 and now CS3 continue to offer this ability — because being able to customize them is key to their being useful, and because a keystroke or combination that's hard to remember or difficult to reach with one hand's fingers is one you won't use.

So now, you don't have to live with the totally illogical and hard to remember strokes, such as J to activate the Healing Brush (J? why J?) or the inscrutable Ctrl+Shift+E (⌘+Option+E) to merge all visible layers. Photoshop CS gave us the ability to simply and easily edit existing keyboard short-cuts, as well as assign shortcuts to commands that formerly had none. CS3 continues to provide this level of customization and has enhanced it to include the ability to customize menus as well. Choose Edit ➪ Keyboard Shortcuts to bring up the Keyboard Shortcuts and Menus dialog box shown in Figure A.3. You can access this command also by pressing Ctrl+Shift+Alt+K (⌘+Shift+Option+K), which ironically is one of the most difficult and convoluted shortcuts in all of Photoshop, but at least you know how to change it now!

Despite its power to really change the way you interface with Photoshop, the Keyboard Shortcuts and Menus dialog box is quite easy to use. First, from the Set pop-up menu, select the collection of shortcuts to which you'd like to make edits. You can modify the default set or create new ones for different users or types of image-editing work. Use the three icons to the right of the Set drop-down menu to save the set, create a new set, or discard the entire set, respectively. From there, select a category from the Shortcuts For pop-up menu, and then simply explore the various sub-sections in the list below. If you dig around enough, you can find almost every single command, function, and filter in the program. Aside from this appendix and references to the shortcuts throughout this book, this might be the best place to find all the shortcuts you never knew existed.

FIGURE A.3

The Keyboard Shortcuts and Menus dialog box lets you change your keyboard shortcuts and menus so that they look and work the way you need them to.

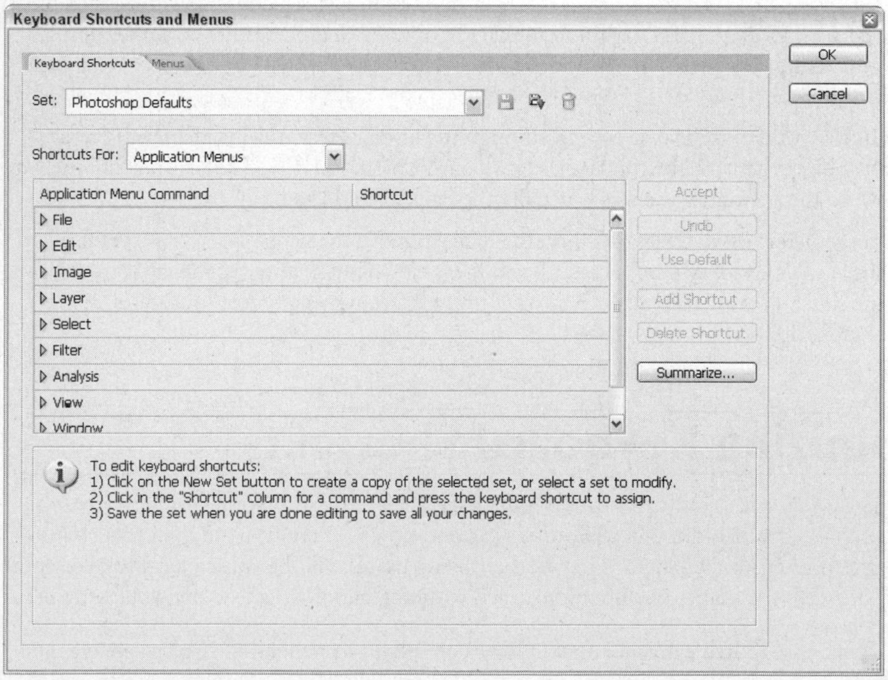

To assign a new shortcut to a command, simply click in the blank area labeled Shortcut to the right of the command name and press the desired shortcut key or combination of keys. As soon as you click the spot in the dialog box, the currently assigned key or combination highlights, so the next thing you type replaces it. If there is no key or combination currently assigned, just type whatever you want to be the shortcut. Then click Accept to make the change/addition permanent.

If you happen to type a keyboard shortcut that is already assigned to another function in the program, Photoshop displays information at the bottom of the dialog box, as shown in Figure A.3, and gives you the option to accept or undo your changes. You also can use the buttons along the right side of the dialog box to save and discard changes, as well as add and delete shortcuts. Lastly, you can click Summarize to generate and display an HTML Web page that lists the currently active keyboard shortcuts, which is a handy list to tack up close to your computer.

Customizing menus

Photoshop's menus also can be made friendlier, using the Menus tab in the Keyboard Shortcuts and Menus dialog box. You can turn on commands that currently have no menu representations so that they do appear in menus, and you can change the color of menu commands so that they stand out for you.

> **TIP** If you want to assign colors to menus and menu commands, be sure that Show Menu Colors is selected in the General Preferences dialog box; choose Edit ➪ Preferences ➪ General to display the dialog box (Photoshop ➪ Preferences ➪ General on the Mac).

To change a menu command's visibility and/or color, choose the Set (Photoshop Defaults or a custom set you or another user who shares your computer may have created), and then choose either Application Menus or Palette Menus from the Menus For list. Application Menus refers to the main menus across the top of the workspace — File, Edit, Image, and so on. The Palette Menus are the menus that are available by clicking the tiny triangle button in the upper-right corner of various palettes.

After you select a Set and a Menu group, choose a particular menu to change. In Figure A.4, the File menu (from the Applications Menus) is chosen, and its commands are displayed by clicking the triangle to the left of the word File. For each menu command, there's an entry in the Visibility and Color columns. Click to insert or remove the eye icon, displaying or hiding that particular command, respectively. If you click the Color option (None, by default), a list of colors appears, also shown in Figure A.4.

Go through and change all the commands you want, hiding some and showing others, changing colors for those you want to have stand out, or grouping related commands by a common color. After you make all your changes, click OK and the changes take effect.

> **TIP** When you hide commands, the Show All Menu Items command is added to that menu. If you ever want to see the hidden commands again, you can Ctrl-click the menu in question, and all hidden commands become visible. Or just click the Show All Menu Items command to redisplay those commands you've hidden.

FIGURE A.4

Use the Menus tab in the Keyboard Shortcuts and Menus dialog box to change the visibility and color of any application or palette menu. Directions remind you how at the bottom of the dialog box.

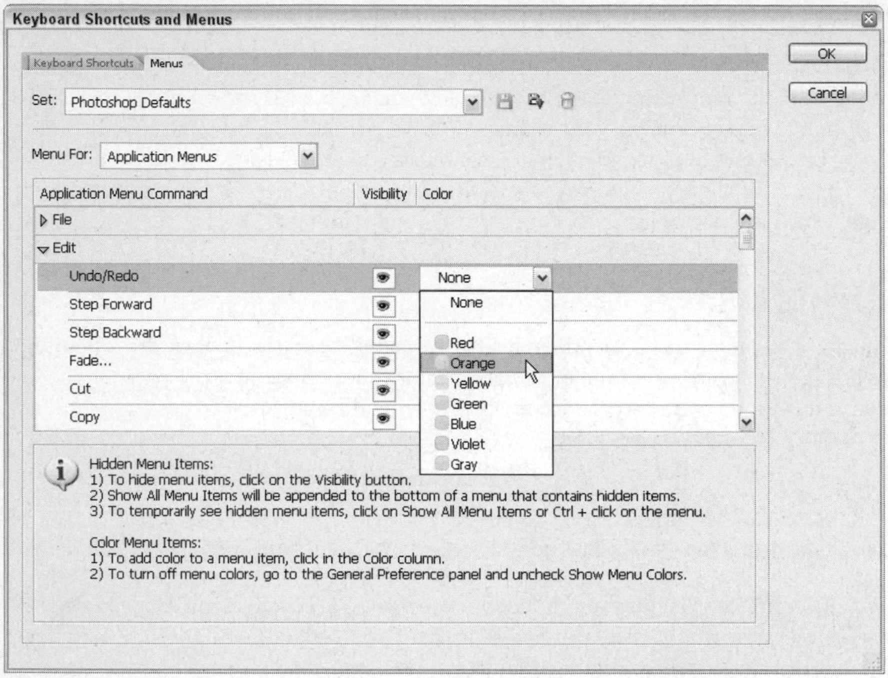

Creating a new menu set

If you want to keep the Photoshop Defaults set of menus just as they are "out of the box," you can create your own custom menu set and customize it instead. Just make your changes — hiding and coloring commands as desired — and then click the second of three buttons to the right of the Set list. This opens a Save dialog box. Name the new set and click Save to make it a reality. The file extension for menu set files is .MNU, and by default, they're stored in the Menu Customization folder, a subfolder of the Presets folder found in your Adobe folder. Don't monkey with the default location for your new .MNU file; if you do, it won't appear automatically in the Set list for future use or modification.

The Great-Grandmother of All Shortcut Tables

A shortcuts table has always been a part of the Photoshop Bible. What kind of Bible would it be if such a handy and powerful list weren't included? The table, however, has grown and improved over the years, and Deke McClelland did a great job of turning it into the fabulous table that it is today.

Any tool is more useful if you know how to use it properly. The table that follows these paragraphs doesn't really need much introduction, but there are a few things to keep in mind. If these reminders seem insulting to your intelligence, we apologize, but ask that you simply skip ahead to the table and don't mutter under your breath. We're just trying to help.

- First, don't press Shift just because a key combination involves a character that normally requires the Shift key. For example, the shortcut for the Zoom In command is Ctrl+plus (⌘+plus on the Mac). Technically, + is the Shifted version of =, so you might think you have to press Ctrl+Shift+= to get this shortcut combination to work. That would be wrong, of course, but we respect that sort of thorough, literal thinking. Remember that the plus sign is used because it implies zooming while the equal sign does not. So when you see Ctrl+plus, just press Ctrl+=.

- Second, if you're a Windows user, note that many of Photoshop's keyboard shortcuts involve both the Ctrl and Alt keys. Ctrl+Alt+O, for example, invokes the Open As command, and Ctrl+Alt+Z undoes an operation from the History palette. Unfortunately, Windows likes to reserve Ctrl+Alt combinations to launch applications, and if you, as a Windows user, set up a keyboard shortcut to invoke a particular application, Windows will commandeer that command and you won't be able to successfully use it within Photoshop. So be careful when creating Windows shortcuts and avoid the following when assigning file-launching shortcuts, which are very much used in Photoshop: B, D, E, F, J, K, L, M, N, O, P, S, T, U, W, X, Z, plus, minus, semicolon, and 0 through 9. This doesn't leave you many other options, but which is more important, Photoshop or Windows? That's right.

> **TIP** Don't know how to create a Windows shortcut to start an application? Here you go: Create a shortcut icon for the application by dragging the Programs menu command and icon from the Programs menu (press and hold Ctrl while dragging so that you make a copy of the command) onto the Desktop. Then right-click the new shortcut icon, choose Properties, click the Shortcut tab, and type the character and modifier key/s of your choice into the Shortcut Key option box.

It's time to wade right into the table and immerse yourself in Photoshop's keyboard shortcuts. Some will be familiar and others won't be. Some will invoke a command or feature you have never used, and others may be the keyboard access to something you do 50 times a day, and now you can't believe how much time you've been wasting clicking buttons and menus. Throughout the table, operations are listed in the left column. Windows shortcuts are in the center column, and Mac shortcuts are in the right column. There is no implied priority in this order — Windows first, or Mac in the "right" column — it's just how it all worked out.

TABLE A.1

Photoshop's Shortcuts and Modifiers

Operation	Windows Shortcut	Macintosh Shortcut
Menu Commands		
Actual Pixels	Ctrl+Alt+0 (zero)	⌘+Option+0 (zero)
Auto Color	Ctrl+Shift+B	⌘+Shift+B
Auto Contrast	Ctrl+Shift+Alt+L	⌘+Shift+Option+L
Auto Levels	Ctrl+Shift+L	⌘+Shift+L
Bring Layer Forward	Ctrl+right bracket (])	⌘+right bracket (])
Bring Layer to Front	Ctrl+Shift+right bracket (])	⌘+Shift+right bracket (])
Browse	Ctrl+Shift+O	⌘+Option+O
Canvas Size	right-click title bar	⌘+Option+C
Clear	Backspace or Delete	Delete
Close	Ctrl+W or Ctrl+F4	⌘+W
Close All	Ctrl+Shift+W or Ctrl+Shift+F4	⌘+Option+W
Color Balance	Ctrl+B	⌘+B
Color Balance, with last settings	Ctrl+Alt+B	⌘+Option+B
Color Settings	Ctrl+Shift+K	⌘+Shift+K
Copy	Ctrl+C	⌘+C
Copy Merged	Ctrl+Shift+C	⌘+Shift+C
Curves	Ctrl+M	⌘+M
Curves, with last settings	Ctrl+Alt+M	⌘+Option+M
Cut	Ctrl+X	⌘+X
Desaturate	Ctrl+Shift+U	⌘+Shift+U
Deselect	Ctrl+D	⌘+D
Duplicate	click left icon at bottom of History palette or right-click title bar	click left icon at bottom of History palette
Exit/Quit	Ctrl+Q or Alt+F4	⌘+Q
Extract	Ctrl+Alt+X	⌘+Option+X
Fade last operation	Ctrl+Shift+F	⌘+Shift+F
Feather selection	Ctrl+Alt+D	⌘+Option+D
File Info	right-click title bar	⌘+Option+Shift+I
Fill	Shift+Backspace	Shift+Delete

Operation	Windows Shortcut	Macintosh Shortcut
Fill from history	Ctrl+Alt+Backspace	⌘+Option+Delete
Filter, repeat last	Ctrl+F	⌘+F
Filter, repeat with new settings	Ctrl+Alt+F	⌘+Option+F
Fit on Screen	Ctrl+0 (zero)	⌘+0 (zero)
Free Transform	Ctrl+T	⌘+T
Free Transform, from clone	Ctrl+Alt+T	⌘+Option+T
Gamut Warning	Ctrl+Shift+Y	⌘+Shift+Y
Group with Previous layer	Ctrl+G	⌘+G
Help Contents	F1	⌘+Shift+?
Hue/Saturation	Ctrl+U	⌘+U
Hue/Saturation, with last settings	Ctrl+Alt+U	⌘+Option+U
Image Size	right-click title bar	⌘+Option+I
Inverse Selection	Ctrl+Shift+I	⌘+ShIft+I
Invert	Ctrl+I	⌘+I
Layer Via Copy	Ctrl+J	⌘+J
Layer Via Cut	Ctrl+Shift+J	⌘+Shift+J
Levels	Ctrl+L	⌘+L
Levels, with last settings	Ctrl+Alt+L	⌘+Option+L
Liquify	Ctrl+Shift+X	⌘+Shift+X
Lock Guides	Ctrl+Alt+semicolon (;)	⌘+Option+semicolon (;)
Merge Down/Linked/Layer Set	Ctrl+E	⌘+E
Merge Visible	Ctrl+Shift+E	⌘+Shift+E
Merge Visible, into current layer	Ctrl+Shift+Alt+E	⌘+Shift+Option+E
New, document	Ctrl+N	⌘+N
New, with default settings	Ctrl+Alt+N	⌘+Option+N
New Layer	Ctrl+Shift+N	⌘+Shift+N
New Layer, skip options	Ctrl+Shift+Alt+N	⌘+Shift+Option+N
Open, existing document	Ctrl+O	⌘+O
Open As	Ctrl+Alt+O	⌘+O
Page Setup	Ctrl+Shift+P	⌘+Shift+P
Paste	Ctrl+V or F4	⌘+V or F4

continued

1083

TABLE A.1   (continued)

Operation	Windows Shortcut	Macintosh Shortcut
Paste Into	Ctrl+Shift+V	⌘+Shift+V
Pattern Maker	Ctrl+Shift+Alt+X	⌘+Shift+Option+X
Preferences	Ctrl+K	⌘+K
Preferences, last panel	Ctrl+Alt+K	⌘+Option+K
Print	Ctrl+P	⌘+P
Print One Copy	Ctrl+Shift+Alt+P	⌘+Shift+Option+P
Print with Preview	Ctrl+Alt+P	⌘+Option+P
Proof Colors	Ctrl+Y	⌘+Y
Redo	Ctrl+Z	⌘+Z
Reselect	Ctrl+Shift+D	⌘+Shift+D
Revert	F12	F12 (reset System Preferences to use this, or you'll open the Dashboard)
Rulers, show or hide	Ctrl+R	⌘+R
Save	Ctrl+S	⌘+S
Save As	Ctrl+Shift+S	⌘+Shift+S
Save as a copy	Ctrl+Alt+S	⌘+Option+S
Save For Web	Ctrl+Shift+Alt+S	⌘+Shift+Option+S
Select All	Ctrl+A	⌘+A
Send Layer Backward	Ctrl+left bracket ([)	⌘+left bracket ([)
Send Layer to Back	Ctrl+Shift+left bracket ([)	⌘+Shift+left bracket ([)
Show/Hide Extras (for example, selection edges, slices, annotation)	Ctrl+H	⌘+H
Show/Hide Grid	Ctrl+Alt+quote (")	⌘+quote (")
Show/Hide Guides	Ctrl+semicolon (;)	⌘+semicolon (;)
Show/Hide Selected Path	Ctrl+Shift+H	⌘+Shift+H
Snap (for example, guides, grid, document bounds)	Ctrl+Shift+semicolon (;)	⌘+Shift+semicolon (;)
Step Backward in History	Ctrl+Alt+Z	⌘+Option+Z
Step Forward in History	Ctrl+Shift+Z	⌘+Shift+Z
Transform Again	Ctrl+Shift+T	⌘+Shift+T

Operation	Windows Shortcut	Macintosh Shortcut
Transform Again, repeat and clone	Ctrl+Shift+Alt+T	⌘+Shift+Option+T
Undo	Ctrl+Z	⌘+Z
Ungroup Layers	Ctrl+Shift+G	⌘+Shift+G
Zoom In	Ctrl+plus (+)	⌘+plus (+)
Zoom Out	Ctrl+minus (–)	⌘+minus (–)
Navigation		
Scroll image with Hand tool	spacebar+drag or drag in Navigator palette	spacebar+drag or drag in Navigator palette
Scroll up or down one screen	Page Up or Page Down	Page Up or Page Down
Scroll up or down slightly	Shift+Page Up or Shift+Page Down	Shift+Page Up or Shift+Page Down
Scroll left or right one screen	Ctrl+Page Up or Ctrl+Page Down	⌘+Page Up or ⌘+Page Down
Scroll left or right slightly	Ctrl+Shift+Page Up or Ctrl+Shift+Page Down	⌘+Shift+Page Up or ⌘+Shift+Page Down
Switch to upper-left corner	Home	Home
Switch to lower-right corner	End	End
Magnify to custom zoom ratio	Ctrl+spacebar+drag or Ctrl+drag in Navigator palette	⌘+spacebar+drag or ⌘+drag in Navigator palette
Zoom in and change window size to fit (assuming default settings)	Ctrl+Alt+plus (+)	⌘+plus (+)
Zoom in without changing window size	Ctrl+spacebar+click or Ctrl+plus (+)	⌘+spacebar+click or ⌘+Option+plus (+)
Zoom out and change window size to fit (assuming default settings)	Ctrl+Alt+minus (–)	⌘+minus (–)
Zoom out without changing window size	Alt+spacebar+click or Ctrl+minus (–)	Option+spacebar+click or ⌘+Option+minus (–)
Zoom to 100%	Ctrl+Alt+0 (zero) or double+click zoom tool icon	⌘+Option+0 (zero) or double-click zoom tool icon
Fit image on screen	Ctrl+0 (zero) or double-click hand tool icon	⌘+0 (zero) or double-click hand tool icon
Apply zoom value but keep magnification box active	Shift+Enter	Shift+Return

continued

TABLE A.1   *(continued)*

Operation	Windows Shortcut	Macintosh Shortcut
Cycle through full screen and normal window modes	F	F
Change screen mode for all open windows	Shift+click screen icon in toolbox	Shift+click screen icon in toolbox
Toggle display of menu bar in full screen modes	Shift+F	Shift+F
Bring forward next open image window	Ctrl+Tab	Ctrl+Tab
Painting and Editing		
Display crosshair cursor	Caps Lock	Caps Lock
Erase to History	Alt+drag with Eraser	Option+drag with Eraser
Select Brush tool or Pencil tool	B or Shift+B	B or Shift+B
Select Airbrush (while Brush tool is active)	Shift+Alt+P	Shift+Option+P
Cycle between Stamp tools	S or Shift+S	S or Shift+S
Select Healing Brush or Patch tool	J or Shift+J	J or Shift+J
Specify area to clone	Alt+click with Clone stamp or Bealing Brush	Option+click with Clone Stamp or Healing Brush
Cycle between Focus tools	R or Shift+R	R or Shift+R
Sharpen with Blur tool or blur with Sharpen tool	Alt+drag	Option+drag
Dip into foreground color when smearing	Alt+drag with Smudge tool	Option+drag with Smudge tool
Cycle between the Dodge, Burn, and Sponge tools	O or Shift+O	O or Shift+O
Darken with Dodge tool or lighten with Burn tool	Alt+drag	Option+drag
Paint or edit in a straight line	click, and then Shift+click	click, and then Shift+click
Change Opacity, Strength, or Exposure in 10% increments	number (1 through 0)	number (1 through 0)
Change Opacity, Strength, or Exposure in 1% increments	two numbers in a row	two numbers in a row
Change Flow in 10% increments	Shift+number (1 through 0)	Shift+number (1 through 0)
Change Flow in 1% increments	Shift+two numbers in a row	Shift+two numbers in a row

Operation	Windows Shortcut	Macintosh Shortcut
Select brush mode	Shift+right-click with paint or edit tool or Shift+Alt+letter	Shift+Control-click with paint or edit tool or Shift+Option+letter
Cycle through brush modes	Shift+plus (+) or Shift+minus (–)	Shift+plus (+) or Shift+minus (–)
Reset to Normal brush mode	Shift+Alt+N	Shift+Option+N
Change brush diameter in increments proportional to brush size	bracket key, [or]	bracket key, [or]
Change brush hardness in 25 percent increments	Shift+bracket, [or]	Shift+bracket, [or]
Cycle between brush presets	comma (,) or period (.)	comma (,) or period (.)
Select first or last brush preset	Shift+comma (,) or Shift+period (.)	Shift+comma (,) or Shift+period (.)
Display Brushes palette	F5 or right-click with paint or edit tool	F5 or Control-click with paint or edit tool
Delete preset brush from Brushes palette	Alt+click preset	Option+click preset
Edit preset name in Brushes palette	double-click preset	double-click preset
Applying Colors and Styles		
Switch foreground and background colors	X	X
Reset foreground and background colors to black and white	D	D
Lift foreground color from image	Alt+click with Paint tool or click with Eyedropper	Option+click with Paint tool or click with Eyedropper
Lift background color from image	Alt+click with Eyedropper	Option+click with Eyedropper
Lift color from different application	click with Eyedropper in image window, and then drag outside window into other application	click with Eyedropper in image window, and then drag outside window into other application
Place fixed color sampler in image	click with Color Sampler tool or Shift+click with Eyedropper	click with Color Sampler tool or Shift+click with Eyedropper
Delete fixed color sampler	Alt+click with Color Sampler tool or Shift+Alt+click with Eyedropper	Option+click with Color Sampler tool or Shift+Option+click with Eyedropper
Display or hide Color palette	F6	F6
Lift foreground color from color bar at bottom of Color palette	click color bar	click color bar

continued

TABLE A.1	(continued)	
Operation	**Windows Shortcut**	**Macintosh Shortcut**
Lift background color from color bar	Alt+click color bar	Option+click color bar
Cycle through color bars	Shift+click color bar	Shift+click color bar
Specify new color bar	Right-click color bar	Control-click color bar
Lift foreground color from Swatches palette	click swatch	click swatch
Lift background color from Swatches palette	Ctrl+click swatch	⌘+click swatch
Delete swatch or style from palette	Alt+click swatch or style	Option+click swatch or style
Add new swatch or style to palette	click in empty area of palette	click in empty area of palette
Add new swatch or style without naming	Alt+click in empty area of palette	Option+click in empty area of palette
Apply style to active layer	click icon in Styles palette	click icon in Styles palette
Add effects in style to those applied to active layer	Shift+click icon in Styles palette	Shift+click icon in Styles palette
Fill selection or layer with foreground color	Alt+Backspace	Option+Delete
Fill layer with foreground color, preserve transparency	Shift+Alt+Backspace	Shift+Option+Delete
Fill selection on background layer with background color	Backspace or Delete	Delete
Fill selection on any layer with background color	Ctrl+Backspace	⌘+Delete
Fill layer with background color, preserve transparency	Ctrl+Shift+Backspace	⌘+Shift+Delete
Fill selection with source state in History palette	Ctrl+Alt+Backspace	⌘+Option+Delete
Display Fill dialog box	Shift+Backspace	Shift+Delete
Select Gradient Tool or Paint Bucket	G or Shift+G	G or Shift+G
Change gradient style	bracket key, [or]	bracket key, [or]
Cycle between gradient presets	comma (,) or period (.)	comma (,) or period (.)
Select first or last gradient preset	Shift+comma (,) or Shift+period (.)	Shift+comma (,) or Shift+period (.)

Operation	Windows Shortcut	Macintosh Shortcut
Type		
Select all text on text layer	double-click T in Layers palette	double-click T in Layers palette
Select all text when already working inside text layer	Ctrl+A	⌘+A
Select single word	double-click word with type tool	double-click word with Type tool
Select word to left or right	Ctrl+Shift+left or right arrow	⌘+Shift+left or right arrow
Increase type size 2 pixels (or points)	Ctrl+Shift+greater than (>)	⌘+Shift+greater than (>)
Decrease type size 2 pixels	Ctrl+Shift+less than (<)	⌘+Shift+less than (<)
Increase type size 10 pixels	Ctrl+Shift+Alt+greater than (>)	⌘+Shift+Option+greater than (>)
Decrease type size 10 pixels	Ctrl+Shift+Alt+less than (<)	⌘+Shift+Option+less than (<)
Kern together 2/100 em	Alt+left arrow	Option+left arrow
Kern apart 2/100 em	Alt+right arrow	Option+right arrow
Kern together 1/10 em	Ctrl+Alt+left arrow	⌘+Option+left arrow
Kern apart 1/10 em	Ctrl+Alt+right arrow	⌘+Option+right arrow
Toggle underlining	Ctrl+Shift+U	⌘+Shift+U
Toggle strikethrough	Ctrl+Shift+slash (/)	⌘+Shift+slash (/)
Toggle all uppercase text	Ctrl+Shift+K	⌘+Shift+K
Toggle small caps text	Ctrl+Shift+H	⌘+Shift+H
Toggle superscript text	Ctrl+Shift+plus (+)	⌘+Shift+plus (+)
Toggle subscript text	Ctrl+Shift+Alt+plus (+)	⌘+Shift+Option+plus (+)
Restore 100% horizontal scale	Ctrl+Shift+X	⌘+Shift+X
Restore 100% vertical scale	Ctrl+Shift+Alt+X	⌘+Shift+Option+X
Tighten leading 2 pixels	Alt+up arrow	Option+up arrow
Expand leading 2 pixels	Alt+down arrow	Option+down arrow
Tighten leading 10 pixels	Ctrl+Alt+up arrow	⌘+Option+up arrow
Expand leading 10 pixels	Ctrl+Alt+down arrow	⌘+Option+down arrow
Switch to Auto leading	Ctrl+Shift+Alt+A	⌘+Shift+Option+A
Raise baseline shift 2 pixels	Shift+Alt+up arrow	Shift+Option+up arrow
Lower baseline shift 2 pixels	Shift+Alt+down arrow	Shift+Option+down arrow
Raise baseline shift 10 pixels	Ctrl+Shift+Alt+up arrow	⌘+Shift+Option+up arrow
Lower baseline shift 10 pixels	Ctrl+Shift+Alt+down arrow	⌘+Shift+Option+down arrow

continued

1089

TABLE A.1 (continued)

Operation	Windows Shortcut	Macintosh Shortcut
Left-align text	Ctrl+Shift+L	⌘+Shift+L
Center-align text	Ctrl+Shift+C	⌘+Shift+C
Right-align text	Ctrl+Shift+R	⌘+Shift+R
Justify all text	Ctrl+Shift+F	⌘+Shift+F
Justify all text except last line	Ctrl+Shift+J	⌘+Shift+J
Insert nonbreaking hyphen	Ctrl+Alt+hyphen (-)	*none*
Insert nonbreaking space	Ctrl+Alt+X	Option+spacebar
Show or hide highlight while editing text	Ctrl+H	⌘+H
Move live text	Ctrl+drag	⌘+drag
Accept changes to text	Enter on keypad or Ctrl+Enter	Enter or ⌘+Return
Cancel changes to text (cannot undo)	Esc	Escape
Highlight font option when Type Tool active but no type highlighted	Enter	Return
Change formatting for multiple linked text layers	Shift+choose setting from Options bar or type value and press Shift+Enter	Shift+choose setting from Options bar or type value and press Shift+Return
Display Character palette	Ctrl+T when text highlighted	⌘+T when text highlighted
Display Paragraph palette	Ctrl+M when text highlighted	⌘+M when text highlighted
Selections		
Select everything	Ctrl+A	⌘+A
Deselect everything	Ctrl+D	⌘+D
Restore last selection outline	Ctrl+Shift+D	⌘+Shift+D
Hide or show marching ants	Ctrl+H	⌘+H
Feather selection	Ctrl+Alt+D	⌘+Option+D
Reverse selection	Ctrl+Shift+I	⌘+Shift+I
Toggle between Rectangular and Elliptical Marquee tools	M or Shift+M	M or Shift+M
Draw out from center with Marquee tool	Alt	Option
Constrain marquee to square or circle	Shift	Shift

Operation	Windows Shortcut	Macintosh Shortcut
Move marquee as you draw it	spacebar	spacebar
Cycle between Lasso tools	L or Shift+L	L or Shift+L
Add corner to straight-sided selection outline	Alt+click with Lasso tool or click with Polygonal Lasso tool	Option+click with Lasso tool or click with Polygonal Lasso tool
Add point to magnetic selection	click with Magnetic Lasso tool	click with Magnetic Lasso tool
Delete last point added with Magnetic Lasso tool	Backspace	Delete
Increase or reduce magnetic lasso width	bracket, [or]	bracket, [or]
Close polygon or magnetic selection	double-click with respective Lasso tool or press Enter	double-click with respective Lasso tool or press Return
Close magnetic selection with straight segment	Alt+double-click or Alt+Enter	Option+double-click or Option+Return
Cancel polygon or magnetic selection	Esc	*None*
Add to selection	Shift+drag (marquee, lasso) or Shift+click (magic wand)	Shift+drag (marquee, lasso) or Shift+click (magic wand)
Subtract from selection	Alt+drag (Marquee, Lasso) or Alt+click (Magic Wand)	Option+drag (Marquee, Lasso) or Option+click (Magic Wand)
Retain intersected portion of selection	Shift+Alt+drag (Marquee, Lasso) or Shift+Alt+click (Magic Wand)	Shift+Option+drag (Marquee, Lasso) or Shift+Option+click (Magic Wand)
Select Move tool	V or press and hold Ctrl	V or press and hold ⌘
Move selection	drag with Move tool or Ctrl+drag with other tool	drag with Move tool or ⌘+drag with other tool
Constrain movement vertically or horizontally	press Shift while dragging selection	press Shift while dragging selection
Move selection in 1-pixel increments	Ctrl+arrow key	⌘+arrow key
Move selection in 10-pixel increments	Ctrl+Shift+arrow key	⌘+Shift+arrow key
Clone selection	Alt+drag selection with Move tool or Ctrl+Alt+drag with other tool	Option+drag selection with Move tool or ⌘+Option+drag with other tool
Clone selection in 1-pixel increments	Ctrl+Alt+arrow key	⌘+Option+arrow key

continued

TABLE A.1   (continued)

Operation	Windows Shortcut	Macintosh Shortcut
Clone selection and move the clone in 10-pixel increments	Ctrl+Shift+Alt+arrow key	⌘+Shift+Option+arrow key
Clone selection to different image	Ctrl+drag selection from one window and drop it into another	⌘+drag selection from one window and drop it into another
Move selection outline independently of its contents	drag with Selection tool	drag with Selection tool
Move selection outline in 1-pixel increments	arrow key when Selection tool is active	arrow key when Selection tool is active
Move selection outline in 10-pixel increments	Shift+arrow key when Selection tool is active	Shift+arrow key when Selection tool is active
Copy empty selection outline to different image	drag selection from one window into another with Selection tool	drag selection from one window into another with Selection tool
Change opacity or blend mode of floating selection, when used immediately after applying a filter	Ctrl+Shift+F	⌘+Shift+F
Paste image into selection	Ctrl+Shift+V	⌘+Shift+V
Paste image behind selection	Ctrl+Shift+Alt+V	⌘+Shift+Option+V
Layers		
Display or hide Layers palette	F7	F7
View single layer by itself	Alt+click eyeball icon in Layers palette	Option+click Eyeball icon in Layers palette
Create new layer above current layer	click Page icon at bottom of Layers palette or Ctrl+Shift+Alt+N	click Page icon at bottom of Layers palette or ⌘+Shift+Option+N
Create new layer below current layer	Ctrl+click Page icon at bottom of Layers palette	⌘+click Page icon at bottom of Layers palette
Create new layer above current layer and assign name	Alt+click Page icon at bottom of Layers palette or Ctrl+Shift+N	Option+click Page icon at bottom of Layers palette or ⌘+Shift+N
Create new layer below current layer and assign name	Ctrl+Alt+click Page icon at bottom of Layers palette	⌘+Option+click Page icon at bottom of Layers palette
Clone selection or entire layer to new layer	Ctrl+J	⌘+J
Clone selection or entire layer to new layer and assign name	Ctrl+Alt+J	⌘+Option+J
Transfer selection to new layer	Ctrl+Shift+J	⌘+Shift+J

Operation	Windows Shortcut	Macintosh Shortcut
Transfer selection to new layer and assign name	Ctrl+Shift+Alt+J	⌘+Shift+Option+J
Convert floating selection to new layer	Ctrl+Shift+J	⌘+Shift+J
Create adjustment layer	choose from Dual-tone icon menu at bottom of Layers palette	choose from Dual-tone icon menu at bottom of Layers palette
Create and name adjustment layer	Alt+choose from Dual-tone icon menu at bottom of Layers palette	Option+choose from Dual-tone icon menu at bottom of Layers palette
Add layer set	click Folder icon in Layers palette	click Folder icon in Layers palette
Add and name layer set	Alt+click Folder icon in Layers palette	Option+click Folder icon in Layers palette
Ascend one layer	Alt+right bracket (])	Option+right bracket (])
Descend one layer	Alt+left bracket ([)	Option+left bracket ([)
Ascend to top layer	Shift+Alt+right bracket (])	Shift+Option+right bracket (])
Descend to background layer	Shift+Alt+left bracket ([)	Shift+Option+left bracket ([)
Go directly to layer containing specific image element when using Move tool	Ctrl+click or Alt+right+click layer in image window	⌘+click or Control+Option+click layer in image window
Go directly to layer containing specific image element when using any tool except Move tool	Ctrl+Alt+right-click layer in image window	⌘+Control+Option+click layer in image window
Select from layers that overlap when using Move tool	Right-click layer in image window	Control-click layer in image window
Select from layers that overlap when using any tool except Move tool	Ctrl+right-click layer in image window	⌘+Control-click layer in image window
Lock transparency of layer	slash (/)	slash (/)
Toggle between current lock configuration and no locks in Layers palette	slash (/)	slash (/)
Convert layer's transparency mask to selection outline	Ctrl+click layer name in Layers palette	⌘+click layer name in Layers palette
Add transparency mask to selection	Ctrl+Shift+click layer name	⌘+Shift+click layer name
Subtract transparency mask from selection	Ctrl+Alt+click layer name	⌘+Option+click layer name

continued

1093

TABLE A.1   *(continued)*

Operation	Windows Shortcut	Macintosh Shortcut
Retain intersection of transparency mask and selection	Ctrl+Shift+Alt+click layer name	⌘+Shift+Option+click layer name
Move layer	drag with Move tool or Ctrl+drag with other tool	drag with Move tool or ⌘+drag with other tool
Move layer in 1-pixel increments	Ctrl+arrow key	⌘+arrow key
Move layer in 10-pixel increments	Ctrl+Shift+arrow key	⌘+Shift+arrow key
Clone and move layer	Alt+drag with Move tool or Ctrl+Alt+drag with other tool	Option+drag with Move tool or ⌘+Option+drag with other tool
Clone and move layer in 1-pixel increments	Ctrl+Alt+arrow key	⌘+Option+arrow key
Clone and move layer in 10-pixel increments	Ctrl+Shift+Alt+arrow key	⌘+Shift+Option+arrow key
Clone layer to another open image	Ctrl+drag layer from one window and drop it into another	⌘+drag layer from one window and drop it into another
Clone layer to new image	Alt+drag layer onto page icon at bottom of Layers palette, choose New from Document menu	Option+drag layer onto page icon at bottom of Layers palette, choose New from Document menu
Bring layer forward one level	Ctrl+right bracket (])	⌘+right bracket (])
Bring layer to front of file	Ctrl+Shift+right bracket (])	⌘+Shift+right bracket (])
Send layer backward one level	Ctrl+left bracket ([)	⌘+left bracket ([)
Send layer to back, just above background layer	Ctrl+Shift+left bracket ([)	⌘+Shift+left bracket ([)
Link layer containing specific image element with active layer	Ctrl+Shift+Alt+right-click layer in image window	⌘+Control+Shift+Option+click layer in image window
Unlink layer that contains specific image element from active layer	Ctrl+Shift+Alt+right-click layer in image window	⌘+Control+Shift+Option+click layer in image window
Unlink all layers from active layer	Alt+click brush icon in front of layer name in Layers palette or Ctrl+Shift+Alt+right-click active layer in image window	Option+click brush icon in front of layer name in Layers palette or ⌘+Control+Shift+Option+click active layer in image window
Change opacity of active layer in 10% increments	number (1 through 0) when Selection tool is active	number (1 through 0) when Selection tool is active
Change opacity of active layer in 1% increments	two numbers in a row when Selection tool is active	two numbers in a row when Selection tool is active

Operation	Windows Shortcut	Macintosh Shortcut
Change opacity of pixels in active layer in 10% increments, independently of effects	Shift+number (1 through 0) when Selection tool is active	Shift+number (1 through 0) when Selection tool is active
Change opacity of pixels in active layer in 1% increments, independently of effects	Shift+two numbers in a row when Selection tool is active	Shift+two numbers in a row when Selection tool is active
Edit layer name	double-click layer name in Layers palette	double-click layer name in Layers palette
Edit blending options for layer	double-click thumbnail in Layers palette or Alt+double-click layer name	double-click thumbnail in Layers palette or Option+double-click layer name
Edit settings for fill or adjustment layer	double-click thumbnail in Layers palette	double-click thumbnail in Layers palette
Change blend mode when Selection tool is active	Shift+Alt+letter	Shift+Option+letter
Cycle between blend modes when Selection tool is active	Shift+plus (+) or Shift+minus (–)	Shift+plus (+) or Shift+minus (–)
Reset to Normal blend mode when Selection tool is active	Shift+Alt+N	Shift+Option+N
Adjust "fuzziness" in Layer Style dialog box	Alt+drag This Layer or Underlying Layer slider triangle	Option+drag This Layer or Underlying Layer slider triangle
Merge layer with next layer down	Ctrl+E	⌘+E
Merge linked layers	Ctrl+E	⌘+E
Merge grouped layers	Ctrl+E	⌘+E
Merge all layers in active set	Ctrl+E	⌘+E
Merge all visible layers	Ctrl+Shift+E	⌘+Shift+E
Copy merged version of selection to Clipboard	Ctrl+Shift+C	⌘+Shift+C
Clone contents of layer into next layer down	Ctrl+Alt+E	⌘+Option+E
Clone contents of linked layers to active layer	Ctrl+Alt+E	⌘+Option+E
Clone contents of all visible layers to active layer	Ctrl+Shift+Alt+E	⌘+Shift+Option+E
Delete active layer	click Trash icon in Layers palette	click Trash icon in Layers palette
Delete active layer without warning	Alt+click Trash icon in Layers palette	Option+click Trash icon in Layers palette

continued

TABLE A.1   (continued)

Operation	Windows Shortcut	Macintosh Shortcut
Delete multiple linked layers and sets	Ctrl+click Trash icon in Layers palette	⌘+click Trash icon in Layers palette
Delete multiple linked layers and sets without warning	Ctrl+Alt+click Trash icon in Layers palette	⌘+Option+click Trash icon in Layers palette
Edit specific layer effect	double-click effect name in Layers palette	double-click effect name in Layers palette
Switch between effects in Layer Styles dialog box	Ctrl+1 through Ctrl+0	⌘+1 through ⌘+0
Save flattened copy of layered image	Ctrl+Alt+S	⌘+Option+S
Brush and Blend Modes		
Normal	Shift+Alt+N or Shift+Alt+L	Shift+Option+N
Dissolve	Shift+Alt+I	Shift+Option+I
Behind	Shift+Alt+Q	Shift+Option+Q
Clear	Shift+Alt+R	Shift+Option+R
Darken	Shift+Alt+K	Shift+Option+K
Multiply	Shift+Alt+M	Shift+Option+M
Color Burn	Shift+Alt+B	Shift+Option+B
Linear Burn	Shift+Alt+A	Shift+Option+A
Lighten	Shift+Alt+G	Shift+Option+G
Screen	Shift+Alt+S	Shift+Option+S
Color Dodge	Shift+Alt+D	Shift+Option+D
Linear Dodge	Shift+Alt+W	Shift+Option+W
Overlay	Shift+Alt+O	Shift+Option+O
Soft Light	Shift+Alt+F	Shift+Option+F
Hard Light	Shift+Alt+H	Shift+Option+H
Vivid Light	Shift+Alt+V	Shift+Option+V
Linear Light	Shift+Alt+J	Shift+Option+J
Pin Light	Shift+Alt+Z	Shift+Option+Z
Hard Mix	Shift+Alt+L	Shift+Option+L
Difference	Shift+Alt+E	Shift+Option+E
Exclusion	Shift+Alt+X	Shift+Option+X
Hue	Shift+Alt+U	Shift+Option+U

Operation	Windows Shortcut	Macintosh Shortcut
Saturation	Shift+Alt+T	Shift+Option+T
Color	Shift+Alt+C	Shift+Option+C
Luminosity	Shift+Alt+Y	Shift+Option+Y
Saturate (Sponge tool)	Shift+Alt+S	Shift+Option+S
Desaturate (Sponge tool)	Shift+Alt+D	Shift+Option+D
Shadows (Dodge and Burn tools)	Shift+Alt+S	Shift+Option+S
Midtones (Dodge and Burn tools)	Shift+Alt+M	Shift+Option+M
Highlights (Dodge and Burn tools)	Shift+Alt+H	Shift+Option+H
Replace (Healing Brush)	Shift+Alt+Z	Shift+Option+Z
Pass Through (layer set)	Shift+Alt+P	Shift+Option+P
Cycle to next mode	Shift+plus (+)	Shift+plus (+)
Cycle to previous mode	Shift+minus (–)	Shift+minus (–)
Channels and Masks		
Switch between independent color and mask channels	Ctrl+1 through Ctrl+9	⌘+1 through ⌘+9
View composite RGB, Lab, or CMYK image	Ctrl+tilde (~)	⌘+tilde (~)
Activate or deactivate color channel	Shift+click channel name in Channels palette	Shift+click channel name in Channels palette
Create channel mask filled with black	click Page icon at bottom of Channels palette	click Page icon at bottom of Channels palette
Create and name channel mask filled with black	Alt+click Page icon at bottom of Channels palette	Option+click Page icon at bottom of Channels palette
Create channel mask from selection outline	click Mask icon at bottom of Channels palette	click Mask icon at bottom of Channels palette
Create and name channel mask from selection outline	Alt+click Mask icon at bottom of Channels palette	Option+click Mask icon at bottom of Channels palette
View active channel mask as rubylith overlay	tilde (~)	tilde (~)
Convert channel mask to selection outline	Ctrl+click channel name in Channels palette or Ctrl+Alt+number (1 through 0)	⌘+click channel name in Channels palette or ⌘+Option+number (1 through 0)
Add channel mask to selection	Ctrl+Shift+click channel name	⌘+Shift+click channel name
Subtract channel mask from selection	Ctrl+Alt+click channel name	⌘+Option+click channel name

continued

TABLE A.1   *(continued)*

Operation	Windows Shortcut	Macintosh Shortcut
Retain intersection of channel mask and selection	Ctrl+Shift+Alt+click channel name	⌘+Shift+Option+click channel name
Enter or exit quick mask mode	Q	Q
Toggle quick mask color over masked or selected area	Alt+click Quick Mask icon in Toolbox	Option+click Quick Mask icon in Toolbox
Change quick mask color overlay	double-click Quick Mask icon	double-click Quick Mask icon
View quick mask independently of image	tilde (~)	tilde (~)
Add spot color channel	Ctrl+click Page icon at bottom of Channels palette	⌘+click Page icon at bottom of Channels palette
Create layer mask filled with white when nothing selected	click Mask icon at bottom of Layers palette	click Mask icon at bottom of Layers palette
Create layer mask filled with black when nothing selected	Alt+click Mask icon	Option+click Mask icon
Create layer mask from selection outline	click Mask icon	click Mask icon
Create layer mask that hides selection	Alt+click Mask icon	Option+click Mask icon
Switch focus from layer mask to image	Ctrl+tilde (~)	⌘+tilde (~)
Switch focus from image to layer mask	Ctrl+backslash (\)	⌘+backslash (\)
View layer mask as rubylith overlay	backslash (\) or Shift+Alt+click layer mask thumbnail in Layers palette	backslash (\) or Shift+Option+click layer mask thumbnail in Layers palette
View layer mask independently of image	backslash (\), and then tilde (~) or Alt+click layer mask thumbnail in Layers palette	backslash (\), and then tilde (~) or Option+click layer mask thumbnail in Layers palette
Add vector mask to layer	Ctrl+click Mask icon in Layers palette	⌘+click mask icon in Layers palette
Convert current path to vector mask	Ctrl+click Mask icon in Layers palette with path active	⌘+click Mask icon in Layers palette with path active
Toggle display of vector mask	click vector mask thumbnail or press Enter when shape or arrow tool is active	click vector mask thumbnail or press Return when shape or arrow tool is active
Disable layer mask or vector mask	Shift+click mask thumbnail in Layers palette	Shift+click mask thumbnail in Layers palette

Operation	Windows Shortcut	Macintosh Shortcut
Toggle link between layer and mask	click between layer and mask thumbnails in Layers palette	click between layer and mask thumbnails in Layers palette
Copy layer mask or vector mask from one layer to active layer	drag mask thumbnail onto Mask icon at bottom of Layers palette	drag mask thumbnail onto Mask icon at bottom of Layers palette
Convert layer mask to selection outline	Ctrl+click layer mask thumbnail or Ctrl+Alt+backslash (\)	⌘+click layer mask thumbnail or ⌘+Option+backslash (\)
Convert vector mask to selection outline	Ctrl+click vector mask thumbnail	⌘+click vector mask thumbnail
Add layer mask or vector mask to selection	Ctrl+Shift+click mask thumbnail	⌘+Shift+click mask thumbnail
Subtract layer mask or vector mask from selection	Ctrl+Alt+click mask thumbnail	⌘+Option+click mask thumbnail
Retain intersection of layer mask or vector mask and selection	Ctrl+Shift+Alt+click mask thumbnail	⌘+Shift+Option+click mask thumbnail
Paths and Shapes		
Cycle between standard, Freeform, and Magnetic Pen tools	P or Shift+P	P or Shift+P
Add corner to end of active path	click with Pen tool or Alt+click with Freeform Pen tool	click with pen tool or Option+click with Freeform Pen tool
Add smooth arc to end of active path	drag with Pen tool	drag with Pen tool
Add cusp to end of active path	Alt+click, and then drag with Pen tool	Option+click, and then drag with Pen tool
Add point to end of active magnetic selection	click with Magnetic Pen tool	click with Magnetic Pen tool
Delete last point added with standard or Magnetic Pen tool	Backspace	Delete
Draw freehand path segment	drag with Freeform Pen tool or Alt+drag with Magnetic Pen tool	drag with Freeform Pen tool or Option+drag with Magnetic Pen tool
Increase or reduce Magnetic Pen tool path width	bracket, [or]	bracket, [or]
Close magnetic selection	double-click with Magnetic Pen tool or click first point in path	double-click with Magnetic Pen tool or click first point in path
Close magnetic selection with straight segment	Alt+double-click or Alt+Enter	Option+double-click or Option+Return

continued

TABLE A.1   *(continued)*

Operation	Windows Shortcut	Macintosh Shortcut
Cancel magnetic or freeform selection	Esc	Esc
Select Arrow tool	A or press Ctrl when Pen tool is active	A or press ⌘ when Pen tool is active
Move selected points	drag point with Arrow tool or Ctrl+drag with Pen tool	drag point with Arrow tool or ⌘+drag with Pen tool
Select multiple points in path	Shift+click with Arrow or Ctrl+Shift+click with Pen tool	Shift+click with Arrow or ⌘+Shift+click with Pen tool
Select entire path	Alt+click path with white arrow or Alt+click path in Paths palette	Option+click path with arrow or Option+click path in Paths palette
Clone path	Alt+drag path with Arrow or Ctrl+Alt+drag with Pen tools	Option+drag path with Arrow tool or ⌘+Option+drag with Pen tool
Access Convert direction tool when Pen tool is active	Alt while hovering cursor over anchor point	Option while hovering cursor over anchor point
Access Convert Direction tool when Arrow tool is active	Ctrl+Alt while hovering cursor over anchor point	⌘+Option while hovering cursor over anchor point
Convert corner or cusp to smooth arc	Alt+drag point with Pen tool	Option+drag point with Pen tool
Convert arc to corner	Alt+click point with Pen tool	Option+click point with Pen tool
Convert arc to cusp	Alt+drag handle with Pen tool	Option+drag handle with Pen tool
Insert point in selected path	click segment with Pen tool	click segment with Pen tool
Remove point from path	click point with Pen tool	click point with Pen tool
Convert path to selection outline	Ctrl+click path name in Paths palette or Ctrl+Enter when Pen or Arrow tool is active	⌘+click path name in Paths palette or ⌘+Return when Pen or Arrow tool is active
Add path to selection	Ctrl+Shift+click path name in Paths palette	⌘+Shift+click path name in Paths palette
Subtract path from selection	Ctrl+Alt+click path name in Paths palette	⌘+Option+click path name in Paths palette
Retain intersection of path and selection	Ctrl+Shift+Alt+click path name in Paths palette	⌘+Shift+Option+click path name in Paths palette
Apply brushstroke around perimeter of path	Enter on keypad when Paint or edit tool is active	Enter when Paint or Edit tool is active
Revert around perimeter of path	Enter on keypad when History Brush is active	Enter when History Brush is active

Operation	Windows Shortcut	Macintosh Shortcut
Save and name path for future use	double-click Work Path item in Paths palette	double-click Work Path item in Paths palette
Hide path (it remains active)	Ctrl+Shift+H	⌘+Shift+H
Deactivate path	click in empty portion of Paths palette or Enter when Pen or Arrow tool is active	click in empty portion of Paths palette or Return when Pen or Arrow tool is active
Cycle between shape tools	U or Shift+U	U or Shift+U
Move shape as you draw it	spacebar	spacebar
Add next shape you draw to active shape layer	plus (+)	plus (+)
Subtract next shape you draw from active shape layer	minus (–)	minus (–)
Adjust roundness of next rounded rectangle you draw	bracket key, [or]	bracket key, [or]
Change number of sides on next regular polygon or star you draw	bracket key, [or]	bracket key, [or]
Change weight of next straight line you draw	bracket key, [or]	bracket key, [or]
Cycle between custom shapes	bracket key, [or]	bracket key, [or]
Cycle between layer styles	comma (,) or period (.)	comma (,) or period (.)
Change color of active shape layer to foreground or background color	Alt+Backspace or Ctrl+Backspace	Option+Delete or ⌘+Delete
Hide shape outlines (shape layer remains active)	Ctrl+Shift+H	⌘+Shift+H
Deactivate shape outlines	Enter when Pen or Arrow tool is active	Return when Pen or Arrow tool is active
Delete shape layer when shape outlines are active	Backspace or Delete	Delete
Crops and Transformations		
Select Crop tool	C	C
Move crop boundary as you draw it	spacebar	spacebar
Move crop boundary	drag inside boundary	drag inside boundary
Scale crop boundary	drag boundary handle	drag boundary handle
Scale crop boundary proportionally	Shift+drag corner handle	Shift+drag corner handle

continued

TABLE A.1 *(continued)*

Operation	Windows Shortcut	Macintosh Shortcut
Scale crop boundary with respect to origin	Alt+drag boundary handle	Option+drag boundary handle
Scale crop boundary proportionally with respect to origin point	Shift+Alt+drag corner	Shift+Option+drag corner
Rotate crop boundary (always with respect to origin)	drag outside boundary	drag outside boundary
Rotate crop boundary in 15° increments	Shift+drag outside boundary	Shift+drag outside boundary
Distort crop boundary	draw crop boundary, select Perspective check box in Options bar, drag boundary handle	draw crop boundary, select Perspective check box in Options bar, drag boundary handle
Constrain distortion effect in Perspective mode	Shift+drag corner handle	Shift+drag corner handle
Scale crop boundary in Perspective mode	Alt+drag handle	Option+drag handle
Accept crop	Enter	Return
Cancel crop	Esc	Escape
Freely transform selection, layer, or path	Ctrl+T	⌘+T
Duplicate selection, layer, or path and freely transform	Ctrl+Alt+T	⌘+Option+T
Move image in Free Transform mode	drag inside boundary	drag inside boundary
Move transformation origin	drag cross-hair target	drag cross-hair target
Scale image	drag boundary handle	drag boundary handle
Scale image proportionally	Shift+drag corner handle	Shift+drag corner handle
Scale image with respect to origin	Alt+drag boundary handle	Option+drag boundary handle
Rotate image (always with respect to origin)	drag outside boundary	drag outside boundary
Rotate image in 15° increments	Shift+drag outside boundary	Shift+drag outside boundary
Skew image	Ctrl+drag side handle	⌘+drag side handle
Skew image along constrained axis	Ctrl+Shift+drag side handle	⌘+Shift+drag side handle
Skew image with respect to origin	Ctrl+Alt+drag side handle	⌘+Option+drag side handle

Operation	Windows Shortcut	Macintosh Shortcut
Skew image along constrained axis with respect to origin	Ctrl+Shift+Alt+drag side handle	⌘+Shift+Option+drag side handle
Distort image	Ctrl+drag corner handle	⌘+drag corner handle
Symmetrically distort opposite corners	Ctrl+Alt+drag corner handle	⌘+Option+drag corner handle
Constrain distortion to achieve perspective effect	Ctrl+Shift+drag corner handle	⌘+Shift+drag corner handle
Constrain distortion to achieve symmetrical perspective effect	Ctrl+Shift+Alt+drag corner handle	⌘+Shift+Option+drag corner handle
Apply specific transformation in Free Transform mode	right+click in image window	Control+click in image window
Apply numerical transformation in Free Transform mode	enter values in Options bar	enter values in Options bar
Accept transformation	Enter	Return
Cancel transformation	Esc	Escape
Replay last transformation	Ctrl+Shift+T	⌘+Shift+T
Duplicate selection, layer, or path and replay last transformation	Ctrl+Shift+Alt+T	⌘+Shift+Option+T
Rulers, Measurements, and Guides		
Display or hide rulers	Ctrl+R	⌘+R
Display or hide Info palette	F8	F8 (be sure to edit your System Preferences or this will invoke Spaces)
Change unit of measure	right-click ruler or drag from X,Y pop-up in Info palette	Control-click ruler or drag from X,Y pop-up in Info palette
Reset ruler origin	double-click ruler origin box	double-click ruler origin box
Select Measure tool	I, I, I (or I, Shift+I, Shift+I)	I, I, I (or I, Shift+I, Shift+I)
Measure distance and angle	drag with Measure tool	drag with Measure tool
Move measure line	drag measure line	drag measure line
Change length and angle of measure line	drag endpoint of measure line	drag endpoint of measure line
Measure angle between two lines (protractor option)	Alt+drag endpoint	Option+drag endpoint
Match rotation of entire image to measure line	Choose Image ➪ Rotate ➪ Arbitrary	choose Image ➪ Rotate ➪ Arbitrary

continued

TABLE A.1 *(continued)*

Operation	Windows Shortcut	Macintosh Shortcut
Match rotation of single layer to measure line	Choose Edit ⇨ Transform ⇨ Rotate	choose Edit ⇨ Transform ⇨ Rotate
Create guide	drag from ruler	drag from ruler
Move guide	drag guide with Move tool or Ctrl+drag with other tool	drag guide with Move tool or ⌘+drag with other tool
Change horizontal guide to vertical or vice versa	press Alt while dragging guide	press Option while dragging guide
Snap guide to ruler tick marks	press Shift while dragging guide	press Shift while dragging guide
Display or hide guides	Ctrl+semicolon (;)	⌘+semicolon (;)
Lock or unlock guides	Ctrl+Alt+semicolon (;)	⌘+Option+semicolon (;)
Display or hide grid	Ctrl+quote (")	⌘+quote (")
Toggle guide and grid snapping	Ctrl+Shift+semicolon (;)	⌘+Shift+semicolon (;)
Edit guide color and grid increments	Ctrl+double+click guide	⌘+double-click guide
Filters and Automation		
Repeat filter with last-used settings	Ctrl+F	⌘+F
Repeat filter with different settings	Ctrl+Alt+F	⌘+Option+F
Fade effect of last filter	Ctrl+Shift+F	⌘+Shift+F
Scroll preview box in corrective filter dialog boxes	drag in preview box or click in image window	drag in preview box or click in image window
Zoom preview box in corrective filter dialog boxes	Ctrl+click and Alt+click	⌘+click and Option+click
Zoom full image preview	Ctrl+plus (+) and Ctrl+minus (–)	⌘+plus (+) and ⌘+minus (–)
Increase selected option box value by 1 (or 0.1)	up arrow	up arrow
Decrease value by 1 (or 0.1)	down arrow	down arrow
Increase value by 10 (or 1)	Shift+up arrow	Shift+up arrow
Decrease value by 10 (or 1)	Shift+down arrow	Shift+down arrow
Adjust Angle value (where offered) in 15° increments	Shift+drag in Angle wheel	Shift+drag in Angle wheel
Reset options in corrective filter dialog boxes	Alt+click Cancel button	Option+click Cancel button or Option+Escape

Operation	Windows Shortcut	Macintosh Shortcut
Create high-contrast clouds effect	Alt+choose Filter ⇨ Render ⇨ Clouds	Option+choose Filter ⇨ Render ⇨ Clouds
Specify numerical center in Lens Flare dialog box	Alt+click in preview	Option+click in preview
Clone light in Lighting Effects dialog box	Alt+drag light	Option+drag light
Delete Lighting Effects light	press Delete	press Delete
Adjust size of footprint without affecting angle of light	Shift+drag handle	Shift+drag handle
Adjust angle of light without affecting size of footprint	Ctrl+drag handle	⌘+drag handle
Select Forward Warp or Push Left tool in Liquify dialog box	W or O	W or O
Select Twirl Clockwise or Turbulence tool	C or T	C or T
Select Pucker or Bloat tool	S or B	S or B
Select Reconstruct or Mirror tool	R or M	R or M
Select Freeze Mask or Thaw Mask tool	F or D	F or D
Change Liquify brush diameter in 1-pixel increments	Bracket key, [or]	bracket key, [or]
Change Liquify brush diameter in 10-pixel increments	Shift+bracket, [or]	Shift+bracket, [or]
Undo last brushstroke in Liquify dialog box	Ctrl+Z	⌘+Z
Undo brushstroke prior to last one	Ctrl+Alt+Z	⌘+Option+Z
Redo undone brushstroke	Ctrl+Shift+Z	⌘+Shift+Z
Select the select image, rotate image, or set vanishing point tool in Photomerge dialog box	A, R, or V	A, R, or V
Select Zoom or Hand tool	Z or H	Z or H
Temporarily access Hand tool	Spacebar	Spacebar
Step backward	Ctrl+Z	⌘+Z
Step forward	Ctrl+Shift+Z	⌘+Shift+Z
Show individual image border	Alt+move pointer over image	Option+move pointer over image

continued

TABLE A.1   *(continued)*

Operation	Windows Shortcut	Macintosh Shortcut
Color Adjustments		
Choose Levels command	Ctrl+L	⌘+L
Switch between channels in Levels or Curves dialog box	Ctrl+1 through Ctrl+3, or Ctrl+tilde (~) for composite	⌘+1 through ⌘+3, or ⌘+tilde (~) for composite
Preview black and white points in Levels dialog box	Alt+drag black or white Input Levels triangle	Option+drag black or white Input Levels triangle
Specify alternate colors for black point, white point, and midtone	double-click black, white, or gray Eyedropper tool	double-click black, white, or gray Eyedropper tool
Invert image in Levels dialog box	swap black and white Output Levels triangles	swap black and white Output Levels triangles
Repeat last Levels correction	Ctrl+Alt+L	⌘+Option+L
Choose Curves command	Ctrl+M	⌘+M
Add point in Curves dialog box	click graph line	click graph line
Add specific color as new point on composite curve in point mode	Ctrl+click in image window	⌘+click in image window
Add color as new point on independent channel curves	Ctrl+Shift+click in image window	⌘+Shift+click in image window
Nudge Input value for selected point	left or right arrow key	left or right arrow key
Nudge Output value for selected point	up- or down-arrow key	up- or down-arrow key
Select next curve point	Ctrl+Tab	Control+Tab
Select previous curve point	Ctrl+Shift+Tab	Control+Shift+Tab
Delete curve point	Ctrl+click point	⌘+click point
Select multiple curve points	Shift+click point	Shift+click point
Deselect all points	Ctrl+D	⌘+D
Repeat last Curves correction	Ctrl+Alt+M	⌘+Option+M
Choose Hue/Saturation command	Ctrl+U	⌘+U
Add colors to Hue/Saturation range when Edit set to anything but Master	Shift+click or drag in image window	Shift+click or drag in image window
Subtract colors from Hue/Saturation range when Edit set to anything but Master	Alt+click or drag in image window	Option+click or drag in image window

Operation	Windows Shortcut	Macintosh Shortcut
Edit all colors in Hue/Saturation dialog box	Ctrl+tilde (~)	⌘+tilde (~)
Edit predefined color range	Ctrl+1 through Ctrl+6	⌘+1 through ⌘+6
Repeat last Hue/Saturation correction	Ctrl+Alt+U	⌘+Option+U
Desaturation colors	Ctrl+Shift+U	⌘+Shift+U
Undoing Operations		
Undo or redo last operation	Ctrl+Z	⌘+Z
Undo operation prior to last one	Ctrl+Alt+Z	⌘+Option+Z
Redo undone operation	Ctrl+Shift+Z	⌘+Shift+Z
Undo to specific point	click item in History palette	click item in History palette
Duplicate previously performed operation	Alt+click item in History palette	Option+click item in History palette
Select state to revert to with History Brush	click in front of item in History palette	click in front of item in History palette
Create snapshot from active state	click camera icon at bottom of History palette	click camera icon at bottom of History palette
Create duplicate image from active state	click leftmost icon at bottom of History palette	click leftmost icon at bottom of History palette
Revert selection to active History state	Ctrl+Alt+Backspace	⌘+Option+Delete
Revert entire image to saved state	F12	F12 (Be sure to edit your System Preferences or this will open the Dashboard)
Miscellaneous		
Display or hide all palettes, Toolbox, and status bar	Tab	Tab
Display or hide palettes except Toolbox, Options bar, and status bar	Shift+Tab	Shift+Tab
Hide Toolbox, Options bar, and status bar	Tab, and then Shift+Tab	Tab, and then Shift+Tab
Display Options bar	Enter	Return
Move panel out of palette	drag panel tab	drag panel tab
Dock palette	drag panel tab into docking well	drag panel tab into docking well
Snap palette to edge of screen	Shift+click palette title bar	Shift+click palette title bar

continued

TABLE A.1   *(continued)*

Operation	Windows Shortcut	Macintosh Shortcut
Fully collapse palette	Alt+click collapse box or double-click panel tab	Option+click collapse box or double-click panel tab
Delete item without warning from any palette that includes trash can	Alt+click Trash icon	Option+click Trash icon
Preview how image sits on printed page	click Doc box in status bar	click Doc box at bottom of image window
View size and resolution of image	Alt+click Doc box in status bar	Option+click Doc box at bottom of image window
View image tile information	Ctrl+click Doc box in status bar	⌘+click Doc box at bottom of image window
Change preference settings	Ctrl+K	⌘+K
Display last-used Preferences dialog box panel	Ctrl+Alt+K	⌘+Option+K
Bring up dialog box with last-used settings	Alt+choose command from Image ➪ Adjustments submenu	Option+choose command from Image ➪ Adjustments submenu
Duplicate image and bypass dialog box	Alt+choose Image ➪ Duplicate	Option+choose Image ➪ Duplicate
Cancel operation	Esc	⌘+period or Escape
Activate No or Don't Save button when closing image	N	D
Activate Don't Flatten button when changing color modes	D	D
Activate Flatten button when changing color modes	F	F

Appendix B

What's on the CD-ROM?

This appendix provides you with information on the contents of the CD that accompanies this book. For the latest and greatest information, please refer to the ReadMe file located at the root of the CD.

System Requirements

Make sure that your computer meets the minimum system requirements listed in this section — these are the same requirements that you'll find for running Photoshop CS3. Of course, you can run the CD-ROM on a computer with lower-end specifications than the one on which you run Photoshop, but we're assuming you're watching the tutorials and opening images from the CD on the computer you use to work with the application. In any case, if your computer doesn't match up to most of these requirements, you may have a problem using the contents of the CD.

For Windows XP or Vista users:

- Processor: Intel Xeon, Xeon Dual, Centrino, or Pentium 4 processor
- System: Microsoft Windows XP with Service Pack 2 or higher
- RAM: 320 MB (384 MB recommended)
- Hard disk: 650 MB
- Monitor: 1024 x 768 monitor resolution, 16-bit video card
- Video RAM: 64 MB
- CD-ROM drive: CD-ROM drive required

IN THIS APPENDIX

System requirements

Using the CD

What's on the CD

Troubleshooting

Customer care

- Browser: IE 6.0, Netscape 4.x, 6.1, 6.2, or 7.0, AOL 6.0 or 7.0, Opera
- Multimedia: QuickTime 7 required for multimedia features

For Mac users:

- Processor: PowerPC G4, or G5 processor, Intel-based Macs
- System: Mac OS X v. 10.3. latest, 10.4. latest, Leopard (10.5)
- RAM: 320MB (384 MB recommended)
- Hard disk: Estimated 1.5 GB
- Monitor: 1024 x 768 monitor resolution, 16-bit video card
- Video RAM: 64 MB
- CD-ROM drive: CD-ROM drive required
- Browser: IE 5.5+, Netscape 8.0+, AOL 5.0+, Safari 1.0+, Opera
- Multimedia: QuickTime 7 required for multimedia features

Using the CD

To use the CD, follow these steps:

1. **Insert the CD into your computer's CD-ROM drive.** The license agreement appears.

   Windows users: The interface won't launch if you have autorun disabled. In that case, click Start ➪ Run (For Windows Vista, Start ➪ All Programs ➪ Accessories ➪ Run). In the dialog box that appears, type **D:\Start.exe**. (Replace D with the proper letter if your CD drive uses a different letter. If you don't know the letter, see how your CD drive is listed under My Computer.) Click OK.

   Mac Users: The CD icon appears on your desktop. Double-click the icon to open the CD and double-click the Start icon.

2. **Read through the license agreement, and then click the Accept button if you want to use the CD.** After you click Accept, the License Agreement window won't appear again.

   The CD interface appears. The interface allows you to view the images and run the tutorials with just a click of a button (or two).

What's on the CD

The *Photoshop CS3 Bible* comes with a CD designed to enhance your experience with the book. In the following sections you learn what we've included, why, and how to make effective use of the content.

Images from the book

Many of the images used in this book are on the CD, found in folders, by chapter. If a photo or other image is used more than once, in more than one chapter, the folder corresponding to the chapter where it first appears is where you'll find it on the CD. Whenever possible, we've provided images in their pristine state — before special filters, color, or light-adjustment tools, and so on were applied to them. For images that appear only after they've been retouched, the final version appears on the CD.

Note that images provided on the CD may include those that are copyrighted by their creators; therefore, any use of any images from the CD for commercial use is prohibited. Feel free to play with the images on your own computer, but do not use them, in whole or in part, in print, Web, or other materials. We ask this out of respect for the photographers and other artists who created them and were gracious enough to allow them to be used in this book. If there's an image you see in the book that you don't find on the CD, the image has not been included because the photographer did not give us the right to distribute it.

Tutorials

We've created a series of tutorials to help you master many of the tools and features of Photoshop CS3, and placed them on the CD. These tutorials consist of movies and onscreen instructions that demonstrate how a given effect is created and/or how various tools and features are used together to achieve interesting results. After viewing the tutorials, you can experiment with the images on the CD to try things out for yourself. We hope, however, that you'll be inspired to not only mimic the tutorials' results but to apply the demonstrated tools and features in new and exciting ways in your own images. Have fun!

Table B.1 identifies the tutorials and the features you'll learn about by viewing them. The easiest way to view a tutorial is to click its title in the CD interface. If you prefer to navigate directly to the tutorial files, you'll find them in a folder called Tutorials.

TABLE B.1

Tutorials on the CD

Tutorial Title	Tutorial Description
Masking a Complex Image	Using the individual channels in an image, along with the High Pass filter and Invert command, you'll discover how to create a very detailed mask that accurately follows the exact edge of selected image content.
Creating a Ringed Planet	Start your own little solar system with Gradient fills and the Radial Blur, Noise, and Lens Flare filters. You'll also play with Levels, Hue/Saturation, and free transformations, along with various layer styles and blend modes. Using gradients to fill your planet and its rings, you'll learn to create selections, fill them, and then apply styles and filters to achieve a surrealistic cosmos.

continued

TABLE B.1   *(continued)*

Tutorial Title	Tutorial Description
Eliminating Background Elements	With expert use of the Clone Stamp, you'll take distracting elements from the background of a photo, replacing them with more neutral, natural-looking content. You'll never miss what's gone, and neither will anyone else who views your "doctored" photo.
Working with the Extract Filter	In this tutorial, the Extract filter is used to take content and pull it out of its existing location for use in another image. You'll learn to use Smart Highlighting and the Fill tool within the Extract filter's dialog box, and then you'll see an object placed in a new image, transformed and made to feel at home in its new surroundings.
Creating a Shadow the Old-Fashioned Way	Rather than live with the limitations of the Drop Shadow you can create with layer Blending Options, try this method that uses the creation and manipulation of layers, fills and filters, as well as creative freeform transformations to create the look of a natural-looking, accurate shadow.
Entering Text Along a Path	Type can follow any path you draw, and in this tutorial, you'll learn to create an elliptical path that surrounds the pi symbol and places the actual value of pi around the symbol, along the path. You'll also learn to manipulate the path to control the flow of text around it, and to apply interesting effects within the path itself.
Working with Edge Masks	Here you'll learn to work with the Unsharp Mask, Find Edges, Maximum, Median, and Gaussian Blur filters in conjunction with an alpha channel to create an edge mask and then convert it to a selection outline.
Healing with a Pattern	In this tutorial, you'll become a plastic surgeon, painting away the years on a man's face with the Healing Brush, the Add Noise filter, and a pattern you create to simulate youthful skin.
Correcting Colors with the Levels Command	The Levels command is used again, this time with the Channels palette and the Hue/Saturation dialog box to correct colors in an image.
Creating a Custom Lighting Effect	As the title implies, you'll learn to create the appearance of light where no natural light existed. Using everything from selection tools to fill tools, from alpha channels to Blur filters and layer styles, you'll create virtual reality and then shed natural-looking light on it, also utilizing the Texturizer and Lighting Effects filters.
The New Vanishing Point	Photoshop CS3's Vanishing Point feature is greatly enhanced, and in this tutorial, you'll learn to create multiple planes and to wrap an image around them — in this case, a series of nations' flags, wrapped around majestic monoliths in a stark landscape.

 For additional Photoshop tutorials, please visit www.photoshopbible.com.

Troubleshooting

If you have difficulty installing or using any of the materials on the companion CD, try the following solutions:

- **Turn off any anti-virus software that you may have running.** Installers sometimes mimic virus activity and can make your computer incorrectly believe that it is being infected by a virus. (Be sure to turn the anti-virus software back on later.)

- **Close all running programs.** The more programs you're running, the less memory is available to other programs. Installers also typically update files and programs; if you keep other programs running, installation may not work properly.

- **Refer to the ReadMe file.** Please refer to the ReadMe file located at the root of the CD-ROM for the latest product information at the time of publication.

Customer Care

If you have trouble with the CD-ROM, please call the Wiley Product Technical Support phone number at 800-762-2974. Outside the United States, call 1-317-572-3994. You also can contact Wiley Product Technical Support at `http://support.wiley.com`. John Wiley & Sons provides technical support only for installation and other general quality control items. For technical support on the applications themselves, consult the program's vendor or author.

To place additional orders or to request information about other Wiley products, please call 877-762-2974.

Index

Symbols and Numerics

G

Wiley Publishing, Inc.
End-User License Agreement

READ THIS. You should carefully read these terms and conditions before opening the software packet(s) included with this book "Book". This is a license agreement "Agreement" between you and Wiley Publishing, Inc. "WPI". By opening the accompanying software packet(s), you acknowledge that you have read and accept the following terms and conditions. If you do not agree and do not want to be bound by such terms and conditions, promptly return the Book and the unopened software packet(s) to the place you obtained them for a full refund.

1. **License Grant.** WPI grants to you (either an individual or entity) a nonexclusive license to use one copy of the enclosed software program(s) (collectively, the "Software" solely for your own personal or business purposes on a single computer (whether a standard computer or a workstation component of a multi-user network). The Software is in use on a computer when it is loaded into temporary memory (RAM) or installed into permanent memory (hard disk, CD-ROM, or other storage device). WPI reserves all rights not expressly granted herein.

2. **Ownership.** WPI is the owner of all right, title, and interest, including copyright, in and to the compilation of the Software recorded on the disk(s) or CD-ROM "Software Media". Copyright to the individual programs recorded on the Software Media is owned by the author or other authorized copyright owner of each program. Ownership of the Software and all proprietary rights relating thereto remain with WPI and its licensers.

3. **Restrictions On Use and Transfer.**

   (a) You may only (i) make one copy of the Software for backup or archival purposes, or (ii) transfer the Software to a single hard disk, provided that you keep the original for backup or archival purposes. You may not (i) rent or lease the Software, (ii) copy or reproduce the Software through a LAN or other network system or through any computer subscriber system or bulletin-board system, or (iii) modify, adapt, or create derivative works based on the Software.

   (b) You may not reverse engineer, decompile, or disassemble the Software. You may transfer the Software and user documentation on a permanent basis, provided that the transferee agrees to accept the terms and conditions of this Agreement and you retain no copies. If the Software is an update or has been updated, any transfer must include the most recent update and all prior versions.

4. **Restrictions on Use of Individual Programs.** You must follow the individual requirements and restrictions detailed for each individual program in the "What's on the CD-ROM?" appendix of this Book. These limitations are also contained in the individual license agreements recorded on the Software Media. These limitations may include a requirement that after using the program for a specified period of time, the user must pay a registration fee or discontinue use. By opening the Software packet(s), you will be agreeing to abide by the licenses and restrictions for these individual programs that are detailed in the "What's on the CD-ROM?" appendix and on the Software Media. None of the material on this Software Media or listed in this Book may ever be redistributed, in original or modified form, for commercial purposes.

5. **Limited Warranty.**

    (a) WPI warrants that the Software and Software Media are free from defects in materials and workmanship under normal use for a period of sixty (60) days from the date of purchase of this Book. If WPI receives notification within the warranty period of defects in materials or workmanship, WPI will replace the defective Software Media.

    (b) WPI AND THE AUTHOR OF THE BOOK DISCLAIM ALL OTHER WARRANTIES, EXPRESS OR IMPLIED, INCLUDING WITHOUT LIMITATION IMPLIED WARRANTIES OF MERCHANTABILITY AND FITNESS FOR A PARTICULAR PURPOSE, WITH RESPECT TO THE SOFTWARE, THE PROGRAMS, THE SOURCE CODE CONTAINED THEREIN, AND/OR THE TECHNIQUES DESCRIBED IN THIS BOOK. WPI DOES NOT WARRANT THAT THE FUNCTIONS CONTAINED IN THE SOFTWARE WILL MEET YOUR REQUIREMENTS OR THAT THE OPERATION OF THE SOFTWARE WILL BE ERROR FREE.

    (c) This limited warranty gives you specific legal rights, and you may have other rights that vary from jurisdiction to jurisdiction.

6. **Remedies.**

    (a) WPI's entire liability and your exclusive remedy for defects in materials and workmanship shall be limited to replacement of the Software Media, which may be returned to WPI with a copy of your receipt at the following address: Software Media Fulfillment Department, Attn.: *Photoshop CS3 Bible*, Wiley Publishing, Inc., 10475 Crosspoint Blvd., Indianapolis, IN 46256, or call 1-800-762-2974. Please allow four to six weeks for delivery. This Limited Warranty is void if failure of the Software Media has resulted from accident, abuse, or misapplication. Any replacement Software Media will be warranted for the remainder of the original warranty period or thirty (30) days, whichever is longer.

    (b) In no event shall WPI or the author be liable for any damages whatsoever (including without limitation damages for loss of business profits, business interruption, loss of business information, or any other pecuniary loss) arising from the use of or inability to use the Book or the Software, even if WPI has been advised of the possibility of such damages.

    (c) Because some jurisdictions do not allow the exclusion or limitation of liability for consequential or incidental damages, the above limitation or exclusion may not apply to you.

7. **U.S. Government Restricted Rights.** Use, duplication, or disclosure of the Software for or on behalf of the United States of America, its agencies and/or instrumentalities "U.S. Government" is subject to restrictions as stated in paragraph (c)(1)(ii) of the Rights in Technical Data and Computer Software clause of DFARS 252.227-7013, or subparagraphs (c) (1) and (2) of the Commercial Computer Software - Restricted Rights clause at FAR 52.227-19, and in similar clauses in the NASA FAR supplement, as applicable.

8. **General.** This Agreement constitutes the entire understanding of the parties and revokes and supersedes all prior agreements, oral or written, between them and may not be modified or amended except in a writing signed by both parties hereto that specifically refers to this Agreement. This Agreement shall take precedence over any other documents that may be in conflict herewith. If any one or more provisions contained in this Agreement are held by any court or tribunal to be invalid, illegal, or otherwise unenforceable, each and every other provision shall remain in full force and effect.